Under the Editorship of

M . F . NIMKOFF

The Florida State University

EXPLORATIONS IN

HOUGHTON MIFFLIN COMPANY

SOCIAL CHANGE

Edited by

George K. Zollschan · Walter Hirsch
PURDUE UNIVERSITY

With an Introduction by

DON MARTINDALE
UNIVERSITY OF MINNESOTA

OSTON · NEW YORK · DALLAS · ATLANTA · GENEVA, ILL. · PALO ALTO

HOUGHTON MIFFLIN COMPANY
PRINTED IN THE U.S.A.

67841   *For Stuart Cleveland*

Acknowledgments

The fact that this book is dedicated to Stuart Cleveland indicates the extent of our obligation to him for his immediate grasp of the potentialities of a volume such as this, and for his continuous, fruitful criticism and personal engagement in our venture up to the time of his tragic and untimely death. David Kirk and Ronald Cohen cooperated with us in the invitation of contributors and in the early stages of planning. Problems of time and distance made it impossible for them to continue their editorial work, but happily both are represented in the volume by their own chapters.

Our contributors as a group were outstanding in the prompt fulfillment of their assumed obligations, and in their gracious response to editorial molestation from us. Some, in particular, took a personal and fatherly interest in the book as a whole. Their encouragement should be appreciated here. The interest of Meyer F. Nimkoff, Editorial Consultant to Houghton Mifflin, must also be mentioned here, as must that of the editors of Houghton Mifflin who succeeded Stuart Cleveland. They have given unstintingly of their enthusiasm and expertise.

Putting together a symposium of this kind is no easy task. Although clerical and typing assistance came from many quarters, special mention should be made of Mrs. Dorothy Butcher, secretary of the Purdue Department of Sociology, who never lost patience with our editorial importunities and harassments.

George K. Zollschan
Walter Hirsch

West Lafayette, Indiana
September, 1963

Contents

Section four · Psycho-social Models of Change

Section five · Broad Historical Perspectives on Change

Section six · Cultural Change, Cultural Contact, and Social Movements

Section seven · Economic Development and Cultural Change

SECTION EIGHT · *Special Areas of Institutional Change*

Don Martindale

Introduction

It is not inappropriate to open the prefatory remarks of this symposium with the observation that in the period following World War II American sociology has itself been undergoing rapid change. Many universities and colleges which formerly offered only a course or two housed in an alien department have added independent departments of sociology, while old departments have been reorganized and expanded. Even so, the harvest of Ph.D.'s in sociology has been insufficient to feed the hungry institutions, and each year attractive positions have gone unfilled. Masses of students have swelled the classes of sociology professors. Editors of textbook publications have scouted the campuses of colleges and universities in search of manuscripts, and have plied prospective authors with all sorts of inducements at publishers' parties given during national conventions. Callow youths with the ink scarcely dry on their diplomas have competed for contracts with eyes bright with the vision of their names in print. And as the market for textbooks has outrun the available talent for unified quality work, a flood of symposia and anthologies has appeared. Foundations have poured millions into sociological research. A generation of sociological entrepreneurs has grown up, adept in soliciting funds, establishing institutes for research, organizing little bureaucracies of secretaries and assistants, and distributing patronage. New professional recognition has been forthcoming as government, industry, and even large hospitals have added sociologists to their staffs. Virtually new areas have developed in sociology itself, as it has sent out colonizing movements into neighboring disciplines (educational sociology, the sociology of health, the sociology of mental health, industrial sociology, and political sociology). And from the midst of all these dramatic transformations in sociology has come the admission that *its theory of social change is the weakest branch of sociological theory.*

This confession by some of the most highly placed persons in American sociology has usually been accompanied by the assurance that sociology's lack of an adequate theory of change is either of no great importance or merely a temporary state of affairs. One cannot but wonder whether this confession and smug reassurance proceed from breath-taking *naiveté* or from an unctuous philistinism.

For man is a bird of passage. To be sure, at times he rides with his head tucked under his wing, asleep on the lifting waves, and on occasion he feeds along the eroding shores of time, stopping to rest on a gray rock or a marine-worm-weakened, weathered piling. But surely he is most fully himself when he lifts his wings and speeds along the buffeting winds of change between the revolving seasons of his spinning-top world as it whirls about its dying star.

To confess that sociology — which was born as a science of interhuman behavior — can account for structure but not for change is like saying that one can account for a bird at rest, but not for a bird in flight. A review of the major substantive issues of contemporary sociology and the major theories may help to clarify some of the reasons why sociology, which arose as a science of social motion, has largely failed in its original intent. It may also assist in evaluating some of the attempts in the present symposium to restore it once more to the status of a science of motion.

The Major Substantive Issues of Contemporary Sociology

As a science, sociology attempts to discover the laws of interhuman behavior. The explanations that compose its theories may be distinguished in terms of the aspect or phase of interhuman behavior to which they are addressed. The most elementary units into which interhuman behavior can be analyzed are single social acts. Since every social act necessarily involves more than a single person, one can observe the arrangement that obtains between the persons involved and carry out an analysis of social action in terms of social relations. One can, to be sure, analyze social actions into their component parts, but when one does, his analysis has moved outside the proper field of sociology into psychology or physiology or biology. This may be valuable, and one may return with new tools to the analysis of social actions and their formation into patterns of varying complexity — re-entering the field of sociology once more.

Social actions are always the behavior of individuals. A human individual entering interaction with others must be calculable and predictable within limits by others, or the interaction becomes impossible. If an individual desires values which he can only obtain in interaction, he must meet the expectations of others. Whether or not they wish it, thus, the parties to human interaction are implicated in a process of reconstructing themselves. It is not possible to create a special system of social life without also creating the personalities that make it possible. A special branch of social theory is concerned with social persons.

At times, considerable advantage may accrue to the parties in a social arrangement if the social actions of a limited number of individuals are stabilized into a reciprocal pattern of some permanence. They then form groups. The members of a group usually symbolize the pattern in which they are participants, sufficiently apart from themselves to permit individuals to leave or join without changing the pattern in any essentials. Conceived in abstraction from any particular group, the pattern is a group institution. The theory of groups and institutions is also one of the basic branches of sociological theory.

Individuals act in numerous groups. The personalities they develop for one may not be completely adequate for another. Moreover, the actions engaged in may partially conflict from group to group. The formation of social persons and social groups thus undergoes a secondary process of reconstruction which adapts them to the requirements of a more or less consistent total way of life. Systems of social behavior sufficiently comprehensive to carry a given plurality of persons through a normal year and a normal lifetime of any given member become a community. The theory of communities is also a basic subject matter of sociology.

Finally, learned modes (cultural forms) play a major role in every aspect of interhuman behavior. Moreover, over and beyond the cultural forms directly instrumental to social arrangements of all types, the creation and synthesis of cultural forms may go on. There is considerable value in the examination of culture in its own right and not simply incidentally to the study of various aspects of social behavior.

From the standpoint of the substantial matters that it attempts to explain, the various branches of sociological theory are:

The Branches of Sociological Theory

Branch	Character
Theory of social action and social relations	Analysis of the nature, elements, types, and operations of social actions
Theory of social persons	Analysis of the nature, component parts, types, and operations of social persons
Theory of social groups and institutions	Analysis of the formation and destruction of groups and institutions from social actions and social relations

Theory of communities	Analysis of the reorganization of groups and institutions into total ways of life
Theory of culture	Analysis of the development of cultural forms within and apart from social structures. Study of the formation of styles and civilizations

Social change can have no other subject matter than the formation and destruction of interhuman arrangements of these various kinds. The individual chapters in the symposium here presented are usually confined to one or a few of the branches of theory outlined above. Together they provide, as I shall attempt to show, a rather complete conspectus of these various theoretical branches.

Major Points of View in Contemporary Sociology

In addition to the branches of subject matter with which it is concerned, sociology offers a number of points of view (theories) of its subject matter. These theoretical orientations differ according to the aspects of social life taken to be fundamental and the kinds of regularities hypothesized among the various aspects of social life.

It is possible to construct a general paradigm of current theoretical orientations on the basis of the aspect of social interaction thought to be most fundamental. From this standpoint the current schools of theory break down into two broad types: holistic and atomistic. Holistic theories assume that the primary human social reality is some more or less comprehensive, organically unified system. There are some differences among holistic theories, depending on their special conceptions of this organic whole. However, the earmark of theories of sociological "holism" is that some type of equilibrium theory is central to their explanations of social life.

By contrast to types of sociological *holism, atomistic,* or elementaristic theories of social life take the various complex patterns of social life to be secondary and derivative. The essential social reality is traced to social actions or social persons or some properties of either. Equilibrium states in the complex byproducts of individual behavior are, from this perspective, "freaks" of social life. At the same time, depending upon the conception of the ultimate unit or atom of social life, different kinds of sociological atomism are possible.

From the standpoint of their basic suppositions about the character of social life, the major contemporary types of sociological theory are as follows:

Major Types of Sociological Theory

General Type	Major Examples	Unit of Social Life Assumed to be Basic
Holistic Theories	Positivistic and pure organicism	Society and/or culture conceived as an organismic unity
	Functionalism and neo-functionalism	Total social systems conceived as organismic units
	Catholic or neo-Thomist sociology	The Church conceived as a spiritual unity
	Marxian and neo-Marxian conflict theory	Society composed of classes or conflict groups
Atomistic Theories	Social behaviorism, symbolic interactionism, pluralism	Social action or some aspects of it
	Formalism	Social forms
	Individualistic forms of conflict theory	Interests

Since social and cultural change is concerned with the formation and destruction of interhuman arrangements, any given approach is inevitably affected by the theoretical perspective (be it consciously or unconsciously held) of the writer. Our outline of the various types of sociological theory can serve to identify the theoretical perspectives of the particular writer. These theoretical perspectives can help to account both for what he assumes to be the basic subject matter for a study of social change and how he handles it.

Some Notes on the Contemporary Crisis in the Theory of Social Change

The two paradigms sketched above on the branches and types of sociological theory and a few historical observations make it possible to locate the source of the crisis in the theory of social change which provided the basic rationale for the present symposium.

The special sociological theories did not emerge all at once. Throughout the nineteenth century sociology was dominated by forms of *positivistic organicism*, considering society as an organic unity and proposing to apply to the analysis of society the positive methods of empirical science. The sub-parts of society were considered in terms of the organs of biological forms. The smallest sub-part, the family, was not analyzed by the positivistic organicists as either social actions or social persons.

Both social structure and social change were analyzed in terms of the predominance of the whole over the parts and the functional relation of parts within the whole. Social structure consisted of the interrelation of parts and whole.

The positivistic organicists were willing to admit that human society was affected by biological factors on the one hand, and environmental factors on the other. However, in its most fundamental nature society was considered an organism which maintained itself in the face of such external factors. The fundamental reasons for what happened to society arose from within it. Evolution was the one notion which permitted positivistic organicism to budget the concept of change in its scheme. If the whole of society was seen as evolving toward ever higher ends, the notion of organicity was preserved while accounting for change in terms of society itself.

Once the positivistic organicists had arrived at this comforting view of social change, they felt free to tear historical and ethnographic materials out of their various contexts and fit them to prefabricated conceptions of progress-evolution. However, such arbitrary procedure permitted so many different and contradictory constructions that the entire enterprise was called into question.

The only major theoretical competitor to positivistic organicism in the nineteenth century was the collectivistic form of conflict theory. As illustrated by Marxism, the idea of a large-scale organic unit moving toward a state of equilibrium also dominated its notion of society. The primary units of social life, however, were not institutions but militantly organized classes. The mechanism of social change was found in class struggle. Class conflicts were resolved by the establishment of ever more comprehensive equilibrium states. The concepts of organicity, equilibrium, and progress-evolutionism were retained by Marxism, which dreamed of a classless society as the utopian fulfillment of history.

However, the multiplication of alternative versions of social evolutionism by the conflict theorists only made the babble of voices more confusing. When exacting standards were applied to social data, the arbitrary procedure of tearing social facts out of context and arranging them into prefabricated patterns became untenable. The failure to establish a mechanism that could adequately account for social evolution (comparable to the genetic changes in biological organisms) destroyed the last vestige of plausibility in the social evolutionary schemes. The entire theory began to collapse, and with it many of sociology's ties with history and ethnology.

Into the vacuum created by the decline of the progress-evolution theory of social change moved the culture lag theory of social change on the one hand, and various cyclical theories of culture on the other. The culture lag theory reconstructed the progress-evolution formula in a disguised and limited form by drawing a distinction between material and non-material culture. Material culture, in turn, was largely identified with technology and viewed as progressive, though usually prevented from bringing about the rapid evolution of society as a whole only by the lag between it and non-material culture.

Upon analysis, the distinction between material and non-material culture broke down. However, so strong was the felt need for the progress-evolution formula that this conception of social change persisted despite the many unanswered criticisms repeatedly made against it.

For the rest, in the period following World War I a series of holistic and cyclical theories of culture appeared. The most famous of these were advanced by Oswald Spengler, Arnold Toynbee, and Pitirim Sorokin. Unfortunately, the evidence for the organicity of culture and for the particular cultural integrations and sequences (cycles) was often as arbitrary as the evidence for the various progress-evolution theories. (The chapter by Schneider and the answer by Sorokin bring this discussion up to date.)

Contemporary functionalist theory in modified manner habilitated the same basic suppositions as positivistic organicism. Step by step these theoretical suppositions have led functionalism down the same road once traveled by its great predecessor. As functionalism runs its triumphant course in the post-World War II period, reconstructing by degrees the same general theory of social structure as its predecessor, difficulty has begun to appear.

What at first was reported as a minor and temporary flaw began increasingly to assume the properties of a major crisis. Functionalism was having trouble with its theory of social change. Functionalist suppositions were, in short, driving their adherents toward a progress-evolution formula such as had ended so disastrously earlier. Understandably, there was much reluctance to take this step. Nevertheless, so powerful is the impetus in this direction that a minor revival of social evolutionary theory in sociology has been occurring in the 1960's. (The chapter by Boskoff in this volume is the latest stage in this development.)

If one applies the paradigm of theory types above to the crisis in the theory of social change, it immediately becomes evident that this crisis is bound up with the fate of a limited number of the types of sociological theories, primarily with holistic types, and especially positivistic organicism in the past and functionalism in the present. It is also evident that the analysis of social change from the standpoint of the various atomistic theories is relatively unexplored.

The present symposium vigorously carries forward the exploration of the problems of social and cultural change from a number of holistic and atomistic positions. From the point of view of holistic theories, the crux of change lies in the larger social configurations: communities, societies, and civilizations. From the point of view of atomistic theories, change is a problem for social arrangements of every level of complexity. In opening its doors to discussion by the theorists of both types, this symposium treats social forms of every level of complexity from social actions to high-order syntheses.

Some Notes on the Organization and Content of
Explorations in Social Change

In sensitive response to aspects of the problem of social change which have dominated discussions in the post-war period, the editors arranged the chapters of their symposium neither in terms of content nor of theoretical perspective, but topically in a manner best calculated to bring unity to the current discussion. Section 1 presents a number of general orientations to the problem; Section 2 presents a new form of social behavioristic theory, and applies it to a number of areas of structure and change; Sections 3 and 4 present a number of collectivist (holistic) and individualist (atomistic) approaches to change; Section 5 presents studies which have made extensive use of historical materials; Section 6 presents approaches which have made use of contemporary and ethnographic rather than historical material; Section 7 takes up various aspects of economic change; Section 8 explores the interaction between various often ignored non-economic institutions and the wider social context. The symposium ends with an essay on the sociology of science, and therewith jauntily sallies forth to meet its critics.

The Section Introductions to the topical organization of the chapters are excellently done, and anyone interested in a general introduction to the symposium would be well advised to read them through as a whole before tackling the individual chapters.

It is possible to describe and trace the operations of social structures without examining social change. However, it is not possible to analyze social change without attention to the problem of structure. Furthermore, one's theory of society has direct bearing upon the kinds of social arrangements seen as primary vehicles of change. Holistic theories, in general, locate the problem of change in the larger interhuman complexes: communities, cultures, civilizations. Atomistic theories locate it in social arrangements of every degree of complexity from social actions to culture. Consequently, the symposium which attempts to do justice to all the major current perspectives inevitably touches every basic category of social structure from all major current points of view.

Three chapters are concerned with social action: that by Zollschan and Perrucci on "Social Stability and Social Process"; that by Barnett on "The Acceptance and Rejection of Change"; and the essay by Hoselitz. The first of these chapters carries out an analysis of the components and processes of social action; the second raises the question as to how innovations which can only begin as psychological phenomena in individuals can become group characteristics. Max Weber, the founder of the social action branch of social behaviorism, analyzed the economic and many

other forms of behavior in terms of a typology of action in which traditional and rational types played a major role. Hoselitz proposes to modify
this kind of analysis by the addition of a new typology of theoretical and
aesthetic types.

Six chapters of the symposium are concerned with problems of the
social person: Zollschan and Gibeau, "Concerning Alienation"; Zollschan,
"Beyond the 'Reality Principle' "; Kirk, "The Impact of Drastic Change on
Social Relations"; Levinson, "Idea Systems in the Individual and Society";
Warshay, "Breadth of Perspective and Social Change"; and Elkin, "Advertising in French Canada." The study by Zollschan and Gibeau explores the consequences of unsolvable needs for the accommodation or
alienation of the social person. The chapter by Zollschan investigates the
possibility of integrating the Freudian theory of personality within his
own sociological framework. Kirk examines the implications of changes
in the social system for social actions and social persons. Levinson
examines autocracy and democracy in personality and culture conceived
as synchronized, boundary-maintaining systems which are most stable
when interlocked. Warshay explores the relevance of persons of broad
and of narrow perspectives for social structure and change. Elkin's study
of the influence of advertising by Anglo-Saxon-dominated corporations
on French-Canadian minority culture in Quebec locates the crux of the
problem in a variety of role and personality adjustments by French
Canadians marginal to both cultures.

A considerable number of the chapters are concerned with one or
another of the major institutions in their interaction with other social
forms. Three major chapters deal primarily with political institutions.
Willer and Zollschan, in "Prolegomenon to a Theory of Revolutions,"
treat revolution primarily as a phenomenon of the rapid and violent transformation of political institutions operating within the wider social *milieu*.
The chapter by Eisenstadt utilizes historical materials on the political
institutions of the ancient bureaucratic empires, tracing their decay to
the effects of conflicting strategies of differently placed groups. The
chapter by Cohen on "Conflict and Change in a Northern Nigerian
Emirate" traces the strategies of native emirates in a political situation
confused by the requirements of the British colonial administration on
the one hand and of the traditional feudalism of the country on the other.

Preoccupation with the role of economics in social change derives both
from classical economics and scientific socialism, particularly Marxism.
The culture lag theory of social change, for example, was rooted in classical economics from which it drew the distinction between material and
non-material culture, identifying the former primarily with technology
and treating its consequences essentially as progressive. In the present
volume, Cottrell's study of "Technology and Social Change on American
Railroads" is a modified version of the culture lag hypothesis in which
"arrangements that maximize energy flow" take the place assigned by

earlier students to material culture, and the simplified contrast between material and non-material culture is replaced by the concept of "a system that reflects the strength of many different groups, operating in different arenas, utilizing different kinds of influence."

The tension between a progressive economy and a traditional society of classical economics was translated by scientific socialism into a conflict of classes. Lockwood's chapter on "Social Integration and System Integration" modifies and brings up to date the theory of change by scientific socialism in much the same manner as is done by Cottrell for the theory of change deriving from classical economic assumptions. Lockwood postulates a fundamental "propensity to social change arising from the functional incompatibility between an institutional order and its material base."

The chapters by Andersen and Eichhorn, Willener, Greenfield, Rosenberg, and Marcus are devoted to specific problems of economic institutions of one sort or another. The study by Banks examines the British feminist movement which followed the radical changes in the status of the family accompanying the rise of the mass society and the migration of many former home industries to the world outside the home. Colvard examines the problems faced by the operators of philanthropic institutions if they are to fulfill their assigned functions without destroying themselves or the interests which established them. Duncan Mitchell examines the evolution of British educational institutions in response to the changing strategies of the social classes.

Three chapters of the symposium are concerned with the problems of the community. Boskoff's chapter on "Functional Analysis" is a modification of the current Functionalist theory of the society or total social system (the functionalist euphemism for community) to accommodate the problem of change. The chapter by Lockwood on "Social Integration and System Integration" also locates social change in a parallel manner. "The term 'social change' will be taken to mean a change in the institutional structure of a social system; more particularly a transformation of the core institutional order of a society such that we can speak of a change in the type of society." Again the neo-Marxian Conflict Theory utilizes the term "society" as a euphemism for community. Thus change, as visualized by Boskoff and Lockwood, despite their very different ways of accounting for it, is change in a community. Finally, my own chapter on "The Formation and Destruction of Communities" is a formulation of the principles of community formation from a different perspective. It treats the community as a grand strategy of life by a plurality. It advances the hypothesis that in the major historical communities of mankind, the collective commitment to the community is so comprehensive that people have been unable to abandon these communities even when they appear to be retrograde. Hence, major transformations in communities have usually been brought about by violence: wars or revolutions.

Finally, four chapters are devoted to problems of culture: Schneider's "Toward Assessment of Sorokin's View of Change"; Sorokin's "Comments on Schneider's Observations and Criticisms"; my chapter on "The Roles of Humanism and Scientism in the Evolution of Sociology"; and Hirsch's "Knowledge, Power, and Social Change."

In his review and criticism of Sorokin's great trilogy of major cultural syntheses, Schneider maintains that holistic theories necessarily employ dialectical methods. Quite apart from his somewhat different interpretations of the dialectic, Sorokin agrees. Moreover, though Schneider is critical of the great trilogy of high cultural syntheses Sorokin isolated (Sensate-Ideational-Idealistic), he agrees as to the value of such discriminations and the reality of such cultural wholes. My essay and that of Hirsch cover cultural configurations of lesser scope: the Sociology of Sociology and the Sociology of Science. The study of the sociology of sociology treats the development of the discipline as the creative achievement of individuals responding, on the one hand, to logical and scientific criteria; on the other, to ideological pressures in the social *milieu*. The study by Hirsch accepts science as a major factor of social change, exploring the potential influences on the freedom and creativity of science and scientists, of the major institutional contexts (educational, industrial, and political) in which the scientist operates.

It is evident, thus, that while the ultimate object of the contributors was to account for various general or specific aspects of change, it was necessary for them to describe social arrangements of every level of complexity. By a different organization of the essays, it is possible to utilize the volume as an original series of discussions of social structure.

An Organization for Use in Courses in Social Structure

Category	Chapter Number
Social Action and Social Relations	1, 4, 14
Social Persons	6, 7, 10, 11, 12
Institutions and Groups:	
Political	5, 17, 19
Economic	9, 22, 23, 24, 25, 29
Philanthropic	28
Educational	30
Domestic	21
Community	3, 8, 9
Culture	15, 16, 18, 31

Through their choice of contributors and their assignment of topics, the editors guaranteed the presence in the symposium of every major perspective of current sociology. However, three of the essays have primarily methodological significance: Sosensky's discussion of "The Problem of Quality," Beshers' study of "Mathematical Models of Social

Change," and Schneider's "Toward Assessment of Sorokin's View of Change." Sosensky carries out an epistemological critique of concept formation in sociology on the basis of a distinction between metaphorical and analogical statements. In his view, metaphorical statements are qualitative assertions of the existence of an identity where none can be specified. Sosensky's critique leads to the melancholy conclusion that nearly all of the most important theories of society are metaphorical and as such not only pre-scientific but pre-logical. Beshers proposes to cut through the conflicting formulations of alternative theories of change to a presumed common sub-stratum of assumptions. Then by a choice of substantive problems simplified for illustrative purposes ("For simplicity consider mobility between generations in a two-class system") and by adding additional assumptions as needed ("The assumption of independence does not reflect a complete social theory, but it does represent a serious theoretical alternative that merits test in empirical situations. Independence is one way to define a classless society.") Beshers constructs mathematical models for hypothetical worlds remote from the pressing exigencies of the actual one. He holds out the hope that "the theory of social change can undergo a metamorphosis from being the most vague of social theories to being among the more precise." Schneider's critique of Sorokin's theories has a general relevance for all holistic theories. He emphatically makes the point that in assigning causal priority to the whole, all holistic theories are inevitably compelled to assume the existence of immanent mechanisms such as some sort of dialectic.

The essays are not always easy to classify with precision, either because a given author is theoretically unself-conscious and fails to clarify his basic assumptions (in which case one must make one's estimates on the basis of internal evidence), or the thinker is deliberately innovating. Such is the case with the chapter on "The Place of the Image in the Dynamics of Society." This delightful essay by Kenneth Boulding with its dancing metaphors and flashing wit identifies what he believes to be the elements of social interaction essential for the study of social change (or for that matter, social structure). These are images, thresholds, and systems. Boulding's *images* (meanings, ideas, symbols, etc.) are the counterpart of what Max Weber described as the "meaningful components of social action," Robert MacIver as "the dynamic assessments of social situations," and Znaniecki as "the humanistic component" of society. In making images a kind of fundamental unit in explaining inter-human behavior, Boulding seems to join the ranks of the social behaviorists. However, he quickly places alongside images "thresholds" and "systems" organismically conceived as basic elements which must be taken into account — ideas which are domesticated in functionalist theory. Boulding's essay thus raises the theoretical possibility of an attempt to bridge across social behaviorist and functionalist theory.

To a lesser extent the essay by Hoselitz is of the same type. By attempting to join in Weber's typology of traditionalist and rationalist social actions and F. C. S. Northrop's continuum of "theoretical" and "aesthetic" cultural systems, Hoselitz is once again proposing to conjoin distinctions domesticated in a form of social behaviorism to others domesticated in a type of cultural holism.

Holistic theories dominated the early stages of sociological development. The original combination of organismic historicism and expiricism has decayed with the strong tendency to separate into pure organicism and pure positivism. At the present time the world's most famous sociological exponent of a purified form of cultural holism is Pitirim Sorokin. His theories of cultural super-systems have been many times attacked and defended. The latest of these attacks and defenses is represented by Schneider's criticism and Sorokin's reply.

Since World War II, Functionalism, a revised form of sociological organicism, has arisen. It has differed from its great predecessor chiefly in being de-historicized. However, it is like its predecessor in joining a theory of organismic system to positivistic conceptions of method. The theories of Talcott Parsons, the single most famous Functionalist in the United States, are ably presented and criticized on the basis of his epistemological distinctions by Sosensky in "The Problem of Quality in Relation to Some Issues in Social Change." The normative character of contemporary Functionalism is clarified by Lockwood in "Social Integration and System Integration." The transition from Positivistic Organicism to Functionalism and the contemporary status of Functionalism is reviewed in my essay on "The Roles of Humanism and Scientism."

A number of essays in the volume attempt to extend Functionalist analysis to correct current weaknesses in it or to apply it to current problems. The essay by Boskoff, "Functional Analysis as a Source of a Theoretical Repertory and Research Tasks in the Study of Change," seeks to demonstrate that if we assign to the institutional leadership in a total social system the function of "filtering and control" of innovations, even though they are antithetical to the system, Functionalism can account for change. Boskoff's metaphor of a "filtering mechanism" places contemporary Functionalism in a position reminiscent of Hegel's; it acquires a function similar to Hegel's heroes of history. Kirk's chapter on "The Impact of Drastic Change on Social Relations" applies Functionalist analysis to the study of the personal consequence of strains in the systems. Strains in the social system are conceived as creating role handicaps to which various adaptations are attempted by differently situated individuals. Levinson's study of "Idea Systems in the Individual and in Society" examines autocracy and democracy in personality and culture conceived in Functionalist manner as synchronized boundary-maintaining systems, each of which is most stable when harmoniously interlocked. The study by Marcus on "Organizational Change: The Case of the American Trade Unions" applies Functionalist principles to the analysis of trade unions conceived as sub-systems operating within a wider external system from which the primary influences to change arise and to which the direction in change in the sub-system (in this case toward democracy or oligarchy) is a response.[1]

Neo-Marxian Conflict Theory, the foremost holistic competitor of Functionalism, is discussed in two of the chapters and is illustrated and extended in another. Just as Sosensky applied the critical implications of his epistemological distinctions to the Functionalism of Talcott Parsons, he also applied them to the form of neo-Marxian Conflict Sociology by Ralf Dahrendorf. In my own chapter on "Humanism and Scientism" Marxian and neo-Marxian Conflict Sociology are historically located. Finally, the essay by Lockwood on "Social Integration and System Integration" represents an original contribution to neo-Marxian Conflict Theory. Lockwood maintains that many of the basic assumptions of Functionalism and Conflict Theory (such as that of equilibrium, immanent development, etc.) are identical. He maintains that these two theories are, in fact, normative and realistic formulations of the same general type. Thus between the contemporary Functionalists and neo-Marxian Conflict Theorists, a drama is re-enacted bearing similarities to the earlier intellectual transition from Hegel to Marx.

Two other forms of holism, neo-Thomism (illustrated by Luigi Sturzo) and left-wing Humanism (illustrated by C. Wright Mills), have sporadically made their appearance. Though there are no representatives of these positions in the volume, both have been briefly discussed and located in my essay on "Humanism and Scientism."

The circumstances surrounding its origin determined that the first phase of the development of sociology would be dominated by holistic theories. However, in the 1890's a variety of atomistic approaches took shape. The three general types to appear were Social Behaviorism, Formalism, and most recently, Existentialism. Formalist theories of social events were strongly anti-historical. This is perhaps one of the major reasons why no chapter representative of Formalism appears in this volume (the theory is briefly discussed in Chapter 18). Moreover, the emergence of an Existentialist theory of social events has only recently got under way, and no extended examples appear in the volume (again, see Chapter 18). However, all branches of Social Behaviorism are represented in the symposium.

One of the major theoretical innovations of the present volume is the appearance in it of a new branch of Social Behaviorism. Because of their novelty and inner theoretical affinity, the chapters by Zollschan and his associates have been grouped into a single section. They stand as the most unified group of essays in the volume. The essays are held together

---

[1] It should be pointed out that underlying the functionalist coloration of Marcus' study is a major explicit stress on dialectics. In a sense his position is halfway between the functionalist and the neo-Marxist.

by, among other things, an unusual talent on the part of the authors for conceptualization and the coining of new terms, and a capacity for extended abstract argument without bogging down in concrete cases. Perhaps the most fundamental of all ideas inspiring the series is that all activity begins with a problem or need or, in the words of the authors, an *exigency*. No better term for this type of Social Behaviorism could be found than *Exigentialism*.[2]

Among the historical predecessors of *Exigentialism*, the most noteworthy is American pragmatism. Except for a difference in terminology and a far more elaborate mechanics of distinctions, *Exigentialism* is quite similar to the social psychology and epistemology of John Dewey, who also argued that all action, social and non-social, begins with a problematic situation. Just as the *Exigentialists* argue that the first phase of integrated action gets under way with *articulation*, so Dewey was fond of arguing that behavior first assumes definite shape with the formulation of a problem. And finally, corresponding to Dewey's solution of the problem and stabilization of habit or custom, is the *Exigentialist's institutionalization*.

The chapter by Zollschan and Perrucci on "Social Stability and Social Process" presents an *Exigentialist* theory of social action. The chapter by Willer and Zollschan on "Prolegomenon to a Theory of Revolution" treats revolution as a quick, violent transformation in political structures, and applies *Exigentialist* theory to groups and institutions. The article by Zollschan and Gibeau "Concerning Alienation" and that by Zollschan, "Beyond the 'Reality Principle'," are primarily concerned with the development of an *Exigentialist* theory of social persons. The first essay explores some of the consequences of unsolvable exigencies for the social person; the second integrates the Freudian theory of personality into an *Exigentialist* framework.

Pluralistic Behaviorism, the branch of theory stemming from Tarde, Giddings, and Ross, is modified, extended, and brought up to date in Barnett's essay on "The Acceptance and Rejection of Change." Social events are reduced to individual acts arising from ideas and beliefs. Social acts, in turn, are either repetitions of previous acts or innovations. Barnett's question as to how an act which is individual can become social is answered by a contemporary parallel of Tarde's original principle, imitation. "How can an individual reaction to an innovation become a social fact? In brief, the answer is that it can and does become a group characteristic when the acceptance or rejection process is duplicated in *n* individuals, the *n* depending on one's understanding of how many and what persons constitute a group." In the statistical-minded tradition of

---

[2] The author introduces the term *Exigentialism* toward the close of Chapter 7 (p. 197) as a metatheoretical rather than a theoretical idea. He would prefer to apply the term to the "metaphysical pathos" underlying his frame of reference, while calling the frame of reference itself *institutionalization theory*. George Zollschan.

the school, Barnett attempts to identify the variables involved and develops "a paradigm with 81 inflections on the acceptance-rejection process. In it each cell symbolizes the acceptance-rejection possibilities in a given situation." Cottrell's study, "Technology and Social Change on American Railroads," modifies and brings up to date the culture lag theory of change which was originally a product of the pluralistic behaviorists of an earlier day.

Two chapters in the symposium are in the Symbolic Interactionist tradition stemming from William James and G. H. Mead, which traces the basic causes of social events to attitudes, worked up in roles and in social persons. Leon Warshay's "Breadth of Perspective and Social Change" questions from a symbolic interactionist point of view which type of person is most significant for social change: one with a broad or one with a narrow perspective. While he seems to be of the opinion that only the person with a broad perspective is competent to deal with social change, Warshay presents the novel argument that the person with the broad perspective "is not necessarily the successful translator of his breadth in bringing about or . . . preventing . . . social change." He is usually "not organic to society." His possible solutions to social problems "are often inconsistent. He is often a problem to himself and . . . a puzzle to others."

Elkin's study of "Advertising in French Canada" examines the conflict of attitudes brought about by the advertising policies of Anglo-American corporations in local and traditional French-Canadian society which attempts to maintain its cultural autonomy in the face of mass trends. Between these two configurations a number of marginal types (reminiscent of Thomas' and Znaniecki's types) arise representing contrasting role adjustments to a marginal situation.

The large majority of the chapters in the book belong to the Social Action branch of Social Behaviorism stemming more or less directly from Max Weber. From this point of view, the basic unit of social life is the social act. All larger formations of social life are seen as strategies by pluralities of individuals in varying stages of organization. The study by Eisenstadt of "Process of Change and Institutionalization of the Political System of Centralized Empires" is close to the Weber tradition. It reduces the politics of the ancient bureaucratic empires to a strategy of control. In turn, it conceives the inner problems of these ancient political structures to be a product of the conflicting sub-strategies of differently placed groups within the control structure. It traces the decay of the ancient empires to consequences of these sub-strategies. The study by Cohen of "Conflict and Change in a Northern Nigerian Emirate" is also best classified as an example of social action analysis. Like Eisenstadt, Cohen traces the political process to strategies of differently located groups (the dual elite, British and native) in Nigeria. In this case, however, in contrast to the situation described by Eisenstadt which led to political decay, Cohen demonstrates how native emirates have devised informal arrangements which permit them to pilot a course between the conflicting requirements of the colonial bureaucracy and the traditional feudal culture.

My essay on "The Formation and Destruction of Communities" develops a social action analysis of community formation and destruction. The study by Hirsch of "Knowledge, Power, and Social Change: The Role of American Scientists" is a social action analysis of the sociology of science. My study of "Humanism and Scientism" is a social action analysis of the sociology of sociology. Finally, a number of studies apply social action principles (that is, an analysis of the problems into social acts and strategies) as special areas of organizational and institutional change. Such are: the Banks' study of British feminism, Colvard's study of the tasks facing philanthropic organizations, and Duncan Mitchell's study of British education.

It is evident that all major positions in contemporary theory are illustrated in the volume. Furthermore, most of the writers indicate their intention either to extend their theories or apply them to new tasks. The book can thus be used with profit in courses in contemporary sociological theory.

Organization of the Essays for Use in Theory Courses

Type of Theory	Chapters Discussing or Illustrating Theory
Holistic	
Old type Organismic	Discussed in 18; illustrated in 15, 16
Functionalist	Discussed in 2, 9, 18; illustrated in 8, 10, 12, 29
Neo-Marxian Conflict Theory	Discussed in 2, 18; illustrated in 9
Neo-Thomism	Discussed in 18
Left-Wing Humanism	Discussed in 18
Atomistic	
Social Behaviorism	Discussed in 18
Exigentialism	Illustrated in 4, 5, 6, 7
Social Action Theory	Illustrated in 3, 17, 18, 19, 28, 30, 31
Pluralistic Behaviorism	Illustrated in 14, 27
Symbolic Interactionism	Illustrated in 13, 20
Formalism	Discussed in 18
Existentialism	Discussed in 18

While the present volume offers a spirited set of essays touching every category of social structure, and while it offers original contributions to all major theoretical perspectives, its most fundamental value lies in its confrontation of the many-sided problems of social change. In the background broods the realization that all man's arrangements are provisional. All things human are only for a little while, and all too often love turns to hate, laughter to tears, friendship to enmity, and the brave battalions of human hope retire in ignominious defeat. The image of society which dominates the pages of this symposium is generally remote from that of the deathless organismic system so popular in the World War II period. It is more akin to a travelling stock company whose players are old and whose scenery is in tatters, playing little one-night stands on forgotten crossroads between nowhere and chaos, lifting actors and audience for a few brief moments into the magic land of illusion, until the battered scenery is taken down and re-loaded, and the wistful caravan rattles off into the night.

General Perspectives on Social Change

Conceptions of social change have been of crucial importance in social thought for quite as long as conceptions of social order, which currently appear to dominate the field. The recent decline of social change in sociological discussion was, in a sense, well deserved. "Social dynamics" of the classical type (irrespective of whether it was dominated by Comtean ideas of evolution or by Marxist ideas of conflict) was haunted by the Laplacean demon. This endearing sprite, conjured into existence by the incredible success of Newtonian mechanics, personified the seeming omnipotence of the principle of determinacy. His demoniac qualities depended in essence upon only one skill, apparently quite reasonable and modest — he knew the nature and disposition of all things present. However, since determinacy stated that the future and the past as well were contained in the present, the Laplacean demon was able to predict (and post-dict) the nature and disposition of all things future and past. The world was a four-dimensional clockwork, governed by reversible time and Newtonian mechanics. Given this picture of the world, science strove for omniscience — omniscience attainable through possession by (or of) the Laplacean demon. And, as most readers of this volume will surely agree, anything the physicists could do, our forbears in the social sciences could do, at least as well.

As the principle of determinacy was abandoned by the physicist for better things, however, its parallel abandonment by the imitative sociologist left the latter with only a clockwork. Sociological theory, particularly in America (the fellows in Europe were still chasing unfashionable demons), became practically synonymous with an emphasis upon the regular and the repetitive — the normative and the functional. The pendulum was left ticking monotonously and soullessly, but the Laplacean demon had been exorcised from the clock. It is not our intention to bring him back into sociological theory with these explorations. His existence, like that of other demons, was predicated upon unrealistic hopes, fears, and assumptions. He could exist only in a world conceived of as a closed system, and such a world has never existed. Microcosmic simulacra of

1

such closed worlds (as, for example, the solar system viewed exclusively from the point of view of mechanics) are freaks of nature. Except in such freak cases in which prediction (say, of eclipses) and prophecy overlap, the future cannot be prophesied — not even by "scientists."

But we may take comfort. As Karl Popper rightly points out: "The main usefulness of the physical sciences does not lie in the prediction of eclipses; and, similarly, the practical usefulness of the social sciences does not depend on the power to prophecy historical or political developments." Neither, we should like to add, does the theoretical illumination shed by either group of sciences depend upon their prophetic powers. Scientific advances depend upon the formulation and testing of conditional predictions. Clarification and elucidation of conditions under which predictions are sensibly made, in other words, are among the primary tasks of scientific endeavor. If we go about this business with energy, imagination, and, hopefully, a modicum of success, the nostalgia for closed systems will be given up without any feeling of loss.

Boulding's discussion begins by examining how much some hypothetical Laplacean demon in the social sciences would have to know in order to reduce the complex flow of historical process to predictability. "The state of affairs on Wednesday," he suggests, "depends not only on the state on Tuesday, but also on the state on Monday." Therefore, the requirement for the demon to know "all" about the state of affairs on Wednesday would not be sufficient in itself. The differential equations governing the real socio-historical system would acquire an entirely new order of complexity — Boulding's demon would be faced by "difference equations of an infinite degree." But these are not the only obstacles in the way of a reduction of human history to something like the celestial mechanics of Newton or Laplace. (Undoubtedly, Professor Boulding would agree that some branches of modern physics also have to deal with more complicated systems than that.) Social systems also have "threshold" characteristics in which outputs are triggered only when inputs of a certain value are achieved. Additionally, social systems differ from mechanical systems in that what Boulding calls "images" produce effects upon the dynamics of society. His concept of "self-justifying images" has found many parallel expressions among social scientists and others; Zollschan and his collaborators in Section Two put image-building ("articulation," as they call it) in an even more central place in relation to social change. Boulding's requirement for the social sciences, in the light of these difficulties, may appear quite modest by comparison with the aim of general historical dynamics. He wants a "guide to present action and certain reasonably secure expectations . . . a reasonably accurate measure of possible futures that we can choose among." Those of us who are engaged with him in seeking these ends know that their achievement is a far from trivial task.

A measure of the magnitude of the tasks that lie before the social

*sciences is given by Sosensky in his highly technical philosophical exam-
ination of the problem of "quality" in relation to some sociological concepts. Quality, as Sosensky uses the term, is a measure of incompleteness
or "primitiveness" of a concept. A term is qualitative "when the necessary
and sufficient conditions for the same attribute of different subjects [or
items] cannot be specified." If he is correct in his analysis, then the area
of inchoate quality, as distinct from formal specificity, in sociological
theory is appallingly large. Sosensky applies his logical tools to the dissection of Talcott Parsons and Ralf Dahrendorf. Happily, both these
gentlemen are alive and can be relied upon to defend their theories with
learning, verve, and elan. Whereas the editors, themselves sociologists,
must confess to a sneaking hope that things are not quite as bad as
Sosensky depicts them, a challenge has been issued which no serious
social scientist can afford to ignore. This is particularly welcome at a
time when most outside criticisms of theory in the behavioral sciences
have degenerated into ignorant and frivolous attacks by persons who have
not bothered to read this theory with care. Certainly, no accusation of
carelessness or superficiality could fairly be leveled at Sosensky. The
field is ripe for a new Methodenstreit, and the issue of metaphoric versus
analogic reasoning Sosensky presents sounds far more promising than
the tired old battle between protagonists of begreifen and verstehen.*

*Boulding and Sosensky are concerned with methodological issues to
be faced in dealing with the subject of social change. Martindale's
chapter, while also most sensitive to methodological issues, gives form
and substance to the idea of social change. Beginning with a characterization of the concerns of the subject as "the formation and destruction of
interhuman arrangements," he focuses on the illustration of these processes
in communities, which are viewed as total systems of social life capable
of bringing their members "through the ordinary problems of a single
year and of a single life." Communities are thus distinguished from
groups (existing for the solution of specific problems) and from culture
(systems and congeries of transmitted traits), whose examination is not
taken up by Martindale in this chapter. He distinguishes three processes
significant for the formation of communities: a stabilization of solutions
to collective problems; the development of consistency among these solutions so as to prevent collisions of the different sets of behaviors; and
closure — the lacing of the whole into a viable arrangement. Martindale's cogently and powerfully argued point of view is that communities,
in his own words, "are ways people act; they do not act themselves." This
viewpoint, which Karl Popper has called methodological individualism,
provides a platform from which an attack on both functionalism and historical materialism is launched, and from which a description of transitions from one type of community to another is derived. Martindale discusses transitions from tribal communities to peasant villages, to cities
and bureaucratic empires, to feudal communities or to nation states,*

relating each transition to the emergence of external problems and problems arising in relation to the integration of component groups of each type of community.

The interpretation of social action in terms of problems reacted to by individual persons is very similar to the formulations of the theory of institutionalization which will be described in the introduction to the next Section. Since the latter was developed quite independently of Martindale's work, the convergence of the two approaches is both remarkable and encouraging. These assumptions may not yield an analogue to anything as simple as classical mechanics but, when fully worked out, promise to furnish alternatives to such a system. With the formal development of these assumptions, we hope, the Laplacean demon may finally be laid to rest.

1

K. E. Boulding

The Place of the Image in the

Dynamics of Society[1]

"The dynamics of society" may seem like merely a pretentious way of talking about history. It is, however, history with a difference; history conceived not as narrative or chronicle, not even as a connected story or tale, but history conceived as a system, that is, as a social system with emphasis on regularities and patterns as well as discontinuities and gaps.

Social systems are, of course, very different from physical systems. The difference is so great that some people have denied that social systems exist at all. This would be a confession of intellectual defeat, however, which I am not prepared to make. The patterns of history may be almost infinitely complex but they are patterns. To deny any pattern to history is to deny any possibility of influencing the future, for influence can only come by following the pattern. In this matter of the interpretation of history, we indeed go between Scylla and Charybdis, the one being the council of despair that refuses to find any pattern or system in the ongoing flux of man and society; the other being the self-assured cockiness that sees patterns where they do not in fact exist. Perhaps the latter is in fact the greater danger. The human mind has a craving for patterns. Anarchy and randomness are abhorrent to us and we have a profound tendency to organize the unorganized, whether this is in sense data, in historical sequences, or in the labor market. We must constantly be on our guard, therefore, against inadequate, incomplete,

[1] An earlier form of this chapter was given as an address before the Public Relations Institute, Cornell University, August 10, 1961.

and premature patternings of history. Nevertheless, without patterns, we cannot live and without some interpretation of history, we cannot guide our actions intelligently. Perhaps even a false guide is better than none at all.

The great difference between social and physical systems is that social systems contain information, images, and symbols as essential elements, whereas physical systems can generally be described completely without these variables and aspects. The basic concept of any dynamic system is that of a succession of "states." A state of the system is a complete abstract description of the relevant variables of a system as they exist at a moment in time. It is like a frame on a reel of film. The dynamics of a system consist, in the first place, of the succession of states, as frames succeed one another in a movie. The system can be dynamically described, that is, reduced to "law" if any one state can be deduced in its entirety from a finite number of preceding states. The simplest case, of course, is where the state on any one day bears a constant relation to the state of the previous day — the "day" here being, of course, any arbitrary unit of time. This is what we mean by a difference equation of the first degree. If there is a constant relation between the state of the world on Monday and the state of the world on Tuesday, and if we are given the state of the world on Monday, we can proceed to deduce the state of the world on Tuesday. Then, given the state of the world on Tuesday, we can deduce the state on Wednesday. Thus we can go on indefinitely and project the whole system indefinitely into the future, or for that matter, back into the past.

In difference equations of the second degree, the state of affairs on, let us say, Wednesday, depends not only on the state on Tuesday, but also on the state on Monday. Systems as simple as this are adequate to describe the whole glorious counterpoint of celestial dynamics. It is little wonder that the success of astronomers in predicting celestial events is the envy of all other sciences. When we are looking for systems and patterns in history, therefore, we are looking for something like difference equations, that is, stable relationships between the past and the present. The economist, for instance, looks for a stable relationship between the household expenditure of today and the income of yesterday. This in one form is the consumption function. In social systems, however, we must reckon with the fact that simple dynamic relationships of this kind do not exist in a truly stable form. There may be temporary stabilities which are helpful in short-run predictions; there are, however, virtually no long-run stabilities of a simple order.

We can, indeed, think of human history as determined by difference equations of an infinite degree. Today depends not only on yesterday or even on the day before yesterday, but on all previous yesterdays. A relationship of this complexity is not only too complex to handle but is theoretically incapable of giving prediction. A dynamic system of

an infinite order is one which we are incapable of discovering because the discovery of stable dynamic relationships can only take place if there is experience over a period of time longer than the order of the relationship. We could never hope to discover, for instance, whether the relationship between Monday and Tuesday was stable if our whole experience was limited to these two days. We never, indeed, obtain certainty in our knowledge of these relationships. There is a small probability, as the philosophers have pointed out, that the sun will not rise tomorrow. The probability of the truth of a dynamic relationship, however, increases very rapidly with an increase in the number of cases. If from our observance of the relation between Monday and Tuesday, we venture to predict on Tuesday on the basis of this relationship what will happen on Wednesday, and our prediction is fulfilled, we will be justified in thinking that this might have been an accident. If, however, our prediction is fulfilled also on Thursday, Friday, Saturday, and on a number of succeeding days, confidence in the original law relating yesterday to today will be strongly fortified.

A single disappointment, however, can shatter a law, and in history (that is, in social systems), these disappointments are extremely frequent. To give but a single example, in the United States and indeed in the Western world generally, it was observed that a peak in the price level came roughly in 1815, in 1865, and in 1919. A long cycle of from 50 to 60 years called the Kondratiev, was postulated on this experience. On the basis of this observation in the *Encyclopedia of the Social Sciences* about 1934, the very distinguished economist, John R. Commons, predicted that prices would continue to fall until 1952, after which they would rise again. Needless to say, this prediction was very far from the truth and it is apparent today that the Kondratiev was largely an accident. To give another example, Mr. Sewell Avery of Montgomery Ward on the basis of the experience of 1919–1920, expected a sharp depression after the end of the second World War. In this expectation, he was disappointed at considerable cost to the corporation which he directed.

The difference between social and physical systems is not confined to the complexity and order of the difference or differential equations which govern them. Social systems are characterized by at least two other peculiarities which differentiate them very sharply from simple physical systems, such as celestial mechanics. The first characteristic is the predominance of "threshold" systems in which small causes can sometimes produce very large consequences. The second characteristic is that social systems are what I call "image-directed," that is, there are systems in which the knowledge of the systems themselves is a significant part of the system's own dynamics and in which, therefore, knowledge about the system changes the system.

In view of the fact that social systems are the creation of the human organism, and especially of the human nervous system, it is not surprising to find that the closest analogue to the threshold quality of social systems is to be found in the neural networks of the human nervous system. The essential element of a threshold system is something like a neuron — an element which has inputs and outputs but in which the output depends upon the sum of the inputs reaching a certain threshold. It would be more accurate to say that some function of the inputs must reach a certain threshold as the function does not have to be simply additive. As long as the threshold is not reached an addition to input produces no output whatever. The moment the threshold is reached, there is an output. In the case of the neuron as far as we know, this output is fairly standardized. We can, however, postulate elements of as great complexity as we wish. A system of this kind is represented in Figure 1 where the square boxes represent "neurons" or threshold elements. The number in each box is the "height" of its threshold elements. Thus, suppose we assume that each of the threshold elements of Row 1 receive 20 units of input. Only Element A will "fire." It will produce an output of 20 which it will pass along the lines marked by the arrows to the next row of threshold elements. As will be seen from the figure, only Element C in Row 2 will fire, and the process will again pass along the lines marked by the arrows to the third row of elements. In this row, both

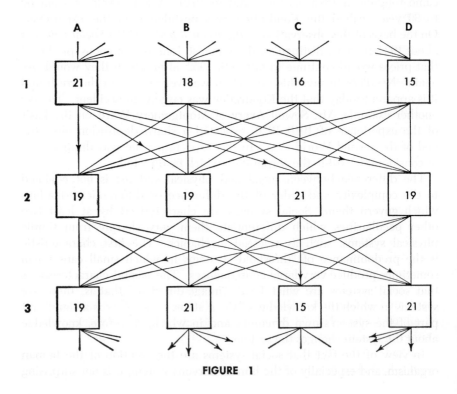

FIGURE 1

Elements B and D will fire, which may mean, of course, that still more elements will fire in Row 4 when this is reached.

It is obvious that systems of this kind are very complex, although some of their properties have been explored by the mathematical biologists. These are systems in which, if I dare quote Browning,

> Oh, the little more and how much it is
> And the little less, and what worlds away!

It was for the loss of a nail, we remember in the nursery rhyme, that the kingdom was lost. There are times in history when a very small change in output can cause one threshold unit to fire which otherwise would not have fired and the whole course of history is changed. It is this among other things which makes prediction so difficult in the social sciences. If we are to be able to predict in social systems, we must know a good deal about the thresholds of the threshold units involved. Unfortunately, this information is often very hard to come by. The higher the threshold, the harder it is to find out where it is. The elements that correspond to neurons in the neural network are, of course, persons in the social system; the firing of a neuron corresponds to the decision of a person — a decision, that is to say, is output of some kind, usually of communication or of information, which follows from the cumulative result of a number of past inputs. These outputs result only, however, when the past inputs accumulate over some threshold. Where the thresholds are low, the behavior is repetitive and easy to find out about. Every morning, for instance, men stagger into the bathroom and shave. This is a very low-level decision. In fact, some people deny the name of decision to these habitual reactions. However, there is input in the shape of the alarm clock and the information which reaches us from our physical surroundings and this is sufficient to carry us over the threshold of behavior. It may be, indeed, that on Saturday morning, the threshold is not reached and we do not shave.

The situation is further complicated in social systems by the fact that the decisions of different persons have different weights. In Figure 1, I have supposed all the threshold elements to be equal in the sense that each one is connected with the next set by an equal number of lines of communication. In social systems, this is not true. There are some elements which are connected to very many others, other elements connected to only a few. The decisions of a sharecropper in Mississippi or a shoeshine boy in New York are communicated to a very small circle of other persons. The decisions of a Kennedy or a Khrushchev are communicated to hundreds of millions of people and may affect the lives of all of them. This is because communication in social systems is neither a uniform nor a random effort but is organized into role structures and organizations. An organization, in fact, has been defined as a set of roles linked by lines of communication.

At this point there are two extreme views of the nature of social systems between which we have to pick our way. On the one hand, there is the purely mechanical view that the nature of a role occupant is quite unimportant and that the decision is determined by the role structure itself. The course of history in this view is determined by great impersonal social forces and the actual decisions of the decision-maker, no matter how exalted, are relatively unimportant. At the other extreme, we have the "great man" theory of history in which the decision of those placed in powerful roles is regarded as all-important and history is written largely in terms of the character and peculiarity of kings, dictators, generals, and prophets. Karl Marx may be regarded as representative of the one extreme and perhaps Thomas Carlyle of the other.

The truth clearly lies somewhere between these two extreme positions. Exactly where it lies, however, is hard to say. We can certainly distinguish large and apparently impersonal forces which operate on the dynamics of social systems. Such things as changes in climate, the discovery of new lands, the accumulation of knowledge and skill, and the growth of population seem at times to be almost independent of the human will. In what Baumol has called "the magnificent dynamics" of the classical economics there is little place for individual decision. In the Malthusian system, for instance, if we once accept the initial premise that the only effective check on the growth of population is starvation and misery, then no matter how grandiose our images or how reasonable our decisions the end is the same. We may illustrate this perhaps in Figure 2. If the system of decision points is triangular in the sense that the number of decision points continually declines in the course of time, then no matter what the path of the system, it all follows down to the same end. It cannot be doubted that systems of this kind exist. It is also clear, however, that the social system of mankind as a whole, up to the present rate, has not been a system of this kind. If anything, indeed, it is a reverse triangle; that is, the number of decision points continually increases with time so that the system becomes less and less determinate in a mechanical sense, hence, the path becomes more and more important.

We now come to the second great peculiarity of social systems, which is that they are to a considerable extent determined by the images we have of them and the knowledge we have about them. They are, that is to say, in part image-determined. It is very important to say "in part" image-determined because there are mechanical elements, independent of the image, of great importance in any social system and we neglect these at our peril. I recall an old Peter Arno cartoon of a very jolly party in an airplane which is about to crash into a cliff, the caption being "My God, we're out of gin!" The future of that small social system could be deduced from its physical environment quite independently of any images of its own future which it might possess. Social systems, therefore, are always mixed systems in the sense that they combine both the

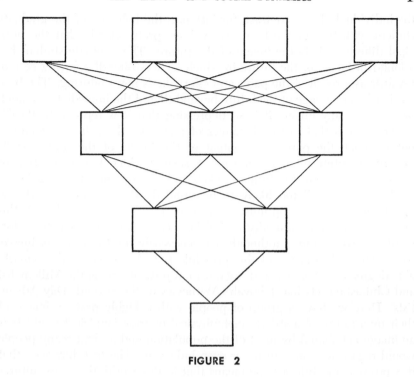

FIGURE 2

mechanical and image-determined elements. One may venture a guess that as the knowledge of society increases, the image-determined elements in social systems becomes more important. That is, as I said in my book, *The Image* (1), there is a strong tendency for the latent to become manifest. Man begins with an image of a world which has really very little to do with his actual environment or the actual system in which he lives. To some extent, these images may be self-reinforcing and where this is the case, he does not change them easily. It occasionally happens, however, that he is disappointed and is aware of his disappointments and, under these circumstances, there may be a change in the image towards "reality." I would rather leave the question of what is meant by reality to another time, or even to another person. Our common-sense notions, however, that some images may be truer than others, are probably not wholly illusory.

Even images which are in some sense false, however, produce marked effects upon the dynamics of society. Dr. Fred Polak in his great book, *The Image of the Future* (2), has brought together an impressive array of historical evidence to indicate that one of the major elements, perhaps indeed the most important single element, which governs the dynamics of particular societies is the nature of the image of the future which prevails in them. One might even extend this concept to the behavior of the individual. If we contrast, for instance, the behavior of the graduate student with that of the bum, we will see pretty clearly that the principal difference is in the image of the future. The graduate student has a long-run image of the future in which he sees himself enjoying certain rewards as a result of the pains and efforts he is now enduring. The bum has hardly any image of the future beyond that of the immediate moment, or if he has any image, it is so depressing that it is repressed. Polak's major point is that in the dynamics of a society, the principal factor is not so much the particular content of the image of the future as its quality of optimism or pessimism. A society which has a negative or pessimistic image of the future is likely to be disorganized and its image of the future is all too likely to be fulfilled. On the other hand, the society which has an optimistic image of the future, even though this image may be quite unrealistic, will be well organized and will go forward into some future, although not necessarily the future of its image. An excellent illustration of this principle is to be found in the remarkable degree of coherence and organization present among the Millenialist and Chiliastic sects like Jehovah's Witnesses or the Seventh Day Adventists. Here we have a group of people with a highly positive image of their own future of a strictly metaphysical or trans-empirical kind. It is an image not shared by most of the population and a great many people would regard it as unrealistic or even ludicrous. The fact, however, that it is positive and full of hope means that in this world, these subcultures are well organized and, in fact, move toward a positive and desirable future even in this world, in spite of the fact that their basic image of the future is other-worldly. The strength of the Communists likewise depends upon their having a highly positive image of the future. This does not differ so much from that of the Millenialist as we might think. Even though the golden future of the Communist image is ostensibly in this world, it is so remote that it might just as well be in another.

Examples of self-justifying images of the future are very common in economic life. It is a commonplace of economics that if everybody expects a rise in prices, everybody will act so as to bring the rise in prices about, and the same goes for the expectation of falling prices. If most businessmen expect a depression, they are likely to behave in such a way as to bring it about. If there is a general expectation of economic development, this is also an important element in bringing it about. And, by contrast, if people have a strong impression that any attempt to better their own position will fail, they are likely to be apathetic and unwilling to exert themselves in new enterprises. The general level of aspiration of the people, as many writers have pointed out, is perhaps the largest single element in the psychological substratum of economic development. In a slightly different area, the expectations of war and peace, likewise, are frequently self-justified. Where we have two countries such as the United States and Canada which are genuinely at peace in the sense that not even the threat of war is used as an instrument in their relationship, the total absence of the expectation of war justifies itself. There are no preparations for war and virtually no possibility of war. On the other hand, the strong expectation of war almost invariably produces it, for this leads to an arms race, which eventually leads to an intolerable situation in which one side or the other precipitates overt conflict.

A question of great importance is the extent to which men's images can be deliberately manipulated and hence, insofar as images determine the future, the future itself can be manipulated. The "cause" of our images is to be found in our total experience. The growth of the image follows a process which is related to biological growth. It is, however, very different from biological growth in the sense that is peculiarly subject to symbolic changes. This is the prime difference between man and the lower animals. The lower animals undoubtedly have images and they may even have dreams. These images, however, are derived from direct experience and are not derived from symbols about experience. A dog can have an image of chasing a rabbit after he has once chased one; he can never derive an image of chasing a rabbit from hearing someone talk about it or reading about it in a book. A human being, by contrast, can derive images of things of which he has no direct personal experience. I have never been to Australia but I have read about it and as a result I have a fairly clear image of what it is like. If I went to Australia I am sure there are some things which would surprise me, for the image derived from symbols is never quite as vivid or as accurate as the image derived from direct experience. I would, however, be very surprised if I was very surprised. It is the essentially symbolic nature of the human image which dominates the social system. It is this which makes human history so profoundly different from any other record of events or any other temporal system. Because of this, the image-makers are a profoundly significant element in society when it comes to the interpretation of social dynamics. These are the writers, the preachers, the teachers, the politicians, the orators — and even the advertising and public relations men!

It is easy to acknowledge the importance of the role of the image-maker in society; it is not so easy to understand or to assess it. The difficulty here is that we are dealing with symbolic systems and these are systems we understand very little. We are unquestionably dealing with threshold systems of a kind, but we do not really know what the inputs and outputs are and we know even less about what determines and constitutes the thresholds themselves. What is it for instance, that gives a symbol power? Duns Scotus "fired France for Mary without spot" and the Virgin, as Henry Adams saw so clearly, built some of the greatest monuments of the human spirit. A Middle-western Protestant of 1961 is not similarly fired. Under the sign of the crescent, the Arabs almost conquered the world, and shifted the center of civilization from the Mediterranean toward the Persian Gulf. I must confess that the Koran which moved so many, moves me very little and I find it hard to enter even by the gates of empathy into an experience that is at the same time so profound and so remote. Now it is nationalism and communism that seem to fire men to devotion and action. Tomorrow, these, too, may seem hollow and unrewarding.

The problem is that the image is not merely an aggregate of information, it is a structure — a structure, moreover, of great complexity and many dimensions. Its complexity is so great that there is a powerful urge to simplify it, and the symbol is the simplification of the image. A symbol, that is, is something which stands for or evokes an image of much greater complexity than its literal self. At a common-place, statistical level, we see it in such concepts as the price level, which reduces a massive list of individual prices to a single number. Similarly the flag invokes a complex and emotionally rich image of national history and the cross invokes a similar rich image of Christian experience, martyrdom, and doctrine. Our image is as frequently clarified and made more powerful as a spring of action by the loss of information as it is by the gain. We have, for instance, a profound tendency to try to reduce a multi-dimensional reality to a single linear dimension. We have a strong urge, for instance, to reduce the almost infinitely dimensioned variety of the human character to a single dimension of good and bad. Even worse, we set up a point on this continuum and divide all mankind into two boxes — the good guys and the bad guys, the right people and the wrong people, the ins and the outs, the good families and the riff-raff, the free world and the Communists, the whites and the negroes. The stereotyping of the image inevitably leads to a loss which can sometimes even be measured in economic terms. The trouble with discrimination is that it is undiscriminating — that is, it discriminates according to an unreal and false set of criteria.

We must, however, at least be modestly humble at this point. There is no litmus paper of truth. There is no simple way of identifying the truth of the image. In theory, indeed, there is no way at all, for images can only be compared with images; they can never be compared with reality. In practice, I think there is a certain skill at truth, and the least we can say is that a demand for it produces a certain supply. One suspects, perhaps, that the main difficulty with the provision of truth is the absence of demand, rather than any basic inelasticity in the supply.

When one thinks of the image-makers, one thinks also, unfortunately, of lies. And the question arises, therefore, what is the power of a lie in determining a course of the dynamics of a society. Goebbels believed, of course, that the bigger the lie, the more often and the more loudly it was shouted, the better chance it had of being believed. There is, unfortunately, a certain amount of evidence to justify this hypothesis. On the other hand, truth has a certain advantage which the lie does not. The lie may be found out, whereas the truth cannot. That is, the lie cannot be found to be a truth and the truth cannot be found to be a lie.

The lie, that is to say, can only be justified within the symbolic system — it cannot be justified outside it in the cold school of hard experience. I think, therefore, that we are justified in assuming a certain "outability" of truth and that Lincoln's favorite aphorism that you can't fool all of the people all of the time is ultimately truer than Goebbel's belief.

One circumstance, however, must require withdrawal at least in part of the optimism of the previous paragraph. When the image is self-justifying, what does it mean to say that it is true or false? In a world of fairy wishing-caps what would happen to the truth? This is a real problem and one stands, indeed, on the edge of an abyss — the abyss of fairyland — a horror where all dreams are true and in which, therefore, there is no truth. The only escape from this nightmare, I think, is the faith that images are self-justified only in the short run. The belief that prices are going to rise may cause prices to rise for a while, but not forever. Eventually, the underlying reality of the world must impose itself on the self-justifying realities of the image. It is a very real problem in social organization, however, as to how we defend ourselves against self-justifying images. These may only be justified in the short run, but the short run can be a desperately long space of time. To paraphrase Lincoln again, we can fool too many of the people too much of the time. The record of history is full of great expectations that were self-justified for a while but which eventually were disappointments.

I may seem at this point almost to be arguing for the mechanical interpretations of social systems which are so attractive in their seeming objectivity, and so free from the corruption of dreams. The image of the social system as mechanical, however, is itself a retreat from reality, for social reality is more complex than any mechanical system can possibly describe. Mechanical views of history, like those of Marx, are therefore likely to lead to results that are as perverse and dangerous as those which stem from the efforts of the liar, the propagandist, and the deliberate perverter of the truth. The Communists are certainly better intentioned than the Nazis, but they may have caused just as great a sum of human misery, and even the most selfless efforts of Christian missionaries have occasionally accomplished disintegration and disaster for the societies which they have influenced. What I am pleading for, therefore, is not a return to clear — and therefore false — mechanical views of history, it is rather that we should dedicate ourselves to a long, slow task, the task of developing true images of social systems, true in the sense that they conform to the nature of man himself and to his potentialities — which I believe are greater than any that we have yet brought to light. They should be true also in the sense of giving us skill in the handling of our society. I do not believe that I have ever asked of the image of a social system that it would enable us to foretell the future. It is not too much to ask of such an image, however, that it give us a guide to present action and certain reasonably secure conditional expectations. What we ask from the image is a reasonably accurate measure of

possible futures that we can choose among. I do not believe either that
we are a helpless pawn of destiny or that we are the masters of our fate.
The truth lies somewhere in between. We have real choices, but the
choices are within a limited menu. The menu perhaps grows longer all
the time, but it is always limited. It should be the great business of the
science of society to learn the limits of this menu — to learn what we cannot have as well as what we can have, and hence, to guide our choice
into those areas which are not only desirable, but realizable.

The most important property of man's image, however, is his ability
to change it. Without this, we may be trapped in images which are
self-reinforcing even though they are not self-justifying. The image,
that is to say, is reinforced in defiance of experience. It is the skill of
learning which is the greatest hope of the human race. It is the will to
learn which is its greatest question mark. If the image-maker conceives
his role as that of the printer, printing his image upon the plastic minds
of mankind, then he betrays his function as a teacher. For the teacher
is not an imprinter; he is one who cooperates with the inward teacher,
the will to learn, the mysterious inner forces of growth and development
of the image within the personality of the individual. Unless there is a
basic respect for the individual image, the image-maker, whether preacher,
politician, writer, ad-man, or even professor, becomes the mere propagandist who may actually destroy the tender buds of true knowledge and
so help to imprison mankind behind the terrible walls of false images. It
may be true that man has mostly lived in these prisons — prisons of
superstition, magic, ideology, priest-craft, party lines, and thought control. But I believe he was not made to be so imprisoned; it is for this
hope that man can and must break out of his image prisons into that
"free world" of the future for which we think he was made and toward
which his potentialities impel him. In this world there is only one loyalty,
loyalty to the truth. It is a difficult and painful loyalty to possess, especially in a world that recognizes it so little. In this loyalty, however,
there lies, it seems to me, the only image of the future which is truly
creative, and it is a future which we do not wholly have to wait to enjoy.
No man, I think, in this world can live wholly free from lies but he can
love the truth and direct the current of his mind and life towards it. If
this sounds like moralizing, I will not deny it; I would only point out that
values are an essential part of the image and constitute, indeed, that
aspect of it which is most influential in affecting behavior and the dynamic course of society.

BIBLIOGRAPHY

1. Boulding, Kenneth E. *The Image.* Ann Arbor: University of Michigan
   Press, 1956.
2. Polak, Fred L. *The Image of the Future,* translated by Elise Boulding.
   New York: Oceana, 1961.

2

Irving Sosensky

The Problem of Quality in Relation

to Some Issues in Social Change[1]

PART 1

The problem of social change, referred to in the title of this volume
and the proposed titles of its chapters, is reminiscent of the earliest formulations of philosophic problems; the titles suggest not merely "change,"
but what does not change while change goes on, i.e., what is referred to
as the "problem of permanence and change." There are various senses
in which "permanence" and "change" can — and have, in the history of
thought — been taken. Aristotle's notions of Substance and Being with
their attendant notions of Actuality and Potentiality represent one kind
of conceptual structuring; Galileo's formulation of the law of free fall as
a proportion between the units of time and the squares of the units of
distance (the units of distance change while the units of time are permanent) represents another. Other formulations may be indicated but
they all entail the question of identity and difference, a distinction whose
vintage is about the same as those of "permanence" and "change," which
will provide us with our conception of quality.

[1] I gratefully acknowledge help from the following: Professor A. C. Benjamin of
the University of Missouri and Professor R. F. Grabau of Purdue University both
criticized an earlier draft of Part I and provided invaluable suggestions; Professor
W. L. Rowe of Purdue University read the present version of Part I and was extremely
helpful; Professors George Zollschan and Walter Hirsch of Purdue University were
uncommonly stimulating and generous with their time; the Purdue Research Foundation awarded me a grant for the summer of 1959 to pursue my interest in "quality."
All instances of error and obscurity are my sole responsibility.

"Quality," if anything, has had more philosophic senses than "permanance" and "change." For Aristotle, quality was "That in virtue of which" something was classified in a certain way; for Locke it meant "power"; for Russell it meant sense-data; for Dewey it was the ineffable and unique; and so on. The non-philosophic occurrences of "quality" are more ubiquitous: it bears on value, standards of workmanship, the *je ne sais quoi* of women, paintings, scenes in the theatre and natural scenery, property (in the sense of "property of a thing"), feelings, and so on. Nevertheless, a certain substratum of sense seems to perdure through all of them. We want to clarify that first.

We shall want to say that logic is irrelevant to quality. To the extent that an issue is determinable by logic, it is non-qualitative; and conversely, to the extent that one is purely in the realm of "quality," it is a realm to which "logic" is unfitted. No logical rule or law can decide issues we shall refer to as "qualitative," although, quality once having been decided, "logic" has to do with sentences about it.

A

Aristotle's law of non-contradiction stated that "the same attribute cannot at the same time belong and not belong to the same subject in the same respect." He held that it is a necessary truth about everything that is. Recently (17, pp. 57–58) it was argued that it does not formulate factual descriptions, empirically or ontologically. In the following way, an objector to the law argues:

> A penny can be said to be sensibly both circular and non-circular; therefore the law of non-contradiction is not a necessary truth about that fact, since this is a violation of the law.

A defender of the law then replies:

> True, but that is in different respects; in the same respect, that is, when the penny is perpendicular at its center to the eye's line of sight, the penny is not sensibly both circular and non-circular. The law is therefore not violated.

The objector, however, may press:

> But within that respect, we may say that a line drawn from the surface of the eye at the point where the line of sight meets it to a point on the edge of the penny both subtends and does not subtend an angle of 30 degrees. The law is therefore violated.

The defender again replies:

> True, but not in the same respect; at a given distance, in that respect, the angle subtended is not both 30 degrees and not 30 degrees.

Two things are noteworthy. First, if the law of non-contradiction is a factual truth, then appeal to the same fact should suffice for its defense. Thus, if anyone were to question the law of gravity by citing a case in which a body attracted to another did not move according to the law of inverse squares, a defender of the law of gravity would point to extraneous changing forces being exerted on the body in the course of its movement, citing the principle of the composition of forces as a reason why the movement of the body in question constitutes merely an apparent violation of the law. The only recourse of the objector would be to show that the defender's evidence is wrong, i.e., that the facts appealed to are really not facts at all. If the objector is wrong, then the defender's appeal suffices, unless the objector cites other facts. But this argument cannot go on indefinitely, for at some point there must be agreement as to what constitutes the relevant facts. But in the argument over the law of non-contradiction, no such agreement can ever be reached, for as soon as a defender cites a respect, the objector can find another apparent violation, and there is no "fact" which will hold as a criterion in the face of all objections.

Second, since there is no fact to which the protagonists can appeal, and there is no other principle analogous to the principle of the composition of forces, it follows that the only place we may look for that to which the defender of the law of non-contradiction may appeal is the principle itself, and this turns out to be the case.

For in order to say whether the penny is either sensibly circular or non-circular, one must first decide what is either sensible or non-sensible; that is, the law of non-contradiction is implicit before applying it to the case; had it not been so, it would not have been applicable. At each challenge the defender must proceed the same way: to decide the penny's sensible circularity, he must decide what is line and non-line, perpendicular and non-perpendicular, center of the eye and non-center of the eye, and so on. The "respect" constitutes the formulation of the total set of conditions which provide for the distinction between the sensibly circular and non-circular. It is implied in the use of "respect" by the defender as a criterion in order to establish itself.

Analogous comments may be made about relations, for which attributes may be regarded as a special case. Of two posts placed on a north-south line, we may say that each is both to the right and left of the other; to which it may be replied that this is not so in the same respect, i.e., not from the same side of the line. Each is both darker and lighter than the other but not in the same respect, i.e., if the light intensity remains constant, and so on. Being on a side or non-side, being on the left or non-left, and being x light intensity or non-x intensity depend on the prior use of the law of non-contradiction.

The foregoing argument is used to demonstrate that the law of non-contradiction is a rule relevant to the formation of sentences about things but does not describe things. The point here is not what the argument is directed for or against, but that it illustrates the meaning of "respect," "attribute," and "subject."

Which of these is crucial to our point may be discovered by changing the strategy of the encounter.

> Objector: A penny is sensibly both circular and non-circular.
> Defender: It is not both in the same respect.
> Objector: In what respect?
> Defender: In the respect that the penny is perpendicular at its center to the line of sight.
> Objector: But a line drawn from the surface of the eye at the point at which the line of sight meets it to the edge of the penny both subtends and does not subtend an angle of 30 degrees with the line of sight.
> Defender: Not in the same respect.
> Objector: In what respect?

And so on. The key term is "respect." An analysis of its usage reveals two distinct relevant definitions:

1) P_i is a respect if it is the only member of a class K of attributes P_1, $P_2, \ldots, P_n$, that is an attribute of the subject S, and A is an attribute of S if P_i is.

For example: in the discussion of the penny, the class K of attributes $P_1, P_2, \ldots, P_n$, is the class of angles at which the line of sight intersects the center of the surface of the penny; the respect P_i is a member of the class K, i.e., the perpendicularity of the line of sight to the surface of the penny at the center; A is the circularity; S is the penny. If the penny is perpendicular to the line of sight at the center (P_i), then the penny (S) appears sensibly circular (A).

Again, "A man is healthy in respect of the functioning of his organs": S is the man: A is "healthy": K is the class $P_1, P_2, \ldots, P_n$: of possible ways in which the organs can function; if they function in a certain way (P_i), then the man (S) is healthy (A).

2) A is a respect if it is an attribute of a subject S, and S is a member of a class of subjects C which A partly specifies.

For example: "A person is a man in respect of courage." The person, S, is a member of the class C of men in respect of the attribute A of courage. The attribute "courage" partly specifies the class of men in this sense (i.e., the moral sense). To specify the class completely, we have to add a number of other respects, such as maturity, judgment, etc. Then we have a number of respects, i.e., a person is a man in respect of maturity, in respect of judgment, etc.: the person is a member of the class of men in *these* respects.

Again, "A person is psychiatrically normal." A person, S, is a member of the class C of normal people, in respect of psychiatric considerations, A. "Psychiatric considerations" partly specifies the class C of normal people, which would be comprised of all those who are medically normal, socially normal, psychiatrically normal, etc. Finally, "A man is intelligent entrepreneurially." A man, S, is a member of the class C of intelligent people in respect of entrepreneurial activities, A. "Entrepreneurial" partly specifies the class of intelligent people, which is comprised of those who are intellectually intelligent, socially intelligent, etc.

We shall refer to definition (1) as the P-respect and definition (2) as the A-respect. The P-respect formulates the necessary and sufficient conditions for the attribute A. For example, we may say that if the penny is perpendicular at its center to the line of sight, then it is sensibly circular, but we can also say that if the penny is sensibly circular, it is perpendicular at its center to the line of sight.

Moreover, an examination of the relations between "subject," "attribute," and "respect" indicates that other employment than that made in the law of non-contradiction, i.e., the *same* subject, the *same* attribute, and the *same* respect, may be considered. We talk about two attributes of the same respect, or one attribute of the same subject in different respects, and so on. Under such circumstances comparison is introduced. Thus, to say that the two subjects S and S' are different in a certain respect is to say one of two things: (1) they have different attributes A and A' if P_i is the only member of a class K of attributes that is an attribute of S and S' (e.g., two coins, S and S', may have the attributes "sensible circularity" (A) and "sensible ellipticity" (A') in respect of their surfaces being perpendicular at the center of the line of sight, P_i, an attribute which is the only member of the class K of angles at which the line of sight may intersect the surface of the coins at the center, $P_1, P_2, \ldots P_n$.); (2) S has a different attribute than S' and both attributes (A and A' respectively) partly define the class C (e.g., S may be a person who has judgment (A) and S' a person who has courage (A'); both attributes partly define the class C of being a "man" in the "moral" sense). But a further discussion of these considerations must be postponed until we discuss sameness and likeness.

B

There are domains where sameness and likeness overlap, and there are domains in which one is applicable and the other is not.

That "sameness" is used under varying circumstances is most firmly attested to by various formulations. Thus,

1) Identity: If JFK is identical with the present President of the United States, then JFK and the present president of the United States are the same.

2) Class: If unmarried mature women are spinsters and vice versa, then the classes are the same.

3) Attribute: If James and Michael are both six feet tall, they both have the same attribute.

4) Class of attributes: If the attributes defining "material object" are the same as the attributes defining "body," then the classes of attributes are the same.

5) Relations: If a is to the right of b, and c is to the right of d, then a bears the same relation to b that c does to d.

6) Classes of relations: If the class of comparative sizes is the class of greater than, less than, and equal to, and vice versa, then each of the two classes is the same.

7) "Sameness" occurs where neither class nor attribute is specified. An example is G. E. Moore's "good," which is "simple" and "unanalyzable," and of which two cases would be said to be the "same," though one could not immediately specify a class of attributes by which they could be said to be "the same."

"Likeness" must be distinguished from "sameness."

1) a is like b if a and b are members of the same class.

2) "Likeness" has to do with including two classes in the same class. The class of cats and the class of dogs are included in the class of animals and are said to be "alike."

3) If two subjects have the same attribute they are said to be alike.

4) "Likeness" is used when two subject-matters have some attributes in common, but not others. Thus, Torricelli introduced the "sea of air" concept, calling attention to the common attributes of water and air. Both have pressure or weight, both are relatively homogeneous, and so on. Nevertheless, they are not the same, for all their attributes are not the same. In this case, we use "likeness" or "similarity" as one does in the case of the dog and cat.

5) There is a sense of likeness which involves neither class nor attribute, e.g., when we speak of "bottling up our emotions": where the likeness suggested is between a bottle containing a liquid and a person "confining" his emotions.

Likeness (4) is the point at which "likeness" and "sameness" overlap. It is often argued that if two subjects are members of the same class, or have the same attribute, they are "the same." But, because in certain respects the subjects are members of the same class and in others they are not, it is clear that the locution "same" is out of place, and "likeness" or "similarity" is apropos. We shall use "same in a given respect" or "same in given respects" as equivalent to "like" or "similar" when it is understood that more than one attribute is relevant to a subject.

C

If a is to the right of b, and c is to the right of d, we speak of a having the same relation to b that c does to d. We speak of "being to the right of" and "being to the left of" as being relations that are "alike" or "similar," i.e., they are "the same in given respects": they may be described as "directional relations," in the same class of relations. If we speak of the "higher" and "lower" notes of the musical scale, we also say that these are "similar" to "directional" relations; but "right" and "left" are alike in a way that "higher" and "lower" notes and "directional" relations are not. The former are analogous and the latter are metaphorical.

An analogy can be spoken of with clarity if we specify the respect in which the analogy holds. A telephone relay system is analogous to a traffic system: electrical impulses enter and leave the telephone system, autos enter and leave the traffic system; a switch holds up the current, the traffic officer holds up the traffic. In each case we may speak of the same relations. But the traffic system has certain relations that the telephone system hasn't: a driver may be arrested.

Or, consider the analogy:

The kidney is the filter of the body.

That it is an analogy implies that there is a comparison; therefore the attributes of each kind must be listed:

The kidney has the following attributes: it is composed of biochemical matter; blood moves through it; it is connected to a system of blood vessels; it has chemicals which eliminate the impurities from the blood; it is a permanent fixture of its system and is never replaced; it is located in a certain place; it has a certain shape.

The filter of a mechanical system has the following attributes: it is metallic in composition; oil or some other fluid necessary to the operation of the mechanical system flows through it; it is connected to a system of pipes or tubes; it has a wire mesh which eliminates the impurities in the oil or other fluid; though it performs a permanent function within the system it must be replaced intermittently; it has a certain shape; it is in a certain place.

We began with an analogy, and "analogy" means "proportion," so the original proposition may be formulated:

The kidney is to the body as filter is to the mechanical system.

Or,

The relation the kidney bears to the body is like the relation the filter bears to the mechanical system.

We may ask:

In what respect?

That this question is permissible shows that the preceding indicative sentence may be formulated:

> The relation the kidney bears to the body is the same as the relation the filter bears to the mechanical system *in given respects.*

The same question may be repeated, and the reply is:

> The kidney bears the same relation to the body that the filter does to a mechanical system in the respects that: both the kidney and the filter trap impurities; fluids move through them; both are connected to a system comprised of tubes, and so on.

"Two things are the same in given respects," then, is the same as "two things have some of the same attributes." In a comparison, "same attribute" has the force that it has in the law of non-contradiction. Therefore, to list the attributes in respect of which the kidney and the filter of a mechanical system is a filter is to list the A-respects.

But there are respects in which they are different. Thus:

> The relation a kidney bears to an animal is unlike the relation a filter bears to a mechanical system.

The same question is permissible; and the reply:

> The relation the kidney bears to the animal body is unlike the relation the filter bears to the mechanical system in the respects that: the kidney gets rid of its impurities and the filter of the mechanical system does not; the filter of the mechanical system must be replaced, and the kidney need not; and so on.

The statement of an analogy requires the formulation of both likenesses and unlikenesses.

But a different strategy may be employed. Instead of listing the A-respects in which the subjects are alike, we select the A-respect in which both subjects are alike and then proceed to ask in which respect the A-respects are alike. The result is a P-respect, thus:

> In what respects is the attribute "trapping impurities" of the kidney the same as the attribute "trapping impurities" of the filter of the mechanical system?

To which the reply is:

> They are the same in the respect that both separate those objects which, if allowed to continue through the system, would render it inefficient.

In what respect would each of the systems be rendered inefficient?

> Each system would be rendered less efficient in the respects that their expected tasks would be performed less rapidly or less precisely, and that more energy would be required for the performance of the tasks.

And so on.

"Trapping impurities" is an A-respect of the filter; it is also an A-respect of the kidney. But asking for the respect in which the A-respect "trapping impurities" of the kidney is like the A-respect "trapping impurities" of the filter is to try to provide a respect in which they are alike, that is, a P-respect. The respect in which "trapping impurities" of the kidney and "trapping impurities" of the mechanical filter are alike is that both the kidney and the filter separate those objects which, if allowed to continue through the system, would render it inefficient. But "separating those objects which, if allowed to continue through the system would render it inefficient" specifies the necessary and sufficient conditions for "trapping impurities." Therefore, we may state:

> If the kidney traps impurities, then it separates those objects which, if allowed to continue through the system, would render the system inefficient.

and

> If the kidney separates those objects which, if allowed to continue through the system, would render the system inefficient, then it traps impurities.

also

> If the filter traps impurities, then it separates those objects which, if allowed to continue through the system, would render the system inefficient.

and

> If the filter separates those objects which, if allowed to continue through the system, would render the system inefficient, then it traps impurities.

Since the same attributes bear the same relations to each other in both cases, it would follow that:

> If the kidney and the filter of the mechanical system trap impurities, then both separate those objects which, if allowed to continue through the system, would render it inefficient.

and

> If both the kidney and the filter of the mechanical system separate those

objects which, if allowed to continue through the system would render it inefficient, they both trap impurities.

What is referred to in the first sentence is the necessary and sufficient condition of that which is referred to in the second.

Nevertheless, each time another respect is asked for, a factual answer can be given. This is not always true of different senses of a word; it is never true of genuine metaphors.

D

Words in a language sometimes mean the same thing and sometimes mean different things. *Prima facie,* it would appear that when the same word "has different meanings," those meanings are analogous in the sense that "kidney" and "filter of a mechanical system" are analogous; but this is not always true.

"Touchstone" originally referred to a piece or block of quartz (named "basanite") easily kept fairly smooth and used to determine how much gold was present in a gold alloy. The following method was used: a piece of alloy whose proportions of gold and other metals was unknown was scratched against a surface of basanite, leaving a streak. The color of this streak was compared to the color of a streak produced by an alloy of known composition, and the expert could tell how much gold was in the unknown alloy. For example, a yellow streak meant more gold; a reddish streak meant more copper.

"Touchstone" is used in other ways, as may be seen from the following quotes from Clive Bell and William Hazlitt: ". . . an original work is the touchstone that exposes educated taste masquerading as sensibility"; and ". . . well digested schemes will stand the touchstone of experience." Another use occurs in a proverb: "Men have a touchstone whereby to try gold, but gold is the touchstone whereby to try men." If we consider the original use and this last use of "touchstone," we would be tempted to say, I think, that the two uses entail different meanings, like "cat" and "concept," but we don't really want to say this, so we use the locution "having different senses," and suggest that there is some connection, unlike "cat" and "concept." We want to say:

Sense *A* (the basanite) is like sense *B* (the gold). But how are they alike? *Prima facie,* the comparison urges that this is an analogy, so, stating the matter as a proportion:

The touchstone is to gold as gold is to men.

Which may then be re-stated:

Touchstone bears the same relation to gold that gold does to men.

And again the question:

> In what respect?

The answer:

> The touchstone tries gold and gold tries men.

And we ask:

> In what respect is the trying of gold by the touchstone like the trying of men by gold?

We propose, in answer:

> In the respect that the touchstone tests gold and gold tests men.

But we are puzzled by "tests"; in what respects are *they* alike? The answer:

> The touchstone "determines the value" of gold, and gold "determines the value" of men.

Yet there is something wrong, for the touchstone does not determine the value of the gold, but of the gold alloy; and presumably it determines its value by determining the proportion of the gold in the alloy. The proverb is confusing. But suppose that the intended phrase is not "gold" but "gold alloy." Then the last comparison reads:

> The touchstone determines the value of the gold alloy, and gold determines the value of men.

Then we ask:

> In what respect?

The answer does not provide us with an unequivocal "sameness of respect." For if we ask in what respect the touchstone determines the value of the gold alloy, and in what respect gold determines the value of men, we don't get the same respect:

> The touchstone determines the value of the gold alloy as an exchange commodity; gold determines the value of men as moral creatures.

The sameness of respect has seemingly eluded us, but let's make another attempt. Is there buried in this last statement a possible sameness of respect?

The touchstone determines the dependability of the gold alloy; gold determines the dependability of man.

But the dependability of the gold in the gold alloy is conditioned by the market and the sharpness of the trader; the dependability of a man's moral qualities may not be conditioned by the milieu in which the moral quality is exhibited. Thus, though a man might not be able to prevent his company from charging exorbitant prices, he himself might be scrupulously honest; he may be persistent in trying to accomplish his purposes though he may fail; he may be dutiful in the performance of tasks for his superiors though those around him are not and he accomplishes nothing: moral dependability is in no specifiable respect like the "dependability" of a gold alloy. On analysis, the "common meaning" of the two "senses" of "touchstone" seem to disappear. Putting the matter in our terminology, on selecting an apparent A-respect in which the different "touchstones" are alike, we can discover no P-respect which enables us to clearly specify what is constituted by the A-respect in which we feel that they are like. But there is a *prima facie* plausibility in the expectation that they are; and that distinguishes this case from the case of "cat" and "concept."[2]

E

This difference makes us look elsewhere, namely, in metaphor, because there neither the sameness nor the similarity is discoverable.

Consider the following rather commonplace metaphor:

The mother is the heart of the family.

Consider it an analogy:

The mother is to the family as the heart is to the body.

And:

The mother bears the relation to the family that the heart does to the body.

To which we may ask:

In what respect?

The answer is difficult to find, so we try an A-respect:

[2] The reader may find the following example more convincing: "stretching the truth is like stretching a rubber band" (from 7, pp. 57–58).

The mother provides the force for the family's spirit and the heart provides the force for the blood's movement through the body.

Again, something is wrong, and it centers on "force." We know clearly enough what is intended by the heart's force: the heart pumps — it compresses, it pushes. But the mother doesn't pump — compress and push; she stimulates, she organizes, she encourages, she prepares. Apparently, we have the "P-respect."

The mother's activities bear the same relation to the family that the heart's activities do to the body.

But again:

In what respect?

And a possible answer:

The mother's activities are responsible for the family being what it is *qua* family, and the heart's activities are responsible for the body's being what it is *qua* body.

But strictly speaking, this is not true. If the mother died or deserted the family, the father or the eldest child would perform the functions that the mother had previously performed, even though not in exactly the same way; but if the heart were destroyed, nothing could replace it. Moreover, while the mother does not maintain herself with the same indispensability as the heart, the functions she performs do often seem all pervading, at least in stereotype; whereas the heart, necessary though it is to the maintenence of life, is not all pervasive. And if we pursue the matter with, "In what respect are they alike?" the "P-respect" we seek will not be found. Nevertheless we are quite willing to argue that the likeness and the sameness do exist.

We cannot specify the attributes by which we have compared the relations, yet we would want to say that they are alike or the same: we would want to say that the mother's relation to the family and the heart's relation to the body are alike, or the same, though we cannot see how. The definitive test has been met: the likeness or the sameness has been communicated. What is said about the metaphor may be said about the likeness — and the sameness too — of the different senses of "touchstone." Why, after all, the same word?

F

We may speak of quality whenever there are subjects that are the same or alike, but where no P-respect in which they are alike may be specified; more explicitly, we may speak of quality when the same necessary and sufficient conditions for the same attributes of different subjects cannot be specified.

This definition excludes, and is specifically intended to exclude, two things, namely, the identity of an individual subject-matter on the one hand, and purely logical properties on the other. Thus, though the previous example of identity, namely, "JFK is the present President of the United States," was in terms of a property, we may wish to say that there is an identity because of the fact that what is referred to by both designations is the same individual. But the "same" individual is not "like" the same individual, because the same individual is identical with the same individual, and to use "like" is to assert or suppose not one, but at least two.

It should be clear also that quality has no dependence on logical issues. That a given instance may be said to be the same sort of thing as another is not a logical rule, though propositions may logically follow from the assertion of sameness. As shown in the discussion about the penny, logical rules cannot determine the selection of subjects or attributes, and therefore respects, unless terms are implicitly defined to include them. Since no respect can be specified, the rules of logic have even less relevance in this context to quality.

PART 2

We began this chapter by juxtaposing "permanence and change" and "quality," then tried to show that quality has to do with "sameness" and "likeness." "Permanence" and "change" also entail "sameness": to be permanent is to remain the same; to change is not to remain the same. We stated then that we are concerned with "what does not change while change goes on"; hence we are concerned with what remains the same while something does not. But, for instance, Aristotle's "substance" and "being" (what "remains the same") and "potentiality" and "actuality" (what does not), and Galileo's units of time (which "remain the same" or are "permanent") and units of distance (which do not), leading to a proportion (which is also "permanent"), exhibit conceptual differences.

Moreover, the sense in which Galileo's units of time "remain the same" and that in which his proportion "remains the same" are distinct. Reflection on the history of, for example, the science of mechanics exhibits the fact that at every conceptual advance the various senses given "permanence" and "change" are altered. In dealing with "social change" it is wise to follow this lead.

But a word of caution is in order. Despite widespread admission that "science" is often a sophomoric encomium for the more formalized empirical disciplines, some "natural scientists" display a contempt for disciplines less formalized than theirs, to which many "social scientists" exhibit sensitivity. Formally, sociological investigation of social change falls short of what sociologists want, but a like condition is true of physics and logic. Sociology falls shorter in this regard, but affirming or denying that it is "science" is irrelevant to honest discussion. Our thesis is that the definition of "quality" we propose is exhibited in sociology by the fact that it is incomplete, as is readily admitted, in a sense or even in various senses that those disciplines more closely allied with classical mechanics are not; but this comparison is not intended to be invidious, for in various ways physics and logic are themselves incomplete.

Our thesis is derived from the fact that the investigators in the field suppose that there is some other way in which sociology can be made a more effective instrument to analyze the phenomena it presently does. It is this point which gives us our interpretation of sociology as to some extent qualitative: there is some presently unknown respect in which it can be said that the data of social change presently under investigation are the same or alike.

What will emerge from our analysis may seem paradoxical: though purely qualitative or metaphorical comparisons do not provide us with clear suggestions as to a line of investigation, nevertheless logically structured, analogical comparisons lead us to claim an unspecifiable respect, however tentatively it may be regarded as unspecifiable; therefore the search for a new respect entails a qualitative sameness or likeness. In many ways this is the permanence that bears on social change.

It may be advisable to indicate what the application of the mode of analysis we have been suggesting is by providing two examples of it before discussing sociological theories themselves. In the first we shall discuss an issue in the history of science. In the second we shall specifically devise a culture hypothesis in order to indicate the bearing of "quality" on theories of social change. After that, the theories of Talcott Parsons and Ralf Dahrendorf will be considered in analogous ways.

A

The discernment of quality by distinguishing metaphor and analogy may be shown in the "plenist-vacuist" controversy about space. This controversy between Torricelli (24, p. 165), Otto von Guericke, Hooke (30, p. 101), and Boyle (2, pp. 26–27) on the one hand, and many Cartesians and those in the Tradition (13, chapter 4), on the other. The seventeenth- and eighteenth-century "principle of plenitude" was that God created a complete world in every respect, which was a *plenum formarum*, or a full scale of forms or beings, admitting no omission. Thus, there was a scale of biological species (or beings) which admitted every possible variation of species or beings and omitted none; a scale for non-living beings, divine beings, etc.; likewise with respect to space

(13, p. 52). No omissions were possible, and Descartes' material substance, defined as extension, was identified with space (10, p. 41). Cartesians in general fused this with an older doctrine, that "nature abhors a
vacuum," *horror vacui*, therefore it is constantly "full" (11, pp. 103–104);
Boyle referred to these men as "plenists," and to himself and others of
like mind who opposed this part of the broader plenist doctrine as "vacuists"; they argued for the existence of a vacuum (2, pp. 26–27).

The plenists argued on the basis of comparisons which were metaphorical, while the vacuists argued on the basis of comparisons which
were analogical. The plenists tended to support their conception of a
non-vacuous space by direct comparison with the plenitude of the world
in other respects. I know of no specific argument to the effect that space
had to be conceived of as a plenum because, for instance, the scale of
biological forms was a plenum; nevertheless, it is clear from the literature
(13, chapter 4) that the conception of both as "filled" was meant to
support the general doctrine of plenitude; which means that both were
conceived of as being "the Same" or "alike." This sameness or likeness is seen to be metaphorical.

The comparison might be formulated in this way:

Position in space is like position in the scale of living things.

If conceived of as an analogue,

Position of a body is to space as place of a species is to the scale of
living things.

And reformulated:

Position of a body bears the relation to space that the place of a species
bears to the scale of living things.

And we ask:

In what respect?

In answer, we try:

In the respect that the body is immediately adjacent to other bodies and
the species is immediately adjacent to other species.

But this is suspicious; it makes no sense to suggest that one species is
next to another in the sense that a body is next to another body; a given
species is "next to" another species because of the way in which we order
our knowledge, and this hardly amounts to the same sense. We may try

other A-respects, but the likeness or the similarity will be discovered to be metaphorical: there is no specifiable respect in which they are alike.

The vacuists argued, quite differently, that there can be a vacuum because air is like water, and volumes devoid of water can be obtained beneath the surface of the sea. Torricelli advanced the hypothesis that there was a "sea of air" surrounding the earth. The implicit comparison was analogical:

1) The sea is a fluid and so is the air.
   In what respect?
2) The sea moves in currents and so does the air.
   In what respect?
3) Portions of a volume of water may move, pushing aside other portions; portions of a volume of air may move, pushing aside other portions.

An A-respect is specified in (1); the P-respect of that A-respect is in (2); and (3) provides a P-respect of (2). In (1) and (2), S and S' are "volume of water" and "volume of air," respectively; both have the attribute of A, i.e., of being a fluid. P_i is "moving in currents," an attribute which is a member of K, the class of various ways of moving, one other of which may be moving in a collection of distinct particles. A is, of course, an attribute of S because P_i is.

There are, of course, various respects in which water and air are not alike, e.g., that the surface of a volume of water is observable and the surface of a volume of air is not, water is virtually incompressible and air (as Boyle discovered) has a "spring."

The likenesses between water and air, then, were not qualitative but could be made explicit in terms of P-respects, and it is this factor which enables the investigator explicitly to formulate, hypothetically, comparisons in other respects, seeking sameness of A-respect formulable in terms of P-respect. In the case of a metaphor, we cannot specify A-respects and P-respects.

And it shows: Torricelli was led to construct a barometer as a result of his speculations about air weight; Boyle demonstrated the existence of a vacuum and formulated Boyle's Law.

The plenist doctrine, on the contrary, provided few consistent or clear explanations of other phenomena. For example, they said that the reason water does not flow out of a narrow-necked bottle held upside down was that the space surrounding it was already occupied, so it had nowhere to go (24, pp. 163–170). But the same would have to be true about a container of water with a broad opening, and it isn't. Or consider another case. If a container with an opening is emptied of air, the opening plugged, and the container plunged into water, then, if the opening is unplugged, the water will rush in. Otto von Guerike had done this, and some plenists might have argued that this demonstrated that nature abhorred a vacuum. What could have been understood by this? That nature will destroy a vacuum? Such an interpretation is contrary to what is suggested in the plenist's interpretation of the above experiment, for it supposes the existence of a vacuum to be destroyed. The principle at this point becomes incapable of application, and does not suggest further ways out.

B

Recently (26) the Pygmies of the great Congo Rain Forest were ascribed the following attributes: they were driven into the forests about a thousand years ago by "the great Bantu invasion"; that now they come out of the forests occasionally to obtain various articles (e.g., knives, clothes) they recognize or suppose to be superior to the articles they might manufacture; that in order to obtain these articles, they hire themselves out occasionally to the Bantu "villagers" who currently live at the edge of the forest; that the "villagers" regard them as inferior; that in order to control the Pygmies, the villagers use various methods: they "adopt" Pygmy families and provide for their initiation, engagement, marriage and death fêtes, i.e., these are the means by which the villagers hope to manage the Pygmies and to keep on good terms with the spirits of the forest. These people of the forest, moreover, are fleet of foot, deft, agile, and camouflage themselves well; they are dangerous to outsiders they consider inimical and therefore the villagers rarely venture there; they have their own forest communities with their own distinctive organization; that in the forest their sustenance comes from hunting, and gathering honey and fruits.

Margaret Murray (16) investigated the witch-phenomenon of the later medieval-early modern period, and discovered, from the literature (e.g., trial reports, personal reports, court records, autobiographies) of the period that those pleasant, relatively harmless creatures referred to as elves, fairies, sprites, pixies, bogies, etc., after the sixteenth century (beginning approximately with Spenser's *Faerie Queen* and Shakespeare's *Midsummer Night's Dream*) were, prior to that period, described in much stronger terms, and indeed were dealt with harshly. Her theory is that these creatures were actually the survivors of a Stone Age culture who had been driven into the forest by invaders who followed and themselves occupied the more fertile agricultural areas, and, of course, built the cities. They were described by the dominant inhabitants of England as being shorter than themselves, fleet of foot, agile, and capable of excellent camouflage. They were hunters, and were regarded as extremely dangerous, especially if met in the forest. They had their own religion (according to Professor Murray, they were worshipers of "the Horned God"), and ecclesiastical authorities violently opposed them, though lay authorities opposed them with considerably less vigor. Hence the violence of the sixteenth- and seventeenth-century witch hunts against fairies or "witches" who had "infiltrated" the dominant society; for, in fact, many of them attained positions of prominence.

Finally, consider the following statement.

> In Greek mythology, Satyrs are sprites of the woodland, in the train of Dionysus, with puck noses, bristling hair, goat-like ears, and short tails. They are depicted as wanton, cunning, and cowardly creatures, and always fond of wine and women. They dwell in woods and on mountains, where they hunt, and tend cattle, dance and frolic with the Nymphs (for whom they lie in ambush), make music pipe and flute, and revel with Dionysus . . . . They were considered as foes to mankind, because they played people all kinds of roguish pranks, and frightened them by impish tricks. . . . In art and poetry they gained a higher significance, owing to the festivals of Dionysus. . . . In early art they are represented for the most part as bearded and old, and often very indecorous. As time went on they were represented ever younger and more graceful, and with an expression of amiable roguishness . . . (25, pp. 559–560).

Given these ideas, a man might be tempted to formulate a culture hypothesis to the effect that if an invading group drives the group from its area into forests and mountains nearby, the relations between the groups proceed from a stage of violent opposition with limited points of contact, through a period wherein the victorious group ascribes supernatural powers to the displaced group, to a period of gradual albeit contemptuous acceptance. Could this hypothesis apply to, say, a given wave of invasion in India where original inhabitants were displaced into the forests, or similar circumstances in Southeast Asia, or to the Slavic displacement of the Finno-Ugrians in the north of Russia? Are the satyrs of Greek art the consequence of a displaced culture?[3] Probably not. Nevertheless, because of the similarities, a clear line of investigation may be formulated in cases of ignorance of the presence or absence of a given attribute. For example;

> The fairies of sixteenth-century England were like the Pygmies of the present-day Congo Rain Forests.
> In what (A-) respect?
> In the respect that their sustenance and dwellings were in the forests.
> In what respect are these alike?
> In the respect that the materials of their sustenance and for their dwellings are obtained within the forests.
> In what respect are these alike?
> In the respect that food was obtained primarily by hunting and the dwellings were constructed primarily out of the soil and vegetation obtainable in the forest.

[3] An alternative theory: Jane Harrison thought that "satyrs" originated in initiation rites, with men dancing in animal skins (8, pp. 341–346).

To ask for the respect in which two subjects have the same A-respect is to ask, of course, for a P-respect. In this sequence each specified respect is the necessary and sufficient condition of the preceding respect.

Since apparently the conditions are analogous, that is, they are the same in certain respects, a clear line of investigation is suggested by the simple question as to whether they are alike in other respects.

Suppose, however, that one were to try to formulate an analogy between the kinds of circumstances just referred to and the relations between minority groups and dominant groups within communities. Merton speaks of the resentment which members of the "in-group" feel toward members of the "out-group"; they are resentful of them, attribute unpleasant characteristics to them, particularly inferior intelligence (for example, Negroes), and where this thesis obviously conflicts with the facts (in the case of Jews), a kind of immorality (15, pp. 182–188).

Could such a theory be maintained on the basis of factual similarity? The facts are, in this case, of different classifications. For example: the Pygmies are not members of the Bantu society, they have no desire to supplant them in terms of leadership in the Bantu society, nor to advance in any way in it; indeed, the contrary phenomenon occurs: the villagers try as much as possible to incorporate the Pygmies into their community practices for their own material benefit, while the Pygmies wish to avoid as much as possible involvement in the activities of the villagers, except those activities which provide them with what they want.

But certain likenesses may be urged. While the Bantus wish to incorporate the Pygmies into their cultural activities, they have no desire that they physically occupy the land that they, the villagers, occupy. It could be urged that the exclusion of the minority-groupers by the dominant-groupers from the status benefits of the society is "like" the exclusion of the Pygmies by the villagers from the occupation of their land. If one asks in what respect the exclusions are alike, the common "respect" is hard to find. To be sure, there would be certain concomitants of the status of power which would render it "like" the exclusion of the Pygmies. For example, the exclusions of minority-groupers from certain neighborhoods in more "civilized" societies is like the exclusion of Pygmies from various villages, but this is not essential to the issue since dropping the bars in one neighborhood results in property depreciation there and raising the bars in a new one. "Social" exclusion is in no respect "like" the physical exclusion of groups of people from the ownership and control of land. Such a suggestion, then, would be a purely metaphorical attempt to render two disparate sets of phenomena the same, hence subject to the same generalization.

For example, what would be the respect in which they would be alike? Consider a factor of more obvious pertinence, namely, the benefits that would accrue if one were to ask in what respect benefits would accrue to the minority-grouper who managed to become accepted by the

dominant-groupers. The benefit would be an improvement in status: he would have access to groups to which he had little or none before; he would enjoy the regard of the dominant-groupers, he would be permitted to enjoy their leisure. "Benefit" in this sense is *toto coelo* different from "benefit" in the sense of an increase of necessities. The senses of "benefit" are metaphorically alike. That every man acts to benefit himself is a recognized truism. We recognize it to be so because those who use it intend the statement as something more than a truism: that the expected consequence of an act is always a benefit. But this would apply to cases of masochism, self-sacrifice, and so on, which would mean that "benefit" in this context is badly defined. To say that "status-benefits" are as different from "necessity-benefits" as I claim, we would have to ask: in what respect are they alike? There is none specifiable, though human talent may perceive "likeness," or "sameness."

My point is that there would (assuming a greater amount of data than presented here) be some justification to seek some of the characteristics of the Pygmy-villager situation in, say, the situation produced by the Indian invasions, or the Slavic displacement of the Finno-Ugrians in the North of Russia. But, on the basis of the similarities presented, there would be no grounds for asserting a similarity between, say, the relations between Negroes and Whites in present-day America on the one hand, and between the pygmies and the villagers on the other. There the similarity would be metaphoric. Since there is no respect in which they are specifically alike, there is no clear line of investigation suggested.

C

In this section and the following ones we shall deal with theories specifically formulated to handle sociological data, concerned with social change. The examples we have already dealt with have been of different sorts: "ordinary" or "common-sense" language was used in the kidney-filter analogy, archaic theoretical language in connection with the plenist-vacuist controversy, and a primitive sort of conceptual jargon ("displacement") in connection with our "culture hypothesis." This section and the ones that succeed will deal with relatively sophisticated concepts deliberately devised and structured to deal with events to which the attention of investigators had already been attracted. But even so, our claim remains the same: that such conceptual structures provide us with analogies and P-respects suggesting possible lines of endeavor; that where there are no P-respects claimed, samenesses or likenesses are purely qualitative; and that the attempt to formulate a general theory provides us with "quality." The theories with which we shall be concerned will be those of Talcott Parsons and Ralf Dahrendorf.

Much of Parsons' theory can be viewed from the vantage point of his

use of the terms "system" (what does not change) and "concrete" (what does). We shall begin with "system." As is well known, Parsons' approach to sociology is "systematic," as evidenced by the frequency with which such terms as "system," "structure," "frame of reference," "organization," "relation," and others appear in his titles and discussions. But the "system" of which he speaks must be thought of in terms of "unit acts" (21, p. 43) or "action" (that is, change) (23, p. 53). In the course of his writings Parsons' definition of these terms differs; in one of his latest works he has defined it as behavior which is (1) oriented toward a goal, (2) in a situation, (3) regulated by norms, and (4) motivated, or involves the expenditure of effort or energy (23, p. 51). Action requires an "actor" in a situation composed of objects (physical, cultural, or other actors). To these he bears "relations," which are "organized" into a "system" of "orientations" (viewpoints, goals, plans of action).

Actions themselves are organized into systems, which Parsons holds are, fundamentally, three: *Personality* systems, which are those actions of an actor which are interconnected and organized by "the structure of need-dispositions," and compatible with the actions and goals of other individual actors; *Social* systems, which are interactions of actors, engaging the focus of their attention, where other actors are the objects of a given actor's cathexis, cognition, and evaluation (in terms of the other's, or "alter's," goals and means thereunto) and engaging in "concerted action" with a common value and "a consensus of normative and cognitive expectations"; and *Cultural* systems, which involve the organization of values, norms, and symbols "abstracted" from the "elements" of the personality and social systems which have a degree of "consistency" with one another, and are "transmissible" from one personality or social system to another (23, pp. 54–55).

All these are involved in the "frame of reference" of the theory of action involving actors which, whether individuals or "collectivities," are "empirical systems of action" — a situation which consists of those objects by which the actor orients himself, and the orientation of the actor to the situation, which involves cathexes, standards, plans by which the actor orients himself. Of these orientations, there are two. The first is *Motivational,* which has to do with the actor's gratifications and deprivations; of these there are three "modes": "Cognitive," which has to do with the various ways in which the actor views the objects in connection with his need dispositions; "cathectic," in which the actor attributes significance to objects in terms of his needs and drives; and "evaluative," which is the means by which the actor "allocates" his activity and energy among the various "cathected" objects (23, pp. 61–63).

The second kind of orientation is the *Value Orientation,* which has to do with norms and criteria of selection relevant to choice. This also has three modes: the "cognitive," which has to do with criteria of the validity of cognitive judgments; the "appreciative," which has to do with

the consistency of the various standards by which cathectic objects are judged; and the "moral" mode, which has to do with the standards by which various types of action and their consequences are judged with respect to their effects on various systems of action (23, pp. 67–76).

Parsons speaks of the "dilemmas" of orientation, and conceives of them in terms of "dichotomies." There are five dichotomies, or "pattern variables," so called because "any specific orientation is characterized by a pattern of the five choices" (23, p. 76). That is, they are the choices an actor must make with respect to a situation before that situation can become determinate and meaningful to him. They are: 1) Affectivity-Affective neutrality; 2) Self-orientation-Collectivity orientation; 3) Universalism-Particularism; 4) Ascription-Achievement; 5) Specificity-Diffuseness. In connection with the situation, these enable a concrete choice of specific action to be made. In connection with the personality system, they enable a choice to be made between habits. In connection with the collectivity, they define a person's rights and duties, i.e., his role. And in connection with the cultural system, the variables enter as a choice between standards of value (23, p. 78). In various ways, the pattern variables are defined with respect to the personality, the social, and the cultural systems.

With these in the background, we shall discuss the personality system first, then the social and cultural systems.

The central notion of the personality system, apart from the idea that it is a system of actions, is motivation. Parsons distinguishes two different meanings of "motivation": "energy" or "drive," and "a set of tendencies on the part of the organism to acquire certain goal objects . . ." (23, p. 111). In this latter sense, it refers to the system of orientations, plans for means and goal reaching with respect to cathected objects. Drives are "innate"; "need-dispositions" are those tendencies which are acquired in the process of drive activity. The latter term has two meanings: (1) the tendency to achieve a certain end; and (2) the disposition to do something with an object designed for the purpose. These may be had with respect to attitudes and relationships to objects (which may, the reader will recall, be other persons as well as oneself), with respect to cultural standards (or "internalized social values"), and with respect to role expectations (e.g., esteem if one has high social status; love, if one is a parent, etc.). With these characteristics in mind, we must conceive of the personality as a system which has a "persistent tendency toward an optimum (as distinguished from maximum) level of gratification" (23, p. 121). This is done by correctly resolving "problems of allocation" and "problems of integration." The former have to do with time and energy, and the latter with drives and need dispositions, i.e., avoiding "conflict" between them.

Parsons, of course, develops his personality system theory in much greater detail than is possible in a short statement of his position.

The difference between the personality system and the social system lies in what Parsons calls the differences of the "foci" of organization. The focus of the personality system is the act and its standards, while the focus of the social system is the role, and the complex of roles in which individuals engage. Most important to roles (undefined, by the way), are the "role expectations," which "organize . . . the reciprocities, expectations, and responses to those expectations in the specific inter-action systems of ego and one or more alters (23, p. 190). It is the reciprocal of the "sanction," which is what the relevant alters expect of the egos, that is, that of the individual in question. Each ego, then, has an orientation role and an object-role; the former has to do with ego's orientation toward alter, and the latter has to do with the fact that alter regards ego as a social object.

In a social system, the roles vary with the institutionalization, i.e., the integration of the role expectations and sanction patterns in accordance with a value system which is common to members of the collectivity. In a collectivity, under these circumstances, action is in concert toward various objects and various sorts of objects. Two other types of "social aggregates" are "categories" of persons (mere classifications) and "pluralities" of people who are ecologically interdependent (as is supposed to happen in the market in perfect competition). The collectivity differs from the category in that the category involves no "action in concert"; it differs from both the social system and the social aggregate in that it has "solidarity," wherein there are tendencies toward shared gratifications.

Inherent, therefore, in Parsons' approach to "the social system" is "the *inter*-action of the individual actors, that it takes place under such circumstances that it is possible to treat such a process of inter-action as a 'system'" (22, p. 1). It is conceived in terms of "the action frame of reference" which has to do with "one or more actors" in a situation that includes other actors. Hence, it is a "relational scheme," requiring situations. Parsons holds that, at some point, "the most elementary components of any action system may be reduced to the actor and his situation" (22, p. 7). For purposes relevant to the social system Parsons describes the situation in the following way:

> The situation is described as consisting of objects of orientation so that the orientation of a given actor is differentiated relative to the different objects and classes of objects, namely, social, physical and cultural objects. The social object is an "actor" which may in turn be an other individual actor (alter), the actor who is taken as a point of reference himself (ego) or a collectivity which is treated as a unit for purposes of the analysis of orientation. Physical objects are empirical entities which do not "interact" or "respond" to ego. They are means and conditions of his action. Cultural objects are symbolic elements of the cultural tradition, ideas or beliefs, expressive symbols or value patterns so far as they are treated as situational

objects by ego and are not "internalized" as constitutive elements of the structure of his personality (22, p. 4).

"The most elementary components of action in general" are formulated in the context of the social system. "Need-disposition system" is the most elementary, of which "the two most primary or elementary aspects" are the "gratificational" and the "orientational." The first concerns the "content" and what the "cost" of the actor's interaction with the world is; the second concerns the how," i.e., patterns of organization with respect to the actions toward the world. The first therefore is cathectic (". . . the significance of the ego's relation to the object or objects in question for the gratification-deprivation balance of his personality."). The most fundamental "orientational" category is the "cognitive" orientation or "mapping," which is most generally treated as the "definition" of the aspects of the situation relevant to the actor's interests . Finally, these entail "an evaluative aspect of all concrete action orientation," which means "an ordered selection among . . . alternatives." The last three are, of course, the modes of motivational orientation, and along with the object-system categorize the elements of action "on the broadest level" (22, pp. 7–8).

These elements are involved in the structure of an "expectation" which has to do with action. Since the reference is to the future, expectation has a time element. That is, it implies a temporal dimension of the actor's concern with the development of the situation. From the point of view of the pattern variables, expectation may be differentiated "along an activity-passivity co-ordinate." The future state which the actor acts to bring about, and hence "expects" is called the "goal." Expecting, then, has to do with activity; "merely waiting," having to do with passivity, is referred to as "anticipation" (22, p. 8).

Further conceptual development runs along similar lines. Parsons goes on to discuss "cognitive," "appreciative," and "moral" standards along with "relational," "regulative," and "cultural" institutions. These merge into the social structure, which he discusses in terms of "relations," "status," and "role" (i.e., the "structure" of relations within which the actor finds himself, the specific "place" he has and the norms according to which he must act). But again, an exhaustive treatment of Parsons is impossible in these pages, and we have discussed enough of the "social system" for our purposes.

Parsons' discussion of the cultural system has not, to date, been extensive. By and large, the cultural system has to do with the "meanings," "signs," or "symbols" which become relevant to the actor's expectations system. When these "serve as media of communication between actors," we have the beginnings of "culture." A cultural system, then, includes "systems of interaction of a plurality of actors oriented to a situation and where the system includes a commonly understood system of cultural symbols" (22, p. 5). The elements of a cultural system are constituted by "symbol systems" of which there are the usual three sorts: cognitive, having a connection with beliefs or ideas; cathectic, having a connection with "expressive symbols," in which the orientation brought about by the object of cathexis is "inward toward the affective state" (23, p. 163), and evaluative, in which "regulatory symbols" or "normative ideas" have the primacy. Each of these provides a corresponding pattern or type of standard of value orientation (referred to also as "normative ideas" and "evaluative symbols"): cognitive, e.g., veridical and non-veridical standards; appreciative, which have to do with standards in connection with art, persons (i.e., personal responses), and collectivities; and moral, e.g., good and bad.

With respect to action-orientations, i.e, actions in which the foci of orientation are standards, ideas, and symbols, the same triad turns up in another guise. They are "instrumental" where the foci are on cognitive problems to be solved by reference to cognitive standards; "expressive," where the foci are on cathectic problems to be solved by reference to appreciative standards; and "moral," where the foci are on evaluative problems to be solved by reference to moral standards (23, pp. 157–159).

Each of these three systems (personality, social, and cultural) is indispensable to the other, though not "derivable" from the other (22, p. 6). There are, however, certain "transformations" (undefined) between one and the other, though on this "theoretical level" they are not a "single system." Finally "it is a fundamental property of action thus defined that it does not consist of ad hoc 'responses' to particular 'stimuli' but that the actor develops a *system* of 'expectations' relative to the various objects of the situation" (22, p. 6). The latter is particularly indicated by the fact that the five pattern variables are applicable in all three systems.

It has been pointed out that Parsons has not developed a "unified deductive system" but that what "derivations" there are are "connotative" (28, p. 93). That is true. Nevertheless, he has worked out a set of terms and statements the nature of which can provide us with a setting for the formulation of analogies. For example:

    A) A university is a social system whose members have roles, and a street gang is a social system whose members have roles.

In what respect are these alike?

    B) In the respect that the members each have role expectations within their respective social systems.

In what respect are these alike?

    C) In the respect that in each social system the role expectations are of love, esteem, and so on.

In this case S and S' are the university and the street gang, A is "a social system whose members have roles," P_i is "having role expectations within the social system," which is a member of the class (of attributes K with members $P_1, P_2, \ldots, P_n$.) of expectations. (A) and (B) are equivalent.

Few people have used the conceptual structure Parsons has proposed as a guide to inquiry, though there are some cases (6, pp. 419–427). Possibly the most successful application of his theory is executed by himself, in Chapter 10 of *The Social System*, which analyzes the medical profession in the light of his concepts. Would casting Parsons' conceptual structure in the above analogical pattern provide a suggestion for a direction of investigation (12, p. 44)?[4] My point is that the pattern suggests further points of comparison between the above social systems; e.g., are role expectations of the same sort in both the university and the street gang?

Likeness sought for may not, of course, obtain in fact. There remains the possibility of a perceived likeness in one A-respect, where no P-respect can be specified. For example:

The child "loves" his father and the gang member "loves" his gang leader.

In what respect are these alike?

The child obeys his father and the street gang member obeys his leader.

This is too often false — in what other respect, then?

And so on with respect to other claimed likenesses. If all of them are discovered to be false and there is yet perceived a likeness or sameness, then the claimed likeness or sameness may be judged to be "qualitative."

There is a legitimate claim to be made for Parsons' "systematic" organization of concepts and statements. Though he does not always distinguish clearly between "action system" and "system of statements and concepts about the action system," there is nevertheless a system of concepts and statements which must be regarded as maintaining a permanent status, in the sense that any kind of social change (action) is ultimately capable of being described by them. A specific actor and action may be described by statements about goals, norms, motivations, and situations as well as by statements about features of the "action system," constituted by the personality, social, and cultural systems. They are or may be persistently used to describe any social change. In order to describe any social change or action, the entire system must be brought to bear.

---

[4] "The use of formalism in sociological data is not yet likely to lead to new findings. But it can disclose unnoticed implications or clarify the relations among propositions" (12, p. 44).

But, first, we want to specify change relative to what does not change; the kind of job for which such concepts as "variable," "constant," and "function" are suited. Parsons does use "variable" and "function." Yet the sense which attends his use of "variable" (in connection with "pattern variables") is only slightly analogous to its use in mathematics and mathematical physics. As for "function," its use in sociology (particularly Parsons' sociology) is merely parallel rather than identical with its use in mathematical physics. Its use in sociology, as distinct from its use in mathematics or formalized physical theory, is to refer to a process which varies on the condition that a number of others do, but the variation is either of a non-formalized sort (i.e., no definite proportion can be formulated between the process in question and those which constitute its conditions), or it is one which cannot be traced in detail.

Second, we want to preclude reference to certain kinds of change. In classical mechanics, for example, a given prediction must be formulated in terms of the fundamental concepts defined in the definitions and the axioms. But if a body is moving because of gravitational attraction, we are not compelled to add that it is moving because of centrifugal force; centrifugal force may be added to the gravitational force but each force may be separately estimated, given certain initial conditions. In Parsons' system the description of an action does not preclude the social system or the cultural system when the personality system is involved; nor, for example, can it be said that when the cognitive elements are present, the cathectic and appreciative elements are precluded. All such elements are involved in every action; we must take into consideration the entire "action system" and recognize that all the concepts and statements constituting Parsons' system are entailed, logically or otherwise. Individuals (or "actors") may be described as changing, but the systematic structure may not; and the system of concepts and statements formulates the respects in which the individuals change. Still, we want, it would appear, other ways of speaking of change than by using "change" or a synonym, as Parsons does with "action."

Parsons is trying to provide a conceptual apparatus in terms of which a theory of "social action" (or change) may be interpreted. Is the specification of "sameness" of any mode of behavior interpretable in these terms? It is instructive to compare Parsons' position with that of physical theorists prior to the formalization of physical theory; as an example, William of Heytesbury (c. 1313–1372).[5] Consider the change in the theory of motion (change of position) between Heytesbury and Galileo, in particular, free fall. Heytesbury believed that motion should be conceived of in terms of a proportion between spaces and times (29, p. 119; 4, pp. 93–95). What distinguishes Heytesbury's theory from Galileo's is the Heytesbury formulation that the spaces traversed were directly

[5] The comparison with pre-Galilean physics is not invidious; it is merely that the examples are simpler.

proportional to the times, rather than the squares of the times. Hindsight guarantees us the falsity of this formulation. Nevertheless, analysis and criticism continued after Heytesbury, so we may presume that the investigators of the time were convinced of the incompleteness of their investigations into local motion. That is, they felt that the correct formula had not been achieved (29, pp. 143–147). On the other hand, they did feel that the phenomena Heytesbury described were alike, but in some other respect than he specified. The respect, was, of course, formulated by Galileo. But since Heytesbury's formulation did not succeed, certainly Galileo and others felt that there must be some other respect in terms of which the instances of "local motion" were alike. Prior to Galileo's formulation this respect was unknown, although sought. And for this reason, it is justifiable to say that, from this standpoint, their physics was "qualitative."

Parsons' position is analogous. He says that if any person is to be described as performing a "unit act," he must conform to all the prerequisites he specifies, otherwise he is not. The assertion of sameness or likeness of the subjects is assumed to be incomplete precisely because the formula in terms of which the sameness and likeness is to be asserted has not yet been found. It is more than possible that the Parsons' concept will not figure in what may turn out to be the successful formulation, but that is what makes his formulations of the various aspects of sociological concepts qualitative: what is being sought is some other respect in terms of which the subjects may be said to be the same; and what is claimed is that they are the same in an unspecified, unknown respect.

This is what strikes us so forcefully about "system." There are few more difficult words in the history of intellectual endeavor than "system." Its extension ranges from purely formal systems of logic to mechanical systems. When we consider the many "systems" we encounter in proceeding from one end to the other (geometrical systems, physical systems, biological systems, organizational systems, personality systems, astronomical systems, and so forth) for which there is no common definition, we may begin to understand the care we must exercise in using the word, and why, ultimately, we can define the word, if at all, ostensively: we may indicate this system or that system by appropriate means and state what properties each has which are responsible for its being a system. That is as far as we can go.

Parsons, at least sometimes, seems to confuse one kind of "system" with another. On the one hand, he talks about the "system" of human actions, each of which conditions and is conditioned by others; on the other, he seems to be talking about a theoretical "system" of propositions (or other symbolic expressions), each of which bears logical relations to the others. Whatever conditions may cause the behavior of certain actions, they do not, except by reference, or the rule-making capacity of propositions, "cause" logical relations to occur.

But, even when *prima facie* consideration of passages he has written suggests that he is dealing with the system of actions (when he writes that the "actor develops a *system* of 'expectations' relative to the various objects of the situation") he is confusing. Does he mean that expectations, anticipations, and preferences can be ordered in terms of their probabilities, and the desired can be ordered in terms of preference, so that some sort of answer can be given to "What is preferred?" by combining the expected and the anticipated? But of course, "needs" must be brought in. To be sure, there is a sense in which Parsons considers this when he says that the system of expectations "*may* be structured only relative to his own need-dispositions and the probabilities of gratifications are deprivations contingent on the various alterations of action which he may undertake" (22, p. 53). Two comments are relevant:

First, Parsons has limited his discussion to situations in which the actor perceives possible gratifications and deprivations (22, p. 4). Why Parsons insists on setting up his system this way is puzzling. Samuel Lubell once suggested that people often conceive their present problems in terms of past problems or conflicts which may have nothing to do with them (14, p. 162). Most people are often positively mistaken or not clear about their need dispositions, i.e., what they need to fulfill certain conditions of their psyche, to eliminate destructive factors in their psyche, or to create circumstances that provide gratification. These are facts of which Parsons must be aware.

Second, respondents to questionnaires provide information in ways other than by explicit replies to questions. More than their explicit answers may be properly inferred, much of which may contradict the explicit answers to explicit questions. The respondent may be lying, but he may also believe what is false.

If the causes perceived by an investigator are different from what a respondent says they are, two possibilities emerge. (1) The interpretation may be made relative to a frame of reference containing factors of which the respondent is not conscious, but which have to do with his behavior. For example, a man may be in a severe state of depression without knowing that the immediate cause of it was the fact that someone he admired was just rude to him; he might even protest that this is not the reason and honestly believe it. (2) The interpretation may be made relative to a frame of reference which has to do with the individual, but only insofar as he is a member of a given kind or class. For example, a dominant-group member may suppose his dislike of a minority-group member stems from the minority group's "infraction" of certain "rules," e.g., working late at night or on Sundays. An investigator might recognize from the pattern of the dominant-group member's attributes and replies that his attitude is typical of dominant group-minority group relations. These suggest that "beginning" with the individual's own perception of his cathexes, rather than with a theoretical structure, is not always the best way.

It is too early to tell which kinds of clues and evidence are less reliable than others, and to preclude still others. If the theoretical structure says one thing and the experimental or investigative techniques another, either the theoretical system must be so defined as not to preclude the techniques (in which case the terms of the system mean something different) or the theoretical system itself has to be replaced or modified. Parsons, by insisting that this "action system" have to do only with perceived gratifications and deprivations, would eliminate much investigation.

It is hard to say with complete conviction what apparently misleads Parsons, but this writer is reasonably sure that one of the most basic reasons is his commitment to what he conceives of as the "concrete." Unfortunately, the word is used in many senses. For our purposes, three may be isolated:

1) The empirical sense — "A concrete name is a name which stands for a thing; an abstract name is a name which stands for an attribute of a thing."[6] Thus, in the sentence, "This paper is white," *this paper* is concrete and *whiteness* is abstract.

2) The poetic sense, involving an evoked image of an object as though directly present to perception, where the image is particularly vivid; in this context, "concrete" is synonymous with "vivid." For example, in "Beauty is but a flower which wrinkles will devour," the image evoked is of a flower losing its firmness in the process of decay. But which flower, in what sort of circumstances, Thomas Nash does not say. To be sure "wrinkling" does occur in individual flowers, but it is the "wrinkling," i.e., the attribute, that one must imagine as well as the flower to which it happens.

3) The Hegelian sense, in which the concrete is that which is immersed in its relations; one must consider the individual in its milieu of relations and connections. In Hegel's philosophy, "concrete" is the opposite of "abstract"; to "abstract" is to consider an object apart from its circumstances, connections, and relations. Perceiving a man, one notes many characteristics displayed in varying circumstances; many men display even more characteristics in even more varying circumstances. To select two, as Aristotle did, and define "man" in terms of the characteristics "rational" and "animal" is to ignore the others, and to abstract "rational" and "animal" from the circumstances, relations, and connections in which they are displayed. In this way Hegel arrives at the "abstract universal," since "rational animal" is an "abstraction" conceived of and attributable to all men. This is the sort of thing to which Hegel was opposed. "Man" must be known in terms of the concrete circumstances in which he develops — in terms of the entire history of circumstances, involving man's trials, victories, hardships, triumphs, and so on. In this case man is known in terms of all the connections and relations in which each circumstance of his development occurs. It is under

[6] J. S. Mill, *System of Logic*, Bk. 1, ch. 2, par. 4. Mill's definition has been a standard one since the nineteenth century.

this condition that Hegel can talk about "man" being a "concrete universal." It is in this context of discussion that Hegel conceived of "concrete" as having to do with that which was not abstracted from its circumstances, connections, and relations.

It would appear, *prima facie*, that Parsons is using the Hegelian sense of "concrete." For he does try to discuss the "unit action" as an act which is exercised only in the "system" he provides. What he apparently is saying is that the "act" takes place only within the "personality," "social," and "cultural" systems. The unit act and the individual actor, then, have to be conceived in these terms.

Two points are relevant. One is that, though Parsons seems to suggest that the unit act can only be understood within the circumstances in which it occurs, he is more interested in "blocking off" the unit act so that any act by a given actor may be completely described. The description of the act is provided by highly abstract terms, e.g., when the motivational orientation is described by the triad of cognitive, cathectic, and evaluative, none of these terms can be said to be "concrete" in any of the current senses. Secondly, if one objects to the above by pointing out that Hegel's classification of knowledge is done this way, it may be replied that this is so only to a limited extent, for Hegel's system had to do with the dialectical ordering — the "unity" of the "thesis" and "antithesis" in a higher "synthesis." Parson's ordering, though often triadic, is not dialectical. Parsons' use of "concrete" seems to be a mixture of the senses we specified; that is what may lead to some of his difficulties. Take, for example, his apparent confusion between the senses of "system." He feels, apparently, that it is necessary to talk about "system" in order to talk about the "concrete," but in doing so, he does not differentiate between the formal requirement of a system of knowledge, and requirements of a system of actions.

Thus, Parsons talks about individuals who conform only to abstract characteristics which he speaks of as being "in the concrete." This is further compounded when he defines "social" and "cultural" in abstract terms different from those in which one is accustomed to hearing them defined. Presumably he would want to argue that these are the characteristics that they do in fact display, and for this reason he can sensibly talk about their being "concrete." But to this there are two obvious answers. For one thing, the terms for characteristics we attribute to individuals on the common-sense level "in the concrete," are not likely to mean the same thing when interpreted in a theoretical context. Thus, "force" was once interpreted in terms of human exertion, but that is far from the meaning the term eventually acquired in classical mechanics (19, p. 118).[7] In this case, the concrete, though it may have enabled the early mechanicians to arrive at a concept of force employable in a theoretical framework, was *toto coelo* different from what its theoretical

[7] An excellent source of similar examples is (27, chapter 3).

requirements demanded — if anything, they demanded a withdrawal from the concrete. For another thing, many central factors used in many classical sciences are not discoverable "in the concrete," e.g., mass.

The previous points about "system" and the "concrete" enable us, I think, to pinpoint one other way in which we can say that the sociology of Parsons is "qualitative." He wishes to argue that what he is providing is a "system." But he always believes his "system" to be incomplete, as is evidenced by the fact that he is continually adding to it. But it is not only from this standpoint that we may regard Parsons' work as incomplete, for if we ask what the criteria for the system of sociology are which would enable us to accept it as valid and composed of true statements, the criteria would be only partly specified. For example, two criteria for the acceptability of a logical system are consistency and completeness; these criteria would apply to the formal system constructed in Newton's *Principia;* but other criteria would have to apply, for one needs "co-ordinating definitions" or "correspondence rules" to relate the terms used in the system and the experimental phenomena. In the case of Galileo's law of free fall, $S = \frac{1}{2}at^2$, we would have to provide a set of rules which would correspond the various computed positions with, say, the various distances a freely falling body moves, starting with 0 velocity along with the positions of the hands on a clock. Undoubtedly correspondence rules would be present in the various areas of a formalized system of sociology. But it is precisely such rules that we do not know, rules which enable us to provide a "definition" of a sociological "system."

We previously pointed out that there is no common definition of "system" applicable to all those entities to which the word refers; we also pointed out that cases into which some rigor has been introduced do provide some criteria, and the criteria of what a system constitutes differ from case to case. Parsons uses "system" in an anticipatory way, for the presumption of his investigation is that there are criteria other than those presently available by which we may decide that the statements which describe the phenomena in question belong to a "system."

If therefore we ask:

In what respect is sociology a system?

the answer that Parsons and many others would give is:

There are many but we don't know some.

That is, there is some respect, presently incapable of being specified, in which the phenomena referred to in sociological statements can be said to be "the same" or "alike"; but a system of statements and concepts, "permanent" and "remaining the same" in the sense of persistent (or possible) reference to objects of social change, cannot be formulated.

D

Dahrendorf tries to approach sociology on a less ambitious basis, for his terms are fewer and more restricted in scope and he combines with this moderate application of Occam's Razor a persistent attempt to state empirical "conditions" for the theoretical terms he proposes. He tries to explain social change in terms of class, and he defines class in terms of "conflict": a "class" is any group of persons whose activities are directed against another person or group of persons. This formulation grows out of Dahrendorf's conception of the opposition between "coercion theory" and "integration theory" respectively, the theory that an ubiquitous social change is to be explained in terms of social conflicts and that social integration is to be explained in terms of the coercion of some members of society by others (5, p. 162), and the theory that social change is to be explained in terms of "functional relations" and the repetition of process patterns (5, p. 159). Each of these is invalid for various purposes, and Professor Dahrendorf wishes to provide a theory in terms of which social change may be conceived as both. That is, patterned group processes do occur, within a functional unity, but the mechanics of this process is conflict.

Individuals have "interests" or "values" impressed upon them by their social milieu; they are exhibited in "associations" where each individual has a "role," i.e., performs a function necessary to the operation of that association. In any society each individual belongs to more than one association and in each he performs no more than one role. His role in the association brings out two kinds of interests: latent and manifest. Latent interests are unconscious but dependent upon his role, and manifest interests are those which are made explicit through the individual's performance in and articulation of his role (5, pp. 172–189).

Dahrendorf then distinguishes between "interest groups," based upon manifest interests which he describes as "psychologically real," in which the association has an explicit and manifest organization of roles ordered in relation of authority and subjection or "imperative co-ordination," and secondary or "quasi-groups," which cannot be said to be groups in any "real" (organized) sense, but which have various latent interests in common, e.g., those occupying correlative positions in different organizations. Inasmuch as latent conflict arises out of authority-subjection, quasi-groups are the area of recruitment for interest groups. To the extent that quasi-groups take on any structure of organization, they become interest groups, e.g., labor unions and employer associations. Classes emerge when an association has groups which develop out of the respective authority-imperative orders of the associations (5, p. 206). By "authority" we are to understand a person's capacity to command someone else, where that capacity depends solely on what the protagonists do in the association.

"Permanence" and "change" have to be understood in this context. What possesses "permanence" here is the "imperatively coordinated association," which Dahrendorf thinks of as "structure." The latter does not have permanence in the sense that, say, an ontologist's conception of "being" may have, but Dahrendorf's conception of "structure" does provide us with a relatively formalized sketch of the permanent elements in a social organization. Yet "structure" is ambiguous; on the one hand, we are required to view the association as a web of interlocking commanding-commanded relationships; on the other hand, "structure" is to be understood as the conflicting groups which compose a given society. "There are, within social structures, certain elements or forces which are at the same time their constituent parts (and therefore 'function' within them) and impulses operating toward their supersedence and change . . . social classes are elements of this kind" (5, p. 123). Dahrendorf is opposed to the biological analogy to be found in "structural-functional" analysis; he finds it too constricting. "Society is process"; and this does not mean that it is a process of specific organs performing various functions, though the constitution of the organs is continually changing. Process in society must be so conceived that we may speak of change, but also so that we may speak of elements which change (i.e., classes, themselves being replaced by others); the mechanism is "conflict." We can understand what Dahrendorf is thinking about; a class conflict between landowners and entrepreneurs was historically succeeded by a class conflict between entrepreneurs and proletarians; and yet the societies within which these occurred remained "the same," e.g., in Germany.

There are three "empirical" (as opposed to "formal") conditions for the formation of interest groups out of quasi-groups: "technical" (those embracing the normative and procedural conditions, e.g., constitution, rules of procedure, norms, etc.); "political" conditions (specifically, political parties); and "social" conditions (communication between the members of a society) (5, pp. 182–189). Since they are the conditions for the formation of interest groups, they are the conditions for conflict. The intensity or violence of conflict varies according to many factors, of which Dahrendorf selects four: the extent to which the many possible conflict-fronts (due to the many imperatively ordered associations in a society) reduce to a few; the capacity of those higher in authority to distribute rewards and facilities; the degree to which associations are "open" or "closed" (and hence the extent to which mobility is possible); and the extent to which conflict is regulated by (not "suppressed," a word Dahrendorf considers "meaningless") the existing associations (5, pp. 210–231). The intensity, so measured, is (Dahrendorf theorizes) directly proportional to the "radicalness of structure change" and the "suddenness of structure change," that is, the extent to which norms are changed, and the extent to which the original occupants of various positions in the imperatively coordinated association are replaced.

What is important here is not society, but the features by means of which Dahrendorf wishes to describe as "the same" society or association. Galileo formulated $S = \frac{1}{2}at^2$ to describe the motion (change) of a freely falling body. The features he isolated were distance and time. Dahrendorf wants to select the features of the replacement of imperative order participants, and the number which are replaced as well as the value change they represent, and to make these the key to social change. For Galileo there was a direct proportion between the distance traversed by the falling body and the squares of the units of the times. Dahrendorf has not formulated a proportion in terms of which the various features of social change may be computed; nor does he claim to, though he does suggest a scale for the intensity and violence of social conflict, from 0 to 1, (5, p. 230), and hence claims to be developing concepts in terms of which various features of social changes might be formulated. Dahrendorf contrives, then, to formulate a conceptual structure in terms of which A-respects and P-respects may be formulated.

A) A strike in the auto industry is a social conflict about wages and working conditions and a strike in the newspaper industry is about wages and working conditions.

In what respect?

B) In the respect that both emerge out of manifest interests about wages and working conditions in imperatively coordinated associations.

In what respect?

C) In the respect that both emerge out of latent interests about wages and working conditions and proceed to manifest interests about wages and working conditions.

S and S' are the strikes in the respective industries, A is the social conflict, P_i is "about wages and working conditions," and K is the class of attributes "issues about which there are social conflicts." (C) is the necessary and sufficient condition of (B), (B) is the necessary and sufficient condition of (A). There is a clear analogy between a strike in the automobile industry and a strike in the newspaper industry, and we may claim the similarities specified on an anological basis. In this case, no reference to quality is required.

Nevertheless for the purposes of a "science" which will enable us to predict relevant differences between times and places, this is less than fully adequate. The discipline may become more adequate in this way when the concepts are more effectively quantized. But part of the trouble is that the concepts are not precise enough.

What does "precise" mean? Aristotle stated that no greater precision should be provided than is required by the subject. As it stands, the statement is merely good advice. Its relevance can be clarified only when "precision" has effects or consequences in a given discipline. Precision affects a given discipline if the refinements introduced by "making precise" are capable of producing refinements in the consequences. If the refinements are such that they either do not show up in the consequences or that the consequences are capable of being formulated in other terms equally well, then the "making precise" is not very good, and might better have been left out.

"Making precise" is the introduction of discriminations which had not previously been an explicit part of the concept in question. The greater the number of refinements, the greater the precision. Obvious examples of this have to do with the divisions that are marked off in an inch on a ruler and the calibrations marked off on a thermometer. But these are not the only kinds of "making precise" that can be attempted; there are others. Torricelli, by insisting that air had "weight," rendered it capable of calibrations it had not been capable of before.

But "making precise" requires caution. William Heytesbury, attempting to discover how the motion of a freely falling body should be determined, discussed, as an example, a freely falling wheel turning as it fell (29, p. 119). Which part of the wheel, he asked, should be regarded as the criterion of its velocity? His answer was that part of the wheel which was moving the most rapidly. It turned out that this refinement was unnecessary for many purposes. If we want to find out where a wheel that is freely falling will be, we simply calculate the time it has been falling; it is unnecessary to raise the question as to which part of the wheel is going fastest at a given moment. On the other hand, if we wish to know how the wheel will bounce, such a determination would have to be made. Heytesbury's attempt was a refinement, but unnecessary.

Medieval physicists distinguished between uniform and diform motion. The distinction, was, essentially, between the motion of an object which is the same distance per unit of time, and motion which is not. Diform motion had not yet been further made precise so as to have something to do with acceleration or deceleration. Yet we would have to argue that it constituted another class of kinds of motion, more precise than those theories which did not make the distinction. The lesson, of course, is that we can't always tell when to apply Aristotle's dictum and when not: the point in introducing a distinction is usually a hope that it will eventuate in an observable or manipulable differentiation in things. But if it doesn't immediately do so, there is no guarantee that it is pointless.

Or consider another case. A seventeenth-century chemist named Stahl distinguished what he thought of as a "fiery substance" in the air, which he referred to as phlogiston (3). Phlogiston was of such a nature that, when a metallic ore was heated, it united with certain substances in the oxide, caused them to leave the ore, and produce the pure metal. But phlogiston was never observed. What later came to be known as "reduction" was explained by it and it explained the occurrence of (relatively) pure metals. The point is that it was a discrimination, a conceptual refinement which had to do with observable phenomena, and in its way it was successful. To this extent it could be said to be more "precise" than the alchemical theories which preceded it.

Other examples may be adduced. But my point is that the establishment of precision is a way of classifying certain subjects as "the same" or "different." To make precise is to add refinements and to eliminate reference to attributes. In the history of the attempts to formulate the laws of motion, weight and impetus were eliminated as primitive concepts, while the remaining primitives were reduced to distance and time, and calibrated into finer subdivisions. New discrimination must be able to select various phenomena or subjects and make them "the same," which is where "quality" comes in. For, apart from the explanatory (and hence, logical) structure which have been imposed upon them, there is no way of discussing things as "non-qualitative."

The medieval physicists correctly (as it later turned out) believed that local motion had to be described in terms of a proportion. They were not clear about what the proportion was between, i.e., what specific criteria to select. Dahrendorf's attempt is to analyze social conflict in terms of "intensity" and "radicalness." But apart from the theoretical attributes he formulates in their connection, specific criteria to show the proportion between them are imprecise. Doubtless an industrial strike is a *prima facie* example of social conflict. Nevertheless we get lost in an endeavor to discover the criteria by which we are to decide that there is a strike. Is it a criterion that there is a work stoppage on a workday? But maybe they are going on their vacations. Is it that the laborers dislike their employers? Often they don't, and in certain cases may dislike their union officers more. Is the criterion of the conflict, then, the discussion of the union officers with the officers of management over the demands of the specific local? But if it is a discussion, why is it necessarily a conflict? Very well, then, it is a discussion of a certain sort, i.e., bargaining. But is bargaining conflict? Two men who sit down to bargain over the price of a commodity would not necessarily be regarded as being in conflict: each, after all, may have decided on the same price without argument, and to use the occasion for bargaining as an excuse to have a pleasant conversation. Why, then, insist upon this in the case of industrial and social phenomena? If the management wants to avoid a long, costly strike and the union officers want to avoid putting their comrades on a starvation basis, and if the management wants to please its stockholders but yet wants to lay off its men for a time because demand is slack, management and labor may agree on a short "strike" because it is advantageous to all to do so.

It is possible to dissolve every suggested criterion in a morass of analysis, unless we know where we are going — unless we already have an idea of what units of analysis will produce clear and dependable knowledge. "Quality" enters because there is no known respect in terms of which we may provide the analysis.

In terms of our example of the auto strike and the newspaper strike:

The auto strike is like the newspaper strike.

In what respect (where "respect" is restricted to an attribute that is a criterion)?

In the respect that in both cases the strikers left their jobs.

But that's no criterion: one group may have left for a vacation and the other may have left over wages and working conditions.

And so on, following the sequence of the previous paragraph. If no common, logically ordered, specifiable criteria (i.e., A-respects with P-respects) may be discovered for calling a given occurrence a "strike," then the only condition for saying that one is "like" another is "quality."

It is true that conflict may be determined by various "indicators" and indices, as Lazarsfeld shows. But the kind of indicators he discusses are not of the sort referred to above. They are such terms as "cohesiveness," "relevant disruptive forces," "location in society," etc. There is no obvious connection between these sets of attributes. We may be tempted to argue that the less the "cohesiveness," the greater the probability that one of the above-mentioned occurrences would indicate a strike. Nevertheless, if we were to seek a relevant respect in which they were alike apart from their connection with a strike, but which would be an indicator of a strike, the likeness would be hard to find, e.g.,

Mr. S and Mr. S′ had common grievances (one "variate" of "cohesiveness") and left the plant.

In what respect are their departures alike?

Apart from certain obvious biological traits common to both occasions but which are irrelevant, we would be hard put to it to state a likeness or sameness, or to formulate a conceptual structure persistently (or "permanently") capable of dealing with the above and other social changes effectively. Nevertheless, there is a claimed likeness or sameness, and this is qualitative.

E

A common concern with many theoretical sociologists, among whom Parsons and Dahrendorf must be numbered, is the concept of "equilibrium."

Both these writers suppose that it is the task of sociological theory to provide a concept of equilibrium for the social order, so that it is possible for us to say under what conditions the community or society maintains itself. That is, they are asking what elements must remain unvarying (or permanent), or what group of elements must remain in an unvarying (or permanent) proportion, in order that the society or community merit some such description as "stable." That is, "equilibrium" is advanced as a means of formulating statements about the permanent features of social change.

Parsons' conception is "functional"; unit acts take place in the personality, social, and cultural systems, hence the "structure" is maintained. In *The Social System*, Parsons distinguishes between "static" and "moving" equilibria; he is concerned with moving equilibria. The concept of the moving equilibrium revolves around notions of two processes: that by which the actor orients himself to his role; and that by which orientations generating deviant behavior are "counterbalanced" by the "mechanisms of social control" (22, p. 482). In *Values, Motives and Systems of Action*, if I understand him correctly, he refers to the first as "allocation," which he defines more generally in the following way: ". . . processes which maintain a distribution of the components or parts of the system which is compatible with a given state of equilibrium." The second he refers to as "integration," which he defines again more generally as ". . . processes by which relations to the environment are mediated in such a way that the distinctive internal properties and boundaries of the system as an entity are maintained in the face of variability in the external situation" (23, p. 108). Though the descriptions of both processes in the different volumes do not seem to me to be strictly consistent, this may be accounted for in terms of a change of mind, or further development of thought. And in any case it is not to our purpose to criticize this aspect of Parsons' theory.

For Dahrendorf, the conception of equilibrium has to do with interlocking imperatively coordinated associations while the participants do or do not shift "places" in the different orders.

In Parsons' terms, this is also a "moving equilibrium," though a more simply conceived one. In order to see what is happening here, it is best to see what meanings are capable of being attributed to "equilibrium." I think five kinds of equilibrium can be distinguished:

1) Simple mechanical, where the balance of equal forces is conceived of in terms of levers, pulleys, screws, inclined planes, winches, and solids immersed in liquids.

2) Equilibrium in a system of moving bodies, where the movements of the individual bodies may be traced in paths that remain the same, as in the solar system.

3) Thermodynamical, where the equilibrium exists when the mean velocity of the molecules in various portions of a volume are the same.

4) Biological, where a given state (often referred to as the "G state") exists in a way such that if some of a number of conditions vary, the G state will vary, and vice versa.

5) The economic, where equilibrium describes the maintenance of supply, demand, and price of a given commodity in a competitive market.[8]

The attempt to discuss sociology in terms of "equilibrium" is not analogical but metaphorical. If one attempts to say that sociological equilibrium is analogous to simple mechanical equilibrium, one may ask in what respect the balance of weights on a lever is the same as or like the "allocation" of roles in society, or the regulation of conflict and coercion. If the claim is that it is like the equilibrium of the solar system, the respect is impossible to find. Parsons tries to "analogize" between the action system and the solar system in terms of "allocation" (23, pp.107–108), and this writer finds it puzzling. In what respect do we say that the distribution of "forces" is "like" the distribution of social roles or factors in a personality? I find the respect impossible to specify, just as some years ago certain sociologists were opposed to the supposed analogy in the term "social forces." There is no explicit respect in which it can be said that social forces and physical forces are the same, or alike. A similar objection occurs to use of the thermo-dynamical conception of equilibrium: society is not conceived of as "homogeneous" in all of its "sectors"; rather it is conceived of as being different in all of its sectors. As to the biological analogy, it has received enough criticism; but as an example it must be pointed out that "the flow of blood" is in no P-respect the same as "the flow of social change." Finally, one wonders indeed just what is being exchanged for what on the sociological scene, since exchange of commodities is central to the notion of equilibrium in the economic sense. To this it may be replied that they are alike because each person does perform an act on the condition that another perform an act, and this, it may be claimed, is "like" exchange of commodities: one person gives another a commodity if the other person gives him another commodity. But this is merely an analogy by courtesy, so to speak, for what is really alike is not the relations which are specified in each of the contexts, but the purely formal structure of the sentence specifying the acts in question, i.e., the propositional form "if . . . , then. . . ."

The attempt to describe society as a whole in terms of a broad concept like "equilibrium" results in the attempt to state the likeness or sameness of all sociological objects of change in terms of an unspecifiable though permanent respect, so that this supports the contention of sociological theorists that their objects are alike in some unspecifiable respect.

[8] Following Pareto's suggestion: sociology ceases to be similar to economics "when we come to the question of correspondences with reality" (20, p. 1291).

F

Considerations of this sort lead us to reflect upon the work of Robert K. Merton. He explicitly attacks the kind of generalizations attempted by Parsons and Dahrendorf, those which are applicable to societies as a whole; he rejects the present or near-future possibility of theories of the broadest range, and advocates "theories of the middle range" to avoid on the one hand, empty formulations, and on the other hand "raw empiricism." That is to say, here one finds the most explicit statement that sociology is a discipline in which the formulations of general statements are recognized to be subject to immanent change.

In his discussion of the codification of laws (15, p. 49) Professor Merton makes reference to the work of B. L. Whorf who, in examining the reasons for various accidents in his capacity as a fire insurance inspector, noted that people reacted to their conceptions of states of affairs rather than to what the states of affairs in fact were. For example, in the presence of gasoline drums people are careful with matches, cigarettes, and other things likely to cause a fire; whereas in the presence of empty gasoline drums people behave carelessly, lighting cigarettes, freely tossing about lighted stubs, and so on, though in fact the "empty" drums are at least as hazardous as the filled ones because they contain highly explosive vapor. "Empty" is ambiguous: it means null and void, and it means devoid of gasoline. To the uninitiate it means the former; to the technical staff it means the latter. Hence conceptualization is different for each, and is responsible for different kinds of behavior. Merton's point is that sociological conceptualization determines an investigator's response to data in a similar way.

There are, then, different respects in which the data of social change may be rendered "the same" or "alike," depending on how the investigator conceptualizes them. But he cannot know antecedently which of many conceptualizations will be successful, if any. If a "theory of the middle range" is proposed, one class of data may be rendered "the same" as another, and formulations are to this extent "the same" relevant to social changes, though, as noted, themselves subject to change. If a theory of Parsonian scope is proposed, formulations are to be regarded as "permanent" relevant to social change. In either case, what is asserted to be the same or alike in given respects is admittedly alike in other respects, presently unknown.

BIBLIOGRAPHY

1. Burtt, E. A. *The Metaphysical Foundations of Physics.* New York: Harcourt, Brace, 1932.

2. Conant, J. B. "Robert Boyle's Experiments in Pneumatics," Case I,

Harvard Case Studies in Experimental Science, Vol. 1. Cambridge: Harvard University Press, 1957.

3. Conant, J. B. "The Overthrow of the Phlogiston Theory," Case II, *Harvard Case Studies in Experimental Science*, Vol. 1. Cambridge: Harvard University Press, 1957.

4. Crombie, A. C. *Medieval and Early Modern Science*, Vol. 2. New York: Doubleday-Anchor Books, 1959.

5. Dahrendorf, Ralf. *Class and Class Conflict in Industrial Society.* Stanford: Stanford University Press, 1959.

6. Gouldner, Alvin W. "Organizational Analysis," in Robert K. Merton, Leonard K. Broom, and Leonard S. Cottrell (eds.), *Sociology Today.* New York: Basic Books, 1959.

7. Hanson, Norbert R. *Patterns of Discovery.* London: Cambridge University Press, 1958.

8. Harrison, Jane. *Themis*, 2nd ed. London: Cambridge University Press, 1927.

9. Hempel, Carl. "The Logic of Functional Analysis," in Llewelyn Gross (ed.), *Symposium on Sociological Theory.* Evanston, Ill.: Row, Peterson and Co., 1959.

10. Jammer, Max. *Concepts of Space.* Cambridge: Harvard University Press, 1957.

11. Koyre, Alexander. *From the Closed World to the Infinite Universe.* New York: Harper Torchbook, 1958.

12. Lazarsfeld, Paul F. "Problems in Methodology," in Robert K. Merton, Leonard K. Broom, and Leonard S. Cottrell (eds.), *Sociology Today.* New York: Basic Books, 1959.

13. Lovejoy, A. O. *The Great Chain of Being.* Cambridge: Harvard University Press, 1936.

14. Lubell, Samuel. *The Future of American Politics*, 2nd ed., rev. New York: Harper Torchbook, 1956.

15. Merton, Robert K. *Social Structure and Social Theory.* Glencoe, Ill.: The Free Press, 1949.

16. Murray, Margaret. *The God of the Witches.* New York: Doubleday-Anchor Books, 1960.

17. Nagel, Ernest. "Logic Without Ontology," in Krikorian (ed.), *Naturalism and the Human Spirit.* New York: Columbia University Press, 1944.

18. Nagel, Ernest. "A Formalization of Functionalism," in *Logic Without Metaphysics.* Glencoe, Ill.: The Free Press, 1956.

19. Nagel, Ernest. *The Structure of Science.* New York: Harcourt, Brace and World, 1962.

20. Pareto, Vilfredo. "On the Equilibrium of the Social System," a selection from *The Mind and Society*, in Talcott Parsons, Edward Shils, Kaspar D. Naegele, and Jesse R. Pitts (eds.), *Theories of Society.* Glencoe, Ill.: The Free Press, 1961, Vol. 2.

21. Parsons, Talcott. *The Structure of Social Action,* 2nd ed. Glencoe, Ill.: The Free Press, 1949.

22. Parsons, Talcott. *The Social System.* Glencoe, Ill.: The Free Press, 1951.

23. Parsons, Talcott, and Edward Shils, eds. "Values, Motives and Systems of Action," Part 2 of *Toward a General Theory of Action.* New York: Harper Torchbook, 1962.

24. Pascal, Blaise. *The Physical Treatises of Pascal. The Equilibrium of Liquids, The Weight of the Mass of the Air,* translated by I.H.B. and A.G.H. Spiers. New York: Columbia University Press, 1937.

25. Seyffert, Oskar. *Dictionary of Classical Antiquities,* revised and edited by Henry Nettleship and J. E. Sandys. New York: Meridian Library, 1956.

26. Turnbull, Colin M. "The Lesson of the Pygmies," *Scientific American,* January 1962.

27. Watson, W. H. *On Understanding Physics.* New York: Harper Torchbook, 1959.

28. Williams, Robin M. Jr. "The Sociological Theory of Talcott Parsons," in Max Black (ed.), *The Social Theories of Talcott Parsons.* Ithaca, N.Y.: Cornell University Press, 1961.

29. Wilson, Curtis M. *William Heytesbury, Medieval Logic and the Rise of Mathematical Physics.* Madison: University of Wisconsin Press, 1956.

30. Wolf, A. *A History of Science, Technology and Philosophy in the Sixteenth and Seventeenth Centuries,* 2nd ed. New York: Harper Torchbook, 1959, Vol. 1.

3

Don Martindale

The Formation and Destruction

of Communities

In the course of the infinitely varied encounters of men with one another and with nature, various arrangements develop and are adhered
to for a time until they are abandoned and replaced by others. The
discovery of the laws of establishment and disestablishment of such arrangements is the primary object of the theory of social change. Sociology
originated in the nineteenth century as a secular theory of history quite
comparable in its comprehensiveness to Augustine's theory of history,
which dominated medieval Christian thought. For Augustine, the history
of the world consisted in the decline of the earthly city and the rise of
the city of God. For Comte, on the other hand, human history consisted
of the decline of a theologically based society and the rise of the positivistic society. To the medieval conception of stages of secular decay,
Comte counterposed his conception of the laws of progress. As early as
the 1880's Nietzsche had discerned that Comte's motivation was essentially religious and his sociology was an inverted form of Catholicism.

> I am told that the most intelligent of Jesuits, Auguste Comte, who wished
> to lead his compatriots back to Rome by the circuitous route of science,
> drew his inspiration from this book (*The Imitation of Christ*) (10, p. 62).

Nietzsche's insight into the non-scientific core of Comte's theory of social
change was increasingly confirmed by later students. However, no one
was to sum up the point with greater accuracy than Bury.

The progress of humanity belongs to the same order of ideas as Providence or personal immortality. It is true or it is false, and like them it cannot be proved either true or false. Belief in it is an act of faith. The idea of human Progress . . . is a theory which involves a synthesis of the past and a prophecy of the future (1, pp. 4–5).

It is unnecessary here to trace the story of the disaster experienced by the progress-evolution theory of social change (7, pp. 60 ff.), or to trace in detail the alternatives to it (9, pp. 4–30). However, when one examines the various theories of social change which have been offered in sociology from time to time, the uneasy sense grows that, over and beyond the limitations of any particular theory, the theorists themselves tend to talk past one another. The advocates of special positions in some measure dispute hotly about different things. The situation in the field of social change has been parallel to the condition in the field of crime, where attempts at formulating a general theory of crime have been foiled by the fact that crime as legally defined comprises behaviors of intrinsically different sorts. In view of this, it is useful to consider (1) the presuppositions of a scientific theory of social change, and (2) the pragmatic considerations most promising for a fruitful attack on its problems.

A scientific theory of social change presupposes that the formation and destruction of interhuman arrangements is a natural process as subject to objective empirical study as the chemical analysis of a compound. The change theorist is no more committed to the view that every interhuman arrangement is identical in structure with any other than a biologist is that a virus and bacterium are identical in structure. Not only does the scientific theory of social change rest on the assumption that interhuman arrangements are "natural" but also on the assumption that lawful regularities occur among them. It is quite possible that human social events can be quite natural and that "causes" can be established for them, but no laws hold between them because each is unique. In this case a social history of social events would be possible, but not a science of social change. Finally, a scientific theory of social change presupposes that a clear line may be drawn between what "is" and what various persons believe "ought to be." The task of a scientific theory of social change is *to explain* and not to prescribe. Prescriptions, normative social theory, belong to ethics or politics. In a sentence, a scientific theory of social change presupposes that social arrangements are natural, recurrent, and subject to non-evaluative analysis which is capable of establishing laws for the recurrent events among them.

The pragmatic considerations suppose that a fruitful attack on the problems of social change involves, in the first place, recognition that not all social happenings are recurrent. The overall drift in human history, for example, is unique. It is a proper subject matter of social

history, not of social change. However, over and beyond this consideration (which Comte, Spencer, and others violated), it is a time-honored
procedure of science to break up the problems into small, related units
rather than to make an attack on the whole of social life on the advance
assumption that everything is similar to everything else. In the hundred
years or so of the history of sociology, abundant evidence has shown that
at least three classes of social events must be kept separate if one is not
to invite trouble: groups, communities, and cultures (9, pp. 39–54).
In this chapter, the focus will be on communities, on the hypothesis
that the formation and destruction of communities is a particularly vigorous problem for the theory of social change.

Unfortunately, the concept of community has slipped from its once
prominent place in the theory of social change.

The Concept of "Community" in Contemporary Sociology

The status of the concept of "community" in contemporary sociology
may be illustrated by the formulations of Maurice Stein and Talcott
Parsons. In the following paragraphs some rather straight-punching
analysis will be made of the works of both Stein and Parsons. This, of
course, is not directed personally at either of these brilliant scholars.
Stein's *Eclipse of the Community* was chosen as a point of attack on the
problems of the community because this chapter is in agreement
with the judgment that it is the outstanding attempt currently to assess
the importance of the community. The problems discovered in its treatment are significant because of the degree to which they typify the status
of the entire area. The works of Parsons, the foremost sociologist in
America today, are of considerable importance as the most authoritative
of all statements of the functionalistic approach to the community.

The following analysis rests on the assumption that the highest respect
that can be paid to a work of science is to take it in a spirit of complete
earnestness.

Stein's study has been extravagantly praised by contemporary social
scientists. Arthur Vidich, for example, maintains that "Stein has accomplished a major synthesis of all the best in the past thirty years of American community studies. In treating the classical community studies as
historical documents he provides us with the main trends in the evolution of American society as a whole. In addition, his method of analysis
stands as a model relating theory to research." Max Lerner forthrightly
pronounces it: "The best critical and theoretical introduction I have
seen to the study of the American community in all its ramifications. . . .
It is a pattern-breaking as well as a pattern-making study" (15, book
jacket). The chief importance of these statements is that in the minds of
some reputable sociologists Stein's treatment of community is the best
there is.

In this extravagantly praised, "definitive" study, no special definition of the community is to be found. Apparently a community is taken to be whatever has been called a community. Moreover, no attempt is made to distinguish the "community" from the "group," other than to suggest that the study of community is large-scale rather than small-scale, and is to be preferred for some rather extraordinary reasons.

> Why study communities when one can much more easily study small groups . . . ? Studies of small groups can sidestep the problem of generalizability simply by defining their objects of study on a sufficiently high level of abstraction. . . . The advantages . . . of small-group research . . . lie largely in the readiness with which observational studies can be conducted and findings generalized. In both these respects, the field of community studies is not nearly as convenient (15, p. 96).

The willing sacrifice of the exactness afforded by small groups is said to be taken because of a sense of "closeness to human reality" to their "appeals to one's appetite for diversity" (15, p. 96), and to a feeling for the variety of styles of living found in complex modern settings" (15, p. 97).

The "pattern-breaking as well as pattern-making" property (in Lerner's words) of Stein's study seems to lie in his hypothesis that communities — whatever they may be — are being transformed by three general processes: urbanization, industrialization, and bureaucratization. On the basis of Park's studies of Chicago, Warner's of New Haven, and the Lynds' studies of Muncie, Indiana, Stein asserts:

> If we use these three sets of studies as points of departure, the foregoing should suggest an interpretive framework for examining other community studies as well as for formulating new ones. The conceptual model rests on the examination of change and assumes that urbanization, industrialization, and bureaucratization . . . plot most of the key dimensions (15, p. 107).

It is unfortunate that Stein has not provided a clear definition of community, for there seems to be a connection between the three processes and the title of his book.

> American communities can be seen continuing the vital processes uncovered in Muncie by the Lynds. Substantive values and traditional patterns are continually being discarded. . . . Community ties become increasingly dispensable, finally extending even into the nuclear family. . . . On the one hand, individuals become increasingly dependent upon centralized authorities and agencies in all areas of life. On the other, personal loyalties decrease their range with the successive weakening of national ties, regional ties, community ties, neighborhood ties, family ties, and finally, ties to a coherent image of one's self. . . . Suburbia is so fascinating just because it reveals the "eclipse" of community at one of its darkest moments . . . (15, p. 329).

It would seem that, after all, the germs of a precise theory of community lie buried somewhere in Stein's account. Although communities are found to be different from groups — in that they have more of the smell of real life about them — communities are taken to be traditional complexes of primary-group qualities. Stein's theory is that the three processes of urbanization, industrialization, and bureaucratization are breaking up such complexes of primary-group qualities, bringing about the "eclipse of the community."

Talcott Parsons, by contrast to Stein, operates with clearly formulated categories. In *The Social System* he developed special versions of the concepts of "community" and "society." "A community is that collectivity the members of which share a common territorial area as their base of operations for daily activities" (11, p. 91). A society, on the other hand, is "the social system which is potentially or, 'in principle,' self-subsistent" (11, p. 113). By the self-sufficiency of a total social system is meant one "which meets all the essential functional prerequisites of long term persistence within its own resources" (11, p. 19). In contrast to such a total social system, a society, all others are "partial" social systems. In this terminology a community is a partial social system. Quite consistently Parsons observes: "We may say that membership in the four types of groupings, kinship, community, ethnic and class, should characterize every individual actor in every society and such groupings should, with the requisite qualifications, be looked for as part of the structure of every society" (11, p. 173).

Parsons' formulation in *The Social System* seems to be a concession to Tönnies dichotomy, *Gemeinschaft* and *Gesellschaft,* frequently translated as "community" and "society." Parsons' discussion is a precise formulation of some of the same ideas that are central to Stein's argument. This, as we have seen, was that communities are complexes of primary-group relationships which are increasingly being liquidated and replaced by secondary relationships. However, had Parsons adhered strictly to Tönnies' formulations, he would have viewed "community" and "society" as alternative types of total social systems without restricting the community to the status of a partial social system of the society.

Even at the time *The Social System* was written, Parsons was in the process of abandoning the notions of both "community" and "society" in place of the conception of "social system." Within the total social system, Parsons distinguished five dichotomously classified types of goals which individuals may pursue. He described these as "pattern variables of role definition": affectivity versus affective neutrality; self versus collectivity orientation; orientation to universal versus orientation to particularistic standards; the evaluation of others in terms of achievement or ascription; and an interest in the object which is specific or diffuse (11, p. 97). One class of these dichotomous pairs conforms to the *Gemeinschaft,* the other to the *Gesellschaft.* In *Working Papers in the*

Theory of Action, Parsons reconceptualized these pattern variables as "dimensions of action space" which were then fused with Bales' conception of four major interaction processes in social systems: adaptation, instrumental control over the situation, expression of sentiment, and integration of the members with one another (12, p. 64). Finally, in *Structure and Processes in Modern Societies* the same concepts were once more reconceptualized as "functional imperatives of social systems" (13, p. 57).

At this stage in his thought, an organization was described by Parsons as "a social system which is organized for the attainment of a particular goal; the attainment of that goal is at the same time the performance of a type of function on behalf of a more inclusive system, the society" (13, p. 56). Three types of successively more comprehensive social systems were identified: the group, the organization, and the society. Not only is it true, according to Parsons, that the group and organization perform essential functions for the society, but they are said to be organized in the same manner. Every social system, according to Parsons, has a value system, adaptive mechanisms, an operative code, and integrative mechanisms.

> The classification used has proved its applicability both for the level of total society and for that of the small group. The present application to an intermediate level [the organization] further increases confidence in its generality (13, pp. 56–57).

Despite the extravagant praise of Stein's study of the community, Parsons' analysis is not only more logically consistent but empirically superior. If we must retain the conception of community as a territorially based social system, Parsons has indicated, it can no longer constitute a total social system. On the other hand, Parsons indicates (as Stein does not) that because the territorially based total social system no longer retains its older meaning, this does not imply that the total social system has ceased to exist. Hence, Parsons, in practice if not in theory, replaces both the concepts of "community" and "society" with that of "total social system."

By contrast, Stein conducts his analysis as if the term "community" refers to everything that has ever been described as a community. Among the examples of communities Stein reviews are numerous cities (New Haven, Muncie, Burlington, Chicago). At the same time, urbanization is inconsistently treated as one of the processes which brings the community into "eclipse." If the city is a community and if urbanization represents the extension of patterns typical of the city, urbanization ought more logically to represent a peculiar kind of community formation rather than community destruction.

Similarly, in handling the relation between the groups and the community Parsons' analysis seems to be unquestionably superior to that of Stein. Stein sees the chief value of community study over the study of groups in the greater sense of reality conveyed by the former. Parsons, on the other hand, contrasts the group and community as partial versus total social systems. At the same time, Parsons treats the partial social system exclusively as performing a single function within the whole. Moreover, his argument proceeds from the premise that the society and the group and organization are identical in structure.

One may formulate these ideas as hypotheses: the group is identical in structure with the community; the sole significance of the group is found in the function it performs for the community with which it is harmoniously integrated. When formulated as hypotheses, these ideas can be proved false. However, the possible difficulties with Parsons' theories of community are as nothing compared with those of Stein. One deals with the community to gain the feel of genuine social life. However, the processes of urbanization, industrialization, and bureaucratization are destroying the community. The real life with which we are encouraged to deal is thus vanishing before our very eyes. *Nevertheless, we are told not to despair.* One of the most astonishing suggestions in contemporary social science is offered for our consolation.

> Each community sociologist is left to work out his own relationship to the community that he studies and the best clues to his solution are contained in the style of the final report. The omnipotent feeling on the part of the reader of a community study can only be a pale reflection of the omnipotence felt by the author as he literally creates the picture of the community while he writes his book. Naturally, this creative process involves exploring the irrational self-images and community images held by his subjects, along with the objective structures that his scientific framework and observational stance enable him to discern (15, p. 319).

Not everyone, incidentally, feels "omnipotent" while reading the community studies. Sometimes one feels bored. And at those times one suspects that the author of a given community study invented the picture he presents; one tends not to feel exalted, but outraged. Nevertheless, we are told that the community is vanishing before our very eyes, but not to despair. The very lack of a community is our opportunity.

> In light of the threatening character of alien meanings, the tendency to employ elaborate technology or elaborate defences against social insight can never be ignored. . . . The development of a dramaturgic frame of reference promises to facilitate research and theorizing in this area as well as in the rest of sociology. From this standpoint, the future of community studies does appear bright. However, the real fate of this subdivision of sociology . . . depends finally upon the state of the sociological imagination (15, p. 337).

"Stone walls," it seems, "do not a prison make." If one has a "sociological imagination" and "develops a dramaturgic frame of reference," one need not be dismayed at the "threatening character of alien meanings" which arise with the eclipse of the community. It is necessary only to conjure up dream images of communities closer to one's heart's desire.

This interpretation of Stein's argument rests on the assumption that he intends to blur the distinction between communities and the descriptions of them, for this is what his words imply. A re-examination of the nature of the community is clearly needed.

The Nature of the Community

The extravagantly praised study of Stein and the treatment by Parsons of the community do not fulfill the promise for the concept developed in the first third of the twentieth century. In a famous study in 1917, MacIver identified the community as a complete system of social life including manners, traditions, modes of speech, and the like. Communities were taken to represent nuclei of common life in varying degrees of integration and intensity.

> In the infinite series of social relationships which thus arise, we distinguish the nuclei of intenser common life, cities and nations and tribes, and think of them as *par excellence* communities (6, p. 23).

In including nations and cities, MacIver's concept of "community" is far more comprehensive than that of Stein, who, at least by implication, includes only complexes of primary relations in his concept. Furthermore, in including the city as a community, MacIver would identify urbanization as a specific community-forming, rather than a community-destroying, process.

Again, in his article for the *Encyclopædia of the Social Sciences* in the early 1930's, E. C. Lindeman was clearly aware of the fact that reference to common territory was not necessary for identifying the community.

> A community, if we define its explicit elements, is any consciously organized aggregation of individuals residing in a specific area or locality, supporting such primary institutions as schools and churches and among whom certain degrees of interdependence are recognized. This definition includes hamlets, villages, towns, and cities. A community, if we define its implicit elements, is any process of social interaction which gives rise to a more intensive or more extensive attitude and practice of interdependence, cooperation, collaboration, and unification. This latter conception omits all consideration of locality (4, p. 203).

This conception would clearly exclude Parsons' reduction of community to the territorial association of a society, and it would clearly include his conception of the society (total social system) as a community.

There is no sound basis in early American sociology for assigning the idea of community exclusively to territorial association nor for withdrawing it from any complete systems of common life. If the concept of community is to preserve its utility in the twentieth century, it is essential that the latter meaning be taken as primary, for occupancy of common territory has lost much of its former importance as a foundation for systems of common life.

The concept of "community" should be kept distinct from those of "group" and "culture." Let us define a *group* as a set of standardized arrangements among a plurality of people for the solution of a specific set of common problems. A family, a state, a corporation, a church, are all examples of groups. Institutions may be defined as the standardized solutions to collective problems which men apply in their group activities. *Culture* refers to the sum total of ways by which men learn to behave in society. The material artifacts produced by these activities are also often included in the concept of culture. Specific items of culture are *forms* or *traits*. Smoking cigarettes, wearing clothing, observing rules of etiquette are samples of cultural traits. A group is an integrated system of interaction: it is *what* a plurality of people do; their culture is *how* they do it.

A community is a set or system of groups sufficient to solve all of the basic problems of ordinary ways of life. As a way of life, a community is complete in two senses: it comprises a set of groups sufficient to carry a plurality of people through all the routine problems of an ordinary year and through the cycle of an ordinary life from birth to death. Once *a plurality* of people possesses a set of groups sufficient to carry it through an ordinary year or an ordinary life, the cycle is complete. If one studies communities at times rather than groups, it is not because one is eager to make the sacrifice of quantitative exactness for a more pungent sense of social reality, but because the group and community are social realities of different sorts.

Every community bears some relation to the natural environment, for a community is a system of common life by a plurality of people who must draw things they require from nature if they are to survive through time. However, this does not mean that the community always or necessarily has some fixed point on the earth's surface with which it is inseparably identified. A community of hunters, for example, does not cease to be a community because it wanders more or less continuously through hundreds of miles of hunting territory. Or again, a gypsy community does not cease to be a true community even though its way of life may lead it to wander over large areas.

In general, the deeper one goes into the past of mankind, the closer the identification of human communities with relatively fixed territories is seen to be, though even in very ancient times this could, as revealed by some hunting and food-gathering communities, be remarkably flexible.

By contrast, although modern communities also draw from nature directly or indirectly the things their members need to survive, identification with some limited territory plays a diminished role in their structure.

The decline of territory as an organizing principle of the modern community is linked to the growth of transportation and communication systems, for the means of transportation and communication available to men implements their relations with nature. While human and prehuman types date back to perhaps 1,500,000 B.C., archaeological and geological evidence indicates that human communities have been in existence since the second inter-glacial period or for at least 150,000 years. However, until around 10,000 B.C. (when the domestication of plants was seriously under way) the communities of primitive hunters-fishers-gatherers were limited in size to the number of men who could be sustained by the natural produce of an area of the earth's surface and from which they could exclude other men. The small communities of men existing at that time must have been forced to move almost continuously through an area capable of sustaining them in a manner not too dissimilar from the hunting territory of a wolf pack. Communications were restricted to oral exchange, and everyone must have known almost instantly about nearly everything happening to other members of the group. The communities of cultivators which arose around 10,000 B.C. were similarly bound by the conditions of their existence into relatively small groups and were even more closely tied to a restricted area than were their predecessors in hunting-fishing-gathering communities.

The ancient oriental city, on the other hand, which arose shortly before 3000 B.C., brought many more people together in a dense settlement at the same time that it freed the community as a whole from the kind of intimate dependence on any specific area of the earth's surface characteristic of previous communities. For one thing, the cities imported the materials they required (metal, wood, stone, and so on) from distant places. For another, the rulers often deliberately founded cities, creating the conditions that made them possible. The ancient oriental kings at times engaged in military activities to secure the labor necessary to undertake extensive irrigation projects which transformed semi-arid lands into gardens to sustain the cities which arose in their midst. Transportation and communications were developed in new forms to make these new communities possible; writing was invented; roads were constructed and paved; and postal systems were established.

In the nineteenth century the most fabulous of all revolutions in communications and transportation was carried through. Contemporary electronic communications and mechanical modes of transportation resting on the employment of inorganic forms of power and machines have transformed man's ancient relation to the environment in a most fundamental sense. The fundamental terms of any system of interhuman life are established not by environment or territory directly but by one's capacity to communicate and to interact on a day-to-day basis. It is possible by means of electronic instruments to communicate immediately with persons thousands of miles away. The jet plane makes it possible to cross the United States and return in a day. A man may sit down to a meal at which there are products from a dozen different parts of the country. Modern men may commute from distant suburbs to their places of business in a central city, daily making a journey which required days for their forefathers.

The essence of the community has always been found in its character as a set of institutions composing a total way of life. In the past when communication and transportation facilities were primitive, such total ways of life were usually confined to relatively restricted areas. It was convenient under such circumstances to view communities as territorially based systems of common life. However, the development of contemporary communication and transportation facilities has rendered such conceptions obsolete. Systems of common life still arise, but they are relatively free most of the time of any narrow dependence on a restricted territory. Perhaps it is not asking too much to expect the theory of community to discover the industrial revolution.

The Principles of Community Formation

There is every reason to believe that Stein and his sponsors (Vidich and Lerner) are mistaken and that Talcott Parsons is correct. The community (Parsons' total social system) has not gone into eclipse; it is a going concern for contemporary man. Only an old-fashioned concept of the "community" has become obsolete. The community has simply lost its old territorial anchorage. On the other hand, there is good reason to question Parsons' notion that the group and community are similarly constituted and that the primary relation between them is found in harmonious service to the community by the group. This may be seen by reviewing the principles of community formation.

Animal communities arise automatically without learning on a foundation of inherited mechanisms. When the proper stimulus is at hand, the creature instinctively does the correct thing. Men, however, have lost the instinctive foundations of their social behavior and hence must learn or invent it from case to case (9, pp. 34 ff.). Though they have no instincts to tell them what to do, it is still necessary for men to solve the problems of adjustment to nature and to one another well enough to survive. In any case, we deal only with those who live to tell the tale. The principles of the formation of human communities have to do with the rise of total systems of interhuman arrangements by creatures who must learn or invent all the behaviors they require to survive. Three such principles are at work in all communities: *stabilization, consistency,* and *closure* (9, pp. 44–49). A variety of secondary principles are discerned (8, pp. 491–493) but are not of concern in the present context.

Three general types of problems must be solved by a human collectivity if it is to survive: *mastery of the material environment, socialization,* or the transformation of pre-social materials into social forms, and *social control,* or the framing of decisions binding on the human collectivity and maintaining the discipline necessary for their execution. The formation of particular arrangements (groups) in which solutions to these problems (institutions) are embodied is the fundamental subject matter of the theory of groups and institutions (9, pp. 39–44). The formation of communities implies, in the first place, the prior formation of groups in all these basic areas of social life. The theory of community proper accounts for how such a set of groups is fashioned into a total way of life.

Stabilization

The first process significant for the formation of communities is the *stabilization* of the solutions to collective problems in the various areas of social life — that is, the formation of groups. Men do not have a dependable set of instincts which provide them with automatic solutions to the problems of collective life. However, they have an unusually comprehensive capacity to invent and to learn. Once a solution to a major problem is arrived at, whether by happy discovery, by patient study and invention, or by learning, it tends to be remembered. The next time the same problem is faced, the remembered or habitual solution comes readily to mind. If it were not for this fact, human social life would be hopelessly inefficient, for each time the problem developed it would have to be solved anew. In any case, the solution to the various problems of collective life tends to stabilize in the habits of individuals (or from the standpoint of the collectivity) the customs of the community.

Consistency

The establishment of solutions to problems in the major areas of collective life and their embodiment in custom do not end the process of community formation. Once the solution to a problem of collective life is embedded in the habits of a plurality of individuals, these habits in turn become preconditions for further actions. The landscape of behavior is quickly plotted and pierced by the established solutions, and as further occasions for action arise the new behaviors arrange themselves around the fixed points.

Sooner or later the nuclei of established behaviors and the concentric rings of consistent activity around them come into contact with the concentric rings of activity around other points.

Even among creatures whose behavior rests on instinct, the possibility of conflict between different spheres of behavior is present. The instinctive activity of a bird in the presence of danger is flight. However, the instinctive activity of a bird toward its young is one of protection. The cunning compromise between the instinct to flee and the instinct to protect its young, also established in the course of biological evolution of the partridge, is for the female to feign an injury, running just out of range of a creature dangerous to its young, until they are safe, whereupon she drums away on powerful wings.

Among human beings, where the solutions to basic problems must be invented or learned, the possibilities for conflicts between alternative behavioral requirements are multiplied. And if conflicting instincts, such as the bird's impulse to flight and to protect its young, may lead to a modified flight which leads danger away from its young, one need not be surprised when the intersection of behaviors proceeding out of different spheres of human life leads to mutual modification.

The characteristics of human groups and organizations described by Parsons as "organized for the attainment of a particular goal," which is "at the same time the performance of a type of function on behalf of a more inclusive system, the society," are a product of the conjoint operation of the two community-forming principles, "stabilization" and "consistency." The first property is a product of the conversion of a successful solution to collective problems into a fixed (habitual, customary, or rational) property of social life. The second property is a product of the re-stylization of groups and institutions in the areas of their primary operation to prevent major collisions with behaviors from other areas.

However, in presenting the relation of groups and communities as harmoniously intermeshed and similarly structured systems, Parsons' theory blurs a social phenomenon of great significance. When a group or institution is re-designed to fit the requirements of the community, the efficiency of the group or institution in the area of its origin may be impaired. A young man who is faced with one of the most bitter choices of his life — to take advantage of a magnificent career opportunity which will take him to a distant part of the earth, or to remain at home and marry "the one and only girl" — need not be told twice that his economic and domestic choices are in tension. Conflicts may arise for individuals not only between the economic and domestic spheres of life but also between any two. Such harmony as exists between the activity of a group and the whole never exhausts the picture, and must always be won at some cost.

Closure

Meanwhile, the cycle of nature and the cycle of organic growth do not permit a collectivity to linger long over the possibilities of recon-

structing the relations between two single areas of social life. Spring
slips into summer, and fall into winter, in the eternal cycle of the seasons,
and individuals are impelled by organic change through the stages of
life. In short, it is necessary to find a formula that without too much
loss not only resolves the conflicts that may emerge between the family
and religion or religion and economic institutions but between a set of
institutions sufficient to the cycle of the year and the cycle of life.

The final major process which completes the formation of a community is the *closure* of the circuit of institutions — the fixing of some
formula which laces the whole into a working arrangement. Sumner
long ago noted that some group habits (customs or folkways) undergo
special evolution and development which raise them to another plane.
"They become capable of producing inferences, developing into new
forms, and extending their constructive influence over men and society.
Then we call them the mores. The mores are the folkways, including the
philosophical and ethical generalizations as to societal welfare which are
suggested by them" (16, p. 30). With special frequency it is the function
of the mores to provide a legitimizing function *in the community as a
whole* which elevates some group habits to the new level of sanctity.

A review of the primary principles of community formation thus
clarifies the fact that one does not study the community rather than
the group because one prefers the color of real life to exactness. Communities are no more and no less real than groups. One studies communities because they are distinctive social phenomena with properties
other than those of groups. Moreover, while a community represents an
integration of groups into a total way of life, a perspective which attends
only to such parallelism of structure as appears between groups and
communities and emphasizes only the harmony between them, misses the
tense interpenetration of the particular group and the whole which
constitutes the drama and life of a community.

The principles of community formation cast into relief the distortions
of the "functionalistic" conceptualizations of communities in organismic
terms. Communities are not organisms nor even like organisms except
on the astonishing hypotheses that the activities of organisms are also
organisms and the actions of a man also act like a man. Communities
are ways people act; they do not act themselves. Communities are not
born, and they do not die; people act, or cease to act, in certain ways.

As a comprehensive strategy of collective behavior, a community involves losses as well as gains. When one area of life is adjusted to another, something will have to change. The formation of a community
involves some impairment of the efficiency of institutions in the areas of
their primary application. To some extent the greater the consistency
and integration in the community, the greater the modification necessary in the primary areas of life. However, a kind of lower limit may
be established beyond which one cannot modify groups and institutions.

In the early days of the Soviet Union, experiments were attempted in the total disposition of the "bourgeois institution of marriage." However, it soon appeared that serious anomic consequences resulted from the replacement of traditional marriage institutions with a companionate marriage scheme, and the traditional family was restored and reinforced. Moreover, not only is there some impairment of groups and institutions by the formation of the community, but considerable flexibility must be sacrificed. A community cannot run smoothly and still tolerate unlimited experimentation in the line institutions.

On the other hand, community-wide arrangements may protect the general welfare against that of the individual. In the years of the buffalo hunt, the Plains Indian police organization had extraordinary powers to prevent anything which might frighten the herd and put it to flight. Women were not permitted to chop wood, and men were not allowed to hunt individually. War parties could be restrained from setting out, and personal hostilities between tribesmen which might precipitate feuds could be arbitrarily terminated. The individualism of the Plains Indians was supplanted at such times by extreme police control (5, p. 385).

The most significant values secured by the fusion of a set of groups into a community are the reduction of conflicts and the securing of stability. The reduction of conflicts has two aspects: the establishment of a legitimate order and the development of institutions (armies, police systems, legal systems) to sustain it. Stability, however, is secured over and beyond the specific maintenance of the legitimate order by sheer pressure of the system as a whole on any single part. Stability is the reverse, the positive side of the loss of plasticity on the part of component groups when they are fused into a community.

A considerable number of hypotheses can be derived from the principles of community formation: (1) an upper limit is placed on the inter-adjustment of the groups of a community by the danger of impairment of basic institutions in the areas of their origin; (2) to the extent that the community formula (a device for transforming a set of groups into an interrelation system) permits groups to retain their original operations, it must accommodate itself to a higher volume of inner-community conflict; (3) to the degree that plasticity is permitted to its basic groups and institutions, a community's capacity to adapt to extra-community crisis is increased; (4) to the extent to which a community forces the total reconstruction of behavior, it becomes virtually indestructible from internal forces; and (5) the unusual internal stability and external resilience of theocratic communities (the Parsees, Jains, and Jews) is bound up in an in-group, out-group ethic which forces rather complete reconstruction of behavior from within while simultaneously freeing the community for adaptation toward the outside.

When the study of the community is brought to full development, hypotheses such as these will be brought out and tested.

A Typology of Historically Significant Communities

While communities form by inter-adjustment of all major institutions to one another, the primary character of a community derives from the institution which more than any other provides the forms for the stylization of the whole. Theoretically, at least, this primary stylization could proceed from any institutional sphere. Among specialized communities which men have formed are religious communities, military communities, ethnic communities, artist colonies, educational communities, communities in pursuit of health, underworld communities. Each specialized community has its unique problems. If one were to analyze community structure in detail, such specialized communities could provide invaluable material. Here, however, the concern is with social change.

In addition to such specialized communities, there are a number which have played a comprehensive role in human history. They are like the mainstreams in human affairs, while the specialized communities have been like branch creeks. Historically, some communities have followed one another in a crude sequence. Such historically significant communities have played a general role in human affairs by paving the way for other communities which followed them. However, no unilinear sequence can be established between such historically significant communities, nor do they form a set of stages in a single development.

Archaeological evidence indicates that human communities have existed from at least the second inter-glacial period; that is, since 150,-000 B.C. It is useful to trace the close of this period of human community formation in terms of the major transformation in the mastery of nature. These early men lived by gathering, by hunting, and by fishing. It would perhaps be useful if the ambiguous term "tribe" were restricted to such pre-cultivating communities. Such tribal communities must, however, have existed in some variety from almost pure food gatherers, hunters, and fishers to combined gathering-fishing-hunting communities. They were also specialized in terms of the kinds of things gathered and the kinds of game hunted or fished.

In the Near East, in some conjoint gathering-hunting-fishing communities around 10,000 B.C., plant cultivation began to transform the fundamental ratio of man to environment. Within 2,000 years after the discovery of plant cultivation, the domestication of animals (beginning with the dog, sheep, and honey bee, around 8000 B.C.) got under way. From 10,000 B.C. to around 3500 B.C., the early communities of plant cultivators and animal breeders represented the most complex communities up to that time. However, here again a considerable variety of subtypes appeared: hoe culture without domestication, amplified by hunting and fishing; plow culture with mixed plant and animal breeding; and pure animal husbandry. Usually the most prosperous and fully developed of the peasant village communities were represented by communities practicing mixed plant and animal breeding.

Though only a fraction of mankind was at first incorporated in them, city communities resting on militarized upper strata and administration consisting in considerable measure of priests, and lower strata made up of an amalgam of free peasants, laborers, serfs, and slaves began to appear shortly before 3000 B.C. Such city life first appeared in the valleys of the Tigris and Euphrates rivers. A wave of city formation soon followed in the Nile Valley. It was not long in appearing in the valleys of the Indus in India, the Yellow River in China, and on the islands of the eastern Mediterranean.

Later waves of city formation such as those of the Mediterranean Sea cities or the cities of the Western Middle Ages had different properties from the ancient oriental cities, but city life never disappeared completely after the beginnings in the Near East.

In many areas of the ancient world, city communities developed imperialistic properties and turned into city empires. When this occurred it was very difficult to retain either the city or the structure which implemented its imperial control against forces which tended to disintegrate it from within. The disintegration of the ancient city imperialism was followed in various times and places by the rise of the communities of a feudal system.

Nothing more quickly disproves the evolutionary or stage theories of human development than the times and occurrences of the rise of feudal systems. A form of feudalism arose in ancient China about 1100 B.C. with the destruction of the ancient city imperialism of the Shang. A feudal system arose in Japan after the fourth century A.D. It also arose in the Moslem world after the eighth century A.D., and in Western Europe after the fourth century A.D.

The distinctive communities of the contemporary world, nation-states, began to form out of elements of European feudal society after the twelfth and thirteenth centuries. Only by the sixteenth century had the emerging national states begun seriously to challenge both the feudal communities of Europe and the city. In the seventeenth, eighteenth, and nineteenth centuries the nation-states began to assume their modern form and to spread in a world-wide movement of community formation which continues in full tide today.

Time Periods and Historically Significant Communities

TIME	DEVELOPED COMMUNITY FORM
150,000 B.C. to 10,000 B.C.	Tribal communities of hunters-gatherers-fishers
10,000 B.C. to 3000 B.C.	The peasant village
3500 B.C.	The city
1100 B.C. to 200 B.C.	Feudal communities of China
400 A.D. to 1900	Feudal communities of Japan
400 A.D. to 1300	Feudal communities of Europe
800 A.D. to 1900	Feudal communities of the Moslem world
1600 A.D.	The nation-state

A number of sociologists in the past and present have offered a far more simple dichotomous typology of communities than the one above.

Traditional Societal Typology

AUTHOR	DICHOTOMOUS TYPOLOGY	
Comte	Theological society	Positivistic society
Spencer	Theological-military society	Industrial-peaceable society
Durkheim	Mechanically-solidary society	Organically-solidary society
Tonnies	*Gemeinschaft*	*Gesellschaft*
Park	Sacred society	Secular society
Redfield	Folk society	Secular society
Parsons	Society resting on ascriptive solidarity	Society resting on functional differentiation

The historical typology of communities reviewed earlier differs from the traditional societal typology in two respects: it abandons its evolutionary assumptions, and it rejects its dichotomous construction.

The Formation and Destruction of Communities

From the standpoint that has been developed in this paper, communities are not born; they are formed or created. They do not die; they are abandoned or destroyed. While acknowledging this, both the theories of the Marxian socialists and the conflict sociologists (such as Gumplowicz and Ratzenhofer) cover only part of the facts. The Marxians treated changes in economic institutions as fundamental, and traced all social change to class struggles. The formation of peasant villages in a world formerly dominated by the tribal communities of hunters-gatherers-fishers seems primarily to have been based on economic changes. The rise of the peasant village may possibly conform to the pattern of Marxian theory. By contrast to the Marxists, the conflict sociologists thought the rise of complex societies was always a politico-military phenomena. The oriental city which supplanted a world of peasant villages was, to Max Weber, a political and military product.

> Irrigation and its regulation presupposed a systematic and organized husbandry. . . . The military campaigns of the Assyrian and Babylonian kings . . . were primarily man hunts for the purpose of securing the human material for building canals and bringing stretches of the desert under tillage. . . . The king retained control of water regulations, but required for its exercise an organized bureaucracy. . . . The result of the system . . . was to place the population in a servile relation to the prince (18, pp. 56–57).

While the formation of the peasant village roughly fits Marxian theory, the formation of the ancient city roughly fits conflict theory. The various historically significant communities do not exclusively fit either the socialistic or conflict sociological conceptions. The one thing that can be accepted without qualification from these theories is that the formation of communities involves destruction as well as construction of social forms.

The Marxians isolated a significant source of social change in conflicts of economic interests internal to the community. They erred, however, in failing to see that conflicts among non-economic interests may be a source of change as well. When they did acknowledge such non-economic interests, the Marxians sought to reduce them to economic terms. The conflict sociologists were correct in seeing inter-community political and military conflicts as a major source of change. However, they tended to minimize the role of inner-community conflicts. To the conflict theorists, the community was a peace group. With the conflict theorists it must be agreed that a variety of internal and external conflicts in varying degrees of importance in the special case have played a role in the formation of the historically significant types of communities. Moreover, the transformations that ensued do not constitute an evolutionary sequence, as the Marxians and also the early conflict sociologists assumed.

Evidences of Upheaval in the Transition from Pre-cultivating Tribes

Although an adequate picture of the community-significant events which occurred with the transition from some pre-cultivating tribes to peasant villages awaits reconstruction largely out of archaeological events, there are a number of indications that this event was no smooth transition; it was made from hunting-fishing-gathering communities to communities resting on hoe culture. This involved not only an economic but a social revolution, for the major components of ancient society were radically re-oriented. The hunting band was bypassed as a primary economic structure, and the women's economy came to the fore. Where a hunting economy was elaborately developed, transition was delayed.

> The revolutionaries were not the most advanced savages of the Old Stone Age — the Magdalenians were all too successfully specialized for exploiting the pleistocene environment — but humbler groups who had created less specialized and less brilliant cultures farther south. Amongst them while men hunted, women . . . had collected among other edibles the seeds of wild grasses, ancestral to our wheat and barley. The decisive step was deliberately to sow such seeds on suitable soil and cultivate the sown land by weeding and other measures. A society that acted thus was henceforth actively producing food. . . . Potentially it could increase the supply to support a growing population (2, p. 41).

Wherever hoe culture spread, the women's group increased its prestige in the councils of the community.

When the point of gravity of economic life shifted to hoe culture in their hands, women also rose to prominence in social and political affairs. "Now woman was far superior economically to man owing to her garden, as long as man remained a hunter. Her permanent plant resources fed the whole family. . . . And so grew a social and political ascendancy of woman over man, and is witnessed, up to today, by the so-called matriarchy" (3, p. 32). However, when the domestication of animals brought men into agriculture, and when animal husbandry became possible, the situation was reversed once more. "Man was by far superior, as a herdsman, to woman as a foodgatherer at this stage or during the mixed herdsmen and planter cultures that followed somewhat later. In a nomadic life, woman very often became a subject being or at least takes second place in the patriarchal social system. Polygamy was considered inevitable because of the increasing demand for men to look after the increasing herds. To have many wives and enormous families was therefore of the highest economic value" (3, p. 40). There were, of course, variations from place to place, however, Heichelheim seems to have located the primary series of revolutions.

Evidences of Upheavals in the Transition from Peasant Villages to Cities

When one examines the ancient oriental city as it appears not only in the archaeological evidence but in its own written records, it is quickly evident that a great economic and social revolution accompanied its appearance. It is a community of greater size than the peasant villages it replaced. Moreover, it has a very different structure: the peasant household has been torn apart, the tribal cults have been abandoned or transformed into minor aspects of a comprehensive city religion, political and military affairs are centralized in a ruling caste, and a large mass of persons at the base of society have been reduced to semi-free or slave status.

The archaeological evidence simply does not bear out the evolutionary assumption that all these changes were brought about by some kind of slow accretion of small changes.

Formerly scholars suggested that there was a gradual development from village and castle to the city proper, and that this first occurred in Mesopotamia. Today we have actual traces of such a change-over from Ur, Kish, Uruk, and a great number of other sites of Mesopotamia, Egypt, Asia Minor, and Syria. But to our surprise there is a sudden transition from village to city to be observed practically everywhere, not a slow growth. The oldest genuine city structures which superseded the primitive village huts with one stroke are often stronger and mightier than the buildings of later town levels. In Uruk, near 3600 B.C. or so, the builders brought stones hundreds of miles down the Euphrates to erect the enormous buildings which are characteristic for the beginnings of this town, our excavations having as yet brought to light no traces of any gradual improvement in technique and culture leading up to this stage (3, p. 103).

This suggests that in a relatively brief time numerous peasant villages were torn to pieces and the ancient oriental cities were formed out of their fragments. Politico-military structures must have played a central role, for when the city is established it bears the scars of past violence with a militaristic and priestly caste at the top and a semi-free and slave stratum at the bottom.

In the peasant village communities that preceded the city, there was at least one frequently institutional development which could have taken over the function of tearing villages to bits and forming their fragments into a new order. When women became able, under hoe cultivation, economically to support the community more effectively than had generally been the case previously, when settlement was consolidated around the gardens of the women, and when the women formed into something of a socio-political unit, the former hunting band was free to develop new forms. In many places around the world under such conditions, the segregated bachelor house or barracks appeared as, for example, in the Andamans and in Australia, or among the Bororo, the Masai, and the Zulu. Among the Masai the bachelors and their paramours were separated from the rest of the community. Every male was circumcised at puberty, marking his transition to warriorhood. For the first two years he had the position of a "shaved one" (apprentice). Thereafter until the age of 28 he was restricted to the bachelors' kraal. After circumcision the bachelor received a sword, spear, club, and shield, and wore a special cap, ostrich-feather headdress, cape, anklets, arm clamp, and a calfskin garment about the loins. For unusual military feats and prowess in their war games the bachelors were given special ranks. At the appropriate time the older warriors celebrated a ceremonial feast and settled in their own homes, assuming the rank of elders (5, pp. 270–275).

Starting with a scheme of bachelor houses (barracks), the Zulu king Chaka showed what could be done. In the early nineteenth century the Bantu king Dingiswayo organized a standing army, conquered numerous tribes, and assumed autocratic powers. Chaka built, on Dingiswayo's system, a militaristic structure which won him the title of "the Napoleon of South Africa." New barracks of adolescent boys were organized each year. Novices were identified by black shields. Once they proved themselves in battle, their heads were shaved, and they received white shields and the title of "men." Though they had love affairs with the women of the community, soldiers were bachelors as far as legitimate matrimony was concerned. Special dispensation of the king was necessary for a warrior to receive permission to marry. The soldiers were maintained at the king's expense. As many as 12 cattle a day might be supplied to a single barracks.

Through such devices, Chaka developed an army of 15,000 men. He organized subjected tribes into units to strengthen his own forces. All people other than boys and marriageable girls from distant tribes were put to death, and the survivors were placed on the level of his former subjects, the girls in his seraglio, the boys in his army (5, pp. 374–375).

Max Weber was convinced that a similar structure was at work in the formation of the ancient oriental city. In the peasant community, corresponding to the house community in which the women's work was carried on, was the men's house. During the period of life from 20 to 30, men lived together in a clubhouse or barracks apart from their families. The men's house was the center of war, hunting, magic, and weapons manufacture. The warriors frequently used captured women as prostitutes, whom they enjoyed in groups.

> Generally the men's house also recognizes a novitiate. At a certain age the boys are taken out of the families, carried through magic procedures (circumcision being commonly included), receive the consecration of young manhood, and take up their life in the men's house. The place is a sort of barracks, a military institution giving rise on its disintegration to various lines of development, as for example, a magical association or a political society on the pattern of the Italian Camorra, the Spartan *andreion*, the Greek phratry, and the Roman *curia* (*coviria*) (19, p. 40).

This primitive military institution, the men's house, was soon replaced by others, but Weber was convinced that it played a historical role first as the institution which permitted the ancient kings to shatter the peasant villages and form their fragments into the first cities of the world.

Whether or not this account is correct in all its details, there is no doubt about the occurrence of revolutionary upheavals in the formation of the ancient oriental city. Moreover, revolutionary upheavals may be discerned in the founding days of later cities. The ancient Mediterranean Sea cities, for example, seem to have originated with revolutionary associations of aristocrats who joined together and forced upon ancient castle-based kings their right to participate in the opportunities for piracy and trade associated with these sea castles. At Athens, Sparta, and many other cities, a kind of founders' day was observed to celebrate the acts of synoecism which had created the city. In Sparta the conquest of Messenia was followed by a rebellion which for a time threatened to throw off the Spartan yoke permanently. In connection with this battle and to prevent any re-occurrence, the Spartans reorganized the community into a permanent military camp. Moreover, not only are revolutionary upheavals evident in the founding of the Mediterranean coastal cities, but the main stages in their development were marked by major internal conflicts, as in the times of Draco, Solon, and Pisistratus in Athens.

While the ancient city appears to have arisen as a warrior community, the medieval city arose as a community of merchants. However, revolutionary upheavals can also be discerned in the early days of the medieval city. These may be illustrated by the conflicts with episcopal authority, though there were also other conflicts with non-religious landed authorities. Many of the medieval cities began to form on the one-time sites of Roman cities which had become (at the time Christianity was made the official religion of Rome) episcopal sees. The bishops were often suspicious of the new merchant formations which began to rise in the tenth and eleventh centuries, and for their part, the merchants staged insurrectional movements against episcopal authority.

The earliest mentioned occurred at Cologne in 1074; two years later in 1076 one broke out at Cambrai. Then about 1080 there followed a revolt at St. Quentin, one at Beauvais in 1099, one at Noyon in 1108–1109; one at Amiens in 1113; one at Laon in 1115. There was no doubt that this tendency to revolt was fomented by the merchants (14, p. 518).

Once again the upheavals bound up with the destruction of old communities and the creation of new ones come into view.

Upheavals in the Formation of Feudal Communities

This is not the place to trace the complex process by which the ancient city so often was transformed into a bureaucratic empire in a process which destroyed the city as an autonomous community at the very time it universalized its influence. The slow collapse of the city which followed was also accompanied by the decay of the bureaucratic empire into local complexes of politics and militarism. When such decay of an imperial structure was accompanied by the invasion of barbarians or of less civilized people, the result could be a typical feudalism.

As the Roman Empire decayed, the time came when the Germanic war organization (*Comitatus*) found it possible to pillage the Roman provinces at will. The relation between the chiefs and the followers of these war bands was one of voluntary loyalty, with the expectation, in return, of maintenance in a style fitting a free warrior. This relationship in the course of time was conjoined to the Roman system of client-patron, in which the client was an economic dependent who in return served in the patron's retinue. Under the Merovingian kings poor men commended themselves for life to powerful persons. From these two sources the medieval lord's men came to include various grades of serfs and peasants as well as armed retainers. Finally to the growing complex a third item was added. As the Roman money economy decayed, often a *precarium* (grant of land) was given at the pleasure of a donor in return for rent or for the performance of specified services. The *precaria* was a *beneficium* or boon of the grantor. With the increasing decay of the money economy, the typical benefice was an agrarian estate (lands organized for subsistence agriculture complete with buildings, tools, domestic animals, and free and servile cultivators).

The communities that emerged had at their top an aristocracy of landlord knights, and at the bottom, a dependent peasantry. The lords and vassals at the top were organized by ties of fealty in return for which they held *benefices* (fiefs) for their subsistence. This system permitted the superior lords to assemble armies of knights, for the chief obligation of the vassal for his benefice was military service.

Once again it may be noted that external military actions and internal upheavals accompanied the rise of typical manorial feudal communities. The role of external conflict in the origin of the feudal community could not be illustrated more clearly than in the experience of England. Before the Norman Conquest a manorial system had grown up under native chiefs, but without the military integration of a lord-vassal type. With the Norman Conquest a typical military stratum of feudal type was clamped on the manorial system, and England was rapidly feudalized.

Social Upheavals Which Accompanied the Nation-State

The military activities, on the one hand, and the revolutions and civil wars on the other, that played a role in the creation and consolidation of the nation-state are too familiar to require specification. The extent of the political revolutions at the threshold of modern times which marked the destruction of old social forms was brilliantly summarized by Tocqueville in his estimate of the French Revolution.

> The French people made, in 1789, the greatest effort which was ever attempted by any nation to cut, so to speak, their destiny in halves, and to separate by an abyss that which had hithertofore been from that which they sought to become hereafter (17, p. vii).

In the eighteenth century, Tocqueville observed, many of the institutions of the Middle Ages were still in existence, though everywhere they were in a state of decay. The manor rolls which in the thirteenth century were masterpieces of methodical conciseness had become obscure, ill digested, and defective. Municipal institutions, once the bearers of a cosmopolitan progressiveness, had collapsed. Where provincial assemblies were still in operation, they acted as if to check rather than further the progress of civilization. Royalty had lost the prerogatives it had enjoyed in the Middle Ages.

In England, where, at the first glance, the ancient constitution of Europe might still seem in full vigour, the case is the same. Setting aside the ancient names and the old forms, in England the feudal system was substantially abolished in the seventeenth century, all classes of society began to intermingle, the pretensions of birth were effaced, the aristocracy was thoroughly open, wealth was becoming power, equality was established before the law, public employments were open to all, the press became free, the debates of Parliament public; every one of them new principles, unknown to the society of the Middle Ages (17, p. 32).

The revolution, Tocqueville observed, was not made to destroy the authority of religious beliefs; it was a social and political revolution not intended to perpetuate discord but to increase the power and rights of public authority. It swept away the remnants of retrograde communities, and formed the nation-state into an integrated community. One must, however, disagree with his observation that:

The Revolution effected on a sudden and by a violent and convulsive effort, without any transition, without forethought, without mercy, that which would have happened little by little if left to itself. This was its work (17, pp. 35–36).

That the revolution represented a sudden violent crystalization of the contemporary nation-state seems undoubted. But that this would have been accomplished "little by little if left to itself" would seem to be doubtful if the evidence assembled for the formative periods of other communities is correct.

Summary

The theory of social change has currently been in crisis, in part because of the attempt to treat the whole of human social life as of a piece in terms of the revolutionary hypothesis. A more promising procedure would seem to be to divide the problem, in time-honored scientific fashion, into smaller units. The problems at least of groups, communities, and culture are sufficiently distinct to deserve separate analysis.

Despite the low estate to which, in current sociology, the theory of community has fallen, there are reasons to believe that the formation and destruction of communities constitutes one of the most vigorous areas of social change. The essence of a community is to be found in the capacity of the members of a collectivity to act and communicate and to form a total system of social life capable of bringing them through the ordinary problems of a single year and of a single life. While in the past such total systems (or comprehensive strategies of collective life) often had narrow territorial locations, the development of contemporary techniques of mechanical transportation and electronic communications has emancipated the contemporary community from narrow territorial dependence.

The primary principles of community formation — of the grand strategies of collective life — are *stabilization* (the fixing of solutions to the primary problems of collective life), *consistency* (the reconstruction of institutions to eliminate conflicts that rise between them), and *closure* (the fixing of a formula binding on the whole or a definition of a legitimate order). The primary principles of community formation call attention to relations between a community and its component groups which are obscured by the notion that groups and communities are similarly constructed and exist only in a condition of harmony. There is, to be sure, some harmony between groups and institutions and the community, for the principles of community formation bring it about. However, in the formation of communities some of the flexibility of groups and communities is inevitably lost. Stability and peace on the whole may not, at times, compensate for the loss of plasticity in line institutions.

Approached from this perspective, it is time to abandon the traditional dichotomous classification of communities (such as *Gemeinschaft* and *Gesellschaft*) with their evolutionary assumptions.

Among the many types of communities formed by men in their ceaseless explorations of the mysteries of experience, some have played more trenchant historical roles than others. Among these are the pre-cultivating tribal communities, the peasant village, the city, the communities of feudalism, and contemporary nation-states. They are not organisms. They are not born, and they do not die like living things. They are strategies of collective life which are formed and destroyed by men. They are primary examples of the ancient truth that "man cannot have his cake and eat it too." To form new communities men must transform their old ones. Revolutionary upheavals are discernible in the formative periods of all of the historically significant communities.

BIBLIOGRAPHY

1. Bury, J. B. *The Idea of Progress.* New York: Dover, 1955.
2. Childe, V. Gordon. *What Happened in History.* New York: Penguin Books, 1946.
3. Heichelheim, Fritz M. *An Ancient Economic History*, translated by Joyce Stevens. Leiden: A Sijthoff, 1958.
4. Lindeman, E. C. "Community," *Encyclopedia of the Social Sciences*, Vol. 1. New York: The Macmillan Co., 1934.
5. Lowie, Robert. *Primitive Society.* New York: Liveright, 1920.
6. MacIver, R. M. *Community.* New York: The Macmillan Co., 1917.
7. Martindale, Don. "Sociological Theory and The Ideal Type," in Llewellyn

Gross (ed.), *Symposium on Sociological Theory.* Evanston, Ill.: Row, Peterson & Co., 1959.

8. Martindale, Don. *American Social Structure.* New York: Appleton-Century-Crofts, 1960.

9. Martindale, Don. *Social Life and Cultural Change.* Princeton, N. J.: Van Nostrand, 1962.

10. Nietzsche, Friedrich. *The Twilight of Idols.* Edinburgh: T. N. Follis, 1915.

11. Parsons, Talcott. *The Social System.* Glencoe, Ill.: The Free Press, 1951.

12. Parsons, Talcott, Robert F. Bales, and Edward A. Shils. *Working Papers in the Theory of Action.* Glencoe, Ill.: The Free Press, 1953.

13. Parsons, Talcott. *Structure and Process in Modern Societies.* Glencoe, Ill.: The Free Press, 1960.

14. Pirenne, Henri. "Northern Towns and Their Commerce," in J. R. Tanner (ed.), *The Cambridge Medieval History.* New York: The Macmillan Co., 1929, Vol. 6.

15. Stein, Maurice R. *The Eclipse of Community.* Princeton: Princeton University Press, 1960.

16. Sumner, William Graham. *Folkways.* Boston: Ginn & Co., 1940.

17. Tocqueville, Alexis de. *On the State of Society in France.* London: John Murray, 1956.

18. Weber, Max. *General Economic History,* translated by Frank Knight. Glencoe, Ill.: The Free Press, 1950.

19. Weber, Max. *The City,* translated and edited by Don Martindale and Gertrude Neuwirth. Glencoe, Ill.: The Free Press, 1958.

Working Papers in the Theory of Institutionalization[1]

The following group of chapters presents a number of contributions by Zollschan and various collaborators designed to explore an orientation to social process — and, in particular, to social change — that may be called the theory of institutionalization. *The reasons for adopting this title should become apparent in the course of our discussion. For the present may it be sufficient to point out that the formation of institutional patterns — patterns of interpersonal action, and of shared and reciprocal expectations — constitutes one of the central problems for the exploration of which our frame of reference is constructed. Before entering into a discussion of the content of these chapters, it will be necessary to present some of the basic assumptions and categories inherent in our orientation, and to develop a terminology that brings these categories and assumptions sharply into focus.*

Whereas it has been customary for some time to begin discussions of social processes with some reference to problems of social order, we start, instead, with the problem of change. Changes in action and, in particular, changes in established patterns of interaction, we suggest, may usefully be conceptualized as responses to exigencies (disturbances of inertia). An exigency we define as a discrepancy (for a person) between *a consciously or unconsciously desired or expected state of affairs and an actual situation. To eventuate in social system changes (or in personality system changes) exigencies must trigger a series of phase processes, namely, articulation — action — institutionalization. Prior to introducing the chapters in this Section of the volume, we wish to classify exigencies and to provide some delineation of the phase processes. We shall also indicate the coordinates involved in the emergence (or abortion) of articulation and action.*

Whereas sources of exigencies are diffuse — all manner of discrepancies

---

[1] This introduction incorporates a modified version of a paper presented before Section K of the American Association for the Advancement of Science, Philadelphia meetings, December 30, 1962. Earlier published expositions of the theory of institutionalization may be found in Peterson and Zollschan (1) and in Zollschan (2).

exist that have the potentiality of presenting themselves to the awareness — three types of discrepancy may be distinguished which, singly or in combination, enter into the constitution of an exigency. The pure types of discrepancy may be enumerated as follows:

Type 1: *Affective or Cathectic: This is a discrepancy between a* desired objective (*absence of an undesired objective*) *and what is actually achieved. "Objective" here may be taken to mean access to a cathected object, a pleasurable feeling, or a desired activity (or, alternatively, avoidance of a "bad" object, unpleasurable feeling, undesired activity). The desired objective may become manifest only in the process of articulation (i.e., when a sufficient discrepancy becomes established) or be consciously present ab* initio.

Type 2: *Evaluative: This is a discrepancy between a* legitimate pattern *or arrangement and an actual situation. The legitimate pattern, again, may be initially present or become manifest in the process of articulation. Both moral and aesthetic principles can be subsumed under this heading; the latter offer us the simplest example and will, therefore, be chosen for purposes of illustration. Thus, for instance, a century ago an unresolved musical discord would have set up a severe evaluative exigency — at least in a musical person in the Western world. Musical folklore abounds with tales of sick or sleepy persons getting out of bed in order to resolve such* discords *as might have occurred in the interaction of, say, a piano and children, or cats.*

Type 3: *Cognitive: This is a discrepancy between a prediction (expectation, explanation) and an observation. The "expectation" may reach awareness only by its disappointment, or alternatively, be fully expressed in hypothetical form prior to the observation.*

Given the presence of an exigency, which is generally some combination of the above three types of discrepancy, the first phase of change in response to the exigency we have called articulation. *Articulation is the recognition (whether correctly or falsely, from the point of view of some all-knowing observer) of the existence and nature of the exigency, and postulation of goals for its removal, prevention, or amelioration.*

Once articulated, the nebulous exigency condenses into more or less stable configurations which we shall call needs; *in the absence of articulation only free-floating discomfort may be experienced. We shall see, when we discuss the coordinates of articulation, that no simple or direct relationship need exist between the composition of an exigency and the expressed form of the need into which it becomes condensed and in which it becomes expressed.*

We shall avoid here the question of whether action can spring directly from an exigency. Certainly, Freud has shown how forms of articulation that do not reach verbal expression as needs — unconscious articulations, as it were — may be postulated as mediating processes between an exigency and the actions evoked by it. Thus action, in our schema, becomes locomotion toward postulated or unconscious goals. Again, the emergence or non-emergence of action, and the forms that action will take, depend upon specifiable coordinates.

The final phase of change we shall term institutionalization. *Institutionalization may be defined as a process consisting of changes in established patterns of interaction and/or the development and substitution of new patterns of interaction for previous ones, resulting from the more or less reciprocal actions of more than one actor. Where only a single or isolated individual is involved in this phase of response to an exigency we may speak, instead, of* personality formation (*or "complex formation" or "habit formation"*). *The conditions for institutionalization and personality formation are rather more complicated than the coordinates involved in articulation and action. They will be examined in the chapters following this introduction.*

The coordinates involved in the emergence of articulation or, more crudely, the requisites for articulation, are salience, specifiability, *and* justifiability. *Salience can be viewed as a measure of discomfort of the individual stricken by an exigency. Such discomfort may be said to be dependent upon the individual's "equilibrium of deprivations," since a greater discomfort can decrease the salience of lesser ones. Insofar as discomfort carries connotations of affect, we have to say that exigencies consisting purely of evaluative or cognitive discrepancies have no empirical bearing on the theory of need articulation. The maintenance of a legitimate or harmonious arrangement or the continual and undisturbed confirmation of a prediction must therefore carry at least a minimal "charge" if discrepancies are either to be noticed at all, or at best, not simply shrugged off with a "so what" reaction.*

The existence of exigencies composed of purely cathectic discrepancies has greater a priori *plausibility, but their emergence into a state of articulation, as we shall see, requires both cognitive and evaluative conditions.*

Specification *consists of an identification or categorization of the elements involved in what will emerge as the need. A hypothetical example might be taken from medical practice. If a patient were to come to a physician and say, "I suffer from general malaise," or perhaps just, "I feel ill," the degree of specification of the need would be very low, although a state of salience would be clearly indicated. The statement, "I have a severe stabbing pain in my right shoulder," on the other hand, would yield a much higher degree of specification.*

This example brings us back to our contention that no simple or direct relation can be specified between an exigency and the need that becomes articulated; that, in other words, there may well be "false specification" (or, in Marx's terms, "false consciousness"). Thus a stabbing pain in the right shoulder may indeed indicate some damage to that part of the anatomy, or, alternatively, be occasioned by a myocardial infarction. The goal of "painlessness," in the latter case, would not be served by treatment of the shoulder. In the absence of a physician (with, presumably, superior diagnostic or "specificatory" competence) it would naturally be the shoulder that should receive such attention as would be deemed appropriate. Any given specification will, of course, be dependent upon an already existing fund of knowledge or what Karl Popper has called, "horizon of expectations." Consequently the nature of a disappointment of a given expectation can only be specified at a given time in terms of the knowledge already available to the actor.

Justification is a process that establishes elements "permissible" in the articulation of a need. It is quite similar to the process of specification except that it rests on a normative rather than an existential basis. Instead of speaking of a "horizon of expectations" in this context, we have to speak of a "horizon of justifications" or ideology existing prior to the articulation of a need; a new justification can only be given in terms of such an ideology.

At rudimentary levels of articulation there may, indeed, be no discernible difference between the processes of specification and justification; but at higher levels a very clear distinction becomes possible and (for purposes of examining certain types of conflict) necessary. Without making such a distinction it would be impossible, for example, to describe the virtually endless number of taboos on the specification of problems which abound in the history of science and medicine. Thus we see that more than just a salient exigency is required if articulation is to take place. There must, in addition, be some possibility of finding a specification of what is "ailing" and of justifying the legitimacy of the need and its associated goal.

This brings us to the question of what happens when the requisites for articulation of a need are not co-present. It should be fairly clear that it is theoretically possible for salience to exist without articulation of what has gone awry taking place. Similarly, where a theoretical potentiality for specification (in the light of existing and manifestly available knowledge) is present, articulation may not take place because of an insufficient degree of salience or because of the inhibitive effects of prohibitions (absence of justification or positive counter-justification).

The problem of strength or degree of salience requires a great deal of further research before much illumination can be shed on the subject. Various thresholds could certainly be indicated ranging from vague discontentment or puzzlement to flooding by uncontrollable affect or total cognitive disorientation. We may ask, in this connection, whether thresholds exist at which processes of specification and justification are aroused, and to what degree such thresholds vary among different persons. A study directed to this question would, of course, have to consider also the contributing influence of specifiability and justifiability.

The presence of a potential for specification of an exigency without the concomitant evolution of articulation has been discussed above in relation to the strength of salience and the inhibitive effects of prohibitions. In regard to the latter relationship, certain questions again arise to which we can only point. They concern the location of equilibrium positions between the facility and "urge" to specify on the one hand, and the strength of the prohibition (or relative lack of any elements that might be used for purposes of justification) on the other. The difficulties of gaining some empirical measure of these relationships are great at the moment, and we are likely to be confined to their ex post facto reconstruction for some time to come.

We may now turn to situations in which the requisites for articulation are present, and needs are expressed (or, at least, may be postulated). Locomotion toward goals associated with these needs is the major concern of what we shall call the theory of action. (We use the term in Max Weber's sense rather than in Parsons'.) Before we come to the coordinates of action, however, a discussion of the conditions under which responses to exigencies become collectivized becomes necessary.

First, it appears to us that exigencies, in their nature, are phenomena touching individual persons. It is, of course, undeniable that a whole category of persons might be confronted by an essentially similar exigency. Indeed, cooperative or collective responses to such an exigency sometimes require a certain degree of similarity in order to appear at all. But the fons et origo *of all action (and thus of responses to exigencies) must always be the individual person or actor, though he may certainly be stimulated to act by other actors and, indeed, have established the forms of his action in intercourse with them. Similarly, expectations, although they may well become "shared," are ultimately only sensible when viewed as individual personal orientations. Certainly, the salience of an exigency can be felt only by the person upon whom it impinges.*

Articulation also, we shall maintain, is a process that can take place only within the individual consciousness. Of course, it is possible that a person in a situation of salience may accept the specifications and justification of need supplied by others, so long as these are moderately congruent with that person's horizons of specifications and justifications. But the process of communicating these elements of articulation we shall describe as a species of action; once a person who has articulated a need attempts to communicate it to others he is engaging in "action" in our sense of the term. The recipient of communications which articulate a need, on the other hand, may accept or reject the communique; acceptance is tantamount to articulation of the same need by him.

The coordinates involved in the emergence of action or, more crudely, the requisites for action, we shall call valence, application, *and* legitimation. *The concept* valence *as used here conforms to the economist's use of "opportunity cost" — alternatives foregone for a particular end. In developing patterns of action of even minimal consistency, some sort of hierarchy of needs or "value ordering" must develop so that "activity" (energy) can be apportioned to minimize the sum total of salience in the individual and/or collectivity. The relative importance of a need in a given value hierarchy we shall term its valence. In the light of the foregoing considerations, it becomes clear that the amount of action generated by a need will vary with its valence. And this condition is complicated where direct contradictions emerge between sets of need-goals that have been separately articulated. It is no accident (as Marx would say) that Freud's term "ambivalence" describes so well (at least, on the intrapersonal level) the situation to which we refer. Where such contradictions emerge interpersonally, we have a situation of* valence dissonance *and a potential for social conflict.*

But valence alone is not enough to evoke action; locomotion towards goals also has a "technical knowledge" component which we shall call application. *Thus where the means of application available are very low, even a need of relatively high valence cannot result in action. Contradictions in what are considered appropriate applications, again, give rise to what may be termed* cognitive dissonance. *Similarly, valent needs and the applications for attaining their associated goals are rendered acceptable by* legitimation. *Where legitimation is not sufficiently strong even highly valent needs with available means of application will not result in action. Contradictions in forms of legitimation give rise to what may be termed* evaluative dissonance. *Valence dissonance, cognitive dissonance, and evaluative dissonance themselves constitute exigencies (second-order exigencies) which may become articulated and result in action and institutionalization.*

It will readily be seen that the coordinates or requisites of articulation and action fall into couplets. Salience and valence, specification and application, justification and legitimation, refer to systems that may, respectively, be called "equilibria of deprivation," "knowledge," and "ideology." Knowledge and ideology are characterized by strain towards consistency; equilibria of deprivations have a tendency to inertia. It is hoped that this model of phases and coordinates will provide a new impetus for the study of social change. Table 1 provides a model overview.

The question of how given sets of action, once evoked by exigencies, become patterned into institutions is examined in the chapter by Zollschan and Perrucci. Beginning with the social generation of exigencies in interpersonal situations, they examine the general conditions under which institutionalization occurs, and go on to depict institutional maintenance as a special case of institutionalization. Instead of regarding social systems as organic and structural-functional entities, they make a case for viewing them as complex and changing instrumentalities of need reduction.

The chapter by Willer and Zollschan takes the institutionalization

TABLE 1

*Phases of Articulation — Activation — Institutionalization
and Their Coordinates*

	PHASES				
	GENERIC FORMS OF EXIGENCY				
COORDINATES	First Order	Second Order: Individual	Second Order: Collective	REQUISITES OF ARTICULATION	REQUISITES OF ACTION
Deprivation Equilibrium	Affective or Cathectic Discrepancy	Ambivalence	Valence Dissonance	Salience	Valence (Institutional Innovation)
Knowledge:	Cognitive Discrepancy		Cognitive Dissonance	Specification	Application (Technological Innovation)
Ideology:	Evaluative Discrepancy		Normative Dissonance	Justification	Legitimation (Ideological Innovation)

frame of reference as a starting point for the study of one specific area of social conflict — that of revolution. By combining some of the categories of the exigency → articulation → action schema with Dahrendorf's formulations on class conflict, they develop the outlines of a general conflict theory, and apply it to the question of under what conditions revolutions come about or fail to come about. In developing their argument they discuss structural positions in society from a novel point of view, namely, as loci of exposure to different kinds of exigencies. Revolutions are described as the culmination of a series of developmental phases in which mutually incompatible complexes of institutionalized actions may ultimately clash in a violent collision of interests.

Viewed together, the Zollschan-Perrucci and Willer-Zollschan chapters may be seen as stepping-stones leading to a set of theoretical formulations in which both the conflict and the consensus models are reduced to the status of special cases of a more general model. Although both chapters exhibit awareness that the exigency → articulation → action sequence is subject to blockages and distortions at many points, they are based upon the rationalistic assumption that the goals associated with articulated needs are unproblematically attainable. This assumption is forsaken in the chapter by Zollschan and Gibeau, which examines, under the general rubric of alienation, *precisely what occurs when goals cannot adequately be attained.*

Zollschan and Gibeau demonstrate the concepts of rationality and of alienation to be theoretically antithetical, and pose the question of whether a rationale cannot be determined for formally "irrational" action. To this end a number of psychiatric diagnostic categories are analyzed from the point of view of the theory of institutionalization. Although this chapter constitutes only the merest beginning, it does assay a step in the direction of a tenable theory of personality formation parallel to, and symmetrical with, the theory of institutionalization. A similar attempt is made from a different direction in Zollschan's chapter.

Zollschan's chapter undertakes to explore the isomorphisms and homeomorphisms of theoretical structure in psychoanalytic metapsychology and the theory of institutionalization. While acknowledging the indebtedness of the theory of institutionalization to Freudian metapsychology, the chapter also attempts to make a contribution — however minor it may be — to Freudian theory itself. Involved in this attempt is a genetic exploration of the development of horizons of justifications and horizons of expectations in the person.

These chapters are all written at high, though varying, levels of theoretical abstraction. They are not, strictly speaking, constituted of congeries of directly testable propositions, although it is hoped that they will give rise to a very large number of such propositions. The editors are greatly indebted to Andersen and Eichhorn for their Appendix which, if it makes no crucial tests of the theory of institutionalization (and, of course, it does not claim to do so), at least demonstrates the applicability and usefulness of some of its concepts for research in an area as empirical as the adaptation to "cardiovascular exigencies" of farmers in Indiana. The next step will be to build several aspects of the institutionalization model into empirical studies in a variety of substantive areas.

Taken together, these chapters and the empirical appendix fall very far short of presenting a fully articulated, consistent, and readily testable body of theory. Few, if any, such bodies of theory are currently extant in the behavioral sciences. But, viewed as working papers — as explorations of concepts which have relevance to the understanding of social change — they will recommend themselves to the reader with sufficient patience and daring to penetrate their fastnesses.

BIBLIOGRAPHY

1. Peterson, Warren A., and George K. Zollschan. "Social Processes in the Metropolitan Community," in Arnold Rose (ed.), *Human Behavior and Social Processes.* Boston: Houghton Mifflin, 1962.

2. Zollschan, George K. "Needs, Interests, and Leaders: Toward a Theory of Occasions for Community Leadership," in Alvin W. Gouldner (ed.), *Studies in Leadership,* 2nd ed. Indianapolis: Bobbs-Merrill. (In press)

4

George K. Zollschan

and Robert Perrucci

Social Stability and Social Process:

An Initial Presentation of

Relevant Categories

"... *Ich ging allen Gestalten, wie sie mir vorkamen, in ihren Veraenderungen nach, und so leuchtete mir ... die* urspruengliche Identitaet *aller Pflanzenteile vollkomen ein....*"

> J.W.v. Goethe.
> (*Geschichte meines Botanischen Studiums*)

The introduction to this Section of the volume has outlined a set of categories for the analysis of social change, as it were, at the source — in the person or persons who begin to articulate exigencies as needs, and act in ways they find appropriate to meet these articulated needs. But these considerations alone can only be viewed as an orientation toward problems of the analysis of social change. They constitute a beginning only, a point of entry into the obscure realm of change processes within the sphere of sociological concerns. The distinctively *sociological* problems of social change require further analysis.

Such an examination, however, necessarily impinges also on problems of social stability since it is our belief that separate and unconnected theories of stability and change are heuristically unsatisfying and logically incomplete. Accordingly, it is our purpose in this chapter to provide categories for the discussion of how patterns of *collective* or *reciprocal* action become established, and how such patterns maintain themselves. Some of the conditions under which such patterns will disintegrate are examined in chapters 5 & 6.

In attempting this task we shall build upon the exigency → articulation → action schema, and develop first the theoretical condition of what we have called *Institutionalization*, namely, the process whereby interpersonal patterns or forms of action become established.[1] Only after these conditions have been outlined will we turn to consideration of why some of these patterns become relatively permanent.

This order of presentation is in accord with the over-arching orientation we represent, namely, that processes of institutionalization are of primary and paradigmatic importance in sociological analysis, and that problems of institutional persistence and disintegration form special cases of the wider theory of institutionalization. Expressed in other words, we are voicing the conviction that states of "equilibrium"are special cases of dynamics in sociology as much as in other scientific fields. But this is not to imply that problems of pattern maintenance are of trivial importance. We shall maintain, on the contrary, that the very real significance of such problems can receive the emphasis it deserves only when these problems are placed within a broader conceptual framework in which the formation and disintegration of institutional patterns, as well as their maintenance, become the central foci of sociological concern.

The Social Generation of Exigencies: A Preliminary Statement

Before proceeding to the main subject of our chapter, however, it would be profitable to examine some of the currently existing statements regarding social change. Our purpose here is to delineate what we have to say about social change by first indicating the relationship our position has with other points of view. It should be kept clearly in mind that we are not necessarily offering an "opposing" theory, but one which appears to be the next developmental stage in the unfolding of a theory of social dynamics.

Much of what has been said in recent years regarding social change consists of sets of orientations toward data. Along with these orientations, we naturally find a development of concepts needed to define the data under observation. The most elaborate statements focus primarily upon the question of *identifying sources of change*.

---

[1] We are using the terms *pattern* and *form* in their most general sense, and intend to include in our discussion all interpersonal systems ranging from spontaneous relationships to highly formalized and organized systems of coordination.

While all these steps are certainly essential in the development of any body of theory, they do not constitute theories in themselves. At best they represent a "map" of the area of social change which directs one where to look for relevant phenomena. Wilbert Moore's recent examination of theories of social change (17, p. 818) clearly points to the fact that, to date, our statements regarding social change have been rather vague about the mechanisms of change themselves.

The task of locating sources of change in current sociological theory is attempted in at least three independent methods of approach. We shall call these three approaches *synergism, culturology,* and *malintegration;* most current statements regarding change fit into one or other of these frameworks. It is our contention that these three approaches can be viewed most fruitfully in terms of their ability to identify those qualities or conditions in the socio-cultural system which are fertile grounds for the emergence of exigencies, those disparities between desired and actual occurrences that may eventuate in change processes. Further, we maintain that what appears to be the terminal stage in these existing frames of reference for the examination of social change — the identification of sources of exigencies — should be the point of departure for a genuinely analytical theory of social dynamics. We shall examine the three frameworks in terms of their contribution to the identification of conditions giving rise to exigencies.

Synergism:

Schneider, in an analysis of some of the assumptions underlying psychoanalytic theory, distinguishes between two levels of analysis: the motivational level and the synergic level. The former refers to what he calls normative prescriptions of behavior, while ". . . the latter refers precisely to the conjoint effects of motivated actions, looked at from the point of view of an observer not directly interested in motivation nor in its effects or results for an *individual,* but rather in its effects or results for the social system" (23, p. 260). While not directly concerned with the generation of change in making his distinction, Schneider provides, in his discussion, the best example of one currently acceptable approach to the study of social change.

Schneider's following example of what he means by the synergic level brings out very clearly the relationship of individual actions and conjoint effects, both as to needs motivating aggregates of individuals to act in similar ways, and as to the exigencies unwittingly produced by the aggregation of their actions: "Assume that I am in a certain income group, say $5,000–$10,000 per year. With an income in this range, I find I can afford a certain make of car, but not a better make which I might wish to have. I wish, at least, to be able to continue getting this make of car, and not a poorer one. I note that my neighbors have a certain kind of house. I wish, at least, not to live in a less adequate one. Given certain standards and a limited income, I decide that my wife and I cannot afford to have more than two children. But I am not alone in this decision. Other men, too, have certain standards and aspirations and similarly limited incomes. . . . Now notice what happens. All I have in mind is to restrict the size of my own family. All Jones has in mind is to restrict the size of his family. . . . But as I limit the size of my family, Jones limits the size of his, Brown the size of his, and so on, the results of our combined actions is a certain (low) birthrate for an entire . . . income group" (18, pp. 94–95.)

What we have in this discussion of the synergic level is the identification of a mechanism by which a certain aggregate of isolated actions produce conditions which could lead to the creation of a new exigency (in this instance, a low birthrate). Individual behaviors of the type described by Schneider can have synergic effects which may eventually lead to significant structural changes in the society. A demographic occurrence of the type just described could result in changes in the composition of the various social classes, in the rates of social and geographic mobility, in the distribution of political power, and in the structure of political institutions. The actual synergic effect of the individual actions cited, however, is not the establishment of the above changes — rather it consists of the creation of exigencies which may, in turn, be changed into needs, actions, and new patterns of institutionalization.

The areas of human events which fit these propositions best are those of economics and demography. The conjoint consequences of individual economic behaviors may, for example, produce an economic depression — an effect quite different from the intended goals of the individuals involved. The consequences of individual demographic behaviors have already been discussed; Sibley's examination of the relation between demographic events and the nature of stratification systems (27, pp. 322–330) is also quite appropriate in this context.

Culturology:

The second currently accepted framework for the identification of sources of change focuses upon the form and content of culture itself as it unfolds, supposedly, according to the dictates of its immanent laws. Cultural forms are viewed as containing, within themselves, the potential for either their further development and elaboration, or for their demise. Here one speaks of contradicting values and norms, the flexibility or rigidity of normative systems, or the potential for change inherent in any cultural system. Leslie White (31, p. 392) provides a rather "pure" or extreme statement of this approach:

> Our sketch of the evolution of culture is . . . wholly culturological. It does not resort to race, physical type, intelligence, a moral sense, the dignity

of man, the spirit of progressive democracy, the individual — genius or otherwise — the rejection of the father, consciousness of kind, a set of instincts or drives, social interaction, a basic personality structure, toilet training in infancy, or breast vs. bottle feeding and weaning, to account for the behavior and growth of this great extra-somatic tradition. We explain it in terms of culture itself. . . .

Culture is . . . a stream of interactive elements; one trait reacts upon others and is affected by them in return. Some elements become obsolete and are eliminated from the stream; new elements are incorporated into it. New permutations, combinations, and syntheses are continually being formed. Whether we deal with a restricted portion of the cultural continuum such as the evolution of mathematics or the genealogy of the steam engine, or whether we envisage culture in its entirety, the principle of interpretation is the same: culture grows out of culture (31, p. 392).

Not every culturologist would give culture a status as disembodied and immaculately conceived as does Leslie White, but the manner in which the (unrevealed) logic of cultural development ineffably grinds out the history of the world[2] should be quite clear from the above quotations. It is the nature of culture itself to produce pressures for change; just how these pressures impinge upon the bearers of the culture is still a question for a theory of change. Actors in socio-cultural situations still have to transform the pressures generated by the logic of cultural development (i.e., exigencies) in order for the culture to change. Thus the culturological framework, even if we were to grant all its manifold assumptions, leaves us with only a map of the territory to be explored.

Malintegration:

This general approach concerns itself with such lack of correspondence between elements of the social structure as are productive of "strain." Inconsistencies are found between "the normative and the factual level,"[3] and these create situations in which individual actors are subject to strain (exigencies). These strains, it is asserted, lead to attempts to bring actual behavior in line with the expressed norms, or to attempts to establish new normative patterns that fit actual behavior.

Within the general framework outlined above, Merton's concept of dysfunction could also be included. Merton asserts: "The concept of dysfunction which implies the concept of strain, stress, and tension on the structural level, provides an analytical approach to the study of dynamics and change" (15, p. 53). Again, even if we were to grant the conception of "integration" as a legitimate starting-point for the analysis of social events, the concept of dysfunction could yield few clues as to the direc-

[2] White, of course, is not the only exponent of a view which sees culture or history as a process in which some kind of laws of development are operative. To some degree he shares this point of view with the evolutionist tradition in sociology and with historicism.

[3] For an example of how inconsistencies between normative and factual levels have been treated, see Mizruchi and Perrucci (16).

tion of change and the question of how dysfunctions become translated into social changes.

We see, thus, that these three frames of reference, taken as exemplary of a great many statements regarding social change, are primarily concerned with identifying the *sources* of change. They tell us little about the mechanisms whereby individual discontent becomes transformed into patterns of collective action. We shall discover that, in attempting to provide a categorical schema for the analysis of these mechanisms, the assumptions, certainly, of the culturological and malintegration approaches to change will have to be greatly modified even if they are to serve merely as maps capable of guiding us to the *caput nili* of change — the substratum of exigencies.

But, independently of their source, or of the conditions under which they are generated, exigencies impinge upon persons, are articulated by them as needs with associated goals, and activate these persons in the direction of the goals. Certain goals require the actions of more than one person to be achieved. We will now examine the types of action for which (and the types of goals for the adequate achievement of which) a plurality of actors are required.

The Conditions for Institutionalization: (How patterns of collective action become established.)

The first, and most directly obvious, case in which action involves more than one person is one where the exigency itself or, at least, the articulated need, implies the response of alters. Here actions will be directed at alters so as to elicit some form of reciprocal response. Thus a lover who directs his activities to the object of his affection is responding to the need to be loved in return by that person and (at any rate, if the activity is sufficiently energetic!) is highly likely to receive some sort of positive or negative response. Generally speaking, where the need is one for a reasonably specifiable range of responses from alters, locomotion to the goal may be either furthered or blocked according to whether alters' reactions do or do not fall within this range of responses. In other words, the reactions of alters may be gratifying or frustrating. It is possible to conceive of limiting cases where any kind of active response from alter would be the goal, e.g., where the alter is a mute, immobile catatonic, or suspected to be dead. A frustrating reaction from alter (where alter's reactions do not fall within the limits of meeting the actor's need) either simply leaves the need unmet or can actually set up new exigencies, particularly where the response is unexpectedly and radically disappointing.

There is, however, a second case where action necessarily involves the actions of more than one person. This is quite simply where more than one person is required for the appropriate action. Clearly, such action is most straightforward where a (sufficient) number of persons (to achieve locomotion) are concurrently faced by the same need. Thus, if an automobile is stuck on a patch of ice and "needs" to be pushed, action is most directly and efficiently achieved when there are a sufficient number of passengers to push the car away from the icy spot (assuming that the driver's unaided efforts were insufficient for this purpose). Where the driver is alone (even though the car were not blocking the passage of others — an eventuality that would spread the incidence of the exigency or need) the nature of the need would extend so as to encompass a need of the type previously discussed, namely, where the appropriate response of a suitable number of alters would, as it were, become a part of the need to move the car. Interest groups and, indeed, all associations formed for the purpose of reaching some goal or goals, are simply variations, at different levels of complexity, of this second type of collective action.

In order for our first variety of collectivization (where there is need for a response from alter) to give rise to a pattern of interaction between ego and alter, one or both of two further requirements must be met. Institutionalization will occur or (more appropriately for an example involving two actors only) a relationship will form where (a) alter brings to articulation similar needs regarding the response of ego (mutual complementarity) and/or (b) where the activation of a suitable response to ego will aid the locomotion of alter to his own, separately articulated goals (manipulative complementarity). A relationship of love or friendship provides the obvious examples. Thus a woman may enter into a relationship with a man either because she develops needs of her own for his response, or because she can use the relationship for, say, financial gain or professional advancement. The two goals (internal and external to the relationship itself) need not, of course, be incompatible and, in practice, most relationships between persons are not unadulterated by external considerations. Indeed, unless the goal in question is an extremely valent one (that is, unless the need is very great and alternative paths to its satisfaction are not readily available) most patterns of interaction between persons will exhibit "overdetermination,"[4] that is to say, they will satisfy a number of goals.

The second variety of collectivization of action, where locomotion to the goal requires the activity of more than one person, will occur (a) where the need with which the persons in question are faced is essentially similar and the goal becomes a shared one (simple cooperation) and/or (b) where activity directed toward the goal will, again, aid the person's locomotion to other, separately articulated goals of his own (transactional cooperation). Here a relationship of production provides the simplest example. Thus a person may play a part in the manufacture

---

[4] Freud, in the *Interpretation of Dreams* (8) introduces the concept of *overdetermination* in connection with dream-content, affect, and hysterical symptoms.

of some item (and this, clearly, involves his involvement in a pattern of relations with others) because he shared the goal of producing this item or, on the other hand, works simply for a salary or wages. Again, these goals are rarely met in their pure and unadulterated form.

These remarks yield a typology of conditions under which institutionalization will occur. Assuming that we may call the need first discussed (which, presumably, initiates the interaction) the *originating need,* its associated goal the *originating goal,* and needs other than this which activate persons to enter the relationship *extraneous needs,* the typology can be schematically represented as follows:

Typology of Conditions under which Institutionalization Occurs

MOTIVATION OF ACTOR:	NEED IS FOR THE RESPONSE OF ALTER:	NEED REQUIRES CONJOINT ACTIVITY OF SEVERAL:
ORIGINATING GOAL:	Mutual Complementarity	Simple Cooperation
EXTRANEOUS GOALS:	Manipulative Complementarity	Transactional Cooperation

It will not have escaped the reader that we are entering this discussion of social change with an implicit "Robinson Crusoe" type of model, postulating responses to isolated needs. We have, however, also stressed the overdetermination of patterns of interaction and implied, thereby, that pure conditions for institutionalization as specified by our typology are not likely to be found with great frequency. Our typology is meant to serve heuristic and simplifying purposes, and not necessarily to provide a description of the formation of actual patterns of interaction as it occurs in the highly complex "real world" of social organization. The existence of social structure and organization obtaining at the onset of an exigency is purposely played down at this point in our exposition. This is to bring into sharp relief the argument that structure and organization are themselves the precipitates of responses to needs. The prior existence of some form of interpersonal structure at the onset of a given need serves, of course, to complicate the goals with which this need is associated. Indeed, we shall maintain that institutionalization patterns of any complexity at all subserve, *ab initio,* what we may call a goal set[5] — a conglomerate of both originating and extraneous goals — and this consideration will lead us to important conclusions with respect to the problem of institutional persistence. But the *fundamental identity* of patterns

[5] Merton (14, pp. 106 ff.) discusses what he calls *role sets* from the point of view of differing sets of expectations by classes of others bearing upon a role or the incumbent of a role. Our use of *goal set* has the pattern of activities as its point of reference, and views such patterns as serving goal sets when a plurality of discrete goals activate the pattern.

of institutionalization, or of their origins, deserves to be stressed as much as their variety and complexity. It is in this connection that Goethe's quotation which heads this chapter becomes relevant.

The Problem of Consonance

There are other complications surrounding the establishment of patterns of collective and reciprocal action which may now be introduced. In general terms, these problems have to do with the mobilization of activity of a number of persons for locomotion to the goal. Up to this point we have assumed perfect agreement between the persons involved on the importance of the goal and the appropriateness and legitimacy of actions taken to achieve the goal. This assumption, however, is open to question.

Let us begin our discussion by assuming that a given person (the "goal originator") has articulated a need and that, moreover, it is a need which, for various reasons such as those enumerated above, requires collective or reciprocal action. For the sake of simplicity, let us also assume conditions of mutual complementarity or simple cooperation.

For the pattern to become mobilized, certain other conditions must simultaneously be met:

1) The goal must be sufficiently valent for additional persons who become involved in the pattern of institutionalization to motivate them to act. This means that the needs they share or reciprocate with the goal originator are sufficiently salient for them, and that no alternative needs of greater salience deflect them to different activities. (Valence Consonance)

2) There must be some similarity of conception regarding the specific activity (or "technique") appropriate for locomotion toward the goal. (Cognitive Consonance)

3) The goal, and the specified activity involved in reaching it, must be justifiable for the persons involved and considered legitimate by them. (Normative Consonance)

Thus, in order to mobilize others to join him in a pattern of collective activity, the originator of the goal must rely on a state of latent (or potential) consonance in those with whom he is to enter into the activity and/ or engage in additional, secondary, pattern-mobilizing activity with the goal of establishing consonance. Where the goal originator cannot mobilize collective or reciprocal activity on the part of alters, a state of latent (or potential) valence, cognitive, or normative *dissonance* is indicated. At this point, the varieties of dissonance assume importance in connection with persons who enter patterns of interaction to pursue extraneous goals.

The conditions of manipulative complementarity and transactional cooperation illustrate an alternative to evoking or establishing consonance that is open for the goal originator. This alternative, of course, consists of wittingly or unwittingly "paying off"[6] others for becoming involved in the institutionalized pattern subserving the originating goal. As pointed out above, for the others who become implicated in the interpersonal pattern under these conditions, the activity presents a roundabout route toward their own extraneous, presumably valent, specified, and subjectively legitimate goals. But even assuming that these extraneous goals are unproblematic for the persons holding them, there must exist, (with certain exceptions to be discussed below) at least a minimal degree of consonance with respect to the originating goal, for them to become involved in the pattern directed toward it.

Where the valence, specificity, and legitimacy of the personal, extraneous goal of a person are so strong as to compensate for lack of consonance with the originating goal, an exception may be made to the requirement of minimum consonance. At this point, internal conflicts, which have previously been designated as ambivalence, cognitive discrepancies, and evaluative discrepancies may arise in these persons (pp. 90, 94). It is under these conditions, in other words, that we find such characters as reluctant prostitutes and pacifist workers in munitions factories, whose subsistence goals outweigh their repugnance for the directer goals their activities subserve.

The problems of consonance are particularly acute where the activity of large numbers of persons is required in order for the goal to be achieved. Here manipulative and, particularly, transactional modes of locomotion to goals become prevalent. The reasons, broadly speaking, are two:

1) Patterns of activity involving large numbers of actors imply that the contributions of any single actor to the goal are so minor, and the connection between a person's activity and achievement of the goal so attenuated, that the goal appears to become the outcome more of "impersonal forces" than of personal striving. This statement is as true of mass action (say, a Mongol horde with the goal of "victory") as it is of highly organized, coordinated systems of divided labor. Where the connection between a person's activity and the originating goal it subserves in the system under consideration is lost, a tendency is released for more immediate personal goals (albeit extraneous to the institutional pattern in which he is involved) to become established. Such a loss of connection is tantamount to alienation — where the contribution of a given person's action to achievement of the originating goal is *meaningless* for that person. Here the inducement to engage in the performances appropriate for meeting the originating goal is liable to come from extraneous goals which, however, retain their immediacy for the person. Few workers on assembly lines are highly motivated by their individual contribution to

---

[6] Coercion may be viewed as an extreme variant of "paying off" a person by withholding punishment. This view will be expanded below on page 120. Dahrendorf's coercion theory of organization (4) is discussed in chapter 5.

the final product the assembly line is organized to turn out, yet it cannot be denied that wages and the fear of unemployment do induce persons to engage in subjectively meaningless activities on assembly lines.

2) Patterns of activity involving large numbers of persons require, for their effective coordination and direction, a hierarchical division of authority. Where such a hierarchy of authority becomes established, the connection between an activity and its goal again becomes attenuated, because the activity has to follow the direction of another.

In mass movements, then, and in complex organizations, the originating goal becomes far removed from the activities of many (and perhaps all) persons involved in them. Where this occurs, it makes sense to speak of *formal* goals rather than originating goals, and of *substantive* goals instead of extraneous ones.[7] This change in terminology is partly justified by the fact that many persons become caught up in these large patterns of collective action without sharing the originating goal in the first place and, perhaps, without even being aware of it — individual goals, as it were, are divorced from pattern goals. It partly provides us with a terminology that will be easier to handle when institutional persistence rather than institutionalization becomes the focus of attention. Certainly, the new terms are *not* meant to conceal a shift away from the genetic methodological frame of reference that we have chosen to adopt, to that of structural-functionalism.

We have seen that the very process of collectivization itself, particularly when large numbers of persons become involved, generates new exigencies. Since these exigencies are incidental to locomotion toward an already established goal we have called them *second-order exigencies*. In their turn, such exigencies can become articulated as needs and call forth action to new goals. In contradistinction to theoretical approaches that postulate relatively fixed and immutable exigencies,[8] we conceive of social process as one involving the continuous creation of exigencies and their articulation into needs, actions, and patterns of institutionalization.

Consideration of the problem of consonance has led us again into the realm of "unanticipated consequences." The assumption with which we started out, that the conscious, or even unconscious, goals activating individuals are simply and directly connected with the emergence of new social forms has had to undergo some modification. The planned

---

[7] Max Weber (29, p. 331) distinguishes between formal and substantive rationality as governing relations between actors in rather similar terms. Substantive rationality is focused upon the requirements of a given relationship and formal rationality upon the requirements of the abstract system of relationships per se. In the same way, our formal goals are the goals of abstract interpersonal patterns while our substantive goals are the goals of individuals caught up in such patterns.

[8] The postulation of fixed exigencies is rather typical of all forms of functionalism. Malinowski's *individual needs* and *integrative imperatives* (12, pp. 90–125) as much as Parsons' *functional imperatives* (system problems) (21, p. 182) share this static quality.

or intended construction of patterns of relations between persons runs into problems whose solutions themselves affect the forms these patterns will take. Collective mobilization toward a goal in itself becomes a factor influencing whether the goal will be reached or not, and even whether it will be, in some sense, exceeded. The various possibilities for the achievement or non-achievement of goals inherent in collectivization may be classified and generalized in the form of a paradigm of originating goals and conjoint consequences.

Originating Goals, Actions, and their Vicissitudes

In his analyses of social action and the unanticipated consequences of social action, Merton (14, p. 50; 13, pp. 894–904) has foreshadowed several important elements of our discussion in his paradigm for functional analysis. Merton makes a clear distinction between the conscious motives and needs of the actors in the situation, and the objective consequences of their action. He stresses the absence of a necessary connection between the intent of the actors involved, and the actual consequences produced by their actions.

While we wish to avoid Merton's stress upon conscious intent in activating a person toward a goal, and thus make a statement referring to action in general, our foregoing discussion amply demonstrates the importance which must be attached to consequences generated by an activity other than the unproblematic attainment of the goal of the activity. In the first place, the goal may or may not be attained. In the second place, and independently of whether the goal of the activity is attained or not, consequences may develop which are additional or extraneous to the mere requirements of locomotion toward the goal. The various possible consequences of the establishment of an interpersonal pattern of action are spelled out below:

1) A "stable" situation in which the pattern of action and the originating goal are, as it were, symmetrical. Simply stated, this means that the pattern of action generated by the originating need serves to attain the goal associated with this need. This condition provides the simplest and most direct "fit" to the institutionalization schema as promulgated above.

2) A situation in which the pattern of action generated by the originating need simply fails to satisfy the goal associated with this need without creating further repercussions for the actors. Here three possible outcomes may be conceived:

    a. The exigency that led to articulation of the need is a transitory one, and the need spontaneously dies out. In this event, the pattern mobilized to meet the need will (always under the assumption that the pattern generates no consequences additional or alternative to reaching the goal) simply be extinguished. The outbreak of a fire in a temporary settlement in the wilderness would constitute such an exigency. (The liability of fire to break out in permanent settlements, on the other hand, tends to lead to the formation of regular fire-fighting agencies.)

b. The exigency remains salient and the need is recognized to have been falsely articulated (i.e., abortive attempts at goal attainment where the action taken is recognized to have no connection with the goal, or where the goal is unachievable). Here rearticulation may take place and lead either to new and different patterns of action associated with the goal, or to new and different goals. The new articulation may be as "false" as the previous one, although the growth of scientific knowledge would appear to indicate a tendency (at least in some areas of need and of action), in the direction of self correction, or movement toward "realistic" actions for the mitigation of the exigency.

c. The conditions of consonance necessary for mobilizing collective or reciprocal activity toward the goal are absent. Here, the lack of these necessary conditions for the mobilization of patterns of institutionalization becomes a second-order exigency (or a set of second-order exigencies having to do with one or a combination of the following: valence dissonance, cognitive dissonance, normative dissonance), and a "need for consonance" will become established leading to activity such as to subserve secondary goals of establishing consonance. "Second-order" activity of this type can serve to complicate and extend very considerably the system of action evoked by the original goal (see page 119 below).

3) A situation in which the pattern of action generated by the originating need fails to satisfy the goal associated with this need, but leads to unanticipated repercussions for the actors. Here again, three possibilities may be set forth:

a. The originating need is not satisfied, but extraneous ones are. The extraneous goals satisfied by the collective pattern of activity may exist for the actors prior to their involvement in it, or may become evoked by their participation in the pattern. This "goal displacement" effect may or may not be recognized by the actors. If the extraneous goals are sufficiently valent, the pattern may persist despite its failure to reach the originating goal. Where the effect is recognized it may lead to changes of detail in the pattern, but the general outline of the pattern will persist. (For example, a male tutor supposed to teach some skill to a lady fails to teach her anything but "falls in love" and therefore continues to go through the motions. In this particular example, we have to assume the additional injunction that an erotic approach to the lady, at any rate in the time period under consideration, is out of the question — otherwise, of course, the pattern of complementarity would take on a different form!) This effect is particularly liable to remain unrecognized in instances where the specificity of the originating goal is low (for example, where the goal is "salvation"). Following Schneider (24, p. 501), we may call this phenomenon "gain through indirection."

   b. The pattern of action embarked upon generates unanticipated exigencies for the actors involved in it. If such exigencies become articulated and the resultant needs are more valent than the need associated with the originating goal, the originating goal will be abandoned.

   c. The pattern of action embarked upon generates exigencies for persons not involved in the pattern. This may lead to articulation of a need on the part of these persons, and action inimical to the achievement of the originally mentioned goal. This process may be viewed as the creation of a *reflective exigency* for the persons involved in the originally mentioned pattern, thus constituting a special instance of 3b above (see also chapter 5).

4) A situation in which the goal of the collective pattern of action is achieved, but the activity itself generates additional repercussions for the actors. Here there are four possible outcomes:

   a. Gain through indirection (see 3a above), in addition to achievement of the goal.

   b. The pattern of action generates unanticipated exigencies which become articulated into needs. The resultant needs, however, are less valent than the need associated with the originating goal.

   c. As in 3c above.

   d. The postulated goal is achieved, but turns out to be irrelevant to the exigency in question. Here again (as in 2b above) the exigency remains salient; there will be re-articulation of the need.

For the sake of brevity, let us attach symbols to the various possibilities enumerated above. Let A stand for the pattern of collective action and an arrow for the consequences of the action. Let G stand for the originating goal; X for unanticipated exigencies resultant from the action; Y for indirect gains from the action; and Z for consequences of the action extraneous or irrelevant to the need. Thus the first possibility considered may be expressed as follows: $A \rightarrow G$; possibilities 2a, b, and c may be expressed as $A \rightarrow Z$; possibility 4d as $A \rightarrow G$, $(G = Z)$; possibility 3a as $A \rightarrow Y$; possibility 4a as $A \rightarrow G+Y$; possibilities 3b and c as $A \rightarrow X$; and possibilities 4b and c as $A \rightarrow G+X$. These various possibilities have a direct bearing upon whether a pattern of action will persist in a changed or unchanged form, or whether it will disintegrate.

The Problem of Pattern Autonomy

Up to this point in our discussion the implicit assumption has been maintained that action has sense and meaning only when viewed as serving the purposes of locomotion toward a goal. We have suggested, furthermore, that interpersonal action — the very "web and tissue" of society itself — comes about where goals imply either the response of others, or where the achievement of goals requires the cooperation of several individuals. Thus we could be accused of promulgating a sociology of associations purely, and of ignoring community patterns of action, since the latter have been defined as being, in some sense, inclusive of *all* goals (11, p. 9).

Additionally, in insisting upon treatment of the social structure as a set of special cases of social process, we lay ourselves open to the accusation of "goal atomism," much as Parsons has accused Max Weber of "type atomism" (20, p. 610; 19, p. 15). Patterns of collectivization, even a sympathetic critic of our approach might say, cannot and do not occur *in vacuo*; there has to be some sense in which they more or less fit into pre-existing patterns.

These hypothetical objections of proponents of "community sociology" and upholders of "system integration," we shall suggest, are fundamentally quite similar. In a social world which becomes increasingly associational, the concept of *system integration* is the legitimate heir to the *Gemeinschaft* frame of reference. In view of the glare given off by the 'Social System', the 'Eclipse of Community', it may well be maintained, need cause no problems of illumination! Both points of view, certainly, conceive of social arrangements as being in some way prior to discrete individual goals. Paraphrasing Spinoza's Ethic, proponents of both views enunciate as their first principle: "*Societas omnibus rebus prior est causalitate.*" Can our categorical system withstand such a critical onslaught?

In answering these objections, it is not our intention to add to the proliferation of myths of human and social origins, but a few brief remarks with a bearing on the question of origins may serve to clarify our stand vis à vis the seemingly perennial issue of individual versus social priority in the analysis of action. If they make a contribution to finally laying this issue to rest, so much the better.

There is no reason to believe that pre-human and pre-social patterns of relations between organisms obey different rules from those we have outlined as governing the formation of associational patterns.[9] If we postulate exigencies and goals for pre-social individuals, some of these goals still require complementary and cooperative behavior. Certain complementary "needs," for example, such as those for sexual contacts

---

[9] Of course, the exigency→articulation→action schema might have to be modified if it were applied to pre-social actions. Thus, while we have found it useful to infer articulation prior to all social action (see pp. 90–91), such an inference might not stand up to criticism in the realm of pre-social action. Fundamentally, our requirement of articulation for social action is analogous to Max Weber's insistence that social action is "meaningful." In other words, we are inclined to attach the same boundaries to social action as does Weber (30, p. 63). We do not insist that animal behavior is the result of articulated goals any more than Weber would insist that it is meaningful.

and those governing the relations between mothers and infants (at least, in the mammalian realm) are built into the biological structure of the organisms under consideration. Where goals associated with these needs are not met, the individuals that fail to meet them die out and leave no descendants, and the species that cannot "adapt" by meeting them becomes extinct.[10]

Once institutionalization patterns involving legitimation and symbolization are established, individuals who are born into the group become caught up in them through processes of socialization. It is in the socialization process that horizons of expectations and horizons of justification are formed in individuals. We are, in effect, suggesting that there exists a feedback process in which institutionalization leads to socialization of the persons who enter into relationships of complementarity or cooperation with others, thereby developing symbol systems (horizons of expectations and horizons of justifications). The horizons of expectations and horizons of justifications of socialized individuals thereupon enter into the determination of new articulations of exigencies and new patterns of institutionalization. Following this line of reasoning, it would appear that the social person and society emerge concurrently. Indeed, any separation of the two is an artifact of inadequate theoretical assumptions.

With the development of symbolization, the previously undifferentiated goal-mass undergoes differentiation, and specialized actions that develop to meet these discriminated special goals generate new exigencies. A spiral of goal differentiation and specialization of action is initiated, and the associational process is under way.

Certain exigencies that arise in this process involve problems of cognitive dissonance and normative dissonance. We may call the patterns of institutionalization arising to meet these exigencies *agencies of consensus* and *agencies of control*. Both agencies of consensus and agencies of control consist of socializing patterns and patterns serving purposes of communication and enforcement of norms. Typically, such patterns, or a large proportion of them, involve the total population on a given territorial base. Thence they are characteristically associated with what has been described as the community type of institutionalization, and not with associations. We have seen, however, that such patterns are actually associational forms involving the total population of a territory. In the nation state which is the closest current approximation to "total

10 When early human groupings become established (or are "inherited" from prehuman ancestors) they become established precisely for the achievement of complementary goals and goals requiring inter-individual cooperation. Goals in these groupings may present themselves as an undifferentiated mass, and the initial patterns of activity that evolve to meet these goals may conform to Durkheim's "mechanical solidarity" (6, chapter 2). It is in the process of collectivization or institutionalization of these activities that distinctively *social* patterns of symbolization and legitimation (norm formation) occur.

social system" as the phrase is used by structural-functionalists, some of the agencies of consensus and control are centralized and form the machinery of law and government.

Any new articulation of needs and their associated goals as it were "filters through" or, more correctly stated, has to be consistent with, individual horizons of expectations and justifications. Insofar as there is indeed a "social order," it rests partly upon relatively common expectations and justifications established in individual persons through processes of socialization, and partly upon the institutionalization of agencies of consensus and of control. To start one's examination of social action with the notion of order, however, (20, pp. 89 ff.) is to obscure the dynamic nature of social process from the beginning.

In any complex society, a given pattern of action directed toward the achievement of a goal is to some degree dependent upon other parts of the "total system," if the total system is defined to include all the elements of which all persons' horizons of expectations and horizons of justifications are fashioned. But such a given pattern may, for all practical purposes, be considered autonomous, since the combinations and permutations of articulations and of patterns of action arising from them are enormous, and since the variability of individual horizons of justifications and of expectations is very great.

In the light of this consideration it is not difficult to share Gouldner's view that "there are *varying degrees* of interdependence which may be postulated to exist among the parts of a system" (9, p. 254) (or *patterns*, in our parlance). The degree of interdependence or *systemness*, we furthermore suggest, is defined by the extent to which a new departure — the emergence of an "original" pattern — generates second-order exigencies. In a system in which interdependence is high, new patterns of institutionalization will generate more exigencies than in a loosely knit system, except in the limiting case where new patterns dovetail perfectly into pre-existing ones. It is our contention that such a perfect fit of new patterns with established ones is likely to be very rare indeed. This contention is open to empirical investigation but, given its validity, it implies that new patterns of institutionalization are less likely to become established in a highly interdependent and integrated system because of problems of consonance. Only in a situation where a substantial degree of pattern autonomy becomes established can heterogeneous and varied needs be articulated in the face of exigencies, and effectively met.

Since the establishment or attempted establishment of any given pattern of collectivization may be examined from the point of view of how many second-order exigencies it generates, the working assumption of pattern autonomy provides a very satisfactory strategy for the description of social process, and the charge of pattern atomism is demonstrated to be misplaced.

The Maintenance of Institutionalized Patterns

Hitherto we have been concerned with how patterns of interaction between persons become established, but the question of why some of these patterns become relatively permanent has been touched upon only very lightly. It is time to turn to an examination of the conditions under which patterns of interpersonal relations, expectations, and norms, once regularized and relatively fixed, come to be maintained.

The simplest instance of interpersonal patterns being maintained may be found where there is a continuous and constant bombardment by the exigencies through which the pattern became evoked. Where a need has become articulated, and its associated goals satisfy the exigency to a reasonable extent, there will be no call for re-articulation and the postulation of new goals. Where these goals, moreover, require or in themselves involve collectivization, the collective patterns that become established will, quite naturally, persist. And such patterns can, and do, persist *apparently* quite independently of any particular personnel who play them out in a given situation and at a given time.

It is precisely this seeming independence of particular persons in patterns of collectivization that leads to descriptions of socio-cultural processes as "super-organic" (10, pp. 23–30), and to assertions regarding social priority such as we have attacked above. But, though the personnel may change, the situation in which exigencies exist continues, and different persons in similar situations, with similar articulations of need, will act to maintain the established pattern. It is situations in which needs persist in a relatively unchanged state that may be characterized, with much justice, as being "exterior and constraining" to individuals in the society (5, p. 13), and not the society itself, which, as we have seen, may more fruitfully be viewed as congeries of interpersonal instrumentalities for the satisfaction of needs. We cannot dismiss even this elementary instance, however, without becoming engaged in a discussion of what is implied by the deceptively simple phrase, "continuous and constant bombardment of exigencies."

Let us return to a simple, almost biological example and consider pain as an exigency liable to impinge on an individual person. Some sort of articulation of a need to be free of pain (or of the goal of "painlessness") can, of course, occur at extremely elementary levels of cognitive organization. It is hardly necessary to add that strategies of action in response to some articulation of this need are very widespead in human history and across cultures, and that such actions quite frequently become interwoven in patterns of institutionalization. In a contemporary society such as the United States, the goal of painlessness (and this goal enjoys widespread legitimation) becomes the focus of a whole institutional complex involving research in the field of analgesics and anaesthetics, the pharmacological industry, advertising, and the multifarious branches of the medical and paramedical professions. The very mention of research in the preceding sentence suggests a situation of change, but even if we were to assume, for the sake of the argument, that the goal of painlessness had been "adequately" met and further research on this specific topic were unnecessary, the "stability of the system" or maintenance of the institutional complex would be upheld by the brute facts concerning the incidence of pain or, at least (in the event of completely effective analgesia) the *onset* of pain in the population. The continuous liability of some members of a sufficiently large population to experience the onset of pain constitutes the "bombardment of exigencies" to which we have referred.[11]

The above instance, then, is simply one where the articulation, action, and particularly, the patterns of collectivization of action consequent to an exigency do not come to a terminus; and persist because the need has not been completely satisfied by the activities that arose to meet it. Where the need is an enduring one, and where patterns of collectivization or institutionalization satisfy it to a reasonable degree for a sufficient number of persons implicated in the need, these patterns will persist. In our notation this case may be expressed in the form $A \rightarrow G$, where the goal is an enduring one.

Where goals are attained by actions not immediately and directly "designed" to reach them, we have another instance of institutional maintenance. Certain goals, indeed, appear to have the quality of being "resistant" to direct attempts at reaching them. Schneider and Dornbusch in their discussion of the *principle of intermediacy* and the realization of, what they call "latent by-products" of certain kinds of goal directed behavior suggest: "If one desires to achieve a goal such as high productivity in a plant or soldiers' willingness to fight, direct exhortations to 'produce' or to 'fight' can be useless or worse. The large ultimate goal often has to be constructed out of relatively modest materials . . . that work toward the large goal intermediately and cumulatively" (25, p. 76 n).

The indirect achievement of goals can have importance for a formal pattern (taking the form of an organization, say) whose maintenance is to some degree dependent upon the achievement of these goals, since otherwise the pattern could be dissolved at the behest of some external authority. The analysis of a state employment agency by Blau furnishes an example (3). One of the formal goals of the agency was the equitable treatment of clients of different racial and ethnic backgrounds. Blau found that the formal bureaucratic requirements designed to assure equitable treatment of clients were less effective in doing so than were statistical records, which were not intended for this purpose. Blau suggests that: "The rule to treat Negroes and whites alike directly conflicts

---

[11] We assume also a reasonable constancy of the incidence of pain over a period of time, since drastic changes in incidence would create exigencies for the institutional structure of "pain relieving" itself.

with a deep seated preferential attitude toward whites in our society. . . . Statistical records, on the other hand, did not arouse this resistance precisely because officials were not aware that their concentration on making placements had any bearing on the problem of discrimination" (3, p. 80). Thus, the instances here described may also be expressed A → G, but by an indirect route.

But the instances outlined by no means exhaust the conditions under which institutionalized patterns will persist as "institutions." The originating needs or goals that activated an institutional pattern do not constitute all of the various needs and goals that may arise for the persons implicated in it. Situations may be postulated in which the actor does not know how his actions support a goal and, additionally, in which the goal constitutes a macroscopic effect of the microscopic patterns implicating actors. Schneider, in an instructive essay concerning the category of ignorance in sociological theory, has the following to say:

> . . . where individual couples desire and have children but there is no contemplation of 'continuance of the personnel of the society' as a goal . . . the conversion from individually realized object to social outcome is contingent on simple additivity. As one female after another gives birth a certain level of births is reached and 'continuance' assured. . . . In Adam Smith's classic effort to show how the desire for individual gain ignorantly and unintentionally brings about general economic welfare, transmutation mechanisms are already more complicated: they work through interactions of individuals on the market, through relations of supply and demand that are certainly not reducible to anything like simple additivity (24, p. 500).

Such "unearned increments," as Becker has called them (1, p. 807), only partially serve to maintain the microscopic patterns of which they are macroscopic effects. They do, however, serve to reinforce the patterns in question and, after being "discovered," serve as powerful legitimations for the maintenance of these patterns. This instance, of course, is one of A → G+Y.

But there are other instances, more directly bound up with the pattern itself, where that pattern leads to the achievement of goals besides the originating goal. We have already seen that certain patterns develop *ab initio* in response to a multiplicity of needs; manipulative complementarity and transactional cooperation were developed as ideal types to fit the existence of a plurality of needs from the beginning. Certainly, institutional patterns of any complexity at all will subserve what we have called a goal set. Zollschan has elsewhere pointed out that the medical profession or schools, viewed as institutional patterns, demonstrably subserve such goal sets: "The needs that the medical profession satisfies differ according to whether you are a physician or a patient; the school satisfies different perceived needs for the teacher, the pupil, the latter's parents, and his potential employers" (32). When a pattern subserves a goal set, not all the goals that put the pattern into motion need remain actual for the pattern to maintain itself; it is sufficient that some of them endure for this to happen.

A related instance to the above is a case in which the pattern becomes diversified in the process of development of second-order exigencies generated by the operation of the pattern itself. As these exigencies become articulated as needs, the pattern of activities, as it were, accumulates goals. The new goals lead to new sets of actions within the original pattern — actions which diversify the pattern. Here again, not all the goals that develop in this process of diversification need remain actual for the pattern to maintain itself. Indeed, in the unfolding of such a process of goal development old goals may become discarded, leading to a situation that may be expressed in our notation as $A \rightarrow Y$.

Another case of goal development and pattern diversification may be found in agencies specifically devoted to planning and research. Here the patterns in themselves embody what one might call the "institutionalization of change" — continuous change in certain specifiable directions becomes the goal itself. Indeed, the major activity discernible in this sort of pattern is devoted to the articulation of exigencies. But such instances of change are consistent with pattern maintenance and pattern diversification rather than with the dissolution of patterns. One reservation must be made regarding the last statement; the structure of knowledge — the collective horizon of specifications and applications, as it were — may undergo revolutionary change in this process. What is important, however, is that the system of relationships in which such changes are created persists relatively unchanged.

The most extreme case of the development of new goals occurs in formalized, highly organized institutional patterns in which publicly stated goals are changed. This process has been called *goal succession* and has been studied in some detail (albeit from a different frame of reference) in recent years (3; 28). A change in the formal goal of an organized pattern of interpersonal action is, of course, highly a propos where the need underlying the old goal becomes less valent or disappears altogether, but where the organization is equipped to serve a variety of goals. As new needs become articulated, the already existing pattern of activity can be deployed for their alleviation. But going beyond this, the atrophy of old goals can create indirect pressures for the articulation of new needs for the pattern to meet. Whereas, as Selznick felicitously remarks "... the needs of individuals do not permit a single-minded attention to the stated goals of the system to which they have been assigned . . ." (26, p. 21), neither does the atrophy of stated goals in formalized patterns permit the individuals, whose extraneous needs are met in these patterns, to ignore the threat to their individual goals posed by the possible dissolution of the pattern. Goals are not always effectively articulated by those most directly faced by given exigencies but, if we may paraphrase T. S. Eliot, the "right goals are often articulated for the wrong reason."

One final question must concern us in this brief exploration of the conditions for interpersonal pattern maintenance, from the viewpoint of a theory of institutionalization. This is the question of coercion or constraint.[12] Our genetic approach to the formation and maintenance of collective patterns of action has led us to adopt a terminology which might, on superficial reading, be taken to imply a rather extremely "voluntaristic" conception of human behavior. Nothing could be further from our intentions than to imply that all persons become implicated in every pattern of institutionalization freely and spontaneously. But a modified voluntarism, freed from utopian implications of the social world as "the best of all possible worlds" (indeed, a powerful case can be made for the proposition that it is very nearly the worst) does, we believe, provide the broadest and most adequate theoretical approach to the understanding of institutional forms.

The categories of transactional cooperation and manipulative complementarity, if fully understood in all their implications, cover all but the direct instances of coercion. This becomes quite clear if we consider the total predicament (or "life space" in Kurt Lewin's terms) of individual persons who become implicated in institutional patterns in order to reach goals extraneous to the purposes for which the pattern exists. The factory worker who submerges his working hours to distaste and boredom prefers this fate to the exigency of unemployment; to earn wages is his "goal." The slave, for similar reasons, if he continues to brave existence as a slave, does so because he is impelled to avoid the exigencies of the whip;[13] his "goal" is to avoid excessive physical injury or pain. Exigencies, it should be remembered, lie at the base of goals in our theoretical approach, and the alternative of human bondage to exigencies is a vacuous Nirvana of purposelessness. Even the victim of torture, bound hand and foot, can swallow his tongue and thus divorce himself from the pattern in which he is implicated (at least, if he has sufficient presence of mind, and when the "goal" of survival has to be relinquished). But perhaps it is inappropriate in this chapter to explore the austere implications of our sober voluntarism to their bitter limits. Beyond these limits lies madness.[14]

Conclusions and Anticipations

In the introduction to this Section, the outlines of a theory of institutionalization were set forth. In its most general form, the theory

---

[12] For the most systematic exposition of a theory of organization based on constraint, see Dahrendorf (4).

[13] Professor Fallding, in a communication to the *American Sociological Review* makes a similar point: ". . . we may bitterly resent the nature of our circumstances, but are prepared to suffer them for the sake of the necessities gained through continuing under them; there being no better alternative before us" (7, p. 778).

[14] Some aspects of these problems are discussed in connection with the question of alienation in chapter 6.

suggested that the emergence of new social forms takes place through a series of conceptually linked and related stages: first is a stage of subjective dissatisfaction experienced by a person or by some aggregate of persons (exigencies); these dissatisfactions must be crystallized and brought to the awareness of the persons involved (articulation); once crystallized, organized individual or collective efforts are directed toward the elimination or satisfaction of the articulated need; the final stage is that of the emergence of a new social form or the modification of an existing one. This orientation, however, contains more than just a specification of processes by which new patterns emerge. An integral part of the institutionalization frame of reference is the view that the operation of socio-cultural systems involves an unending process of the production of exigencies, their transmutation into expressible needs, and the mobilizing of action to satisfy these needs. The existence of a stable state or equilibrium is viewed as a special case, since the actions — and particularly collective patterns of action — which are directed toward the alleviation or elimination of a need will themselves create new exigencies along the way.

The inherently dynamic nature of this institutionalization framework — reflected by the conceptual tools utilized in its description — has led us to explore the distinctively sociological problems involved in such a theory of change. Thus we have taken the first and most general steps in exploring (1) the conditions in, or qualities of, socio-cultural systems that produce exigencies. This becomes the motivational base upon which subsequent actions are built; (2) the conditions under which institutionalization occurs, given goals that require the responses of others or the cooperation of others; (3) the extent to which persons involved in patterns of institutionalization either have, or develop, shared orientations and expectations. Thus we have spoken of normative, valence, and cognitive consonance as supporting conditions for the emergence of collective action. Problems of dissonance have been viewed as second-order exigencies giving rise to new or additional goals; (4) how additional consequences, other than those sought within the pattern, develop. Such consequences were viewed as either supportive of, or inimical to, the originating goal; (5) the extent to which the emergence of new patterns is related to existing social systems. The crucial question examined here concerned the degree of autonomy of discrete patterns of institutionalization and their relationship to some more or less systematic "social system"; (6) maintenance as a special case of institutionalization in which patterns persist primarily because of the continued existence of needs and/or because of pattern generation of unanticipated consequences supportive of the persistence of the pattern.

A classification of types of patterns of institutionalization (forms of organization) has not been attempted in this chapter. Our propositions in their highly general form are meant to apply to interpersonal patterns ranging from the informal and spontaneous development of relations between persons, to legalized, highly formalized, organizational systems of coordinated activity. The extent to which our original propositions would have to be augmented to do justice to the entire range of levels of organization remains a matter for further exploration.

One of the persistent problems in current sociological writings has been the attempt to reconcile explanations of how social order and stability is possible with the irrefutable evidence of all-pervasive conflict and change. Sociological concern with equilibrium, as evidenced by the structural-functional school, has produced a conceptual apparatus of powerful impact on the establishment of sociology as a respectable intellectual discipline. Certain inadequacies of this framework for the exploration of social events have given new strength to opposing frames of reference, emphasizing, in particular, conditions for the emergence of conflict and the generation of change. It has been our ambition in this chapter to take some initial steps toward the demonstration of structural and conflict views of social action as special cases of a more general theory of institutionalization.[15]

In a recent article, Professor Black concludes that Parson's theory, in its present stage of development, should be regarded primarily as a theory about social statics. Black adds: ". . . we may well remind ourselves . . . that what is called the 'statics' of material bodies (the theory of bodies under equilibrium) has to be supplemented by independent mechanical principles before we are in a position to say anything about [their] motions . . ." (2, p. 275). Thus, he implies, we should not expect a theory like Parsons' to predict how systems change.

The present chapter has reported on an attempt to supply some of the "independent principles" necessary for the consideration of the dynamics of social systems. It should be stressed that the kind of predictions that may ultimately be derivable from the principles proposed will be conditional predictions — not the unconditional prophecies of historicism.[16]

Finally, it should be stressed, that while our suggestions have been for a theory of social change, they may also illuminate the currently highly obscure mechanisms whereby social systems maintain stability. Parsons asserts that in order to maintain stability, social systems must meet what he has called the "functional problems" (21, p. 183). We propose that social systems continue to satisfy functional requirements such as these only as long as potential failures to meet them become exigencies for actors and are transmuted (by the processes we have outlined) into patterns of institutionalization. States of equilibrium are special cases of dynamics at *all* levels of scientific analysis.

[15] A fuller examination of the bearing of the categorical framework we have outlined to the theory of conflict may be found in chapter 5.

[16] Karl Popper (22, p. 43) has made this distinction between prophecy and prediction. We feel it should be stressed in our chapter, as our emphasis upon social dynamics is not meant to imply predictions of "the future" in open systems.

BIBLIOGRAPHY

1. Becker, Howard. "Normative Reactions to Normlessness," *American Sociological Review*, Vol. 25, No. 6 (December 1960), pp. 803–810.

2. Black, Max. "Some Questions about Parsons' Theories," in Max Black (ed.), *The Social Theories of Talcott Parsons*. Englewood Cliffs, N.J.: Prentice-Hall, Inc., 1961.

3. Blau, Peter M. *The Dynamics of Bureaucracy*. Chicago: University of Chicago Press, 1955.

4. Dahrendorf, Ralf. *Class and Class Conflict in Industrial Society*. Stanford: Stanford University Press, 1959.

5. Durkheim, Emile. *The Rules of the Sociological Method*, G. Catlin (ed.), Glencoe, Ill.: The Free Press. 1938.

6. Durkheim, Emile. *The Division of Labor in Society*, translated by George Simpson. Glencoe, Ill.: The Free Press, 1947.

7. Fallding, Harold. "Towards a Reconciliation of Mills with Parsons," *American Sociological Review*, Vol. 26, No. 5 (October 1961), pp. 778–780.

8. Freud, Sigmund. "The Interpretation of Dreams," in *The Complete Psychological Works*. London: Hogarth Press, 1953, Vols. 4 and 5.

9. Gouldner, Alvin W. "Reciprocity and Autonomy in Functional Theory," in Llewellyn Gross (ed.), *Symposium on Sociological Theory*. Evanston, Ill.: Row, Peterson and Co., 1959.

10. Kroeber, Alfred L. *The Nature of Culture*. Chicago: University of Chicago Press, 1952.

11. MacIver, R. M., and Charles H. Page. *Society*. New York: Rinehart and Co., 1953.

12. Malinowski, Bronislaw. *A Scientific Theory of Culture and Other Essays*. Chapel Hill, N.C.: University of North Carolina Press, 1944.

13. Merton, Robert K. "The Unanticipated Consequences of Purposive Social Action," *American Sociological Review*, Vol. 1, No. 6 (December 1936), pp. 894–904.

14. Merton, Robert K. "The Role Set: Problems in Sociological Theory," *British Journal of Sociology*, Vol. 8, No. 2 (June 1957), pp. 106–120.

15. Merton, Robert K. *Social Theory and Social Structure*. Glencoe, Ill.: The Free Press, 1957.

16. Mizruchi, Ephraim H., and Robert Perrucci. "Norm Qualities and Differential Effects of Deviant Behavior," *American Sociological Review*, Vol. 27, No. 3 (June 1962), pp. 391–399.

17. Moore, Wilbert E. "Theories of Social Change," *American Sociological Review*, Vol. 25, No. 6 (December 1960), pp. 810–818.

18. Ogle, Marbury B., Louis Schneider, and Jay W. Wiley. *Power, Order, and the Economy*. New York: Harper and Bros., 1954.

19. Parsons, Talcott. Introduction to *The Theory of Social and Economic Organization*, by Max Weber, translated by A. M. Henderson and Talcott Parsons. Glencoe, Ill.: The Free Press, 1947.

20. Parsons, Talcott. *The Structure of Social Action*. Glencoe, Ill.: The Free Press, 1949.

21. Parsons, Talcott, Robert F. Bales, and Edward A. Shils. *Working Papers in the Theory of Action*. Glencoe, Ill.: The Free Press, 1953.

22. Popper, Karl R. *The Poverty of Historicism*. Boston: Beacon Press, 1957.

23. Schneider, Louis. "Some Psychiatric Views on 'Freedom' and the Theory of Social Systems," *Psychiatry*, Vol. 12, No. 3 (August 1949), pp. 251–264.

24. Schneider, Louis. "The Category of Ignorance in Sociological Theory," *American Sociological Review*, Vol. 27, No. 4 (August 1962), pp. 492–507.

25. Schneider, Louis, and Sanford Dornbush. *Popular Religion*. Chicago: University of Chicago Press, 1958.

26. Selznick, Philip. "Foundations of the Theory of Organization," *American Sociological Review*, Vol. 13, No. 1 (February 1948), pp. 25–35.

27. Sibley, Elbridge. "Some Demographic Clues to Stratification," *American Sociological Review*, Vol. 7, No. 3 (June 1942), pp. 322–330.

28. Sills, David L. *The Volunteers*. Glencoe, Ill.: The Free Press, 1947.

29. Weber, Max. *From Max Weber*, translated and edited by H. H. Gerth and C. Wright Mills. New York: Oxford University Press, 1946.

30. Weber, Max. *Basic Concepts in Sociology*, translated and with an Introduction by H. P. Secher. New York: Philosophical Library, 1962.

31. White, Leslie A. *The Science of Culture*. New York: Farrar Straus, 1949.

32. Zollschan, George K. "Needs, Interests, and Leaders: Occasions for Community Leadership," in Alvin W. Gouldner (ed.), *Studies in Leadership*, 2nd Ed., Indianapolis: Bobbs-Merrill. (In press)

5

David Willer

and George K. Zollschan

Prolegomenon to a Theory

of Revolutions

*"Die Ermittlung der Sozialstruktur der revolutionaeren Situation ist
das Kernstueck der Theorie der Revolution; sie bedeutet zugleich
einen Betrag zur Erforschung der Faktoren, die eine allgemeine
Theorie des sozialen Wandels konstituiren."*[1]
(Dahrendorf, 9, p. 159)

Traditionally, the study of revolutions — forcible overturns of governments — has belonged to the fields of history and political science and,
it would appear, quite justifiably so. After all, revolutions are unique,
often extremely complex, concrete historical phenomena and, as such,
"naturals" for the ideographic methods and concerns of the historian.
What is more, revolutions are defined by their relationship to governmental or political structure, and thus form part of the subject matter of
political science. What justification, then, can the sociologist find for
entering an edifice of learning heavily populated with ideas and, indeed,
overcrowded with learned and not so learned works? There are several

---

[1] The elucidation of the social structure of revolutionary situations is the core of
the Theory of Revolutions. It involves, at the same time, a contribution to the
discovery of elements constituting a general theory of social change.

answers to this question; some of them, we hope, will be clearly implied in the burden of our argument. One general answer to justify sociological concern with the topic may, however, be given at the outset. For several decades the main stream of sociological endeavor (at least, in America where the subject has prospered most) has been diverted from the subject's long-standing concern with social change. The difficulties of generalizing across historical instances appeared too great to yield scientifically acceptable evidence; the early ambitions of some "historicist" sociologists who tended to see the task of sociology as prophecying historical events, much as astronomy was predicting eclipses of the sun and moon, were seen to be unrealistic and, indeed, methodologically preposterous (31, pp. 35–54, pp. 105–130). A much readier avenue to the advance of knowledge in the field appeared to be provided by the synchronic approach — concerned with the delineation of social structures and speculation regarding their "functions" — and this approach is still on the ascendant. There is, however, a rising chorus of criticism of structural-functionalism, and the dominant voices to be discerned are those of theorists who espouse sociologies of interests and dissensus of values, of coercion and of conflict — in short, of social change, or at least, of conditions for social change.[2] It is thus quite clear that in contemporary discussions of social change, clashes of interests and instances of interpersonal conflict must have a prominent place. For concerns of this nature the study of revolutions is virtually paradigmatic.

A simple assertion that the study of revolutions is central to a current tendency in sociological thinking, however, still cannot justify the entry of the sociologists into this field. Could not the sociologist leave descriptions of revolutions to historians and use their discoveries (or inventions) for purposes of illustration? To some degree this is bound to happen, but we believe the sociologist also has a distinctive contribution to make to the study of revolutions, a contribution for which the training and orientation of historians are not entirely adequate. This contribution lies in the systematic explanation of elements that enter into historical situations in theoretical terms. We believe, in other words, that the time has come again, after the sociological moratorium of the structural-functionalist period, to attempt the sociological analysis of the components of concrete historical events, like revolutions, and to assay generalizations regarding these components. To be sure, the analytic tools and concepts developed by structural-functionalists will help us in this effort.

Before we enter a discussion of these sociological components of revolutions and their analysis, it is proper to pause and to discuss how the term "revolution" will be used. Here Arthur Hatto (18, pp. 498–499) can come to our aid. The original use of the term, he tells us, is bound to the image of a revolving wheel. It occurs in Polybius' account and

[2] We may single out for special mention the work of Lockwood (22), Dahrendorf (7; 8), Coser (6), and Mills (26).

embellishment of Plato's cyclical theory of social change in the *Republic*.
". . . alleging that he is giving his busy readers a conveniently brief account of what Plato has said, Polybius makes kingship pass into tyranny,
tyranny into aristocracy, aristocracy into oligarchy, oligarchy into democracy, democracy into mob-rule, and mob-rule into that state of nature
which . . . must inevitably produce kingship and a new cycle." It is not
until the pre-revolutionary writings of Montesquieu, Rousseau, and Voltaire that some implicit cyclical theory of history (or, at least, reference
to the re-establishment of a real or hypothetical previous state of affairs
that had undergone change) is given up in the use of the term. The
image of a turning wheel is replaced by these writers with the image of
an "overturning" object — the "object" in question being, of course, the
extant power structure.

This new usage of "revolution" is the one we shall adopt; it is succinctly defined in the *Oxford English Dictionary* (1961) as follows:
"A complete overthrow of the established government in any country or
state by those who were previously subject to it; a forcible substitution
of a new ruler or form of government." Of course, revolutions in this
modern sense of the word took place long before its new usage had been
established. Thus Hatto for example, tells us that "though the Greeks
had their fill of revolution they had no single word for it" (18, p. 498)
and goes on to describe similar states of affairs up to the establishment
of the term's current meaning.

We shall concentrate on those species of revolutions which have a
fundamental impact on the structure of government and the society as
a whole. For "Latin-American" types of revolution — where the revolution can take place "in one corner of the market place while life flows on
peacefully in the other" (18, p. 514) — we shall reserve the term "coup
d'etat."

The stress we have placed upon the justification of sociological concern
with the subject matter of "revolution" is not meant to imply that we
are alone among contemporary sociologists in our interest. Recently,
James Davies has put forward a theory of revolution based on the relationship between curves of actual and of expected "need satisfaction"
plotted over time. In brief, Davies' theory postulates "a period of rising
expectations and a succeeding period in which they are frustrated . . ."
(10, p. 17). More specifically, the article contains both the notion that
revolutions do not occur where there is an unimpeded opportunity to
satisfy developing expectations, and the idea that revolutions require
rising expectations, since they do not occur "where there is no hope."
The hypothetical instance where the base line is one of fairly high expectations, and where such expectations meet with increasing frustration, is not considered by Davies. He assumes, in other words, that the
level of expectations for "need satisfactions" at which any time-curve
plotting the development of a revolution should be started is necessarily
a very low one.

Davies chronicles a number of revolutions and rebellions[3] to illustrate his hypothesis, and is quite honest in taking note of certain contrary instances, although he is content to attach ad hoc explanations to some of the latter.[4] All in all, his formulation, although interesting as a discussion of historical uniformities, fails to live up to the designation "Theory." For it to do so, Davies would have to furnish, at the least, certain hypotheses governing the extent of the gap between expectations and satisfactions at which the revolution would become triggered, for example, or alternatively, relate the outbreak to the rapidity with which the gap develops. But a more fundamental criticism may be leveled at Davies' formulations, at least, insofar as they contain pretensions of constituting a theory of revolutions. Basically, this is the same criticism expressed by Dahrendorf (9, p. 158) concerning the contributions of Gottschalk (16) and Brinton (4). In brief, Davies ignores the fundamental structural conditions under which a revolution comes about. He concentrates, rather, on the short-run, immediate processes in which a revolution is precipitated.

We will propose a set of structural categories going beyond the mere description of uniformities discoverable in cases where revolutions are precipitated. In so doing, we hope to lend a new sharpness of definition to accounts of historical uniformities of the revolutionary process that are currently extant. In some respects this approach parallels Blumer's formulations on collective behavior (3, pp. 202–205).

Some Fundamental Categories for the Analysis of Revolutionary Situations

In his *Class and Class Conflict in Industrial Society,* Dahrendorf (8) proposes a theory of conflict that serves as a point of entry into the problematics of category construction for a theory of revolutions. Dahrendorf assumes that the "distribution of authority is the ultimate 'cause' of the formation of conflict groups" (8, p. 172). Further, he suggests that, within any given imperatively coordinated association (by which he means, roughly speaking, both hierarchically organized associations such as industrial enterprises, and political units such as states or municipalities), authority is dichotomously distributed. There is domination and subjection in an imperatively coordinated association; *tertium non datur.* Thus the category of authority becomes the "structural determinant of conflict groups" (8, p. 173).

We shall have occasion to question this assumption as we develop our categories for a theory of revolution. But a slight variation of Dahrendorf's subsequent discussion of the phases of conflict group formation

[3] He gives particular attention to Dorr's Rebellion of 1842, the Russian Revolution of 1917, and the Egyptian Revolution of 1952.

[4] In this connection Davies becomes involved in a lengthy discussion of the depression of the 1930's in the United States as an instance of "a revolution that did not occur" (10, p. 16).

will form the basis of our analysis of the emergence of revolutionary groups and, therefore, deserve rather full exposition in this context.

Dahrendorf adds to his assumption of dichotomous distribution of authority ". . . the proposition that differentially equipped authority positions in associations involve, for their incumbents, conflicting interests" (8, p. 174). His delineation of the phases of conflict group emergence is sufficiently terse to permit their quotation in full:

> Orientations of behavior which are inherent in social positions . . . (role expectations), and which oppose two aggregates of positions in any imperatively coordinated association, shall be called *latent interests.*
> *Quasi-group* shall mean any collectivity of individuals sharing positions with identical latent interests without having organized themselves as such.
> *Manifest interests* shall mean orientations of behavior which are articulate and conscious to individuals, and which oppose collectivities of individuals in any imperatively coordinated association.
> *Interest group* shall mean any organized collectivity of individuals sharing manifest interests (8, pp. 237–238).

Like Dahrendorf, we are especially interested in the action potential inherent in occupying a position. Dahrendorf's implication, however, that a given structural position is *directly* connected with a given set of actions strikes us as rather naive. The relationship between a "position," however defined, and specific actions — or even the possible emergence of specific actions — is by no means as simple as he wishes to imply.

Social positions and especially socio-economic positions can be defined in either of two ways: first, in terms of their structural relationship to other positions; or second, in terms of actions, typical or potential. Weber's well-known definitions of class and status are essentially of the former type. An individual's chance in a market, his effective demand, and his ability to receive social honor form the basis for Weber's conceptions.[5] Marx, on the other hand, emphasizes certain action potentials in his conception of class. This is clear, for when discussing peasants in France he states, "In so far as there is merely a local intercommunication among these small peasants and identity of interests begets no unity, no rational union, and no political organization, they do not form a class" (23, p. 109). While both Marx and Weber include components of structure and action, the emphasis of each is clear. For Marx, unless common actions are expected, a collectivity is not considered to be a class; while for Weber, class interest does not stem directly from his more structural conception.[6] Dahrendorf's formulations regarding position clearly follow the Marxian emphasis on action potentials; ours will attempt to take the emphases of both Marx and Max Weber into account.

[5] For Weber's concepts of class and status see (35, p. 181, pp. 186–187).

[6] In relation to this question Weber states that the concept of class interest is highly ambiguous unless it is understood to mean the "factual direction following with a certain probability from the class situation for a certain 'average' of those people subjected to the class situation" (35, p. 183).

Let us consider a structural position to be a person's totality of statuses relative to others within organizations and other institutional patterns. Taking the concept of exigency (as introduced on page 89) as an intervening variable between structural position and interest position, we should be able to give better definition to the problem of the conditions under which certain types of action will be touched off. A structural position, in our scheme, may be a source of diverse exigencies for its incumbents — subjection in an imperatively co-ordinated association is clearly not the sole exigency of which any position can be the source. Thus even Marx considers levels of consumption, in addition to questions of what Dahrendorf calls domination and subjection, as being important in the generation of situations of conflict, and Sombart (33, p. 192) explains the absence of a socialist movement in the United States partially by reference to the high standard of living of the "subjected" (although the extent of social mobility is the major prop of his argument). A theory of conflict based upon subjection as the sole exigency is too narrow to account for the rich and varied subject it sets out to explain.

We may thus reformulate Dahrendorf's account of conflict group emergence and broaden it so as to include a suitably modified version of the exigency→articulation→action schema (pp. 90–91). In so doing, we suggest that a more adequate theory of group conflict becomes possible, and greater candlepower may be deployed to illuminate revolutions which, of course, become special cases of the general theory of conflict:

An *exigency* is a feeling of unease in the person and the occurrence of unrest in a collectivity stemming from a differential between the person's definition of the relevant social situation as it is and as it should be. Typically an exigency as such is on a pre-verbal level.

An *articulation* is any verbal statement capable of translating an exigency into an expressed need. Articulations may range in complexity from simple statements to elaborate ideological systems. They may arise from a single individual or simultaneously from numerous individuals faced by an exigency. Articulations need not have any empirical validity: the definitions of the situation they contain may be unacceptable to an observer possessing a wider range of relevant knowledge, and the programs they imply or propose may not satisfy the exigency. In the latter case we shall speak of "false" articulation.

A *need* is an articulated exigency involving the desire of an individual or group to modify the relevant state of affairs in line with their accepted values. Like exigencies, needs are usually composed of situational and ideal components, and contain explicit or implicit programs for bridging the gap between these two sets of components. Thus a need has a dual base in the exigency itself (via salience) and in articulation.[7]

[7] A full description of the role of salience and the question of articulation in general is furnished on pp. 90–93.

An *interest* is a need specific to a group or collectivity which is perceived as being contrary to the interests of other groups or collectivities.[8]

A *latent interest position* is a position involving exposure to a set of exigencies and also to a set of items of information which may be used for purposes of articulation.

A *latent interest group* is any collectivity of incumbents of latent interest positions.

A *manifest interest* is defined by a set of articulations accepted by incumbents of this position. The probability is put forward that those sharing exposure to similar exigencies and having similar sources of information will develop or accept similar articulations.

A *manifest interest group* (for the sake of brevity we shall use the generic term "interest group" for this, except when otherwise stated) is any collectivity of incumbents of manifest interest positions, whose interests are common,[9] and form a possible basis for collective action.

A *complex interest group* is composed of persons who may not occupy similar (or identical) manifest interest positions, but whose interests are none the less common in relation to a given situation. Complex interest groups may be considered as combinations of simple interest groups.

An *organized group* is a simple or complex interest group organized to undertake collective action in support of interests common to the group.

We shall maintain that revolutionary movements share, with other movements based upon interests and ideologies, certain relatively clear-cut stages which we shall describe as: the stage of latency, the manifest stage, and the organized stage. These definitions will be employed in following the emergence of revolutionary movements through these stages. Before we procede to analyze this sequential progression of stages preceding revolutions, however, some implications of our categorical scheme should be brought out.

When considering the complexity of any person's structural position, the task of discovering groups faced by similar exigencies may appear impossibly difficult. This, we assume, is why Dahrendorf has recourse to but one structural differentiation; that between domination and subjection. In our view, a structural position may be the source (or the mirror) of diverse exigencies. For each of these — when considered in relation to the "means of legitimation" and the "means of specification" — a latent interest position may be postulated. Given a concrete situation, this may not be easy to do; certainly it is simpler (although not necessarily more precise) to attach labels like "dominant" and "subjected" to various positions, but the problem of exactly locating exigencies and latent interests prior to their articulation and emergence into the

---

[8] Such contrariety may involve the direct opposition of two groups or may arise from a mutual struggle for limited resources.

[9] Common interests are those which form a basis for non-contradictory actions. Clearly, given substantially diverse interests, the extent of communality will depend upon the structure of the situation as well as upon the particular issues in question.

arena of conflict does not concern us here. We *are* concerned with the
establishment of a set of categories that shows some promise of doing
justice to the richness and variety of conflict relations as they play themselves out on the stage of history and in the social realm.

It has already been implied that structural positions are not simply loci
of differential exposure to certain kinds of exigencies; they may also be
positions governing possibilities of gaining access to certain kinds of information. The eventuality may even be considered that, given the
"means of articulation" available to the incumbents of a set of structural
positions, only one latent interest position exists for them, regardless of
the possible diversity of exigencies with which they are individually
faced. In the case of Nazism in Germany the diversity of interests is
striking. From frustrated civil servants to *Junkers*, from displaced re-
turnees from the First World War to the miscellaneous *lumpenprole-
tariat*, the movement, with its patchwork ideology, formed a socially
unifying (if not logically unified) set of ideas. No other ideology could
be found in Germany at that time to appeal to all these groups.

Another obstacle to relating structural and interest positions concerns
the role of "false" articulations, which we have briefly mentioned. A
need falsely articulated in a manner that does not adequately and without distortion reflect the exigency leading to its articulation we shall call
a *pseudo-need*. Similarly, interests based upon false articulation we shall
call *pseudo-interests*. Terminology such as this implies something like
privileged access on the part of the "scientific observer" to the nature of
the raw exigency — access from which the actors in the situation themselves are, presumably, excluded — and is therefore open to question.
Although Marx's rather similar use of the term "false consciousness" has
been widely criticized (8, p. 14, p. 114), we would still maintain that
some terminology such as we have suggested is necessary to reach an
acceptable description of historical instances where manifestly declared
interests were clearly self-defeating and absurd to all except those proclaiming them. That Dahrendorf and Geiger, who were both only too
well acquainted with events in Germany in the years 1933 to 1945, should
be willing to dismiss a concept such as this so summarily is surprising,
to say the least. A frame of reference imputing rationality[10] to all actors
in every social situation (and particularly in situations of conflict) contents itself with a chaste kiss for its subject matter and believes that a
marriage has been consummated! All this is not to say that the problem
of determining what is a pseudo-interest is easily solved in relation to
every interest group. But clear instances of the latter are so easily found,
and are often so overwhelmingly convincing, that any denial of the
desirability (nay, necessity) of such a concept cannot be seriously entertained.

[10] A distinction between the concepts of "rationality" and "rationale" is attempted
in chapter 6.

The Structural Preconditions of Revolutions

Our foregoing set of categories is designed to have the potential of being developed into a general theory of conflict, but this necessarily would exceed both the scope and the intentions of this chapter. Nonetheless, a general treatment is justified if revolutions can be shown to be the resultant of special limiting conditions surrounding conflict situations. We shall now consider the special structural conditions necessary for a revolution to take place.

The first and most general condition — a rather trivial one, since it is bound up with the definition of revolution that has been presented — is that the revolutionary situation must contain a centralized government. Violent conflict can be found at all levels of political organization, from the most archaic to the most complex and highly developed, but for revolution to occur at least something approaching a nation-state with a centralized government must exist. Quite simply, where no centralized and separate organization — the "government" — exists, nothing exists for the revolution to overturn. Thus violent conflict which does not have the potentiality (at least, in principle) of overthrowing a government will be excluded from consideration.

But, given the existence of a specialized association in the society with the task of government — however this task may be defined in the society in question — other, less trivial conditions for the rise of revolutionary situations must be considered. Such conditions inhere in the social structure of the society and may fruitfully be discussed in connection with a typology of government based upon the degree to which clear-cut, legitimate channels exist for various groups and associations in the society to participate in, or otherwise directly affect, the decisions made by the government. The extremes of the resulting continuum of governmental types we may call unitary and pluralistic governmental structures.[11]

At the unitary extreme, one group, an elite, holds a monopoly of all significant power positions, their legitimation, and the means of access to them. Such a group attempts to maintain itself through monopolization of the means of violence and legitimation. The form of legitimacy typical of the unitary extreme may be "traditional," or "ideological." In either case, those in positions of political dominance claim they, through the existing system, embody the higher ideals represented in the tradition or the ideology. Furthermore, they claim a monopoly of interpretation of the set of ideals in relation to everyday activities. Thus, whatever the present policy may be, it is always to be viewed as the best of all possible embodiments of those ideals and is always interpreted in relation to

[11] The unitary extreme of this continuum corresponds with Mosca's discussion of elite political structures (27, pp. 50–53). Bentley's views on government (1, pp. 270–71) conform very closely to the pluralistic extreme.

them. Stability at this unitary extreme depends upon the acceptance by all potentially powerful groups of the ideals and their embodiment in the existing system.

At the pluralistic extreme, access to centers of political power and to the means of legitimation is allowed to all groups wishing to organize within the society. The real center of power is not the governmental structure itself but the diverse groupings pursuing their interests within it. While each competing group may claim a special ideological legitimation in relation to its own particular interests, the legitimacy of the political structure as a whole is "legal-rational." Thus within stable pluralistic systems proper actions are limited to non-violent ones. Pressure upon decision-makers rather than power over them is the rule. Violence remains monopolized by the official political hierarchy (the official representatives of the "state"), while the hierarchy remains a clearinghouse for underlying interests.

A smoothly working monolithic (unitary) system is most easily maintained within a relatively stable, relatively simple society. In such a situation, existing exigencies are easily recognized and controlled. Increasing complexity gives rise to a highly differentiated and varied complex of exigencies and raises the problem of establishing new modes for channeling and controlling their articulation. Rapid social change, itself the product of diversifying exigencies and multiplying means of their articulation as needs and interests, will tend to outrun the established means of social control. With increasing complexity and change, the rise of organized groups capable of opposing the government or of competing with it becomes very difficult to stop. Rather than crush all opposition, those in power often prefer to allow the organization of special interests to take place in subgroups controlled by the elite. Where formal education, at least to the level of literacy, is general, as in industrial societies, the ideological expression of the educated majority must be channeled and controlled. While traditional despotisms and modern totalitarian structures differ in the complexity of the means of control necessary for their persistence, and at their disposal, both nevertheless are monolithic.

The type of society underlying a monolithic government determines the extent to which totalitarian means of control are necessary. Modern technological developments not only make totalitarian structures possible through rapid means of communication and techniques of propaganda and mass persuasion, but also *require* the existence of such devices if the monolithic system is to be maintained. The stability of any monolithic political structure is a complex balance between the volume of exigencies generated together with the means available for their articulation and translation into organized action, and the means available to those in power to channel the articulation of these exigencies, to minister to the articulated needs, or to destroy the means of alternative articulation and action. Traditional despotism in a relatively simple society may not be threatened by sudden increases in the volume of exigencies as commonly as ideological totalitarianism. However, as in Imperial China during times of great floods (36, p. 171), when the level of exigency increases so does the potentiality for revolt. Totalitarian rule is an adaptation of monolithic governmental organization to a complex social structure, a sophisticated population, and a high or oscillating volume of exigencies.

At the other extreme of our continuum of governmental structures, pluralistic political systems have much greater flexibility and adaptability to the range of exigencies that can become articulated as needs by various elements in the population, and the varieties of action possible to meet, alleviate, or prevent these needs. But still there is no guarantee that all persons or groups will be successful in pursuit of their interests; some will find their actions blocked by competing groups with opposing interests. Pluralistic political systems themselves include patterns of institutionalization of non-violent conflict and engender a generally shared ideology of compromise, but compromise is not always enough for meeting the valent needs of a highly frustrated group. The myth that the existence of every successful interest group brings forth an equally strong and, presumably, equally successful opposing group[12] has no theoretical justification and no basis in historical fact. Even in pluralistic societies certain groups are able to further their interests to an adequate degree; others are not.

The various types of political organization which exist between these two ideal-typical extremes need not be fully spelled out for our present purposes; it will be sufficient simply to point in their direction to illustrate their range. At times a pluralistic society can become dominated by a concert of a few powerful interests while others remain too weakly organized or too divided among themselves to reach even compromise goals. Here, clearly, we have a departure from the ideal-type of pluralism with high incidence in many modern, formally pluralistic, systems of government. Periclean Athens, again, though "democratic" by constitution, was pluralistic only within the confines of its relatively broad elite. Slaves, foreigners, and the like were disenfranchised, and their interests remained mute. Early Western democracy exhibits a mosaic of monolithic and pluralistic elements, becoming more pluralistic as suffrage and the right to organize became more widespread. The true medieval ideal was pluralistic, but it was rarely realized in practice. Modern totalitarian states, though containing overtly pluralistic elements, are very close to the unitary extreme in their functioning. Independently of their position on the continuum, political systems contain the potentiality for the emergence of interest groups, and the possibility that such interest groups should be frustrated in reaching their aims by non-violent means. These two elements constitute the major general conditions for the occurrence

[12] See for example Galbraith (14).

of revolutions, but the particular and specific conditions surrounding the formation of revolutionary groups are dependent to a large extent upon the position of the political system in question on the monolithic-pluralistic continuum.

In outlining the stages and sub-processes typical of revolutions, we shall have to concentrate upon the development of those interest groups whose goals are opposed to goals sought and permitted by the existing powers. We shall maintain that, to a large degree, the delineation of revolutionary phases is determined by the stage of development of competing groups. It should be clear that the diverse groupings which can be involved in any particular revolution may well be at different stages of development. Thus some groupings may remain at a latent stage throughout the revolution while others remain only manifest and do not organize. Some may organize only during the last stages of revolt, while others may form an organized vanguard active throughout the revolution. For purposes of exposition, however, we shall speak of the latent, manifest, and organized stages of the revolution as a whole, measured by the stages of development of the most significant groups involved.

The Phase of Interest Group Incubation

We have spoken of a latent interest group when referring to any specifiable aggregate or collectivity of persons faced by similar exigencies. For a latent interest group, concerted action, which requires articulation of an interest and organization in service of the interest, is impossible by definition — but mass actions,[13] particularly random ones, may be presumed to be quite common when shared exigencies are salient. Without full articulation of a common interest such mass actions may vary from individual acts of violence to collective disturbances. Thus, unless we are willing to accept interpretations of persons not involved in the given situation or, perhaps, some psychological measures of states of saliency, we often gain our first indication of the existence of salient exigencies in certain collectivities by noting the occurrence of such instances of unorganized, seemingly irrational, collective unrest.

Not all exigencies, of course, lend themselves to articulation as group interests. Some exigencies strike sporadically at isolated individuals and can, at best, be articulated simply as needs. Whether these needs can be adequately met or not, and even when their satisfaction conflicts with established interests, they are not likely to become the basis for the formation of an interest group. Other needs (whether correctly or incorrectly defined from the point of view of reaching goals associated with the need) are not perceived as being relevant to the formation of an

---

[13] We adopt Max Weber's term here which means "similar reactions to a given stimulus" (35, p. 183).

interest group. The need for food and shelter may be highly articulate among an aggregate of paupers, but this need may not be seen as being relevant to development of an organized interest group dedicated to the alteration of the prevalent system of wealth distribution. It may express itself instead as isolated individual (or, for that matter, as organized collective) action directed to need alleviation within the existing system of distribution. On the other hand, certain exigencies may never come to articulation as simple "interest-free" needs at all, but may be articulated from the beginning as interests. This is liable to happen when there is differential access to generally accepted goals — where the need itself, as it were, has to do with the perception of inequitable distribution of "rewards," that is, of access to goals (see also 35, p. 184).

The means of articulation available also determine whether an interest can or cannot be formulated. In our pauper example above, it may be assumed that the articulation of the need for food and shelter that has taken place, is insufficiently specific to connect the need with an inequitable system of wealth distribution to be understood by those concerned. Or alternatively (or, perhaps, additionally) it may be assumed that the legitimacy of the distribution system is not questioned, or even cannot be questioned, by the persons faced by the exigency. Inadequate means of articulation among those stricken by exigencies may, indeed, become the basis of a conscious policy of *divide et impera* by those in power who recognize the dangerous potentialities of interest group emergence. No starker instance is conceivable than that provided by slave traders, who put together their human cargoes in such a manner that different linguistic and cultural groups were mixed. Thus, while all members of a given consignment of slaves may be faced with strictly similar and powerfully salient exigencies, the means of articulation of interests and of consequent organization are almost completely lacking (12, p. 91). But, quite generally, and not only in slave ships, it is rare for the most underprivileged persons in society to be capable of articulating common interests. As L. P. Edwards has noted, the rise of revolutionary movements more often than not is based upon the "fusion of ideas propounded by the revolutionary intellectuals with the elemental wishes of the oppressed" (11, p. 91).

Quite aside from the least favored persons in society, it is quite clear that the means of articulation are not equally distributed throughout social systems. In most societies of any complexity, not only is there an unequal distribution of property, but also of education, and thus of access to ideas. Consequently there is also a highly unequal distribution of the level of saliency of an exigency that will be borne by an aggregate of persons without articulation of a need taking place by any of the persons involved (this being, as has been pointed out on page 91, a partial function of the breadth of the horizons of specifications of the persons involved). If inarticulate collectivities are to be active in the revolutionary process, they must be guided to the manifest realization of common interests by articulators outside the group.[14]

Articulators (or, as we have elsewhere called them, "articulation leaders" (38) are typically from different and more advantaged backgrounds than average participants in revolutions. In modern times the most important source of articulation leaders has been that group of intellectuals or semi-intellectuals who hold marginal positions in the social structure. The exigency they face is the second- or third-order exigency of alienation — inability to reach goals which may originally have little to do with the alleviation of the needs later formulated and espoused as interests. Thus, the "overly" educated son of the civil servant has very often been the true modern revolutionary.[15] Not being advantaged in other ways, but often highly skilled in speech and writing, he takes it upon himself to articulate the interests and espouse the cause of other, less articulate collectivities faced by exigencies. The presence of a large number of these articulate types of persons in India predetermined independence for that country, and the same may be said for other colonies that have shaken off imperial ties. The lack of such types (or their absorption into the bureaucracies of state and party) is one of the most significant bases for stability in totalitarian societies.

"Free-floating" articulators, however, cannot make revolutions from whole cloth. If an exigency is not sufficiently salient to justify interest group formation on the part of the stricken public, or if the exigency is not sufficiently widespread, their attempts at articulation cannot lead directly to revolution. If the time is not ripe the articulator may attempt to create conditions which can later be exploited by him. This role of the articulator may be demonstrated by the case of Russia during the "migration to the people" by the Populists (Narodniky) (17, pp. 81–96). Without elaborate or formal organization, the Populists (primarily students but with an admixture of other middle-class elements) migrated from the cities in 1873–1874 to lead the peasants in revolt against the Czar. While the revolt failed, even when the appeal was directed toward the peasant class who were in sporadic rebellion at the time, the seeds of a new interest base, so important in 1905 and 1917, were established.

While all societies contain aggregates of persons whose exigencies are unarticulated, it is often the special prevalence of such groups that typifies pre-revolutionary eras. In societies with monolithic political systems which strictly circumscribe groups which can legitimately pursue

---

[14] In relation to articulation carried to inarticulate groups Edwards makes the point that, "one great service which the . . . [articulators] render to the revolutionary movement is that of concentrating the general irritation which is spending itself thus wastefully" (11, p. 46).

[15] From Thomas Paine, an English exciseman, to Robespierre, a lawyer, to Lenin and Hitler, each sons of civil servants, the middle class and especially the lower professions seem to be the major source of revolutionary leadership.

their interests, the sporadic oscillation of numerous uncoordinated group-ings from latency to a quasi-manifest stage, and back again to latency, is to be expected.[16] The attempt to build a simple interest group with a single set of articulated interests and goals under these conditions more often than not proves futile. The early articulations of such groups, being too limited, die with the failure of the groups. It is the widespread ac-ceptance of a single set of ideas among such frustrated tributary groups that forms the impulse needed for the growth of a fully fledged move-ment. This is the work of ideology — ideology being viewed as a system of articulations. A major source of the complexity of historical ideologies springs from the necessity of appealing to diverse types of people faced by different exigencies. In order to appeal to these groups, an ideology must minimize differences between them. This is achieved by ideologies that emphasize some shared characteristic (real or fictional) which all the groupings concerned have in common. Thus Marx, by claiming that a future polarization of society would reduce nearly all unpropertied persons to a state of proletarianization, could appeal to white-collar workers, professionals, and small capitalists. Nationalistic movements in colonies manage to appeal to the majority of persons upon ethnic (and thus national) grounds, and by emphasizing the evils of foreign capital and government.[17] Whether the characteristic emphasized is class, na-tion, race, religion, or a combination of these, the major effect is to define a group in which internal differences are minimized.

The playing down of differences in complex interest group ideologies can be carried only to a point. Beyond this, the ideology will lose its appeal. Thus a labor movement, for example, is based mainly upon a limited set of related but not identical exigencies connected with a social-structurally defined "working-class" position. All persons faced by such a set of exigencies, however, need not accept the proffered articu-lation of an ideology. Conversely, of course, some persons who are not structurally defined as working class may well accept such an ideology as the basis for the expression of their own interests.

One of the factors aiding the general appeal of ideologies is their complexity and "face consistency." Ideologies are rarely espoused for their total content but rather for their appeal in some specific area. The very complexity of the ideology thus presents diverse aggregates of persons faced by respectively different exigencies, with special appeals. But because of its face consistency, there is a tendency for a person who accepts a part to accept the whole. Of course, the question of whether the consistency is inherent in the ideology itself or whether it exists only in the eyes of the believer remains unanswered. The acceptance of an

[16] Oscillations of this variety include the great European peasant revolts (32) and rebellions such as the *Tai Ping* in China (19, p. 123). Examples of insurrec-tions following this description in Cuba may be found in Phillips (29).

[17] As Eric Hoffer notes, "common hatred unites the most heterogeneous elements" (19, p. 89).

ideology presenting a ready-made world view is simpler than piecemeal analysis and specification of a situation of exigency.

In the incubation stage of interest group development, therefore, ideologies are first formulated which may have to compete on an "idea market" for acceptance. As concensus increases, so do possibilities of communal action.[18] The function of such ideologies is to act as vehicles of interest aggregation, so that the possibility is established of developing a heterogeneous complex interest group with sufficient backing to effect revolutionary action. In cases where the aggregate of persons faced by a similar exigency is sufficiently large to effect such action by itself, the development of a simple interest group greatly lessens the problem of ideology with which we have been concerned. But, irrespective of the homogeneity or heterogeneity of interests represented in the revolutionary ideology, it is the development of such an ideology that constitutes the incubation phase of revolution.

The Phase of Interest Group Development

When a relatively high level of ideological concensus is established — or, in other words, when a manifest interest group is in existence — the question of implementation of the interest arises. Early in the phase of interest group development, active participation in revolutionary groups is usually quite small. Such groups, organized as independent or semi-independent circles, may exist within established "parliaments" as in the American and French revolutions, and in the English civil war (4, p. 11). In totalitarian settings, such groups have to operate "underground." Cohesion among individual groups rests not so much upon central control as upon a developing consistency of ideology and recognition of the primary spokesmen of the ideology. The limited number of active participants at this point in the revolutionary process is not the true reflection of the strength of the rising movement. The major organizational aim of movements in their earliest stages is as much the gaining of supporters as the recruitment of members. When membership expands, it is enlisted from the more enthusiastic and potentially "useful" supporters. The enlistment of a mass membership, however, is typically accompanied by formalization of the organization of the movement.

In order to understand the process of formalization that takes place when the membership of an organized interest group increases, one has only to note the problems of communication; these increase with increasing size of membership. When only two persons are involved there is one line of communication; where there are three persons involved, three lines of communication exist. As the size of the group increases, the

[18] By *communal* action we mean action based upon a mass stimulus but, going beyond that, "oriented to the feeling of the actors that they belong together" (35, p. 183). Clearly, such action falls short of rational calculation.

possible lines of communication increase exponentially.[19] There are, thus, only two possible alternative solutions when the number of persons becomes unwieldy; either to divide up into smaller circles or to institute hierarchical communications. We have observed that, as an interest group emerges from latency to a manifest stage, the first alternative is commonly chosen. But as the need for unity and concerted action increases, so does the likelihood that there will be a shift to hierarchical forms of communication. At times this shift is hardly realized by the average participant but his group — no longer an independent circle — becomes a "cell" in the larger structure.

Concurrently with the development of hierarchical lines of communication there naturally arise differentials in the decision-making power or authority vested in active members of the interest group. The leaders of interest groups, and particularly of developing revolutionary movements, must base their claims for compliance on somewhat different grounds than those regularly employed in bureaucratic organizations. While the members of a bureaucracy often serve the formal goals of the bureaucracy largely for extraneous, personal goals such as social standing and economic gain (by way of promotion, for example), the members of a social movement — at least, in its early, pre-bureaucratized stages of development — serve the ideological goals of the movement largely for their own sake. Using the terminology proposed by Zollschan and Perrucci in chapter 4, the compliance of supporters of a revolutionary movement conforms to *simple cooperation* rather than to *transactional cooperation*.

The peculiarly marked adherence of interest group members to the originating goals of their organization leads to special problems in connection with leadership of these groups. The basic aims of interest group ideologies are long-range, and do not give unambiguous guidance as to actions appropriate in specific situations encountered along the way. Those in positions of leadership must make short-run pragmatic decisions. Compliance to such decisions can only be expected when articulation or ideological leadership is merged with organizational leadership. The more complex the situation in which concerted action is required and the greater the requirement for quick tactical decisions, the greater becomes the need for the majority of the members to relinquish independent action and independent interpretation of tactics in relation to the strategic goals of the movement to a central body or individual. Since extraneous, "rational" rewards cannot be given by the leadership for compliance, an occasion is created for the emergence of charismatic leadership.

[19] The formula relating the possible number of lines of communication to persons is, of course, $\frac{n\,(n-1)}{2}$. Thus, as the number of persons reaches 20, no less than 190 lines of communication are possible.

Clearly, we cannot do justice to the phenomenon of charismatic leadership in a few paragraphs; the topic deserves an exhaustive examination in its own right. Let it suffice, here, to point out some of the conditions under which occasions for charismatic leadership[20] lead to the emergence of a charismatic leader. As is well known, instead of being delegated ideological authority, the charismatic leader claims it as a right, and this right is incorporated into the system of legitimations embodied by the ideology. The mystique of the leader, as it were, becomes part of the ideology.[21] But the above remarks provide only considerations of what might be called "demand" for charisma — that an *occasion* exists for charismatic leadership. Its supply is related in some way to the originality or aptness of a charismatic leader's articulations as perceived by the group he comes to lead. If, as Zarathustra exhorts, "values are the result only of value-giving: without value-giving the nutshell of existence would be hollow" (28, p. 63), then an articulator who can come to be perceived as a value-giver has a *prima facie* chance for recruitment to a position of charismatic leadership.

The relative prevalence of charismatic leaders in revolutionary situations must be left for further exploration. We would, however, propose the tentative hypothesis that the occasion for charismatic leadership varies in strength inversely with the level of formalization and the means of organization available to the interest group (the demonstrated ineffectiveness of non-charismatic leadership can serve as a functional equivalent of difficulty in organizing). Whether the occasion itself can lead to the actual emergence of a charismatic leader will then depend upon two sets of mutually interdependent variables. One of these, as already indicated, is the prevalence and valency of infantile needs for a "strong father" or the like. The other set of variables consists of considerations affecting the availability of a "value-giver" who can supply

---

[20] The distinction between an occasion for leadership and the actual kinds of leadership experienced appears to us to be an important and neglected one. It is considered in some detail in Zollschan (38).

[21] We suggest that this may be explained by reference to exigencies of early socialization in members of the aggregate which become re-articulated so as to form part of the interest group ideology. It does not really matter, from the point of view of the outcome, whether these infantile exigencies which lend themselves to articulation as the "need for a strong father" (or as something which could be so interpreted) have persisted since infancy in members of the group, or whether there is a regression to such a need under conditions leading up to the revolution. We would agree with Erich Fromm's statement that "the function of an authoritarian ideology [or, in our use, a leadership mystique] can be compared to the function of a neurotic symptom" (13, p. 238). Salient exigencies such as those experienced in periods leading up to revolutions, when experienced in a state of relative helplessness and isolation — as the concentration camp literature amply attests (2; 5; 21) — are very liable to lead to regression and infantilization of persons in even the most highly sophisticated groups. The articulation of a leadership mystique may include sado-masochistic elements or may be relatively free of these, and the style of charismatic leadership that results (or the recruitment of the kind of person who becomes a charismatic leader) is partly dependent upon this articulation.

what appears to his followers to be the *mot juste* for the exigency. The extent of such needs, and the extent of availability of individual suppliers of the "means of articulation" (value-givers), also become matters for further exploration.

The development of revolutionary movements, of course, never occurs in a power vacuum. It requires, by definition, an established regime which (whether correctly or incorrectly) becomes viewed by members of the movement as, either directly or indirectly, the source of their frustration. At the same time the nature of the political structure, conversely, sets the environment in which interest group development can or cannot occur. Where combination is illegal, as in totalitarian governmental structures, and the movement is forced underground, efficient organization becomes very difficult. We have seen that the difficulties surrounding problems of organizing under these circumstances can help create the occasion for charismatic leadership. Where the interest group can develop in the open (although it would probably have to develop under a non-revolutionary guise in most political structures), effective organization without a leader mystique at least becomes a theoretical possibility.

Once an interest group with a revolutionary ideology exists, communal actions are possible, but such actions are inefficient where they are not centrally organized and concerted. The revolutionary movement which remains fixated at the manifest interest group level without achieving a high degree of organization has only the strategy of sporadic terrorism at its command. The limitation of such a strategy, except where the prevailing government is weakened by internal dissension or for external reasons such as war, are evident. Mass organization, however, may develop very rapidly when internal dissensions in the government, or external threats to the government, weaken the latter's position. Thus the abortive Hungarian revolution broke out in reasonably organized form, after a split had occurred within the leadership of the Hungarian Communist party.[22] A manifest interest group opposed to the regime had existed for some time before this event.

The question of possibilities of organized interest group development in different kinds of political structures is a complicated one. We can discuss it most fruitfully in connection with conditions for the outbreak or prevention of revolutions.

Conditions for the Outbreak or Prevention of Revolutions

The transition from the phase of group development to the outbreak of revolution marks the final development of organized revolutionary groups. In successful revolutions this transition is accompanied by one or both of the following processes: the coalescence of numerous manifest or even organized interest groups into one (or a limited number) of

[22] For some recent discussions of the Hungarian revolution see (20; 37).

revolutionary organizations, and the establishment of organizational leadership (if this has not occurred previously).

The coalescence of numerous relatively ineffectual groupings (all of which need not have the aim of revolution) into a few comparatively large revolutionary organizations is typically accompanied by the formalization and final crystalization of ideologies. The more marked the coalescence into highly organized movements, the greater is the formalization of ideology. These two processes not only occur together, but are mutually supportive. The ideological formalization allows clear-cut recruitment and forms a basis for compliance to leadership, while the consolidation of organization provides places of leadership from which the ideology can be impressed upon the followers.

If the rise of mass organization opposing the existing powers does not soon bring success to the movement but results in a relatively stable balance of antagonistic powers, the equilibrium of forces is accompanied by a rift in the normative system of the society. In the extreme case, such a rift may wreck so many of the shared legitimations providing a basis for normative consensus that, whether the revolution occurs or not and whatever its outcome, stability will come to rest essentially upon powers of coercion alone. Though complicated by numerous other factors, a comparison between the Russian and American revolutions is pertinent here. The frustration of groups already in process of emergence in Russia lasted more than 20 years. The lack of success of moderate proposals drove both sides to more extreme stands. The relatively quick success of the American revolution, however, left the moderates firmly in power. The frustrations suffered by the revolutionary groupings were cut short by success before a moderate-radical split became unbridgeable. What is more, the day-to-day activities of the populace as a whole were not disrupted. Even the revolutionary leadership in America considered itself a group of revolutionary amateurs rather than professionals. While terror was experienced in America during the revolution, it soon abated. Terror, however, became the rule in Russia, at least until the death of Stalin. Given the alternative political techniques available in a modern totalitarian society, the terror can only be explained by a deep and unbridgeable rift in the underlying normative structure. Normative splits are furthered when ideological enthusiasts break their "normal" associations and isolate themselves from everyday affairs in favor of total involvement in the movement. The prevalence of ideological fanaticism is an index of the valency of the revolutionary group's interest — in other words, it is a measure of frustration.

The probable success of revolutionary movements, and also the exact form taken by revolutions, depend upon the type of governmental structure against which the revolution has taken place. It is not at all surprising that most successful revolutions in modern times have been against monolithic, but non-totalitarian (or pre-totalitarian), governmental structures. King Charles' claims to divinely sanctioned absolutism,

British rule of the American colonies which blocked access of the colonials to policy decisions, the centralized Bourbon monarchy, and the despotism of the Czar and the traditional Russian aristocracy were the structural situations preceding the four great modern revolutions in the western world. Monolithic governmental structures provide the likeliest situations for an accumulation of blocked, valent, oppositionist interests to take place and to reach "critical mass." It is interesting to note that, with the possible exception of the Russian instance, totalitarian means of control were not used, or for that matter, available. Totalitarian control was, however, on the increase between the English civil war and the Russian revolution.

The question arises as to what extent modern totalitarian rule is proof against revolution. In a totalitarian state virtually all the necessary means for the development of interest groups and for conduct of the revolution are monopolized by the persons in power. Education and the means of mass communication can, under the technical conditions available to the modern state, be centralized and effectively made subservient to the wishes of the prevailing government. The right to combine or organize, in addition, may be withheld, and modern governments do have means of discovering illicit attempts at combination or organization. Thus both the means of articulation and the means of organization are not available to persons outside the totalitarian elite. The conclusion might appear justified that organized autochthonous rebellion in a closed totalitarian system is, in principle, impossible. For the sake of logical completeness, however, an ideal-typical extreme case of the dissolution of a totalitarian regime without the occurrence of an organized revolution may be proposed.

Assuming that the salience and prevalence of unarticulated exigencies or uncommunicable needs in a totalitarian society become sufficiently great and sufficiently widespread, a situation is conceivable in which (consequent upon some sudden precipitating event) the whole society could explode, and the entire population run amok. No actual historical examples of such an event, affecting the whole society, are available, but on a smaller scale, approximations to such unorganized collective upheavals occasionally occur in microscopic "total systems" such as slave or prison compounds. But a reasonably well informed totalitarian regime would be abundantly aware of the likelihood of such explosions on the level of collective behavior long before their occurrence. Faced by such a possibility, totalitarian governments may take a number of steps to counter the danger. Such steps, to be discussed below, may be combined in our analysis with steps designed to prevent the development of interest groups and the occurrence of organized revolutions. Before methods of preventing collective explosions or organized revolutions are examined, however, another possibility of revolution in totalitarian governmental systems should be discussed.

As already indicated in connection with the Hungarian instance, dissension within a totalitarian regime may sufficiently weaken its control to allow an incipient revolutionary movement to come into the open. A totalitarian regime may also lose control when faced by an external attack. The existence of foreign states whose regimes are hostile to that of the totalitarian state under consideration may foster revolution in the latter state in more ways than merely by frontal assault. Antagonistic countries can present suitable locations for the development of revolutionary interest groups composed, perhaps, of émigrés from the totalitarian state in question, and for the formation of "governments in exile" which are ready to assume leadership of, and provide resources for, a revolution when opportunities arise. Thus given the existence of several states, the prognosis for revolution, even in the most effective totalitarian system, is not entirely hopeless.

Turning now toward the pluralistic end of our continuum of governmental structures, the point can be made that unsuccessful revolutions are, paradoxically, most typical of pluralistic structures. We have observed that there is no guarantee that all interest groups will be even minimally successful in a pluralistic system. There is, however, a thorny dilemma that faces frustrated interest groups in such a state. As long as they work within the system, only some groups may be opposed to them, while, if they attempt to overthrow the system, they are likely to be opposed by a coalition of all other groups. What is more, the means used in operating within the system are very similar, if not identical, to the means necessary for overthrowing it. Organizational ability, financial support, effective leadership, a mass following, and so on are all requirements for the effective action of parties and pressure groups as well as of revolutionary organizations. Under these circumstances it is, of course, highly questionable whether revolution can succeed where other methods, requiring similar resources, cannot. The American Civil War and Shay's Rebellion (also in the United States) provide illustrations of the difficulty of opposing a reasonably efficient pluralistic regime by revolutionary action.

All this does not mean to imply that pluralistic systems of government are unlikely to be overthrown — such an hypothesis would have been amply falsified in recent history. We do assert that pluralistic political structures[23] are not susceptible to overthrow by outright revolutionary means. Pluralistic systems are liable to fall to interest groups identical or, at the least, similar to revolutionary ones; but they fall not by revolution but by the regular election of members of the frustrated interest group to positions of power, or by their co-optation. At that point, the

---

[23] We are not talking, in this connection, of specific governments which may rise and fall within the legitimate framework of a pluralistic order, but of the pluralistic order itself. It is, of course, the form of government, not a specific government, that a revolutionary group in a pluralistic structure would want to overthrow since, by definition, legitimate access to the interest-goals of the group are blocked in the structure.

revolution is initiated, as it were, from the seat of power, rather than from below. A formal overturn of the prevailing government by violent means thus becomes unnecessary. A case in point is provided by the Weimar Republic. The Nazi Party, while remaining formally legitimate and, initially, operating much as any non-revolutionary interest group, was able to seize control of the machinery of state and — within a few years of accession to power — to dismantle the pluralistic structure of the Weimar Republic entirely and substitute for it a totalitarian regime. The success of this operation, and the total ineffectuality of any existing opposition, was due more (in the stage of the take-over, at any rate) to the threat of violence than to its use.

Prevention of revolution may be accomplished by a variety of means. The most direct consists of elimination of the revolutionary leaders and, for that matter, of their followers. Where imprisonment or execution cannot legitimately be defended (assuming that the government is not an absolute one, in which case "legitimacy" is readily transformed into governmental fiat), the revolutionary leadership may be subverted by bribery or co-optation into the existing elite. The latter means is not very effective, since it leaves the frustration of the opposing interest group unabated (although it may force a regression from an organized stage to a previous one), and since it opens the door to a possible take-over by the newly co-opted members. The danger of co-optation is clearly illustrated in the case of Germany, where the Nazis were brought into the Hindenburg government and "took over" shortly thereafter.

Another means of preventing revolution consists of providing access to a suitably modified version of the goals of the interest group so as to lessen the saliency of the exigencies that lend it motive power. The introduction of social legislation in Germany under the regime of Bismarck (thereby "stealing the thunder" of the opposing interest group) provides a good example.[24] Certainly, this is the most effective means of eliminating the opposing interest group, but it is also the most difficult, since the structure of rewards in the society may have to be modified in this process, thereby creating exigencies for those who are already in advantaged and powerful positions.

A third method for preventing revolution consists of channeling the articulation of the exigencies of a latent interest group into pseudo-interests. Thus the action of frustrated groups may be directed to attacks upon ethnic or religious minorities of foreign powers, who have been defined as the source of frustration. The difficult question of the conditions under which such manipulative pseudo-articulation can be successfully employed remains a matter for further analysis.

We have been concerned with the underlying causes of revolution and, very briefly, with the prevention of revolution in the light of such under-

[24] The English Reform Bill of 1832 is also generally agreed by historians to have forestalled insurrection.

lying causes. Precipitating causes of revolutions (the actual forms taken by individual revolutions, as well as their aftermath) do not belong to our analysis. Implicit in our foregoing discussion there have, of course, been a number of relevant theoretical consequences to be taken into account in the study of the immediate processes involved in the outbreak of a revolution and in its aftermath. We shall not bring out these consequences in any length, but will simply point and recommend them to the attention of students of revolutions in the traditional manner. That revolutions tend to be touched off at times when the dominant powers are permanently or temporarily weakened is a commonplace. That the frustration of rising expectations constitutes a more clear-cut and salient exigency than the mere unaltered persistence of accustomed misery is inherent in the definition of the term *exigency* as we have presented it. The concomitant relationship between the degree of ideological and normative bifurcation in the society in which the revolution occurs, and the severity of the subsequent reign of terror, may be less obvious. Given the intentions of our chapter, it is not necessary to expatiate at any length upon these issues; nonetheless, we trust that our analysis of the fundamental structural conditions of revolutions will also aid those students for whom the immediate, concrete, revolutionary event will remain the focus of attention.

Conclusions: "The Realm of Freedom"

In developing our prolegomenon to a theory of revolutions we have been initially concerned with general theoretical issues affecting the sociological theory of conflict. In confronting these issues we have found that a combination of a modified version of Dahrendorf's categories with the exigency → articulation → action schema proposed in the introduction to this Section yielded the outlines of a conflict theory having potential utility for the explanation of phenomena such as revolutions. Given particular social structures, we have asserted, positions in these structures are, among other things, loci of exposure to particular sets of exigencies. Some of these exigencies lend themselves to articulation as interests, that is, as needs contrary to the needs of specifiable other groups in the society.

Narrowing down these general categories of a theory of conflict so as to give it specific relevance to political revolutions, we have proposed a continuum of governmental structures ranging from monolithic to pluralistic, in relation to which the analysis of various forms of revolution, and of problems attending the conduct of revolution, could be carried out. In outlining this typology of political structures we have been able to present theoretical grounds for denying the alleged immunity of pluralistic structures to the liability of experiencing revolutions. Turning to the development of revolutionary, or potentially revolutionary, interest groups, we have described them as forming in reaction to needs related to diminishing perceived inequalities in the distributions of rewards.

The special role of interest articulators was discussed, and the interest aggregating functions of ideologies indicated. The necessity of organizing for revolution, and the special problems of revolutionary interest group formation and organization were outlined, and the creation of occasions for charismatic leadership established in the light of these problems. The special problems related to the conduct of revolutions in totalitarian and in pluralistic structures have been examined, and prescriptions for the prevention of revolutions offered in a rather Machiavellian manner. Without maligning Machiavelli (as is currently the fashion) or belittling his outstanding appreciation of the sociological problems faced in a discussion such as ours, we may, to conclude our examination, turn to the question of whether revolutions are necessary.

For Karl Marx the history of class struggle, although characteristic in one or another form of "all hitherto existing societies" (25, p. 125), was to come to an end in a post-apocalyptic *realm of freedom* in which productivity would so outstrip wants that "labor under the compulsion of necessity and of external utility" would cease (24, vol. 3, p. 954). Thus, Marx considered "economic necessity" the root exigency at the base of all human articulation and action. This exigency would evaporate, leaving ". . . complete harmony of interests sustained without any resort to force, although brought about by force — the provisional dictatorship" (34, p. 252). Whether Marx was correct in his optimism, even if his "exigency monism" were granted, is not central to our argument, although the validity of his views have been put severely to question. Our criticism is more fundamental; we conceive of Marx's concept of the economic substratum as being simplistic, and, quite simply, untenable.[25] The mind and society generate exigencies in the course of their operation — exigencies that are inexhaustible in both variety and number. In this profusion, certain goals associated with needs articulated from exigencies are bound to clash with other goals, or with the goals of others. Thus either alienation (which is treated in chapter 6) or conflict are inescapable features of the human condition.

So long as the clash of goals can generate interests, and so long as the expression of these interests can be blocked by government, the theoretical possibility of revolution remains alive. There is no cheap and easy way out of the "paradox of freedom" (30, pp. 112–113, p. 541n.). Certainly, it is possible to devise political structures in which the development of articulation is untrammelled; certainly, it is possible to mitigate the clashes of interests by finding means for the taming or institutionalization of conflict without the use of force. Ultimately, no political system

---

[25] This must not be interpreted as detracting from Karl Marx's importance as one of the principal forerunners of the exigency→articulation→action schema (although he would have placed the category of action before that of articulation).

can be specified such that action supporting any interest would not be blocked. And, as long as actions in support of certain interests can be blocked and frustrated, revolution remains a modality of action *in extremis,* whose possibility cannot be circumvented.

BIBLIOGRAPHY

1. Bentley, Arthur F. *The Process of Government.* Evanston, Ill.: Principia Press, 1949.

2. Bettelheim, Bruno. "Individual and Mass Behavior in Extreme Situations," in *Journal of Abnormal Psychology,* Vol. 38, No. 4 (October 1943), pp. 417–452.

3. Blumer, Herbert. "Collective Behavior," in Alfred McClung Lee (ed.), *Principles of Sociology.* New York: Barnes and Noble, 1953.

4. Brinton, Crane. *The Anatomy of Revolution.* New York: Vintage Books, 1957.

5. Cohen, Elie. *Human Behavior in the Concentration Camp.* New York: W. W. Norton, 1953.

6. Coser, Lewis A. *The Functions of Social Conflict.* Glencoe, Ill.: The Free Press, 1956.

7. Dahrendorf, Ralf. "Out of Utopia; Toward a Re-orientation of Sociological Analysis," in *American Journal of Sociology,* Vol. 64, No. 2 (September 1958), pp. 115–127.

8. Dahrendorf, Ralf. *Class and Class Conflict in Industrial Society.* Stanford: Stanford University Press, 1959.

9. Dahrendorf, Ralf. "Ueber Einige Probleme Der Soziologischen Theorie Der Revolution," *Archives Europeenes de Sociologie,* Vol. 2, No. 1 (1961).

10. Davies, James C. "Toward a Theory of Revolution," in *American Sociological Review,* Vol. 27, No. 1 (February 1962), pp. 5–19.

11. Edwards, Lyford P. *The Natural History of Revolution.* Chicago: University of Chicago Press, 1927.

12. Elkins, Stanley M. *Slavery.* Chicago: University of Chicago Press, 1959.

13. Fromm, Erich. *Escape from Freedom.* New York: Farrar & Rinehart, 1941.

14. Galbraith, John Kenneth. *American Capitalism; the Concept of Countervailing Power.* Boston: Houghton Mifflin, 1956.

15. Geiger, Theodor. *Die Klassengesellschaft im Schmelztiegel.* Koeln: Hagen, 1949.

16. Gottschalk, L. "Causes of Revolution," in *American Journal of Sociology,* Vol. 50, No. 1 (July 1944), pp. 1–8.

17. Gross, Feliks. *The Seizure of Political Power in a Century of Revolutions.* New York: Philosophical Library, 1958.

18. Hatto, Arthur. "Revolution: An Enquiry into the Usefulness of an Historical Term," in *Mind*, Vol. 58 (October 1949), pp. 495–517.

19. Hoffer, Eric. *The True Believer; Thoughts on the Nature of Mass Movements*. New York: Harper and Bros., 1951.

20. Kecskemeti, Paul. *The Unexpected Revolution: Social Forces in the Hungarian Uprising*. Stanford: Stanford University Press, 1961.

21. Kogon, Eugen. *The Theory and Practice of Hell*. New York: Farrar, Straus, 1946.

22. Lockwood, David. "Some Remarks on the 'Social System'," in *British Journal of Sociology*, Vol. 7, No. 2 (June 1956), pp. 134–146.

23. Marx, Karl. *The Eighteenth Brumaire of Louis Bonaparte*. New York: International Publishers, 1898.

24. Marx, Karl. *Capital: A Critique of Political Economy*, translated by Ernest Untermann. Chicago: Charles H. Kerr, 1909.

25. Marx, Karl, and Friedrich Engels. *The Communist Manifesto*. London: George Allen & Unwin, 1948.

26. Mills, C. Wright. *The Sociological Imagination*. New York: Oxford University Press, 1959.

27. Mosca, Gaetano. *The Ruling Class*, translated by Hannah D. Kahn. New York: McGraw-Hill Book Co., 1939.

28. Nietzsche, Friedrich Wilhelm. *Also Sprach Zarathustra*. New York: Ungar, 1930.

29. Phillips, R. Hart. *Cuba; Island of Paradox*. New York: McDowell, Obolensky, 1959.

30. Popper, Karl R. *The Open Society and its Enemies*. Princeton, N.J.: Princeton University Press, 1950.

31. Popper, Karl R. *The Poverty of Historicism*. Boston: Beacon Press, 1957.

32. Postgate, Raymond. *Revolution from 1789 to 1906*. Boston: Houghton Mifflin, 1923.

33. Sombart, Werner. *Warum gibt es in den Vereinigten Staaten keinen Sozialismus?* Tuebingen. Siebeck, 1906.

34. Talmon, J. L. *The Origins of Totalitarian Democracy*. London: Secker & Warburg, 1955.

35. Weber, Max. *From Max Weber*, translated and edited by H. H. Gerth and C. Wright Mills. New York: Oxford University Press, 1946.

36. Wittfogel, Karl August. *Oriental Despotism; A Comparative Study of Total Power*. New Haven: Yale University Press, 1957.

37. Zinner, Paul E. *Revolution in Hungary*. New York: Columbia University Press, 1962.

38. Zollschan, George K. "Needs, Interests, and Leaders: Toward a Theory of Occasions for Community Leadership," in Alvin W. Gouldner (ed.), *Studies in Leadership,* 2nd ed. Indianapolis: Bobbs-Merrill. (In press)

6

George K. Zollschan

and Philip Gibeau

Concerning Alienation:[1] A System

of Categories for the Exploration

of Rational and Irrational

Behavior

> *"When I make a word do a lot of work like that,*
> *I always pay it extra."*
> Humpty Dumpty (Alice in Wonderland)
> *"The investigations which lay at the root of Breuer*
> *and Freud's studies led to . . . [the result] that*
> *. . . symptoms have sense and meaning."*
> (Freud, 4, p. 108)

It is the essence of the human tragedy that there exist goals for persons which cannot be reached or, if they can be reached, exact a heavy price in their pursuit. This chapter is concerned with such goals, and with the persons for whom such goals exist.

[1] Many of the ideas in this chapter grew out of a number of discussions between one of the authors (George K. Zollschan) and Professor David Kirk of McGill University. The latter's contribution to the chapter, both by the generous sharing of his ideas and his stimulating comments, is gladly acknowledged.

In tracing the evolution of goals out of exigencies in the introduction to this Section, we postulated that the latter achieve conscious or unconscious representation by way of the articulation of needs. A need, it has been assumed, once articulated, gives rise to goals of action associated with the satisfaction, mitigation, or prevention of the need. But there are goals toward which action is highly problematical. For example, where death is an exigency[2] and some kind of need not to die, or "goal" of immortality, becomes articulated, there is ultimately nothing that can be done to maintain the life of an individual indefinitely. Similarly, where a need for the response of another specific person becomes articulated and such a response is not forthcoming, the activity is "frustrated" and the goal cannot be reached.

There are other needs associated with goals attainable, at least, in principle, where action in the direction of the goal is subject to disapproval of, or punishment by, others. Here also, action toward the goal may become fraught with problems. Similar problems are raised by actions which serve immediate goals uncongenial to the person, which he is forced to engage in for the sake of reaching his own goal by an indirect route. Both these cases may be viewed as constituting special instances of conflicting goals, the latter quite overtly, the former because avoidance of disapproval by others may be assumed to be a fairly general, if often latent, need.[3]

Let it be granted then, that there are insoluble, or at least, unsolved, problems in existence for a variety of persons — problems associated with reaching a variety of goals. In relating such problems to *alienation* we begin by following Seeman's analysis of the varying uses made of this concept in the history of social thought (16, pp. 783–791).[4] We intend to provide a systematic interpretation, critique, and extension of Seeman's analysis of the meanings of alienation, and to relate the resultant system of categories with discussions of *rationality* by Pareto and Weber. Finally, we intend to try out our ideas on some diagnostic categories in

[2] Death is not believed to be an exigency in all cultures. Thus, for example, Kardiner (6, p. 260) maintains that the Tanala fear neither death nor the dead. Whether this actually means that death simply is not an exigency in Tanala culture, or whether it means that a need "not to die" cannot become articulated in this culture, is a nice question. It should be remembered that an exigency can only be postulated when *some* person exists who is capable of finding an articulation for it. Cross-cultural need articulation raises many fine problems which would require a close study of given situations for their resolution.

[3] Generalized "needs" of this kind, which cut across the pursuit of specific goals, have been described by McClelland (8) and Shipley and Veroff (18), who have studied what they call "achievement motivation" and "need for affiliation" respectively. We will return to consideration of such general motives below.

[4] In his analysis, Seeman identifies five meanings that have been attached to "alienation": *powerlessness, meaninglessness, normlessness, isolation,* and *self-estrangement.* Seeman's definitions of the first four of these meanings are presented elsewhere in this volume (chapter 10, pp. 271–273); self-estrangement is defined by him as ". . . dependence of the given behavior . . . upon rewards that lie outside the activity itself" (16, p. 790).

psychiatry and to raise some questions of interest to the behavioral sciences in general. It cannot be sufficiently stressed that this exploration is a "working paper" in the fullest sense of the term, and makes absolutely no pretence to any kind of finality.

A System of Categories for the Exploration of Alienative Predicaments

Seeman states his purpose in distinguishing between five usages of the term *alienation* as it crops up, in one form or another, in the history of sociological thought very clearly. He sees his task as being "a dual one: to make more organized sense of one of the great traditions in sociological thought; and to make the traditional interest in alienation more amenable to sharp empirical statement" (16, p. 783). His efforts are thus directed at logical clarification and the production of instruments of measurement such as scales to measure powerlessness, normlessness, and so on (2, p. 849). While these aims are, of course, perfectly legitimate, it is equally permissible to take these five "meanings" of alienation and interrelate them in a unified system of categories in which various combinations and permutations of alienative situations can be simultaneously examined. This course is the one we shall take in this exploratory analysis.

Alienation may be viewed either as a variety of "estranged" behaviors or as a set of predicaments in which alienated behaviors may become aroused. The meanings of alienation isolated by Seeman, we suggest, lend themselves better to the analysis of predisposing conditions for alienation than to the description of the behavioral forms it actually takes. The forms may usefully be viewed as varieties of accommodation to alienative predicaments. We will return to the examination of forms of accommodation later in our discussion: at this point we begin by outlining a set of possible predicaments associated with any specified goal.

Since Seeman has brought together categories derived from different sources and periods, it is not surprising that he has — in places — incongruent definitions of a particular type of alienation. This occurs, for instance, in the case of meaninglessness, where he appears to be talking about two different things, goals and appropriate means (16, p. 786). In order to make the types of alienation conceptually discrete and to sharpen them somewhat, we have taken the liberty of modifying them slightly. Powerlessness we have converted into the issue of the achievability of the person's goal; meaninglessness into the issue of the goal's predictability, providing the person takes action to achieve it. These two predisposing conditions of alienation thus become unachievability and unpredictability with respect to a given goal. These two types of alienation are in the *instrumental* realm in the sense that they lie within the actor's personal range of competence. Seeman's concept of normlessness we are taking to mean a subjective predicament in which legitimate means are not available or effective in the pursuit of the goal. Isolation, on the other hand, is the condition under which the goal in question is not commonly shared in the person's society or group. The last two categories are less instrumental in character, since they depend not so much upon the competence of the person as upon the reactions and dispositions of others; we may describe them as *institutional* types of alienation.[5] The distinction between instrumental and institutional conditions determines opportunities for accommodation available to the person, particularly since institutional conditions for alienation, by themselves, do not directly affect the possibility of achieving the given goal.

Self-estrangement can occur when the goal towards which action is directed is an intermediate one, not directly desired in itself. The existence of intermediate goals of this kind for some persons is not, of course, a sufficient predisposing condition to alienation, it is merely an indication of deferred gratification. But where the intermediate goal clashes with the ultimate goal, or with other more personal and direct goals (or where, using the terminology of chapter 4, an extraneous goal clashes with an originating one), a condition for alienation may definitely be said to exist. But, it is the conflict of goals that predisposes to alienation. Self-estrangement per se appears rather to have the characteristics of an end-state of alienation — of an "unsuccessful" or alienated accommodation to alienative conditions — than of a set of predisposing circumstances. Logically, self-estrangement is not in the same category as the other meanings of alienation, but we may add *goal conflict* (in cases where one of the conflicting goals is an extraneous or intermediate one) to the previously enumerated types of conditions for alienation. Later, we shall see that goal conflict is of the greatest importance for alienation in general. For the sake of simplicity, however, a model of alienative predicaments in relation to a *single goal* is first presented. Such a model operates with the four types of conditions that can be satisfied where only one goal is under discussion, namely, unachievability, unpredictability, illegitimacy, and non-sharedness.

We begin by making a number of assumptions, some of which may be lifted after the model has been described. The first assumption (and one we do not intend to lift on this occasion) is that achievability, predictability, and so on, are dichotomous categories and not continua. Although such an "all or nothing" (zero sum) assumption is patently false, and ignores all the work that has been done on the construction of measuring scales, it adds substantially to the simplicity of exposition and detracts nothing from the argument, at least, at the rather humble level of theoretical precision attempted here. The second starting assumption, and one which will certainly have to be re-examined, is that the person's assessment of his predicament vis-à-vis the given goal is a "correct" one,

[5] We are indebted to Professor David Kirk for the instrumental-institutional distinction. The concepts "shared goals" and "legitimate means" are employed by Zollschan and Perruci in a paper (23).

consonant with the actually obtaining state of affairs. The third assumption is that the person cannot (or refuses to) relinquish the goal as an objective — that he cannot, in other words, "leave the field." This implies that acceptable substitutes for the goal in question are not available, or alternatively, that such substitute goals pose no relief from the conditions for alienation surrounding the originally considered goal. Following economic usage, we may call goal substitutability the *elasticity of valence* of that goal; thus, much as unsubstitutable goods ("necessaries") create inelasticity of demand,[6] so unsubstitutable goals create inelasticity of valence. Inability to leave the field where a goal is surrounded by the pitfalls of alienation itself implies, besides inelasticity of the goal's valence, at least a minimum degree of intensity of salience of the exigency which the goal is set up to relieve. In order to bring the issue of salience in its relationship to alienation into sharp focus, we can make a final assumption, namely, that the exigency underlying the goal in question has a high degree of salience. Without this assumption, the affective and behavioral concomitants of alienation could be so mild as to be negligible. With these assumptions in mind, we turn to a description of the model.

Diagram 1 represents a map of all combinations of alienative conditions facing persons in relation to the attainment of a given goal. The horizontal axis consists of a subdivision into legitimate (L) and non-legitimate (NL) means, each further subdivided into achievable (A) and non-achievable (NA) access to goals. The vertical axis, similarly, comprises a division into shared (S) and non-shared (NS) categories, each further subdivided into predictable (P) and non-predictable (NP).

No alienative predicament is present for Box 1 in this diagram, since

DIAGRAM 1

Combination of Alienative Conditions Facing Persons
with respect to a Given Goal

		L		NL	
		A	NA	A	NA
S	P	1	2	3	4
	NP	5	6	7	8
NS	P	9	10	11	12
	NP	13	14	15	16

[6] "Elasticity of Demand" is a concept introduced into economics by Alfred Marshall (10, pp. 102–113, also pp. 839–840) to account for continued purchases of certain goods under conditions of increases in the price. A mathematical demonstration of the relations between Marshall's formulation and our more general one must be left for a future occasion.

here the goal is shared and its attainment is predictable, legitimate, and within the province of confident achievement. The remainder of our diagram represents conditions of different types, and varying degrees of alienative potential. The following listing presents the types and degrees:

Alienative Potential of the First Degree

Box #		Type
2	Instrumental {	Powerlessness
3		Normlessness
5	Institutional {	Meaninglessness
9		Isolation

Alienative Potential of the Second Degree

Box #		Type
6	Instrumental: {	Powerlessness and Meaninglessness
11	Institutional: {	Normlessness and Isolation
4		Powerlessness and Normlessness
7	Mixed: {	Meaninglessness and Normlessness
10		Powerlessness and Isolation
13		Meaninglessness and Isolation

Alienative Potential of the Third Degree

Box #	Type
8	{ Powerlessness, Meaninglessness, Normlessness
12	{ Powerlessness, Normlessness, Isolation
14	{ Powerlessness, Meaninglessness, Isolation
15	{ Meaninglessness, Normlessness, Isolation

Alienative Potential of the Fourth Degree

Box #	Type
16	{ Powerlessness, Meaninglessness, Normlessness, Isolation

A logical difficulty arises in the "boxes" in which both unachievability and unpredictability are combined (Boxes 6, 8, 14, and 16), since unachievability implies that an unsuccessful outcome of any goal-directed action toward the given goal is clearly predictable. In a map of all possible predicaments that can face a person in the pursuit of a given goal (under the limiting assumptions we have outlined above), these four boxes would therefore have to be blocked out. But, the distinction between unachievability and unpredictability remains a valuable one. It

should be noted that conditions where a goal is achievable but not predictable (as in Boxes 5, 7, 13, and 15) can occur, and modes of adaptation to such conditions may be found. Thus the conditions prevailing
in Boxes 5 or 13 may elicit "fatalistic" activity in pursuit of the goal; those
in Boxes 7 and 15 can lead to modes of adaptation which might be described as "risk-taking innovation" (or "risk-taking criminality").

Thus far, not much more has been done than to modify Seeman's
meanings of alienation somewhat, and to combine them in a paradigm of
conditions for alienation with respect to a given goal, under limiting assumptions. By itself, such a procedure would be nothing more than
elementary exercise in model construction, suitable, at best, for peda-
gogical purposes. In stating that we have found examples of adaptations
for each of these sets of alienative conditions,[7] nothing is added; we have
just another workable system of classification. What is especially interesting about the mapping of alienative predicaments, from our present
point of view, however, is that some of these predicaments may be interchangeable with respect to a given goal. In other words, if a person is
confronted by barriers of the kind described above in relation to the
achievement of a given goal, he may (at least within specifiable limits,
and with certain goals) choose the form of alienation that appears to be
least damaging to him. This possibility of "choosing one's box" under
certain circumstances is of the greatest importance in the discussion of
forms of accommodation to alienative predicaments.

The Problem of Accommodation to Alienative Predicaments

We have stated that the categories of alienation discussed above create
(singly or in combination) 12 predicaments (or "boxes") in which a
person may find himself with respect to the pursuit of a given goal. We
have also implied that any given box may, at least in the case of some
goals, admit of a variety of accommodations. Finally, we have suggested
that, again in the case of some goals, a choice of boxes is possible for the
person. Thus the whole question of *accommodation* is closely bound up
with the relationship of goals either with the means to achieve these
goals, or *with the means of adaptation to situations in which these goals
cannot be achieved.* Now, the "adequate or efficient employment of
means to attain ends [or goals]" (15, p. 14) has been proposed as a definition of rationality; it would appear that rationality and alienation are

---

[7] To indicate at least two of the more unlikely possibilities, let us suggest that the
caption "ritualistic eccentricity" might well be applied to one form of adaption to
conditions in Box 10. Here we meet with the spectacle of Bertrand Russell pursuing
the generally non-shared goal of pacifist ban-the-bomb views, without a high degree
of expectation that the banning of thermo-nuclear weapons is indeed achievable. Or
take Box 15, in which one form of adaptation might be called "risk-taking perversion."
Here we see the homosexual deviate in prison where he believes he can achieve
non-legitimate access to his generally non-shared sexual goal, but with low predictability of the outcome of any given attempt in its pursuit.

closely related concepts, overlapping in certain respects; incompatible in others. The overlap, of course, has to do with their common concern with the relationship between means and ends. Their incompatibility stems from the implicit assumption in the conception of rationality that "adequate or efficient" means to the attainment of goals are necessarily in existence (if only in some Platonic heaven). The basic assumption inherent in the notion of alienation, as we have presented it, is that such means are, under certain (alienative) conditions, lacking. Any adequate examination of action, therefore, requires that both rationality and alienation be taken into account.

It is quite clear that the category of unachievability (Seeman's "powerlessness") is logically incompatible with rationality; indeed, it is the direct converse of rationality, since it implies total lack of any effective means to the goal. Under conditions of unachievability, therefore, rational action in pursuit of the specified goal is impossible. The other conditions of alienation logically set less absolute limitations upon rational action, but the concept of alienation implies interferences with the adequacy with which the goal can be attained. The question arises; if the actions of a person in an alienative predicament cannot be rational (in the sense of being adequate for the attainment of the goal in question), are they devoid of sense and meaning? Max Weber insisted that any analysis of social action is bound to the categories of *means* and *end* (purpose); in order to explain socially relevant behavior we require these categories (20, p. 149). What is more, the concept of rationality, by requiring some "adequate" activity to bridge the gap between means and end, provides the social sciences with an analogue to *direction* in classical mechanics. Goals *direct* actions. Our question may therefore be rephrased: where no adequate activities are available for the attainment of a goal, does action become directionless? Freud's early psychic determinism (as exemplified by the quotation at the head of this chapter) implied an attempt to give a negative answer to this question, and his clinical findings provided strong support for this methodological position. By combining the point of view implicit in early Freud with that explicitly presented by Max Weber, we arrive at an important distinction. If the term *rationality* characterizes actions directed at a goal and adequate for its attainment, another term, *rationale*, may be proposed for goal-directed actions in cases where there are barriers to the adequate attainment of the goal.

Perhaps an analogy with physics may be illuminating at this point. If not taken too far, it may help to clarify the distinction attempted above. Let us liken a goal to a magnet, and actions to iron filings. The arrangement of the filings, when brought into proximity with the magnet, would be an analogue to rationality. Now, let a physical barrier (which does not, however, break the magnetic field) be interposed between magnet and filings. The arrangement of the filings, when brought into proximity with the magnet, will be different, but they will still arrange themselves in certain patterns according to the nature and disposition of the barrier. This latter arrangement or pattern will still exhibit some sort of "rationale." The various conditions of alienation are analogous to physical barriers between the magnet and the iron filings. The nature of these barriers may be more adequately explored if we regard them as second-order exigencies attendant upon the articulation of our problematic goal.

For the sake of simplicity we may give names to the second-order exigencies associated with the various conditions for alienation: unachievability gives rise to *frustration*, unpredictability to *anxiety*, non-shared goals to *shame*, and non-legitimate actions in pursuit of the goal to *guilt* and *fear of punishment*. The mode of accommodation to whatever box one may be in (or the rationale of one's actions in the given situation) is thus compounded both of the goal whose attainment is problematic, and of the second-order exigency occasioned by the problems associated with the attainment of the goal. The saliency of these second-order exigencies with respect to the goal barriers may, of course, vary widely from person to person. Some persons may have a low tolerance for frustration, others for guilt, and so on. Second-order exigencies of this character may be articulated as needs for achievement, security, affiliation, and approval, respectively.

We may now examine modes of accommodation in each of the boxes with alienative potential of the first degree (Boxes 2, 3, 5, and 9). Situations in which more than one condition for alienation are present can be dealt with more efficiently with the help of mathematics. We will not attempt their examination here. Let us begin by assuming that there is no choice of boxes; that the particular problem confronting the person in pursuit of the goal in question cannot be exchanged for another one. (Such an assumption, for example, excludes the case of a person who finds the acquisition of wealth unachievable by legitimate means, turns to illegitimate means, and is thus able to become wealthy.) In each of these boxes accommodation may be more or less difficult. Thus in Box 2, ritualism may provide a perfectly adequate adaptation; "going through the motions" may itself be sufficient to keep the person from exploding in a paroxysm of frustration and vanishing from our analysis. Ritualism, if insufficient by itself, is greatly aided where the goal is repressed, but the mechanism of isolation (where only the affect normally attached to the goal, and not the representation of the goal, is repressed) may serve as an adequate substitute. Naturally, where the attainment of the goal is necessary for biological survival, the person will die — otherwise he may continue to act in a manner that combines the motions that would be necessary if the goal could be obtained with those necessitated by the experience of frustration in itself. In the analysis of the actions of a person in Box 2, the Lemurs in Goethe's *Faust* spring irrepressibly to mind.

With their rhyme we may leave the successful ritualists, fully adapted to his box:

> "Our pointed staves, we have them here,
> Our chain to measure sections,
> But why you called on us, we fear,
> Has slipped our recollections."[8]

In Box 5 a perfectly comfortable adaptation can be made by a person able to tolerate uncertainty; but where anxiety is very salient (or where the "need for security" is very great), clinical reactions to anxiety may come to dominate a large part of the person's behavior. It is, indeed, possible for the salience of the anxiety to outweigh the salience of the exigency underlying the goal whose unpredictability occasioned the anxiety. In this event, it may be less damaging for the person affected to take up position in Box 2 (where the goal is subjectively unachievable) than to remain in Box 5. Similar considerations hold for a person in Box 3, where the goal requires non-legitimate or illegitimate action for its attainment, and in Box 9, where the goal is an "off-beat" or idiosyncratic one. The saliency of the guilt (or fear of punishment) and of shame can outweigh the saliency supporting the goal. Here also, a subjective change of the predicament to that of unachievability appears to be in full accordance with the rationale of the situation.

It is clear in the above-mentioned instances of movement from Boxes 3, 5, and 9 to Box 2, that the single-goal assumption is, in a sense, inadequate.[9] It cannot be maintained except, perhaps, in the case of unachievability, since in every other instance, a *situation of goal conflict* is at hand (or at least, would be at hand if anxiety, guilt, and shame could be articulated as needs for security, approval, and affiliation). Interestingly enough, all of these cases of goal conflict are strictly symmetrical with the category of self-estrangement. While the latter involves the pursuit of a punishing goal (or a goal with negative valence) in order to attain a rewarding one, unpredictability, non-sharedness, and non-legitimacy involve the relinquishing of one (possibly pre-articulate) goal like predictability, sharedness, and legitimacy (security, affiliation, and approval) for the sake of another one. One could as well say that, in order to achieve the original goal, the punishing goals of insecurity,

---

[8] This is Louis MacNeice's translation of the lines from *Faust*, Part 2 (Great Forecourt of the Palace) which runs as follows:
> "Gespitzte Pfaehle, die sind da,
> Die Kette lang zum Messen,
> Warum an uns der Ruf geschah,
> Das haben wir vergessen"

[9] So, to some degree, is our assumption that the person's subjective assessment of the situation is correct. Certainly, if a person subjectively assessed himself as in a particular box with respect to a given goal, and his assessment were consonant with reality, no movement to another box would be possible. We shall return to this point.

dis-affiliation, or disapproval have to be courted (at least, in cases where there is a choice of boxes).

Our account up to this point has been concerned only with choices in favor of Box 2, with respect to a given goal. In a sense such choices do have logical priority, if our single-goal assumption is relaxed so as to permit consideration of a two-goal case. Thus, if Box 2 is not chosen with respect to Goal A, the person finds himself in this box with respect to the second-order goal (Goal B) which may be security, affiliation, or approval. In other words, if we admit the latter as goals, our person is bound to end up in Box 2 either with respect to them, or with respect to Goal A. But unachievability with respect to these second-order goals may be less punishing for the person than unachievability of Goal A. In such a case, other boxes may be chosen by the person with respect to Goal A. An illustration may help to give our argument a certain degree of concreteness.

Let us begin by specifying the goal in connection with whose attainment conditions for alienation arise. An example might be the goal of academic distinction. If the person holding this goal believes it to be unattainable, yet cannot relinquish it, he is in Box 2 with respect to this goal. He can continue with his studies or academic career, accepting his undistinguished "place in life" and relegating his goal to the realm of phantasy or subjecting it to total repression. If, however, the frustration implicit in this mode of adaptation is too great, the person in question can move into one of the following boxes:

a) He can choose a means of access to the goal which is achievable but not legitimate. For example, he can cheat in examinations or hire a "ghost writer." This is tantamount to moving into Box 3 from Box 2.

b) He can involve himself in tremendous exertions and in academically risky ventures in the belief that the goal, though unpredictable, may, with sufficient work and risk, be attained. This is tantamount to moving into Box 5 from Box 2.

c) He can redefine the goal of academic distinction slightly in such a way as to make it attainable. Thus, for example, in an academic climate of "dustbowl empiricism," our ambitious person can set himself up as a theoretician. This can be seen as moving into Box 9, where a non-shared goal of academic distinction — "great theoretician" (as distinct from the shared one, "great researcher") — is achievable.

d) He can decide to aim for a goal sufficiently akin to academic distinction to enable successful self-deception, by striving for administrative responsibilities in the academic field. If administrative goals, however, are uncongenial to him, this course of action is tantamount to a choice of Seeman's category of self-estrangement.

Whereas the above example may help to illustrate what is involved in the process of "choosing one's box," its exposition does stretch our starting assumptions somewhat. When assumptions threaten to burst their bounds, the time has come to relax them. It is our hope that their relaxation, while enabling us to retain the analytic insights initially gained by entertaining them, will open the way to a better understanding of alienated (that is, non-rational) behavior.

The Concept of Rationality and the Conditions for Alienation

Two of the assumptions found expedient for the development of a modified general model for Seeman's meanings of alienation are rather closely related to some of the most important discussions of the concept of rationality extant in the field of sociology. The assumption requiring the person to make a correct subjective assessment of an alienative predicament is closely akin to Pareto's classification of logical and non-logical actions (11, paragraphs 150–151, pp. 77–78). The assumption that acceptable substitutes for the goal are not available, we shall discover, comes close to some of the theoretical concerns at the root of Max Weber's distinction between *Zweckrationalitaet* and *Wertrationalitaet* (21, pp. 12–13). By digging up the foundations of these classifications of rational action, a more satisfactory basis for the explanation of the rationale of action in alienative predicaments may be discovered.

Pareto refers to rational (his term is "logical") action, as action which is appropriate (and, presumably, adequate) to the attainment of ends *both* from the subjective point of view of the persons engaging in the action *and* "objectively."[10] It takes no great intellectual leap to extend this kind of analysis to assessments of whether an end is, indeed, subject to conditions of alienation in relation to the means available for its attainment.[11] For the sake of brevity, let us call a goal which is necessarily subject to alienative conditions a *problematic* goal. Diagram 2 presents the various combinations of subjective and objective assessment in answer to the question "Is the goal problematic?" (for the actor).

Where both actor and observer regard the goal as being problematic,

DIAGRAM 2

Is the Goal Problematic?

	Subjectively (Actor)	Objectively (Observer)
Alienation		
Proper	Yes	Yes
Inhibition		
(Pseudo-alienation)	Yes	No
Pseudo-potency	No	Yes
Potency	No	No

[10] From the point of view of an observer with more extensive knowledge, as Parsons suggests (12, p. 190), or, ideally, from the point of view of some "all-knowing" observer *a la* Leibnitz.

[11] To put the question in this general way is preferable to asking whether the goal is achievable, predictable, and so on, since, as we have seen, it is occasionally possible to "choose one's box" in relation to a problematic goal.

a state of objective alienation with respect to the goal in question may be said to be in existence. Where both view it as non-problematic there is, of course, no question of alienation. In the two remaining cases, where objective and subjective assessments are at variance, the actor has an unrealistic assessment with respect to his goal. An unrealistic assessment may be due to mere ignorance — the unavailability of information necessary to make a correct assessment of the adequacy of available means to the desired end — or it may be due to some pathology in the articulation of the goal. Pathology is of greater interest to us here than ignorance, since it makes action resistive to the "corrective" influence of added information. When pathology leads a person to assess a goal as problematic unrealistically, we may speak of *inhibition;* when it leads a person to assess a goal as unproblematic unrealistically, we may speak of *pseudo-potency* with respect to that goal. Where a person exhibits pseudo-potency with respect to a large number of goals (or, better still, "all" goals), he may be described as *pseudo-omnipotent.* We will return to these categories after subjecting Weber's discussion of rationality to a certain amount of scrutiny.

A severe difficulty in Weber's distinction of the types of social action lies in the degree to which they are overloaded with meanings. The terms *Zweckrationalitaet* and *Wertrationalitaet,* in particular, exhibit such a syncretism of possible meanings as to make them fair game for any social scientist who desires to be learnedly obscure. Weber describes wertrational action as: a) constituting an end in itself; b) without consideration of its consequences; c) in obedience to principles held by the actor; and d) involving some "cause" and/or having to do with values such as "duty," "honor," "beauty," or "piety." Zweckrational action he describes as action that weighs against each other: a) ends and means; b) ends and side consequences; c) ends and other ends. The choice between competing and conflicting ends may itself be made in relation to *wertrationalitaet* or according to their subjective "urgency." We may follow Parsons (22, p. 115n; 12, pp. 640–649) in considering the essential distinction between these two concepts as lying in the attainment of an "absolute" end (*wertrationalitaet*) versus the weighing and ordering of alternative ends (*Zweckrationalitaet*). To be sure, this simplification cuts through the Gordian knot of means, ends, side consequences, "urgencies," and "principles," in which Weber contrives to entangle himself, and has some consequences that Weber himself would not have anticipated,[12] but it does provide a unitary conceptual dimension on which the two terms can be contrasted. If we accept this somewhat cleansed and purified definition of Weber's distinction, we discover that it becomes none other than the distinction between action in pursuit of goals that can be

12 For example, "food" becomes, if anything, a better illustration of a wertrational goal than, say, "honor." Although decisions between "bread" and "cake" (assuming both are available at a price) are, of course, zweckrational.

substituted for or replaced by others, and action toward goals that cannot be. Zweckrational action enables the person to establish priority among goals according to their relative valency (urgency); wertrational action impels the person to a goal irrespective of the existence of other goals. In other words, the valence of a goal of wertrational action is inelastic.[13] Weber's conception of *wertrationalitaet* as governing the choice between competing or conflicting goals provides us with a second meaning of the term that ties in with his linkage of it to values such as honor, piety, beauty, and so forth. We suggest that Weber might have been trying to arrive at a categorization of second-order ends here, of the kind exemplified by our achievement, security, approval, and affiliation, which come into operation where the direct (first-order) goal is a problematic one. Be that as it may, however, it does not change our characterization of the goals of wertrational action as having inelastic valences.

The phrase "competing and conflicting ends" that may be glimpsed fleetingly — slipping through the tangled undergrowth of Weber's sentence constructions — is a very telling one. It deserves more of our attention. Not only does its closer scrutiny spur us to jettison our single-goal frame of reference, it takes us back to the source of all goals — the process of articulation.

Given that we have a "person" (a human creature with existing horizons of justifications and expectations), we may start out with the somewhat zweckrational assumption that the person's actions are determined by need-goals arranged according to their relative valence. Now let our person be faced with a new exigency. The need-goal that will become articulated draws its valence from the saliency of the exigency. The other (already existing) goals which compete for the person's activity, if already articulated and being attained without excessive problems, may be viewed as serving the purpose of keeping other exigencies at bay. They derive their valence from the actual or potential salience of the latter exigencies. Under conditions of perfect elasticity of valence, it would be possible to maintain that an equilibrium of deprivations at any moment of time can establish itself without any problems. To give some examples under this assumption: when one's house is on fire, the goal of, say, "resting" loses its valency and putting out the fire takes up all one's time and energy. To go even further, when one has a kidney colic, an ordinary toothache, far from attracting some kind of mitigating activity, may not even be "noticed" (that is, may not even have enough relative salience to reach articulation).

Where goals have inelastic valences, however, the automatic equilibration of deprivations cannot occur. Under these circumstances, competing

---

[13] It is for this reason, we would suggest, that the goals of wertrational action are the ones that are liable to become surrounded by conditions of alienation, and the actions may continue — ritualistically — apparently self-contained and in disregard of consequences.

goals become transformed into conflicting ones, where attainment of one goal makes the other goal a "problematic" one in our technical sense of the term. Here a variety of possibilities are open to the person affected: he can strive for the attainment of one goal and relegate himself to alienation with respect to the other; he can vacillate between conflicting goals; or he can sink into a state of alienation with respect to both goals.[14]

At this point, we may diminish the complexity (and, hopefully, increase the clarity) of our discussion somewhat by making very explicit the re-evaluation of the paradigm of alienation implied by the lifting of our starting assumptions. The admission of *security, affiliation,* and *approval* as competing (and potentially conflicting) goals with the achievement of our original, arbitrarily chosen goal leaves one residual category that is truly alienative. This is failure to achieve the original goal — unachievability. It is true that there is yet another category that must be accounted for, that of *self-estrangement.* Here, as we have seen, the original goal requires for its attainment an intermediate goal (or "means"[15]) that is uncongenial to the person. But we will demonstrate that this may be re-interpreted as simply another special instance of competition between goals.

Another way of saying that an intermediate goal (B) must be achieved in order to attain the original goal (A), is to link the achievement of Goal A with the obverse of Goal B, namely, with the goal of *avoiding* the actions associated with the attainment of Goal B. If we call the goal of avoiding the actions with Goal B, Goal β, we may (borrowing again from elementary economics) describe Goals A and β as *complementary* goals.[16] The situation of self-estrangement therefore may be defined more rigorously by characterizing it as one where goal β is unachievable. In more generalized terms, self-estrangement becomes any situation in which there are two complementary goals, one of which is unachievable.

Thus we finally arrive at a general and irreducible definition of alienation as a *condition in which one or more goals are unachievable in a situation of goal conflict* (that is, where the goals involved are *both*

[14] As is the case with the famous donkey of the psychologists, positioned between a pile of carrots and a pile of hay, who starves to death in contemplation of these two "incompatible" goals. But let it be remembered that the donkey may be "better off" dead than regretting the hay while eating the carrots.

[15] At the present stage of development of the theory of institutionalization we prefer to retain the term "goal" as a primitive concept, differentiated only by reference to levels (that is, whether the goal is an originating goal or a second-order goal). It will not have escaped the careful reader that any distinction between goals (ends) and means has been avoided. This avoidance, of course, has been intentional. No purpose is served, in our view, by making such a distinction *in abstracto,* since both "means" and "ends" in the traditional sense of these words seem to be no more than analogs of "direction" in classical mechanics. Insofar as separate meaning for the term "means" may be distinguished by us, it appears to be precisely the concept of "intermediate goals" as we present it here.

[16] The concept borrowed here is "Complementarity of Demand," which describes parallel fluctuations in demand for two goods as, for example, "bread" and "butter."

competing *and* inelastic). Alienation, furthermore, becomes the direct obverse of rationality, which may be defined as the *attainment of goals with elastic valencies in an order of priority set by their relative valencies.*

An Application of the Concepts "Alienation" and "Rationality" to the Field of Mental Health

"Psycho-analytic descriptions of health . . . developed in two divergent directions. One was the goal of rational man ('where id was, there shall ego be') stemming from the philosophic roots of [psycho-]analysis in the rationalism of the age of enlightenment. The other and contradictory goal was that of instinctual man (unhampered by neurotic inhibitions) stemming from the philosophy of the romantics" (19, p. 33). Our foregoing remarks and, indeed, all the tenets of the theory of institutionalization would seem to indicate that the traditional dichotomy between the rational man and the uninhibited one in psychoanalytic theory, to which Wallerstein refers in the above quotation, is a false one. It is precisely the rational man, in our view, who is able to order his urges and therefore to bring them to expression without excessive problems. Such problems, we have seen, arise from the existence of conflicting goals. One of the goals of psychotherapy, in the light of this orientation, would appear to be the reduction of conflicting goals to merely competing ones, or, in other words, the reduction of inelasticities in the valencies of goals.

These considerations lead us to assay a definition of psychological health in terms of the theory of alienation. The condition under which the valencies of *all* the goals of the healthy person would be relatively elastic is clearly a *reductio ad absurdum*. The very feel and savor of the human condition, in any culture, seems bound up with the existence of inelastic goals — without them the human tragedy would become a well-ordered and rather uninteresting farce. We have, in any event, already observed that some goals of this type are dictated by biology. But there is one particular kind of approximation to this condition which is both cogent and realistic. It is reasonable to require as a criterion of mental health that, with respect to any first-order goal, the second-order goals of *security, affiliation,* and *approval* should be elastic. Returning for one moment to our abandoned single-goal case, the foregoing implies that, with respect to the problematic goal, the healthy person always chooses Box 3, or 5, or 9, in Diagram 1, in preference to Box 2. This does not imply, of course, that the healthy person rushes wildly to Box 15 every time he encounters a problematic goal. It means only that the mentally healthy person has the willingness and ability to take risks, tolerate disapproval, and court isolation in order to achieve his goals, at least, if this is justified by their valency.[17]

[17] This definition of mental health is quite similar to the *engagement* (commitment) of the existentialists and to Maslow's "self-actualization" (7, pp. 232–234, p. 378).

But elasticity of the aforementioned second-order goals alone is not a sufficient condition of mental health in a person. To it we would have to add the requirements that the person should have the capacity for *progressive articulation* (to be described below), and that pathological (as distinct from merely ignorant) false articulation should be avoided by him. These requirements we may now discuss.

Clearly, if (as the Freudians aver) little boys indeed have the goal of acquiring the mother as a sexual object, it would hardly be a sign of health if a given little boy were to press for achievement of this goal at the expense of social approval. Indeed, the condition of infantile dependence is such that the little boy (however able or energetic he might be) would not get very far with his goal. It is a peculiarity of infancy, in other words, that the institutional and instrumental dimensions of goal achievement are merged during that period. Within the family setting an illegitimate goal for the infant (lying outside the immediate bodily processes of the infant) is *ipso facto* an unachievable one; a non-shared goal necessarily becomes unpredictable. Except with respect to vegetative processes such as elimination (and, in early infancy, even with respect to these) instrumental potency comes only with the passage of time. This means that, with respect to certain goals (such as the one we have suggested), there simply does not exist any choice between boxes — the goal is unachievable and that is that. In such predicaments of unachievability, mental health would appear to depend upon the articulation of the problematic goal in such a way as to minimize the consequences of frustration, particularly over the passage of time. In contradistinction to "regressive" articulation, we may call this form of articulation *progressive* (innovative). Although nothing approaching a full elucidation of progressive articulation will be attempted here, the term should become clearer when discussed in connection with the concepts *fixation* and *regression*. Before we come to these concepts, however, a discussion of *false articulation* is necessary.

The field of false articulation, and of the rationale underlying it, is a vast one. We can barely touch upon it here. Certain types, however, have a particularly close bearing to established modes of interpretation in psychiatry, and we briefly indicate them for that reason. Some of the strains of a headlong conflict between goals may be avoided by means of false articulation, and even by means of non-articulation of one or both of the goals. *Inhibition*, we have already seen, consists of the false articulation of a goal as a problematic one. The rationale of such a false articulation is to give free rein to a competing goal and to prevent it from becoming a conflicting one. *Pseudo-potency*, on the other hand (which we have described as consisting of false articulation of a problematic goal as unproblematic), has the rationale of avoiding frustration; if necessary, at the price of distorting the horizon of expectations. Failure to articulate a goal which, if attained, would mitigate the saliency of the underlying exigency (a goal, so to speak, "doing justice" to the exigency) also exacts a price in mental health. It leaves the person flooded with "free-floating" saliency, which can form inchoate apprehensions, involuntary and aimless aggression, and somatic symptoms.

Consideration of the time dimension which we have thus far neglected in our discussion, provides us with another set of distinctions in the area of false articulation. We may assume that as the psyche develops, well-trodden pathways towards goals, or "modes" of goal attainment, become established. False articulations may occur because of the person's inability to leave the "beaten track" with regard to the establishment of new goals. Where it is impossible for the person to get off well-traveled roads to goal attainment, atavistic or *fixated* articulation is likely to occur. Indeed, sometimes the person exploring previously untrodden paths will, when confronted by some fearsome obstacle to the attainment of his goal, scuttle back to the main artery of articulation, and engage in degenerative or *regressive* articulation. By contrast to fixated or regressive articulations, progressive ones point in hitherto untraveled directions.

All these points regarding the process of articulation should, of course, be greatly expanded. Our purpose here has only been to indicate the contours of a problem. Nonetheless, even these few pointers and allusions may be used for the interpretation of various forms of psychopathology within the frame of reference of the theory of alienation. The following discussion of a few common diagnostic categories in psychiatry is meant to illustrate how this may be done. Quite clearly, our explorations in this area are in their earliest infancy, and our remarks are meant to be tentative and hypothetical in the extreme.

Before we enter this discussion, a few cautionary points should be made. The goals imputed to persons in the following account may be viewed as goals articulated by the observing psychiatrist rather than by the "sufferer" himself. The psychiatrist argues that the patient is acting "as if" a particular goal had been articulated by him; and it does no damage to our interpretation if we give the psychiatrist the benefit of the doubt. Furthermore, we have been quite ruthless in translating a variety of psychiatric terminologies into the language of the theory of institutionalization. Clinicians who do their work on the battlefronts of psychopathology may, perhaps, be forgiven for their cancerous overproduction of primitive terms. In cutting through the chaotic bombardment of their terminology, we may have dispelled some of the smoke of battle, but the diagnostic types as briefly described by us should still be clearly recognizable to one acquainted with the field of mental health.

Hysteria:

Both Abse (1, pp. 272–293) and Fenichel (3, pp. 216–236) see hysteria as being related to the oedipal situation, that is to say, the implicit goal of sexual gratification with a parent of the opposite sex. Shaffer and Shoben (17, p. 257) describe the hysterical personality as being characterized by four features: 1) what they call "social immaturity" —actions inappropriate for situations as they exist, but, presumably, appropriate for previous situations; 2) strong needs for affiliation and approval (an "outward orientation"); 3) poor integration of behavior; and 4) ready suggestibility.

If we accept the contention of Abse and Fenichel that the problematic goal in hysteria is the oedipal one, there are two sets of questions that must be asked. First, what is the nature of previous articulations occurring before the goal arises (if any); and second, what reaction occurs in face of the problematic oedipal goal? In view of psychoanalytically oriented psychiatrists, articulate (although not necessarily conscious) goals exist prior to the emergence of the oedipal situation. In the case of hysterics, they hypothesize "parental overindulgence" with respect to the child's goals. We may take this to mean not only that pre-oedipal goals are unproblematic for the child, but that their attainment is not connected by the child with any great effort on his part. His previous attainment of goals has been such that the expectation is engendered that need satisfaction comes from, and is given by, others.

With the onset of oedipal exigencies, the accessibility of need satisfaction in general (at least, insofar as it emanates from the primary sources of all previous goal attainments — the mother and father) becomes problematic. Thus the rationale of hysteric behavior is partly explicable in relation to the problematic oedipal goal, and partly to the characteristics of previous modes of goal attainment to which the person (because of the frustration of the oedipal goal) becomes fixated. In this manner, the characteristics noted by Shaffer and Shoben acquire sense and meaning.

Anxiety Reaction and the Sociopathic Character:

Rather than being associated with specific direct goals, the exigencies at the base of these nosological entities appear to be of a generalized or "second-order" nature. The aetiology of the anxiety syndrome, in particular, has received a great deal of attention in recent years: Portnoy talks of it as a consequence of frustration in the process of growing toward "self-realization" (13, pp. 307–324); Fromm speaks of a "separation from others and from nature" (5); and Rollo May of a "loss of self" and "loss of meaning" (9). Upon closer examination of these descriptions, we suggest, what really appears to be involved is a set of problems to do with the choice between goals of affiliation and approval versus achievement ("autonomy") goals.

The pattern of anxiety develops when the child desires both to be independent and loved. In early stages of personality development, the

goal of being loved is more easily accessible to the future anxiety neurotic than that of being autonomous, and compliance becomes the dominant mode of articulation. But while self-subordination and dependency
become the dominant modes of action, the goal of independence is not
given up entirely (such a goal is apparently inelastic, at least, in the potential anxiety neurotic). It continues to operate in the anxiety neurotic
in the form of ideal and unreachable standards of achievement, whose
unattainability is reacted to by hatred and contempt of self. This self-
punishment for the inability to reach idealized goals manifests itself in
anxiety symptoms such as apprehension, uneasiness, cardiovascular
hyperactivity, gastro-intestinal reactions, and disturbances of sleep. Fundamentally, we interpret the situation with regards to idealized derivatives of the independence goal as one of *unpredictability*, since, on some
level, they are not viewed as being totally *unachievable*. Thus the anxiety neurotic manifestly strives for reachable goals of affiliation and approval, and latently is in Box 5, vis-à vis the goal of independence.

Where the goal of being loved and cared for is not more easily accessible, and where the manifest mode of goal satisfaction becomes one of
autonomy, we find certain types of sociopathic characters. It would appear that the competing dependency goal is less inelastic with these persons, or at least, does not manifest itself in as clear a manner as the problematic autonomy goal manifests itself with anxiety neurotics. Problems
in connection with the attainment of the independence goal in sociopaths
are typically avoided by means of false articulations taking the character
of pseudo-potency or pseudo-omnipotence.

Obsessive-compulsive Neurosis:

The exigencies at the base of the obsessive-compulsive personality
structure are much the same as those involved in anxiety neurosis and
sociopathic reactions. What differentiates the obsessive or compulsive
neurotic from the two previously described types is that, instead of being
either dependent or autonomous, the obsessive-compulsive is essentially
in a condition of continuous vacillation between the two goals.

The dynamics of compulsive behavior are interpreted by Rado as beginning at the time bowel training is initiated by a demanding mother,
and the situation resolves itself into one of "obedience" versus "defiance"
(14, pp. 324–345). Whereas the anxiety neurotic at this stage in his
development sees affiliation and parental approval as an achievable goal,
and the sociopathic character is able to articulate his goals of defiance
in such a way as to make them appear achievable to himself, the compulsive sees both autonomy and dependency as equally problematic.
From this peculiarity stems the symptomatology of the condition.

There are three patterns of thought and action associated with obsessive-compulsive neurosis: 1) apparently irrational or silly repetitive

thoughts and acts, 2) obsessive fears, 3) compulsive ritualistic structuring of one's life. These three groups of symptoms have in common the characteristics associated with Box 2 of Diagram 1. Obsessive thoughts are indicative of a process of continual ritualistic scanning for a not really achievable goal. Compulsive actions, at base, are actions to cope with a situation in which goals in general appear to be unachievable. Behavior becomes a clockwork process of going through the motions.

Conclusion

Our exploratory study of alienation leaves us with many unanswered questions. This is entirely as it should be, since little more has been attempted than merely an application of some of the general principles of the theory of institutionalization to instances where duly articulated goals cannot be attained. It is meet and proper, in our submission, to release an article with a "rough finish," while still in the formative stages of theoretical development, particularly if the issues raised for future research and study are clearly and honestly confronted. One group of issues, in particular, should concern us in this chapter, and we confine ourselves to them in our conclusion. It contains questions that have been raised in connection with the substantive area to which our analysis was applied — that of mental health.

If we maintain that alienation is ultimately reducible to situations in which given goals are unachievable, and that, empirically, such situations are most often created by goal conflict, then a virtually unlimited variety of alienative predicaments is theoretically possible. Yet the psychiatric literature appears to be rather specific about a limited number of goal clusters which involve alienative predicaments. In a sense, this is not surprising. The established modes of articulation in a person are formed in the first few years of life, and fixation at, or regression to, these modes of articulation is liable to occur in problematic situations later in life. But the question arises as to what happens to *progressively* articulated goals if they are discovered to be unachievable. Do persons afflicted with such goals simply freeze into replicas of Michelangelo's slaves, looking only inwards and gritting their teeth? Or do they spend themselves in endless, useless, and, possibly, heroic agitation? Or does the frustration of one goal lead them to the exuberant articulation of other (possibly achievable) goals, mysteriously transmuted out of the frustrated goal by the arcane processes of "sublimation"? And, if all these things occur — under what conditions do they manifest themselves? The question remains, stark and uncompromising, what does a "sane" person do when he has an inelastic goal which cannot be achieved? Or is one to join the throng, and uphold an ideal of mental health where inelastic unachievable goals simply are not articulated? The last-mentioned ideal appears to us as a sort of witless, lackluster, unimaginative psychiatric paradise which even the psychiatrists are in process of abandoning. One thing is certain, research into the alternatives of regression in alienative predicaments is badly needed.

BIBLIOGRAPHY

1. Abse, D. Wildred. "Hysteria," in Silvano Arieti (ed.), *American Handbook of Psychiatry*, 2 vols. New York: Basic Books, 1959, Vol. 1.

2. Clark, John P. "Measuring Alienation Within a Social System," in *American Sociological Review*, Vol. 24, No. 6 (1959), pp. 849–852.

3. Fenichel, Otto. *The Psychoanalytic Theory of Neurosis.* New York: W. W. Norton, 1945.

4. Freud, Sigmund. "Psycho-analysis," in James Strachey, (ed.), *Collected Papers.* London: Hogarth Press, 1950, Vol. 5.

5. Fromm, Erich. *Escape from Freedom.* New York: Rinehart, 1941.

6. Kardiner, Abram. *The Individual and his Society.* New York: Columbia University Press, 1939.

7. Maslow, Abraham Harold. *Motivation and Personality.* New York: Harper & Bros., 1954.

8. McClelland, David C. *et al. The Achievement Motive.* New York: Appleton-Century-Crofts, 1953.

9. May, Rollo. *Existence.* New York: Basic Books, 1958.

10. Marshall, Alfred. *Principles of Economics.* London: Macmillan, 1927.

11. Pareto, Vilfredo. *The Mind and Society (Trattato di Sociologia generale),* translated by A. Bongiorno and A. Livingston, Arthur Livingston (ed.) London: Jonathan Cape, 1935.

12. Parsons, Talcott. *The Structure of Social Action.* Glencoe, Ill.: The Free Press, 1949.

13. Portnoy, Isidore. "The Anxiety States," in Silvano Arieti (ed.), *American Handbook of Psychiatry*, 2 vols. New York: Basic Books, 1959, Vol. 1.

14. Rado, Sandor. "Obsessive Behavior," in Silvano Arieti (ed.), *American Handbook of Psychiatry*, 2 vols. New York: Basic Books, 1959, Vol. 1.

15. Schneider, Louis. *The Freudian Psychology and Veblen's Social Theory.* New York: King's Crown Press, 1948.

16. Seeman, Melvin. "On the Meaning of Alienation," in *American Sociological Review*, Vol. 24, No. 6 (1959), pp. 783–791.

17. Shaffer, Laurance, and Edward Shoben, Jr. *The Psychology of Adjustment.* Boston: Houghton Mifflin, 1956.

18. Shipley, T. E., and J. Veroff. "A Projective Measure of Need for Affiliation," in *Journal of Experimental Psychology*, Vol. 43, No. 5 (1952), pp. 349–356.

19. Wallerstein, Robert S. "The Problem of Assessment of Change in Psycho-

therapy," in *International Journal of Psycho-Analysis*, Vol. 44, No. 1 (1963), pp. 31–41.

20. Weber, Max. *Gesammelte Aufsaetze zur Wissenschaftslehre*. Tuebingen: Mohr (Paul Siebeck), 1922.

21. Weber, Max. "Wirtschaft und Gesellschaft," in *Grundriss der Sozialoekonomik*. Tuebingen: Mohr (Paul Siebeck), 1925, Vol. 3, Parts I and 2.

22. Weber, Max. *The Theory of Social and Economic Organization*, translated by A. M. Henderson and Talcott Parsons, Talcott Parsons (ed.). New York: Oxford University Press, 1947.

23. Zollschan, George K., and Robert Perrucci. "Notes Toward a Clarification of the 'Conflict' and 'Consensus' Models," paper read at the annual meetings of the American Sociological Association in Los Angeles, August 28, 1963. (mimeo)

7

George K. Zollschan

Beyond the "Reality Principle"

Problems and Perspectives Leading to the Theory of Institutionalization

> *"The demiurge spoke, and poured into the crater*
> *the mixture . . . and composed the universe."*
>   Plato. (Timaios 41d)
> *". . . the stream which perennially flows drew forth*
> *the divine spirit from the tree of life and poured*
> *it into the tree which contains death, and, . . . [the*
> *strife]has been continued in the body of man."*
>   Zohar. (Bereshith 37b)

Apologia:

In this chapter many things are attempted. First, it is meant to provide some intellectual ancestry for the theory of institutionalization
which is tentatively formulated in the introduction to this Section, and
which finds its clearest source in Freudian speculations. This implies, of
course, the existence of fundamental isomorphisms of structure in social
change theory and in psychoanalytic theory. Second, the chapter provides another addition to the growing philosophical and scientific literature accumulating on the subject of Freud's duality of "Eros" and the
"death instincts." Finally, I hope to take some steps along the long and
difficult road of adding depth and substance to the formulations of the
theory of institutionalization. There are other things in this chapter, as
there must be in any piece of writing composed, as it were, *de profundis.*
These I shall allow to speak for themselves.

Certainly the chapter is not representative of a cross-section of current sociological writing in America. Consequently, it requires an *apologia*. It will be accused of being overly ambitious but, like Freud, "I like to avoid concessions to faintheartedness" (15, p. 91), and will be prepared to take the consequences for any mistakes that I may have made. It tries to say a lot in few words and, therefore, may be somewhat obscure. It lies wide open to accusations of levity and playfulness — unseemly, in the view of so many, for as sober and responsible a profession as sociology. But Freud himself discovered (or rediscovered) that it is necessary to be playful in order to be profound; and, in order to be profound, I am prepared to add, it is worth taking risks.[1] The list of things for which apology should be made would probably fill a chapter in its own right. Let me conclude this recitation of *mea culpa* with a defense against the most unfashionable of all my crimes — that of being "metaphysical." Here, also, Freud stands arraigned with me in the dock.

Like David Bakan, I "believe that . . . [the] pattern, from mysticism to science, is one of the more important historical characteristics in the development of general science. We have but to think of such major scientists as Newton, Kepler, and Fechner, who, deeply immersed in theological traditions, succeeded in so rationalizing the phenomena with which they were concerned, that the supernatural elements which were an integral part of their thought, could be abandoned as gratuitous" (1, pp. 25–26). It is my fondest hope that specific hypotheses may soon be derived from the theory of institutionalization and put to rigorous (and, preferably, crucial) test. But to succumb too early to *methodological inhibitions* would dry up the well-springs of invention — and theories, like works of art, have to be invented. What a disaster in the history of ideas it would have been if Freud had allowed himself only "explicit treatment of behavior as a datum, of probability of response as the principal quantifiable property of behavior, of learning and other processes in terms of changes of probability . . ." (37, p. 84). Indeed, it is pleasing that Mr. Skinner does not actually trammel and confine his own work in such a manner (see 36, pp. 88–130), for otherwise we should lose the productivity of quite an able psychologist.

But enough of apologies; Sigmund Freud's protean theoretical and speculative outpourings do not make a systematic account of psychoanalytic theory easy to present. Let this more important and more difficult task take up our energies. The discussion will begin with an attempt to outline the Freudian model of personality formation. The exposition will, initially, be confined to certain selected, but crucial, aspects of the Freudian model: those aspects having to do with excitation of the psyche (or behavior system) and with the formation of ego structure. My very

---

[1] On second thought about the last point; let those who would accuse me of levity turn to their collections of Nietzsche's works (and to their dictionaries) and ponder on the following words: "im echten Manne ist ein Kind versteckt, und es will spielen." I remember this quotation from my Viennese childhood and regret that I simply cannot find the reference!

brief account draws heavily upon Rapaport's heroic attempts to bring simplicity and order to the rich profusion of Freud's thinking (30; 31), but a careful rereading of the relevant Freudian literature has not been avoided.

The Freudian Model of Personality Formation

"If, about the generation of the universe, I cannot present notions that are in every way exact and internally consistent . . . do not be surprised"

Plato (Timaios 29c)

The first distinction necessary for this account is between *primary process* and *secondary process*. Primary process, which describes the earliest modes of behaving, is viewed by Freud as occurring more or less "automatically" without the intervention of psychic structures. It consists, as it were, of actions exhibited by (or, at least, inherent in) the psychic organization of the human organism prior to the formation of personality structures. Secondary process, on the other hand, is action mediated by personality structure. Secondary process and, indeed, personality structure as such, are precipitates of primary process. The manner in which this precipitation takes place in the area of cognition (and which may be allowed to illustrate this transformation in general) is described by Freud as follows:

> . . . first the apparatus's efforts were directed towards keeping itself as far as possible free from stimuli. . . . But the *exigencies of life interfere with this simple function* [our italics]. The exigencies of life confront it first in the form of the major somatic needs. The excitations produced by internal needs seek discharge in movement, which may be described as an "internal change" or an "expression of emotion." A hungry baby screams or kicks helplessly. But the situation remains unchanged, for the excitation arising from an internal need is not due to a force producing a *momentary* impact but to one which is in continuous operation. A change can only come about if . . . an "experience of satisfaction" can be achieved which puts an end to the internal stimulus. An essential component of this particular experience of satisfaction is a particular perception . . . the memory image of which remains associated thenceforward with the memory trace of the excitation produced by the need (12, p. 565).

Thus, "all our psychical activity starts from stimuli (whether internal or external) and end(s) in innervation" (12, p. 537). "Innervation" literally means the distribution of nerves in an organism or organ; Freud means by it what I shall call *structure*.

The Freudian models of conation, cognition, and affect, as they apply to primary process are lucidly presented by Rapaport (31, pp. 71–73). Essentially, my account is a précis of Rapaport's description. These models take the form of processual sequences which may, respectively, be depicted as follows:

a) Restlessness→sucking→subsidence of restlessness ("gratification").
   This model describes the *pleasure principle*.
b) Drive→absence of drive object→hallucination of gratifying object.
   This model describes *wish-fulfillment*.
c) Drive→absence of drive object→discharge of affect. In the last-
   mentioned model, affect may be discharged in outward behavior
   (alloplastically) by means of some expressive act such as howling
   or kicking, or inwardly (autoplastically) through somatization or
   the establishment of anxiety. It will be observed that both the
   cognitive and affect models require for their activation the absence
   of a drive-object, and thus we may formulate a combined model of
   affect and cognition (d).
d) Drive→absence of drive object→hallucination of gratifying object
   and/or affect discharge.

We have seen above that delay of gratification of a drive (as in the
case of the hungry baby) results in the accumulation of memory traces.
Such representations carry drive energy which is, however, "mobile" —
that is to say, the energy can be shifted (displacement) or compounded
(condensation). Rapaport suggests that "the free displacement [of
energy] is a corollary of the unrestrained tendency towards full discharge by the shortest path . . . characteristic of primary process behavior" (30, p. 694). When drive tension mounts and the drive object
is absent and if, in addition, discharge into affect or ideation (hallucination) are not sufficient to make the tension tolerable, then there develop
"control and defense structures" (31, p. 73). These structures raise the
drive-discharge threshold; they imply "an experiential connection-
system of progressively more differentiated and discrete ideas" (30, p.
696). The delay itself, as it were, becomes "structuralized." Initially
there are two outcomes of the delay: "binding," whereby the drive discharge becomes transformed into quiescent energy which becomes available to the secondary processes (to be discussed below); or "primary
repression," whereby the drive and its ideational representation are denied
access to motility and consciousness (30, p. 695). Repressed ideational
representations were conceptualized by Freud as the *Unconscious*. Where
only the affect charge is repressed, but the ideational material is not,
Freud speaks of *isolation* (18, pp. 120–121).

The position of external excitations in Freudian theory is a somewhat
peculiar one. Although Freud clearly implies that external excitations
and drives are not qualitatively different, that drives, in fact, are
varieties of excitation of somatic (or "internal") origin — he suggests that
"the excitations coming from within are, however, . . . more commen-
surate with the system's method of working than the stimuli which stream
in from the external world" (14, p. 29). To deal with the excitations
emanating from the "outside world" the psyche, as it were, develops a
crust — a *stimulus shield* that serves to reduce their impact. Internal

excitations or drives, on the other hand, are not subject to the interposition of such a stimulus barrier, and thus take primary place in the Freudian conception of "psycho-dynamics." Thus Freud maintains that "feelings of pleasure and unpleasure . . . are an index of what is happening in the interior of the apparatus" and "predominate over all external stimuli" (14, p. 29). Drives and external stimuli may, however, undergo a sort of transposition through the agency of the mechanisms of *projection* and *introjection*. Internal excitations producing an "excessive" quantum of unpleasure are, by projection, treated as if they were acting from the outside so that it becomes possible to bring the stimulus shield into effect against them. Introjection is a mechanism whereby the stimuli emanating from the earliest drive objects are experienced as drives and where, moreover, these pseudo-drives continue to operate in the absence of the drive object.[2]

Where the excitation emanating from the environment is such as to render the stimulus shield (or functional equivalents of the stimulus shield, as the capacity to utilize mechanisms of withdrawal such as *flight*, *undoing*, or *denial*) inadequate, Freud speaks of *trauma*. The personality attempts to master traumata by repetition (in motor behavior or hallucination analogous to that consequent upon the experience of a drive) "with a view to the psychical binding of traumatic impressions" (14, p. 33). Thus, I assume, the excitation that has breached the stimulus barrier is considered by Freud as acting like a drive which, however, has no drive-object and is discharged through the *repetition compulsion*, whether the energy freely discharged in this form of repetitive behavior can indeed become bound energy, Freud does not say. The casual manner in which he handles this hypothesis (it is only mentioned once) must give us reason to pause. Equally surprising is the scantiness of his discussion of introjection to which we have referred in footnote 2. Before these questions can be clarified, it is necessary to discuss Freud's conception of the psychic structure which mediates secondary process.

In *The Ego and the Id*, Freud makes a distinction between three structural entities of the psyche: id, ego, and super-ego (ego ideal). The id, essentially, is the repository of drives and the seat of primary process behavior. The ego is viewed in this book as consisting essentially of a conception of one's body (body ego), plus "that part of the id which has been modified by the direct influence of the external world" (19, p. 25). The latter phrase would imply that the ego also includes the

[2] Freud nowhere makes an explicit statement such as I have made above regarding introjection and I am not aware of any such statement in the psychoanalytic literature. But whereas a search of Freud's writings on the subject of introjection or identification, its "later" equivalent (see for example, Bronfenbrenner, [5] reveals little by way of elucidation of how introjection operates, there can be no doubt of the importance of early introjection in the formation of the super-ego. Thus introjection tends to be treated as a primitive concept and described, residually, in terms of its outcome. The discussion of psychic structures, which follows below, will provide justification for the way in which introjection is characterized here.

stimulus shield and mechanisms associated with secondary process such as repression, isolation, and projection.[3] "By virtue of [the ego's] relation to the perceptual system it gives mental processes an order in time and submits them to 'reality testing.' By interposing the processes of thinking, it secures a postponement of motor discharges and controls access to motility" (19, p. 55). The super-ego, conceived of as the source of conscience, is a precipitate of early introjection. "The super-ego owes its special position . . . in relation to the ego to . . . [the fact] that it was the first identification and one which took place while the ego was still feeble . . . it is a memorial of the former weakness . . . of the ego" (19, p. 48).[4]

The function of the ego as the mediating agency of secondary process is made quite explicit in the allusion to reality testing quoted above. In his later writings (for example, [18, p. 90] and [19, p. 56]), Freud is equally explicit in ascribing to the ego a mediating role between impulses emanating from the id, the super-ego, and "reality" (viewed as the current environment). Drives emanate from the id, external excitations from the environment, and "punishments" from the super-ego. The super-ego thus assumes the characteristics of a second reservoir of impulses, additional to the id, and situated "within" the psyche. In view of these conclusions of Freud concerning psychic structure, my previous description of introjection would appear to supply a missing link in the systematization of psychoanalytic theory. Prior to the development of the ego (secondary process), external excitations have the force of drives, and their representations are incorporated into the psyche (behavior system). What is more, the capacity of some persons to exercise rational conscience without experiencing an excessive amount of punishment from the super-ego (guilt) would suggest that the energy connected with introjected excitation, as much as the energy connected with drive excitation, is capable of becoming "bound." Thus the compulsion to repeat is an analogue of drive-discharge obeying the "pleasure principle," and like such drive-discharge, is liable to become subject to the defenses and controls of reality testing. Certain traumatic excitations experienced after the secondary process is established do not become bound but continue to press for direct discharge through behavior Freud described as the compulsion to repeat. But then, some persons also continue to follow

---

[3] Anna Freud (although, following in her father's footsteps, she tends to be somewhat indiscriminate in lumping together different orders of phenomena as "mechanisms of defense") does acknowledge something like Rapaport's distinction of the types of "mechanisms" involved in primary process and those involved in secondary process. Thus she suggests: "It is meaningless to speak of repression when the ego is still merged with the id"; and "such processes as . . . reversal, or turning round upon the self are . . . as old as the instincts themselves" (8, pp. 55–56).

[4] Freud's interchangeable use of the terms *introjection* and *identification* is somewhat confusing. Since he himself makes a distinction between early identification, which forms the super-ego, and later identification, which modifies the ego, (see, for example, Freud, [17]) I suggest that the term *introjection* be reserved for the former process, and the term *identification* for the latter. Such a terminological distinction is in line with the attempt at theoretical clarification which follows below.

directly the dictates of certain of their drives, without the drive becoming subjected to detours and postponements typical of secondary process.

Some further evidence for such an equation of drive discharge and the repetition compulsion, and for the contention that both are capable of psychic binding, is provided by Fairbairn, who speaks of the Freudian super-ego as an "internalized object," and notes that this is the only "truly dynamic endo-psychic structure" for Freud (6, p. 126). Since Fairbairn, on the same page, equates impulse with what he calls "dynamic structure," we may assume that he would agree with my characterization of the super-ego as a reservoir of impulses.[5] Particularly interesting in Fairbairn's discussion is his view that "it is always the 'bad' object that is internalized in the first instance" since "it is not the satisfying object that the infant seeks to coerce" (6, p. 110). If we equate the terminology of "bad" objects and "good" objects with satisfying drive-objects and sources of painful external excitation respectively,[6] and if Fairbairn's felicitous use of the term "coercion" is agreed to refer to binding, it is easily seen that Fairbairn is moving towards a point of view similar to mine. Unlike Fairbairn, however, I do not believe it is necessary to discount somatic excitation as an independently active reservoir of impulses. In connection with his studies of victims of sexual assault, Fairbairn finds that they do not repress that trauma because of guilt concerning "forbidden" gratifications (a hypothesis that would be in line with the Freudian view), but because of the unavoidable relationship with a bad object (6, p. 63). He suggests, in fact, that "what are primarily repressed are bad internalized objects"[7] (6, p. 62). If indeed traumatic external stimuli are capable of repression or some other form of "coercion," then my contention that external excitations are capable of psychic binding would appear to be upheld.

It would therefore appear that any wide and sweeping claims concerning a qualitative difference between external excitations and drive excitations (which, it must be remembered, Freud conceives of as sexual) and their respective modes of expression would require skillful and consistent advocacy. Freud, of course, makes such a claim, characterizing the libidinal emanations of the id as *Eros* (14, p. 58), and the compulsion to repeat activated by external excitations (as indeed the functions of the ego in general) as the *death instinct* (14, pp. 36–38). But even in the work in which the above distinction is promulgated certain confusions arise. Early in the book, Freud says that the "pleasure principle follows the principle of constancy [that is, inertia]" (14, p. 9), but

[5] Fairbairn more or less denies the importance of the id as a reservoir of energy, maintaining that "libidinal 'aims' are of secondary importance in comparison with object relationships" (6, p. 60). Hence he ascribes only one legitimate reservoir of impulses to Freudian theory.

[6] Such an equation would appear to be quite justifiable. See in this connection, Klein (24).

[7] Freud himself suggests in a late work that guilt is repressed in hysteria (see 19, pp. 49–50).

later he links tendencies to inertia with the death instincts (14, p. 36). This is confusing because the pleasure principle is supposed to obey libidinal (sexual, erotic, "life") urges alone, but the confusion becomes chaotic in later works, and in *The Ego and the Id* we find a complete reversal from his former position; there he is capable of proclaiming "it would be possible to picture the id as under the domination of the mute but powerful death instincts, which desire to be at peace and (prompted by the pleasure principle) to put Eros, the mischief maker, to rest . . ." (19, p. 59)! It would be easy to "rest" one's case at this point, and to conclude that Freud, in his old age, reverted to methods of argument reminiscent of the "mechanisms" of primary process. But such a course of action would, I believe, be a grave mistake. Sigmund Freud's intellectual achievement, however "untidy" it may be, is so colossal that anyone who would deride him for inconsistencies can make only himself ridiculous.[8] I shall follow a more plausible course, and assume that whatever Freud was trying to say was so important that he felt impelled to publish his gigantic struggle for both clarity and faithfulness to the enormous subtlety of his subject matter, prior to being able to reach a consistent formulation. The primary process-like character of the "reversals," "condensations," and "displacements" displayed by his argument, I shall furthermore assume, was intentional and not the consequence of some involuntary cognitive "regression." The conceptual rubble field he left after *Thanatos*[9] won the battle, can fill one only with astonishment and awe,[10] both for its scope, and for the superbly brilliant execution of the fragments with which it is littered. In order to piece some of these fragments together it is necessary to turn to the consideration of the nature of "reality" in the Freudian system.

The Nature of "Reality"

"Our god *Logos* is not perhaps a powerful one . . . we shall not thereby lose our interest in the world, for . . . we believe that it is possible for scientific work to discover something about the reality of the world."

Freud (11, p. 95)

[8] To cite an example of how rash it is to dismiss Freud lightly, David Bakan in his remarkably profound book (1, pp. 137–143) takes *Moses and Monotheism*, superficially the weakest and most fantastic example of the much-attacked "pseudo-anthropology," as the fulcrum of his discussion of Freud's association with the Jewish mystical tradition. He is able to demonstrate the importance of its double content for understanding Freud's place in the history of thought and, indeed, for understanding the essence of the Freudian theory itself. See also my review of Bakan's book (40).

[9] *Thanatos* is the Greek angel of death — occasionally the Freudian death instinct has been called by this name; just as Freud chose to refer to the "life instinct" by the name of the Greek god of love.

[10] In relation to feelings of astonishment and awe the reader may be directed to Freud's essay *The Uncanny* (9), and also to Bakan's discussion of this essay (1, pp. 303–319). Especially noteworthy, in the light of the foregoing discussion, is the peculiar allusion to the repetition compulsion as uncanny (9, p. 391).

It has already been implied that "reality," for Freud, consists of the external environment of the psyche. Thus far this environment has been considered solely as a source of current excitations (as distinct from drive excitations or introjected external excitations in the past), but it is also the realm in which drive objects are located; objects in which tensions may find a terminus and resolution. The secondary process, in which drive tensions do not press for direct or immediate discharge, is frequently characterized by Freud as "reality testing" (as in 17, pp. 244–245).

For a systematic account of secondary-process models of action (or conation, cognition, and affect), recourse may again be made to Rapaport's account (31, pp. 73–78). The secondary model of action may be depicted as follows: Drive→derivative drive→structuralized delay→detour activity (searching for) and means activity (reaching for) the drive object→satisfaction. Derivative drives are drives altered by defenses; where such alteration is not necessary, this step in the sequence is bypassed. Structuralized delay and detours enable the theory to account for tension maintenance and tension increase. The shift in terminology from "gratification" (in the primary model) to "satisfaction" in the secondary model, indicates that complete tension discharge upon reaching the drive object gives way to discharge compatible with the maintenance of tension — tension which is inevitable because of the existence of structure.

The secondary model of cognition is fundamentally quite similar to the action model: Drive (or derivative drive)→structuralized delay→experiment in thought with small amounts of energy to anticipate, plan, locate the drive object, and act upon it. Here structuralized delay prevents the shortcut to hallucination and is productive of ordered thinking. For the secondary model of affect, reference may be made to Rapaport's account (31, p. 79); its exposition would add little of direct relevance to this discussion. What strikes one about the secondary-process model is the emphasis on detours, delays, and above all, on activities involving *searching* for drive objects. Thus reality becomes more than merely the realm in which drive objects are located, and from which external excitations emanate. It becomes also a sort of map on which the location of satisfying drive objects (or derivative drive objects which have the capacity of satisfying), and presumably also the location of sources of painful excitation can be more or less specifically fixed. The secondary process is one of mapping sources of painful excitation and satisfying objects; reality, presumably, is the "true" location of these excitations and objects.

If secondary process can be seen as obeying the reality principle, the inconsistency of Freud's statements on Eros and the death instincts, to which allusion has been made, can admit of partial resolution. Freud says that "from the point of view of preservation of the organism among the difficulties of the external world [the pleasure principle] is from the very outset inefficient and even highly dangerous" (14, p. 10). Thus one may infer that, although he sets out by viewing sexual drives as being of the essence of Eros, Freud considers the primary process mode of their gratification highly inept for the expression of Eros. The formation of ego structure, adaptive to "reality," is a prerequisite of "viability," and hence the only proper medium for the expression of Eros. Paradoxically, it is only the delay of gratification which, by creating structure, can lead to satisfaction. But this formulation still clashes with Freud's earlier linkage of the ego (the organon of secondary process), with the death instincts (14, p. 39). He retracts this view, however, suggesting "we were prepared . . . to include the so-called preservative instincts of the ego among the death instincts, but we subsequently corrected ourselves on the point and withdrew [this view]" (14, p. 53). At the end of his discussion in *Beyond the Pleasure Principle,* Freud leaves us with a somewhat ramshackle conception of sadism-masochism as a derivative of the death instincts (14, p. 53; see also 19, p. 41), and an inadequately developed idea of Eros as "combining substances into ever larger unities" (14, p. 42) and as similar to the "Eros of the poets and philosophers which holds all living things together" (14, p. 50).

I shall attempt to show that these somewhat unsatisfactory conclusions spring from defects in the Freudian conception of reality. A more adequate discussion of reality may help to illuminate the kind of problems with which Freud was struggling when he arrived at these unpersuasive formulations. The startling similarity of Freud's conception of secondary process with the theory of capital accumulation proposed by the Austrian economist Boehm-Bawerk provides a useful starting point.

In his *Positive Theory of Capital,* first published in 1888,[11] Boehm-Bawerk sees man (labor) and nature (land) as the aboriginal factors of production. Initially, labor and consumption are virtually equivalent, as in his example of "some Robinson Crusoe thrown on a lonely shore without either tools or weapons" who "must support life . . . by gathering berries which grow wild" (4, p. 101). Capital formation (as, for example, Crusoe's fabrication of a bow and arrow) is seen as a roundabout way of increasing the number of goods to be consumed. The time that Crusoe has to spend on fabricating the bow and arrow cannot be used for gathering (and consuming) berries. He has to delay the immediate gratification of eating berries in order to construct the bow and arrow, a process which Boehm-Bawerk characterizes as *saving* (4, p. 103). To give a cognate example, if one can delay the immediate maximum gratification to be obtained, for example, in the consumption of fresh water by carrying buckets from a well, sufficiently long so as to construct a

---

[11] A few years before the appearance of Breuer and Freud's *Studies of Hysteria* (1893–1895), with which psychoanalysis was inaugurated. This is not to imply that Freud was consciously modeling his ideas on Boehm-Bawerk's, but these ideas must have been "in the air."

water pipe, the supply of water at home (the locus of consumption) will ultimately — after completion of the pipe — be enhanced.[12] Thus *capital* (the bow and arrow, or the pipe) is roundabout labor, labor that has undergone a "detour" in order to increase utility (consumption potential). It requires no great act of the imagination to substitute the term *drive energy* for *labor, environment* for *land,* and *detour activity* for *saving.* Indeed, by analogy to Breuer and Freud's *bound energy, capital* in Boehm-Bawerk's sense may be viewed as *bound labor.*[13] To follow the analogy further, Boehm-Bawerk does go beyond Freud in one important respect; namely, in his formulation that the accumulation of capital increases productivity and "utility." Freud could not bring himself to the point of stating unequivocally that the binding of drive energy, and the formation of the ego, may actually increase the total quantum of satisfaction available to the person. Undoubtedly, his reluctance to do so was due to his primary interest in pathology, which he saw as an outcome of drive inhibition — something to do with the development of the ego. But then, the early critics of "capitalism" (or, for that matter, current critics of communist programs of capital formation at the expense of producing consumer goods), who saw labor inadequately rewarded by opportunities for consumption consequent upon capital formation, were also far from laudatory concerning the benefits of capital. Freud did grope towards a recognition that the existence of ego structure increases the total satisfaction available to the person. Every schoolboy knows his oracular pronouncement "where id was there shall ego be" (10, p. 111). I shall go further and attempt to show that Freud was trying to arrive at a conception of Eros as the principle underlying the creation of structure, both in the personality and in society.

There can be no question but that Freud saw the formation of ego structure as depending in some degree upon the environment. For structuralized delay to occur in the first place, there must, at the very least, first be an objective absence of the drive object in some "real" environment. But Freud nowhere concerns himself with the characteristics of real environments; such characteristics have to be inferred from his statements regarding the development of ego structure. To take up the capital formation analogy again, this time finally, it is as though capital were to be explained by the idea of "frozen labor" alone. But it is, of course, the characteristics of the land with which Crusoe's labor, dedicated to saving instead of immediate consumption, must interact in the creation of primeval capital. Where there are no trees or bushes in "objective" existence, no (wooden) bows and arrows can be contrived.

---

[12] I am indebted for this example to Professor Lionel Robbins, whose Lectures at the London School of Economics I attended in 1948.

[13] For the sake of simplicity, my discussion is confined to Boehm-Bawerk's notion of real capital (machinery and the like, not money). I must hasten to add that Boehm-Bawerk's work on capital is by no means limited to the examination of real capital.

No one could blame Freud for failing to conform to the tenets of some variety of *naive realism;* the problem of reality as it faces the infantile psyche is more subtle by far than the problems ostensibly confronting some adult marooned Crusoe with an already developed system of knowledge. But still, it would have been desirable if some more concrete hypotheses concerning the environment could have been formulated by Freud. As it is, reality remains a residual category in Freudian theory — colorless, and somewhat chimerical, a tissue of memory traces and undefined "searching."

For a more adequate epistemology to deal with the impingement of reality upon thought and behavior — which goes further than Freud's hints and yet does not consider knowledge of reality as something just lying "out there," ready to be picked up by any person with an unimpeded perceptual apparatus — I shall turn to methodology, the "logic of science," and particularly to the work of Karl Popper. My assumption is that the experimental sciences constitute reality testing at its most consistent and articulate level. Popper's model of reality testing as employed in empirical science provides a more convincing description of epistemological process than either Freud's evasions and hints, or positivistic descriptions postulating the wholesale swallowing of pre-digested reality in a gingerbread fool's paradise of ontological plenty.

Popper asks: "How is the system that represents our world of experience to be distinguished? The answer is: by the fact that it has been submitted to tests and has stood up to tests." " 'Experience,' on this view, appears as a distinctive *method* whereby one theoretical system [or, for that matter, a single idea] may be distinguished from others." "The theory of knowledge whose task is the analysis of the method of procedure . . . [of] empirical science, may accordingly be described as a theory of the empirical method — *a theory of what is usually called experience"* (29, p. 39). Thus Popper's methodology contains the implicit view that ideas ("hypotheses") are prior to observations. Observations are the experiences against which ideas are tested. Given that a *realistic* theory (or, on a pre-scientific level, realistic knowledge) is to be obtained, ideas should be given up if they do not match with observations. Regarding the problem of an "empirical basis," Popper maintains: "Perceptual experiences have often been regarded as providing a justification for basic statements [in my terminology; statements of an idea]. It was held that these statements are 'based upon' experience. . . ." As against this, Popper suggests (and I am changing the terminology very slightly, but not the meaning) that any idea of an object or of relationships between objects can become, as it were, *objective* only when it pushes up against falsifying observations. Thus falsification of an idea is the only real way we have of coming into direct contact with *reality.* Reality, in words which I shall long remember,[14] is for Popper akin to

14 From a personal conversation with Karl Popper in 1949 or 1950.

the experience of a "blind man who walks into a wall." Or, in other words: "my proposal is based upon an asymmetry between verifiability and falsifiability . . ." (29, p. 41).

The similarity of Popper's conception of an hypothesis (what I call an idea) with Freud's conception of a drive, cannot escape attention. For Freud, as we have seen, a representation of an object depends upon delay of gratification. For Popper, a change in the representation of an object in the direction of empirical reality depends upon the "falsification" of the original idea concerning the object. Freud sees gratification after delay as precipitating a memory trace. Popper would surely speak of such a representation as an untested hypothesis — a "basic statement" which must undergo testing in order to be either confirmed (it can never be "verified") or rejected. Popper's conceptions, moreover, augment those of Freud; they look at the other side of the coin. Thus while reality testing is, for Freud, inextricably connected with the formation of ego structure, testing for Popper is the process whereby we discover (or "create") structure in empirical reality. Both ego formation and theory formation are thus "dynamic" processes; both involve the creation of structure.

This point of view is at variance with Hartmann's conception of the "conflict-free ego sphere" (23, pp. 3–21). Hartmann avers: "not every adaptation to the environment or every learning . . . process, is a conflict. I refer to the development outside of conflict of perception, . . . object comprehension . . . [and] thinking" (23, p. 8). The proposition that "we can think even when no fundamental need activates us" (30, p. 704), which follows Hartmann's formulation, depends entirely for its veracity upon a somewhat whimsical definition of what is supposed to be a "fundamental need." Perception and object comprehension (wherever they are not illusory), we learn from Karl Popper, develop precisely because of conflict; conflict with "reality" which impinges upon us in the guise of falsification. It is surprising that Freud did not characterize the regressive formulation of Hartmann, whose major concern is with *adaptation* (that is, inertia), as a derivative expression of the death instincts.[15] Had his conception of reality been as dynamic and as cogent as his conception of psychic structures, he would surely have done so.

Although the image Freud presents us of "reality" is not a clear one, it is possible to piece together his conception of the "environment." Peculiarly enough, in view of criticisms which accuse him of biological

---

[15] Concepts such as *adaptation, adjustment,* and *function* have exercised a truly pernicious influence in the study of behavior. They appear to be hanging on in psychology and sociology, although biology is on the verge of abandoning them. Some of the salutary changes in biology are exemplified in Oppenheim and Putnam's account of developments in genetics and evolution theory (28, pp. 20–26). I must hasten to add that I consider Oppenheim and Putnam's general conclusions regarding the "unity of science" premature, and their emphasis on what they call *micro-reductionism* misplaced.

determinism, Freud's conception of the environment is almost exclusively "social." Freud speaks of this environment as though it were "filled" with persons and little else. The early drive objects to which Freud typically refers, are the mother or her surrogates. It is typically a representation of the father or his surrogates that is introjected when the super-ego is formed. Thus guilt, stemming from the super-ego, has to do largely with interpersonal relations or interpersonal wishes, at least, when it is not concerned with auto-erotic sexuality. Freud states that "Religion, morality, and a social sense, . . . were originally the same thing" (19, p. 37). And, for Freud, the reality principle itself seems to consist mainly of methods whereby satisfaction (if not direct gratifications) can be obtained from other persons. Hartmann, who is more explicit on this point, says ". . . to conform to reality, that is to fit into the social situation . . ." (22, p. 378). Even had Freud made no excursions into anthropology, it would not be surprising under these circumstances, that Marcuse can quite effectively document Freuds reality principle as being a "performance principle" relative to a particular social system (27, pp. 44–47), or that Stoodley can make a brave attempt to find "a road from the libidinized ego to the collective representations of Durkheim" (39, p. 259). Even Hartmann's "conflict-free ego sphere" becomes intelligible insofar as this relates to the neglected section of reality which, in some sense, is extra-social and which, therefore, by extension of Freud's implications, is affected by no "fundamental" needs.

If we augment Freud's conception of the formation of structure in the personality — in human behavior — with Popper's conception of the formation of representational structures ("theories") of reality (those representational structures, that is to say, which are "realistic" and not pathological), we may arrive at a preliminary reformulation of the conception of Eros in Freudian theory. Eros who "unbounded presses ever forward" (14, p. 42);[16] Eros the "breaker of the peace" (14, p. 63); and, finally, Eros who "holds all . . . things together" (14, p. 50); all these manifestations become unified when we view them as *disturbances of inertia which have the effect of creating or elaborating structures.* Both *sexual excitations* (which, as Freud so often suggests, are "hard to tame") and *falsifications* qualify for such a definition; at whatever level of organization their impact becomes felt, they upset the existing equilibrium and press toward the elaboration of organization at a higher level of structure (be it of the personality, or of systematic knowledge — science). By contrast, the so-called "death instincts" may be interpreted as *reactions resultant upon disturbances of inertia which lead to rigidities and strains in existing structures, or in their disintegration.* In order to provide a better foundation for these assertions it becomes necessary to formulate their relationship with the theory of institutionalization.

[16] I am here providing a translation of Freud's quotation from Goethe's Faust (Part 1, Scene 4): ". . . ungebaendigt immer vorwaerts dringt."

The Theory of Institutionalization

"Es ist so gut, als waer es nicht gewesen
Und treibt sich doch im Kreis, als wenn es waere"
(Mephisto)
"Nur der verdient sich Freiheit, wie das Leben
Der taeglich sie erobern muss"
(Faust)
Goethe. (Faust Pt. 2)[17]

In the foregoing discussion, two additions have been made to Freud's views on personality formation and on reality. The first is an explicit statement regarding the role of external excitations that occur before the development of an adequate stimulus shield, or that are sufficiently powerful to breach the stimulus shield once it has come into being. I have suggested that some derivatives of these early or traumatic excitations are experienced as analogues of drives or drive derivatives. This statement is more general than what may be pieced together from Freud's inconsistent and scattered assertions regarding the super-ego, and the impulses emanating from the super-ego, which he typically considers as consisting of self-punishments taking the form of guilt. The second addition to the Freudian world view has been an emphasis upon the importance of falsification (cognitive discrepancies) in the development of a person's conception of reality, and upon the "dynamic" nature of this reality for the person. To be sure, there have been other attempts to develop less inadequate formulations of reality than Freud's within the general Freudian framework. Both Schilder (34, pp. 178–179) and Schachtel (33, pp. 309–324) make some approximation to the views I am presenting, and Helen Lynd is rather emphatic in her assertion that "the development of individual identity must be understood . . . in a world conceived in its full dimensions — personal and nonpersonal" (26, p. 160). What is original in my formulation is the juxtaposition of Freudian and Popperian views of reality, and the emphasis upon falsification as a special variety of "external excitation" of paradigmatic importance in the development of a conception of reality.

If the proposed additions to Freudian theory are to be accepted, we emerge with a conception of three systems operative in the psyche, each of which tends to a form of equilibrium. First, of course, there is the internal system, liable to disturbance by somatic excitation; inertia is restored by means of gratification. This is the system with which Freud is primarily concerned. Secondly, there is a system created by the impingement of the environment upon (or the intrusion of the environment

[17] My translation of these lines, both sets from Act Five, "the great forecourt of the palace," would run something as follows:
"It is as good as had it never happened/And still it mills around as though it had" and "He only earns his freedom or his life
Who's forced to take them every day by storm"

into) the infant's behavior. We may call this the *introjected system.*
Equilibrium here consists of environmental constancy, disturbances of
which are internalized, or perhaps "assimilated," by repetition. Conceptions of *pattern* and *order,* both in the behavior (or "conduct") of
objects — including the self as an object — and in their form and arrangement, are outgrowths of the attempt to master such disturbances.
When *either* gratifying objects are absent, *or* when the earliest stable
conceptions of order — *proto-patterns,* as it were — are in their turn
disturbed, a third system develops. This system may be called the
ideational system or "knowledge." I am suggesting that the ideational
system is the offspring of both the internal and the introjected systems.
The tension arising in the absence of gratifying objects which, as Freud
has shown, gives rise to memory traces and hallucinations, interacts with
the earliest conceptions of order imposed by the obtrusion or intrusion
of the environment, to give rise to ideas or expectations. Once conceptions
or expectations are established, they can undergo "disappointment" or
falsification. When this occurs the ideational system becomes modified.
But the ideational system, although produced by the interaction of the
internal and introjected systems, does not completely annex the latter —
after it begins to make its appearance it co-exists with them, and continues to co-exist with them throughout the history of the person.

It is not difficult to see that the disturbances of the three systems I
have outlined correspond to the types of discrepancy proposed in the
sketch of a theory of institutionalization that precedes this section of
the volume. A disturbance of the inertia in the internal system produces
an affective discrepancy. A disturbance of the introjected system of
proto-patterns, in a sense, "offends" the person; it may be viewed as an
evaluative discrepancy. Falsifications — disturbances of the ideational
system — I have called cognitive discrepancies. As the personality becomes complex, the internal system ceases to constitute merely a state
of affective inertia which is disturbed by drives. It becomes a balance
of competing disturbances; an equilibrium of deprivations. The melange
of primeval proto-patterns also becomes differentiated, giving rise to a
horizon of justifications (or counter-justifications), at least in relation
to concrete and actual situations. As far as expectations are concerned —
perhaps it is somewhat rash to characterize the jumble of expectations
constituting most persons' knowledge as anything as regular and consistent as a "horizon." Still, let us be charitable in the terminology proposed. In specific fields, or in situations in which a given person's cognition is heavily employed, something like an approximation to a horizon
of expectations will come to be. A global horizon of expectations, ordering all possible expectations in a world which is so rich in baffling experiences, either is the resultant of an extremely limited environment,
or paranoid, or, finally, approaches Spinoza's *cogitatio mentis dei* as an
unreachable ideal of completeness.

It must be stressed that the three systems to which reference has been made cease to be simply inert after the initial disturbances, but develop structure and, in the Freudian sense of the term, "dynamics." The equilibrium of deprivations tends toward an even distribution of levels of excitation; the horizons of justifications and expectations are subject to "strains toward consistency." The interaction of these systems, as has already been implied, is of particular importance. A disturbance of the equilibrium of deprivations, where it cannot be directly rectified by gratification, arouses searching or "scanning" activities along the horizon of expectations (once the latter has come into existence) with a view to finding routes toward satisfaction. An evaluative discrepancy, whether it is encountered directly, or as a result of the aforementioned scanning for routes to satisfaction, may also result in the modification of the horizon of expectations in two ways: by *repression*, in which parts of the horizon of expectations become blocked out, and by *rationalization*, in which the horizon of expectations becomes elaborated and reorganized so as to integrate the "unjustifiable" experience.

In the case of repression, the inactivation of certain segments of the horizon of expectations implies also a damming of certain pathways to satisfaction. The mapping of resultant devious routes to satisfaction (or attempted re-equilibration of the equilibrium of deprivations) is, without doubt, the crowning glory of Freud's clinical achievements. But the very power of his model and the illumination with which it flooded areas of behavior that had been outside the purview (or, at least, peripheral to the formulations)[18] of previous students, had the effect of a sort of intellectual "fixation." Freud was struggling to get beyond this model in his later "metapsychological" works, but he was never again able to generate explanatory candlepower to equal that of his early formulations on hysteria and on dreams. Consequently, he felt himself unable to make sufficiently radical reformulations of this model — to transform it, as it were, into something else that was not as "good."

There appear to be instances in which evaluative discrepancies exert direct influence upon the equilibrium of deprivations without the mediation of repression (that is, inactivation of segments of the horizon of expectations). Certain evaluative discrepancies occur with specific modes of gratification which do not result in the inactivation of segments of the horizon of expectations but which, nonetheless, result in the avoidance of the still available cognitive pathways to satisfaction, and the

---

[18] Of the large number of gropings in the direction of foreshadowing some aspects of Freud's model of dreams, the following, isolated prophecy of Nostradamus is perhaps the most direct:
"Gynique sexe captive hostage
Viendra de nuict custodes decevoir" (32, p. 124)
I would translate this: "The 'sex female' held captive as a hostage, shall come by night to deceive her warders." This refers, of course, to dream symbolism, but could equally well describe the "return of the repressed" in symptoms.

seeking of satisfaction by other, more tortuous, routes. Such instances illustrate what Freud was talking about when he used the term *isolation*. Here the cognitive pathways appear to be intact, yet the route to satisfaction along them is not taken. May I be forgiven if, like Freud, I "cannot as yet grasp" (18, p. 164) the exact mechanism involved in this functional equivalent of repression in which the horizon of expectations remains active.

Falsifications, or cognitive discrepancies, alongside affective and evaluative discrepancies, may also have repercussions in any of the psychic systems I have outlined. A falsification, whether it is encountered directly (as where one unanticipatedly puts one's foot into a hole in the floor while walking) or in the processes of rationalization and scanning, "knocks a hole" as it were, into the horizon of expectations. This hole may be bridged by the process I have called *specification*. Thus falsification may lead to modifications in the equilibrium of deprivations in that new specifications have the effect of rerouting pathways to satisfaction. But it may also be traumatic in nature, requiring more than cognitive patchwork, or even cognitive reorganization.[19] In such cases one may view the falsification as being akin to an evaluative discrepancy, and as leading to the same kinds of consequences. Scanning leads to an elaboration of the horizon of expectations, specification and rationalization to both its elaboration and reorganization. In discussing scanning and specification processes in the developed personality, it appears legitimate to use "specification" as the generic term. Rationalization, although in many respects akin to specification in its effect upon the horizon of expectations, is a more direct derivative of the horizon of justifications, and expresses itself more properly as what I have called *justification*.

It will readily be seen that the internal system or equilibrium of deprivations roughly corresponds with Freud's conception of the *id*, the introjected system with his conceptions of the *super-ego* and of the *archaic ego* (*censor, stimulus shield,* "agency of primary repression," and so forth), and the horizon of expectations with his *perceptual-conscious* and *preconscious* systems or, in other words, with "higher" parts of the ego. Indeed, the correspondence is sufficiently close for Freud's terminology to be worth retaining within the framework of the theory of institutionalization, where infantile personality development or clinical (psycho-therapeutic) processes are under discussion, even though the structural distinction between the super-ego and the archaic ego is dissolved in the theory of institutionalization, and even though nontraumatic falsification is given the status of an independent dynamic force. But in the explanation of sociological phenomena (as should become clear in chapters 4 and 5), the new terminology is more apropos.

The rather early interdependence of the equilibrium of deprivations

---

[19] Freud's discussion of the castration complex in males provides a case in point. (See, for example, 13, p. 195.)

and the horizons of justifications and specifications in the development of the personality, renders it difficult, in practice, to isolate affective, evaluative, and cognitive discrepancies. For that reason they may all be subsumed under the general rubric of *exigencies*. Most exigencies, indeed, because of the interdependence of these systems, may be assumed to be compounded of the different types of discrepancy in varying proportions. Where a more or less developed personality — obeying "secondary process" types of thought and action — is under consideration, any exigency will lead to articulation, or at least, to attempts at articulation. As has been pointed out in the introduction to this Section of the volume, articulation determines needs and associated goals in relation to their salience, justifiability, and specifiability. Articulation, in other words, refers to the establishment and development of secondary-process thinking and behavior. It is the master process whereby excitations, whatever their nature, and falsifications are channeled, confined, and reacted to in a manner that defines them and that is consistent with the establishment of a more or less unified personality and a more or less unified view of reality. Given the occurrence of an exigency, its articulation will, as has been indicated, depend upon specifiability, justifiability, and salience. The first two elements mentioned are, of course, properties of the currently existing horizons of expectations and justifications respectively. The question arises whether salience is purely a property of the equilibrium of deprivations; this question may be combined, in this discussion, with the more general question of the concept of *energy* as it applies to behavior.

In the history of science, and of pre-scientific speculation, *motion* and *change* have always been connected with some concepts such as *energy* or *force*. Thus Frank H. Knight in a preface to his famous early work laments: "There is nothing in economics corresponding to either momentum, or energy, or their conservation principles in mechanics . . ." (25, p. xxiii), yet he finds notions like force, resistance, and equilibrium, unavoidable in interpreting economic phenomena. Freud found himself equally unable to do without the concept of energy in the attempt to explain psychological changes. Initially Freud equated psychological energy with affect, but by the turn of the century it had become firmly associated by him with drive energy (*libido*). (See, for example, 11, p. 599, p. 610.) This energy he conceived of as being displaceable from the drive to which it had originally been attached. Thus he speaks of the energy available to the ego as consisting of "narcissistic libido" (19, p. 44), it being transferred to the service of the ego as a result of the early choice of the self as a drive object. Along similar lines, Rapaport suggests that the relationship between primary process and secondary process as regards the use of energy is like that between power engineering and information engineering respectively (31, p. 91). Freud sees the same energy source activating also the super-ego, and is quite emphatic in stating that ". . . energy does not reach . . . the super-ego from . . . perception . . . but from sources in the id" (19, pp. 52–53). Translating this idea into my terminology, it would appear that Freud insists on viewing the equilibrium of deprivations as the sole source of behavioral energy or, in other words, of behavior. If we accept this point of view, it follows that salience is generated by disequilibration of deprivations alone, and that any changes or "motions" detectable in the horizons of justifications and expectations must borrow their energy from that source. Such an approach is entirely consistent with an equation of energy with entropy — the establishment of thermodynamic equilibrium.

If a somewhat far-fetched analogy[20] may be allowed, behavior may be likened to a substance, and excitation to heat. "At the absolute zero point of temperature . . . the entropy of any substance is zero" (35, p. 72). Similarly, we may assume, there will be no behavior in the total absence of any excitation. Given the addition of heat to the substance, it will tend toward "decay in thermodynamical equilibrium (death) which may also be described as an "inert state of maximum entropy" (35, p. 74). Given the occurrence of psychic excitation, similarly, primary process discharge — action obeying the pleasure principle — will also tend toward inertia. But neither the horizon of justification nor, still less, the horizon of expectations appear to be subject to some principle analogous to the second law of thermodynamics. If anything, they appear to be systems of tension designed to uphold something like a steady state. However, if the conception of the psyche as a closed system, and the functional equivalence of energy and entropy are upheld, then, clearly, there can be no energy save that "radiating" from the processes of equilibration of excitations (deprivations). My emphasis on external excitations and, particularly, on falsifications, betrays a bias in favor of viewing the psyche as an open system feeding, as it were, upon negative entropy. Could not Schroedinger's following remark regarding biological organisms be applicable also to the organization of thought and behavior: "the device by which an organism maintains itself stationary at a fairly high level of orderliness (fairly low level of entropy) really consists in continually sucking orderliness from its environment" (35, p. 75). Positively no process in the realm of biology approaches as closely to the idea of "sucking orderliness from the environment" as does falsification, and the consequent reorganization of the horizon of expectations. Thus the possibility, at least, arises that reorganizations of the horizons of expectations and justifications, obeying their strains towards consistency (a "steady state"), can occur "on their own steam." Certainly, this theoretical possibility would save us from the awkwardness

---

[20] I want to stress, rather emphatically, that I am making an analogy between behavioral and physical energy (or "change potential") and not the kind of equation that is sought and implied in Bernfeld and Feitelberg's discussion (2, pp. 137–206). As Rapaport points out: ". . . psychological energies are not equated with any known kind of biochemical energy" (31, p. 93).

of having to postulate energy cathexes from the equilibration of deprivations necessarily, and always, becoming attached to the horizons of justifications and expectations. It could also be used to give the *coup de grace* to Hartmann's clumsy formulation of the conflict-free ego sphere. All this is not, of course, meant to deny the peculiar importance, sensitivity, and intimate connectedness with the equilibrium of deprivations, of those segments of the horizon of expectations having reference to "self."

Although the foregoing discussion has not really solved the problem whether evaluative or cognitive discrepancies in their pure form can generate salience — Freud's conception of cathexis deserves a more careful examination before it is either accepted or rejected — it has opened an avenue to the consideration of processes of articulation and institutionalization. These appear to be analogous to (if not isomorphic with) Bertalanffy's ". . . irreversible processes in open systems [which] cannot be characterized by entropy . . ." (3, p. 127). Bertalanffy goes on to speak of ". . . the revolutionary consequence that in the transition to a steady state within an open system there may be a decrease in entropy and a spontaneous transition to a state of higher heterogeneity and complexity." The development of institutionalized patterns of thought and action in persons, and of interpersonal patterns of institutionalization constitute, I submit, an analogue of precisely this emergence of states of higher heterogeneity and complexity that Bertalanffy is trying to describe. But it is possible to go further than this; these processes constitute what Freud was groping for in his formulation of Eros. With his inimitable, almost prophetic, speculative flair, Freud foreshadowed modern discussions by biophysicists of "life" by almost a generation. Only the few minor changes necessary for an adequate formulation of a theory of institutionalization eluded him.

The conclusion thus becomes tenable that what I have called *institutionalization* coincides with Freud's conception of Eros or, more properly, constitutes a clearer statement of what Freud was trying to move towards when he proposed the concept of Eros. Exigencies reveal Eros in the guise of the 'disturber of the peace'; patterns of institutionalization describe Eros as the principle holding things, and persons, together; institutionalization as a general process — that is, the total exigency→articulation→institutionalization sequence — is the 'forward pressing' Eros, for ". . . it is the difference between . . . [what] is demanded and . . . [what] is actually achieved that provides the driving factor which will permit of no halting at any position attained . . ." (14, p. 42).

This still leaves us with the problem of the so-called death instincts. It has been suggested that unimpeded motion in the direction of inertia in the equilibrium of deprivations is akin to entropy, and thus constitutes something like a tendency towards death. But Freud also speaks of sadism and masochism (see especially 20) as though they were independent drives with the aim of attaining "pain" or, more properly, of attaining the destruction of objects (including, as in the case of masochism, the self as an object), and views them as derivatives of the death instinct which become "fused" with erotic (sexual) elements. It would appear, however, that the linkage of some teleological aim with drive excitations prior to the formation of psychic structure is logically unsound. To be sure, "goals" appear with the development of psychic structure, and, in particular, in connection with higher-order processes of articulation, and certain of these goals may be, in some sense, "destructive." But the only *aim* of which it is legitimate to speak prior to secondary-process thought and action, is the general aim of "gratification" (in other words, "removal of the excitation"). It would seem that Freud got himself into something of a semantic muddle with his death "instincts." The real problem he is facing is not one concerning the existence of inherently destructive drives, but whether it is possible to speak of tendencies in the direction of entropy *where psychic structures are in existence.*[21] Such tendencies could be in operation in cases where the structure, at some juncture in its development, becomes involved in destructive conflict, or when it rigidifies and simply runs itself down without either achieving satisfaction or structural elaboration. Thus sadism and masochism could be interpreted as conflict phenomena deriving from considerations such as the following: "During the oral stage of organization of the libido, the act of obtaining erotic mastery over an object coincides with that object's destruction . . ." (14, p. 54). Rigidification and "running down" are, of course, exemplified by the repetition compulsion. On the level of articulation these phenomena may be stated as incompatible needs or goal conflicts, and as alienation respectively. They are considered in chapter 6.

The quotations from *Faust* which preceded these remarks concerning the connections between Freudian theory and the theory of institutionalization do better justice to the conceptions of Eros and Thanatos than did Freud himself. Eros is the process of institutionalization — the process of creating freedom and life itself; a forced process set in motion by exigencies. Thanatos is not a set of destructive drives, but an abstract principle which renders things, persons, and events as "good as though they had never existed." The theories of institutionalization and of alienation can be viewed as attempts at the explanation of Eros and Thanatos in the personality and social realms.

Postludium

"Freud deserves better than followers who can only parrot his jargon. He needs a Galileo, gifted in method and language."

Livio C. Stecchini (38, p. 16)

Both the protean range of Freudian speculation, and the Promethean challenge facing the student of behavior in constructing a tenable ap-

[21] Compare Fenichel's discussion of this question (7, pp. 59–61).

proximation to anything resembling a theory of social change, do not really permit the dismissal of the subject matters of this chapter within its confines. Nonetheless, the chapter had to be written. It has been my contention that Freud was struggling semi-articulately to find formulations for a general theory of behavior. If the reformulations at which I have here hinted fail to achieve greater clarity in the establishment of such a theory, they will have failed in the most excellent company.

One thing is beyond dispute — the demands that a Freudian type of sociological theory could satisfy are widely felt and stated. To provide one example, Gouldner refers to the possibility of establishing a ". . . 'Theory of Organization' *methodologically* modeled. . . . along psychoanalytic lines" (21, p. 662).[22] Gouldner is suggesting in this passage that the phenomenon of succession in organizations is analogous to a "diagnostic concept" with a highly visible symptomatology. Whether we agree with this metaphor or not (and I find it a highly questionable one), it is rather strange that the exploration of methodological and theoretical analogues of sociological and psychoanalytic theory has not been seriously taken up in the literature. This is all the more strange since the problems of the articulation of personality and social systems have occasioned a vast amount of research and theoretical speculation in several disciplines in recent years. Typically, this kind of work has looked for bridge concepts, such as *role* for example, rather than for fundamental isomorphisms of theoretical structure. Whatever else its merits or failures may be, the theory of institutionalization sharply emphasizes such structural isomorphisms.

The philosophical implications of the theory of institutionalization are also more akin to those of Freudian theory than they are to the "metaphysical pathos" of other sociological orientations, particularly structural functionalism. It is entirely open to question whether such implications should be drawn and developed by proponents of the theory. Such philosophical biases and assumptions, I believe, are better left to be "unmasked" by critics. And as for those who would wish to espouse "exigentialism" as a philosophy of life — to them one can only quote Freud: "I am not at all partial to the fabrication of *Weltanschauungen*" (18, p. 96). Certainly, the theory of institutionalization is not intended as a Baedeker to guide any person's journey through life; if it has any validity, this will be established by its heuristic value as a set of sensitizing concepts and orientations and as a seedbed for testable hypotheses.

It need hardly be repeated that the foregoing exploration into Freudian metapsychology and its connection with a developing theory of institutionalization and alienation falls far short of constituting anything like a definitive and complete account of Freud's reasoning and its "vicissitudes." Still less can the foregoing discussion lay claim to constituting an

---

[22] The passage omitted in this quotation is ". . . as Parsons and Selznick have suggested. . . ." There is no reference to published sources of this suggestion.

adequate presentation of a general theory of personal and social change, even by the merest implication. Yet the problems and perspectives that have been faced and (perhaps equally importantly) winked at, are too exciting and too imperious to be suppressed. May this first faltering effort, pulled together though it may be from stolen odds and ends, set the direction for further exertions.

BIBLIOGRAPHY

1. Bakan, David. *Sigmund Freud and the Jewish Mystical Tradition.* Princeton, N.J.: Van Nostrand, 1958.

2. Bernfeld, S., and S. Feitelberg. "Der Entropiesatz und der Todestrieb," in *Imago*, Vol. 17, No. 2 (1930), pp. 137–206.

3. Bertalanffy, Ludwig von. *Problems of Life.* New York: John Wiley & Sons, 1952.

4. Boehm-Bawerk, Eugen von. *The Positive Theory of Capital,* translated by William Smart. New York: G. E. Stechert, 1891?

5. Bronfenbrenner, Urie. "Freudian Theories of Identification and Their Derivatives," in *Child Development*, Vol. 31, No. 1 (March 1960), pp. 15–40.

6. Fairbairn, William R. D. *An Object Relations Theory of the Personality.* New York: Basic Books, 1952.

7. Fenichel, Otto. *The Psychoanalytic Theory of Neurosis.* New York: W. W. Norton, 1945.

8. Freud, Anna. *The Ego and the Mechanisms of Defense,* translated by Cecil Baines. New York: International Universities Press, 1946.

9. Freud, Sigmund. "The Uncanny," in *Collected Papers.* London: Hogarth Press, 1925, Vol. 4.

10. Freud, Sigmund. *New Introductory Lectures in Psychoanalysis.* New York: W. W. Norton, 1933.

11. Freud, Sigmund. *The Future of an Illusion.* New York: Liveright, 1953.

12. Freud, Sigmund. "The Interpretation of Dreams," in the Standard Edition of *The Complete Works of Sigmund Freud,* translated and edited by James Strachey. London: Hogarth Press, 1953, Vols. 4 and 5.

13. Freud, Sigmund. "Three Essays on the Theory of Sexuality," in *Complete Works.* London: Hogarth Press, 1953, Vol. 7.

14. Freud, Sigmund. "Beyond the Pleasure Principle," in *Complete Works.* London: Hogarth Press, 1955, Vol. 17.

15. Freud, Sigmund. "Group Psychology and the Analysis of the Ego," in *Complete Works.* London: Hogarth Press, 1955, Vol. 17.

16. Freud, Sigmund. "Studies on Hysteria by Josef Breuer and Sigmund Freud," in *Complete Works.* London: Hogarth Press, 1955, Vol. 2.

17. Freud, Sigmund. "Mourning and Melancholia," in *Complete Works*. London: Hogarth Press, 1957, Vol. 14.

18. Freud, Sigmund. "Inhibitions, Symptoms, and Anxiety," in *Complete Works*. London: Hogarth Press, 1959, Vol. 20.

19. Freud, Sigmund. "The Ego and the Id," in *Complete Works*. London: Hogarth Press, 1961, Vol. 19.

20. Freud, Sigmund. "The Economic Problems of Masochism," in *Complete Works*. London: Hogarth Press, 1961, Vol. 19.

21. Gouldner, Alvin W. Theoretical Addendum to "The Problem of Succession and Bureaucracy," in Alvin W. Gouldner (ed.), *Studies in Leadership*. New York: Harper and Bros., 1950.

22. Hartmann, Heinz. "On Rational and Irrational Action," in Geza Roheim (ed.), *Psychoanalysis and the Social Sciences*, An Annual. New York: International Universities Press, 1947, pp. 359–392.

23. Hartmann, Heinz. *Ego Psychology and the Problem of Adaptation*. New York: International Universities Press, 1958.

24. Klein, Melanie. *New Directions in Psychoanalysis*. New York: Basic Books, 1955.

25. Knight, Frank H. *Risk, Uncertainty, and Profit*. Boston: Houghton Mifflin, 1921.

26. Lynd, Helen Merrell. *On Shame and the Search for Identity*. New York: Harcourt, Brace, 1958.

27. Marcuse, Herbert. *Eros and Civilization*. Boston: Beacon Press, 1955.

28. Oppenheim, P., and H. Putnam. "Unity of Science as a Working Hypothesis," in H. Feigl, M. Scriven, and G. Maxwell (eds.), *Minnesota Studies in the Philosophy of Science*, 3 vols. Minneapolis: University of Minnesota Press, 1958, Vol. 2.

29. Popper, Karl. *The Logic of Scientific Discovery*. London: Hutchinson, 1959.

30. Rapaport, David. *The Organization and Pathology of Thought, Translations and Commentary on Selected Sources*. New York: Columbia University Press, 1951.

31. Rapaport, David. "The Structure of Psychoanalytic Theory: A Systematizing Attempt," in Sigmund Koch, *Psychology: A Study of a Science*, 3 vols. New York: McGraw-Hill Book Co., 1959, Vol. 3.

32. Roberts, Henry C. *The Complete Prophecies of Nostradamus*, translated and edited by Henry C. Roberts. New York: Nostradamus, 1949.

33. Schachtel, Ernest. "The Development of Focal Attention and the Emergence of Reality," in *Psychiatry*, Vol. 17, No. 4 (November 1954), pp. 309–324.

34. Schilder, Paul. *Goals and Desires of Man: A Psychological Survey of Life*. New York: Columbia University Press, 1942.

35. Schroedinger, Erwin. *What is Life?* New York: The Macmillan Co., 1945.

36. Scriven, Michael. "A Study of Radical Behaviorism," in H. Feigl, M.

Scriven and G. Maxwell (eds.), *Minnesota Studies in the Philosophy of Science,* 3 vols. Minneapolis: University of Minnesota Press, 1956, Vol. 1.

37. Skinner, B. F. "Critique of Psychoanalytic Concepts and Theories," in H. Feigl, M. Scriven, and G. Maxwell (eds.), *Minnesota Studies in the Philosophy of Science,* 3 vols. Minneapolis: University of Minnesota Press, 1956, Vol. 1.

38. Stecchini, Livio C. "On Scientific Language," in *American Behavioral Scientist,* Vol. 5, No. 1 (September 1961), pp. 14–16.

39. Stoodley, Bartlett H. *The Concepts of Sigmund Freud.* Glencoe, Ill.: The Free Press, 1959.

40. Zollschan, George K. Review of David Bakan, "Sigmund Freud and the Jewish Mystical Tradition," in *Sociological Quarterly,* Vol. 1, No. 4 (October 1960), pp. 253–255.

Ronald M. Andersen

and Robert L. Eichhorn

Appendix

Application of a Theory of

Social Change to Heart Disease

and Its Consequences

Data from the Purdue Farm Cardiac Project provide an opportunity to apply Zollschan's scheme for the analysis of social change to empirical findings.[1] Since the data were not gathered in terms of Zollschan's categories, actual testing of hypotheses derived from the scheme is not possible. However, we can look at the process whereby an "exigency" has resulted in a behavioral change. Various aspects of the change situation can also be examined and categorized in terms of "articulation," "action," and their components as defined in the theoretical frame of reference. This exercise indicates how the scheme might be used to explain an actual process of change and hints of its potential for developing hypotheses in other situations.

The exigency considered is heart disease. The potential change

[1] The data used in this paper were collected as part of the Purdue Farm Cardiac Project co-sponsored by Purdue University, Indiana Heart Association, American Heart Association, Indiana State Board of Health, and the National Heart Institute. For a more complete description of the project see Morris (2). The authors are indebted to G. J. Kallas, W. H. M. Morris, and D. C. Riedel for their assistance in either the collection, analysis, or presentation of these data.

triggered by heart disease is in work behavior. A group of Indiana farmers, some diagnosed as having arteriosclerotic heart disease (ASHD) and others considered normal, make up the sample used.[2] More specifically, the farmers are divided into three groups after being medically examined in two time periods:

1) Old Cardiacs: 67 cases diagnosed as having ASHD in both 1956 and 1960.
2) New Cardiacs: 52 cases diagnosed as having ASHD in 1960 only.[3]
3) Normals: 107 cases diagnosed as having no form of heart disease or high blood pressure in 1956 or 1960.[4]

Work behavior, in terms of hours spent working each day and acres farmed, is measured for each of these groups. This overall design allows us to consider two effects: (1) the tendency which the exigency (heart disease) creates for a farmer to change his work behavior over a period of time (determined by comparing cardiacs and normals with respect to changes in work); and (2) the differences in change in work caused by the onset of the exigency for different periods of time (determined by comparing old cardiacs with new cardiacs). Using Zollschan's model, we attempted to show some ways in which heart disease articulated the problem and motivated men to action.

Assuming the exigency is present, the other components of the model are outlined below. Each of these components of articulation and action will be operationalized in terms of the problem described above. The relevancy of each component will be shown by differences found to exist between cardiacs and non-cardiacs.

TABLE 1. *Phases of Articulation — Activation and Their Coordinates*

Coordinates	Requisites of Articulation	Requisites of Action
Deprivation		
Equilibrium	(1) Salience	(4) Valence
Knowledge	(2) Specification	(5) Application
Ideology	(3) Justification	(6) Legitimation

1. *Salience:* One measure of the saliency of a problem is the extent to which an individual realizes that it exists. Diseases, especially such in-

[2] Arteriosclerotic heart disease (ASHD) was the most prevalent type among farmers of the sample and the most debilitating. See Chapter 22 for a more complete description of the Purdue Farm Cardiac Project sample as a whole.

[3] The number of new cardiacs, diagnosed as ASHD's in 1960, is larger than could be expected to develop during a four-year period in a sample of this sort. Some of the new cardiacs are genuine. Others, judged normal in 1956 but ASHD in 1960, fall into this group as a result of different interpretations of the medical history and electrocardiographic results by physicians on the two occasions.

[4] In the tables the totals for each group are not always the same as the figures shown here. Each respondent did not answer every question.

capacitating ones as heart disease, become known as problems to their victims through their symptomatology. Each farmer was asked if he experienced any of five symptoms commonly associated with heart disease.[5] Those mentioning two symptoms or less were defined as having a problem of low saliency; those with more than two were considered to have a problem of high saliency.[6] Degree of saliency compared to the groups in the sample provided the results shown in Table 2.

TABLE 2. *Salience*

SALIENCE	OLD CARDIACS	NEW CARDIACS	NORMALS
Low (two symptoms or less)	37%	42%	83%
High (three symptoms or more)	63%	58%	17%
Total Per Cent	100%	100%	100%
Number of Cases	(67)	(51)	(106)

(P < .001)*
*All tests of significance in this paper were computed by Chi Square.

Cardiacs are much more likely to experience a large number of symptoms. These symptoms are often produced by the vigorous activities associated with farm work. The cardiac farmer may realize that a problem exists because of the excess of his discomforts. He may also relate his work to these discomforts in some fashion.

2. *Specification:* Specification of a problem includes knowledge about the various aspects of that problem and the fact that these aspects are related to one another. The more a farm cardiac knows about heart disease, the greater would be the expectation that he would be able to associate his health-related difficulties to heart disease — the greater would be the specification of his problem. Each member of the sample under study was asked to name as many kinds, symptoms, and treatments of heart disease as he could. From this a knowledge index was constructed. If cardiacs are found to have more knowledge about heart disease than normals, then cardiacs as a group would have means to specify their problems not available to people without heart disease. Low specification was defined to be four or fewer kinds, symptoms, and treatments named. High specification was defined as five or more.

The results, as shown in Table 3, indicate that cardiacs do have more

---

[5] These symptoms were fainting spells or dizziness, pains in the chest, shortness of breath, swelling in the ankles, and persistent headaches.

[6] It should be realized that these symptoms can be associated with ailments other than heart disease.

general knowledge about heart disease. To the extent that this helps them to specify, and in general to articulate the problem they face, we might expect behavior change to alleviate needs created by heart disease.

TABLE 3. *Specification*

SPECIFICATION	OLD CARDIACS	NEW CARDIACS	NORMALS
Low (four answers or less)	37%	47%	65%
High (five answers or more)	63%	53%	35%
Total Per Cent	100%	100%	100%
Number of Cases	(67)	(51)	(106)
		(P ≈ .001)	

3. *Justification:* According to Zollschan's theory, articulation of a problem previous to action involves not only salience and specification but also a willingness to admit a problem exists and a justification for possible subsequent action. For our sample such a justification might be represented by agreement with the statement: "There is no way to avoid heart disease — if you are going to have it, you are going to have it." A man who feels himself unable to avoid a problem, it could be argued, has every right to admit his problem, and to consider action to resolve it (in this case, modification of work). If cardiacs are looking for a justification for acknowledging their disease, a greater portion of them than normals would probably agree with the above statement.

Table 4 shows that cardiacs are, indeed, more likely to agree with a statement implicitly justifying their acknowledgment that heart disease is unavoidable — and thus, presumably justifiable. This table, as well as the two previous tables, also indicates that, in general, older cardiacs are

TABLE 4. *Justification*

JUSTIFICATION *There is no way to avoid heart disease — if you are going to have it, you are going to have it.*	OLD CARDIACS	NEW CARDIACS	NORMALS
Agree	43%	34%	16%
Disagree	57%	66%	84%
Total Per Cent	100%	100%	100%
Number of Cases	(67)	(50)	(107)
		(P < .001)	

better able to articulate their needs than are new cardiacs. For each co-ordinate of articulation, the degree of articulation for new cardiacs appears to be somewhat less than for old cardiacs, but more than for normals. These results might be attributed to two factors: (1) the exigency or need (heart disease) has existed for a longer period for old cardiacs; and (2) the older cardiacs in general have more severe cases of heart disease — the exigency is of greater intensity and thus, the motivation for articulation is greater.

4. *Valence:* Assuming that the problem of heart disease has been sufficiently articulated for cardiacs, consideration must be given to the requisites for action or the actual change in behavior itself. First among these is valence. For the sample of farmers we seek some indication that the need created by heart disease is sufficiently important to cause these men to give up something they value. Generally, these men hold their work in high regard — they tend to value it as an end in itself (1). We would expect them as a group to wish to continue working at a normal pace. If cardiacs admit that they have slowed down in their work habits lately, to a greater extent than do normals, we postulate that the exigency of heart disease forces them to admit a necessary change. Each man was asked if he had been cutting down on work recently.

TABLE 5. *Valence*

VALENCE CUTTING DOWN ON WORK	OLD CARDIACS	NEW CARDIACS	NORMALS
Yes	52%	67%	36%
No	48%	33%	64%
Total Per Cent	100%	100%	100%
Number of Cases	(60)	(52)	(107)
		(P<.001)	

That cardiacs are more likely to admit cutting down work is evident from Table 5. The fact that new cardiacs are more likely to admit cutting down than old cardiacs is probably related to old cardiacs having had longer to adjust — some of their work changes may have taken place long ago.

5. *Application:* Even though a man may understand his problem (articulation) and admit a needed change in behavior, there may still be some doubt as to whether he has the wherewithal to implement his decision. For the cardiac farmer, we have tried to show that the exigencies of heart disease point to a need to reduce work activity. The farmer's information sources (doctor, mass communication, etc.) as well as his own symptom-

atology guide him in this direction even though such a step may be opposed to his own value system and economic condition. As a measure of actual work change, consider the difference in acres farmed in 1956 and in 1960 (Table 6).

TABLE 6. *Application: Acres Farmed*

APPLICATION ACRES FARMED IN 1960	OLD CARDIACS	NEW CARDIACS	NORMALS
Decreased from 1956	54%	42%	32%
Equal to 1956	16%	25%	20%
Increased from 1956	30%	33%	48%
Total Per Cent	100%	100%	100%
Number of Cases	(67)	(52)	(107)
		(P<.05)	

Cardiacs do tend to reduce the amount of land they farm more than do normals. In order to eliminate the effect of outside help let us consider the hours the farmer himself puts in on an average harvest work day.

TABLE 7. *Application: Hours Worked*

APPLICATION HOURS OF FIELD WORK (1960)	OLD CARDIACS	NEW CARDIACS	NORMALS
Ten or less	97%	84%	64%
Eleven or more	3%	16%	36%
Total Per Cent	100%	100%	100%
Number of Cases	(61)	(51)	(105)
		(P<.001)	

Table 7 shows that cardiacs are much more likely to work a shorter day than are normal farmers. These results show that a behavioral change for the farmer with heart disease — which might be expected and better understood by looking at the other components of Zollschan's model as applied to this particular case — does in fact take place. All that remains to round out the scheme is some "legitimation" for the change which has taken place.

6. *Legitimation:* The fact that the cardiac farmer probably wished to continue to work as hard as his normal counterpart, yet was forced to ease up by heart disease, will probably lead him to adopt some attitude which would justify his change in his own eyes and in the eyes of others. If such

is the case, this should distinguish the cardiac from the normal farmer who has no need to develop such an attitude.

A person who agreed with the statement, "If you wait long enough you can get over most any illness," would seem to be advocating a status quo position in the face of illness. That is, one should continue his daily pattern of living, ignoring the consequences of the illness besetting him. Such a position might well be unacceptable to the cardiac farmer who suffered an illness which forced him to alter his daily pattern of life — he has reduced his work activity. To justify his change he might be expected to advocate necessary change in the face of illness and disagree with the statement. However, the normal farmer, not having been forced to such a change, would be more likely to agree with the statement.

TABLE 8. *Legitimation*

LEGITIMATION If you wait long enough you can get over most any illness.	OLD CARDIACS	NEW CARDIACS	NORMALS
Agree	24%	28%	32%
Disagree	76%	72%	68%
Total Per Cent	100%	100%	100%
Number of Cases	(67)	(50)	(107)
		$(P \approx .50)$	

While the relationship in Table 8 is not statistically significant, the cardiacs do show a greater tendency to disagree with the statement than do normals, as we might expect.

This chapter has been an exercise, applying Zollschan's theory of change to empirical data drawn from the Purdue Farm Cardiac Project. Since the data were not gathered to fit the model, the theory as a whole could not be put to the test. However, the ready applicability of the model to empirical data and its utility in explaining a process of change is a hopeful sign. We can expect more cogent and precise results when the model is employed in the methodological as well as the analytical stage of an empirical study.

BIBLIOGRAPHY

1. Goldstein, B., and R. L. Eichhorn. "The Changing Protestant Ethic: Rural Patterns in Health, Work, and Leisure," *American Sociological Review*, Vol. 26 (1961), pp. 557–565.
2. Morris, W. H. M. (ed.), *Proceedings of the Purdue Farm Cardiac Seminar*. Lafayette, Ind.: Purdue Agricultural Experiment Station, 1959.

SECTION THREE

Social System Models of Change

A major strength of structural-functionalism is its vue d'ensemble —
the panoramic view of social events considered so crucial by Durkheim
and, before him, by Comte who, if not the initiator of the intellectual
endeavors here represented, at least concocted their barbaric appellation.
Although this visual strategy of taking in the whole in one glance admittedly avoids the well-known pitfall of "not seeing the woods for the
trees," it is difficult to see how one can "find a way through the woods"
without having an equally acute perception of the individual trees. The
opening skirmishes of the theory of institutionalization, some of which
were presented in the previous Section, have knowingly, deliberately,
and (we hope) provocatively, eschewed such a vue d'ensemble. There,
attention is focused upon the "individual in society," stricken by exigencies and articulating goals. Social structure is seen as a product of
the interaction of such persons seeking their goals, and also as a system
(or, perhaps, a congeries) of loci of exposure of persons to different exigencies.

Such an approach — Kingsley Davis' claims that functionalism and
sociology are equivalent notwithstanding — is truly sociological without
being either functionalist or reductionist in character. It has some similarities, to be sure, with the so-called micro-reductionism of contemporary
molecular biology (that is, if one allows a somewhat generous analogy
between real organisms and merely conceptual "social systems"), but it
certainly is not reductionism in Davis' sense of reducing the level of
sociological analysis to what he understands to be a "psychological" one.
It may be viewed as reductionist in the special sense of reducing both
"functional sociology" and "functional psychology," in his terminology,
to something akin to what we may call the "rationale of the situational
field." These "democratically imperialistic" claims of functionalism are
strongly reminiscent of a Viennese working-class jingle of the pre-Hitler
era (too simple to translate) which goes: "Ich bin kein Jud, ich bin kein
Christ, ich bin ein Kommunist." Of course, one adds to this the further
benevolent injunction — "and so are you." The resulting "universalistic"
professions have the potential of becoming rather dangerous. Another
Viennese working-class jingle springs to mind, which replaced the aforementioned one after the advent of Hitler: "Willst du nicht mein Bruder

209

sein, dann schlag ich dir den Schaedel ein," ("If you don't want to be my brother, I'll smash your skull.") .Over-exuberant members of the functionalist school (and a special school it was, is, and remains) should take this warning to heart, as indication of what can happen to people who do not distinguish between fish, flesh, and fowl.

Certainly Boskoff's brand of structural-functionalism is far from over-exuberant. Indeed, serious concern with problems of social change appears to bring out the best in members of the structural-functional persuasion (for reasons which are not at all mysterious, at least to their critics). The trouble appears to be that so few of them have allowed themselves concerns of similar gravity. At the risk of indulging in some editorial over-exuberance of our own, we pronounce Boskoff's learned and deeply concerned contribution surely one of the clearest, best, and (not least important) most concise statements of the structural-functional position ever published. After erecting the customary scaffolding of functions, levels, and mechanisms, he adds a time dimension, reducing this to "sources of," "filtering or control of," and "reverberation to" innovative values and behavior. But only then does he take his really major step, and effectively use the ingredients of his system for the systematic production of hypotheses that, in principle at least, have the potential of being put to test. This move, in his own words, "from the comfortable level of formulation to the exciting but often disquieting level of demonstration" is cause for congratulation. There are two questions to be asked about Boskoff's ambitious program for research. First, is the structural-functional scaffolding particularly crucial for any of the hypotheses put forward; could they not have been equally well constructed by a conflict theorist, or a formalist, or a social behaviorist, or what have you? Second (and independent of the first question), does his scaffolding lead to the production of more and "better" (that is, more readily testable) hypotheses? Boskoff, we know, will be the first to agree that these two independent questions provide the surest touchstones for future judgment of his ambitious exploratory formulation.

David Lockwood, one of the earliest and boldest critics of structural-functional theory, with a swift and sure grasp comes, inter alia, *to the conclusion that dialectical materialism is merely one variant of "functional" theory! But Professor Davis should mix his triumph with caution; Lockwood claims dialectical materialism forms a part of a very special and purified kind of functional theory. He sets his course with a distinction between two elements of functional theory: normative integration, and what he calls system integration. The first, which he suggests has drawn the fire of some of the critics of functionalism, emphasizes "common value elements" and insists that the "study of social stability must precede the study of social change." This variant of functionalism Lockwood rejects. The second contains the potentiality of "strain, tension, or contradiction"; it consists of the compatibility or incompatibility "between the dominant institutional order of a social system and its material base." Well — all this may be functionalism, but it "sure ain't" what Professor Davis means by it. Lockwood takes Marx's theory as his first illustration of this highly original sort of functionalism and attempts to show that it constitutes a special case of system mal-integration (the "production crisis" of capitalism.) He then proceeds to compare this with the "taxation crisis" of patrimonial bureaucracies and what we may call the "embourgeoisement crisis" of the communist state. Translate his somewhat volatile "material base" into a "substratum of exigencies," and you get something very similar to the theory of institu-tionalization. Zollschan readily acknowledges Lockwood's paternity: whether Lockwood wishes to do the same is for him to decide.*

Kirk's chapter, by contrast, provides a very explicit link between functional theory and something very much like the theory of institu-tionalization. Starting with a concept he calls situational discrepancy *(very much akin to the* exigencies *of the last Section), Kirk moves on to another concept,* role handicap *(interferences with role performance) which he links with the foregoing. He then examines typical means of (attempted) adaptation and asks to what extent, if at all, these means serve the desired end. The various phases of this model are illustrated with references to the relocation of Japanese-Americans during World War II, and the case of families with adopted children. His conclusions are applied to yet another case, that of the family with a retarded child. Although the emphasis of this chapter is primarily upon application, it has been included in this Section both because of the intrinsic theoretical interest of the model employed, and because of the model's potential for bridging some of the gaps between the foregoing chapters in this Section and those contained in the previous Section of the volume.*

In the Elysian Fields of Pythagorean number mysticism there must surely be an enclave reserved for the followers of Professor Markov. This is a very important area for behavioral scientists, for it is one of the few in those heavens populated by members of their own kind. From among their number, Beshers, superbly indifferent to the rival claims of functionalism and alternative theoretical formulations, makes his pro-nouncements in these pages. His remarks defining what he means by social change contain the statement that an effective causal analysis must be able to predict "no change" following the same laws with which we predict "change." Hence the mechanism governing both social change and social stability operates something like a "balance of forces." All our authors would appear to be in agreement with these statements. Holding out the prospect of future mathematical conquests in such realms as the transmogrification of the "protestant ethic" into capitalist production and exchange, Beshers confines himself to a somewhat simpler problem, namely, that of inter-generational social mobility. Although (like all mathematical writings) slow reading, the chapter is a model of lu-cidity and simplicity, and implications for more ambitious kinds of for-malized problems of social change are clearly and temptingly spelled out.

8

Alvin Boskoff

Functional Analysis as a Source

of a Theoretical Repertory and

Research Tasks in the Study

of Social Change

Among sociologists and other social scientists, there is considerable disquietude about the prevailing inadequacies in analyzing and explaining social change (10; 48; 61, chapter 7; 45, pp. 810–818; 40, chapter 1). The problem of change, both in its theoretical and practical forms, has achieved an urgency for which scholars and administrators have been largely unprepared, except on an intuitive basis. Consequently, in recent years a variety of social scientists have re-focused their efforts on devising appropriate concepts, hypotheses, and related methods of gathering and analyzing crucial data concerning social change as a problem in its own right (74, pp. 18–33; 64; 18; 37; 77; 45; 69).

While it is perhaps too early to evaluate the results of this revivified concern, it may be in order to indicate briefly what seem to be the most disturbing shortcomings in theories of social change in the recent past. In fact, since this paper reflects another attempt to contribute to a theoretical renaissance, perhaps this summary critique can also provide an implicit set of standards for evaluating the discussion to follow. I believe five related points can be made:

213

1) Theories of social change have traditionally been too grandiose, too general, and therefore too simplified in their attention to the complex variables of social behavior. In trying to explain all social changes in all known societies for all historical periods, theorists have inevitably set forth over-extended and mutually competitive principles of change. Some well-known items would include: diffusion theory; imitation; invention; increasing heterogeneity; evolutionary stages; challenge and response; class conflicts; and inner or immanent tendencies (35, chapters 10, 14; 70; 71, chapter 5; 66). In reaction to such theories, some theorists have transferred their efforts to more restricted empirical levels, such as population change, marriage and family dynamics, social aspects of change in industrial systems, religious organization, and racial and ethnic relations. But often — and understandably — these specialized areas contain important substantive problems that deflect attention from social change per se.

2) Ever since Comte made the analytical distinction between social statics and social dynamics, sociologists have tended to erect a thick and impenetrable wall between analyses of structure and change. In practice, this meant either (a) ignoring one problem for the other, or (b) postponing analyses of change until problems of social organization (socialization, differentiation, stratification, power, and so on) could be defined and properly studied (10, pp. 260–262). Indeed, the textbooks in introductory sociology (even such outstanding ones as Kingsley Davis' *Human Society* or Bennett and Tumin's *Social Life*) generally treat social change as an uncomfortable appendage. As a result, change seems to be epiphenomenal — an accident, intrusion, or catastrophe — and sometimes a mystery (as "the little man upon the stair").

Furthermore, the controversially prominent structural-functional approach in its early development also seemed to emphasize structural problems. Its critics have rashly concluded that such an approach is therefore inherently incapable of analyzing change without horrendous damage to its conceptual structure (48; 61; 20; 34). But I shall later seek to show that the analysis of social change is not only feasible but theoretically and empirically enhanced by a modified structural-functional framework — a sociological equivalent of retaining the engine but shifting into higher gear.

3) A related difficulty of theories of social change is the failure to develop a distinctive (but not isolated) conceptual kit. On the one hand, change is not clearly defined in relation to such kindred concepts as social process, development, cycle, evolution, and adaptation, though MacIver, Znaniecki, and others have provided quite workable distinctions (36, pp. 405–415; 78, pp. 326–328; 10, p. 266). An equally gnawing problem has been an absence of general or specific concepts appropriate to change itself. Until recently, sociologists seemed to work primarily with *synonyms* — "dynamics," "variation," "alteration," "deviation" —

adding little to the *analysis* of change. Now we are beginning to exchange synonyms for such analytically promising concepts as "dynamic assessment" or "definition of the situation," "innovation," "transitional periods," "radical opposition," and "types of deviant behavior" (37; 3; 11). However, a minimal set of concepts for describing social change seems to await a systematic analysis of change, which is a major tenet of this chapter.

4) In view of the preceding criticism, it is not surprising that much confusion exists concerning the proper units of analysis. What should be the focus of study, observation, and measurement? The theoretical literature is all-encompassing; it includes personality types, social relationships, technology, value systems, institutionalized activities, control systems, stratification systems, communities, and politically or culturally organized societies. But what is (or are) the *crucial* unit(s) of analysis, as derived from theory and/or experience?

5) The last difficulty to be considered at this point is slowly receding: the traditional (and sometimes unconscious) concern with examining the *direction* or *trend* in social change, rather than a search for the "mechanics" or basic processes and conditions of change. Certainly, it is desirable to search for evidence of increasing rationality, variations in types of solidarity, processes of secularization, or alternations of Ideational, Idealistic, and Sensate supersystems. But the *conditions* of such changes have often been considered either in an a priori manner or as theoretical afterthoughts of a vague and non-empirical nature. As a result, change has tended to assume an inevitable, irreversible cast that precludes analysis of periods of little significant change or of successful resistance to change.

Fundamental Problems in Analysis of Social Change

On the basis of the preceding discussion, and given the evolving nature of sociology and related disciplines, the fruitful study of social change appears to require attention to several basic problems. This is not a matter of demonstration, but rather one of probable utility — to be tested and revised through application and further discussion.

1) Analysis of social change is probably inseparable from prior identification of *analytically separable social systems* (54, pp. 3–5, pp. 68–81; 78, pp. 12–13; 79, p. 164; 13, pp. 95–98), preferably communities and national or "cultural" societies. The study of "dynamics" in *specific organizations* (e.g., an industrial firm or a government agency) or in *isolated institutional areas* (e.g., religion, family and kinship, art, education) is almost bound to ignore the operation of some important interrelations with influential groups. Thus, changes in family structure require close attention to the operation of the local status structure, the economic system, the politico-legal system, and perhaps educational and medical trends.

"System" is a concept easily misunderstood or taken with humorless literality. For most sociological purposes, a "system" may be simply conceived as an analytically isolated set of interrelated variables whose "identity" is sufficiently clear to permit a base point from which to study the operation of any implicated variable (6, pp. 125–134; 7, pp. 58–75; 32). Social systems, therefore, refer to socially relevant sets of behavioral variables that can be identified with concrete, relatively continuous interaction networks (groups, communities, societies). Note that living systems are inherently "dynamic" rather than marked by "true" or "stable" equilibrium, since "perfect" equilibrium is incompatible with action, reaction, or work (6, p. 132). Furthermore, it is neither logically nor empirically necessary to exclude or ignore from the concept of system such phenomena as tension, strain, and conflict — or even the presence of semi-autonomous units (53, chapters 12–14; 54, chapter 7; 26, pp. 241–270). But the notion of a "system" does involve the crucial assumption that the operation of these system-challenging phenomena does not interfere with the identifiability of the system over some time interval.

2) Once social change is identified with social systems, the distinctive nature of social change can be clarified — as compared with such concepts as "process," "development," and so on. Whereas "process," "development," and "cycle" deal with predictable variations in the operation of social systems (that is, in terms of the strength of the variables and their demonstrable interactive effects), based on study of *previous* phases of their operation, social change may be defined as significant variations from processual and developmental patterns (37, p. 27, pp. 63–65, p. 176; pp. 326–327; 79, p. 164; 10, pp. 263–266).

For example, a given community may experience growth in population, area, and number of organizations as a consequence of a healthy economic base. With increasing prosperity, congestion develops and the social and economic elites relocate themselves beyond the municipal boundaries. One result may be a diminution of local leadership, expressed in inadequate attention to recurring civic problems. This in turn may be followed by withdrawal of some firms to more "progressive" communities and thus an eventual population decline. While this is a somewhat fictitious illustration, it should be clear that the hypothesized "variations" are (1) highly significant for the entire system, and (2) not easily foreseeable or extrapolable from earlier processes or trends.

3) A third problem to which a theory of social change must give serious attention derives from the nature of change as significant but "unpredictable" variations in social systems. As MacIver and Znaniecki (among others) have persuasively argued, these interruptions in established patterns of social systems require a type of explanation different from that used for the genesis and development of social systems. Such an explanation must deal with social *causation,* that is, those processes that account for the *production* of significant variations and also for the *application*

or *containment* of such variations (37, pp. 63–65, p. 123, p. 176; 79, p. 164, pp. 224–231). Earlier theories of social change had either approached causation from a non-social standpoint (geography, race, destiny, divine will) or had prematurely fixed upon single social or psychological variables (for example, imitation, diffusion, "the great man," technological development [65, chapters 1, 2–7, 10, 11]). A more fruitful approach might redefine the problems of causation as marked by an interdependent series of decision-making processes in component social units of social systems. In this way, causation need not be the stepchild of assertion and vague generalization, but a product of statements faithful to fact about conscious and unconscious, direct and indirect, evaluative actions of identifiable persons, role-clusters, and organizations.

4) [Although the two are undeniably interrelated, it is particularly important to distinguish between social change and cultural change] (10, pp. 263–264; 74, p. 27; 79, p. 336, pp. 396–398; 23, p. 6; 75). A basic reason for this distinction is that the nature of these interrelations may and does vary and thus presents problems in causal analysis. [If we define the cultural aspect as involving values and techniques approved for human adaptation to the socio-physical environment, and the social aspect as comprising the patterns of association and reciprocal influences connected with group formation, persistence, and change, then the complex interdependence-independence of social and cultural dimensions can be explored.]

It can be generally accepted that, for a given population, associational patterns and value systems rarely develop at comparable rates or with great logical consistency. Instead of analyzing these differential rates in terms of cultural or social *lag*, perhaps it makes more sense to point to the flexibility of these dimensions. In research terms, both the social and the cultural can operate with respect to each other either as independent or dependent variables. For example, we know that persons in regular association generate "new" values or standards (for instance, work groups and informal quotas, scientific groups and "new" hypotheses). On the other hand, the application of a strongly held set of values can produce important alterations in pre-existing social relationships (for example, the abolition of slavery or the development of representative government). However, it is also evident that social and cultural variables *fail* to achieve significant effects in the other sphere. Reform movements (segmentally organized expressions of value systems) often eventuate in little or no genuine changes in the organization and operation of governmental, educational, and economic groups. And, as industrial sociologists have shown, organizational change may not be followed by desired valuational shifts among group members.

The import of this variety of interrelationships seems reasonably clear: it is unwise to treat social and cultural variables interchangeably or as consistently interdependent. Instead, we must view these dimensions and their operation as an important aspect of the causal analyses of social change, seeking types of variables that help to distinguish the emergence of each of the above-mentioned interconnections between social and cultural variables. Theories of social change will thus be enabled to unite hypotheses, inference, research techniques, and data with greater fidelity to the complexities of the phenomena of change.]

A Structural-Functional Orientation to Social Change

At the present stage of development in the social sciences, the most promising avenue to a comprehensive and workable theory of social change appears to be a suitably modified structural-functional approach (45; 15; 64). The prevailing opinion to the contrary stems, I believe, from a fixation on one or two characteristics of earlier formulations of this approach — characteristics that do not seem basic or inherent in modern structural-functionalism. The remainder of this chapter will therefore be devoted to: (1) a summary of fundamental postulates that define the nature of structural-functionalism; (2) a conceptual framework which provides an initial orientation toward social change; and (3) a set of researchable hypotheses derived from this framework.

General Orientation

Since statements about structural-functionalism vary with each proponent and critic, a definitive formulation that cites chapter and verse is not possible. The interpretation that follows tries to avoid both the earlier exuberance of its champions and the tangential inadequacies pointed out by its critics. Consequently, my interpretation must in fairness be labeled a *modified structural-functionalism,* which can be sketched in a series of postulates.

1) The first requisite is the notion of conceptually closed systems of variables. Simply stated, this involves two further assumptions drawn from experience and pre-existing theory. First, it is assumed that the most crucial variables can be separated for analysis from the total complex of variables presumed to be relevant to some problem. The crucial variables are taken to represent aspects of *association* among persons — not biological traits, personality characteristics, or most categories of cultural patterns. Second, it is assumed that the crucial variables are sufficiently interrelated with one another to permit the analyst to construct an identifiable and meaningful entity (76, pp. 90–100; 4, chapter 5; 68, chapter 26).

2) Once identified in this manner, the system is presumed to operate in time and space through the working of its component variables. However, these variables over time are conceptualized in terms of patterned clusters or differentiated substructures, whose interdependent operation

is fundamental to the continued viability of the system. Furthermore, and this is a disputed point, the component structures of a system comprise a starting-point both for analysis of relative stability *and* change.

3) These substructures are conceived as specialized (but not necessarily rational or perfect) "solutions" to a repertory of "needs" of the system (31, chapter 4; 1). But it is misleading to refer to "needs" of a system; and it is equally unprofitable to speak of "needs" of individual members without a reductionism that logically precludes the concept of a social system. Instead, I would suggest that these needs have reference to problems of *relating* the performance of individuals to the interactive social networks (groups) in which they must act. It follows that the system is marked by an empirically definable range of adjustments of individuals to social networks, and vice versa. The relative importance of these types of adjustment is a painfully moot question in the annals of social theory.

4) The functional relations postulated as basic to social systems may be defined as (a) the demonstrable effects of one substructure on the operation of one or more other substructures in the same system, or the simple co-variation of two or more "parts" — for example, a change in the allocation of library space in a university and a consequent alteration in the availability of reserve readings for some courses, but with little or no noticeable effect on the university as a social system, and (b) the effect of any combination of substructures on the operation of the system as a whole, particularly with respect to other systems. Plainly, two methodological consequences should be pursued. First, to remove functional analysis from the realm of intuitive judgments, a *causal framework* (14, p. 173; 28; 47) and the investigation of *alternative causal sequences* in system variables and structures seems not only desirable but imperative. Second, the latter type of functional analysis provides a logical and practical justification for a structural-functional analysis of change.

5) Change *in* a system (process, development, differentiation) is equivalent to the first type of functional analysis. But change *of* a system (Type 2) — or social change — is likewise an integral part of the conceptual-theoretical kit of structural-functionalism.

6) The analysis of change (change of systems) follows an explicit bias that is consistent with previous postulates, but may be modified without destroying the fundamental thrust of this orientation. In general, the analyst first seeks for sources and precipitants of eventual change *within* the system (67, chapters 43–46; 54, pp. 201–207). Contrary to recent criticisms, this requires a *diachronic* or *historical* approach to systems, in order to locate (a) temporal points at which substructures may be shown to reflect altered operation or "new" (unpredictable) effects on other substructures, and (b) the *emergence of conditions* that help account for such shifts in operation and/or consequences. Since systems are

conceptually or analytically "closed," "external" variables often must be investigated. However, the analyst must demonstrate the significance of these external variables by investigating their effects upon specific substructures and upon the larger system.

The conceptual ingredients for a structural-functional analysis of social change have been available in various forms for more than a generation; they are basically simple and familiar, requiring no esoteric language or tortuous exposition, as some critics assert.

First, the operation of social systems is conceived as comprising four fundamental and interrelated processes (or system needs and functional problems). These processes can be investigated at the system level and also with reference to component structures or subsystems (55, chapter 4; 56, pp. 13–15). These are:

1) *The Adaptive Function.* The adaptive or instrumental function, through appropriate roles, serves to create and apply technical means through which aspects of the environment (physical and social) can be converted into objects and mechanisms suitable for the satisfaction of goals identified with systems or substructures. Adaptive structures therefore tend to exhibit a high degree of rationality, since judgments of efficiency and effectiveness can be quantitatively made and compared. Economic sectors of societies are largely adaptive, as are the breadwinner role in the family system, the purchasing office of universities, fund-raising committees of churches, and so on.

2) *The Goal-Attainment Function.* Each system (and in varying degrees, each subsystem) possesses a set of declared or implicit objectives which its representatives seek to achieve. These goals may be realizable or illusory; they may be variably beneficial or harmful to the system or to significant components of the system; and the source of these goals may range from rational discussion to charismatic imposition. In any case, the creation and pursuit of this function are major attributes of *political phenomena* in every compartment of human association.

Essentially, *political* aspects of behavior may be identified in those activities which organize or manipulate the behavior of others in order to realize some objectives for a social system. Thus, we may recognize "politics" not only in the maneuverings of public officials, but also in the choice of a desirable family vacation, in the revision of a college curriculum, and in price-fixing among competitive firms. Goal-attainment in each case is inherently "political" because the differential interests and values of the participants are *temporarily aligned* by the mechanisms of *power* (or infallible persuasion) to produce an artificial consensus reflected in behavior directed toward a common goal. In terms of this approach, all political phenomena represent the goal-attainment function. But not all goal-attainment is necessarily political, since a prior consensus (whatever its source) does not require the use of power as a leveler of difference or a dissipator of resistance.

3) *Tension-Management and Pattern-Maintenance.* The preceding two functions deal principally with the system's relation to its environment. "Internal" relations are of course interdependent with "external" relations, but the former may be analytically distinguished from the total operation of social systems with some profit. One extremely important "problem" in this regard is that of proper *motivation* of members to perform roles predictably. This is not merely a matter of learning role specifications; in addition, (a) members must often perform without immediate prospect of reward (that is, gratification must be deferred), and (b) members must retain in *latent* form appropriate attitudes and skills in the intervals between performances. The problem of deferred gratification, which has been called "tension-management," is normally handled by such mechanisms as discipline, graded and predictable sets of rewards (promotion, seniority, career patterns), formal education, and approved forms of tension reduction (sports, recreation, out-group aggression, and so on). The closely related problem of pattern-maintenance has been resolved in varying degrees by rehearsals and practice sessions, interim or "brush-up" training, pep talks, and other organized forms of exhortation.

4) *Integration.* The problem of integration is essentially one of maintaining the identity of a system and the attraction of its over-arching goals, which might otherwise be threatened by the necessary pursuit of adaptive, tension-management, and goal-attainment functions. In short, successful internal specialization may create narrowed and contradictory allegiances. Integrative processes serve to demonstrate or assert the common underlying interests and values of the members in component structures, as well as their collective difference from other systems. Some examples are the broad appeals of certain charismatic leaders, ceremonial occasions (in every cultural sector), and the use of "central" organizations with representation from constituent groups in a community.

A Structural-Functional Hierarchy of Organizational Levels

We may now turn to a conceptual scheme that defines characteristic substructures for the operation of social systems, as formulated in recent years by Parsons (57, chapter 2). Essentially, Parsons has developed a functionally relevant typology of levels of group organization *within* societies. Each level of organization possesses: (a) a distinctive subsystem of social relationships; (b) some effective radius of responsibility; and (c) a special concern for one (or two) functional problems.

1) *The Primary-Technical Level.* The most basic operational unit is a relatively small group with clearly defined, rather narrow objectives. These objectives normally involve effective adaptation of persons and the physical environment to one another in order to make some predictable contribution to other units and thus to the larger system. In general,

these technical units are dependent on other units for equipment, standards of operation, and controls. Some illustrations are shop or factory crews, primary-school classes, nuclear family units (particularly during child-rearing periods), professional sports teams, symphony orchestras, and actors' companies.

2) *The Managerial Level.* To mediate and control the operations of several specialized but interdependent technical units, a managerial system normally develops. Essentially, managerial roles take as given some set of goals or policies, which guides processes of supervising technical units. Groups with managerial responsibilities therefore are extremely goal-oriented, but serve to achieve significant goals (for example, profit, educated persons, national aggression) by (a) providing tension-management and pattern-maintenance "services" to subordinate technical units, and (b) sustaining a "low-level" routine integration among such units. A bureaucratic system, which we can find in governmental, economic, religious, educational, and recreational spheres, is in these terms an ascending series of managerial units.

3) *The Institutional Level.* The operations of managerial units require support and legitimation in the form of: (a) goal specification; (b) development of some hierarchy or priority of goals; (c) "lending" superior prestige and authority to strengthen managerial decisions when challenged. This "policy-making" role complex is the property of the *institutional level* of organization, which is reflected in such concrete groups as boards of trustees, appellate or superior court systems, professional licensing organizations, independent regulatory commissions, and monocratic political systems. Normally, institutional groups coordinate managerial units within a *single* sector of cultural activities. As far as the four functional problems are concerned, however, institutional groups seem to focus on "internal" issues. A predominant concern is apparently with *integration* on the philosophical-abstract level (leaving its translation into profane operations to managerial units), with secondary emphasis on educational and honorific activities (pattern-maintenance).

4) *The Societal Level.* The most inclusive and complex organizational level is the societal, which provides coordination among specialized units at the institutional level as the latter provide coordination among managerial units. Conceptually, the societal level should be independent of specific institutional units, representing an inter-institutional core of values. In practice, however, societies have always witnessed the ascendancy of one of three types of institutional groups — governmental, economic, or religious — to the societal level. At the same time it should be noted that the assumption of full responsibility on the societal level is immeasurably difficult, as even despotic dictatorships have discovered. This simply means that complex social systems cannot achieve: (a) *parity* among specialized institutional groups; (b) *coherence* in interests and values of institutional groups; or (c) an *autonomous, socially impartial*

body that can long remain above the narrower socio-cultural bases of institutional levels — in short, the ideal of the philosopher-king. Consequently, some institutional groups may be said to achieve the quasi-societal level. This is particularly reflected in responsibility for relations with other systems.

A third important element in this conceptual framework, already strongly implicit in the preceding typology, is the patterns of control and coordination as these affect (a) the maintenance of action systems and the production of innovative behavior, and (b) the relative flow of innovative patterns to various subsystems. But a conceptualization of the *variety* of controls from a structural-functional standpoint has only recently been suggested by Parsons (57, chapter 5) and should be incorporated (on a trial basis, at least) in our framework.

Briefly, the coordinative-control complex is centered in the operation of the institutional level of organization. In practice, institutional controls are translated into *specialized functional mechanisms* that help maintain such key institutional tasks as (a) making binding policy decisions, and (b) implementing these decisions through allocating facilities and responsibilities to subordinate levels. These functional mechanisms are:

1) *Authority.* This concerns the right to make decisions on specific matters that are morally and practically unquestioned by subordinates.

2) *Authorization.* Obviously dependent on the prior existence of a system of authority, authorization refers to the process by which subordinate units are permitted to use authority for application to specifically defined situations or problems included within the radius of the superordinate authority. Thus, a department chairman in an American university may hire a staff member (a delegation of authority vested in the board of trustees and appropriate deans), but he may not in most instances compel the staff member to join a particular religious group.

3) *Regulation.* Unlike authorization, regulation involves a restricted type of control. Essentially, it involves general supervision of subordinate (usually technical) units by setting more or less definite "limits of acceptable action" for such units.

4) *Legitimation.* This is a broad, complementary process in the coordinative-control complex. Legitimation is a *sanctioning-evaluative* process, in which the actions of any social level are judged with reference to the *sacred core of values* in the total system, for which the institutional level is major representative and interpreter.

5) *Power.* According to the rather unique formulation by Parsons, and yet in line with the general orientation of structural-functionalism, power can be simultaneously viewed as a basic process of social systems and as a product of their operation. In the present context, power is primarily regarded as the generalized process by which the various resources of a social system are organized for achieving system goals. Thus,

power includes all the previously discussed functional mechanisms, which may be conceptualized as various legitimized patternings of power. A variable residue of force, coercion, threats, and unique manipulative practices is of course inherent in power. But *at the institutional level* this residue is taken to be small, by definition.

A Structural-Functional Schema of Social Change: Analytical Phases

From these conceptual materials, we can derive at least two fundamental propositions concerning social change.

1) *Analytic stages in social change as a process.* In view of the earlier definition of social change ("significant variations from processual and developmental patterns of operation" of social systems), the description and explanation of change require an *historical* dimension so as to encompass the full course of processes of change. A structural-functional orientation toward change therefore posits a tentative three-phase sequence (10, pp. 289–302):

a) *Sources of innovative values or behavior.* In terms of the preceding framework, these sources are most likely to be technical and/or managerial levels of organization, or external sources (that is, derived from interaction with other systems). By its very nature, the institutional level is uncongenial to innovative roles *for itself.* This is of course in sharp contrast to theories of elites and leaders as initiators of change (52, pp. 1689–1694; 40, chapter 3; 71, chapter 11); but it is important to note that the statement asserts only that institutional levels do not participate *in the earliest stages* of innovation.

b) *The filtering process, or control of contributed innovations.* Because of the great significance of all four functional problems and the hierarchical system of social levels, innovations have little intrinsic meaning. They must be recognized, tried, and evaluated — a set of tasks which innovators themselves are largely unprepared to perform. In the social system, the major responsibility for such judgments is vested in the institutional level and its representative groups.

c) *Derivative structures and functional reverberations.* When innovations receive the sanction of control groups, attempts are inevitably made by subgroups at the managerial and technical levels to accommodate these innovations to any of the structural or functional components of the social system that seem to be significantly affected (in the form of pressures, threats, or extended opportunities) by the innovative practices (50, pp. 265–280; 49, chapters 12, 19) . Thus, for example, the adoption of the wet rice system by the Tanala was followed by understandable adaptations in family structure, property, warfare and defense, and formal political organization (33, pp. 349–356).

2) The crucial stage is therefore phase (b), since phase (a) provides *possibilities* of significant change and phase (c) comprises the implemen-

tation of critical decisions (positive and negative) that are made during phase (b). In other words, phases (a) and (c) provide *necessary* components of social change, while phase (b) involves both *necessary* and *sufficient* conditions for given sequences of social change.

Two corollary propositions may be suggested at this point:

a) The process of social change reaches a significant point when the institutional level is ineffective in controlling the cumulation of variations and the strains of inconsistencies derived from such variations. This may be called *change by institutional default*. For example, modern metropolitan areas represent case studies of extensive and relatively uncontrolled change processes in which technical innovations (communication and transportation), changes in housing and space demands, and various permissible "inventions" in land subdivision and building have created severe challenges for institutional or policy-making groups. With negligible exceptions, these problems have not been successfully resolved in American urban regions because responsible leadership has failed to establish workable controls. Of course, this failure is essentially in line with the thinking of most urbanites. But the constantly evolving set of consequences is a transformation of urban living. One result is a sharpened segregation of status categories and associated styles of life. Another effect of institutional default is what Odum called "achievement lag," that is, an intensified insistence on realizing goals (gracious living, more land, spiritual progress, and other abstract ideals) for which the current technical-organizational facilities are unsuited. Change by institutional default is therefore experienced as "social problems," persistence of generally shared frustrations, and the temporary appearance of aimlessness that superficially resembles *stasis*.

b) The process of social change reaches a significant point when the institutional level undergoes significant variations in personnel and/or motivation in applying the functional control mechanisms. In this case, the institutional level has redefined its functional responsibility to include facilitation of proposed changes, with or without ulterior motives. This may be called *change by institutional acquiescence or facilitation.* A contemporary example of the effects of personnel change on the institutional level is the general shift to "liberal" interpretations in United States Supreme Court decisions. This may be traced to the New Deal period, but succeeding appointments (both Republican and Democratic) have largely altered the social philosophy of the Court. On the other hand, we may point to a motivational or valuational shift in an institutional elite in the case of the Japanese leadership less than 100 years ago. The Meiji Restoration adopted a formal political change (the revised role of the Emperor) and the technological bases of Western industrialism, but this was carried out by the prevailing leadership, which was thereby confirmed in its position in Japanese society.

Toward a Theoretical-Research Repertory: Translating a Conceptual Scheme into Testable Propositions

The pursuit of these propositions requires considerable specification so that the theoretical import of this approach may be converted into researchable problems. Furthermore, it is important to underscore the interrelation of these research problems (and associated hypotheses) for an adequate theoretical system of social change. Consequently, each phase in the process of change will be translated into a series of hypotheses drawn from the initial framework and designed to explain the basic contribution of that phase to the overall process of social change.

Sources of innovative values or behavior

Hypotheses for this stage must deal with the conditions associated with structural and/or functional *opportunities* for variation, as well as the *motivations* for variation that can be attributed to structural and/or functional features of social systems. A representative set of such hypotheses might well include the following:

1) The greater the specialization of roles for discharging the four functional needs of social systems, the greater the opportunity for variation and innovation among technical and managerial persons in each functional division (adaptation, goal-attainment, pattern-maintenance, and integration) (57, pp. 62–66; 22, pp. 147–174, pp. 283–303). Thus, sacred societies (in which religious, political, economic, and socialization roles are concentrated in kinship groups) provide less evidence of innovation than that found in "civil," complex societies. The period of greatest experimentation in classical Greece — in government, art and literature, and religious cultism — followed the "reforms" of the sixth and seventh centuries B.C., which loosened the power of kinship, and permitted greater scope for military and economic enterprise. Similarly, innovations of a technical and organizational nature in industrial and commercial firms have increased in volume as an accompaniment of the shift from the small, partnership type to the complex corporate hierarchies of the present, with their internal specialization of production, personnel training, public relations, research and development, legal affairs, and political influence.

2) Other things being equal, adaptive and goal-attainment functions provide more opportunity for variation than the pattern-maintenance and integrative functions. As Merton, following Weber, has shown, once the impetus to innovation had been provided by the religious changes of the seventeenth century in England, the surge of scientific inventions in ensuing years was largely responsive to felt needs in industry and navigation. Of course, it is extremely difficult to compare — in a strict quantitative manner — economic and political innovations, on the one hand,

and artistic, educational, and familial innovations, on the other hand, during this period. However, it seems likely that seventeenth-century England was marked more by political and economic ferment than by changes in other spheres of activity.

3) The opportunity for adaptive and goal-attainment variations is directly related to complexity of societal types, with significant differences between folk and advanced secular types (49, chapters 14, 20; 59, chapter 12). For example, we would expect greater innovation and experimentation in technological aspects, forms of exchange and distribution, and in mechanisms of power and authority in complex, urbanized societies than in preliterate or "underdeveloped" societies. Not only are adaptive and goal-attainment functions more clearly specialized in complex societies; they are also assigned a special importance which, in practice, encourages "improvements."

The preceding hypotheses assume both constancy of motivation and some continuity of relations among the four functional needs. Since these are sometimes unwarranted assumptions, the following hypotheses may be tentatively offered:

4) The opportunity for variation is directly associated with significant shifts in the proportional effort (resources, time, personnel, verbalization, imagery, and so on) devoted by the social system to the four functional problems (29, chapter 32). As an illustration, Bales' study of small experimental groups seems to suggest that interaction focuses initially on appropriate ideas and a task-orientation (adaptive), then on organization of the group process to implement these ideas (goal-attainment). This is followed by indications of both hostile and amiable attitudes towards participants and by processes of composing these differences (tension-management); and subsequently by periods of common appreciation of the varied individual contributions toward solving the assigned task (integrative phase) (55, chapter 4). In a general way, but with considerably less precision in determining these "phases," American history reflects gross shifts in focus. The early republic was concerned with carving out and taming half the continental expanse, while a series of *policy* issues (the United States Bank, political rivalry, slavery, and so on) marked the period 1820–1860. The Civil War and Reconstruction reflected imperfect solutions to societal integration. By the '90's the adaptive emphasis became dominant again and soon questions of internal power struggles and then major foreign policy matters became insistent. After World War I, adaptive problems shifted somewhat to emphasis on socialization and broad educational problems (witness the growing importance of advertising, public relations, mass communications, and the seemingly incessant wrangles over educational philosophy and practice), while intermittent concern for national morale can be noted during the Great Depression and World War II.

a) One such pattern of shifts, analyzed by Sorokin, Toynbee, and

Parsons, involves a developmental, cyclical alternation of dominant societal concerns. Parsons and Bales (55, chapter 5) identify a "phase movement" pattern, for example, in which adaptation gives way to goal-attainment, then to pattern-maintenance and tension-management, to integration, again to adaptation, and so on. This of course assumes a relatively autonomous system. In any case, variant behavior is hypothesized to alter in intensity according to changing dominance of the four functions. An independent indication of functional dominance seems to be most imperative to prevent this from becoming a circular statement.

b) Significant shifts in the dominance of functional problems are (or can be) related to contacts with or pressures from other social systems and/or physical catastrophes, such as floods, earthquakes, drought, fires (24; 67, chapter 28).

5) Opportunity and motivation for innovation are directly related to the amount of interpersonal and intergroup conflict within each of the four functional areas, whatever the underlying reasons for such conflict (3, chapters 10, 14). Thus, innovations in industrial technology in Western nations have coincided with periods of heightened conflict between technical and managerial-institutional levels — though innovations can also be shown to be a source of such conflicts, as for example, the effects of commercial expansion on political divisions between aristocratic families and the new merchant families of classical Athens.

6) The opportunity and motivation for innovation within one or more functional areas are directly related to the amount of intergroup competition for dominance on the institutional level. For example, municipal inventions of the medieval period were a result of controversy between the previously dominant institutional leadership (clerical and noble-military) and the rising "technical" level of merchants (58). Similarly, "progressive education" is a set of innovations created by representatives of rising lower-middle-class and acculturating lower-class groups in opposition to the curriculum and philosophy of an aristocratically oriented (but socially "upper-middle class") elite (43). The adoption of "progressive" measures was dependent on prior change in the thinking and personnel of school boards (the institutional level) and superintendents (upper managerial level).

7) The opportunity and motivation for innovation are inversely related to *perceived* levels of efficiency in meeting specific functional needs. This of course involves the general problem of the relation between deviation and dysfunction. However, the concept of dysfunction needs greater empirical orientation, as suggested in the following subsidiary hypotheses:

a) The level of innovation or deviation within a given functional area is directly related to the *perceived* failure of existing practices in meeting that functional problem. In general, the effective motivation for innovation in this situation is more likely to be found among the "producers" of the "service" than the "consumers," though there is varying communication between consumers and producers. A tentative explanation for this locus of motivation may be the greater awareness of the availability of workable alternatives among technical and managerial units, and perhaps the seductive possibility that responsible (and approvable) variations can enhance status without directly challenging the position of the institutional level.

Martin Luther's famous assault on abuses in the Catholic church was an ideological innovation, not intended as a revolutionary thrust, from the "managerial" level. The same dependence on technical or managerial levels for innovation may be found in the military realm, particularly in the case of such originally contested innovations as the airplane, the tank, the aircraft carrier, and the atomic submarine. Finally, in the twilight zone between material and ideational inventions, mention might be made of the modern city-planning movement, which was (and is) largely an amalgam of notions and theories from architects, engineers, and a representative sprinkling of academic disciplines in close touch with local government (for example, economics and political science).

b) The level or amount of innovation within a given functional area is directly related to the perceived degree of overemphasis (in terms of allocated time, personnel, and resources) on otherwise legitimate objectives. Perception of overemphasis may occur at any of the organizational levels, but two foci of innovation responsive to this perception may be suggested.

(i) Technical units, by virtue of their specialized nature and subordinate position, are more likely to interpret the operations of managerial and institutional levels as "overemphasis" than *vice versa*. In a pattern-maintenance function such as formal education, for example, administrative (managerial) policies are often viewed by teachers (technical level) as beyond the bounds of necessity or wasteful of time more properly applied to more legitimate tasks. Innovative (deviant) responses are well-known to teachers: ignoring certain regulations or interpreting them to minimize paper work, political maneuvering by informal groupings of teachers, suggestions for shifting work to an available functionary, appointment of a special committee to "study the matter." Note that we are not required to evaluate the *utility* of innovations.

(ii) But a second source of innovation derives from technical (and managerial) units *outside* the area of perceived overemphasis. Because of the interrelated nature of the four functional problems, overemphasis in one area is sooner or later translated into indirect or direct interference with the operation of other subsystems. For example, much of the complex legal and administrative apparatus of the federal government during the past generation may be interpreted as necessary innovative reactions to the *perceived* autonomy or unbridled "imperialism" of an otherwise technically proficient and desirable economic system. Similarly, we may point to the perceived overemphasis on recreation and economic success asserted by many religious groups and the various non-religious attempts by such groups to attract and retain members, such as sponsored recreation, professionally conducted fund-raising, and baby-sitting facilities.

c) Finally, the level of innovation is directly related to perceived threats to the traditional operation of all organizational levels within a functional area that stem from changes introduced by other subsystems or by external systems. An excellent series of examples is surely the numerous and temporarily ingenious mechanisms by which judicially approved desegregation of public schools in the United States has been resisted in a number of Southern states by such tactics as pupil placement, tuition grants, privately operated grade schools, and even discontinuation of public schools. For this type of innovative situation, both experience and deductions from the general theoretical framework indicate that sources of innovation are likely to be found on several levels, including the institutional. This is of course a partial exception to the general hypothesis concerning the relative rarity of innovation among institutional groups. But it may be suggested that such "exceptions" occur when there is a high level of *consensus* (and therefore common perception of threat) among the various organization levels. Though evidence in these comparatively rare cases is understandably scanty, a plausible hypothesis can be advanced. We would expect that *initial innovations* derive from technical and managerial levels, while groups at the institutional level tend to innovate in response to perceived threats at a later period, in modification of earlier innovations, rather than as competitors or independent innovators.

None of these hypotheses seeks to identify highly specific categories of persons as predominant sources of deviation or innovation. The structural-functional framework thus far is restricted to concern with structural conditions favorable to innovation and to motivational patterns that enable broad categories of system members to perceive and utilize these structural opportunities. It is obvious that personality variables should also play some significant role in the operation and variability of social systems. In particular, personality variables should enable us to understand *why some but not all* persons in the preceding "innovative situations" respond in innovative or deviant ways. Some valuable clues may be found in the work of McClelland (41), Hagen (27), and Barnett (3). In the meanwhile, let us turn to the second phase.

Control and Facilitation of Innovation

The basic propositions for this phase, as discussed previously, are: (1) that the control phase is the key to the overall process of social change, since the reception and derivative effects of innovation are largely determined during this stage; and (2) that the operation of the institutional levels is crucial to the facilitation or suppression of innovative behavior. Consequently, hypotheses directly concerned with the major factors in the structure and functioning of groups at the institutional level — as these contribute to promoting or arresting change — are extremely significant for a theory of social change.

1) Control or containment of innovations within any functional area — or within the system as a whole — is directly associated with success in pattern-maintenance and tension-management. In other words, the extent to which the institutional level can provide rewarding motivations to support existing practices and forms of relationships helps determine the diffusion and import of alternative (innovative) forms. Thus, it is suggested that the crucial function of institutional groups, as far as potential change is concerned, is neither goal-attainment nor integration, but "proper" socialization and motivation. Change is therefore indirectly but significantly fostered by prolonged deficiencies in performing the latter function.

2) Control or support of innovations by institutional groups is likewise related to characteristic patterns of interaction with subordinate levels. More specifically:

a) Control or promotion of innovation is associated with differentials in the bureaucratization (specificity of hierarchically-ordered responsibilities and control) of subsystems. In general, the more diffuse and the more flexible the system of interaction, the greater the opportunity for diffusion of innovations and the greater the likelihood that these will be ignored by personnel at the institutional level.

b) Closely related is the hypothesis that perception of innovations by institutional groups is conditioned by existing patterns of formal and informal communication (with respect to policy, orders, suggestions, grievances) with subordinate levels. Temporarily disregarding the personnel composition of the institutional level, we may suggest that one-way communication (from the top downward) reduces *perception* of innovation, and also serves to reduce potential diffusion of available innovations. Conversely, two-way communication may be expected to increase not only the likelihood of perception by the institutional level (and therefore opportunity for control) but also opportunities for the lower levels to influence superordinate levels to accept or approve innovations.

c) The response of institutional groups to innovation or deviation is associated with the selective pattern of control techniques adopted by such groups as a consequence both of (i) a previously preferred or legitimized range of techniques, and (ii) the relative security and prestige of current occupants of institutional roles. Institutional groups which rely on the more *direct* control mechanisms (for example, force or threat of force, personal influence over subordinates, prompt reward for prescribed actions or punishment for disapproved actions) tend to be uncomfortable and uncertain in their superordinate positions and therefore are more likely to feel uncongenial to innovation — unless it is under their own auspices. On the other hand, use of more *indirect* mechanisms of control (persuasion, manipulation, "divide and rule," political interchanges, and self-confirmatory compromises) may well indicate greater assurance and flexibility in assessing the responsibilities of the institutional level. In this case, innovations are more likely to be judged for their functional consequences (for a subsystem or the overall system). Of course, the probability of *correct* (pragmatically speaking) functional evaluations of innovations is a problem of great difficulty, part of which will be treated later.

3) Previous hypotheses have assumed a relatively invariant set of abilities, motivations, and socially relevant characteristics among members of institutional groups. However, historical data and the work of such theorists as Mosca (46), Pareto (52), Mannheim (39), Toynbee (71), Mills (44), and Dahl (19) strongly suggest not only recurrent changes in the composition of these groups — variously known as elites, power elites, top leaders, or influentials — but consequent changes in receptivity to innovation. Several specific applications of this theme seem to present possibilities of clarifying situations of potential change that remain unexplained by the previous hypotheses.

a) Changes in the criteria of recruitment into institutional elites help account for otherwise unpredictable reactions to innovations. Drawing upon clues contributed by Pareto (52) and Mannheim (39, pp. 86–96), we may analytically separate these criteria into two categories: one emphasizes ascribed qualities (such as race, family, inherited property), parochial interests, tradition, and direct controls; the other emphasizes previous achievement in some specialized endeavor, cosmopolitan interests, and the value of discussion, manipulation, and experimentation. Consequently, the latter would be more receptive to innovation than the former.

b) The relative *permeability* of institutional elites is likewise related to their general attitudes toward innovation. Those elites that restrict replacements to specific social categories, such as occupational or religious groups, without reference to internal differences in the above-mentioned qualities of members of such categories, tend to resist the diffusion of innovation, while elites with more varied social composition (other things being equal) are more exposed to divergent perspectives and thus view innovation with less hostility.

c) This of course raises the familiar problem of co-optation, the relatively voluntary process of absorbing socially and politically subordinate persons into the policy-determining level as a means of avoiding threats to its stability (62, pp. 217–226, pp. 259–261). In particular, what is the likelihood that innovative persons from technical and managerial levels will be co-opted by institutional groups and, more important, retain an innovative perspective?

Theoretical answers to this crucial problem have been few and rather inadequate, principally because relevant data have not been gathered. Since one function of hypotheses is to suggest some definite pattern or regularity, however incorrect later investigation may prove it to be, the following hypothetical statements may be of some value:

(i) Co-optation of managerial and/or technical levels by institutional elites is more likely in social systems that are characterized by comparatively specialized subsystems of power. "Democratic," "representative" systems (in government, economics, family affairs, and the like) carry on a structural dialogue between institutional and subordinate levels that limits the essentially sacred, arbitrary nature of institutional groups. For example, the traditional patriarchal family in Europe and America was marked by concentrated authority, as were the merchant guilds of latter-day feudalism. Co-optation was extremely difficult, for the existence of a serious challenge to incumbent policy-makers in either case was unthinkable. However, in the liberated middle-class family, both subtle and obvious forms of co-optation may be found in the wife's and the children's (managerial and technical levels) decisive influence on purchase and use of automobiles, family budget revisions, choice of vacation locales, family recreation patterns, and selection of proper mates for marriageable sons or daughters.

Furthermore, as Mosca (46, p. 244, p. 460) somewhat overextends a reasonably acceptable compound of fact and inference, in the long run there is a tendency for *all* "ruling minorities" to be recruited in terms of generally desired qualities that are appropriate to the needs of a given historical era. By implication, co-optation is a realistic necessity of social survival, regardless of differences in ideology and formal structure.

(ii) Co-optation is, from a structural-functional standpoint, a process associated with unique functional emphases characteristic of certain types of institutional groups. In general, it may be suggested that conditions which compel institutional groups to emphasize goal-attainment likewise create greater *access* of already innovative persons to the institutional level. Essentially, groups with prominent adaptive and goal-attainment functions tend to give more attention to the latter aspect during crisis situations — either when persistent failures accumulate or when new opportunities for success present themselves (the *windfall* situation). Crisis normally places an additional premium on *achievement,* to which the institutional level is particularly attuned, not only for the future of the system, but also to sustain the prestige of institutional personnel. Consequently, in view of the structural limitation on innovation among persons at the institutional level (previously discussed), it becomes necessary to seek fresh assistance from subordinate levels. Failure to do so is not unknown (for example, Hitler and the Romanovs),[1] but co-optation in one form or another is widely practiced in industrial organization, political parties at many levels, and sometimes in academic settings.

Parenthetically, it is quite probable that the general lack of co-optation (and, comparatively, of change) in religious, familial, and legal realms stems from a characteristic emphasis on *integrative* and *pattern-maintenance* functions. Indeed, under these conditions, change seems to require "social movements," which normally base their appeal on a goal-attainment theme, bolstered by charismatic persons who promise higher fulfillment of "neglected" values. Charisma, in this context, may be simply defined as an effectively personal attempt at innovative goal-attainment.

An Empirical Typology of Social Change Situations

The range of hypotheses presented for the innovative and control-coordinative phases of social change gives some indication of the *complexity* that inevitably accompanies processes of social change. One aspect of this complexity implicit in our discussion thus far concerns the *alternative empirical courses* (direction, rate, and amount of resistance) that potentially and actually develop in social change phenomena. For convenience, then, let us construct an empirically relevant typology of social change situations that may be conceived as products of phases (a) and (b). This typology may well be based on four interrelated variables or dimensions:

    1) The relative autonomy or vulnerability to external influences of the social system.

    2) The *source* of innovation — internal or external.

---

[1] For example, the breakdown of Nazi Germany can in part be attributed to Hitler's refusal to accept competent military advice from professional officers. Many of his decisions from 1941 to 1945 were based on improvisation and an essential distrust of his General Staff. See H. R. Trevor-Roper (72, pp. 7–11, pp. 28–30, pp. 233–236); and Walter Ansel (2, pp. 76–86, chapter 10). Likewise, the Romanov Tsars during the period 1870 to 1914 steadily weakened their positions by failing to adopt rather mild political reforms which would have given more responsibility and a sense of identification with the government to various strata. In particular, the shackling of the powers of the Duma opened the way for subsequent revolutions. See Hugh Seton-Watson (63, pp. 48–49, chapters 2, 5, 8, epilogue); and Richard Charques (16, chapters 1, 7, 10).

3) Dominant response patterns of the institutional level — rigidity, passive acquiescence, active facilitation.

4) Short term effects of (2) and (3): strain, inconsistency, and limited change; relatively orderly change; rapid and disorderly change.

Out of the numerous logical combinations of these dimensions, however, four types seem to be most frequently encountered:

1) Gradual, orderly change in social systems marked by relative isolation and stable institutional groups.

2) Structured strains in social systems with rigid containment or suppression of innovation by dominant institutional levels.

3) Externally imposed innovations in social systems whose institutional groups are unable to channel or control the consequences of innovation.

4) Planned, internally based change in social systems characterized by unchallenged institutional groups operating on the societal level and either developing their own innovations or sponsoring specialized, technical units designed for solicited innovations.

Derivative Consequences.

From either a theoretical or empirical standpoint, it is abundantly clear that the development and legitimation of innovations are followed by a variable amount of secondary or "unanticipated" effects — both cultural and social organizational — on implicated social systems. One portion of the efforts of sociological and anthropological theorists in the past has been devoted to providing a generalized explanation of these consequences, with uncomfortably mixed results. This is of course an exceedingly difficult problem, one for which monistic determinisms of any sort cannot adequately supply a solution. However, once again the data of ancient and recent history, and a structural-functional framework, can be interpreted to give promise to several theoretical points.

a) Following the approved, institutionally sanctioned practice of some innovation, or the satisfactory but unsanctioned dissemination of an innovation, there is some alteration in the relative efforts given to the four functional problems, either in the overall system or in a significant subsystem. In short, the process of change encourages revised functional emphases, which are expressed in new skills and "knowledge," new or expanded roles and groups, and a new or heightened attraction of persons with appropriate characteristics. Innovation therefore furnishes opportunities for previously unused or unrewarded skills and thus increases potentialities for new organizational forms. Thus, the military, political, and economic changes of the tenth through the fourteenth centuries in Western Europe opened the way for merchant organizations and urban changes (that is, a shift from integrative to adaptive and goal-attainment emphases), just as the changes embedded in the failure of the Weimar Republic soon eventuated in the Nazi movement and the dominance of the lower-middle class in the German bureaucracy — a shift from adaptive to goal-attainment and integrative emphases (25, pp. 517–541).

b) Though there are undoubtedly pockets of autonomy in every social system, the fact that at least some integration exists among the component groups of society and among the functional problems the society has to solve insures that an approved innovation in one activity will have effects on one or more other functionally significant activities. The *typical direction* of these adaptations has long been a moot question in sociological theory — perhaps, from the present framework, a misleading and fruitless question. In general, however, complex societies may exhibit a certain priority in adaptive and goal-attainment functions, with derivative changes in pattern-maintenance (family, education) and integrative functions (law, religion). For simpler societies that retain cultural-geographic isolation, it is even more difficult to detect regularities of this sort. We can venture a plausible guess: by the debatable evidence of differential complexity, both religion and kinship provide greater opportunities for initial or "trigger" innovations, with derivative effects on economic systems, "power structure," and "science."

c) Intimately connected to (b) is the widespread phenomenon of relatively uneven processes of derivative change, which demonstrates that societies cannot be perfectly integrated in practice, or that some segment recurrently diminishes coordinative or integrative relations when the process of change attains an advanced state. But the presence of "lag" or differential rates of change is unquestionable. Two crucial theoretical problems arise at this point, for which the structural-functional schema may furnish useful clues.

First, what conditions contribute to uneven change? Though other explanations have been presented by Veblen (73), Ogburn (50, Part III), and Odum (49), the differential emphasis on functional problems — found in all social systems as a matter of practicality — is inevitably expressed in differential application of resources toward adjusting other areas to legitimized innovation. In addition, there is normally some competition among institutional groups representing the major specialized activities of complex social systems. Finally, uneven change results from the varied maneuvers of institutional groups engaged in contests for a *societal level* of functioning.

The second problem concerns the "normal" consequences of uneven change. In the most general terms, uneven change both produces and reflects a period of transition (9; 10, pp. 297–299), in which the most visible signs are a range of social problems and a continued incapacity to diminish the personal and social inefficiencies that accompany such problems. More specifically, periods of transition are marked by: (1) significantly reduced satisfaction of one or more societal functions; (2) uncertainty in the operation of institutional, managerial, and perhaps the technical levels; (3) one or more attempts to provide integration by direct mechanisms (force, fear, hysteria, witch-hunting, tightened controls, and the like) operated by institutional and managerial levels; (4) a derivative motivation for change (rather than for specific innovations) among technical and some managerial groups; and (5) a series of variably spaced "social movements" which do not seek fundamental, radical innovations, but rather innovations — in personnel and in responsibilities of institutional and managerial levels — that permit the consolidation and effective operation of previously sanctioned innovations. For example, the agrarian movements in the United States from 1870 to 1924 or so were basically devoted to obtaining greater political representation and more equitable economic returns ("parity") from a society in which desired technological change and organizational developments seemed to favor the urban segments of the nation.

Thus, in the structural-functional approach, change and tension (dysfunction) are reciprocally intertwined. Innovations initially arise in "normal" and/or disturbed functioning of social systems. When accepted, these in turn create further tensions, traceable to uneven derivative adjustments. And these tensions — expressed in social problems — incite further, presumably stabilizing changes.

d) A highly significant consequence of the preceding processes is, eventually, a corresponding change in the system(s) of stratification 8, pp. 124–125, pp. 130–131). This appears to be a complex and partly invisible or latent set of interrelations. The following simplified analysis is therefore presented provisionally, with the hope that its theoretical components provide a base for inevitable improvements.

Regardless of source or motivation, innovations devised in the first phase create new or greatly revised social roles for some members of a system. These roles may be associated either with a *shift* in functional emphasis (the scientific or research administrator is a recent and somewhat poignant example of such a shift) or with the attempt to discharge some consistently evaluated function (for example, pattern maintenance and the "progressive teacher" role). In either case, new roles and their occupants come to be evaluated in terms of (1) relative efficiency in providing solutions to a major functional problem, and (2) the organizational level at which the role is performed. According to prevailing general patterns of evaluation, new roles (and their occupants) likewise acquire special rewards, privileges, opportunities, and levels of prestige. Change processes, then, spawn roles that confer status, while in stable periods given status levels selectively entail certain role obligations or role-sets (42).

However, new roles and statuses also create new interactional possibilities, most significantly with traditional status groups. The result is some degree of status inconsistency (5; 30), which to some participants and observers seems to mean diminished stratification. Over longer periods, however, status inconsistency seems to reflect the changing relations among the four functional problems and the concomitant variations in the hierarchical and power position of competing institutional groups. Changes is social class systems can be charted, therefore, in terms of the weight assigned to ethnic background, family name and inheritance (pattern-maintenance), religion (integration), occupational type and earned income (adaptation), political influence and opinion leadership (goal-attainment).

e) A final and admittedly broad category of derivative consequences is *cultural,* comprising a range of demonstrable adaptations to change in the form of value systems, shared attitudes and opinions, and common aspirations — as these are expressed in philosophies, theologies, literature, recreation, and the arts. Essentially, derivative cultural changes perform two important tasks for participants in social systems. On the one hand, they provide a practical response to the altered "balance" of functional problems, as *rationales,* apologies, or sanctifiers. Alternatively, they serve as coherent protests (direct or indirect) to such changes. The relation between these types of cultural adaptation and Mannheim's (38) analysis of "ideologies" and "utopias" is immediately apparent. But the problem of demonstrating unambiguous relations between adaptive cultural productions and functionally differentiated social segments remains a formidable one for the sociology of knowledge and an overall theory of the process of social change (42, chapter 12; 17; 21).

Conclusion

The analysis and understanding of social change are probably the most crucial task of sociology, both in its relation to other social sciences (12) and in its overall contribution to modern society and its problems. Consequently, whatever label is applied, any theoretical scheme that seeks to provide a detailed examination of the basic mechanisms of social change merits some attention and the leaven of criticism. I believe a modified structural-functional scheme constitutes the most promising available means of analyzing change. With the kinds of modification and explication suggested throughout this chapter, it is perhaps time to stop the oft-repeated but unexamined criticisms of structural-functionalism — in particular, the untenable assertion that functionalism contains a static model inapplicable to conflict, external factors, or change. Instead of a priori judgments, I suggest that sociologists put functional concepts and hypotheses to the test of use; only then can needed improvements be made.

What, briefly, are the potential contributions of this approach?

First, social change may be theoretically linked with its alleged "opposite" — order, stability — as extremes of the same continuum: the operation of social systems. Change, therefore, cannot be viewed as either inevitable or impossible.

Second, social change may be approached, not as a morass of seemingly vagrant processes, but as a product (along with stability) of the *variable capacity of social systems for generating and channeling innovative processes*. This compels us to approach change and order as probabilistic alternatives, as contingent effects of interrelated system components in their "historical" operation. And this in turn requires a renewed concern for usable classifications of social systems, in contrast to the traditional attraction for dichotomous societal types.

Third, the postulates and hypotheses discussed previously, despite their limitations, enable us to identify different types of change situations and, ultimately, to relate these types to a typology of social systems. In this way, the general explanatory value of our approach can be adjusted to the empirical variety of historical and contemporary social changes without yielding to the twin dangers of fragmentation or the reactive arbitrariness of Procrustean generalization.

Finally, this approach — and any alternative, coherent theoretical orientation — requires us to move from the comfortable level of *formulation* to the exciting but often disquieting level of *demonstration*. With some such scheme, sociologists can develop a growing fund of comparable, theoretically informed case studies of social change — in communities and societies — and for any historical period for which reasonably adequate data exist.

BIBLIOGRAPHY

1. Aberle, David, *et al.* "The Functional Prerequisites of a Society," *Ethics*, Vol. 60 (1950), pp. 100–111.

2. Ansel, Walter. *Hitler Confronts England.* Durham, N.C.: Duke University Press, 1960.

3. Barnett, Homer G. *Innovation: The Basis of Cultural Change.* New York: McGraw-Hill Book Co., 1953.

4. Becker, Howard. *Through Values to Social Interpretation.* Durham, N.C.: Duke University Press, 1950.

5. Benoit-Smullyan, Emile. "Status, Status Types, and Status Interrelations," *American Sociological Review*, Vol. 9 (1944), pp. 151–161.

6. Bertalanffy, Ludwig von. *Problems of Life.* New York, N.Y.: John Wiley and Sons, 1952.

7. Bertalanffy, Ludwig von. "General System Theory," in Richard W. Taylor

(ed.), *Life, Language, Law: Essays in Honor of Arthur F. Bentley*. Yellow Springs, Ohio: Antioch Press, 1957.

8. Boskoff, Alvin. "Negro Class Structure and the Technicways," *Social Forces*, Vol. 28 (1950), pp. 124–131.

9. Boskoff, Alvin. "Postponement of Social Decision in Transitional Society," *Social Forces*, Vol. 31 (1953), pp. 229–234.

10. Boskoff, Alvin. "Social Change: Major Problems in the Emergence of Theoretical and Research Foci," in Howard Becker and Alvin Boskoff (eds.), *Modern Sociological Theory*. New York: Dryden Press, 1957.

11. Boskoff, Alvin. "Social Indecision: A Dysfunctional Focus of Transitional Society," *Social Forces*, Vol. 37 (1959), pp. 305–311.

12. Boskoff, Alvin. "Recent Theories of Social Change," in Werner J. Cahnman and Alvin Boskoff (eds.), *Reader in Sociology and History*. New York, N.Y.: The Free Press of Glencoe. (In press)

13. Blumer, Herbert. *An Appraisal of Thomas and Znaniecki's The Polish Peasant in Europe and America*. New York: Social Science Research Council, 1939, Bulletin 44.

14. Bredemeier, Harry C. "The Methodology of Functionalism," *American Sociological Review*, Vol. 20 (1955), pp. 173–180.

15. Cancian, Francesca. "Functional Analysis of Change," *American Sociological Review*, Vol. 25 (1960), pp. 818–827.

16. Charques, Richard. *The Twilight of Imperial Russia*. London: Phoenix House, 1958.

17. Child, Arthur. "The Theoretical Possibility of the Sociology of Knowledge," *Ethics*, Vol. 51 (1941), pp. 392–418.

18. Cottrell, Fred. *Energy and Society*. New York: McGraw-Hill Book Co., 1955.

19. Dahl, Robert A. *Who Governs?* New Haven: Yale University Press, 1961.

20. Dahrendorf, Ralf. "Out of Utopia," *American Journal of Sociology*, Vol. 64 (1958), pp. 115–127.

21. DeGré, Gerald L. *Society and Ideology*. New York: Columbia University Press, 1943.

22. Durkheim, Emile. *The Division of Labor in Society*. Glencoe, Ill.: The Free Press, 1947.

23. Eggan, Fred. *Social Organization of the Western Pueblos*. Chicago: University of Chicago Press, 1951.

24. Firey, Walter. "The Responsiveness of Interaction Patterns to Emergency," *Social Forces*, Vol. 21 (1942), pp. 17–21.

25. Gerth, Hans H. "The Nazi Party: Its Leadership and Composition," *American Journal of Sociology*, Vol. 45 (1940), pp. 517–541.

26. Gouldner, Alvin W. "Reciprocity and Autonomy in Functional Theory," in Llewellyn Gross (ed.), *Symposium on Sociological Theory*. Evanston, Ill.: Row, Peterson and Co., 1959.

27. Hagen, Everett E. *On the Theory of Social Change.* Homewood, Ill.: Dorsey Press, 1962.

28. Hempel, Carl G. "The Logic of Functional Analysis," in Llewellyn Gross (ed.), *Symposium on Sociological Theory.* Evanston, Ill.: Row, Peterson and Co., 1959.

29. Herskovits, Melville J. *Man and His Works.* New York: Alfred J. Knopf, 1947.

30. Lenski, Gerhard E. "Status Crystallization: A Non-Vertical Dimension of Social Status," *American Sociological Review,* Vol. 19 (1954), pp. 405–413.

31. Levy, Marion J. *The Structure of Society.* Princeton, N.J.: Princeton University Press, 1952.

32. Lillie, Ralph Stagner. *General Biology and Philosophy of Organism.* Chicago: University of Chicago Press, 1945.

33. Linton, Ralph. *The Study of Man.* New York: D. Appleton-Century, 1936.

34. Lockwood, David. "Some Remarks on 'The Social System'," *British Journal of Sociology,* Vol. 7 (1956), pp. 134–146.

35. Lowie, Robert H. *The History of Ethnological Theory.* New York: Rinehart and Company, 1937.

36. MacIver, Robert M. *Society.* New York: Farrar and Rinehart, 1937.

37. MacIver, Robert M. *Social Causation.* Boston: Ginn and Company, 1942.

38. Mannheim, Karl. *Ideology and Utopia: An Introduction to the Sociology of Knowledge.* London: Kegan Paul, Trench and Trubner, 1936.

39. Mannheim, Karl. *Man and Society in an Age of Reconstruction.* New York: Harcourt, Brace, 1940.

40. Martindale, Don. *Social Life and Cultural Change.* Princeton, N.J.: D. Van Nostrand Company, 1962.

41. McClelland, David C. *The Achieving Society.* Princeton, N.J.: Van Nostrand, 1961.

42. Merton, Robert K. *Social Theory and Social Structure.* Glencoe, Ill.: The Free Press, 1957.

43. Mills, C. Wright. "A Sociological Account of Some Aspects of Pragmatism." Ph.D. dissertation, University of Wisconsin, Madison, 1942.

44. Mills, C. Wright. *The Power Elite.* New York: Oxford University Press, 1956.

45. Moore, Wilbert E. "A Reconsideration of Theories of Social Change," *American Sociological Review,* Vol. 25 (1960), pp. 810–818.

46. Mosca, Gaetano. *The Ruling Class.* New York: McGraw-Hill Book Co., 1939.

47. Nagel, Ernest. "A Formalization of Functionalism," in *Logic Without Metaphysics.* Glencoe, Ill.: The Free Press, 1956.

48. Nisbet, Robert A. "Social Structure and Social Change," *Research Studies*

of the State College of Washington. Pullman, Wash.: Vol. 20 (1952), pp. 70–76.

49. Odum, Howard W. *Understanding Society.* New York: The MacMillan Co., 1947.

50. Ogburn, William F. *Social Change.* New York: B. W. Huebsch, 1922.

51. Ogburn, William F., and Meyer F. Nimkoff. *Technology and the Changing American Family.* Boston: Houghton Mifflin, 1955.

52. Pareto, Vilfredo. *Mind and Society,* 4 vols. New York: Harcourt, Brace, 1935, Vol. 4.

53. Parsons, Talcott. *Essays in Sociological Theory Pure and Applied.* Glencoe, Ill.: The Free Press, 1949.

54. Parsons, Talcott. *The Social System.* Glencoe, Ill.: The Free Press, 1951.

55. Parsons, Talcott, Robert F. Bales, and Edward A. Shils. *Working Papers in the Theory of Action.* Glencoe, Ill.: The Free Press, 1953.

56. Parsons, Talcott. "The Role of General Theory in Sociological Analysis," *Alpha Kappa Deltan,* Vol. 29 (1959), pp. 12–38.

57. Parsons, Talcott. *Structure and Process in Modern Societies.* New York: The Free Press of Glencoe, 1960.

58. Pirenne, Henri. *Medieval Cities.* Princeton, N.J.: Princeton University Press, 1925.

59. Redfield, Robert. *The Folk Culture of Yucatan.* Chicago: University of Chicago Press, 1941.

60. Redfield, Robert. *The Primitive World and its Transformations.* Ithaca, N.Y.: Cornell University Press, 1953.

61. Rex, John. *Key Problems of Sociological Theory.* London: Routledge and Kegan Paul, 1961.

62. Selznick, Philip. *TVA and the Grass Roots.* Berkeley, Calif.: University of California Press, 1949.

63. Seton-Watson, Hugh. *The Decline of Imperial Russia.* New York: Frederick A. Praeger, 1952.

64. Smelser, Neil J. *Social Change in the Industrial Revolution.* London: Routledge and Kegan Paul, 1959.

65. Sorokin, Pitirim A. *Contemporary Sociological Theories.* New York: Harper & Bros., 1928.

66. Sorokin, Pitirim A. *Social and Cultural Dynamics,* 4 Vols. New York: American Book Co., 1937–1941.

67. Sorokin, Pitirim A. *Society, Culture, and Personality.* New York: Harper & Bros., 1947.

68. Spiethoff, Arthur. "Pure Theory and Economic Gestalt Theory: Ideal Types and Real Types," in Frederic C. Lane and Jelle C. Riemersma (eds.), *Enterprise and Secular Change.* Homewood, Ill.: Richard D. Irwin, 1953.

69. Steward, Julian. *Theory of Culture Change.* Urbana, Ill.: University of Illinois Press, 1955.

70. Tarde, Gabriel. *The Laws of Imitation.* New York: Henry Holt, 1903.

71. Toynbee, Arnold J. *A Study of History.* Abridged by D. C. Somervell. New York: Oxford University Press, 1947.

72. Trevor-Roper, H. R. *The Last Days of Hitler.* New York: The Macmillan Co., 1947.

73. Veblen, Thorstein. *The Theory of the Leisure Class.* New York: The Modern Library, 1934.

74. Vogt, Evon Z. "On the Concepts of Structure and Process in Cultural Anthropology," *American Anthropologist*, Vol. 62 (1960), pp. 18–33.

75. Weber, Alfred. *Fundamentals of Culture-Sociology.* New York: Columbia University (mimeographed), 1939.

76. Weber, Max. *The Methodology of the Social Sciences.* Glencoe, Ill.: The Free Press, 1949.

77. Wilson, Godfrey, and Monica Wilson. *The Analysis of Social Change.* Cambridge: Cambridge University Press, 1945.

78. Znaniecki, Florian. *The Method of Sociology.* New York: Rinehart, 1934.

79. Znaniecki, Florian. *Cultural Sciences.* Urbana, Ill.: University of Illinois Press, 1952.

9

David Lockwood

Social Integration and

System Integration

The term "social change" will be taken to mean a change in the institutional structure of a social system; more particularly, a transformation of the core institutional order of a society such that we can speak of a change in type of society. I do not believe that it is necessary to reach agreement on what is meant by the "core institutional order" of a society or on how a typology of societies is to be differentiated before there can be meaningful discussion of how the process of change takes place. That is, unless there is some a priori commitment to a "dominant factor" theory of social change; in which case the wrangle about whether change has "really" taken place can be endless.

The main purpose of this chapter is to discuss some of the implications of recent criticisms of functionalism, especially those which have a bearing on how social change is internally generated in a society. The thesis is that, in concentrating their fire on a special, albeit prominent, version of functionalism ("normative functionalism"), critics have become over-involved with what may be called the problems of "social integration." As a result, they have tended to ignore what is just as relevant to their central interests in conflict and social change, namely, the problem of "system integration." And here the perspective of general functionalism would still seem to be the most useful instrument.

I

In a recent article, Kingsley Davis (6) has proposed such a catholic definition of functionalism as to make it virtually indistinguishable from the most basic presuppositions of contemporary sociology. This is all very comforting. But if by functionalism nothing more were meant than seeing society as a system of interdependent parts, and an aversion to "reductionism," then most of those who have been engaged in criticism of functionalism would be proselytized overnight. How many would accept the attendant ideas, such as that of "functional requisites," is more debatable, and would probably depend on how they were interpreted. Again, exactly what elements are included as "parts" of a social system, and the exact implications of the idea of "interdependence" itself, are obviously areas of potential disagreement (10).

But, omitting these considerations, surely the "general" functionalist standpoint which Davis has restated must be distinguished from its more specific and controversial form. Davis avoids mentioning precisely those characteristics which are now widely associated with, though not logically entailed by, a functionalist orientation: first, the emphatic role attributed to "common value elements" in the integration of social action; and second, the unwarranted assumption that the study of social stability must precede the analysis of social change. Both these predispositions, but especially the first, typify what we wish to speak of from now on as normative functionalism.[1]

Before going on to examine the position to which we are led by the critics of normative functionalism, one further distinction is relevant to the subsequent argument. It is the wholly artificial one between "social integration" and "system integration." Whereas the problem of social integration focuses attention upon the orderly or conflictful relationships between the *actors*, the problem of system integration focuses on the orderly or conflictful relationships between the *parts*, of a social system.

It may be said at once that the connection between these two aspects of integration is neatly made by normative functionalism. The logic is simple. Since the only systematically differentiated parts of a society are its institutional patterns, the only source of social disorder arising from system disorder is that which takes the form of role conflict stemming from incompatible institutional patterns. If, however, it is held that such institutional patterns do not exhaust the generally relevant "parts"

---

[1] Gouldner quite properly points out that this tendency has amounted to what is in fact "implicit factor-theorizing": "Although the methodological position of the earlier functionalists commonly affirmed an amorphous interdependence of parts within a social system, it does not follow that the specific empirical analysis in which they engaged actually utilized this principle. In particular, the classic contributions, from Comte to Parsons, have gone out of their way to stress the significance of 'shared value elements' in maintaining the equilibrium of social systems" (10, p. 265).

of a social system, then this particular articulation of system and social integration is only one way of relating the phenomena of "deviance" and "conflict" to the operation of the system as a functioning entity. To this point we shall return later. For the moment, what needs stressing is that the critics of normative functionalism have devoted their critique entirely to the way in which this theory handles the problem of social integration; and particularly to the ambiguities of the concept of "institution."

II

The leading exponent of the general functionalist school, Robert K. Merton, has already drawn attention to the static connotation of the term institution: "It is not enough," he writes, "to refer to the 'institutions' as though they were all uniformly supported by all groups and strata in the society. Unless systematic consideration is given to the *degree* of support of particular 'institutions' by *specific* groups we shall overlook the important place of power in society" (15, p. 122). The major criticism of normative functionalism which has frequently been made is that it treats institutions primarily as moral entities, without rigorously exploring the interplay between norms and power that is universally present in major institutional contexts. This weakness has been seized upon by such writers as Dahrendorf (5) and Rex (19). Their basic theses are sufficiently similar to be treated jointly. For the sake of convenience, their ideas may be called "conflict theory."

The conflict theorists have pointed out first that norms and power must be considered as general alternative modes of "institutionalizing" social relationships. To quote Rex:

> We have also to recognise that some of the ends which the actors in our system pursue may be random ends from the point of view of the system or actually in conflict with it. If there is an actual conflict of ends, the behaviour of actors towards one another may not be determined by shared norms but by the success which each has in compelling the other to act in accordance with his interests. Power then becomes a crucial variable in the study of social systems (19, p. 112).

Second, potential conflicts of interest are seen as endemic in all social systems which "institutionalize" power relationships,[2] because power

[2] Briefly, to define authority as institutionalized power is to beg exactly the question that Merton raises, if the line between authority and power is drawn in terms of the presence or absence of a claim to legitimacy, not in terms of the sentiments of those (principally) over whom authority is exercised. Perhaps the most general consideration which makes the "de-institutionalization" of authority an ever-present possibility is the fact that, whereas the legitimacy of authority tends to take the form of general principles, acts of authority are always specific; and they are always more specific than derived rules of authority, no matter how well developed the latter. Thus, the "exploitable" ambiguity surrounding the derivation and interpre-

(authority) over others is the most general form of "scarce resource" and one that is inherent in society itself. "The distribution of authority in associations," writes Dahrendorf, "is the ultimate 'cause' of the formation of conflict groups" (5, p. 172). Thus, if potential conflicts of interest between those who exercise authority and those over whom authority is exercised are a "normal" feature of social organization, the de-institutionalization of power, and the use of power to maintain institutions, are ever present possibilities. In any realistic and dynamic view of institutionalization, the role of power, both in the generation and control of conflict, is of prime concern.

At first sight, it would seem that the image of society constructed by normative functionalism has given rise to counter-arguments which bring us round full circle to the polemical starting point of modern sociology, namely, the debate on social contract. But fortunately both normative functionalists and conflict theorists are not prepared to recognize as a real issue the Greenian dichotomy of "Will" versus "Force" (11). The themes of norms-consensus-order, and power-alienation-conflict are not regarded as viable sociological alternatives.[3]

It is, therefore, a little surprising to find that both Dahrendorf and Rex consider it necessary to develop their antitheses to normative functionalism in a *systematic* form. These take the shape, respectively, of a "coercion theory of society" and a "conflict model of society".[4] For this strategy they give reasons which are even more surprising. The first is that they both feel their "models" or "frames of reference" are specially suited to certain problem areas in sociology, particularly to the study of industrial societies (5, pp. 161–164; 19, p. 112, p. 114). And, second, Dahrendorf feels that the unification of the "integration theory" (normative function-

---

tation of the legitimacy of specific acts means that authority is never given, but is always contingent upon its exercise. It is precisely with such conflicts arising within the interstices of institutionalized power that "conflict theory" is concerned; and not simply with the more unusual approximations to "unstructured" power conflicts.

[3] At any rate, in formal terms. For instance, Parsons: "I do not think it is useful to postulate a deep dichotomy between theories which give importance to beliefs and values on the one hand, to allegedly 'realistic' interests, e.g., economic, on the other. Beliefs and values are actualized, partially and imperfectly, in realistic situations of social interaction and the outcomes are always codetermined by the values and realistic exigencies; conversely what on concrete levels are called 'interests' are by no means independent of the values which have been institutionalized in the relevant groups" (18, p. 173). See also Dahrendorf (5, p. 159, p. 163) and Rex (19, p. 112). But while there is formal agreement on this point, both the normative functionalists and the conflict theorists fail to explore in any rigorous way the interrelationship of "normative" and "realistic" elements of social systems.

[4] Both authors state their propositions in summary form (5, pp. 236–240; 19, pp. 129–131, p. 195, pp. 236–240; 19, pp. 129–31). Their premises are very similar: "Every society displays at every point dissensus and conflict; social conflict is ubiquitous" (5, p. 162); "Instead of being organised around a consensus of values, social systems may be thought of as involving conflict situations at central points" (19, p. 129). The major disagreement between the two would seem to be how far, *in fact*, lines of social conflict overlap. See Rex (19, pp. 117–118).

alism) and the "coercion theory" is unlikely and probably impossible (5, p. 164).

Neither of these reasons is very compelling. You cannot assert that society is unthinkable as either a purely moral or a purely coercive entity, and then suggest that a vocabulary built around one or the other of these unthinkable premises is necessary because some societies are manifestly more orderly or conflictful than others. To be sure, the degree to which power enters into social relationships is a factor indispensable for the understanding of both the "imperfection" of consensus and the propensity to conflict. But even in situations where power is very evident and conflict endemic, it is doubtful whether the phenomena of conflict can be adequately grasped without incorporating into conflict theory many of the concepts and propositions concerning the dynamic properties of value systems (or ideologies) which have been developed, or taken over, by normative functionalism. For, given the power structure, the nature of the value system is of signal importance for the genesis, intensity, and direction of potential conflict. Particularly crucial is the way in which it structures the levels of aspiration of different social strata. It may, of its own accord, create aspirations which generate demands for change, or add fuel to the fire of conflicting material interests. It may be sufficiently open and ambiguous to be exploited simultaneously by different conflict groups; or, contrariwise, be capable of absorbing counter-ideologies within itself. Or, sudden change in the relative material positions of different groups may result in widespread conflict as a consequence of what Durkheim calls "moral de-classification." It could, therefore, be argued that even the analysis of that facet of social integration to which Dahrendorf and Rex consider their theories to be especially relevant — namely, social conflict — requires nothing less than a systematic extension of their framework to take explicitly into account the variable properties of value systems that have been the focus of normative functionalism.[5] To the extent that this is done, their conflict theory ceases to be a "special" approach. That status is reserved for the unmodified version of normative functionalism.

Finally, both normative functionalism and conflict theory quite obviously utilize many sociological concepts (which are the property of neither the one perspective nor the other for the solution of their respective problems). Witness only Dahrendorf's (5, pp. 213–218) extensive use of the concept of "multiple group relationships" to account for the variability of class conflict in a way that is not at all dissimilar from the way it is used, for example, by Williams (24, pp. 560–561). Surely it is in the active use of precisely such common concepts and propositions, rather

---

[5] To take an actual example, compare the explicit use of the idea of the "exploitability" of the common value system by Parsons (17, p. 293, p. 355) in accounting for the intensification of "deviance" with the implicit reference to such an idea by Rex (19, p. 125) in discussing class conflict.

than in procuring an agreed definition of "institution" or "society," that the desired unification of which Dahrendorf is so sceptical is constantly being achieved. In actual fact, the divergence between what he calls "integration theory" and "coercion theory" is much more evident in defining problems than in solving them.

Why, then, the concentration on the development of alternative conceptual schemes in which the ideas of power and conflict play a central role? Partly because the recognition given by normative functionalism to the arguments put forward along these lines has so far amounted to nothing more than lip service. More fundamentally, perhaps, it is because, in seeing equilibrium analysis combined in normative functionalism with a focus on shared value elements, Dahrendorf and Rex, with their manifest interest in social change, have as a consequence sought the key to this problem in the area of power and conflict. If this is so, how far do the conflict theorists take us in the analysis of social change?

Dahrendorf and Rex assert that social change is a result of the shifting balance of power between conflict groups (5, pp. 231–236; 19, p. 196). Now, while social change is very frequently associated with conflict, the reverse does not necessarily hold. Conflict may be both endemic and intense in a social system without causing any basic structural change. Why does some conflict result in change while other conflict does not? Conflict theory would have to answer that this is decided by the variable factors affecting the power balance between groups. Here we reach the analytical limits of conflict theory. As a reaction to normative functionalism it is entirely confined to the problem of social integration. What is missing is the system integration focus of general functionalism, which, by contrast with normative functionalism, involves no prior commitment to the study of system stability.[6]

This is exceedingly interesting because both Dahrendorf and Rex arrive at their respective positions through a generalization of Marx. Yet it is precisely Marx who clearly differentiates social and system integration. The propensity to class antagonism (social integration aspect) is generally a function of the character of production relationships (e.g., possibilities of intra-class identification and communication). But the dynamics of class antagonisms are clearly related to the progressively

[6] I may refer here once more to the excellent essay by Gouldner (10) and especially to his idea of the "functional autonomy" of parts. This concept provides an obvious link between social and system integration. He explicitly points out that "the concept of the differential functional autonomy of parts directs attention to the need to distinguish between parts having a greater or lesser vested interest in system maintenance," and that "not only efforts to change the system, but also those directed at *maintaining* it are likely to entail conflict and resistance" as a result of differential functional autonomy. What I find a little ambiguous, however, is his use of the term "parts" of a system: at one stage they seem to mean structural aspects (e.g., ecological conditions); at another, actual groups (the French bourgeoisie). The "parts" which may become functionally autonomous are surely *groups*; the "parts" whose interplay conditions their functional autonomy are the *structural* elements of the system. I hope this will become clear in the subsequent argument.

growing "contradictions" of the economic system. One might almost say that the "conflict" which in Marxian theory is decisive for change is not the *power* conflict arising from the relationships in the productive system, but the *system* conflict arising from "contradictions" between "property institutions" and the "forces of production." Though definitely linked, these two aspects of integration are not only analytically separable, but also, because of the time element involved, factually distinguishable. Thus it is perfectly possible, according to this theory, to say that at any particular point of time a society has a high degree of social integration (e.g., relative absence of class conflict) and yet has a low degree of system integration (mounting excess productive capacity).

Further interest attaches to the fact that the idea of structural contradictions is central to the general functionalist view of change:

> The key concept bridging the gap between statics and dynamics in functional theory is that of strain, tension, contradiction, or discrepancy between the component elements of social and cultural structure. Such strains may be dysfunctional for the social system in its then existing form; they may also be instrumental in leading to changes in that system. When social mechanisms for controlling them are operating effectively, these strains are kept within such bounds as to limit change of social structure (15, p. 122).

The vital question is, of course: what are the "component elements" of social systems which give rise to strain, tension, or contradiction? General functionalism, as I understand it, does not attempt to formulate an answer to this question (10, pp. 244–248). It is, by contrast, in normative functionalism that institutional patterns emerge as the only generally identified and systematically differentiated components of a social system between which there can be conflict and resultant strain. Since social systems are differentiated only along the institutional axis, there can be no place for the kind of contradictions which Marx envisaged, contradictions which are obviously relevant to the problem focus of conflict theory. We may ask, therefore, does the Marxian view contain the elements of a more general sociological formulation?

III

Criticism of the Marxian interpretation of society and social change has focused on the meaning and importance attributed to the "material mode of production." Sometimes, this has been simply and erroneously interpreted as technology. Yet it is quite obvious that in the Marxian schema technological change is not regarded as the prime mover, but as a force which operates interdependently with the productive relations of the society, that is, the prevailing organization of property and labor. The inclusion of productive relationships in the concept "mode of production" lays the theory open to the criticism that the degree of differentiation and independence of such relationships from other social structures in the same society varies very considerably; and that in particular, the saliency of the economic system under capitalism is not at all characteristic of most historical societies in which the mode of political organization heavily conditioned the structure and potential change of productive relationships.[7] Marxian theory has not, for fairly obvious reasons, been overmuch concerned to rebut such criticisms of its basic sociological assumptions. Given its premises about the general long-run decisiveness of the economic order for social change, it has quite logically confined its discussion of system integration to the *internal* dynamics of the mode of production itself — to the economic theory of the contradiction between "forces of production" (technological potential) and the "relations of production" (property institutions).[8]

While this narrowing down of the problem of system integration is highly questionable, the idea of a contradiction between the material conditions of production and the productive institutions of the economic system has a more general relevance that should not be ignored.

First, contradiction implies that the material means of production (e.g., industrial technology) favor a set of potential social relationships (socialist ownership) which constitutes a threat to the existing social relationships institutionalized in the property system (private ownership). Now, whatever reservations one may have about the specific linkage of industrial production with socialist property relationships, there is nothing metaphysical about the general notion of social relationships being somehow implicit in a given set of material conditions. Material conditions most obviously include the technological means of control over the physical and social environment and the skills associated with these means. They include not only the material means of production, but also what Weber frequently refers to as the material means of organization and violence. Such material conditions must surely be included as a variable in any calculus of system integration, since it is clear that they may facilitate the development of "deviant" social relationships which run counter to the dominant institutional patterns of the system. Michels' study of oligarchical tendencies is only the classic example.

Second, according to Marx, the actualization of these potential counter-relationships is determined by the success with which those with vested interests in the existing order are able to resolve the functional incompatibility between the material means of production and the property framework. In the capitalist case, this incompatibility arises from the inability of private property institutions to accommodate the productive capacity of the industrial system. The focal point of strain is "overproduction." The argument, of course, goes further than this. The theory of the "crisis mechanism" not only postulates dysfunctionality but attempts

---

[7] See especially, Weber (22, pp. 739–43).

[8] See, for example, Baran (1) and Sweezy (20). For the difficulty of locating the "crisis mechanism" of feudalism, see Dobb (7).

to demonstrate how the internal contradictions of the mode of production are endogenously intensified to the point of system breakdown by the inherent development of productive forces. This mechanism, most fully elaborated in the case of capitalist societies, is the conveyor belt which moves a society from one stage of its historical evolution to the next. But in order to use the idea of a functional incompatibility between the dominant institutional order of a social system and its material base, it is not necessary to assume that the system must inevitably break down or that it must inevitably be succeeded by another system of a given type.[9]

We now have a view of system integration, particularly relevant to conflict theory, which may be summed up as follows:

1) One generally conceivable source of tension and possible change in a social system is that which arises from a "lack of fit" between its core institutional order and its material substructure.

2) The material substructure in such a case facilitates the development of social relationships which, if actualized, would directly threaten the existing institutional order.

3) The system will be characterized by a typical form of "strain" arising from the functional incompatibility between its institutional order and material base.

4) The actualization of the latent social relationships of the system will depend on the success with which groups having vested interests in the maintenance of the institutional order are able to cope with the dysfunctional tendency of the system in the face of particular exigencies.

5) If these exigencies lead to an intensification of the functional incompatibility of the system, and if compensating measures by vested interest groups lead (unintentionally) to a further actualization of the potential social relationships of the system, a vicious circle of social disintegration and change of the institutional order is under way. If, on the other hand, compensating measures are effective, the institutional order will remain intact, but the focal point of strain will continue to be evident so long as the functional incompatibility of the system persists.

These propositions do not limit the analysis of system integration to the productive system of a society. Nor do they imply a differentiation of types of societies primarily in terms of their modes of production. Such problems cannot be settled a priori. Consequently, the "dominant" or "core" institutional orders may vary from one type of society to another; and the identification of such institutional orders would seem to be first and foremost a way of defining what is meant by saying that a society has changed.[10] There are, however, certain problems which arise

---

[9] See the instructive remarks of Coulborn (4, pp. 254–269).

[10] Thus differences of opinion about the endurance of Western feudal society depend very largely on whether the military, the political, or the economic aspect of this institutional complex is singled out as the "core" order. See Hintze (13).

when the concepts of "dominant" institutional order and material base are applied to social systems. It may make sense to apply such a distinction to some particular subsystem of a society or to some particular type of corporate group; is it equally relevant, in the case of a society, to regard, for example, the productive system as a "material base" from the point of view of the "dominant" political system, even though the productive system manifestly includes institutional elements? Insofar as the predominant concern is with the way in which the material preconditions of a certain type of political action are, or are not, to be found in a given economic order, there would appear to be good reason for answering this question in the affirmative.[11] Such an answer would, of course, in no way prejudice the further explanation of how such a *given* economic order came about; the problem of the "causes" of the type of system instability under consideration is, anyway, a quite separate issue. It should also be noted that the degree of institutional differentiation of economic and political structures varies very considerably. In cases where the relations of production and the relations of political power are not institutionally very distinct, and especially where the relations of production are institutionalized to a considerable extent around political goals, it would seem reasonable to regard the economic order much more directly as a "material base" of the "dominant" political institutions. A brief reference to Weber's discussion of patrimonialism may serve to illustrate these points as well as the propositions previously advanced.

Although Weber's concept of patrimonialism, and especially that of patrimonial bureaucracy, refers primarily to a type of political structure, it is clear from his remarks that this structure might well be regarded as the "core" institutional order of the society and as a major point of reference for societal change. Moreover, Weber's analysis of the material preconditions of bureaucratization clearly indicates the nature of the functional problems facing societies of the patrimonial bureaucratic type. These center on the relationship between the institution of bureaucracy and the material substructure of a subsistence economy. After setting out the general rule that: "A certain measure of a developed money economy is the normal precondition for the unchanged and continued existence, if not for the establishment, of pure bureaucratic administration," Weber goes on to note that historical cases of "distinctly developed and quantitatively large bureaucracies" may be found which "to a very great extent, partly even predominantly, have rested upon compensation of the officials in kind." This he explains by arguing that "even though the full development of a money economy is not an indispensable precon-

---

[11] What else does Weber imply when he writes: "Der Zerfall des Reichs war die notwendige politische Folge des allmaehlichen Schwindens des Verkehrs und der Zunahme der Naturalwirtschaft. Er bedeutete im wesentlichen nur den Wegfall jenes Verwaltungsapparats und damit des geldwirtschaftlichen politischen Ueberbaus, der dem naturalwirtschaftlichen oekonomischen Unterbau nicht mehr angepasst war" (21, p. 308).

dition for bureacratization, bureaucracy as a permanent structure is knit to the one presupposition of a constant income for maintaining it," and that "a stable system of *taxation* is the precondition for the permanent existence of bureaucratic administration." But again: "For well-known and general reasons, only a fully developed money economy offers a secure basis for such a taxation system" (23, pp. 205–209).

The strategic functional problem, then, is one of maintaining a taxation system that can effectively meet the material needs of a bureaucracy in the context of a subsistence, or near-subsistence, economy. The centralizing goal of bureaucratic institutions is constantly liable to sabotage by the potential social relationship structure of the subsistence economy which favors the decentralization and "feudalization" of power relationships.[12] As Weber himself says: "According to all historical experience, without a money economy the bureaucratic structure can hardly avoid undergoing substantial internal changes, or indeed, turning into another type of structure" (23, p. 205). The relationship between bureaucracy and taxation is a highly interdependent one. The efficiency of the bureaucracy depends upon the effectiveness of its taxation system; and the effectiveness of the taxation system depends on the efficiency of the bureaucratic apparatus. Thus, for whatever reason, any increase in the bureaucratic load or decrease in taxation capacity may generate a vicious circle of decentralization of power. Indeed, it might be argued that the "taxation" crisis of patrimonial bureaucracy is essentially analogous to the "production" crisis of capitalism. At any rate, the focal point of strain in this type of society is taxation capacity relative to bureaucratic needs.

This strategic functional problem sets the stage for the characteristic conflicts of interest that arise between the bureaucratic center, the officialdom, landed magnates, and peasantry. The points of tension are those which represent an actualization of the potential for "feudalization": the tendency of officials to "appropriate" the economic and political resources of the office; the struggle of large landowners to gain immunity from taxation and/or usurp fiscal and political functions; and the local relationships of economic and political dependency into which the peasantry are forced in seeking protection against the tax burden of the bureaucratic center. These "centrifugal" tendencies may be seen as both a cause and a consequence of the possible failure of mechanisms for maintaining effective taxation capacity and central control. The outcome of such struggles, and the success with which the functional problem is solved by the bureaucratic center, is, of course, decided in each historical case by the particular circumstances facing the patrimonial bureaucracy. These may vary very considerably; but whether they make for stability

---

[12] The logic of this is succinctly argued by Bloch (3, p. 68) and Hartman (12, p. 19).

or breakdown of bureaucratic institutions, all societies of this type may be studied from the point of view of their common contradiction.[13]

Another example of a not too dissimilar kind is that of the functional tensions arising from the relationship between the totalitarian political system and the industrial economy of the Soviet Union. It is noteworthy in this connection that many who would deny the relevance of the idea of "internal contradictions" to capitalist societies have only too readily exaggerated the incompatibility of industrialism and the institutions of a one-party state. Be this as it may, it would seem that the type of contradiction envisaged here is one which those having an interest in the dominant political institution have thus far successfully controlled, but which nevertheless is likely to remain as a focal point of strain and potential change. It arises from the tendency of an industrial mode of production to create latent interest groups of a class character. This tendency must be "dysfunctional" for a totalitarian political system, one precondition of which is a "classless" society, i.e., an absence of bases of potential social organization outside the party bureaucracy.

Such a contradiction could manifest itself either by such latent interest groups striving for an autonomous corporate existence (which seems unlikely given the nature of party control) or by their subversion of the party organization from within. Of such groups, associated with industrialization, the least potentially threatening is that of worker opposition. Using Weber's typology of class formation, worker protest hardly advanced beyond the stage of "mass reactions of a class character" (labor turnover and so on) in the early phase of Soviet industrialization; and, while disruptive to the economy, it was not allowed to develop into a more politically dangerous "societal" action. More of a threat from this point of view, however — and this is the element of truth in Burnham's otherwise extravagant thesis of a "managerial revolution" — is the so-called "Soviet bourgeoisie": the functionally important quasi-group of predominantly industrial bureaucrats which has emerged as a result of rapid industrialization (9).

The focal point of strain for the totalitarian political system is not simply that this latent class tends to develop vested interests in its position and privileges, but that it has an organizational capacity and cohesiveness that could form the basis of a political opposition. And, given the nature of the political system, such an interest group would be most

---

[13] On the particular conditions favoring the stability of patrimonial bureaucracy in Egypt and China, see Weber (22, pp. 706–709 ff.). The most famous instance of breakdown, that of the later Roman Empire, is a case where the "defense mechanisms" introduced by the bureaucracy (aptly described by Lot as the "regime of castes") intensified the trend towards subsistence economy and actualized the potential for "feudal" relationships. See Weber (21); Lot (14, pp. 62–153); Bloch (2); and for the Byzantine case, Ostrogorsky (16). The general problem of "feudalizing" tendencies in patrimonial bureaucratic societies is discussed in Coulborn (4). On the major lines of conflict in such societies, see Eisenstadt (8).

likely to take the form initially of cliques within the party bureaucracy. Therefore, the strategic functional problem of the dominant institutional order, from this point of view, is that of maintaining the control of the party bureaucracy over the industrial bureaucracy, and more especially of securing the party against infiltration by vested interest groups of the managerial elite (which includes insulating the latter from any wider support in the society). Most fundamentally, the party must develop means by which it can systematically "de-classify" the lines of stratification and interest-group formation that have their basis in the industrial substructure. At the same time, however, (and here arises the point of system tension) such de-classification must not undermine the conditions of industrial efficiency.

IV

The foregoing examples have been all too sketchy, but perhaps they may serve the purpose of illustrating the viewpoint advanced in the main body of the chapter. It has not been the intention to claim that this perspective is the only possible way to approach the problem of social change, still less to imply that there is anything other than a polemical advantage to be gained by focusing on system integration *as opposed* to social integration. What has been suggested, however, may be summed up as follows:

1) The propensity to social change arising from the functional incompatibility between an institutional order and its material base has been ignored by normative functionalists because of their concentration on the moral aspects of social integration.

2) It has been equally ignored by conflict theorists, who, in concentrating on the weakness of the normative functionalist approach to social integration, have failed to relate their interest in social change to the problem of system integration.

BIBLIOGRAPHY

1. Baran, Paul A. *The Political Economy of Growth*. New York: Monthly Review, 1957.

2. Bloch, Marc. "The Rise of Dependent Cultivation and Seigniorial Institutions," in J. H. Clapham and Eileen Power (eds.), *The Cambridge Economic History*, Vol. 1. Cambridge: Cambridge University Press, 1942.

3. Bloch, Marc. *Feudal Society*, translated by L. A. Manyion. London: Routledge and Kegan Paul, 1961.

4. Coulborn, R. *Feudalism in History*. Princeton, N.J.: Princeton University Press, 1956.

5. Dahrendorf, Ralf. *Class and Class Conflict in Industrial Society.* Stanford: Stanford University Press, 1959.

6. Davis, Kingsley. "The Myth of Functional Analysis as a Special Method in Sociology and Anthropology," *American Sociological Review,* Vol. 24, No. 6 (December 1959).

7. Dobb, M. H. (ed.), *The Transition from Feudalism to Capitalism: A Symposium.* Patna, India: People's Book House, 1957.

8. Eisenstadt, S. N. "Political Struggle in Bureaucratic Societies," *World Politics,* Vol. 9, No. 1 (October 1956).

9. Feldmesser, Robert A. "Equality and Inequality under Khrushchev," *Problems of Communism,* Vol. 9, No. 2 (March–April 1960).

10. Gouldner, Alvin W. "Reciprocity and Autonomy in Functional Theory," in Llewellyn Gross (ed.), *Symposium on Sociological Theory.* New York: Harper and Bros., 1959.

11. Green, T. H. *Principles of Political Obligation.* London: Longmans, 1906.

12. Hartman, Ludo Moritz. *The Early Medieval State.* London: The Historical Association, 1960.

13. Hintze, Otto. "Wesen und Verbreitung des Feudalismus," *Staat and Verfassung.* Leipzig: Koehler and Amelang, 1941.

14. Lot, Ferdinand. *La Fin du Monde Antique et le Debut du Moyen Age.* Paris: Michel, 1951.

15. Merton, Robert K. *Social Theory and Social Structure.* Glencoe, Ill.: The Free Press, 1957.

16. Ostrogorsky, Georg. "Agrarian Conditions in the Byzantine Empire in the Middle Ages," in J. H. Clapham and Eileen Power (eds.), *The Cambridge Economic History,* Vol. I. Cambridge: Cambridge University Press, 1942.

17. Parsons, Talcott. *The Social System.* London: Routledge, 1952.

18. Parsons, Talcott. *Structure and Process in Modern Society.* Glencoe, Ill.: The Free Press, 1960.

19. Rex, John. *Key Problems of Sociological Theory.* London: Humanities Press, 1961.

20. Sweezy, Paul M. *The Theory of Capitalist Development.* New York: Monthly Review, 1942.

21. Weber, Max. "Die Sozialen Gruende des Untergangs der antiken Kultur," in *Gesammelte Aufsaetze zur Sozial- und Wirtschaftsgeschichte.* Tuebingen: Mohr (Paul Siebeck), 1924.

22. Weber, Max. *Wirtschaft und Gesellschaft.* Tuebingen: Mohr (Paul Siebeck), 1947.

23. Weber, Max. *From Max Weber: Essays in Sociology,* translated and edited by H. H. Gerth and C. Wright Mills. London: Oxford University Press, 1948.

24. Williams, Robin M., Jr. *American Society, A Sociological Interpretation.* New York: Alfred A. Knopf, 1960.

10

H. David Kirk

The Impact of Drastic Change

on Social Relations—A Model for

the Identification and Specification

of Stress

Men are creatures of habit. Habits are formed and reinforced in social contexts. Habituated modes of conduct, directed and sanctioned by group norms, lend continuity to social relations. When a situation is subjected to sudden or drastic change, the socii in it can no longer rely on each other's habituated responses to role expectations. Role performances will then be to some extent disordered. In the simplest sense this is the kind of structural stress which drastic change engenders in social systems.

When policy-makers and administrators occupationally concern themselves with social change they typically do so along two lines: (1) They tend to ask how the behavior of the men they govern can be changed in certain particular directions, or, (2) they may ask how their organizations can best cope with stresses that derive from change brought about by external or internal forces. This chapter is addressed to the second of these administrative considerations. It proposes a frame of reference

258

for conceptualizing stresses derived from drastic change and for determining procedures capable of alleviating these stresses.

In outline this frame of reference consists of five parts. In the case of any particular actor, drastic change implies a discrepancy between the situation he expected to experience (part 1) and the situation as he actually encounters it (part 2). As long as the discrepancy is not too great the actor may continue to perform his role more or less adequately, but at some point the discrepancy will become too severe and will seriously interfere with role performance. This interference with role performance, following upon a "situational discrepancy," is here called "role handicap" (part 3). Discrepancies between culturally induced expectations and subsequent encounters with a drastically changed situation are illustrated by sudden illness, severe accidents, death, and disasters. Bereavement, for instance, involves role handicap in that it interferes with the pursuit of an established relationship. Similarly, disasters frequently prevent victims from carrying out important role obligations.[1] Role-handicapped persons typically seek some means of coping with the handicap. A wide range of social and psychological mechanisms can become means of adaptation (part 4). These adaptive steps are intended, or unconsciously set in motion, to give support to role performances which have been interfered with by drastic change. But it must not be assumed that such means of coping necessarily serve the desired end. The question must be raised to what extent, if at all, they function as "role supports" (part 5).

The concepts of Situational Discrepancy and Role Handicap resemble those formulated by other investigators, notably Relative Deprivation (16), Cognitive Dissonance (2), Interpersonal Competence (3), and Alienation (13). However, only the last mentioned has directly influenced and aided the construction of our model. The model evolved in the course of analysis of data from studies of two social systems which had been subjected to drastic change. In both cases the object of study was in part to discover how the observed changes affected the performance of crucial roles. The two systems studied are structurally so different that the pertinence of our concepts suggests that these may have wider applicability in the analysis of the impact of change on social relations. We shall now inspect our analytic model in the context of the two studies which gave rise to it. Such an inspection will facilitate demonstration of the utility of the concepts as well as their further elaboration as instruments of sociological analysis.

---

[1] Interestingly, several of the disaster studies sponsored by the National Research Council foreshadow parts of this model. Thus Beach and Lucas (1, pp. 136–137) have drawn attention to the importance of role preparedness as a basis for coping with the problems brought on by the disaster. Perry, Silber, and Bloch (10, pp. 35–38) have inquired into patterns of communication about the disaster within the affected group, and have sought to evaluate the relative utility of different approaches to communication as means of adaptation. Perry and Perry (11, p. 30) have suggested that the acquisition of new skills as part of a realignment of role obligations tends to supply functional role supports.

Case 1: Drastic change and its behavioral consequences in a large social system

Several years ago this writer was able to study the detailed reports of the Community Analysis Section of the Manzanar Relocation Center, assembled at Cornell University. These records bore testimony to the stresses which resulted from the evacuation of the Japanese minority from the West Coast states. The loss of effective civil rights by the Japanese Americans forcibly removed from their homes in 1942 will here serve as an instance of "drastic change." Their responses to an official demand for the expression of unqualified loyalty will serve as an indication of civic role performance under stress.

Early in 1942 more than 111,000 persons of Japanese ancestry were forcibly evacuated from California, Oregon, and Washington. They were sent to "relocation centers" farther inland. These centers, under the administration of the War Relocation Authority, were relatively makeshift assembly camps, intended as points from which the evacuated people could be relocated in other parts of the United States. The circumstances of wartime fear of a Japanese invasion of the West Coast and the long-standing pattern of anti-Oriental agitation there combined to delay speedy relocation and to make the bleak, isolated desert and mountain camps into places of detention.

While the Japanese on the West Coast had had some warning of the brewing storm, the danger signals had been ambiguous. Some groups pressed for their immediate removal after the attack on Pearl Harbor; other groups urged them to stay. Few among the Japanese-American minority had financial resources outside of small businesses, farms, or jobs. They were largely dependent on a Caucasian market. But a small minority left voluntarily. Most stayed on; some planted new crops. No evidence existed that they posed a threat to the safety of the United States. But the irrational power of fear-propelled stereotypes nevertheless deprived them of their civil rights as legal residents and citizens of the United States. The ultimate blow was struck by General John L. deWitt, Commanding General of the Western Defense Command. On February 14, 1942, he sent a memorandum to Secretary of War Henry L. Stimson, recommending the "immediate evacuation of all persons of Japanese lineage," aliens and citizens alike, from the "entire strategic area" of California, Oregon, and Washington. In this document the General not only gave expression to the most virulent racism but did so with the help of a most remarkable syllogism:

> . . . In the war in which we are now engaged racial affinities are not severed by migration. The Japanese race is an enemy race and while many second- and third-generation Japanese born on United States' soil, possessed of United States' citizenship, have become "Americanized," the racial strains

are undiluted. . . . *That Japan is allied with Germany and Italy in this struggle is no ground for assuming that any Japanese, barred from assimilation by convention as he is, though born and raised in the United States, will not turn against this nation when the final test of loyalty comes. It, therefore, follows that along the vital Pacific Coast over 112,000 potential enemies, of Japanese extraction, are at large today. There are indications that these are organized and ready for concerted action at a favorable opportunity. The very fact that no sabotage has taken place to date is a disturbing and confirming indication that such action will be taken* (12, emphases added).

This line of reasoning, based on the assumption that where there is no smoke a very dangerous fire is just about to break out, was not of the General's own making. Paradoxically, Walter Lippmann, who first used the term stereotype (8) in a psychological sense, had apparently been responsible for it. A few days before the General's letter Mr. Lippmann had gone to California to learn at first hand about the situation of the Japanese Americans. On February 12 his nationally syndicated column, written in San Francisco, was entitled "The Fifth Column on the Coast." In it he said:

> . . . since the outbreak of the Japanese war there has been no important sabotage on the Pacific Coast. From what we know about Hawaii and about the fifth column in Europe, this is not, as some have liked to think, a sign that nothing is to be feared. *It is a sign that the blow is well organized and that it is held back until it can be struck with maximum effect* (9, pp. 126–127)

Lippmann then continued by advocating that the civil rights of citizens of Japanese ancestry be set aside for the duration of the emergency. On the basis of such thinking, subsequently reflected in General deWitt's document and in Westbrook Pegler's column ("the Japanese in California should be under armed guard to the last man and woman right now and to hell with habeas corpus until the danger is over") the evacuation of the Japanese-American minority was instituted by Executive Order.

Late in March of 1942, the first large group of Japanese residents and American citizens of Japanese ancestry was moved from Los Angeles to the Manzanar Reception Center in Owens Valley, California. The majority of the immigrant generation (Issei) were middle-aged or old. To be torn out of their life seemed to most of them economic extinction in America. In the rush of events preceding evacuation they frequently sold farms, equipment, and household goods at great loss, or abandoned them. Although the federal government had set up channels through which goods might be stored, the legal machinery was slow in developing.

The first shock of camp life was tremendous, but since the camps were initially regarded as way stations to a more settled life elsewhere, the shock was absorbed. In spite of adverse physical and psychological conditions of camp life many of the young citizens (Nisei) at first insisted that a better life was in store for them. But the insidious racist propaganda against them led to demands by chauvinistic newspapers and organizations for further restrictions against the evacuees. Thus work furloughs away from the camps were ended and the evacuees were restricted to a limited camp area which was surrounded by wire fence and guarded by soldiers. The conditions were those of internment and they were indistinguishable for aliens and citizens.

Two well-meant but badly calculated administrative acts further aggravated the situation and led to the events which provide the basis for a study of response to drastic change. The first of these administrative acts called for the establishment of community councils for whose offices only Nisei would be eligible. This idea had originated in Washington in the hope that the Nisei could thereby be partially compensated for the loss of status and the ineffectiveness of their citizenship. It was a vain hope. In some centers, notably Manzanar, plans for community government were being foiled. Feelings ran high. Not until May 1943, when the official policy was altered to include Issei in the community councils, did some of the camps, which had refused to do so previously, set up such governments under charter. But the effect of the crisis had been that the Issei, who had gradually been gaining in power and prestige among the young under the impact of total experience in center life, had really come to take a central position. The crisis had forced some Nisei to an unconditional support of administrative policies, however unreasonable they might be. And it had delivered others to the values and controls of the traditional Japanese family. These events set the stage for the second and decisive crisis in the camps.

As a result of Director Dillon Myer's hope for a speedier resettlement of the evacuees, a plan for leave clearance proceedings was made. This plan was joined to another one for voluntary enlistment of the Nisei. The enlistment policy was announced by the Secretary of War on January 28, 1943. Specially instructed officers visited the camps, addressed the evacuees, and sought to answer their questions. All evacuees of 17 years and over were asked to register. Two types of questionnaire were set before them. One was for male citizens of Japanese ancestry, the other for female citizens and aliens of both sexes. The first one was headed "Selective Service System," the other "War Relocation Authority Application for Leave Clearance." The questionnaires were similar — there were some 30 items dealing with personal and family history and status. It was a complicated and lengthy document, but truly troublesome were Questions 27 and 28 which read, for male and female citizens respectively:

Male Citizens

No. 27: Are you willing to serve in the armed forces of the United States on combat duty, wherever ordered?

No. 28: Will you swear unqualified allegiance to the United States of America and faithfully defend the United States from any and all attack by foreign or domestic forces, and forswear any form or allegiance or obedience to the Japanese Emperor, or any other foreign government, power, or organization?

Female citizens and aliens of both sexes:

No. 27: If the opportunity presents itself and you are found qualified, would you be willing to volunteer for the Army Nurse Corps or the WAAC?

No. 28: Will you swear unqualified allegiance to the United States of America and forswear any form of allegiance to the Japanese Emperor, or any other foreign government, power, or organization (15)?

The position of the Issei was a difficult one throughout. It became intolerable when they were asked to swear loyalty to the United States from whose citizenship they were barred by United States law. Under these circumstances most of them thought it necessary to do nothing that would invalidate their citizenship obligations toward Japan. At the same time they wished to assure the American authorities of their harmless intentions. One of them put it this way:

No Issei would disobey the laws of the United States. They've always been law-abiding. In that sense they can be called loyal to the United States. On the other hand, none of them are disloyal to Japan. *You can't use the word "loyalty" or "disloyalty" for Issei because it just doesn't apply to them* (17, p. 101, emphasis added).

When this situation came to be understood in Washington, an inoffensive question was substituted for use by the Issei. The new question read:

Will you swear to abide by the laws of the United States and take no action which would in any way interfere with the war effort of the United States?

Now the vast majority of them proceeded to answer in the affirmative. But the damage had been done. Many Nisei had joined their parents in saying "no." When their elders were given the opportunity to change their answers, the Nisei were left with non-affirmative replies. From figures published by the Statistics Section of the Relocation Planning Division of W.R.A. (14, p. 165) we obtain a picture of the final registration results for all the centers combined, and for Manzanar separately. Of the total number of aliens who registered, barely 2 per cent said "no," whereas of the total number of citizens who registered, 12 per cent said "no" to Question 28. At Manzanar the ratio was even more extreme; there 1 per cent of the aliens and 22 per cent of the citizens gave non-affirmative replies.

The plan was to segregate the disloyal from the loyal elements. But the results of the leave clearance registration were soon understood to be a poor indicator of the evacuees' true attitudes. The citizens who had given non-affirmative replies to Question 28 were therefore to be given a chance to change their minds. For this purpose, hearing boards were established in the camps.

At Manzanar two such boards met simultaneously. Morris E. Opler, Community Analyst at Manzanar, attended as many of the hearings as he could, shuttling back and forth between the two boards. His hearing records of 479 cases, somewhat more than half of all the cases being reviewed at Manzanar, represent a close approximation to a random sample. They provide insight into the differential impact of the drastic changes involved in evacuation, internment, and registration. Let us inquire of these records how different categories of internees responded to the boards' inquiry as to why they persisted in their non-affirmative replies. In Opler's group of 479 cases there were 24 aliens. Only the citizens are of interest to us because we have asked how drastic change affects the role enactment of citizenship. More specifically, we shall now ask whether different degrees of commitment to American institutions are associated with differential response patterns to the loyalty question. Opler's records supply only a very crude index of "commitment to American institutions." His procedure had been to note whether an evacuee had ever resided in Japan. For lack of a more satisfactory index, we shall take "no residence in Japan" to mean that such persons were more likely to be committed to American institutions than persons who had resided in Japan.

The records were thus coded for foreign residence, and also for the reasons these evacuees gave for their persistent refusal to swear unqualified loyalty to the United States. These reasons were grouped:

* — Fear of forced relocation
* — Family decision
* — Marriage or engagement to person saying "no"
* — Abridgement of citizenship
* — Race discrimination
* — Property loss (no future in the U.S.)
— Generally angry at evacuation
— Wanting to live in Japan
— Loyalty divided or for Japan
— Uncertainty
— No information or report incomplete

Table 1 shows the frequencies with which citizens who had never been to Japan, and those who had been there, gave explanations of this order to the hearing boards.

* starred categories are mentioned in Opler's unpublished report "Segregants at Manzanar"

This table shows that in each category of citizens reasons of the order of "Family Attachment" accounted for over 40 per cent of the replies. Likewise, uncertain and incomplete replies in each case accounted for nearly 20 per cent of the total. When these categories of "Family Attachment," "Uncertain," and "No Information" are removed from the table, the remaining four-fold table clearly shows a relationship between the index of "commitment to American institutions" and the manner of response to drastic change.

TABLE 1

Citizen Evacuees at Manzanar Maintaining Non-Affirmative Replies to Question 28: By Residence and Reasons Given to Hearing Boards.

Type of Reason Given for Retaining Non-Affirmative Reply	Citizens Who Have Resided Only in the United States		Citizens Who Have Resided in Japan	
	Number	*Per Cent*	*Number*	*Per Cent*
Fear of Forced Relocation	12	5.5	2	.8
Family Decision	56	25.8	40	16.8
Marriage or Engagement to Persons Wanting to Go to Japan	22	10.1	60	25.2
"FAMILY ATTACHMENT" total		41.4%		42.8%
Abridgement of Citizenship	9	4.2	4	1.7
Race Discrimination	12	5.5	1	.4
Property Loss (no future in U.S.)	14	6.5	1	.4
Generally Angry at Evacuation	29	13.4	5	2.1
"PROTEST" total		29.6%		4.6%
Want to live in Japan	15	6.9	64	26.9
Loyalty Divided or for Japan	5	2.3	15	6.3
"ORIENTATION TOWARD JAPAN" total		9.2%		33.2%
Uncertain or Ambivalent Reply	3	1.4	11	4.6
Information Incomplete	40	18.4	35	14.7
"RESIDUAL" total		19.8%		19.3%
All cases	217	100%	238	100%

Chi square $= 77.32$ $p < .001$

While both groups of citizens retained their non-affirmative replies to Question 28, and thus seem superficially to have responded identically to the drastic changes to which they were subjected, we have now found that their response patterns apparently served quite different functions. In the case of the citizens whom we judged to have the lesser attachment to American institutions, we found a considerably lower tendency to protest the loss of effective citizenship rights than in the case of citizens

TABLE 2

*Differential Commitment to American Institutions
and Response to Drastic Change*

TYPE OF REASON GIVEN FOR RETAINING NON-AFFIRMATIVE REPLY:	RESIDENCE ONLY IN U.S. (*Interpreted as high commitment to American institutions*)		SOME RESIDENCE IN JAPAN (*Interpreted as lower commitment to American institutions*)	
	Number	*Per Cent*	*Number*	*Per Cent*
"PROTEST"..........	64	76	11	12
"ORIENTATION TOWARD JAPAN"....	20	24	79	88

Phi. = .81
p < .001

whom we believe to have the greater commitment. The citizens who were most deeply committed to the political institutions of America were also by definition the most deprived by the withdrawal of their citizenship rights. If they knew the Constitution of the United States they were aware that the Fifth and Fourteenth Amendments specifically guarantee that no person shall be "deprived of . . . liberty, or property, without due process of law." But they and their families had in fact been deprived of liberty and property by executive order, without due process of law. The rights which they had fully expected to be theirs by the fact of their birth in the United States proved worth little or nothing when most needed. They were therefore deprived of their capacity to enact their citizenship role. Finally, when asked to declare their loyalty to the nation which had handicapped them in this way, they were more inclined than their brethren with lesser expectations, to say "no" in protest. In other words, they came to consider illegitimate means (the refusal to swear unqualified loyalty) as offering them opportunities for asserting their rights to the institutionalized goals of citizenship.

We have thus seen our model emerge from the data of an empirical study. We learned that the citizen generation had been socialized in American schools and that most of them had not visited or lived in Japan. Therefore they had to have certain definite expectations for their role performances as American citizens, based on constitutional guarantees of rights to liberty and property, as well as on more diffuse values of equal opportunities without regard to ancestry. With the outbreak of hostilities between Japan and the United States, anti-Oriental agitation and invasion fears combined to produce the evacuation and relocation camp problem. Under these conditions the citizenship rights of Americans of Japanese ancestry had been voided in fact if not in principle.

The situational discrepancy experienced by the Nisei meant that, shorn of the powers of citizenship, they could not carry out their civic roles in sanctioned ways. They were also unable to perform their filial roles which called for acts of shielding alien parents against defamation, loss of home, livelihood, and life earnings. Under these conditions of role handicap some Nisei sought to adapt themselves by rationalizing the adverse circumstances as unavoidable and temporary. They looked to the future. Others turned to the traditional values of their parents, thereby looking to the past for stability and role support. A third group, which we studied in some detail, took their stand in the present, refusing to accede to government demands for an expression of unqualified loyalty when reciprocal rights were witheld. Although we have here interpreted certain behavior patterns as mechanisms of adaptation we shall for the moment refrain from an assessment of these mechanisms as functional role supports. To this we shall return after a consideration of the impact of change on another social system, in the context of which we can refine our concepts and procedure.

Case 2: Drastic change and role handicap in a small social system

The data from studies of the Adoption Research Project at McGill University have made possible the further development of the concepts under consideration. The small system to be investigated now is that of the husband-wife dyad. The drastic change to which it is subjected is the spouses' discovery that their union is childless and that they must depend on adoption if they are to have a family. This situation lends itself to an enumeration of various expectations which become frustrated; in other words, it permits a point-by-point dissection of the situational discrepancy. The following listing represents that enumeration of the parts of the discrepancy as far as it has been learned. Within this enumeration we shall try to locate different dimensions of role handicap.

THE SITUATION OF BIOLOGICAL PARENTHOOD WHICH TYPICALLY SERVES THE HUSBAND-WIFE DYAD AS THE FRAME OF REFERENCE FOR ROLE EXPECTATIONS

THE SITUATION CONFRONTING THE NON-FECUND COUPLE DESIRING FAMILY LIFE.

1. Preparation for adult life presumes that there will be children. This implies that persons moving into marriage ordinarily take for granted their potential fertility. They have thus a mental link between marriage and the ability to have offspring.

While the cultural script prepares people to expect fertility, for sterility and its interpersonal consequences there is little if any preparation. Interviews with 70 adoptive parents have shown that only 13 per cent could recall ever having considered the possibility of childlessness before they encountered it in their marriage.

2. The vast majority of people have been raised by their biological parents. They are aware of models for parenthood which fit the circumstances of fecundity.

Adopters have seldom had intimate contact with adoptive parents who might serve them as role models.

Preparation for parental roles, especially the mother role, is aided by childhood play. During courtship and early marriage, aided by the assumption of potential fertility, the couple recall their experiences while discussing what they will do when their own first child comes — their hopes and plans are partly cast in terms of their own experience.

The pre-adoptive parents will find that their recall will not be fully suited to the preparation for substitute parenthood.

4. Preparation for biological parent roles is *gradual* — the period of pregnancy provides the couple with a known timetable which moves them imperceptibly toward progressive involvement in their coming parental tasks.

Preparation for adoptive parenthood tends to be *abrupt*, with no clear-cut timetable by which they can shape their feelings and thoughts about their hoped-for parenthood.

5. Maternity clothing begins to be worn about the mid-term of pregnancy. This clothing is an external sign to others and to the couple of their changing position. It thereby assists the couple in moving into the path of developing parenthood. (Note also the folklore about irrational food cravings which suggest that the culture gives the pregnant woman much latitude in her concern for herself and her role.)

For adopters there are few signs to impress on others and on themselves the changing position for which they are reaching.

6. The biological parents are ultimately *independent* in the procurement of their child. However much they may utilize the technological services of medicine, surgery, and hospital, they know that procurement is possible without all

Adopting couples are ultimately *dependent* on the services of a middle man, whether this helper is professional, or friend, social worker, physician, lawyer, minister, or black marketeer. (Note that relative dependence may be increased in agency adoptions, partly because there is

these services. Essentially they are *not in need of a middle man.* (Note here the importance of relative independence and autonomy in the middle-class value system.)

7. The biological tasks of gestation are entirely those of the female and this "division of labor" aids the process of solidifying marital roles. Division of labor makes for interdependence and therefore leads to social solidarity.

8. At the birth of their first child parents are typically in their twenties, the wife in her early twenties. Further, the time between marriage and the birth of the first child tends to be short, i.e., between one and two and one-half years. Both of these factors, the spouses' ages and the length of their marriage at the birth of the first child, are in favor of rather easy transition from married-pair living to life with a child.

9. People in their twenties have typically a relatively high level of energy for the chores of infant care.

10. Because parental obligations are total and unqualified, parents are expected to accept all deficiencies in their offspring. This obligation of unqualified acceptance means that they are not allowed to be preferential, but that they must consider every child equally desirable and a proper member of their family permanently, "for better or for worse."

here no direct transaction between parent and adopters, but also partly because the latter are frequently not clear about the agency's criteria for evaluating applicants.)

In the preparation for adoptive parenthood, both spouses have biologically inactive roles, approximating that of the male in the biological situation. This state therefore precludes ready role differentiation in preparation for later family living.

At the coming of their first child adopters are typically in their thirties, at least seven to eight years older than their biological counterparts. Furthermore, there is a wider age range for adopting than for natural parents, i.e., there are proportionately far more adopting parents over 40 than natural parents, at the time of the arrival of the first child. This, plus the fact that they have had a long, and frequently frustrating time between marriage and adoption, implies that the shift to parenthood will involve greater difficulties for them than for natural parents.

People in their thirties have probably a somewhat lower level of energy for these same tasks.

Adopters are apparently expected to be qualified in the connection they make with the child before the adoption is legalized. The fact that they may not be allowed to keep the child probably keeps some adopters from making as firm a feeling connection with the child as they otherwise would. Some adopters have been counseled by doctor or agency to return a child found to be defective. Since such rationality and qualifications are clearly not applicable to parenthood as they have learned to think of it, the adopters are likely to be at a loss as to the meaning of their position. This element of rationality, as an expectation of adoptive parenthood, is reflected in laws which provide for the possibility that an adoption, once legalized, can be set aside.

11. With the child's coming, parents are fully expected to do everything in their power to make him one of their group, to integrate him into their midst. Only after he has become fully a member need they give any thought to his participation in groups outside the family circle.

For over two decades, adopters have been advised that they must tell the adopted child about his adoption. Although this professional prescription has been surrounded by assurances that it will not be a problem if started very early in the child's life, this very aspect of the prescription makes it especially problematic. It means that adopters are confronted by conflicting role obligations — the first to integrate the child fully before he is allowed to find other membership and reference groups; the other to begin his differentiation out of their midst simultaneously as they are seeking to integrate him.

12. Once licensed to marry, the couple have no further requirements to meet to make them eligible for parenthood.

Adopters have to show authorities that they are fit for parenthood. Eligibility must usually be proved along lines of economic, psychological, and marital stability, and membership in religious organizations.

13. Parental status is initiated during pregnancy and fully secured at birth. All rights, duties, and privileges of parenthood accrue to the new parents at that time. This fact aids them in directing all their feelings to the infant as a *member* of their family unit.

Parental status is not fully secured at the arrival of the child in the adoptive household. Adopting parents are responsible for the child's maintenance and safety, but guardianship rights remain in the hands of others who are still *in loco parentis*, i.e., either the natural parent(s) or the agency.

14. The relative certainty of the child's coming makes possible an early sharing of news with parents and friends. Their rejoicing will be supportive dur-

The considerable uncertainty connected with adoption plans frequently inhibits sharing of plans with family members or friends. Thus, at the time of the adopting couple's other difficul-

ing some of the trying times which may be part of the pregnancy.

ties, there is the additional fact that others, through ignorance, may be unable to rally and support them.

15. At the time of the child's birth the family usually gathers around the new parent couple, looking for family likenesses in the newborn, remarking on the choice of name, and are frequently participants in religious ceremonies whereby they assert the new member's part in the group.

In adoption there are no ceremonies of this order to mark the new member's arrival in the family. Knowledge of the rupture of the family line precludes looking for family likenesses.

16. In our society, biological parenthood is sanctioned and rewarded by a variety of benefits which are conferred on the new parents. For instance, medical and hospital care plans recognize and help pay for certain costs involved in the child's arrival. Further, federal and state tax laws allow medical costs of pregnancy and birth to be deducted from taxable income.

For adopting couples there is no equivalent arrangement to take care of the costs of the child's arrival. Tax laws do not uniformly make provision for the deduction of expenses involved in adoption. Thus while California income tax law permits such expenses as legitimate deductions, federal law does not do so. (In 1960 former California Congressman Kasem sought unsuccessfully to introduce such a bill [HR 9333].)

17. If the child dies, even shortly after birth, the parents are given the support of understanding and sympathy of their friends and the community, just as would occur in the case of the death of a member of longer standing.

When an adoptive couple loses a child prior to legalization, either by death or by removal and return to the natural parent, there is no great likelihood that they will receive an equivalent support from others.

This listing of 17 deprivational circumstances associated with family formation by non-fecund couples was given its present ordering with the aid of Seeman's typology of alienation (13). I have argued that alienation represents the subjective concomitant of the objective condition called role handicap. This correspondence between alienation and role handicap is revealed in the list of items that constitute the situational discrepancy of non-fecund adopters. To enable us to inspect this concept relationship we shall first briefly summarize four of Seeman's five types of alienation.

Powerlessness: "This variant of alienation can be conceived of as the expectancy or probability held by the individual that his own behavior cannot determine the occurrence of the outcomes, or reinforcements, he seeks" (13, p. 784).

Meaninglessness: "We may speak of high alienation, . . . when the individual is unclear as to what he ought to believe — when the individual's minimal standards for clarity in decision-making are not met. [Alienation in this sense is also] characterized by a low expectancy that satisfactory predictions about future outcomes of behavior can be made" (13, p. 786).

Normlessness: "Following Merton's lead, the anomic situation, from the individual's point of view, may be defined as one in which there is a high expectancy that socially unapproved behaviors are required to achieve given goals" (13, p. 788).

Isolation: "The alienated in the isolation sense are those who, like the intellectual, assign a low reward value to goals or beliefs that are typically highly valued in the given society" (13, pp. 788–789).

Powerlessness is thus experienced by an actor when the situation which confronts him does not furnish him with the minimum of *autonomy* he had expected for the performance of his role. Meaninglessness is experienced when the actor finds that the *role preparation* he had been given is insufficient or misleading in the situation encountered. An actor experiences normlessness when he finds himself in a situation in which he cannot carry out his *role* obligations by normatively sanctioned means.

The listing of 17 aspects of the non-fecund adopters' situational discrepancy reveals that 11 of them pertain to these types of role handicap. Points 1–5 each indicate handicap in the area of *role preparation*, Points 6–9 refer to handicaps in *role autonomy*, and Points 10 and 11 are instances of handicaps in meeting *role obligations*. Seeman's fourth type of alienation as defined by him, has not appeared in this listing of the situational discrepancy of non-fecund parenthood because of the characteristics of adoption. By definition, non-fecund adopters assign a high reward value to the goals of family and children. Non-fecund people would be isolated in Seeman's sense, if they rejected the culturally given values of fecundity and family life. What we have found is a type of role handicap apparently not covered by Seeman's definition of *Isolation*. Our adopters lack sanctions which fully legitimate their role. Although this type of role handicap and its concomitant sense of estrangement may appear quite different from the isolation which derives from an actor's rejection of cultural values, both types have in common the problem of value sharing. For purposes of our analysis we shall therefore enlarge the concept of *Isolation* to include estrangement that results from lack of shared values and sanctions as well as from their rejection.

We have now identified some of the types of role handicap which at least, in the system currently under consideration, represent the focal points of strain derived from drastic change. Now we must address ourselves to the question of the differential distribution of these handicaps in the system. Two questions must be raised with respect to differential distribution of strain: First, how are the handicaps distributed among the different positions in the system? And second, what handicaps appear to be most pressing? In order to answer, a recent study of the experiences of adopters asked 283 husbands and wives separately:

> Looking back over some of the experiences you had in becoming an adoptive parent, which of the following experiences did you at the time find rather difficult or hard, and which not so difficult or hard?
> — Learning that you would probably not have a child born to you.
> — Having to depend on the assistance of outsiders (agency, doctor) in getting a child.
> — Having to prove to the authorities (agency and/or court) that you were suitable for raising children, something biological parents don't have to prove.
> — Having no dependable timetable (such as a nine-month's pregnancy) for knowing how soon the child would arrive.
> — Knowing, that even when the child came to you, and until legal adoption, you would not be full parents.
> — Discovering that among your family and friends there are those who are ill-informed about the meaning of being an adoptive parent.

Sixty-nine per cent of the wives and 37 per cent of the husbands said they found the experience of childlessness very difficult. Forty-two per cent of the wives and 28 per cent of the husbands deplored the lack of a timetable in family formation by adoption. Thirty-one per cent of the wives and 20 per cent of the husbands mentioned three or more items as having been difficult or hard. The distribution of role handicap in this marital system thus appears to be uneven. Non-fecundity has evidently more disastrous consequences for the interpersonal expectations of wives than of husbands.

In addition to the question of distribution of role handicap among different positions, we can pose the question of the relative importance of different types of role handicap in a system. Table 3 shows the frequencies with which non-fecund wives identified various role-handicapping events as difficult or hard. It indicates that the meaning and importance attached to different aspects of role handicap differs within the same position.

TABLE 3

Frequencies With Which Wives Identified Role-handicapping Experiences as Difficult or Hard

EVENT:	TOTAL NUMBER OF WIVES REPORTING EVENT:	PER CENT REPORTING THE EVENT TO HAVE BEEN DIFFICULT OR HARD:
Discovery of Infertility	224	69
Lack of Known Timetable	255	42
Lack of Parental Status at Coming of Child	263	31
Dependence on Outsiders	272	28
Having to Furnish Proof of Eligibility	268	19
Other People Ill-Informed	235	16

Any analysis of the impact of change on social organization should then take account of the distribution of stress among positions and among different aspects of role performance. Thus questions of autonomy may weigh more heavily in some situations than questions of clarity and predictability. Where it is possible to study the distribution of such stresses empirically, that will be preferable. In the case of changes to be introduced intentionally their impact will have to be anticipated in the light of knowledge about the organization in question. Where the organization is large and complex and the role relations share in that complexity, studies of the actual or expected outcome of change will have to take into consideration the perspectives in which different groups see the organization. If, for instance, a state or provincial administration plans to introduce the drastic changes involved in a medicare program, it will have to anticipate the impact of the changes from the perspectives of the medical profession as well as of the organizational machinery within which the program is to be administered. Chart 1 lists some rudimentary questions meant to guide inquiries into the distribution of stress in consequence of organizational change.

Assessing the Means of Adaptation

Questions concerning the distribution of stress lead to the related issues of means of adaptation. If we learn where social relations are likely to be most strained we can more readily look to the ways in which role incumbents seek to cope with the strain. For the Nisei in relocation camps various means of adaptation seemed possible. Some sought to accept traditional Japanese family values. Others resisted this kind of cultural capitulation and sought to maintain faith in American institutions, going along with the requirements of the federal government and

CHART 1

Questions to Guide the Analysis of the Distribution of Stress in Complex Organizations involving Professional Activity and Subjected to, or Anticipating, Change

QUESTIONS IN THE PERSPECTIVE OF ORGANIZATIONAL (ADMINISTRATIVE) INTERESTS:	QUESTIONS IN THE PERSPECTIVE OF PROFESSIONAL INTERESTS:
Do the means of control in the hands of the administration suffice for the pursuit of administrative ends under changed conditions?	Do the professional participants have sufficient power to pursue their interests under changed conditions?
Are professional attitudes, skills, and knowledge specific enough to permit the administrators to predict the outcome of administrative action under changed conditions?	Is the organizational structure well enough defined to give unambiguous directions? Is the changed organizational context such as to permit predictability of outcome of professional activity?
Are there organizational norms which do not sanction certain professional techniques or procedures and which therefore invite deviant behavior on the part of the professionals?	Are there professional norms which do not sanction organizational requirements and which therefore tend to call forth repressive or underhanded administrative action?
How do professional goals under changed conditions affect the security of the administrative officers?	How do the organizational goals under the changed conditions affect the morale of the professional personnel?

its War Relocation Authority. Finally, there were those who voiced their protest over the loss of their citizenship rights through the paradox of a "loyalty of disloyalty." It was a mode of adaptation by which the role-handicapped actors sought to recover some degree of power or autonomy. While one may doubt the effectiveness of this method as a role support for the Nisei who took this position, it is also likely that the collective impact which their "conscientious objection" had on their fellow Americans was not inconsiderable in the long run.

In the case of the adopters it was found that the most typical mode of adaptation was through denial of differences between adoptive and natural parenthood. This mode of coping is one by which the role-handicapped actors seek to increase the clarity and predictability of their situation. A theoretical analysis of the adoptive situation (5) suggests that coping through denial is inimical to the long-term interests of the adoptive parent-child relationship. More recent research findings (6) factually bear this out. In other words, in this situation the most prevalent mode of adaptation does not serve as a functional role support.

An assessment of the relative utility of different coping behavior calls for a number of analytic steps. *Firstly,* it requires a theoretical listing of possible means by which role-handicapped actors could respond adaptively to the changed situation that confronts them. *Secondly,* there needs to be an accounting of observed patterns of behavior which arise with the change in situation and to which coping functions can be imputed. *Thirdly,* the behavior should be inspected for the facet of role handicap toward which it seems directed. Does it look as if it could serve as a device for dealing with a lack of autonomy, predictability, common norms, or shared ends? *Finally,* each behavior pattern is evaluated in terms of its function as a role support. Thus, if it seems addressed to powerlessness, does the mechanism employed actually aid in reconstituting some degree of the actor's autonomy? If addressed to meaninglessness, does it help the actor in redefining the situation toward greater clarity in his role performance?

The assessment of the relative utility of coping behavior is now to be illustrated with reference to problems involved in mental retardation. The question to be posed concerns the relative utility of associations, by parents of retarded children, as role supports. We will assume that this question comes from previous cataloguing of possible modes of adaptation and observed behavior arising from the change which discovery of a child's retardation brings to the family.

Case 3: Role handicap in the husband-wife relationship where there is a retarded child, and the relative utility of a parent association as furnishing supports for familial roles

The cultural script normally available to parents consists of the values, beliefs, sentiments, and directives to action they began to learn as children. While for different groups the script supplies somewhat different cues, it nevertheless possesses considerable uniformity. This family behavior script says, for instance, that marriage should lead to children, that children must be sheltered during infancy but be given increasing opportunities for independence as they grow older, and that they will eventually have to compete with other children. The script sets out an array of physical, social, and intellectual achievements toward which children's development ought to be directed. Such value-laden directives are among the points of reference which are common for parents, especially in the middle class.

The cultural points of reference become role expectations for the parent actors. They come to expect as part of their own situation what they have learned to think of as generally applicable. Given a script which emphasizes competition and achievement, parents expect their children to be able to perform according to the script. Retardation is therefore not something that is ordinarily thought about or expected for one's own offspring.

Let us now take the situation of two actors — husband and wife — who encounter a discrepancy between their expectation of normal development in their child and their actual experiences.

Situational Discrepancy

(1) Role Preparation

The parent actors have expected offspring capable of various achievements.	They encounter in their offspring disabilities which will interfere with such achievements.
The parents have had experience with relatively normal growth and have expected such growth patterns in their offspring.	Finding that their child is handicapped, they must learn to deal with growth patterns of which they know very little.

(2) Role Autonomy

The parents have expected to fulfil the tasks of parenthood relatively independently.	They find that they have become dependent for the enactment of their role on medical, psychological, and possibly custodial services.

(3) Role Obligations

They had expected to carry out a series of unqualified obligations to their child.	They may find that some of the specialists they consult will counsel them to limit their obligations. For instance, some parents may be advised to place their child in institutional care, thereby transferring some of their own parental activities to others.

(4) Community of Interests

They expected sympathy and understanding from other people in the enactment of their parental roles.	They may find that other people do not readily understand their predicament and that some may actually appear brusque and unmannered.
They expected public interest through tax-supported services such as schooling.	They discover that new financial burdens for needed services add to existing emotional strains.

(Because this is an abbreviated hypothetical situation considerations of the distribution of stress in this system will be omitted.)

The Mutual Aid Association as Mechanism of Adaptation

1) Along Lines of Role Definition

Parents of retarded children, when on their own, are typically uncertain as to proper performance of parental roles. The association provides (a) technical information about types and aspects of retardation, (b) models for reconstructed parental roles through contacts with other members who have already progressed in their role learning, and (c) opportunities for trying the changed role definitions on for size in a protected setting, among people similarly handicapped.

2) Adaptation Along Lines of Role Autonomy

Parents who have been dependent on professionals can now gain new understanding of their plight from people "in the same boat." Through planned action not only on behalf of their own retarded child but of other children similarly stricken, the parents can establish new areas of autonomy.

3) Adaptation Along Lines of Role Obligations

Parents of retarded children who seek to act on their own are typically dependent on the standards of conduct prescribed by the cultural script. This script directs parents to provide increasing opportunities for independence for their children. A parent who seeks to act in accordance with such standards of good parenthood will let his child move increasingly away from him and his controls into those of the group of age mates. The parents of the retarded child cannot so readily do this. If guided only by the cultural script of the wider society they are liable to feel that they are not doing right by their child, evoking in them feelings of guilt. But the new or modified script evolved through the activities of the association will give the parent members new assurances, new sanctions for the requirements of their special parental roles. This means that parents will now be able to evaluate themselves and their performance by new and more appropriate standards.

4) Adaptation Along Lines of Common Interests

The parents of retarded children who are on their own find themselves relatively isolated from the interests of parents with normal children. Participation with parents similarly handicapped supplies bases for the establishment and expansion of common interests. Jointly they can create schools for their children, and act on the political front to press for tax support for these schools and for other services which their special plight requires. In this setting they can be mutually helpful by letting each other know of their sympathy and understanding. Such a community of interests tends to buttress the performance of roles not similarly understood in the community at large.

This hypothetical listing of various ways in which the mutual aid association can be used by parents of retarded children suggests that it can indeed provide considerable role support. With the elaboration of the analysis of the adaptive phase completed, we can briefly summarize the steps involved in our model.

Summary of the Model

The analysis of the impact of change on social relations calls for:
1. Identification of the relationship affected
2. Specification of the expectations held by the actors before the onset of change
3. Specification of the points of discrepancy between expectations and encounter with the changed situation
4. Noting the aspects of role performance with which the discrepancy interferes
5. Noting distribution of role handicap among positions involved.
6. Noting the distribution of handicap for various aspects of role performance
7. Listing of theoretically possible modes of adaptation
8. Listing of observed behavior to which coping functions are being imputed
9. Identification of the facet of role performance toward which each mechanism in question seems to be directed
10. Evaluation of the relative utility of each observed mechanism as a role support.

This model is primarily intended as a heuristic device. Its major utility probably lies in its potential for generating hypotheses which can be tested by empirical research.

BIBLIOGRAPHY

1. Beach, H. D., and R. A. Lucas (eds.). *Individual and Group Behavior in a Coal Mine Disaster*, Washington, D.C.: National Academy of Sciences-National Research Council, Publication 834, 1960.

2. Festinger, L. *A Theory of Cognitive Dissonance.* Chicago: Row, Peterson and Co., 1957.

3. Foote, N., and L. A. Cottrell, Jr. *Identity and Interpersonal Competence.* Chicago: University of Chicago Press, 1955.

4. Kirk, H. D. "The Loyalties of Men in Crisis." Unpublished Master's thesis, Cornell University, 1950.

5. Kirk, H. D. "A Dilemma of Adoptive Parenthood: Incongruous Role Obligations," *Marriage and Family Living*, Vol. 21 (1959), pp. 316–326.

6. Kirk, H. D. *Parent-Child Relations in Adoption.* Montreal: McGill University School of Social Work, 1961, (mimeo).

7. Kirk, H. D. *Shared Fate: A Theory of Adoptive Relations.* New York: The Free Press of Glencoe (in press).

8. Lippmann, W. *Public Opinion*. New York: The MacMillan Co., 1922.

9. McKee, R. E. *Wartime Exile*. Washington, D.C.: War Relocation Authority, U.S. Government Printing Office, 1946.

10. Perry, E. S., E. Silber, and D. A. Bloch. *The Child and His Family in Disaster: A Study of the 1953 Vicksburg Tornado*. Washington, D.C.: National Academy of Sciences-National Research Council Publication 394, 1956.

11. Perry, H. S., and S. E. Perry. *The Schoolhouse Disasters*. Washington, D.C.: National Academy of Sciences-National Research Council Publication 554, 1959.

12. Roche, J. P. "Justice and Ancestry." Unpublished Master's thesis, Cornell University, 1947.

13. Seeman, M. "On the Meaning of Alienation," *American Sociological Review*, Vol. 24 (1959), pp. 784–791.

14. Statistics Section, Relocation Planning Division, War Relocation Authority, United States Department of the Interior. *The Evacuated People-A Quantitative Description*. Washington, D.C.: U.S. Government Printing Office, 1946.

15. Spicer, E. H., *et al. Impounded People*. War Relocation Authority. Washington, D.C.: U.S. Government Printing Office, 1946.

16. Stouffer, S. A., *et al. The American Soldier*, 2 vols. Princeton, N.J.: Princeton University Press, 1949, Vol. 1.

17. Thomas, D. S., and R. S. Nishimoto. *The Spoilage*. Berkeley, Calif.: University of California Press, 1946.

11

James M. Beshers

Mathematical Models of

Social Change

We shall explore the mathematical representation of theories of social change in two steps. First, we shall examine the assumptions of the classical theories of social change.

A critique of these assumptions will provide the substantive basis for our formalization efforts.

Second, we shall consider the mathematical formulation of these assumptions. Several models that illustrate an increasing complexity of assumptions will be presented. A variety of mathematical approaches will be suggested in this way.[1]

Three criteria can be brought to bear on all model construction:

(1) Deductive criteria — does the model in fact yield unambiguous predictions? (2) Substantive criteria — does the model represent a reasonable substantive argument in the light of past theory and research in the area? and (3) Testability criteria — do there exist research procedures, or is it possible to indicate the nature of appropriate research procedures, such that the predictions of the model may be empirically tested? Our discussion will center on (1) and (2), with (2) receiving the heaviest emphasis. We wish to establish that models currently available and under development can express the substance of classic theories of social change.

[1] See Kaplan (13, pp. 1294–1313); some useful definitions are given in Beshers (3).

Classical Theory

Three closely related classic problems in the theory of social change deserve our immediate attention. These are: (1) the distinction between social statics and social dynamics; (2) the notion of "equilibrium"; and (3) the notion of dialectical social change.

The distinction between statics and dynamics has been made in all the social sciences. This distinction can serve a useful purpose, but it has more typically served to obscure theoretical questions. Several issues arise. Let us agree on the setting for our problem in order that these issues be carefully distinguished.

We are studying a social unit — group, organization, community, society. We observe events in the passage of time. We discover regularities in these events. Certain patterns of events recur. Thus we might define social statics as the study of recurrent events — essentially a descriptive endeavor. In parallel one would then have two choices — social dynamics could be defined as the descriptive study of non-recurrent events, or social dynamics could be defined as the analysis of patterns of occurrence of events. The latter approach is more useful.

Another definition arises if we focus our attention upon certain events that exhibit great regularity over long periods of time, then seemingly shift or become irregular, but stabilize later in a new pattern of regularity. The study of the first and last situations is then defined as social statics whereas the study of the intermediate situation is called social dynamics. We may call this case "transition" theory.

A third definition, closely related to the second, is arrived at if we suppose that the occurrence of the events under study is the result of the interplay of several mechanisms. One may then classify mechanisms into those that tend to preserve a particular pattern of regularities, and those that tend to alter it. The study of the former mechanisms is called social statics whereas the study of the latter mechanisms is called social dynamics. This approach relies on the mechanical analogy of centrifugal and centripetal forces. We may call this a "balance of forces" approach.

A main difficulty that runs through all these definitions is that the causal, or analytic, aspect of the problem tends to become confused with the descriptive aspects. From the point of view of causal analysis the occurrence of any event, new or repeated, is supposed to be due to certain relationships with other types of events. It is the regularity of relationships among events in time that causal inquiry seeks to establish, not the simple descriptive recurrence of certain types of events.

Thus if an effective causal analysis has been carried out, the case "no change" should be predicted from the same laws from which the case "change" is predicted. The same causal analysis leads to both predictions as possibilities arising from the relationships among events; Kurt Lewin properly underscores this point (15). The descriptive classification of events into "change" and "no change" cannot serve as an explanation of these events, and must not lead to the belief that two entirely different sets of causal mechanisms are operating in the two cases.

With these strictures in mind the second and third definitions may serve as a basis for theories of social change. However, one must be aware that most of the writing on both topics is of a metaphorical rather than an analytic character. The mechanisms of the balance of forces approach must be spelled out specifically — preferably mathematically.

The notion of equilibrium is often used to describe either the "transition" or the "balance of forces" definitions of social statics given above. Here again, we must be cautious to differentiate between a descriptive equilibrium that may be implied by the transition definition and an analytic or explanatory basis for equilibrium that is implied by the "balance of forces" definition. In effect, this view suggests that the descriptive aspects of transition theory may be explained by the balance of forces approach. Description yields data, analysis provides explanation.

The dialectical theory of social change contains many of the elements in our previous discussions. Hegel, Marx, and Weber viewed social change as the resultant of conflict or contradiction among mechanisms in the system. Absence of change was also a resultant of these mechanisms. The time span, however, was viewed as broken into discrete units, or epochs, within which the mechanisms resulted in slight change but between which there was a complete change of mechanisms themselves (relativism of social laws). It is important to note that directionality may be implied in the sequence of epochs, as by Hegel and Marx, or that cyclical possibilities could occur, as by Weber and Sorokin. In either case we note the dissimilarity with the linear theories of evolution — with the assumptions of a continuous directionality of social change.

Especially from Weber we learn the essentially paradoxical nature of social change. The charismatic leader breaks tradition, yet becomes the inspiration of a new traditional bureaucracy (17, pp. 196–251). The compulsive psychological elements of modern capitalism stem in part from the other-worldly, antimaterialistic doctrines of Calvin (18). Such complex possibilities must not be dismissed out of hand as being too difficult to formalize, and therefore irrelevant to mathematical model construction. On the other hand, let us not expect the simpler mathematical models to do justice to such complex reasoning.

Mathematical Models

Let us select a substantive problem in social change to illustrate mathematical methods. The classic problem of social mobility lends itself to our purposes. For simplicity consider mobility between generations in a two-class system, class C_1 and class C_2.

We shall employ several models to analyze this problem. All of them, however, will be of the stochastic process type — probability models for describing and analyzing processes (14, p. 177). First we establish the mathematical concepts and give them substantive interpretation. We say that our system always has two "states," C_1 and C_2. We say that our system has "elements" that are in either of the states, say, fathers and sons. We choose a finite time interval to describe the process — the generation.

We now describe the process as it passes through two successive time units, t and $t + 1$. We form a matrix with two rows and two columns. The two rows represent C_1 and C_2 at time t. The two columns represent C_1 and C_2 at time $t + 1$. The entries in the matrix are probabilities that describe the change of state of elements between the two time periods. Thus $p_{11} \equiv$ the probability of an element being in state C_1 at time $t + 1$ given that the element was in state C_1 at time t. The matrix so defined is a "transition" matrix. Note that the row probabilities add up to unity.

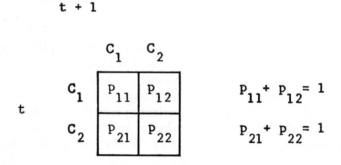

Besides the transition matrix we need a distribution vector that describes the *number* of elements in each state at each time. Let the vector be designated $m(t)$ with elements $(m_1(t), m_2(t))$ such that $m_1(t)$ is the number of elements in C_1 at time t while $m_2(t)$ is the number of elements in C_2 at time t. Let us suppose that there are 100 males in our society and that they exactly reproduce themselves in each succeeding generation. For an initial distribution at t let us take 50–50, $m_1(t) = 50$, $m_2(t) = 50$.

In applications we must specify the transition probabilities. They may be estimated directly from empirical data or supplied by theoretical considerations.

Let us probe another possibility. We wish to write down a theory from which we can deduce the whole history of the process — that is to say, the distribution vector $m(t)$ for any time period t. Several different assumptions yield several different models from which deductions can be obtained.

The first assumption we consider is that there is no historic effect, that the probability of a person being in C_1 at $t + 1$ is independent of whether he was in C_1 or C_2 at time t. Thus we reduce the problem of the distribution of persons by classes to the problem of flipping a coin — with heads equivalent to C_1 and tails equivalent to C_2. We note that the coin may be biased; so long as the bias is consistent throughout history, the assumptions of the binomial distribution are still met in this case.

The situation can be represented by a tree diagram of a branching process. We enumerate the possible paths that can be taken and then assign probabilities to each. For our problem two branches occur at each time interval, one to C_1 and one to C_2.

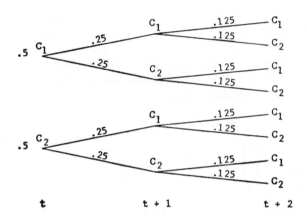

$$
\begin{array}{c}
t + 1 \\[4pt]
\begin{array}{cc}
 & C_1 \quad C_2 \\
\begin{array}{c} C_1 \\ C_2 \end{array} &
\left(\begin{array}{cc} .5 & .5 \\ .5 & .5 \end{array} \right)
\end{array}
\end{array}
$$

Suppose there is an even chance of ending in either class. Then the probability of a C_1 father having a C_1 son = the probability of a C_1 father having a C_2 son = the probability of a C_2 father having a C_1 son = the probability of a C_2 father having a C_2 son = .25. The analysis can be carried forward and we see that the expected distribution of persons by classes at any time is 50–50.

In terms of our previous notation: $p_{11} = p_1 \cdot p_1$, $p_{12} = p_1 \cdot p_2$, $p_{21} = p_2 \cdot p_1$, and $p_{22} = p_2 \cdot p_2$. The distribution vector $m\ (t) = (m_1\ (t),\ m_2\ (t))$ $= (50, 50)$ for all t.

The assumption of independence does not reflect a complex social theory, but it does represent a serious theoretical alternative that merits test in empirical situations. Independence is one way to define a "class-less" society mathematically. It implies that class membership has no influence on mobility.

The next assumption is that history has an effect, but each time period only affects the succeeding time period. For time periods that are not adjacent there is no historical effect assumed. This assumption defines a Markov process.[2]

Our illustration is a special case, a first-order Markov chain. We assume that the same historical effect links each pair of adjacent time periods. Thus the transition probabilities for any pair of adjacent time intervals also hold for all pairs of adjacent time intervals. We need only study the long run effects of a single transition matrix.

For the case of the Markov chain we can represent several aspects of classical social theory. First let us choose several different values for the probabilities. Here are three cases.

$$\begin{pmatrix} 1 & 0 \\ 0 & 1 \end{pmatrix} \qquad \begin{pmatrix} .8 & .2 \\ .4 & .6 \end{pmatrix} \qquad \begin{pmatrix} .5 & .5 \\ .5 & .5 \end{pmatrix}$$

$$(1) \qquad\qquad\qquad (2) \qquad\qquad\qquad (3)$$

Case (1) would be called a caste system; Case (2) an "open" class system; and Case (3) is equivalent to the case of independence discussed above.

The long run effects of Case (3) have already been noted. If we examine Case (1) however, we see that the long run also implies a 50–50 distribution. Thus we see that the fact of a 50–50 distribution does not allow us to infer mobility rates of the social system. Quite often in sociology it is noted that an event is compatible with one hypothesis when in fact the event is compatible with a large number of hypotheses. Mathematics can help us successfully resolve such theoretical issues.

The long-run effects of Case (2) bring new complications. In a two-class system with both upward and downward mobility permitted, the long-run distribution of persons is in proportion to the ratio of the two

[2] Markov chains have been used in sociology in the following works: Blumen, Kogan, and McCarthy (7); Cohen (9, pp. 69–81); Prais (16, pp. 56–66); Anderson (1); and Goodman (12, pp. 57–78).

"change" probabilities, p_{12}/p_{21}. In Case (2) this ratio is one-half, and therefore, a ratio of 1 to 2 is implied, or approximately 67 to 33 in C_1 and C_2 respectively. Clearly C_1 will be largest, as it will initially receive twice as many as it gives up.

But Case (2) also has another interpretation. We note that the father-son mobility will never be "classless." But the possibility still exists that the grandfather-grandson mobility will be "classless" or some even more greatly attenuated ancestor-descendant relationship may be "classless." For Case (2) the grandfather-grandson, or two-step mobility relationship, is given by:

$$\begin{pmatrix} .72 & .28 \\ .56 & .44 \end{pmatrix}$$

and the four-step mobility relationship is given by:

$$\begin{pmatrix} .68 & .32 \\ .65 & .35 \end{pmatrix}$$

We note that the four-step chance to become a C_1 starting from C_1 is almost equal to the four-step chance to become a C_1 starting from C_2, i.e., ending up in C_1 is almost independent of four-step origin. In this sense our system is four-step classless. Note that the two rows of the four-step transition matrix are similar to the long-run distribution. As the number of steps increases the multi-step transition matrix will converge to (.67, .33) in each row. If each of the four probabilities in the transition matrix is not zero, then the method given here correctly deduces the long-run result.

We may complete the discussion with Case (4):

$$\begin{pmatrix} 1 & 0 \\ .4 & .6 \end{pmatrix}$$

Clearly in the long run everyone will be in C_1. Thus we discover another interpretation for a "classless" society — a society with only one class.[3] The rate at which this takes place can be computed, but we shall not pursue the matter here.

We have studied the situation in which a single transition matrix governs the entire history of the process. This case is sometimes called a "stationary" stochastic process. Now we turn our attention to the case in which the transition matrix itself becomes a variable dependent on time, the "non-stationary" case. We will continue, however, to use the Markov assumption that the historical effects extend only to adjacent time periods.

In order to trace out the history of the non-stationary process a definite mathematical formula or rule must be provided that permits us to calculate each transition matrix from the transition matrix and distribution vector of the preceding time period. An example of such a model is provided by Beshers and Reiter (6). The transition probabilities are made dependent upon the distribution of "power" among the classes. Power itself is distributed according to certain fixed parameters and according to the varying numbers of persons in each class.

At each time period we compute the number of persons in each class from a transition matrix, then we compute a new transition matrix from the number of persons obtained. Since this model assumes that the social mobility rates are determined by the balance of power, this model has classic substantive interpretation.

Another example of such non-stationary Markov processes lies in the field of contagion or epidemic models (2). Instead of two social classes changing in a generation we have two health categories, say measles or not measles, and a week for a time unit. We may study the distribution of the number with measles over time as a result of the distribution of contacts among persons in the population. We want to know the probability of contacts between those who have not yet had measles and those who are currently infectious. Thus our system depends upon the number of persons in particular categories — specifically, the rate of infection, the transition probabilities, will vary according to the numbers of persons in the categories. We are assuming that the number with measles is the number infectious in this model. More realistic models have been constructed.

The contagion model can be interpreted in general as a diffusion model — diffusion of artifacts or diffusion of behavior throughout a population. This type of model of social change is under investigation by Coleman and his students. Sociometric measures must be used to supply empirical contact data in this approach (10, pp. 253–270). Another approach to

---

[3] The two concepts of "classlessness" presented in this chapter are completely different; no particular definition of this concept is adhered to. What I am trying to show is that the mathematics can be employed for any definition. In one case there are two "classes," but they do not serve to constrain mobility — any classical theorist would say that classes that do not have mobility effects are in fact not "social classes" and that a society with such classes as in fact a classless society. The issue turns on whether classes are defined by status symbols or by social mechanisms.

diffusion models can be made using the notion of social structure. The rate of diffusion of behavior among social "classes" may depend upon the amount of contact between the members of the various classes. The rates of intermarriage may serve to index such contact, or more general behavioral measures of the "social distance" between classes can be constructed. The probabilities of contact can be studied under the Markov assumptions (4, chapter 7 and appendix), also Beshers (5).

The non-stationary Markov processes we have been discussing all require a specification of the formula by which the new transition probabilities are calculated. This formula can be regarded as an extended "memory" of the system. As a memory, however, it is quite static in that the parameters are constant over time. Such systems are determined by their initial conditions, with no variability allowed for "experience."

One might well ask if a "learning" mechanism could be developed. Selective "recall," transitions to novel "response" patterns, or "insight" are all suggestive of the kind of mechanism that might be desirable. In effect, this raises the question of a cumulative culture — is Pareto correct in asserting that no essential change occurs in cultural history, or is Cassirer's view of the evolution of symbolic manipulation in culture more adequate?

Questions of this sort can be approached in several ways. Let us return to the basic branching process. The elements are traveling along the various paths. Now, let us regard the presence of an element on a path as the result of a "decision." We assume the existence of a "criterion" for selection of the path. Suppose further that during the journey down the path there is some "test" of the criterion — in the crudest case, a reward or punishment. The result of the test can influence the selection of path at the next "trial" of the experiment.

There are several different possibilities within this general situation. First, the probabilities underlying the "test" can be manipulated in various ways. If these probabilities are held constant during the experiment, then one might predict the "response" pattern on the basis of Markov chain theory as presented above. This is the basis for the Estes-Bush-Mosteller approach to psychological learning theory (8).

Second, we may regard the "test" as an introduction of new information into the system. Thus the criteria for decision may be fixed, but the alternative selected may depend upon the availability of "new" information during the process.

This case may be illustrated as a non-stationary process in which the formula for computing the new transition matrix contains fixed parameters. The formula is re-estimated from a sequential sampling of "new" information. In effect the formula is re-estimated by a least square procedure in which the parameters determining the general nature of the formula are fixed, but the new data also have an effect on the precise definition of the formula.

Third, we may have both "new" information and "new" decision criteria during the process. This is the possibility of "insight." In effect, the formula by which the transition probabilities are computed has fewer constants, or parameters, than in the previous case. Depending upon the relative weight assigned to new information as against past information, the change of the parameters themselves may be slow or rapid. If great weight is given to new information then a continuous "memory decay" takes place.

These last two types of models are not easily constructed. Yet great effort is being invested in this area and results pertinent to theories of social change can be expected from this effort (11). The more subtle theories of social change may hope to find mathematical representation in these developments.

Let us now indicate some problems not readily handled by mathematical methods. Generally speaking, the dialectical theories mentioned earlier cause the greatest trouble. The difficulties in formalizing such theories stem from two features.

First, the transitions from epoch to epoch in classical social theory often imply the emergence of entirely new relationships among variables. This view may be entirely realistic, but it provides little guidance for theory construction. Just how one is to deduce the form of this system is not suggested, save that certain variables, say, the economic or the technological, are assumed to have over-riding significance. The sequentially revised models mentioned above have some applicabilities, but if the change in system is radical then much time will pass before a suitably revised model is constructed.

Second, the emergence of new variables themselves creates difficulties. This is not a hypothetical question. Take the case of occupation. Any system of variables that includes occupation, either as a dependent or independent variable, has to contend with the fact that entirely new occupations have developed in the last 150 years. Only the grossest of classifications of occupations can be used to compare the new system with the old. Such gross classifications may, in fact, obscure essential features of the new system of variables.

Some other special problems can be noted in passing. Often short-run fluctuations are of interest, in contrast to long-run equilibrium analyses. Computer methods can be devised for this situation but it is not simple.

Cyclical equilibrium processes can be studied fairly easily. One can study the period of the cycles on a statistical basis, or one can investigate the mechanisms that bring about the cyclical behavior. In the latter case the mechanism must be explicit if formalization of the theory is to be undertaken. Note that we do not have to deal with the emergence of new relationships or new variables that can occur in certain transition problems discussed above.

Summary

In summary, the study of social change can be aided by various mathematical methods. These methods make possible unambiguous deductions as to the course of social change. Quite a number of these methods are currently available, others are under development.

With these new methods the theory of social change can undergo a metamorphosis from being the most vague of social theories to being among the more precise social theories. Greater precision of theoretical statement makes possible more refined empirical testing.

BIBLIOGRAPHY

1. Anderson, T. W. "Probability Models for Analyzing Time Changes in Attitudes," in Paul F. Lazarsfeld (ed.), *Mathematical Thinking in the Social Sciences.* Glencoe, Ill.: The Free Press, 1954.

2. Bartlett, M. S. *Stochastic Population Models in Ecology and Epidemiology.* New York: John Wiley & Sons, 1960.

3. Beshers, James M. "Models and Theory Construction," *American Sociological Review,* Vol. 22 (February 1957), pp. 32–38.

4. Beshers, James M. *Urban Social Structure.* New York: The Free Press, 1962.

5. Beshers, James M. "Urban Social Structure as a Single Hierarchy," *Social Forces,* Vol. 41 (March 1963), pp. 233–239.

6. Beshers, James M., and Stanley Reiter. "Social Status and Social Change," *Behavioral Science,* Vol. 8 (January 1963), pp. 1–13.

7. Blumen, I., M. Kogan, and P. J. McCarthy. "The Industrial Mobility of Labor as a Probability Process," *Cornell Studies in Industrial and Labor Relations,* Vol. 7 (1955).

8. Bush, Robert R. "Mathematical Learning Theories," in R. Duncan Luce (ed.), *Developments in Mathematical Psychology.* Glencoe, Ill.: The Free Press, 1960.

9. Cohen, B. P. "A Probability Model for Conformity," *Sociometry,* Vol. 21 (March 1958) pp. 69–81.

10. Coleman, James S., Elihu Katz, and Herbert Menzel. "The Diffusion of an Innovation Among Physicians," *Sociometry,* Vol. 20 (1957), pp. 253–270.

11. Ferguson, Charles E., and Ralph W. Pfouts. "Learning and Expectations in Dynamic Duopoly Behavior," *Behavioral Science,* Vol. 7 (April 1962), pp. 223–237.

12. Goodman, Leo A. "Statistical Methods for Analyzing Processes of Change," *American Journal of Sociology,* Vol. 67 (July 1962), pp. 57–78.

13. Kaplan, Abraham. "Sociology Learns the Language of Mathematics," in

James R. Newman (ed.), *The World of Mathematics*. New York: Simon and Schuster, 1956.

14. Kemeny, John G., Laurie J. Snell, and Gerald L. Thompson. *Introduction to Finite Mathematics*. Englewood Cliffs, N.J.: Prentice-Hall, Inc., 1956.

15. Lewin, Kurt. "On Aristotelian and Galilean Modes of Inquiry," in Kurt Lewin (ed.), *A Dynamic Theory of Personality*. New York: McGraw-Hill Book Co., 1935.

16. Prais, S. J. "Measuring Social Mobility," *Journal of the Royal Statistical Society*, Vol. 118 (1955), pp. 56–66.

17. Weber, Max. "Bureaucracy and the Sociology of Charismatic Authority," in Hans Gerth and C. Wright Mills (eds.), *From Max Weber*. New York: Oxford University Press, 1946.

18. Weber, Max. *The Protestant Ethic and the Spirit of Capitalism*. New York: Charles Scribner's Sons, 1958.

SECTION FOUR

Psycho-Social Models of Change

Established definitions of the terms "social" and "psychological" have been breaking down in recent years. Almost anyone who reads this book will be able to remember some occasion — an examination perhaps — when he or she was called upon to provide a demarcation for these "levels" of scientific explanation. Yet it should be kept in mind that Auguste Comte saw no necessity for distinguishing between two such levels in his hierarchical system of classification of the sciences, and his disciple, Durkheim, found a reluctant place for "social psychology" in his own, very similar classification of scientific levels, only toward the end of his life. Perhaps the distinction of "levels," like many other spurious demarcations in human knowledge, has been no more than the resultant of traditional disciplinary boundaries and of the clash of academic vested interests. When social change (or personality change) becomes the focus of attention, rigid distinctions of such levels melt in one's gaze. Perhaps the very idea of "static" systems of society or of the personality, is bound up with overt or covert attempts to maintain such distinctions. How otherwise could something as "unnatural" as a static system be conceived? Under the demanding discipline which requires one to account for changing situations, the traditional "levels" give way to a variety of interlocking systems, neither entirely "social" nor entirely "psychological" in the established senses of these words.

All this is rather reminiscent of the Angelology of Duns Scotus, in which the weighty question posed in the Liber Sententiarium of Petrus Lombardus (Bishop of Paris) concerning the number of angels who could dance on the head of a pin was tempered by consideration of whether angels might interpenetrate. (To the best of our recollection, the question of angelic "saturation points" went beyond even the brilliant and prophetic imagery of John the Scott.) Later on, with Descartes, the question of angels became "immaterial" in more than one sense of the word. Materiality and extension were "self-evidently" co-terminous, and angels (if indeed they existed), were again forced to jostle cheek by jowl (if indeed they had cheeks — or jowls), just as they were by the unimaginative Bishop of Paris. Our readers should not jump to the unwarranted conclusion, at this point, that we prefer the outpourings of the Scottish spirit to distillations of the French; simply that we believe an interpene-

tration of fields of forces (or, for that matter, of angels), is vastly superior to cramped vortex motions in Descartes' "pushy" world. Many conceptual angels dance on the pinhead of human thought and action — and they interpenetrate!

Our authors in this Section view the traditional boundaries of learning with a healthy and peremptory disdain. For Levinson, an "idea system" interpenetrates with personalities and with social structures. Warshay draws a broad rainbow of perspectives across our vision; iridescent with sportive hues and shades. Finally Barnett, who earns his bread in the workshops of anthropology, strides magisterially through the thickets of both psychology and logic, leaving a path which can be followed in safety, if not with ease. It may all be very puzzling to university administrators and their kind, but none of our contributors can be chided for "narrowness of perspective," and those who lament the passing of Renaissance man should take both pause and courage.

Levinson's points are brought out very concisely in a series of propositions, which he embroiders in the body of his chapter. To paraphrase these propositions here would be pointless, but he presents leads for further research to which attention may fruitfully be brought. His first proposition emphasizes the importance of autocracy and democracy for the characterization of idea systems. It follows that the transformation of an authoritarian personality into an egalitarian one (or vice versa), or of an autocratic social structure into a democratic one (or vice versa), becomes a question of some importance for the study of social and personality change. The conditions under which such changes could occur are implied by Levinson. They have to do with the number and variety of ideological alternatives available in the socio-cultural matrix, in their legitimation, in the sanctions supporting the legitimized ideologies and discouraging non-legitimized ones, and, perhaps, in other elements as well. A model that could formally relate these elements and give them relative weight would be of the greatest importance in the study of ideology. Another question raised by Levinson that whets one's appetite for further researches concerns the feedback (if any) that exists to the socio-cultural matrix from the personalities of strategically placed persons in the structure. For example, could the accession to leadership of an egalitarian person in an autocratic society increase the availability (or, perhaps, the production) of ideological alternatives? Thus Levinson's discussion, though basically theoretical, is fecund in the empirically testable questions it raises, and this enhances its importance.

Out of the welter of "all possible character types," Warshay isolates what must surely be not only the "best" but also the most novel — the person of broad perspective. When we become thoroughly introduced to this character we discover (not, perhaps, with too much surprise) that he is a symbolic inter-actionist with interests ranging all the way from demography to the "perception habits" of experimental psychology. But he takes other forms as well. That such a person is better able to bring change about than are others is highly probable (although, as Warshay demonstrates, this occurs only under specifiable conditions). "Aye, there's the rub," for the question then arises as to whether such a person is likely to be in a structural position to influence change. Here the answer is, generally speaking, negative, although exceptions to this rule are, again, subject to enumeration and specification. Although much more work is freely acknowledged by Warshay to be necessary before the relationships between perspective breadth and social change are fully disentangled, the delicate whimsicality of his characters, both broad-perspectived and narrow (as well as the predicament of his "house fly with its twenty-four hour cycle"), cannot but broaden the perspective of any whose eyes light on this essay.

While Warshay is concerned with his "wide-eyed" protagonist as an agent of change, Barnett's actor accepts, or rejects, innovations impinging upon him from outside. In common with the other scholars represented in this Section, Barnett proclaims that there is "no antithesis between a psychological and a sociological treatment" of his problem. Instead of Levinson's relatively organized conception of an idea system interpenetrating with individuals and social structures, however, Barnett is concerned with the partial and differential interpenetration of systems of meanings and understandings — of communications. Every "message" or stimulus, as it were, has the qualities of a "multiple entendre," and every perceiver may receive the message in its entirety, selectively, in distorted form, or not at all. With great originality and logical acuity, Barnett develops a paradigm in which the acceptance-rejection possibilities in any given confrontation of a person with a message may be systematically and exhaustively explored, and reports on a test of its empirical applicability.

12

Daniel J. Levinson

Idea Systems in the Individual

and in Society*

Ideas have long been recognized as a moving force in the lives of nations and of individuals. Many of the sciences and humanities are concerned with the nature of man's thought, with his ideational productions, and with the causes and consequences of man's conceptions of himself and the world he lives in. The inquiries have been conceptualized in various forms: the sociology of knowledge; the psychology of attitudes; analyses of ideology, public opinion, cultural values and value-orientations, political and religious movements, themes in intellectual history, and the like.

The starting point for all such analyses, the phenomenal stuff on which they work, I should like to call the "idea system." By this I mean the total manifold of concrete ideas by means of which an individual or social group defines its reality and guides its affairs. For certain purposes it is useful to distinguish various types of idea systems according to the sector of the social world, or of human experience, with which they deal. Thus, there are idea systems concerning religion, politics, education, international relations, and so on.

* An early version of this paper was presented in 1954 at the Founders Day Institute of Boston University. The present version, developed after a period of gestation, follows the same line of reasoning but incorporates some recent trends in my own thinking and in the literature. For useful suggestions and criticisms I am indebted to Professors Gordon W. Allport, Alex Inkeles, and Robert W. White. Work on this study was facilitated by research grants M–687 and M–1000 from the National Institute of Mental Health, U.S. Public Health Service, and by a grant from the Foundations Fund for Research in Psychiatry.

For purposes of analysis, the idea system can be regarded as an aspect of the individual or as an aspect of a collective unit (community, class, nation). Every collectivity develops a limited number of viewpoints or rationales that justify and make meaningful its social structure, traditions, and modes of operation. Its idea systems are contained in "collective documents" such as constitutions, official statements of policy, folklore, newspapers, and other mass media. They are presented to children and to new members of adult groups by a variety of formal and informal indoctrination agencies. The collectivity provides, as it were, an ideological environment for its members — an environment that facilitates certain ideational learnings and impedes others. The collectivity, like the individual, must have ideational rationales that help in maintaining its integration and in meeting its day-to-day problems.

Every individual forms his own idea systems, utilizing passively or creatively the viewpoints available in his social environment. His idea systems have a particular content; they also reflect his modes of thinking, his character traits, his unconscious fantasies, and the like. A general theory of idea systems must take account of their functions for, and their impact upon, the individual as well as the collectivity.

The distinction between the concrete idea system and the analytically derived characteristics such as attitudes or values is an important one, for two main reasons. First, it serves to emphasize that terms such as "values" or "ideology" are analytic constructs selectively imposed by the social scientist for theoretical purposes. Since no one analytic device can ever take account of the full complexity of the phenomena being investigated, and since our theories are still of such limited power, we ought to be alert to new variables and new modes of analysis. Second, the distinction between ideational phenomena and analytic constructs is a reminder that seemingly disparate analyses of ideology, of social attitudes, public opinion, cultural values, and intellectual history, all deal with the same order of phenomena. The various modes of analysis should certainly not be combined or reduced to a single master plan. In these days of attempted synthesis in the social sciences, the distinctiveness of the single disciplines has also to be acknowledged. However, if we cannot have full synthesis we can at least strive for a kind of coordinated autonomy.

This chapter seeks to bring together, in a single framework, modes of analysis derived from sociology and from dynamic psychology. Its guiding concepts are *ideology*, *personality*, and *social structure*.

In ideological analysis, the idea system is characterized with regard to the type of social structure it supports and rationalizes. Thus, when we say that a man has a "fundamentalist Protestant" religious ideology, we mean that his idea system regarding religion is most consistent with, and gives the greatest support to, a fundamentalist Protestant form of religious organization. Again, various concrete idea systems concerning international relations can be classified according to the types of foreign policy they envisage. Ideology is a "type" concept; for example, "fundamentalist Protestantism" is a construct that will be approximated but seldom fully exemplified in any particular case.

Ideological analysis takes into account the scope and organization of the idea system. In this respect it differs from the mode of analysis used in many current studies which focus on a single, narrowly defined "attitude" or "opinion" concerning a specific social issue. Analysis in terms of broad ideological patterns would seem of greater value from a socio-psychological point of view. By viewing the individual's idea system as corresponding roughly to a currently available ideology, we are in a good position to "move outward," to coordinate the study of individuals with the study of social structures. At the same time, having thus characterized the idea system in terms of its relation to the external social world, we are in a better position to "move inward" and to analyze it in terms of its relation to the intra-psychic world. That is, we can consider the personal meanings, motives, and modes of functioning expressed in a given ideological pattern. This mode of analysis, which I should like to call *personological*, takes as its starting point the assumption that an idea system has expressive, adaptive, and defensive functions for its adherents — in short, that the idea system is an aspect of personality.

Ideology and personality thus constitute two distinct but interrelated analytic frameworks that can be applied to a common phenomenal reality, the idea systems of individuals or collectivities. Ideological analysis tells us about the kind of social world its adherents want to live in. Personological analysis tells us about the kind of person who prefers one rather than another social world. The influence of deeper-lying aspects of personality upon ideological preference will be considered below.

This chapter offers a theoretical approach to the analysis of ideology and of its interrelations with personality and social structure. We begin with a particular set of ideological orientations — "autocratic" and "democratic" — and relate these to a corresponding set of personality constellations — "authoritarian" and "equalitarian," respectively. Following this, we present a more general formulation of ideology viewed as an aspect of personality. Finally, relations among ideology, personality, and social structure are considered. The major elements of the theoretical argument will be stated as a series of theses or propositions.

Autocratic Ideology and Authoritarian Personality

Proposition I. The concepts of autocracy and democracy are widely applicable and of fundamental importance in the analysis of ideology.

Autocratic orientations may be characterized briefly as follows. They emphasize, and seek to maximize, status and power differences in social life. They involve a hierarchical conception of society — "a place for everyone and everyone in his place." Status considerations permeate social interaction. There is great emphasis on authority. It is regarded as both natural and right that social power be concentrated in the hands of a few authorities or elites. An authority (higher-status) figure has the right, indeed the obligation, to dominate those in a subordinate position, in whom obedience and respect are the cardinal virtues. In more structural terms, an autocratic group is characterized by a unilateral, downward flow of power, the low-status roles having little opportunity to initiate or control in matters of group policy. This conception of social structure is applicable to small, face-to-face groups, to single institutions and organizations, to massive social structures within a nation, and to international relations.

It is more difficult to characterize the democratic orientations, whose ideal of societal patterning tends to be more open-ended, more predicated on "variousness" and change. In general, they are inclined to minimize control, to conceive of authority as temporarily delegated rather than permanently established, and to minimize the existing differentials in power and formal status. They may take an extreme libertarian or even anarchistic form in which all direct forms of authority and control are opposed, or they may attempt various forms of synthesis of the often conflicting demands of individual self-determination and collective integration. Clearly, to be democratic one need not in principle oppose the institutionalizing of authority nor the requirement of some degree of individual conformity as such. Democrats seek, however, to minimize these requirements, to replace "arbitrary" with "rational" authority (12), and to eliminate conformity based primarily on fear and on self-deception.

The autocratic-democratic distinction is a generic one in numerous analyses of the history and present characteristics of Western civilization. Thus, in describing the evolution of the Western intellectual climate since the Middle Ages, Crane Brinton (7) finds as perhaps the dominant trend the development of the democratic spirit, nourished first by humanism, Protestantism, and rationalism, and modified in various forms in the nineteenth and twentieth centuries. There is always a congeries of democratic orientations, for democratism is in principle individualistic, change-seeking, inductive rather of multanimity than of unanimity. Nor can any single democratic variant rightfully claim to be the ultimate or final realization of democratic ideals. In Parrington's (28) analysis, a dialectic between democratic and autocratic modes of thought is seen as fundamental in American intellectual history. Lionel Trilling (33), from a slightly different vantage point, writes of the "liberal imagination" on the assumption that liberalism constitutes a single, though diversely motivated and manifested, approach to life. A distinction between democratic and autocratic approaches underlies Fromm's (11) treatment of European history, Almond's (4) discussion of American foreign policy, the analyses of industrial firms by Gouldner (16), Argyris (6), MacGregor (24), and others, and various treatments of "modern" as contrasted with "traditional" approaches to the penal, educational, and mental hospital systems (e.g., Ohlin, [27]; Goffman, [14]; Greenblatt, Levinson and Williams, [15]).

Proposition II. Consistency: Individuals are relatively (though by no means entirely) consistent from one ideological domain to another in their tendency to think autocratically or democratically.

For example, persons who hold an autocratic ideology regarding the family will, according to this hypothesis, tend also to be autocratic in their views on intergroup relations, religion, education, and the like.

There are various lines of empirical study along which this hypothesis can be investigated. One may, for example, analyze the writings of various individuals who have played an important part in history. Thus, in our own country, we find variegated forms of democratism expressed in the ideas of such men as Roger Williams, Benjamin Franklin, Whitman, and Thoreau. Conversely, we find contrasting, autocratic conceptions variously expressed by Increase Mather, Alexander Hamilton, and Henry Clay, and more recently by a number of political and military figures well known for their extreme nationalism, anti-intellectualism, and propensity to limit civil liberties. C. H. Pritchett (29) has shown that our Supreme Court justices during the late 'forties can be divided into fairly clear-cut "liberal" and "conservative" factions in accord with their stand on a series of civil liberties cases. It would be of interest to determine whether this consistency extended to other ideological domains. There are, of course, national leaders who have shown conflict over, and attempted compromise between, autocratic and democratic modes of thought. They are in accord with the above hypothesis as long as their "intermediate" position between the two extremes is maintained in various ideological domains.

For more general theoretical purposes, however, it is important to determine whether the "consistency" hypothesis holds among ordinary individuals in various walks of life, and to test it in a more rigorous manner. Evidence of this kind is given by research reported in *The Authoritarian Personality* (1) and other related studies. I can attempt only the briefest summary here. It should be noted that the subjects for these studies are primarily of the urban middle class, and that the specific ideological content and techniques of measurement may have to be modified in other groupings. It should also be noted, however, that similar results have been obtained on highly diversified groupings in several regions of this country and in several other countries.

There appears to be a significant though imperfect relationship among the following ideological orientations. That is to say, an individual's tendency to support or to oppose an autocratic position in one ideological domain corresponds roughly to his position in the others.

a) In the domain of *intergroup relations,* autocracy is represented by *ethnocentric* ideology (1). Ethnocentrism, in our definition, "is based on a pervasive and rigid ingroup-outgroup distinction; it involves stereotyped negative imagery and hostile attitudes regarding outgroups, stereotyped positive imagery and submissive attitudes regarding ingroups, and a hierarchical view of group interaction in which ingroups are rightly dominant, outgroups subordinate." This conception of ethnocentrism as an ideology encompasses a variety of tendencies usually considered in isolation. It includes anti-minority prejudice, anti-intellectualism, illiberalism regarding civil rights, and that form of nationalism in which other nations are regarded as inferior and threatening and one's own nation is glorified (23).

b) Autocratic ideologies regarding the *family* most often take a relatively traditional, patriarchal form (even though the actual family structure may in some respects be matriarchal) (22). The husband is regarded as formal head of the household, and the wife is ultimately more responsible to him than he to her. Automatic acceptance of parental standards and discipline are of primary importance in the conception of a "good" child. The requirements of various roles, particularly the lower-status ones, tend to be concretely specified and conformity to them demanded. The conceptions of masculinity and femininity are disparate to the point of dichotomy; males and females are conceived of as made out of different stuff, and a double standard of sexual morality and social responsibility is held. The democratic family orientations are more variable. Concerning child-rearing, they may involve an easy-going informality, an anxious permissiveness in which difficulty in accepting the authority functions of the parental role may be discerned, or an attempted synthesis of the control-inducing and the individuality-supporting functions of parents. Similarly, concerning husband-wife relations and masculinity-femininity generally, the democratic orientations may attempt totally to equate or partially to differentiate the roles and personal characteristics of men and women.

c) In the case of *religion,* the autocratic ideologies tend to be either fundamentalistic (especially in rural and in lower-class urban settings) or "conventionalistic" — the somewhat diluted fundamentalism often found in middle and upper class urban settings (5; 21). The approaches conceived of here as more democratic are those which, broadly speaking, are more humanistic. These viewpoints tend to be associated with democratic viewpoints in other spheres. They ordinarily conceive of God in abstract terms or not at all; they emphasize the ethical more than the supernatural aspects of religion, and they view religion in individualized terms rather than as a matter of institutional allegiance and adherence to tradition (2).

d) Finally, the autocratic orientations take the form of traditionalism or *"custodialism"* in such diverse institutional settings as *mental hospitals, prisons, schools,* and *wartime relocation centers* (e.g., Leighton,
20). In each of these settings there is a massive membership — patients,
criminals, pupils, or "enemy aliens" — who are in some sense being
"treated" and cared for by employed personnel. The autocratically-
minded personnel tend to conceive of the institution in hierarchical
terms, to be mainly concerned in their work with maintaining order and
efficiency, and to relate to the "inmates" in a stereotyped, essentially
anxious and suspicious manner. The more democratic personnel, on the
other hand, seek to minimize rules, to equalize the rights of all concerned,
and to deal with the members on an individualized basis. Various forms
of this approach have guided the development of rehabilitation-oriented
policies in prisons and mental hospitals, and of the modern educational
system.

I have briefly described prototypic autocratic and democratic positions
in several ideological domains. I have suggested that the several autocratic viewpoints constitute a broad ideological syndrome in the sense
that they tend to co-exist in the same individuals. And I have described a
corresponding but contrasting democratic syndrome. Having stated a
proposition in its most general form, let me add a few qualifications.

First, the world is not to be divided simply into democrats and autocrats. These terms refer not to simple categories but to opposing extremes of a continuum on which there are numerous intermediate positions. Moreover, the continuum is internally complex; at each point it
contains a series of qualitatively distinctive variants. Although the distinction between autocratic and democratic viewpoints is of fundamental
importance, the qualitative differences among democrats and among
autocrats are also significant and worthy of investigation.

Second, I wish to emphasize both that the correlations among the several constellations are *significant* and that they are *imperfect.* At their
best, the correlation values reach .8, at their worst perhaps .3. Few are
the individuals who are ideologically all of a piece; and small wonder, in
view of the internal contradictions and complexities of both individual
personality and social milieu. Let us avoid, then, all spuriously homog-
enized conceptions, whether of individual ideology, of individual personality, or of sociocultural matrix. We shall consider presently conditions that make for more or less ideological consistency in the individual.

Third, the constructs of democratic and autocratic outlook regarding
any institutional sphere are theoretical prototypes and are only approximated in any concrete individual case. This is particularly true of individuals assessed as "democratic" by our measures or by other, reasonably
meaningful criteria. Ask a number of persons whether they have prejudices and, as several studies have shown, those who are relatively the
most open-minded will answer most often in the affirmative. To be rela-

tively low in prejudice and to be ready to oppose it in oneself and others, is not necessarily to lack prejudice. In attempting, however crudely, to measure a given democratic-autocratic continuum, we must keep in mind the range of possibilities to be found in the particular cultural setting. In our society, where the cultural diversity is so great and the ambivalence about it even greater, not many of us can get through childhood without forming some stereotypes about our own and other groups, some anxieties about our own identities, and some tendencies to project onto various groups what we cannot integrate in ourselves. However, some persons try harder than others to outgrow these early difficulties.

Proposition III. The individual's readiness to hold an autocratic or a democratic ideology in one domain, and his relative consistency across domains, depends in large part on generalized, enduring personality characteristics.

Authoritarian personality constellations make for receptivity to autocratic ideology, while *equalitarian personality* is associated with democratic ideology.

Authoritarianism and equalitarianism are conceived of as opposite poles of a broad continuum along which personalities differ. Each polar extreme is to be thought of not as a homogeneous entity but rather as a complex syndrome of dynamically interrelated characteristics. Each syndrome is defined broadly to allow for numerous individual and subtype variations, and enough component variables can be measured so that individuals can be crudely assessed with respect to their qualitative patterning and their quantitative position along this continuum. Although empirically derived, both syndromes are theoretical models or prototypes seldom found in their pure forms, at least in our society.

The numerous features of each constellation can be given only the briefest summary here. (The interested reader is referred to the work of Stagner [32], Fromm [11], Reich [30], Maslow [25], Dicks [8], and the collaborative research of Adorno, Frenkel-Brunswik, Levinson, and Sanford [1]). At one level, authoritarianism includes the values and conceptions of social symbols noted earlier in the generalized formulation of autocratic orientations (Proposition I): for example, a preference for hierarchical status structures and for strict conformity to established modes, and a conception of the "alien" as threatening to ingroup integrity. In addition, authoritarianism comprises other characteristics which underlie, and are reinforced by, the autocratic values and conceptions. These include: unconscious fear of weakness and immorality in oneself and the wish for a powerful, protecting-controlling authority; extreme self-deception concerning one's own impulses and feelings; a tendency to displace aggression from its early-childhood familial objects to others conceived of as immoral or weak; rigidity and intolerance of ambiguity in cognitive functioning and in the handling of inner conflicts; punitiveness as a favored way of dealing with value-violations; and others.

It is not necessary to continue the listing of specific characteristics. What we need, and what we do not yet have, is a well substantiated, theoretical formulation of the fundamental underpinnings of authoritarianism. Let me suggest the following as a tentative start in this direction: (a) Much of the early-childhood fantasy life of authoritarian personalities has become ego-alien and has continued in an extremely primitive form. Comparatively, the fantasy life has been unable to develop, to enrich the individual's conception of himself and his capacity for imaginative understanding of self and others. (b) The super-ego — the intrapsychic moral agency established in early childhood — has also remained strong but ego-alien. It continues as a source of threat to the ego-organization, imposing the absolutistic demands of childhood morality which the ego either accedes to (as in the case of compulsive conformity) or rebels wildly against (as in criminality and other anti-social rebellion). (c) As a corollary of the first two: the ego has been largely unable to fulfill its synthesizing functions, that is, to achieve a meaningful identity, a mature conscience, a capacity for genuinely loving relationships to self and others, and a freeing of the imagination and intellect for constructive, complex pursuits.

The various equalitarian syndromes merit fuller analysis than they have yet received. In their values, equalitarian individuals show an opposition to rigid hierarchy and a preference for self-expression, self-understanding, and affectional mutuality in human relationships. In comparison with authoritarians they tend, on the average, to be more insightful, flexible, autonomous, unvindictive, love-oriented and change-seeking. They have, by and large, come farther in the direction of moral integrity and personal maturity. Yet it would be an oversimplification to identify equalitarianism with maturity or mental health or total freedom from irrationality. The differences between the two constellations are in part quantitative; one might say that equalitarians are in many ways like authoritarians, only less so. In a more important sense, however, their values, conceptions, modes of ego functioning, and forms of irrationality differ qualitatively. For example, in contrast to authoritarians, relatively equalitarian persons may tend unrealistically to idealize the disadvantaged and to reject the legitimate authority.

There is considerable evidence that the authoritarian-equalitarian continuum of personality is associated to a significant degree with autocratic-democratic continua in the various ideological domains mentioned earlier in Proposition II. Measures of personal authoritarianism have been shown to correlate appreciably with measures of autocratic ideology regarding intergroup relations, the family, religion, education, the mental hospital, and other institutional structures. We thus have empirical support for the proposition that individual ideology has internal as well as external sources. What a man believes about the external world depends, in part at least, on what he *is* within himself.

The qualifications stated earlier with regard to ideological consistency hold also with regard to ideology-personality consistency. Authoritarianism and equalitarianism are not homogeneous entities or simple categories into which people can be neatly placed. Although we can for certain purposes speak of a single (quantitative) continuum and construct theoretical prototypes at each extreme, we must keep in mind that few individuals actually exemplify a given prototype in its entirety. Individual personality, like individual ideology, is seldom made of a single cloth. This is particularly true of relatively equalitarian persons, in whom opposing tendencies are more the rule than the exception. Moreover, the correlations between general authoritarianism and the several ideological orientations, though moderately high (of the order, .5 to .8), are by no means perfect or invariant. Ideological inconsistency in the individual is partly a reflection of deeper-lying contradictions of personality; but it is also due in part to contradictory ideological demands and opportunities in the social milieu. Finally, the depth of the psychic roots of ideology — the degree to which an ideology expresses, and has functions for, other aspects of personality — undoubtedly varies from individual to individual and from one ideological domain to another within a given individual (see Proposition VI, below).

Formation of Ideology in the Individual: The Influence of Social Structure and of Personality

Our discussion has thus far centered on one particular set of ideological orientations, seen in relation to a corresponding set of broader personality constellations. However, the study of autocratic ideology and authoritarian personality is derived from, and has implications for, a more general theory of ideology and its relation both to personality and to social structure. This theory is broadly outlined in the remaining propositions.

Proposition IV. The socio-cultural matrix of the adult plays an important part in establishing and maintaining his ideology.

Every social milieu presents, explicity or implicitly, directly or indirectly, a patterned set of general values and specific norms that defines the rights and obligations of the individuals within it. These values and norms legitimize certain kinds of behavior. They set limits on what may be regarded as acceptable behavior; beyond these limits behavior will be considered "eccentric," "criminal," or "subversive." An ideology is, in socio-cultural perspective, a *rationale* that serves to justify, interpret, and integrate the structurally-given norms.

The stability of any social order depends not merely on the inducing of behavioral conformity to its normative requirements, but also on the

inducing of some degree of ideological conformity. That is to say, societal stability requires that the most common (*modal*) ideologies held
by its individual members shall be congruent with, and thus serve to
maintain, the norms of the existing social structure. The greater the
prevalence of structure-congruent ideology, the greater the likelihood of
structure-supporting behavior. While societies differ in the degree of
ideological diversity they produce and tolerate, every society has, as part
of its apparatus of social control (stability-maintenance), numerous
means of encouraging individual ideology-formation in "appropriate"
directions and of hindering development in other ideological directions.

The following are but a few of the ways in which the social order
exerts an influence on individual ideology. It limits the number and
variety of ideological alternatives available to its members. It legitimizes
only those alternatives which are reasonably congruent with the existing
social structure and policy. Through an intricate system of sanctions,
it supports the holding of legitimized viewpoints and punishes ideological
deviance. The societal elite groups, which are likely to be identified with
the prevailing system, can exert great conformity-inducing influence as
a result of their prestige, their control over the indoctrination and communication media, and their politico-economic power. In every society
there are greater or lesser limitations on the range of available experiences. Very often, individuals are systematically prevented from having
experiences that might lead them to question the dominant ideologies;
for example, the idea that Negroes are uneducable is reinforced in the
deep rural South by a system that hinders the Negroes' intellectual development at every turn.

Many social scientists have been so impressed with the number and
pervasiveness of the mechanisms of ideological control, and with their
system-stabilizing value, that they have made rather generous assumptions about the degree of ideological uniformity achieved among the
members of any given society. They have tended also to assume that
such uniformities as do exist are brought about directly by social pressures of the kind listed above and they have given little consideration to
the part played by personality factors in this process. My position, to
be developed below, is that (a) the degree of ideological diversity in
most social systems is greater than most social scientists have recognized,
and (b) personality influences ideology-formation in all societies, whether
the ideological diversity among their members is small or great.

**Proposition V. The formation of ideology in the individual involves
numerous aspects of personality and is not a matter of simple imitation
or pure reason.**

Two conceptions of the process of individual ideology-formation
are rejected by this proposition. The *imitation* theories are represented
in caricature by Will Rogers' facetious expression, "All I know is what I

read in the newspaper." According to these viewpoints, people acquire their opinions and values by absorbing, in a more or less automatic fashion, those ideas which their environment presents most often and with the greatest pressure. It is only a moderate distortion to call them "sponge" theories, for they conceive of the individual as a passive material that soaks up whatever ideological liquids the environment provides. These theories have been historically useful in emphasizing the importance of learning and of the social environment in ideology-formation. They have been simplistic and dreadfully limiting, however, in their neglect of the complexities in the external "stimulus field" and in their failure to grasp the varied psychological processes involved in the selection, organization, and creation of ideas. In particular, they have overlooked the role of reason and the more complex conceptual-imaginative processes, as well as the myriad ways in which man's intellectual operations are influenced by non-rational and irrational processes. More on this shortly.

In the more *rationalistic* theories, "self-interest" becomes a primary basis for the formation of ideology. It is assumed that an individual's general orientation, or his stand on a particular issue, will be determined primarily by a more or less rational appraisal of his personal interest or the interests of the groups to which he belongs. This approach has been especially prominent in economics and political science, where the conceptions of "economic man" and "political man," each hedonistically and rationally pursuing his practical goals, have until recently prevailed. It has had value in pointing up the social functions of ideology and the role of social forces in the formation and change of ideology.

There are, however, several major inadequacies in this approach. First, it cannot account for those cases — too numerous to be lightly passed over — in which an individual's (or group's) ideology is not in accord with his immediate interests, and indeed may be antithetical to them. A few contemporary examples: anti-Semitism in Jews, the acceptance of chauvinistic ideologies against their own group interest by Negroes and women, the existence of extremely conservative, pro-business political ideology among workers, and the phenomenon of the upper-class radical. Second, it is often difficult to say what is the "true" interest of a given group. Every group has multiple aims and interests, some of which may limit or preclude the realization of others. Again, since each individual belongs to, and is identified with, a variety of groups whose interests are not likely fully to coincide, his ideology cannot serve all of them equally well but must reflect his personal attempts at compromise or synthesis. Given the existence of multiple groupings in society, of multiple group-memberships and group-allegiances in the individual, and of individuality in the synthesis of one's social outlook, it is almost inevitable that there should be alternative interpretations within any large group concerning its true interests and the best way to implement them. Those white employers who would hire Negroes (without discrimination), and equally those who would not, believe that their policy preferences best serve the economic interests of industry.

Clearly, imitation, reason, and group interest often play an important part in the formation and maintenance of ideology by the individual. However, none in itself, nor the three in combination, provide an adequate basis for the understanding of individual ideology. The first requirement, in my opinion, is a conception of individual personality within which ideology can be seen as an intrinsic, functional component. Seen in *personological* perspective, as an aspect of personality, ideology can be related to other cognitive-affective-conative processes (including the appraisal of reality-interests and the readiness to accept various kinds of conformity demands). This approach will, I believe, facilitate the effective meshing of psychology with the various social sciences.

Various theories of personality are available as starting points for a personological approach to ideology. My own preference is to start from psychoanalytic theory while utilizing concepts from other theories as well. For related though different approaches, see Flugel (10), Murray and Morgan (26), and Smith, Bruner, and White (31). The formation of ideology may be regarded as an *external function* of the ego, that is, as one of the means by which the person structures social reality, defines his place within it, and guides his search for meaning and gratification. Other external ego functions include the choice of an occupation, the development of a characteristic "style," of preferred modes of thinking and relating to others.

Like the other external ego functions, ideology-formation is related to the ways in which the ego carries out its *internal functions* — that is, to the ego's ways of coping with, and attempting to synthesize, the demands of ego, id, and super-ego. These internal activities, the "psychodynamics" of personality, include among other things: the individual's unconscious fantasies; his unconscious moral conceptions and the wishes against which they are directed; the characteristic ways in which these tendencies are transformed or deflected in his more conscious thought, feeling, and behavioral striving; his conception of self and his ways of maintaining or changing that conception in the face of changing pressures from within and from the external world. I am proposing, then, that *the ways in which the ego carries out its internal functions will heavily influence, though not entirely determine, the individual's selection, creation, and synthesis of idea systems.*

This general formulation implies a postulate of *receptivity:* the individual will be most receptive to those ideologies that have the greatest functional value in meeting the requirements of the personality as a system. He will prefer those ways of dealing with external religious, political, or other social issues that best mesh in with his preferred ways of dealing with internal issues of impulse control, maintenance of self-esteem, fulfillment of esthetic urges, and the like. We would make, also, a postulate of *immanence:* many of the personality characteristics that have influenced the individual's ideology-formation are directly reflected (immanent) in his idea system. It is possible through psychological analysis of the idea system to derive many of the personality features that have helped to establish and maintain it. As Lowell observed, "Truth is said to lie at the bottom of a well for the very reason, perhaps, that whoever looks down in search of her sees his own image at the bottom, and is persuaded not only that he has seen the goddess, but that she is far better-looking than he had imagined."

In summary, I have suggested that ideology is an aspect of personality and that central and enduring personality characteristics are often expressed directly or indirectly within it. The non-ideological aspects of personality influence ideological choice: they hinder the acceptance of "unappealing" (dynamically incongruent) orientations, and they facilitate the acceptance or creation of others that are personally meaningful.

However, there are important variations from one individual to another, and from one ideological domain to another within a given individual, in the degree to which psychodynamics influence the choice and the specific content of ideology. Clearly, no single set of ideas ever engages all of the personality. Ideological choice is affected from within not by the "total personality," but primarily by the particular facets of personality that are engaged at a given period of time. Moreover, inner compulsions and rigidities are seldom so strong that they permit acceptance of, and total involvement in, only one viewpoint. Most individuals have multiple ideological potentials and are capable of some measure of ideological change. Such change may come about not only through new knowledge and external circumstances but also as a result of inner changes in ideology-relevant aspects of personality. While acknowledging the importance and durability of the personality structure established by the age of five or six, we must still allow for important new developments and partial restructurings after that time and throughout life.

Relatively fundamental personality changes may occur at various ages through maturation and intense growth-inducing experiences. Also, changes in defensive equilibrium (e.g., from submission to rebellion, or from projective to introjective defenses against anxiety) and in involvement in social issues may alter the person's ideological receptivities. Adolescents, for example, commonly exhibit marked instability in their relationships, interests, and ideological preferences; their awkward, shifting attempts to find a meaningful and satisfying *modus vivendi* in the external world are closely and reciprocally related to equally difficult attempts to master anxieties and to outgrow infantile dilemmas in the intra-psychic world. After adolescence, however, both ideologies and personalities tend to become more stable, more resistant to change. The very limited effects of most efforts to induce ideological change in adults give evidence of this. When marked ideological change does occur in adults, it is ordinarily precipitated by equally marked change in external setting (e.g., depression, war, prosperity, drastic social-structural changes, tragic or euphoric personal experiences), *and* in internal equilibrium.

Finally, in emphasizing the intimate relation between internal dynamics and ideology, we must keep in mind that this is a two-way process. Ideology is not a "mere epiphenomenon" or superstructure, caused but having no causal force of its own, a simple instrument of the fundamental substructure. Ideas play their causal, dynamic role in individual personality as in social structure. They may promote change or they may serve to maintain the status quo; individual personalities, like societal orders, vary in this regard. To the extent that his ideology is personally congenial, it has significant equilibrium-maintaining functions for the individual: it helps to consolidate his ego defenses, to maintain control over fears and conflictful wishes, and to impel him in lines of activity that are morally appropriate and emotionally gratifying. This is true equally of the liberal and the conservative, the scientist and the artist, the businessman and the religionist. However, an individual's ideology may not be entirely congenial to him; the fit between ideology and dynamics is seldom perfect. A partially incongruent ideology perpetuates and perhaps intensifies inner conflicts and anxieties.

In addition, ideological change often has important system consequences. New ideological trends in a society, which emerge in part out of its social structure, have a serious impact on that structure. The same is true for ideological change in the individual. Although the gradual acceptance of a new ideology depends in part upon the individual's dynamics when the change began, it may very well have major re-equilibrating effects on the dynamics. For example, the availability of a chauvinistic nationalistic ideology during a period of international crisis may lead, in some of those who accept it, to the active use of projective, aggression-releasing defenses that might, in another ideological climate, be more controlled. Again, the new worker in a mental hospital is likely to be worried about the possibility of aggressive, homosexual, or otherwise threatening behavior from patients. The "humanistic" ideology available in some modern hospitals (13) may permit him not only to relate more constructively with patients but also to gain greater insight into, and control over, the inner sources of his anxieties regarding his own aggression and homosexuality. He must have some readiness to accept a humanistic ideology — something that depends in part on his personality when he comes into the hospital — but as he assimilates it, this ideology can have significant intra-psychic effects.

To sum up: I have argued against the sponge theories which regard ideology-formation as a process of mechanical absorption, and against the rationalistic theories in which ideology is conceived of solely as a tool serving group interests. In supporting a personological approach to the study of ideology in the individual, I have cautioned also against "mirage" theories according to which ideology is seen primarily as a psychic by-product, a result of inner defense maneuvers, with no (conceptualized) relation to social reality, and with no effects on the inner man. A more complete approach must take into account the interplay between the intra-psychic influences — rational as well as non-rational and irrational — the socio-cultural opportunities and demands, and the ideology itself.

Proposition VI. The degree to which an individual's ideology is congruent with, and embedded in, other aspects of personality depends on both intra-personal and external socio-cultural conditions.

In taking a personological approach, I have tried to indicate the value of studying individual ideology in relation to other aspects of personality. There is, of course, considerable variation in the degree to which ideology is immixed in the total personality. Allport (3) has proposed a distinction between "functional" prejudice and "conformity" prejudice, the latter referring to ideas which are passively accepted from the cultural environs and which have only the most shallow personal roots. Given this distinction, it becomes important to understand the conditions which maximize the role of personal characteristics in determining the choice and content of ideology. Here are two hypotheses.

a) The greater the *effective range of ideological alternatives*, the greater the role of personality as a determinant of choice. Personality is likely to be of particular importance in modern, continually changing societies, where the number of ideological alternatives available is greater than in non-literate societies, and where the effectiveness of the conformity-inducing pressures is somewhat reduced. The greater the richness and complexity of the external stimulus field, the more will internal organizing forces operate in determining the individual's adaptation. This postulate has found considerable support in laboratory investigations of relatively simple cognitive processes. It promises to be equally valuable, though more difficult to apply, in more macrocosmic studies of complex cognitive-motivational processes taking place in a societal stimulus field.

b) The greater the degree of *personal involvement* in a given ideological domain, the greater the part played by personality in ideology-formation. Conversely, the less salient the issues involved, the less one cares about the problems in question, the more likely one is to accept or reject ideas on the basis of immediate external pressures. When a personally congenial ideology is not readily available to an individual, and he cannot create one for himself, he may nominally accept an uncongenial ideology, but without commitment or involvement. However, he is likely to be characterized by apathy or anomie and to have a strong potential for change to a new and more functional ideology.

Ideological Unity and Diversity in the Collective Unit:
The Influence of Personality and of Social Structure

Proposition VII. Within a total society, the degree of ideological diversity among the members is related to the degree of diversity in individual personality and to certain characteristics of the social structure.

a) Let us first consider personality-ideology relations in *monolithic* societies where the social order remains relatively constant over several generations and a high degree of ideological uniformity has apparently been achieved. I have in mind certain cohesive, encysted subcultures within modern nations, and various non-literate societies prior to foreign invasion, undisturbed by international pressures or internal technological changes. They are characterized — if we can believe the ethnographers — by a rigidly codified system of norms, effective systems of indoctrination and sanctions, a modal ideology that supports the overall structure, and minimal ideological deviance.

The monolithic society, if it is to be stable, requires uniformity in personality as a psychological substratum, a foundation for the maintenance of ideological and behavioral conformity (17). Personality is as important an element as ideology in the dynamics of social control. If its personality-forming devices, particularly the child-rearing system, are effective, the monolithic society may achieve a high degree of personality standardization. In this case, there will be a modal personality congruent with the modal ideology. This does not mean complete psychological uniformity; it does involve the widespread occurrence of those personality characteristics that make the dominant ideology seem reasonable and generally appealing.

However, it is conceivable that a society may induce ideological conformity on a large scale, without a corresponding modal personality. In this hypothetical case, many individuals accept the prevailing outlook although they do not have the personality to go with it. These individuals, already alluded to in Proposition VI, have a "conformity-based" ideology that has few functional roots in personality. As long as they continue to hold the required views, their system-incongruent personalities may be unnoticed. However, they have a strong potential for ideological change and are therefore of great strategic importance in social change. Under changed personal or social circumstances, they may play a key role in innovating structural change or in furthering change once it is begun by others. Conditions of social unrest contain numerous possibilities of institutional restructuring; which of the possibilities are implemented, and the degree of leadership and support for each, will depend in no small part on the psychological potentials — of which many may until then have been dormant — available for activation.

b) Most of the modern industrial nations are *pluralistic* societies in which individual differences seem to be relatively great with regard to both ideology and other aspects of personality. There are a number of major competing ideologies in almost all social domains — politics, religion, education, international relations, and the like. In addition, the variations in personality are sufficient to make things extremely difficult for the students of national character and culture-personality relations. The Soviet Russian regime, even after applying the most elaborate conformity-inducing pressures for over 30 years, has not been able to achieve anything approaching ideological uniformity (19). And the American South, despite its traditional, institutionalized subordination of Negroes, is showing an ideological diversity concerning educational desegregation that strongly contradicts a simple social-deterministic point of view.

The overall psychological diversity in these societies is, of course, related to their structural complexity and continual change. Continual technological change in industrial societies makes some degree of structural change inescapable. Moreover, ideological innovation is encouraged and to varying degrees legitimized by widely-held assumptions concerning the increasing perfectability of man and his institutions, and by the value for diversity as a good in itself. However, the ideological differences among individuals in each society are, according to the present hypothesis, associated with corresponding variations in individual personality. Thus, as Dicks' (9) research suggests, the Soviet government's difficulty in achieving ideological uniformity is due in large part to the uncontrolled and perhaps uncontrollable diversity in personality. And in the American South, I would expect the greatest uniformity of anti-Negro ideology in those states that have the most firmly-established authoritarian modal personality.

Proposition VIII. Within a single social organization or institution, the existence of a structure-congruent modal ideology depends in part on the existence of a corresponding modal personality.

The referent here is not a total society, but rather a specific organized group (such as a social club, a political party, or the staff of a hospital or school) in which appreciable consensus of outlook prevails. The achievement and maintenance of ideological unity depend in part on the effectiveness of the group structure. They also require certain psychological conditions within the individual members. Let me suggest two.

a) The members will have joined the group voluntarily, as a matter more of personal choice than of external compulsion. The more weighty the internal determinants of choice, the greater the psychological homogeneity of the membership.

b) The members will have had, prior to joining, personality characteristics congruent with the dominant ideology, and perhaps certain explicit or implicit ideological tendencies which are further developed and articulated in the group setting. The group presents to its members various opportunities and demands for the formation of certain viewpoints; but the degree to which these external availabilities are "consumed" by individual members is strongly influenced by the psycho-ideological characteristics they bring to the group situation. A necessary though by no means sufficient condition for group unity is that the entering members have personality characteristics and ideological readinesses appropriate to the existing group aims.

While individual psychological characteristics provide an initial basis on which the group process develops, the member's participation in the group may then become a basis for significant changes in these characteristics. As I have already noted in Proposition V, the causal connections among personality, ideology, and system pressures are multilateral. With group support, an individual may be enabled actively to utilize an ideology that he would otherwise have been too timid to accept. Since most individuals have multiple ideological potentialities, group memberships are often of crucial importance in determining which potentials are actualized. Group participation helps the individual to articulate, legitimize, and find meaning in a given viewpoint; and it provides the ego-supports and external facilitations of which some minimum is necessary for the active maintenance of conviction. Finally, experiences in the group setting may affect deeper-lying personality characteristics. For example, going to a morally and intellectually "narrow" college is likely not only to prevent a broadening of the student's intellectual horizons but also to affect the way in which he deals with the central inner problems of adolescent development. To perhaps a lesser but still significant degree, group participation during the adult years will determine which of the individual's psychodynamic potentials are more fully realized and which are hindered or left dormant.

Summary and Conclusions

The study of idea systems has been a major concern of psychology, social science, and the humanities. This concern is represented in the considerable work on ideology and public opinion, on the sociology of knowledge and communication, on culture as a system of values and orientations, on intellectual history and the role of ideas in massive social change. There has, however, been relatively little communication or intellectual exchange among the various disciplines. This chapter presents an initial step toward the coordination of psychological and socio-cultural approaches to the study of idea systems. Its theses are conveyed through a series of propositions:

I. The concepts of autocracy and democracy are widely applicable and of fundamental importance in the analysis of ideology.

II. Consistency: Individuals are relatively (though by no means entirely) consistent, from one ideological domain to another, in their tendency to think autocratically or democratically.

III. The individual's readiness to hold an autocratic or a democratic ideology in one domain, and his relative consistency across domains, depend in large part on generalized, enduring personality characteristics. Authoritarian personality constellations make for receptivity to autocratic ideology, while equalitarian personality is associated with democratic ideology.

IV. The socio-cultural matrix of the adult plays an important part in establishing and maintaining his ideology.

V. The formation of ideology in the individual involves numerous aspects of personality and is not a matter of simple imitation or pure reason.

VI. The degree to which an individual's ideology is congruent with, and embedded in, other aspects of personality, depends on both inner psychological and external socio-cultural conditions.

VII. Within a total society, the degree of ideological diversity among the members is related to the degree of diversity in individual personality and to certain characteristics of the social structure.

VIII. Within a single social organization or institution, the existence of a structure-congruent modal ideology depends in part on the existence of a corresponding modal personality.

Idea systems are at once individual and collective phenomena. They are aspects of individual personality and of socio-cultural milieu. They are to be seen *both* as superficial effects of more fundamental psychological and sociological processes, and as primary causal agents in individual and societal stability or change. This chapter has pointed to the need for a theoretical framework encompassing these several perspectives. Such an approach would take account of man's docility and of his creativity. It would comprehend man as a "social product," a "culture carrier," shaped and standardized to varying degrees by social, cultural, and ecological forces over which he has little control. It would also comprehend man's individuality, his capacity for re-interpreting himself and his world, and for influencing his own destiny. Finally, it would seek to grasp both the conformity- and the individuality-inducing features of societal patterning. Applied to collective policy, it might provide increasingly adequate answers to an old utopian problem: What forms of social organization (economic, familial, political, and the like) are best contrived to produce and sustain individuals who can make maximal use of the cultural past and yet be able as well to transcend the limitations of growing up within a single cultural form?

BIBLIOGRAPHY

1. Adorno, T. W., Else Frenkel-Brunswik, D. J. Levinson, and R. N. Sanford. *The Authoritarian Personality.* New York: Harper and Bros., 1950.

2. Allport, G. W. *The Individual and His Religion.* New York: The Macmillan Co., 1950.

3. Allport, G. W. *The Nature of Prejudice.* Cambridge, Mass.: Addison-Wesley Publishing Co., 1954.

4. Almond, G. A. *The American People and Foreign Policy.* New York: Harcourt, Brace, 1950.

5. Alven, W. C. "An Investigation of Patterns of Protestant Religious Ideology." Unpublished doctoral dissertation, Western Reserve University Library, 1950.

6. Argyris, C. *Personality and Organization.* New York: Harper and Bros., 1957.

7. Brinton, C. *Ideas and Men.* Englewood Cliffs, N.J.: Prentice-Hall, Inc., 1950.

8. Dicks, H. V. "Personality Traits and National Socialist Ideology," *Human Relations,* Vol. 3 (1950), pp. 111–154.

9. Dicks, H. V. "Observations on Contemporary Russian Behavior," *Human Relations,* Vol. 5 (1952), pp. 111–175.

10. Flugel, V. C. *Man, Morals, and Society.* New York: International Universities Press, 1945.

11. Fromm, E. *Escape from Freedom.* New York: Farrar and Rinehart, 1941.

12. Fromm, E. *Man for Himself.* New York: Rinehart, 1947.

13. Gilbert, Doris C., and D. J. Levinson. "Ideology, Personality, and Institutional Policy in the Mental Hospital," *Journal of Abnormal and Social Psychology,* Vol. 53 (1956), pp. 263–271.

14. Goffman, E. "Characteristics of Total Institutions," *Symposium on Preventive and Social Psychiatry.* Washington, D.C.: Walter Reed Army Institute of Research, 1958.

15. Greenblatt, M., D. J. Levinson, and R. H. Williams (eds.). *The Patient and the Mental Hospital.* Glencoe, Ill.: The Free Press, 1957.

16. Gouldner, A. W. *Patterns of Industrial Bureaucracy.* Glencoe, Ill.: The Free Press, 1954.

17. Inkeles, A., and D. J. Levinson. "National Character: The Study of Modal Personality and Sociocultural Systems," in G. Lindzey (ed.), *Handbook of Social Psychology.* Cambridge, Mass.: Addison-Wesley Publishing Co., 1954.

18. Inkeles, A., Eugenia Hanfmann, and Helen Beier. "Modal Personality and Adjustment to the Soviet Political System," *Human Relations,* Vol. 11 (1958), pp. 3–22.

19. Inkeles, A., and R. A. Bauer. *The Soviet Citizen.* Cambridge, Mass.: Harvard University Press, 1959.

20. Leighton, A. H. *The Governing of Men.* Princeton, N.J.: Princeton University Press, 1945.

21. Levinson, D. J., and P. Lichtenberg. *Authoritarian Personality and Re-*

ligious Ideology. Boston, Mass.: Center for Socio-psychological Research, Massachusetts Mental Health Center, 1950 (mimeo).

22. Levinson, D. J., and Phyllis E. Hoffman. "Traditional Family Ideology and its Relation to Personality," *Journal of Personality,* Vol. 23 (1955), pp. 251–273.

23. Levinson, D. J. "Authoritarian Personality and Foreign Policy," *Conflict Resolution,* Vol. 1 (1957), pp. 39–47.

24. McGregor, D. M. *The Human Side of Enterprise.* New York: McGraw-Hill Book Co., 1960.

25. Maslow, A. H. "The Authoritarian Character Structure," *Journal of Social Psychology,* Vol. 18 (1943), pp. 401–411.

26. Murray, H. A., and Christine Morgan. "A Clinical Study of Sentiments," I and II. *Genetic Psychology Monographs,* Vol. 32 (1945), pp. 3–311.

27. Ohlin, L. E. *Sociology of the Field of Corrections.* New York: Russell Sage Foundation, 1956.

28. Parrington, V. L. *Main Currents in American Thought.* New York: Harcourt, Brace, 1927.

29. Pritchett, C. H. *Civil Liberties and the Vinson Court.* Chicago: Chicago University Press, 1954.

30. Reich, W. *The Mass Psychology of Fascism.* New York: Orgone Institute Press, 1946.

31. Smith, M. B., J. S. Bruner, and R. W. White. *Opinions and Personality.* New York: John Wiley & Sons, 1956.

32. Stagner, R. "Fascist Attitudes: Their Determining Conditions," *Journal of Social Psychology,* Vol. 7 (1936), pp. 438–454.

33. Trilling, L. *The Liberal Imagination.* New York: Viking Press, 1950.

34. Weber, M. *The Theory of Social and Economic Organization,* edited by T. Parsons. New York: Oxford University Press, 1947.

13

Leon H. Warshay

Breadth of Perspective and

Social Change

The writer, in introducing *breadth of perspective* as of relevance to
social change, presents in this chapter a character type who only infrequently is in an effective position to influence social change directly.
This is the man with broad perspective, i.e., capable of redefining situations in radically different ways by alternately changing means, goals, and
values and by not being too satisfied with any given formulation for long.
The "broad" man is seen as often "inorganically" related to society; as
tending toward the informal and categorical (or "lightly-patterned")
sphere of social life; as being at best only a temporary participant in
legitimate seats of power and influence. His role in social change, a
complex one, tends to be tangential.

It would seem that the person with a greater diversity of perspective
would be better able to bring change about. Analysis of the problem,
however, not only raises the question as to whether this is true (for our
broad actor may, after all, value the status quo, or value something else
that requires the status quo), but the following questions as well:

1) Is the broad (or narrow) person likely to be in the *position* to influence, even to recognize, change?

2) If not, under what circumstances is he likely to enter such a position?

3) If relatively "sealed off" from said position, under what circumstances may he actively influence change from the outside?

9

19

4) Given a relatively powerless and isolated position, what kind of relationship to change does he then have?

5) What relation does his entrance into, or absence from, the legitimate centers of decision-making have to social change?

6) What other mechanisms and relationships embrace perspective breadth and social change?

The relationships are complex. They involve questions and issues having to do with the nature of perspective, of change, and of personal and societal processes that serve as context for perspective and change. Before discussing these processes, a preliminary outline of breadth of perspective and of social change will be presented.

Breadth of Perspective: Preliminary Outline

Breadth of perspective is a relatively stable "capacity" of the actor to think of *alternate* kinds of solutions to problem situations presented to him. In fact, it is the capacity to see *new* problems in *old* situations (rather than only in situations "presented to him" as such) — by changing the focus or context, by seeing new goals, new means, and new contingencies as relevant (or as conceivably relevant) — that is being delineated here. It is more than mere volunteering of countless solutions that hover around the same theme — a sign more of verbal fluency than of breadth; Turner's (70, pp. 319–321) use of perspective in the plural is closer to this chapter's usage in that he sees each perspective as a standpoint from which to observe and interpret the world.

This concept refers, therefore, to the broadness or scope of perspective, to the relative richness of meanings and ideas that people bring to situations that enable varied, concurrent definitions and namings for the "same" situation. The concept does *not*, therefore, deal with: (1) the single overt response *actually* made; (2) the *probability* of any response being made; (3) the consequences of an overt (or covert) response; or (4) the *efficiency* of an overt (or covert) response. On the contrary, perspective breadth refers to the covert rather than the overt, to possibility rather than probability, to more than one of these, and to range rather than consequence. In brief, it is the range and variety of angles or standpoints of the several possible alternate "solutions" that the actor is able to think of, that is of interest.

An additional point needs to be made, that of self-propulsion, i.e., the broader the actor's perspective, the more of a self-stimulator, self-organizer, and self-initiator he can become. Not only does he excel at manufacturing alternate solutions to a problem, but he also manufactures alternate problems, unasked. And he often does this for no apparent or compelling reason, and in areas that he does not necessarily value; is often, in fact, irreverent. All humans do this but some more than others; perspective breadth is therefore a variable in that some "have" more of it than others. In an earlier, more eloquent, moment, the writer put it this way (77, p. 172):

> The person with broad perspective is not necessarily . . . the successful problem-solver in immediate situations; breadth of perspective is not analogous to social intelligence or even to intelligence in general. He is one who learns ideas, meanings, and values — but not for immediate use; they might be useful some time in the future, or perhaps never. He . . . [is] not . . . practical in the usual sense and is not, therefore, rewarded by others in the usual way. The tests and criteria for selecting the successful do not usually fit him very well nor is he likely to have much value for them.
>
> He has a variety of potential responses in his arsenal and these are often inconsistent. He is often, as Strauss (66, p. 28) says, a problem to himself and, therefore, a puzzle to others.

Plato might have sympathized with some of the above in defining the role of aristocratic ruler as that of propeller, initiator, or beginner — though the ruler would remain master over what he had begun, the actual carrying out of the activity being the responsibility of the ruled. Hanna Arendt (3, p. 199) writes that the Greek verb, *archein*, means to begin, i.e., to lead, whereas *prattein* means to act, i.e., to achieve and finish, Plato having thus opened up a gulf between knowing and doing "which according to Greek understanding were interconnected."

This gulf has seldom been appreciated in the past. The same seems true in the current political world — Helen Fuller drawing from Jesse Unruh, California Democratic leader, the idea that "The man who succeeds in politics . . . is a self-starter who follows through on whatever he begins: 'To have one of those qualities is good — with both you are sure to be a comer'" (27, p. 65).

In fact, the doer is the more valued of the two, judging from current leadership emphases in educational institutions, corporations, and the military; it is the executor of predetermined goals — whether he be called functional leader, empathic leader, employee-centered supervisor, executive, manager, or bureaucrat — who is at a premium. Even a "humanist" of the John Ciardi stripe speaks deprecatingly of the writer who "is out for release, not for containment . . . is a self-expresser, not a maker" (14, p. 12). Traits of responsibility, decision, and effectiveness — of acting quickly and with dispatch on the basis of necessarily incomplete and imperfect information — are demanded; but these are *not* likely to characterize broad perspective.

The broad-perspectived is a more "sticky" type, usually holding back and, while he may sometimes play the role of agitator and — in rare moments of grace — respected and/or effective manipulator, refraining from finishing or achieving the enterprise. Inwardly, he is often characterized by wide associations, fleeting images, dissonance, obsessions, and even conflict; overtly, by occasional hesitancy, immobility, lack of confidence, impatience, and/or compulsiveness. In many cases, to be discussed further below, he gravitates toward the serene, the subtle, the ambiguous, and the untimely.

He functions best where there is the time and room to think, rehearse, change viewpoints and sides, and change even goals, means, values, and the like, without the continual necessity of *public appraisal, justification,* or *validation.* Bolt argues for the freedom of the good Hollywood screen writer from having to meet continual quizzing by directors and producers. There is the danger that if "the discussion is intense and serious, he (the writer) will enter in wholeheartedly and be convinced, and leave the conference having undertaken to do things he feels, vaguely but passionately, he ought not to do" (8, p. 15).

Up to very recently, little or no attempt has been made to study this phenomenon in a conscious and systematic manner[1] — not even in studies of problem-solving in general, or of thinking, memory, self-concept, creativity, flexibility, empathy, and the like. It is only in the past few years that any empirical work has been attempted, not to mention theoretical development.[2]

The student of social change may be interested in this mechanism, i.e., the possible relevance to change of the range of solutions, ideas, and radically differing standpoints that people have, of impractical ideas, and of the tendency to see new problems — all these in relation to anticipating, fomenting, carrying through, opposing, or forestalling social changing. It might be that the person with breadth is better able to start social change when it is not occurring, guide it once it has begun, slow or stop it after it has begun, or be overrun by it.

Social Change: Preliminary Outline

Before attempting to place social change and breadth of perspective within the same intellectual context, it appears necessary also to delineate social change. One useful method appears to be to ask a number of questions that not only might aid in understanding change but that will also suggest some possible or likely relationships between change and perspective. Some issues to be raised are: what is changing; change versus variation; short-term/long-term change; the form of change; its rapidity, its causes and consequences, and, probably embracing the above, its significance. (The question of what change itself *is*, apart from what one might infer from the answers to the above issues, is being conspicuously omitted, partly because that is the crux of this paper. Apart from a hasty explicit definition of change as something that is both new and

---

[1] Combs (16) is a possible exception.

[2] The writer's chapter (77, pp. 149–151) and especially his doctoral dissertation (75, pp. 5–15) contain a more full delineation of the concept. For discussion of problems of measurement, there is the writer's unpublished paper delivered at a professional meeting (76, pp. 2–4), dittoed copies available upon request.

important to the observer, it is well to point out that this varies with breadth of perspective.)

What is Changing

Social organization is assumed to be changing, and is of relevance here, rather than people, behavior, or process. The trend of recent years and decades, perhaps because of the influence of contextualism, pragmatism, behaviorism, and general semantics, has been to emphasize process. Criticism of "structure" as static, however, has frequently led to the reification of process, one consequence of this being the formulation of abstract laws of change regardless of what it is that is changing (as if looking for Lewis Carroll's "grin without the cat"). In this chapter, the emphasis is upon change in structures such as social relationships, groups, institutions, classes, communities, and the like.

Change versus Variation and Short-term versus Long-term Change

No clear answer to this problem appears except as each student of change decides for himself what is *significant* change. To argue, for example, that the daily, weekly, and even yearly activities of people are merely variation or fluctuation with no significance for change may seem reasonable. That approximately three million Americans enter marriage each year and the better part of a million leave it can be similarly interpreted since all this motion may still leave monogamy essentially unscathed. The molecules may move but the mass remains stationary.

Further, the time-span of an activity may be involved — though hardly relevant in itself — a 24-hour cycle (probably significant to the house fly), a yearly cycle or change, the course of a career or a marriage, the life of an industry, the life of a civilization, the creation and evolution of life, and other "long-term" changes in matter. The significance of any of the above would appear to depend upon the perspective of the observer — be he passerby, participant, or student of change.

Form of Change

Related to the above considerations is the question of the form of change. Given the above reluctance to posit abstracted change laws and curves, and the reasons for the reluctance, this question becomes less crucial. It seems less important, therefore, whether one expects a *unilineal* shape (from a biblical "fall from high perch" to some kind of "progress" assumption as in the work of St. Simon, Comte, Spencer, Marx, Darwin, Morgan, Tylor, Fiske, Ogburn), a *cyclical* one (e.g., Machiavelli, Vico, Pareto, Spengler, Toynbee, Sorokin), or some variation or compromise such as a *rising* or *descending cycle*, or *spiral*. Chapin's "synchronous culture cycles" of differing orders and degrees of "generality" (13, pp. 207–214) suggest that it is at least partly a matter of the observer's outlook. What *is* a whole cycle from one view is part of the beginning (or end) of a larger cycle from another view; and what appears, therefore, to be unilineal may be seen as but one portion of a huge cycle that the study of change has as yet been unable to perceive or name (and a "changeless" state may be its middle portion).

The other social change issues mentioned above — its rapidity, perhaps its direction, and its causes and consequences — depend on the scholar's theoretical and methodological scheme that determines what he deems significant change. Two issues that are not being raised directly are the distinction between cause and mechanism and the prospect of some change as a restraint upon further change.

In relating perspective to change, therefore, a crucial variable is the answer that various participants, or potential participants, in the drama give to the above questions. It may or may not matter whether some have a unilineal or a cyclical view of change; it is more likely to be important — in asking the perspective question — which variation, fluctuation, or time span is considered significant. The relation of perspective breadth to the anticipating, as well as the answering of the above, is one indication of what the present discussion is about.

Perspective and Change: Four Ideal-Type Relationships

At the beginning of this chapter, the varying role of degree of breadth of perspective to social change was briefly indicated. Figure 1 presents the broad limits of the relationship in simple form.

	CHANGE LIKELY	CHANGE UNLIKELY
Person with Broad Perspective	a	b
Person with Narrow Perspective	c	d

FIGURE 1

Box "a" above presents the relationship between perspective breadth and social change that would occur first to many, i.e., it is the broad person with alternate perspectives, foci, goals, and the like who is most likely to think of new social values and arrangements — be he reformer, agitator, radical, innovator, utopian, schemer, creative man, or whatever, he can at least *recognize* that changes are on the way and can prepare to guide and/or stimulate them further. A continually changing urban-industrial society with a sufficiently pronounced productive capacity, and perhaps a consumption emphasis, is likely to stress the role of broad knowledge and of education in bringing about change, if only in its sermons.

Box "b" suggests the less obvious relationship between breadth and change, i.e., the broad-perspectived person who can prevent change because he is better able to anticipate it. He may be one in a position of power and/or prestige, perhaps at a major communication network junction, this question being obviously relevant to the earlier raised problem of the broad man's relative access to positions of influence. If he has also a conservative orientation — in the classic Edmund Burke sense — then he is able to foresee the many possible changes and their pitfalls (he interprets "short-term" trends or fluctuations as "significant" potentially for the long-run) and move to forestall them; even if he should eventually fail, as in the example of gaslight interests opposing the introduction of electric lighting. Often, an "enlightened conservative" will prevent change by solving a limited set of problems which, left to themselves, would lead to others and, perhaps, to more momentous change.

This is not to imply that perspective breadth always leads to more "correct" or "efficient" decisions, even when its possessor is located in a strategic position. As will be shown below, short- and long-term success depend also on the *remaining* elements of the "social equation."

In Box "c," change occurs because of *narrowness* of perspective; change is "inorganic," in the sense that it is an accidental, unanticipated, and often unwanted, development. The actor unwittingly causes it to happen:

1) In the case of the *planner* or *reformer* with narrow perspective, it is the unforeseen outcome of a purposely carried out change — such as the drop in the English birthrate following institution of child-labor legislation in the first half of the nineteenth century; this appears to be the fate of many new proposals, programs, doctrines, and philosophies.

2) In the case of the narrow *non-actionist*, much of what he defines as merely variation or fluctuation turns out to be significant change (as in the case of "cultural drift") — but he was not broad enough to anticipate, or recognize, it. Change, when it in fact does come, is therefore the more likely to be violent.

Lastly, Box "d" presents the perhaps curious, and at least intriguing, phenomenon of change not occurring until and unless people envision it. Change is therefore slow, or left at the post, because elites, people in key positions, or significant numbers of the population at large, are too narrow to perceive, much less appreciate, the potentialities in a *possible* situation; they do not see that they are "at the flood." A new world would be theirs, were they but to grasp it.

What often happens is that, in the case of the narrow, both "c" and "d" are occurring, i.e., they do not get what they want and what they do not want or anticipate, they get.

Personal Considerations: The Relevant Behavioral Process

1. Habit in Relation to Perspective and Change

The crucial question therefore appears to be: Under what circumstances are people likely to anticipate a trend as *significant* change rather than merely as variation or fluctuation (and vice versa) and/or as a long-term rather than short-term trend (and vice versa)? And relevant to this chapter is the following question: What difference does variation in breadth of perspective make to the above? A preliminary answer appears to be that the person with narrow perspective tends to see "new" situations in "old" terms whereas the broad person is more likely to see both old and new situations in new terms. Strauss has written that "what is ambiguity or problematic is in relation to what is known or taken for granted" (67, ix). But this is oversimplification.

Everyone's world contains ambiguity, whether in the classic folk village or in the modern metropolis. Social life, however, must go on as if most social forms and social "others" will continue to be stable and, therefore, more "predictable" — even where the basis for interaction becomes "superficial" and less "relevant" (this is referred to below as "categorical association"). Even the most rapidly changing society provides the setting that rewards the person *without* extremely broad — though not with very narrow — perspective, for, to survive and be effective, one must needs ignore much change or variation, or perhaps never notice it.

Dewey (18; 19) points to the tendency of humans to treat each new situation as if it were similar to the old, i.e., to respond habitually until and unless habit is persistently blocked. Firemen are more likely to treat a fire in routine fashion when they believe they have the skills and equipment with which to cope with the fire (36, pp. 42–43). Experimental support is given this idea by research such as Luchins' classic water-jars studies of rigidity, the *"einstellung* effect" where subjects continued to apply techniques to new problems that were relevant to older ones, except where forewarned (43); Bruner and Postman (10) showed experimentally people's tendency to reject an "incongruous" physical pattern and to fall back upon already existing perception habits. Shibutani writes that "although reference group behavior is generally studied in situations where choices are possible (i.e., to the investigators), the actor himself is often unaware that there are alternatives" (62, p. 565).

The person with narrow perspective is therefore less likely even to recognize the existence of a new situation, let alone see it in complex, or contingent, terms — and even less likely to anticipate its arrival. On the other hand, not only is the broader-perspectived person likely to see the new in the old, but also to seek out the new and the different *actively*.

Moreover, people tend to avoid, or resist defining as such, situations containing stress and threat. Camilla Anderson emphasized the very tendency of people to maneuver themselves into comfortable, habitual, and familiar situations "and thus avoid the anxiety that would otherwise be their lot" (2, p. 236); Rue Bucher, in her analysis of people's reaction to disaster (a plane crash), points to their immediate tendency to seek, and content themselves with, familiar explanations that enable them to rest "because their world was still in order" (11, p. 468). That emotional shock or trauma (such as death of husband) tends to narrow one's perspective was indicated in the writer's previous research on perspective (77, pp. 159–160).

The above is less true of broad people who, for whatever reason, more often maneuver themselves into the threatening or stressful. And often, as indicated below, uncertainty and anxiety are built into their way of life without socially patterned devices for meeting these stresses; hence there is room, if not necessity, for innovation.

To many, this is indeed a moral world where what "ought" to be "will." The Millerites in nineteenth-century America continued to believe, even after their prophecy had failed, as did many other religious sects, including the more recent case of the Lake City believers (22). Bettelheim (6) reports that inmates of a Nazi concentration camp at first believed that outsiders were doing their utmost to free them, that the world would not sit by and let them suffer.

Much orderly and regular change is precluded by narrow perspective, and moral blinders make this all the more true. To the degree that people, or people in crucial places, are ignorant and/or committed to particular values and situations, change does not occur, except in fits and starts, as in the case of Boxes "c" and "d," above.

2. Later Stages of Habit and Thought

What happens, finally, when the situation is actually *defined* as "new" by the actor, i.e., he admits, to himself at least, that there is a *structural* difference in the situation (whether it be a three-car accident, a complex murder trial, a business upturn, or a new civilizational direction)? The one with broader perspective had already so defined it earlier, perhaps had created it, certainly saw more in it, and perhaps no longer is excited by it — compared with the narrower person. It is at this point that he is ready to bring about, or to assist others to bring about, change.

If the new situation is not very stressful, threatening, or urgent, but simply unfamiliar and puzzling, there is the tendency to *interaction*. One seeks to talk the situation over with others, exchange hypotheses and facts. The formation of publics, and perhaps of social movements, is likely, except for the "isolate" for whom mass participation might substitute. Bucher wrote that "When the disaster cannot be assimilated to a conventional frame of reference, the cause of it becomes a prolonged and serious issue. People continue to puzzle over what kind of disaster it was, why it happened, and under what conditions it may happen again" (11, p. 468). Experimental evidence tends to support the proposition that people are most suggestible in situations that they have defined as "ambiguous" (cf. 59; 41; 15). Sherif and Harvey (60) demonstrate, further, that ambiguous situations make for decrease in norm-governed behavior and an increase in unpatterned behavior (see the later discussion on "categorical" association).

The narrower person is thus very capable of instituting, or at least engaging in, change (Box "c" above). However, his thoughts and actions are not likely to be very creative or far-reaching, nor is the change likely to be very clear or gratifying to him.

For the broad person, on the other hand, the problem is at a higher level, perhaps related by him to areas that narrower people do not see as relevant or problematic; he may have similar confusion about change, but on a different level. And having gone through such excitement or turmoil before, he is perhaps better prepared for others so doing (as in Box "b," above) and may therefore be better able to prevent the incipient change if he wishes. If he is not in a position to do so, on the other hand, then heavy thinking and perhaps creativity and fantasy will have to substitute.

When the situation is seen as *threatening* and perhaps *urgent,* the first reaction appears to be rigidity, in both thought and action. Without redefinition by others, one is likely to be "frozen in one's tracks"; with redefinition by others, little or no intelligent calculation is likely to follow — and one may become susceptible to confident leads and calls to action, perhaps even to participate in such leadership. With prolonged threat, increasing flexibility and permissiveness, even imagination and creativity, are likely; and, therefore, an increase in the degree and relevance of breadth.

Support for the first generalization in the above paragraph is given by accounts of response to sudden disaster, such as paralysis during the Halifax explosion of 1918 (53, p. 36), the narrowing of focus during a tornado in a Southwestern state (35, p. 42), and panic at the Iroquois Theater fire in Chicago in 1903 (24, pp. 96–97) or the Cocoanut Grove night club fire in Boston in 1942 (72, pp. 197–207). Crowd behavior other than panic is likely, including mobs and riots. Experimental evidence in less momentous circumstances also supports the above: Cowen (17) gave the Luchins water-jars problems to subjects and found that increasing stress increased rigidity; Pally (50) achieved the same by increasing threat; Mintz induced panic, or "non-adaptive group behavior," by introducing "competitive stress" (47).

Then, as further stated above, the *prolongation* of stress, threat, and the like tends to make for change, both in the personal and in the social order. Vinacke paraphrases O. H. Mowrer as suggesting that anxiety "has an adaptive function in preparing the individual for threatening situations . . . (stimulating him to) adopt new and acceptable modes of behavior" (74, p. 285). Symonds (68, p. 156) sees the tension state associated with anxiety as interfering with efficient response to current demands of the external world and, while it tends to lead to personal discomfort and even disorganization, yet may also stimulate the inner mental processes — especially in the direction of fantasy; Hagen (31, pp. 141–143), on the other hand, gives aid and comfort to a frequently expressed tendency among men of letters to point out the advantages of personal difficulties in that he sees anxiety as a more facile and direct motivator of innovation. Allport, Bruner, and Jandorf (1) studied the responses to deprivation, frustration, and persecution in Nazi Germany, finding not only that — as the subjects later reconstructed their feelings — there had been resignation, regression, security-striving, and conformity (findings compatible with those of Bettelheim [6]), but also eventual adoption of temporary frames of reference, increased planning, and increased problem-solving.

Similarly, the broad-perspectived person sometimes finds himself in a position cut off from the usual sources of societal reward and satisfaction; though bombarded by stimuli he cannot respond in any satisfying, effective, or far-reaching manner. He then develops his thinking processes further, at the expense of other things.

3. Conclusion

The foregoing attempted to delineate the main kinds of relationships between breadth of perspective and social change, on the one hand, and the thinking and feeling human being, on the other. It not only sought to outline the structural elements of perspective and change, but also raised the question of the cognitive and emotive processes that the various participants in the drama undergo. We have now to turn to a further, and perhaps broader, analysis of the larger context within which this occurs — society at large.

Societal Considerations: Social Engagement and Alienation of Perspective

Social change is, presumably, societal, i.e., change in society or of some portion thereof — institutions, groups, classes, communities, and other social relationships, as indicated in a previous section. The person with narrow or broad perspective, on the other hand, is a psychological organism — he has personality or personal organization and/or values, motives, perceptions, identities, anxieties, and other organizing characteristics; he is partly the product of past socialization and is behaving within a present social situation. It therefore appears incumbent upon the writer, at this point, to develop the social and/or societal, context within which perspective breadth and social change are related.

A number of generalizations will now be made and treated in turn:

1) The broad-perspectived person is not usually "organically" related to society and does not usually find himself in positions of authority or prestige that enable him either to bring about orderly change (Box "a" above) or to forestall it (Box "b").

2) He often finds his comfortable relation to society, therefore, to be informal and, in many cases, "categorical" (to be described below).

3) Therefore, he appears to fit some of the "social types" and "character types" developed by Thomas, Park, Riesman, Fromm, Jung, Stern, and others.

4) He usually, therefore, finds himself either withdrawing "inwardly," ranging from mild "privatization" to psychosis.

5) He may turn "outwardly," but outside traditional or formal organization, into sectarianism, social agitation, and the like.

6) When the broad-perspectived person is located in a position of authority and influence, he can then become more effective socially — if only temporarily — because he is organically related to society.

1. Inorganic Relation to Society

The man with broad perspective is less likely to "flow" organically in relation to his society. This is used both in the sense of (1) his personal history, and (2) his contemporary relation to society.

In the first sense, the broad man is less likely to have grown to become what his family and community anticipated, and is therefore the result of much unanticipated socialization. He has probably had more "habit blockage" than most, and more ambiguity, stress, and threat during growth.

In the second sense, therefore, he is not as likely to become the "child of his time," to have a basic personality that fits his society. The broad man is less likely to have been satisfied or successful with what will below be called the main traditional, formal, or at times even the informal, relationships of society, nor is he as likely to influence change through them. Instead, he appears satisfied, or compelled, to function through what will below be called *categorical* associations (and, at times, the informal as well). If he is to influence social change under normal conditions, he will gradually do so, if at all, largely through categorical and informal associations, by either his writing or personal influence.

2. "Categorical" Relation to Society

In the usual course of events, the person with broad perspective is unlikely to be found influencing change in the *traditional* (unplanned, publicly legitimatized and honored relationships that develop over a long time) and *formal* (planned, publicly legitimatized relationships set up for a specific purpose) centers of power and influence. He is not likely to be a leader or important functionary in any of the major institutions nor is he to be found in the ranks of celebrities attuned to a mass audience. Instead, there is the tendency to confine his traditional and formal associations to the minimum necessary and to gravitate toward informal and categorical relationships.

By *informal* association is meant a relatively unplanned and not necessarily publicly legitimatized association, as a sewing circle or friendship group; it may be legitimatized within a narrow circle only. The influence of any of its members upon social change is likely to be minute, and indirect at best, except when the members begin to coalesce into something on the order of a social movement.

By *categorical* association, the writer refers to social association that is only "lightly patterned" (one interacts with others in terms of the barest social identities). Such association is unplanned, unorganized, and sometimes not even privately legitimatized and, of the four relationships, is the only one at all not likely to be "shared" with others. It is thus social in the barest sense in that interaction with others is in terms of categories such as age, sex, race, clothes, and/or manner; these usually present very surface, and often inaccurate and irrelevant, bases for social intercourse and accustom one to living with and manipulating ambiguity.[3]

Yet the latter two relationships abound in modern life with its rapid urbanization and changing identities (filling the gaps left by the first two relationships) and they are characteristic of many with broad perspective. The danger is, however, that where the broad person has not succeeded in establishing satisfactory informal contacts in society — and since he tends to restrict his traditional and formal associations as well — categorical ties are all that remain. The problem with categorical associations is that, when exclusive, they tend to narrow perspective through "desocialization," as the following discussion concerning isolation and privatization will attest. While he might then be seen by some as a lower-class type, because of his outward life style, he would certainly not exhibit the unimaginativeness, suggestibility, concreteness of thought, intolerance of the different, or the orientation toward the present that seem to be true of the industrial lower class (42, p. 115) and also of the village peasant (61, pp. 692–703). Nor is he ever likely to become "massified" since his breadth would be incompatible with the shallowness and passivity of the mass.

[3] The above four forms of association broaden the primary-secondary group distinction (or several of its other versions: gemeinschaft-gesellschaft, mechanical-organic, folk-urban, sacred-secular, multibonded-unibonded, nonsegmented-segmented) by presenting *four* types of secondary relationships (traditional, formal, informal, categorical) and *two* types of primary (traditional, informal). Examples of the four secondary relationships in modern society are: rural Southern Negro-White relations, bureaucratic organization, calling a new acquaintance by the first name, and a bargain-counter riot, respectively. Examples of the two primary relationships are: the patriarchal conjugal family and the friendship group, respectively. This broadens especially the concept of secondary relationship — of particular relevance to modern social life — and ties it further to the conceptually more clear primary relationship by seeing "traditional" and "informal" association as common to each. Gregory Stone (64, p. 94) has developed a four-type classification — human (universal) relations, structural (titled) relations, interpersonal (names and nicknames) relations, and masses (anonymous) — which strongly resembles the traditional-formal-informal-categorical scheme; the main differences are this writer's explicit emphasis on the traditional character of the first type and his relating of the scheme to the primary-secondary dimension.

Social change issuing from traditional or formal centers without broad perspective is more likely to be unintended, misdirected, and/or sudden and violent. A significant question therefore occurs here: Under what set of circumstances does perspective attach to centers of power and prestige; and under what circumstances does it promote, or prevent, change outside of these centers (in areas of non-legitimate power)? This point will be discussed further below.

3. Social Type and Character

Though he is clearly socialized — since broad perspective implies a well-developed set of ideas, values, goals, and the like — there still is an aspect of isolation and privatization as used by Lang and Lang (40, pp. 101–103) about the man of broad perspective. He will sometimes avoid the public arena and may be said to be more *enculturated* than *socialized* (he has a good sense of the culture but not of the social skills).

In the extreme case, perspective is acquired at a cost, following the path of a turning inward in the face of stress, threat, rejection, or disappointment. A number of "character" analyses appear to point to the heightened creativity, insight, imagination, fantasy, or obsession that often results. Personality or character typologies such as Jung's introvert, Stern's subjective, Rorschach's introversive, Kretschmer's schizothymic, Gross's deep-narrow, and Jaensch's disintegrate seem to emphasize several similar characteristics, e.g., inwardly directed interest and experience, responsiveness to inner stimulation, less immediate adaptation to reality, greater creative ability, and more theoretical persevering (44, pp. 17–23).

Moreover, many of the social types and social characters would appear relevant, though privatization would hardly be characteristic of some. Included here might be Park and Stonequist's marginal man and Becker's in-between adjusted or marginal, representing broad withdrawn types, and Thomas's bohemian, Rank's neurotic, and Merton's retreatist as examples of the more narrow. Less withdrawn and more successful might be Becker's liberated, Thomas's creative, Rank's creative man, Fromm's productive, Merton's innovator, Riesman's autonomous, Foote and Cottrell's autonomous, the humanistic scholar of Hutchings, Barr, and Adler, and the conservative of Kirk, Rossiter, and/or Viereck.[4]

The next two sections will compare the "inward posture" of the more recluse broad type, largely outside the institutional structure, with the "outward posture" of the more effective broad-perspectived person who may become part of the structure.

---

[4] The relevant citations are: Park (51 and 52), Stonequist (65), Becker (5, pp. 217–19 and pp. 221–24), Thomas (69, pp. 159–61), Rank (54, pp. 263–68), Merton (46, pp. 153–55 and pp. 141–49), Fromm (26, pp. 82–85 and pp. 90–106), Riesman (55, Part III), Foote and Cottrell (23), Kirk (37), Rossiter (56), and Viereck (73).

4. The Inward Posture

The social science literature is amply endowed with analysis of socialization, of degrees of it, and of courses it might take. Whether in the philosophic vein of a Dewey (18) or Mead (45) or in the more empirical studies of isolation (e.g., feral man, solitary confinement, schizophrenia in urban "transition areas"), the ideas behind concepts such as "autistic," "unsocialized," and "desocialized" indicate the general processes that are assumed to be involved in an "inward posture."

The broad-perspectived person who gravitates toward the "lightly patterned" social life — probably because he is less comfortable in the general swim and because the latter is not very comfortable with him — finds himself in dire straits. If genuine isolation sets in, or even *privatization* (defined by Lang and Lang [40, p. 83 and pp. 264–265] as a breaking off from social ties, especially primary, affective ones and the increased concern with one's own needs), one is very likely to remain ineffective with reference to social change and is also in danger of perspective eventually atrophying.

An extreme case of withdrawal with pathological overtones, though not one of narrow perspective, is the *obsessive-compulsive*. Fenichel (21, pp. 46–51, pp. 296–300) writes that the obsessive is one who takes flight in the purely cognitive, at the expense of emotion; who, rather than using thought as part of a total act, falls back instead upon continual, repetitive, rehearsal of ideas. He seeks flight from the flesh and blood of realistic grappling with his problems into the shadowy world of words and concepts — into fantasy. There is regression, according to Freud, into an earlier state of magical belief that the name, the word, the symbol is all one needs for the control of situations. It is the *omnipotence* of words — expressing itself for the normal person in obscenities, swearing, poetry, and logical exercises — which for the obsessive becomes the major orientation.

The obsessive may retain some broad perspective. In fact, the latter may have been a necessary condition for the former — whatever other personal "defects" may be present, these by themselves may not be sufficient to make a person of *narrow* perspective an obsessive-compulsive. The narrow person can eventually develop many maladies, but obsessive-compulsive neurosis may very well *not* be one of these.

5. The Outward Posture

Lang and Lang present an alternative to privatization: instead of responding with apathy and a withdrawal from the ambiguous and the anxious, one may seek a "positive solution" (40, pp. 264–265). Accepting some higher authority, mortal or not, one then becomes an agent of extreme change by identifying with and attempting to follow causes and social movements — particularly of the "value-oriented" type (71, chapter 15). Cantril, Fromm, Gilbert, and Hoffer discuss similar seeking of the dramatic, secure, and sweeping positive solution, as does the literature on the "sect"[5] and, to a degree, Lipset's analysis of political "extremism" (42, chapter 5).

Blumer's second kind of *agitator* fits here, — not the one who is excitable, restless, and aggressive and who infests people already disturbed and unsettled; but one who, more calm, quiet, and dignified, raises doubts in the minds of people who take the status quo for granted. Foreseeing a possible future that his listeners do not, he is "likely to be a man sparing in his words, but capable of saying very caustic, incisive, and biting things — things which get 'under the skin' of people and force them to view things in a new light" (7, pp. 204–205).

Among other outward postures might be social and spatial mobility, and other kinds of moving of the broad, sensitized person into new positions. Examples of this would be migrants, emerging family types, new occupations, and the entrance of women and minority groups into the arts and professions — and therefore into a somewhat better position to influence social change.

Before moving to examine the broad-perspectived man who is more securely ensconced in society, it is interesting to note that four of Seeman's (58) five senses of *alienation* fit the types and processes discussed above. Powerlessness and value isolation, for example, fit "categorical association," meaninglessness fits the "agitator," and normlessness and the above three fit one or another of the social types and social characters. It is only self-estrangement, in the Marxian-Frommian sense, that appears to have no clear application here.

6. Organic Relation to Society

When broad perspective is found in high places, "intelligent" manipulation of social change is more likely, either to bring it about (Box "a" above) or to forestall it (Box "b"). While continual occupancy of legitimate centers of decision-making is not usually conducive to broadening perspective further, or even to maintaining its intensity, there is at least the means for its translation into effective action.

One example of this is the leader, whether formal or traditional, who finds himself in new and changing situations which present continuing and persistent challenges to his outlook — thus keeping him aware of new definitions, foci, goals, and the like. He tends to have a self organized broadly around the "near and familiar," one whose major activities and commitments are likely to have been *publicly recognized* and *vali-*

---

[5] The relevant citations are: Cantril (12), Fromm (25), Gilbert (28), Hoffer (32). For a representative analytic literature on the sect, see Gillin (29), Niebuhr (48), E. Faris (20), Becker (5, chapter 23), and Kornhauser (38).

dated; he is also likely to be industrious, indefatigable, and, within socially tolerable limits, opportunistic. Franklin D. Roosevelt, probably comparatively broad when he assumed the presidency, engaged in continual, pragmatic reformulations in peace and war. But whereas he found himself periodically challenged to think and act radically during turbulent times, he otherwise relaxed by "riding the waves" during the relatively tranquil times between. An Edison or a Ford appears to have been a similar type in a similar time. These three examples perhaps indicate something about the decision-making centers of American society.

On the other hand, there is the leader who, like the agitator referred to above, has long tried to cajole a sleeping potential followership and then suddenly finds himself in power. This leader — more officious than the one above — has a self organized around the "strange and distant" and many of his activities and commitments were *privately recognized and validated.* Before his rise to respectability, this leader's viewpoint is likely to have been more widely accepted than was publicly recognized or conceded — a condition akin to Floyd H. Allport's "pluralistic ignorance" (34, pp. 174–175) having existed. The example of Winston Churchill may fit here, as may that of Charles de Gaulle — although more pure examples would be preferred. Such a person has very broad perspective and, in an emergency, finds himself catapulted into a position of authority; when the emergency is seen as over, he is likely to be removed, as was Churchill in July, 1945 (Churchill's own history for several decades had included several long periods away from vital centers of power.)

The more desperate the followers, the more likely they are to turn to the second type of leader. However, both *imply change* since one or the other is permitted to lead only where the more commonly found leader — whether traditional, formal, or informal — has been socially defined as inadequate to the new situation. Where followers see a clearly new, and perhaps threatening, situation, they are more ready to turn to the previously humored, distrusted, and/or despised for leadership; if the latter should then also be broad, then a more smooth and organic process of change, or its prevention, is likely. Sanford's work is relevant here when he distinguishes between the "functional" leader, corresponding somewhat to the above, and the "nice guy" leader. The former arises in "a life-or-death situation [where] the follower's need for warm approval is likely to be less important than his need to survive" (57, p. 339). The previous experience of the latter (the "nice guy" leader), on the other hand, is "dangerous because it easily induces habits of sheer mechanized action, blindness, tendencies to perform slavishly, instead of thinking, instead of facing a problem freely" (78, p. 62).

At most, then, the functional leader is called in when radical *adaptation* to the "new" appears needed, but released when *integrative* functions become paramount. When society is falling apart, this less comfortable type may be called in but, as the physician in cases of illness, he is less appreciated when society is "on the mend."[6]

Most leaders, therefore, in politics or not, and in upper or in middle executive levels (and whether or not they really are "nice guys"), would appear to be in situations which do not call for, and would often not tolerate, very broad perspective; they often make decisions without quite verbalizing or knowing much of what went into their making. Yet they could not be very narrow-perspectived either since, having to participate in diverse activity, mental variety is also assured. However, having to act makes a formulation that is radical, creative, and/or fantastic a luxury and a severe handicap; the active leader cannot normally have much tolerance for "inefficiency." Hence, whereas "followers" may be found to be distributed across the entire range from narrow to broad perspective, leaders might be expected to fall closer to the middle of the range, probably a bit above it.[7]

When the broad-perspectived finds himself in a position of legitimate power, and especially where this fits the logic of the times (more in the case of Churchill than of F. D. R.), vast social changes, fluctuations, or resistances to change are likely. That the broad person can never be too comfortable when "organically" related to society may be seen by the relatively short and precarious tenure in office of a Churchill. Only in this uneasy manner does he become a child of his time.

Perspective therefore appears to be in continual danger of narrowing at the poles of a *social contact* continuum, with isolation at one end and continual habitation of legitimate power and influence centers at the other.

Sequential Analysis of Perspective and Change

It may prove useful at this point, though admittedly premature theoretically and skeletal in form, to treat the relation of perspective to change sequentially, thus putting together many of the above ideas. The analysis assumes a dialectic framework with cyclic modifications; and it begins from a rather static *traditional* social setting, though a beginning could have been made from any of several points.

First, the existence of a traditional society is assumed — either all of it or a part — implying heavy reliance upon custom, particularly in the economic realm and in other areas defined as vital. Change is generally absent or is unnoticed by a populace with generally narrow perspective.

[6] Hogbin presents an interesting analysis of "disintegration and reintegration" in primitive society that is of some relevance to this chapter (33, pp. 46–54).

[7] Gouldner's (30, p. 33) statement that leaders generally are a bit more intelligent than the average of their followers may be relevant here even though intelligence and perspective breadth are not synonymous; Krout's statement that great men range between extremes of dull normal and genius (30, p. 34) can perhaps be explained by the "extremes" being recognized and/or utilized only during crises.

Then, some important change — caused internally or from without — occurs and is so perceived by a few but not noticed by the majority. The change can be either a misfortune or even sudden good fortune, but only a minority even suspects its implication. For some of the few, "categorical association" — and some loosening of the norms — arises, tending to isolate somewhat those not already in and around central, legitimate power positions. A breach in tradition comes into existence.

Should this process continue, more people — or their offspring — gain broader perspective and the fact, or possibility, of change becomes *publicly* recognized and legitimatized. This is accompanied by rapid development of new social types — both of the inward and outward "posture" — and of new subcultures not necessarily ethnic-based. A potential exists for crowd formation, the rise of publics, rumor spread, fashion, and perhaps the rise of new sects. People may still ask the "wrong" questions but there is "the new" in the very asking — in that the great degree of "variation" and "fluctuation" is seen by some as possibly implying "significant," and perhaps long-term, change. The broad person may then be utilized — either to create and guide change or to prevent it — and not only do *categorical* associations (and normlessness and feelings of powerlessness and meaninglessness) increase, but also tendencies arise toward filling the newly-created "structural gaps" with *formal* and *informal* organization, i.e., since *traditional* organization no longer "suffices."

In time, diversity and complexity increase and there is continuous change, with all it implies for the increased ambiguity and stress in social life. With a general increase in perspective breadth, there is the anticipation of future change and increased planning, and some discomfort at the idea of blind change — whether or not one favors change. Reformism, radicalism, conservatism, and reaction all take to the arena, often in turn; propaganda and social movements are likely to be added — if they have not indeed already made their appearance — to the aforementioned forms of elementary collective behavior. While there is greater existence and use of perspective, much of the more radical, and isolated, perspective breadth is omitted, coming to the fore at infrequent intervals largely via sudden and violent mechanisms.

If all goes well, a heightened period of change, creativity, florescence, and disorganization, alternating with attempts at reorganization, ensues. This is typified by strong secularity, relativism, a new conception of "freedom" perhaps,[8] and a greater turning toward abstractions — toward the "just possible." It is at this point that the *very broad* person, not just the moderately broad, is most "needed," i.e., the one who can reorient his

[8] The concept of freedom as "absence of restriction" — i.e., defined negatively — becomes the "presence of more possibilities and opportunities" — i.e., defined "positively." This represents movement from a society with few restrictions but few opportunities to a more complex one with more restrictive organization but more choice; and from relatively narrow persons to those with a richer mental life.

definitions of reality in radically new, and often amoral, ways. His utilization or the lack of it helps determine the next condition of society.

Gradually, however, tendencies toward traditionalization (orthodoxy, reaction, or even a strong moderation emphasis) begin to supersede the other three relationships (formal, informal, and categorical); this may occur in the society generally or in selected portions.[9] Perspective breadth is less likely to be sought; narrower, more effective, leader types and character structures develop and prosper, the broad person gravitating more and more to the periphery and/or to an appreciative subculture.

Eventually, however, tradition — and perhaps the still existing formal and informal organization — begins to be beset by stresses and changes, and categoricalization begins to increase. The process, an essentially *dialectic*[10] one with reference to the four relationships, begins again, but sooner this time and from a new base.

A more concrete example of this sequential process, one more easily examined within the present intellectual apparatus, is the development of new areas of social contact. As examples, we shall take social contact within a new geographic setting — as in a frontier town — or in the interstices of tradition and formal organization — as in nineteenth-century capital-labor conflict — in the more recent examples of school integration, and in the rise of the urban fringe (9, pp. 140–142). Under all these conditions, categorical contacts are plentiful, in the absence of more organized relationships. In time, both formal and informal arrangements arise, as the development of law-enforcement agencies, labor and race legislation, industrial pacts and understandings, and eventual informal understandings with one's neighbors indicate. In more time, these will tend to take the character of *tradition*, with the informal being more likely to do so, sooner, than the formal. With traditionalization, a relationship more organic to society, and embodying social respect and even honor, has been built within each of the above areas of contact. Then, however, tradition (or either of the other two) eventually starts to break down and people again begin to interact more and more in ambiguous or lightly-patterned situations, i.e., categorical associations, and the process begins anew. Here is the best opportunity for the gravitation of broad perspective to traditional and/or formal centers of power (if the breakdown is the beginning of a new social arrangement) or to the creation of new power positions, as indicated above.

[9] Kroeber's historical studies suggested to him that all periods of florescence end in either disorganization or traditionalization (39, pp. 773–77) and Sorokin's "idealistic" middle point of the cycle of societal change eventually "descends" to the less creative sensate or ideational polar extremes (63). It is only fair to state, however, that more optimistic formulations exist, usually of a more positivistic nature. Apart from a St. Simon or a Comte, one may point to a Barnett "piecemeal" view of change as inherent in the interactive process (4) or to Ogburn's "exponential" pattern that results from an ever enlarging and self-generating "culture base" (49).

[10] That the four types of association — traditional, formal, informal, categorical — are related to one another over time in *dialectic* fashion was suggested to the writer by Carolyn Furr Levy, University of Kansas City sociology department.

The foregoing has been an attempt, first, to outline, then to illustrate, application of the conceptual tools of this chapter to a sequential analysis of perspective and change. This is one way to organize the contribution of the chapter. The conclusion that follows is a second.

Conclusion

To paraphrase the quoted two paragraphs in the early portion of this chapter (page 321):

> The person with broad perspective is not necessarily the successful translator of his breadth into the bringing about or the preventing of social change; breadth of perspective is not easily translatable into the process of social change, or even into orderly social process in general. He is one who has ideas, meanings, and values — but not easily channeled into the traditional or formal social process; they might be so channeled at some time in the future, or perhaps never. He is not organic to society in the usual sense and is not, therefore, utilized by others in the usual way. The groups and institutions that affect and control social change do not usually fit or select him very well nor is he likely to gravitate toward them.
>
> He has a variety of potential reformulations of social life in his arsenal and these are often inconsistent. He is often a problem to himself and, therefore, a puzzle to others.

In capsule form, the following generalization's appear to reflect the above discussion:

1) Both broad and narrow perspective may, under differing circumstances, either bring about or prevent change.

2) Perspective breadth is seen as affecting the likelihood of the actor's recognizing and distinguishing between "significant" change and mere "fluctuation," and between long-term and short-term change.

3) Perspective thus helps to account for why "the new" does or does not catch hold, as well as it does for why it is created or prevented.

4) The person with broad perspective is usually not found in the position to influence change, though this is less true in advanced societies.

5) Advanced societies, more inclined to social change, are also more likely both to create and to appreciate, to value, and to utilize breadth.

6) Even in advanced societies, however, the broad man is not likely to be called upon by the legitimate power centers (unless, of course, he is already part of such centers), nor to gravitate toward them, until the situation is defined by the powers that be as one of crisis.

7) Part of the reason for the above is that the broad man's outlook is often less utilitarian, conscious, disciplined, or circumspect.

8) Much of the time, therefore, the broad man is either left out of the swim of things (in the area of the lightly-patterned) or he seeks substitute power centers, often helping to create them.

9) While tending toward the societal periphery, then, broad perspective

is found all along the line from isolation to influence — and in many social "postures" and character types — affecting change differently at each point.

10) Therefore, unless and until broad perspective is utilized, the portending signs for significant social change are likely to be missed, thus making said change all the more likely to be unanticipated, sudden, violent, and misdirected or unwanted when it comes.

11) In accounting for the relationship between perspective and change, therefore, the nature of existing societal relationships and of the personal experiences of its members become of crucial importance, with elements of isolation, inorganic ties, categorical association, and mental distress and confusion figuring prominently in the outcome.

Social change is affected by breadth of perspective and is also unaffected, directly at least. It both creates the broad man and is also, at odd times and often tangentially, created by him — or at least is recognized, and sometimes prevented, by him. In tranquil times society tends both to ignore and tolerate him and is likely to cough him up in times of crisis when even he may be too late. At times he will not wait and thus helps bring change about, whether from within the institutional structure or from without. At other moments, he may not exist at all, and neither will social change — except violently, whence the broad man will also be created. Formal organization excludes him, informal organization tolerates, and tradition sees him not; he is most likely to be ensconced in the categorical, or lightly-patterned. Hence, or hence not, social change.

In conclusion, the specific relationships between breadth of perspective and social change are imprecisely known and stated.[11] But the nature of these relationships — in both promulgating and preventing change — is perhaps better understood when one notes the inorganic relation between the broad-perspectived and society, and the conditions under which the broad man leaves the area of the lightly-patterned in order to participate, however briefly and anxiously, in the legitimate mechanisms of the social process.

BIBLIOGRAPHY

1. Allport, Gordon W., Jerome S. Bruner, and E. M. Jandorf. "Personality under Social Catastrophe," *Character and Personality*, Vol. 10 (1941), pp. 1–22.

[11] This undoubtedly is partly the result of the *idealistic* emphasis of this chapter (e.g., emphasis upon ideas, meanings, values, motives, perceived goals) and, to some degree, *rationalistic* as well. Perhaps more *positivistic* (i.e., more nominalistic, elementaristic, microscopic concepts that would be more easily operationalized, e.g., stimulus-response, imitation) and *emotive* emphases (e.g., emotion, temperament, mood) should be pursued.

2. Anderson, Camilla M. "The Self Image," *Mental Hygiene,* Vol. 36 (1952), pp. 227–244.

3. Arendt, Hanna. *The Human Condition.* Garden City, N.Y.: Doubleday Anchor Books, 1959. (First published 1958.)

4. Barnett, Homer G. *Innovation.* New York: McGraw-Hill Book Co., 1953.

5. Becker, Howard P. *Man in Reciprocity.* New York: Frederick A. Praeger, 1956.

6. Bettelheim, Bruno. "Individual and Mass Behavior in Extreme Situations," *Journal of Abnormal and Social Psychology,* Vol. 38 (1943), pp. 417–452.

7. Blumer, Herbert. "Social Movements," in *New Outline of the Principles of Sociology,* revised edition. New York: Barnes & Noble, 1946.

8. Bolt, Robert. "The Playwright in Films," *Saturday Review* (Dec. 29, 1962), pp. 15–16.

9. Boskoff, Alvin. *The Sociology of Urban Regions.* New York: Appleton-Century-Crofts, 1962.

10. Bruner, Jerome S., and Leo Postman. "On the Perception of Incongruity," *Journal of Personality,* Vol. 18 (1949), pp. 206–223.

11. Bucher, Rue. "Blame and Hostility in Disaster," *American Journal of Sociology,* Vol. 62 (1957), pp. 467–475.

12. Cantril, Hadley. *The Psychology of Social Movements.* New York: John Wiley & Sons, 1941.

13. Chapin, F. Stuart. *Cultural Change.* Dubuque, Iowa: William C. Brown Co., 1928. (First published by The Century Co.)

14. Ciardi, John. "On Writing and Bad Writing," *Saturday Review* (Dec. 15, 1962), pp. 10–12.

15. Coffin, Thomas E. "Some Conditions of Suggestions and Suggestibility," *Psychological Monographs,* Vol. 53 (1941), No. 4.

16. Combs, Arthur W. "Intelligence From a Perceptual Point of View," in E. L. and R. E. Hartley (eds.), *Outside Readings in Psychology.* New York: Crowell-Collier Publishing Co., 1957. (First published 1951.)

17. Cowen, Emory L. "The Influence of Varying Degrees of Psychological Stress on Problem-Solving Rigidity," *Journal of Abnormal and Social Psychology,* Vol. 47 (1952), pp. 512–519.

18. Dewey, John. *Human Nature and Conduct.* New York: Henry Holt, 1922.

19. Dewey, John. *How We Think.* Boston: D. C. Heath & Co., 1933.

20. Faris, Ellsworth. "The Sect and the Sectarian," *American Journal of Sociology,* Vol. 60 (1955), pp. 75–89.

21. Fenichel, Otto. *The Psychoanalytic Theory of Neurosis.* New York: W. W. Norton, 1945.

22. Festinger, Leon, Henry W. Riecken, and Stanley Schachter. *When Prophecy Fails.* Minneapolis: University of Minnesota Press, 1956.

23. Foote, Nelson N., and Leonard S. Cottrell, Jr. *Identity and Interpersonal Competence.* Chicago: University of Chicago Press, 1955.

24. Foy, Eddie, and Alvin F. Harlow. "The Iroquois Theatre Fire," in R. H. Turner and L. M. Killian (eds.), *Collective Behavior.* Englewood Cliffs, N.J.: Prentice-Hall, Inc., 1957.

25. Fromm, Erich. *Escape From Freedom.* New York: Farrar & Rinehart, 1941.

26. Fromm, Erich. *Man for Himself.* New York: Rinehart & Co., 1947.

27. Fuller, Helen. "The Man to See in California," *Harper's Magazine,* Vol. 226 (1963), pp. 64–72.

28. Gilbert, G. M. *The Psychology of Dictatorship.* New York: Ronald Press, 1950.

29. Gillin, John L. "A Contribution to the Sociology of Sects," *American Journal of Sociology,* Vol. 16 (1910), pp. 236–252.

30. Gouldner, Alvin W. (ed.). *Studies in Leadership.* New York: Harper & Bros., 1950.

31. Hagen, Everett E. *On the Theory of Social Change.* Homewood, Ill.: The Dorsey Press, 1962.

32. Hoffer, Eric. *The True Believer.* New York: Harper & Bros., 1951.

33. Hogbin, H. Ian. *Social Change.* London: C. A. Watts & Co., 1958.

34. Katz, Daniel, and Richard L. Schanck. *Social Psychology.* New York: John Wiley & Sons, 1938.

35. Killian, Lewis M. Unpublished material summarized in R. H. Turner and L. M. Killian (eds.), *Collective Behavior.* Englewood Cliffs, N.J.: Prentice-Hall, Inc., 1957.

36. Killian, Lewis M., and James R. Griffin. Unpublished material summarized in R. H. Turner and L. M. Killian (eds.), *Collective Behavior.* Englewood Cliffs, N.J.: Prentice-Hall, Inc., 1957.

37. Kirk, Russell. *The Conservative Mind.* Chicago: H. Regnery Co., 1953.

38. Kornhauser, William. "Social Bases of Political Commitment," in A. M. Rose (ed.), *Human Behavior and Social Processes.* Boston: Houghton Mifflin, 1962.

39. Kroeber, Alfred L. *Configurations of Culture Growth.* Berkeley and Los Angeles: University of California Press, 1944.

40. Lang, Kurt and Gladys E. *Collective Dynamics.* New York: Thomas Y. Crowell Co., 1961.

41. Lewis, Helen Block. "Studies in the Principles of Judgments and Attitudes: IV. The Operation of 'Prestige Suggestion,'" *Journal of Social Psychology,* Vol. 14 (1941), pp. 229–256.

42. Lipset, Seymour M. *Political Man.* Garden City, N.Y.: Doubleday & Co., 1960.

43. Luchins, Abraham S. "Mechanization in Problem Solving: The Effect of Einstellung," *Psychological Monographs* (1942), No. 248.

44. Mackinnon, Donald W. "The Structure of Personality," in J. McV. Hunt (ed.), *Personality and the Behavior Disorders* (2 Vols.), Vol 1. New York: Ronald Press, 1944.

45. Mead, George H. *Mind, Self, and Society,* edited by C. W. Morris. Chicago: University of Chicago Press, 1934.

46. Merton, Robert K. *Social Theory and Social Structure,* rev. ed. Glencoe, Ill.: The Free Press, 1957.

47. Mintz, Alexander. "Non-adaptive Group Behavior," *Journal of Abnormal and Social Psychology,*" Vol. 46 (1951), pp. 150–159.

48. Niebuhr, H. Richard. "Sects," *Encyclopedia of the Social Sciences,* Vol. 13 (1937).

49. Ogburn, William F. *Social Change.* New York: B. W. Huebsch, Inc., 1922.

50. Pally, S. "Cognitive Rigidity as a Function of Threat," *Journal of Personality,* Vol. 23 (1955), pp. 346–355.

51. Park, Robert E. "Human Migration and the Marginal Man," *American Journal of Sociology,* Vol. 33 (1928), pp. 881–893.

52. Park, Robert E. "Cultural Conflict and the Marginal Man," by E. V. Stonequist, Introduction to *The Marginal Man* (1937). (See 65 below.)

53. Prince, S. H. *Catastrophe and Social Change.* New York: Columbia University Press, 1921.

54. Rank, Otto. *Will Therapy and Truth and Reality,* translated by J. Taft. New York: Alfred A. Knopf, 1945.

55. Riesman, David, Nathan Glazer, and Reuel Denney. *The Lonely Crowd.* New Haven: Yale University Press, 1950.

56. Rossiter, Clinton. *Conservatism in America.* New York: Alfred A. Knopf, 1955.

57. Sanford, Fillmore H. "The Follower's Role in Leadership Phenomena," in G. E. Swanson, T. M. Newcomb, and E. L. Hartley (eds.), *Readings in Social Psychology,* rev. ed. New York: Henry Holt, 1952.

58. Seeman, Melvin. "On the Meaning of Alienation," *American Sociological Review,* Vol. 24 (1959), pp. 783–791.

59. Sherif, Muzafer. *The Psychology of Social Norms.* New York: Harper & Bros., 1936.

60. Sherif, Muzafer, and O. J. Harvey. "A Study of Ego Functioning: Elimination of Stable Anchorages in Individual and Group Situations," *Sociometry,* Vol. 15 (1952), pp. 272–305.

61. Sherif, Muzafer, and Carolyn W. *An Outline of Social Psychology,* rev. ed. New York: Harper & Bros., 1956.

62. Shibutani, Tamotsu. "Reference Groups as Perspectives," *American Journal of Sociology,* Vol. 60 (1955), pp. 562–569.

63. Sorokin, Pitirim A. *Social and Cultural Dynamics,* 4 Vols. New York: American Book Co., 1937–41.

64. Stone, Gregory P. "Appearance and the Self," in A. M. Rose (ed.), *Human Behavior and Social Processes.* Boston: Houghton Mifflin, 1962.

65. Stonequist, Everett V. *The Marginal Man.* New York: Charles Scribner's Sons, 1937.

66. Strauss, Anselm L. "Identification." Unpublished manuscript (revised to *Mirrors and Masks,* Glencoe, Ill.: The Free Press, 1959).

67. Strauss, Anselm L. *The Social Psychology of George Herbert Mead.* Chicago: University of Chicago Press, 1956.

68. Symonds, Percival. *The Dynamics of Human Adjustment.* New York: D. Appleton-Century Co., 1946.

69. Thomas, William I. *Social Behavior and Personality,* edited by E. H. Volkart. New York: Social Science Research Council, 1951.

70. Turner, Ralph H. "Role-taking, Role Standpoint, and Reference-group Behavior," *American Journal of Sociology,* Vol. 61 (1956), pp. 316–328.

71. Turner, Ralph H., and Lewis M. Killian. *Collective Behavior.* Englewood Cliffs, N.J.: Prentice-Hall, Inc., 1957.

72. Veltfort, Helene R., and George E. Lee. "The Cocoanut Grove Fire," in R. H. Turner and L. M. Killian (eds.), *Collective Behavior.* Englewood Cliffs, N.J.: Prentice-Hall, Inc., 1957.

73. Viereck, Peter R. E. *Conservatism.* Princeton, N.J.: Van Nostrand, 1956.

74. Vinacke, W. Edgar. *The Psychology of Thinking.* New York: McGraw-Hill Book Co., 1952.

75. Warshay, Leon H. "Breadth of Perspective, Culture Contact, and Self." Doctoral dissertation, University of Minnesota libraries, Minneapolis, 1959.

76. Warshay, Leon H. "Breadth of Perspective: Further Thoughts." Unpublished paper presented at Midwest Sociological Society meetings, Omaha, April 28, 1961. (Dittoed)

77. Warshay, Leon H. "Breadth of Perspective," in A. M. Rose (ed.), *Human Behavior and Social Processes.* Boston: Houghton Mifflin, 1962.

78. Wertheimer, Max. *Productive Thinking.* New York: Harper & Bros., 1945.

14

H. G. Barnett

The Acceptance and Rejection

of Change

Several years ago I proposed a scheme for systematizing reactions to innovations. It conceptualized positive and negative responses to new things, behaviors, and ideas as processes; that is, as controlled and limited sets of interrelations between variables in a closed system of events. Under this interpretation a process is a generalization from particulars and can be expressed as a formula. Its specific manifestations are regarded as action complexes, or mechanisms, with definite beginning and end points which will repeat themselves when the appropriate initiating conditions recur. In the present instance these action systems are psychological, that is, they are mental operations activated by sensory stimuli. Consequently, the acceptance or rejection of an innovation is essentially, and sometimes solely, an internal reaction which cannot be directly observed but can be inferred or postulated and which often becomes manifest in verbal or other behaviors.

Whether or not an acceptance or rejection becomes manifest is an important question because it bears directly upon our main concern, which is with social change. It is, however, another problem with its own set of variables which can be investigated in addition to, but not in place of, those conditioning the psychological reactions to innovation. This aspect of the problem is set aside in the interests of clarity and in order to focus attention upon what is believed to be the source and genesis of social change.

The same must be said with respect to an intimately related question,

345

namely, how can an individual reaction to an innovation become a social fact? In brief, the answer is that it can and does become a group characteristic when the acceptance or rejection process is duplicated in n individuals, the n depending upon one's understanding of how many and what persons constitute a group. In other words, and contrary to common supposition, there is no antithesis between a psychological and a sociological treatment of this problem. One does not need to appeal to a transcendent or a reduction mechanism to get from one of these alleged "levels" of analysis and interpretation to the other. The social "leap" occurs when one individual does what another does, and imitation is one manifestation of the acceptance process.

The acceptance-rejection process, as here proposed, is an explanatory concept and cannot claim to be anything more. It has been abstracted from external events which are accessible and which therefore can be verified by repeated observations. As in all conceptualizations, however, the observable data have been interpreted and organized in a particular way, that way being determined by the objective of comprehending change systematically. The demands of the system must be specified before an attempt is made to demonstrate its applicability.

In a presentation such as this it is necessary at the outset to identify clearly the referents of the discussion because one set of symbols must be employed to designate other symbols, as well as concepts and things. The statement, "Women are inferior to men," for example, can be simply a particular assortment of black lines on the white paper of this page, as it would be to an illiterate person. It can be a sentence, that is, a grammatical phenomenon with a subject, a copula, and a predicate in that restricted order. It can be a communication, a piece of information in which inferiority is attributed to women by comparison with men. It can be a proposition, a statement which is either true or false and which presumably can be demonstrated. Finally, it can be a description in writing of an existing situation in which women are actually treated as the inferiors of men. Unless otherwise noted, the illustrative statements in the following discussion fall in this last category; that is, they are intended to be descriptions of situations with physical referents.

Structuralization

Let us suppose that this headline appears in a reputable newspaper: "Scientists to Experiment on Condemned Criminals." Let us suppose further that it is intended to report an actual situation; it is not a verbal innovation, a plea, an announcement of a subject for debate, or a description of what scientists do. Even assuming that no reader questions the truth of the report, it is almost certain that individual reactions to the situation it describes will differ. One reason for this is that no sensory field is ever completely or unalterably structured in one way only (1, pp. 442–445). Its content, limits, and other properties may be more or less determined by the manner in which it is presented or approached; but by the same token, every experience is divisible, extensible, and partial. All of us are blind men groping around elephants, but many times the ears and tails we feel are not even connected. Indeed, they may be parts of other animals. Those who advocate an innovation, and those who report or describe it to others, exercise some control over the apperception of it by others, but never entirely so. Moreover, their structuring of it is subject to significant variation. The complex of events which inspired the hypothetical headline above could be reported quite differently: "Lifers to Become Guinea Pigs," "Incorrigibles May Redeem Selves," "Cure For Murder is Sought," "Drastic Therapy Legalized," or, most improbably, "Lobotomists Tackle Recidivism." Often there is no such intermediation, and one individual will apprehend a change in a way which its advocate or some other person would regard as grotesque or as nothing new at all. It may very well be perceived not as a unit, but as a chaotic assemblage of discrete and unrelated events, or as an undifferentiated mass in the background of more interesting things. It cannot be denied that there are newspaper accounts which produce this effect, and also that newspaper reporters are not the only people who fail to "make sense" or make the "wrong" kind of sense out of a "complicated" situation.

Utilizing letters of the alphabet, we can symbolize the latent possibilities in a stimulus field thus: P Q R S . . . . . X Y Z. If the field is an innovation, it is possible for a given observer to attend to it selectively, regardless of the way in which it is presented. One reader of the news reported under the first headline above may be so concerned about the criminals, whom we shall call Y, that he gives little or no attention to other components of the situation. His preoccupation may be so preclusive that he skims over, or does not read, the particulars about the scientists, the X component, nor those pertaining to the types of experiments to be conducted. For him the saliency of Y suppresses attention to X. Another reader may be concerned exclusively about the involvement of scientists in this kind of research, and so opposed to it that he does not care either about the subjects or the nature of the proposed experiments. For him just who the Y's are is unimportant; they could be criminals or any other people. For both readers, X and Y are independent.

There is a third possibility. It is realized when an observer attends to more than one component in his perceptual field. In terms of the symbols used above, both X and Y register with him. If they do, there must be some recognized connection between them; otherwise they will divide and divert his attention. He may supply the connection himself or he may accept the one given by someone else such as a newspaper reporter. In conceptual terms these connections are called relationships. They are extremely important in both innovation and the acceptance process; yet we have only a limited and imperfect terminology with which to communicate about them. They are significant because they reflect and govern our comprehension of the modes and dimensions by and through which we conceive our experiences to be linked. We have names for some of them: temporal, spatial, causal, predicative, affective, filial, genetic, subordinate, correlative, and so forth (1, pp 411–432). Each of these has an indefinite number of named and unnamed nuances and inflections, and there are many more which we intuit and act upon without being able to verbalize them.

In our language, relationships often take the form of verbs and prepositions; but they can be expressed by other grammatical devices as well. Nouns, pronouns, and adjectives which name a state or a property of something usually denote the referents between which a relationship is asserted. Thus in "Man is sinful," man is X, sinful is Y, and is, the relationship asserted to obtain between them. In "Scientists to Experiment on Condemned Criminals," the scientists are X, the condemned criminals Y, and the rest of the sentence defines the relationship between them. The lack of precision with which relationships are stated in instances such as the last example is due in part to the grammatical requirements of our language — or any other language. Conventional speech forms have their own structural demands and these seldom conform to the conceptual framework of other systems. In addition, the relationships between persons and things are seldom simple, although a single strand in a complex set can be selected as the most important one.

This leads to the statement of an important assumption which is implicit in the foregoing, namely, that every innovation can be structured to conform to the pattern of X R Y; meaning that, however it might be stated linguistically, any given sectioning of a stimulus field is specific and polarized such that it consists of two and *only* two components with one and *only* one relation per section existing between them. This does not forbid multiple sectioning; in fact, this frequently happens. Moreover, a shift from one sectional axis, plane, or perspective of the field to another can occur instantaneously, as it does in the fluctuations of ambiguous figures (1, p. 437, pp. 445–447).

Contact

The absence of rigidity in a stimulus field must be considered in conjunction with other factors in order to comprehend the diversity of reactions to new things and proposals (1, pp. 204–207). One of the most fundamental is the requirement that an innovation, or a part of it, make psychological contact with some antecedent experience of its potential acceptor or rejector. This factor is so intimately connected with structuralization that the one does not occur without the other. Structuralization operates selectively upon the inventory of past experiences of the acceptor-rejector, and the particular experience which it evokes, let us say, A, reacts upon its instigator to stabilize or to modify it. New experiences do not simply imprint themselves on a blank mental field; they must revive a component of the memory record if they evoke a reaction. If the words "incorrigibles" or "recidivism" are alien to the vocabulary of a reader, and if their referents in the newspaper story are puzzling, contradictory, or ambiguous, he is likely to turn to something else or to seek clarification from other sources. On the other hand, it is not essential that both the X and the Y components of an innovation evoke the recall of something familiar. Some readers may not know what "incorrigibles" or "lifers" (X's) are and get no illumination from a newspaper description of them, but may still have a basis for reacting through their familiarity with the concepts of redemption or guinea pigs (Y's). In this case we can say that X has failed to evoke an A out of the past experience of a reader but that Y has made contact with something else which can be labeled B. Failing that, the encounter has been sterile; both X and Y are psychologically inert.

Frequently an innovation directly recalls a past experience through the intermediation of an identical part of each. Identity in this sense means absolutely co-existent; X *is* A (or Y *is* B), not as members of a class or by definition, but because they are presumed to be simultaneously and co-extensively present. One and the same set of scientists X are to experiment on criminals Y as they do in training or performing surgery on rats B. We may symbolize identities of this kind by X O A, or alternatively as Y O B, signifying that it does not matter whether the contacting element is designated as X or as A, or, alternatively, as Y or B. Both sets, X O A and Y O B, cannot, in any given instance, have this property. If they could there would be no innovation.

It is important to bear in mind that identities have limits. Scientists may be regarded as an indiscriminate set in one context, such as Y, but not so in another context such as B; similarly for kidnappers and murderers as criminals, and guinea pigs and rats as experimental animals. Total and undeviating identity is a function of other constants.

A less direct means of establishing contact between the new and the old is by appeal to definition, consensus, or conventional dictate; X is A or Y is B by assertion or by tacit agreement. If our reader of headlines does not know what a "recidivist" is, he might resort to a dictionary or derive his own definition of it from such information as is provided in the text of the news story. Or he might guess what it is, which amounts to his projecting some familiar conception into the context of the account. The possibilities for structuring the stimulus data — sometimes called "distortion" — are evident here just as they are with identities. Except for logical definitions, which only partially relate to the world of sense experience, all definitions have elastic limits, and the identities among natural phenomena are always subject to redefinition.

Another way to bridge the gap between the new and the old is by means of their respective and overlapping analyses. This possibility requires that X and A or Y and B have some property in common. There must be something about individual X which recalls individual A, something which puts them in the category or class of scientists, for example; or some characteristic of a scientist which permits him to be equated with, let us say, a biologist or a psychologist. Alternatively, a conceptual analysis of the guinea pigs and rats with which these scientists work can be made, leading to their equation.

Equation by analysis is an extremely common reaction to new experiences as well as to a vast number which are not considered to be new. Very often it is not recognized because it is accomplished almost instantaneously and without awareness. Summarizing the results of some of his experiments on perception, Bartlett concluded that:

> the experiments show that the common method of an observer, in the absence of special conditions, which may be either objective or a matter of temperament and training, is to respond to whatever is presented as unitary. Nevertheless, there is no perceptual situation in which some detail does not stand out and influence what is perceived more than the rest. With structurally simply material, such dominant detail may be: gaps; odd and disconnected features; simple spatial references — above, below, right, left; light and shade. With structurally complex material it may be plan of construction; disposition of figures which are themselves given scant notice; general topic and representational significance. Thus, although perceiving is rarely analytical or piece-meal in its method, yet it *is* a kind of analysis, since always there are some features of the perceptual situation which take a lead over the others. These dominant details are a kind of nucleus about which the rest cluster. They set the stage for remembering (2, pp. 31–32).

It will be noted that equation by analysis is an expedient for locating identity in diversity. It is an indispensable operation because we live in such a constantly changing environment that it is doubtful whether any two of our experiences are absolutely identical, yet we must treat many of them as if they were. The discrepancies may be so microscopic that they elude all but the closest examination. Or they may be gross and easily located, their neglect being due to pragmatic considerations, to bias, to disinterest, or to a variety of other controls. In any event, there is some loss of fidelity in equating things, acts, and concepts, and considerable individual variation in the toleration of it. It is difficult to escape the conclusion that falsification is inevitable with the lapse of time, that there is always some difference between the mental record and the experiences which later impinge upon and activate it. When recall occurs and a present stimulus set is recognized, it is due to only a partial overlap, a common denominator, and not to complete correspondence. This would appear to be true even when a definition provides a bridge between old and new, because even though it translates a new experience into familiar terms, the latter must still be judged to be familiar.

While it is true that memory is fallible and that sense data are often unwittingly altered to make them fit a familiar pattern, it is not true that the lack of complete correspondence between X and A or between Y and B always goes unnoticed by the person who analyzes and equates them. On the contrary, he is often aware that his equations are only approximations, especially when they are challenged by other people or when a close inspection is necessary in order to establish them. In these instances X and A or Y and B are understood to be similar but not identical, their differences being considered to be immaterial for present purposes. In other words, they are enough alike that one can function in a given context of the other, but they may not be universally interchangeable.

Equation can be achieved, not only by the analysis of X and A (or Y and B), but by incorporating in each some referent to which both have the same relationship (1, pp. 189–202). Factitious as this may seem to be, it frequently happens under the pressure of bias, demands, training, or special interest. When it occurs, the saliency of the common referent obscures and belittles the differences between X and A (or Y and B). Psychologists and biologists may be equated, not because both are regarded as scientists but because both are associated with the same project, such as experimenting on criminals, the character and purpose of that research being the predominant concern of their classifier. In other words, he may not care whether psychologists are scientists or whether they have any other property in common with biologists, the relevant consideration is that both are going to experiment with human beings.

We can symbolize equations arrived at by identification, definition, analysis, or incorporation by $X = A$ and $Y = B$. Care must be exercised not to view them as truisms. $X = A$ is not a tautology but a conclusion or an assertion, a fact which this alphabetic means of expression is intended to emphasize. Yet when words are substituted for these letters confusion begins to creep in. "Psychologists = biologists" preserves the significance of their equation, but "scientists = scientists" can easily obscure it. What the latter equation signifies is that a specific group of persons denoted by the term "scientists" is judged to be the same as a second specific group designated by the same term. Furthermore, each group is a unit and, as such, is equated with the other despite the fact that they carry labels which are linguistic devices for characterizing pluralities of individuals.

It is assumed that it is impossble for an X or a Y to contact directly or spontaneously an A or a B which is totally unlike it in the estimation of the acceptor-rejector. Speaking more generally, some degree of similarity between experiences is essential for a present one to recall a previous one. Nevertheless, dissimilar concepts, things, and behaviors do at times confront each other. They may be juxtaposed by accident, or upon the suggestion of someone who thinks that they are similar or the same.

Just as often, however, their apposition is the result of an analysis which begins with a question about their similarity. Thus, a reader of the head-line "Scientists to Experiment on Condemned Criminals" may wonder what kinds of scientists could be involved. He may mentally try out a list of the kinds with which he is familiar, including chemists and physicists, but in the end exclude chemists and physicists as possibilities in this con-text. He may also reflect upon what kinds of criminals are to be subjected to experimentation and reach the decision that even though children may commit crimes they cannot be included in the class of condemned crimi-nals. Conclusions reached in these ways can be expressed symbolically as $X \neq A$ and $Y \neq B$.

Assimilation

The union of a new with a familiar experience may terminate with identification, definition, analysis, or incorporation; but if it does, the acceptance-rejection process is incomplete. That is tantamount to re-jection because the new, even though it has gained an entree, has not been located and fixed in the cognitive network of the potential acceptor. This is the outcome when he loses interest or patience in trying to de-termine what X or Y is, or when he is distracted by something else. Most often, however, it happens because the A or the B image, concept, or im-pression evoked by X or Y is vague, fluctuating, evanescent, or isolated from other past experiences; in short, because no part of the innovation has meaning. Any new thing or idea must be fitted into the context of the known in some fashion if it is even to be recognized; it is what it is understood to be only with reference to the associations of its familiar counterpart. Every new experience presents an observer with this prob-lem of relating present to past experience; and whether he is aware of it or not he must find a solution to it if the new is to have meaning for him. Bartlett describes the situation thus:

> Because this task factor is always present, it is fitting to speak of every
> human cognitive reaction — perceiving, imaging, remembering, thinking and
> reasoning — as an *effort after meaning*. Certain of the tendencies which
> the subject brings with him into the situation with which he is called upon
> to deal are utilized so as to make his reaction the 'easiest,' or the least
> disagreeable, or the quickest and least obstructed that is at the time pos-
> sible. When we try to discover how this is done we find that always it is
> by an effort to connect what is given with something else. Thus, the im-
> mediately present 'stands for' something not immediately present, and
> 'meaning,' in a psychological sense, has its origin. As we have seen, in cer-
> tain cases of great structural simplicity, or of structural regularity, or of
> extreme familiarity, the immediate data are at once fitted to, or matched
> with, a perceptual pattern which appears to be pre-existent so far as the
> particular perceptual act is concerned. This pre-formed setting, scheme,

or pattern is utilized in a completely unreflecting, unanalytical, and unwitting manner. Because it is utilized the immediate perceptual data have meaning, can be dealt with, and are assimilated (2, pp. 44–45).

In terms of the symbolism adopted here this paragraph can be condensed to read: when $X = A$, X can be assimilated to some context B, this context being the idea of anything associated with A in the past experience of an acceptor-rejector; or alternatively, when $Y = B$, Y can be assimilated to context A, which is a familiar associate of B. One significant interpolation is necessary in order to fulfill a requirement of the acceptance-rejection process, namely, that some specific relationship exist between components A and B to make it possible for assimilation to occur. The recall of one component is contingent upon the activation of the other, and the relationship between them is the vector which makes their interaction possible. Together with their relationship they constitute a unit which can be analyzed, but at the instant of its activation it is an undifferentiated whole. It is a redintegrated section or slice of past experience, and on that account it has the character of a prototype (1, pp. 207–210).

The relationships which link A and B have the same characteristics and scope as do those already described as connecting elements for the X and Y components of the innovation which evokes A and/or B. In some instances they are identical, but this is by no means always so. In fact, differences between them are often the basis for the acceptance or rejection of something new. It is therefore important to indicate whether they are the same or different in any given case. Subscripts will serve this purpose. Thus $X_1 = A_1$, $X_2 = A_2$, $Y_1 = B_1$, and $Y_2 = B_2$ signify that the relationships are identical in equated experiences, while $X_2 = A_1$ and $Y_2 = B_1$ mean they are different. If the components and their relationships are both different, then $X_2 \neq A_1$ and $Y_2 \neq B_1$.

When A is activated by X, it can arouse B on the axis of their relationship, and since X is equivalent to A it can stand in the same relationship to B as does A. This means that it can be substituted for A in the context of B in the same manner and to the same degree to which A is related to B. In other words, B assimilates X. The assimilation can be preclusive in that X can displace A completely in the context of B. If lobotomists X are fully equated with psychologists A, who train rats B, they can take over that function entirely from the psychologists. On the other hand, A can share its relation to B, making X its alternative: either psychologists or lobotomists may experiment with rats. The same assimilative mechanism can bring Y into relationship with A through the activation of B: if condemned criminals Y can be equated with guinea pigs B, then biologists A can mate them as they do guinea pigs, either abandoning their experiments with guinea pigs in favor of the criminals or carrying on comparable research with both categories of subjects.

It is evident that X can be assimilated only if there is a context B into which it can be fitted. It should be made explicit, however, that the necessary condition for this is that A have its relationship to B, so to speak, attached to it. The satisfaction of this requirement can be indicated by writing A with its subscribed number 1 in this fashion: A_1. The same requirement holds for the assimilation of Y. That can happen only if Y can be connected with A through the intermediation of B and its attached relation, a condition symbolized as B_1.

Assimilation occurs when one or both components of an innovation X Y are so pronounced and demanding in the estimation of an acceptor-rejector that they contend with or assert their superiority over their familiar counterparts A and B. Sometimes it is believed by the acceptor-rejector that they *are* A and/or B; that is, he completely identifies them with what they bring to mind: lobotomists *are* psychologists. In other instances, and for a variety of reasons, the X and/or Y of an innovation appeal to an acceptor-rejector because they make at least as good if not a better fit in the framework of the prototype than do A or B or both. Also, as noted earlier, he may take a partial and selective view of the relative significance of the X and Y components of an innovation. The structuralizing capacity of his prototype may be such that X dominates his attention to the exclusion of Y and X's relationship to it. In common parlance, he "lifts X out of context," or "fails to take all of the facts into account." Stated in terms of our symbols, $X = A_1$. Alternatively, Y may command his attention exclusively, in which case $Y = B_1$. Both X and Y can be taken into account, and they frequently are. In that case the relationship between them, and between A and B, are important considerations, as is noted in the third paragraph above.

Projection

In assimilation a relatively unfamiliar stimulus is absorbed into a familiar framework. The opposite effect is also possible. It is realized when, in the estimation of an acceptor-rejector, one (or both) component(s) of his prototype A B has a pre-emptive character about it (them) vis-à-vis the innovation counterparts X and Y. Components mentally contend with or displace their counterparts by what might be called a mechanism of projection, meaning simply that the acceptor-rejector can visualize them in place of their equivalent X and/or Y, or that he believes that they *are* X and/or Y: Christian Scientists A = scientists X; therefore they can experiment with condemned criminals Y along with, or to the exclusion of, other scientists. Or, the parents B of condemned criminals Y are equally criminal and so should be subjected to experiments by scientists X instead of, or along with, their offspring.

As with assimilation, projection may be selective and partial. In some instances this means that the prototype of the acceptor-rejector is not actually such because its A and B components must be completely disassociated. They may have been connected to begin with, but more often they are not components of the same system. Moreover, they are not firmly embedded in any system. We can represent this condition by X_2 = A and Y_2 = B, to signify that A is projected into the context of Y in the same relationship that X has to Y, and that B is projected into the context of X in the same relationship that Y has to X. If the acceptor-rejector does not admit to the equality of X and A, then $X_2 \neq A$, and if Y and B are not alike in his estimation, then $Y_2 \neq B$.

If A and B do constitute a prototype, that is, are members of one related system, projection is still possible, or impossible, depending upon the acceptor-rejector's conception of equivalence. In either case, the relationship between A and B is a factor contributing to his decision. If he regards the compared components and their relations as equivalent, we can characterize his reaction as $Y_1 = B_1$, $X_2 = A_2$, $Y_2 = B_2$, or $X_1 = A_1$. Contrariwise, if the components *and* their attached relations are judged to be different, then $X_2 \neq A_1$ and/or $Y_2 \neq B_1$.

Projection can occur with or without an awareness of it. All of us resort to it when we see or hear something which to our private way of thinking is incomplete. Incompleteness in this sense "raises questions" and we fill in the blanks with whatever A's and B's we have at our command from past experience, sometimes tentatively, sometimes confidently, without a moment's reflection. This mechanism also represents an "effort after meaning." One reader of "Scientists to Perform Experiments on Condemned Criminals" may spontaneously and directly project "physiologists" A into the X_2 position occupied by the ambiguous term "scientists," and may perhaps in the same way assume that "murderers" B are the "condemned criminals" Y_2 intended by the report, and project accordingly. Other readers may wonder, that is, vacillate with tentative projections of physicians, physical therapists, psychiatrists, etc., into the X_2 position; with kidnappers, embezzlers, traitors, etc., into the Y_2 position; and with surgery, shock treatment, survival tests, etc., interpolated as the action which relates the scientists to the criminals.

Assimilation and projection are extremely common occurrences, not only with respect to innovations but to everyday experiences. They have been demonstrated experimentally and they can be identified in the daily course of our lives. The conditions which contribute to the one as opposed to the other, or to their partial as distinct from their complete manifestations, are complex and it is not possible to enlarge upon them here. Suffice it to say that the variations upon the interactions between an innovation and the prototype which it evokes are governed by the interplay of many variables deriving from the background of the acceptor-rejector as well as the circumstances which confront him at the moment he makes his decision.

Values

This leads to one further matter which requires discussion before we can deal with the acceptance-rejection process as such. This is the bearing which individual values have upon it. From what has been said so far it is easy to assume that a familiar practice, custom, ideal, behavior, or concept, and the prototype which represents it, is approved by the person who thinks of it upon his encounter with an innovation. The mere statement of the problem in this way is sufficient to dispose of the assumption. Nevertheless, the treatment of contacts between innovations and the prototypes which they call to mind in terms of equality and inequality may give the impression that this settles the question of acceptability, and it is now necessary to explain why it does not. The reason is that the decision in favor of or in opposition to an innovation is made in consequence of an interaction between the values placed on familiar patterns and the similarity, or the lack of it, which these patterns have with the innovation. Thus $Y = B_1$ signifies acceptability only if the acceptor-rejector places a positive value on B. If he approves of B, then more of it (or a very similar alternative to it), Y, is agreeable to him — discounting considerations which may moderate or adversely affect this conclusion but which are external to this key issue. If, on the other hand, he objects to B, he is likely to object to something as similar to it as Y. If he sanctions experimental research on rats B by psychologists A, and if he thinks criminals Y make subjects as good or better than rats, he is led to the conclusion that psychologists should be permitted to conduct the same type of research on criminals as they do on rats. He has a basis for rejecting the suggestion if he is averse to experiments on rats in the first place, even though he might agree that criminals could be used as subjects just as well or perhaps better than rats. This same pattern holds for other equations, as $X = A_1$, $X_2 = A$, $Y_2 = B$, $Y_2 = B_1$, and $Y_1 = B_1$.

The issues are not so clearly defined when there are significant differences between X and A or between Y and B; that is, when $X_2 \neq A$, $Y_2 \neq B$, $X \neq A_1$, $Y \neq B_1$, $X_2 \neq A_1$, and $Y_2 \neq B_1$. In these instances the value placed upon the prototype by the acceptor-rejector may or may not dispose him to accept the particular innovation represented by X Y. He will not, for example, accept just any change from something which he dislikes. He may be opposed to capital punishment B_1 and be no less averse to a proposal to brand Y criminals A as an alternative form of punishment. On the other hand, he may favor the stigmatizing of criminals because it accomplishes something which their execution does not. Differences are thus a minimal basis for rejecting an innovation as a substitute for, or as an alternative to, an existing mode which is already personally rejected. The issue is likewise indecisive when a prevailing mode or some personal standard of thought or behavior has a positive value. A proposal to replace it with something different may be rejected because of the difference, but not necessarily so. An advocate of capital punishment may nonetheless be receptive to an alternative or to a substitutive form of punishment, such as exile or ostracism, which he regards as different but more effective, humane, or economical; but he may reject it because it lacks something which capital punishment has and which he regards as essential.

It seems that the only definitive acceptance-rejection situation is one based upon an equivalence. That circumstance reduces the ambiguity inherent in the perception of any unfamiliar configuration; and when such reduction operates in conjunction with a positive or a negative evaluation of its familiar equivalent the issue of acceptance is most clearly defined. It also appears that this manner of dealing with something new is a typical maneuver. That is, an acceptor-rejector tends to base his position on similarities rather than on dissimilarities. Thus, if an opponent of capital punishment is confronted with the alternative of a law which would permit criminals to go free but would make it illegal for anyone to associate with or assist them in any way, his reaction to it is more likely to depend upon his attitude toward something with which he is familiar that resembles it, such as exile, than upon the difference between it and capital punishment.

An innovation may be accepted or rejected in part only, or with reservations, because differential values are attached to components of the prototype with which it is compared. This must mean that the innovation and the prototype are analyzed in order to yield or exhibit their parts. Thus a rejector of experimentation on criminals may be such because to him the only permissible subjects for experimentation are dumb animals. He may at the same time be ambivalent about just which scientists should be involved. On the other hand, he may accept experiments on criminals if he can specify their nature and scope; or he may insist that clergymen and not scientists should attempt to treat criminals as they do other unfortunate individuals. These specifications and reservations amount to a subdivision or an amalgamation of classes of persons, procedures, and things which have saliency because of the values the acceptor-rejector feels compelled to assign to aspects of his experience. Their referents can be selective: some criminals, experiments, and scientists are admissible but not others. Their referents can also be most specific, even to the point of being individualized: the self, *this* criminal, or *that* scientist may be the only acceptable or unacceptable case among those encompassed by an innovation. At the other extreme are value emphases on categories of A's or B's or relationships that are total, exhaustive, and mutually exclusive: all or no scientists, or all or no criminals, always or never certain relationships, etc. These are variations upon the acceptance-rejection process which logicians deal with under the headings of quantity, quality, exclusion, and the distribution of terms in their traditional analysis of categorical propositions. As will be indicated shortly, their treatment of the validity of inference is directly relevant to this process.

When no aspect of an innovation is more salient than another to a given acceptor-rejector he reacts to it in its entirety in terms of its equivalence or non-equivalence with some prototype and the value he assigns to the latter. For him it is all or nothing. This reaction is typical of a special but significant case of the general scheme. In it the prototype is not a record of an observation with external referents; it is a statement of a principle, a law, an ethic, or a moral postulate. It is therefore a value declaration in itself and in its entirety, and upon it an acceptor-rejector frequently takes his stand. He does this as in the other cases, that is, by either agreeing or disagreeing with it and then transferring his evaluation to the innovation which it either resembles or does not. Thus some people will assert in effect that any tampering with human life is presumptuous, if not immoral, and that experimentation with criminals is tampering with human life. Others will either disavow the dictate, or the equation, or both. These are syllogistic arguments, and as might be expected, often resorted to by partisans and opponents of innovations.

Acceptance and Rejection Possibilities

The chart on page 360 represents an attempt to incorporate most of the variables discussed in a general statement. It has been generated by a systematic permutation of these variables; consequently, it is a paradigm with 81 inflections on the acceptance-rejection process. In it each cell symbolizes the acceptance-rejection possibilities inherent in a given situation. The box of letter symbols in the left half of each numbered cell brings together the various combinations of elements in terms already defined. The conclusions which they embody can be determined by following the "rules" indicated by the foregoing discussion or by reference to their condensation in the chart explanation on page 361. The arrows to the right of the boxes do this graphically. Those in solid line which are directed to the left indicate projection possibilities; those to the right, assimilation. Arrows in solid line curving to the left and downward signify that B can replace Y in the context of X; those curving to the left and upward, that A can substitute for X in the context of Y; those curving to the right and downward, that Y can replace B in the context of A; and those curving to the right and upward, that X can replace A in the context of B. The dotted arrows mean an operation cannot take place because of an inequality between paired components. The absence of arrows signifies that the substitution which their presence would suggest is impossible because there is no relationship to provide a link with the context. *In all cases the indicated operations presume that a positive value is attached to the involved parts of the prototype.* If the prototype or a part of it is not valued, some of the solid lines will become dotted and some of the dotted ones solid in accordance with the preceding discussion of the acceptability of differences.

It should be emphasized that the chart does not assert that there are 81 acceptance and rejection possibilities. On the contrary, each curved line represents such a possibility. There are eight of these (four solid and four dotted), but they occur in varied combinations resulting from varied patterns of equivalences and differences between an innovation and some past experience with which it is compared. Each cell therefore represents a *situation* with a greater or lesser number of possibilities. Furthermore, not all of the potentials of a given situation are necessarily realized. Cell 41, for example, has the potential for four positive reactions but only one, two, or three of them may be activated in any particular individual's response to the situation it defines. In brief, each cell is unique in the pattern of opportunities for interaction which it provides, not by the number which are actually perceived and given effect.

A full exposition of the chart is not intended, but a few features of it may be pointed out. Row 1 and Column 1 are the zones with the fewest possibilities, the reasons being the failure, or rejection, of contacts between familiar and unfamiliar components and the lack of a relationship between them. Cell 1 represents a situation in which nothing can happen because its components are unrelated, independent, or identical, however one might wish to describe a situation which does not initiate a response. The rest of the cells in Row 1 and Column 1 embody deductive reasoning wherein there are only three terms. In them there is a major and a minor premise, which means that one term of the general scheme is either identical with another of the four, or it is completely disassociated from it. X O A, for example, signifies either that X and A are completely independent or that they are identical. Thus, by assimilation (Cell 3) it does not matter what else X scientists Y are or do, they are equal to all biologists B_1 as far as experimentation with rats A is concerned; and by projection (Cell 4) it does not matter what else A biologists B are or do, inasmuch as they are equal to scientists Y_2 they can experiment with condemned criminals X. In the terminology of logical analysis (3, p. 82) this is called a syllogism of the "first figure" wherein the subject of the major premise, i.e., the B of the prototype or the Y of the innovation, is the predicate of the minor premise, which is Y = B. A reversed up-for-down reading of the content (scientists, biologists, etc.) assigned to X, Y, A, and B components in this example would put it in Cells 19 and 28. Cells 7, 8, 55, and 64 accommodate syllogisms of the "second figure" wherein the middle term is the predicate of both premises. Thus to refer to Cell 7: all experimentation with human lives A is interference with God's will B_1; no scientist Y may act in a manner which constitutes interference with God's will; therefore no scientist may experiment with human lives. Acceptance of this conclusion presumes a positive evaluation of both premises. Which of these several ways of stating the syllogism is adopted is a matter of cognitive structuring by the acceptor-rejector; subject and predicate designations depend upon the focal point of his attention; pro-

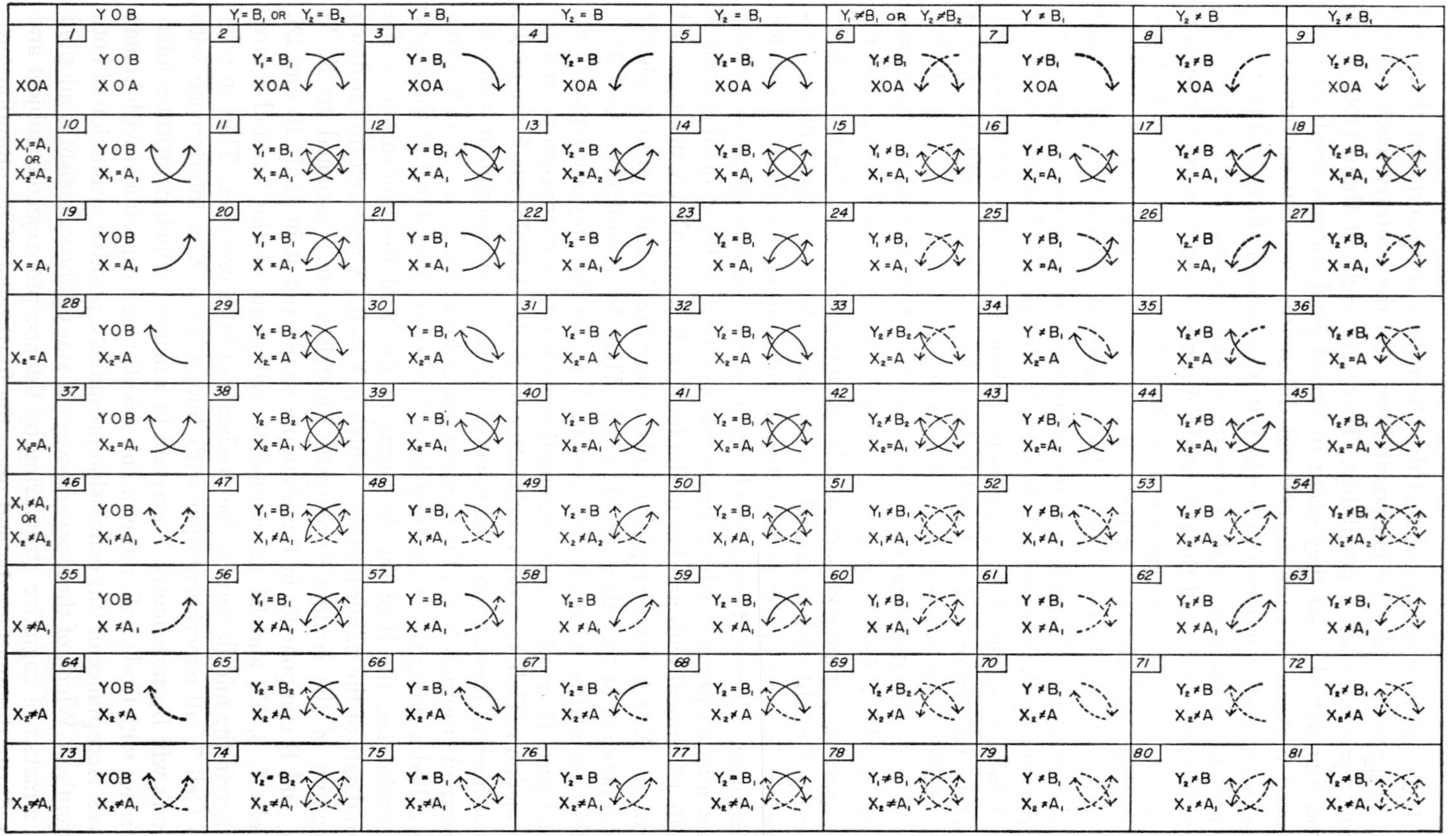
YOB
$Y_1 = B_1$ OR $Y_2 = B_2$
$Y = B_1$
$Y_2 = B$
$Y_2 = B_1$
$Y_1 \neq B_1$ OR $Y_2 \neq B_2$
$Y \neq B_1$
$Y_2 \neq B$
$Y_2 \neq B_1$
XOA
$X_1 = A_1$ OR $X_2 = A_2$
$X = A_1$
$X_2 = A$
$X_2 = A_1$
$X_1 \neq A_1$ OR $X_2 \neq A_2$
$X \neq A_1$
$X_2 \neq A$
$X_2 \neq A_1$
1 YOB XOA
2 $Y_1 = B_1$ XOA
3 $Y = B_1$ XOA
4 $Y_2 = B$ XOA
5 $Y_2 = B_1$ XOA
6 $Y_1 \neq B_1$ XOA
7 $Y \neq B_1$ XOA
8 $Y_2 \neq B$ XOA
9 $Y_2 \neq B_1$ XOA
10 YOB $X_1 = A_1$
11 $Y_1 = B_1$ $X_1 = A_1$
12 $Y = B_1$ $X_1 = A_1$
13 $Y_2 = B$ $X_2 = A_2$
14 $Y_2 = B_1$ $X_1 = A_1$
15 $Y_1 \neq B_1$ $X_1 = A_1$
16 $Y \neq B_1$ $X_1 = A_1$
17 $Y_2 \neq B$ $X_1 = A_1$
18 $Y_2 \neq B_1$ $X_1 = A_1$
19 YOB $X = A_1$
20 $Y_1 = B_1$ $X = A_1$
21 $Y = B_1$ $X = A_1$
22 $Y_2 = B$ $X = A_1$
23 $Y_2 = B_1$ $X = A_1$
24 $Y_1 \neq B_1$ $X = A_1$
25 $Y \neq B_1$ $X = A_1$
26 $Y_2 \neq B$ $X = A_1$
27 $Y_2 \neq B_1$ $X = A_1$
28 YOB $X_2 = A$
29 $Y_2 = B_2$ $X_2 = A$
30 $Y = B_1$ $X_2 = A$
31 $Y_2 = B$ $X_2 = A$
32 $Y_2 = B_1$ $X_2 = A$
33 $Y_2 \neq B_2$ $X_2 = A$
34 $Y \neq B_1$ $X_2 = A$
35 $Y_2 \neq B$ $X_2 = A$
36 $Y_2 \neq B_1$ $X_2 = A$
37 YOB $X_2 = A_1$
38 $Y_2 = B_2$ $X_2 = A_1$
39 $Y = B_1$ $X_2 = A_1$
40 $Y_2 = B$ $X_2 = A_1$
41 $Y_2 = B_1$ $X_2 = A_1$
42 $Y_2 \neq B_2$ $X_2 = A_1$
43 $Y \neq B_1$ $X_2 = A_1$
44 $Y_2 \neq B$ $X_2 = A_1$
45 $Y_2 \neq B_1$ $X_2 = A_1$
46 YOB $X_1 \neq A_1$
47 $Y_1 = B_1$ $X_1 \neq A_1$
48 $Y = B_1$ $X_1 \neq A_1$
49 $Y_2 = B$ $X_2 \neq A_2$
50 $Y_2 = B_1$ $X_1 \neq A_1$
51 $Y_1 \neq B_1$ $X_1 \neq A_1$
52 $Y \neq B_1$ $X_1 \neq A_1$
53 $Y_2 \neq B$ $X_2 \neq A_2$
54 $Y_2 \neq B_1$ $X_2 \neq A_2$
55 YOB $X \neq A_1$
56 $Y_1 = B_1$ $X \neq A_1$
57 $Y = B_1$ $X \neq A_1$
58 $Y_2 = B$ $X \neq A_1$
59 $Y_2 = B_1$ $X \neq A_1$
60 $Y_1 \neq B_1$ $X \neq A_1$
61 $Y \neq B_1$ $X \neq A_1$
62 $Y_2 \neq B$ $X \neq A_1$
63 $Y_2 \neq B_1$ $X \neq A_1$
64 YOB $X_2 \neq A$
65 $Y_2 = B_2$ $X_2 \neq A$
66 $Y = B_1$ $X_2 \neq A$
67 $Y_2 = B$ $X_2 \neq A$
68 $Y_2 = B_1$ $X_2 \neq A$
69 $Y_2 \neq B_2$ $X_2 \neq A$
70 $Y \neq B_1$ $X_2 \neq A$
71 $Y_2 \neq B$ $X_2 \neq A$
72 $Y_2 \neq B_1$ $X_2 \neq A$
73 YOB $X_2 \neq A_1$
74 $Y_2 = B_2$ $X_2 \neq A_1$
75 $Y = B_1$ $X_2 \neq A_1$
76 $Y_2 = B$ $X_2 \neq A_1$
77 $Y_2 = B_1$ $X_2 \neq A_1$
78 $Y_1 \neq B_1$ $X_2 \neq A_1$
79 $Y \neq B_1$ $X_2 \neq A_1$
80 $Y_2 \neq B$ $X_2 \neq A_1$
81 $Y_2 \neq B_1$ $X_2 \neq A_1$

ACCEPTANCE AND REJECTION POSSIBILITIES

Explanation of the Chart

X O A — Signifies that X and A are identical or independent. They are also isolated unless Y or B respectively bear some relation to them.

$X_1 = A_1$ — and $X_2 = A_2$ signify that X is equivalent to A and that their relationships to Y and B are the same.

$X = A_1$ — Signifies that X is equal to A and that Y and the relationship of X to it are ignored. Only assimilation is possible.

$X_2 = A$ — Signifies the opposite of $X = A_1$. Only projection is possible.

$X_2 = A_1$ — Signifies that X equals A and that their relationships are different. Both assimilation and projection are possible.

$X_1 \neq A_1$ — and $X_2 \neq A_2$ signify that X is not equivalent to A, but that their relationships to Y and B are the same.

$X \neq A_1$ — Signifies that X and A are not equal. Projection is ruled out, and assimilation is impossible because of the inequality of X and A.

$X_2 \neq A$ — Signifies opposite of $X \neq A_1$. Assimilation is ruled out, and projection is impossible because X does not equal A.

$X_2 \neq A_1$ — Signifies that X is not equivalent to A and that their relationships to Y and B are different.

The combinations of Y and B symbols have parallel meanings.

jection and assimilation depend upon his frame of reference; and these have their own determinants. The cells just discussed also characterize situations in which internal conflict is produced by the identity of one component and the non-equivalence of the other two. They symbolize what are sometimes called conflicts in space, time, activities, and other needs and demands. In Cell 7, for example, employers are likely to agree that idleness Y is not an acceptable substitute for labor B_1 as a source of income A. Cell 41 takes all four components of an innovation into account and indicates that it is acceptable; Cell 77 does the same but indicates a basis for either acceptance or rejection because of the internal conflict produced by equivalence and non-equivalence of paired components. Cells in the last row and column appear to be relatively sterile but are such only when the prototype or its parts are valued over parts of the innovation. They are so apparently unproductive because either a component or its relation may come in conflict with its paired component and its relationship.

Application

Recently an opportunity arose to test the applicability of this formulation systematically as a part of an investigation into "the nature, function, and control of resistance to education by television" in a population residing in the combined urban-suburban area in which the University of Oregon is located.[1] The inquiry was undertaken over a three-year period by an interdisciplinary research unit at the University of Oregon. The major part of it was conducted by recognized survey techniques using structured interviews and has resulted in several preliminary papers.[2] That part of it which is relevant here consisted of 178 unstructured interviews with individuals who were known or suspected of being "low consumers" of television output, including educational television. The interviews lasted from one-half to four and one-half hours, with an average of around two. They were free-ranging with unobtrusive steering by the interviewer to keep television the topic of the discussion.

The investigation concentrated its efforts upon a definition of the acceptance-rejection situation rather than upon the characteristics of the respondents. It sought to identify the psychological components of

[1] This research was supported by a grant from the U.S. Office of Education under the provisions of Title VII, National Defense Education Act of 1958 (P.L. 85–864).

[2] These have been mimeographed under the auspices of the Institute for Community Studies of the University of Oregon under the project title of *Studies in Resistances to Cultural Innovation.* They include "Preliminary Report Number One" by Marshall Goldstein, Walter R. Martin, and John R. Shepherd (no date); "A Study of Some Aspects of KOAC-TV Programming and Its Audience," by John R Shepherd, issued May 3, 1961; "A Sequence of Proposed Research Designs Relating Program Structure to Resistance to ETV," by John R. Shepherd and Thomas M. Scheidel, issued September 1, 1961; and "Problems in the Measurement of Educational Television Consumption," by Martin Meissner, issued November 1, 1961.

decisions in favor of or in opposition to television and gave only peripheral attention to the sociological characteristics of the decision-makers.
It endeavored to elicit undirected responses to some form of the general
question, "Why do you or do you not like television?" and accepted them,
without interpretation, as the data to be analyzed. Inferences from the
responses, from the contexts in which they were offered, and from other
information forthcoming during the interviews were not incorporated
in the analysis. They were recorded and constitute a body of information
that is reserved for another treatment of the problem.

It is evident that this approach was designed to get people to state, in
their own words, their reasons for liking or not liking television. It was
adopted with full awareness that such responses are notoriously difficult
to treat objectively and systematically. They can be untrustworthy, irrelevant, thoughtless, superficial, placatory, and many other things which
vitiate their utility as indicators or measures of motivation. The inescapable question they raise is when or whether the reasons given are the
"real" ones; there appears to be no way of answering it to the satisfaction
of those who have seriously concerned themselves with it. Nevertheless
it must be admitted that people do think in terms of reasons for their
actions and that the reasons therefore constitute a significant dimension
in human relations. This being so their analysis and interpretation may
be regarded as an important problem and the question becomes one of
how to deal with it (4).

The view adopted here is that reasons are more or less satisfying ways
of structuring situations, whether familiar or unfamiliar. They are not
simply expressions of approval or disapproval. Rather they are cognitive
organizations of a field of experience which are reinforced by a positive,
a negative, or a null affect. Since they are verbalizations, and since
language is an imperfect means of representing many structural possibilities, it is not surprising that the reasons given for adopting a position are
frequently at variance with how a person apperceives an experience, and
consequently why his public reasons are often not his "real" reasons for
doing something. He is and must be inarticulate about most of his cognitive organizations because he has no words to describe them. Moreover, he is not encouraged to find accurate expressions for his sense data.
In the interest of common understanding he has been conditioned to
justify the positions he adopts by resort to certain conventionalized organizational patterns which amount to a system of folk logic with premiums attached to its use, the premiums of being generally understood,
supported, followed, and defended.

The 178 interviews produced many more than that number of reasons
for liking or not liking television. This was not only because each respondent gave his own verbalization of his conceptualization of television
— which accounts for the 178 — but because many of them multiplied
their reasons. This is not to say, however, that each reason represents a

different structuring of the phenomenological field the focal point of which is television. Rather, it means that they are more or less articulate statements about it, that "it" being a universe with many and diverse facets which are nonetheless amenable to classification. There is no single way to effect this classification, but it is suggested that it can be done in terms of the preceding analysis. In other words, the many specific reasons for accepting or rejecting television, including educational television, can be construed to be exhibits of one or another of the 81 situations constituting the paradigm on page 360.

Adopting this approach, it can be said that there are three categories of responses to the question, "Why do you or do you not like television?" They may be characterized as the two-, the three-, and the four-component structuring of the constellation of things, persons, and events called to mind by that question. The two-component structure is represented by Cell 1 of the paradigm wherein "television," Y or X, registers, either positively or negatively, as A or B, but as such is psychologically isolated and inert. This is practically a null category as far as commercial television is concerned, because among the respondents in this inquiry there was no one who had not heard of it and who therefore did not have some associations which gave it meaning for him. It is, however, a significant category with respect to educational television because there were many respondents who in one manner of speaking or another attested to the fact that such television presentations as a Shakespearean play or a laboratory demonstration of a chemical reaction had little or no meaning to them. They expressed their reactions in such terms as, "That's over my head," "It's too deep for me," "That's long-haired stuff." For such people, A and B do not constitute a prototype. The evoked A (or B) is fragmentary, diffuse, incomplete, unstable, or vacillating; or it is incapable of activating a clear or consistent B (or A): Elizabethan English strikes them as being ridiculous, precious, or contrived; and "an electrically charged atom or group of atoms" is just so many words which might as well be said in another language — as they are in equally unintelligible Italian operas.

The remainder of the cells in Row 1 and in Column 1 are three-component structurings of television, half of them acceptable, half not, if we continue to assume that a positive value is placed on A B. A large number of responses fall into this category, which as we have seen is the one comprising syllogisms. It is understandable that many reactions conform to this pattern because not only is it a common way to justify a position, it is also the one which is readily summoned by a question such as, "Why do you or do you not like television?" The same circumstances account for the fact that complete expressions of syllogisms occur only rarely. In part, this is because the question itself supplies the conclusion. Thus, to take an example exhibiting the pattern of Cell 3, *with a negative value placed on B:* "I (A) do not like violence and immorality (B_1), and there is too much of it on television (Y)." It is unnecessary and would seem pedantic to add "that is why I do not like television." Incompleteness also occurs because elliptical statements of this kind frequently occur in ordinary speech. Logicians call them *enthymemes*. They are characterized by the omission of one of the premises or the conclusion on the assumption that the listener takes the missing part for granted.[3] Thus, to illustrate with another negatively valued B in Cell 3 again: "I (A) cannot afford to waste time (B_1), and watching television (Y) is a waste of time," is an enthymeme with the conclusion omitted. But another respondent gave the same reason in a manner which conforms to Cell 55: "People (A_1) who watch television are wasting their time (B)." He tacitly assumed the negative minor premise "I (X) am not one of those people" ($X \neq A_1$). To take another example, one respondent said that she did not like a certain professor or his manner of presenting Shakespearean plays on television because he tried to act the parts of the characters in the play instead of lecturing about them as did a former college professor of hers. In this reasoning we have a case conforming to Cell 9 in which the television plays X were regarded as identical with those A studied in a college class, but both the television professor Y and his treatment (relationship 2) of the plays were considered to be significantly different from the admired former professor B and his manner of presenting (relationship 1) the plays; that is, $Y_2 \neq B_1$. Had the television professor's personal qualifications Y been acceptable to this respondent by comparison with her college professor B, but his role playing (relationship 2) still distasteful, her rejection of the programs would be described by the arrow directed to the left in Cell 5, but it would be dotted, not solid.

A few respondents categorically dismissed commercial television with a peremptory statement that *all* of it is undesirable. They used such terms as "trash," "horrible," "childish," "moronic," and even "vidiotic" to characterize its productions. They were in effect, and sometimes explicitly, equating television content X with that of books and magazines A_1, which they regard as sensational, inartistic, lurid, hackneyed, and blatant B. In so doing they were asserting that the Y component of Cell 19 is inconsequential or non-existent, for if *all* commercial television X is said to be trash, there can be no Y remainder.

There were a number of cases conforming to the three-component pattern which seemingly are not syllogisms, but are such in fact with their

[3] "The following are familiar illustrations of enthymemes: *This medicine cured my daughter's cough; therefore this medicine will cure mine.* The inference is valid on the tacit admission of the major premise: *Whatever is a cure for my daughter's cough is a cure for mine.* An enthymeme in which the major premise is unexpressed is of the *first order. All drunkards are short-lived; therefore John won't live long.* Here the missing premise is the minor: *John is a drunkard.* Enthymemes suppressing the minor premise are of the *second order. Usury is immoral, and this is usury.* The conclusion *This is immoral* is here left unexpressed. Such an enthymeme is of the *third order*" (3, p. 78).

minor premises expressing a denial of equality, as in Cells 7, 8, 9, 55, 64, and 73. They arise when mutually exclusive choices between X and A or between Y and B must be made. Thus, some respondents said that they could not view regular educational television programs because they were presented at the identical time when the respondents must do something else, such as work, prepare meals, take care of their children, have coffee with their neighbors, go fishing — or sleep. There were others who said that they could not afford a television set or a subscription to a cable service. Further inquiry revealed that what they meant was that they preferred to spend that part of their budget which they could have used for a set or service on such things as clothing, food, books, or recreational activities.

Four-component structurings of television and its offerings are often expressed in elliptical responses comparable to enthymemes. Thus, when one respondent was asked a question about television he replied, "I like television because you can see the people who are doing the talking." His unexpressed prototypes, as was soon verified, were the plays, newscasts, and speeches presented by radio. Thus, television X_1 was equated with radio A_1, and the audio-visual presentations Y_1 associated with television were equated with comparable presentations B_1 on radio, and a lesser value was placed on the latter. This situation is represented by the assimilation possibilities (the arrows directed to the right) in Cell 11. If the respondent had preferred radio to television in spite of their resemblances he would have rejected the substitution and his decision would be indicated by dotted instead of solid-line arrows to the right in the same cell. If the differences between the two media and their outputs had impressed him, and had he valued radio, Cell 51 would represent his rejection of assimilation. If he had preferred the programs on television but not that medium as contrasted with radio, Cell 47 would represent his partial acceptance by selective assimilation, not projection.

Many of the four-component responses were such only by implication, but the implications were clear. Thus it was evident that many respondents equated education X_1 with work A_1, and in effect said that the place for the latter was not in the home but in an office, shop, or school. Others made it plain that education is for children, not for adults, and that educational television was therefore not for them; or that educational television is for specialists, such as accountants, teachers, and engineers, therefore not for them. In all these instances there is an equation of two of the components and rejection of an equation of the other two, the results being selective assimilation as represented by the dotted and solid arrows curving down and up to the right in Cells 47 and 15.

Before leaving these illustrations it should be pointed out that something can substitute for "nothing," and vice versa (1, pp. 222–223). This becomes an entirely reasonable statement when it is realized that what is commonly called "doing nothing" is only a figure of speech. We never do absolutely nothing, but at times we do things which are not highly valued. Consequently televiewing can take the place of relaxing, conversing, dawdling, or drowsing. Furthermore, since we are dealing with ideas, educational television can take the place of an unrealized hope of getting an education in school, and many acceptors of it are explicit in acknowledging this substitution.

The foregoing illustrations could be multiplied, but to do so would become tedious. The examples above are intended only to indicate the flexibility of the model. It is believed that all the responses obtained in the course of the television interviews have a place within its framework.

The television research began with the notion that it was to be an inquiry into the reception of an innovation, i.e, educational television. For a time the question of whether educational television was in fact an innovation or not was a troublesome one, for it was evident that many respondents were familiar with it in some fashion, and therefore, with regard to them at least, our inquiry was more comparable to one which seeks to find out why some men prefer Camel to Chesterfield cigarettes. As it turned out this was not a significant question because with the analysis here employed it does not matter how familiar a person is with something toward which he takes a receptive or a non-receptive position. He in any case proceeds in accordance with one or another of the variations on the acceptance-rejection process.

BIBLIOGRAPHY

1. Barnett, H. G. *Innovation, The Basis of Cultural Change.* New York: Mc-Graw-Hill Book Co., 1953.

2. Bartlett, Frederick C. *Remembering. A Study in Experimental and Social Psychology.* New York: Cambridge University Press, 1950.

3. Cohen, Morris R., and Ernest Nagel. *An Introduction to Logic and Scientific Method.* New York: Harcourt, Brace & Co., 1934.

4. Sills, David. *A Sociologist Looks at Motivation.* (Bureau of Applied Social Research, Reprint #298.) New York: Columbia University Press, no date.

SECTION FIVE

Broad Historical Perspectives

on Change

A few years before his death Albert Einstein remarked ruefully that when he was a young man he could easily keep up with developments in the entire field of physics, but at the end of his career he could not even assimilate what was going on in the area of his special competence. In spite of the relatively recent birth of sociology its practitioners are also faced with the specter of specialization; several generations ago even great scholars like Max Weber were castigated for their inadequate grasp of specialized historical materials. One possible solution to the problem is interdisciplinary team work — an approach which however raises additional questions relating to creative scholarship. Yet even at this stage of development of the social sciences there are men willing and able to sacrifice the safety of specialization for a greater though riskier task. In this Section we present authors who may be said to stand with one foot in the realm of the traditional Geisteswissenschaften, *and the other in the realm of contemporary "social science." We need not review here the controversies about the differences between history and sociology; suffice it to say our authors do not believe history is "just one damned thing after another," nor that contemporary social changes can be adequately conceptualized and described without a knowledge of past events.*

Future students of the history of sociology (and some present ones as well) will not find it difficult to show that "it is no accident" that a veritable Sorokin revival is taking place at this time. The "dialogue" between Schneider and Sorokin which initiates this Section is ample evidence of the viability of Sorokin's contribution to the study of large-scale sociological change. Like all "grand theorists," Sorokin has to pay the price for the grandeur of his enterprise, and although Schneider does not insist on exacting the last ounce of flesh, neither is he willing to let Sorokin get away with logical inconsistencies or doubtful empirical documentation.

Schneider sees Sorokin's major contribution in his use of the dialectical mode of analysis, but at the same time he seeks to show that more explicit and rigorous use can be made of this method. (Our readers will

368

note the ubiquity of the dialectical approach throughout this volume, often by implication, as in the chapter by Eisenstadt in this Section, or explicitly as in Marcus' chapter in Section 8.) Schneider is critical of Sorokin's triad of the major cultural systems, including his tendency to fall back upon the invocation of what in pre-social science days would have been called the Zeitgeist. *Among the many problems raised by Schneider we may single out one which has an important bearing on the analysis of social systems at the "micro" as well as the "macro" level — the relation between the degree of integration of a system and its ability to withstand disruptive influences from without. Here, as in several other instances, Schneider proposes an alternative hypothesis to Sorokin's "self-evident" axioms.*

Sorokin, in his characteristic "inner directed" and vigorous manner stands up to Schneider's criticisms, and we leave the reader to decide who has the better of the intellectual combat. Let us simply add our own adage to that with which Sorokin closes what he is pleased to call his "yarns": "Si monumentum requiris, circumspice!"

As already mentioned, Eisenstadt's study of institutionalization in the political system of centralized empires makes use of a dialectical frame of reference, though implicitly so. He is not concerned with finding the magic key to change, but jumps right in medias res: empire builders find it necessary to co-opt certain strata of the societies they seek to "integrate," and these strata, once having been invested with power, must be adequately controlled lest they turn it against their overlords. Often the exhaustion of the supply of able and reliable members of the native population requires the importation of foreign "mercenaries" to fulfill various functions. The foreigners enjoy certain immunities, but at the same time run considerable risks because of their conspicuousness, often serving as scapegoats when things go wrong.

Eisenstadt's seeming neglect of traditional theories in his discussion is of some interest. Others dealing with the same data would find the invocation of, say, Machiavelli, or Marx, or Pareto, or Mosca well-nigh irresistible. It is most unlikely that Eisenstadt is unaware of the work of these men, nor is he intent upon promulgating his own "system." Whatever his reasons, he escapes the danger of "premature closure" by avoiding the use of ready-made formulations. While basically concerned with the disruptive forces operating within the centralized bureaucratic regimes, he does not neglect the fact that some of them have been remarkably stable, and he adduces reasons for this. Thus the lack of a pre-conceived rigid theoretical scheme enables him to do justice to the multiform possibilities of social and historical development in this type of society, while his implicit conceptual framework saves him from the pitfalls of "arid empiricism."

Martindale's analysis of the evolution of sociology can be conceived of as an exercise in the sociology of knowledge. He starts out with two sets of "perspectives": the individualist-collectivist and the humanistic-scientific, which serve as the matrix within which sociology develops, along with other systems of thought. In so doing he takes account of both the "immanent" changes within the discipline and of the "existential conditions" which impinge upon the growth and decline and permutations of various combinations of the perspectives. He then proceeds to close the circle by showing how subtypes within the matrix of perspectives have developed from the impact of the preceding interactions.

Martindale's procedure tends to be more empirically oriented than Sorokin's in several respects, and avoids some of the question-begging aspects which Schneider criticizes in Sorokin's approach. Thus Martindale adduces specific reasons for his assertion that "sociology arose under conditions which virtually guaranteed that it would be a form of scientism," rather than falling back upon a generalized "sensate factor." Similarly, in discussing contemporary sociological frames of reference he shows that the reaction against "scientific collectivism" may take the alternate forms of either existentialism, with its individualistic orientation, or of "humanistic collectivism." Whether or not one accepts Martindale's formulation, it is evident that he has gone far beyond the facile proposition that there are "two cultures" which are either at war or exist in blissful ignorance of each other. If nothing else, he makes plain that there is a "third culture" with some claim to recognition, along with the natural sciences and the humanities.

15

Louis Schneider

Toward Assessment of

Sorokin's View of Change

Pitirim A. Sorokin's *Social and Cultural Dynamics* is certainly one of the most interesting, as it is one of the most elaborate, efforts of a contemporary sociologist to analyze socio-cultural change. But it is not an easy effort to assess. It is spread over nearly 3,000 pages. It contains material of very varying value, ranging through both doubtful and suggestive statistical data and exhibiting both a determined effort to fit cultural materials into a certain framework, come what may, and inordinately acute and illuminating observations on philosophic, scientific, and religious positions that have been held from antiquity on. Sorokin himself refers (23, vol. 1, p. 84; vol. 4, p. 65, p. 755) to an interesting work by Wilhelm Ostwald[1] in which the latter distinguishes between classical and romantic types of scientists, the main point of differentiation between the two, from which in Ostwald's view others follow, being speed of reaction. The classical type is slow and the romantic fast. The great speed of reaction of the romantic type occasions much breadth of interest, abundance of ideas, and high productivity. The romantic is also less likely than the classical type to tidy up ideas very carefully and present them solely in finished form. Ostwald contends that a greatly effective stimulator of science in the field of sociology can scarcely be conceived as other than a romantic type, while a romantic type of mathematician is precluded, although there were still such mathemati-

[1] The reference is to (16, esp. pp. 371–378).

cians in the nineteenth century. Whether Ostwald is right on this last point or not, Sorokin certainly appears to incline toward the romantic side. The consequence is that the would-be critic, unless he has a range comparable with Sorokin's and the space of a sizable monograph at his disposal, confronted as he is with a tremendous quantity of material, sometimes superb in quality and sometimes exasperatingly defective, soon finds himself utterly frustrated unless he chooses to confine himself to a decidedly limited number of things.

The decision to be very selective in the present effort at assessment of Sorokin's work has perforce been made. At the same time, no attempt to assess the contribution of the work as a whole to the theory of socio-cultural change can afford to bypass its central features. The best solution I can offer is to treat Sorokin's work in rather broad terms as presenting two main aspects: a perspective on change which, following Sorokin's own usage, will be designated as dialectical; and a view of culture and the movement of Western history set out in the well-known language Sorokin employs: the language of "Sensate," "Ideational," and "Idealistic" culture forms. If a great deal is necessarily bypassed by treating the work in this way, at least the procedure allows a clear statement of the theme of this chapter, which is basically quite simple. The theme is that Sorokin's main contribution to the analysis of change lies in his employment of a dialectical approach to change, that this approach has significant foundations in the history of social science and is susceptible of further development, and that this approach, finally, can be seen as largely independent of the merits or shortcomings of Sorokin's contentions with regard to the triad of cultural forms which he sees as central in the socio-cultural realm. Some scepticism about the latter contentions will be expressed.

Two other things should be said at this point. First, much of the peculiar character of the present chapter is to be explained by the circumstance that it is conceived as an item in a kind of debate with Sorokin, while at the same time it is addressed to a wider audience. Thus, for example, a brief summary of the main theme of the *Dynamics* follows. Sorokin hardly needs instruction in the content on his own major work. Readers, on the other hand, may be unfamiliar with it in varying degrees and may find a résumé helpful in following the subsequent argument. Also, it will be noted that the chapter has been entitled "Toward Assessment." A "definitive" evaluation of Sorokin's work is not even remotely thought of for present purposes, if this is not already sufficiently clear. It will be enough if the chapter in some degree sharpens a few of the questions that must be asked about his theory of socio-cultural change. Procedurally, the chapter goes on from the summary of Sorokin's argument to a discussion of dialectic and change and then to some observations on Sorokin's culture forms and a few final words toward assessment.

The Argument of the *Dynamics*

A culture, for Sorokin, is above all a system of meanings organized about and to an appreciable extent (not wholly) derivable from premises about the character of ultimate reality. What Sorokin calls logico-meaningful method is in his view accordingly necessary for the comprehension of culture, and the method is designed to probe for "the central principle (the 'reason') which permeates all the components" of a culture, "gives sense and significance to them, and in this way makes cosmos of a chaos of unintegrated fragments" (23, vol. 1, p. 32).[2] Actually existing empirical cultures will never show perfect integration. The central principle(s) will *not* be all-pervasive. Empirical cultures are, rather, likely to represent some degree of fusion of or compromise on premises not completely reconcilable. However, it does appear that there are two main empirical cultural forms that show considerable integration or consistency, and one compromising or intermediate or synthetic form that shows sufficient stability (although it is less stable than the other two) to be fairly readily discernible as at least an incident in the alternations of the other two main forms in the course of Western history since the Greeks. The two main forms are Sensate and Ideational culture; the intermediate form is Idealistic.

A major premise of Sensate culture — indeed, it is fair to say, *the* major premise — is that "reality" is what can be perceived by the sense organs and that there is no reality beyond this. In Ideational culture, on the other hand, reality is taken as non-Sensate and non-material, as a form of transcendent or everlasting Being. While Sensate culture is concentrated upon this world and its goods and engaged in striving in and with this world, for Ideational culture this world is snare and delusion, and the man cognizant of true reality will disdain it. Sensate culture (at least in its Active form) typically seeks to solve a variety of problems presented by and in this world by onslaught on the world itself and modification thereof, as it might try to solve a public health problem by improving sanitation. Ideational culture seeks to solve a variety of problems less by onslaught on the world than by addressing the human agent who faces the world, as it might try to solve a public health problem by fortifying the inner man in a conviction that health is in any case ultimately vanity and a this-worldly good with which one should not have excessive concern. The intermediate Idealistic culture by definition compromises on or fuses or synthesizes the distinctive outlooks of the other two. In detail, Sorokin discriminates seven types, but he is ordinarily preoccupied with the three main ones.[3]

---

[2] The quoted words are italicized in the original.

[3] Within Ideationalism, Active is distinguished from Ascetic Ideationalism. The latter is bent upon maximizing spiritual ends and minimizing carnal ones and seeking detachment from this world. The former, while sympathetic with ascetic impulse,

The culture forms or types are recurrent in history. Hence a characterization such as Sensate will be applied to the early centuries of Greek culture *and* to the period roughly between Alexander the Great and the fourth century A.D. *and* to the West from about the beginning of the thirteenth century until the present. The three main types follow one another in what Sorokin regards as a rather reliable sequence, such that Sensate will be followed by Ideational and the latter by Idealistic culture forms and so on. Since early Greek times, Western culture has completed two cycles of this sequence and is ostensibly in the Sensate and perhaps already even incipiently Ideational phase of a third. (We are at present destined to live in a time of Sensate decline, amid wars and rumors of wars and numerous other untoward circumstances, but Sorokin's "pessimism" is only interim, for he believes he already discerns the outlines of a new Ideational culture to be the possession of Western man.) A very large portion of the *Dynamics* is devoted to tracing fluctuations in a variety of fields, from the arts to forms of social relationships, in the double sequence in Western history of Sensate-Ideational-Idealistic. The "portions" or "sectors" (art, religion, science, etc.) of the cultures developmentally traced are in at least rough accord with one another, "integrated" and informed by dominant outlooks (as Sensate outlooks). They are also more or less temporally aligned with one another.

All cultural forms are in endless flux. And they change by what Sorokin regards as a kind of inner destiny. Thus, integrated cultural systems "change according to the course of life which is predetermined for them by their very nature." Or as regards a single system, Sorokin asserts that "at a certain point in its history (slightly accelerated or retarded by . . . external circumstances) the cultural system must undergo its inwardly ordained change." And again he avers that "a cultural system has its own logic of functioning, change, and destiny, which is a result not only (and regularly not so much) of the external conditions, but of its own nature" (23, vol. 1, p. 50, p. 51, p. 53). This view is often reiterated. It is in virtue of the principle of immanent change that "each of the three

---

seeks to change the world of culture and society by moving it toward the demands of the spirit; it is bent on the salvation of others as well as the self and must operate in the world. Within Sensate culture, Active Sensate, Passive Sensate, and Cynical Sensate forms exist. The first transforms the outer world and is exemplified by the outlooks and actions of the great executives, conquerors, and empire-builders. The second takes the world as a set of given instrumentalities for the enhancement of sensual pleasures. The last encourages hypocritical conformity and quick "adjustment" in any direction that will "pay off." The intermediate Idealistic form gives a sixth type. And Sorokin adduces a Pseudo-Ideational form. For the Pseudo-Ideational culture mentality, which is "unintegrated," needs and ends are predominantly physical and reality is largely felt as Sensate. The mode of satisfaction of needs is "neither an active modification of the milieu to any appreciable degree, nor a free modification of self, nor a search for pleasure, nor successful hypocrisy." Representatives of this culture mentality are imposed upon by an external agency which they cannot resist. Slaves working under cruel conditions and harshly dominated persons in general exemplify this mentality or cultural form (see 23, vol. 1, p. 76).

integrated forms, or phases, of the Ideational, Idealistic and Sensate supersystems cannot help changing; rising, growing, existing full-blooded for some time, and then declining" (23, vol. 4, p. 737).[4] Sorokin relies on the notion of the immanent necessity of change and on the notion of limited possibilities to account for change and recurrence. As regards limited possibilities, he believes that there are only five basic answers to the question of the nature of true reality — that it is supersensory; that it is sensory; that it is supersensory-sensory; that it is unknown and unknowable; that it is phenomenally known and transcendentally unknowable (23, vol. 4, p. 738). Cultural systems must change, but as they change they are confronted only with limited possibilities soon enough exhausted. Hence change as it goes on must involve recurrence.

It is also true that cultural systems are internally constrained by a principle of limit. A certain kind of truth, by way of example, will stand only so much stress and development. It becomes richer and more productive up to a point and produces good sounds, as it were, up to that point, but beyond that it becomes decreasingly productive and emits bad or feeble sounds or none at all. Cultures are indissolubly wedded to systems of "ultimate" truth. Again they appear as phenomena that develop from premises about true or ultimate reality. The cognitive character of culture could hardly be contended for more emphatically. Each of the three main systems of truth (the first three of the above five) is in the end "partly true and partly false, partly adequate and partly inadequate," and the same kind of assertion is applicable to the culture associated with it. As a cultural system rises and becomes powerful and monopolistic, "its false part tends to grow, while its valid part tends to decrease." Indeed, the system becomes more and more "inadequate," and inadequacy, although undoubtedly intended in a philosophical sense, is clearly also intended in an "institutional" sense, for Sorokin writes that, with inadequacy, the system "becomes less and less capable of serving as an instrument of adaptation, as an experience for real satisfaction of the needs of its bearers; and as a foundation for their social and cultural life" (23, vol. 4, pp. 742–743). The time comes when the false outweigh the true parts of the system. The dominant system, as it were compulsively exaggerating, and thereby in an ultimate view distorting, the portion of truth of which it has hold, immanently prepares its own demise and clears the path for one of the rival systems. "All the forms of truth are subject to . . . 'dialectical destiny' and are hardly exempt from a self-preparation of their own decline in the course of their development" (23, vol. 2, pp. 121–122).

Dialectic and Change

It is not by accident that the above summary has been ended with a quotation relating to "dialectic." I hold to the view that it is in connec-

[4] Italicized in original.

tion with dialectical notions that Sorokin makes his largest contribution to the theory of change — at the very least in a *sociological* perspective. There is one other line of thought with regard to change (aside from the whole matter of the Sensate-Ideational-Idealistic forms and recurrences) which is arguably quite important in Sorokin's work, namely, his treatment of the relations of vehicles, agents, and meanings, but even this is in part handled dialectically, as will appear below.[5] The object of the present section is to stress Sorokin's own dialectical bent and to suggest, by reference, at least, to some of the more obvious sources, that this bent has been and continues to be an important one in the history of both social and specifically sociological thought. Also, I want to stress that dialectical insight is in principle subject to further development. And the dialectical stress is not an *incidental* part of Sorokin's work. As the above has, hopefully, already made clear to some extent and as should become clearer shortly, dialectical argument is a very significant aspect of what Sorokin has to say.

Certain understandings are needed with regard to what is done in the present section. Dialectic is taken as a rather "de-philosophized," even, if the reader will, in a "naive" sense and with an admitted "social science" bias.[6] It is taken as a set of insights with regard to how change takes place, although it is not necessary to argue that *all* change must have dialectical form. It is taken, in particular, as a set of insights, then, with respect to the *manner* of socio-cultural change. It is taken heuristically or, in a loose sense of the term, experimentally, and most certainly not as a set of revealed truths. It is *not* taken as something that can perform all the functions of a rounded sociological theory of change. That would be quite impossible. Indeed, the severance I suggest between dialectical thought in Sorokin and the latter's conception of the Ideational, Sensate, and Idealistic would seriously affect the structure of the *Dynamics* as a sociological theory of culture (or as a "philosophy of history"); I have no doubt whatever that he will be inclined to resist the severance precisely on this ground, if on no other. Dialectic, as here understood, definitely cannot perform a variety of significant functions. But it can perform some others, and, if it is indeed susceptible of further development in heuristic use I suggest that it may in time become a very useful

---

[5] On vehicles, agents, and meanings, not only the *Dynamics* should be consulted but also other work of Sorokin's, particularly the brief but very able presentation in (21, pp. 51–63).

[6] In other words, there is much of the historic philosophical background of the whole notion of dialectic which is given no room in the conception here set out. This is quite deliberately done, but it does not mean that I would necessarily contend that various philosophical problems not touched upon here but often touched upon in connection with some past presentations of dialectic are either useless or reducible to sociological propositions or insights. Thus, in the past the notion of dialectic has at times been associated with critical stances toward existing schemes of society and culture. Whether these stances were justifiable or not, I would regard any effort to *dissolve* ethical standpoints by tracing them to such social foundations as they may have, as a particularly unfortunate form of "sociologism."

instrument, conceivably even of greater help in the formulation of more or less rounded sociological theories than appears likely at first blush. Finally, the meaning here attached to the notion of dialectic need not be formally announced as a prelude to the argument, but may be allowed to "unfold" in due course.

As it happens, in Sorokin the dialectical outlook may be said to develop in three phases. This is only a rough view of the matter, but it seems to me useful in following the trend of his thought. The first phase perhaps has no necessary connection with dialectic, but it is unmistakably present and significant in Sorokin's work and it could very easily be one important source of motivation for adopting a dialectical outlook, even if it does not "determine" such an outlook. It may be called a phase of *general vision of change.* (The other phases may be called *dialectical bent or bias* and *stress on dialectically relevant mechanisms.*) In the phase of general vision of change, Sorokin's view is indeed a broad, general one, as it is also a very old one. It ultimately comes to an insistence that the things of this sensory realm are transitory. This sometimes appears tinged with a suggestion of near-melancholy and it evidently gives Sorokin a special sympathy with Ideational outlooks that point toward "the eternal" and away from the circumstances of this evanescent world. The insistence undoubtedly antedates the Buddha, who, however, provides a very clear statement of it and already affords it in such fashion as to shadow forth the second phase just mentioned. Thus, the Buddha is represented in an eloquent rendering of his life as saying to his favored disciple Ananda, as that life draws to an end: "But now, Ananda, was I not wont to declare to you that in the very nature of things we must separate ourselves from all things that are near and dear to us, and leave them? For how, Ananda, can it be otherwise? Everything whatsoever that is born, brought into being, and organized, carries within itself the inherent need for dissolution. How therefore can such things not be dissolved? Ananda, it must be so" (2, p. 44).

The Buddha thus not only expresses a view of the transitoriness of the things of this sensory realm, including humans, but refers to "inherent dissolution." Underlying all Sorokin's central theses about change, underpinning all his elaborations, it is certainly not difficult to discern his general vision by the light of which all systems to be found in this world are involved in endless change, renewal, and decay; but he also has given marked stress to immanent or "inherent" dissolution of systems. One of the indicators and components of dialectical thought as here understood is a pronounced readiness to exploit the possibilities of "immanentalist" views of change. Further, in dialectical perspective, change works by processes such that we can see that the seed of death is in the thrust of life and the price of success is failure. (The "poetry" here involved does not inhibit the possible conversion of statements such as these into sociologically significant propositions.) Sorokin would agree that in the

inner development of a system the very component that originally guarantees the system viability or success may become the source of its downfall or destruction (and sometimes he would undoubtedly say *must*
rather than *may*, for, as in the case of a culture's system of truth, he
would insist that its hold of a portion of truth would bring it "success"
but the further development of the very component guaranteeing success would bring "failure" or downfall). He concurs with Marx in the
view that "the capitalist system bears within itself the seeds of its own
destruction," perhaps less because he has various specifically Marxian
leanings than because he thinks this kind of assertion is safely made
about any system. And he notes also his agreement with the claim of
"the dialectic logic" that "every concept contains in itself its own negation, that in its full form any concept is a *coincidentia oppositorum* . . .
that a thesis passes into its antithesis and this into a synthesis which as
a new thesis contains again its antithesis and passes into it" (21, p. 327,
fn. 3, p. 704).

This kind of statement makes it easy to infer that the Sensate-Ideational-Idealistic triad was originally conceived as a form of thesis-
antithesis-synthesis. But such observations are of limited utility, and
it will be more helpful to adduce some of the detail of dialectical process
Sorokin offers when he deals with somewhat less ambitiously large entities and phenomena, or at least with other phenomena even if they may
be said to be equally "large." In the following illustrative matter from
Sorokin's work it will be quite evident that he is well launched beyond
his general vision of change and into the phase of dialectical bent or
bias. The third phase of stress on dialectically relevant mechanisms is
also, at the very least, adumbrated in some of the following. What is
meant by the third phase is simply this: it is possible to stop at a still
rather vaguely "poetic" or "general" level in the course of dialectical
thought; but to take dialectical hints and insights seriously for purposes
of sociological analysis is to go on beyond this level and examine in
rigorous detail how a dialectical movement takes place. Thus, I argue
in the first illustration from Sorokin that follows that in effect he approaches the phase of stress on dialectically relevant mechanisms by
indicating that the immanent movement from Ascetic Ideational to Active Ideational culture discernibly operates in a *variety* of ways. In the
third phase, the hard work of "locking in" dialectical mechanisms is
done (insofar as it *can* be done, so that the *probability* of "escape" from
dialectical effect becomes low, other things being equal) through careful
and comprehensive specification of how the dialectical movement occurs.
What follows represents a selection from Sorokin's work and does not
offer an exhaustive view of instances of his dialectical perspective on
change.

1) Sorokin contends that "it is the tragic and immanent destiny of
the Ascetic Ideational culture system to turn into the Active Ideational."
As the followers of an Ascetic Ideational way increase and an organiza-

tion arises, organizational necessities impose "the world," and, with organization, there comes movement toward the Active Ideational.[7] For success in the world, some of the ways of the world must be adopted, and these are bound to compromise or endanger the original ascetic ideals: "When we read about the activities of St. Paul, the great organizer of Christianity, we notice at once how he had to busy himself with worldly matters and how the empirical world caught him more and more in its web . . . most of the matters in which his flock involved him, from riots and politics to property and wealth, were of this world" (23, vol. 1, pp. 135–136). This is *one* way, one mechanism, whereby Ascetic Ideationalism turns into its "opposite," the Active variant. If it had no worldly "success," this transformation would not occur. What appears to be a somewhat different mechanism comes from the circumstance that saints can and often do become objects of veneration that draw crowds, stimulate markets and trade, and create prosperity, so that thereby asceticism is again jeopardized or destroyed (23, vol. 3, pp. 223–224). The contrast need not be over-strained, but there is evidently a difference between a situation in which there is a threat to the asceticism of men who themselves become directly involved in organizational circumstance and one in which the total quantum of asceticism is reduced by unforeseen consequences of saintliness even if the saints themselves remain intact. A third mechanism is suggested by the view that large numbers of followers cannot in any case attain or long remain at the Ascetic Ideational level (23, vol. 1, p. 135). Success of a church or religion brings increase of adherents, but the increase guarantees that that to which there is adherence will change significantly.[8] Sorokin is clearly probing for a "full" specification of the meaning of his proposition about Ascetic and Ideational culture. Yet just here he offers little that would suggest specific dialectically relevant mechanisms. Do masses flatly reject prophets? Are kindly leaders perhaps indulgent of ignorance, lack of understanding, and inveterate magical bias until there is a certain fatal cumulation of consequences? The dialectical bias has to pay its way by presentation and analysis of dialectically relevant mechanisms. (Even these simple questions may be allowed to indicate that the bias is "sensitizing" and susceptible of elaboration through examination of specific mechanisms.) Sorokin is, I believe, already effectively aware of this necessity, although he gives it no formal stress.[9]

[7] Cf. the stimulating discussion by Thomas F. O'Dea (15).

[8] This theme has been developed in the specific sphere of religion by Gustav Mensching. See (13, pp. 132–160). Mensching notes (p. 155): "We must . . . take into consideration an inner dialectic of universal religion. On the one hand, universal religion, as its name indicates, aspires to make good its universal claim through the greatest possible expansion and thereby through incorporation of the masses. But on the other hand this expansion is possible only at the price of the depth and distinctiveness of the high religion — and in turn this outcome produces criticism and protest from the side of pure high religion." Mensching presents some historical and comparative evidence to support this generalization.

[9] (23, vol. 3, pp. 221–224) seems to me to reinforce this assertion.

2) In further illustration of his dialectical bent, Sorokin *generalizes* the assertion about the involvement of failure in the success of religion or church. He claims that like phenomena are at work far beyond the sphere of religion alone. Thus: "Quantitative success of almost any system of meanings is bought at the cost of its identity, purity, and adequacy." Or: "Qualitatively, the greatest religious, philosophical, ethical, scientific, or artistic systems are at their best and purest when their followers are limited to a small group of faithful, competent, and understanding apostles. When they are diffused among vast millions, their purity, verity, adequacy is lost, disfigured, and vulgarized." And again Sorokin writes of "the tragedy of vulgarization and decisive disfiguring of any complex and great and sublime system of cultural values when it infiltrates and roots itself among the large masses." He adds: "Such a success is invariably bought at the cost of . . . simplification and distortion" (23, vol. 4, p. 82, p. 84, p. 259, fn. 83). Sorokin does not push these rather general observations into the area of dialectically relevant mechanisms, nor does he care to make the obvious point that democratic concern might well seek ways to blunt the effects he observes and thereby come upon close acquaintance with relevant mechanisms, but it would be easy enough to outline a few such mechanisms and it is not unreasonable to suppose that analysis of the workings of mass culture will in time yield a large number of them.

3) Even before widespread adoption of a religion, doctrine, art form, or the like has occurred, there are at work processes that subtly change the cultural phenomena of doctrine or form or the like, in Sorokin's view. There is a "tragedy of culture" which shades into the tragedy of popularization and is connected with the latter in that popularization may greatly enhance it, but it is not the same as the tragedy of popularization. Sorokin's position here may be put as follows. "Pure" cultural phenomena, to have effect in the world, need some kind of initial "embodiment" (and socialization or diffusion). The embodiment is vehicular, i.e., in the form of what Sorokin calls "vehicles." Language functions as a vehicle when, say, the inventor of an idea gives it its first embodiment in words (and its first socialization and diffusion to another) by expounding it to a friend. "Pure" cultural meanings are constantly influenced by the vehicles used to carry them. Language as a vehicle has its inadequacies and human agents have their imperfections, and cultural systems in their "pure" form are subject to the inadequacies and imperfections. One may say that culture is, paradoxically, "imperfectly" realized because the vehicles it must have to be other than pure, to be involved in empirical human existence, change it and decrease its original purity. In this connection, it has constantly to be kept in view that not only does culture influence vehicles but vehicles influence culture. An elevated conception of a deity may suggest an originally symbolically conceived artistic representation of that deity, but the repre-

sentation may quickly become an idol worshipped for itself and, so treated, influence the initial lofty conception retroactively. This suggests the process when it is perhaps already far advanced in vulgarization, but it may serve to clarify Sorokin's basic notion. "Defeat" of pure culture may occur just at that point of "success" where it finds a vehicle, or at the point where the vehicle begins to influence that which it conveys.

Sorokin, also, refers to Simmel in this general connection and apparently takes the phrase "tragedy of culture" from a paper by the latter (20, pp. 236–267). Simmel's paper is concerned with the "alienation" between man or personality and "objectified spirit." He examines this alienation in some detail and is especially concerned with what he regards as the circumstance that the realm of cultural objects has "its own logic of development." He gives the case of a writer's having proposed a riddle with a specific solution when another solution should be found, fully as apt and meaningful as the writer's own. The latter becomes just as "correct" as the writer's and exists as "ideal objectivity." "As soon as our work," Simmel says, "stands out, it has not only objective existence and a life of its own, which have detached themselves from ourselves, but it contains in this self-sufficiency strengths and weaknesses, components and significances, for which we are not accountable and by which we ourselves are often surprised." There thus arises opposition between man and his cultural world, and, interestingly, Simmel remarks that the "fetish-character" which Marx attributed to economic objects is but "a specially modified case of this general fate of the content of our culture" (20, pp. 259–260). Whatever the precise value of these observations of Sorokin's and Simmel's, they foreshadow the significant dialectical play whereby something generates or develops into its own "opposite" — in the specific sphere of the relation between intention and outcome, for the former often is oriented in one direction but leads to an outcome that points in a very different direction. Human intention for the cultural sphere is one thing, but that sphere has some tendency to confront man as a world he never made even if its origins in his own strivings are undeniable.

4) The third set of phenomena just referred to, then, suggests discrepancy between initial intentions and final outcomes.[10] This in turn suggests the dialectical play referred to, involving the creation of outcomes "opposite" to those intended.[11] In regard to Mandeville's paradox whereby public virtue arises out of private vice, Weber writes pertinently of "that power 'which constantly seeks the bad and constantly creates the good'" (29, p. 33). Sorokin is interested in much the same

[10] That it suggests this to Sorokin himself is clearly indicated in the footnote in (23, vol. 4, p. 43).

[11] I mark the dialectical process (or processes) here involved without prejudice to the question of just what its (or their) status in relation to others might be found to be after intensive analysis.

thing, although he might wish to say that when, for example, he indicates how Ideationalism, despite its indifference to wealth, brings wealth into being or increases it, he is talking about a power which "constantly seeks the good and constantly creates the bad." Sorokin notes: "Like any other variable or process, Ideational and Sensate cultures generate in the course of their existence a series of characteristic consequences that follow inevitably from their individual natures. Some of these consequences may operate in the direction of weakening and destroying the culture that generates them." And he adds that "thus, in the field of economic conditions, some of the consequences of Ideational culture may, in spite of its negativistic attitude to 'prosperity,' work toward an accumulation of wealth, careful and successful organization of economic activity, and therefore toward 'prosperity'" (23, vol. 3, pp. 222).[12]

The entire basic phenomenon of discrepancy between intention and outcome, between purpose and consequence, which Robert K. Merton has suggested in his phrase "the unanticipated consequences of purposive social action" (14, pp. 894–904), is of really major interest for Sorokin insofar as he is constantly concerned to note how actions undertaken in the terms of the norms and premises of one cultural system immanently generate effects that encourage movement to an "opposite" or radically different cultural system. The focus in this shifts somewhat from the matter of how success involves failure — but, clearly, only somewhat — toward the matter of how an "opposite" of a strategic element in a system arises from within the system itself. This kind of concern is also an old one on the part of social theorists. Mandeville has been mentioned in passing. Adam Smith's awareness of the discrepancy between individual intentions on the line of making profits and the general prosperity of the community that he claims comes out of the myriad individual efforts to make gain is one of the best known intellectual achievements of any social scientist. The eighteenth century was apparently quite rich in this particular cognizance of discrepancy between intention and outcome. Vico gave the discrepancy a significant twist in connection with his entire notion of "a rational civil theology of divine providence," for providence so acts that "out of the passions of men each bent on his private advantage, for the sake of which they would live like wild beasts in the wilderness, it has made the civil orders by which they may live in human society" (26, p. 56; see also pp. 3–4, p. 21, p. 210, p. 382).[13]

[12] The treatment in (23, vol. 3, pp. 221–224) is one indication of Sorokin's interest in dialectical or dialectically relevant mechanisms.

[13] Fisch has noted that Vico's notion of a rational civil theology of divine providence may be compared with Wundt's idea of the heterogony of ends, Mandeville's private vices-public virtues, Smith's invisible hand, and Hegel's cunning of reason. He has even suggested that Vico may have been thinking of Mandeville when he averred that the public virtue of the Romans was but a good use that providence made of their "grievous, ugly and cruel private vices." See Fisch's "Introduction" to (28, pp. 54–55) and his "Introduction" to (27, p. xxxii.)

For Turgot, also, men's "blind passions" were unwitting instrumentalities that functioned to bring about excellent ends.[14]

Sorokin's cognizance of the intention-outcome discrepancy clearly puts him in the line of a very significant tradition. Certainly, the whole notion of this discrepancy has long since been secularized: its present-day neutrality or independence in relation to theologically tinged thinking is quite plain in social science; but this does not remove the provenience of the notion in older social science. Neither in the history of social thought *nor* in Sorokin's views on socio-cultural change has the notion been an incidental one.

On broader fronts of dialectical thought, stress on dialectical modes of change again antedates Sorokin's *Dynamics* (and also postdates it). Thus, the fourth volume of the *Dynamics,* in which the theory of change is most extensively presented, is replete with references to Ibn Khaldun (the index shows eleven references), Pareto (thirteen references), and Toynbee (forty-five references). Ibn Khaldun shares Sorokin's very general vision of the impermanence of the things of this realm: "It should be known that the world of the elements and all it contains comes into being and decays." Indeed, "duration belongs to God alone." As if for good measure, Ibn Khaldun adds: "This entire world is trifling and futile. It ends in death and annihilation" (7, vol. 1, p. 278, p. 301, p. 386). But, as is well known, what is in effect clearly a dialectical view of change goes along with this. Dynasties come and go. They dissolve and rebuild in a repeated cycle from hardy desert virtues and solidarity to the decay of virtue, the development of luxurious ways of life, and financial troubles. Among other things, the dilemma of wealth for Protestant sects that Wesley and Weber recognized is foreshadowed. Conquest brings wealth, but wealth breeds luxury and luxury corrupts the virtues of hardiness that enabled conquest in the first place, much as the old Protestant virtues of thrift, frugality, and industry were later represented to bring about a wealth that reacted disintegratingly on the virtues that produced it. That which enabled conquest in the end turns on itself when its consequences are fully developed, and a kind of dialectical suicide takes place. The flower destroys the seed from which it came. Ibn Khaldun is so keen on dialectical process and suggests it so variously that one is almost tempted to attribute to him a specific awareness of the need to go on for purposes of close analysis to the examination of dialectical or dialectically relevant mechanisms.

For Pareto, it will suffice to recall that in the circulation of elites one notable process is that whereby, once lions are in power, it becomes evident that leonine virtues are not adequate for the running of a govern-

---

[14] The reference is to an often quoted passage in Turgot's *Oeuvres.* The passage is translated in Karl Löwith (9, p. 103). For an indication that Turgot here only states a rather general eighteenth-century theme, see F. E. Manuel (10, pp. 46–47).

ment, and clever foxes, full of chicane, must be returned to various offices as they begin a new infiltration (changing the distribution of residues in the ruling group) that finally occasions a new lion revolt. The governmental system changes out of itself and by internal processes a governmental form constantly generates its own "opposite" (17, vol. 4).

The dialectical mode of thought is certainly not uncongenial to Toynbee. Immanent development is given its measure of stress by him also. "In demonstrating that the broken-down civilizations have not met their death from an assassin's hand . . . we have been led . . . to return a verdict of suicide." And Toynbee quotes Meredith: "In tragic life . . . no villain need be. . . . We are betrayed by what is false within." The theme of the failure of success is a very important one for Toynbee. He contends that the successful creator is handicapped by his success, and remarks that if this is true, "so that the chances are always against 'the favorite' and in favor of 'the dark horse,'" when it comes to writing a new chapter in creativity, "then it is plain that we have run to earth a very potent cause of the breakdown of civilizations." Toynbee goes on at once to note that this nemesis of creativity would operate in two ways: "On the one hand it would seriously diminish the number of candidates for playing the creator's role in the face of any given challenge, since it would tend to rule out those who responded successfully to the last challenge and these . . . were potential creators before their very success in turning promise into achievement threatened to sterilize their creativity in the act of demonstrating it." And in the second place, the past creators, by virtue of their past achievement, have come to hold "key positions where their senile impotence to create is aggravated by their lasting potency *ex officio* to thwart and hinder." (Toynbee holds that this nemesis of creativity can be averted.) This specification of two kinds of possibilities also suggests possible ease of transition to the notion of working out dialectically relevant mechanisms. Another instance of the "law" that success leads to failure (or that nothing fails like success) is found in those "fumbling and irresolute" animal adaptations which, just because they are indecisive, leave open possibilities of change and adjustment which are closed off for organisms that have worked out "perfect" and detailed solutions to particular problems in evolutionary course — and of course the "law" has its human applications of main interest to Toynbee (24, p. 120, p. 260, pp. 423 ff.)[15] For Toynbee, as for others, so very bare and partial an indication must suffice.

[15] The points involved here have been interestingly developed by Elman R. Service, in (19, chapter 5). Service holds that "the more specialized and adapted a form in a given evolutionary stage, the smaller is its potential for passing to the next stage," and that "the evolution of species takes place *because* of adaptation; the evolution of the total system of life takes place in *spite* of adaptation." Service applies this view to socio-cultural development and accordingly writes of "the privilege of backwardness." Being unstabilized and relatively amorphous and uncommitted in ways in which more advanced countries are stabilized and specifically formed and committed, the backward country may move ahead more quickly at cru-

The dialectical approach to change as here taken exploits the possibilities of understanding change immanently. It is willing to take assertions such as "the seed of death is in the thrust of life," "the price of success is failure," or "the flower destroys the seed whence it came," and explore the prospects of developing these into sociologically relevant propositions that go carefully into the detail of what is initially intimated by rather "poetic" assertions. It involves interest, therefore, in dialectically relevant mechanisms. It is further concerned with the possibilities of understanding change suggested by notions that may be crudely rendered as follows: the very "factor" that brings strength or viability or success to a system will also bring its downfall; "elements" at work in a system are likely to engender their own "opposites" (the intention-outcome discrepancy being a special case of this); in a process of realization (as of realization of culture in the sense that it gets launched into the world through receiving vehicular expression), realization is baffled as soon as it occurs.

Sorokin's thought has been richly dialectical when dialectic is thus understood. It would also appear that this kind of thought is susceptible of further development. It postdates Sorokin's work as surely as it antedates it. Further development need not be understood as mere further illustration, which obviously would hardly be development at all, but as movement into detailed analysis of dialectically relevant mechanisms, which may also be enriched through exploration of the relations of such mechanisms to phenomena such as feedback.[16] Again, although I acknowledge freely that a dialectical bent renders no rounded sociological theory, I would suggest tentatively that it may in time be more helpful for a rounded or full-scale theory, even of the "grand" type that Sorokin seeks to afford, than at first appears. Presumably no adequate view of socio-cultural change will ever develop that does not pay attention to "structures" or "forms" or the like that are in process of change. And here dialectic as it has been taken in this chapter seems not to be of much help. Yet a medical analogy, if I may be permitted it, may suggest a slightly brighter prospect. Ambitious analysts of socio-cultural change may evoke the picture of physicians who have begun to show a shrewd eye for symptoms and pathological process, who are not as yet ready to say just what the symptoms are symptoms *of* and are therefore not prepared to set out definite disease entities, but whose incipient understanding of process already gives promise that disease entities will in time be well discriminated.

---

cial junctures. The privilege of backwardness is inevitably reminiscent of Thorstein Veblen's idea of "the penalty of taking the lead." Cf. Veblen (25) and Dowd (3, chapters 15 and 16) for pertinent efforts to apply Veblen's ideas.

[16] Reference has been made above to the Protestant virtues of thrift, frugality, and industry as creating wealth that reacted disintegratingly on the virtues themselves. This is one among many dialectically significant phenomena that may be thought of as exhibiting "feedback that works the wrong way."

If this analogy may be continued for a moment, Sorokin has already proposed "disease entities," mainly in the form of his Sensate, Ideational, and Idealistic cultures. Whether or not these are useful for purposes of sociological analysis — and this is the focus of my concern with them — it seems evident that Sorokin's illuminating work on dialectical process has no necessary relation to them, in the simple sense that one may be quite willing to explore the possibilities of a dialectical approach to change while perhaps casting about for very different "entities" from those Sorokin proposes and being measurably skeptical about the latter. It will be clear by now that I am proposing that, despite inevitable limitations, Sorokin's application of dialectic is a very considerable contribution to sociological thought. I am less sure about the contribution made by his main "entities."[17] It is as well to turn to what I indicated, in beginning, as the second aspect of Sorokin's work.

The Culture Forms

This section takes the form of some reservations bearing on the value, for purposes of describing and analyzing culture, of Sorokin's cultural terms or units. In one way or another, Sorokin himself concedes a good many of the difficulties that will be indicated in the following. He evidently concedes them, however, in the conviction that his basic terms or units — Ideational, Sensate, Idealistic — remain illuminating and useful. Of course, much depends on what meaning one assigns to "illuminating and useful" or like phrases. It should be clear that I am not contending in what follows that Sorokin's cultural theory is lacking in all merit. This is far from true. Many of his sets of data are undoubtedly of real help in piecing out his general characterizations of culture, and his essential triad (Sensate-Ideational-Idealistic) describes many phenomena quite aptly. But no one, even today, I submit, can read, let us say, Comte's *Positive Philosophy* or his *Positive Polity* without acknowledging that the categories Comte applies to Western history "describe many phenomena aptly" (as they also fail to describe numerous other phenomena aptly). It is a measure of the standards one is tempted to bring to bear on Sorokin's work that one wants more than this from him — something closer to a rather rigorous sociological theory of culture.[18]

---

[17] The circumstance that I am rather skeptical of Sorokin's main culture "entities" of course does not mean that I would be equally skeptical of other "entities" that have been proposed in the social sciences or in sociology in particular (and, indeed, by Sorokin himself).

[18] It is possible to see in the *Dynamics* elements of three kinds — "sociological" in a rather limited sense, "culture-analytical," and "philosophical" (as bearing on philosophy of history). A philosophy of history is clearly not the same as a sociology in a contemporary sense. But I am here presuming that sociological and culture-analytical enterprise can be conceived as very close to one another and that it makes sense to speak of "a sociological theory of culture." An example of the distinguished sterility that may emerge from a learned effort to fence off carefully from one another the three elements in the *Dynamics* just mentioned is afforded by Anton Hilckman, in (6, pp. 405–420).

In a mood of impatience because of a feeling that he does not offer this, one might get out of humor with him and echo Manuel, who refers to Vico's adoption of Varro's scheme of three ages of gods, heroes, and men and writes of this "rather hackneyed triad," already old in Vico's day, and "worn even thinner by a long line of philosophers of the rise, maturity, breakdown, and disintegration of nations, states, societies, civilizations" (10, p. 151). In other moods, one can certainly be more admiring. But even then reservations must be made. The following notes set out some of them under three headings.

1) The first heading may be designated as "facts and data." The task Sorokin confronts in the *Dynamics* (as well as the task of any critic) would have been considerably eased had Sorokin always had "hard" data at his disposal. I have asserted that many of his sets of data are helpful to him, as indeed they are. But there are also many occasions when he has genuine and perhaps insuperable difficulties with them. It should be pointed out that some of the easiest and most obvious criticisms of Sorokin can be levelled at the quality of his data. He tends to make the task rather easy himself by frequent acknowledgement of difficulties. (This is a merit of his work complemented by that other high merit of the relative clarity of his exposition — which involves the great advantage that his mistakes are relatively easy to discover.) But the difficulties remain, and they touch on essential themes of Sorokin's with sufficient frequency to cause him embarrassment. Comprehensive criticism of his data would be beyond the limits both of this chapter and of my competence, but I may allude to a few typical problems.

Sorokin's data on art may be cited as exemplifying some of his problems. These data are often unique, and good checks on them are generally not available, to the best of my knowledge. Something of the pressure the difficulties these data put upon Sorokin may be inferred from his evidently rather less than joyous comment, with respect to the materials he uses to exhibit fluctuations in Western European art, that these materials "may be unreliable but they are more reliable than any data presented up to the present time, so far as the general course of art fluctuation in the countries studied is concerned" (23, vol. 1, p. 375).[19] When discussing medieval literature from the fifth to the tenth centuries, a literature which he regards as strongly Ideational, Sorokin remarks in a footnote that "there is no doubt that on the lower levels of literature there existed a great many pagan and partly heroic, partly Sensate, and even indecent songs, poems, stories, tales. But . . . these levels are beyond the scope of this work" (23, vol. 1, p. 612). Should they be beyond the *scope* of the work? Evidently one hardly proves that the most important or characteristic literature of the Middle Ages is the Ideational literature Sorokin stresses without seriously considering how important the more vulgar literature may have been. The art historian, Hauser, remarks that "even in epochs in which the most influential work is founded

19 Italicized in original.

on a single class, and from which only the art of this class has come down to us, it ought to be asked whether the artistic products of other groups may have been buried or lost," and he adds that "in the Middle Ages the creations of secular art must have been, at any rate, more significant in relation to ecclesiastical art than the works that have survived would lead us to expect" (5, vol. 2, pp. 179–180). If fuller evidence than Sorokin affords were in fact afforded, medieval art might well appear less "monolithic" and less Ideational than he represents it to be. If we assume that there are close affinities between Sensate culture and achievement motivation, a not unreasonable assumption, there are some interesting discrepancies between Sorokin's work on Greek culture and work that has recently been presented by McClelland (12, pp. 108–129). The detail cannot be reviewed here, but it may be noted that in a period of Greek history (about 900 to 500 B.C.) which Sorokin regards as dominated by Ideational art, McClelland's materials suggest rather the existence of an art which reflects achievement motivation, which in turn may be broadly construed as involving strong preoccupation with this world and drive toward mastery thereof.[20]

If the example of discrepancy just given (assuming that it is indeed allowed to constitute an example of discrepancy) does nothing else, it reinforces the point that Sorokin's data often need checks that are still to be made and may well never be made. Again, there should not be misunderstanding. I do not really doubt that there are occasions when Sorokin's categories apply well to his data and when the data themselves are meaningful. But there are occasions when one must be more dubious. It is very likely that there are points where errors balance out or cancel one another, but there are also chances of systematic bias. In the absence of a careful and comprehensive evaluation of Sorokin's various data, one is constrained to say that the difficulties with his data and the uncertainties bearing on them that are now discernible make it the harder to assess the overall organizing or explanatory power of his basic cultural terms.

2) A second heading may be designated as "the relation of premises and norms and behavior." There is considerable evidence in the *Dynamics* of struggle on Sorokin's part with the problem of the relation of ideas and norms to behavior or conduct. It has been noted in the summary how strong a stress he puts on cognitive premises in the determination of the character of a culture. Yet he makes constant qualifications in the sense of indicating that conduct will not follow the pure line of premises (even if premises are themselves pure and unmixed in the first place). Again he admits a great deal that a critic might say in this matter. But the question is where the admissions leave his final stand. Let us mark some illustrative statements. "Historically, there has probably never existed in pure form in a single individual, group, or culture, any one of the unmixed types of culture mentality. . . . Even the most ascetic,

[20] See McClelland's review (12, p. 124–127) of Aronson's work on Greek vases.

the most austere, mystic cannot help changing his empirical milieu or satisfying to some extent his bodily needs. Otherwise he would die. . . . Sometimes even those of Sensate mentality modify themselves, and not their milieu; satisfy their spiritual, instead of their material needs." Again: "All the earmarks of the mentality of a given culture may appear to be Ascetic Ideational, and yet it is thinkable that the external aspect of such a culture may be a shocking contrast to such a mentality: materialistic, comfortable, luxurious, ostentatious, mercenary." And we are warned that "we must not postulate, without a test, that mentality and actual behavior of human beings are always clearly integrated and logically consistent" and that "a man may agree with and extol the Christian principle of loving one's neighbor as oneself, and yet in his actual behavior be the most egotistic of individuals" (23, vol. 1, pp. 77–78, p. 101; vol. 3, p. 221, p. 510).

Thus there is, after all, a considerable margin of indeterminacy, a considerable number of degrees of freedom (or, if one will, a considerable number of variables not specified and perhaps not even recognized) in the relationship between over-arching, ultimate cultural premises and behavior or conduct. The more "free" conduct is from determination or constraint by the premises the more one may question their significance for purposes of cultural analysis.[21] (They *could* finally appear as philosophical irrelevancies or near-irrelevancies so far as a great deal of conduct is concerned.) How *much* freedom is there? One feels almost guilty about asking such a question, which is so easy to ask, since it would be so hard to answer in any case and since Sorokin's own relevant data and lines of argument are far from strong enough to bear its burden.

Sorokin concedes that the existence of like rudimentary biological needs for participants in all cultures will lessen behavior contrasts, and he states: "The members of the Ideational and Sensate societies must eat, drink, have shelter, sleep, work, reproduce their kind, defend themselves against agencies and forces menacing their existence" (23, vol. 3, p. 511). He has already been quoted as saying that even the most ascetic or austere mystic must satisfy his bodily needs to some extent. To this extent, minimally, the Sensate-Ideational contrast is irrelevant to conduct. It is theoretically possible, in Sorokin's scheme of analysis, that in con-

---

[21] Obviously, this statement implies a certain view of culture. In a highly "idealistic" or "normativistic" notion of culture, the relative freedom of conduct from constraint by ideas or norms would not be of great "cultural" importance. But Sorokin himself clearly desires to demonstrate that his basic categories are relevant to conduct. And it is fair to add that at least in contemporary anthropological and sociological conceptions of culture, exclusion of conduct would on the whole be quite unacceptable. This is not to deny that culture may be analyzed "on its own" as a distinctive realm of meanings, values, and symbols, for such abstraction, undertaken for particular purposes, is not incompatible with a lively sense of the actual influence of culture on conduct. Bidney's critical tone would be widely echoed when he writes that "normative idealists tend to define culture in terms of social ideals and to exclude the actual practices as not constitutive of culture," and accordingly marks a "normativistic fallacy." See David Bidney (1, p. 32).

trasting cultures one might begin with a sharp differentiation (on the basis of ultimate premises and norms) of some as Sensate and others as Ideational and yet come around to the final view that, by the criteria of conduct, there is nothing of importance to distinguish the one set of cultures from the other.[22] The matter of degrees of freedom referred to above is again relevant. There can be no question of a rigorous specification of the factors that might bring about practical identity of conduct in the cultures with the different premises, but three roughly distinguishable sources of the outcome of conduct resemblance, in effect suggested by Sorokin himself, may be noted. The constraint toward likeness across cultures exercised by like biological needs may be put together with constraints exercised by strictly "social" interaction.[23] Even if one begins with a sharp differentiation of Sensate and Ideational cultures, in Sorokin's views there are likely to appear in empirical cultures all sorts of "admixtures" and "impurities," intrusions of alien premises and norms that would mitigate the effect of the initial differentiation. This is a second source (although it may be fed from the first) of elements bringing different cultures about to likeness of conduct in their carriers. Finally (and without comment on the relation of this source to the others), there would be gaps or lack of carry-over or absence of permeation from one "portion" of a culture to another, such that premises and norms that would otherwise have a differentiating effect on conduct would "skip" or "miss" and thereby leave conduct unaffected.

Sorokin often seems to me to allow this third source of conduct-convergence through lack of permeation of otherwise differentiating premises and norms, by implication if not directly. The notion of this third source is closely related to one or more of the various senses in which he uses the term "integration." It may be remarked, incidentally, that a careful analysis of this term as Sorokin employs it would be most interesting. Such analysis would surely reveal that some of the propositions that appear in intimate connection with the term are quite vulnerable. Thus, Sorokin claims that "the greater and better" the integration of

[22] I indicate this as a possibility. It is true that Sorokin's general bias would be toward seeing effective pervasion of a culture by ultimate premises. But I take it that this is an empirical issue. If so, the possibility indicated remains open. It has also been noted above that Sorokin himself makes statements such as: "All the earmarks of the mentality of a given culture may appear to be Ascetic Ideational, and yet . . . the external aspect of such a culture may be a shocking contrast to such a mentality. . . ." Sorokin's own argument in regard to relationships of culture and conduct will be considered below.

[23] It is commonplace to make distinctions between "biological," "social," and "cultural" spheres. Sorokin distinguishes social from cultural (23, vol. 3, p. 3). Franz Zwilgmeyer is particularly aware of the distinction between the social and cultural (see his article [30]). Kroeber makes one of numerous statements that might be cited which suggests limits on cultural elaboration exercised by social and biological factors: "Since human culture cannot be wholly concerned with values, having also to adapt to social (interpersonal) relations and to reality (survival situations), the totality of a culture can scarcely be considered outright as a sort of expanded style" (8, p. 152).

social and cultural systems, the greater their length of life, among other things. His criteria for integration at this point in his argument are: amount of causal and meaningful interdependence of the components of a system, so that the system whose components are highly integrated causally and in terms of meanings is in this regard highly integrated; second, the "solidary" character of relationships among the members of a system, a criterion which may be roughly understood by noting that at an extreme of non-integration there would not even be quite impersonal or contractual contacts among the human members of a socio-cultural system (although this extreme might raise problems of definition: would there still be a "system" in the extreme case? — but this and other questions may be left aside); third, as Sorokin puts it, "consistency between the components of the system." Highly integrated systems of philosophy, religion, art, or law will definitely tend to outlast less highly integrated systems. "The same," says Sorokin, "is true of the social systems. Unintegrated armies have always been beaten by integrated ones. Unintegrated states have always been short-lived compared with the integrated ones. A poorly integrated family, or business organization, or any 'eclectic social organization' has . . . as a rule, more quickly and frequently . . . come to an end. . . ." The argument has a suspiciously "abstract" flavor and does not carry conviction. Taking Sorokin's criteria for integration, one could equally well argue that the more highly integrated social and cultural systems are the more liable to shortness of life and to destruction. In case of a threat or danger from outside or inside such systems, that threat or danger will sweep through the entirety of the systems the more quickly and the more devastatingly the more integrated the systems are — precisely because of high conductivity (see also 4, p. 253). Lower conductivity would increase the chances of localizing danger or "infection." What might be regarded as a possibly significant qualification, to the effect that integration should not be identified with "plasticity" or "rigidity," is too vague to be of much help. A variety of considerations might lead one to the tentative view that on the whole an "Idealistic," compromising, fusing sort of structure (of organizations if not of culture-meanings, and perhaps of the latter also) might be most viable.[24]

To revert to the general matter of the factors that baffle or stultify the differentiating effect on conduct of different (Sensate and Ideational) premises with which one may start, it seems that these factors may come to a great deal. At least this can be said, even if it is hardly a precise statement. Moreover, on the whole, little is known about these several sources of de-differentiation. It is possible to get beyond a few wholly rudimentary statements (of the type that even ascetics must eat to live), but it is not clear that it is now possible to get far beyond them. Yet

[24] The material from Sorokin quoted in the above paragraph is contained in (23, vol. 4, p. 610, pp. 613–614).

Sorokin, because of the character or structure of his system, is in effect responsible for handling the exceedingly difficult problems of analysis all this suggests. His theory of culture becomes very hard or impossible to work out in rigorous fashion. His often fine sense for the character of systems at large (both social systems, in the very broadest meaning, and non-social systems) affords him good insights, but these remain rather "Platonic" in that he cannot carry them forward into a precise handling of the interaction of ultimate premises and norms and the de-differentiating factors that have been noted. Evidently, too, the sheer theoretical possibilities of conduct-convergence despite initial premise-norm differentiation may be quite embarrassing to his outlook. And, given the complexity of the process whereby one may have to get around to strong conduct resemblance after initial premise-norm differentiation, it may be asked whether other ways of handling the relevant problems than those Sorokin proposes may not be better. If strong conduct resemblance is taken as a consequent, it may be variously interpreted, may have more than one antecedent. Simply as a possibility, one might suggest that there is much more central tendency (*Idealistic* bias) across cultures than Sorokin's scheme allows and that it might be feasible to derive a large part of conduct resemblance more or less directly from this, instead of through a cumbersome and most-difficult-to-handle set of factors mitigating an otherwise supposedly expectable conduct-differentiation.[25] (Even if it be granted — as I think it must — that problems of culture analysis, at least on occasion, have to be handled in rather cumbersome fashion, this is plainly no guarantee of rigor. Conflicting "themes" may have to be posited and treated, but the power of analysis in treating them has not been conspicuously high.)

It is only fair to note that Sorokin seeks to face up to the problem indicated. He presents a brief treatment of the "relationship between types of culture and types of personality and behavior" in the fifteenth chapter of the third volume of the *Dynamics*. Here he contends that there will be a *closer* relationship between the character of a dominant culture and the "mentality" of its carriers than between the character of culture and the conduct of its carriers. But he adds that "though the relationship between the dominant culture and the behavior of its bearers is not always close, nevertheless, it does exist," and further affirms: "In application to the various types of culture, this means that the bearers of the Ideational and Sensate cultures differ from one another not only in their mentality (ideas, opinions, convictions, beliefs, tastes, moral and aesthetic standards, etc.) but also in their behavior and personality" (23, vol. 3, p. 512).[26] Sorokin's data, however, for so important a point are meager and quite crude. Thus, for example, he puts a good bit of stress

---

[25] I am well aware that this statement regarding alternative possibilities of explanation might be extended and refined and particularly regret that this cannot be done here, for the whole matter of alternative possibilities of explanation for various phenomena Sorokin seeks to explain seems to me to be extremely important.

[26] The two statements quoted are italicized in the original.

on a table of geometric means for participation in religion by contrast with participation in business, the data being derived from materials on historical personages, from 900 B.C. to 1849 A.D., included in the *Encyclopedia Britannica*. Religion and business are two of ten fields of activity covered (geometric means for participation in each field being converted into percentages, the total for all fields coming to 100 per cent). Others include statesmanship, literature, scholarship, and fine arts. No specific data are given for fields other than religion and business. Sorokin remarks that activity in these other fields "may, by their nature, be either Ideational or Sensate" (23, vol. 3, p. 527). Very plainly, it would be important to know something about the character of conduct in these other fields, more particularly since religion and business, taken together, appear to constitute less than 25 per cent of total activity in more than 40 per cent of 55 fifty-year periods, on the face of Sorokin's materials.[27] Moreover, there is no measure of the character of conduct in religion and business; there is only an indication of amount of participation in each, which is perhaps suggestive, but far from conclusive for what Sorokin wishes to show. The trends from one time period to another indicated by these data in detail also raise very ticklish questions. On the basis of data such as these, Sorokin cannot get far, granted that they may have been the best data available to him. If the relationship between dominant culture, as Sorokin understands it, and behavior is in principle susceptible of some sort of determination by measurement and can be adequately treated only through measurement, much better measurements will have to become available before the relationship can be convincingly set forth.[28]

Sorokin clearly wishes to vindicate the notion that ideas and norms are not mere epiphenomena, but have genuine independent efficacy in shaping conduct, even conduct close to the level of biological needs (23, vol. 3, p. 529). He breaks a lance for human rationality. One may sympathize with his endeavor to do this. (Also, by the way, one may grant him whatever he might want granted in favor of the notion of the independent efficacy of ideas and norms and yet wish to stress *different* ideas and norms from those he sees as crucial.) At the same time it is quite evident that the analysis of ideas and norms in relation to conduct presents great complexities. Sorokin is most certainly aware of this, but he often presents solutions to a variety of pertinent problems that are not compelling. Thus, he contends that the existence of magic and supersensory religion among primitive and prehistoric peoples argues the presence of "a variety of the Ideational conception of causality" and then avers that these peoples "have also a Sensate form of causality

[27] See the table in (23, vol. 3, p. 527). Sorokin comments that what activity in the fields of statesmanship, literature, etc., was like in any specific case "we cannot know without further details. . . ." The admission is significant.

[28] Taken individually and together Sorokin's indices bearing on culture and behavior or conduct exhibit considerable insensitivity and may at the very most be said to be "suggestive."

applied to many daily experiences where the connection between the phenomena is explained sensately and 'experimentally' as a result of the 'natural' properties of the variables involved" (23, vol. 2, p. 389). This is a particularly interesting assertion because it suggests that one may have to infer "ideas" themselves from conduct. (If there is little explicit primitive formulation of "experimental" notions and yet appreciable adherence to such notions implicit in conduct, the matter of deciding on the character of primitive "thought" becomes the more complex.) Is it satisfactory to conclude from Sorokin's observations about primitives' ideas that they have, say, a "mixed" form of culture mentality? This would be to take two sets of "ideas" with equal seriousness, which may or may not be warranted. Sorokin's brief treatment of culturally variant conceptions of number (23, vol. 2, pp. 433–437) bears on number symbolism or a kind of number poetry among the Chinese and others. Sorokin himself suggests something similar can be found in Western culture. How large a role did the variant conception of number play in China? Is it a variant conception of *number*, anyway, or a superadded kind of play with numbers of which some signs can also be found in the West? If the Chinese in important parts of their numerical "behavior" act much as we do — if, for example, in the simplest terms, they demonstrate behaviorally that they fully accept such notions as the notion that two and two make four; and it is hard to see how they could do otherwise, on pain of certain unhappy results — we may well allow their behavior to influence our own views as to what their very *"ideas"* of number are. Certain kinds of variant verbalizations, even certain kinds of variant styles, may well conceal a common substance. The philosopher Woodbridge somewhere has a remark to the effect that when a man of the eighteenth century referred to the woman he loved as "a handmaiden of the Lord" he "meant" she was "a darn fine girl." The "Sensate" and the "Ideational" cannot always be allowed to go on their own most obvious appearances and persuade us that they do not need further interpretation.

It is pertinent to note that no effort is made in the *Dynamics* to develop anything like a systematic psychological theory. Psychological observations are made *ad hoc* in the course of Sorokin's major work.[29] It may

---

[29] When Sorokin is annoyed with psychoanalysis, as he often is, he is likely to refer to its image of man as one that represents the latter as a "bag" filled with libido, lust, and aggression. Sorokin's own "man," as he appears in the *Dynamics*, seems to be largely an imprint or reflex of Sensate or Ideational or Idealistic culture — a "bag" filled with the appropriate premises and values. He seems to have no motors, no insides that work on the materials given him by his cultural environment. This should not be taken to mean that Sorokin never has anything of interest or cogency to say on psychological matters. (Note, for example, his useful discussions of fundamental and conditioned, normative, and purposive motivation in [21, pp. 45–46, pp. 96–97]). In recent years, he has shown an interest in creativity that was already foreshadowed in the *Dynamics* (see 23, vol. 4, pp. 747 ff.), and has observed: "No one is entirely passive. Every person selects, combines, and sometimes even creates, and to that extent he is an active agent in the social process" (22, p. 93). It remains true that in the *Dynamics* there is no interaction worth noting of psychic and socio-cultural stuff in the sense of systematic psychological treatment.

at least be suggested that an effort to develop something on the order of a socio-psychological theory might have given Sorokin considerable help with some of the problems above indicated. I do not pursue the matter further. But this particular omission, whatever its effect for Sorokin's work may have been, suggests a few others worth noting.

3) Under a final heading of "undeveloped themes," I wish merely to indicate several points that Sorokin has evidently left in incomplete form and the elaboration of which might have brought greater conviction on the part of his reader of the organizing or explanatory power of his basic cultural terms. The points indicated may be taken as a short listing of examples of undeveloped themes.

While in very broad terms Sorokin contends that the "portions" or "sectors" of the cultures he treats are in accord with one another, "integrated" and informed by dominant outlooks (as Sensate outlooks), this is indeed only a loose way of rendering his notion on the matter. He contends that in Sensate cultures and periods, art, by way of example, understood as a value area, is "separated" from other value areas, but so are other value areas separated from one another. Religion, morals, science, philosophy, and so on, are united in Ideational culture, but apart and even in conflict, in Sensate culture. Sorokin does say that the Sensate culture is also "an integrated culture," but it is "integrated around the principle of diversity, and the mutual independence of its main values and compartments" (23, vol. 1, p. 672).[30] He adds of Sensate culture that "it is not an absolute 'patriarchal monarchy' with one 'we' of its values, but a federal republic based upon the principle of the separation and division of its main states" (23, vol. 1, pp. 672–673, p. 677). Problems are thus raised about the character of the connections between "sectors" of culture on which Sorokin does not satisfy us. His entire treatment suggests unequivocally that there is "unity" in Sensate culture in that its painting is like its architecture, its literature like its music, and so on. These and other fields share Sensate characteristics: preoccupation with the world of sense instead of the transcendent world, with Becoming rather than with Being, with the immediate rather than with the eternal, and others. Whence *this* unity? and just how shall it be described? Perhaps Sensate culture gets a distinctive kind of unity from some form of consensus that its diverse "sectors" shall be allowed autonomy — and perhaps this is what Sorokin means by his analogy with a "federal republic." This, however, would be unity at one level only. It might help account for, or at least point to, "unity in diversity," unity despite independence and even unity based on independence. But there remains to be explained the unity that comes from the culture-content resemblance of the various "sectors" to one another. Perhaps the "government" holds together on the basis of an agreement that the "states" shall be allowed to go very much on their own, but why do the states turn out to be so like another (in Sensate culture)? The whole matter is left unexplored,

[30] Italicized in original.

to the possible impoverishment of Sorokin's differentiation of his two fundamental terms and of his theory of culture.

A second point is that Sorokin does not systematically collate all the elements in his work that bear on the like or common and the unlike or uncommon in various cultures, to reach a thoroughly reasoned judgment about the extent and importance of resemblances and differences. Undoubtedly, this would have been a herculean task; I suggest nevertheless that it might have aided his basic cultural analysis greatly. It has already been noted that he acknowledges minimum-like biological needs across cultures (so that, by way of example, there always has to be some provision for acquisition of food and the rudiments of an economy, and a culture must ordinarily stop short of prohibiting all sexual intercourse). He contends that forms and categories of thought are profoundly shaped by cultures and will differ appreciably as the latter do. But he does not contend this without reservation. He seems to stop short of a relativism that would take the extreme form of the contention that there is no truth except "truth" so conditioned culturally that it is not truth at all. He both allows a measure of independence of culture to some branches of scientific thought and appears not unwilling in principle to concede the substantial independence of culture of the formal laws of logic and mathematics (23, vol. 2, chapter 12, esp. p. 466). In his study of "ethicojuridical mentality in criminal law (23, vol. 2, chapter 15) he finds in the criminal codes of five leading European countries some 16 types of criminal actions which he calls "absolute crimes," criminal and punishable in all the codes analyzed. Sorokin is thereby prompted to think in terms of something like an approximation to "moral consensus" (23, vol. 2, pp. 577–578), which further investigation might well show to be more extensive. These and other elements of the like or common are not taken up in a rigorous overall accounting, balancing the like or common against the dissimilar across cultures, with particular reference to Sensate and Ideational forms. Again, I recognize that the job involved would have been very considerable, and resources for doing it were even less when Sorokin wrote the *Dynamics* than they are now. It is still unfortunate that the job could not be done.

Finally, Sorokin never develops his original seven-fold typology in any detail. He operates, as has been noted, mainly with his three grand types. There are various points in his work where it appears likely that a further development and refinement of his entire typology would have been helpful. He inclines to think we are now in transition from a Sensate to an Ideational form. Granted that his theory allows for differences between Sensate-turning-to-Ideational, on the one hand, and Idealistic, on the other, there also seem to be considerable resemblances between these two. In this case, as in others, his sheer description shows a crudity that might have been mitigated by a conscientious elaboration of subtypes and careful assignment of subtypes to various portions of the social structure, including social strata. I recognize again that this is to ask for a good deal, which it may simply have been impossible to offer.

The reservations suggested will indicate why I am not convinced that Sorokin has "cut" the socio-cultural universe in a theoretically very useful way — to be sure, judging by high standards. His "blocks" or "wedges" (or, if one will, his "disease entities") would, minimally, appear susceptible of very much refinement.[31] I remain unconvinced, in particular, that he has locked in the whole historical process with his view that there are only five basic answers to the problem of the nature of true reality and that these must recur. If we grant that these five answers are "basic" and recur, it is still quite possible (as has already been intimated) that each, first developed, then exhausted and rendered effete in turn, and in turn paradoxically generative of one of its own siblings, might have considerable irrelevance to the concerns, character, and conduct of the majority of mankind.

Final Remarks toward Assessment

I may summarize and extend slightly by some additional remarks the view of Sorokin's work that has been proposed.

I have indicated that I regard Sorokin's dialectical approach to change as very valuable and that it appears to me to have further potential for illuminating change. Nevertheless, it remains an *orientation* to change, a set of shrewd notions of how change takes place that still needs a great deal of checking and should be frankly recognized as "experimental." It does not in itself constitute a theory of change. When to it are added, as Sorokin does add, the scheme of Sensate-Ideational-Idealistic culture forms and the hypothesis of few and recurrent basic views of truth inseparable from and informing whole cultures, and the whole scheme is given historical application, then something on the order of a theory of change with empirical reference is undoubtedly offered. But I have tried to show there is reason for much skepticism about such additions and applications. If there is justification for this view of the matter, is the outcome not quite disappointing? But it may be proposed, once more, that one should not expect too much from exceedingly ambitious

---

[31] It may be argued that in this section I have tried to judge Sorokin's work by standards that should not be applied to it. Here, after all, one may say, in the form of the *Dynamics*, is another imposing culture theory and philosophy of history, to be regarded critically, yet, in a sense, not too critically. One may expect knowledge and sagacity from a Vico, a Hegel, a Comte, a Sorokin, but not an authentic and resounding scientific triumph in a strict sense. If one applies certain strict criteria, one is adopting a rather unimaginative and perhaps even humorless attitude. An organism that may be expected to have certain notable frailties (even if along with sturdy qualities) need not be stretched on a rack. I am not at all averse to taking Sorokin's work in the "tolerant" way suggested. But clearly it would not follow that the theory of culture forms he offers would then fare better: one would merely expect less of it.

and difficult enterprises in the understanding of entire cultures and all history.

For the near future, at any rate (and pending a time when perhaps further patient dialectical — and other — work may give us more aid), we may not be able to achieve a great deal more in the field of qualitative macro-culture analysis helped out by statistical data than has been achieved by a work of the type of, say, Kroeber's *Configurations of Culture Growth*. Kroeber's work is based on much learning and is carried through with characteristic care. While the patience and caution and immense common sense manifested in it are wholly admirable, the results *are* rather modest. Kroeber's conclusions about the clustering of cultural achievement in particular times and places and some of his leading concepts, such as the concept of pattern saturation, are, with the best will in the world, less than overwhelming. Sorokin does try to do more. He is much more adventurous — and is bound to make many more mistakes. The matter might be let go at that, but one other point should be suggested. It is often the mark of a man of stature that he takes chances and ventures on matters from which others would shrink. Sorokin is at one with many of the leading figures in the history of the social sciences (or, for that matter, in other disciplines) in displaying an audacity that simultaneously gets him into trouble and ensures that he is likely to be worth listening to even when he is in trouble.[32] His struggles with a large variety of problems, such as, say, the problems of the relation of ideas to conduct, may yet yield more, however subject to criticism they may be, than I am inclined to think at present. Nevertheless, and at least for the present, I, for one, remain convinced that his largest contribution is in the immense suggestiveness of his dialectical outlook on change.

Since I have stressed that Sorokin makes errors, it is only appropriate to add that this effort at assessment has been so conceived and deliberately limited that it has not been possible to give recognition to some of his outstanding virtues. It has not been possible to do justice to the circumstances that he is most extensively and brilliantly informed about numerous aspects of the history of social thought;[33] that he often presents issues on the borderlands between sociology and philosophy in a fresh, sharp, distinctive way;[34] that his specifications of significant terms can be extraordinarily apt;[35] that he is capable of powerful cultural portraiture;[36]

---

[32] It is worth recalling that Robert E. Park, in a review of the first three volumes of the *Dynamics* (18, pp. 824–832), remarked that his teacher, Windelband, had observed that "in the realm of philosophy it was not those who were right who contributed most, but those who had been wrong."

[33] See (23, vol. 4, chapter 8) on theories of rhythm and phases in socio-cultural change.

[34] See (23, vol. 2, chapters 6 and 7) on realism, conceptualism, and nominalism, and on universalism and singularism.

[35] Note, e.g., the descriptions of "fideism" in (23, vol. 2, passim).

[36] See (23, vol. 1, chapter 12) on music.

that, more broadly, the *Dynamics* abounds in insights some small portion of which many a social scientist would be happy to claim as his own. Judged by the standards set by rather similar enterprises, his *Dynamics* is a tremendous achievement.

BIBLIOGRAPHY

1. Bidney, David. *Theoretical Anthropology.* New York: Columbia University Press, 1953.

2. de Silva-Vigier, Anil. *The Life of the Buddha.* Great Britain: Phaidon Publishers, 1955.

3. Dowd, Douglas F., ed. *Thorstein Veblen: A Critical Reappraisal.* Ithaca, N.Y.: Cornell University Press, 1958.

4. Gouldner, Alvin W. "Reciprocity and Autonomy in Functional Theory," in Llewellyn Gross (ed.), *Symposium on Sociological Theory.* Evanston, Ill.: Row, Peterson & Co., 1959.

5. Hauser, Arnold. *The Social History of Art*, 2 vols. New York: Alfred A. Knopf, 1951, Vol. 2.

6. Hilckman, Anton. "Geschichtsphilosophie-Kulturwissenschaft-Soziologie," *Saeculum*, Vol. 12 (1961).

7. Khaldun, Ibn. *The Muqaddimah*, 3 vols., translated by Franz Rosenthal. New York: Pantheon, 1958.

8. Kroeber, Alfred L. *Style and Civilizations.* Ithaca, N.Y.: Cornell University Press, 1957.

9. Löwith, Karl. *Meaning in History.* Chicago: University of Chicago Press, 1949.

10. Manuel, Frank E. *The Eighteenth Century Confronts the Gods.* Cambridge, Harvard University Press, 1959.

11. Manuel, Frank E. *The Prophets of Paris.* Cambridge: Harvard University Press, 1962.

12. McClelland, David C. The Achieving Society. New York: D. Van Nostrand, 1961.

13. Mensching, Gustav. *Soziologie der Religion.* Bonn: Ludwig Röhrscheid, 1947.

14. Merton, Robert K. "The Unanticipated Consequences of Purposive Social Action," *American Sociological Review*, Vol. I (December 1936), pp. 894–904.

15. O'Dea, Thomas F. "Five Dilemmas in the Institutionalization of Religion," *Journal for the Scientific Study of Religion*, Vol. 1 (October 1961), pp. 30–39.

16. Ostwald, Wilhelm. *Grosse Männer*, 5th ed. Leipzig: Akademische Verlagsgesellschaft, 1919.

17. Pareto, Vilfredo. *The Mind and Society*, 4 vols., translated by Andrew Bongiorno and Arthur Livingston. New York: Harcourt, Brace, 1935, Vol. 4.

18. Park, Robert E. "Review of *Social and Cultural Dynamics*, Vols. 1–3," *American Journal of Sociology*, Vol. 43 (1938), pp. 824–832.

19. Sahlins, Marshall D., and Elman R. Service (eds.), *Evolution and Culture*. Ann Arbor: University of Michigan Press, 1960.

20. Simmel, Georg. "Der Begriff und die Tragödie der Kultur," *Philosophische Kultur*. Potsdam: Gustav Kiepenheuer, 1923, pp, 236–267.

21. Sorokin, Pitirim A. *Society, Culture, and Personality*. New York: Harper and Bros., 1947.

22. Sorokin, Pitirim A. *The Ways and Power of Love*. Boston: Beacon Press, 1954.

23. Sorokin, Pitirim A. *Social and Cultural Dynamics*, 4 vols. Totowa, N.J.: Bedminster Press, 1962.

24. Toynbee, Arnold J. *A Study of History*, 12 vols. London : Oxford University Press, 1939.

25. Veblen, Thorstein. *Imperial Germany and the Industrial Revolution*. New York: Viking Press, 1939.

26. Vico, Giambattista. *The New Science of Giambattista Vico*, translated from 3rd ed. by Thomas G. Bergin and Max H. Fisch. Ithaca, N.Y.: Cornell University Press, 1948, pp. 3–4, p. 21, p. 56, p. 210, p. 382.

27. Vico, Giambattista. *The New Science of Giambattista Vico*, revised and abridged, Thomas G. Bergin and Max H. Fisch. Garden City, N.Y.: Doubleday Anchor, 1961, p. xxxvii.

28. Vico, Giambattista. *The Autobiography of Giambattista Vico*, translated by Max H. Fisch and Thomas Bergin. Ithaca, N.Y.: Cornell University Press, 1944, 1963.

29. Weber, Max. *Gesammelte Aufsätze zur Wisschenschaftslehre*, 2nd ed. Tübingen: J. C. B. Mohr (Paul Siebeck), 1951, p. 33.

30. Zwilgmeyer, Franz. "Kultur," in Werner Ziegenfuss (ed.) *Handbuch der Soziologie*. Stuttgart: Ferdinand Enke Verlag, 1956, Pt. IV, Chapter 3.

16

Pitirim A. Sorokin

Comments on Schneider's

Observations and Criticisms

Preliminaries

I find Professor Schneider's dissection and criticism of my views of socio-cultural change most thoughtful, competent, and admirable in many respects. Since his analysis deals with the basic problems in this field the importance of his observations and criticisms goes beyond virtues and vices of my views: his insightful remarks become relevant for all investigators of socio-cultural change. In this sense his paper is a real contribution to our knowledge of the how and why of change. So much for my general reaction to his paper.

As to Schneider's *diagnosis of myself as a Romantic type of a scholar* (in terms of W. Ostwald's typology), *the diagnosis appears to me essentially correct.* Perhaps it would be still more accurate to say that predominant Romantic characteristics are mixed up with some Classic features such as: re-issuings and translations of my works without any change some 30 years after their initial publications; the term "classic" applied to my *Social Mobility, Contemporary Sociological Theories, Source Book in Rural Sociology,* and the *Dynamics* by a number of fellow-sociologists, and so on. In Ostwald's typology these features are assigned to the Classic rather than to the Romantic type.

Roughly accurate is also Schneider's summary of the main themes of the *Dynamics.* However his outline needs a few corrections. They will be made farther on when I shall deal with his criticisms of the Ideational,

01

Sensate, and Idealistic supersystems of culture. After these preliminary
remarks, we can pass to the main themes and criticisms of Schneider's
chapter.

Dialectic Method and Dialectic Models of Socio-cultural Change

The section dealing with Dialectic is one of the most important parts
of Schneider's essay. He is not only the first to discover an important
role played by dialectical method in my theories of change[1] but — what
is more important — he forcefully brings the fruitfulness of this method
to the attention of American sociologists who, with a few exceptions, have
largely neglected it. I completely agree with most of his observations
concerning this method. First, he is quite right in stating that this
method had a long, venerable, and cognitively fruitful history.

Indeed, we find its skillful and extensive use in the early texts of Taoism,
Hinduism, and Buddhism[2] by the Greek pre-Socratic thinkers like Hera-
clitus, by Plato, Aristotle, Plotinus, and other Neoplatonists.[3] In the
period of the first seven centuries of our era, it finds a magnificent development by the great Mahayana Buddhist logicians: Nagarjuna, Asanga,
Vasubandhu, partly Gotama, Dignaga, and Dharmakirti.[4] In about the
same period and later on, dialectical logic is well used by Damascius and
by some of the Church Fathers, such as Clement of Alexandria, Origen,
Tertullian, St. Augustine, Pseudo-Dionysius, Erigena, and others up to
Nicolas of Cusa.[5] Subsequently in various forms, including Kant's "dialectic of a radical negation of dialectic," this method and logic have
been skillfully applied by many eminent philosophers, natural and social
scientists such as Fichte, Hegel, Proudhon, K. Marx, and Lenin,[6] to mention but a few names.

This sketch shows that the dialectic method has been fruitful not only
in philosophy but also in the social and humanistic sciences because,
largely through its use, many of these thinkers made their significant contributions to our knowledge of psycho-social and cultural phenomena
generally and of cosmic and socio-cultural change specifically. Schneider
is quite correct in his statement that the dialectic method can perform
a number of important cognitive functions and that "it is susceptible of
further development in heuristic use . . . and may in time become a
very useful instrument, conceivably even of a greater help in the formulation of more or less rounded sociological theories than appears likely at
first blush."

[1] His paper well supplements the essays of some 25 eminent scholars dealing with
my various theories in P. Allen's volume (1) and E. Tiryakian's volume (35).

[2] See a brief sketch of a history of dialectical logic in P. Sorokin (24, pp. 364 ff.).

[3] See an outline of dialectics of Plato and Plotinus in G. Gurvitch (6, pp. 30–44).

[4] See on this the excellent work of Th. Stcherbatsky (33), also (32); see also
R. G. H. Siu (15).

[5] See on the dialectics of Damascius and Pseudo-Dionysius, Gurvitch (6, pp.
44–49).

[6] See on their dialectics, Gurvitch (6, pp. 50–156).

As a matter of fact, his prognosis is already being realized by the natural as well as by the social sciences. Surprisingly, for many a too-narrow empirical sociologist who still regards the dialectical method as sterile speculation, the recent decades have been marked by a strong resurgence of dialectic method in the social as well as in the natural sciences. A galaxy of eminent physicists and mathematicians such as Niels Bohr, Louis de Broglie, F. Gonseth, J. L. Destouches, G. Bachelard, W. Heisenberg, and others have introduced it, in the form of "a dialectic complimentarity," into microphysics, nuclear physics, the mathematics of the infinitely great and the infinitely small, and so on for reconciliation of the opposite theories in these fields.[7] Likewise in recent years we observe an increasing number of works devoted to the dialectic in philosophy and the social sciences and a still more rapidly increasing use of this method in research of social, cultural, and psychological phenomena. As representative examples of such works, besides the works of some of the Marxians, the recent monographs of M. Merleau-Ponti, J. P. Sartre, and G. Gurvitch can be mentioned here.[8]

These concise comments show a complete agreement between Schneider's and my views concerning the cognitive functions of the dialectical method in a study of natural and socio-cultural processes.

Turning now to Schneider's comments on my use of dialectic, I find his interpretations essentially correct and insightful. Their only shortcoming is that he concentrates his analysis almost entirely on one — the "immanentist" — variety of dialectical method[9] and passes by without examination other forms of this method used in my works.

Whatever the reasons for this oversight, it may be responsible for Schneider's "severance" of my dialectical method from my conception of the Ideational, Sensate, and Idealistic supersystems of culture. This severance, as he correctly expects, I find unwarranted. In other words, in the construction of my Integral system of sociology and in my analysis of culture as systems, supersystems, and congeries I continue to use the dialectic method in its different forms (tempered and tested by empirical verification and combined with "postulational-deductive" and inductive methods).

[7] Instead of giving the titles of the respective works of these and other eminent scientists I simply refer to the international review, Dialectica, established in 1947, where the scientists of diverse exact sciences endeavor to find through dialectic method a solution of various (conceptual and experimental) difficulties confronting them in their research.

[8] Cf. M. Merleau-Ponti (10); J. P. Sartre (13); G. Gurvitch calls his system of sociology "dialectique empirico-réaliste." He developed it in a number of his works. His Dialectique et Sociologie gives a summary of his views of cultural and psychological phenomena. Resurgence and refinements of dialectic method and of the philosophy of dialectic materialism among the Marxians can be observed by reading Voprosy Filosofii, the main philosophical and partly sociological journal of the U.S.S.R. Almost in each copy of this journal several studies devoted to dialectics are published.

[9] Schneider himself quite skillfully uses this variety of dialectic in his study of "the Role of the Category of Ignorance in Sociological Theory," in (14, pp. 492–508).

Dialectic and Ideational-Sensate-Idealistic Supersystems

To show this, I shall remind the reader of two things concerning dialectic method. First, as Gurvitch correctly states, "The dialectical method is first of all the method of adequate cognition of the *real* social and historical" totalities (or unified systems in contrast to congeries). Second, that it involves at least five different operational procedures: (1) dialectic complementarity; (2) mutual dialectic implication; (3) dialectic ambiguity; (4) dialectic polarization; (5) dialectic reciprocity of perspective.[10] At least four of these dialectic procedures have been used in construction of my Integral system of philosophy, sociology, and personality structure;[11] of my conception of the superorganic as the form of being different from the inorganic and the organic forms of reality; of three-dimensional (social, cultural, and personal) aspects of the superorganic; and especially for construction of my theory of social, cultural, and personal systems (including Ideational-Sensate-Idealistic supersystems) and congeries.[12]

Without a use of dialectic procedures of complimentarity, mutual dialectic implication, dialectic polarization, and dialectic reciprocity of perspective, it is hardly possible to define and study adequately social or cultural systems as *Ganzheiten* (quite different from congeries); their three-componential structures, their three-dimensional aspects, their meaningful causal unity, their triple interdependence of parts upon the whole, upon each other, and of the whole upon the parts, and other basic characteristics.[13] Anyone who carefully examines either the *Dynamics*

---

[10] Gurvitch (6, pp. 27 ff., pp. 184 ff.). Gurvitch correctly states that a study of the movements of the real social and historical totalities is a common characteristic of all diverse forms of dialectic.

[11] See for my Integral system of philosophy (27); also (30); for my system of sociology cf. (29); for my theory of personality structure cf. (24); also (38).

[12] May I be permitted to state that already in (17) and then in (18), I introduced and delineated the concept of social and cultural *systems* vs. mechanistic, nominalistic, atomistic, and organismic conceptions of society and culture. In (19) and then in (29), the conceptions of *social systems* vs. unorganized and semi-organized groups and *cultural systems* vs. congeries were fully developed and built in their concrete, empirical, historical manifestations and forms. At the present the concept of social or cultural system has become quite popular but most of such concepts are still permeated by nominalistic and atomistic fallacies that rob such "systems" of their unity and other inalienable characteristics of the real systems as *Ganzheiten* quite different from a nominalistic group of interacting individuals or congeries of cultural phenomena unrelated to each other either meaningfully or causally.

[13] When definition and analysis of social or cultural system is attempted without use of the mentioned dialectic operational procedures, the invariable result is either a mere nomenclature of various interactional or even singularistic activities of individuals like: "knowing, feeling, achieving, norming, ranking" and so on, which completely miss a social or cultural system as *Ganzheiten*, as unified reality different from these activities; or a semi-nominal and semi-atomistic pseudo-unity of actors and roles without delineation of the play they are supposedly playing together. Charles Loomis's books (8; 9) give an example of such a nomenclature and T. Parsons (11) supplies an example of semi-nominalistic pseudo-social system.

or *Society, Culture and Personality* and who is versed in the mentioned operational procedures of dialectic method can easily see my use of these procedures throughout my Integral system of philosophy, sociology, and psychology. This explains my rejection of Schneider's severance of my dialectic from my theory of social and cultural systems and congeries, including the Ideational, Idealistic, and Sensate supersystems. Contrary to his statement that in a study of socio-cultural structures and forms "The dialectic seems not to be of such help," I think that without a skillful use of the dialectic in its various forms no adequate theory of the socio-cultural structures and forms is possible.

We can now pass to examination of Schneider's criticisms of the Ideational, Idealistic, and Sensate supersystems of culture.

Corrections

But before answering the criticisms I have to make two corrections in Schneider's outline of the main themes of the *Dynamics* and *Society, Culture and Personality*. First, my conception of culture or of the superorganic socio-cultural world is not "derivable from premises about the character of ultimate reality" and not "indissolubly wedded to systems of ultimate truth." These statements of Schneider are accurate only in regard to the Ideational, Sensate, and Idealistic supersystems of culture, as the specific and vastest forms of its integration. In my conception the whole realm of the superorganic or socio-cultural reality represents an incomparably vaster universe than these supersystems. This reality is basically different from the inorganic and the organic forms of being. In contradistinction to the inorganic phenomena that have only one physico-chemical component, and to the organic phenomena that have two components — physical and vital (life) — the socio-cultural or superorganic phenomena have the "immaterial" component of — conscious, rational, and superrational — *meaning* (or meaningful value and norm) superimposed upon the physical and vital components. This component of "meaning" is decisive in determining whether a phenomenon is socio-cultural. All phenomena that have the component of meaning are cultural phenomena. Such phenomena are found only in the world of mindful human beings who meaningfully interact with one another and create, operate, accumulate, objectify, and "materialize" their meanings in and through an endless number of physical and biological media ("vehicles"). To sum up: the totality of the "immaterial" meaning-values-norms, not objectified as yet through the material vehicles but known to some members of mankind; the totality of already objectified meanings-values-norms with all their physical and biological vehicles and energies; finally, the totality of interacting mindful individuals and groups — past and present — these inseparable totalities make up the total man-made socio-cultural world, superimposed on physical and biological realms of the total reality

of the universe.[14] This definition of culture shows that the total cultural
reality is neither "derivable" from, nor "wedded" to, the Ideational-
Sensate-Idealistic forms of its integration.

In a systematic and detailed way this superorganic universe is studied
in my works in its main structural and dynamic, as well as in its social,
cultural, and personal aspects; in its ideological, behavioral, and material
forms, as well as in its social and cultural systems basically different
from unorganized collectivities and cultural congeries.

It is precisely my study of cultural systems which attracted my attention to the reality of the Ideational, Sensate, and Idealistic supersystems.
The point is that in the *total* culture of any population or even of an
individual, there exist a multitude of cultural congeries and of causal-
meaningful (logically or aesthetically) consistent systems. These range
from the smallest systems of meanings like "A is B," or "Two and two
make four," to ever vaster ones. The "two by two is four" is a little cultural system; the multiplication table is a larger system; arithmetic is a
still larger system; all mathematics (arithmetic, algebra, geometry, calculus, etc.) is yet a vaster system; the entire field of science is a still more
embracing system. Similarly, we find a wide range of systems, beginning
with the smallest and ending with the vastest, in other fields of cultural
phenomena.

Since in the total culture of any population there are millions of
various cultural systems and congeries, a study of all the millions of
small systems (and congeries) would give, at best, only a knowledge of
diverse, infinitesimal fragments of the total cultural universe. It never
can give an essential knowledge of the basic structural and dynamic
properties of this superorganic reality. As any nomothetic (generalizing)
science, sociology endeavors to overcome this bewildering diversity of
the millions and millions of systems and congeries in two different ways
of its cognition: first, by concentrating our attention on the generic
static and dynamic properties of *all* socio-cultural phenomena; second,
by particular and intensive study of the *main* social and cultural systems.
Cognition of the generic properties and relationship of *all* socio-cultural
phenomena gives us a knowledge of their basic properties, relationships,
and uniformities. Cognition of the main socio-cultural systems delivers to
us a substantial knowledge of "the main continents" or "galaxies" of the
superorganic universe and — through that — the knowledge of its total
structure, of the relationships and configurations of these continents to
each other, of the main processes and uniformities in the life history of
each of these main systems and — through that — of the whole cultural
world. Even more, as an adequate cognition of each of the main systems
is impossible without a cognition of the subsystems of which each main
system is made up, a thorough knowledge of all the main systems and

14 P. T. de Chardin aptly calls the superorganic reality by the term of "noosphere"
in difference from the "biosphere" and physical classes of reality. Cf. his (4).

especially of the vastest supersystems (if a given total culture reaches this highest form of integration) provides us with macro-sociological as well as with micro-sociological knowledge of the total superorganic universe.[15]

Exactly these two ways — a study of the *generic* characteristics of *all* socio-cultural phenomena as well as an investigation of the structural and dynamic properties of the main social and cultural systems and, among them, of the vastest — Ideational, Sensate and Idealistic super-systems (supplemented by a study of the unorganized social groups and cultural congeries) have been used in my works for obtaining a basic knowledge of the superorganic or socio-cultural universe.

These remarks explain why in the *Dynamics,* side by side with a study of the basic properties of the generic socio-cultural phenomena, of cultural systems and congeries, I concentrated on a study of the Ideational, Sensate, and Idealistic supersystems. As mentioned, my investigation of these supersystems has led me to a systematic study of the systems of science, philosophy, religion, fine arts, ethics, law, and the vast derivative systems of applied technology, economics, and politics with their sub-subsystems and congeries. In this way the *Dynamics* represents a nomothetic, macro- and microsociological investigation of the many-dimensional superorganic universe in its cultural aspect.

These remarks show why my conception of culture is not "derivable . . ." and is "not indissolubly wedded to systems of ultimate truth." The *Dynamics* clearly states that only a few total cultures of a few societies and periods reach the highest possible integration into the Ideational, Sensate, and Idealistic supersystems. Even in such *Hochkulturen* these supersystems unify only their significant part, and not their total culture. In other words, these supersystems are neither coextensive nor equivalent with the total human culture.

Finally, one more correction. Schneider, like many other commentators on the *Dynamics* states that "the three main types (of culture) follow one another in what Sorokin regards as a rather reliable sequence, such that Sensate will be followed by Ideational and the latter by Idealistic culture forms and so on," and that the present disintegrating Sensate culture will be replaced by a new Ideational culture. This statement is incorrect. "I nowhere claimed that such an order of succession is a universal uniformity . . . I do not think the sequence observed in the history of the Greco-Roman and the Western cultures is universal or uniform for all societies and at all times." These remarks, and those in several other places of the *Dynamics* make my position clear. I do not have any sufficient logical ground on which to contend that the observed

---

[15] A detailed descriptive cognition of some of the unique, concrete fragments — persons, groups, events, etc. — of this superorganic universe is given to us by the ideographic disciplines of history, anthropology, and other ideographic sciences. See on this P. Sorokin (28, pp. 235–254).

order is invariable. Neither is there a sufficient empirical evidence for such a claim. Neither have I claimed that the dying Sensate order of our time would be necessarily followed by a new Ideational order (19, vol. iv, pp. 770–773).

After these corrections we can turn to an examination of Schneider's thoughtful criticisms of the supersystem of culture.

Reply to Schneider's Criticisms of the Concept of Supersystems

1. Argument of "Hackneyed Triad"

Schneider's first criticism suggests that my triad of the Ideational-Sensate-Idealistic supersystems is "a rather hackneyed triad, already old in Vico's day." The criticism is partly correct: even before Varro and Vico a number of known and unknown thinkers of ancient Egypt, India, China, Persia, Greece, and Rome formulated several cyclical and rhythmical theories somewhat resembling my triad. The *Dynamics* gives an extensive survey of these theories; it indicates the points of resemblance between these theories and my "triad."[16] However, from the fact that atomic theory was formulated long ago, even before Demokritos and Leukippos, and has been reiterated since many times in subsequent centuries, it does not follow that the atomic theories of the contemporary physicists are "hackneyed stuff." From the fact that many of the basic concepts and principles of physical and biological sciences such as "number," "time," "space," "causality," "emanation and undulatory theories of light," vitalism, mechanism, abiogenesis, struggle for existence, determinism, indeterminism, geocentric, heliocentric, and other cosmogonies[17] were conceived centuries before our era, the conclusion does not follow that the respective theories of today's physicists, chemists, astrophysicists, and biologists are "hackneyed stuff . . . worn even thinner by a long line" of the scientists who have dealt with these problems. The same argument still more applies to philosophy and the psychosocial sciences: these disciplines are still busy mainly with the problems and theories formulated two or three millenia ago.

When one compares today's and the early theories of each of the main problems of physical, biological, psychological, and philosophical disciplines, one cannot fail to notice that the contemporary theories, though remotely resembling their ancient predecessors, nevertheless are quite different from their great-grandfathers. The same is true in regard to many a predecessor of my theory of the Ideational-Sensate-Idealistic supersystems. Using the term of the detective stories, one can say that their remote resemblance is largely coincidental. These remarks are sufficient to dismiss the argument of "a hackneyed triad."

---

16 See (19, vol. 2, chapters 10, 11, 12; vol. 4, chapters 7, 8, 9, 10, 11. See also G. C. Cairne (3).

17 See on the genesis and fluctuation of these theories in (19, vol. 2, chapters 11, 12); cf also (20).

2. Defective Quality of My Data

The next and more important criticism consists of the indication of the defective quality of some of my data. As an example of such questionable data, Schneider mentions my data on art, particularly on literature. Again in a small degree his criticism is correct: in comparison with the *ideally* complete, precise, and thoroughly verified data, my data are, of course, deficient. I myself repeatedly stress their shortcomings and inadequacies in almost each chapter of the *Dynamics*. But Schneider knows well that the ideally perfect data may exist only in the Platonic world of ideal forms and (unless they concern elementary platitudes) they are unobtainable for a mortal investigator of real, everchanging, and many-dimensional empirical phenomena. For this reason defectiveness of my data should be decided not by comparison with the ideal *but with the obtainable empirical data used by other sociologists and scholars working on similar problems.* If and when the only such possible, fair, and real comparison is made, I am ready to reiterate my statement that my data "are more reliable and complete than any data presented up to the present time, so far as the general course of art fluctuation in the countries studied is concerned." The same contention I am ready to make in regard to my data concerning the forms and fluctuation of materialism, idealism, nominalism, realism, rationalism, mysticism, temporalism, eternalism, movement of scientific discoveries and inventions, oscillation of main ethical theories, changes in the codes of law, movement of wars, internal disturbances, fluctuation of theocratic and secular governments, of governmental regimentation, and of all the other socio-cultural processes studied in the *Dynamics*.

The main reasons for this contention are as follows:

a) Even the best sociological works dealing with the long-term fluctuations or formulating some uniformities in the relationship of the studied socio-cultural variables give for empirical verification of their hypotheses only a few illustrative cases (for example, Max Weber's empirical corroboration of his theory of Protestantism-Capitalism, or Marx's opposite theory in this field, or A. Toynbee's unduly generalized Hellenic model of civilization in the first six volumes of his *Study of History*, or Durkheim's generalization that "the intensity of punishment is proportional to the degree of absolutism and unlimitedness of the central government" (5, pp. 65 ff.), or they use so-called "representative samples" (whose representativeness ordinarily remains unproved and questionable). In contrast to these doubtful procedures, I give, instead of a few cases or samples, *the complete known series* or *the total known universe of the relevant empirical facts;* not just samples, but *all known* scientific discoveries and inventions; *all* Greco-Roman and Western philosophers, mentioned in the fullest histories of philosophy; *all* historical persons mentioned in the *Encyclopaedia Britannica; all* ethical thinkers; almost *all* European pictures and sculptures (more than 100,-

000) known to the most complete histories of European painting and sculpture; almost *all* the French, the German, and the Russian codes of criminal law beginning with the Barbaric codes of the fifth-sixth centuries and ending with the Soviet, the Nazi, the Fascist codes; *all* Greco-Roman and Western wars and internal disturbances recorded in historical persons mentioned in the *Encyclopaedia Britannica; all* ethical urement of a *complete universe* or of the *total class* of the phenomena investigated gives a more adequate knowledge of the movement of these phenomena in time and space than a study and measurement of *a mere fraction* or *a mere sample* of these facts. Even the best sampling techniques, when applied to a study of long-term fluctuations of many-dimensional, somewhat abstract and discrete phenomena, are liable to yield but fragmentary, inadequate results, since they are based on cases selected in an unsystematic or biased manner.

b) To reduce the elements of subjectivity and incompetence in the collection of the relevant empirical data for verification of my hypotheses, I intentionally eliminated myself from this collection in all quantitative series of the *Dynamics* and arranged this enormous spadework done by *the internationally known specialists in the field of each series, without telling them for what purposes or hypothesis each of the factual series was needed.*[18] This simple procedure more efficiently eliminated the element of subjectivity and at the same time secured a more competent collection of the relevant empirical data than could be done by myself or by ordinary research assistants (graduate students and the like) who are not eminent specialists in these fields.[19]

c) Contrary to Schneider's statement that my data "are often unique, and good checks on them are generally unavailable," *I give a complete possibility of verification of every detail of my procedures and summary tables.* In many long appendices to each volume of the *Dynamics*, there are given detailed lists of all the wars, revolutions, philosophers, ethical thinkers, scientists, painters, sculptors, and so on, with all the details of quantitative evaluation of each person or event. In this way any competent scholar is given a complete opportunity to check each detail of factual accuracy of my quantification procedures, of all the summary tables, and all the main conclusions and generalizations.

[18] Professor N. S. Timasheff, who was one of the collectors of the series of all the known internal disturbances in the history of Greece, Rome, and the Western countries, testifies to this fact in his essay in (34).

[19] The danger of subjective biases and incompetence in collection of the empirical facts studied (for substantive and verificatory purposes) is not eliminated by the modern "data collecting and processing technique," neither by the techniques of sampling or item analysis or paired comparison and others. In many empirical studies using "the modern techniques" this phase of research is often entrusted to incidental and hardly competent agents without an effective control of the competence of their operations. The material presented by them to the researcher-scholar is frequently "processed" without a sufficient test of its accuracy, completeness, and so on. As a result many an empirical research is vitiated already at this early phase and yields therefore doubtful conclusions based on defective data.

d) A further precautionary measure in my quantification of the many-dimensional, qualitative-quantitative phenomena has been my preferential use, whenever possible, of the *simplest quantitative procedures involving either none or the minimum of arbitrary assumptions, ranking, scaling, complex formulae, and other intricate manipulations with figures and facts.* The scientific reason for this preference is almost axiomatic: the less arbitrary assumptions, ranking, scaling, estimates, and other arbitrary manipulations a measurement or quantification contains, the more roughly reliable and correct the results of the quantification are likely to be.[20] This explains why most of my tables give just the actual number and percentage of the counted — and countable — items obtained through simple arithmetic computation.[21] Side by side with these tables there are also tables involving several assumptions, estimates, ranking, and other arbitrary operations in quantification of their not completely scalar data. The tables giving the movement of the internal disturbances from 600 B.C. to A.D. 1925 are a conspicuous example of such tables. But just because, for their construction, several arbitrary assumptions were made, such tables appear to me less reliable than the simple "arithmetic" tables free from most of the arbitrary manipulations.

e) As an additional measure for securing a comparative reliability, completeness, and adequacy of my quantitative data and of my conclusions derived from them, I regularly checked these conclusions by logical (including dialectical) analysis and supplemented them by a qualitative description and interpretation of additional points not shown by the quantitative indexes.

f) Perhaps as a further evidence of a comparative accuracy of my data I can mention the fact that, when some of my pioneering studies like the movement of wars in Greco-Roman and Western populations from 600 B.C. to A.D. 1925 were repeated along somewhat similar lines by Quincy Wright and B. Urlanis, their results happened to be in essential agreement with my results, indexes, and curves of war movement.[22] If this agreement happened in regard to the time-series of wars in which several arbitrary assumptions were made, I am reasonably certain that

[20] A more developed criticism of these assumptions, ranking, and other arbitrary manipulations with figures is given in (25).

[21] This straightforward arithmetic counting seemingly is responsible for several criticisms of my "statistical methods" by the devotees of the complex, statistical manipulations infected by a legion of the arbitrary assumptions, subjective scalings, and other simulacra of "refined and precise" statistical procedures with impressively looking pseudo-mathematical formulae having in fact no relationship to real mathematics and sound statistical operations. Cf. for substantiation of this statement (25, chapters 7, 8, and also 4, 5, 6).

[22] See (19, vol. 3, chapters 9, 10, 11; 40; 37). Despite Urlanis' criticism of some of my procedures and assumptions — which criticism reproduces mainly my own warnings of the deficiency and inadequacies of the available data and of the assumptions made in my study — nevertheless his main indexes and curves of the movement of wars of the seventeenth, eighteenth, nineteenth, and twentieth centuries are in essential agreement with my indexes and curves.

my tables and curves obtained through a mere arithmetic computation of the items counted will be still better confirmed by future competent studies of the same phenomena along similar lines.[23]

The totality of considerations (a), (b), (c), (d), (e), (f), explain why I do not agree in this point with Professor Schneider and why I do not hesitate to contend that, though from the ideal standpoint, my data "may be unreliable but they are more reliable than any data presented up to the present time, so far as the general course of art fluctuation (and also of fluctuation of other variables) in the countries studied is concerned."

After these considerations we can turn to Schneider's case of an alleged deficiency of my data. I myself state that it is probable that during the early Medieval period "on the lower levels of literature there existed many pagan, partly Sensate and even indecent songs, poems, and tales." "But," I add, "these levels are beyond the scope of this work." Schneider seems to have failed to pay attention to this addition. In the *Dynamics* I study not "*the lower levels*" of science or philosophy or religion or fine arts or other cultural congeries and primitive systems of the Greco-Roman and the Western total cultures, but precisely their highest levels — the levels that give individuality and creative originality to these (or other) cultures: their greatest and highest systems and supersystems. And these "highest levels" are studied throughout the whole existence of these cultures. If therefore my study shows that the grand literature, grand sculpture-architecture-philosophy-science-religion-ethics-law-politics-economics of these cultures were in some periods predominantly Ideational, while in other periods they became predominantly Idealistic or Sensate; if, in addition, my study shows that in these transformations all these great systems of these cultures have been changing "in togetherness," in mutual interdependence — then the demonstration of these metamorphoses clearly testifies that, on their highest levels, these cultures have indeed undergone respective Ideational or Idealistic or Sensate transformation and that, on this high level, their main cultural systems have indeed been integrated into respective dominant supersystems. The existence of all sorts of cultural congeries and "vulgar" systems on the lower levels of these cultures in no way damages or cancels the accuracy of my data and the validity of my conclusions concerning the high levels or the dominant grand systems and supersystems of these cultures.

---

[23] The comparative accuracy of my data has been confirmed even by vitriolic critics of my *Dynamics*. "In general, Mr. Sorokin appears to have been most conscientious about his facts" (2, p. 252). On the other hand, several eminent historians like M. I. Rostovtzeff, and sociologists like L. von Wiese found "the factual framework of the *Dynamics* so solidly built that its essentials are unlikely to be changed by future investigators; they certainly will correct here and there some sidewalks and secondary streets of the city of the *Dynamics* but its main features are likely to remain unchanged" (12). "In comparison with Sorokin's great work, the works of Comte, Spencer, Pareto and Spengler appear to be arbitrary and fanciful" (39). See also (36).

Furthermore, in contrast to the Danilevsky-Spengler-Toynbee theories of complete integration of their *Hochkulturen*[24] or "Civilizations," I persistently contended that *the total culture* of any group or even of any individual is hardly ever completely integrated, that it always represents a co-existence of various, sometimes even contradictory, congeries and systems; that in each of *the total Hochkulturen* there exists, side by side with the dominant supersystem, the other supersystems as minor structures. For this additional reason, the existence of a vulgar Sensate literature on lower levels of cultures which on their higher levels have been dominated by grand Ideational literature in no way damages my data or contradicts my conclusions concerning the fluctuation of Ideational, Idealistic, and Sensate literature on the higher levels of the cultures studied. This argument alone is sufficient to negate Schneider's criticism.

Several additional reasons and empirical evidence notably reinforce my argument. First, we should not exaggerate the contrasts between the cultures of the higher and the lower levels of the same total culture, or between the cultures of the higher and lower classes and groups of the same society. Despite ever present differences of higher and lower levels of the same total culture, or the differences of cultures of different strata and groups of the same society, the dominant forms of the culture of the higher levels or of the dominant classes, as a rule, greatly influence and mold the culture of the lower levels or strata. With the exception of the periods of disintegration of the culture of the higher levels or of the dominant, upper classes, in normal periods the culture of the lower levels or classes largely imitates that of the upper levels or classes (see 19, vol. 4, chapter 5; 29, pp. 568 ff.). During a vigorous domination of Ideational (or Sensate, or Idealistic) culture on the higher levels or in the dominant classes, a simplified version of Ideational (or respectively Sensate, or Idealistic) culture usually becomes dominant also on the lower levels of the same total culture or in the culture of the lower classes of the same society. For this reason the scarcity of Sensate literature in the early Mediaeval Ideational period may be due not only and not so much to the hypothetical factor of such a Sensate literature "being buried and lost," but also and mainly to the factor of an insignificant production, diffusion, and use of such a literature in a culture dominated on its higher levels, or in its dominant classes, by an Ideational supersystem. The validity of this last hypothesis is supported by the fact that in the periods of domination of a given culture by the Sensate supersystem, a vast production of Sensate culture on its lower levels and classes does not become "buried and lost": it leaves abundant evidence of its wide

---

[24] See my criticism of their theories of complete integration of the total *Hochkulturen* and of similar theories of the German "holystic morphologists" and of other "total integralists" in my (23, chapters 3, 4, 5; 21, chapter 43; 19, vol. 4, chapter 3; 30).

diffusion, popularity, and use; many samples of it enter and are preserved in the annals of history; many forms of it survive in its "vehicles" and in the historical traditions of subsequent generations. This means that the very hypothesis of Schneider and Hauser about the Sensate literature of the early Middle Ages "being buried and lost" is quite doubtful: it is supported by practically no empirical evidence. Neither is an explanation offered for why Sensate literature of the lower levels or classes at some periods becomes "buried and lost" leaving few, if any, traces of its existence, and why at other periods it leaves a vast body of evidence of its vigorous life and does not become "buried and lost." To take other examples from the data, tables, and curves of the *Dynamics*: glancing at the tables of the movement of scientific discoveries and inventions, we see that in Greece their number and curve decline after the fourth century B.C., in Rome after the first century A.D., and in Europe they remain at exceedingly low level throughout the period from A.D. 700 to 1200.[25] Can these (and many other) declines and scarcities of scientific discoveries and inventions in these periods be explained by the hypothesis of "being buried and lost"? Hardly; at least I do not know any competent historian of science and technology who advances this sort of explanation. Generally accepted explanations account for the declines and scarcity by the fact that in such periods actually only a few discoveries and inventions were made.

Or glancing at the tables of movement of idealistic and materialistic philosophies in the history of the West, we see that in the period of A.D. 580 to 1280 there is a zero index for all kinds of materialistic philosophy: the annals of history of philosophy do not register any single materialistic philosophy having emerged, diffused, and socialized during this period.[26] Again can this disappearance of materialistic philosophy in the total philosophical thought and culture of Europe of this period be accounted for by the hypothesis of "being buried and lost"? If someone would try to account for it by this hypothesis then he has to explain the still more formidable problem of why materialistic philosophies have not been buried and lost but on the contrary have prospered and become dominant at other periods of the Western or Greco-Roman cultures. I am reasonably certain that neither of these two questions can be satisfactorily answered by the hypothesis of "being buried and lost." With these remarks I can wind up my reply to this criticism of Schneider.[27]

[25] See the detailed tables and curves in (19, vol. 2, chapter 3).

[26] See for the tables and details (19, vol. 2, chapter 4).

[27] I pass by without comments Schneider's reference to D. C. McClelland's work because his "achievement motivation" is too generally defined without differentiation of Ideational or Sensate or Idealistic "achievement motivations." McClelland's interpretation of some parts of Greek art for the period 900–600 B.C. can hardly be interpreted as Sensate art. Even if they are interpreted in this sense, they represent only a fragment not representative of the total Greek art of these centuries. As a minor part of this art, it does not contradict the theory of the domination of Ideational art of the upper levels as well as of the total Greek art culture of this period.

3. Influence of the Ideological Systems and
Supersystems on Behavior

Schneider's next criticism is still more serious than the preceding ones. Boiled down, it aims to show that I have not given sufficient evidence that the Ideational-Sensate-Idealistic supersystems of culture exert tangible influences upon the overt behavior of individuals living in such cultures: "By the criteria of conduct, there is nothing of importance to distinguish the one set of cultures from the other." Therefore if the overt behavior of persons living in predominantly Ideational culture does not differ tangibly from that of the persons living in predominantly Sensate culture, then these supersystems and their premises "could finally appear as philosophical irrelevancies or near-irrelevancies so far as a great deal of conduct is concerned."

This main criticism implies two other shortcomings of my theory of culture: first, that it seemingly excludes the conduct-phenomena from my conception of culture, which "exclusion would on the whole be quite unacceptable"; and second, that "no effort is made in the *Dynamics* to develop anything like a systematic psychological theory."

"Not guilty" is my plea in regard to both these charges.

a) That I do not exclude behavior-phenomena from my conception of culture follows from my very definition of the superorganic in its cultural as well as in its social and personal aspects: "All empirically rooted socio-cultural phenomena are made up of three components: 1. meanings-values-norms; 2. physical and biological vehicles objectifying them; 3. *mindful human beings (and groups) that create, operate, and use them in the process of their interaction*" (19, vol. 4, pp. 46 ff.). Conduct or behavior phenomena are discussed throughout all volumes of the *Dynamics*, and Chapter 15 of Volume Three: "Relationship Between Types of Culture and Types of Personality and Behavior" is specially devoted to this problem. Furthermore, behavior or conduct phenomena enter my very definition of culture in its differentiated forms as "Ideological, *Behavioral* and Material Cultures of Individuals and Groups." Here is my definition of these forms: "1. the totality of meanings, values, norms possessed by interacting individuals and groups make up their 'ideological' culture; 2. the totality of their meaningful *actions-reactions* through which the pure meanings, norms, and values are objectified, conveyed, and socialized make up their *behavioral* culture; 3. the totality of all the other vehicles, the material, biophysical things and energies through which their ideological culture is manifested, externalized, and socialized make up their 'material' culture. Thus the total empirical culture of a person or group is made up of these three levels of culture: ideological, behavioral, and material" (29, p. 313). Subsequently, in several chapters of this work, each of these forms of culture, including the behavioral one, and their relationships to each other are analyzed in considerable detail. For these reasons I find this charge of Schneider unwarranted.

b) Unwarranted also is his charge that I failed to develop a systematic psychological theory (of human personality and behavior). It is true that, though in various parts of the *Dynamics* such a theory is given, it is not summed up in a systematic form in special chapters. However, in my *Society, Culture and Personality,* in my *The Ways and Power of Love,* a systematic theory of the mental structure of human personality and of human behavior is clearly outlined and in several important points investigated in considerable detail. The gist of my theory of man, personality-structure, and behavior can be summed up as follows. I find the prevalent theories in this field grossly defective and offer my "integral" version, considerably different from these prevalent (unduly Sensate) theories. The prevalent Sensate theories view man mainly as an animal organism of the *homo sapiens* species. They tend to interpret his nature and behavior predominantly in mechanistic, materialistic, reflexological, and other "physicalistic" terms.

"The depth psychology" of these theories "either flattens the mental structure of personality to the level of the unconscious or subconscious, with a sort of epiphenomenal and vague 'ego' and 'superego,' or just depicts it as a "two-story building" — the unconscious (subconscious) and the conscious (rational). They see mainly the lowest forms of man's energies (the unconscious and subconscious) and are blind to man's rational and supraconscious genius." Among other blunders they "merge into the category of the 'unconscious' or 'subconscious' (E. von Hartmann, P. Janet, S. Freud, and others) two radically different energies of man: *the biologically unconscious* that lies below the level of the conscious state of mind and *the supraconscious* ("genius," "creative plan," Greek *nous,* Pneuma, 'Creative self,' 'Tao,' 'jnana,' 'prajna,' etc.) that lies above the level of any rational thought or energy."

In contrast to this "physicalistic," "animalistic" conception of man the Integral theory of man views *homo sapiens* not only or mainly as an animal organism, but especially as a mindful rational thinker and doer and as a supersensory and super-rational creator (genius). It is in the rational and the supra-conscious levels of man that the answer may be found to the ancient question: "What is man, that thou shouldst magnify him?" In contrast to the shallow "depth psychology" of personality structure, the Integral "height psychology" (as it is aptly called by Björn Sjövall, using Franz Kafka's dictum: *"des Menschen Tiefe ist seine Höhe,"* — "the deepest in man is his highest"[28] distinguishes in the total human personality and behavior "four different forms of energies — four mental levels and activities: (1) *the biologically unconscious;* (2) *the biologically conscious;* (3) *the socio-culturally conscious;* and (4) *the supraconscious.*"

1) Man is an animal and all the hereditary anatomical properties,

[28] See (16, pp. 48 ff., also 38).

physiological processes, reflexological, instinctive and unconscious excitations and inhibitions, drives and activities of the human organism necessary for animal life and survival make up the biologically unconscious matrix of human personality. Activities and processes determined by anatomical and physiological constitution of our organism, like breathing, eating, drinking, micturition, defecation, sleeping, rest after fatigue, sexual conjugation, avoidance of pain, cooperating with and fighting other human beings in the struggle for existence, reflexological crying, laughing, yelling, or growling and so on — such are the main biological drives, needs, and activities. This biological part of a human individual manifests, and is conditioned, by the biophysical properties of the organism and of the total cosmos. Being unconscious, this part of the personality's psyche does not have a conscious experience of "ego" or "I." Strictly automatic reflexes and activities of breathing, heart-beating, or digestion proceed without any consciousness of ego. This unconscious part of our mental apparatus and the reflexological-instinctive activities of the human personality are something much more complex and manifold than Freud's unconscious 'id,' 'libido' and complexes. . . .

2) Next to the unconscious energies and activities come the bioconscious ones associated with a set of biological egos and roles in personality. When a person becomes aware of his biological tension and the tension enters the field of consciousness (e.g., "I am hungry," "I have pain in my arm," etc.), the biological energy becomes bioconscious and leads to bioconscious activities on the part of the corresponding biological ego ("hungry ego," "sex ego," "thirsty ego," "urinating ego," "physically painful ego," and so on). Side by side with these short-term replacements of one biological ego by another in the course of each day, there is an irreversible long-time succession of the biological age — egos of the individual: the egos of a child, adolescent, mature man, old man. It is determined by biological forces and is accompanied by a legion of anatomical, physiological, and psychological changes in the individual, in his behavior, his relationships with others, and his position in his social groups.

3) Above this bioconscious stratum lie the *conscious socio-cultural energies, activities, egos, and roles.* They are generated by the conscious, meaningful interaction of mindful persons in their collective living, experience, and learning. Through their collective experience, they are accumulated and transmitted from person to person, group to group, generation to generation. In the process of this interaction, they are patterned into scientific, philosophical, religious, ethical, artistic, political, and technological forms of socio-cultural thought, norms, values, activities, and institutions. *A person possesses as many socio-cultural egos, roles, and activities as there are socio-cultural groups with which, voluntarily or not, he is connected.* Most of us have our *family ego* and activities, our *national, occupational, recreational, religious, political* egos and activities and the *lesser egos* and activities of the societies, clubs,

associations to which we belong. Each of these egos is a reflection of the meanings, values-norms of the particular group it represents. The activities and the role of each of our socio-cultural egos are defined by their respective social group. . . . Each of the groups seeks to impress upon a person its own image, in the form of a particular ego; each attempts to mold the individual after its own pattern; each prescribes to him a detailed course of his conduct; each demands a portion of his time and energy, a pound of flesh and a part of his soul or conscious mind. This explains the proposition that *each of us has as many conscious socio-cultural egos as there are organized groups with which we are in contact. The totality of these egos occupy almost the whole field of our conscious mentality, and the totality of these roles and activities fill a major part of our time, activities, and life. . . . If the groups to which a given individual belongs are in a solidary relationship with one another, if they all urge the individual to think, feel, and act in the same or concordant way, push him towards the same or concordant goals and prescribe to him the same or concordant duties, rights, then the different egos of the individual which reflect these groups will also be in harmony with one another, unified into a single, large harmonious ego.* (On this socio-cultural level) *he will be blessed with peace of mind and consistency in his conduct. . . . If on the other hand the groups to which an individual belongs are in conflict; if they urge him to contradictory ideas, values, convictions, duties and actions, then the individual's respective egos will be mutually antagonistic.* The individual will be a house divided against himself and split by inner conflicts. His conduct will be irresolute, inconsistent, and contradictory, as will also be his thoughts and utterances. The conscious, socio-cultural part of our mentality and behavior is directly connected with the socio-cultural human world.

4) Finally, there is a still higher level in the mental structure of man, a still higher form of energies and activities realized in varying degrees by different persons — namely, the *supraconscious* level of energies and activities. These constitute the fourth and highest stratum of man's personality, energies and activities. . . . At its purest and best, the supraconscious manifests itself in the greatest discoveries and creative achievements of men of genius in all fields of creative activity: science, philosophy, fine arts, religion, technological inventions, law, ethics, politics, and economics. These men of genius unanimously testify to the fact that their discoveries and creations have been inspired and started by the supraconscious flash of enlightenment — quite different from sensory observation and rational logico-mathematical thought — and then developed and tested by the sensory and rational methods of cognition and creativity.[29]

---

[29] The outline and quotations are taken mainly from my (24, chapter 5). For a developed form of this theory of personality structure see (24, chapters 5, 6, and 7),

This sketch of my Integral theory of personality-structure and behavior shows that contrary to Schneider's statement, I have a systematic psychological theory in this field, fairly well developed and verified by a substantial body of empirical evidence.

Now, having in the background the outlines of my theory of the Ideological Behavioral and Material forms of culture of individuals and groups and the Integral ("Height-psychology") theory of personality structure and behavior, we can turn to a concise examination of Schneider's main criticism that I have not given sufficient evidence that the Ideational-Sensate-Idealistic supersystems exert a tangible influence upon the overt behavior of individuals and groups living in such cultures. If by sufficient evidence he means perfectly apodictic or unquestionably certain evidence, then his criticism is largely correct. But again in all empirical sciences and particularly in psychosocial disciplines there are very few, if any, theories and propositions that are apodictically certain. Instead of this ideal — hardly ever realized — standard of sufficiency of evidence, we must take the obtainable, comparative standard of adequacy of empirical corroboration as it is given by almost all psychological and sociological theories in this field. Measured by such a standard my main propositions concerning the influence of the cultural supersystems upon the mentality and overt behavior of individuals living and acting in the atmosphere of predominantly Ideational-Sensate-Idealistic cultures have a fairly substantial logical and empirical corroboration. These main propositions (developed in the *Dynamics*, in *Society, Culture and Personality*, and the *Ways and Power of Love*) are summed up as follows:

1. In accordance with my theory of personality structure and behavior the *actual overt behavior of a person is a resultant of the bio-physical-unconscious, the biologically-conscious, the socio-culturally conscious, and for especially creative men of genius, of the superconscious forces, incorporated in the individual himself, and of his — physical, biological, social, and cultural — worlds in which he is born, reared, lives, and acts.* Each of these factors generates and determines a set *of specific activities of an individual and no one of them can be regarded as the generator and determiner of the total behavior of a human being.*

2) This means that only a part of the total behavior of an individual is tangibly influenced — generated, molded, and patterned — by his culture, particularly by his cultural systems and supersystems and by the totality of social groups of which he has been and is a voluntary or involuntary member.

3) Each of the above five factors may generate in and "urge" the individual to the activities mutually antagonistic to each other (for instance, the biological sex drive may urge him to commit a sex act while

also (21, chapters 17, 18, 19, and 35). For a detailed analysis of the supraconscious and for an empirical evidence of its difference from sensory perception and rational thought, cf. also (19, vol. 4, chapter 16).

his religious-ethical "ego" may oppose it). Therefore the activities generated by each of the mentioned five factors may be — and often are — in conflict with each other.

4) In accordance with the theory of the Ideological, Behavioral, and Material cultures of an individual, his total Ideological culture contains many ideas, values, norms, which are not realized in his behavioral or material cultures. One may know a great deal about Communism or Buddhism or Shintoism or homosexualism without practicing their teachings in his behavior or objectifying these "ideologies" in any material vehicles of his total "material culture."

5) "There has hardly ever been any single individual whose total sum of meanings, values and norms (the total ideological culture) has been either completely integrated or completely contradictory. . . . There has hardly been an individual whose ideological culture has been either fully and closely integrated with his behavioral and material cultures, or entirely unintegrated with these. . . . Therefore the total (ideological, behavioral and material) culture of a person either in each or on all three levels is never completely integrated, nor completely unintegrated and contradictory."

6) "A human being is neither perfectly logical and rational, nor entirely nonlogical, illogical, nonrational and irrational. He is partly both."

7) "The degree and amount of integration of all three forms of culture in their meaningful-causal connections fluctuate from person to person, from group to group."[30]

From these general propositions, as their detailed form, follow the propositions formulated in the *Dynamics*, namely:

8) "The dominant type of culture tangibly molds the type of mentality (the Ideological culture) of human beings who are born and live in it. . . . Other conditions being equal, the mentality of a person will be predominantly Ideational if he has had a contact only with the Ideational culture." The same is true with regard to the Sensate, Idealistic, or Mixed type of culture.

9) "It is quite another matter with the problem of the relationship between the dominant type of culture and the actual behavior or conduct of the persons who are a part of it. . . . The relationship between the character of the dominant culture and the conduct of the persons who live in it either cannot be very close or cannot be as close as the correlation between the dominant culture and the mentality (Ideological culture) of these persons."

10) "Though the relationship between the dominant culture and the behavior of its bearers is not always close, nevertheless, it does exist. . . . The bearers of Ideational and Sensate cultures differ from one another not only in their mentality (Ideological culture) but also in their

---

[30] (21, pp. 325 ff.) contains the development and substantiation of these generalizations.

behavior and personality. All in all, the conduct and personality of the Ideational man would be more Ideational than that of the Sensate man, and vice versa. . . . The difference between the bearers of the Ideational and Sensate cultures is less great with respect to conduct and personality (their Behavioral and Material cultures) than to mentality (their Ideological cultures); nevertheless, the difference exists and is quite readily perceptible" (19, vol. 4, pp. 509 ff.).

Schneiders' criticism concerns mainly Propositions Nos. 9 and 10 in the sense that I have not given a sufficient evidence of their validity. Therefore my whole theory of the Ideational, Sensate, Idealistic, and Mixed types of culture may amount merely to a sort of "philosophical irrelevancies or near-irrelevancies so far as a great deal of conduct is concerned."

As I mentioned already I cannot agree with him on this point. First, he does not give practically any — logical or empirical — corroboration of his challenge: it remains a purely dogmatic statement. Second, his main argument consists essentially of an unduly exaggerated reiteration of my own statements that the predominant types of culture determine the overt behavior of their bearers much less than their mentality (Ideological culture). Even his considerations of the main factors of this lesser determination of the conduct of persons and groups by the predominant types of culture correctly outline my own factors of: an incomplete integration of ideological-behavioral-material cultures in individuals due to the frequent mutual conflicts of various biologically unconscious and conscious parts in their personality structure; the socio-cultural factor of affiliation of most of the individuals with different and often mutually contradictory social groups — the affiliation producing, in an individual, conflicts and inconsistencies among his socio-cultural egos and the activities required by each of them; and the conflicts between the demands of the biological, the socio-cultural, and the supra-conscious forces in the human personality. As can be seen from the above sketch of my theory of personality structure and of the ideological, behavioral, and material cultures of a person, there is no disagreement between Schneider's considerations and my fairly fully developed theories in this field. For this reason, Schneider's considerations of this point become irrelevant as an evidence against the Propositions Nos. 9 and 10. Third, in the *Dynamics* and in my subsequent works I give, if not apodictic then, at least, a comparatively substantial body of empirical evidence corroborating the Propositions Nos. 9 and 10. In the first place, insofar as the *Dynamics* has demonstrated the existence of Ideational-Sensate-Idealistic types of mentality (Ideological supersystems) and the existence of vast Ideational-Sensate-Idealistic systems of truths, philosophy, religion, fine arts, ethics, law, even politics and economics, and so far as it has demonstrated an interdependent change in togetherness of these systems and supersystems in time in the total cultures of Greece, Rome, and the West (and more cursorily in several other cultures), the very demonstration of these cardinal facts (which none of the critics has been able to disprove) represents a most substantial empirical corroboration of Propositions Nos. 9 and 10 as well as other propositions sketched above. Why? *Because all these empirically rooted Ideational-Idealistic-Sensate systems and supersystems of "fine arts, systems of truth (science, philosophy, religion) moral systems, systems of law; forms of political, social, and economic organizations; and so on are not only the phenomena of mentality (Ideological culture) but also the phenomena of behavior in the most overt, 'behavioristic' sense.* Their creation, existence and functioning in any culture presupposes an incessant stream of actions and reactions — that is, of behavior — on the part of the members of the culture. The creation of the Parthenon or the Chartres Cathedral (as well as that of the Empire State or the Wall Street buildings) involved the capital and labor (that is an enormous amount of activities) of thousands of persons for a notable length of time. The creation and functioning of any institution, be it the Roman Catholic See or the New York Stock Exchange, are carried on through incessant activities, i.e., through certain forms of behavior, of a few or of many human individuals. Since these activities assume one (behavioral and material) form in an Ideational and a quite different form in a Sensate society in all the socio-cultural compartments, this means that a very large part of the conduct of the members of an Ideational culture assumes Ideational forms, while that of the members of a Sensate society take on Sensate forms" (19, vol. 4 pp. 511 ff.) It is not a phenomenon of mentality only, but also of behavior that members of Medieval society build a multitude of cathedrals, churches, and abbeys as their greatest buildings outlining the skyline of their cities and villages, while the members of Sensate society build the Empire State, Radio City, and other commercial and secular buildings towering above all churches and cathedrals lost among these secular giants. It is not merely a phenomenon of ideological culture but no less a very solid and massive manifestation of behavioral and material culture that in the dominant Ideational culture its artists paint, sculptors sculpt, musicians compose their masterpieces almost entirely on religious topics, while in Sensate society they do so on perfectly Sensate themes. The same is true of literature and drama. The same is to be said of the Ideational-Sensate-Idealistic codes of law and ethics (with the behavior of their judges and violators, with the court buildings and systems of punishment), of the theocratic and secular governments, of respective systems of philosophy and theology, of their economic systems, of prevalency of respective familistic, contractual and coercive forms of social relationships, even of their modes of wars and revolutions. The *Dynamics* has fairly conclusively demonstrated the existence and fluctuation of Ideational-Sensate-Idealistic forms in practically all compartments of culture and organized social systems in the Greco-Roman and the

Western social worlds. Millions and millions of these "materialized and congealed objectifications" of Ideational-Idealistic-Sensate ideological systems represent uncontestable, massive empirical evidence of quite a tangible and unquestionable influence of these ideological systems upon the behavior and "material culture" of these populations. "To the extent that the *Dynamics* has shown that Ideational, Idealistic, Sensate and Mixed cultures have their own forms of mentality in all the main fields of cultures and social relationships; to the extent that any phenomenon of this culture mentality is at the same time a phenomenon of overt behavior (of the respective populations) — to these limits the conduct and behavior of the members of any such culture is quite tangibly conditioned by it, and stands in a consistent and clear association with it."[31]

This massive evidence, underestimated by Schneider, fairly convincingly repudiates his charge.[32]

As to the additional statistical evidence given in the *Dynamics* for a supplementary corroboration of the discussed Propositions Nos. 9 and 10, there are the tables of the Ideational-Sensate-Mixed types of personality of the Roman Catholic Popes from the year 42 to 1937; of the types of French-Russian-Austrian-English kings from 800 to 1917; of the percentages among all the historical persons listed in the *Encyclopaedia Britannica* of the persons who became historical through their religious (Ideational) or their business (Sensate) activities and achievements at the specified periods from 900 B.C. to A.D. 1849. Each of these tables alone would indeed be insufficient evidence for confirmation of Propositions Nos. 9 and 10, but taken together they significantly reinforce my main evidence to an extent to which a significant coefficient of correlation may be taken for a proof of a validity of a proposition.[33] So much for this criticism.

[31] See (19, vol. 4, p. 514). See there a development and specification of this influence upon the forms and patterns of respective behavioral actions, stimulation or inhibitions of certain forms of actions in conformity with the nature of each of these cultures; influences on the frequency of commission or non-commission of the favored and prohibited activities, and so on.

[32] This sort of evidence anyone can observe daily by visiting and studying the ideological, behavioral, and material cultures of, say, a monastic community and that of a night club; or of the Dukhobor, the Mennonite, the Hutterite village communities and those of secularized farmers; of a typical Catholic or of a Southern Baptist college and the non-denominational, secular college. Even in the case of the colleges a number of differences in the courses, in the attendance of religious services, and in dozens of other behavioral and especially material cultural traits can be easily observed.

[33] Since writing the *Dynamics* two additional statistical series showing the number of the saints sanctified by the Christian church (before its splitting into different denominations and after its split) by the Roman Catholic and the Russian Orthodox churches from the first to twentieth century, and the statistics of the number of the Christian and Roman Catholic Popes sanctified at various periods of existence of the Papacy from 32 A.D. to 1823 reinforce the testimony of the mentioned three tables. Taken together, all five statistical series corroborate the main evidence discussed. For these additional two statistical series see my (22, chapters 37 and 38; 31, pp. 80–82).

I do not have space to examine carefully other, somewhat casual, critical remarks of Schneider concerning the Ideational and Sensate meanings of such concept as causality and number. I can only state that the distinction of these forms is not invented by me but is pointed out and carefully analyzed by the most competent historians of these concepts. All I did was to apply to their forms the terms Ideational and Sensate, which accurately fit these forms. Yes, in many operations the Chinese count "Four plus four makes eight," and "Eight is a bigger number than three," but in a number of operations when they attach a "mystic" meaning to a certain number then, as my quotation from Granet testifies, "Number three becomes greater than the number eight," because "Three means 'unanimity' while eight means only a 'majority.'" Precisely when an ideational meaning is attached to this or that number — and such "numerological" attachment has been prevalent in the predominantly Ideational cultures and periods and sometimes its survivals are found even in a Sensate culture (like the unlucky number thirteen in our Sensate culture, a replica of Hesiod's "calendar of the lucky and unlucky days": the sixth day in each month unpropitious for the birth of a female, the thirteenth, for sowing; the fourth day for good marriage, etc.) — many small numbers become in their value larger than quantitatively bigger numbers, and vice versa. The numbers with the ideational meaning attached to them influence the behavior of their believers in different ways than purely quantitative numbers affect Sensate behavior. This Ideational meaning sometimes makes three greater in its mystic power than eight or 100 and for that reason more desirable than many quantitatively bigger numbers.[34] To these remarks I add the observation that Schneider does not give any evidence for his contention. To sum up: even the Ideational or Sensate conception of numbers exerts a tangible influence on the behavior of their partisans and sometimes Ideationally makes a greater number of what, from a purely quantitative Sensate standpoint, is a smaller number, and vice versa.

With a slight modification these remarks can be applied to Schneider's statements concerning the psychology and behavior of the pre-literate peoples and the Ideational and Sensate concepts of causality.[35]

Finally, acknowledging the subtlety of Schneider's analysis of my concept of "integration," I cannot accept his replacement of my proposition by his two propositions. My proposition states that "other conditions being equal, the highest amount of self-determination belongs to those

---

[34] See the details in (19, vol. 2, pp. 433–437; vol. 4, chapters 9, 10, 11. In these chapters many examples of "mystic interpretations" of numbers like 3, 7, 12, and others are given. The to us more familiar Jewish cabala contains many samples of an Ideationally-esoteric interpretation of numbers.

[35] See for the definitions of Ideational and Sensate causality and also of time and space, for fluctuation of these two forms in history of the Greek, the Roman, and Western thought, and for their behavioral effects in (19, vol. 2, chapter 11; vol. 4, chapters 9, 10, 11; also 20, passim).

social and cultural systems which are most perfectly integrated, causally and meaningfully." Additionally I warn not to mix "integration" or lack of it with "plasticity," "rigidity," and similar meanings. Schneider finds this proposition doubtful and replaces it by two propositions: (1) "the more highly integrated social and cultural systems are the more liable to shortness of life and destruction"; and (2) "on the whole an 'Idealistic,' compromising, fusing sort of structure might be more viable."

As to his second proposition, with a proviso that his "compromising and fusing" do not undermine the integration of the system, it does not necessarily contradict my generalization; a well-integrated system may be plastic and elastic. As to his first proposition, since he does not give any proof of it except an abstract consideration of a faster sweeping of danger or threat throughout the whole integrated system, instead of a long argument I simply say that, despite his proposition, I still (and I suspect he also does) prefer to drive a well-integrated automobile to a poorly constructed or dilapidated jalopy; I still believe that other conditions being equal, a well-organized army or a football team will defeat a poorly-trained and unintegrated army or team. And I do not criticize our military authorities for installation of a radar system immediately able to inform the defense authorities and the whole nation about the enemy's missiles and bombers. I think that fast communication to the whole nation of the danger helps but does not hurt the nation's defense or survival. Likewise the longevity, survival, and self-determination of well-integrated scientific, philosophical, religious, or artistic systems on the whole has been much greater than those of the eclectic "too much compromising and fusing" congeries. Since Schneider does not give any other evidence, and since the *Dynamics* furnishes a considerable number of cases corroborating my proposition, I can refer the reader to my work (19, vol. 4, pp. 604–620) and with these remarks can end my reply to this section of Schneider's criticism.

4. Shortcomings of the "Undeveloped Themes"

In this section Schneider points at a series of themes touched in my works but left without a sufficient analysis and development. His charge is correct to the extent that my analysis of these problems neither gives an adequate knowledge of, nor makes unnecessary further research for a better understanding of these themes. Acknowledging this shortcoming, at the same time I think that my analysis of the themes gives at least a rough approximation to such an understanding. As a thorough discussion of these problems here is impossible, I may be excused for the sketchiness of my answers to the critical remarks of Schneider.

a) His first question is, what really unites various Sensate systems or "value areas" into one Integrated Sensate culture (supersystem) since these "value areas," according to my own statements, are separated from one another. "Whence this unity? And just how shall it be described?" My answer in black and white is: they are united into a Sensate *Ganzheit* by the identity of their ultimate premise that the true reality (and value) is sensory and by empirical grounding of this premise in the material vehicles and behavior of a respective population.

This premise in its manifold differentiations unifies, and is articulated by, all Sensate "value-areas"; Sensate arts, science, philosophy, religion, ethics, law, economics, politics in their ideological, behavioral, and material forms. From this premise also follow similar, predominantly utilitarian, hedonistic, and sensate value systems, motivations, social tasks, "ethos and pathos" permeating and animating all the systems or "value-areas" of Sensate culture; like Sensate art they all endeavor to serve mainly the Sensate "life, liberty, and pursuit of happiness." For this purpose Sensate science studies only the sensory empirical reality, Sensate philosophy philosophizes about mainly empirical forms of Becoming, Sensate ethics prescribes utilitarian and hedonistic rules of conduct aimed at "the maximum of Sensate happiness for the maximum of human beings"; likewise Sensate codes of law, Sensate economics and politics aim to realize the same objectives, if not for all human beings then, at least, for the respective "power elite" that controls legislation, economics, and politics. From the same premise issue the Sensate "unity in diversity" or "*ex pluribus unum*," relativity, and the incessant change of Sensate values and norms of conduct and many other characteristics of Sensate culture analyzed in great detail in the *Dynamics*.

b) Schneider's second charge is that I do not give a systematic classification of the resemblances and differences of Ideational-Sensate-Idealistic and other cultures. My answer is: in my system of general sociology that deals with the *generic* characteristics of *all* superorganic phenomena, of *all* organized social systems, unorganized social groups and nominal social plurels, and with generic traits common to *all* integrated cultural systems and unintegrated congeries and in my general and differential theory of personality structure, *the generic resemblances of all varieties of socio-cultural phenomena in their structural and dynamic aspects are listed, classified, and analyzed*.[36] In still greater detail are classified and analyzed the differences of main social systems and of their strata (in my systematic theory of social differentiation and stratification),[37] of main cultural systems,[38] and particularly of Sensate-Ideational-Idealistic systems and supersystems.[39] For this substantial reason I do not think that this charge is correct.

c) If this charge means that I did not give a systematic theory of the factors of these multitudinal resemblances and differences — their reasons or sources — then the charge is partly correct, but only partly,

[36] See for that (21, chapters 3, 4, 5, 8, 9, 17–34).
[37] See for this (21, chapters 10–17).
[38] See (21, chapters 17, 18, 35–39, 44, and 45).
[39] See (21, chapters 40–43), and then all volumes of the *Dynamics*, passim.

because in my theory of the *generic* "resemblances" and "differences" in personality structures, in social and cultural systems, the main reasons for their similarities and dissimilarities are indicated. In shortest form "the resemblances" in personality structure and behavior, in various social and cultural systems, including the Ideational-Sensate-Idealistic supersystems, are due to the common biological and psychosocial properties of human nature or of the species *homo sapiens*.

Biologically all members of this species (with the exception of a few biologically defective individuals) have basically similar anatomical structure, physiological processes, neurological mechanisms of unconditioned reflexes, and other biological properties, needs, and "drives." Psychosocially, likewise, they are equipped with essentially similar "mechanisms" of sensations-perceptions-reproductive imagination, feelings, emotions, volition, conditioned reflexes and associations, elements of rational thought and potential creativity. In the terms of my theory of personality structure, almost all human beings have many basic resemblances in the "biologically-unconscious," the "biologically-conscious," "the socio-culturally conscious," and, to a lesser degree, even in the "supra-conscious" parts of their total psyche. These biological and psychosocial basic similarities largely account for the *generic* similarities of all social and cultural systems, including the Ideational-Sensate-Idealistic supersystems built upon these similarities. Then, once created, these cultural and social systems of interacting human beings often increase these basic similarities by adding to them many similarities created and imposed by the culture and social systems themselves.

On the other hand, side by side with these similarities there exist many biological and psychosocial dissimilarities of individuals and groups: biological differences of sex, age, race, inherited constitution, health, nervous system, reflexes, needs, and others; and psychological differences in their intellectual, affective, emotional, volitional and creative equipment; plus the differences in the cosmic, biological, and psychosocial environment of their rearing and living. These differences make up the first basis for emergence of many differences of various cultural systems and supersystems.

These initial similarities and differences are continuously modified and transformed by the incessant process of interaction of the person and groups in social living together, by their changing environment, and by the factor of the manifold possibilities of solution of their problems. These factors generate several additional differences and resemblances superimposed upon the inherent bio-psychological ones.

Such in black and white are the sources of similarities and differences of various cultures, including the Ideational-Sensate-Idealistic ones. In each of these cultures, members satisfy their basic biological needs and each culture has complex systems of scientific, economic, political, legal, religious rules and institutions that regulate the activities and relationships of their populations involved in the satisfaction of these needs. In each of these cultures their members manifest and, in accordance with the nature of the culture, satisfy their quest for knowledge, wisdom, goodness, beauty, and other "super-biological" values by creating their systems and congeries of science, philosophy, religion, ethics, law, fine arts, political, economic, and other "value-areas." A long series of essentially the same activities, cultural systems, institutions, and "value-areas" are found practically in *all human societies and cultures*, beginning with the paleolithic and ending with the contemporary ones.

On the other hand, on account of biological and psychosocial differences, and different environments of individuals and groups, and of the manifold possibility of achievement of these tasks in different ways, each and all of these activities, systems, and institutions have assumed *concretely different forms and contents*, including the differences of Ideational-Sensate-Idealistic-Eclectic cultures. They are similar in having their systems and congeries of science, philosophy, religion, fine arts, ethics, politics, and economics, but the concrete Ideological, Behavioral, and Material forms and contents of these systems are different. Such is the gist of my answer — extensively developed and documented in my works — to this question.

d) This answer leads us to the pointed question of Schneider: if each of these cultures has its own system and criteria of truth (or of beauty or goodness), then does this mean there are only perfectly relative truths and no universal, perennial, or absolute Truth (and ethical and aesthetic standards) whatsoever? No. First of all, as Schneider himself correctly observes, there is a large "area of consensus" among the Ideational-Sensate-Idealistic systems of truth, of aesthetic, ethical, legal, even political and economic systems. Even beyond this "area of consensus" there is "an area of mutual complementarity" of these systems. Only in part are these systems mutually incompatible and contradictory. While this "incompatible and mutually contradictory" area embodies perfectly relative, local, temporary, evanescent, "small" truths, "small" ethical and legal norms, aesthetic, economic, and political values, the cognitive-aesthetic-ethical-legal-political-economic and other systems that lie in the "areas of consensus and mutual complimentarity" are much closer and truer approximations to the universal and perennial values-standards-norms which in their turn are a still truer approximation to the Absolute Truth, Absolute Beauty, Absolute Goodness.[40] In other terms, each of the Ideational-Idealistic-Sensate cultures creates and contains the values that approach

---

[40] In the terms of St. Thomas Aquinas the "area of mutual contradiction" somewhat corresponds to what he calls "human law" (relative, changeable, temporary); the areas of "mutual complementarity and consensus" correspond to what he calls "natural law" and my Absolute Truth-Beauty-Goodness is congenial to his "divine law" of to the Platonic ideal forms and values. In the terms of the Integral system of socio-cultural time the area of contradictions lies in *tempus*, the area of consensus and complimentarity in *aevum*, the absolute values in *aeternitas*. Cf. on this my (20, chapter 4).

the universal and perennial values side by side with the temporary, local values and plain pseudo-values. None of these cultures embodies "the whole truth and nothing but the Truth" or immortal values. Exactly for this reason when each of these cultures realizes its limited fund of the real values, it is bound to decline and be replaced by another form of culture pregnant with its own fund of the real values.[41]

Such is my answer to this question of Schneider.

Leaving his minor remarks without a reply,[42] in conclusion I thank Professor Schneider for his most thoughtful observations and criticisms of my "yarns" and the editors of this volume for their willingness to publish my "Reply." I can finish it by quoting the old adage: *Feci quod potui faciant meliora potentes.*

BIBLIOGRAPHY

1. Allen, Philip. *Pitirim A. Sorokin in Review.* Durham, N.C.: Duke University Press, 1963.

2. Brinton, C. "Socio-Astrology," *The Southern Review* (Autumn 1937), p. 252.

3. Cairne, G. C. *History of Cyclical Theories.* New York: Philosophical Library, 1963.

4. de Chardin, P. T. *The Phenomenon of Man.* New York: Harper & Bros., 1959.

5. Durkheim, E. "Deux lois de l'evolution penale," *L'Annee sociologique*, Series 1, Vol. IV, pp. 65 ff.

6. Gurvitch, G. *Dialectique et Sociologie.* Paris: Flammarion, 1962.

7. Kroeber, A. *Configurations of Culture Growth, Style and Civilizations.* Berkeley: University of California Press, 1947.

8. Loomis, Charles. *Social Systems.* New York: Van Nostrand, 1960.

9. Loomis, Charles. *Modern Social Theories.* New York: Van Nostrand, 1961.

10. Merleau-Ponti, M. *Les aventures de la dialectique.* Paris: Flammarion, 1955.

11. Parsons, Talcott. *The Social System.* Homewood, Ill.: The Free Press, 1951.

12. Rostovtzeff, M. I. Personal letter to P. A. Sorokin, dated Dec. 1, 1937, in which Rostovtzeff gives his evaluation of the *Dynamics.*

[41] This answer is connected with my Integral system of philosophy — in its ontological and epistemological parts. Cf. an outline of my Integral philosophy, ontology, and theory of cognition and creation in (26) and in (27). See also (30).

[42] There are many similarities between A. Kroeber's theories of culture developed in (7) and my theories. My analysis and appraisal of Kroeber's theories are given in (23, chapters 9 and 13).

13. Sartre, Jean Paul. *Critique de la reason dialéctique*, Tome I. Paris: Gallimard, 1960. "Theorie des Ensembles pratiques."

14. Schneider, Louis. "The Role of the Category of Ignorance in Sociological Theory," *American Sociological Review*, Vol. 27 (August 1962), pp. 492–508.

15. Siu, R. G. H. *The Tao of Science*. New York: John Wiley & Sons, 1957.

16. Sjöval, Björn. *Hojdpsykologi*. Stockholm: Svenska Kyrkans, 1959.

17. Sorokin, Pitirim A. *Sistema Soziologii*, 2 vols. St. Petersburg: isdatelstvo Kolos, 1920.

18. Sorokin, Pitirim A. *Contemporary Sociological Theories*. New York: Harper and Bros., 1928.

19. Sorokin, Pitirim A. *Social and Cultural Dynamics*. New York: American Book Co., 1937.

20. Sorokin, Pitirim A. *Sociocultural Causality, Space, Time*. Durham, N.C.: Duke University Press, 1943.

21. Sorokin, Pitirim A. *Society, Culture and Personality*. New York: Cooper Square Publishers, 1947.

22. Sorokin, Pitirim A. *Altruistic Love: A Study of American Good Neighbors and Christian Saints*. Boston: Beacon Press.

23. Sorokin, Pitirim A. *Social Philosophies of an Age of Crisis*. Boston: Beacon Press, 1951.

24. Sorokin, Pitirim A. *The Ways and Power of Love*. Boston: Beacon Press, 1954.

25. Sorokin, Pitirim A. *Fads and Foibles in Modern Sociology and Related Sciences*. Chicago: H. Regnery, 1956.

26. Sorokin, Pitirim A. "This is My Faith," in S. G. Cole (ed.), *This is My Faith*. New York: Harper and Bros., 1956.

27. Sorokin, Pitirim A. "Integralism is My Philosophy," in Whit Burnett (ed.), *This is My Philosophy*. New York: Harper and Bros., 1957.

28. Sorokin, Pitirim A. "Theses on the Role of Historical Method in the Social Sciences," *Transactions of the Fifth World Congress of Sociology*. Washington, D.C.: International Sociological Association, 1962, Vol. 1.

29. Sorokin, Pitirim A. *Society, Culture and Personality*. New York: Cooper Square Publishers, 1963.

30. Sorokin, Pitirim A. "Reply to My Critics," in Philip Allen (ed.), *Pitirim A. Sorokin in Review*. Durham, N.C.: Duke University Press, 1963.

31. Sorokin, Pitirim A., and W. Lunden. *Power and Morality*. Boston: Porter Sargent, 1959.

32. Stcherbatsky, Th. *The Central Conceptions of Buddhism*. London: Royal Asiatic Society, 1923.

33. Stcherbatsky, Th. *Buddhist Logic*, 2 vols. Leningrad: U.S.S.R. Academy of Science, 1932.

34. Timasheff, N. S. "Sorokin on Law, Revolution, War and Social Calami-

ties," in Philip Allen (ed.), *Pitirim A. Sorokin in Review.* Durham, N.C.: Duke University Press, 1963.

35. Tiryakian, E. *Sociological Theory, Values and Sociocultural Change,* Essays in Honor of P. A. Sorokin. New York: The Free Press of Glencoe, 1963.

36. Toynbee, Arnold J. "Professor Sorokin's Philosophy of History," in Philip Allen (ed.), *Pitirim A. Sorokin in Review.* Durham, N.C.: Duke University Press, 1963.

37. Urlanis, B. *Voiny i narodonaseleniye Evrope.* Moscow: Isd. Soz. Ekon. Literatury, 1960.

38. Vexliard, A. "Psychological Theories of P. Sorokin," in Philip Allen (ed.), *Pitirim A. Sorokin in Review.* Durham, N.C.: Duke University Press, 1963.

39. von Wiese, L. "Ideenkultur und Sinnenkultur," in *Archiv für Rechts und Sozial Philosophie,* Band XXXI, Heft 3.

40. Wright, Q. *A Study of War,* 2 vols. Chicago: University of Chicago Press, 1942.

17

S. N. Eisenstadt

Processes of Change and

Institutionalization of the Political

Systems of Centralized Empires

The present chapter[1] will attempt to shed some light on problems of social change through the analysis of the processes of change in one specific type of political *system* — the so-called centralized bureaucratic empire. This type of political system comprises the major historical societies, namely: (a) the ancient empires — especially the Egyptian, Babylonian, and, possibly, the Inca and Aztec as well; (b) the Chinese empire from the Han period to the Ch'ing; (c) the various Iranian empires, especially the Sassanid and, to a smaller extent, the Parthian and Achmenid; (d) the Roman empire and the various Hellenistic empires; (e) the Byzantine empire; (f) several ancient Hindu states, especially the Maury and Gupta, and Mogul empires; (g) the Arab Caliphate, especially from the reign of the Abbassides and Fatimids, the Arab Muslim states in the Mediterranean and Iran, and, finally, the Ottoman empire; (h) the West, Central, and East European states from the fall of the feudal systems through the Age of Absolutism; (i) conquest-empires — that is, the various political systems established in non-European countries as a result of European

[1] This analysis is based on a broader work by the author on the political system of centralized empires (13). For preliminary formulations see Eisenstadt (9; 10; 11; 12), where full bibliographical references are given. Several parts of this chapter have been published before in *Diogène* (11) and are reproduced here by permission of the editors.

expansion, colonization, and conquest, especially the Spanish-American and French empires and the British Colonial empire in India.

The theoretical focus of the analysis will be an attempt to investigate the extent to which such problems of change can be analyzed within the framework of a systematic sociological approach and not only as cases of discrete historical developments. From this point of view these empires are of special interest, as they have been to historians at least from Gibbon on up to such modern historians as Baynes (2), Lewis (15), Cahen (5; 6; 7), Ostrogorsky (16; 17; 18), Jones (14), and Boak (4). An analysis of these historial works, especially the more recent ones, shows that some recurring general theses about the causes of change in these empires or their decline — beyond the description of the details of development of any specific society — are applicable to most of them (see in greater detail Eisenstadt [11]).

Among these general causes of change, the most important are the emphasis on the growing burden of bureaucracy, the shrinkage of economic resources and manpower, and the loss of civic spirit. While some of these "causes," such as the importance of civic spirit, seem — at least at first glance — to apply to all political systems, most of the other causes listed by these historians are more closely related to problems that were specific to the political systems of the centralized empires.

Thus the work of these historians, each of whom has been mainly interested in the development of a particular society, indicates that we are dealing with a certain general type of political system with its own characteristic problems and that the processes of change and decline which may seem unique to each society are to some extent rooted in the nature of the political system common to all these societies. It is here that a sociological approach to political systems in general and to the specific systems of these empires may attempt to analyze in a systematic way the processes of change taking place in them.

The Establishment of the Empires

The basic characteristic of the political systems of these empires was the co-existence within the framework of the same political institutions of traditional, undifferentiated types of political activities, orientations, and organizations, and of more differentiated, specifically *political* ones. In order to understand these characteristics, it will be best to describe briefly the concrete processes of development by which these empires were established.

The majority of these centralized bureaucratic empires developed from either: (a) patrimonial empires such as Egypt, or the Sassanid Empire; (b) dualistic nomad-sedentary empires (necessarily sharing many characteristics with the patrimonial ones); (c) feudal systems, such as the

European absolutist states; and (d) city-states (the Roman and Hellenistic Empires).

These empires were characterized on the one hand as relatively differentiated, autonomous, centralized political structures, by a well developed bureaucracy and by a relatively direct approach of the rulers to the subjects. On the other hand, this differentiation of the political structure was limited by the traditional legitimation of the rulers and by the lack of any political rights of the subjects.

Despite the great variety in historical and cultural settings, certain common features in the first stages of establishment of polities may be found. The initiative for the establishment of these polities came in all cases from men already in power — emperors, kings, or members of a patrician ruling elite (like the more active and dynamic element of the patrician ruling elite in Republican Rome). In most cases, the rulers were either members of established patrician, patrimonial, tribal, or feudal families or were usurpers, coming from lower-class families, who attempted to establish new dynasties or to conquer new territories. In some cases, such rulers, whatever their origin, were conquerors who attempted to vanquish foreign territories and establish their rule over them. In most cases such empires arose in periods of unrest, turmoil, or dismemberment of the existing political system — a patrician city-state, a tribe, a patrimonial empire, or a feudal system — or of acute strife within them. Usually the rulers' aim was the re-establishment of peace and order. But at the same time, they did not attempt to restore the old order in its entirety, even though for propagandist and opportunistic reasons they sometimes represented the new regime as a restoration of the old order. They always had some vision of unity. They aimed to establish a more centralized, unified polity in which they could monopolize political decisions and the setting of political goals without being bound by various traditional aristocratic, tribal, or patrician groups. Even when they were conquerors — as in the case of the Roman, Islamic, or Spanish-American empires — they also had some such vision of unity and attempted to transmit it to at least segments of the conquered population.

These aims were very often oriented against, and encountered the opposition of, various social and political groups. However great the turmoil, unrest, and internal strife may have been, some groups always existed who either benefited from such states of unrest, or hoped to do so, or aimed to re-establish the "old" order in which they themselves had held positions of power and influence. These groups — typically consisting of aristocratic, patrician, or more traditional urban and cultural elites — usually felt themselves menaced by the new aims and activities of the rulers. They believed that their position was threatened by the trend toward political centralization and they were not willing to help in the implementation of this trend. Therefore they frequently withdrew their political and economic support from the rulers, plotting and working against them either in open political warfare or by sleight of hand, infiltration, and intrigues.

Against these aristocratic or patrician forces, the rulers had to find allies, whether passive or active, in order to implement their policies. They had to forge instruments of power and policy with which to mobilize the resources they needed — economic resources, manpower, or political support. The rulers naturally tried to find such allies among the groups and strata whose interests were opposed to those of the more traditional and aristocratic groups and who could benefit by weakening them and by establishing a more unified polity. These allies were, basically, of two kinds. The first were more active (mostly urban) economic, cultural, and professional groups, who, by origin and/or by their social interests and orientations, were opposed to the aristocratic-traditional groups. The second were the wider, politically and socially more passive strata — especially peasants and to a smaller extent lower-class urban groups who could benefit, even if indirectly, from the weakening of the aristocratic forces and from the establishment of peace and order by the rulers. It was from these groups and strata that the rulers hoped to mobilize the resources they needed.

In order to mobilize these resources and to implement their policies, the rulers also had to forge reliable instruments of political and administrative action through which they could provide various services to the major strata which were their potential allies or supporters. In most instances, the rulers could draw on some existing administrative and political organs and personnel. But even when such organs of administration were available — with the personnel to staff them — the rulers had to transform these administrative organs in order to adapt them to their own purposes. Insofar as the existing personnel were related to the aristocratic forces opposing the rulers, they often had to be replaced. But changes of personnel were not enough. The rulers also needed some assurance that the new personnel would remain faithful to them and dependent on them, that they would not be won over by the opposing forces. Moreover, the rulers had to make sure that these administrative organs would be so set up as to be able to perform various functions, both for the rulers themselves and for their supporters among the major strata in the society. To this end, the rulers attempted to concentrate in their own hands the nominations to these positions. They tried, as far as possible, to appoint persons who were both loyal to them and qualified to execute the necessary tasks. The rulers also attempted to control the budgets of these administrative organs and to have enough resources at their disposal to provide for the expenses of maintaining the officials. The rulers tended to stress that these officials were either their own personal servants, or servants of the polity which they wanted to establish, but not representatives of any particular groups or strata in the society.

In general, then, the rulers tried to make these organs as independent as possible of the more traditional and aristocratic strata and groups, and to give them power and prestige vis-à-vis these strata. Here the rulers had, necessarily, to allow these administrative personnel some measure of autonomy and independence to enable them to perform services for the population at large.

True, the rulers very often wanted to use these organs only — or mainly — for exploitative purposes so as to tap the resources of the population. But even in conquest empires, if the rulers wanted to perpetuate their rule, they had to allow these services to take into account the needs of the major social groups — if only to provide them with peace, security, and some minimal services.

It was out of the interplay of the various forces described above that the basic characteristics of the political system of these empires — the co-existence of traditional and differentiated political activities and organizations and the development of a *limited* tendency to autonomy of political institutions — were shaped. This development was manifest, first, in the tendency toward political *centralization*, second, in the development by the rulers of autonomous political goals, and, third, in the relatively high degree of organizational autonomy of executive and administrative activities.

But the extent of differentiation of political activities, organizations, and goals was still limited by several important factors. First, the legitimation of the rulers in these regimes was usually couched in traditional-religious terms, even if the rulers tended to stress their own ultimate monopoly of such traditional values and tried to deny that other (traditional) groups could also share in this monopoly. Second, the political role of the subject was not fully distinguished from other basic societal roles — such as, for instance, membership in local communities; the individual's political role was often defined almost totally by membership in such groups, and the citizen or subject did not exercise any direct political rights through a system of voting or franchise. Third, many traditional ascriptive units, such as aristocratic lineages or territorial communities, performed a number of crucial political functions and served as units of political representation. As a consequence, the scope of political activity and participation was far narrower than in most modern and contemporary political systems.

The existence of both traditional and differentiated political orientations, activities, and organizations created within these empires a complex interrelation between the political institutions and other parts of the social structure. The rulers were in need of both "traditional" and more complex, differentiated political support and were dependent on both. Their "traditional" dependence on other parts of the social structure was manifest in their need to uphold the traditional legitimation and the traditionally defined "unconditional" political attitudes that identified them with many groups. On the other hand, the rulers' tendency to political independence and autonomy forced them to rely on types of resources not available through ascriptive-traditional commitments and relations. The rulers were here, as shown above, in need of a more flexible means of support than the revenues and other resources embedded in traditional, ascriptive groups and committed to more or less fixed goals; what they needed was resources that could be used to implement their varied goals according to their own political consideration.

Similarly, the political demands made on the rulers by different groups in the society were both of the traditional, "ascriptive" type, consisting of demands to uphold the fixed traditional rights and benefits of various groups, and of more complex and differentiated types of demands. For example, a group might demand participation in the formation of different economic or social policies of the society or it might even demand the right to play a part in the legitimation and accountability of the rulers. Because of all these factors even the "traditional" legitimation of the rulers was, in these societies, no longer based on "automatic," "fixed" support.

These two types of political orientation did not co-exist in these political systems in separate "compartments," bound together only in some loose and unstable way. Rather, they operated within the same institutions, and the continuity of each type of political activity was dependent on the existence of both types of political orientation. For this reason, the activities of the rulers were, paradoxically, oriented to maintaining basic *traditional* legitimation through manipulation not only of traditional but also of non-traditional support, and also to mobilizing, through non-traditional channels, "traditional" resources for politically autonomous goals.

As a result, the political system of these empires could subsist only insofar as it was possible to maintain, simultaneously and continuously within the framework of the same political institutions, both the traditional and the more differentiated levels of legitimation, support, and political organization. The continuity of these systems was dependent on the uninterrupted existence of a certain balance between political activity and involvement on the part of certain elements of the population, and of political non-involvement or apathy toward central political issues by the majority of the population. This limited political involvement could assure some of the more flexible political support required by the rulers, while the apathy of the majority was necessary for maintenance of the traditional legitimation of the rulers.

Contradictions Within the Empires

The preceding analysis is admittedly a somewhat overgeneralized summary of complex historical events, but it does serve to shed some light on the processes of institutionalization of these — and perhaps also of other — types of political systems, as well as directing attention to the problems of their continuity and change. These political systems became institutionalized through the juxtaposition of two different types of conditions: first, the existence or appearance of political leaders or rulers with strong political aspirations to establish wider, centralized political entities; and, second, the existence of appropriate social conditions — such as certain levels of social and economic differentiation — which could assure resources necessary for the development and maintenance of the institutions organized by the rulers and for the implementation of their policies. Indeed, the likelihood that the characteristics of a centralized bureaucratic empire would be institutionalized seems to have increased in direct proportion to the degree that both of these conditions existed at any given time.[2]

However, the mere institutionalization of these characteristics did not in itself guarantee the *continuity* of the system. In principle, the perpetuation of the system was dependent on the continuation of the same conditions that enabled its institutionalization in the first place — that is, the availability of rulers with strong political vision and strong ambitions for political autonomy, as well as a degree of social differentiation that would assure the provision of resources to the rulers and their institutions. But the persistence of neither of these two conditions could be taken for granted: methods had to be devised to guarantee an adequate supply of personnel for the central political positions, whether from within the ruling houses or through recruitment from other groups and strata; and special policies, activities, and organizations had to be set up to guarantee the *continuous* willingness and ability of various strata to provide the resources necessary to the ruler, be they economic resources or a certain level of political support.

Moreover, the very establishment of special institutional devices to guarantee the persistence of these conditions created potential contradictions within the new political systems — contradictions that could easily be starting points of processes of change within them. One set of contradictions arose from the fact that the rulers had to pursue continuously certain policies that were oriented against some social groups while favoring others, thus intensifying potential opposition to their basic premises among important sectors of the society. Another set of contradictions centered on the fact that the personnel of the very organs created for the implementation of the policies of the rulers necessarily developed special orientations and interests of their own which often conflicted with the interests of the rulers and led these personnel to challenge the basic premises of the system. To make these contradictions clearer, let us examine in more detail the policies of the rulers.

The rulers of these empires tended to develop three basic political orientations toward resources. First, they were interested in the limited promotion of *free* resources — in freeing them, that is, from commitment

[2] For a fuller exposition of this hypothesis see Eisenstadt (12).

to traditional aristocratic groups. Second, the rulers were interested in *controlling* these resources — in committing them, as it were, to their own use. Third, the rulers tended to adopt various goals — military expansions, for example — which might in themselves exhaust many available free resources. The contradictions among these different orientations toward resources, though not always consciously grasped by the rulers, were nevertheless implicit in their structural position, in the problems and exigencies with which they dealt, and in the concrete policies they employed in order to solve these problems (see in detail Eisenstadt [10]).

The area where these contradictions were most pronounced was that of legitimation and stratification. As we have seen, the rulers often attempted to limit the aristocracy's power and to create new status groups. But these attempts faced several obstacles. Regardless of the extent of the monarchs' independent activities in this field, of the number of new titles created, or of the degree of encouragement of new strata, the symbols of status conferred by the rulers were usually very similar to those already borne by the landed, hereditary aristocracy or by some religious elites. The creation of an entirely new secular and "rational" type of legitimation based upon universalistic religious or socio-political principles was either beyond their horizon and/or against their basic political interest. It would necessarily involve extending the sphere of political participation and consequently the growing influence of various strata in the political institutions. Therefore, the rulers were usually unable to transcend the symbols of stratification and legitimation borne and represented by the very strata whose influence they wanted to limit. For this reason, the ability of the rulers to appeal to the lower strata of the population was obviously restricted. Even more important, because of the emphasis on the superiority and worth of aristocratic symbols and values, many middle strata and new groups tended to adopt them and consequently to "aristocratize" themselves.

Contradictions in the rulers' policies and goals could also develop from other sources. However tradition-bound the ruling elites may have been, their policies required the creation and propagation of more flexible free resources in various institutional fields. The propagation of such free resources strengthened many religious, intellectual, and legal groups like the urban bourgeois, religious and secular intelligentsia, professional lawyer associations whose value orientations were much more flexible than the traditional ones. Moreover, the orientations and values of the broader middle strata of the society were often similar to those propagated by these more active elite groups. Although in many cases, as in Byzantium and especially China, these middle strata were weak and succumbed to the influence of the more conservative groups and policies of the ruling elite, in other cases — as in Europe — they developed into relatively independent centers of power, whose opposition to the rulers was only stimulated by more conservative policies.

Similar contradictions may also be discerned in the activities of the rulers in the economic field. First of all, the main economic aims of the rulers of these empires — mobilization of resources for implementation of any one policy at any given moment of time, and maintenance of conditions maximizing the availability of independent "free" resources — posed for the rulers a series of dilemmas which could be extremely acute in relatively undifferentiated economic systems and which could give rise to intense contradictions between the long-term and short-term economic policies of the rulers. The continuous need to mobilize extensive resources could often exhaust the available "free" resources and make the rulers dependent on the more traditional forces. The big landowners and merchants, who constituted important centers of economic power, quite often tried to intensify this contradition by providing the government with short-term allocations at the price of buttressing their own positions and at the expense of the rulers. The rulers had to accept the services and resources of these groups, giving them in turn concessions like exemptions from taxes or permission to levy their own troops that often tended to undermine the long-run availability of various free resources and to weaken the position of the rulers.

A similar contradiction existed between the long-range and short-range policies dealing with problems of administrative manpower. In many cases there was not enough manpower available for the execution of various administrative and political tasks or, because of inadequate communication and technical facilities, it was very difficult to supervise such personnel effectively. It then became necessary to "farm out" various functions and positions, either to local gentry and landowners or to officials who used these state functions as a means of entering the aristocracy.

The best example of how the social groups created by the ruling elite became partially opposed to its aims and basic political premises is the development of the system of selling offices, a practice which was closely connected in these empires with the entire process of recruitment into the bureaucracy (19). At first, this practice was usually introduced by the rulers as a means of solving their financial problems and admitting new, non-aristocratic elements into their service. But in time, in most of these societies, the bureaucracy came to regard its offices as possessions and either transmitted them in the family or sold them in the market. In this way the rulers, despite many efforts to the contrary, slowly lost an important measure of control over these offices. This was only an instance of the more general tendency of the bureaucracy — the very instrument of power of the rulers — to "aristocratize" itself, to acquire symbols of aristocratic status, and to ally itself with older aristocratic forces. When this happened, the bureaucracy was likely to replace its goal of service to the rulers with the goal of self-aggrandizement — its members using their positions for enriching themselves and their families, thus losing their efficiency for the rulers and becoming a growing burden on the economy.

As the process of aristocratization intensified, the supply of political leaders for the central political institutions dwindled. The more active members of the bureaucracy became alienated from the regime, either succumbing to the aristocratic forces and to complete political apathy, or becoming centers of social and political upheaval and change.

Just as contradictions developed in the political orientations of the rulers, so too they tended to develop in the political attitudes and activities of the members of different strata of these societies. We can distinguish several characteristic attitudes of these strata toward the basic premises of the empires and the aims of their rulers.

The first attitude (evinced chiefly by the aristocracy) was one of opposition to these premises. The second attitude, that of relatively passive and conditional acceptance of the system, was manifested mainly by the peasantry and, sometimes also, by other groups interested only in maintaining their own limited local autonomy and their immediate economic interests. The third attitude, found mostly among the bureaucracy and parts of the urban groups and professional and cultural elites, consisted of a basic identification with the premises of the political system and a willingness to fight for its interests within the existing framework of political institutions and the polities set up by the rulers. The fourth attitude, developed mainly by the more differentiated urban groups and professional and intellectual elites, favored changes in the scope of the political system. This attitude, most clearly evinced by European middle-class and intellectual groups at the end of the eighteenth century, was manifested in various attempts to change the basic premises of the political system, to widen the patterns of political participation within it, and/ or to find new symbols and criteria of political activity and commitment which transcended the given political system.

These attitudes often overlapped in particular instances, and the concrete attitudes of each group and stratum varied in different societies and periods. Moreover, the attitudes of any one group were never homogeneous and stable; they could change significantly according to the demands of the rulers and other conditions. The concrete constellations of these different political attitudes of the major social groups greatly influenced the extent of their political participation and the scope and the nature of political leadership that tended to develop from within these groups. Here, again, the most significant trend from the viewpoint of continuity of these systems was the bureaucracy's tendency to aristocratize itself and thus undermine the very conditions of such continuity.

Trends Toward Bureaucratic Autonomy

But the contradictions in the activities of the rulers and the various strata were not the only important foci of potential change in these political systems. Of no less importance was the possibility, already mentioned, that the very organs created to implement the rulers' policies could develop orientations and activities opposed to the basic premises of these political systems. The most important possibility of this kind was rooted in the tendency of the bureaucratic personnel to develop autonomous political orientations and activities of their own.

This tendency had several causes. First, the power these bureaucracies acquired in societies where few "constitutional" limits were placed on power and in which access to power was relatively limited put the members of the bureaucracy in an especially privileged position (see 20, pp. 122–166; 21; 8; 3). Second, the great emphasis in these societies on ascriptive symbols of status necessarily "tempted" the members of the bureaucracy to use their position to acquire such symbols or to make the positions themselves the basis of such symbols. Third, the relatively low level of economic development and social differentiation permitted very little specialization of professional roles and inadequate remuneration for them. The fact that in most of these societies the selling of offices was a very common expedient fully attests to this.

For all these reasons, the different echelons of these centralized bureaucracies may often have tended to distort many of the system's customary or explicit rules, diverting its services to benefit either themselves or some social group with whom they had become identified, and becoming alienated from other strata and groups in the society and oppressive toward them. In other words, they might displace their service goals to the rulers and/or to given social strata and emphasize goals of self-interest and aggrandizement instead.

On the other hand, the relative political weakness of many political groups and the great dependence of the bureaucracy on the kings could often have the effect of undermining the relative autonomy of the bureaucracy through its total subjugation to the rulers. The rulers often had the power to divert all the activities of the bureaucracy to their own exclusive use without allowing it to perform any continuous services to different strata in the society or to follow any general rules for providing services.

Consequently, the bureaucratic administration in these societies could develop political orientations that were to some extent opposed to the basic premises of the rulers' politics, and which would undermine their foundations and generate processes of change that could not be contained with the existing framework.

The most important types of political orientation developed by the bureaucracies in the historical bureaucratic empires were: (a) maintenance of service orientations both to the rulers and to the major strata (with usually greater emphasis — in the societies studied here — on the services to the rulers); (b) development into a passive tool of the ruler with little internal autonomy and few services to the different strata of the population; (c) displacement of its service goals to the various strata and to the polity in favor of goals of self-aggrandizement or usurpation of power exclusively in its own favor and/or in favor of a group with which it had become closely identified; and (d) displacement of its service goals to the major strata in favor of goals of self-aggrandizement and attainment of political power *together with* maintenance of service goals to the polity and the rulers. All the bureaucratic administrations in the historical bureaucratic empires usually evinced some mixture of all four tendencies, although a particular tendency usually predominated for at least part, if not the whole of the history of a particular historic polity. As we shall see later, these different orientations of the bureaucracy were of great importance for the continuity of these political systems — or for the processes of change which took place.

Processes of Change and Disintegration

The possibilities of change were thus built into the nature of these systems. The very process by which the special characteristics of the systems were institutionalized not only failed to assure the continuity of the system but tended also to create additional systemic "pushes" toward change. The interplay of the rulers' policies and the political orientations and activities of the major social groups constituted the crux of the political processes of change within these societies and could bring about the development of conditions leading to the downfall of the empires. The concrete constellations of these various factors greatly influenced both the *extent* of the changes that took place and the *ability* of these systems to develop various mechanisms which could counteract the impending changes and absorb them.

Specifically, the main factors generating processes of change were: (a) the continuous needs of the rulers for different types of resources and especially their great dependence on flexible resources; (b) the rulers' attempts to maintain their own positions of control, both through traditional legitimation and effective political control over the more flexible forces in the society; (c) the possibility of the development in most of these societies of what has been called "primacy of foreign policy" (1) and consequently great and continuous sensitivity of the internal structure of the empires to external pressures and to political and economic developments in the international field; (d) the consequent needs of the rulers to intensify the mobilization of resources in order to deal with problems arising from changes in military, diplomatic, and economic international situations; (e) the development of autonomous orientations and goals among the major strata and their respective demands on the rulers. Insofar as strong contradictions developed among these several factors, and especially insofar as the rulers emphasized very "expensive" goals that exhausted the available economic and manpower resources, or if there developed strong, autonomous political orientations among dif-

ferent strata, the rulers were often caught on the horns of the basic dilemmas inherent in their own political orientations, goals, and policies and
were unable to absorb political systems resulting from these different developments.

In such situations, the special sensitivities were brought out, and forces
were generated which could undermine the delicate balance between
political participation and apathy on which the continuity of these systems depended. When the balance was threatened, the rulers' tendency
to maintain active control over different strata could become predominant,
thus increasing the power of traditional forces, sharpening the conflicts
between them and the more flexible, differentiated strata, and either destroying or alienating the "free" groups and strata from the rulers. The
excessive demands of the rulers that developed in such situations, the
growing public expenditures, and the consequent increase of taxation and
inflation, if not checked, often struck hardest at those groups whose economic structures were based on the more flexible resources and tended
to deplete them. This depletion may have taken on different, varying
forms: outright apathy and consequent shrinking of manpower; weakening of the more independent economic elements and their subordination
to more conservative, aristocratic-patrimonial (or feudal) elements; and
depletion or flight of mobile capital. It is important to note that these
processes were usually closely related to the "aristocratization" or ossifi-
cation of the bureaucracy, with its growing parasitic exploitation of the
economy, and — equally important — to a sharp decline in the supply
of active political personnel loyal to the regime.

In the face of such depletion of native manpower, there often developed a continuous flux of foreign elements into the centers of the realm.
In the military sphere, these foreign groups initially were mere mercenaries and personal helpers of the rulers. Gradually, however, as the supply of reliable native personnel was exhausted, and as a result of growing external and internal exigencies, these foreign mercenaries succeeded
in infiltrating into some of the most important political posts (in such
roles as eunuchs, military commandants, and viziers), and finally in totally usurping the ultimate political power. Nor was foreign manpower
important only in the military sphere: there could be a similar influx of
foreign merchants, who sometimes, as in Byzantium or the Ottoman
Empire, succeeded gradually in monopolizing all the tradeposts abandoned by the depleted indigenous merchants.

In some cases — Europe, for example — in which the economically and
socially more active strata were depleted, they became alienated from
the rulers and their policies and from the political institutions of the society, and became hotbeds of revolt and changes.

Such developments usually intensified the great sensitivity of the
rulers and the society to external economic and political changes. Such
economic disturbances, for example, as changes in trade routes or inter-

national prices, along with constant political changes such as the immigration of foreign groups or outright invasion, tended to lessen the rulers' capacity to cope effectively with domestic events. It was in such cases that the rulers often tended to adopt short-sighted policies, based mostly on experience of the past and on their own limited and contradictory perception of the situation. These policies were aimed chiefly at increasing centralized control through progressive restriction of the main social groups — as if such restriction would somehow solve the problems posed by the changing situation of these societies.

As we have said, the development of different political orientations by the bureaucracy was an important impetus to change in these political systems. Insofar as the bureaucracy maintained its basic service orientations both to the rulers and to the major strata, it usually contributed to the continuity and stability of the regimes and especially to the maintenance of the basic conditions of the centralized bureaucratic regimes. In those societies or periods in which such service orientations were maintained by the bureaucracy, the rulers were able, with the help of the bureaucracy, to maintain their own positions and those of those strata who supported them, and to keep in check the strata who were opposed to the basic prerequisites of the centralized political systems. But insofar as the bureaucracy was able to monopolize the highest social, political, and economic positions and to minimize its political responsibility and responsiveness to the rulers and/or the major flexible strata, it often contributed to the weakening of the social structure.

In day-to-day terms, this means that the total subservence of the bureaucracy to the ruler, as in the cases of Prussia and the Ottoman Empire, was usually associated with the use of force to a very high degree in implementing the rulers' goals against strong opposition. At the same time, there was relatively little direct support for the rulers from those types of group (such as urban classes, the free peasantry, and so on) who were in the best position to provide the resources needed for the implementation of the rulers' goals and the development of centralized, bureaucratic polities. Ultimately, because of the paucity of requisite free resources and because of their strongly prescriptive orientations, the rulers had to turn to the more traditional and ascriptive (aristocratic) groups, had to make use of their social prestige, and eventually had to come to some sort of stable *modus vivendi* with them. But by turning to the aristocracy, the rulers were constantly in danger of weakening and alienating the more flexible groups and strata, who were themselves aspiring to some *entente* with the rulers. This in turn was a contributory cause of the gradual disintegration of these empires either through the strengthening of the aristocratic, ascriptive elements and the consequent development of a pre-bureaucratic (patrimonial or feudal) system (as the feudal system which developed gradually in Europe after the downfall of the Western Roman Empire, or the patrimonial system that developed after the downfall of the Egyptian Empires), through outright disintegration and dismemberment of the polity under external pressure, or, finally, through the development, usually by some revolutionary movement, of a still more differentiated "modern" type of political structure, as was the case in most Western European countries.

The preceding analysis indicates that the bureaucracy, by virtue of its central regulative functions in these systems, performed very important tasks in the regulation of free-floating power in the historical bureaucratic societies and in the maintenance of a continuous and regulated flow of such power and resources. But to the extent that the bureaucracy became a semi-independent stratum or was not effectively controlled in the political field, it may itself have become an omnivorous consumer of the available free resources, and it may greatly have impeded the functioning of the basic institutional framework of these societies and thus constituted a stumbling block to the continuous flow of regulated generalized power.

The general problems outlined here were rooted in the basic characteristics of the social and political structures of all these empires. They were common, if only in varying degrees, to all of them. However, the exact ways in which these problems developed, and the exact processes which caused them, varied in different empires according to the specific constellation of the structural characteristics already discussed. For any particular case, various external processes and unique historical circumstances also played their part in forcing any one empire into the course of development it took.

The *internal* aspects of the social structure of these empires that influenced the processes of development and disintegration within them can now be summarized. (1) The nature of the goals of the rulers is crucial. It is essential to know whether they were chiefly military and expansionist or whether they were oriented more to the maintenance of a cultural order or to economic advancement. Furthermore, the demands which the implementation of these goals made on the various types of resources available in the society was a force to bring about change. (2) Processes of change and disintegration were greatly influenced by (a) the major policies developed by the rulers for the implementation of their goals and the repercussions of these policies on the relative strength of different strata; (b) changes in the relative strength of such strata as a result of internal economic, religious, or political developments; (c) the development of internal and external exigencies and the ways in which the policies developed to deal with them influenced the strength of different groups. (3) The initial level of social and economic differentiation in any given society. (4) The initial social composition of these societies. Development was necessarily influenced by the relative strength of different social groups — the aristocracy, the various urban groups, and the peasantry — and the extent to which the rulers could find enough supporters among them. (5) Of particular importance was the extent to which there existed common cultural and political bonds encompassing the major social groups and the rulers (as, for instance, in the case of the Confucian order in China) or, on the other hand, the extent to which various social and cultural groups were bearers of independent values and orientations not entirely identified with the rulers and the polity.

Among the more *external* or "accidental" causes of change, we should mention different degrees of external pressure, major movements of population, conquests of nomads, international economic fluctuations, or the degree to which there existed from the beginning ethnic heterogeneity in a given society. Also of crucial importance was the specific geopolitical situation of any polity. Thus, the geopolitical position of Byzantium at the crossroads of Europe and Asia, of East and West, greatly influenced both its vulnerability to invasions and its political self-constellation.

In general, it was some combination of the kinds of external and internal exigencies summarized above that precipitated change in the political systems of these empires. Hence, the greater the intensity of the internal contradictions discussed and of the pressure of external exigencies that could not be dealt with by the internal forces of the society, the quicker and more intensive was the accumulation of processes of change in these societies.

Thus, to give only a few examples (for fuller exposition see Eisenstadt [13]), the fact that in China various invasions, rebellions, and the famous "dynastic cycles" never undermined for very long the basic institutional structure of the Chinese empire (from the Han to the Ch'ing), can be understood if one is aware of three crucial factors. First, its geopolitical position made it to some extent immune from the heavy impact of external forces. Second, the relative weakness of the aristocracy, and the predominance of the gentry, tended to enhance the position of the centralized rulers. Third, the Confucian literati and bureaucracy, who constituted the backbone of the social and political structure and intervened between the central government and the major social strata, provided an indispensable framework of continuity and unity of the empire. When we compare these features of China with the geopolitical vulnerability of the Byzantine Empire, its strong sensitivity to invasions and internal developments, the continuous struggle between the aristocracy and the free peasantry, or with the great importance of the autonomous religious and cultural groups in the Roman and Arabic empires, as well as the different geopolitical position of these empires, we may in turn understand their greater vulnerability to external pressures and the inability of their rulers to cope with the internal forces which developed within them.

Conclusion

The preceding analysis of the processes of change in the centralized bureaucratic empires may provide a general notion of the ways in which the problem of change can be analyzed within a systemic-structural framework and applied to historical entities. Perhaps the first important upshot of our analysis is that it is impossible to analyze processes of change systematically without full explication of the political (or social, or economic, or cultural) system with reference to which the analysis of change is undertaken. Furthermore, because any process of change is a historical entity, it is obviously necessary to describe the development of the process within the concrete entity. But once we are interested in going beyond such idiographic description, and try to make explicit the analytical assumptions that are only implicit in the individual histories, it becomes necessary to specify clearly *which* structural or systemic aspects of a historical entity are being analyzed in any given case.

Our analysis also shows that within the system analyzed here (and, I would venture to say, within any institutional system, whether political, economic, or cultural) there exist inherent predilections to change — that is, the very establishment or "institutionalization" of such a system creates several inherent possibilities of change. These inherent predilections to change are rooted in the fact that any "system" denotes a certain level of institutionalization of social activities, roles, and organizations which necessitate, for their establishment and maintenance, the provision of various resources from different parts of the society. Such resources have to be mobilized from different groups whose activities are organized not only in the framework of the given institutional system under analysis (for example, a given political system) but also of other institutional systems (for example, economic or cultural systems).

These facts create several problems from the point of view of full institutionalization of any given structural system. In the first place, differences may exist among various groups in the extent of their willingness or ability to provide the resources needed by the system and in the ability of the system to mobilize these resources from them. Second, various contradictions may also develop between the demands of the given institutional system and those of other institutional systems in which these groups are organized. Thus the process of institutionalization of any system is never complete and necessarily contains several possibilities of conflict and change.

But not only is the process of institutionalization never complete (in the sense that the articulation and upholding of its norms are never full or the same in all parts of a society); it also necessarily involves several additional contradictions which tend to become foci of conflict and change. The very process of institutionalization of any social system, the establishment of specific norms and organizations, creates new forces which generate pressures on the resources needed by the system. Moreover, organizations created by such institutionalization may easily develop independent needs, orientations, and demands of their own, which may in themselves create demands and pressures on the resources needed for the maintenance of the larger system. These organizations, having independent needs, may also ally themselves with some of the groups antagonistic to the larger system of which they form a part or unwittingly reinforce such groups and antagonistic orientations.

But if such predilections to change are necessarily built into any system, the direction and scope of such change is not entirely random but is greatly dependent on the nature of the system from which they are generated. Thus, although all political systems are necessarily influenced by external exigencies and pressure, the special sensitivity of the centralized bureaucratic empires to such exigencies and pressures and to international economic fluctuations was rooted, first, in the great emphasis of their rulers on military and expansionist goals, and, second, in the dependence of these rulers on various resources the availability of which was itself dependent on such international economic situations. The dangers to these political systems from excessive taxation and inflation were again rooted in the high expense of implementing the rulers' goals and in the great importance of various flexible resources for the general political position of the rulers of these empires.

Similarly, while all political systems are influenced by, and dependent upon, the efficiency and political loyalty of whatever administrative personnel exists within them, the special sensitivity of these empires to the working of the bureaucracy and to the possibility of its becoming "aristocratized," parasitic, and overswollen was rooted, first, in the fact that the bureaucracy was the main instrument of the rulers in the implementation of their goals and in their struggle with their political opponents; and, second, in the constant danger of depletion of free resources by the encroachments of various aristocratic or traditional groups. Finally, the sensitivity of these political systems to an excess of political passivity or "other-worldliness" — or a lack of what some of the historians have called "civic spirit" — was rooted in their dependence on the maintenance of a certain extent of *active* political participation, and not only on general identification with the regime or the rulers. It was these specific sensitivities that constituted the foci from which the impetus to change or the ability to contain such changes within these systems developed.

It can be claimed that any process of institutionalization of a social, political, or economic system creates the possibility of the development, within it, of several "anti-systems," of institutional foci and groups which tend to develop relatively negative, ambivalent, or contradictory orientations towards the premises of the system. While the strength of such "anti-systems" may vary greatly and they may, in any society, often be latent for very long periods of time yet they may also, under propitious conditions, serve as important foci of change.

While the existence of such contradictions or conflicts between the different institutional spheres and different groups of any society does not preclude the possibility of relatively continuous maintenance of the boundaries of a system through a hierarchy of norms, accommodation, or partial insulation of different subsystems, yet it always emphasizes the possibility of conflict and of potential changes.

In the political systems of the centralized empires, the chief focus of potential change was the possibility of development of levels of social differentiation which could generate political demands and pressures that the rulers were either unable to absorb within the framework of the existing system or which undermined the resources needed by the rulers and the system.

Such developments here stemmed mainly, though not exclusively, from two spheres. One was the sphere of economic and social organization. The level of differentiation of this sphere and the nature of its internal, autonomous organization was of crucial importance for the development of different levels of resources, on the one hand, and of political demands, on the other. The other sphere was that of values. The critical importance of values lies in the fact that they provided the legitimation of the systems and their rulers and that they regulated many aspects of communication and may therefore have greatly influenced the level of demands and the expectations of different groups from the central political institutions. While in many cases the sphere of values could have guaranteed that the level of such demands remained within the confines of the system, on the other hand it might also become a very important focus of new developments, such, for example, as the charismatic innovations in the Islamic and European countries which may easily have been responsible for undermining the existing system and creating entirely new perceptions of the political sphere among many social groups.

Both spheres have therefore been of great importance from the point of view of the specific sensibilities of these systems and of the generation of change within them. Their impact on the destiny of these political systems has been of crucial significance when developments in the two spheres have combined in the same direction — either in the direction of increasing or of diminishing differentiation.

BIBLIOGRAPHY

1. Altheim, F. *Gesicht von Abend und Morgen.* Frankfurt: Fisher Verlag, 1955.

2. Baynes, N. H. "The Decline of the Roman Power in Western Empire," reprinted in *Byzantine Studies and Other Essays.* London: Oxford University Press, 1955.

3. Beloff, M. *The Age of Absolutism.* New York: Hillary, 1954.

4. Boak, A.E.R. "The Role of Policy in the Fall of the Roman Empire," *Michigan Alumnus Quarterly Review,* Vol. 56 (1950), pp. 291–294.

5. Cahen, C. L. "L'Histoire economique et social de l'Orient musulman medieval," *Studia Islamica,* Vol. 3. Paris: Maisoneuff, 1955, pp. 93–116.

6. Cahen, C. L. "Les facteurs economiques et sociaux dans L'Ankylose culturelle de L'Islam," in R. Brunschvig and G. E. von Grunebaum (eds.), *Classicisme et decline culturel dans l'historie de L'Islam*. Paris: Besson Chantenerel, 1957, pp. 195–217.

7. Cahen, C. L. Lecons d'histoire musulmane, Cours de la Sorbonne, Vol. 1–3. Paris. (mimeo)

8. Eberhard, W. "The Political Function of Astronomy and Astronomers in Han China," in J. K. Fairbank (ed.), *Chinese Thought and Institutions*. Chicago: University of Chicago Press, 1957.

9. Eisenstadt, S. N. "Political Struggle in Bureaucratic Societies," *World Politics*, Vol. 9 No. 1 (1956), pp. 15–37.

10. Eisenstadt, S. N. "Internal Contradictions in Bureaucratic Politics," *Comparative Studies in Society and History*, Vol. 1 No. 1 (1958), pp. 58–76.

11. Eisenstadt, S. N. "The Causes of Disintegration and Fall of Empires," Sociological and historical analyses, *Diogene*, No. 34 (1961), pp. 82–107.

12. Eisenstadt, S. N. "Religious Organization and Political Process in Centralized Empires," *The Journal of Asian Studies*, Vol. 21 No. 3 (May 1962), pp. 271–295.

13. Eisenstadt, S. N. *The Political System of Empires*. New York: The Free Press of Glencoe, 1963.

14. Jones, A. H. M. "The Decline and Fall of the Roman Empire," *History*, Vol. 40 No. 140 (1955), pp. 209–226.

15. Lewis, B. "Some Reflections on the Decline of the Ottoman Empire," *Studia Islamica*, Vol. 9. Paris: Maisoneuff, 1958, pp. 111–127.

16. Ostrogorsky, G. "Die wirtschaftlichen und sozialen entwicklungsgrundlagen des Byzantinischen reiches," *Vierteljahrschrift fuer Sozial- und Wirtschaftsgeschichte*, Vol. 22 (1929), pp. 129–143.

17. Ostrogorsky, G. "Die perioden der Byzantinischen geschichte," *Historische Zeitschrift*, Vol. 163 (1941), pp. 238–254.

18. Ostrogorsky, G. *History of the Byzantine State*. New York: Oxford University Press, 1956.

19. Swart, K. W. *Sales of Offices in the 17th Century*. The Hague: Nijhoff, 1949.

20. Weber, M. *Wirtschaft und Gesellschaft*. Muenchen: C. Mohr, 1920.

21. Wittfogel, K. *Oriental Despotism; A Comparative Study of Total Power*. New Haven: Yale University Press, 1957.

18

Don Martindale

The Roles of Humanism and

Scientism in the Evolution

of Sociology

In the curriculum of the modern university the courses fall into three clear divisions: the humanities, the sciences, and the social sciences. Even persons who have not attended closely to the development of Western intellectuality are well aware of the fact that the humanities are the oldest, and the social sciences are the youngest of the trilogy. Moreover, one can quickly assure himself that the social sciences are insurgent between the humanities and science, borrowing from each and somewhat in tension with each. Many a hard-headed physical scientist of the old school will exclaim, if pressed, that the social sciences "are not even sciences." And many a traditional humanist is so sure that social concerns belong properly in the humanities as to find the very idea of a social science "revolting." The social scientists, for their part, often smugly consider themselves as the true synthesizers of the thought and experience of modern man, as the bearers of the discipline which fused the humanistic and scientific poles of Western thought. Auguste Comte thought sociology was the queen of the sciences, and C. Wright Mills observed:

> It is *not* true, as Ernest Jones asserted, that "Man's chief enemy and danger
> is his own unruly nature and the dark forces pent up within him." On the

contrary: "Man's chief danger" today lies in the unruly forces of contemporary society itself, with its alienating methods of production, its enveloping techniques of political domination, its international anarchy — in a word, its pervasive transformations of the very "nature" of man and the conditions and aims of his life.

It is now the social scientist's foremost political and intellectual task — for here the two coincide — to make clear the elements of contemporary uneasiness and indifference. It is the central demand made upon him by other cultural workmen — by physical scientists and artists, by the intellectual community in general. It is because of this task and these demands, I believe, that the social sciences are becoming the common denominator of our cultural period, and the sociological imagination our most needed quality of mind (18; p. 13).

In this forthright statement sociology is the true synthesis of the intellectual currents of the West, and only in the hands of sociologists may its affairs be trusted. "To be aware of the idea of social structure and to use it with sensibility is to be capable of tracing . . . linkages among a great variety of *milieux*. To be able to do that is to possess the sociological imagination" (18, pp. 10–11).

The rise of sociology as a discipline which sought to substantiate claims such as those of C. Wright Mills to be the representative outlook of contemporary man is intimately bound up with its relation to the intellectual currents and the substantive issues of Western man. Humanism and science — the two main streams of Western thought — summarize the alternative ways by which Western man solves the problems of his social and natural world. The two most comprehensive substantive problems which Western man must solve are those of the individual and those of the collective (society). No orientations to the problems of existence are more fundamental than those which take the individual as primary (individualism) and those which take the collective as primary (collectivism). It is not misleading to take these two methodological orientations (the humanistic and the scientific) and substantive theoretical alternatives (individualism and collectivism) as the primary compass points of Western thought.

If we pass quickly in review the main methodological orientations of Western thought and the major substantive theoretical alternatives, it is possible to employ the resultant sketch to map the evolution of sociology. The primary forces playing upon sociology arise out of the experience of Western man.

Humanism as the Pioneering Outlook of Western Man

The distinctive communities of the Middle Ages were agrarian and religious in character: peasant villages, feudal manors, and monasteries (15, pp. 409–415). Though they have roots in the Middle Ages, the first

Main Compass Points of Western Thought

P		SUBSTANTIVE ALTERNATIVES	
e		---	---
r		*Individualism*	*Collectivism*
s p e	Humanistic	Humanistic Individualism	Humanistic Collectivism
c t			
i v e s	Scientific	Scientific Individualism	Scientific Collectivism

of the distinctive communities of the contemporary world were cities (15, pp. 415–418). Humanism, the pioneering outlook of Western man, was born in the city. Early civic humanism can be most simply defined as a secularized, man-centered outlook and methodology developed for the needs of civic man in contrast to the God-centered outlook and salvation technology of the members of typical medieval communities.

The most highly valued types of men of the Middle Ages were chivalrous knights and ascetic monks. The most meaningful life was one devoted to God's work, whether this consisted of vigils, fasting, ascetic privations, prayer, or engaging in military activities in the name of the faith. The most sanctified of all modes of deportment were those of the monastic recluse. The technology of the religiously significant life centered in withdrawal from sensual pleasure, fasting, privations, and prayer — especially in contemplation of the holy.

In the rising cities the modes of deportment associated with chivalrous adventurers or contemplative ascetics were retrograde. In the streets of the city, knights and monks rubbed shoulders with new commercial and industrial types: plutocrats rich from international trade and able by their new wealth to deck themselves out with fineries from afar in a manner that outshone the poor knight and poorer monk. Moreover, in the streets there appeared a variety of others: traders from afar speaking strange tongues, craftsmen, former serfs enjoying the freedom of the city. While knight and monk lost comparative status with the rise of the new commercial types, they lost it also with the rise of the new freemen from the base of society. In these cities a new thriving secularity was evident. The silent watches and vigils of the knightly novitiate or the silence of the monastic chamber had no place. The religious structures serving the city were propelled to a new grandeur. In the cities the magnificent Gothic cathedrals were being subscribed and constructed. The humble monasteries were withdrawing to a vine-draped countryside as the tides of life surged away from them.

The overpowering sense of the evil of the secular world which had sent

Christianity into the monastery in the days of the decay of the Roman cities was replaced by a new optimistic sense of abundant life. In the cities Western man even began to re-tool his religion to correspond to the new secular optimism that fired his aspirations. In the cities men were individualized, cast upon their own resources, and compelled to employ their own talents to construct the institutions they needed:

> In the Middle Ages both sides of human consciousness — that which was turned within and that which was turned without — lay dreaming or half awake beneath a common veil. The veil was woven of faith, illusion, and childish prepossession, through which the world and history were seen clad in strange hues. Man was conscious of himself only as a member of a race, people, party, family, or corporation — only through some general category. In Italy this veil first melted into air; an *objective* treatment and consideration of the State and of all the things of this world became possible. The *subjective* side at the same time asserted itself with corresponding emphasis; man became a spiritual individual, and recognized himself as such. In the same way the Greek had once distinguished himself from the barbarian, and the Arab had felt himself an individual at a time when other Asiatics knew themselves only as members of a race (1, p. 81).

In the twelfth century, in response to the need for guidance in their new civic communities, the humanists had begun to examine the classics of antiquity. It was not the slightest intention of the persons engaged in this enterprise to deify the past: quite the contrary. They recognized in the literature produced in the ancient *polis* the writings of people with experience in many points similar to their own. In the course of their interest in the exploitation of classical sources, they pioneered an elaborate array of new skills: they acquired the classical languages and began to insist on the study of the classical texts in the original; they developed philological techniques; they began to elaborate the standards of historical criticism in a manner not seen since the days of the classical Greeks.

The humanists belonged to the civic types responsible for developing the institutions of the city: corresponding secretaries, the tutors in important political and merchant families, advisors of princes, and, at times, even the princes and popes themselves, rich merchants with strong voices in the councils of the cities, and professors in the newly forming universities (1, pp. 128–136). While a single coherent philosophy cannot be assigned to the humanists as a whole, they were characterized by their optimistic theory of human nature, the employment of scholarship as a device for the solution of contemporary problems, the evaluation of classical learning as a source of guidance in social and intellectual affairs, and the development of alternatives to medieval theological explanations of the world (2, pp. 47–133, pp. 223–254).

By the twelfth century the traditional powers of the medieval world had become fully aware of the new spirit that was breaking away from their control. At the University of Paris in 1210, 1215, and again in 1231, professors and students were excommunicated for having disobeyed orders of the Church by reading Aristotle (21, pp. 460–461). In the cities the new social and intellectual ferment so completely eluded traditional structures as to lead to the formation of a wide variety of voluntary associations. Some of the new formations were eventually taken over by the Church, and made into new official monastic movements like the "Four Orders," the Dominicans, Franciscans, Carmelites, and Austin Friars (12, p. 727). But other semi-religious social movements such as the Beguines and Beghards of the Low Countries, the Humiliati of Italy, and the Poor Men of Leon were not blessed with Church approval.

Representatives of the new mendicant orders pressed their way into the newly forming universities and took up the battle against the new intellectual ferment. It was quickly perceived that one could not destroy the new intellectual currents. The task was to turn them to the religious advantage of the Church. If masters and students were going to read Aristotle at the risk of excommunication, the task was to take over Aristotle and purge the texts. The reconciliation of Aristotle with Christian theology was urged by great Franciscan scholars such as Robert Grosseteste, and by even more prominent Dominicans such as Albert the Great (1200–1280) and Thomas Aquinas (1225–1274). In the thirteenth century the Benedictine orders won the day and clamped an official scholasticism down on the universities.

With this development, the humanists were forced to minor positions in the universities and to purely private circles, where at times, like Ficino, they established private academies, and at times promoted the cause of Platonism against the official scholasticism and Aristotelianism that were becoming dominant in the universities (2, pp. 4–6, pp. 185–186). By the fifteenth century in private circles of the Italian cities, the tide turned again. Humanism broke through the spell of official scholasticism and achieved a kind of classic fullness.

The Emergence of Western Science

In the same civic world where humanism had formed, Western science emerged. Humanism arose in circles of cultivated social and political strata; science arose in the circles of artists and craftsmen. Humanism pioneered a new mode of deportment in the social and political world, while science pioneered a new method of procedure toward the world of physical things.

The peculiarities of science are found in its fusion of a rational conception of knowledge with a systematic experimentalism toward the world of facts. From the ancient world the West inherited the rational proof and the dream of systematically transforming all thought into a comprehensive rational unity (14, pp. 6–10). Social developments in the ancient *polis* had cast its citizen-intellectuals on their own conceptual resources without the opportunity for recourse to institutional devices to settle differences of opinion. Under these circumstances, the philosophers of ancient Greece began to analyze the thought process in the attempt to establish rules which would automatically guarantee the truth without the need to appeal to any agency outside the thought process itself. The unique place of Socrates among the Greek philosophers was bound up with the self-consciousness he brought to this search for an autonomous thought process. The great monuments to the search for the rational proof were Euclidean geometry and Aristotelian logic.

However, the rational proof and the dream of the rational integration of all knowledge born in Greek philosophy was restricted from any extensive application to the world of fact by the social situation of the ancient philosopher. The ancient philosopher was a citizen-soldier (15, pp. 353–355) in a society where the status of work was determined by slavery. Wherever slavery appears, the conduct of practical activities tends to be technologically unprogressive. While the ancient world supplied the rational proof to science, it could not supply the progressive technology which science also needed.

Contrary to those historians of science who see no contribution at all to science from the Middle Ages and the Renaissance, they supplied it with the technology that science required. The decline of slavery in the Middle Ages freed technology from its bondage to that unprogressive system. The new progressiveness has been skillfully phrased recently by Lynn White, Jr. The heavy-wheeled plow which was invented and developed to cultivate the heavy soils of northern Europe in turn sustained developments critical to the emergence of the modern world:

> The increased returns from the labour of the northern peasant raised his standard of living and consequently his ability to buy manufactured goods. It provided surplus food which, from the tenth century on, permitted rapid urbanization. In the new cities there arose a class of skilled artisans and merchants, the burghers who speedily got control of their communities and created a novel and characteristic way of life. . . . In this new environment germinated the dominant feature of the modern world: power technology (26, p. 78).

It was of crucial importance for the rise of science that when the medieval cities arose, they grew out of and continued to evolve on the basis of the free technologies of the medieval world:

> The later Middle Ages that is, roughly from A.D. 1000 to the close of the fifteenth century, is the period of decisive development in the history of the effort to use the forces of nature mechanically for human purposes. What had been, up to that time, an empirical grouping, was converted with increasing rapidity into a conscious and widespread programme designed

to harness and direct the energies observable around us. The labour-saving power technology which has been one of the distinctive characteristics of the Occident in modern times depends not only upon a medieval mutation of men's attitudes towards the exploitation of nature but also, to a great extent, upon specific medieval achievements (26, p. 79).

Under a slave economy, the capitalist owns both slaves, as a kind of human cattle, and the tools with which they work. It is usually to the advantage of the slave to work as little as possible to keep the level of demands on himself reduced. He has no incentive either to preserve the tools with which he works or to improve them. He is far more inclined to express his resentment for his condition by sabotage of his tools. However, men working for themselves and in possession of their own equipment consider their tools as a virtual extension of their personalities. Moreover, any improvement they make in their tools or in the use of non-human forms of energy eases the burden of their labors and increases the supply of the material things which enhance their styles of life. The conditions of a free economy, thus, may promote an attitude of systematic instrumentalism toward tools and the material conditions and things of life. Pragmatic instrumentalism has appeared frequently among pre-literate peoples. The technology of the Eskimo, for example, is dominated by a hardheaded pragmatic instrumentalism:

> The physical environment of the Eskimo is so forbidding and its peculiarities so extreme that a human group, finding itself in this environment, would perish unless it achieved a very special adjustment to environmental conditions. This is precisely what has happened in the case of the Eskimo. By means of a large number of special devices they have managed to make the inhospitable Arctic their home, and so well have they solved this difficult problem that occasional visitors from the outside world, such as white traders or ardent anthropologists, have been known to accept the Eskimo mode of life rather than, in usual fashion, impose theirs upon the Eskimo (9, p. 74).

Boas' studies of Eskimo technology showed that there were times in the past when the Eskimo's fascination with tools and implements led to surprisingly delicate elaborations which adapted them to tasks of a refinement that could not possibly have had survival value. Needles, for example, were developed for tasks of such refinement that they could only have had aesthetic use. Such periods of empirical tool and implement refinement are invariably followed by a reaction in the direction of practical efficiency once again. In the end pragmatic instrumentalism always dominated the Eskimo's orientation to nature.

However, pragmatic instrumentalism in man's orientation to his tools and to nature is not, per se, science. Science presupposes a rational ideal of knowledge conjoined to a method of establishing "truths" in the world of fact comparable to the role played by logic and mathematics in establishing truths in the world of ideas. The rational proof in the world of ideas was recovered from antiquity by the humanists. The breakthrough from the pragmatic instrumentalism of the medieval rural and urban worlds to the rational ideal of knowledge was the work of the Renaissance craftsman-artist.

When the artist is a slave, as he often was in antiquity, he can hardly be expected to pioneer a new orientation in thought binding on his times. The free artist of the Western city, on the other hand, operating with a free technology, was in quite a different position. The artist worked in a world of material things and tools. His competence was related, in the first instance, to his knowledge of and control over them. When in addition the artist was expected to create new patterns with his materials and tools, he had only one recourse. It was necessary to experiment. The Renaissance artist ever and again had recourse to experimentalism and to explore the possibilities of materials. He often found himself in a position where he had to invent new instruments for his researches. Systematic instrumentalism was being transformed into a general procedure as fundamental for the investigation and establishment of "truths" in the empirical world as logic and mathematics were in the world of thought.

In the medieval and Renaissance cities, where systematic instrumentalism was emerging as a basic method for the investigation of nature, the humanists had recovered the rational proof from antiquity. In the instant these two configurations (rational proof and empirical experimentalism) were linked, science was born. Their conjoint operation in the minds of the Renaissance artists is evident in the notebooks of Leonardo da Vinci. Leonardo went to considerable lengths to recover mathematical treatises from antiquity. In the world of thought, he argued, mathematics provides certainty:

> He who blames the supreme certainty of mathematics feeds on confusion, and will never impose silence upon the contradictions of the sophistical sciences, which occasion perpetual clamour (5, p. 83).

To anyone who wished to understand the world, he advised: "O students study mathematics and do not build without foundations" (5, p. 82). But, at the same time Leonardo recognized that some knowledge has a non-mathematical origin in the world of fact. "All our knowledge originates in our sensibilities" (5, p. 67). However, the world of fact, knowledge of which is gained by experience, also has an order. By means of experiment, experience can be made to yield up its certainties:

> Experience is never at fault; it is only your judgment that is in error in promising itself such results from experience as are not caused by our experiments (5, p. 64).

When one undertook to experiment with nature, he was convinced that
it was advisable to proceed by the most direct and least complicated
route possible. "When you wish to produce a result by means of an
instrument, do not allow yourself to complicate it by introducing many
subsidiary parts, but follow the briefest way possible" (5, p. 64). And
once one has ascertained natural causes, the need for further experiment
ceases. "There is no result in nature without a cause; understand the
cause and you will have no need of the experiment" (5, p. 64). In short,
nature presents a lawful world.

Contrasts between Humanism and Science

Humanism arose in educated and politically responsible circles of the
medieval and Renaissance cities; science arose in artistic and industrial
circles. Humanism arose as a new secular orientation toward social and
intellectual affairs; science arose as a new orientation toward instruments, material things, and the physical world.

The methodological differences between humanism and science are
of considerable interest, since they supplied the major disciplines of the
university. Humanism developed a series of techniques for exploring
ancient literature and contemporary experience for guidance in current
affairs. It elaborated the techniques of philological criticism and historical research. Science, on the other hand, developed systematic experimentalism into a general procedure for the investigation of nature.

The sharpest of differences, however, appear in the objectives of humanism and science. Humanism was a man-centered (secular), normative orientation intended to justify as well as implement the new kinds of
individuality and community represented by the citizen and the medieval
city. Humanism was inspired by an optimistic view in contrast to the
pessimistic medieval view of human nature. Humanism saw the fullness
of man's powers in terms of his achievements in secular contexts. Science,
on the other hand, arose as a non-normative method for investigating
nature. Its objectives were not to establish a particular state of natural or
social affairs but to acquire the most exact knowledge of nature possible
and to increase to the maximum man's ability to control the material
world (15, pp. 424–458).

The elements of the fundamental polarity in Western thought, humanism, and science, arose in the city, the first distinctive community of Western men. However, the initial polarity was between humanism and
theology. In the sixteenth century the new community represented by
the nation-state (15, pp. 418–421) had begun to replace the city as the
primary community of Western man. Humanism gravitated to the new
national communities, where it became foundational to seventeenth- and
eighteenth-century rationalism (15, pp. 440–443). At this time the old
tensions between humanism and theology began to break down. Theol-

ogy was beginning to cast its lot with the humanities. Science began to display its unparalleled powers to increase men's objective knowledge of nature. It was found to be invaluable in the new military and economic contexts associated with the rise of the nation. With this development the basic polarity of Western thought achieved its classic form.

Individualism and Collectivism in Western Thought

There are no more basic problems to men attempting to account for themselves and for their social world than the comparative significance to be assigned to the individual and to the collective. In the medieval monastic communities there was even a hermitic (individualistic) and cenobitic (communal) theory of monastic life. The major contrast between the forms of Eastern and Western monasticism was in the hermitic character of the former — a property which transposed Eastern monastic establishments into *laissez-faire* communities of competitive religious virtuosos. In Western monasticism, stemming from St. Benedict, on the other hand, cenobitic patterns prevailed and individual ascetic virtuosity was always subordinated to the collective requirements of the monastery as a whole under the abbot. Eastern monasticism, in short, rested on the theory and practice of ascetic individualism; Western monasticism rested on the theory and practice of collective asceticism.

The individualistic or collectivistic orientations emerge in every community. When these perspectives are raised to the level of systematic philosophies of the importance of the individual and of the group, they formulate a very fundamental ideological contrast. Individualism is an ideology which maintains that the person is the highest of all values and the vindication of a society is to be found in its assistance in the maximum unfolding of the individual's potential. Collectivism is an ideology which maintains that the highest of all values is the society (and the peace and harmony it guarantees). While individuals are important, they are second to the community, for without the community the individual is insignificant.

Individualism leads naturally to the assumption that society and institutions are instrumental — institutions are made for people, not people for institutions. Collectivism leads naturally to the position that internal peace is the highest of all values, without which only chaos ensues. Hence, collectivism maintains that people must order their behavior to the priority of the community.

As shown by the hermitic and cenobitic theories of monasticism, there is an individualism and collectivism in the monastic community as well as in any other type of community, be it a rural community, a city, or a nation-state. As these ideologies have developed in Western thought, the individualistic position has been most closely linked with liberalism; the collectivistic position has been most closely linked with conservatism.

However, because liberalism and conservatism are not consistently linked with individualism and collectivism, this terminology is avoided in the present chapter.

While individualism and collectivism represent alternate categories of life in every community, and while they are never completely absent as alternative perspectives, they are very often present in quite different proportions. Without attempting to account for minor cycles in the alteration of individualism and collectivism in the course of the development of a community, it can be noted that individualism tends to be strong in the periods of the formation of a community. Collectivism, on the other hand, tends to dominate the period of a community's maturity. The reasons for this are not far to seek.

At the time people are in the process of creating a new community, they are forced to solve problems which are quite new. This is what it means to create a new community. Since there are no established patterns to go by, individuals must be free to create new ones. At such times the average age of the community's leaders tends to be lowered. The outstanding individual is followed because of his creativity, without regard for external qualifications (such as derivations from an old or an outstanding family). It is the time of the charismatic leader. Every community tends to remember from its formative period an array of charismatic leaders whom it may apotheosize as cultural heroes.

On the other hand, once the new community has been formed and its institutions stabilized, there is a tendency to discourage individualism, which can, at this time, appear only as a disruptive principle. The age of a community's leaders is often raised, for people prefer the stable older men and not the young hotheads. Anti-individualistic, collectivistic ideologies enjoy greater popularity during the maturity of a community.

The rhythm of an early individualism followed by a mature collectivism is discernible first in the Western city and later in the nation-state. In the formative period of the Western city (in the eleventh and twelfth centuries), a new spirit of individualism was apparent in the works of the first wave of humanistic intellectuals. A new, impudent note of social criticism was manifest in the songs of the jongleurs. In the same period the universities were beginning to take shape out of voluntary associations (guilds) of scholars and teachers. Famous teachers wandered from place to place with remarkable independence, and were often followed by their students. By the end of the twelfth century most of the institutions of the city had been established, and the process of perfecting them into an urban synthesis was under way. At this very time, the counterattack on the individualism which had been released in the city was launched by the mendicant friars, particularly the Dominicans and Franciscans. The counterattack was successful. The method of Abelard, who had been a spokesman for the newly powerful secular clergy, and the method of dissolving all issues into a conflict between equally impressive authorities and freeing thought for a new formulation, was transformed into the procedure of scholasticism for disposing of the objections of the opposition. Aristotle, for the reading of whom scholars and masters at Paris had once been excommunicated, was fused with medieval theology and lifted into the position of a dogmatic authority.

Without tracing the cycles more closely, in the early city the humanistic individualism of the eleventh and twelfth centuries was followed by the scholastic collectivism of the thirteenth and fourteenth. Unfortunately, the analysis of the individualistic and collectivistic aspects of the civic humanism of the fifteenth- and sixteenth-century city has never been carried out.

Again in the formative period of the nation-state, when it was fusing into an integrated community (in the seventeenth and eighteenth centuries), the wave of philosophy from Descartes to Kant reflects a powerful upsurge of individualism. Even Descartes' formula, which is frequently taken as the starting point of modern philosophy, *cogito ergo sum*, expressed the assumption that the one indubitable reality is the individual. The indisputable reality (unquestioned assumption) of the collectivistic medieval world was *God is*, but in Descartes' world one starts with the individual. All other realities, including God, were to be established by a chain of logical reasoning beginning with the first reality of individual thought.

However, once the revolutions of the nineteenth century had brought the modern nation-state into existence, collectivistic philosophies (Hegelianism, Absolute Idealism) became popular. Within the nation-state the individualistic ideologies of the seventeenth and eighteenth centuries were thrust into the background by the comparative dominance of collectivistic ideologies in the nineteenth and twentieth centuries.

Some Important Subdivisions in the Modern Individualistic and Collectivistic Ideologies

Recent individualism and collectivism have been subdivided in further ways. Individualism has taken two major forms, depending on whether the forms of rationalism were or were not made central. One may agree that the individual is the most significant of all realities without considering men to be primarily distinguished by their reason or rationality. It is possible to distinguish rationalistic and non-rationalistic forms of individualism even at an early period. In the cities, for example, a form of theological collectivism, scholasticism, (Aquinas) attempted to press the forms of ancient rationalism to the support of scholasticism. In reaction to this attempt, many humanists fused their humanistic individualism with a non-rational (mystical or emotional conception of the individual (Ficino). On the other hand, eighteenth- and nineteenth-century rationalism detached rationalism from scholastic contexts, and found the essence of the individual in his rational faculties (Voltaire). On the other hand, various forms of nineteenth-century romantic individualism found the essence of the individual to be in his feeling and his emotional life, (Victor Hugo) not in his rationality. Western individualism has alternated between rational and non-rational forms.

Collectivism, too, has significant subtypes. Collectivism is identified by its establishment of the primacy of the community over the individual. However, the collective has different implications, depending on whether it is under the control of the upper or lower classes. In the nineteenth century a basic division appeared in the contrast between Hegelianism and Marxism. The Hegelians were spokesmen for middle- and upper-class collectivism; Marxism, together with other forms of so-called scientific socialism, was spokesman for a collectivism for the lower classes.

It is possible to diagram some of the major positions in recent Western thought in terms of their humanistic and scientific components and their positions with respect to one or another of the individualistic or collectivistic ideologies.

Some Major Intellectual Positions in Terms of Their Humanistic-Scientific and Individualistic Collectivistic Components

METHODOLOGICAL PERSPECTIVES		SUBSTANTIVE ISSUES			
		INDIVIDUALISM		COLLECTIVISM	
		Rationalistic	*Non-Rationalistic*	*Left Wing*	*Right Wing*
	Humanism	17th- & 18th-Century Rationalism	Phenomenology Existentialism	Radical Romanticism	Neo-Thomism
	Science	*Laissez-faire,* Neo-Kantianism Utilitarianism		Marxism, Scientific Socialism	Hegelianism, Absolute Idealism

Early Sociology: Science or Scientism

From the time of Francis Bacon there were sporadic suggestions for the application of science to social phenomena. However, a number of factors in Western thought and social experience prevented this for a time. In the first place, sometimes a possible line of intellectual development is frustrated by the prior occupancy of the field. The scientific analysis of social phenomena was prevented in the city from the twelfth to the sixteenth century by the fact that the interpretation of social phenomena was virtually monopolized by the theologians (the Roman Catholics in Southern Europe and, somewhat later, the Protestant theologians in Northern Europe) and the humanists. Comparable to the division of the sphere of thought between the humanists and the scholastics in the early period (twelfth and thirteenth centuries) was the division of the sphere of social thought between the northern humanists and such Protestant leaders as Luther and Calvin in the later period (fifteenth and sixteenth centuries).

Meanwhile, also operating against the application of science to social affairs was the adaptation of science to the study of physical things. Science had developed as a form of non-evaluative instrumental knowledge. Human social experience, on the other hand, was traditionally a sphere for evaluation. To extend science to social phenomena meant, literally, that one had to treat men "like things." This was a notion for which humanists and theologians (both Roman Catholics and Protestants) had an almost instinctive repugnance. Hence, one could expect a science of social phenomena to be seriously proposed only if science had proved, beyond any question, its value for the study of the physical world, while the humanistic and theological interpretations of social affairs had been brought into serious question. Both contingencies came to pass.

The religious and nationalistic wars of the sixteenth and seventeenth centuries shook European man, and left many persons for a time determined to avoid all forms of religious excess. Meanwhile, the primary arena of social development was shifting to the nation-states. The religious wars powerfully promoted their formation. In the newly forming nations, a reconstituted humanism was taking shape in which rationalism (which had been torn loose from its anchorage in scholasticism) was conjoined to humanistic values. However, the thought of the enlightenment gradually evolved the social criticism that provided the rationalizations for the revolutions which rocked eighteenth-century society.

The French Revolution terminated in the Terror, and then in the dictatorship of Napoleon. The whole of European society was shaken, first by the example of the Revolution, and then by the force of French arms. When the storm of revolution had passed, responsible groups in European society were sick to death of revolution and everything it signified. Above all, there was a profound repugnance on the part of many people for those ideas which had justified revolution and provided its program.

However, the reaction to the excesses of revolution occurred in a world which revolution had brought into being. Medieval institutions had been swept away. The new mass societies of the contemporary world had made their appearance. In the nations of Western Europe and in the United States, the middle classes had been thrust into a central position. At the same time, the continuing revolutionary ferment which had brought the middle classes to power was setting in motion the laboring classes of the rising nation-states. Once the friend of the middle classes, revolution had become their enemy, for if revolution had given birth to middle-class democracy, it had also spawned socialism.

The Western world was at last ripe for an attempt to employ science for the analysis of social phenomena. The theological interpretation of social events and the humanistic program for them had both been cast into disrepute. However, if science was to take over the ancient role of theology and humanism, it would be expected to do more than analyze in a spirit of complete neutrality. Nevertheless, in the instant that science undertakes the task of *justifying* one social arrangement rather than another, it ceases simply to be science. Whenever science becomes normative and assumes tasks that exceed empirical explanation, it is, perhaps, best described as *scientism*. Sociology arose under conditions which virtually guaranteed that it would be a form of scientism.[1]

However, the fact that sociology arose under conditions which tended to subordinate it to ideological requirements of special social groups does not eliminate the possibility of a scientific sociology. Whenever it abandons normative objectives and devotes itself purely to the task of investigating and explaining social phenomena, sociology is on the road to science. It was a foregone conclusion that whatever ideological elements were present in early sociology would eventually come into conflict with scientific requirements.

From Positivistic Organicism to Functionalism

The three persons conventionally viewed as the founders of sociology — Comte in France, Spencer in England, and Ward in the United States — were spokesmen for nineteenth-century middle-class groups in their respective nations. France in the early nineteenth century was fresh from the throes of revolution. The nation had glided into the hands of the new middle classes. But as an earthquake that sends out minor tremors after the main shock waves, the revolutionary ferment continued. Comte turned his face against the scientific socialism he had flirted with as a young man (as a disciple of Saint-Simon). In England the country had come into the hands of the middle classes by more peaceable means. Spencer opposed the forces of radical democracy and socialism which represented English parallels of the French scientific socialists. In America the Revolution had also placed the nation in the hands of the middle classes. Coming from the middle-class stratum of the American Midwest,

---

[1] The term "scientism" is here being applied to all attempts to settle questions of value by means of scientific methods. This usage should be distinguished from that of F. A. Hayek who employs the term to refer to the "slavish imitation of the method and language of science." Hayek continues: " 'scientism' or the 'scientistic' prejudice . . . describe . . . an attitude decidedly unscientific in the true sense of the word, since it involves a mechanical and uncritical application of habits of thought to fields different from those in which they have been formed" (10, pp. 15–16).

Ward was spokesman for those groups pressing the federal government for assistance in opening the West. Inasmuch as Spencer was opposed to government interference in social affairs while Ward urged it, the mistake has occasionally been made of supposing that they were intrinsically opposed: quite the contrary. In Spencer's nineteenth-century England, social reform meant a movement in the direction of radical democracy and socialism. But in the American Midwest the efforts to secure government assistance meant the promotion of the interests of the same groups that Spencer wished to protect with his policies. When it was suggested that Ward's program was identical with socialism, Ward was — quite correctly — thoroughly shocked. Comte, Ward, and Spencer were all spokesmen for the middle classes of their own countries. Differences were related to the peculiar problems of the middle classes in each country.

In any case, Comte, Spencer, and Ward subscribed to an organismic theory of society and attempted to found it on a scientific methodology. They were quite aware that they were recombining the traditions of Western thought in an essentially new manner. They conceived sociology as the great intellectual synthesis of the West. They proposed to take materials from the humanistic disciplines — above all, from history, the discipline which had come more than any other to combine humanistic perspectives. At the same time they all proposed to analyze historical (and ethnographic) materials by means of the methods of the physical sciences.

The more fully Comte developed his system, the clearer it became that a specific normative intent lay at the foundation of his thought. He proposed to establish a new religion of humanity in a society under the guidance of sociologist-priests. The secular affairs of society were to be placed in the hands of businessmen who would possess so much power that they would no longer be greedy. Women would be returned to the home. Some 20,000 sociologist-priests, Comte thought, would be required for the administration of social affairs in Europe alone. He generously suggested his own services as chief high priest with his headquarters in Paris. Historically, Comte's idea was most clearly approximated by the Indian caste system, whose stability he praised. He evidently conceived of sociologists as the Brahmins of his sociocracy (4).

Not all adherents of the Positivistic Organismic position expressed its normative presuppositions with so much clarity. However, a strong normative orientation remains characteristic of a large number of Positivistic Organicists even into the period of its decay. According to Lundberg, science operates as a kind of mental hygiene: "The mere possession of scientific knowledge and scientific habits of thought regarding the natural universe relieves us of a world of fears, rages, and unpleasant dissipations of energy" (13, p. 2). The lines between normative theory and empirical theory are erased in the instant one speaks of "scientific solutions of social problems." This Lundberg does in a forthright manner:

> It is not true . . . that scientific solutions of social problems face a peculiar situation in that large numbers of people do not want such solutions and would be under no compulsion to accept them. Scientific solutions, in the long run, carry with them their own compulsions for acceptance. The demonstrated superiority of scientific methods has been, in the last analysis, the major reason why they have triumphed. Also, once scientific criteria are accepted in a community as the final arbiters, no one challenges their decisiveness (13, p. 8).

This formulation of Lundberg represents scientism in relatively pure form. His position rests on the notion of the self-evident superiority of the value of the community over individuals:

> There can be no doubt at all that the authority of a properly *constituted state* is preferable to what seems to be the alternative, namely, private and self-constituted legislatures, police, and courts, as they occur today among all kinds of organizations, seeking to impose their private wishes upon the larger public (13, p. 54).

Lundberg's sociologist is not far removed from Comte's sociologist-priest:

> When people are in trouble, they will look for a savior. . . . They are likely to surround themselves with seers, poets, playwrights, and others alleged to possess . . . powers of "seeing." The idea is a sound one. The only reform needed is a substitution of scientists for these soothsayers and soothseers (13, p. 54).

Toward the end of the nineteenth century competitors of Positivistic Organicism began to appear on the scene. Nevertheless this first school of sociological theory retained much of its original prestige and only began to disintegrate into its component parts (positivism and organicism) in the interwar period (14, pp. 110–121). It is quite possible that the world-wide depression of the 1930's which shook people's confidence in the self-evident superiority of the modern nation-state played a role in the decline of Positivistic Organicism. However, after World War II the Functionalistic school of sociological theory rapidly took shape, combining an organismic theory of society with a revised positivism of method, once again making it the true heir of Positivistic Organicism (14, pp. 446–450).

Beyond any question the dean of contemporary Functionalism is Talcott Parsons. Hence, if there are still elements of scientism in Functionalism, his work offers the most authentic of all sources for their study. In 1961 Talcott Parsons, Edward Shils, Kaspar D. Naegele, and Jesse R. Pitts joined their talents to bring out the most ambitious selection of readings in sociological theory ever attempted. The result appeared in two large volumes, together with long introductions by the editors. In all, several hundred fragments of early sociological writings were cut and pasted into a framework provided primarily by Parsons' Functionalistic theory.

Rarely has a monument of such proportions been erected to a scholar while still alive, for the big two-volume assemblage of elements from early sociology are organized into the form of an anticipation of Parsons. Moreover, his theories are stated to be the great climactic synthesis of sociology. The reason why 1935 is the break-off point for the assemblage of readings in sociological theory seems to be explained by the conviction of the editors that since 1935 Parsons' Functionalism is the only theory that counts. In Shils' apotheosis of the dean of Functionalism, these points are explicitly stated:

> The Structure of Social Action was the turning point. It was this work that brought the greatest of the partial traditions into a measure of unity. It precipitated the sociological outlook that had been implicit in the most interesting of the empirical inquiries; it made explicit the affinities and complementarity of the sociological traditions that had arisen out of utilitarianism, idealism, and positivism. It redirected sociology into its classical path, and in doing so, it began the slow process of bringing into the open the latent dispositions that had underlain the growth of sociological curiosity. Abstract and complicated though its argument was, The Structure of Social Action laid out the main lines of the concrete sociological outlook that has come forward in academic study and in the public appreciation of sociology since its appearance (22, pp. 1406–1407).

Shils too frequently and too emphatically emphasizes the fact that Functionalistic sociology intentionally eliminates the lines between normative and empirical explanation to permit the possibility that this is unintentional:

> Sociology has come into its present estate because its own development bears a rough correspondence to the development of the consciousness of mankind, its moral progress (22, p. 1410).

A few pages later Shils formulates the relation between the sociologist and his objects of study as priest-like:

> Sociology is not a purely cognitive undertaking. It is also a moral relationship between the human beings studied and the student of the human being (22, p. 1413).

And finally Shils blurs the lines between sociology and the reality it studies:

> Sociological theory is not just a theory like any other theory; it is a social relationship between the theorist and the subject matter of his theory. It is a relationship formed by the sense of affinity.

The sociological theory that grows from the theory of action is simply a
more forward part of a widespread consensual collectivity (14, p. 1420).

In a word, morally and ethically sociology is itself the best that contemporary society has to offer.

Once this extraordinary position has been put forward, Shils hence-
forth speaks of the sociological position that he shares with Parsons as
Consensual Sociology. He describes its operation as follows:

> The content of a human life flows outward into other minds and lives
> through the medium of sociology. The "larger mind" is extended and
> deepened through the program of the sociology that moves in the direction
> of the theory of action. . . . The consensual impetus to sociological inquiry
> is . . . something new in the world, and a positive addition to the moral
> progress of the race (14, p. 1430).

All sociology which does not accept the "consensual" position is described by Shils as oppositional sociology. Those who accept oppositional sociology, he argues, are often "former or quasi-Marxists — who,
without giving their allegiance to Marxism, wish nonetheless to retain
its original disposition" (14, p. 1422). Such sociology, he insists, has an
"alienated outlook" and the analyses of its members have "an overtone
to the effect that those in authority have acted wrongly, out of incompetence, blindness, or disregard of the good. . . . The result is an outlook that radically distrusts the inherited order of society" (14, p. 1422).
Having hung the stigma of "Marxists" on all who disagree with Functionalism, Shils summarizes his view that "consensual sociology is alone
capable of satisfying the requirements of an adequate theory and a
proper relationship to policy" (14, p. 1440).

The Scientific Impulse in Sociology

In its first theoretical school, Positivistic Organicism, sociology attempted to synthesize a scientific method for the study of social phenomena with a collectivistic theory of society. The humanistic individualism of the Enlightenment had lost prestige by its association with the
Revolutions which ushered in the mass democracies. Besides, the rationalistic impulse of the Enlightenment had been borne in large measure
by the advisers to and critics of the Enlightened Despots, who proposed
to reform the monarchies, not replace them with democracies. In the
nineteenth-century world, the point of gravity had shifted to the middle
classes, who had never been the primary bearers of the humanistic outlook. Moreover, the intellectual program of the middle classes in the
post-revolutionary period was the reverse of their program in the pre-
revolutionary world. They now had the task of conserving and justifying

a social and political order that had been taken over into their own hands, whereas in the pre-revolutionary period, their objective had been to eliminate the remnants of medievalism and other obstacles in their path.

At the time of its origin, thus, Positivistic Organicism was structurally parallel to Hegelianism. As a matter of fact, when Hegel's work was called to Comte's attention, Comte saw the essential similarity between their positions. To Comte, Hegel's Absolute Idealism was merely a more metaphysical form of his own position (14, p. 156). In his youth Comte had dallied with the brilliant scientific socialism of Saint-Simon, but soon reacted powerfully against it, though he did not hesitate to appropriate large blocks of Saint-Simon's ideas. There is little question that in Comte's own mind sociology was a conservative answer to scientific socialism, as it still is for Shils and Parsons.

Positivistic Organicism numbers powerful figures among its adherents: Comte, Spencer, Ward, in the early period; Tönnies, Pareto, and Durkheim, later; and Sorokin, Lundberg, and Redfield in the modern period. When contemporary functionalism thus conceives of itself as the legitimate heir of the whole of sociology, it must be admitted that it is at least the heir of the single, most pervasive of the early positions. And when some contemporary functionalists automatically identify anyone who disagrees with them as a "Marxist," they are repeating a drama as old as Comte's denunciation of Saint-Simon and the reaction of some Hegelians to the Marxists.

However, there was no reason why the scientific impulse in sociology should be exhausted by the combination of Positivism and Right-Wing Collectivism in the manner of Positivistic Organicism and Functionalism. From an analytic point of view, the most obvious second school of scientific sociology to develop should have been a form of positivistic, left-wing collectivism. In view of Comte's self-conscious opposition to Saint-Simon and the scientific socialists, this would seem doubly probable. When Marxian sociology eventually developed, this possibility was finally realized. However, it was a late rather than an early development.

The slowness of a positivistic form of left-wing collectivism to develop must be sought in social conditions. Schools of thought do not develop among the sociological theorists simply because they are abstractly possible in the panorama of intellectual positions. Positivistic Organicism had developed because it was needed by the middle classes, in whose hands the modern nation-state had formed. Left-wing collectivism, on the other hand, was put forth to satisfy the needs of the modern proletariat. In the nineteenth century at the time sociology arose, it was practically impossible for a sociology representing a positivistic form of left-wing collectivism to make its way alongside Positivistic Organicism and be heard in the same forums. While the middle classes were sponsoring the development of the social sciences in the colleges and universities, the lower classes were in no position to place their versions of social science in competitive position with them. Only in the twentieth century have academic versions of the sociological counterpart of scientific socialism appeared. Moreover, it is more frequent in Europe than in America.

It was quite possible, however, that various forms of sociological theory representing combinations of positivism and individualism should appear. As noted earlier, in any given community a differentiation appears between the collectivists and the individualists. Once the nation-state had begun to assume its modern form and find its point of gravity in the middle classes, a new differentiation could be expected among the middle classes between collectivists and individualists. Two schools of sociological theory combining scientific positivism and individualism (a non-rational and rational form) eventually made their appearance: Conflict Theory and Neo-Kantian Formalism.

Conflict Theory developed first. A number of persons in different countries such as Bagehot in England, Gumplowicz and Ratzenhofer in Austria, and Small in America were thoroughly convinced that a science of social phenomena was not only possible, but necessary. If anything, they found themselves opposed to the Positivistic Organicists on the grounds that they were too lax in their positivism. However, they found themselves far more dissatisfied with the organismic theory of society. This theory, they believed, obscured the fluid dynamism that everywhere came into view whenever one actually looked at social life. To the conflict theorists society is not an organism; it is a process. Its events consist of endlessly varied encounters between people as individuals and in groups. Each is in hot struggle to advance its own peculiar interests (14, pp. 127–211).

However, Conflict Theory was no return to the optimistic individualism of the Enlightenment. It had no faith in human reason, and had serious doubts about the doctrine of progress sponsored by Positivistic Organicism. Peace was a kind of treaty marking an interval between the wars and contests of groups. Most individuals, according to its view of things, are weak and sheep-like. It is only in groups that the fundamental combativeness of the individual is able to manifest itself in full force. *Conflict Theory, thus, was a positivistic form of non-rational individualism.*

Although there was a sharp impact of realism about Conflict Theory, it presented some anomalies. It was a form of individualism hardly calculated to appeal to the ordinary individual, who was conceived of as sheep-like (as by Gumplowicz for example), but inwardly aggressive. Society was visualized as a series of major and minor arenas of conflict. Both pictures are rather unappealing. The case was different with Sociological Formalism.

In the course of the continuing differentiation of individualistic perspectives within the nation-state, it was perhaps a foregone conclusion that the pessimistic formulas of the Conflict Theorists would satisfy few. Toward the end of the nineteenth century a neo-Kantian revival took place not only in Western philosophy, but also in a number of other humanistic disciplines. It carried with it strong impulses toward rationalism and optimism. Sociological Formalism reflected this movement in sociology. The movement in sociology sustained an optimistic outlook toward the individual — an outlook far more attractive to most people than was Conflict Theory. The rationality of the individual had not received equivalent emphasis since the eighteenth century. At the same time, this rationalistic revival occurred in a framework of science rather than of humanism.

Social life was conceived by the neo-Kantian Formalists as distinguishable into form and content. Sociology was visualized as a discipline, like geometry, and concerned with the forms of social life in separation from their content. Such forms, moreover, were conceived as in some respect directly accessible to man's reason. Sociological Formalism seemed to offer the prospect of integrating the whole of social life in terms of forms of varying degrees of comprehensiveness. For a time, it appeared that Formalism would sweep the entire field.

The Humanistic Counterattack on Sociology

As has been observed, from the time of Comte to the contemporary Functionalists, there have been strong normative elements in sociology which in any strict construction have no scientific standing. The Humanists who were skilled in analyzing value suppositions at an early date brought the value premises of the new science of society under critical review. In 1887 Isabel Hapgood brought out a volume of Tolstoy's essays, which were at the time circulating in Russia in manuscript form. In one of them Tolstoy analyzed the evaluative elements of the sociology of Comte and Spencer.

> The justification of all persons who have freed themselves from toil is now founded on experimental, positive science. The scientific theory is as follows:

> "For the study of the laws of life of human societies, there exists but one indubitable method — the positive, experimental, critical method.

> "Only sociology, founded on biology, founded on all the positive sciences, can give us the laws of humanity. Humanity, or human communities, are the organisms already prepared, or still in process of formation, and which are subservient to all the laws of the evolution of organisms.

> "One of the chief of these laws is the variation of destination among the portions of the organs. Some people command, others obey. If some live in superabundance, and others in want, this arises not from the Will of God, but because the empire is a form of manifestation of personality, but because

in societies, as in organisms, division of labor becomes indispensable for life as a whole. Some people perform the muscular labor in societies; others, the mental labor" (24, p. 169).

Tolstoy formulated the central argument of the Positivistic Organicists:

> The theory is as follows: All mankind is an undying organism; men are the particles of that organism, and each one of them has his own special task for the service of others. In the same manner, the cells united in an organism share among them the labor of the fight for existence of the whole organism; they magnify the power of one capacity, and weaken another, and unite in one organ, in order the better to supply the requirements of the whole organism. And exactly in the same manner as with gregarious animals — ants or bees — the separate individuals divide the labor among them. The queen lays the egg, the drone fructifies it; the bee works his whole life long. And precisely this thing takes place in mankind and in human societies. And therefore, in order to find the law of life for man, it is necessary to study the laws of life and the development of organisms (24, p. 175).

It is on this new doctrine, Tolstoy observes, "that the justification for men's idleness and cruelty is now founded" (24, p. 176).

> From this view of science, it appears that all previous knowledge was deceitful, and that the whole story of humanity, in the sense of self-knowledge, has been divided into three, actually into two, periods: the theological and metaphysical period, extending from the beginning of the world to Comte, and the present period — that of the only true science, positive science — beginning with Comte (24, p. 178).

This whole edifice, Tolstoy argues, rests on an error — that of conceiving humanity as an organism. "In humanity itself all actual signs of organism — the center of feeling or consciousness — are lacking" (24, p. 178).

Comte's work, Tolstoy observes, had two parts: his positive philosophy and his positive politics. Both had evaluative aspects. However,

> Only the first part was adopted by the learned world — that part which justified, on new premises, the existent evil of human societies; but the second part, treating of the moral obligations of altruism, arising from the recognition of mankind as an organism, was regarded as not only of no importance, but as trivial and unscientific (24, p. 179).

Tolstoy's argument was sound. There were evaluative elements in both aspects of Comte's sociology.

Some 15 years, at least, after Tolstoy had written these lines, he summed up his estimate of the sociology deriving from Comte and Spencer in an essay on "The Restoration of Hell." In it Beelzebub, the chief of the devils, received reports on the state of the contemporary world from various of his cohorts. To distract men from spiritual things, one reports:

> "I have devised for them . . . sociology, which consists in studying how former people lived badly. So instead of trying to live better themselves according to the teaching of Jesus, they think they need only study the lives of former people, and that from that they will be able to deduce general laws of life, and that to live well they need only conform their life to the laws they thus devise. . . .

> "And as soon as those who are considered the promoters of science become persuaded of their infallibility, they naturally proclaim as indubitable truth things that are not only unnecessary but often absurd, and having proclaimed them they cannot repudiate them" (25, pp. 326–327).

Tolstoy's comments on Comte's and Spencer's Positivistic Organicism may illustrate how devastating the humanistic critique of the ideological elements of early sociology could become. But it was perhaps to be expected that the humanities should also mount a methodological counterattack on sociology. After all, Comte had proposed taking over bodily the materials of history. However, Comte brushed aside the assumptions on which the study of history had traditionally rested — that it was a manifestation of men's ideas, thoughts, and feelings, in short, of the human spirit. In accord with his positivism, history was reduced by Comte to the overt happenings in human behavior. The existence of the human spirit behind them was denied (4, vol. 1, p. 9). Sociology analyzed such occurrences with the methods of natural science and the notions of succession, co-existence, and cause, thereby establishing the general laws of social evolution (4, vol. 4, p. 17). Comte's arguments were reinforced by John Stuart Mill, who also hoped to improve the state of the social sciences by application of the methods of natural science. Mill thought it possible to deduce the successive states of consciousness from the physiological functions of the brain. This was the first step, Mill believed, in establishing the natural laws of activity of human pluralities (16, pp. 529–532).

Comte, Mill, Henry Thomas Buckle, and others not only developed a collectivistic view of society and man which was radically in opposition to the traditional humanistic and individualistic conception, but which brushed aside the methods by which the humanists had studied man and society. Sociology might claim to be the queen of the sciences, but history was the queen of the humanities. If a counterattack on sociology were to proceed out of the humanities, it was most plausibly to be expected from history. When this counterattack came, as it did, it would be expected to be from a historicism different from its eighteenth-century rationalistic forms, for the rationalistic humanism of the eighteenth century had seriously suffered from its identification with revolution. Moreover, the rationalistic impulse in Western thought was being pre-empted by science. Rationalism, thus, was twice damaged in the view of many humanists: first by its identification with the cause of revolution, then by its role in the social sciences, where it seemed to many persons to be bringing about a wholesale destruction of spiritual values.

A major attempt to combat positivism by means of a reconstructed historicism was made by Johann Droysen, who in 1852 developed a course at the University of Berlin on the "Methodology and Encyclopedia of the Historical Sciences," which sought to study history on historical foundations (11, p. 31). Droysen drew a sharp distinction between the methodology of the natural and historical sciences (8, pp. 307–342), and argued (7) that the spheres of history and science are quite distinct: history deals with the sphere of moral judgment which eludes statistical and causal study. However, statistical and causal methods are appropriate to the study of *things*.

The scholar who more than any other came to synthesize the counterattack by a reconstituted historicism was Wilhelm Dilthey. Without tracing the steps by which he arrived at his final position, it may be noted that Dilthey took history, not sociology, to be the most fundamental of all disciplines. Positivism, in Dilthey's opinion, was not new. Comte's positivism was merely the culmination in modern times of the materialistic explanation of events running through d'Alembert and Hobbes to Comte (6, p. 357). The peculiarities of the materialistic philosophy of history are its attempts to explain mental and spiritual events in terms of categories originally developed to explain things.

However, if we cut beneath such gross materialism as that of Comte and Mill, which would explain spiritual events by categories appropriate to things, we must still recognize that their materialism is an outlook (*Weltanschauung*), a form of analysis, and an activity of mind. History is more fundamental than sociology or any science because its subject matter is not one or another of the products of mind (of which Positivism is only one), but because *its subject matter is life itself*. Yet this does not mean that Rationalism or Idealism are more fundamental than Positivism. They, too, are world views, the ultimate source of which is life.

> The ultimate root of any world view is life itself. Life is present all over the globe in innumerable particular lives, and is lived and re-lived by every individual. Being but an instant of time present, it eludes strict observation. But in retrospect and in its objective manifestations Life is better capable of being fully grasped and meaningfully interpreted than life according to our personal knowledge and in its countless forms today, and thus it reveals everywhere the same identical traits and common features (6, p. 21).

History, to Dilthey, was the most fundamental of all disciplines, because its subject matter is the mind. History is meaningful, because it is the product of the forms of the mind. The ultimate category of mind is meaning, and history is the study of the manner in which the mind objectifies itself according to its own principles.

Thus it may be seen that Dilthey shares with the eighteenth-century rationalists the conception (humanistic) of a universal human nature manifesting itself according to its own principles. However, since Dilthey has treated rationalism as merely one of the products of the human mind, and reason as only one of its capacities, he was not in the position to derive the forms of human life as manifest in history from man's reason or from the categories of the mind in the manner of Kant or any other of the rationalists. Rather, Dilthey followed a suggestion contained in Schopenhauer and in his one-time associates at Basel, Burckhardt and Nietzsche. Poetry may be more revealing than logic as a source of insight into the forms which come to serve as the receptacles for systems of ideas in which human life ultimately objectifies itself.

In the Basel *Introduction* (1867) Dilthey declared that poets had taught him to understand the world.

> The systems of Schelling, Hegel, and Schleiermacher were but logical and metaphysical translations of a *Lebens- und Weltansicht* of a Lessing, a Schiller, and a Herder. The poet is the interpreter of a state of mind, which permeates a generation and crystallizes it into a system. A system lives or dies, not according to reasons of logic, but by virtue of the duration of that state of mind which has originated it (11, p. 75).

If history is to yield its richness for the study of man, some method other than that of the physical sciences is essential. Moreover, such analysis cannot proceed simply on the basis of logical forms, which are appropriate to only one of the basic aspects of life (its cognitive aspect). In addition, life has affective (emotional) and conative (moral) dimensions. Depending on which one of these basic properties of experience is uppermost, the mind objectifies itself in different ways. These objectifications, in turn, become the vehicles of world views which define immediate experience and give them form. There are three fundamental world outlooks: objective idealism, the idealism of liberty, and naturalistic realism. The third of these is contained in the view of Comte and Spencer. "The Naturalistic concept of 'type' not only renders historiography schematic, but reduces it to sociology" (11, p. 97).

Dilthey's methodological attack on sociology led him to offer typology as the peculiar method of the spiritual (historical) sciences.

The Humanistic Impulse in Sociology

The foregoing sketch of some of the forms of the humanistic counterattack on sociology was not intended to set up a particular sequence of influences. An essay is not the vehicle for such an enterprise. Tolstoy's and Dilthey's reactions to sociology were selected, not because they brought about changes in sociology, but because they typify some of the forms of the humanistic reaction to sociology's value commitments and positivistic method. Tolstoy's critique of sociological collectivism and the philistine support of the status quo by the Positivistic Organicists may dramatize the fact that so far as sociologists remained sensitive to the humanistic critique of their theories they would find reason for a shift to more individualistic orientations. On the other hand, Dilthey's vigorous criticism of the positivistic analysis of social phenomena and his development of typology as an alternative method for the analysis of socio-historical events, could well force some sociologists to re-examine their methods.

As time has gone by a number of forms of humanistic individualism and collectivism have appeared. These, however, developed in very different degrees and at different times. Forms of humanistic individualism developed first and most completely; forms of humanistic collectivism have developed only recently and rather sporadically.

It could, perhaps, be assumed — if abstract possibilities were the primary consideration — that humanistic collectivism would have developed in sociology before humanistic individualism. After all, the oldest school of sociological theory was Positivistic Organicism. The organicism of the early sociologists so strongly sustained the need of the new middle classes to justify the status quo (which had recently come into their hands) that a non-positivistic organicism would seem to have been a logical product the moment the application of physical science methods to social events was questioned. However, until such time as sociology was firmly established, the reaction to the physical science bias of early sociology tended rather to take the form of rejection of sociology altogether rather than of the establishment of a new school of sociology. It was only after sociology became indubitably established and had made its way into the universities as one of the basic academic disciplines that it became desirable formally to establish a kind of right-wing humanistic collectivism which still described itself as a sociological theory. When, eventually, the attempt was made in Roman Catholic circles to establish sociology on a basis of Neo-Thomism, this possibility was realized. Perhaps the main stream of what is, at times, called Roman Catholic sociology fits this category.

The conditions for the development of a humanistic form of left-wing collectivism which still described itself as a form of sociology are even more difficult to realize. For this to occur, the given individual would have to reject both right-wing collectivism (Positivistic Organicism and Functionalism) and science; otherwise the thinker would fall into the camp of Marxism or of other scientific socialists.

This seems to be the precise description of the form of sociological theory which was being embraced by C. Wright Mills at the time of his death. In his impressive major works, *Character and Social Structure* (with Hans Gerth), *White Collar*, and *The Power Elite*, Mills conducted his theorizing within the framework of Social Behaviorism (14, pp. 430–433). However, in his later works Mills increasingly subscribed to a collectivistic position which was combined with a forthright anti-empiricism. In an essay for Llewellyn Gross' *Symposium*, Mills stated:

> Now I do not like to do empirical work if I can possibly avoid it. . . . Besides, and more seriously, in the social sciences there is so much to do by way of initial "structuring" . . . that "empirical research" is bound to be thin and uninteresting.
>
> In our situation, empirical work as such is for beginning students and for those who aren't able to handle the complexities of big problems; it is also for highly formal men who do not care what they study so long as it appears to be orderly. All these types have a right to do as they please or as they must; they have no right to impose in the name of science such narrow limits on others. Anyway, you ought not to let them bother you (17, p. 35).

Later in the same year, Mills generalized his opposition to physical science.

> The cultural meaning of physical science — the major older common denominator — is becoming doubtful. As an intellectual style, physical science is coming to be thought by many as somehow inadequate. The adequacy of scientific styles of thought and feeling, imagination and sensibility, has of course from their beginnings been subject to religious doubt and theological controversy, but our scientific grandfathers and fathers beat down such religious doubts. The current doubts are secular, humanistic — and often quite confused. Recent development in physical science — with its technological climax in the H-bomb and the means of carrying it about the earth — have not been experienced as a solution to any problems widely known and deeply pondered by larger intellectual communities and cultural workmen have come to feel that "science" is a false and pretentious Messiah, or at the very least a highly ambiguous element in modern civilization (18, pp. 15–16).

Mills' powerful impetus in the direction of left-wing collectivism was made fully manifest in his passionate propaganda tract in defense of the Cuban revolution and in his apotheosis of its leader in *Listen, Yankee*.

> My major aim in this book is to present the voice of the Cuban revolutionary, as clearly and as emphatically as I can, and I have taken up this aim because of its absurd absence from the news of Cuba available in the United States today. You will not find here The Whole Truth about Cuba, nor "an objective appraisal of the Cuban revolution." I do not believe it is possible for anyone to carry out such an appraisal today, nor do I believe that anyone — Cuban or North American — can yet know "the whole

truth about Cuba." That truth, whatever it turns out to be, is still being created, and every week it changes. The true story of the Cuban revolution, in all its meaning, will have to wait until some Cuban, who has been part of it all, finds out the universal voice of his revolution (19, p. 8).

At no time does the slightest hint of criticism of Fidel Castro ever creep into Mills' account. Castro looms through the pages of *Listen, Yankee,* as an apotheosized superman.

> When men seize an opportunity, they make history; this man has. And he is. He is the most directly radical and democratic force in Cuba. He has always appealed, at every juncture, to public opinion, on the TV and also in person. Before any problem is solved, Fidel spends long hours on the TV. In the last eighteen months the power in Cuba has rested upon the people. He explains and he educates, and after he speaks almost every doubt has gone away. Never before has such a force of public opinion prevailed for so long and so intimately with power. So close, for example, that even a weak rumor sends Fidel to the TV to refute it or to affirm it, to explain what it is all about. So long as Fidel is there, we are going to be all right. His speeches actually create the revolutionary consciousness — and the work gets done. It is fantastic to see how, as it goes along, the revolutionary process transforms one layer after another of the population. And always, there is Fidel's anti-bureaucratic personality and way of going about things, of getting things done, without red tape and without delay and in a thoroughly practical and immediate way (19, pp. 122–123).

In his last book, *The Marxists,* Mills divided the most vital of the intellectual currents of modern times into Marxism and liberalism. They are, he argued, animated by common ideals.

> Both Marxism and liberalism embody the ideals of Greece and Rome and Jerusalem: the humanism of the Renaissance, the rationalism of the eighteenth-century enlightenment (20, pp. 13–14).

Of these alternatives, Mills emphatically preferred Marxism.

> What is most valuable in classic liberalism is most cogently and most fruitfully incorporated in classic Marxism. Much of the failure to confront Marxism in all its variety is in fact a way of not taking seriously the ideals of liberalism itself, for despite the distortions and vulgarizations of Marx's ideas, and despite his own errors, ambiguities, and inadequacies, Karl Marx remains the thinker who has articulated most clearly — and most perilously — the basic ideals which liberalism shares. Hence, to confront Marx and Marxism is to confront this moral tradition (20, p. 14).

A few pages earlier, Mills had formulated the reasons for his preference for Marxism over current social science.

> The social scientists study the details of small-scale *milieux;* Marx studied such details, too, but always within the structure of a total society. The

social scientists, knowing little history, study at most short-run trends; Marx, using historical materials with superb mastery, takes as his unit of study entire epochs. The values of the social scientists generally lead them to accept their society pretty much as it is; the values of Marx led him to condemn his society — root, stock, and branch (20, pp. 10–11).

These passages from Mills, to be sure, contain a fuzzy bundle of half-truths. It is not true, for example, that classic liberalism and Marxism share the same values: classic liberalism is individualistic; Marxism is collectivistic. It is not true that all social scientists study only the details of small-scale *milieux* and have no mastery of historical materials: some do, some do not. Marx's mastery of historical materials — far from being "superb" — has been seriously questioned by some scholars. The ambiguous statement that both Marxism and liberalism embody the ideals of Greece, Rome, and Jerusalem, humanism and rationalism, fails to discriminate the very different aspects of Western thought which are distributed among these positions. Finally, Mills has himself emphatically rejected the linkage between his left-wing collectivism and science — a link which Marxism resoundingly affirmed.

The important point for the present context is this: Mills cast his lot simultaneously with left-wing collectivism and against the linkage between it and science. In his last years, there has been some seething ferment around Mills. If this ferment should condense into a new school of sociology with C. Wright Mills as its charismatic founder, its distinctiveness will be seen to lie in its unique combination of humanism and left-wing collectivism.

Far more important (in terms of numbers of adherents and richness and variety of works) than either right-wing, humanistic collectivism (Neo-Thomistic sociology), or left-wing, humanistic collectivism (the position of C. Wright Mills), are the sociological forms of humanistic individualism represented by Social Behaviorism and Phenomenological Sociology.

Social Behaviorism, the powerful school of sociological theory which acts as the great counterweight in American sociology to Functionalism, represented a reaction both to collectivism (of both right- and left-wing varieties) and to what it conceived to be the excessively rigid positivism which stood in the way of an adaptation of physical methods to the unique properties of social life. All three branches of Social Behaviorism (Pluralistic Behaviorism, stemming from Tarde, Le Bon, Giddings, and Ross; Social-Action Theory, stemming from Max Weber, Robert MacIver, John R. Commons, and Thorstein Veblen; and Symbolic Interactionism, stemming from William James, Cooley, George Herbert Mead, and W. I. Thomas) represented positions in sociology which combined humanistically modified methods with an individualistic approach to social events. Social Behaviorism, thus, is the nearest approach to eighteenth-century rationalism that sociology offers (14, pp. 285–440). It should be noted, however, that the Social Behaviorists actually tried to find a common ground between the methodological perspectives of humanism and science. It thus represented what might be described as either a humanized positivism or scientific humanism. Social-Action Theory, for example in its methodological perspectives, attempted to press to scientific account the typological procedures which Dilthey had offered as an alternative to scientific methods.

Finally a non-rationalistic form of humanistic individualism took shape as a departure from Neo-Kantian Formalism (14, pp. 267 ff.). On analogy with a procedure of Kant, who had treated science as the empirical study of experience but had drawn a distinction between mind-given forms and empirical content, the neo-Kantian Formalists in sociology drew a distinction between the form and content of social life. The content was studied by other social sciences, but sociology was argued to be similar to geometry. It was said to be a study of pure social forms in separation from their content.

However, if one examined the Kantian view carefully, it quickly became apparent that although both form and content were said to be objects of scientific study, they were assigned very different properties. Since forms are present from the moment experience occurs, and since they are present as possibilities before experience occurs, it is not necessary to employ experimental methods to discover social forms. In fact, experiment is of no help in studying forms, since they are present from the beginning of experience. It should only be necessary to examine experience carefully though introspectively to discover social forms. There was a potential crisis for scientific methodology buried in Neo-Kantian sociology, for the most significant of all methods would seem to point toward introspection.

Long before Neo-Kantian sociology came face to face with its methodological problems, other developments had been occurring in Western thought which were to offer a possible solution to the Sociological Formalists. The ferment in the methodology of the humanists of the nineteenth century (in part illustrated by Dilthey above) was forcing them to look to alternatives to science for the analysis of social phenomena. Dilthey, it was noted above, had thought that poetry could be more valuable in the understanding of the operations of the human mind than logic. A primary product of the search during the nineteenth and early twentieth centuries for a non-logical (non-rational in this sense) procedure for analyzing the events of human experience was phenomenology. In its most rudimentary sense, phenomenology may be described as a new method of controlled or directed introspection that was believed by its proponents to be more fundamental than either logical analysis or empirical-scientific procedures.

Once it became completely clear that the methodological status being assigned to social forms was potentially quite different from that of social content, phenomenology offered itself as a natural method. Phenomenological sociology, pioneered by Alfred Vierkandt, was developed with particular brilliance for the analysis of various social and cultural forms by Max Scheler (14, pp. 267–281).

Existentialism and Sociology

With phenomenology, sociology had already entered the edifice of Existentialism. However, a fully developed Existentialist sociology is only now under way. This is no place to consider these problems in detail, but it is useful to sketch some of the major elements of Existentialism and indicate the direction of their possible influence on sociology.

It has been argued that the essence of Existentialism is found in a profound sense of alienation from their society and their traditions by Western men. However, Marxism, too, has argued that modern workers are alienated by the methods of production and the operation of those forces which separate them from ownership of the instruments of production. It has been argued that the essence of Existentialism is found in the formation of an outlook resting on a profound sense of dread. Some Existentialists (Kierkegaard, Heidegger) fulfill this definition, but some others (Ortega y Gasset and Jaspers) seem basically to have had Apollonian dispositions. It has been argued that the essence of Existentialism is a powerful subjective religious sense (Kierkegaard and Jaspers qualify on this standard), but some persons accepting the label of Existentialism have been quite irreligious (Sartre and Ortega y Gasset for certain, Heidegger perhaps). Hence it has finally been argued that Existentialism has no coherent position and is, in fact, indefinable (Walter Kaufmann).

However, there are a number of things shared by those to whom the label of Existentialism has been applied. None of the Existentialists is collectivistic. A powerful anti-collectivism runs through them all in two respects: they radically reject the collectivistic philosophies of both right and left wing; they are powerfully opposed to collectivistic trends in contemporary society. Whatever else may be true of it, Existentialism is, first, a powerful individualistic reaction in an age of collectivism.

In its individualism, Existentialism finds a deep echo from ancient traditions of the West, from the civic humanism of the earlier period, and from the tradition in its period of maturity from Descartes to Kant, reaching a kind of culmination in eighteenth-century Rationalism. However, Existentialism represents an individualistic reaction in an age of collectivism in a world disillusioned with the individualistic rationalism of its classic period. The rationalistic traditions had operated like dissolving acid on the traditional faiths of Western man. When the traditional faiths declined, they left in their place only the unstable compound: faith in Reason. But Reason rationalized the Revolution which ushered in the mass world — a world that powerfully thrust Reason aside.

The new individualism that arose in the collectivistic world was disillusioned with the rationalistic formulas of the earlier age. It had no confidence in the products of reason. All "systems" cast up by the thought process in the course of experience were now conceived ultimately as mere "rationalizations" of a more fundamental psychic reality. The new individualism thus rejected the rationalism that had served as so powerful a tool for the individualism of the seventeenth and eighteenth centuries. This means, however, that the new individualism was automatically pressed into the situation where it had to develop a new analysis of experience. It explored not logic, but the non-logical areas of individual activity for a method of personal orientation. When personal experience is examined, it presents no clear, logical distinctions and organized sequences of thought, but an amazing complex of ambiguities, doubts, anxieties, and uncertainties. When thought intervenes in personal experience it often imposes a set of categories as if from the outside, categories which force the ill-fitting densities of experience into a condition of half-fittedness. Hence, the exponents of the new individualism looked to areas thrust into the background by men who had thought that the essence of man was his reason: to poetry, to art, to the experience of the religious mystic, to mythology. And when phenomenology attempted to gather these many impulses into a single procedure for a new analysis of experience, the Existentialists were powerfully influenced by them.

Finally, it may be noted, there was good reason why the new individualism might not wish to arm itself with science. For one thing, the rationalistic impulse in Western thought was in considerable measure taken over by science. But more importantly, the great collectivistic movements in modern times had taken over science as a powerful instrument. Science had been used with great efficiency by the large business and industrial combinations of modern industry, by the big states and powerful armies. Science was the great implement of collectivism!

There was a time when the peculiar ingredients of Existentialism would have been quite impossible to assemble in the West. However, a series of powerful individualistic figures responding both to the social trends and to the traditions of the West gradually pulled these ingredients into its eventual synthesis. Perhaps most noteworthy were Schopenhauer, Kierkegaard, Burckhardt, Nietzsche, Dilthey, and Edmund Husserl. Near the turn of the century several of these influences were woven into systematic interpretations of modern man and his times. Among the persons playing a major role in bringing about the Existential synthesis are Bergson, Ortega Y Gasset, Heidegger, Jaspers, Berdyaev, and Sartre.

It is not unfair to conceive the social doctrines of the Existentialists as constituting an Existentialist Sociology. An able young writer, Edward A. Tiryakian, accurately summed up the general social doctrines of the Existentialists as follows:

From Kierkegaard's *The Present Age* to Jaspers' *Man in the Modern Age*, the existentialists' evaluation of the individual-and-society relationship remains strikingly the same. What stands out in particular is their rejection and condemnation of modern society as an impersonal environment antithetical and inimical to the development of authentic selfhood. While some thinkers stress the importance and the positive aspects of the inter-subjective relations, there is none who looks with favor at society itself. Everything societal is considered either an unauthentic, unreal abstraction, or a sort of technological Chronos devouring the personality by means of an implacable, devastating levelling process (23, p. 144).

Tiryakian maintains that there is a need for a reunion of sociology and philosophy, and proposes bringing about this union by a fusion of *sociologism* and *existentialism* on the ground that the contemporary predicament of the individual and of society is their common concern. "Basically both are reactions to the disorganization of the modern world" (23, p. 151). It should be noted that, even in the unlikely event that one were able to unite Existentialism and what is called sociologism, one could still not claim to have united philosophy and sociology. Existentialism is only one — though a vigorous one — of the traditions in contemporary philosophy. What Tiryakian calls sociologism is only one of the traditions (again, though, a vigorous one) of the recent forms of theory. By *Sociologism* Tiryakian means Positivistic Organicism and Functionalism. Durkheim is his favorite illustration.

Tiryakian accurately sums up the difference between Existentialism and this type of sociology in the following passages:

Durkheim stressed the reality of society as a psychic entity, a collective consciousness produced by the association and interaction of individuals. Gabriel Marcel warns against the notion that elements A and B, endowed respectively with consciousness C' and C'' may form a whole having a synthetic consciousness C''' (23, p. 151).

Durkheim saw no fundamental conflict between the individual and society. . . . Heidegger regards the social self as the unauthentic part of human-being, but Durkheim considered it that which gives us true humanity, because it makes us civilized (23, p. 152).

In Durkheim's thought . . . the end of moral action is the collectivity. . . . In contrast to Durkheim, the existential perspective on morality is . . . ambiguous and ambivalent. . . . For Nietzsche, the utility of social morality is no proof of its validity. . . . Kierkegaard also took an ambiguous position on morality. The ethical, for him, is a higher realm of existence than the aesthetic (23, p. 152).

Unlike Kierkegaard, Durkheim did not perceive any opposition between morality and religion (23, pp. 153–154).

Durkheim believed emphatically that society pervades the individual: he cannot, without contradicting his nature, liberate himself from the limits imposed upon him by his participation in the social world. . . . The authentic selfhood of the person is to be found only through participation in a collectivity, in social reality. This view is antipodal to that of existentialism. . . . Beginning with Kierkegaard all existentialist thinkers have been aware of and disturbed by the levelling process of civilization. The existential perspective sees this process as a threat to the individual, robbing him of authentic, unique existence. The levelling process effects equality by obliterating individual differences. Kierkegaard, Nietzsche, Marcel, Heidegger, and Jaspers, holding social equality to be tantamount to mass mediocrity, make a common front in decrying both the process and the advocates of egalitarianism (23, p. 155).

After detailing the contrasts between existentialism and the form of sociology he describes as sociologism, Tiryakian proposes that they be fused in a single perspective. The first step in such synthesis is to conceive Existentialism and sociology, simply, as alternate responses to the same problem.

If sociologism and existentialism have a common source in their awareness that the modern world is in a state of moral crisis, are they irrevocably apart because of their contrasting evaluation and approach to the relation of the individual and society? Stated in somewhat broader terms, are sociology and philosophy to remain in a state of "cold war" (23, pp. 162–163)?

By an extraordinarily simple re-interpretation, Tiryakian seeks to reduce sociologism and Existentialism to complementary rather than contrasting perspectives.

We propose that Durkheim's fundamental concern was really to study objectively a *subjective* reality, not, as is sometimes assumed by existentialists among others, an *objective* reality (23, p. 163).

And by one blow Tiryakian claims to have cut the Gordian knot, to have synthesized sociologism and existentialism and reunited sociology and philosophy.

It would surely be a triumph of dialectical reasoning if, in this manner and at one blow, one were able to synthesize scientific, right-wing collectivism with humanistic, non-rational individualism. However, it is not true that a common moral crisis produced sociologism and Existentialism and that these are merely different evaluations of the same crisis. Decisives to act come first: moral crises may or may not ensue. Nor does one wipe away the collectivistic theories of Durkheim or any other Positivistic Organicist by such a device as discovering that Durkheim was simply trying to treat a subjective reality objectively. One has merely equivocated on the meaning of individuality by reducing it to subjectivity.

There is an Existentialist sociology or at least an Existentialist interpretation of social phenomena, but any such fusion of contradictory positions such as those of the Existentialists and the Functionalists is out of the question. One is reminded of the old story of the two Russians who found themselves on a train, one going to Minsk, the other to Pinsk, and broke into hot argument, since they were in opposite directions. Peace was restored only when one suggested — "it must be the dialectic."

Sociological Theories in Terms of Their Humanistic-Scientific and Individualistic-Collectivistic Components

M e t h o d o l o g i c a l	P e r s p e c t i v e s		SUBSTANTIVE ALTERNATIVES			
			INDIVIDUALISM		COLLECTIVISM	
			Rationalism	*Non-Rationalism*	*Left Wing*	*Right Wing*
		Humanism	Social Behaviorism	Phenomenological Formalism Existential Sociology	The Sociology of C. Wright Mills	Main Stream of Catholic Sociology
		Science	Neo-Kantian Branch of Sociological Formalism	Conflict Theory	Marxian Sociology	Positivistic Organicism Functionalism

Summary

The most fundamental of all perspectives in Western thought are those of humanism and science. Humanism arose as a man-oriented secular outlook in the dawn period of the Western cities, when offspring of medievalism were cast as orphans into a new world and forced to exploit the resources of their own natures to solve the unprecedented problems of their existence. Humanism arose in politically-responsible (elitist) circles: the advisors or princes, the tutors in eminent households, diplomatists, secretaries, and university professors. In the attempt to solve their problems, the humanists searched through the literature of the past, developing philological methods and techniques of historical research. They left a permanent heritage in the humanistic disciplines of the present day. Later, when the city began to crystallize and the rising nation-state took up the curve of development, the humanistic skills and techniques were transferred to the sphere of the nation-state. Perhaps their highest and fullest expression was achieved in seventeenth- and eighteenth-century Rationalism. However, another phenomenon accompanied this transition. In the course of the shift from the city to the nation-state, the old polarity of humanism and theology of the city was lost, and theology was shifted into the sphere of the humanities.

Western science, which fused the rational proof discovered and worked up by man in the classical polis with systematic experimentalism — the world of things — was also born in the Western city. It emerged in quite different circles from humanism, and had, originally, a different intent. It proceeded out of the circles of craftsmen and artists. It was intended, not to solve problems of man's social experience, but to discover new things about the world of physical things. Science powerfully implemented the free technology which formed its medieval birth matrix, and in whatever sphere it was released it worked revolutions.

The primary substantive issues of human social life are formed by the relation between the individual and the collective (society). In every society, including the Western city and later the nation-state, individualistic and collectivistic theories have developed. Individualistic theories see the highest human values in the most harmonious and smooth-running society possible.

In the period of the Western city, individualistic theories were most frequently advocated by the humanists, while collectivistic theories were most often advocated by the theologians (of both Roman Catholic and Protestant persuasion, though more frequently by the former).

In this early period there were only the most sporadic suggestions for lifting science from the world of physical things and applying it to human affairs.

When the curve of development shifted to the nation-state, the early division between humanism and theology was wiped away, and humanism and theology often found themselves making common cause against the forces of a new world. Moreover, a re-division in the forms of individualism and collectivism was carried through and the lines between rationalistic and non-rationalistic individualism and left- and right-wing collectivism were crystallized.

Perhaps the single most dramatic intellectual event of the nineteenth and twentieth centuries has been the rise of the social sciences with their attempt to transplant techniques which proved so powerful in dealing with the physical world to the social world. While the social sciences held out the promise of fusing the scientific and humanistic poles of Western thought, they have carried with them the danger (from some points of view) of permanently transforming the ratio between individuality and collectivity and carrying through an unprecedented curtailment of the sphere of individual freedom. Against the forces moving in this direction, Existentialism has represented an insurgent protest. Its essence is found in a new anti-rational and anti-scientific individualism.

Some of the major ways in which sociology has evolved under the strains of these diverging forces have been traced. Sociology is a dynamic development opened by the establishment of Positivistic Organicism, dividing into many contrasting and, in part, complementary forms, and continuing in the present with the emergence of an Existentialist sociology, on the one hand, and forms of left-wing, humanistic collectivism on the other.

BIBLIOGRAPHY

1. Burckhardt, Jacob. *The Civilization of the Renaissance.* New York: Oxford University Press, 1945.

2. Cassirer, Ernst, Paul Oskar Kristeller, and John Herman Randall, Jr. *The Renaissance Philosophy of Man.* Chicago: University of Chicago Press, 1958.

3. Comte, Auguste. *Cours de Philosophie Positive.* Paris: Au Siege de la societe positiviste, 4 vols., 1892.

4. Comte, Auguste. *Systeme de politique positive* or *Traite de la Sociologie instituant la Religion de l'Humanite,* 4 vols., translated by John Henry Bridges as *System of Positive Polity.* London: Longmans, Green, 1875–1877.

5. Da Vinci, Leonardo. *The Notebooks of Leonardo Da Vinci,* edited by Edward MacCurdy. New York: Braziller, 1956.

6. Dilthey, Wilhelm. *Dilthey's Philosophy of Existence,* translated by William Kluback and Martin Weinbaum. New York: Bookman, 1914.

7. Droysen, Gustav. *Grundrissder Historik,* translated by E. B. Andrews as *Outline of the Principles of History.* Boston: Ginn & Co., 1893.

8. Droysen, Johann Gustav. "Zur Characteristik der europaischen Krisis," in Felix Gilbert (ed.), *Politische Schriften.* Munich, 1933, pp. 307–342.

9. Goldenweiser, Alexander. *Anthropology.* New York: F. S. Crofts, 1937.

10. Hayek, F. A. *The Counter-revolution of Science.* Glencoe, Ill.: The Free Press, 1952.

11. Kluback, William. *Wilhelm Dilthey's Philosophy of History.* New York: Columbia University Press, 1956.

12. Little, A. G. "The Mendicant Orders," in *The Cambridge Medieval History,* 8 vols. New York: The Macmillan Co., 1929, Vol. 6.

13. Lundberg, George Andrew. *Can Science Save Us?* New York: Longmans, Green, 1947.

14. Martindale, Don. *The Nature and Types of Sociological Theory.* Boston: Houghton Mifflin, 1960.

15. Martindale, Don. *Social Life and Cultural Change.* Princeton: Van Nostrand, 1962.

16. Mill, John Stuart. *A System of Logic.* New York: Longmans, Green, 1949.

17. Mills, C. Wright. "On Intellectual Craftsmanship," in Llewellyn Gross (ed.), *Symposium in Sociological Theory.* Evanston, Ill.: Row, Peterson & Co., 1959.

18. Mills, C. Wright. *The Sociological Imagination.* New York: Oxford University Press, 1959.

19. Mills, C. Wright. *Listen, Yankee.* New York: Ballantine Books, 1960.

20. Mills, C. Wright. *The Marxists.* New York: Dell Publishing Co., 1962.

21. Munro, W. G., and George Sellery. *Medieval Civilization.* New York: Century Co., 1910.

22. Shils, Edward A. "Epilogue: The Calling of Sociology," in Talcott Parsons, Edward Shils, Kaspar D. Naegele, and Jesse R. Pitts (eds.), *Theories of Society,* 2 vols. New York: Free Press of Glencoe, 1961, Vol. 2, pp. 1403–1449.

23. Tiryakian, Edward A. *Sociologism and Existentialism.* Englewood Cliffs, N.J.: Prentice-Hall, Inc., 1962.

24. Tolstoy, Leo. *What to Do?* translated by Isabel F. Hapgood. New York: Thomas Y. Crowell, 1887.

25. Tolstoy, Leo. *On Life,* translated by Aylmer Maude. London: Humphrey Milford, 1934.

26. White, Lynn, Jr. *Medieval Technology and Social Change.* Oxford: Clarendon Press, 1962.

SECTION SIX

Cultural Change, Cultural Contact, and Social Movements

In the Section to follow we present four chapters involving the inter-action of value systems and structural elements in society. The reader will recognize phenomena which not long ago would have been de-scribed in terms of "assimilation" or "acculturation" in some of these chapters. The fact that these concepts are not used by the present authors indicates another facet of cultural change which calls for analy-sis, namely, the creation and disappearance of concepts, frames of refer-ence, models, and systems. Is this merely a matter of "fads" and "fashions," dependent partly on the need for innovators to make their mark by the creation of neologisms and the pouring of old wine into new bottles, or does this signify a real inadequacy of the old concepts in the light of the accumulation of new knowledge and superior insights? The question is more threatening and less easily answered for the social than for the natural sciences, and we shall not pursue it further, if only for these reasons. Instead let us see how the material to follow illuminates some basic problems in cultural change, by dint of intensive analyses of specific situations in a variety of settings, utilizing a number of more or less explicit frames of reference.

In his analysis of the political operations of a dual elite (the British and the native) in Nigeria, Cohen tests a set of hypotheses previously applied to the study of the Soviet industrial system. These hypotheses are based on a "conflict" model, which would seem to be the most mean-ingful kind in view of the fact that the native definition of the goals and methods of political rule differ substantially from that of the colonial administrators. Cohen shows that in spite of this the system has been viable, partly because of the adroit use of informal arrangements which often deviated from the traditional formal norms of both cultures. The ability of the British to "muddle through" has often been commented upon; one might add that the success of their Commonwealth depended in equal measure on the same ability among the relevant counterparts among the "lesser breeds." In the case described by Cohen the existing conflicts, far from producing disorganization and anomie, were "utilized"

491

by the society to meet new exigencies with a high degree of flexibility. The native emirates learned to adopt mechanisms for their own transformation, thus obviating the "need for revolution." Other societies have been less successful in this respect; for a systematic treatment of the reasons for this we refer the reader to the chapter on revolution by Willer and Zollschan in Section Two.

A somewhat similar situation is described by Elkin in his study of the role of advertising in French Canada. Though in this case the British culture is not represented by colonial administrators who rule the French "natives," the general dominance of the former over the latter is patent. Elkin views advertising as a "key to change," in that it serves as a source of both information and education. The fact that it does not have formal standing as an educational institution makes it all the more difficult to control on the part of the French minority intent on maintaining or increasing its cultural autonomy. In addition the "natives" (or at least certain important power groups among them) are aware that the only hope for survival lies in adapting their culture to the prevalent trends, i.e., in "modernization." However, for the most part the members of the French minority who would be most instrumental in making this possible have other fish to fry: they are concerned with maximizing their socio-economic status. In the case of advertising (as well as business life in general) the rising specialists must operate within Anglo-Saxon dominated corporations, thus undercutting the strengthening of French culture. This of course has been a fairly prevalent pattern in the assimilation of minorities, and unlike Nigeria, the Province of Quebec is not likely to have its flag flying among those of the newly created independent nations.

The desire for political and cultural autonomy and dominance has been among the most powerful forces for change in recent human history (unless we follow the theorists espousing extreme formulations of historical or cultural determinism). J. A. and Olive Banks address themselves to the questions of how British feminism differed from other social movements, and why it "petered out" in a relatively short time.

As to the first question, they show that "sex consciousness" paralleled class consciousness to some degree, but lacked the systematic blueprint for utopia found among most socio-political movements of the nineteenth century. With reference to the second question, the authors search for "structural" origins of women's dissatisfaction with their lot, and in this context challenge certain assumptions made by the Parsonian school regarding women's role in childrearing. (The reference here is to Talcott, not Elsie, the American anthropologist. One hesitates to predict the consequences for structural-functional theory if Talcott Parsons had been a woman.) They also raise the problem of why female dissatisfactions "withered away" in view of the continued existence of the double standard. Has the battle of the sexes been won by the "weaker" sex on the non-political level, as many American observers (mostly male) main-

tain? Or have modern women been lulled to sleep by the opiates of the affluent society? (It should be pointed out that the level of levity inherent in these questions is the responsibility of the editors, not the authors.)

In a more serious vein we should draw attention to the fact that the Banks are concerned with several of the most problematic aspects of social movements, namely, those relating to the mobilization of values and motivations of collective action. We need to refer here only to the concept of false consciousness, or to Ferdinand Lassalle's complaint about "the damned wantlessness of the poor." The other side of the coin is represented by the fanaticism of the "true believers," whose involvement in collective action is reduced by some observers to a kind of irrationality or other manifestation of pathological needs. Finally we should mention one of the most challenging statements made by the authors, namely that "the most significant change in the position of women during the last hundred years" was connected with the fall of the birth rate, and that this was not at all an explicit goal of the feminist movement. Apparently Lysistrata had few adherents among the suffragettes.

The study by Andersen and Eichhorn can be conceived as starting out at the opposite pole from the one just discussed. Their subjects are only dimly aware, if at all, of being members of a "community of fate" and of the potentialities of collective action for the prevention or mitigation of heart disease. But what Durkheim has called the "constraining role of social facts" operates nevertheless, limiting and determining to a high degree the decisions which they make within their "life space." Using a basically Lewinian model, the authors show that the combination of poverty and ill health minimizes the degrees of freedom available to Indiana farmers, no matter how individualistic their ideology. In the past, American farmers have organized to protect their economic interests and social status — through the cooperative movement and pressure groups, and when these proved insufficient, the creation of Populist political parties. It remains to be seen whether they will recognize illness as an exigency requiring collective action, as did their counterparts in Canada, for example.

19

Ronald Cohen

Conflict and Change in a

Northern Nigerian Emirate[1]

I

Up until recently much of the descriptive work of the ethnographer, especially in dealing with African societies, has been carried out by placing a great deal of reliance on the assumption, often implicit, that action follows from institutionalized patterns. Because many of the institutions in the African societies are unfamiliar and exotic, it has always been a primary responsibility of the anthropologist to discover what these are, and to describe them in a systematic fashion. This is often an arduous task which requires detailed observation and long, hard hours of analysis. By the time it is completed, however, the anthropologist is often oriented to the social behavior he has observed in terms of the institutions he has outlined.

Several factors have conspired to turn the attention of anthropologists in other directions. Studies of African peoples are now much more common, and the overall structural types of the segmentary and non-segmentary societies are widely understood. This has allowed us to concentrate more attention on the details of social life within these now familiar types of social structures. Furthermore, the rapid social change taking

[1] Revised version of a paper entitled, "The Analysis of Conflict in Hierarchical Systems," in *Anthropologica* n.s., 4, 1, 1962, pp. 87–120; based upon a paper presented at the Annual Meeting of the Canadian Political Science Association, Kingston, Ontario, June 1960.

place in Africa is pointing our attention more towards the behavior of persons in new situations, rather than at the varieties and interrelations of traditional institutions. Finally, at the theoretical level, a number of workers in both anthropology and sociology have been discussing the limitations of the social system model in which man lives in a group with a tradition such that the rules are functional and the entire system is a nicely balanced, self-supporting, integrated whole.[2] Social life in this model revolves around the internalizing of norms so that the individual can take his place in the system and play out the part tradition has ordained for him. Activity not functionally directed is labeled deviant, dysfunctional, or disequilibrating, and often put forward or selected as a major cause of social change. However, as Buckley (2) has pointed out, this carries with it a danger that we may negatively evaluate change, since the model stresses stability and persistence in its analytic perspective. Because change is separated from the integrated model as a kind of irritant which forces the system to adjust, it is difficult to use it in a rapidly altering situation where change is a primary characteristic of the social situation under observation. What is needed then is a theoretical perspective which attempts to order the changing situation *while it is changing.*

To begin such an approach, it is necessary to assume that the institutionalized social structure is only one among many facets of social reality which determines the course of social life.[3] This leads us to a more complex, but perhaps more realistic, view of social process, in which man is seen as an actor who acts and reacts in relation to a multitude of pressures and stimuli. These are internal and external to himself in origin; traditional and novel in time depth; interpersonal, supernatural, material in substance. In this chapter we shall deal with only one facet of these stimuli — that of the exigencies or pressures, and the reaction to these, which result from a hierarchical political organization.

The situation chosen is one in which there are conflicts among the standards governing behavior. This forces us to pay attention to the adjustive responses of the actors instead of looking out for the "functional" or "integrative" qualities of the cultural norms which pertain to behavior. If an actor in a given context is institutionally enjoined to behave in a certain way, and not to behave in this manner — all at the same time — then a description and analysis of the rules governing behavior cannot give us any adequate predictive conclusions about the resultant action. What is obviously necessary is an analysis of the resultant behavior itself.

The analysis to follow has been organized with the aid of a theoreti-

[2] See for example, Dahrendorf (5), Epstein (6), and Leach (10).

[3] Compare this with Radcliffe-Brown's assumption that "the social life of the community is here defined as the functioning of the social structure" (14, p. 180). A more extreme example of this approach can be seen in Levi-Strauss' statement that social anthropology consists "exclusively of the study of rules" (11, p. 538).

cal schema first put forward by Frank (8) as a method for the description and analysis of conflicting standards. He developed the theory as a result of his interest in the Russian industrial system, but suggests that it is more widely applicable. The following discussion therefore has a two-fold purpose: first, to present material on the Kanuri political system using a new approach, and second, to test the applicability of Frank's theory to an entirely different cultural context.

The Theory

Frank (8) feels that if three conditions are present in a social situation, it is possible to predict a series of behaviors which are of necessity associated with them. These conditions are (1) conflicting standards, (2) ambiguous goals, and (3) selective enforcement.

Conflicting standards are rules or prescriptions for conduct which are enforceable through formal or informal sanctions. Their distinctive feature is that they pertain to rules or prescriptions which cannot be satisfied simultaneously, since compliance with one involves the failure to meet another equally enforceable standard.

Goal ambiguity refers to the state of affairs in which it is difficult for members in the system, or indeed for any observer viewing the system in part or as a whole, to ascertain clearly the desired ends towards which everyone should be striving. Thus the social structure cannot in any empirical sense be made to resemble a simple means-ends scheme.

Selective enforcement is the process by which the model is put into operation. It postulates a differential enforcement over time of the total gamut of enforceable standards so that not all standards must be conformed with to the same extent.

Frank puts it this way:

> Multiple and at least in part conflicting standards are set by superiors for subordinates. More than one hierarchical channel of communication is maintained. Conflict may arise among standards set within each hierarchy as well as among those set by different hierarchies. Subordinates are free to decide which of the conflicting standards to meet, if any. However, subordinates are responsible to superiors for their performance with respect to all standards; and subordinates may be held accountable for failure to meet any standard. The relative importance of standards is neither well, nor completely defined, nor is it entirely undefined. The priority among standards is ambiguous. Subordinates make their assessment of priority to guide their decision-making and task performance. Each subordinate appeals to those standards which are most in accord with his incentives and the circumstances of the moment and to those which are most likely to be invoked by superiors in evaluating his performance. Superiors in turn make their assessment of priority to guide their necessarily selective evaluation of subordinates' performance and enforcement of standards. The entire process is

continuous: superiors modify the set of standards to comply with their changing objectives; subordinates adapt their decisions to changing standards and to changing circumstances; superiors enforce standards in accordance with changing priority (8, p. 11).

The author of the theory goes on to suggest that if the above conditions are present, then the following behavior can be observed:

A. Member Behavior

The more the system relies on conflicting standards organization, the more the members will:

1) Fail to meet all standards and exhibit differences in selection of the standards they do meet.

2) Change the selection, over time, of the standards they do meet.

3) Simulate or feign meeting of standards.

4) Provide themselves with safety factors for contingencies.

5) Have recourse to (and become) intermediary dealers in information, influence, and any other organizational resource which enhances a particular member's ability to meet standards by eliminating some of the conflict (for him) among standards.

B. System Organization

The obstacle to formal rationality entailed by conflicting standards suggests that:[4]

6) The more conflicting standards there are the more the system will be oriented toward substantive rationality.

The system will also exhibit:

7) Changing standards for members.

8) Ready adaptation to changes of environment by system members at the system-environment boundary.

9) Widespread member initiative as a possibility (but not a necessity). Where this is not expressed in a standard, Frank suggests that a "let sleeping dogs lie" policy can be expected.

10) Widespread information about standards and system goals among members.

11) Strong incentive to, and evidence of, member use of information and attempted compliance with standards.

[4] Frank uses the Weberian terms *formal rationality* and *substantive rationality* to mean roughly what anthropologists imply by the terms *ideal* and *real*, respectively. For our purposes here, formal rationality refers to a means-end schema in which stipulated ends are achieved through a set of stipulated means and these rules are the only ones used by actors to achieve their agreed-upon ends. Substantive rationality refers, here, to a system in which actors are oriented to situations rather than to ends or means. They achieve ends through their understanding and reaction to a situation, and whether or not this situation has within it formally recognized and culturally acceptable means is immaterial, or at least less important than the fact that the actor is reacting to his perception of the situation and its constituent social, cultural, and psychological ingredients. In other words, a shift from formal to substantive rationality is a shift from an emphasis on rules to one in which there is an emphasis on the social situation itself.

C. System Change

The flexibility of a conflicting standards system, particularly changing standards and initiative (Hypotheses 7 and 9, respectively), should:

12) Permit substantial change or variability within the given systematic structure.

13) Render a conflicting standards system continuously receptive and responsive to external pressure for systemic change; and, *ceteris paribus*, to change by small steps, rather than (pressure having built up on the outside and finally breaking through) by a few big steps or by evolution rather than revolution.

The possibility of institutionalizing initiative (Hypothesis 9):

14) May result in internally (as well as externally) generated system change.[5]

II

Turning now from theory to data, it is necessary first to indicate the context in which the conflict takes place. It is then established that the three premises of the theoretical model are present in this context. Finally data are presented to illustrate the presence or absence of the theoretically predicted behavior said to be associated with the premises.

The Context[6]

The Kanuri of Bornu province of northeastern Nigeria have been organized as a Muslim emirate in the Chad basin for many centuries. Their language classification by Greenberg (9), early Arabic sources, and the scattered work of a few interested scholars, supports the notion of their continuity in the region, with possible origins somewhere to the northeast of their present habitat. The pre-colonial emirate kept up continual trade and cultural contacts with the Maghreb during its long history as an organized state.

The Kanuri number about one and one-half million with a population density of 50 to 60 per square mile. There is no pressure on farmland, which can be extended simply by clearing new bush areas farther away from the population settlements. The majority of the people are farmers who carry on three analytically separable economic activities. These consist of (1) farming (primarily millet and guinea corn, supplemented

[5] These hypotheses have been taken, for the most part, verbatim from Frank (8, p. 13).

[6] The field data were collected in Bornu Province, Nigeria, between January 1956, and August 1957, with the financial assistance of the Ford Foundation Area Training Fellowship Program. The author would like to express his thanks to Professor C. W. M. Hart, under whose guidance field research among the Kanuri was planned and carried out. Professor A. G. Frank has read and commented on previous drafts of this chapter. The writer would like to express his appreciation to Professor Frank for many useful hints and suggestions.

by maize, beans, squash, cucumbers, and groundnuts), (2) cash crop-ping (mostly groundnuts), and (3) a dry season non-farming activity connected with the market. Market activities are in turn divided into craft work, sales of agricultural products, and a complex middleman trade between markets. There is much variation in the dependence of each household upon farming as compared to market activity, although some farming is carried on by almost everyone except a few full-time specialists.

In pre-colonial Bornu the Kanuri were ruled by a monarch, the Shehu, and his nobles. These latter were given fiefs. Taxes were levied, and men conscripted for wars which involved punishing or subduing vassal states, and/or taking slaves to be used for agricultural labor and servants. There were courts and an independent or specialized judiciary, although all political leaders served in a judicial capacity as well. Stability was maintained through the tight control exerted on the society by the Shehu and his followers. All followers who were titled fief-holders, except one — the Galidima was almost a vassal lord of his own sub-state — had to remain in the capital under the eye of the monarch, while the fiefs were run for them by subordinates. Internal political instability resulted from the competition for kingly office which followed the death of the Shehu. Segments of the royal lineage and their followers became factions in the state and vied with one another for the supreme power. Stability en-sued when a faction emerged whose members were able to organize a strong central government under their royal leader.

The society has been stratified for a long time, with status differences based on tribal membership, occupation, birth, age, wealth, and, to some extent, urban residence identifications. The people recognize two major class divisions — the upper or ruling class (*kantuoma*) and the broad base of the peasant class (*tala*) under the autocratic hegemony of the rulers. This is complicated by the recognition that there is a royal group within the nobility, and that the low status of slaves may vary and cross-cut other rankings through achievement and appointment to high office. In analytical terms, the stratification system is a highly complicated resultant of the interplay of status determinants. Rosman (15) uses eight separate categories of social status in his work on Kanuri acculturation. Cohen has used status gradients and their interre-lationships to explain social differentiation, upward mobility, and class structure (3).

Today, the Shehu (King or Emir) of Bornu lives in his capital city of Maiduguri. There is a courtly life with titled nobles, including *Ajia* (District Heads) who live in their own District capitals as sub-rulers of 21 segments of the emirate under the Shehu. District heads, in turn, have under their jurisdiction a group of contiguous Village Area units headed by *Lawan* (Village Heads). Under these latter are Hamlet Heads (*Bulama*), in charge of small settlements of contiguous compounds. Peasants call themselves the peasants of such and such a *Lawan*. Today the Native Administration departments have their personnel stationed throughout the district. Along with the district head and his chief followers, they form an urban upper class living in the districts throughout the state.

At the interpersonal level of village and city life, social relations are governed by the organization of households. These vary enormously in size, although the usual peasant household is often not more than four to eight people. However the households of very wealthy men, or more especially, politically important men, can be as large as 50 or 60. These units are regarded *as if* they were kinship organizations and indeed, for peasants, they often are nuclear, polygynous, or patrilocal extended family groupings. However in a large number of cases totally unrelated persons live in the compound as the subordinate of the compound head. Marriage is polygynous for all classes and the usual Muslim custom of allowing up to four wives is followed, although political leaders often have a small number of concubines, as well as male slaves. Divorce is common and household units break up continuously, either through divorce or through the death of the household head which can provoke competition and conflict among his heirs. The household is regarded as the basic social unit in the society and relations to the household are modeled on the father-son relationship for all males in the organization. It is this relationship, that of household head to household (male) member that provides the model for proper superior/subordinate relations in the political system. Traditionally, the superior gives the subordinate economic security, social status, and a role in the community, and may even provide the subordinate with a wife in return for disciplined loyalty and obedience.

For purposes of clarity and expression, and because most of the conditions described here are still present in Bornu society, this chapter was written in the present tense, although the data were gathered during 1955–57 when the country was not yet an independent state.

III

Establishment of the Theoretical Premises

In order to establish that "goal ambiguity," "conflicting standards," and "selective enforcement" do occur in Kanuri society, it is necessary to take a detailed look at behavior in the system. Although these processes are present at all levels of Kanuri social organization, documentation of this contention would carry us well beyond the limits of one chapter. Therefore, our attempt to establish the relevance of the premises of the theory to Kanuri society will concentrate on the role of the district head. The same purpose would have been served just as well, however, by focusing on the role of district officer, Native Administration official, village area head, or indeed of the Shehu (Emir) himself.

The District Head

The appointment of district heads is officially made by the Shehu in consultation with his Waziri (chief minister) and Council. In practice, it is agreed upon by both the Native officials and the British administrative personnel present in the area. This means that a district head owes his appointment to both these sources. Furthermore, the deposition or re-stationing of a district head can be traced to complaints coming from either of these central agencies.

Traditionally, the district head collected taxes, and raised militia for his superior from his fief. Taxation was a form of tribute in kind given to superiors for the privilege of holding office. The subordinate raised enough to support himself and his dependents, as well as to pass on a surplus to those above him in the hierarchy to whom he owed security of tenure. During 1956–57, although direct evidence was scarce, tribute was referred to as normal by the population at large, by junior Native Administration officials, and among several close associates of district heads, throughout the emirate. Periodic gifts of horses, foodstuffs, and cash were the items most often referred to by informants as the kinds of tribute normally sent by district heads to powerful Kanuri leaders above them in the hierarchy. One high-placed Kanuri official at the capital told the writer that all district heads are "corrupt" (he used the English word). However, during the same interview, this official received and accepted a presentation of several goats and sheep, and two bags of millet sent to him by a district head.

The office of district head is a pivotal one in the political structure of the Emirate. Although others at the district level, such as the Native Administration departmental personnel, and the village area heads are also responsible for carrying out various aspects of emirate governmental action, the district head is the person to whom all attention at the capital turns if something goes wrong. This is reflected in the dependence that local Native Administration officials have upon his cooperation. Thus a young agricultural extension worker found that he could not obtain any participation in his departmental program in the district until the district head sent word to the village area heads concerned, to the effect that they must arrange for a certain number of household heads to take part in the program. When programs fail, officials at the center, aware of the widespread power exerted by the district head in his own domain, tend therefore to suspect him of either active or passive disobedience to the central organization of the state.

Difficulties in the system are reflected in the rate of turnover of district heads per district. Figures from four of the 21 districts of the emirate indicate that in the six decades of colonial rule, the range of district head tenure is between five and nine years in any one district, for two-thirds of the cases, even though tenure is potentially for life. Of the 38 persons who held the post of district head in each of the four districts during the colonial period, three retired, five died, 14 were dismissed, and 16 were transferred to other districts. In other words, 79 per cent of all turnover was due to dismissals or transfers. The figures are probably higher for the emirate as a whole when it is realized that retirement is often "suggested" by the senior British officials, as a means of replacing a district head.

Dismissals from the position of district head are always due to some continued infringement of rules, and follow a series of warnings by the colonial and Native Administration officials at the center. Thus between 1929 and 1932, a district head was warned continually to stop using followers as village area heads instead of the officially recognized ones. These followers were raising their own taxes and levying court fines for adjudication. Finally, the British officials recommended to the Shehu and his Council that this particular district head be dismissed, and the Bornu annual report of 1932 stated that the Shehu-in-Council had deposed the district head in question. During 1956–57 the writer observed the series of warnings by British district officers delivered to one district head because of tax irregularities. He was warned that a recommendation for his dismissal might have to go to the Shehu-in-Council if the irregularity continued. Letters from the area since that time indicate that he was sent to a low-salary district — a "punishment station."

District head salaries are a function of the tax receipts and population size of their districts, standardized at some date and adjusted from time to time. Districts are ranked in the minds of district heads and their subordinates, as well as by a large part of the population, as "better" or "worse" in relation to one another. Transfer from a high-paying district to a low-salary one is seen as a punishment, while movement to a higher-salaried district headship is seen as a reward. British officials agree with this interpretation and feel the same way about district head transfers. Thus the high turnover of district heads due to transfers and dismissals is associated with action by superiors in terms of rewards and punishments in relation to standards of district head performance.

Orientation and Goal Ambiguity

It is now a commonplace in the acculturation literature to think of culture contact as involving some ambiguity or ambivalence, and writers like Fallers (7) and Mair (12) have emphasized this point for the African chief. The term "orientation" is used here to refer to a syndrome of goals derived from one cultural tradition. Bornu displays two major orientations, derived from differing cultural backgrounds. The British conceived of political behavior as involving a very high degree of public responsibility, personal integrity, and slow but steady progress in economic and social development. Consequently, they looked forward to decreasing corruption, introduction or extension of Western schooling, higher productivity, democratic government, and all the paraphernalia required by Western-European socio-cultural values. In contrast, the Kanuri think of their political organization in feudal and Muslim terms. The social order is regarded as the result of divine will; and attempts to change it, although conceivable, are not morally defensible. Thus, the opposition party in modern Bornu is regarded not merely as a result of the new contact situation but also as an heretical group whose aims are said to be the perversion of the moral universe of traditional society. Kanuri concepts of social interaction, from the Shehu down to the lowly peasant, are feudal; loyalty and obedience are exchanged for various economic and political functions performed by the superior. District heads, like other political functionaries in Bornu, occupy roles which combine these diverse British and Kanuri orientations.

Possibly less obvious, and we suggest insufficiently emphasized in the above-cited literature on the African chief, is the ambiguity of orientation and the conflict among standards *within* each of the cultural traditions. The British administration was committed to the "peace, order and good government" of the area. The exact meaning of this phrase is open to various interpretations. On the one hand, much was said officially and privately about "progress" and "economic and political development," while *slow*, steady, but *well considered*, progress was held to be better than rapid growth. Initiative and innovation were often approved officially, and privately condemned. Or again, while colonial officials publicly accepted eventual self-rule, many of them privately admitted that the Nigerian (including the Kanuri) was unable to govern himself.

Kanuri leaders are committed to the political and economic development of the area, but they value their traditional political system and their religion and hope to keep these unchanged now that self-government has been achieved. Although most political leaders fervently wanted an end to colonial rule, they did not intend to abandon the political structure of colonialism. Many young Western-educated Kanuri, as well as high-placed officials, said that self-government will not mean an end of district officers, residents, *et al.* It will mean, merely, that these jobs would be filled by the Kanuri themselves.

These ambiguities within and between orientations (and many others not mentioned here) mean that the Bornu political organization cannot be seen in terms of a single means-end schema in which the entire system is committed to a simple set of formally-stated ends or goals. The orientations are not clear-cut; the inconsistencies tend to make the objectives of the political structure vague and indistinct. Thus "progress" is often discussed by both British and Kanuri leaders in terms which sound as if it should be negatively valued, while at other times it is obviously positively valued.

District heads, being Kanuri, are variably committed to Kanuri value orientations. However, they are also committed to maintaining their roles and minimizing the danger of dismissal or transfer to a district of less prestige. This means that all district heads are aware, again to a greater or lesser extent, of the ambiguities in objectives present in Bornu politics. In day-to-day terms, these ambiguities are translated into action through the conflicting standards under which district heads operate, particularly in their relations with the capital.

Conflicting Standards

There are three agencies at the capital which exert pressure on the district head in his rural district. These are the Native Administration, the colonial administrators, and the colonial government technical departments. At the top of the Native Administration is the Shehu, the traditional head of state, and his council. This council, under the chairmanship of the Waziri, forms a cabinet, with the Waziri as chief minister and with each cabinet member serving as the nominal head of one of the Native Administration civil service departments in the emirate.

The differences in orientation between British and Kanuri culture are reflected in the conflicting standards of performance which govern the behavior of the district head. Perhaps the most common of these is the clash between British colonial and Kanuri feudal standards of tax collection. The British regard the district head as a salaried agent of government who performs a public service by collecting taxes. Many members of the Kanuri hierarchy at the capital see him as a feudal fief-holder who collects tribute and passes surpluses to his superiors in the organization. Since delivery of taxes to anything but the Native Administration treasury is illegal under colonial law, the payment of tribute to the Shehu and other members of the royal family, as well as to other high-ranking officials, is conducted in secrecy. But failure to meet either of these tax standards could lead to punishment.

Much conflict in standards of performance emerges for the district head because of the colonial orientation towards Western democracy. Thus, he is pressured to introduce and support "democratic" elections and local councils which violate traditional standards of autocratic political behavior. Similarly, some of the British disapprove of chiefs, rather than the Muslim judges, adjudicating legal cases, even though adjudication is part of the chief's traditional power. The British pressure the district head to reduce his large group of followers, fearing he may have to embezzle tax funds to maintain this group. These and many more standards of performance are promoted and enforced by the British. If the district head submits to these demands, he weakens his traditional role, thus making his job of political control more difficult.

Consistent with the British orientation, colonial officials demand that the district head maintain his tax receipts at a constant or rising level. The British do not officially recognize subordinates of the district head as active members of the revenue collection system; and yet to be able to collect taxes at all, he must support these men and their families and give many of them horses. These men ride out annually over the district in several groups to collect *Jangali*, the cattle nomad tax which accounts for approximately two-thirds of all emirate tax revenues. If the district head succumbs to British demands to reduce his following, the efficiency and numbers of his tax collectors, hence his total receipts, decline.

To add to the incongruity, the British expect district heads to put on large displays periodically. If the Queen or any senior colonial official from outside the province visits the area, district heads are called to the capital to take part in a large *durbar*, (a horse show, and parade). Competition among district heads for prestige demands that they spend a good deal more on these events than the allowance allotted for such exhibitions. The British thus discourage large followings on the one hand, and demand them as part of the local scene on the other, without, however, affording the district head the necessary support for this traditional institution.

As noted earlier, conflict among standards is not confined to differences between the colonial and native administrative demands; conflict is similarly common among standards set *within* each of the administrations — as well as, indeed, with some of the minor administrative organs. Conflicting standards often arise from the partial separation of the various departments of the colonial government. For instance, technical service officers try to enforce their own program objectives in public works, education, or agricultural improvements, while at the same time the administrative officers demand that the necessary resources be devoted to meeting other objectives. Thus, if the education officer wants more children in the district school during the several months of the tax-collecting period, the district head has to deflect some of his followers from tax work to rounding up children to meet the demand.[7]

In the Native Administration, constant transfers, dismissals, arrests, and retirements produce changes in the personnel of superior/subordinate relations. Village area heads, although formally subordinate to their local district head, often have ties to other district heads in the Emirate.[8] In

---

[7] In parts of Bornu the district head must force parents to give up their children for Western schooling because of the unpopularity of the schools, especially for girls. To do so, the district head's followers ride out over the district and obtain a few children by methods that are most aptly described as capture.

[8] The British set up this conflict at the beginning of the colonial era by appointing district heads from the capital on the advice of the Shehu, and appointing village

one district, five village area heads were strongly loyal to a previous district head, and the present office-holder enforced his authority with great difficulty. He could not easily get rid of these five, since their real superior belonged to a very powerful faction in the state that could bring pressure to bear on him. On the other hand, he could not allow the five complete freedom since he is officially responsible for the affairs of the district. Somewhat the same thing occurs at the capital. The district head carefully cultivates personal relationships (through gift-giving and tribute) with high-placed officials at the center. He hopes these will protect him against other leaders in the Native Administration and/or the British. However, rapid turnover of personnel counteracts this process, leaving the district head constantly searching for supporters in the capital.

Social and cultural change has also introduced conflicting standards into the district head's role in the Native Administration. This is easily exemplified in the literacy campaign strongly supported by high-placed officials at the center. The district head knows he must support literacy campaigns and uses the Native Administration propaganda when doing so. This propaganda, originally inspired by the British, tells of the benefits to be gained from learning to read. The peasant is told that literacy will allow him to check on district heads and village area heads who give tax receipt slips indicating a smaller amount than the actual tax collected. But peasants believe that this practice is widespread among chiefs. Thus, the district head must persuade peasants to learn to read so they can undermine his customary tax collection procedures.

Another conflict in standards occurs when Native Administration personnel come to the district. Each district has its complement of young semi-educated civil service personnel from the various departments of the Native Administration. Traditionally, a fief-holder controlled his fief completely; everyone in the area was *ipso facto* his political subordinate. The Native Administration personnel, however, are less easily turned into subordinates. They have departmental responsibilities as well as traditional links of loyalty and respect for the positions of the district head. Thus a district head may find his attempt to win the affections of nomad cattle-herders in the area is being subverted by the ardor of a young Native Administration member from the Veterinary Department who is condemning many of the cattle in the area and forcing herders to give up some of their stock for quarantine.

Not all pressures exerted upon the district head originate from his superiors in the political organization. The district head is a local potentate and must act like one. He lives in a much larger compound than other people in the district, and supports a large number of dependents

---

area heads on the basis of some hereditary claim to local leadership. Traditionally, district heads appointed their own village heads; thus making sure of a loyal political machine in their fiefs.

and their families. He must maintain his own band of praise-singers and his own group of Koranic *malams* (teacher-priests). Periodically he feeds the local Native Administration personnel and gives out money to wandering players who come into his town to entertain the populace and to sing his praises. His dependents, many of whom he supplies with horses, must have dress costumes for ceremonial occasions and gifts from him at times of *rites de passage* in their families and at annual religious festivals. All of these things must be done and "done well" if the district head is to be judged by himself and others as a successful chief. Common people, Native Administration personnel in the bush, and district heads often discussed or made allusions to the relative merits of one district head's chiefly attributes as opposed to another's. Since widely-known cultural values define what is meant by "good" district head behavior, the person in this role constantly feels pressure, both from his own values and the demands of those under him, for proper chiefly activity.

In sum, it should be realized that the salary given the district head by the Native Administration is never sufficient to allow him to maintain his social role. He must give gifts to many above and below himself in the political structure; he must support a large following; and he must live in a style which befits his high-ranking position in the state. As a result, he must constantly devise means of support which lie outside the formal rules of the political organization, reliance on which makes him vulnerable to criticism at all times.

Selective Enforcement

Although many of the standards of performance to which a district head must accede conflict with one another, all standards are not equally enforced. Personnel changes in both the Native Administration and the colonial government produce changing emphases among the district heads' superiors. One district officer may be interested in roads, while his predecessor pressed for an improvement in the tax collection system. Others might keep aloof from innovation and simply carry on what they think are the current policies of the agency. Furthermore, as time passes, both the Native Administration and the colonial government recruit their staff from approximately the same age range, and from slowly changing worlds. The young colonial servant of today, and his Native Administration counterpart even more so, have somewhat divergent views from those of their respective forbears at the turn of the century.

It should also be realized that Bornu Emirate is only a part of a much larger political unit. The government of Northern Nigeria and the Federation of Nigeria have been moving towards self-government for some time. With this development, new bodies of African legislators, cabinet members, and high-level bureaucrats are all vying for the furtherance of their pet schemes. In such a rapidly changing situation it is often difficult to maintain consistency among all directives coming into the province. This means that the district head experiences unequal pressures from the capital, not only as a result of the personnel priorities of superiors, but also because of the demands on these superiors themselves.

IV

Kanuri Political Organization: The Test of the Hypotheses

Having established that goal ambiguity, conflicting standards, and selective enforcement occur in Bornu political organization, it is now possible to test whether or not the limitations they impose on individual behavior and the social consequences they produce are those hypothesized by the theory. Since the hypotheses are given in full above, they are referred to below by number. It should be noted that, for the sake of clarity in presentation of the data, the original order has not been adhered to in the test. Several of the hypotheses have been found to allude to similar behaviors, and have been treated together.

Hypotheses 1 and 2 (Selection and Change of Standards that Are Met)

One of the most obvious responses among district heads to Bornu political organization is the widespread practice of simply not living up to all standards of performance. All district heads attempt to collect enough taxes to keep their superiors happy. Some accomplish this objective by maintaining large groups of horsemen, some by working in close collaboration with village area heads, and some work out close ties with Fulani headmen[9] and agree on cattle counts below the actual number but in excess of the district head's treasury commitments. Others use all these methods. One district head decided to reduce the number of his followers and thus lower his own expenditures. He also hoped that by complying with administration demands on the size of his following, he would avoid pressure from this source and be congratulated for complying with official demands. Instead his tax receipts fell drastically, which brought threats of dismissal from his superiors. The following year he reversed his decision and worried about tax collections rather than the size of his following. Some district heads station followers in each of the district towns in order to ensure some measure of control when they have no long-term superior/subordinate relations with the village area heads of the district. This is illegal, and several district heads do not

[9] Under the authority of their local headmen, Fulani pastoralists move through Kanuri territory annually in small bands for transhumance purposes.

use their followers in this way. Nevertheless, no one can possibly meet all standards in such situations, and breakage of certain rules has become almost a commonplace occurrence. Consequently, all district heads mulct some tax money or they could not possibly afford to maintain their social positions or the organizations necessary for tax collection. For the same reason, all district heads adjudicate cases, levy court fines, and accept tribute from the people of their districts.

Hypothesis 3 (Simulation of Standards)

One of the most widespread kinds of behavior among district heads, and indeed among many of the Native Administration officials, is feigning or simulating British standards of performance. Whenever the author met district heads or other top Kanuri officials for the first time, attitudes towards standards of performance and goals were universally fairly accurate reflections of the official colonial government policy in the area. Besides the dangers implicit in not simulating British standards, it should be noted that in traditional Kanuri society it is considered bad manners to disagree with superiors. Thus when a district head speaks, listening persons keep repeating *nam, nam* (yes, yes) to show their assent and unanimity. When the district head is in the presence of his superiors in the political organization, he behaves in the same way.

Another example of this simulation of standards occurs in the district council meetings. In order to maintain their autocratic leadership and yet comply with the British standards of parliamentary procedure, some district heads rehearse the meeting before the British official who is to witness it arrives in the district. Others run a second meeting after the official leaves, re-arranging a few of the decisions, and ordering out of, or into, existence other matters which have been democratically accepted or declined at the formal meeting. This helps maintain the district head's status as an autocratic leader and gives traditional force to unaltered decisions of the "democratic" council.

Hypothesis 4 (Safety Factors)

District heads also tend to provide themselves with safety factors for unforeseen emergencies. Excuses like sickness are often used. Thus one district head often had a "fever" on occasions on which he anticipated some threats from his superiors. At a ceremony, another district head announced to a district officer that it was now time for him and the other Kanuri present to go into another courtyard and say their prayers. The district officer politely excused himself and a part of the ceremony which involved the giving of money to the district head continued without out the district officer present.[10]

[10] I am indebted to Professor A. Rosman for this information.

The operation of safety factors can also be seen in the contacts that many district heads maintain among the wealthy traders. These relations are due partly to the traders' desire to be friendly with a political leader who often borrows money from them. However, another aspect of these links is their possible usefulness to a district head if he is dismissed or retired from his political position. Several ex-district heads in the capital are making a profitable living from trade. One of these remarked on several occasions that most of his present suppliers of goods and credit are men whom he had known and befriended during his years as a district head.

One of the most interesting safety factors is that of factional membership. District heads not only cultivate office-holders in the capital but also maintain traditional links with segments of the royal lineage. Groups of district heads, like other high-status nobles of the realm, inherit relationships to one or another of the living male heirs to the throne. Tribute in cash and kind is delivered by district heads (not all) to their royal faction whether or not this person holds a Native Administration office. It is believed that the royal person argues for, and helps protect, his faction members in the higher councils of the emirate. Although the evidence is far from clear on this point, it may be that the linkage of some district heads to their royal factions is maintained as a safety factor resulting from inability to obtain protection and permanent or stable factional links with other high-ranking officials at the capital, because of the high turnover of these latter personnel.

Hypotheses 10 and 5 (Information and Dealers in Information)

One of the important ways in which a district head alleviates the tensions inherent in conflicting standards and ambiguous goals is to have as many sources of information as possible. Indeed, information in Bornu is a valuable commodity. District heads lavish hospitality on messengers, native police, and Native Administration officials from the city who pass through the district. Touring British officials are listened to intently so that currently stressed goals and standards may be discerned. One district head knew English but kept this knowledge to himself, that he might appear ignorant and catch stray pieces of information from local and touring Europeans. Each district head keeps a compound in the city with a *Wakil* (chief follower) heading up a group of his subordinates. A major task of these followers is to maintain a steady flow of information on town affairs to the district head out in the bush. One district head kept a follower continually travelling back and forth from city to bush. This man visited town houses of other district heads, the Shehu's court, the Shehu's Council, and houses of rich traders, picking up information for his superior about the state of politics in the emirate. Almost everybody in Bornu seems to be in the information business; and all peasants know that every follower of a district head is an informal seeker of information for his superior. Very often persons who are not district head clients but have aspirations in that direction, or who are hoping for some other favor from him, try to win his affections by bringing information of a political nature to him.

The results of all this are twofold. First, most news travels quickly throughout the emirate. Indeed, the transfer or dismissal of a district head is usually known before the event occurs, because of leaks in and around high places in the Native and Colonial Administrations. A Kanuri messenger working for the Colonial Administration is a man cultivated by many of the richest and most successful district heads, especially if he has some knowledge of English. Second, gossip and rumor about the goals and enforcement of standards of political behavior in the state can be heard at almost every level of society. As much of the information is false as it is true, and a successful district head tries always to check and recheck a piece of information before relying on it. This widespread interest in political news and the endless search by district heads for information gives to Bornu political life a strong quality of intrigue. However, underlying this surface quality is the lack of adequate information in the system, and the end result of this fact is that the district head with the most reliable sources of information is able to predict more accurately what standards are most likely to be enforced.

Hypotheses 11 (Incentive to Use Information and Comply with Standards)

Related to the widespread scarcity of information and its use by district heads is the strong incentive to obtain and use good information. This varies from one district head to another. Some may have very good sources of information already, and are only mildly interested in additional knowledge from new sources. Others felt the lack of information about policy enforcement by superiors so strongly that, after very little acquaintance with the anthropologist, they would move the conversation towards a discussion of goals and standards and future enforcement by this or that agency at the capital. In these situations it was difficult to tell who was conducting the interview, the anthropologist or the district head. One district head asked a district officer, who had threatened him with transfer, to "Tell me what to do, and I will do it," when the officer hinted that punishments might ensue because of the lowered tax revenues in the area. The district officer replied that it would be wise for the district head to go out and tour his district on horseback as well as sending out his followers. A few days later the district head left on the proposed tour.

Hypothesis 9 (Sleeping Dogs and Initiative)

One of the most widespread consequences of conflicting standards and scarce information is the general acceptance by everyone in the Bornu political system of a policy of "let sleeping dogs lie." British officials know that local troubles require reports to their own superiors in the regional capital, followed by multitudes of questions, and often some sort of inspection and increased supervision of the local scene. A senior official explained his own aversion to trouble by saying that "agitators" were everywhere. Any irregularity could therefore, he claimed, reach "international proportions" and would undoubtedly be distorted if given any publicity. On the other hand, no trouble can always be alluded to as "steady progress" in reports. Furthermore, colonial officials and senior officers in particular are often held responsible (officially or unofficially) for any sizable disorder within their jurisdictional area. Thus a recently retiring officer in Bornu was described by one local district officer as having "left somewhat under a cloud" because of the political riots which broke out just before his last days in a senior position. Native Administration officials, including the district head, all recognize that any trouble may bring an investigation by the colonial administrators who, although reluctant to start anything really serious, will enforce their standards when matters are brought to their attention. This always opens the possibility that more trouble will result. In 1956 a Native Administration treasury official, angry over organizational matters, suddenly took the Bornu treasury records to the Colonial Administration. Before very long an investigation was ordered which was followed by a long series of dismissals, arrests, and jail sentences which reached into every department of the Native Administration. The British attitude to this kind of apprehension was summed up by one British official who claimed that all Kanuri are "corrupt," i.e., that they do not believe in British standards of political responsibility in public office. Since there are so few educated Africans it would be folly, he said, to be investigating all the time since "corrupt" officials would only be replaced by less well-trained ones who were also "corrupt." Nonetheless, initiative by district heads towards the realization of the policy objectives of the central government is formally encouraged. Speeches by visiting officials, and the official literature of the Northern Nigerian government constantly stress the district head's role as a progressive leader. He is regarded as the link between the past and the future, as a man who has a place of traditional leadership and who should also lead the way towards higher living standards, modern democracy, and the spread of Western education. On the other hand, as a result of goal ambiguity and conflicting standards (some of which are not even officially recognized), initiative is dangerous unless it is carried out under the aegis of extremely good information. Generally speaking, only highly acculturated district heads can afford the luxury of initiative towards official goals. Only those persons who can discriminate which goals can be achieved without any danger from the relinquishing of other goals are safe. One district head has previously been headmaster of the European School in the capital; he knew much about both Kanuri and Western culture. Consequently, he knew that his project to improve the water supply in the district, which he had cleared with the proper authorities, was unassailable by anyone. Most district heads do not have so clear an understanding of what they can and cannot do; as we have seen, information is scarce, goals and standards often difficult to pin down and/or reconcile with one another.

Furthermore, like officials everywhere, the colonial government personnel, especially the older ones in the more senior positions, resent disturbances. Initiative can very often be confused with disturbance or at least the unsettling of the status quo. Thus, several young officials complained to the writer that they had been squelched in development schemes because they had not consulted higher-ups first before going ahead with their plans. Higher-ups were angry at such initiative since the junior members of the political organization were subordinates, and the higher-ups would be responsible if anything went wrong.

Hypotheses 7, 12, and 14 (Changing Standards and Internal Variability)

Changes in colonial government staff are frequent. District officers and technical staff are often moved from one part of Northern Nigeria to another every time they start an 18-month tour of duty. Indeed, in several instances colonial officials were re-stationed within one tour. Previous writers have commented on this practice so that we can safely assume that it has been a characteristic of Nigerian administration for a long time (13). It is beyond the scope of this present chapter to discuss the pros and cons of this mobility; for our purposes it is sufficient to mention its presence and note one of its major effects — the variation in standards and their emphases resulting from the continuous movement of colonial personnel.

In Bornu a young energetic official can easily institute innovations by simply proclaiming his goals widely and making sure that none of his superiors disapprove of his actions. Because district heads are used to changing standards and selective enforcement, they are generally receptive to new pressures from the top of the political structure. More emphasis on schools, roads, or taxation can easily be instituted. Some of these trends, once begun, are not terminated even when pressures ease off due to the transfer of the official originally responsible for the innovations. New roads built under pressure from one particular official must be maintained, as are schools and medical dispensaries.

It is becoming more and more common among district officers to narrow down the broad general range of their duties and specialize in only one or two branches of administrative work. Thus, one district officer in Bornu specialized in local government, another in fiscal policy and revenue collection, and so on. Furthermore, young assistant district officers often attempt to initiate changes in various sectors of the emirate government under their jurisdiction.

One young district officer started a race track up in a bush district as his pet project. The local district head approved of the idea, probably because it kept the officer busy. As a distraction for touring officials from the capital and for local entertainment, the race track has become a local institution. This same district head institutes formal, and public, Friday services in the local mosque no matter what district he is stationed in, and no matter what the previous practices in the area have been. On the other hand, others merely continue to stress those areas of the administration program about which their superiors on the local scene are enthusiastic. One district officer carried on the policy of his superior concerning the alleviation of cruelty to animals. Because of the constant shifts in personnel, it is not always a simple matter for the district head to know far ahead just what part of the administration goals will be stressed, since the emphasis can quite easily change with the personnel.

In the technical departments one education officer may spend more of his time at the provincial capital looking after matters there; others spend much time going around the province. Both tasks are performed by all officials, but stress on one or the other area of work varies. This means that with changing personnel, the district head must expect changes in the amount of pressure applied locally by the technical officers. When an officer spends more time in the capital, power is delegated to the Native Administration officials and much of the departmental pressure felt by the district head comes from the Native Administration. If the officer tours out in the districts a great deal, then his personal policy preferences become more important pressures.

In the Native Administration, center officials tend to exhibit constant and often unpredictable job turnover. Only three of the dozen or so chief councilors of the emirate retained their positions during the period 1956–57, and letters from the area since then indicate that the rate of personnel shifts and depositions has remained much the same. Illicit practices, which come to light periodically, can bring a quick series of removals, and even a jail sentence, to what seem to be a random assortment of positions throughout the Native Administration.

Hypotheses 8 and 13 (Adaptability to Externally-initiated Change)

As a result of the high amount of conflict in the Bornu political organization, social and cultural change has an ever-ready route into the society. It has already been noted that goals as well as enforcement of standards may change over time.

A major change was the very introduction of the British rule itself, and the Kanuri political system's adaptation to that externally induced change. The colonial era has served to complicate the traditional obligations of district heads to members of the hierarchy. That the district head should pay heed to the wishes of officials at the center such as the Shehu, the Council members, and other high-placed persons in the Native Administration departments is easily understood, since these persons are engaged in tasks that require the cooperation of the district head and these responsibilities are backed up by the colonial officials. It is somewhat surprising, however, to find other nobles who, like top Native Administration personnel, also receive gifts but have no officially recognized high office in the contemporary political organization. Thus the writer, having promised his kerosene refrigerator to a district head at the end of the field trip, was asked to deliver it to a member of the Bornu royal family who has no Native Administration position whatsoever. This is explained by the fact that the district head involved has a client relationship which he inherited from his father with this particular segment of the royal lineage. That is to say, this district head feels that he is a part of the faction in the state as whole which is allied to a particular heir to the throne. He also feels that this royal person is still a power in the state and will help protect him against other factions and authorities in the political organization. To a certain extent this is true. When this district head is to be disciplined for some misdemeanor, the head of his faction pleads his case before the Shehu and as many Council members as he can contact. Thus the older traditional factions and their leaders still perform some political functions in the emirate, in addition to the officially recognized Kanuri hierarchy above the district head at the capital. Lack of support by all these people, or at least a majority of the most powerful among them, leads to easy punishments when district heads are accused of breaking the rules. On the other hand, informants feel that delivery of gifts to faction leaders, as well as to high-placed Native Administration officials, ensures the district head of some support by traditionally powerful persons as well as the official hierarchy recognized and supported by the colonial government.

Externally originated change still finds ready reception in Bornu today. A Kanuri agricultural officer, after traveling to Israel and Pakistan, has decided that Bornu, especially its southern portions, can support a citrus-growing industry. By utilizing the British-inspired goal of economic development and his own authority, as well as his friendship links with both British and Kanuri leaders, he has been able to introduce citrus growing into the Bornu economy. That is to say, Kanuri leaders, whether they be district heads or other officials, can usually find some goal or standard which gives jural support to the acceptance of innovations brought in from the outside world. It should be noted at this point that all the top Kanuri leaders spoken to during the field trip are to a variable degree committed to the goal of economic development. Many of them feel that the two biggest blocks to this end are (a) the poverty of the area, and (b) the conservatism of the senior British officials. They are not at all worried over the traditionalism of the people. This is due to their own stated understanding that innovation is not excessively difficult in a system in which people react to pressures more often than to rules.

Hypothesis 6 (Substantive Rationality)

The discussion of Bornu political organization indicates that jural rules are hardly the primary guides for individual conduct, or the sources of social integration in the system. In Frank's Weberian terms, the Kanuri do not place substantial reliance on formal rationality. District heads who do, usually get into some kind of trouble, and are either punished or eliminated. One district head is reported to have behaved as if there were no conflicts in the system. He ruled his district autocratically, extorted large amounts of excess taxes from its inhabitants, and even tried to buy up the surplus millet at low harvest prices to sell later in the year. He was soon apprehended and transferred out of the district. He is said by those who have worked under him to be contemptuous of modern times, and to prefer traditional pre-colonial rules of political behavior. Most district heads know that they must accommodate to the real system rather than any idealization of it, and in so doing the sets of jural rules (derived from Kanuri and British orientations) governing their political roles become merely a backdrop against which a real system political action is played out. In this "real" system it is pressures and information that form the basis for active political response and initiative. Thus in more theoretical parlance the structural features of the political system in terms of its formal rules are less important than its constituent interpersonal and hierarchical relations.

V

Conclusion

This chapter has dealt with organization of political activity among the Kanuri of Northern Nigeria by approaching the behavior of one political role, that of the district head, as if this person's actions were responses to a series of conflicts. In so doing, we have demonstrated that conflicts do in fact exist in the situation, and that the activity of persons occupying political roles is predictable within the limits outlined in a theory of conflict derived from a study of Russian industry.

Concerning the theory itself, Frank's schema has come from empirical data, but it is in itself a deductive system in which certain behaviors follow logically from the basic premises. In using it, we have found that several of the predicted behavioral correlates associated with the premises actually deal with the same events. Thus, Hypotheses 10 and 5, dealing with information and dealers in information, refer to the same area of political behavior in the district head's role. Similarly, and perhaps more importantly, all hypotheses dealing with change focus on the same mechanism: the response to, and desire to comply with, known pressures from higher-ups, rather than any idealization of the traditional rules. This is due to Frank's (8, p. 13) deductive separation of the hypotheses into levels of "member behavior" and "system" consequences, when in fact the only material available for study is the response by members of the hierarchy to conflicts among standards. Recently Berliner (1, p. 102) has commented that anthropology has no detailed theories of self-generating internal change such as the economists have in their conceptualization of the dynamics of the business cycle. A close look at the way in which change has been treated in this chapter shows that the change mechanism being discussed is indeed "internal" and "self-generating." Because actors in the hierarchy are more concerned with compliance to superiors than they are with the essentials of tradition, there is a ready avenue for change to enter the society, from within or without, at all times.

This brings up another point of theoretical interest. What do the terms "internal" and "external" actually mean in the context of this analysis? The author has had a number of long discussions with Professor Frank over this point and we find it difficult to resolve the problem. As it is used here, the term "internal" really refers to the political hierarchy itself as a distinct and analytically separate phenomenon in comparison to other systems of social action and cultural traditions in which it is embedded in everyday life. In other words, this chapter suggests by its method of analysis that the boundaries of different systems of social action within social and cultural systems of much greater complexity should not be considered coincident to one another in the culture contact situation. The political hierarchy dealt with in this work included both British and Kanuri officials. At the time of fieldwork research (1955–57) and even more so today, after the achievement of Nigerian independence, all these leaders were part of the same political structure. It is within this system of political action that change can be said to be internal. In other words, as I have pointed out elsewhere (4), the comprehensive inclusion of all facets of a society and its cultural traditions within a unifying set of boundary conditions can lead to an oversimplified view of any social situation, especially when we are interested in change and the forces that bring it about. Thus we should think about the boundaries of much more limited sets of activities, such as the economic system, or the moral order, or the political system, or even sub-sections of these, and make no assumptions about the congruency of any of these systems and their boundaries.

It is also of note in view of the contemporary interest in evolution that this method of presenting and analyzing data approaches in many major respects a genetic model of evolution. This model depends basically on two conditions. First, the evolving phenomenon must be shown to be variable in terms of its constituent units, and second, there must be analytically distinct selective factors which operate on the variation within the phenomenon to produce a constantly adapting and thus an evolving history of development. Although there are more or less stable orientations of tradition present in Bornu, conflicts in the political organization produce a variability of response by the actors upon which selective pressures exerted by superiors in the political hierarchy may operate to bring about innovations and changes that are incremental in their nature, i.e., evolutionary rather than revolutionary.

The rate of change has not been established in this study, but it is possible to make some theoretical statements about the rate on the basis of this analysis. Factors which promote change, such as the ones isolated here, when intensified should hasten the rate of change. Thus we can hypothesize that the greater the intensity of conditions which promote the conflicts described here, then the greater will be the rate of change. In the Bornu situation the conditions most likely to produce conflicts are the differences in orientation of superiors and subordinates, the differences in interests and goals of superiors, and the rate of turnover amongst superiors. These will be summarized in Hypothesis 9 below.

Summing up the discussion of the theory we can now re-state it in light of its submission to the Kanuri material.

If it is established that there are present in any hierarchical social situation differences in cultural orientation which create goal ambiguity, and/or goal ambiguities are present for any other reason, as well as conflicting standards, and selective enforcement of these standards, then the following may be predicted to occur:

1) Members (of the hierarchy) fail to meet all standards, exhibit differences in selection, and change the selection, over time, of standards they do meet.
2) Members simulate or feign the meeting of standards.
3) Members provide themselves with safety factors for contingencies.
4) Information is a scarce and positively valued commodity in the hierarchy, and members are motivated to use any and all methods to obtain information on enforcement policies. This may or may not become institutionalized so that professional information seekers may or may not be present. If not, then the social organization takes on an atmosphere of intrigue.
5) Widespread member initiative is possible; but unless it is incor-

porated into standards, individuals will "let sleeping dogs lie." That is to say, the failure to comply with some standards is widely known within the hierarchy, and members are prone to overlook this fact for the sake of making the organization work on a day-to-day basis.

6) Standards change continually, thus re-orienting and possibly changing the organizational form of social life.

7) Conflicting standards generate innovations and selective enforcement provides for their acceptance.

8) Conflicting standards and selective enforcement make for ready adaptation to changing circumstances.

9) The rate of change in a hierarchy is a function of:
   (a) The differences in orientation of superiors and subordinates,
   (b) The differences in interests and goals of superiors to one another,
   (c) The rate of turnover among superiors.

The greater any of these factors are, the more rapid will be the rate of change.

One final conclusion of a practical nature emerges from this analysis, especially from Hypothesis 8 above. Many observers of the modern Nigerian scene attribute a conservative, anti-progressive character to the emirates of Northern Nigeria. If our analysis is correct, these emirates have within themselves well-developed mechanisms for their own transformation. That is to say, it is predictable that, given a continuation of conflicting standards, and selective enforcement, along with changing and more modern goals emanating from the top of the political hierarchy (which is a very likely occurrence, given the increasing amount of Western education amongst top officials), these societies will incorporate and accept modern developments. This means that it will not be necessary to change and modernize the northern emirates by a drastic revolutionary measure, but merely by continued and constant pressure, to which, as has been shown, they are definitely responsive.

BIBLIOGRAPHY

1. Berliner, J. S. "The Feet of the Natives are Large: An Essay on Anthropology by an Economist," *Current Anthropology* Vol. 2, No. 5 (1961), pp. 90–103.

2. Buckley, W. "Social Stratification and the Functional Theory of Social Differentiation," *American Sociological Review*, Vol. 23, No. 4 (1958), pp. 369–375.

3. Cohen, R. "The Structure of Kanuri Society." Ph.D. thesis, University of Wisconsin, University Microfilms, Inc., Ann Arbor, mic 60–986.

4. Cohen, R. Comment on "The Feet of the Natives are Large: An Essay

on Anthropology by an Economist," J. S. Berliner. *Current Anthropology,* Vol. 2, No. 5 (1961).

5. Dahrendorf, R. "Out of Utopia: Towards a Reorientation of Sociological Theory," *American Journal of Sociology,* Vol. 64, No. 2 (1959), pp. 115–127.

6. Epstein, A. L. *Politics in an Urban African Community.* Manchester: University of Manchester Press, 1957.

7. Fallers, L. "The Predicament of the Modern African Chief," *American Anthropologist,* Vol. 57, No. 2 (1955), pp. 290–305.

8. Frank, A. G. "Goal Ambiguity and Conflicting Standards: An Approach to The Study of Organization," *Human Organization,* Vol. 17, No. 4 (1959), pp. 8–13.

9. Greenberg, J. H. "Studies in African Linguistic Classification; VIII. Further Remarks on Method: Revisions and Corrections," *Southwestern Journal of Anthropology,* Vol. 10 (1954), pp. 405–415.

10. Leach, E. R. *Political Systems of Highland Burma: A Study of Kachin Social Structure.* London: G. Bell and Sons Ltd., 1954.

11. Levi-Strauss, C. "Social Structure," in A. L. Kroeber (ed.), *Anthropology Today.* Chicago: University of Chicago Press.

12. Mair, L. P. "African Chiefs Today," *Africa* Vol. 28, No. 3 (1958), pp. 195–206.

13. Perham, M. *Native Administration in Nigeria.* London: Oxford University Press, 1937.

14. Radcliffe-Brown, A. L. *Structure and Function in Primitive Society.* London: Cohen and West Ltd., 1952.

15. Rosman, A. "Social Structure and Acculturation Among the Kanuri of Bornu Province, Northern Nigeria," *Transactions of the New York Academy of Sciences,* Ser. II, Vol. 21, No. 7 (1958), pp. 620–630.

20

Frederick Elkin

Advertising in French Canada:

Innovations and Deviations in the

Context of a Changing Society

Advertising in French Canada,[1] as elsewhere in the Western world, is rather taken for granted. The mass of people in French Canada assume that, in one form or another — in newspapers, magazines, radio, television, billboards, or window displays — they will be exposed to hundreds of advertisements a day. Some they are interested in and seek out; most pass them by as part of the background of daily living.

Because advertising is so all-pervading and so readily and unquestionably accepted, we are likely to recognize its importance as a source of information and education (18). By the same token, it may be viewed as a key to changes occurring in the society. In French Canada, particularly in Quebec, this seems especially true. In recent years, French Canada has been in ferment, with striking changes in education, religion, industry, communication, and politics. The traditional picture of a relatively stable, politically conservative, church dominated, and economically retarded province — which was only relatively true — is now completely irrelevant. The reasons behind these changes are legion and the

[1] French Canada, literally, refers to those sections of Canada in which those of French origin are distinct and numerically superior. However, in ordinary parlance, French Canada means Quebec, with focus on the French population in distinction from the English. In this chapter, we shall — unless the context clearly indicates otherwise — use the latter meaning.

part directly played by advertising is undoubtedly small; yet, in various ways, the questions that have arisen in advertising point up many of the broader problems. The strategic importance of advertising derives essentially from its many-sided implications — it is a technique essential to the operation of the commercial and industrial world, an instrument of mass culture, the primary means of support for the mass media of communication, and, in Quebec, it is a bicultural operation in a bicultural setting. Thus advertising may be viewed as a key to recent developments in the society and to the struggles being waged between the intellectual and commercial communities, the protagonists and antagonists of "Americanization," and especially between ethnic groups.

This is our perspective. In this chapter, through discussing advertising in its social context, we hope to understand better both the developments in advertising and social change in French Canada. This report is part of a larger ongoing study of advertising in French Canada based, so far, on about 85 interviews with English and French advertising personnel, a questionnaire distributed to almost 200 French Canadians in advertising, and a study of those bicultural advertising campaigns in Canada that have the largest budgets. Communications with French Canadians were in French and with English Canadians in English.

Historical Perspective

The cultural development of Quebec has been unique in North America. The French Canadians were the charter members of Canada, the explorers, pioneers, and first settlers. The English came later and superseded them in numbers and power. The French Canadians — at least, those who remained in Quebec where they still make up over 80 per cent of the population — remained relatively isolated from the main streams of cultural influence in the United States and English Canada. They never acknowledged for themselves the model of the subsequent immigrant groups who were culturally absorbed into the Anglo-Saxon society. So, through the generations, the French Canadians have maintained their own language, version of Catholicism, and school system; loyalties, mythology, and heroes of history; and certain traditions in food habits, customs, and holiday celebrations (12; 7; 8).

The French Canadians who, in search of employment, left Quebec for New England or western Canada — a process which began early in the nineteenth century — present a different picture. In a few places — as well as in certain nearby sections of Ontario and New Brunswick — they were sufficiently concentrated and circumstances were sufficiently favorable for them to maintain many traditional patterns of behavior and thought, but generally they have become merely one ethnic group among many, gradually losing their language and their uniqueness (19).

Economically, too, the development of French Canada has its distinctive elements. Until a few years ago, Quebec was akin, in some respects, to an underdeveloped area. The British, Americans, and English Canadians introduced industry, bringing in the required capital and developing the primary resources of aluminum, mining, and pulp and paper. These same English-speaking groups also maintained the managerial and technical expert positions while the French Canadians, often happy to find jobs for the numerous children, were the workers in the forests, mines, and mills. Other French Canadians who drifted to the city became white-collar clerks and salesmen and filled the numerous unskilled and semi-skilled jobs necessary for the maintenance of urban concentrations. Over the years, many French Canadians became foremen, personnel directors, and managers of branch operations; but few obtained positions with major decision-making powers (16; 17; 5). Many smaller businesses developed by French Canadians, such as retail shops, laundries, and trucking companies, were successful; but these were often family businesses and did not — because of the large families, the reluctance to take risks, and the competition from American and English-Canadian companies — develop into larger industries. Thus the opportunities for the mass of French Canadians were limited.

The elite of the French-Canadian society, following century-long traditions, were the professional men — the priests, doctors, and lawyers — and the system of higher education was directed towards the training of this elite. The educational system, long after adaptations were made in the English-speaking world, continued to give a minimum of education to the mass and a good classical education to the potential elite. Education and training for a world of commerce and technical achievement were virtually ignored.

Political control in the province and municipalities, with such a small proportion of English, was in the hands of the French Canadians, but the political leaders made few attempts to modify the basic economic pattern. On the whole, they tended to welcome and work hand in glove with English-Canadian and American business interests.

Off and on through the years, movements did develop among French Canadians protesting against their subordinate position. But the movements were directed less against the economic domination, or their own institutions which accepted this situation, than against the federal political realm, and took such forms as resisting military conscription during both world wars or demanding political independence for Quebec.

The Current Ferment in Quebec

Quebec has never been static. In past generations, the population grew, the children of farmers moved to the cities, cities developed the necessary new services. Many moved to western Canada and the United States, women came to participate more in public affairs, leisure activities became more organized, modern inventions and appliances were adopted, and there were no end of political crises. However, no short period of time seems to have aroused as much ferment among so many people and in so many areas of life as that of the past decade. This ferment comprises three general overlapping areas — nationalism, modernization, and the revitalization of French culture.

Nationalism

French Canada has always had undercurrents of nationalistic movements and, often in its history, strong and active groups have battled on behalf of certain issues. The most recent upsurge of nationalism probably focuses less on any single issue than earlier movements and is more broadly based. The immediate sources of this latest movement are many — including the independence movements in Asia and Africa,[2] an increasing freedom of expression and aggressiveness among journalists, political leaders, and intellectuals, and new exposés of the superordinate positions of the English and the deprived positions of the French Canadians.

Most of the forms which nationalization has taken have set the French Canadians, indirectly if not directly, against the English Canadians. The Liberal party of Quebec campaigned successfully in 1962 with a slogan, "Maîtres chez nous," advocating that the French Canadians become "Masters in their own house," and demanded, with no serious opposition, that the "province's natural resources be returned to the people of Quebec" through nationalizing the English-controlled electric utilities, the "trusts."

Editorial writers and public speakers constantly cite the discrimination in the officially bilingual government. French Canadians are not sufficiently represented in the Cabinet and have few high posts in the Civil Service. Military units operate in English. Reports are not always issued simultaneously in both languages. French Canadians who seek public information are asked to communicate in English. Until 1961, government checks were written only in English. Industry also discriminates — labor contracts may be written only in English; few French Canadians achieve top executive positions and, when they do, the jobs are often "window dressing"; letters are written to French Canadians in English; and the companies, including French-Canadian ones, insist on using English names to designate themselves and their products. The criticisms against such forms and symbols of discrimination are often bitter.

This nationalism implies a strong sense of identity to Quebec. In

---

[2] An advertisement of a Separatist group advocating political independence for Quebec reads, "In 1951, Gabon was a colony and Quebec was demanding bilingual checks; in 1961, Gabon is an independent state and Quebec is demanding bilingual checks."

previous years, the governing National Union Party, under the battle cry of autonomy (although patronage and other factors were involved) refused grants from the federal government for education, highway construction, and hospital insurance. Officials now speak of Quebec as a center for French Canadians and French-Canadian culture everywhere and when Quebec's Premier met Premier de Gaulle in France, the French-Canadian press alluded to the meeting of "two heads of state."

Modernization

Closely linked with nationalism and also giving a spirit of identity and direction is the movement for modernization. Quebec has lagged behind most of the United States and some provinces of Canada in such spheres as education, medical care, political reform, and highway construction. Over a certain opposition from previously established groups and institutions, movements have been in full swing to bring Quebec up to date. Education, with strong government support, is perhaps the most striking area of radical action. For the first time, instruction is completely free and compulsory up to the age of 15 and parents of older students are given financial assistance. Schools of commerce and science are being constructed and enlarged; academic facilities and personnel have grown at a remarkable pace; and provincial scholarships permit an increased equality of opportunity based on ability. It is generally expected, following the report of a Quebec Royal Commission in preparation, that the entire system of education will be revamped and modernized.

Moral reform underlies many of the projects. The provincial police has been reorganized and cleaned up; the distribution of liquor and beer licenses is less arbitrary and politically motivated; Montreal's reform administration has reorganized its police force and is vigorously fighting corruption. Scandals in the building of hospitals, "cut-backs" in awarding construction contracts, inefficiency and irresponsible administration of mental institutions and prisons, and secret purchases of stocks by government officials of a newly-organized utility have all been exposed with great fanfare.[3]

Development and social welfare are other key concepts. Montreal, after years of indecision, has a subway under construction and will play host to the World's Fair of 1967. Skyscraper and highway construction projects are changing the face of Montreal and the Province. The provincial government has established a central bank to assist the development of industry, while trade and promotion offices in New York, London, and Paris are seeking to lure capital and tourists and further missions are

---

[3] The questions cited have been widely discussed in the newspapers *La Presse* and *Le Devoir* and the magazines *Cité Libre* and *Le Magazine Maclean* — all recognized forums of discussion for problems of French Canada. See also Peter C. Newman (14, pp. 21 ff.).

planned for Milan, Chicago, and Boston. With new insurance laws, almost all automobile owners have liability insurance whereas a few years ago, less than 50 per cent had this coverage. Free hospital care is available to all Quebec residents, and leading church officials are rethinking the role of the church in Quebec society (15; 10).

Revitalization of French Culture

This modernization in Quebec — at least to its leaders and intellectual elite — does not just mean catching up to, and becoming like, other Canadian provinces. Accompanying this movement is a resistance to "Anglicization" or "Americanization" and a renaissance of French culture. To the elite, the "Anglicization" of the culture is a menace to be fought with vigor. They regard with apprehension the popularity of American hit parade songs and magazines, the penetration of such holidays as Mother's Day and Valentine's Day, the wide use of English language textbooks in colleges and universities, and especially the hundreds of Anglicisms in everyday language. Pointing out this menace also implies an attack on the traditional institutions, especially the school system, which did not sufficiently forearm the mass of French Canadians against these influences.[4]

The revival in part stresses the links with the civilization of France. Many departments at the Université de Montréal and Université Laval have closer links with French than with English-Canadian and American scholars. Artists and students in humanities and science are flocking to France to study. The Province's "Maison du Québec" in Paris which, among its other functions, serves as a student center, is moving into a new building costing a quarter of a million dollars. Dozens of French entertainers and scholars come to Quebec each year and, on the whole, are enthusiastically received. Montreal is one of the world's best markets for French books and phonograph records and the sale of French magazines and newspapers has been increasing from year to year. And, in selecting equipment for its subway, Montreal selected Paris as its model rather than other Western cities.

An intellectual revival in the province itself is also in full swing, with many French Canadians exhibiting a new spirit of freedom and achievement. The intellectual and cultural reputation of the French network of the Canadian Broadcasting Corporation far exceeds that of its English and American counterparts. As evidenced in exhibits, sales, and publicity, French artists and musicians are becoming better known to the public. Small magazines which discuss public affairs and literature,

---

[4] A book by a Church Brother, *Les Insolences du Frère Untel*, which sharply criticizes the popular language and the schools which are judged to be primarily responsible, has sold over 120,000 copies, more than any other book published in Quebec.

small theater groups, film theaters specializing in European artistic films and encouraged by an annual film festival — all have achieved a success unimaginable ten years ago. The Provincial Government has helped this revival. Its film censorship board, with new personnel, has relaxed the formerly strict controls; the Ministry of Cultural Affairs awards prizes to Quebec authors and buys and distributes some of their books. An Office of the French Language has been established to encourage the use of standard French in the province.

French Canadians do not all agree on the directions these movements of revival should take, who should take the lead, or the emphasis to be given to its various dimensions; yet pervading all the movements is a stronger spirit of freedom and sense of identity and direction than ever before.

The Role of Advertising

What is the role of advertising amidst all these changes? Historically advertising was represented by the dominant English-Canadian and American culture. The French Canadians, besides being the major suppliers of labor, were also the major consumers. The products they bought came ordinarily not from French-Canadian, but from American and English-Canadian industry. The major advertisers, then, were also English and American. Since advertising on a large scale was not part of the traditional French-Canadian culture, the English-Canadian and American companies, and their advertising agencies — the first English-Canadian agency began operations in Quebec in 1889, the first American in 1930 — were entering a new and unfilled field. They did not have to replace or fight any traditional or distinctive French-Canadian patterns. In fact, national advertising was welcomed by the French-language media — radio, newspapers, magazines, and billboard landowners — as a source of income, and, with this type of publicity, with its distinctive design and language, was the consumers' first experience. The local French Canadians did relatively little advertising and, when they did, generally followed the model of the English media.

Thus the English-Canadian and American advertisers had a relatively free hand in introducing advertising into Quebec. Their only concern was with the language, since the advertising had to be in French. They saw no reason why advertising carefully prepared and effective for the English should not be equally effective in another language. Therefore they followed the simplest and cheapest policy; they used the same illustrations and hired translators. Translation was assumed to be a relatively simple task which any French-speaking person could handle. The translators had little prestige and no power; their job was to translate as literally as possible. Some had little education or writing ability, some were from France, with scant knowledge of French Canada; they often made egregious errors or wrote advertisements that were just incomprehensible. Or, if they did seek to do free translations, they risked losing their jobs. To quote one informant:

> The French specialist in an advertising agency was a young chap who knew English well and came from Quebec. They gave him a little corner with a typewriter on his knees and a pile of texts to translate. They said to him: "My boy, translate that, translate that, and translate that." This fellow couldn't be himself at all. On the contrary, if ever he tried to interpret instead of doing a foolish translation, he was in danger of losing his job.

Every French-Canadian veteran in advertising can cite a host of badly written, although often literal, translations.[5]

On the whole, the mass of French Canadians seemed to accept these advertisements in the same way that they accepted English and American products. It was not their role to create a disturbance or make decisions in such areas. At the same time, they were becoming familiar with the style and manner of the American and English-Canadian advertisements. Perhaps the one effective protest group was the Church and advertisers did, in deference to the power of the clergy, tone down advertising displays of girls in underclothes or bathing suits. Certain intellectuals and minority groups occasionally protested, but without much effect either on the English-Canadian and American advertising directors or the French-Canadian consumers.

The changes since these early days have been considerable, with much more initiative and responsibility now being given to French Canadians. Within the past few years, at least four French Canadians have become vice-presidents in English-Canadian or American-controlled advertising agencies. Others have become officers or directors of advertising in large companies producing beer, textile products, and flour. Currently, in the preparation of advertisements, the most common pattern is first to develop quite carefully an English campaign. Then the French department or advisor is asked whether the same campaign is more or less acceptable in French and, if so — which is generally the case — the advertisements are sent to a translation agency and reviewed for correctness and clarity by the agency's French department. For television, the comparable pattern is to have the same video while a French sound track replaces the English. There are variations of this pattern. Perhaps minor modifications are required in the copy; perhaps the copy is acceptable, but the accompanying illustration is not; perhaps the whole campaign is judged not suitable and the French department is given leeway, with a certain budget, to develop its own campaign. And oc-

---

[5] For example, "They (refering to fountain pens) are terrific," translated into French, became "Elles sont terrifiantes," which means literally, "They are terrifying." Or "(Product X) is first with me," is translated "X est premier avec moi," which means literally, "X and I are first together."

casionally, especially for the breweries, new and original Quebec campaigns are developed in French which in turn may even be adapted into English.

For American companies with Canadian subsidiaries, such as automobile, gasoline, soft drink, and large food companies, the campaigns in the two countries, more often than not, have the same basic themes and sometimes are precisely the same. But the variations are many, depending on the medium and the particular campaign. The directors of Canadian subsidiaries generally affirm that they are autonomous and are free to use, or not use, the American-developed campaign. Sometimes — and this has the important advantage of being least expensive — the Canadian office judges the American campaign to be satisfactory for the Canadian market and adopts it, with only minor modifications to meet Canadian measures or Canadian food and drug or broadcasting regulations. In other instances, the Canadian companies may not even seriously consider the American-developed campaigns, but prepare their own. The Canadian advertising agencies, probably more than the companies, advocate independent Canadian campaigns, but the companies pay the bill and consequently make the final decisions.

The companies which do the largest amount of advertising — automobile manufacturers, breweries, soft drink, cigarette, and large food producers — are almost all controlled by American or English-Canadian interests and use English-Canadian, or branches of American, advertising agencies. The subsidiaries of American companies, with a few exceptions, are free to choose, and do not use the same advertising agencies as their parent American companies. The advertising agencies in Canada — even those that are branches of American concerns — are staffed almost entirely with Canadian personnel.

French Canadians, we observed, have few positions of major influence in the largest companies. They are more influential in the advertising agencies although the patterns within agencies vary considerably and change from year to year. A few small agencies are completely French-owned and controlled, but do not have many large accounts, even of French-Canadian companies. Some of the smaller agencies employ one French Canadian who advises on all French advertising, while a number of the larger agencies have separate French departments, with account executives working on those accounts for which language is particularly important. A recent development is the all-French branch office in Montreal handling French language advertising, while the Toronto head office handles the English.

Current Questions at Issue

The increasing prosperity of Quebec and the extensive social transformation of the past few years have had their effect on the manufacturing companies. The companies are now competing more intensively for the Quebec market and are anxious to win French-Canadian good will. Crucially affected are both the personnel of the advertising world and the content of advertising.

Personnel

Advertising is a relatively new occupation to French Canadians. The French Canadian who worked on the farm, in the factory, or in a lower white-collar job had little opportunity to become aware of the positions or skills required in marketing or advertising and few aspired to such posts. Those who first came into advertising did so more or less by chance. Some were stenographers, clerks, or translators who, when the need arose, were given assignments writing copy, evaluating French language advertising, or analyzing media statistics. Others worked for newspapers or radio stations and, when satisfactory jobs were not available in these fields, accepted jobs in advertising. In time, in the course of these new jobs, these men came to know the field of advertising and became the specialists on French Canada.

In recent years, with the increasing demand for trained personnel, the pattern of recruitment has become more like that of the English world. The now experienced French Canadians began to give lectures and evening courses for students and others who were becoming aware of career possibilities in the commercial world. The relatively new French-language schools of commerce in Montreal and Quebec have included courses in marketing and advertising in their curricula, courses which essentially follow American and English-Canadian models. Thus the younger men are more likely to have come into advertising by choice, at a younger age, and to have had some formal instruction in the field. Our questionnaire to French-Canadian advertisers also demonstrates these points (Tables 1 and 2).

The French Canadian who aspires to promotion and a successful career in advertising, as in many other occupational worlds, may follow one of three basic models — Assimilationist, Separatist, or Distinctive Component.

The *Assimilationist* model, in its extreme form, is basically no different from the pattern of adaptation followed by ethnic groups in the United States and the rest of Canada. The traditional culture and personal relationships recede into the background and the key reference groups become those in the English world. Perhaps the French Canadian moves into an English section of the city, sends his children to an English school, joins an Irish instead of a French-Canadian church, gives his name an English pronunciation, participates in English lodges and charity campaigns, and gives up former friends and family ties. Relatively few French Canadians in advertising, especially in Quebec, have seriously

TABLE 1

Question: *Did you come into the field of advertising by choice
or by some chance development?*

AGE	BY CHOICE %	BY CHANCE %
Below 35	56	44
35–44	46	54
45 and over	33	67

$X^2 = 6.15$ $P < .05$

TABLE 2

Question: *At what age did you get your first job related to
advertising?*

AGE	BELOW 25 %	25 AND OVER %
Below 35	80	20
35–44	44	56
45 and over	44	56

$X^2 = 20.66$ $P < .001$

followed this model; but those who have may still, because they know
French, see themselves, and be seen by their English associates, as expert advisers on the French market. To quote one informant:

> Let me tell you what the companies do. They come here to look for a
> French Canadian specialist. They find someone and send him to Toronto
> to work in an exclusively English group. Our poor little French Canadian.
> After two or three years, he becomes English. All that he has left is the
> French language, and that is no longer very good; it is a mixture of the
> two languages. He has lost his French soul; he has assimilated. They al-
> ways refer to him there as a specialist. Well, they lie. Mr. X is no longer
> French, he is a hybrid.

At the other extreme is the *Separatist* model in which the key identifications, associates, and loyalties are completely French-Canadian. This
is a primary pattern, especially in radio and newspapers outside of
Montreal, and in a few relatively small advertising agencies in Montreal
and Quebec City. Contacts with the English world may be important,
particularly in contracting and placing of advertisements; and the
personnel, especially in Montreal, almost all know English well. But the
language of the office is French, the personnel are completely, or almost
completely, French-Canadian, and the career lines are within the French-

Canadian world. Quoting one manager in a small French-Canadian advertising agency:

> If you want to compare us to the large English agency, you can say that here we have a family-type enterprise, each person can do everything and, indeed, we do all work together. . . . There are even some here who don't speak a word of English. If people work here, it is because they want to. Some just prefer a French company rather than a large agency like J. Walter Thompson.

The third model, the *Distinctive Component,* with a number of subvariations, is the most common. These French Canadians work in an English- or American-controlled firm but, in their personal lives, inhabit a French-Canadian world. They live in a French section of the city, speak French at home, give their children a French education, read French magazines and newspapers, and participate with other French Canadians in informal groups and associations. In their ideology they emphasize, and sometimes even brandish, their French-Canadian distinctiveness. They affirm that French Canadians have different interests, behavior patterns, and sentiments than the English Canadians. They fear that French-Canadian traditions and civilization are in danger of being overrun and accept, in most cases quite wholeheartedly, the recent movements of nationalism and cultural revival. The ordinary English Canadian, they say — and no doubt with some truth — knows little of their culture and does not understand or appreciate the traditions and sentiments of French Canada. It is this particular specialized knowledge and sympathy, affirms the French Canadian in advertising, which makes him so valuable and necessary to the English and American companies seeking French-Canadian customers. The following statements are typical of comments by French Canadians about the situation:

> It is here that you run into the contrary phenomenon: the inability of the English-speaking people to understand the viewpoint of the French (4, p. 77).

> It is currently believed by some who neglect to dig under the surface that educated French people have a tendency to be more like the English-speaking Canadians. This is absolutely false. *French Quebec is evolving in the furrow which is French culture* (20, p. 7).

> Translators must also take into account the deeper psychological factors which determine the essential differences in individuals and groups, even within one nation. *The awareness of these differences in mentality and ethnic character is the key to successful mass selling in Canada, as it is the key to individual sales* (3, p. 5).

> Thrifty, cautious, money-minded, the French-Canadian woman may seem somewhat austere. . . . (Yet she has) in addition . . . an obvious taste for

frivolity. . . . (She) has two main weaknesses: she is "gourmande" and "coquette," two untranslatable words . . . and qualities! . . . She also likes "chatoyant" materials, lively colors, jewelry, exotic articles, and rich perfumes, showing by these tendencies that she remains very Latin even in a North-American environment (13, p. 58).

The French Canadian who fits the distinctive component model wants to succeed in the English business world. The English and American companies offer the best paying positions, the best chances for learning specialized skills, the greatest opportunities for advancement, and the greatest possibilities for influencing the public. To this end, the French Canadian must be somewhat Anglicized. Since English is the language of these firms, he must know English well enough to speak it freely and prepare reports.[6] Psychologically, he must feel adequately at ease among the English managers and executives to express his opinions, participate in their pleasantries, and not act unduly defensive. He must feel, or at least manifest, a certain loyalty to his company's goals. Ordinarily his progress and potential career line are determined by the degree to which he is successful in selling American and English-Canadian made products to French-Canadian consumers.

Yet this French Canadian must avoid becoming too Anglicized. If he becomes too involved in the English world and views problems from its point of view, he will lose touch with the developments and changing sentiments of French Canada and approach the less valuable, and disparaged, assimilationist model. At the same time, and this is personally more important, he may lose the esteem of his own ethnic reference group. Many French-Canadian spokesmen and intellectuals, who affirm that French Canadians should have opportunities equal to the English in achieving executive positions, are already quite suspicious. It is of little importance to them that the American and English-Canadian manufacturers of cars, beer, cigarettes, soft drinks, and a host of other products, prosper through selling to French Canadians. And more important, they look — as do many intellectuals throughout the world — with a certain disdain on American-type commercials, jingles, and slogans and, in Quebec, on some glaring examples of a distorted French. These are, in fact, among the very forces they are fighting. The French Canadians in advertising do not all deny these attacks. In response to a question which asked whether French Canadians were justified in fearing that English-Canadian and American influences might gradually absorb their culture and identity, about 70 per cent of our questionnaire respondents replied, "Yes." And as many as 58 per cent said French Canadians in advertising were partly responsible for this situation.

Thus becoming too Anglicized is a danger to avoid; but so too is

[6] For an analysis of certain dilemmas accompanying bilingualism in the work world, see E. Jacques Brazeau (1, pp. 532–540).

identifying too closely with the French-Canadian world. Many an English Canadian is wary and suspicious; he is aware of the social ferment in Quebec and the ever-pressing demands of the French Canadians in advertising. Ideologically, he may suspect that the French-Canadian participant in this ferment may have interests which extend beyond the commercial interests of the organization. Perhaps the French Canadian makes exaggerated demands to increase his influence and gain a more important position. To quote an outspoken English-speaking president of a tobacco company:

> . . . . to spend days and weeks, and perhaps months, trying to split hairs, trying to survey and analyze, trying to devise and determine what exactly are the peculiarities and the differences in the Quebec market, would, I respectfully submit, be a sheer waste of time. . . . Too much is being made of the so-called deep-seated differences and peculiarities of the French market and . . . this has become a bit of a professional game.[7]

So the French Canadian who wants to succeed in the English work world must beware, in his ultimate demands, of veering so close to a French-Canadian nationalist position that he fails to see the perspective, or loses the basic confidence, of the English. The French Canadian who concluded a public address with, "After all, profits are the reason you and I are in business," was aware of this danger.[8]

To the French Canadian in advertising, the dilemma of living in one ethnic world and working in another must not be left to resolve itself. The few lone-wolf critics of the past have been superseded by dozens of active and vigorous French Canadians who speak up either as individuals or as members of a professional association, *Le Publicité Club de Montréal.* This Club, formed in 1959 to focus attention on problems distinctively French-Canadian, has regular meetings. It presents awards for the best French advertisements and commercials, sponsors courses in collaboration with the French school of commerce, and prepares economic reports on the province.

The French Canadian in advertising is waging his battle both among the French and the English. Among the former, he seeks primarily recognition and prestige. Some 90 per cent in our survey acknowledge that the French-Canadian advertising man has more prestige among his compatriots than he did ten years ago, but over 55 per cent say that he still is not sufficiently respected, and almost as many believe that the French Canadian in advertising receives less esteem from French Canadians than does the English advertising man from English Canadians. The *Publicité Club* manifests the struggle in its aim "to familiarise

[7] Talk given before the Canadian Association of French Radio and Television Owners in Montreal, Nov. 6, 1962, by W. Tennyson, President, Rock City Tobacco Co. Ltd. This statement is relatively extreme and not often expressed in public.

[8] Talk given before the Canadian Association of French Radio and Television Owners in Montreal, Nov. 6, 1962, by Yves Menard.

the public with advertising" and, as one of its first projects, sponsored a "Semaine de la Publicité," with radio talks and publicity releases in honor of "Le Publicitaire Inconnu" (The Unknown Advertising Man).

The more important struggle is waged in the English world where, again, it is acknowledged that conditions are much better now than five or ten years ago. Quoting a former president of the *Publicité Club*: "I would say that the most practical goal of the *Publicité Club* is to make the French market known in the English-speaking milieu, both Canadian and American." And to this end, French Canadians constantly speak to the English of the need for more and better advertising campaigns in French, and the *Publicité Club* sponsors the French Marketing Month with public releases, special articles, and speakers. This struggle takes on various forms, underlying all of which is the affirmation of difference between the French and English Canadians — not only in language, but in traditions, tastes, feelings, and emotional expression. To ignore these differences, they affirm, means to expose oneself not only to blunders, but also to be ineffective in communicating a message and in selling to French Canadians.

Since adapting advertisements to the French Canadians implies an avoidance of English forms of expression, the advertising man can flourish this cause before the French as well as the English, thus participating in French Canada's cultural revival. The French Canadians are constantly affirming this point and the *Publicité Club* expresses it in its aim, "to maintain the quality of French language advertising."

The struggle with the English world is manifested most directly in the arguments about advertising content, but no less important is the power struggle which, so far, has been successful. In recent years, French Canadians in advertising agencies have become not only account executives and media directors, but also Directors of French Services and officers. A few have become directors of advertising in manufacturing firms. In most instances the high level positions given to French Canadians are new and have not involved the direct replacement of English Canadians. However, when an advertising agency in Montreal, for example, becomes a completely French organization, French Canadians do replace, or at least take on positions which formerly would have gone to the English. Such changes have far-reaching implications, for the higher and more responsible the positions of the French Canadians, the more they can influence the major areas of decision.

But the very success of the French Canadian introduces a potential problem for the future. In the present struggle, the most the French Canadian can ordinarily hope for is to be accepted as an expert on French Canada, with offices in Montreal. But assuming that French Canadians achieve this goal and do have a decisive influence on the content of advertising in Quebec, will they have no higher aspirations? It seems unlikely. The ultimate decision-making positions — where budgets, major appointments, and policy decisions are made — are in still higher echelons, in the officerships and boards of directors, with offices often in Toronto, New York, or elsewhere. This means living and moving in an English-speaking world and extending one's range of concern and responsibility beyond French Canada to national and international considerations. But since the success of the cultural revival of French Canada depends on a segregated environment, this means that those very French Canadians who will be most influential economically will withdraw from participation in the revival and, perhaps, even serve as models of success to other French Canadians. If we generalize, the very success of the members of a minority group in the majority group's large corporations carries with it the risk of retarding, or even obstructing, the maintenance and development of the native culture.

Advertising Content

The content of advertising takes on a significance which extends far beyond the immediate practical problem of communicating a message and, in the minds of many French Canadians, is the central issue. Advertising content, in part, has become a symbol of the questions surrounding cultural assimilation. If the content is a routine translation, more or less literal, of the advertisements prepared in English, it suggests that the French-Canadian market is not large enough for special consideration — which becomes less defensible with the increasing development of Quebec — or that the two ethnic cultures in recent years have become very much alike, a position which the French Canadians strongly deny. A routine translation of English advertisements of course would also reduce the role of the French Canadians to mere language technicians, a position which hardly befits their aspirations in the current effervescence in Quebec.

Differences between the groups in purchasing habits are acknowledged. Marketing research studies, for example, show that French Canadians, compared to the English, patronize independent stores more and supermarkets less. They buy more ale (and less lager), mayonnaise, and wine, and thicker soups. They buy less dog food, peanut butter, chocolate chips, and frozen vegetables. Also some particular manufacturers of common products do well; others do badly.

Nor are the two groups always exposed to the same advertisements. The products that sell better to French Canadians are likely to be advertised more in French and vice versa. The English, according to one study of English and French newspapers, are exposed to more advertisements of hotels and of a financial nature such as dividend notices, financial statements, and company appointments. The latter reflects the dominance of the English in the business world and the former, the presumption that they travel in the United States. More French Canadians, in turn, are exposed to more advertisements for medical products and services, supporting a popular view that the French Canadians are more receptive to traditional home remedies and are generally less sophisticated about medical matters (6). Department stores too take differences between the group into consideration. In English advertising, greater emphasis is given to higher-priced clothing, furniture, and gifts; while in French, more advertisements stress religious goods, pets, rocking chairs, and lower-priced clothing (11). There are also some companies whose products, such as paint or soup, are well known only in Quebec and who advertise almost entirely in French; there are also English companies known only in English Canada who advertise only in English media. But most national companies advertise in both languages to both groups, following one of three general patterns: translation, adaptation, or separate campaigns.

Translation

By far the least expensive technique for any company is translation. The advertisements are prepared in English and then translators convert the copy into French for newspapers, magazines, radio, or television. No changes are made in illustrations, labels, or actions. This approach, at one time employed by practically all national advertisers, is still most common. In printed media, such translation is standard procedure for local advertising of supermarkets and department stores; for the relatively technical advertising in business, industry, and professional magazines; and for most newspaper and magazine national advertising. In the study of Montreal newspapers, close to 90 per cent of the comparable national advertisements were essentially translations of this type.

Direct translations occur less often in radio and television advertising. Estimates by advertising men of translated commercials (that is, translated and read, or occasionally dubbed, in French) range about 50 to 60 per cent. It is also not uncommon for English packages to be illustrated on French television commercials since French packages are often not available.

There are variations in the translation procedure. Almost all the large English companies — and also some French-Canadian ones, to the annoyance of newspaper critics — have legally registered only their English names. So at the bottom of French advertisements may be seen such names as Canadian Kodak Co., Limited, or Aluminum Company of Canada, Limited, or Champion Spark Plug of Canada Limited. A few companies, however, especially the banks, have also registered French versions of their names for use in French advertisements. And, with the recent nationalistic pressures in Quebec, the number of companies registering French versions of their names is increasing.

Many companies have given English brand names to their products, for example, a tire is called, "Royal Safety 800," a whiskey, "Royal Command," and a cough syrup, "Jack and Jill";[9] and these companies have traditionally used these English names in their French advertisements. In choosing names or symbols for new products, Canadian companies often seek versions acceptable in both English and French, such as Matinée, Belvedere, or CN which might represent Canadian National or Canadien National. In the past few years, a few companies have also translated the brand name. So "Mr. Clean" of the English advertisement is "Monsieur Net" in the French, and "Red Kettle" soup in English is "Chaudron Rouge" in French.

More and more, too, companies are tending to use bilingual packages, with the French side of the package shown in the French advertisement. But it is still common to see advertisements with such English phrases as "king size," "filter tip," or "custom blended," or with such English trade marks as "keyed for speed," or "They grip because they CLAW."

In the aforementioned study of newspaper advertisements, over three-fifths of the French advertisements had at least one word of English somewhere in the advertisement. However, with the changes taking place in company and product names and especially in packaging and labeling, this proportion is steadily decreasing. The greater concern with the French market, the wish not to prejudice their advertising campaigns, and the clamor of French-Canadian spokesmen have had their effect.

For a variety of reasons, companies have come to realize that translations cannot be literal. Sometimes they still insist on literal translations or, to the annoyance of their translators and French-Canadian advisors, demand considerable convincing before accepting any proposed rewording, but, on the whole, the battle of the French Canadians for free translations is being won.[10] Thus the English idiom, meaningless in translation, the testimonial by English-speaking celebrities unknown to French Canadians, or the irrelevant theme, such as an advertisement for pancakes on Shrove Tuesday (which to French Canadians is a feast day), are much less common than in the past.

French-Canadian translators and advertising personnel, to whom language is a significant element of the cultural revival, are ordinarily careful to write a good French. Slang expressions such as "one-of-a-kind" or "tops-in-value," Anglicisms such as "plywood" or "switchboard," or coined expressions such as "rainettes" or "baby-dolls" are — with the exception of certain local shops and media which seek a "common man" appeal — quite scrupulously avoided. Advertisements in French therefore are often more conservative in style than the English advertisements

[9] The company chose this name despite its English connotation. The French pronunciation becomes Jacques and Gilles, two boys' names (2).

[10] The term "translation" still carries a strong stigma among French Canadians in advertising and, except when literal and badly done, has been replaced by the more acceptable "adaptation."

from which they are translated (11). When the French Canadians in advertising were asked in the survey whether they considered it acceptable to use "joual" (the term for the somewhat distorted language of the man in the street) in advertisements if "joual" would be better understood by the audience the advertiser wanted to reach, over 75 per cent said "No." But occasionally, "joual" is preferred by English who make the final decisions and the French-Canadian adviser is overruled.

Adaptation

The line between translation and adaptation is blurred but, in general, adapted advertisements are derived from the English, but have additions or are significantly different in design or meaning. These changes, for any particular advertising campaign, may occur in one or more media and may vary in their degrees of importance. Adaptations may occur in the illustrations, the ideas of the copy, or both.

Occasionally an illustration in the English advertisement is considered inappropriate for the French and another is substituted. In an English bank advertisement, for example, a well-to-do middle-aged man is shown sitting in a chair in contrasting moods, happy and dejected; in the French advertisement, the illustration, with essentially the same copy, shows a young man waiting for a bus. The difference, reflecting the positions of the English and French in the occupational hierarchy, presumably makes for easier identification by the respective ethnic groups. In an English television commercial, a cleaning woman with a strong Scotch accent demonstrates and describes the virtues of Spic and Span; in the French commercial, the very same ideas are expressed by a cleaning woman with a strong working-class accent.

The adaptations in the copy sometimes involve a phrase or two. A Florida hotel adds "ici on parle Français"; the girl at the typewriter is called Betty in the English advertisement and Blanche in the French; a man buying a car in an English advertisement is Jim Roberts, in the French, he is Jacques Robin. Occasionally the French advertisement is directed to a lower economic level, so an English advertisement gives the full price of a car while the French advertisement refers to a time-payment plan (6).

Radio jingles, of which — according to one respondent — some 80 to 90 per cent are first written in English and have the same music and sound track, almost always necessitate some form of adaptation in the lyrics. It is almost impossible to translate and carry over the same syllable emphasis.

The adaptations in slogans, based on idioms and variations of company trade marks, are sometimes striking. Thus added to the French Jello ad is "Jell-O à la bouche," a variation of the common French idiom, "J'ai l'eau à la bouche." Shell Gasoline's "Shell que j'aime" is a variation of "Celle que j'aime." Labatts brewery adds its symbol of a French-Canadian lumberman and "Y a rien qui la batte!" Coca Cola replaces "Zing" with "Y a d'la joie," with appropriate changes in the copy. One beer company puts in a nationalistic flavor in replacing "Canada's largest selling ale" with "La bière de chez nous." Such adaptations, depending on the emphasis given to them, may be relatively minor or they may significantly change the tenor of the advertisement.

Some adaptations duplicate an original English style, but are almost different enough in illustration and copy to be considered original. A notable series which gave a great impetus to both distinctive French campaigns and the positions of French Canadians in advertising was developed during the Korean war when Canada's Department of National Defence sought more French-Canadian recruits. Formerly advertisements were directly translated from the English. The new campaign, with appropriate illustrations and copy, especially stressed the French-Canadian pioneers and heroes of the past and the protection of their heritage. An Army advertisement, for example, pastoral in atmosphere and with a blazing religious cross in the foreground, was headed, "Protegera nos foyers et nos droits" ("Protect our homes and our rights"), a line from the French version of the anthem *O Canada*. A Navy advertisement, with a heading from a folk song about French fishermen, discussed the sailors of Brittany who founded French Canada. Another example of a major adaptation was a breakfast cereal jingle which, in English, was based on English nursery rhymes, and, in French, on such rhymes as *Cadet Rousselle* and *Le roi Dagobert*. Testimonials too may involve major adaptations, with a substitution of French celebrities for the English and appropriate modifications in the copy.

Separate Campaigns

The sophisticated French Canadian is very much aware that no necessary relationship exists between the original campaign, conceived and developed by French Canadians in French, and its effectiveness; and also that original advertisements may or may not refer to distinctive elements of French-Canadian culture. Nevertheless, the original campaign has become, for many French Canadians, the symbol of their battle for equality. A former French-Canadian program producer writes:

And the light (referring to a previously cited anecdote) . . . rests entirely upon the French-Canadian planners, writers, and producers. They are the ones who can give the proper voltage required for a complete illumination of the message you wish to convey. Literal translation is taboo, "adaptation" is, at times, acceptable, but CREATION . . . original CREATION is the answer to a perfect solution of the problem (9, p. 21).

Advertising prepared in French is not uncommon in Quebec, especially for local shops, for goods and products intended primarily for a French market, and for such services as charity and political campaigns. However, relatively few national companies have developed original French campaigns. In some instances, these companies acknowledge that a separate and original French campaign may be more effective than the translation or adaptation, but doubt that the size of the French-Canadian market merits the extra cost. Of the national companies that do sometimes prepare original campaigns in French, the most common are breweries. The explanation lies in their more or less autonomous provincial organization, the intense competition, the unique beer-drinking pattern in Quebec, and the restrictions on beer advertising which forbid the companies to discuss the merits of their products.

By viewing the advertisements themselves, we cannot always distinguish the original French campaign from the translation or adaptation. Most of the original French advertisements, for example, of department stores, specialty shops, automobile dealers, and restaurants, especially in printed media, are essentially no different from comparable advertisements in English. Perhaps the only valid generalization is that advertisements created in French avoid certain representations and symbols of a distinctly English or American type, for example, the Union Jack or the ever smiling blonde who often demonstrates soap or cosmetics. (A comparable model for French Canada would probably be dark, chic, and more pensive.) Also, of course, in radio and television, the announcers and characters in commercials are clearly French-Canadian in appearance, manner, and expression.

The French advertisements that are distinctive fall into three groups. The first appeals to a spirit of nationalism. A paint manufacturer, for example, advertises: "It is in buying products manufactured here by French Canadians that we help ourselves economically." A brewery advertisement shows pictures of its French-Canadian managing personnel and says, "A Quebec company since 1790," and "At the service of Quebec." A department store, in a full-page advertisement on June 24, the provincial holiday honoring Quebec's patron saint St. Jean Baptiste, salutes the French-Canadian population and the "épanouissement" (the flowering) of French Canada. A political party, in its French campaign — which is quite different from its English counterpart — blazons the slogan, "Maîtres chez nous." A brewery introduces a new beer which sells "everywhere in Quebec and only in Quebec."

A second group of distinctive advertisements are not strictly nationalistic, but sentimentally appeal to an identification with the province and, by implication at least, differentiate the English from the French. Soups or teas are prepared "au gout québecois"; jingles advertising coffee are based on French-Canadian folk songs; a flour company presents a traditional cake recipe of old Quebec; television commercials present scenes or vignettes of village life, sports, occupations, or business enterprises in the province; a brewery, recognizing the wide interest in family names — of which there are a limited number since the original settlers were so few — displays drawings of the pioneering and heroic activities of the family's first Quebec settlers.

A third type of distinctive advertisement does not refer to Quebec, but is based on traits unique to the French Canadians. A Chinese man, advertising a restaurant, speaks French with a Chinese accent; a French shipping line stresses its French food, language, and services; a Belgian airline describes the pleasures of visiting French-speaking countries of Europe; a local political campaign, in French only, promises special treatment to hospitals founded by religious orders; beer advertisements, based on market research, stress, in a style which is more lighthearted than that of the English advertisements, the delights of drinking a particular brand.

For the large English and American advertisers, the originality of the campaigns prepared in French is never complete. Budget limitations are still imposed by the English-speaking directors; the basic conception of much of the advertising, for example, the jingles or premiums, is American in origin; and no subsidiary or branch is free to discard or adapt the basic trade marks and symbols of the companies.

In analyzing social change, a crucial question becomes: Does advertising function as an "Anglicizing" or "Americanizing" force contributing to a common culture among the ethnic groups or does it function to reinforce traditional cultures and differences? In French Canada, both are true, depending on the aspect of the communication and culture being considered.

In some respects, the ways of expression and patterns of thought of the French Canadians are reinforced. The language is French and French Canadians are exposed to some advertisements not shown to the English. In radio and television, the characters and models are French-Canadian types, and — which is relatively recent — the French Canadians see and hear more advertisements with a nationalistic flavor and identification. However, in other basic respects, the values and references are no different in French Canada than in English Canada. In the vast majority of national and local campaigns, the style and content of the advertisements is basically the same for both groups. To what extent, we may ask, can significant cultural distinctions, ethnic and otherwise, be maintained in areas strongly influenced by advertising? Modern advertising, which seems to incorporate the development of large, centralized industry, the growth of the mass media of communication, and the generally similar demands of all peoples who are earning more money and have more leisure time, would seem primarily — except for its emphasis on national identification — to be a force making for a common culture, teaching common values, ideals, and patterns of behavior.

Conclusion

Our picture of advertising in French Canada does not lend itself to any neat and simple explanatory model of social change. In part, no doubt, there is a power struggle. The English Canadians and Americans seek to maintain their dominant position and the French Canadians demand more opportunities and rights for themselves. But this is too facile a picture. In both groups, the movements are diverse and of varying strengths, and the values and sentiments far from integrated. Sometimes the English Canadians and the Americans, rather than presenting a united front, take opposing stands and the French Canadians may be called on to join forces with one side or another. Nor within the English and American companies is the perspective the same at the various hierarchical levels. An apparent struggle within an agency or firm in Montreal, or even between the offices at Montreal and Toronto, may be quite differently viewed in the highest echelons where the basic decisions are made. What at one level is a victory or a concession, at another may be a means of maintaining control or a relatively minor personnel change to ensure the prosperity of the company.

Differences within the French-Canadian group contribute to the blurring of the picture. The French Canadians are actively seeking to change the status quo, but efficiency is hampered by differences in perspectives — between those who want a tight professional organization and those who want one more broadly based; between those who espouse a free enterprise approach and those of a more radical economic ideology; between those who work for and are loyal to one company and those who work for and are loyal to competing companies; between those with universal skills and those whose knowledge and usefulness is limited to Quebec; between those who are more and less Anglicized. And also, as we have observed, the continued success of the French Canadians — since it can lead ultimately to posts in the national and international decision-making echelons — carries with it the seeds of destruction of that which is distinctly French-Canadian.

This research has implications for the study of social and cultural change elsewhere in the world. The major producing countries of the world, with their own definition of civilization and in competition with each other, introduce in less-developed areas, their products, personnel, and ideas — in all of which advertising is a potent factor. To what degree do these new elements, both in their content and their new occupational patterns, function to standardize the way of life and values of these groups and to make them similar to people in other parts of the world? To what degree, by appealing to nationalistic sentiment and traditional culture, do they encourage differences? To what degree do the indigenous collaborators accept the positions and values assigned to them and to what degree do they participate in resistance movements and fight for the maintenance of their culture and their "rights"? A pertinent theory of social change must encompass both the broader developments and the range of dimensions and alternatives.

BIBLIOGRAPHY

1. Brazeau, E. Jacques. "Language Differences and Occupational Experience," *Canadian Journal of Economics and Political Science*, Vol. 24 (1958), pp. 532–540.

2. Buckley, F. C. "Marketing a New Proprietary Medicine," in E. J. Fox and D. S. R. Leighton (eds.), *Marketing in Canada*. Homewood, Ill.: Richard D. Irwin, Inc., 1958, pp. 363–372.

3. Champagne, Henault. "Translation Won't Score a Bull's-Eye in French Market," *Marketing*, Sept. 25, 1959, p. 5.

4. Coté, Paul. "Mental Blocks Distort French Market Evaluation," *Marketing*, June 8, 1962, pp. 76–78.

5. Dofny, J. and M. Rioux. "Les Classes sociales au Canada francais," *Revue Française de Sociologie* Vol. 3 (1962), pp. 290–300.

6. Elkin, Frederick. "A Study of Advertisements in Montreal Newspapers," *Canadian Communications*, Vol. 4 (1961), pp. 15–22, p. 30.

7. Falardeau, Jean-Charles, ed. *Essais sur le Canada français*. Laval, Quebec: Les Presses Universitaires Laval, 1953.

8. Garigue, Philippe. *Etudes sur le Canada français*. Montreal: Université de Montréal, 1958.

9. Goulet, Barney. "Don't Be a Monkey," *Canadian Broadcaster*, Nov. 1, 1962, p. 21.

10. Gzowski, Peter. "The Cardinal and His Critics," *Maclean's*, July 14, 1962, pp. 13 ff.

11. Hill, Mary B. "Bilingual Advertising in the Retail Enterprise." Master's thesis, McGill University, Montreal, 1963.

12. Hughes, Everett C. *French Canada in Transition*. Chicago: University of Chicago Press, 1943.

13. MacKay, Suzanne Thiboutot. "Madame, Who, What Is She?" *Marketing*, June 8, 1962, pp. 56–58.

14. Newman, Peter C. "The French Revolution, Quebec, 1961," *Maclean's*, April 22, 1951, pp. 21 ff.

15. Pelletier, Gérard. "La Société çanadienne-française et L'Eglise," *Le Magazine Maclean*, Sept. 1961, pp. 37 ff.

16. Porter, John. "The Economic Elite and the Social Structure," *Canadian Journal of Economics and Political Science*, Vol. 23 (1957), pp. 377–394.

17. Porter, John. "Higher Public Servants in the Bureaucratic Elite," *Canadian Journal of Economics and Political Science*, Vol. 24 (1958), pp. 483–501.

18. Sandage, C. H. and Fryburger, V. (eds.). *The Role of Advertising.* Homewood, Ill.: Richard D. Irwin, Inc., 1960.

19. Wade, Mason, ed. *Canadian Dualism.* Toronto: University of Toronto Press, 1960.

20. Waiter, Maurice. "The Difference Isn't So Vague — It's Vital," *Marketing*, Sept. 25, 1959, pp. 7–8.

21

J. A. and Olive Banks

Feminism and Social Change—A

Case Study of a Social Movement

Sociologists have, on the whole, been remarkably uninterested in feminism, and it is rare, even in books about social movements generally, to find the subject dealt with in any detail. Yet, changes in the status of women have occurred in all countries where there are sociologists, and feminist organizations have been and often still continue to be associated with the movement towards emancipation which those changes in status are usually held to connote. Feminist literature, moreover, can hardly be said to be lacking in quantity, and the social historian or historically-minded sociologist who is concerned with relating social ideologies and organized social movements to contemporary shifts in the balance of social, economic, and political power, cannot be excused on this ground for failure to consider the subject. The contrast between the attention paid to feminism and to other social movements, such as socialism or trade unionism, is sufficiently striking for a plea to be entered here that there is good cause for an inquiry to be directed towards this subject.

Such lack of interest becomes all the more surprising when we realize that it is relatively easier for the scholar to identify separately the movement of organized bodies, deliberately established and developed to foster the rights of women, from that of the processes of change in the relation between the sexes which appear to have taken place at about the same time. It is also true of feminism, in a sense that is the case with very few other social movements for which as much documenta-

547

tion is extant, that to all intents and purposes its whole lifetime is complete. Socialist organizations and trade unions, however much they have evolved since their inception in the nineteenth century, still continue to find sufficient adherents in the second half of the twentieth to hold out the promise that their impact may be world-shaking even yet; but the organized feminist movements, if they continue at all today, can only be counted alongside vegetarianism and nudism as bordering on the cult. The movement's decline in this respect is the sociologist's gain, for only in situations of this kind is it possible for him to estimate the degree of its success. It is the main task of this chapter to provide a brief discussion of what is implied by such an investigation in this field.

Since in the view of the present writers, feminism has so much to offer to both sociologist and social historian which is of considerable theoretical importance, it is of some interest to consider why it has been for so long neglected. McGregor has suggested that the reason, or part of the reason, might be in the nature of feminism itself: "It is not a subject on which men and women easily find their way to rational views" (16, p. 48). This is true, but it would seem to apply equally to other social movements. The long debate over socialism has hardly been notorious for its level-headed reasoning. A similar objection would also seem to apply to McGregor's alternative suggestion — "a formidable obstacle to serious investigation is the vast, repellent literature raised by the hagiographers of the 'women's movement'" (16, p. 49). All partisan literature includes a fair share of the repellent which will be particularly obnoxious to those who are not themselves parties to the controversy. Rather it would seem that a fundamental reason for the neglect of the feminist movement by historians, at any rate, is the belief that the emancipation of women has been of little historical importance. This attitude of mind is the product of a number of influences not least of which is the fairly widespread acceptance of a Marxist or quasi-Marxist interpretation of history which sees all struggles for power in economic terms. Nor does feminism fit easily into the traditions of political or constitutional historiography which tends to concern itself, if it concerns itself with women at all, only with the struggle for the suffrage, a spectacular but comparatively minor aspect of the feminist endeavor. It might not indeed be too fanciful to ascribe the neglect of feminism on the part of historians to their more general neglect of genuine *social* history.

Sociologists, it is true, have been far more concerned than historians with the position of women in society but they too have ignored its possible relationship with organized feminism. This seems to be because they have approached the subject, in the main, as part of the study of the family. They have tended, therefore, to see women primarily as wives and particularly as mothers. Other roles which women may from time to time fill are regarded, somewhat askance, as liable to be in conflict with what Parsons has called "root functions" — "which must be found wherever there is a family or kinship system at all" (17, p. 8). There has been accordingly a kind of reproductive determinism underlying the structural-functional approach which is analogous to the economic determinism of the Marxist writers, and which has led it to overlook feminism and organized feminist movements as impotent to achieve changes in role and status where these are conceived to be incompatible with woman's "root" roles in the family. It must also be admitted that the structural-functionalists, who have been responsible in recent times for a good deal of work on the family, have been notoriously uninterested in the more general problems of social change. They have been more interested in the history of sociology than in the sociology of history, and with a few exceptions, they have preferred to gather data from contemporary society or to rely on the work of historians, rather than to conduct their own researches into the past. These two dominant trends in their thinking have predisposed them to ignore a movement which has few adherents today. Nevertheless, the protagonists of an alternative sociology which would give pride of place to the study of changes in ideology, social systems, and personality have so far not proceeded much beyond the kind of alternative to structural-functionalism which is presented by conflict theory, with its emphasis on clashes of material interests. In their turn they have dismissed feminism, ruling it out of account almost, by the very way in which a social movement has been defined. For example, its main criterion, it has been said by a textbook writer on the subject, "is that it aims to bring about fundamental changes in the social order, especially in the basic institutions of property and labour relationships" (12, p. 6). There is a sense, of course, in which the feminist movement could be included under this definition, but Heberle does not mention it, although he lists proletarian, fascist, peasants', and farmers' movements as examples. The efforts of women to change their status vis-à-vis men does not fit easily into the categories of analysis customarily employed by historians and sociologists; to argue a case for the study of feminism is in fact to assert the validity of a different set of categories.

Indeed, perhaps one of the most valuable contributions to sociology which can be performed through an investigation of feminism and its correlate, the emancipation of women, is the correction it offers to some of the stereotyped thinking about social movements which arises from equating them with socialism. Thus, one of the easiest traps into which the sociologist or the social historian may fall is that of assuming all social movements to display the same kind of thoroughly articulated ideology which characterizes socialist movements. There is, that is to say, good ground for accepting Sombart's argument that the writings of Utopian socialists, Marxists, and revolutionary syndicalists — "the spiritual precipitate of the modern social movement" — attempt to realize in the world of thought what the organized socialist movement undertakes to realize in the world of reality; but it by no means follows from this that all social movements will necessarily possess "not only an economic and social-political programme but almost a whole *Weltanschauung*" (23, p. 1, p. 15, p. 25). Feminism, to be sure, has its *Vindication of the Rights of Women* (Wollstonecraft: 1792) and its *Appeal of One Half of the Human Race, Women* (Thompson: 1825) to put alongside the *New View of Society* (Owen: 1813) and the *Manifesto of the Communist Party* (Marx and Engels: 1848), but the literature of the "cause" is on the whole poor in messianic and utopian content when compared with the flood of socialist aspirations for a new world order. It tends moreover to be concerned with particular abuses and to become indignant about wrongs for the organized movement to put right, rather than with fashioning the blueprints of a new society for it to achieve. There is in this respect, superficially at least, a closer relationship between ideology and achievement than obtains with socialism. At the same time, it should not be assumed that feminist writers are solely concerned with practical reforms. They too have ideals to sustain them. The point is that emancipation for them means more often than not emancipation from the restrictions of the existing order, without a very clear idea of some other order which will take its place; equality means equality with men, irrespective of the economic, social, and political systems which exist.

There is one quite obvious reason why this should be. Unlike the advocates for class warfare who are always subject to the danger of confusing the role of the capitalist with the person of the individual businessman and who are easily led into the position of seeking the abolition of the former through the liquidation of the latter, it is far more difficult for feminists to preach sex warfare with the intention of exterminating men. However much it was believed by an extreme wing of the English movement, for example, that sexual desire was a sign of the moral inferiority of men and that women were happier and better if they remained spinsters, parthenogenesis was never seriously advocated as a practical possibility within the foreseeable future, whatever was thought to be the rapidity of evolutionary development or the advance of biological technology (2, pp. 111–113). Socialists might dream of a world without a boss class, but a world without men was not part of the feminist conception of the millenium. On the contrary, the ideal was one of comradeship between the sexes — a new woman matched with a new man — and for this there was no need to counsel revolutionary upheaval. Feminists believed that all they needed concern themselves with was the development of a general recognition that the widespread material advance of their time required fresh intellectual, emotional, and moral attitudes to what had been the traditional roles of the sexes. The old division of labor could be seen as no longer making sense (20, chapter 6).

The fact that the ideological expression of feminism has stopped short of that kind of revolutionary chiliasm which is a marked feature of many types of socialist propaganda, is related to another aspect of difference between social movements which is often overlooked. There is in feminism little tendency towards what the Dutch refer to as *verzuiling* — the forming of columns or blocs. Applied primarily to the contemporary religious scene in Holland it is, nevertheless, capable of generalization to all kinds of social ideology and organization. The main point is that *verzuiling* permeates every aspect of life. For example, in Holland "alongside the central organizations such as the party and the trade union, there was a strong socialist youth movement, a socialist people's school, press and radio, socialist sports leagues and holiday camps, publishing and scientific institutions" (7, p. 43). People of the same faith, people with the same dream of a better world order, can through this proliferation of organizations prepare themselves regularly for it and in the meantime more easily sustain the period of waiting. *Verzuiling* is thus to be seen as a form of isolation within an existing society, the consequence of techniques employed to build up solidarity among the committed by concentrating upon their ideological similarity and emphasizing their lack of genuine dependence upon the "enemy." It is significant that among feminists the clearest signs of *verzuiling* tendencies were demonstrated by those who rejected men outright — a section of the movement in Great Britain which has been accused of homosexuality (6, p. 142), and this section apart, the most striking feature of feminism was indeed its attack on sex segregation. A world denied to women, in the universities and in the professions, was a citadel to be stormed. There can be little doubt that most feminists saw the Victorian society of their day as composed of two vertical strata — *verzuiling* carried to the extreme — and the movement was in consequence organized deliberately to break down barriers rather than to build them up.

Of course, it goes without saying that from the point of view of developing a satisfactory sociological theory of the part played by social movements in social change, it is insufficient merely to point out where stereotyped thinking persists and to show empirically that various types of social movement occur. It is also necessary to develop an explanation for the variations. Underlying the assertion that separatism was not appropriate for tackling the situation in which feminists found themselves, is the hypothesis that the way in which a social movement is organized depends on the problems it has to solve. Both ideology and organization are in their different ways responses to the issues people have to face. A satisfactory theory of social movements must show how such responses occur.

A challenge and response theme of this kind, however, is not the only one to be considered. Even if it can be shown that an ideology and an organized social movement are the results of dissatisfactions with an existing order, no matter how those dissatisfactions arise, it should not be too lightly assumed that any changes which afterwards occur in the circumstances of the dissatisfied must necessarily have been produced in response to their demands. There is always the possibility that ideologies and organized movements are in this respect epiphenomena. The sociology of social movements accordingly requires that empirical evidence be provided for the alleged translation of ideology into effort and for the asserted consequences of that effort, whether it is held that such consequences were intended or not. In the present context this means that the organized movement for reform of the position of women in society be distinguished from those changes in their position with which it is customary to associate the term "emancipation" and that other possible explanations of emancipation be considered alongside the exertions of the feminists. It cannot be denied that this demand implies a much larger program of research than is usually thought necessary in this area, but at the same time, even a slight familiarity with the literature on social change shows that it has been for the most part hastily conceived and even more hastily executed (1, pp. 61–65). The alternative to superficiality is either to embark on more ambitious long-term projects or to limit the field to aspects of the problems which are manageable in size. Thus, the authors have studied the relationship between the feminist movement and the decline of family size in Britain in the late nineteenth century, demonstrating that the advent of the smaller family, with all its consequences for the position of women, was not only unrelated to feminist propaganda but was not even perceived by them as a desired goal, before the actual change in family size had occurred. This study, it is true, was developed as part of a larger inquiry into the genesis of family planning and was not conceived with the present issue in mind, and for that reason, it can be of limited relevance only. Nevertheless, in the absence of meticulous sociological studies of feminism it may be referred to as an example of the kind of work which might be undertaken, and the present chapter read as a sketch of the lines on which a more detailed account of the relationship between feminism and the emancipation of women, or between a social movement and the processes of social change, for that matter, might proceed. While it is hoped that it will have a general applicability, for reasons of convenience the empirical evidence has been taken largely from British experience. American data on some comparable points may be found in (10, pp. 227–302).

"At its inception the feminist movement was essentially a middle-class movement. Nor could it have been otherwise. Power machinery was no respecter of sex. It drove women and children into factories where the privilege of sharing the right to work with their menfolk was the privilege of basic subsistence. Only among those exempt from the choice between wage work and starvation did the social status of women emerge as a challenge to self-regard" (11, p. 315). An interpretation such as this is commonplace. Feminism is usually regarded as a protest movement of middle-class women, a part of the general rise to importance of the middle classes as a consequence of what, for the sake of brevity, may be called the capitalist industrial revolution. Yet, although the evidence superficially supports this point of view, it cannot be accepted at its face value. Of course, it is true that the feminist movement was led by middle-class men and women, but this was also true of most other protest movements in the nineteenth century. More important is the fact that feminism never seemed to appeal to the working classes. This is not to suggest that organized working-class opinion has necessarily been anti-feminist. It has, rather, been indifferent to the claims of women as such, in spite of support given to the feminists by prominent individuals within the labor movement, such as Keir Hardie (9, p. 134), and in spite of occasional working-class support for certain of the feminist goals, such as the Trade Union Congress resolution in favor of equal pay in 1885 (25, p. 52).

It is also true that, for their part, feminists have not been interested *as feminists* in those hardships suffered by working-class women solely as a consequence of their class position — hardships, that is to say, which they have shared along with working-class men. Nor did the feminists, in their organized movement, ally themselves with working-class protest movements or with left-wing political parties. Even when, from time to time, the feminists were associated with radicals of the Liberal Party, it was an alliance of expediency rather than of principle, and many of the well-known feminists were Conservative in politics (24, pp. 264–285). At the same time, it would be a serious mistake to assume that feminists have been concerned only with issues affecting middle-class women. They were ready and eager to take up cases of every type of exploitation of women by men, some of which applied almost exclusively to women of the working or, at the most, of the lower-middle classes. A most interesting example of this — and one which is extremely revealing of the nature of feminism — is the agitation conducted for the repeal of the Contagious Diseases Acts of 1864–69. These Acts required, in 17 garrison towns of Great Britain, that women suspected of being prostitutes should be registered and supervised by the police, should be periodically medically examined, and should, if found suffering from venereal disease, be compulsorily detained in special hospitals. It is hardly likely that these Acts affected any of the women who were active in the feminist organizations which existed while they were on the statute book, and it is clear that the leaders of the organized protest movement had no personal interest in the outcome. They saw the Acts moreover as genuine examples of double-standard legislation.

As Strachey has put it, in the opinion of Josephine Butler and her colleagues the evils and misfortunes suffered by prostitutes arose from the fact not that they were prostitutes as such, but that they were women. "It was actually because of their sex that they were outcasts, not because of their behaviour. The men who did as they did, and who shared their vice and their degradation, were not dealt with in the same manner, nor held in the same disgust. The double moral standard allowed to men what it forbade to women, and it was from this root that the worst of the evil grew" (24, pp. 189–190). The fight for repeal was, accordingly, conducted in terms of a struggle between the sexes in which class issues were largely irrelevant.

It is, however, when we come to look more closely at those changes in the social structure which helped to produce feminism that we see how misleading it can be to think of it as an exclusively middle-class phenomenon. The industrial revolution, it is true, "transferred an increasing number of productive activities from the home to the factory and thereby relieved women of many household burdens." It is also true that in some degree "it excluded the women of the middle-class from the economic process and made their lives idle and futile" (15, p. 263). But it would be an error to think of feminism on that account as the middle-class woman's answer to idleness and boredom. Of really much greater importance was the change in her role and status as housewife which had resulted from the separation of home from work. From being a partner, although certainly never an equal partner with her husband, when the family was organized as a production unit, she had rapidly become dependent in the course of the late eighteenth and of the nineteenth centuries upon some other person's earning capacity for the income she spent as the family representative. What the organized feminist movement was connected with in consequence was the plight of single, widowed, divorced, and married women who were exploited as a result of this dependency. It should be obvious that the new methods of production which, by enlarging the scope and scale of industry, had taken it out of the middle-class home into the factory had had precisely the same effect on the working class. The family system of domestic production gave way, first to the employment of the whole family in the factory and later to the partial, although never wholly complete, removal of the married working-class woman from the industrial scene. The situation in her case was, however, complicated because the position of working-class women as members of the working class appears to have often overshadowed their position as women. As employees or potential employees, they more often had interests in common with the men of their own class in conflict with their employers than they had interests in common with the women of other classes. As a result we can find examples of members of the working classes and their sympathizers asking for the protection of working-class women in industry or for their removal from it altogether, rather than, as did the feminists, demanding equal rights for women in industry. Yet this interpretation should not be pressed too far. The spokesmen of the organized working class for most of the nineteenth century were men and may well have expressed only their own point of view. We do not always know how working-class women responded to the various attempts made to protect them. There is, indeed, some evidence that on occasions they reacted to such protection precisely as their middle-class counterparts might have done and even joined with the feminists to help voice their disapproval. Ray Strachey cites two examples of this, both in 1887, when the effort to restrict women's employment in the interest of their health was actually resisted by the women involved, and with the support of middle-class feminists the proposed legislation was abandoned (24, pp. 236–238). It is quite possible therefore that there was more support for feminist goals among working-class women than the attitude of the organized working-class movement would lead us to suppose, and it is to be regretted that newspapers and other sources of local protest on the part of such women, as women, have not been subjected to the same intensive scrutiny as has been employed for the study of class conflict. All we can conclude is that middle-class women were more acutely aware of the problems which arose from their role as consumers in a world dominated by men as producers than were working-class women; but at the same time all women had interests in common as a result of the industrial revolution which the organized feminist movement sought to realize.

Yet it is unsatisfactory to attempt to understand the nature of feminism by looking only at the effect of industrialization on the role of the housewife. Alongside the recognition of particular disabilities, such as the restriction of employment opportunities for women, and the desire for certain legal reforms (as, for example, the right of a married woman to her own earnings), went a general consciousness amongst feminists of, as they put it themselves, the rights of woman and her wrongs. There was within the organized movement, and particularly in its leadership, a sense of sex consciousness which paralleled the developing class consciousness of the labor movement at the same time. This consciousness of great exploitation by men led the movement far beyond the formulation of specific remedies for particular wrongs into the more radical claim for equality between men and women, in every sphere, from the vote to the standards of sexual morality. It was this essentially ideological position which drew the various "causes" together and made what might otherwise have been a series of pressure groups into a single movement, just as socialism united and gave direction to the various aspects of the working-class struggle for social and economic improvement in conditions of life.

What significance such an ideology has is not so clear. Was it entirely created and sustained to provide a rationale to justify the demand for the reform of particular wrongs — a rationale to match the cry of "woman's place is in the home" with which these reforms were resisted? Or had it an independent source in a general surge towards legal, political, economic, and social equality which is characteristic of all social movements in the nineteenth and twentieth centuries? Either view of feminism is plausible, although the evidence of the rise and fall of feminism seems rather to support the first hypothesis. Each successive campaign, from that of the 1850's and 1860's to improve the education of girls, to the final tumultuous fight for the vote, ended successfully for the feminists; those who took part in the struggle could look back as at a war in which they were at long last victorious. Yet, a quarter of a century or more later, it is still pertinent to question how far the *ideology* of feminism has become reality. Old attitudes have persisted in spite of changes which have freed women from the legal domination of husbands and fathers. It is still true, as it was in the nineteenth century, that "the husband is head of his family, its main economic support, and its representative in the larger community. Women, consigned to domesticity, are mothers and homemakers" (21, p. 301). In the occupational sphere, too, in spite of near-equal educational opportunities and the opening up of professional employment, women are still limited in the main to occupations of lower skill, pay, and prestige. "The assumed progress towards occupational equality between the sexes becomes, upon closer examination, a change in the form of inequality" (4, p. 234).

The inference is obvious: the absence of sex equality in itself has not been sufficient either to prolong the life of feminist organizations or to give rise to a new movement. There are some — we do not know how many — who still subscribe to a feminist ideology, and others who feel a vague but unfocused discontent, but the majority in Britain and, we believe, elsewhere, consider that women are already fully emancipated or, if they are more sophisticated about such things, that emancipation has gone far enough. It would seem that an ideology cannot win the backing to sustain a social movement unless it can center upon a series of practicable reforms urgently desired by those to whom it sets out to appeal.

It remains to consider briefly how far the changes in the position of women over the past hundred years have in fact been the achievement of the feminists and how far they have been brought about by social and economic changes independent of feminist agencies. This, the role of social movements in producing social changes, is an important theoretical issue in the study of social movements, and it is, perhaps, the greatest methodological difficulty in disentangling cause and effect in any historical process which has made it so consistently neglected. Given the requisite research it is, however, possible to make some approach to this problem, although its full solution depends upon a detailed comparative study of feminism and other social movements. Certainly it would be fairly straightforward to discover those feminist campaigns which have been unsuccessful, or only partially successful. The opening of the professions to women is such an example, for while there are few professions which are either legally or customarily barred to women altogether, in most women enter only in small numbers and rarely rise to the top.

It is also possible to discover changes of great significance for the status of women which owe nothing to feminist influence. In some cases, and these are the most straightforward methodologically, the feminists have not even tried to bring about such a change; in others, although the movement has campaigned long and constantly, the change itself has been brought about in other ways. The nineteenth-century fall in the birth rate, in Britain, is one very striking example of a change which does not seem to have occurred to the feminists as either necessary or desirable before the new trend in family size had already established itself (2, pp. 9–10). On the other hand, although the feminists were very anxious about the limited opportunities for women, the great expansion of non-manual work which provided so many jobs for girls and women was a consequence not of the efforts of the feminists but of the technological and social diversification of industrialism and its demand for cheap labor (16, pp. 54–55). The same is true of the tremendous expansion in the proportion of married women at work at the present time. Although of obvious significance for the position of women in society, and although to some extent in line with feminist ideology, it has been brought about entirely by demographic and industrial changes.

There are other aspects of feminism which still remain so little investigated that we can do no more than guess at their relationship with social change. How far, for example, are the changes in sexual morality over the past hundred years a consequence of feminist propaganda? We know so little about this that it is not even clear whether the result of feminine influence, where it has occurred, has been in the direction of a tightening or a loosening of the allegiance to Puritan morality. In spite of the allegations of its opponents that feminism was equivalent to free love, there is more evidence that the organized movement as a whole interpreted a single standard of morality in terms of male chastity rather than female licence (2, pp. 109–111).

This is not to suggest that the feminist movement was without effect, but rather that its effect was both more subtle and more complicated than might be supposed. It was the feminists and their allies, for example, who persuaded the House of Commons to change the law with respect to married women's property and the custody of children. It was also mainly, if not predominantly, feminist influence which abolished state-regulated prostitution in Britain. Further research might well reveal many more such examples.

What we do not know, and what we, as sociologists, need to know is the kind of reform a social movement can achieve, and the kind of reform which is outside its scope and power. The evidence we have is severely limited, but there is sufficient to make it worthwhile to suggest some generalizations which should serve as useful pointers in future research. In the first place, it would seem that feminism has not succeeded in making great or wide-sweeping changes in the status of women. Reforms that we can genuinely attribute to feminist efforts have been small in scope, even if of considerable importance to those affected by them. A typical example is the law relating to married women's property or earnings. This has been of enormous benefit to divorced and separated wives without making any *fundamental* difference to women's subordinate role in society. Even in the United States where women own about two-thirds of all wealth, "it must also be conceded that they neither control nor manage the organizations maintaining and producing that wealth" (10, p. 278). Moreover, studies of married women at work in Britain invariably indicate not only that they subordinate the job to the needs of their family but also that their earnings are spent on home and children, rather than on themselves (14, pp. 120–122). The same may be said of the opening of the universities to women, the repeal of the Contagious Diseases Acts, or any other of the successful campaigns waged by the feminists. The most significant change in the position of women during the past hundred years, the fall in the birth rate, was not produced by feminism at all.

It seems likely, therefore, that the role of the feminist movement has been a two-fold one. Firstly, it has acted as a pressure group, representing certain classes of women and providing them with relief from particular disabilities. Its work for the middle-class spinster is perhaps the example that springs most to mind, for it was this particular issue that lay behind the campaign for improved education for girls and the opening of employment opportunities for women. This was not, however, its exclusive concern, and the same year saw the struggle to give deserted wives some share in the custody of their children, and the campaign for the repeal of the Contagious Diseases Acts. Moreover, as is the case with all pressure groups, it has operated most effectively when the reform has been a simple and straightforward one; a change in the law or in the rules governing some particular organization.

Secondly, the feminist ideology has provided justification for these reforms by challenging the traditional attitude towards women in society. This was done by arguing that the old view of women as inferior, dependent, and subordinate was no longer relevant to contemporary problems. By a series of propaganda devices the feminists sought to show the *consequences* of women's dependent and subordinate role in the situation of spinster or prostitute, or tried to prove, by achievements in previously masculine spheres, that women were capable of equality with men. We have already suggested that in its fullest expression this ideology was never realized in practice and was indeed probably not shared by even the bulk of those who called themselves feminists, but this is not to argue that the ideology was not immensely important, if only to give direction and courage to the leaders of the movement and misgivings to its enemies. Indeed, this propagandist and educational aspect of an ideology would well repay further study if we are ever to understand the process by which the values of a social system are changed.

What general, if tentative, conclusions emerge from this necessarily sketchy treatment of a movement which still remains to be more thoroughly investigated? Our main assertion has been that feminism constituted a genuine movement, rather than a series of pressure groups, because it possessed a unifying ideology which was shared by the separate "wings" of the movement, even though this ideology was limited and did not take the *Weltanschauung* form, typical of messianic and utopian movements generally. The methodological point of importance here is that such an ideology, if it is to be regarded as characterizing a social movement, must not be simply inferred by later sociologists and historians from the activities of the individuals who are members of the various organizations associated with it. It must be consciously formulated as an ideology by those who have committed themselves to the movement's goals and activities. They must have deliberately created it, that is to say, in order to foster and sustain the solidarity of the adherents to the movement, both positively and directly, by giving them a slogan to work with — in this instance, "equality in all things with men" — and negatively and indirectly, by providing an antidote to the counter-ideology of those who opposed the movement's particular aims — "woman's place is in the home" (2, pp. 33–67). It is possible, indeed, that ideologies are necessary to social movements because people are unable to nerve themselves for the task of carrying out what may become a long and bitter struggle with others for the reform of "abuses" as they see them, unless they are able to couch their demands in the form of deductions from more general ethical principles, perhaps even from a *Weltanschauung* or a whole cosmography, although the study of feminism suggests that such refinements are not essential. Moreover, the fact that such ideologies are related in this way to particular "abuses," accounts for another characteristic feature, namely, that no matter how fantastic they may become in the hands of some of their propounders, they are never pure fantasy. The core of feminist thinking, for example, was intimately concerned with the real situation in which women found themselves, that of persistent inequality in all their relations with men, and in this respect it is relevant to consider the parallel situation of the working classes with which the socialist ideology has been concerned. We may then ask whether the predominant aspect of a social system which provides the *sine qua non* for the emergence of movements of social protest is the existence of latent conflict between those with authority and those without, between the legitimate makers of decisions and those who are constrained to submit to them. Of course, it may be that not every social movement is necessarily built up around inequalities between social roles and around the potential conflicts between individuals which these role inequalities imply. Some purely religious movements may obtain the allegiance of their adherents primarily from the uncertainties of man's place in nature, rather than from the certainties of his place in society; but even here the sociologist must proceed with caution. The messianic movements of the Middle Ages, for all that their eschatology was fantastic and their leadership possessed of megalomania, obtained their impetus from the desperation of "the surplus population living on the margin of society" (5, p. 314); while those of contemporary Melanesia are impelled by the native's consciousness of a discrepancy between his possessions and those of the white man who "perversely" denies him cargo (26, p. 246). Whether an explanation of social movements which confines itself to the sociologically relevant is likely to be ignoring a theoretically important issue is not a question which can be answered one way or the other, given the current state of knowledge of such movements. For our present purpose it seems not unreasonable to claim that one powerful source of the drive behind them is to be found in the persistence of conflicts in society.

Yet, the subordinate position of women existed long before a feminist movement came into being to campaign about it, and it has continued long after the movement's strength has ebbed away. Clearly, it is not enough that potential conflicts should exist for an organized social movement to occur. Some further condition is necessary, and it is with the nature of this condition that the sociology of social movements should be most concerned. What the study of feminism may contribute most to theory in this regard is the demonstration that this condition cannot be equated with the actual making manifest of conflict or inequality. Mary Wollstonecraft, William Thompson, and many others (2, pp. 136–137) developed a feminist ideology many years before organized movements for reform agitated Victorian complacency, and feminists occasionally emerge today to protest at the continued inequality of the sexes. Nor is it satisfactory to attempt to avoid the issue by tracing a thread of continuity from the *Vindication* or the *Appeal* to the articles in the *Englishwoman's Review* and the *Victoria Magazine*. The pages of these feminist journals indicate, on the contrary, that the ideological output of the second half of the nineteenth century was built around the problems women of that time had to face; where their authors repeated what had been written before them by the so-called precursors of the movement, it was not because they were familiar with their works — the evidence on this point is obscure — but because the same fundamental fact of inequality had impressed them all. If we take the trouble we can trace the course of socialist ideology from Plato to the present day, but we miss the significance of the exercise if we think of the historical continuity as of itself one of the causes of socialism. What still has to be accounted for is how it comes about at a given period of time that a large number of people become sufficiently intolerant of their own circumstances to seize upon slogans such as "from each according to his ability, to each according to his needs," and to apply them to themselves in such a degree that they become moved to attend and organize meetings, devise petitions, and enter generally into the struggle with the "enemy." The sociology of social movements still needs to determine whether deviants such as Wollstonecraft and Thompson, and perhaps even the leaders of a movement which has obtained some popular support, are deviants in some basic personality sense. It also needs to consider means whereby the expression "a large number of people" may be given a more precise, numerical magnitude. We can do no more at the present time than to notice such tasks in passing. More immediately manageable is the consideration of theoretical positions, taken generally from sociology, which may be employed to account for the spread of awareness through a subject group that its situation is open to improvement through a challenge being offered to those who take advantage of it.

The Marxist conception of class consciousness seems obviously pertinent here. Marx, it will be recalled, not only emphasized that society was divided into conflicting classes, he also asserted that class consciousness on the part of the eventually victorious class was inevitable once certain conditions were fulfilled, these conditions being the development of easy communication between individuals in the same class position and their continuous record of failure in struggles with the ruling class over economic rewards (3, p. 30). There could be no successful revolution without class consciousness and no class consciousness without both the dissemination of ideas and programs of action amongst the working class and a realization of their position through unsuccessful attempts to improve their economic situation. The non-Marxist sociologist may treat these hypotheses for what they are, and regardless of whether they are validated by the evidence of trade union and socialist organizations of the nineteenth and twentieth centuries, consider in the present context whether they are applicable to feminism. This approach does violence, of course, to the Marxist interpretation of capitalism which conceives of the emancipation of women as the inevitable outcome of the replacement of the domestic economy by large-scale industry (8, pp. 210–219, p. 282). Hence it would probably explain the organized struggle of the feminists as part of the wider class struggle, or dismiss it as a sign of inner contradictions in the position of the bourgeoisie; but in the absence of convincing demonstration that feminism can be explained in this way, we have no alternative as sociologists than to use it in our own way. This means that we should consider whether the evidence of feminism supports the view that sex consciousness appeared, not because a few feminists were articulate about it, but because a number of women became involved in unsuccessful struggles with men over economic issues, such as the right to determine how their own earnings were to be spent, and because as members of a literate and mobile section of the community they regularly came into contact with women involved in a similar conflict to their own. The Marxist conception of class consciousness, modified in this way to refer to the growth of self-consciousness on the part of any social group, seems especially fruitful in the present instance, since it would go far to explain why the great bulk of the feminists were likely to be members of the middle rather than of the working classes, and why women employed in factories alongside men were more likely to become involved in class rather than in sex warfare. At the same time, it also seems unnecessarily restrictive in its emphasis on struggles over economic rewards; for the long struggle of the feminists to put an end to the double standard of sexual morality was undoubtedly of considerable significance in the development of sex consciousness on the part of the women of the day, and that struggle had only a very tenuous relationship with economics. While it is true that Victorian men often took advantage of the weak economic position of women to exploit them sexually, the advantages they gained were not economic. The Marxist conception needs to be broadened to allow for different kinds of exploitation which can give rise to conflicts of interest other than those which center upon the extortion of surplus labor, if it is to be of use to the sociologist who wishes to develop a general theory of social movements.

The general Marxist formulation, as applied to feminism, may be said to be found wanting in another respect. As applied to trade unionism and to political socialism, it can still make some pretension to maintaining the inevitability of revolution on the grounds that these are movements still involved in struggle and the conditions for a change of system are not yet ripe. But feminism has withered away without a revolutionary upheaval and a dictatorship of the second sex. Group consciousness, in this instance, has faded before the full promise of the movement has been realized. How can this be? The obvious answer would seem to lie in the essentially pressure-group type of allegiance given to a social movement by the great bulk of its members. If it is always the case, as we have attempted to show through this brief account of feminism, that widespread adherence to the ideals of a movement occurs only where and when the shoe pinches, it would follow that as this pressure is reduced, a more general apathy will return. Erstwhile active members of the movement lose interest, the older ones die, and the younger generation, from whom the newest recruits might be expected to come, will not have the same urgent need to take part in the campaigns which so preoccupied their elders. The real problem for the sociologist is that of ascertaining the factors responsible for those changes in the circumstances of broad categories of people — in this instance, of single, widowed, divorced, and married women — which create dissatisfaction with their lot sufficient to drive them to look for leaders to voice their discontent, or, on the other hand, which so lessen their sense of being the victims of exploitation that they cease to feel the urge to combine.

It is here that a reference to Smelser's attempt to develop a structural-functional type of explanation in working-class history seems not only relevant, but imperative, and not least because among other qualities, it claims to avoid the shortcomings of the Marxist concept of exploitation, and hence of class conflict, as an explanatory principle. From Smelser's point of view, "it is less embarrassing analytically to interpret cases of outright conflict between the classes as disturbed reactions to specific structural pressures rather than as manifestations of a permanent state of war between them" (22, p. 394). To the extent that this position is valid it would follow that feminism should be seen as a reaction to structural pressures operating on the family, and the explanation for the rise and decline of the feminist movement should be sought for in the sequence of events by which these structural pressures were relieved and a new family system became institutionalized. There is, to be sure, little reference to feminism in Smelser's work. This is mainly because it is a study of the Lancashire cotton industry between 1770 and 1840 and stops before the organized movement of feminists began. It is also partly because it is confined to the separation of home from work as it applied to the working-class textile family. Hence the only feminist writing referred to, William Thompson's *Appeal* (1825), is classified along with Owenism and early Co-operation generally, as among examples of what Smelser regards as "unjustified" negative, emotional reactions to pressures on the family economy and as "unrealistic aspirations on the part of various elements in the population," produced as a response to the dissatisfactions which these pressures had created (22, p. 170). Thompson's plea for the ending of the inequality between the sexes is seen, that is to say, as an attempt to minimize conventional differences between the sexes through "a massive de-differentiation of roles," a feature of the demand for a return to a simple way of life, so characteristic of the social movements of this time (22, pp. 254–257). Early feminist ideology, from this point of view, at least in its implied application to the problems of working-class women, is to be regarded as no more than a "symptom of disturbance."

Smelser's hypothesis for the explanation of structural changes in social systems asserts that in "growing and developing social systems" seven definite steps of change which follow each other in sequence are discernible. "Symptoms of disturbance" occur early on, occupying only the second step of the sequence, which is said to begin with "dissatisfactions with the goal-achievements of the social system . . . and a sense of opportunity for change in terms of the potential availability of facilities." The disturbances produced by these dissatisfactions are thereupon " 'handled' by mechanisms of social control and 'channelled' into mobilization of resources." This leaves Smelser with four more steps to cope progressively with the conversion of these resources into "more and more specific proposals to innovate. Favourable innovations are rewarded by extraordinary sanctions and then gradually routinised" (22, p. 15). The organized feminist movement, and the feminist ideology of the second half of the nineteenth century, can be interpreted in terms of this approach, provided that the symptoms of disturbance are read as a reaction, not to the problems which faced working-class mothers employed in the textile factories, but to those which faced the unemployed women of all classes who depended on the goodwill of others for their livelihood. As we have seen, the real drive behind feminism came from those single, widowed, divorced, and married women who were exploited in various ways as a result of this dependency. The organized feminist movement may accordingly be interpreted as finding its place on step five of Smelser's sequence — "positive attempts to reach specification of the new ideas and institutional patterns which will become objects of commitments" (22, p. 15) — soon to become routinized into the form of new types of employment for women, in hospitals and in offices, accompanied by the legal right to determine for themselves what might be done with their earnings. Indeed, the decline of feminism would appear to be reasonably well accounted for by this hypothesis, since it is to be expected that some of the support for the organized movement would die away by step seven, once these aims had been achieved.

There are, it must be admitted, certain discrepancies between this account and the strict Parsonian line taken by Smelser. For example, the outcry, "Woman's place is in the home," is regarded by him as a realistic reaction to the legislation which forbade the employment of children; it is placed in step six of his sequence, on the ground that the separation of adult from child at work "gave commanding importance to formal education and to the role of women in the socialization of children *in the home*" (22, p. 299). It is, however, not difficult to show that the slogan, "Woman's place is in the home," was far more characteristic of the anti-feminist ideology of the 1850's and later, than it was of the factory agitation of the earlier period. It was applied, moreover, not to mothers who were employed in the factories, but to single women who were never likely to get married while monogamy lasted, because of the preponderance of women of marriageable age. In terms of the realities of their situation, it was an "unjustified negative, emotional reaction" to the development of the nuclear family amongst both middle and working classes — a family which had no place for unmarried aunts and sisters if they were unproductive in the industrial sense of income earning — and the later steps of the sequence should be more correctly interpreted as the process whereby the contemporary nuclear family became the institutionalized form for an industrial society. Clearly, whether an ideology is to be classified as positive rather than negative, as realistic rather than fantastic, and hence placed on steps four or six of a sequence rather than on step two, depends on a prior decision about the nature of the new institutionalized forms which are "consolidated as permanent features of the institutionalized family" and which constitute the seventh and last step in the sequence of structural change experienced by the household (22, p. 164). It is pertinent to consider, therefore, what there is about the structural-functional approach which led Smelser to conclude his sequence in the 1840's. As he has presented the argument, he has implied not only that the new family system of the Lancashire cotton workers was one in which the function of socialization was performed in the home, but also that the women came out of the factories to perform it, whereas in point of fact all evidence suggests that the employment of wives and mothers in textiles continued right through the nineteenth century (13, pp. 1–18), and that the new family system which has appeared under industrialization has been one in which accommodation has been made to permit women to combine the two roles of wage-earner and housewife.

It can hardly be doubted that the root of the difficulty is to be found in the tendency towards reproductive determinism which characterizes the structural-functional approach to the family. This may perhaps be best seen in Parsons' treatment of the modern household, where he differentiates between sex roles along "instrumental-expressive" lines and justifies the differentiation on the ground that "the bearing and early nursing of children establish a strong presumptive primacy of the relation of mother to the small child and this in turn establishes a presumption that the man, who is exempted from these biological functions, should specialize in the alternative instrumental direction" (17, pp. 22–23). Feminist ideology, from this point of view, is unrealistic as applied to equality between the sexes, because it must either deny the essentially biological difference between them, or refuse to admit that the allocation of roles is, as a matter of fact, determined by the consequences which flow from these differences. It is, of course, notorious that this latter argument was precisely the one which the organized movement sought to combat, asserting that some women would never become mothers, and that others would be obliged to combine the role of mother with that of income-earner, and that *for these women* is was absurd to deny them occupational opportunities on the ground that they ought to be in the home. In effect, what the feminists asserted was that the simple Victorian identification of role differentiation within the household with biological differentiation between the sexes was nothing more than ideology, a negative reaction to the everyday demonstration that women were quite obviously filling instrumental roles on behalf of the family. It is indeed open to inquiry whether one of the successes of feminist agitation might not have been the acceptance by the twentieth century of the position that the rigid differentiation of sex roles within the household along "expressive-instrumental" lines is an anachronism. As compared with the Victorian era it is now accepted that women may adequately fill a number of roles on behalf of the household, some expressive and some instrumental, and that for those which may be performed only within the home — those concerned with the "maintenance of integrative relations between the members, and regulation of the patterns and tension levels of its component units," which is Parsons' way of describing expressive roles (17, p. 47) — men have comparable roles to perform which were below the dignity of their grandfathers. Husbands, that is to say, now provide "solid, reliable help" to their wives in homemaking (14, p. 126) and fathers are expected to participate to a large extent in the early socialization of the child, so that the residual tasks of actual childbearing and breast feeding have been relegated to a very minor place in the functions performed.

It should be understood that we have called the Parsonian approach "reproductively determinist" not merely because it takes sheer reproduction to be a "root" function which differentiates social roles along sex lines, but also because it would account for the differences between the roles performed by men and women in the occupational sphere on the same basis. "The distribution of women in the labor force," he has asserted, "clearly confirms this general view of the balance of the sex roles. Thus, on higher levels typical feminine occupations are those of teacher, social worker, nurse, private secretary and entertainer. Such roles tend to have a prominent expressive component, and often to be 'supportive' to masculine roles. Within the occupational organization they are analogous to the wife-mother role in the family" (22, p. 15 n. 13). It can hardly be denied that in general women are employed in "supportive" occupations and that in this respect the feminist dream of equality has not been realized. Yet, we suggest this is not because the demand was unrealistic in the light of the biological function of women in the family, but because the whole trend of industrialization has been in the direction of the increasingly hierarchical organization of roles within the economy. Women worked as "assistants to their husbands and fathers" before the Industrial Revolution (19, p. 2); their subsidiary role was perpetuated afterwards in the factories and in the offices. But whereas previously their menfolk had been able to make authoritative decisions on behalf of the family enterprise, only amongst the power elite is it now possible for them to determine their own economic destinies. For the men of the middle ranks of society, industrialism has replaced the uncertainties of market fluctuations and climatic conditions by the specified certainties of subsidiary roles in the large bureaucracies and has inserted a host of new supervisory and managerial roles between the manual workers and their employers. A large number of modern occupations filled predominantly by men, that is to say, are not merely subordinate and supportive to others. They are concerned with the internal affairs of the enterprise, with coordinating the activities of the manual and clerical labor force employed, and with handling tensions between subordinates. They are, in the language of the Parsonian calculus, primarily "expressive." Hence it may be questioned whether industrialism might not have been responsible for weakening the traditional association between biological differentiation and the differentiation of roles along "expressive-instrumental" lines by requiring more and more men to fill expressive roles. Indeed, it is a matter of further research to ascertain whether this, rather than the efforts of the feminists, has been the reason why men have come increasingly to perform expressive roles within the household.

Of course, it still remains true that, however much men's occupations in our bureaucratically organized society may be said to have become expressive, they still remain differentiated from those of women in that in general those of the latter are less skilled. Women tend also to perform work which is subordinate to that of a man, as in the case of a nurse or a private secretary. Moreover, and in the opinion of the authors this is the most significant fact of all, where women have succeeded in gaining entry to a predominantly male profession or occupation they tend, with certain individual exceptions, to remain on its lower rungs. This is true, for example, in medicine, in politics, and even in schoolteaching. At the same time, this general subordination of women to men in the occupational sphere has not, as we have argued earlier, been able to activate a vigorous feminist movement. While we could perhaps speculate, as others have done, on the reasons for this, speculation is no substitute for research, and it is in this area that further work could be most fruitful. We need to know in particular why women acquiesce in this occupational subordination, as the absence of any sign of disturbance or agitation suggests that they do, and we need to know why the drive behind feminist organizations seems to have come to an end once the formal right of entry to the professions was attained.

This brings us back, indeed, to the central problem of this chapter, circumstances which activate a social movement. Neither the Marxist interpretation of history, understood in a very broad sense, nor the Parsonian interpretation of social equilibrium, also understood broadly, provides a very satisfying explanation for the rise and decline of feminism, although both in their separate ways illuminate aspects of it. We can hardly escape the conclusion, therefore, that what the sociology of social movements most lacks at this time is not general theory but empirical research conducted in the light of some middle-range hypotheses, developed perhaps through submitting general theory to the kind of empirical challenge we have attempted here. In particular, there is a need for systematic studies of movements in decline and vigorous examination of those changes in their social environment which are conceived to be responsible for fluctuations in their fortunes. This is why we have sought to argue the case for the treatment of feminism as a critical instance in this field. The accumulation of historical and contemporary data on the position of women and on women's organizations in a great variety of countries is one of the most obvious next steps for sociologists interested in social change.

BIBLIOGRAPHY

1. Banks, J. A. "Social Implications of Technological Change, Some Reflections on Historical and Social Research on the Impact of Technological Change on the Local Community, the Enterprise and the Family," in *Les Implications Sociales du Progrès Technique*. Paris: Conseil International des Sciences Sociales, 1962.

2. Banks, J. A., and Olive Banks. *Feminism and Family Planning*. Liverpool: Liverpool University Press, 1963.

3. Bendix, Reinhard, and Seymour Martin Lipset. "Karl Marx' Theory of Social Classes," in R. Bendix and S. M. Lipset (eds.), *Class, Status and Power, A Reader in Social Stratification*. London: Routledge and Kegan Paul, 1954.

4. Caplow, Theodore. *The Sociology of Work*. Minneapolis: University of Minnesota Press, 1954.

5. Cohn, Norman. *The Pursuit of the Millenium*. London: Mercury Books, 1962.

6. Dangerfield, George. *The Strange Death of Liberal England*. London: Constable, 1936.

7. van Doorn, J. A. A. "Verzuiling:een eigentijds systeem van social controle," *Sociologische Gids*, Vol 3 (1956), pp. 41–49.

8. Engels, Friedrich. "The Origin of the Family, Private Property and the State," in Karl Marx and Frederick Engels, *Selected Works in Two Volumes*. Moscow: Foreign Languages Publishing House, 1949.

9. Fulford, Roger. *Votes for Women, The Story of a Struggle*. London: Faber and Faber, 1957.

10. Green, Arnold W., and Eleanor Melnick. "What has Happened to the Feminist Movement?" in Alvin W. Gouldner (ed.), *Studies in Leadership*. New York: Harper and Bros., 1950.

11. Hamilton, Henry. *History of the Homeland: The Story of the British Background*. Primers for the age of plenty, No. 4. London: Allen and Unwin, 1947.

12. Heberle, Rudolf. *Social Movements: An Introduction to Political Sociology*. New York: Appleton-Century-Crofts, 1951.

13. Hewitt, Margaret. *Wives and Mothers in Victorian Industry*. London: Rockliff, 1958.

14. Jephcott, Pearl. *Married Women Working*. London: Allen and Unwin, 1962.

15. Klein, Viola. "The Emancipation of Women; Its Motives and Achievements," in *Ideas and Beliefs of the Victorians*. London: Sylvan Press, 1949. (B.B.C. Publication of a series of talks on the "Third Programme.")

16. McGregor, O. R. "The Social Position of Women in England, 1850–1914: A Bibliography," *The British Journal of Sociology*, Vol. 6 (1955), pp. 48–60.

17. Parsons, Talcott. "The American Family: Its Relations to Personality and to the Social Structure," in Talcott Parsons and R. F. Bales *et al* (eds.), *Family, Socialization and Interaction Process*. Glencoe, Ill.: The Free Press, 1955.

18. Parsons, Talcott. "Family Structure and the Socialization of the Child," in Talcott Parsons and R. F. Bales *et al* (eds.), *Family, Socialization and Interaction Process*. Glencoe, Ill.: The Free Press, 1955.

19. Pinchbeck, Ivy. *Women Workers and the Industrial Revolution*. London: Routledge, 1930.

20. Schreiner, Olive. *Woman and Labour*. London: R. Fisher Unwin, 1911.

21. Sirjamaki, John. "Culture Configurations in the American Family," *American Journal of Sociology*, Vol. 53 (1948). Reprinted in N. W. Bell and E. F. Vogel (eds.), *A Modern Introduction to the Family*. London: Routledge and Kegan Paul, 1960.

22. Smelser, Neil J. *Social Change in the Industrial Revolution*. London: Routledge and Kegan Paul, 1959.

23. Sombart, Werner. *Sozialismus und soziale Bewegung*. Jena: Gustav Fischer, 1908.

24. Strachey, Ray. *The Cause, A Short History of the Women's Movement in Britain*. London: Bell and Sons, 1928.

25. Trade Union Congress. *Women in the Trade Union Movement*, issued on the occasion of the 25th Annual Conference of unions catering for women workers, May 1955.

26. Worsley, Peter. *The Trumpet Shall Sound, a Study of 'Cargo' Cults in Melanesia*. London: MacGibbon and Kee, 1957.

22

Ronald M. Andersen

and Robert L. Eichhorn

Health and Retirement Among
Farmers: A Panel Study[1]

Illness interferes with the routine of everyday behavior. More frequent contact with doctors, changes in personal habits (eating, smoking, resting), altered relations with family and friends, and an inability to go to work may all result from feeling ill. These changes may be of a temporary nature resulting from a cold, or some short-lived infectious disease, which causes no permanent damage to the body. They may be of longer duration for the victims of polio or rheumatic heart disease where impairment may date from childhood, or for those suffering from degenerative diseases which are more commonly associated with old age (arteriosclerotic heart disease, nephritis, diabetes). These degenerative diseases can sometimes be arrested but rarely completely cured.

Chronic or persistent illness can radically change the course of one's life. Goals may have to be abandoned, as illustrated by the farmer forced to quit work, thereby giving up the income, security, and the sense of personal fulfillment that continued work could give. New means for attaining life goals may have to be sought: a farmer may be compelled to change his accustomed methods of work to continue farming.

These changes result, obviously, from the restrictions upon physical

[1] The data used in this paper were collected as part of the Purdue Farm Cardiac Project co-sponsored by Purdue University, Indiana Heart Association, American Heart Association, Indiana State Board of Health, and the National Heart Institute. For a more complete description of the project see Morris (15).

activity that diseases impose. Persons with arteriosclerotic heart disease, for instance, often cannot work as hard as they have in the past because of anginal pains. We have shown that even undiagnosed cardiacs, ignorant of the true meaning of the pains they experienced, avoid symptom-producing activities and tend to reduce the amount of work they do (21; 7). However, cutting down on activities or quitting work completely to avoid symptoms of disease is especially likely when the person has been apprised of his condition by a physician and, therefore, recognizes the symptoms as danger signals. In his desire to get well and forestall a grim prognosis, he changes his behavior. Even iatrogenics, persons who mistakenly think they have heart disease, often alter their work behavior and increase the precautions they take.

How a person behaves in response to the onset of disease, then, is only partially explained by the direct limitations imposed by the disease itself. The psychological characteristics of the individual, his goals, the nature of his relations with others, his values, his perception of the disease, and the physical and financial resources for coping with the problems created by disease all play important parts. These factors do not act singly in determining response to disease but together interact to determine the outcome.

Individual Changes in Behavior and Their Impact on Social Change

Each of the farmers whose behavioral changes are analyzed in this chapter would regard his own circumstances as unique. In some respects we, as social scientists, would agree that they are. The importance a particular farmer attaches to work, his preparation for and conception of retirement, and the course of his disease would be peculiar to him and different from that of any other person. Thus, a clinical approach would be necessary to explain completely why a single farmer behaved as he did after he was confronted by serious illness. Yet, we know that while individuals do differ in the forces that determine their behavior (or in the weights of the various forces that are common to them all), much is shared. For instance, arteriosclerotic heart disease has a somewhat uniform symptomatology, occurs generally after middle age, and often restricts particular types of activity. Older farmers face similar farm production problems and tend to have similar orientations toward work. Thus, while the impact of disease and the forces that determine response to it are unique for the individual, there is enough shared among those in the same occupation, at the same stage of life, and threatened by similar diseases, that group data for individuals can be meaningfully analyzed to predict and better understand behavior.

While we will be content to present a social psychological analysis of changes in work behavior among a group of farmers, we suggest the following: social changes are resulting from the sheer magnitude of individual changes as well as from institutional and group activity.[2] We can thus vault from this social-psychological level to a plane of discourse appropriate for dealing with the dramatic social changes occurring in American agriculture today.

As an example, let us consider the decision of the older farmer whether to retire or remain active. The high price of land and equipment, and the low margin of profit adequate for the efficient mass producer tend to force the older, often less efficient, farmer to make a major occupational decision. He is reluctant at his age to go into debt to get more land or to modernize his equipment. This results in an even less efficient operation, paying little in return for much hard work. Contrary to the desires of the farmer, the pressures all encourage him to get out of agriculture. The illnesses associated with older age only speed up this process. The realities of the market place, of old age, of the nature of farm work, and of degenerative diseases, while affecting each individual in some singular fashion, are sufficiently uniform in their impact that there has resulted a mass exodus of older farmers from agriculture in recent years.[3] Accompanying this exodus are significant social changes and correlated problems generated by thousands upon thousands of individual decisions.

Two distinct types of changes are emerging with their attendant problems: one is concerned with whether to (or how to) keep the older man farming; the other grows out of the large number of farmers who have actually retired.

The first type includes questions of national farm policy as it affects "marginal" farmers with all the intricacy, ambiguity, and confusion surrounding price supports, the soil bank, tariffs, and taxes.[4] The farm implement industry has also reacted with new equipment engineered to help the older, sometimes disabled farmers. There are sun shades, air-conditioned tractors, power steering, cushioned seats, and a host of automatic or partially automatic items to reduce the stress and strain of farm labor. Another related development is the emergence of "rehabilitation schemes" designed to help the chronically diseased farmer adjust his behavior so that he may continue to farm without cost to his health.

Changes of the second type have resulted from the retirement of a large number of people, including farmers. There has grown up in recent years in the United States a "retirement industry" geared to cater to the retiree's special needs, hopes, and fears. Retirement communities,

[2] This proposition corresponds closely to the concept of "synergic level" which refers to the uncontemplated results emerging as the combined effect of many individual human actions (19, p. 95). It is also related to Sumner's description of "crescive" as opposed to "enacted" institutions (23, pp. 53–54). While enacted institutions are "products of rational invention and intention," crescive institutions have their beginnings in "folkways" and "customs" and finally develop from mores.

[3] Some preliminary research done by the Purdue Farm Cardiac Project indicates farmers' eligibility for Social Security benefits has influenced them to retire at an earlier age.

[4] Within this "marginal" group are many older and/or chronically diseased men.

plans for investing retirement savings for the highest and safest returns, and much literature on how-to-be-happy-though-retired have all come into being. As a further illustration, the Social Security Administration has made accommodations for the special problems of farmers, who were recently included under the provisions of the Old Age and Survivors Insurance Plan. In the wake of this change, many farmers came out of retirement, returning to work temporarily to accumulate larger Social Security benefits. Finally, the nature of landholding, inheritance, and the character of the rural dweller himself are all being influenced by the pattern of retirement from farming. More and more retired farmers or urban commuters live in the farm houses, while the land is rented to the few remaining farmers who must have larger landholdings to stay in business.

In sum, the individual decision we will discuss appears to have consequences extending far beyond the individual who makes them. We have mentioned a few; there are undoubtedly many more. These retirement decisions of farmers, made independently of each other, when taken collectively can bring about fundamental social changes.

Illness Among Farmers as a Cause of Change

The peculiarities of farming as an occupation make illness especially threatening to the farmer.[5] The farmer himself provides most of the labor required to operate the typical family farm in the United States, therefore, his business is in jeopardy when he cannot work. The physical and environmental demands of the job are great. The cycle of farm work often requires long hours of grueling work during the peak of the summer's heat and repeated exposure to the severe weather of winter.

The "alienated" assembly line worker is often contrasted to the farmer, who sets his own pace, works at home plainly visible to his family and neighbors, and performs a more complete task involving knowledge of mechanics, agronomy, animal husbandry, finance, and management. Because of the foregoing, farmers are thought to have a better conception of the final product and greater identification with their jobs, which leads to a deeper sense of personal satisfaction. Therefore, economic, social, and psychological reasons motivate the farmer to continue in much the same way he has worked in the past.[6]

In spite of the fact that farmers can voluntarily retire at any time they feel able, they do tend to work more years than persons in urban occupations. Farmers and farm managers are three times as numerous among employed men 65 and over as they are in the male working force as a

[5] Farm and factory work have been compared in greater detail in Gripe, Klatch, Rothrock, Morris, and Eichhorn (10, pp. 354–364).

[6] While the opportunities for farmers to move into other lines of work or to make changes in their current practices that would permit them greater economic rewards in farming are more numerous than they suspect, farmers are neither easily shunted into other lines of work nor guided by outsiders in farming methods.

whole (22, pp. 42–43). This means that the farmer, who in some respects can afford illness less than the urban worker, is especially liable to be plagued with those diseases characteristically associated with older age. The ill farmer may have to give up work completely, reduce the level at which he works, alter his methods of work, or look for some other kind of job. These changes can affect his livelihood, his status in the community, and the sense of achievement that comes from productive work. Since farming usually involves strenuous labor, which illness can make impossible, often the only alternative is retirement.

In this chapter the effects of poor health upon changes in work behavior among farmers will be examined along with other factors that operate in conjunction with it. The onset of illness among older workers has special relevance for the study of change in behavior from both practical and theoretical points of view. The increasing prevalence of the chronic diseases associated with a longer life span makes long-term illness a pressing social problem. Those who would rehabilitate the chronically ill need guidance in the engineering of planned change. Theoretically, illness offers rare opportunities for testing crucial hypotheses about change and resistance to change. For instance, the fear of death itself becomes a variable in the hands of the social scientist permitting more definitive statements than before about the relationship of a man's confrontation of death in his illness and subsequent behavior modification.

Nature of the Study

The Objectives

Here we propose to examine the factors that influence change in work behavior. From among the many alterations in work behavior that can occur in farming (changes in methods, adoption of new technology, reduction in size of enterprise, alterations in the crop or animal systems), the analysis will be limited to perhaps the most dramatic of all — completely quitting work, or retirement. Among the influences leading to retirement, health will receive major consideration. However, changes in level of health do not act alone in impelling retirement but, in conjunction with other factors. Thus, the farmer for whom work is central to his self-image might be less likely to retire than the farmer for whom it is less crucial. The influence of illness and physical well-being as they interact with other factors upon the decision to retire will be examined.

Theoretical Considerations

Following Lewin, we will regard retirement as the result of the field of forces that impinge upon the person at a given time period (11, pp.

66–113; 12). This field includes goals toward which the person strives. Goals may be specific or diffuse, conflicting or consonant, realistic or admittedly unattainable, few or numerous. Many of the dominant goals around which farmers in our sample ordered their lives were attainable only if the men were able to continue work. These were farm ownership, providing for children, and the realization of some idealized standard of living.[7] Continued work, itself, was a goal toward which farmers strived. These goals create forces in the life space of the farmer.

Few farmers actually look forward to retirement.[8] The compulsion to work is quite pronounced and is directly related to age and poor health. The older the farmer and the poorer his health, the less attractive retirement is to him. We, therefore, assume that "all other things being equal," these farmers would continue to work if they were able. Yet we see that farmers differ in the number of years that they do work. Of 369 farmers who were actively operating a farm in 1956, 61 had retired by 1960. Of the 308 farmers still active, 89 were of ages similar to those farmers who had retired. (Sixty years or over.)

The work behavior of these farmers before their decisions to retire was a function of their psychological field at that prior time. Their goals, age, health, economic resources, and the influence of others all entered in to make continued work the outcome. As these influences were modified, some of the farmers retired. Illness is one factor which might bring about a change in the field. The modal tendency was for healthy farmers to remain active and sick farmers to retire. But illness may have different consequences for the person who is financially prepared for retirement in contrast to the one who is not. That some healthy farmers retired while a portion of the ill farmers remained active may well reflect financial situations. Thus, we will consider in addition to the effect of health, the interaction of health with other factors which influence retirement in agriculture. In this manner, the changes that result from poor health will be better understood.

The Means of Data Collection and Classification

In 1955 all men in a five-county area of Central Indiana, whose names were listed in rural directories, were sent a mail questionnaire to ascertain the nature of their farm operation, age, and self-reported health (16, pp. 51–52). From this population, 435 farmers were selected by a stratified sampling method to increase the proportion with heart disease. An attempt was made to interview and examine these men medically. Of the 435, 413 were interviewed and 397 medically examined. In 1960 these 397 farmers were again contacted for interview and examination.

---

[7] Other important goals included the retention of life, earned leisure, and, for some, an earned retirement (13).

[8] This conclusion was substantiated in our study as well as in McKain (14).

The 369 who cooperated in the second phase of the panel study provided the data used here.

To qualify as a farmer in 1955 a man must have been 65 years of age or younger, must have farmed 80 acres or more before any heart disease became manifest, and must not have worked more than 100 days per year off the farm. From the sample two groups were selected according to age and occupational status after the 1960 restudy:

1) Retired farmers: This group contains all those men who stated in 1960 that they were not actively managing a farm. Men who stated that they were engaged in only light or supervisory farm work were also included. Sixty-one men were classified as being retired.

2) Active men 60 years of age and over in 1960: This group includes active farmers and also those found to be in other occupations in 1960. There were 89 active men in this category.[9] Only two of the retired farmers were under the age of 60. Therefore, the retired farmers and the active group are roughly age-matched.[10]

As part of the medical examination in 1956, every farmer filled out the Cornell Medical Index Questionnaire (CMI).[11] This questionnaire asks about symptoms of poor health in general, as well as symptoms related to specific diseases. A "yes" answer to a question indicates that the respondent has experienced the symptom. The farmers were divided into two groups according to the number of affirmative answers they gave. Those farmers who answered 25 or more questions affirmatively were considered to be in "poor health." Those giving fewer than 25 "yes" answers were defined as being in "good health."[12]

Practically all measures of those forces which we expect to influence retirement were taken in 1956 when the men studied were active farmers. The occupational status of the farmer (whether or not he had retired in a four-year interval) was then determined through the 1960 survey. Our plan for analysis, then, is to look for the influence of various forces on the farmers' decision to retire through a four-year interval. Controlling for the obvious influence of age, the first of the major forces

[9] The remaining 219 farmers of the 369 total were all active in farming or other occupations and under the age of 60 in 1960.

[10] The retired group had a higher mean age. However, the difference was not considered large enough to negate the assumption of age control. Mean age of the retired group in 1960 was 65.15; for the active group it was 63.98.

[11] Items 1–138 were used to measure the health status of the respondent (3). It should be noted that this is a subjective measure of health. It is not based upon a clinical diagnosis but on symptoms *reported* by the respondent.

[12] Dichotomizing the CMI scores to measure health admittedly has weaknesses. The dividing point between "good" and "poor" health was necessarily an arbitrary selection from a rather grossly defined continuum of health. An individual may be classified as being in good health when he mentions very few symptoms, which may, however, indicate a serious disease. Conversely, an individual may be considered to be in poor health because he reports a large number of symptoms, which, nonetheless, stem from minor ailments. However, validity studies do show that this index indicates relative health status of different groups (3, pp. 13–15).

upon retirement to be considered is *health*. Subsequently, the influence of health is "held constant." Then, comparing separately those farmers who were in good and poor health in 1956, the influence of heart disease, socio-economic status, attitudes toward work and leisure, work efficiency, and the influence of family and community upon retirement will be considered.

Analysis of Data

Health Status in 1956 and Retirement[13]

Apart from the influence of age, health is regarded as the most important factor influencing the decision to retire in much of the literature (2; 4; 17; 24; 25; 26; 27; 28). Using the responses to the CMI as a measure of health, our findings were consistent with this general conclusion. The more symptoms farmers reported in 1956, the more likely they were to retire by 1960. Table 1 shows that 61 per cent of those farmers reporting 30 or more symptoms in 1956, in contrast to only 19 per cent of those reporting fewer than ten symptoms, retired by 1960.

TABLE 1

*Retirement Status of Farmers by the
Number of Symptoms of Illness Reported**

OCCUPATIONAL STATUS (1960)	NUMBER OF SYMPTOMS OF ILLNESS (1956)		
	0–9	10–29	30+
Retired	19%	34%	61%
Active	81%	66%	39%
Total Per Cent	100%	100%	100%
Number of Cases	(16)	(80)	(46)
		(P < .01)**	

* Taken from responses to the Cornell Medical Index Questionnaire.
** All significance levels in this paper were computed by Chi Square.

Hereafter, those farmers in poor health and those in good health will be treated separately to see how other factors interact with health to influence retirement.

More Recent Changes in Health

Since an individual's health can change rapidly (as after a heart attack), a measure of health from the 1960 data was included to see how

13 The data presented in this chapter are taken largely from Andersen (1).

recent health status affected the decision to retire. The farmer who saw his doctor six or more times in the year preceding the interview in 1960 was judged to be in poorer health. In order to ascertain the influence of more current health status, apart from or in conjunction with earlier health conditions, health status was controlled by the 1956 CMI scores. Table 2 shows that recent changes in health play an important part in a farmer's decision to retire regardless of his initial health status. Among individuals judged to be in poor health in 1956, 68 per cent of those seeing their doctors six or more times a year retired, compared to 36 per cent who saw their doctors less often. Among those farmers in good health in 1956, 55 per cent of those seeing doctors over five times a year, compared to 25 per cent of those seeing doctors five times or less, had retired by 1960. Those initially in poor health, who continued to be in poor health, were most likely to retire. Those initially in good health, who retained their health, were most likely to be active. Thus, states of health in both periods are important, but recent health changes do influence retirement regardless of earlier health status.

TABLE 2

Retirement Status by the Number of Times Farmer Saw a Doctor in the Last Year

OCCUPATIONAL STATUS (1960)	POOR HEALTH (1956) *Times Saw Doctor* (1960)		GOOD HEALTH (1956) *Times Saw Doctor* (1960)	
	Five or Less	*Six or More*	*Five or Less*	*Six or More*
Retired	36%	68%	25%	55%
Active	64%	32%	75%	45%
Total Per Cent	100%	100%	100%	100%
Number of Cases	(28)	(31)	(61)	(22)
		(P < .05)		(P < .05)

Impact of Heart Disease

The uncertain prognosis and the fear of sudden death associated with heart disease can have special significance in the decision to retire. Retirement or sharp curtailment of physical activities may be part of the doctor's prescription. We, therefore, attempted to ascertain the separate and compounded effects of heart disease and general health level.

The farmers in the sample were typed by a team of physicians using the New York Functional Classification System (18). On this basis, farmers were divided into two groups: (1) those having abnormalities of the circulatory system, including heart disease; and (2) those with normal circulatory systems. Table 3 shows that among those in poor health, no meaningful difference was found in the tendency to retire between persons who were normal and those with circulatory disorders. However, a difference was found among farmers who were in good health in 1956. Twenty-one per cent of the normals, compared to 39 per cent of those with a heart condition, retired.

TABLE 3

Retirement Status by Presence of Circulatory Disorder

OCCUPATIONAL STATUS (1960)	POOR HEALTH (1956)		GOOD HEALTH (1956)	
	Circulatory Disorder (1956)	No Circulatory Disorder (1956)	Circulatory Disorder (1956)	No Circulatory Disorder (1956)
Retired	55%	47%	39%	21%
Active	45%	53%	61%	79%
Total Per Cent	100%	100%	100%	100%
Number of Cases	(23)	(19)	(29)	(54)
		(P < .70)		(P < .20)

Heart disease is more likely to lead to retirement in the absence of a host of other disabling symptoms. If a farmer had reported many symptoms of poor health, his tendency to retire was not greatly strengthened by heart disease. Still, the cardiac farmer of 1960 who was also in poor health in 1956 was most likely to retire; the healthy farmer of 1956 who remained free of heart trouble was most likely to be active.

Socio-economic Status

Along with health, socio-economic status has been regarded as most important in determining retirement (27; 20; 5). Financial reserves and a more positive regard for the leisure that retirement affords leads higher-status workers to retire earlier than lower-status workers. To measure socio-economic status for the farmers in our sample, a Guttman-type scale was constructed. This scale included information about land ownership, education, community leadership, value of farm produce, and an interviewer's evaluation.[14]

While others have found that higher socio-economic status facilitates earlier retirement, our data indicate that among farmers in poor health it has no statistically significant effect. There is little difference in tendency to retire between high- and low-status groups (Table 4). Among farmers in good health, however, a definite trend is in evidence. The percentage retiring increases from 26 per cent in the lower category to 50 per cent among those in the higher category.

[14] The coefficient of reproducibility for this scale is .90 (1, p. 166).

TABLE 4

Retirement Status by Socio-economic Status

OCCUPATIONAL STATUS (1960)	POOR HEALTH (1956)		GOOD HEALTH (1956)	
	Lower SES (1956)	*Higher* SES (1956)	*Lower* SES (1956)	*Higher* SES (1956)
Retired	55%	50%	26%	50%
Active	45%	50%	74%	50%
Total Per Cent	100%	100%	100%	100%
Number of Cases	(47)	(12)	(65)	(18)
	(P < .80)		(P ≈ .05)	

We can assume that no one likes to retire when he foresees economic hardship as a result. However, poor health forces some low socio-economic status farmers into retirement. Some of these people would probably remain working if they were in comparatively good health. Thus, the influence of socio-economic status on retirement, so apparent for farmers in good health, is nullified by poor health.

Work as an End in Itself

Work has meant different things to different societies, to different generations within our own society, to those in different occupations, and to different individuals. Work can be a means to an end or an end in itself; an unpleasant activity rewarding only on payday or a source of inner calm and personl fulfillment. However a man regards his work, other areas of his life are influenced. Goldstein and Eichhorn have shown that those farmers who are high work-oriented are less likely to make rational economic decisions (9). High work-oriented farmers are also less likely to comply with their doctors' advice to slow down (6, pp. 65–68). With respect to retirement, Friedman and Havighurst have shown that a man who regards his work primarily in economic terms tends to retire early; if he emphasizes values other than economic, he will probably retire late (8). Here, we are interested in the relation of high work-orientation to retirement of farmers in good and poor health.

Farmers in our sample were divided into high, medium, and low work-oriented groups using a scale designed to measure their inclination to view work as an end in itself rather than as a means for attaining other ends.[15] Among farmers in poor health, the tendency to retire among high work-oriented farmers was almost as great as among low work-oriented farmers. (Table 5).

[15] The scale is described in Riedel (21, p. 98).

TABLE 5

Retirement Status by Degree of Work Orientation

OCCUPATIONAL STATUS (1960)	POOR HEALTH (1956) Work Orientation (1956)			GOOD HEALTH (1956) Work Orientation (1956)		
	Low	Medium	High	Low	Medium	High
Retired	53%	62%	46%	38%	35%	17%
Active	47%	38%	54%	62%	65%	83%
Total Per Cent	100%	100%	100%	100%	100%	100%
Number of Cases	(19)	(16)	(24)	(42)	(23)	(18)
		(P < .70)			(P < .10)	

However, high work-orientation seemed a deterrent to retirement among farmers in good health. Thirty-eight per cent of the low work-oriented farmers as opposed to only 17 per cent of the high work-oriented farmers were retired by 1960. Where good health permits, work values exert an influence; a farmer may continue to work or retire as his values dictate. But poor health tends to force high and low work-oriented alike to retire.

Work Efficiency

Confronted by rising costs for the things he buys and lower prices for the things he sells, the inefficient farmer is being forced out of agriculture today. The farmer whose efficiency has been reduced by poor health may be especially hard pressed if he is unable to adjust to the lower standard of living which accompanies decreased efficiency.

A farm efficiency index was developed that reflected the amount of work accomplished as a function of the total amount of time spent in doing it.[16] The efficient farmer has a higher ratio of tasks accomplished to time expended.

Greater efficiency in doing farm work helps to postpone the retirement of all farmers, but especially those in poor health (Table 6). Sixty-six per cent of the less efficient farmers retired by 1960 compared to 37 per cent for the high efficiency group. The same pattern holds to some extent for those in good health; the less efficient farmer tends to retire. The efficient, healthy farmer is more likely to remain active.

Influence of Others

Doctors, friends, and family members are all likely to give the chronically ill person advice. The extent to which a farmer is told to slow down, get out of farming, or quit working may strengthen his own

[16] For a description of this index, see Andersen (1, p. 90).

TABLE 6

Retirement Status by Farming Efficiency

OCCUPATIONAL STATUS (1960)	POOR HEALTH (1956) Farming Efficiency (1956) Low	High	GOOD HEALTH (1956) Farming Efficiency (1956) Low	High
Retired	66%	37%	40%	27%
Active	34%	63%	60%	73%
Total Per Cent	100%	100%	100%	100%
Number of Cases	(32)	(27)	(35)	(48)
	(P < .05)		(P < .30)	

inclinations to retire. A scale was constructed to measure the amount of such advice.[17] Table 7 shows that among farmers in poor health those receiving the most advice were most likely to retire.[18] The sheer quantity of such advice seemed to have little effect upon farmers in good health.

In addition to differences in exposure to advice about continuing work or retiring, farmers differ among themselves in their dependency upon the advice others give them. Most ill persons receive some counsel from their doctors or families to "take it easy." We would expect the person accustomed to depending upon others to be most likely to act upon this suggestion: he might be more inclined to retire.

TABLE 7

Retirement Status by Work Reduction
Advice Scale* (Cardiacs Only)

OCCUPATIONAL STATUS (1960)	POOR HEALTH (1956) Work Reduction Advice Low	Medium	High	GOOD HEALTH (1956) Work Reduction Advice Low	Medium	High
Retired	36%	56%	65%	37%	25%	33%
Active	64%	44%	35%	63%	75%	67%
Total Per Cent	100%	100%	100%	100%	100%	100%
Number of Cases	(11)	(18)	(17)	(16)	(16)	(15)
		(P < .40)			(P < .80)	

* Although the level of significance for the poor health group is low, there is a difference in significance between the groups. Also the direction of percentages for the group in poor health supports our argument.

[17] For an explanation of this scale, see Andersen (1, p. 169). The coefficient of reproducibility is .93.

[18] In Table VII only cardiacs are considered since they are much more likely to receive advice to change their work behavior.

A scale was constructed to measure the extent to which a farmer depends upon others in making a decision. With this scale, farmers were separated into those who seldom make decisions alone, and those who make most decisions by themselves. These decisions ranged from buying farm equipment to buying appliances for the kitchen.[19]

Farmers in good health, who depended upon others to aid in making decisions, were no more likely to retire than more independent farmers (Table 8). However, among farmers in poor health, 68 per cent of those judged to be dependent had retired by 1960 in contrast to 32 per cent of the more independent farmers.

TABLE 8

Retirement Status by Degree of Dependency

OCCUPATIONAL STATUS (1960)	POOR HEALTH (1956) Dependency (1956)		GOOD HEALTH (1956) Dependency (1956)	
	Low	High	Low	High
Retired	32%	68%	30%	35%
Active	68%	32%	70%	65%
Total Per Cent	100%	100%	100%	100%
Number of Cases	(25)	(34)	(13)	(40)
	(P < .05)		(P < .90)	

In summary, the farmer in poor health who (1) receives more advice to quit work or slow down, and (2) has depended upon others to help him make decisions is more likely to retire than the farmer in poor health who receives less advice and has made decisions in the past by himself. Neither the amount of advice received nor the degree of dependency upon others helps us understand the decision to retire among farmers in good health.

Retirement and the Farm

Most farmers in Central Indiana retire on their farms, often retaining the house while renting out the land. They are thus able to retain neighborhood associations, have access to familiar surroundings and the opportunity for meaningful work, and can perpetuate the family name in the community. The penalties of retirement would be less for the farmer who is more deeply rooted in the community and is able to remain there after he quits work. However, other farmers are not so committed to the community of their residence. For them, retirement on the farm has

---

[19] This scale is described by Andersen (1, p. 168). The coefficient of reproducibility is .95.

little reward since the work itself and the income the work provided were their major reasons for being there. These farmers may, therefore, resist retirement on the farm and also retirement to any other place, since the satisfactions of the latter are unpredictable.

Attachment to the community and the farm as a place of residence was measured by a scale that included items about the number of years the farmer had lived in the area, whether or not he had inherited the land from his father, and how long he had lived on his present farm.[20] High residential stability, measured by this scale, was related to the tendency to retire among farmers in good health. Those farmers in good health, who seemed most tied to the community, were most likely to retire (Table 9). Among farmers in good health, 8 per cent of the least committed farmers retired, while 43 per cent of those most committed retired. The farmer least committed to the community may continue to work in his quest for financial security. The farmer with strong ties to his farm and the neighborhood may derive security and other satisfaction from sources other than money.

The farmer in poor health does not appear to retire as a consequence of his relationship to the community and his farm. Poor health can force retirement for the uncommitted farmer as well as the one with local ties.

We supposed that the tendency for farmers to retire would be strengthened if they knew that someone in their own family would take over the operation of the farm after retirement.[21] The farmer who did not expect his children to take over the farm would continue to work rather than sell or even rent his farm to outsiders. This supposition is borne out for farmers is good health only (Table 10). Among healthy farmers, 38 per cent of those who were certain in 1956 that their children would

TABLE 9

Retirement Status by Residential Stability Scale

OCCUPATIONAL STATUS (1960)	POOR HEALTH (1956) Residential Stability			GOOD HEALTH (1956) Residential Stability		
	Low	Medium	High	Low	Medium	High
Retired	56%	50%	52%	8%	40%	43%
Active	44%	50%	48%	92%	60%	57%
Total Per Cent	100%	100%	100%	100%	100%	100%
Number of Cases	(16)	(20) (P < .95)	(23)	(13)	(28) (P < .05)	(42)

[20] For a description of this scale, see Andersen (1. p. 177). The coefficient of reproducibility is .92.

[21] This view is supported by Nelson (17).

TABLE 10

Retirement Status by Degree of Certainty
That Children Will Take Over the Farm

OCCUPATIONAL STATUS (1960)	POOR HEALTH (1956) Will Children Take Over (1956)			GOOD HEALTH (1956) Will Children Take Over (1956)		
	Yes	*Uncertain*	*No*	*Yes*	*Uncertain*	*No*
Retired	50%	50%	57%	38%	29%	19%
Active	50%	50%	43%	62%	71%	81%
Total Per Cent	100%	100%	100%	100%	100%	100%
Number of Cases	(28)	(12)	(14)	(39)	(14)	(27)
		(P < .99)			(P < .30)	

take over the farm had retired by 1960, while 29 per cent of those who were not sure, and only 19 per cent who knew that their children would leave the farm, had retired.

On the other hand, the expectation of a family successor on the farm was not related to the retirement of farmers in poor health. Again hopes, plans, and preferences can enter into the retirement decision of a well man but such considerations give way in the face of poor health.

Summary

Illness results in major changes in people's behavior and goals. Illness also interacts with, and modifies, other forces which are capable in their own right of bringing about change. Here, we have studied retirement among older farmers who we assumed, as group, wished to continue farming. However, some of them had retired since 1956. Recent changes in health, farming efficiency, relations with others, work orientation, and socio-economic position were all considered as they interacted with the initial health status of the farmer in bringing about retirement. Table 11 shows the factors influencing farmers in good and poor health in their decision to retire.

We found that farmers in poor health in 1956 were much more likely to retire by 1960 than were farmers in good health. Furthermore, recent illness exerted an influence on both groups, resulting in retirement. However, heart disease tended to lead those who had previously been in good health to retire but did not influence those already in poor health. The perceived consequences of heart disease may appear more threatening to the man who has not already experienced a large number of symptoms associated with illness.

In general, the state of the farmer's health is the most important

TABLE 11

A Summary of Some Forces Influencing the Retirement of Farmers

FORCE	POOR HEALTH (1956)* Active (1960)	Retired (1960)	GOOD HEALTH (1956) Active (1960)	Retired (1960)
Health (1960)**	Good***	Poor	Good	Poor
Heart Disease	Does not differentiate active from retired		Absent	Present
Socio-economic Status	No differentiation		Low	High
Farming Efficiency	High	Low	High****	Low
Work Orientation	No differentiation		High	Low
Advice to Retire	Low	High	No differentiation	
Dependency on Others	Low	High	No differentiation	
Residential Stability	No differentiation		Low	High
Family Successors for Farm	No differentiation		No	Yes

    * Those in poor health in 1956 had a greater tendency to retire than those in good health.
    ** All subsequent forces are measured by 1956 data.
    *** These descriptions refer to relative modal tendencies of the group — not to particular individuals.
    **** Farming efficiency does not differentiate retired from active farmers in good health as much as it does those in poor health.

factor in determining whether or not he will retire. For farmers in good health, however, other factors enter the picture. These men have more opportunities to give their values and goals free play than do those in poor health whose range of alternatives is reduced by illness.

Thus, farmers in good health tended to retire if they valued their work less (low work-oriented), if they had a satisfying future to anticipate in the community upon retirement, and if there would be a successor from within the family to operate the farm. The farmer in good health was not influenced in his decision to retire by either the degree of his dependency upon others or the encouragement he received from others to retire. Farmers in poor health, on the other hand, seemed especially susceptible to the influence of others. Both farmers in good and poor health tended to retire if their operations became inefficient. Farmers in poor health, whose efficiency was decreased by illness, were especially likely to retire.

In summary, the forces that bring about change in this limited instance operate selectively and seldom alone. While we have considered change in terms of individual behavior, the sheer magnitude of this change, often induced by similar external forces, has general social implications for farming as an occupation and as a way of life, and for society as a whole.

BIBLIOGRAPHY

1. Andersen, Ronald M. "Retirement Decision and Satisfaction: A Study of Cardiac and Non-cardiac Farmers." Unpublished Master's thesis, Purdue University, Lafayette, Ind., 1962.

2. Anderson, W. F. "Work and Retirement: Influences on the Health of Older Men," *Lancet*, Vol. 2 (1956), pp. 1344–1347.

3. Broadman, K., *et al. Cornell Medical Index Questionnaire Manual*. Ithaca, N.Y.: Cornell Medical College, 1949.

4. Delbert, A., *et al.* "Personal and Social Adjustments of Forty-nine Retired Rural Men." Pennsylvania Agricultural Experimental Station Progress Report, No. 19. State College, Pa.: Pennsylvania State University, 1950.

5. Donahue, W., *et al.* "Retirement: The Emerging Social Pattern," in C. Tibbits (ed.), *Handbook of Social Geronotology*. Chicago: University of Chicago Press, 1960.

6. Eichhorn, R. L., D. C. Riedel, and W. H. M. Morris. "Compliance to Perceived Therapeutic Advice," in *Proceedings of the Purdue Farm Cardiac Seminar*, Agricultural Experiment Station. Lafayette, Ind.: Purdue University, 1959.

7. Eichhorn, R. L., and R. M. Andersen. "Changes in Personal Adjustment to Perceived and Medically Established Heart Disease: A Panel Study," *Journal of Health and Human Behavior*, Vol. 3 (1962), pp. 242–249.

8. Friedman, E., and R. J. Havighurst. *The Meaning of Work and Retirement*. Chicago: University of Chicago Press, 1954.

9. Goldstein, B., and R. L. Eichhorn. "The Changing Protestant Ethic: Rural Patterns in Health, Work and Leisure," *American Sociological Review*, Vol. 26, No. 4 (1961), pp. 557–565.

10. Gripe, R. P., B. Z. Klatch, P. W. Rothrock, W. H. M. Morris, and R. L. Eichhorn. "Returning the Farmer with Cardiac Disease to Work," *The American Journal of Cardiology*, Vol. 7, No. 3 (1961), pp. 354–364.

11. Lewin, Kurt. *A Dynamic Theory of Personality*. New York: McGraw-Hill Book Co., 1935.

12. Lewin, Kurt. *Field Theory in Social Science*. New York: Harper & Bros., 1951.

13. Ludwig, E. G. "Goals, Values and Rehabilitation: A Case Study of the Goals and Values of Cardiac and Non-cardiac Farmers and their Relevance to Rehabilitation." Unpublished Master's thesis, Lafayette, Ind.: Purdue University, 1961.

14. McKain, W. C., Jr. "Old Age and Retirement in Rural Connecticut." Agricultural Experiment Station Research Bulletin, No. 299. Storrs, Conn.: University of Connecticut, 1956.

15. Morris, W. H. M., ed. *Proceedings of the Purdue Farm Cardiac Seminar*. Agricultural Experiment Station. Lafayette, Ind.: Purdue University, 1959.

16. Morris, W. H. M., and R. L. Eichhorn. "Sampling Procedure Used in the

Farm Cardiac Survey," in *Proceedings of the Purdue Farm Cardiac Seminar.* Agricultural Experiment Station. Lafayette, Ind.: Purdue University, 1959.

17. Nelson, L. "Farm Retirement in Minnesota." Agricultural Experimental Station Bulletin, No. 394. Minneapolis: University of Minnesota Agricultural Experimental Station, 1947.

18. New York Heart Association. *Nomenclature and Criteria for Diagnosis of Diseases of the Heart and Blood Vessels,* 5th ed. New York: New York Heart Association, 1953.

19. Ogle, M. B., Jr., Louis Schneider, and J. W. Wiley. *Power, Order and the Economy.* New York: Harper & Bros., 1954.

20. Parron, T., *et al.* "Retirement From the Point of View of the Worker," in G. Mathiasen *et al,* (eds.), *Criteria for Retirement.* New York: G. P. Putnam's Sons, 1953, pp. 61–118.

21. Riedel, D. C. "Personal Adjustment to Perceived and Medically Established Heart Disease." Unpublished Ph.D. dissertation, Purdue University, Lafayette, Ind., 1958.

22. Sterner, P., and R. Dorfman. *The Economic Status of the Aged.* Berkeley and Los Angeles: University of California Press, 1957.

23. Sumner, William Graham. *Folkways.* Boston: Ginn & Co., 1906.

24. Taitz, P., *et al.* "Adjustment to Retirement in Rural New York State." Agricultural Experiment Station Bulletin, No. 919. Ithaca, N.Y.: Cornell University, 1956.

25. Thompson, W. "The Impact of Retirement." Unpublished Ph.D. dissertation, Cornell University, Ithaca, N.Y., 1956.

26. Thompson, W. "Pre-retirement and Adjustment in Retirement," *Social Issues,* Vol. 14 (1958), pp. 35–45.

27. Thompson, W., and G. F. Streib. "Situational Determinants: Health and Economic Deprivation in Retirement," *Social Issues,* Vol. 14 (1958), pp. 18–34.

28. Tuckman, J., and I. Lorge. *Retirement and the Industrial Worker.* New York: Columbia University Press, 1953.

SECTION SEVEN

Economic Development and

Cultural Change

While Adam Smith was writing The Wealth of Nations, *James Watt was perfecting the steam engine, that diabolical machine which would ultimately blow up the Professor of Moral Philosophy's harmonious model. Can current models of economic behavior be perfected fast enough to lead to an understanding, and perhaps even to rational control of these processes?*

There is one hopeful sign: economists are increasingly becoming aware of the institutional (sociological and cultural) variables impinging on economic life. As Rosenberg points out in his chapter, the classical economists were quite aware of the crucial role of these variables, but their epigoni tended to "forget" the teaching of the founding fathers. The reasons for this constitute a fascinating and largely unexplored chapter in the sociology of knowledge, and both Rosenberg and Greenfield have some apposite thoughts on this.

A related problem, touched upon in all chapters in this Section, concerns the causal relations between economic ideology and economic practices. Classic formulations regarding this can be found in the works of Marx, Weber, Veblen, and Schumpeter, to mention a few well-known and outstanding examples. The present contributors, rather than explicitly espousing a systematic theoretical approach, address themselves to the problem in a more limited way, stressing empirical observations of contemporary economic changes (though they are by no means oblivious of the need for perfecting systematic theory). Thus Willener analyzes the relation between technological change and the methods for paying workers in certain French industries. His results show that traditional values persist among both management and workers in the face of changes in methods of production. Both sectors recognize the existence of "lag," but they differ as to the most desirable means for "adjustment." Both management and union representatives tend to consider themselves more progressive than their antagonists, whose backward mentality they hold responsible for the inadequate development of productive enterprise. Furthermore (shades of Veblen!), the managers who

589

are engineers appear to be the most "tradition-bound" in their attitudes, in that they are least willing and able to recognize the "human" aspects of production, while steadfastly marching in place under the banner of Zweckrationalität. *In accounting for the sources of these attitudes Willener specifies the need for looking both inside and outside the organizational system and in this connection raises important issues relevant to the methodology of structural-functional analysis. The reader need hardly be reminded that this is one of the crucial problems with which the entire volume is concerned.*

Greenfield's case study of the sugar economy of Barbados, though concerned with a different type of economic enterprise than that discussed by Willener, also involves the relation between economic ideology and behavior. The phenomenon he seeks to account for is the "underdevelopment" of a one-crop economy and the persistence of traditional attitudes towards the ownership and use of land which appears to fly in the face of a more rational exploitation of resources and investment of capital. Greenfield shows that we are not dealing here with the stereotyped peasant who is "wedded to the land," but with people whose chief social goal is occupational mobility. They use the production of sugar as a means for not being tied down, using the product as readily convertible capital analogous to stocks and bonds. Consequently Greenfield argues that attempts by American and British experts to "rationalize" the Barbadian economy would disrupt the indigenously developed system and the entire social organization of Barbados. This constitutes of course another instance of the criticism of the more or less forcible imposition of "outside" ideologies upon ongoing institutions, a criticism paradoxically found among both the "conservative" advocates of laissez faire of the Spencer-Sumner school and the "liberals" who espouse the doctrine of cultural relativism. It remains to be seen whether a dialectic synthesis can be produced which will satisfy the demand for both cultural autonomy and maximum economic and social "efficiency."

Rosenberg, though less concerned than Greenfield with the breaking-up of existing social structures and more with the problem of optimizing economic growth, is necessarily dealing with the same set of variables. He argues that W. W. Rostow's theory of take-off, involving a sudden rise in the rate of savings and net capital formation, is unduly simplistic and neglects the role of equally essential socio-cultural variables. Rosenberg's model of economic growth involves positive and negative "feedback" mechanisms. For example, he points out that the Midwestern American farmer has developed in the course of his operations managerial as well as technical skills which are readily transferable to non-farm enterprises. The same conditions do not hold for the type of farming which requires essentially unskilled labor. Rosenberg suggests that the failures in livestock production in the Soviet collective farms can be attributed to the lack of managerial skills and related motivations among the rank and file. In this case the skills had to be imposed "from the top," rather than operating "naturally." In general, Rosenberg goes on to point out, this is the problem of the "underdeveloped" countries which rely on a large, unskilled labor force whose very existence inhibits the adoption of labor-saving devices. (One is reminded of Engels' apostrophe to the bourgeoisie: "Your very ideas are the result of your bourgeois conditions of existence . . ."). His explanation appears to have much in common with the well-known thesis that the economic backwardness of the American South resulted from the institution of slavery and its later transmogrification into the tenancy system. Rosenberg also points out the strategic importance of government policies and expenditures in raising the cultural base for innovation, notably via the support of education and scientific research, as well as the impact of changing consumer wants due to participation in specific types of productive enterprise. Somewhere Alfred N. Whitehead has said that "a science which hesitates to forget its founders is lost." Considering the use made by Rosenberg of the insights of the classical economists we might add that a science which forgets its founders fails to maximize its economic potential.

Like the other contributors to this section, Hoselitz jumps across disciplinary fences to investigate the role of social values in economic growth. He considers the Weberian dichotomy of traditional and rational systems, and the assumption of a unilinear historical change from the former to the latter as inadequate for a description of the multiform behavior patterns actually or potentially existing. Consequently he adds another continuum, borrowed from F.C.S. Northrop, with Western "theoretical" and Oriental "aesthetic" belief systems at its poles. He then proceeds to use the resulting four-fold table as an instrument for the delineation of the conditions under which various combinations of value systems may produce maximum economic performance. Like Rosenberg, Hoselitz invokes a "feedback" mechanism; that is, he considers the impact which economic behavior has on the prevailing value system and vice versa. Like Willener, he is concerned with the fact that value systems and technology do not change at the same rate, and with the differences in values and attitudes among various segments of the population.

The fact that all contributors to this Section tend to be preoccupied with the same basic problems without having been briefed by the editors in this respect lends support to the belief that the current emphasis on an interdisciplinary approach can lead to important breakthroughs in this area.

23

Alfred Willener

Payment Systems in the French

Steel and Iron Mining Industry:

An Exploration in Managerial

Resistance to Change

This chapter constitutes a report on research findings and a discussion of some major research problems in the analysis of resistance to change in a specific empirical case. The still debatable issue whether social change is more usefully conceived in terms of development or in some other way, we also intend to illustrate in our discussion. We should be clear about exactly what questions we are trying to explore. We need to know how the participants in a process of social change interpret their situation; how they define the situation; and what it means to them.

The particular case under consideration is change from incentive to non-incentive systems of payment in two industries in France — iron-ore mining, and steel production. Perhaps an even more far-reaching question, but one which may logically be regarded as a preliminary one, is to what extent the researcher's bias — his use of sociological perspectives and selection of certain data — leads to a particular kind of study. The researcher is also, and necessarily, "interpreted" by those he interviews in the research situation, and this, too, may influence his inquiries and his findings.

1. Our Previous and Present Research Problems

At the outset, it is appropriate to state the source of the research problem. In the present case, three successive research projects were sponsored by the European Steel and Coal Community (C. E. C. A. Luxemburg).[1] This body was, more specifically, a "joint consultation" board, gathering governmental, labor, and management representatives from all six countries in the community who recommended support for research which would clarify the relationship between technical and social change. The major concern was the changing *influence* workers had on production. Characteristically, in this case as in several others in post-war Europe, international agencies were interested in initiating sociological research on aspects as "technological" as possible; the only directly "social" element was the interest in payment systems.

The first study, carried out in various works in France and all the other countries of the Community, met considerable difficulty in defining just what would be understood by "change." It was of course obvious that mechanization was to be regarded as an evolutionary process, involving gradual as well as radical *changes* of various types. Fortunately, in the French study, we had the opportunity of examining both production and payment in three factories containing rather "typical" steel mills. The first factory still had a workshop with a very old hand-rolling mill. There the workers were craftsmen, involved in heavy and continuous physical work, thus controlling their output in a most direct way. In the second factory (a nearly automatic workshop), where steel was laminated in a continuous flow through a dozen successive mills, surveillance, rather than direct control of output, was the workers' contribution to production — they had to prevent stoppages and interruptions and to give close attention to the machines. The third factory presented an intermediate case. The *incentive* payment system seemed adapted to situations of control, but not of surveillance, since in the latter case the workers' efforts do not significantly affect output. This first study arrived at the conclusion that fundamental technical changes had been accompanied by only minor alterations in the payment systems. This made it clear how unrealistic it would be to assume that technical change necessarily accompanies, and therefore explains, organizational changes, especially in a study of short-term developments in industry.

In the second study, all the materials gathered in the various countries were examined, and general evolutionary trends were sketched. On the whole, the more mechanized production was, the less sensitive to varia-

[1] See especially Durand *et al.* (7), Lutz *et al* (13), and Dofny *et al.* (6). I am much indebted to my colleagues, especially to J. Dofny, for many of the results, ideas, and suggestions here presented, which were developed in team work. Of course, my colleagues cannot be held responsible for any shortcomings in this chapter. The research was undertaken at the *Institut des Sciences Sociales du Travail, Université de Paris.*

tions in production was the payment system; in other words, variations in the workers' pay were less frequent and less directly tied to production where the latter was highly mechanized. One exception to this trend was documented in the French study; the only two cases of straight piece-rates encountered were in France. The payment system of the most modern, highly automated production unit also was shown to include an important percentage of variable pay (salaire variable). On the other hand, French payment systems tend to involve rules of greater severity than those elsewhere.[2] The major result of this European comparison turned out to be the diagnosis of a kind of crisis in incentive payment systems and, perhaps, an indication of their decline. The way in which they functioned seemed generally to contradict their basic principles.

In a (third) follow-up study we then proceeded to explore, in France, the process of resistance to change, and to describe the extent of this phenomenon. In this study we made a special effort to widen the empirical basis in order to get at the sociological variables; we decided to work on a sample of enterprises (not just of individuals). But we still had to conform to the limitations already mentioned: we had to focus on payment systems. Obviously this was a severe limitation, but since we had decided on an ambitious sample, the effect was salutary, opening up a practicable way for studying a specific kind of social change. We found that payment systems were, and still are, an important method of control which manifests technical and economic aspects, as well as psychological and sociological ones. Here the *total* perception of the industrial context yielded by the sample of enterprises was of major significance in reading our results.

To sum up: technical change was seen as something of a liberating force from intricate, unsolved social worries. At last industrial problems were becoming scientific problems, to be expressed in technical terms; similarly, the specific area of workers' payment systems could also be reduced to technical terms.

Since we were observers interested primarily in exploring change and resistance to it, we did not consider that it was our role as sociologists to express either optimistic faith or pessimistic doubt about the future prospects of increased industrial rationality in Max Weber's sense of the term. In fact, at the beginning we were rather inclined, as were some other institutes and some representatives of the European agency, to stress the importance of technical progress as a factor in the reduction of social problems. But the actual history of these three studies itself displays our gradual recognition of the socio-political side of technological change which, after all, necessarily occurs in a complex pre-existing social context.

[2] In French payment systems, for example, there is a greater percentage loss in payment than in most other countries, for an equivalent loss of production.

Our next step is a short description of the research setting in France. In French industrial research the points which follow are well recognized, but may be less commonplace for American readers.

The Research Context and Design

a) The Conflict Setting

It is a well-known fact that industrial sociologists in general find it easier to study management problems and labor problems separately, rather than in combination. This is perhaps even more distinctively true of France than elsewhere. The standard procedure used in our Institute was to ask management to give the research team an opportunity, at the outset of the investigation, to make clear the aims of the research and to emphasize that it had university backing. This was done at a special meeting of the *comité d'entreprise* where representatives of both management and trade unions discussed the project.

In spite of the sponsorship of the European Agency and the backing of the principal national association of managers, we could not introduce the study by following this procedure. Our project, since it focused attention on resistance to change of payment systems, was obviously of great interest to management, but the majority of directors did not welcome the idea of a study which might later be published. On the other hand, the trade unions were not only interested in this project, but showed themselves rather eager to push it forward. Trade unions in France are often not very well informed about even a vital subject such as payment systems (which very often they know about only by hearsay, "through a worker's brother who works in the factory payment department"). They were therefore interested to learn more about them.

In this situation of divergent interests, then, we had to cope with two sides who naturally saw the problem from their own point of view, even though they did not deny its importance to the other side with whom they are accustomed both to struggle and to cooperate. We planned a first phase as the study of management's opinion, and separated it from a second phase, the study of union delegates' and workers' opinions. Such a procedure, as compared to the procedure of conducting the study simultaneously with both sides, has a different influence on the interview data; instead of stressing the consensual aspects, it tends to delineate the aspects of conflict in the situation. As a matter of fact, in the conflict setting, especially in such a case, where interviewing was carried out in two distinct phases, the observer is perceived, by both sides, as an expert who is on their own side.

We had not, in fact, expected this, at least not on the management side. We had intended to use a non-directive type of interview for the managers but later developed a semi-directive interview of a special kind, featuring 12 forced-choice responses, with an A and B alternative for each and asking at the same time for a choice and comment.

The interview, as it turned out, was usually rather lengthy, ranging from one to five hours. Loquacious managers felt inclined to lecture extensively, to show their vast, complex, and often well structured general knowledge and overall interpretation of the situation. Others, more down to earth and disliking the painting of wide vistas, were prepared to go into specific areas of limited scope in great detail.

In nearly all these cases the interviewer, although not confining himself strictly speaking to the non-directive attitude in Rogers' sense of the term, was usually perceived as a welcome visitor who really wanted to understand and who helped the interviewee express himself completely. We came to notice gradually to what extent our desire for rapport was interpreted as sympathy. Except for a very few cases, the interviewed representatives of management nearly came to consider the interviewer as some sort of involved expert — as somebody taking sides with them much as do management consultants (in France the "organisateurs conseils"). This was the response to our non-active, but receptive, attitude and to the conflict setting.

The same thing happened on the workers' side. The French trade unions still have more in common with an underground organization than with a bureaucratic, efficiently formalized, and public organization. Once we had met the major figures of each of the three national workers' trade unions (CGT, CFTC, and FO) in Paris, introductions to the locals and also the factory delegates were easily gained. As can be expected in organizations with only a small amount of formalization, the visitor was either accepted or rejected at the top level of the organization, since the top officials cannot afford to rely on lower-level members to exercise discretion in dealing with certain types of visitors. Hence, once accepted at the top, there were no difficulties lower down. The visitor was then in possession of two names — that of the well-known top official, and that of the first-level delegate. Thus, workers, unions, and managers could only regard the interviewer as an allied expert — or, of course, an enemy, but hardly "a neutral."

In this research setting of implicit conflict — and since we could not undertake direct observation of inter-actional behavior — it seemed wise to make the best of this open-mindedness of both sides as we met it. We therefore, particularly in the study based on an extensive sample, focused attention on the general image each group had of industrial evolution. Even in a short visit it appeared possible to gather sufficient data on the perceptions of the situation entertained by both sides — including those of workers as well as of union delegates.

b) The Research Definitions

Exploring resistance to change in one particular element in a social situation, particularly if it happens to be a fairly central element, may be regarded as defining resistance or acceptance of change vertically. In principle, it cannot be said that resistance along one vertical dimension (in this case on payment system) is correlated with resistance on another, nor can it be considered as necessarily indicative of general resistance. This fact must always be borne in mind, although there is some reason to believe that definite patterns of "conservative" and "liberal" orientations can sometimes be discerned.

Management's resistance to changes in payment systems may be nominally defined as the desire to maintain incentive; we define it operationally by their actually observed decision to apply (or to go on applying) hourly wage rates of which more than one-third is incentive bonuses. In defining this resistance operationally, we relied on three criteria,[3] all of a rather general nature, but sufficient for the heuristic purpose of classifying the factories in the study according to the relative payment pressure which they exerted on production workers. Our most general hypothesis was that this resistance was correlated with management's image of industrial development.

The earlier studies concluded that there was little technical justification for an incentive system and that the functioning of the actual payment systems was often blocked or maintained artificially by various practices of "cheating."[4] In other words, the incentive system had more dysfunctions than functions for the total operation of the factory, as well as for the productive process.

It was therefore important to allow management to convey as extensively as possible their conception of the industrial situation so that those elements of the situation which a sociologist might regard as the "latent functions" of the traditional payment systems might appear.

Management's strategy has to be understood as action — potential or actual — *for* the organization, *in* the organization, but also *through* the organization. Using these three types of strategy we can depart from the usual organizational frame of reference. Management obviously seeks to maintain the organization; it works toward its goals and much of its action must be conceived as directed to this specific end. But management also has goals formulated to serve its individual or group interests which it can promote within the organization, and this too determines some of management's action. Finally, management uses the organization for the realization of yet another set of goals which transcends the organization itself, but for which the organization becomes an instrument. This we may call the more general level of social strategy at large, be-

---

[3] Incentive bonus as a percentage of total pay; the way non-productive time (that is, during stoppages) is treated; and the size of the work group (small team of workers, shop, factory as a whole) used as a basis for incentives. In factories of the type studied, group incentives rather than individual incentives are the general practice.

[4] Cheating may occur not only in "go-slow" tactics by workers, but also in management "fiddling" with production figures, in order to equalize discrepancies in output and pay between groups.

tween individuals and social categories in the total society. We shall designate these three types of strategy as (1) *functional*, (2) *sectional*, and (3) *social*.

1) *Functional Strategy.* The goal of the industrial enterprise, whether defined as production or as profit, is the primary justification — and usually the official justification — of the working organization (2), and also the justification for the exercise of authority. The payment system is one method of translating authority, in one way or another, into action, especially in the case of variable incentive pay. Payment by output is manifestly related to the goal of the enterprise: it stimulates motivation, rewards performance, and it also punishes failure to perform. A manager who resists change toward the abolition or transformation of such a system may, therefore, be emphasizing as a primary consideration this particular function of the payment system. Its function is clearly *zweckrational* in relation to the organizational goal — it operates "for" the organization.

2) *Sectional Strategy.* Because role-occupants in an enterprise inevitably engage in primary relationships, a second kind of strategy "in" the organization is probably in universal operation, even though it may take a variety of forms. It has recently been stressed that even in a highly formalized organization where impersonal regulation reduces involvement and prescribes the functions of each role-occupant, there are still extensive possibilities for a strategy which operates in the interests of sections of the total population employed in the organization, whether these sections be individuals, groupings, or simply categories such as those enjoying similar status. A more or less intensive conflict between the functional strategy and the sectional strategy[5] can develop.

3) *Social Strategy.* This type is carried out "through" the organization; the industrial enterprise is patterned by the social and cultural setting and is at the same time an outcome of purposive social action. On the one hand, in Harbison and Meyers' terms the industrial manager is an "organization builder" (10). If the organization is socially and culturally conditioned, it is also partially determined by the free, untrammeled actions of management. But the organization is also affected by the counterpressure of other social movements, workers, or even manager's associations, and influenced by political and other pressure groups. Various interests may succeed — at least partially — in carrying out their own strategy "through" the organization.

No doubt the functional, sectional (or micro-political), and social (or macro-political) strategies are more or less confused in actual everyday

[5] For a clear analysis of organizational, sectional strategy, in an instance taken from French industry, see Crozier (3).

behavior. Their distinction is analytic (even though it might happen that at times, for instance in a speech outlining management's policy, or in parts of an interview record) reference is made exclusively to one of them. In this research project we were primarily concerned with resistance to change in payment systems. This resistance appeared as a complex totality. Our narrow focus of concern — whatever its disadvantages — did enable us to discern and to illustrate concretely these various types of strategy.

The social meaning of a situation for the actors is often simply an interpretation provided by the investigator in the form of a frame of reference which he assumes has relevance for all the persons involved. This is, at times, a completely synthetic reconstruction, particularly when the observer assumes that all the actors are disposed to interpret their situations and behavior in the same terms. Such an assumption seems to be more common in sociology than in social psychology. The difficulties of discovering the actual types of social frames of reference (for example, those of the upper and lower classes) obviously discourage investigation of this kind. As a step toward the exploration of actual perceptions we decided, instead of superimposing a unifying frame of reference at the stage of analysis (a posteriori, as it were) to submit one a priori to both groups.

Our hypothesis was that perceptions of industrial development are progressively more impeded as one moves from questions of technical change to questions of change in the economic, psychological, and sociological spheres.[6] Rather than using the idea of *progression* of the expected opinion distribution (in the Guttman-scale sense),[7] the distribution can be conceived of as scaling levels of industrial development. This is not the place to reproduce our material in great detail. Nevertheless, a

[6] Twelve questions were formulated, three each for the technical, economic, psychological, and sociological spheres. These questions were presented on a questionnaire form and drew on materials from newspapers and periodicals which seemed to indicate typical stages of industrial development. We called the traditional stage A, and the more recent or "modern" stage B. Since the heavily idiomatic phrases are difficult to translate, we can give only two examples here. These, however, should give a good indication of the general gist of the questionnaire.

Question 1 in the technical area of the questionnaire presented the following alternatives: A) The worker has a good deal of influence on the flow of production; he is the dynamo that produces output. ("L'ouvrier a une influence directe sur la cadence, il a un rôle moteur.") B) The worker has a less direct influence on production flow, mainly of a supervisory type. For instance, he has to prevent accidents. ("L'ouvrier a une influence moins directe et plutôt du type surveillance ou prévention d'incidents.")

Question 2 in the sociological area of the questionnaire presented these alternatives: A) On the whole, the workers' delegates have only the workers' interests in mind. They do not worry about the plant. ("Dans l'ensemble les délégues ouvriers ne pensent qu'à l'intérêt des ouvriers, sans se préoccuper de celui de l'entreprise.") B) On the whole, the workers' delegates tend to see the connection between the workers' and the plant's interests. ("Dans l'ensemble les délégues ouvriers tendent à comprendre que l'intérêt des ouvriers et celui de l'enterprise sont liés.")

[7] We adopted the method of facet analysis (9).

few quotations of some rather typical comments on the questionnaire may be illuminating.

II. The Image of Industrial Development

1) Management's Views

a) *The Backward-looking Type.* Those managers who systematically selected the A alternative on all our questions answered and commented in terms of the status quo. To them things have not been transformed, or at least, not transformed sufficiently to justify an overall image departing from the status quo; they tend to focus on those aspects which have not changed.

Technically, "the workers still have great influence on production and its variations remain very important. You only have to introduce an incentive in order to get higher output. This is the proof of the worker's influence"[8] (that is, control over production).

"The workers still regulate for themselves the amount of work they do; they succeed in establishing a sort of balance between pay and work." Other respondents speak of two distinct types of situations: "They slow down as long as we are establishing a new set of time allowances; then, when the incentive is introduced, they get moving."

"On the whole work is changing: some time ago, work was a matter of muscles, now it is a matter of nerves," but the "effort is still felt at once; we have not yet reached the stage where the quantity of work is no longer of relevance."

The working and technical organization, as stated in our third A alternative and respondent's comments, are not yet formalized and planned to a point where varying and sporadically maximized amounts of production would be a nuisance.

Economically, "wages continue to be an important factor in the total budget." "In the iron-mines the wages are still the most expensive item."

The other alternatives and comments show that there is no general and long-term calculation of wages; these cannot, in the view of those who gave this first type of answer, be calculated in advance.

Individually, there is no "psychological" change; the workers, in the managers' standard expression, have not "changed their mentality," "they are not mature enough" to work on fixed pay schedules. The incentive is "the spice of life." Some respondents analyze the situation in more detail. Quite a number consider that "a minority of workers have undergone a change of mentality, but on the whole, as a *mass* they remain incapable of understanding anything other than the principle of pay tied to output."

---

[8] Each sentence in quotes is from a comment in various interviews, often directly paraphrasing the selected alternative (A or B; in this case A).

"The mentality of blue-collar and white-collar workers is still very different." "If all the workers simply became (monthly) salaried, we (management) would have nothing left with which to force them to work; one must not forget either that the incentive is a means of control over their behavior in general." "In the case of a strike we take away parts of their wage bonus."

Collectively, there is no general change in the worker's mode of life. The worker "lives from hand to mouth" (au jour le jour). He is not "asking for a fixed wage" — the only thing he is interested in is the "amount of pay."

The workers' trade unions still are the same; they "have no eyes for anything but their own interest." Some of our respondents think that some union delegates hesitate to press their claims: "They would like to take account of the factory's interest, but as soon as they present their demands they forget all about it and think exclusively of the workers' interest."

"On the whole the workers are still attached to the idea of the class struggle." Here again a category of respondents have some comments to add; they perceive a slight, but superficial change in ideology: "As soon as a little quarrel comes up, they start again with their business of class struggle." "If you take them individually, they are reasonable, but collectively they are different." Frequently this is commented on in terms of political influence "coming in from the outside."

Let us turn now to the diametrically opposite pattern of answers of those choosing the B type of responses.

b) *The Forward-looking Type:* In this case, the respondent selected systematically all B alternatives and commented on them. These alternatives are intended to describe a higher stage of industrial development.

Technically, the worker's influence has considerably declined. At one modern rolling-mill the response is that "the steel flows with never changing speed," the engineers have arranged "regular and automatic dispatching, for instance, every 45 seconds" in one illustrative case. At the furnaces "there is a pre-determined program to be fulfilled." "Output is a matter of engineers, not of the crews." "Productivity? We get it through better working organization."

There is no longer a special problem of effort; "we do not push anybody to the point where they sweat." What is looked for is planned, stable, and coordinated production, instead of maximization with its implied unexpected variations.

Economically, there is change; "the prices no longer depend on how much wages we pay, they are in the hands of the engineer and the salesman."

"Stability (that is, low turnover) of the personnel is more and more important."

Individually, "there is a new mentality amongst the workers." "The amount of production does not go down when the incentive payment system is dropped." "No doubt, people understand more and more the necessities of regular functioning of the enterprise and we get, in many respects, better understanding." "The salaried white-collar type of mentality is spreading among workers."

Collectively, respondents frequently give optimistic accounts of recent changes. "The worker wants to be salaried, to have a fixed steady income; his standard of consumption has undergone considerable change."

Between management and the labor delegates "a more confident climate" is developing. The delegates show more understanding of what is in the own interest of the enterprise; "they have come to know what investment is." Finally, the workers "are not as revolutionary as it seemed, all they want is cars, television sets, and so on." There is a trend toward *embourgeoisement.* "You can see how petit-bourgeois the wallpaper and furniture are in their apartments."

c) *The Main Types of Managers' Opinions.* We did not find the scale-type of distribution that was one of our hypothetical expectations and, therefore, turned to a typological analysis (11). We sought to discover inductively whether a discernable relationship between the patterns of ideas we have discussed and the *existential basis* could be established. This can hardly be an elaborate or exact procedure in industrial sociology, when one is dealing with a sample of factories. Nevertheless, in the face of the very strong prevailing stereotypes, the following results have some overall value.

Since the type of industry is usually considered as a major determinant of payment systems, we started by analyzing managers' images of development in terms of the type of work under consideration. We found no close or constant relationship on the basis of our admittedly limited data. It appears that there is no necessary and all-pervasive relation between image and specific types of industry, nor is there a relationship between image and specific stages of development of which these types are examples.

Regional conditions, which were expected to be of extreme importance in view of management's policy and outlook, did not yield a clear picture either. The resemblance of the managers' opinion profiles in each particular region was not greater than in each particular type of industry. Even holding these two situational variables constant, the variation of opinion was still too great and demanded some other explanation than that of "situation."

Finally, in a three-dimensional analysis, individual firms being added to the two former variables, negative results were still obtained. There was no apparent relationship between management's image and affiliation to a particular industrial firm.

2) Trade-union Delegates' Views

We were able to gather a much larger sample of trade-union delegates than of managers. Three times as many delegates as managers were interviewed, but we discovered that a considerable degree of consensus prevailed among the former. The greatest possible similarity of formulation was maintained between the questionnaires for delegates and managers, with the exception of some questions relating to *perspective;* we had, of course, to reformulate some of the alternatives in terms of workers. The great homogeneity of opinion was an unforeseen result.

As the specialized reader knows, there are three more or less competing national trade unions in France:[9] The Communist-led *Confédération Générale du Travail* (C.G.T.), the largest of the three; the Catholic, but progressive, *Confédération Française des travailleurs chrétiens* (C.F.T.C.); and the smallest, but not unimportant, *Force Ouvriére* (C.G.T.–F.O.), grouping together former members of the C.G.T. who split away. We expected to find some differences between them, but it turned out that the opinion profiles, with only rare and minor exceptions, were the same for delegates of the C.G.T., C.F.T.C., and C.G.T.–F.O. We did not find any significant differences between delegates from various industries either.

Concerning trends *inside* the enterprise,[10] the union delegates rarely stressed the importance of advances in technology. "Work is still done with our hands." "It is not the machine that makes any decisions: the worker decides on how fast you have to go." "There is a beginning of technical change, but it hasn't really happened yet." On the whole, we think that the importance of technological development tended to be underestimated by these respondents. Sometimes the delegate suggested that the pace of work had increased, the major change being one from muscular to nervous exertion. The organization of production has not yet developed to the stage where only coordination, as distinct from maximization, is essential. "Everything pushes you to maximum production, the payment systems and the foreman." "Nobody turns his head, to see whether those behind are following."

According to the delegates themselves, the worker's "mentality" has not developed either. They generally argue that the worker's attitude towards production is far too intimately related to the payment system imposed on him. Therefore no "psychological" development in the direction of greater understanding of the enterprise's need for cooperation can take place. "If the worker is asked to do a fair amount of work, if he is free to stop when he likes to, he can produce without control. But now, he tries all possible tricks in order to get a higher wage."

---

[9] For a good comparison between the French and American labor movements see Lorwin (12).

[10] Questionnaire areas 1 (technical) and 3 (psychological).

The imposed organization being what it is, "the only thing the worker really does understand is the relationship between production and pay." In other words and more generally, the delegates held that the system was responsible for a tendency toward individualism and sectional particularism. "The worker is preoccupied only with his own little corner, he is not sensitive to any general point of view that concerns the enterprise." "The worker is terribly down to earth: all the claims are limited, they are claims of a particular shop, often even of a particular team." The standard local union's type of strategy is the "snow-ball" method: once management yields satisfaction to a particularistic claim, other groups or sectors of the enterprise will try to get the same, and so on. This strategy and its success reinforce the habit of particularism.

Fairly clearly, the interviews with delegates led to the conclusion that in their view, due to the "reactionary" methods of management, the enterprise and also the worker's "mentality" had not developed. This is parallel to the views held by some managers that organizational methods cannot change as long as the personnel maintains its "backward mentality."

Concerning trends *outside* the enterprise[11] the delegates are optimistic to the point not only of believing in the reality of change, but also in overestimating it. They contend that the cost of the technical equipment has increased so much that wages and salaries, as a proportion of production costs, seem negligible. Therefore it is no longer the worker's effort, but "responsibility that is essential." And quite a number of delegates expressed astonishment "that management did not make the best of this evolution (by changing antiquated payment systems)." This trend is said to be parallel to another one toward "planning." "Production is planned in advance by the top management of the firm in Paris." "The gross amount of the wages is calculated in advance." Obviously many of the delegates distinctly feel that in the national economy "something has changed, but our management does not want to follow." Even though the same interviews contain a whole collection of unmistakable anti-capitalistic remarks such as "our capitalistic economy cannot be totally planified," the delegates tend to adopt a forward-looking view.

A similar belief in development is found at the social level, but with more restraint and expressed with accompanying remarks on management's resistance to change. Is there any change in working-class consumption patterns? Does the worker's family live "from hand to mouth"? Do the workers strive for fixed (non-incentive) pay? Here the answers show some variations. They stress, first of all, the worker's claim for a steady wage, with no variations based on incentives. "People like regular pay, rather than getting a few additional francs by dint of extra effort." This response again, as compared to traditional patterns, is indicative of a change. But to the claim of regularity there is usually more or less

[11] Questionnaire areas 2 (economic) and 4 (sociological).

explicitly added the claim of predictability of earnings. "I want to know in advance what I am going to earn, what I can spend." "The workers want to make predictions, they always ask the foremen how much they'll earn." In other words, the applied incentive payment system is criticized against the background of changed ("new") consumption habits. In their comments a few delegates go as far as describing an alleged current tendency among workers to save money.

Do delegates view management as something which has "changed"? In this crucial question "internal" and "external" trends of industrial development are intermingled. About three-quarters of the answers were negative. Some of the more extreme answers were quite vehement. "They (the managers) are not at all bothered about the workers' interests." "They would rather save a machine's life than a worker's life." "They force you to work at a speed that shortens your life." "He (the manager) is a carpet-bagger." But not only did one-third of the delegates choose the opposite alternative answer, indicative of a change, but a great many of the others mentioned a difference in styles of management or the "climate" of industrial relations. "The management is quite different now from the gangsters we used to have before the war." "They are not inhuman, the situation is to blame." At least a large minority of statements, then, attack management less directly.

Our last question contrasted individual action with collective action. A majority of answers used the second alternative, with comments describing change hopefully and in bright colors. One type of comment in this vein is that the working class is "getting more and more homogeneous." Another type suggests a recent change in the collective bargaining process: more and more it is said that the non-manual workers and even supervisors and lower management show solidarity and support labor claims together with the manual workers. But the comments indicate how "new" this trend appears to be to the respondents. "The horizon is more and more open; this is due to automation, to the improved standards of living and the breaking down of some barriers."

Contrasting with these, a minority of answers pessimistically describe the other alternative, in terms of individual action. Thus, "the workers think the only way to get ahead is through individual effort." They try to earn more through overtime hours. And the union delegates of course heavily condemn all sorts of "tricks" leading to social stability in individual rather than collective terms.

Although the local delegates of different geographical regions, different industries, and even of different national union affiliations answered in the same way to a surprising degree, some differences in the style of the comments and a few variations in the choice of question alternatives appeared. But on the whole, the major trend was the same for all categories of delegates; they have generally the same image of change. They nearly all agree that the incentive payment system should be abandoned.

Now this rather large area of agreement could, of course, be said to be due to the union delegates' specific position in the enterprise. We do not think, however, that this is a sufficient explanation. Being generally manual workers themselves, in the plant, except for a few hours a week, the local unions' delegates tend rather to respond as do most workers, faced with autocratic social structures (or what they conceive of as being autocratic from their vantage point, a position without authority).

In order to check to what extent the interviewed delegates' preference for change in payment systems was also the wish of workers themselves, we added a short study on the workers' ideas for change.

We can only briefly summarize some of the major trends of the workers' own image here, but a few of these results will help illuminate aspects of the social meaning of change, a subject which has not received much empirical treatment (see also 18).

III. The Workers' Image

A great majority of respondents express an optimistic desire for a change of payment systems; a smaller majority tend to think in terms of a "conflict" image of both society and the plant.

1) On Payment Systems

In this country automation, or advanced mechanization, has not been introduced very generally and the traditional contrast between office and shop workers is still a very vivid one. The question whether the difference between monthly salary and hourly wage is perceived as legitimate, justified by technical differences of function, is therefore an interesting indicator of the workers' readiness to accept existing organization.

Results show that the interviewed workers[12] do not conceive of the salary/wage distinction as a legitimate functional one. They do not regard the tying of pay to production as a legitimate technical device. Only a small proportion of the total sample held this view. Thirty-two per cent believe the workers' effort is the important factor; 8 per cent hold that the workers are in no way responsible for variations in two-weekly output. On the other hand, 77 per cent express the opinion that they have no influence on their own pay (Question 6).

Asked (Question 9) to choose between the job of skilled *maintenance work* — in a position when the workers are already paid on a non-incentive basis — and the job of *bookkeeper*, both earning the same amount of money, 91 per cent of all respondents express preference for the latter, the monthly paid job.

Asked to justify the existence of a system distinguishing between sal-

[12] The data come from 289 interviews of young skilled workers constituting a random sample for steel works and iron mines.

aries and wages, 30 per cent accepted it; 43 per cent rejected it; and 27 per cent were undecided, or did not find any reason.

The main types of comments on this alternative in terms of some degree of agreement concerned the following:

1. The social prestige or social organizational legitimation — "Those who have the responsibilities are salaried"; "Those who are educated and who are managers get the monthly pay"; "The workers are not worthy of it."

2. Technical or economic legitimation — "It is necessary in order to adapt the amount of work to the demand of a certain product"; "The monthly paid work is more regular"; "It would cost too much to pay everybody salaries."

3. Resignation to tradition or law — "It has always been so"; "This is the law."

The more frequent disagreement with the proposition was usually phrased with reference to management's power strategy — "It breaks the solidarity of the personnel"; "It forces the worker to keep quiet in the hope that he will get a promotion." Even the more technical or economical sides of the arguments were frequently and rather clearly expressed in terms of control, or coercion — "it is in order to push production."

Finally, 75 per cent of the respondents (Question 11) say they personally feel they should be paid by monthly salary. Hence it appears that the union delegates' aspiration towards a new form of payment system is paralleled by workers' aspirations of similar nature and intensity.

In order to come to a closer understanding of the social meaning of this response, we presented other questions to help us elaborate the respondents' image of society and the enterprise.

2) On Hierarchy and Conflict

Three types of questions were designed to focus on hierarchy in terms of earnings, of prestige, and of stratification in the plant, in the town, and in the country. Are these differences perceived as continua or as dichotomies?

a) Our first indicator was the guesses the respondents were asked to make on how much a director (top manager of a plant), an engineer, a foreman, and a skilled worker earn per month. The results displayed a rather distinct gap between the average figures of engineer's and director's imputed earnings. Whereas the curve representing the average guesses for the worker, foreman, and engineer levels rises at an even rate, there is a sharp increase in the angle between the last two. Although we do not know the exact amount of directors' salaries ourselves — precise figures are practically never published or talked about in public in France — they may reasonably be said to have been greatly exaggerated, especially in the small mines. We rely, in making this judgment, upon our own guesses which are partly based upon comparisons with the national statistics on earnings of salaried management. This particular finding holds true not only for the average figures of the whole sample, but also for each particular plant. Within each plant there is, of course, a variation of responses. We interpret this as indicative of a felt and resented class difference.

b) Our second indicator was the answers to a set of questions on social participation. In order to get some measure of the perceived hierarchy of prestige and the actual pattern of social relations outside the plant we asked the respondents to evaluate the frequency of informal contacts, of children's intermarriage, of friendship ties between skilled workers and unskilled workers, foremen, office workers, and engineers, and the frequency of their affiliation with the same union. The results again revealed a dichotomy, the cutting point occurring one level lower — between the engineers and the three lower categories.

c) Our third indicator was the choices made by the respondents between a differentiated, continuous social hierarchy and a discontinuous hierarchy.[13] Respondents were asked to describe alternatives for the plant, for a middle-sized town, and for the whole country. To what extent is there, in this population of young skilled workers, a preference for the integrated image of a continuous hierarchy as against a discontinuous, simplified conflict image?

The results showed that two-thirds of the respondents selected the list with the non-continuous hierarchy and one-third the continuous (integrated) one. This trend was consistent for the three types of areas, the plant, the town, and the nation. This stress on division rather than unity is also consistent with the results already mentioned.

In order to touch in a more direct way on the difficult problem of integration and conflict we submitted two further questions designed in terms of the industrial enterprise.

Again, about two-thirds of the respondents say they think "what the managers and what the workers want" (Question 19) is (or is mainly) in opposition.

And to the following Question 18, "Some people say that the plant and the manager are like a football team and its captain, they are both

---

13 *Plant:* Alternative A (integrated image):
The director, the engineers, the white-collar staff, the skilled workers (ouvriers professionels), and the semi-skilled workers (ouvriers spécialises).
Alternative B (conflict image):
The "boss" ("patron" has a rich social connotation which cannot be adequately translated), the staff ("collaborateurs"; this is also a sociologically interesting term, impossible to translate), and the workers.
Country: Alternative A (integrated image):
The professions, the businessmen, the technicians, clerks (employés de bureau), and the workers.
Alternative B (conflict image):
The ruling class (classe dirigeante), the middle class, the working class.

interested together to shoot as many goals as possible," the answers were again distributed in accordance with the preceding trends (sample of 289 interviews):

Strongly agree	12%	28%
Agree	16%	
Disagree	28%	69%
Strongly disagree	41%	
No answer	3%	
	100%	

The Social Meaning of Resistance to Change

Geographic and industrial variables had, as we have seen, no significant consequences for the image of industrial development held by either managers or delegates. Two other modes of analysis still were available: the comparison between management's and the delegates' images, and the comparison of the images of different kinds of management according to the degrees of their resistance to change. We finally added a third, the content analysis of the expressed meaning of change in the field of payment systems and of authority as expressed in the review articles of management associations.

Three modes of analysis have thus been employed. We do not claim anything more than exploratory value for our techniques and conclusions.

1) Image Discrepancy and the Tension Cycle

Up to this point we have been describing the views of change of management and of union delegates separately. In these descriptions the other party was more or less explicitly present in quite a number of comments. If we put these images side by side, we see not only the expected conflict, but, in addition, we get a measure of relative discrepancy. This discrepancy of the two images was then compared to the relative resistance to change of payment systems, as indicated by actual practice in the plant.

The result of this comparison — which is still crude and tentative — may be briefly summarized: the greater the observed resistance to change (as established by the payment system in operation), the greater the discrepancy between management's image and the union delegates' image of industrial development (as measured by the interview scheme). This relationship is definite and linear.

On the basis of image discrepancy, especially as there are no differences according to technical or geographical background or even to union doctrines for the delegates' image, we think it can be reasonably assumed that a kind of *structural strain* is measured by these questions. We would like to outline as an extension of the preceding summary statement the following model of interrelation:

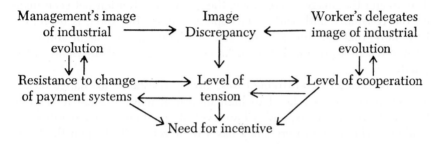

FIGURE 1

The lower half of Figure 1 represents a version of the vicious circle process as it has been elaborated by Myrdal and used in many of the applications of the idea of circular causation between repression and rebellion (14, pp. 37–47; 16). The greater the tension between management and workers, the lower the level of consent, the more necessary the incentive payment system appears. Thus management exerts a kind of social pressure upon the workers through incentives and naturally resists changes in this kind of payment system. On the other hand, the workers react against the use of this device by lowering their level of cooperation. Thus managerial resistance and lack of cooperation by workers reinforce each other.

The importance of adding image discrepancy to our model lies in the fact that the idea of the vicious circle does not, by itself, increase our understanding of change. In order to clarify why there are different degrees of resistance to change and why some managers may pass from a greater to a lesser degree of resistance, we introduce image discrepancy in the upper half of Figure 1. Two consequences follow: a) The level of tension influences the image the social actors have of industrial development. This proposition suggests that a general view of industry and society is not independent of the internal life in a particular organization. It contradicts one of management's central beliefs, namely, that the worker's political orientation is exclusively determined by influences external to the plant. But, to state the perhaps even more important complementary proposition: b) the level of tension is influenced by the view of industrial development, itself the outcome of a number of factors — complex causes from outside the limited area of the organization (for example, class structure, social movements, political parties), as well as the actor's more or less free decisions, either as a member of the organization, or more broadly (and this is a most neglected aspect), as a member of a particular society and historical tradition. Thus, if the image discrepancy intervenes in the interactions between managerial resistance and worker cooperation, it becomes relevant for our model. We conclude that image discrepancy operates as an inhibitor of change. The greater the image discrepancy, the greater the tension between managerial resistance and worker uncooperativeness. But there is no reason to believe that the image could not accelerate a movement toward a tension relaxing process if it were "in advance" of actual situations in the plant.

Let us consider two extreme cases. Strong resistance to change on the management side is related to high industrial tension, a great need to use incentive payments, and a low level of spontaneous cooperation by workers. The image discrepancy has a reinforcing effect upon the backward-looking outlook of the managers and the forward-looking outlook of the workers, and hardens their respective positions. Low resistance to change, on the other hand, would seem to be related to relatively low tension and a high level of cooperation by workers. In this case the small image discrepancy will have an accelerating effect upon the process of industrial development.

At this point we may indicate the special interest of a study of resistance to change in incentive payment systems from the point of view of social control. For management, incentive payments are clearly a governing device, an instrument for controlling the workers' production behavior. Management can either perceive it as an indispensable tool, without which the very existence of industrial authority is threatened, or simply as a device which may be replaced by some substitute. There is, in principle, no reason to believe that the degree of management influence could not be approximately the same in the extreme cases outlined above. Management using a strongly authoritarian payment system has to contend with a very low level of worker cooperation. Management using little economic pressure through incentive payment systems, on the other hand, can count on a much higher voluntary level of worker compliance. The degree of management's control may well remain about equal in both situations.

While this kind of reasoning, although oversimplifying processes which are very complex in actual industrial situations, may appear quite reasonable to the detached observer, it is not adopted by a great number of French managers. In the conflict-ridden industrial setting there is fear of change in any event, but whereas some managers fear only a *relative* loss of control over the workers, others fear an *absolute* loss of control, involving something like the total disintegration of the authority structure. The managers who resist change most strongly believe that an absolute loss of authority will occur if the incentive payment system is abandoned, involving a paralysis of managerial action as a whole. For them, resistance means opposing changes capable of effecting a major transformation of the social structure.

The manager who resists less strongly has either come to the conclusion (having agreed previously to introduce a less radical incentive payment system) that there is no loss, or only a relative loss of management's influence and that change does not necessarily mean transforming the social structure.

What, then, can be said about the reasons for which some of the managers adopted strong resistance and the backward-looking view of industrial evolution, and others lesser resistance and a more forward-looking image of development?[14]

2) The Forward-looking Entrepreneur and Change

A great majority of the managing directors whom we met in the steelworks and iron mines were engineers. They were engineers by training and they clearly conceived of themselves as engineers. This is a fact of prime importance. The fact that they managed the human and economic aspects of their companies was of lesser importance to them.

The main feature of the opinion distribution is a cutting point between the technical and non-technical questionnaire areas; more generally, if we take the whole population of the interviewed managers, the opinion profile is:

TABLE 1

Questions in	Management's Answers	
	Backward-looking	Forward-looking
Technical terms		x
Economic terms	x	
Individual terms	x	
Social terms	x	

The pattern reflects the director's professional pride as an engineer. If we look closely at the interview reports, we notice how much the respondents liked to discuss the technical aspects of the enterprise. It is difficult for them not to yield to the temptation of overestimating the stage of technical development of the plant.[15]

This tendency reflects professional pride, but also the fact that the

14 It has recently been pointed out (17) that the study of social change through resistance to it is not the most direct way of gaining insight into this general problem. Unfortunately it is often the only way open for research.

15 In saying this we do not want to imply that the technical area is not in fact, relatively speaking, the most advanced area in the industries under consideration.

manager is an engineer. It is also a way of avoiding the discussion of more "delicate" social problems. The engineer seems often to have a distinct dislike for the "unscientific" human side of production; he would like to produce without the troublesome and sometimes hostile semi-assistance of men, especially of manual workers.

In order to understand how it happens that a minority of managers adopt a forward-looking image of the industrial scene, and especially why there is a cutting point between the technical and the non-technical, as well as an unexpected regularity in the answers to the non-technical social question-area, we observed one additional and seemingly relevant difference in the interviews.

The relatively rare managers who have the forward-looking attitude answer in more personalized terms than the others. They consider the social climate less as a given external structure. Talking about the workers' attitudes they comment: "One can transform the personnel's 'mentality'" (by changing the payment systems). "If we let them have more and better information, we get more understanding," or, "We can create a better social climate in the plant."

Thus it seems that the manager accepts, and even tends to overestimate, technical change as soon as he believes that he is the technical innovator. Two consequences follow from this principle of entrepreneurial initiative. Not only does the manager-engineer know the problems of technical innovation and manipulation better than those in the social realm, but, in the social area, innovation is more relevant to questions of power. Strong resistance is likely to arise both out of management's ignorance of social manipulation and from fear of changes not introduced by management itself. Absence of, or low resistance, on the contrary, is likely to imply both knowledge of social manipulation and the desire to introduce changes controlled by management (or at least perceived as controlled by them).

It remains to be stated more completely why the most resistant managers are more inclined than their "progressive" colleagues to oppose change, which they see as something driving towards a dangerous evolution.

3) Backward-looking Managers and Change

Our findings suggest that management's resistance to change is remote from any purely functional, goal-oriented strategy. One of the top executives analyzed the situation as follows: "If you take away something in the system of a plant, all the rest of it runs the risk of falling to pieces. If you change something in one plant of the same company, or the same geographical area, all the other plants are going to be influenced. Everything holds together." This prediction surely could only hold if "the thing" to be taken away were of relatively central importance, and providing there were a low level of consensus.

Industrial goals, whether defined as profit or production, are of course directly related to the level of productivity, hence the central relevance of payment systems which have the effect of regulating, stimulating, and compelling productivity. The strongly resistant manager therefore considers that without incentives as a managing device he would, generally speaking, be in trouble.

This, in the observer's eyes, may be a false appraisal of the situation, since management could well use quite a number of alternative devices for controlling workers. But it is considered by management as a realistic assessment. The main reason, we suggest, why management holds such a view is to be found in the social meaning of resistance *as holding up development*, not just any change. This meaning being tied to the whole pattern of interacting images and tensions, the only major additional concept to be added to our model is that of conflict in a situation where there are no shared expectations. It is at this point, in our view, that the description of the image held by both sides in the enterprise, and in society at large, becomes necessary and leads beyond the traditional functionalist frame of reference which views social systems in terms of consensus alone. The perceptions of industrial development of trade-union delegates as well as of workers imply both consensus on some major features of the social structure, and considerable dissensus on others. They are at variance with management views — very often in direct opposition — and their homogeneity suggests that a class-linked perspective is in operation here.

So long as our model is one of a closed system, be it the goal-oriented organization, the enterprise, or, on a more abstract level, the society dominated by consensus (and conforming to the functionalist model), neither resistance to change nor aspirations towards alternatives to existing situations can be adequately understood.

We may conclude by drawing attention to some types of legitimations recently given in the publications of French management, in discussions on payment systems. The core of the argument is: if traditional payment systems are too clearly or too rapidly abandoned, the workers are likely to break the traditional rules of accepting unilateral managerial authority. This, in other words, opens the discussion on legitimation of unilateral authority. And the "functional" legitimation ("somebody must command") is usually not given without additional or extraneous arguments.

The maintenance of the right of property[16] is, of course, one of the arguments. The manager's authority "has its source in the Supreme

---

[16] In a jointly directed enterprise the right of property would be destroyed, and "this right is a direct outcome of the human person's nature" (1).

Legislator" (1). The more industry develops towards concentration, the more a centralized authority and a strong hierarchical system is necessary (5).

Some articles also stress the absence of a problem: there is no real need for legitimation, this problem has been introduced from the outside by those who "invented" the idea of class antagonism (15).[17]

Conclusion

The main difficulty in understanding social change in the French industrial situation lies perhaps in the fact that the social actors are neither completely divided, nor completely united. On the one hand, change is likely to be understood as a modification of the present pattern of *interactions*; a certain degree of resistance or acceptance of change is therefore functional to the maintenance of this pattern or essential parts of its structure (i.e., the structure of authority). On the other hand, change is likely to present another face, in terms of *action*, as re-interpretation of the present pattern of interactions. It is also understood as development or retrogression on a more general level. The social actors live to some extent in the same world, but they also live in a partially different world: they interact in an organizational context, but this has different social meanings, according to the positions of the actors who perceive it.

We suggest that neither the goal-model, nor the system-model (8) of the theory of organizations permits us to understand all cases of social change. The particular case presented here was only a study in resistance to change; but even in this limited context it is difficult to explain the various degrees of resistance (or acceptance) of change as functional or rational in terms of an organizational system model. We therefore introduced the actors' image of change at a general level in order to permit at least a glance at the non-functional aspects of the organization.

The actor's social image synthetizes the following contents: it is determined by the actual situation, the present pattern of interactions, and the perspective a particular actor has, looking (upward or downward) from his organizational position; it is at the same time determined by the actor's aspirations (forward- or backward-looking) toward the traditional situation or toward a different situation and another pattern of interactions, and these aspirations further guide his selective perception and interpretation of present and future reality.

We also suggest that the non-organizational social positions, as well as the cultural background of the actor (omitted here), have to be introduced if we want to analyze further the meaning of the actor's image of change.

---

[17] On the other hand, quite a number of managers among those who publish articles in rather liberal journals, themselves analyze industrial problems in terms of social classes (4).

BIBLIOGRAPHY

1. Editorial, "L'autorité légitime du patron," *Professions*, No. 394 (July 1956).

2. Burns, Tom, and G. M. Stalker. *The Management of Innovation*. Chicago: Quadrangle Press, 1961.

3. Crozier, Michel. "Human Relations at the Management Level in a Bureaucratic System of Organization," *Human Organization*, Vol. 20, No. 2 (1961).

4. De Longevialle, M. Editorial, ACADI (December 1953). (Monthly bulletin published by Association de cadres dirigeants de l'industrie pour le progrès social et économique.)

5. Demonque, M. "Réflexions sur la civilisation moderne," *Jeune Patron*, No. 61 (January 1953).

6. Dofny, J., J. Duplex, M. Maurice, and A. Willener. "Evolution des modes de rémunération," a follow-up report to the European Coal and Steel Community. Paris: C.E.C.A. 1962.

7. Durand, C., C. Prestat, and A. Willener. "Niveau de mécanisation et modes de rémunération," (French report on an international project sponsored by the European Coal and Steel Community). Paris: C.E.C.A., 1958. (mimeo)

8. Etzioni, Amitai. "Two Approaches to Organizational Analysis," *Administrative Science Quarterly*, Vol. 5, No. 2 (1960), pp. 257–278.

9. Guttman, Louis. "A Structural Theory for Intergroup Beliefs and Action," *American Sociological Review*, Vol. 24, No. 3 (1959), pp. 318–328.

10. Harbison, Frederick H., and Charles A. Meyers. *Management and the Industrial World*. New York: McGraw-Hill Book Co., 1959.

11. Lazarsfeld, Paul F., and Allen H. Barton. "Qualitative Measurement in the Social Sciences," in Daniel Lerner and Harold Lasswell (eds.), *The Policy Sciences*. Stanford: Stanford University Press, 1951.

12. Lorwin, Val R. "Reflection on the History of Two Labour Union Movements: France and the United States," *Journal of Economic History*, Vol. 17, No. 1 (1957), pp. 25–44.

13. Lutz, B., and A. Willener. "Niveau de mécanisation et modes de rémunération," (Report to the European Coal and Steel Community High Authority.) Paris: C.E.C.A., 1960.

14. March, James G., and Herbert A. Simon. *Organizations*. New York: John Wiley & Sons, 1958.

15. Mijola, L. "Dialogue entre chrétiens, in ACADI (December 1952). (Monthly bulletin published by Association de cadres dirigeants de l'industrie pour le progrès social et économique.)

16. Myrdal, Gunnar. *An American Dilemma*. New York: Harper and Bros., 1944.

17. Orzack, Louis H. "Role Implications of Change in a New Organization," a communication read at the Fifth World Congress of Sociology, Washington, D.C., September 1962. (mimeo)

18. Willener, Alfred. "L'ouvrier et l'organisation," *Sociologie du Travail*, Vol. 4, No. 4 (1962), pp. 332–348.

24

Sidney M. Greenfield

Stocks, Bonds, and Peasant Canes

in Barbados: Some Notes on the

Use of Land in an Overdeveloped

Economy

Evolution, Development, and Functional Analysis

A student of social change in the 1960's learns rather quickly that there are at least two meanings generally attributed to the term "social change" by scholars writing on the subject. On the one hand, there is the traditional concept associated with the broad problem of social dynamics and the evolution of society and culture — as first posed in sociology by Comte and Spencer and in anthropology by Tylor and Morgan. As developed by these nineteenth-century scholars, the key issue or problem was an academic and theoretical one — specifically, that of attempting to understand and account for the emergence and growth of human society and culture. On the other hand, especially in the literature of the post World War II period, there has been a tendency to restrict the usage of the concept "social change" so that it refers to the singular process of development, or modernization. This is a more delimited usage that implies something different from the classical meaning. Thus, while the work of the nineteenth-century scholars was primarily academic and theoretical, the efforts of most modern writers are in the direction of application, specifically, planning.

One possible explanation for this shift in interest may be that the nineteenth-century studies in change were conducted by sociologists and anthropologists who were struggling to establish generalizing sciences of society and culture. Though interested in the possibility of application, their primary concern was historical reconstruction and theoretical understanding. This interest induced them to take as their empirical subject matter — and point of departure for research — the cumulative evidence of man's past on the earth. Their specific contributions often took the form of establishing a series of evolutionary stages and positing the possible means of movement that carried given peoples from one stage to the next.

The modern studies, however, have been stimulated, at least at first, by economists and others acting as advisors and consultants to the governments of industrially advanced nations interested in helping former colonies, dependencies, and poor neighbors. Sociologists and anthropologists have come into the picture only recently — to apply their skills in getting the plans of the economists and policy-makers across to the people. The theoretical generalizations being worked on appear to be more in the nature of recipes as to how to implement policy effectively, than as tested hypotheses on social process. Upon examination it is quickly apparent that the modern studies in development are in fact illustrations of a special case of the broader conceptualization of social dynamics. Whatever light they shed, therefore, should be expected to be of limited utility with respect to the formulation of scientific generalizations. However, though to the knowledge of this writer they have not been examined thus far, there are interesting parallels between the work done in development in the twentieth century and the nineteenth-century studies of social dynamics — specifically, studies in social and cultural evolution.

The concept of evolution has been used to mean many things. There are, however, two key ideas that may be taken as central. The first is the notion of transformism, and the second, the idea of progress (see 10). Transformism implies that when a series of similar forms are found in any substantive field they may be explained by the hypothesis that they are "historically connected in the dynamic process of growth" (10, p. 57). The concept of transformism then is the logical opposite of what is generally referred to as creationism — that each related form is the result of a separate creation.

Nineteenth-century studies in social dynamics took as one of their basic assumptions the idea of transformism. When similar social and/or cultural forms — invariably institutions — were found in human history it was assumed that they were historically connected. A number of stages — composed of complexes of similar forms — were posited and growth, development, and change were taken to be the process of transforming the institutions in one stage to those in the next — i.e., evolution.

The second and logically distinct idea was that of progress — that things get better. Just as it was accepted in the biology of the period that man was more advanced or higher (had progressed farther) than, let us say, an amoeba, it was assumed in sociology and anthropology that modern man's society and culture was more advanced than that of his early ancestors. Man evolved from the amoeba by the process of transformism and was an improvement. In the same way, it was believed, modern man's institutions had evolved from those of early man and, by analogy, they too were more advanced and consequently better.

The dynamics of the universe, as conceived by the nineteenth-century evolutionists then, were that human culture and society were improving all the time and that the better forms in the later stages were related, or "historically connected in the dynamic process of growth" to the earlier ones. The process of growth of society and culture, as conceptualized at that time, may be compared to the act of climbing a ladder. The most advanced forms were believed to be those found at the top, with the least advanced on the bottom. The only way to get to the top was to climb the ladder, and, so to speak, duplicate the development of the more successful forms at the top. Today we refer to this view as straight line, or unilineal evolution.

Many modern evolutionists still accept both the ideas of transformism and progress. The ladder analogy, however, has become the issue upon which they split. Evolutionists, as Steward (30) has indicated, take one of three positions as to how development or advancement may be achieved. The first is the traditional nineteenth-century position — straight line or unilineal evolution. The second, expounded for example by White (31), eliminates the concern with specific stages by concentrating on the world's supply of Culture — as opposed to specific cultures. Thus the whole ladder — actually the top step — as it goes higher and higher is the object of interest, not any one step. The third position, which may be referred to as multilineal to distinguish it from the unilineal assumption of the nineteenth century, is that although there are stages, and the top one is acknowledged to be better than the ones below, there are several alternative ways to get to the top.

Students of development in the twentieth century, like the evolutionists of the past, appear to accept the assumptions of transformism and progress. In this respect they may be said to believe in evolution. They, however, have focused their attention on the top step, and take as their problem the processes that will enable all people to advance to the pinnacle. They appear to believe rather strongly in the idea of progress and take it to be their basic value and the goal toward which their efforts are directed. The top step is the best and their job is to help all the occupants living on lower steps get to the top, as rapidly as possible.

In addition to progress they also seem to accept the idea of transformism. Thus the means of attaining the top and most advanced step is to transform the social and cultural forms on the lower steps so that they become like the ones found at the top. Interestingly enough, the means of accomplishing this is diffusion, the very mechanism seized upon by critics to refute the works of the nineteenth-century evolutionists.

Students of development today, then, like students of evolution in the past, believe in both transformism and progress. Though the interests of the former are applied in contrast with those of the latter, which are academic, the values and assumptions of both appear to be strikingly similar.

There are at present two basic and contrasting approaches to the problem of how development is to be achieved. One, as represented for example by Slotkin (28) and Hoselitz (15), is that "culturally speaking the so-called 'underdeveloped areas' are those which have not adopted the body of customs constituting industrialism" (28, p. 9). This "implies that the process of modernization of poor and economically little advanced nations may be interpreted principally as a process in culture change and cultural *diffusion*" (15, italics mine). That is, to achieve progress (which is taken to be desirable), the occupants of all steps on the ladder must be transformed — by means of directed diffusion or "assistance" — so that they manifest the social and cultural forms found on the top step. Then and only then, it is maintained, will development be achieved.

The alternative point of view accepts the notion of progress and the desirability of "development." Its proponents, however, maintain that the actual process of industrialization and growth for each country or area of the world follows, or should follow, a limited number of dissimilar patterns in accordance with the existing differences in culture, social structure, values, and so forth, of the country, or area concerned (see for example 19, pp. viii–ix; 17, pp. 15–32, pp. 266 ff.)

The two positions mentioned bear a strong resemblance to the unilineal and multilineal alternatives that split students of evolution. Belief in development and in evolution both imply transformism, but in each pair of alternatives one segment maintains that the only way to get to the top is to go up the ladder and become like the occupant of the top step, while the second argues that progress is desirable, but there are several ways of getting to the summit. Those who take the latter position also maintain that it is possible to invent new forms that may be even better than those presently found on the top step of the ladder. Also, implicit in this assumption is the belief that it is at times possible to skip or bypass altogether many steps (forms) found on the ladder.

Contemporary sociological thinking and research has developed in a direction that is distinct and separate from that taken by students of both evolution and development. While change and process have been the key issues discussed by writers on evolution and development, structure and system are the most important concerns in sociology. The so-called structural-functional approach has, so to speak, abstracted from time — stopped the clock — so that systems of relationships could be intensively investigated and analyzed.

The tentative conclusions of modern structural-functional sociology, however, point out certain factors of relevance to students of evolution and development. For example, social systems do "hang together" with some degree of functional integration, though not to the degree assumed by some sociologists. There appear to be forces in operation that tend to keep each given social system going and, therefore, "behaving" or "functioning" as it had been in the past. The concept of "boundary maintenance" has been developed to emphasize this empirical tendency toward equilibrium. In summary, it appears that in every social system there are forces, often very strong, that mitigate against the occurrence of change. In the absence of powerful forces to the contrary, it appears that systemic equilibrium may safely be assumed. This finding — the tendency toward system maintenance — is of extreme relevance to the study of evolution and development. One might assume, for example, that in spite of diffusion — in the direction of the social and cultural forms to be found on the top step of the assumed evolutionary ladder — that has characterized modern history, there are strong tendencies to maintain, in some degree, traditional systems and forms.

The material from Barbados, a small island in the West Indies, presented below provides one example in which the system of agriculture being diffused from western Europe and North America is being resisted. We shall show that the system developed on the island is retained because it is a functionally effective solution to the requirements of the local setting.

Specifically, the unique function of the rights of possession in land will be described. These rights in the principal source of wealth in this agricultural society will be shown to be the functional equivalent of the ownership of stocks and bonds in the United States. Consequently, an individual possessed of such rights can earn income from them without the performance of any activity such as those generally associated with labor or management. Rights of possession in land then, are, in themselves, an income-earning asset and may be viewed as a form of capital investment.

This unique situation requires explanation since rights of possession in land do not customarily contain such implications in agricultural societies. The explanation presented will be related to the generally "overdeveloped" nature of the Barbadian economy — which is based upon wage labor and the market-exchange system of distribution — and, more specifically, to the markets for land and sugar, and the desire for more efficient production on the part of the island's sugar factories.

The Island: History and Development

At the eastern edge of the lesser Antilles there lies the small coral island called Barbados, named, according to legend, by a Portuguese seaman because when first sighted it resembled a bearded fig tree. The island, relatively flat, measures only 166 square miles in size but today is one of the most densely populated areas in the world (20). In 1957 it was inhabited by approximately 230,000 persons, a density of 1,380 persons per square mile. As the old man in George Lamming's novel summed it up:

> . . . 'twas more people in this island than the lan' could hold or the law allow. 'Twas a high burnin' shame to put on a piece o' land no more than a hundred an' something square miles, . . . two hundred thousand people . . . when you put us together from top to bottom was . . . a record population for the size o' the piece of land anywhere in this God's world" (18, p. 83).

The island has long been faced with the task of supporting a large population. Though, today, the economy must be viewed in terms of its ability to provide for the masses, historically the large numbers are a consequence of the economic forces that shaped the island. Barbados in the sixteenth and seventeenth centuries was the heart of Great Britain's sugar empire in the Carribbean. Sugar, which brought wealth, fame, prestige, and power to the plantation owners, required large numbers of resident laborers in addition to land and capital to be cultivated efficiently. Labor, throughout the Americas, as is generally known, came in the form of Negro slaves who performed the tasks necessary for the production of agricultural staples. Barbados, for many reasons, was ideally suited to the cultivation of the most valuable crop of the period. Consequently, hundreds of thousands of Africans were forced to reside on the island and to work, as slaves, in the canefields.

With the decline in importance of sugar in the world economy in the nineteenth century and with the associated end of slavery and the classical plantation system, Barbados was left with the problem of a large number of former slaves who were no longer useful in producing great wealth for its ruling classes. To the dismay of this latter group, however, the Negroes required subsistence after emancipation just as they did at the height of slavery. When they were valuable factors of production this requirement was satisfied — at least in part — by the planters, who imported provisions for their sustenance that were doled out in accordance with the traditions of the slave plantations. With emancipation, some economic arrangements were called for whereby the large population of former slaves could obtain support. The details of the new arrangements are revealing because they provide the basis for the contemporary system of sugar-cane farming to be described presently.

After emancipation many of the former sugar colonies abandoned the cultivation of that crop as their primary economic mainstay. In several areas the former slaves abandoned the estates to become peasant farmers in the mountains or forested interiors. There the former great plantations were also abandoned or, at times, sold or left to the Negroes to be partitioned and cultivated in subsistence crops as peasant holdings. This, however, was not the case in Barbados. To quote Beachy, "Barbados swam against the tide in the nineteenth as she had in the eighteenth century. In a period generally ruinous for British West Indian sugar interests, Barbadian planters made more money than ever before. . ." (4, p. 8). In fact, conditions were so well suited for the cultivation of the saccharine staple that down to the present day it has remained as *the crop* on the island.[1]

At emancipation there were approximately 82,000 former slaves in Barbados. There were no mountainous interiors nor uninhabited forest reserves. On the contrary, almost every inch of arable land was owned, occupied, and under cultivation.[2] For the freedmen this meant that there was no place to go — other than to emigrate, an outlet that has in the past century prevented a bad situation from becoming intolerable (22). With no land available to make peasant farming possible and the continuation of the sugar plantations as going concerns, the former slaves, who were now presented with the necessity of providing for their own needs, had little choice but to accept positions as wage laborers on the estates they formerly served in bondage.

The Contemporary Sugar Economy

The Barbadian economy has maintained, in gross form, the same basic features that characterized it in its golden age. The most significant change has been that the segment of the population who labored then as slaves now perform many of the same tasks as wage earners. Sugar, however, still dominates the economy since it is by far the most important source of wealth on the island. With the full development of wage labor and the market-exchange system,[3] the need for money income by the inhabitants to meet their subsistence requirements became magnified so that, as in most other areas where this form of economic integration is to be found, money became an end valued, so to speak, in itself. The attainment of money, therefore, is a very important goal towards which the vast majority of Barbadians consciously and actively strive.

Barbados has maintained, then, a very specialized place as part of the world economy. As in days of old, it has continued to concentrate almost all its productive capacity on the growth of sugar cane to be sold on the world market. The money thus obtained is used to purchase almost all of the goods and services consumed on the island. Unlike most

[1] The authors of *A Ten Year Development Plan for Barbados 1946–56*, for example, refer to it as "the life blood of the island" (1).

[2] As early as 1677 Governor Atkins reported that "there is not a foot of land in Barbados that is not employed even to the very seaside . . . so that whoever will have land . . . must pay for it dearer than for land in England." Quoted in Starkey, (29, p. 79).

[3] Prior to emancipation, only a fraction of the island's population was involved in this extension of the economic system of western Europe. In spite of this, however, the market-exchange system has always been, and still is, the form of institutionalized behavior that has dominated economic activity on the island.

other agricultural areas of the world, very little in the way of foodstuffs and other subsistence goods are produced locally. The imported goods, however, are expensive and Barbadians, in order to obtain them, must earn money. Though several other economic activities are performed on the island, all, in the final analysis, are dependent on the income earned in the sale of sugar. As recent national income studies have revealed (6; 7), sugar is the cornerstone of the entire economy. A corollary of this statement is that the island's fortunes fluctuate as precariously as does the price of sugar on the world market.[4]

Of the various factors of production that go into the Barbadian sugar economy perhaps the most interesting and important, because of its fixed supply, is land. Labor, as we have seen, traditionally has been, and still is, available in excessive quantities. The same may be said to a lesser degree of capital, managerial skills, and technological creativity. The primary factor that sets limits on the growth of the island's economy then, is the limited supply of land.

In a highly efficient economy such as that of Barbados it is interesting to note that the production of the one and only crop is not, generally speaking, economically rational in the sense that output is not responsive to the forces of supply and demand and the price established on the world market. That is, the volume of production — best measured by the area planted in cane — does not increase or decrease as the market price goes up or down.[5] The total of volume of sugar produced, however, does vary with the amount of annual rainfall.[6] Following years of abundant precipitation, per acre yields increase and the volume of sugar produced is greater than it is in the years following periods of drought. This fluctuation, though, is independent from variation in price.

Landholdings

Given the strategic position of land in the economy, let us now examine its distribution and the use to which it is put by its owners.

There are approximately 106,000 acres of land on the island. Of these a little under 70,000 are arable. Sugar cane is grown on almost all of this. The total acreage may be divided into two principal categories of holdings. Plantations over ten acres in size control more than 76,000 of the total acres — which includes almost 80 per cent of the arable acres (8, p. 1). There are between 350 and 375 estates in this category which average between 250–350 acres in size. Most cluster around the average and there are very few at the lower extreme and even fewer at

[4] "Barbados produces less than ½ per cent of the world's annual crop of sugar. It is, therefore, entirely dependent on the outside world for markets and prices" (25, p. 9).

[5] Since the end of World War II, however, as a result of the Commonwealth Sugar Agreement, which will extend at least until 1963, there has been a sure market for Barbadian sugar with a consistent, relatively high price.

[6] Irrigation is not generally considered feasible; therefore, rainfall is the only source of water for the crops.

the upper end — the largest estate containing a little over 800 acres.

Smallholders, on the other hand, control approximately 18,000 acres of which 14,500 are considered arable (9, p. 1). The number of small-holdings — approximately 30,000 — contrasts sharply with the number of plantations, just as their average size of one-half an acre contrasts with the area of the latter. The parcels in this category vary from a few square feet to the ten-acre limit. More than 72 per cent, however, are less than the one-half acre average. On the other hand, less than 5 per cent are two acres or larger (13). The landholdings in Barbados then, are either relatively large or very small. The plantations, which contain most of the acreage, are run very efficiently by a class of professional managers who work for both resident and absentee owners. They concentrate on the cultivation of sugar cane for profit, growing other crops only when required to do so by the government.

Sugar Cane Farming on Smallholdings

The smallholdings, for the most part, tend to be worked by their proprietors in very much the same manner as are plantations. This has resulted in considerable inefficiency and one of the major tasks set for itself by the Department of Science and Agriculture is to improve the level of cultivation on the small plots.

What then is the principal system of farming practiced by the small-holders in Barbados and why do they continue its practice if it is as inefficient as the experts say?

The predominating system of cultivation has been described by Skeete (27) and Halcrow and Cave (13); and since it varies at times from the pattern observed by the author in 1956-57,[7] the earliest published account, as modified by my own field observations, will provide the foundation for the description to be presented.

Sugar cane, as has been indicated, is the main crop, but certain other subsidiary crops are also grown. According to Skeete (27, pp. 2-5), the plot of land is divided in half. Each half is cropped with sugar cane to be reaped in alternative years so that each year there is a crop of sugar cane to be reaped on one half of the holding. Between the end of the crop (February–April) and the beginning of the rainy season (June–July), the soil is forked and prepared for the planting of other crops: old cane stumps are removed and new cane holes dug.

At the beginning of the rainy season, a variety of crops such as yams, sweet potatoes, corn, eddoes, etc., are planted in the piece from which sugar canes were reaped earlier in the year. They are planted either on the banks between cane holes or in the corner of the hole, but never in the center (see Diagram 1). Other minor crops (okras, pigeon peas,

[7] The fieldwork was made possible by fellowships from the Social Science Research Council and the Institute for the Study of Man in the Tropics, for which I express my deepest gratitude.

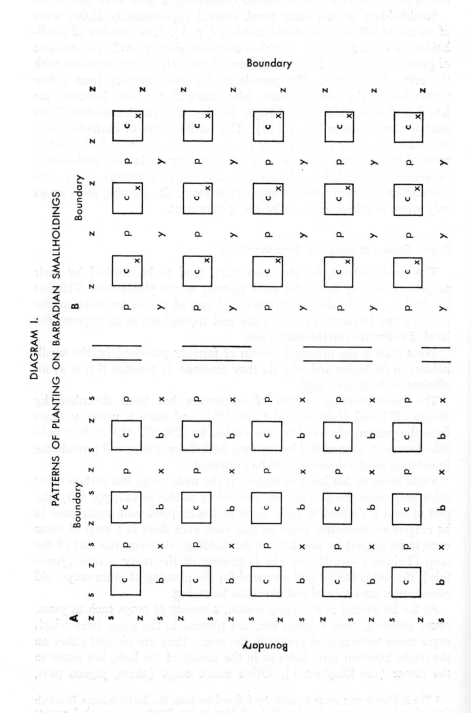

DIAGRAM I.

PATTERNS OF PLANTING ON BARBADIAN SMALLHOLDINGS

The diagram above illustrates two of the several ways of planting sugar cane and subsidiary crops by cultivators of smallholdings in Barbados. The squares represent the cane holes which are used by almost all small-scale cultivators on the island. The holes are approximately two feet square and six inches deep. The soil from the holes is heaped up on the banks between the holes. There are usually between five and one-half and six feet between the holes. Though some cultivators — to increase the number of holes in which they can plant, a practice that is harmful to the cane — use five-foot linings. Though one plant is shown at each location on the diagram, in the majority of the cases there may be two, i.e.,

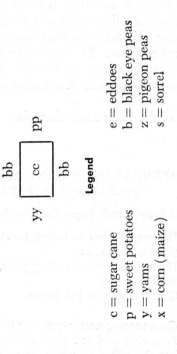

bb

yy | cc | pp

bb

Legend

c = sugar cane   e = eddoes
p = sweet potatoes   b = black eye peas
y = yams   z = pigeon peas
x = corn (maize)   s = sorrel

sorrel) may be grown around the edge of the patch, but are seldom planted as a crop.

There seems to be no special policy adopted in the selection of the varieties of these "provision" crops to be planted. The rule appears to be the cultivation of whatever is easily available. The time for reaping varies according to the crop (see Calendar of Activities below).

Fertilizers — natural and/or artificial — are generally applied to the cane plants, but only in rare cases are they used on provisions. The majority of cultivators try to keep — either their own or borrowed — a cow or at least a donkey or possibly a sheep, goat, or pig to make pen manure. This compost is applied to the cane crop just before planting or in its early stages of growth, but always after the provision crops have been harvested. Generally, it is distributed over the field either in manure holes alongside the cane holes or is broadcast on the surface between the holes. Artificial fertilizers are, usually, applied at the beginning of the rainy season. These are obtained, mostly, from the sugar factories — from the merchants in Skeete's time — on credit, to be paid for when the crop is harvested. A calendar of activities is presented below (13, p. 12).

The planting of the sugar cane takes place usually in November. Cut-

CALENDAR OF PEASANT AGRICULTURAL
OPERATIONS IN BARBADOS

(1) Predominant System with Sugar Cane as the Main Crop

January ...... Harvesting roots including yams, sweet potatoes. Potash applied to plant cane.

February ..... Harvesting roots including yams, sweet potatoes. Start reaping sugar cane.

March .... Cane reaping in full swing.
April
May .... Cane reaping nearly completed by the end of the month.

June .... Preparing land and planting yams, sweet potatoes, corn, etc. Potash applied to ratoon cane. Reaping cassava.

July .... Continuing as in June. Sulphate of ammonia applied to cane with the advent of the rains. Planting cotton, peanuts, corn, cassava, etc.

August ...... Weeding and cultivating the annual crops.
September
October ...... Planting sugar cane through the yams. Reaping and planting sweet potatoes, corn, beans, peas, shallots.

November .... Main planting of sugar cane through the yams. Reaping of sweet potatoes, corn, etc. Planting cabbage, tomatoes, sweet potatoes, and vegetables generally.

December .... Reaping minor crops and planting vegetables.

tings are made from other plants and placed in the center of the cane holes — one or two per hole according to the desire and ability to obtain plants — in the middle of the other crops if they have not already been harvested (see Diagram 1). Where the provision crops have been delayed, at times the planting of canes is deferred until as late as January or even February. The quality of the planting material is highly variable. In the worst cases, old stumps, left over from the previous year, are used. Where possible, however, cultivators obtain — "through purchases or otherwise," to quote Skeete (27, p. 4) — good planting materials from the nearby plantations. Slips can also be obtained from the several experiment stations of the Department of Science and Agriculture. Relatively few small-scale cultivators, however, go directly to this source. Generally, the plantations obtain materials from the experiment stations, and several years later distribute them to the smallholders.

The provision crops — and some vegetables which at times are also planted in these patches — are generally harvested as they become ripe. An attempt is made to reap them as needed for consumption, but due to the fear of spoilage and theft, most individuals reap the entire crop. They use what they can and sell the excess — which frequently turns out to be most of the crop — to hawkers for cash that, according to my own observations, is often used to purchase the same kinds of produce from neighbors at a later period when the latter's crops are ripe. The hawkers take the produce into the city of Bridgetown where it is sold primarily to the members of the urban middle class.

When the time comes for harvesting the cane crop the smallholder usually hires labor — either to assist him or, as is often the case, to do the entire job. The cut canes are then hauled to the neighboring factory by freightermen who receive a price per ton that varies according to the distance between the plot and the factory. In recent years both the labor for cutting and loading the cane — the price being so much per ton — and the transportation for freighting it, is more and more being provided by the sugar factories. The details will be presented below.

The major distinction between Skeete's 1930 description and the observations made by the present writer over a generation later[8] is that today comparatively few plots of land are halved. That is, very few cultivators divide their plots in half, growing cane on each section in alternative years. The probable reasons are related, at least in part, to increased fragmentation of holdings so that the average parcels are now too small to be divided. But an even more important factor appears to be the improved technology of the past 25 years. There are two basic aspects to the improved technology: (1) better varieties of cane that permit more ratoons; and (2) greater use of fertilizers that

[8] Though made primarily in the Parish of St. George, most of the details of my observations were corroborated for other areas by the members of the extension staff of the Department of Science and Agriculture and others.

have a similar effect.[9] In addition, the general market situation and the specific relationship between small cultivators and the sugar factories (see below) leads the small proprietor to choose — whenever possible — not to take any land out of cane. Thus, the smallholder attempts to obtain as many years of production as possible from one planting, thereby ending the older pattern of replanting in alternate years.

Today, then, a field would be planted, let us say, in November to be reaped approximately 15 months later. When canes are first planted, therefore, one season of harvesting must be lost, since the new plants will not be ready until the second cutting season after the last crop has been reaped from the plot. During the time the young canes are developing, several crops of provisions can also be grown. Since the slips are placed in the center of the cane hole, the provision crops can be cultivated on the banks and cross-sections between holes (see Diagram 1). It is only after the canes begin to grow tall that the sides of the caneholes are cleared of other crops.

Following the harvest of the first planting, the stumps that remain after cutting are allowed to spring back to give a second crop or ratoon. Cane stumps will grow again — yielding decreasing sugar content and tonnage per acre, of course — until they are dug up. In the second year, then, a crop is reaped and the same in the third, fourth, fifth, and so forth. With ratoons no complete season is ever lost. Cultivators, therefore, try to get as many crops as possible before replanting. Not only is a season not lost, but ratoons require much less labor than do cane plants.

At times, some smallholders try to reap their last crop of ratoons at the beginning of the harvest or, as it is called locally, "crop" so that they can prepare the land and plant new canes — say, in March or April — that will be at least partially mature — but ripe enough to cut — by the end of the following crop. In this way there is no lost reaping season.

When the land is ratooned or when plants are rushed so as not to miss a season, provisions are still grown. Instead of having half the field devoted to this, however, the subsidiary crops are grown between the canes in the period between the harvest and the time the following season's canes are tall. Here the entire plot — which, we repeat, may be as little as a quarter of an acre or less — is worked as a unit, but still produces both cane and provision crops.

Sample income and expense summaries for experimental plots in various parts of the island are presented by Halcrow and Cave (13, p. 22) and summarized in Table 1. Though considerable inflation has occurred since the time of the survey, their conclusion that per acre profits are small is still true. In addition, as Skeete has pointed out, "There is a tendency, as the minimum size limit . . . is approached, for the average

---

[9] For an expanded analysis in which nine basic factors are presented for the increase in sugar yields in the last century, see Simon of Wythenshawe (25).

TABLE 1

Sample Income and Expense Summaries for Experimental
*Plots in Various Parts of the Island**

	YIELD (tons)	EXPENSES	RETURNS
		$	$
Christ Church Station:			
Sugar Cane —			
(i) Plant cane	17.5	92	160
(ii) 1st Ratoon	12.0	58	108
Yams	5.0	60	222
Potatoes & fodder	3.0	83	50
Average		73	135
St. Philip Station:			
Sugar Cane —			
(i) Plant cane	11.0	79	99
(ii) 1st Ratoon	14.0	71	126
Yams	1.5	68	100
Potatoes & fodder	8.0	60	113
Average		69	109
St. George Station:			
Sugar Cane —			
(i) Plant cane	44.0	236	396
(ii) 1st Ratoon	30.0	104	270
Yams	4.5	122	195
Potatoes & fodder	5.5	93	114
Average		139	244
St. Peter Station:			
Sugar Cane —			
(i) Plant cane	25.0	92	225
(ii) 1st Ratoon	7.0	46	63
Yams	2.25	57	120
Potatoes & fodder	10.0	73	161
Average		67	142
Average per Acre over all		$86.00	$158.00

* Source: Halcrow and Cave (13, p. 22).

standard of cultivation to be lower. The smaller the holding," he adds, "the less are the gross profits and quantity of food crops produced . . ." (27, p. 7). In spite of this, however, the system of sugar cane farming is practiced on even the smallest size holdings. To again quote Skeete for a generalization that is still true today: "The planting of sugar cane as the main crop persists down to the smallest farm in almost every district, and apart from a moderate or low yielding crop of sugar cane, on the average not more than a few small potatoes and a few handfuls of such other crops as beans, pigeon peas, and okras during the wet season are obtained from these holdings" (27, p. 7).

Why Practice Uneconomic Behavior?

Why then, it has been asked, do Barbadian smallholders continue with this inefficient, poorly rewarding practice? Why do not more individuals cultivate their tiny holdings, let us say, as market gardens as suggested by the experts of the Department of Science and Agriculture?[10]

Skeete, over a generation ago, presented one reason that is still verbalized by many Barbadians — both expert and layman — today:

> The fact must not be lost sight of that peasant farming in Barbados has only been established in comparatively recent years, that the peasant farmers have had no other agricultural training than that associated with the cultivation of sugar cane with its subsidiary crops already referred to. The peasant, like other classes of farmers on the Island, has acquired a "sugar cane sense" after nearly 300 years of sugar cane cultivation in Barbados. From the earliest days of his youth, he has heard about and learned to speak about "the crop," meaning the sugar cane crop or harvest, and has looked forward to the day when he could refer to his own "crop." This stage of peasant agriculture, although still persisting among the smaller and less educated proprietors, will pass with increasing knowledge of agriculture, and with new and extended markets (27, p. 13).

A "sugar cane sense," however, is a very questionable explanation. In addition, it is interesting to note that in spite of almost three decades of education — both formal (Barbados is generally acknowledged to have the best school system in the Caribbean) and informal (through the work of the Agriculture Extension staff) — not only has the system of sugar cane farming persisted, but it has, according to informants, increased to a point where more sugar and less food is being grown today than a generation ago at the time of Skeete's report.

Perhaps a better explanation for this apparently inefficient system of farming is to be found by examination of the island's productive enterprise. As mentioned above, the emancipated slaves were incorporated into the wage labor, market-exchange system of economic organization in the first half of the nineteenth century. Production and distribution of almost all the goods and services necessary for life was, and

---

[10] The advantages of market gardening and other systems of farming on smallholdings has been demonstrated by Jolly and others in experiments conducted at the Imperial College of Tropical Agriculture in Trinidad. See Jolly (16).

is today organized in the form of occupational positions or jobs that pay money income or wages, in return for the performance of specified behaviors or meeting of role expectations by those who occupy the positions. The money, of course, becomes the means of obtaining the other available goods and services. Barbadians, then, for more than 125 years have been, and still are, primarily wage laborers. First and foremost in their schedule of activities is the need to obtain a job; all else is secondary. Both Skeete and Halcrow and Cave were aware of this. As the latter state, ". . . more than 83 per cent of the peasants (smallholders with 1 to 10 acres) were only part-time cultivators. For holdings under one acre," which represents 83 per cent of the total of smallholdings, therefore they conclude, "it can be assumed that practically all the occupiers were part-time cultivators" (13, p. 7).

The Barbadian smallholder then is first off a wage earner whose behavior must be guided primarily by the demands of his employment. Overpopulation, however, has resulted in a condition of chronic unemployment and underemployment in the island (8). Most individuals, consequently, in order "to get by" must have several sources from which to earn income. The trick, so to speak, is to be able to move from one source of income to another in such a way that the requirements of all the jobs are satisfied. The average Barbadian, therefore, becomes a master at having "several things going" simultaneously. He also learns how to avoid having to be in two places at precisely the same time.

When the system of farming practiced on smallholdings is viewed within the context of the general economic and social life of the cultivators it begins to take on a new meaning. The Barbadian value system stresses the importance of social mobility. The means of achieving mobility are through the occupational system. Devotion to agriculture on a full-time basis, even if it is as profitable as, for example, Jolly (16) and the staff of the Department of Science and Agriculture believe it to be, means that the individual must give up his hopes and dreams of achievement and success. Becoming a full-time cultivator, in effect, means that the individual must retire from the battle for prestige, status, and success — the goals of the society. It is interesting to note in terms of this that with the exception of one individual, all of the full-time agriculturists that I met during my stay in Barbados were either elderly, lame, or otherwise incapacitated and, therefore, were unable to fill any of the normal range of employment categories.

The system of sugar cane farming as practiced by the vast majority of landholders, however, fits very well with the goals, values, aspirations, and occupational organization of Barbadian society. Sugar cane, in the system previously described, can be cultivated in addition to holding a full-time job or several part-time ones. Skeete recognized this when he wrote, ". . . sugar cane cultivated at the average standard attained by the Barbados peasant proprietor is a crop which needs but relatively little attention and is well suited, but not economically, to the grower whose time is otherwise employed" (27, p. 13). The price paid for the canes — no matter how little it may be — can be added to the income earned from other sources. It functions somewhat as an extra dividend, which, unlike wages, is paid in a lump sum.

In addition, as soon as an individual plants cane on a plot of land it becomes a negotiable security which he can use to obtain credit. Ownership of the land is not required. All that is necessary is that it be generally known that the individual in question has the right — in law or custom — to reap a crop from the property. Possession of a parcel of land with a cane crop on it is all that is usually called for in obtaining credit and cash advances. The sources of credit are the sugar factories which generally provide substantial advances to smallholders in return for the latters' promise to deliver their plants for processing when "the crop" begins. In 1956, for example, the factory near the village in which I worked had extended almost $50,000 worth of credit and cash advances to smallholders prior to the harvest.[11] This figure was considered not above normal and I was told that all of the other 20 or so factories on the island also extend substantial, but not such sizeable sums.

In the case for which I have detailed records, the credit and advances were given to individuals numbering in the thousands. The amounts varied from a few dollars to, in rare cases, in excess of $1,000. The creditors, at times, had as little as a ton or less of cane to be delivered in the crop. But in spite of this, they could present themselves periodically for small loans.

The bookkeeping is done by the factory staff and interest is not charged. At the beginning of the crop, agreement is reached by representatives of the factories, the plantations, and the government to pay a specified price per ton of cane delivered to the factory, subject to adjustment at the end of the harvest according to a previously agreed upon formula. Upon presenting a receipt indicating the delivery of canes to the factory, a credit is placed in the individual's account and he is paid the balance left after his advances are deducted. At this point he can obtain a further advance, if he so requires it, against the "preference" — the additional price per ton adjustment that is not calculated and paid until the November following the crop.

Obtaining credit on a sugar crop is a practice that goes back a considerable number of years in Barbadian history. The advantage of the custom to a wage earner with a piece of land is considerable. This is especially true on an island like Barbados where employment opportunities are so limited. In any emergency such as the loss of his job or during illness or if he has the need or just plain desire to make some

---

[11] This information was obtained from the manager of one of the plantations owned by the factory who, though not directly associated with the factory, kept all of the records concerning loans to smallholders.

additional purchase, the working man can obtain extra funds without any added hardship. His land — no matter how large or small — planted in sugar cane provides him with a security that can be converted into cash whenever needed.

In recent years, however, the factories have added other services besides credit, of which the smallholder can avail himself. Many owners of land are often so tied up with their occupational activities that they have difficulty finding time to perform the minimal labor required by the system of cultivation described above. Many persons, especially those who have had land in their family for several generations, have become moderately successful occupationally. In terms of the general insular value system, such upwardly mobile individuals are not expected to perform agricultural labor. The area in which my fieldwork was done, for example, was one of the oldest "freeholds" on the island. Most of the adult males, at the time of the research, were employed as skilled — by local standards — craftsmen in the construction field or held governmental posts such as policemen, teachers, and so on. According to local custom these individuals hired labor to work their land. Though the system of farming was the same as the one already discussed, the manual labor was performed by what may be termed as a professional agricultural worker. The landowner, however, often supervised the job in much the same manner the plantation owners, managers, and overseers supervised the work performed on their estates.

To this segment of the population, labor has become a problem. They repeatedly expressed concern over the difficulty they had in obtaining laborers. Moreover, they constantly complained about how little work the people they hired performed and how they were forced to "see after them" lest the worker would "give them nothing for his day's pay." Constant supervision of workers, however, impinged upon their own occupational activities, thereby presenting them with a dilemma. A solution is to be found in the traditional pattern of delegating the task of supervising the cultivation of the land to the womenfolk. The sugar factories, however, have come to provide an even better way out.

Today, in addition to providing credit to all individuals with a right to raise a crop on a piece of land, many of the sugar factories will also provide the necessary laborers and "see after" management of the property. A wage earner, then, if he has rights of possession to a parcel of land, can go to the nearby factory owner or manager[12] and arrange for the services of the plantation laborers and supervisor to work on his property. Workers will come at a scheduled time and do as much or

---

[12] Each factory has what may be considered a number of home plantations that supply it with canes. In most cases, the estates are owned by the same companies that own the factory. Though the administration is generally kept separate, the overlapping administrative personnel can control and coordinate the activities of each phase of the industry. Thus, the factories can make arrangements committing the use of the services of the labor force of the estates.

as little as they are instructed. At times they do everything, including preparing the ground, planting the slips, weeding and fertilizing the growing plants, cutting the ripe crop and transporting it to the factory. The property owner can simply go about his other business. If he needs extra cash he can obtain it from the factory. At the end of the crop he need only present himself to the person handling the accounts and receive the income from his property, which is the total price paid for his tonnage less the cost of labor, machinery, transportation, and the total of the advances he has taken.

In one case a school teacher who owned approximately one acre of land was leaving the island to study elsewhere for a year. Before departing he arranged with the factory representative to obtain all the labor necessary to cultivate and harvest his cane crop.[13] When he returned home the following year all he had to do was to visit the factory administrator and pick up his money. This is not to say that his net return could not have been higher if he had been at home to perform some of the labor or supervision. What is significant is that even though he was not on the island his land was earning income for him.

The additional services available from the sugar factories have created the unique situation presented at the beginning of this paper. An individual with rights of possession in a parcel of land has, therefore, an economic asset that can work for him — even without any activity on his part — and thereby earn income. Though he can increase his total return from the land by adding his own labor or managerial skills, he can, if he so wishes, choose to take his income without the performance of any tasks. In addition, his asset is highly negotiable in that it can be sold with ease or used as a security in obtaining credit. In function, then, the rights of possession in land are analogous to the ownership of stocks or bonds in our own economy. The Barbadian landholder, however, has a share not in a particular industry but rather in the entire economy of the island. His rights of possession, so to speak, function as a share in the insular economy that earns an income for him as long as he makes sure that sugar cane, the basic crop, is cultivated.

This situation, as indicated earlier, is somewhat unique. Rights of possession in land do not customarily function in this manner in agricultural societies. In Barbados, however, unlike most agricultural areas of the world, the cultivation of the land is a commercialized activity governed by the laws of supply and demand and the rules of the market. Wage labor and not subsistence production is, and for many years has been, the rule. The productive enterprise is organized in much the same manner as it is in the industrialized, "developed" societies of Western Europe and North America. Wage labor, a highly stratified occupational system, and what may be considered a commercialized money-oriented

---

[13] In this situation, no provisions were planted since there would be no way of his administering their sale in *absentia*.

set of values dominate economic activities. Production, which is for sale on the world market, is specialized and the entire economy is geared toward the growth of sugar. The strength of the total economy, in fact, can best be measured by the amount of sugar produced. National income, consequently, tends to vary directly with the size of the crop now that a stable price has been assured — at least until 1963. But as it is now constituted, very little, if any, growth is possible for the Barbadian economy. As long as she remains a one-crop, one-industry island, Barbados may best be considered to have an "overdeveloped" economy. The reason for this is that she has most of the organizational characteristics of a developed economy but is unable to expand specifically because her only natural resource, land upon which to grow sugar cane, has been exhausted. The addition of investment capital does not seem to increase productivity or, more specifically, to provide additional jobs for the overabundant population and still provide satisfactory returns to investors.[14] This situation is not new for the island. Barbados has probably had an overdeveloped economy for a century or more. Emigration and technological development, however, have helped to increase per acre and per capita returns in the past and, therefore, have made for some growth (25). But contemporary forecasters do not see this continuing in the future. The system of sugar cane farming by smallholders, however, has also made possible some additional expansion. This relationship to economic growth will provide the explanation for the contemporary situation in which the rights of possession in land function as the equivalent of the ownership of stock in the insular economy.

The Growth of the Sugar Industry in the Twentieth Century

At emancipation, as was pointed out earlier, all the land on the island was owned and cultivated by plantations of various sizes. There were very few, if any, smallholdings. Land, however, was extremely valuable and sought by the former slaves for reasons other than its cultivation.

[14] According to Lord Simon of Wythenshawe (25, p. 2), "Barbados can hardly be called an underdeveloped country. It has no resources, in form of land or minerals, which could be developed by applying capital to them." Beasley agrees with this but adds, "On the other hand, Barbados is not a 'developed' country in the ordinary sense" (5, p. 6). His reasons relate specifically to the colonial status of the island and the management of commercial and monetary activities from abroad. He, therefore, prefers neither the designation underdeveloped nor developed. He does, however, agree that, "its basic resources are fairly fully exploited and that there is no urgent call for capital equipment to expand primary production. . . ." In addition, "Savings derived from the earnings or profits of the inhabitants disappear for the most part into securities abroad. . . ." The reason for this, I suggest, is that the capital cannot be invested locally at a profit anywhere near what it can earn abroad. Barbados, then, is neither underdeveloped nor developed. It is overdeveloped, a designation to my knowledge not applied to any other economy thus far. As stated by Lord Simon "Barbados is perhaps unique among the countries of the world in having a permanently limited income and a rapidly increasing population" (25, p. 26).

The so-called "located labor law" severely restricted the movement and activities of the freedmen (see 14 for details). The only escape from located labor was the possession of land (see 12). Though the price was exorbitant in terms of local earning ability — £100 per acre for most of the nineteenth and early twentieth centuries — many former slaves had managed to purchase holdings.

In 1840, according to Schomburgk (23, p. 153) there were 1,874 proprietors on the island. Of these, 940 had holdings in excess of ten acres — that is, they could be considered plantations. Of the remaining 938 proprietors, more than 83 per cent held less than five acres. Within two decades, however, this total of 780 small proprietors with five acres or less had increased to more than 3,500 (24, p. 39). In the following century the number expanded almost tenfold, according to the figures presented earlier (see page 624).

At the beginning, just as today, the Barbadian smallholder was primarily a wage earner. The principal function of his land was that it freed him from the constraints of the located labor laws which existed in Barbados until the last World War. In general, however, the ownership of land became a prerequisite to social mobility and movement up the occupational ladder. This general condition also survived until the war (11).

In the period immediately following emancipation the estates on the island continued to produce sugar. The techniques of production used in the mid-nineteenth century, however, differed little from those used a century or so before. As late as 1884, for example, most muscovado estates still employed the open pan system described by Pere Lobat 150 years earlier. The inefficiency of the operation can be seen from the fact that the first grinding process of the single three-roller mill extracted only approximately 50 to 60 per cent of the weight of the cane in juice though 87 per cent of the plant could be obtained in the liquid by more efficient techniques (4). Furthermore, the two major phases of the sugar industry — cultivation and processing of cane into sugar — were both handled by every estate as they had been traditionally. Each plantation, no matter how large or small, had a windmill and a set of works. In a competitive market this was a rather inefficient way of doing things. Operating a complete set of works to produce 15 to 20 hogsheads of sugar raised the unit cost of the product considerably since the equipment for manufacturing sugar was expensive.

At this time steam power was being introduced into Barbados as a more efficient means of operating sugar mills. In some instances, however, the steam engines were not sufficiently powerful for the mills and this reduced their efficiency and the rate at which steam replaced wind as the source of power. In 1862, for example, out of 500 estates with mills, only 30 mills were operated by steam. Thirty-five years later, in 1897, the number had increased to only 90 (4, p. 63). The big advantage of steam was its consistency. Windmills provided a cheap source of power, but a sudden calm, such as occurred in March 1892, reduced all production to a snail's pace. The steam engine, however, though more efficient and reliable, spread slowly for two reasons. In the first place, it was expensive and the planters, especially as hard times set in as a result of the competition from the beet sugar industry later in the century, were faced with a lack of capital. The plantations in Barbados were comparatively small, as plantations go, and there was no tendency in the direction of large companies, either local or foreign, accumulating extensive holdings. Individual plantation owners with 200–300 acres could not afford the machinery needed to convert their mills. In addition to the initial expense, fuel presented a problem since there were no local sources of supply. The only means of rationalizing the entire industry was in the development of central factories.

In the 1840's Barbadians began to discuss the possible advantages to be derived from the separation of the cultivation of the cane from its manufacture into sugar. As outlined by Schomburgk:

> The manufacturing department on a sugar-estate is connected with very heavy expenses, and it would prove more to the advantage of the cultivator if he could sell his canes, and leave the manufacturing to those who would devote their whole attention to the means of extracting the largest quantity and the best quality of sugar out of the raw material. The central manufactories (sic) in Guadaloupe and Martinique in the West Indies, and in Bourbon in the Indian Ocean, have realized every expectation; and a company has just been formed . . . , to undertake the separate manufacture of sugar in central establishments, on principles similar to those adopted in the "Usines Centrales" in Guadaloupe (23, p. 527).

The creation of central factories in Barbados presented a means of increasing the efficiency of the total economy. By 1913, however, very little progress had been made in this direction. According to Sinckler (26) almost every plantation still had its own set of works — some run by steam but most by wind — for manufacturing sugar. Even though steam power was gradually replacing wind power each estate still had its own complete factory.

The reasons for the reluctance to establish this division of activities that would increase the efficiency of the entire economy are many. Land in Barbados, in contrast with the English method of concentrating it, was held in widely scattered holdings. It had always been expensive and therefore it was difficult, if not impossible, to acquire enough contiguous tracts to support a large mill at a price within the means of any individual or family. Since the vast majority of estates were owned by individuals and their market price prohibited the organization of a company to purchase sufficient acreage to operate a central factory, the only alternative was cooperation on the part of the planters. Such cooperation by the estate owners, however, presented several problems. In the first place, it would have required a "charge on their estates as security for loans raised and mortgages, attorneys and managers were opposed to a scheme which, it was considered would adversely effect their positions" (4, p. 83). Even with agreement on this, however, it would have been difficult to obtain a consensus favorable to supporting a central factory in any one block of estates of sufficient area to maintain it. Cooperation is not a virtue of the Barbadian plantation owner. In addition to affecting his financial position, the cooperative venture would have meant that the profits would have to be shared with others. Furthermore, each planter was for the creation of a central factory if *his* mill could be expanded to become the center of production for his area. The difficulty appeared when it was suggested that someone else might get the plum. Thus, each refused to let the next gain the advantage and, therefore, each continued to grind his own cane in his own small mill. Thus, to this day, there are still more factories on the island than are needed for the sake of economic production.[15]

In spite of the difficulties, however, something approximating central factories and the separation of cultivation and manufacture did take place on the island beginning in the early part of the present century and continuing up to today. The conditions that made at least minimal centralization possible, though, were not at the time advantageous to the islanders. Barbados had prospered for several decades following the termination of slavery. For a while it appeared that good times would go on indefinitely, for sugar continued to bring good prices on the world market. Toward the end of the last century, however, Barbadian sugars began to lose their traditional market. The United Kingdom had continued to import West Indian sugar in the post-emancipation period. Prices tended to remain high and Barbados was able to maintain a competitive advantage since labor and other costs were low. With the development of the beet sugar industry in Europe and the subsidies of the various governments to stimulate its export, however, "West Indian producers of sugar from 1876 onwards were faced with increasing competition from raw beet sugar which came into the United Kingdom

---

[15] This is true though the number has been reduced to approximately 20. But as the authors of the *Ten Year Development Plan for Barbados, 1946–56* stated, "under modern conditions of extraction the number of factories now operating in the Island is not the most economic organization for the present output. There is no doubt that in the long run the Island would be better served by fewer but bigger and, more efficient factories. The most obvious remedy for this state of affairs would be a scheme of consolidation of factories but there are a number of serious obstacles in the path of such a scheme. One is that sugar machinery is expensive and it would require a large amount of new capital, the interest of which would tend to increase costs of production, or at any rate to offset the benefits to be derived from the more efficient methods of production. Another is that many of the factories are old established family concerns the proprietors of which have operated them for generations and are naturally very reluctant to amalgamate with larger concerns and thus lose their individuality and special personal interest."

at prices below any hitherto experienced, and which quickly prejudiced the refiners of soft moist sugar in favor of beet sugar" (4, p. 41). By the end of the century the cheaper beet sugar had all but driven the producers of cane out of the market. Hard times followed in Barbados.

Beginning at the end of the nineteenth century and continuing up to the last World War, Barbados experienced continual difficulty that was accentuated by a series of periodic depressions that coincided with the periods of economic decline in the great nations of Europe and North America. As a result of the depressions, many plantations went bankrupt. When relative prosperity returned for at least brief periods — such as the time during World War I when beet sugar sources were inaccessible to the United Kingdom and the price of West Indian sugars soared — energetic and speculative individuals were able to acquire plantations whose former owners had gone bankrupt. Thus, sizeable holdings of property were accumulated by either individuals or families. At the beginning each estate still operated its own mill. But soon the equipment from the several works was brought together at a convenient location and, with the assistance of borrowed capital, larger steam driven factories began to appear. It was soon recognized by the factory owner that production costs could be reduced considerably by expanding the growing factories even further. A shortage of land, however, was still the major drawback. At times agreements were reached with the owners of smaller plantations who could not make ends meet if they continued to maintain their own sugar mills. The factories offered to pay cash for the cane plants and assume the risk of selling the manufactured product. In other cases, neighboring planters were offered shares in the factory, which was then set up as a limited liability company independent of the plantations. The former sole owner of the factory remained as the principal and controlling stockholder in the new company, as well as the outright owner of a number of the plantations that supplied the mill. The factory company then paid him in cash for his plants just as it did the other planters. But still sufficient land could not be obtained to permit the really efficient expansion of the factories.

All this time the owners of small plots had been cultivating sugar cane and subsidiary crops in much the manner described above. When the cane plants were ripe, however, by contrast with the patterns described, they were taken to the nearby mill where they were ground into sugar and molasses. In payment the mill owner took 25 per cent of the sugar obtained from the smallholder's plants. The landowner then, was left with three-fourths of the sugar and the molasses. To obtain any revenue, however, he then was obliged to transport his sugar to the main city of Bridgetown and sell it to a merchant. This was a burdensome and time-consuming activity that did not fit with the other activities performed by the smallholder. It is interesting to note, therefore, that for a considerable period of time during the early years of the twentieth century — especially during periods of depression — sugar cane did have a significant rival as the principal crop produced by the islanders. "Nearly every landowner in Barbados," wrote McLellan, "cultivated potatoes, . . . no sweet potatoes," he concluded, "no Barbados" (21, p. 52).

His description of the organization of sweet potato cultivation and distribution elaborates upon the importance of the crop at the time in which he wrote:

> Tons upon tons (of potatoes) were there, and a whole industry seemed concerned in sending prices down to zero with a stupendous over-supply. The output is eminently an over-supply and that is why nearly all the year round schooners freighted with the vegetable sail out of Carlisle Bay. Along the great trunk roads which approach Bridgetown little box-carts hauled by donkeys, big box-carts hauled by mules, and other kinds of carts and hybrid gigs laden with potatoes stream in disorderly procession. Up hill, down dale they go, all in their courses verging to the great central market for export and distribution for town consumption (21, p. 50).

Though much of the over-supply was produced by the plantations — who, at times, were in desperate need of the additional revenue — the organization of the marketing arrangements sheds considerable light on the behavior of the small cultivator. While sugar had to be processed and carried to town to be sold, potatoes were convertible into cash while still in the ground. The distribution of the root crop was conducted by a class of highly astute hawkers and speculators. These individuals, who were invariably of African origin and in most cases the children or grandchildren of slaves, would go from field to field as the potatoes ripened. There they would purchase the crop. According to informants who had spent most of their lifetime in the business, there were two methods employed to purchase the staple. The preferred means was "by the hole." Since all the land in Barbados was cultivated in cane holes — the potatoes were grown on the bank of the hole — a price was paid by the speculator for each hole. Then the speculator, assisted invariably by the members of his family, would dig the plants from the ground. As the number of pounds of potatoes varied from hole to hole and from field to field, the speculators, to earn a profit, of necessity had to know prices, market conditions, and the qualities of various soils. Where either of the parties preferred, the crop could be sold at an agreed upon price per pound. Here, though each party was more sure of his possible profits, the landowner was at a disadvantage because he had to dig the potatoes.

The Barbadian small cultivator, then, was able to grow potatoes on his land and receive a sum of money when the crop was ripe. Also, he could either delegate the task of supervising the digging or do it in his spare time. Once the price per hole had been agreed upon, the speculator assumed all the responsibility and the associated work needed to market the crop. The system for distributing a crop of potatoes then, for a period of time, was better adapted to the life of the wage-earning smallholder than was the system of converting sugar cane into currency. Consequently, it is not surprising that both informants and observers of the times report the importance of sweet potatoes in the Barbadian economy.

As the newly created steam mills expanded, however, there were developments which resulted in the deposition of potatoes, and for that matter, all other crops, as a serious threat to sugar cane as *the crop* to be cultivated on all holdings, large and small.

Several plantations acquired by a single owner during hard times had provided the basis for the development of larger factories that could specialize in the manufacture of the sugar and thereby become more efficient. Some additional canes, necessary to run an expanding factory at peak conditions, were obtained from other small estates as the result of negotiations and advantageous offers to their owners. When no more plantations could be brought under the influence of the expanding factory, it appeared that a limit in size and efficiency of production had been reached. Then, however, a new practice began. Several far-sighted individuals realized that considerable acreage had been and was being sold to "peasant proprietors" in one- and two-acre lots. This practice, which began immediately after emancipation, was accentuated in the first two decades of the twentieth century. Many persons who had participated in the great emigrations to Trinidad and Demerara and more significantly to Panama (to work on the canal) returned to the island with sufficient wealth to purchase land at figures in excess of the already high market rates that prevailed. These individuals were not farmers. But they did cultivate the land, and in accordance with the traditional practices on the island, they did grow at least some sugar cane.

A growing factory could increase its capacity if it could be assured of the cane plants of a large number of small landholders. The extra acreage needed to utilize at least some of its excess capacity could be obtained from the "peasants" if the latter could be induced to cultivate canes and to send them to the specific factory.

In the second decade of the present century, according to my informants, the owner of the factory referred to above — which today is one of the largest on the island — initiated the hitherto untried practice of paying smallholders for their plants in cash, rather than renting them use of his factory equipment for a percentage of the sugar produced.

The advantage to the smallholder was immediate. He no longer was obliged to spend the time and energy required to transport his canes to the factory and the processed sugar and molasses home and then into the city to be sold to the merchant. Now all he had to do was to deliver his plants to the mill and he would receive some money. Since all the other responsibilities were now assumed by the factory, the smallholder could quickly return to his occupational pursuits — with some extra cash in his pockets.

The advantage to the factory was that it received additional cane — that could not be obtained elsewhere — and, therefore, it could expand and make more sugar efficiently. In the same factory referred to above, for example, in the years 1932 to 1935, an average of a little less than 50,000 tons of cane were ground per year. Of this, approximately 69 per cent was supplied by the home plantations. Eight outside plantations added another 18 per cent, while the remaining 13 per cent was obtained from smallholders. Small proprietors, then, added an average of almost 6,600 tons of cane to total production each year.

Other expanding factories soon recognized the advantage to be derived from "wooing" peasant canes. Within a few years after the custom of paying cash for canes to smallholders was introduced, almost every factory on the island was practicing it. At the beginning the price paid per ton was low and at times smallholders complained of collusion on the part of all the factory owners in their area. The competition between the expanding factories for this new source of canes — which, to the total economy, was the equivalent of finding additional land — was, however, so intense that the hard bargaining factory owners tended to offer a price to small cultivators that was generally in line with market conditions. The extent of this competition is to be seen in the relationship established between factory owner and the smallholders of his area. The patronage system, so well known in the areas of the world dominated by large plantations, assumed a specific form. The factory owner became the patron, or "godfather," to use the local term, for most of the landowners in his area. The latter would turn to him for assistance with most of their problems, which were generally confined to questions of the legal implications of transactions involving land, obtaining credit to pay liens on land or to pay for other large irregular expenditures, or obtaining assistance in finding jobs for their children. The numerous individuals assisted at one time or another by the factory owner assumed a feeling of loyalty and obligation and repaid him in the only way they knew how: by sending their canes to his factory.

The Barbadian sugar industry has expanded considerably in the last century. Improved varieties of plants and other technological innovations have seen total production increase by approximately 300 per cent during the period — from 43,000 tons of sugar per year in 1852 to a crop in excess of 200,000 tons in 1957 — in spite of an inexpandable supply of land. In addition, the sugar factories have grown from tiny mills of limited capacity to large, modern, efficient units. A factor that made this development possible, we submit, was the incorporation of smallholdings into the industry in the manner described above. In the 15-year period (1940–1955) for which records are available smallholders contributed an average of 14 per cent of the total annual crop (13, p. 13).

The larger factories, such as the one discussed above, however, generally obtained more than 14 per cent from smallholders. In the 1957 crop, for example, the factory just mentioned had expanded so that it processed slightly more than 140,000 tons of cane. Of these, a little more than half (75,000 tons) came from the home estates. The remainder were purchased from outside estates and from smallholders. More than 21 per cent, in excess of 30,000 tons of cane, were obtained from small-holders who supplied almost as many canes as the outside estates. These figures seem sufficient to justify economically the $50,000 paid in advances and the bookkeeping expenses incurred by the factory.

Summary and Conclusions

In conclusion, the system of sugar cane farming by smallholders in Barbados, in which we have likened the rights of possession in land to the ownership of stock in the island's economy, is an outgrowth of attempts to rationalize production in the sugar industry within a context of economic overdevelopment. Modernization in the growth and processing of sugar, which has remained the economic mainstay of the island, as it was at the height of the colonial period, required the creation of central factories. The development of the latter, however, was retarded because sufficient land could not be accumulated by any individual or group to supply a large modern mill with canes. All the land on the island has been owned and has produced income for several hundred years. At emancipation the plantations were not abandoned; they continued to operate in spite of the change, as profit-making concerns. The market value of land tended to remain high. Thus, central factories, and even steam-driven machinery, were slow to make their appearance on the island.

The economic decline that followed the emergence of beet sugar as a more efficient competitor for traditional markets set the stage for the appearance of true sugar factories in Barbados. During periods of relatively good times some individuals succeeded in enlarging their holdings. Around these groups of estates under a single owner were established larger factories that continued to grow in size as other estates were induced to supply them with canes. Administrative reorganization soon established these as developing central factories. There were, however, more factories expanding and modernizing than were needed on the island. Competition soon developed between factories for sources of canes.

Within this historical context the system of sugar cane farming on smallholdings took root. The 18,000 acres of small plots represented a significant source from which expanding factories might obtain additional canes, that is, if the proprietors of the land could be induced to continue growing sugar cane. The inducements offered by the factories constitute the essentials of the system described above. The successful establishment of the system also is related to the occupational organization of the island's productive enterprise. Individuals obtain provender in the form of wages earned at a job. The arrangements that developed were adaptive and functional for the wage-earning landowners of the island. Therefore, though the system appears uneconomic and disfunctional to agricultural experts who view it in the abstract, it appears that in the absence of gross changes in the Barbadian economy — that do not seem imminent — the system of sugar cane farming, with rights of possession in land functioning as the equivalent of the ownership of stock in the total economy, will continue to thrive rather than change in the direction suggested by the agricultural experts.

The system of farming being diffused from western Europe and North American then, is being resisted in Barbados. The tradition of sugar-cane farming that developed on the island is retained because it is an apparently satisfactory solution to the demands of the local situation.

This system, however, is in fact a modification, or variation of the very pattern being diffused. The island of Barbados was settled originally by colonists from Great Britain. The insular socio-cultural tradition was the same as that of the first great industrial power. Barbadian institutions, therefore, may be characterized as "modern" or "developed." But, since the island's resource base has been exhausted, her economy may best be characterized today as being overdeveloped. Hence institutional adjustments were required, and the system of land use and sugar-cane farming described above developed.

As a final point, we may note that while the structural-functional emphasis of contemporary sociology can benefit from the infusion of historical and developmental thinking, the study of growth, evolution, and development can also profit from an awareness of the structural-functional orientation.

BIBLIOGRAPHY

1. *A Ten Year Development Plan for Barbados 1946–1956.* Bridgetown, Barbados: The Advocate Co., Ltd., n.d.

2. *Annual Report of the Department of Science and Agriculture 1954–1955.* Bridgetown, Barbados: The Advocate Co., Ltd., 1955.

3. "Barbados — Present and Future," *West Indian Economist*, Vol. III, No. 1 (1960), pp. 15–21.

4. Beachy, R. W. *The British West Indies Sugar Industry in the Late 19th Century.* Oxford: Basil Blackwell, 1957.

5. Beasley, C. G. *A Fiscal Survey of Barbados.* Bridgetown, Barbados: Cole's Printery, 1952.

6. Bethel, Jeanette. "A National Accounts Study of the Economy of Barbados," *Social and Economic Studies*, Vol. 9, No. 2 (Special Number 1960).

7. Bonnett, R. L. "The National Income and National Accounts of Barbados," *Social and Economic Studies*, Vol. 5, No. 3 (1956), pp. 213–260.

8. Cumper, G. E. "Employment in Barbados," *Social and Economic Studies*, Vol. 8, No. 2 (1959), pp. 105–146.

9. Foster, C. B. *The Yield of Sugar Cane in Barbados in 1956*. Bulletin No. 24 (New Series) of the Department of Science and Agriculture. Bridgetown, Barbados: The Advocate Co., Ltd., 1956.

10. Greenberg, Joseph H. *Essays in Linguistics*. Chicago: University of Chicago Press, 1957.

11. Greenfield, Sidney M. "Family Organization in Barbados," Unpublished Ph.D. thesis, Columbia University, New York, 1959.

12. Greenfield, Sidney M. "Land Tenure and Transmission in Rural Barbados," *Anthropological Quarterly*, Vol. 33, No. 4 (1960), pp. 165–176.

13. Halcrow, M., and J. M. Cave. "Peasant Agriculture in Barbados," Bulletin No. 11 (New Series) of the Department of Science and Agriculture. Bridgetown, Barbados: The Advocate Co., Ltd., 1947.

14. Hamilton, Bruce. *Barbados and the Confederation Question 1871–1885*. London: Crown Agents for Oversea Governments and Administrators, 1956.

15. Hoselitz, Bert F. "Advanced and Underdeveloped Countries: A Study in Developing Contrasts." Unpublished paper, n.d.

16. Jolly, A. L. "Small-Scale Farm Management Problems," *Tropical Agriculture*, Vol. 32, No. 2 (1955), pp. 80–87.

17. Kerr, Clark, John T. Dunlop, F. H. Harbison, and Charles A. Meyers. *Industrialism and Industrial Man: The Problems of Labor and Management in Economic Growth*. Cambridge: Harvard University Press, 1960.

18. Lamming, George. *In the Castle of My Skin*. New York: McGraw-Hill Book Co., 1953.

19. Levine, Solomon B. *Industrial Relations in Postwar Japan*. Urbana, Ill.: University of Illinois Press, 1958.

20. Lowenthal, David. "The Population of Barbados," *Social and Economic Studies*, Vol. 6, No. 4 (1957), pp. 445–501.

21. McLellan, George. *Some Phases of Barbados Life*. Demerara: The Argosy Co., Ltd., 1909.

22. Roberts, G. W. "Emigration from Barbados," *Social and Economic Studies*, Vol. 4, No. 3 (1955), pp. 245–288.

23. Schomburgk, Sir Robert. *The History of Barbados*. London: Longman, Grown, Green and Longman, 1848.

24. Sewell, William G. *The Ordeal of Free Labor in the British West Indies*. New York: Harper and Bros., 1859.

25. Simon of Wythenshawe, Lord. *Population and Resources of Barbados*. Bloomcroft: Didsbury, 1954.

26. Sinckler, E. Goulburn. *Handbook of Barbados.* London: Duckworth & Co., 1913.

27. Skeete, C. C. *The Condition of Peasant Agriculture in Barbados.* Bridgetown, Barbados: The Advocate Co., Ltd., 1930.

28. Slotkin, James S. *From Field to Factory.* Glencoe, Ill.: The Free Press, 1960.

29. Starkey, Otis P. *The Economic Geography of Barbados.* New York: Columbia University Press, 1939.

30. Steward, Julian H. "Evolution and Process," in A. L. Kroeber (ed.), *Anthropology Today.* Chicago: University of Chicago Press, 1953.

31. White, Leslie A. *The Science of Culture: A Study of Man and Civilization.* New York: Farrar, Straus, 1949.

25

Nathan Rosenberg

Neglected Dimensions in the

Analysis of Economic Change

The purpose of this chapter is essentially exploratory. Its central analytical focus will be upon certain dimensions of the process of economic development which are, as yet, only very imperfectly understood. It is hoped that the formulation presented below will encourage students of disciplines outside economics to undertake research which may, eventually, make an important contribution to our understanding of what economic growth is all about.

I

A convenient starting point will be to refer to the results of some recent research which has attempted to quantify the contributions of various factors to American economic growth during the past 90 years or so. Conventional economic theory suggests that the output of the economy at any point in time is a function of factor inputs and that, therefore, it ought to be possible to relate *changes* in output over time to systematic changes in factor inputs. An important segment of economic theory is devoted to exploring the relationships between variations in inputs and the associated variations in outputs — these relationships being summarized in the term "production function."

A plausible inference of this approach is that one can explain economic growth as resulting from an acceleration in the economy's rate of capital formation. According to this view, the rise in human productivity

651

which is a central aspect of the development process is attributable to an increase in the rate at which the economy makes additions to its capital stock, that is to say, that the rise in output per man is essentially a function of a "capital-deepening" process. One of the most widely popularized theories of the "take-off" into economic growth in fact identifies this take-off with a sudden rise in the rate of saving and net capital formation (32).

The results of a recent study by Moses Abramovitz, however, raise serious questions concerning the adequacy of such an approach. Abramovitz set out to determine how much of the rise in per capita incomes in the United States between the decades 1869–78 and 1944–53 could be attributed to changes in the capital and labor inputs, as these inputs are conventionally defined and measured. Although his technique was necessarily based on some rather heroic simplifying assumptions, his results were nevertheless startling. It appears that changes in capital and labor inputs can account for only a very small fraction of the quadrupling of per capita incomes which took place during the period examined. During a period in which output per capita increased four times over the base decade, a weighted index of capital and labor inputs per capita rose by only 14 per cent (1, p. 11).[1] If we look upon economic growth, then, as a mere piling up of additional factor inputs, we have scarcely made a dent in the magnitude of the rise in per capita incomes. As Abramovitz so aptly puts it, what his calculations provide is a measure of our ignorance, which is large indeed.

The startling nature of these results has triggered numerous attempts to measure the growth in output which can be attributed to technological change, i.e., to *shifts* in the production functions, as opposed to mere movements along an existing production function. This constitutes a significant and long-overdue change in the direction of analytical effort, since economists, with few exceptions, have long tended either to exclude technological change from their theoretical work or to treat it as a purely exogenous variable.

The deficiencies of the conventional approach to economic growth which are so effectively highlighted by the Abramovitz study bring us to the central problems posed in this chapter. The economy's output may be raised not only by increasing the supply of inputs (movements along an existing production function) or by technological change (shifts in the production function) but also by numerous kinds of alterations in the *qualities* of the inputs of a sort which typically escape the scrutiny of the economic theorist.[2] It is apparent that economic development

---

[1] Broadly similar results were reached, for a different time period and employing a different technique, by Robert Solow (40).

[2] It is possible, of course, to *define* technological change in such a manner as to include all alterations in the relationship between inputs and outputs, but it is difficult to see what would be gained thereby. Definitions ought to assist in the clarifica-

is associated with important qualitative changes in the human agent as a factor of production. These improvements take such forms as changes in knowledge, technical skills, organizational and managerial abilities, levels of economic aspiration, responsiveness to economic incentives, and capacity to undertake and to adapt to innovation. The nature of the mechanisms by which these alterations take place is as yet only very imperfectly understood.

It is suggested here that a major neglected source of these improvements has derived from participation in economic activity itself. That is, the quality of the human agent as a factor of production is decisively affected in a variety of ways by the nature of his production and consumption[3] activities, which in turn appear to change in fairly systematic fashion as a result of economic development itself. The manner in which different patterns of economic activity (including both production and consumption) affect the human agent in any time period t may be of critical importance in determining the output of the economy in subsequent time periods $t_{+1}, t_{+2}, t_{...n}$.

These feedback[4] phenomena upon the human agent have been neglected in part because of the long disinterest of the economist with questions dealing with economic growth and his preoccupation with problems of an essentially short-run nature. From the time of the so-called "marginal revolution" of the 1870's until recent years the central tradition in economics has been primarily concerned with problems revolving around the conditions of optimum allocation of a fixed stock of resources.[5] As Jevons stated it in 1871: "The problem of Economics may, as it seems to me, be stated thus: — Given, a certain population, with various needs and powers of production, in possession of certain lands and other sources of material: required, the mode of employing their labour which will maximise the utility of the produce" (11, p. 267).

It is not our purpose here to minimize the importance of the problem of maximization of output from a fixed stock of resources which is, of course, fundamental. The point is, rather, that when we turn our attention to the problem of the *growth* of output over time, we are compelled to consider new problems of a sort not illuminated by static analysis.

---

tion and classification of phenomena, whereas such a definition would serve to blur and obscure important differences in the sources of productivity change, and implications drawn from such a definition could never be disproved.

[3] We should include, as part of this consumption, an increase in the availability of leisure time which, historically, has been one of the major "outputs" of a successfully developing economy. This has been one of the most important factors which has transformed the whole pattern of life in high-income countries.

[4] In this chapter we use the term "feedback" to refer to any process whereby the future quality of the human agent as a factor input is altered as a result of current participation in economic activity.

[5] Even where it dealt with questions of growth this tradition was wedded to the point of view — already discussed — that the process of growth can be explained in terms of changes in the supplies of homogeneous capital and labor inputs.

Economic growth is, in many important respects, a learning process, a process whereby the human factor acquires new skills, aptitudes, capabilities, and aspirations. And the pattern of resource use which may maximize output from a given stock of resources may or may not generate the qualitative changes in the human agent which are most conducive to the growth of output in subsequent time periods.

Neo-classical economics fails to capture much of the explanation for the growth in productivity because of the failure to consider a variety of feedback mechanisms. We fail to consider, for example, the impact upon productivity of certain kinds of economic activities as opposed to others — such as manufacturing versus agriculture. Different kinds of economic activities have different kinds of effects upon the productivity of the human agent. Moreover, we regard the household, as a unit of ultimate consumption, with excessive sanctity, and thereby fail to raise the question of how different consumption patterns (including leisure-time activities) within the household react upon its members in their capacities as (present or future) producers. Posing questions of feedback in this fashion opens the door wide to the ministrations of the sociologist, and suggests a possible fruitful area of interdisciplinary research.

The theory of international trade centering upon the theory of comparative advantage is subject to the same strictures as the comparative statics of neo-classical economics, of which it is indeed merely a special case. This theory demonstrates how, given a fixed factor endowment in each country, total world output at any time is maximized through regional specialization and trade. A previously closed economy which is opened up to trade will undertake to re-allocate its resources between production for domestic purposes and for export purposes in a manner based upon differences in initial factor endowment and therefore relative costs and prices. It is at least conceivable that the reluctance of many countries to conform to the role of primary product exporters, which the theory of comparative advantage frequently appears to impose on them, may reflect an intuitive perception that such activities fail to generate the secondary feedback effects conducive to economic growth (25; 26).

II

The role of feedbacks from economic activity in determining the future growth of the economy was a problem to which the classical economists attached great importance. They were very much concerned with the individual's role in productive activity and the manner in which such activity created pressures and inducements which in turn formed his character, led to the acquisition of skills and inventive ability, created a system of values, determined his relative preferences for work and leisure, and so on. A thorough examination of this embryonic economic sociology is eminently worth undertaking, but would reach monographic length, and cannot be attempted here. Some brief references, primarily to the works of David Hume and Adam Smith, must suffice to give some indication of the content and direction of this analysis.

The early classical economists — especially Hume and Smith — were very much interested in the process of economic evolution. In particular, they were concerned with the manner in which a predominantly agrarian society transforms itself into one where commerce and industry flourish. Both agreed that there were inherent limits to the development of an agricultural economy — especially one dominated by a large landowning class — and that a predominantly agricultural economy was likely to remain a backward and stagnant one. Hume and Smith were agreed that men possess a certain predisposition to indolence[6] and that an agricultural society does not furnish sufficient motive to overcome this indolence. As Hume states:

> Where manufactures and mechanic arts are not cultivated, the bulk of the people must apply themselves to agriculture; and if their skill and industry encrease, there must arise a great superfluity from their labour beyond what suffices to maintain them. They have no temptation, therefore, to encrease their skill and industry; since they cannot exchange their superfluity for any commodities, which may serve either to that pleasure or vanity. A habit of indolence naturally prevails. The greater part of the land lies uncultivated. What is cultivated, yields not its utmost for want of skill and assiduity in the farmers (10, p. 10).

Not only do indolence and lethargy prevail in such a society in general; the habits and manners of the class of large landed proprietors which frequently dominates such a society are such that the potential economic surplus which might be devoted to productive investment is squandered in a display of idle dissipation and profligacy.

> . . . as the spending of a settled revenue is a way of life entirely without occupation; men have so much need of somewhat to fix and engage them, that pleasures, such as they are, will be the pursuit of the greater part of the landholders, and the prodigals among them will always be more numerous than the misers. In a state, therefore, where there is nothing but a landed interest, as there is little frugality, the borrowers must be very numerous, and the rate of interest must hold proportion to it. The difference depends not on the quantity of money, but on the habits and manners which prevail (10, p. 50).[7]

[6] Indolence is not, however, an inborn human trait. As Rotwein points out in his valuable introduction, Hume regards indolence and the pursuit of "the pleasures of idleness" as a symptom of frustration (10, pp. 48–49).

[7] Smith's position is the same. "In a country which has neither foreign commerce, nor any of the finer manufactures, a great proprietor, having nothing for which he can exchange the greater part of the produce of his lands which is over and above the maintenance of the cultivators, consumes the whole in rustic hospitality at home" (Smith 38, p. 385). Smith also remarks on the pernicious influence of court society

Rental incomes in a predominantly agricultural society are squandered on the maintenance of a large class of footmen and retainers, quite simply, because alternative forms of goods are, in large measure, not available (17, p. 227).

While an agricultural society without a growing commercial sector will be merely one where stagnation is self-perpetuating, the growth of a commercial and industrial sector is likely to generate numerous positive feedbacks conducive to continued growth. Not the least of these is the capacity and inducement to introduce progressive methods into agriculture itself. "When a nation abounds in manufactures and mechanic arts, the proprietors of land, as well as the farmers, study agriculture as a science, and redouble their industry and attention" (10, p. 11, p. 22).[8]

More generally, the growth of commerce and industry introduces the public to a wide assortment of new consumer goods which provides a major incentive to industry and effort, thus overcoming the languor and indifference characteristic of a purely agricultural society and precluding the possibility of a backward-sloping supply of labor at relatively low levels of income.

> The most natural way, surely, of encouraging husbandry, is, first, to excite other kinds of industry, and thereby afford the labourer a ready market for his commodities, and a return of such goods as may contribute to his pleasure and enjoyment. This method is infallible and universal (10, p. 146; cf. 29, pp. 102–103).

It is in part this "demonstration effect" which accounts for the importance attached to foreign trade in an early stage of a country's development.

> . . . this perhaps is the chief advantage which arises from a commerce with strangers. It rouses men from their indolence; and presenting the gayer and more opulent part of the nation with objects of luxury, which they never before dreamed of, raises in them a desire of a more splendid way of life than what their ancestors enjoyed (10, p. 14; see also pp. 21–22; cf. 23, p. 581).

Equally important, Hume argues, is the fact that commerce begets both industriousness and frugality, qualities indispensable to the achieve-

---

upon character and industry: "Our ancestors were idle for want of a sufficient encouragement to industry. It is better, says the proverb, to play for nothing, than to work for nothing. In mercantile and manufacturing towns . . . they are in general industrious, sober, and thriving. . . . In those towns which are principally supported by the . . . residence of a court . . . they are in general idle, dissolute, and poor" (38, p. 319).

[8] Adam Smith makes the same point: "We may observe that the greater number of manufacturers there are in any country, agriculture is the more improved, and the causes which prevent the progress of these react, as it were, upon agriculture" (39, p. 230).

ment of economic growth. For a commercial society provides a combination of inducements and opportunities not available in an agricultural society and thereby redirects the human agent from the casual pursuit of pleasure and diversion to the active pursuit of business profits.

> There is no craving or demand of the human mind more constant and insatiable than that for exercise and employment; and this desire seems the foundation of most of our passions and pursuits. Deprive a man of all business and serious occupation, he runs restless from one amusement to another; and the weight and oppression, which he feels from idleness, is so great, that he forgets the ruin which must follow him from his immoderate expences. Give him a more harmless way of employing his mind or body, he is satisfied, and feels no longer that insatiable thirst after pleasure. But if the employment you give him be lucrative, especially if the profit be attached to every particular exertion of industry, he has gain so often in his eye, that he acquires, by degrees, a passion for it, and knows no such pleasure as that of seeing the daily encrease of his fortune. And this is the reason why trade encreases frugality, and why, among merchants, there is the same overplus of misers above prodigals, as, among the possessors of land, there is the contrary.
>
> Commerce encreases industry, by conveying it readily from one member of the state to another, and allowing none of it to perish or become useless. It encreases frugality, by giving occupation to men, and employing them in the arts of gain, which soon engage their affection, and remove all relish for pleasure and expence. It is an infallible consequence of all industrious professions, to beget frugality, and make the love of gain prevail over the love of pleasure (10, p. 53).

Smith is in essential agreement with Hume on the character-forming impact of commercial activity on the commercial classes. "The habits, besides, of order, oeconomy and attention, to which mercantile business naturally forms a merchant, render him much fitter to execute, with profit and success, any project of improvement" (38, p. 385). Moreover, "Whenever commerce is introduced into any country probity and punctuality always accompany it. These virtues in a rude and barbarous country are almost unknown" (39, p. 253).

Smith goes beyond Hume, however, by adding more specific dimensions to the impact of wealth, class, and occupation upon the human actor. Although the *desire* for affluence is one of the fundamental propelling forces of all mankind, the *attainment* of great wealth is likely to corrupt the effectiveness of its possessor. This is so because ". . . a man of a large revenue, whatever may be his profession, thinks he ought to live like other men of large revenues; and to spend a great part of his time in festivity, in vanity, and in dissipation" (38, p. 766).[9] Moreover, if profit opportunities are so structured — for example, through monopoly or special privilege — that high profits are easily earned, this too

9 For a more extended discussion see Rosenberg (31).

destroys the effectiveness of the capitalist by releasing him from the disciplining forces of the competitive marketplace and corroding those characteristics which constitute the chief economic virtues of this class. "The high rate of profit seems every where to destroy that parsimony which in other circumstances is natural to the character of the merchant. When profits are high, that sober virtue seems to be superfluous, and expensive luxury to suit better the affluence of his situation" (38, p. 578; cf. 19, p. 192).

For similar reasons, large landowners are likely to possess personal attributes inimical to growth:

> It seldom happens . . . that a great proprietor is a great improver. . . . To improve land with profit, like all other commercial projects, requires an exact attention to small savings and small gains, of which a man born to a great fortune, even though naturally frugal, is very seldom capable. The situation of such a person naturally disposes him to attend rather to ornament which pleases his fancy, than to profit for which he has so little occasion (38, pp. 363–364).

The behavioral characteristics most conducive to a growth in agricultural productivity, Smith argues, are likely to be produced by a system of small proprietorships with security of tenure.

> A small proprietor . . . who knows every part of his little territory, who views it all with the affection which property, especially small property, naturally inspires, and who upon that account takes pleasure not only in cultivating but in adorning it, is generally of all improvers the most industrious, the most intelligent, and the most successful (38, p. 392, see also pp. 368–369).

We add one final point on the impact of productive activity upon the human agent, as conceived in classical economics. It is well known that Adam Smith placed enormous emphasis upon the role of the progressive division of labor as the main engine of economic growth (38, Book I, chapter 1). Less attention has been devoted to the fact that Smith also argued that this same division of labor, if left to itself, exerted a devastating effect upon the minds and character of the great mass of the population, i.e., the "labouring poor."

> In the progress of the division of labour, the employment of the far greater part of those who live by labour, that is, of the great body of the people, comes to be confined to a few very simple operations, frequently to one or two. But the understandings of the greater part of men are necessarily formed by their ordinary employments. The man whose whole life is spent in performing a few simple operations, of which the effects too are, perhaps, always the same, or very nearly the same, has no occasion to exert his understanding, or to exercise his invention in finding out ex-

pedients for removing difficulties which never occur. He naturally loses, therefore, the habit of such exertion, and generally becomes as stupid and ignorant as it is possible for a human creature to become. . . . His dexterity at his own particular trade seems . . . to be acquired at the expence of his intellectual, social, and martial virtues. But in every improved and civilized society this is the state into which the labouring poor, that is, the great body of the people, must necessarily fall, unless government takes some pains to prevent it (38, pp. 734–735).[10]

Smith was content to argue that public education was necessary to offset these deleterious effects, but, if he took his own observations seriously, it is difficult to understand why they did not disturb him even more than appears to have been the case. It is hard to conceive of such workers playing the major role which Smith earlier attributes to them as sources of technological innovation — even within their own narrow, subdivided range of productive activities (38, Book 1, chapter 1).

III

The classical economists were much concerned with the sort of feedback phenomena we have discussed because they were deeply interested in problems of economic evolution and change. With the emergence of neo-classical economics in the latter part of the nineteenth century, interest in such phenomena was very largely submerged as the central theoretical interests of the economics profession were directed to the problem of optimum allocation of a fixed amount of resources. A serious assault upon the analysis of growth, which is once again a major preoccupation of economists, would appear to require that feedback phenomena again be explored, but in a more rigorous and systematic way.

We have now arrived at a critical juncture in our analysis. Neo-classical economics examines the conditions under which output from a given volume of resources will be maximized. But it does not examine the manner in which different patterns of resource use — production and consumption — affect the future quality of the human input as a productive agent. And, whereas for the former problem (output maximization) one may legitimately regard all economic activities as being on an equal footing, the critical growing points for subsequent economic growth may well be determined by the manner in which current economic activity modifies the character of the human input. This range of feedbacks deserves careful exploration. It may further serve to illuminate the widely-held belief that, once development has proceeded to a certain point, it

10 In his earlier lectures Smith had stated: ". . . in every commercial nation the low people are exceedingly stupid. The Dutch vulgar are eminently so, and the English are more so than the Scotch. The rule is general; in towns they are not so intelligent as in the country, nor in a rich country as in a poor one" (39, p. 256).

appears to acquire a momentum of its own and becomes, as it were, self-generating.

There now exists considerable empirical evidence suggesting that rising per capita incomes are associated with certain systematic alterations in the composition of resource use as well as the composition of output. The inadequacies of the data, the conceptual problems involved in interpreting them (14, chapters 6 and 7), and the obvious diversity in the historical experiences of different countries and regions all caution against hasty and premature generalization. In particular, much of the data available are cross-sectional by country, rather than long-time series for each country, and the attempt to draw inferences about historical patterns from cross-sectional data is fraught with hazards. Some long-term secular trends, however, are fairly clear. Countries which have attained high levels of per capita income have experienced rather drastic changes in the relative importance of different industrial sectors — a sharp decline in agriculture, a growth in the manufacturing sector, and a later, more pronounced expansion of transportation, communication, and the service sectors generally (retailing, finance, government, and so on). Associated with this have been declines in numbers of unskilled workers, proprietors, and managers (largely in the farm sector) and increases in numbers of clerical, professional, and technical workers. These input changes in large part reflect the differential impact of technical change and the changing composition of output associated with rising incomes, such as the rising proportion of government expenditures in total output and the major compositional changes in consumer expenditures — growth in the relative importance of durable goods and in the provision of services, such as education, medical care, and recreation. Superimposed on these changes are the decline of the household as a nucleus of productive activity and the increasing importance of the market nexus, an increase in leisure time, and a massive shift of the population from a primarily rural to a primarily urban environment. Phenomena such as these transform the human agent in ways about which we know relatively little, but which are obviously linked with growth as a continuous (and perhaps in some ways self-reinforcing) process.

With respect to the impact of productive activities, one important area of exploration is the differential consequences of different sorts of employments. It is, for example, a widely held view that specialization in agriculture and primary production generally is less beneficial to the human agent than participation in manufacturing (37). This is so, it is held, because manufacturing activity creates skills, secondary educational effects, and external economies which, in their diffusion, are responsible for widespread future increases in productivity.

There may be a good deal to be said in favor of such a point of view, but on reading the arguments of its proponents, it is difficult to avoid the feeling that the generalizations are too sweeping and that the invidious comparison of agriculture in general with manufacturing in general is conducted on far too gross a level.

In considering the alleged failure of agriculture to generate beneficial secondary effects, it is important that we isolate those forces inherent in agricultural production from other forces which happen to be associated with agriculture in any particular geographic or historical context. For instance, relative factor endowment and therefore relative factor prices may be expected to be critical in determining the choice of productive techniques. A highly labor-abundant economy, *ceteris paribus*, will adopt labor-intensive techniques not only in agriculture but in industry and the service sector as well. This may be the dominant consideration in explaining the limited secondary benefits generated throughout much of the tropical and semi-tropical regions of the world which have concentrated on primary product extraction and export. Many of the human skills and aptitudes vital for growth are acquired in the production and employment of a (generally capital-intensive) machine technology, but a labor-abundant society will have minimum incentive to introduce such technology either in agriculture *or* industry. A highly elastic supply of labor at or near the prevailing wage has undoubtedly been a pervasive force in densely populated regions in accounting for both the productive methods employed as well as for the failure of wages to rise with the expansion of activity in the primary sector resulting from the "opening up" of these regions to world trade (16).

It is highly important, furthermore, that we should distinguish clearly between underdevelopment of resources and backwardness of population, especially since it is a frequent practice to regard low-income countries as possessing both characteristics. For, historically, many of the low-income tropical countries experienced a highly intensive exploitation of their natural resources, but in a manner which has left the human agent virtually untouched. As Hla Myint has expressed it:

> . . . in spite of the striking specialization of the inanimate productive equipment and of the individuals from the economically advanced groups of people who manage and control them, there is really very little specialization, beyond the natural adaptability to the tropical climate, among the backward peoples in their roles as unskilled labourers or peasant producers. Thus the typical unskilled labour supplied by the backward peoples is an undifferentiated mass of cheap manpower which might be used in any type of plantation or in any type of extractive industry within the tropics and sometimes even beyond it. . . . Thus all the specialization required for the export market seems to have been done by the other co-operating factors, the whole productive structure being built around the supply of cheap undifferentiated labour (25, p. 153).

This failure to acquire economically relevant skills has frequently been further reinforced by factors not immediately resulting from the preoccupation with primary products itself. For, we might ask, since the growth of such activities necessarily requires a further growth of skilled supervisory and technical personnel, as well as a variety of middlemen and other business and marketing functions, why have native populations typically failed to acquire the skills these important roles would seem to offer?

The answer to this question is complex and urgently requires further study, but it appears to be associated, at least in part, with the compelling pull, certainly during the early stages, of village or tribal communities, such that the native worker remains essentially a migrant, participating only on a temporary basis in the plantation or mine economy (3). Thus, labor turnover rates are high and the worker does not remain long enough to acquire the skills and disciplines required for upward mobility. This is further reinforced by the impediment to upward mobility of discriminatory practices (official or unofficial) and their corrosive effects upon incentives and aspirations. Under these circumstances it may not be primary production as such, but the specific role of supplier of unskilled labor which is imposed upon the native work force, which accounts for much of the failure to acquire skills of future economic usefulness (25, pp. 152–159; cf. 26).

A closely related set of considerations is the specific institutional context within which primary production takes place. Land tenure arrangements and marketing and credit systems may easily structure the framework of incentives and opportunities in such a way as to predetermine the nature of the impact of agricultural activity upon the human agent (41; 7).

A further point of major importance is the specific incidence of different kinds of crops. Agricultural products differ drastically in the kinds of knowledge, technical competence, and even social systems required for their successful cultivation, and the secondary effects they generate may also differ significantly. Kindleberger has noted the contrast between sugar and tobacco in countries like Cuba:

> Sugar is produced on a sizable scale with capital and unskilled labor in a highly seasonal burst of work, followed by a "dead season" of four or five months. Tobacco, on the other hand, calls for skilled labor, working a year round; a worker has a chance to develop his creative powers. In sugar, the land is owned by large companies, and it is impossible for a worker to move up on the economic scale through acquiring land (13, p. 30; cf. 20).

It is clear — and important — that the kinds of skills generated by agriculture depend very much upon the type of agriculture one has in mind. Some crops require an unskilled labor input performing nothing but simple, routinized, repetitive tasks — e.g., cotton.[11] Where this is the

[11] It is only in very recent years that mechanical techniques for the picking of cotton have been developed, by contrast with the mechanization of grain harvesting

case the plantation system has been a logical development, since it is possible to centralize decision-making and to supervise the activities of large numbers of unskilled workers.

But Midwestern United States agriculture has provided a radically different experience. The pattern of agricultural activity in the American Midwest was of such a nature that it developed a high degree of commercial and technical sophistication on the part of the labor inputs. Much of the explanation lies in the fact that this was an agriculture centered on livestock husbandry, which required a highly efficient and sophisticated system of managerial decision-making. Midwestern farming has been, to a considerable extent, an example of a complex system of vertical integration on the part of the individual producing unit — the individual farm typically produces the food-cereal products which constitute the basic food input of its livestock population.

The Midwestern farm is often a fairly elaborate enterprise in which the decision-maker must be close to the detailed day-to-day operations of the farm and which demands a familiarity with market phenomena and a wide range of technical skills.[12] Midwestern farming has therefore produced effective managers and people well versed in mechanical skills who have successfully transferred these skills to other sectors of the economy during the prolonged secular decline of the agricultural sector in the American economy.

One may suggest, then, that the system of small family proprietorships developed in the Midwest was a logical outgrowth of the complex technical and managerial requirements of an agriculture centering on livestock husbandry. By contrast, monoculture patterns such as prevailed in the American South and in many tropical countries generated a wholly different pattern in part because of the unskilled labor it required.

The ramifications of these suggested contrasts extend even further. Many of the spectacular failures of the Soviet collectivization of agriculture can be attributed to factors such as have been suggested here. The contrast between Soviet and American agricultural performance reflects, to be sure, numerous differences in soil, climate, factor endowment, and so on. Yet it is no accident (as Marxists themselves are fond of saying) that their comparative failures have been greatest in livestock husbandry.[13] These failures are, in large part, attributable to the attempt to impose a highly centralized management structure upon the production of agricultural products which, to be successfully raised, require a care-

---

which has been going on for over a century. The nature of the cotton crop made its mechanization inherently a much more difficult technical problem. It is interesting to speculate on the final outcome of the slavery issue had mechanized cotton-picking developed along with mechanized grain-harvesting in the 1840's.

[12] The extreme sensitivity of Midwestern farmers in transferring resources from one use to another in response to market forces is embodied in the so-called "corn-hog cycle."

[13] See the succinct presentation of comparative figures in Campbell (5, pp. 70–77).

ful balance of strong personal interest and incentives with decentralized, "on-the-spot" managerial decisions.[14]

Further aspects of the possible impact of productive activity upon the human agent are illuminated when we focus our attention explicitly upon the fact that successful economic development necessarily involves continuous *alterations* both in the pattern of resource use in response to the changing composition of aggregate demand and in the kinds of technology employed in the productive process. Perhaps one of the most serious problems involved in primary product specialization as it has been carried out in many low-income countries is that such skills as are involved are typically attached to the exploitation of particular primary products and frequently cannot be employed in doing other things. They possess, as it were, little transfer value to other uses and therefore provide little capacity for shifting effectively to new products in the event of a decline in the demand for the product. Technologically speaking, they are "dead ends." Such economies, therefore, are likely to be highly vulnerable to changing world demand and to technological change in advanced countries which often involves the development of synthetic substitutes or techniques which make it possible to reduce primary input requirements per unit of final output. It is this limited capacity to adapt to change, rather than primary product production per se, which is likely to prove fatal.

Here again it is important that our assertions not be too sweeping and categorical and that further research be directed toward isolating the more specific factors and mechanisms which limit the capacity for adaptation. Not all primary production, as we have already argued, is equally deficient in generating technical skills, nor is all manufacturing activity equally successful in producing them. For example, one particular sector of the economy stands out in its role as a source of new technology appropriate to a country's factor endowment and in its ability to facilitate the adaptation to changing output: the capital goods producing sector. This sector — aside from construction — is usually undeveloped, or even non-existent, in primary producing countries, and its undeveloped state would appear to constitute a handicap of enormous proportions. It is probable that one of the most important factors contributing to the viability and flexibility of industrial economies is the existence of a well developed capital goods sector possessing the technical knowledge, skills, and facilities for producing machinery to accommodate the changing requirements of productive activity *plus* the ability and incentive for rais-

[14] It has recently been suggested that Asian collectivization may come to grief because of its inability to cope with the extreme delicacy of the rice plant. The great care and personal effort and attention involved in its cultivation make it a recalcitrant candidate for the rigors and centralized discipline of collectivization. "Plants . . . stand in no awe of Communism. In the whole of the vegetable kingdom, it is the rice plant which possesses the most 'bourgeois background' and which is proving the most 'reactionary' in the face of the policy of collectivization which has been applied in Asia during the past few years. Rice may well be the factor which brings about the downfall of Asian Communism" (6, p. 104).

ing productivity of machinery production itself, thereby reducing its cost and encouraging its further adoption. Herein may lie the most important feedback of all which is central to explaining the differences in behavior between industrial and primary producing economies. Industrial societies, through the role of their highly developed capital goods producing industries, have, in effect, internalized in their industrial structure a technological capacity which undertakes technological change and adaptation almost as a matter of course and routine. Underdeveloped economies, of course, import much of their capital goods from abroad, but this expedient deprives them of a learning experience in the production, improvement, and adaptation of machinery which may be vital to economic growth.

Even if the position taken here is valid, however, its policy implications are by no means obvious. For, by and large, the currently industrial countries developed under historical conditions of comparative labor scarcity and their capital goods sectors grew, in part, because the comparatively high price of labor provided a continuous inducement to the adoption of capital-intensive methods of production.[15] By contrast, entrepreneurs in the labor-abundant economies of most of the underdeveloped world possess a strong inducement to perpetuate labor-intensive techniques, as well as to undertake other forms of economic activity which may make little further contribution to the growth process (30).

The abundance of labor in primary producing countries is likely to generate growth-inhibiting forces in other ways as well, via what may be referred to as "negative feedbacks." Extreme labor abundance not only induces adoption of labor-intensive techniques but also leads to development of attitudes and social institutions which, in turn, create a preoccupation with work-spreading arrangements and with aspects of productive activity which are simply irrelevant to growth and may easily constitute obstacles to it. Such an environment has led to make-work techniques and arrangements for spreading work among the largest number of people which are such a familiar feature of densely-populated low-income countries. The virtual social obligation for the wealthy Indian to employ a large number of functionally-specialized domestic servants is a case in point (24, pp. 49–50). Furthermore, such environments are highly conducive to the proliferation of traditions and standards of craftsmanship — virtuoso performances of painstaking care and effort reflecting many years of patient apprenticeship and training — which are, at best, simply irrelevant to the skills required for adaptation and growth. At worst, such attitudes and interests discourage the exploration of new methods and techniques and constitute a powerful obstacle to innovation.

In contrast with the "negative feedbacks" which appear to play such an important role in primary producing low-income countries, it appears

[15] See the highly suggestive comparison of Britain and the United States in Habakkuk (9).

that, during some stages in their development at least, high-income industrial countries enjoy beneficial feedbacks from a rapid rate of growth of "knowledge-producing" occupations. Professor Fritz Machlup has recently completed a study of what he calls knowledge-producing occupations. Although there are many serious objections which may be raised concerning his definitions and criteria for classification, his conclusions nevertheless command considerable interest.

These are the trends read from the statistical series: (1) The knowledge-producing occupations have grown over the last 60 years much faster than occupations requiring manual labor. (2) The share of knowledge-producing occupations in the total labor force tripled between 1900 and 1959. (3) The share of these occupations in total employment has increased even more. (4) While in the first part of this century growth was fastest in clerical occupations, the lead was then taken by managerial and executive occupations, and more recently by professional and technical personnel. (5) The share of knowledge-producing occupations in total income has increased during the last decade. (6) The share of professional and technical personnel in total income has increased during the last two decades (18, p. 396).

We conclude on the basis of the preceding discussion that the impact of productive activity on the quality of the economy's future input is of decisive importance in determining the future growth of the economy.

IV

The final considerations to which we shall address ourselves can be dealt with more briefly, because they are admittedly even more speculative and less familiar than the subjects of the preceding discussion. Our general argument here is that a whole range of feedbacks are produced not only by the pattern of productive activity but by the pattern of consumer goods and services and, moreover, by the composition of the economy's entire range of final output — not only consumer goods and services but also investment goods and goods and services produced in the government sector. Indeed, it is necessary to go further and insist that, for many of the problems connected with the growth process, it is becoming increasingly artificial even to maintain a rigid distinction between production and consumption. An important implication of this position is that we can no longer maintain a sharp separation between the firm and the household, regarding the former as the center of productive activity and the latter simply as the place where the output of the economy is passively consumed (4). For what goes on in the household may provide the key to important productivity changes, and it may well be that the limited success of the economist thus far in accounting for the extent of the rise in per capita incomes lies in an excessive preoccupation with the economic activity within the firm as the sole source of productivity improvements.

In one important respect economic analysis is currently attempting to incorporate some of the phenomena referred to here. It is now generally recognized that economics has, in the past, operated with a highly restricted concept of capital formation, confining itself to tangible capital of the kind purchased by business firms for direct use in the productive process.[16] Much of society's "investment" (if the term is used in the only meaningful sense of any current use of resources which increases future output) consists in investment in human capital; and a significant portion of the apparent discrepancy between the growth in output per capita and the growth in measured inputs, referred to earlier, is attributable to the exclusion of all capital which becomes embodied, so to speak, in the human agent. Such investments become increasingly important as an economy achieves higher levels of per capita income, and it is apparent that the failure to include the expenditure of resources upon such activities as formal education and on-the-job training has imparted a major downward bias to our measure of capital formation and to our measures of growth-inducing forces generally.[17]

It is suggested that the notion of investment in human capital, although it constitutes an important corrective to an excessively restrictive concept of capital formation, is nevertheless merely a special species of a much larger genus. What now requires exploration is the multitude of ways in which resource use in the government and household sectors results in outputs which, through their feedback effects, modify the character of the human agent in ways further conducive to economic growth.

An adequate discussion of the role of the government sector would take us far beyond the limits of the present chapter, and cannot be attempted here, but a few brief comments are in order. As Kuznets has persuasively argued, many expenditures of government in an industrial, urbanized society should be regarded as cost outlays necessary to the smooth functioning of such a complex society, and not as part of the flow of net final product (14, chapters 6 and 7). On the other hand, a functional analysis of government expenditures will also reveal major growth-inducing activities financed (although not necessarily performed) within that sector. For example, the percentage of gross national product devoted to all research and development activities in the United States has risen abruptly over the past decade, rising from 1.4 per cent to 2.8

[16] Even though Adam Smith had long ago included in his definition of fixed capital ". . . the acquired and useful abilities of all the inhabitants or members of the society. The acquisition of such talents, by the maintenance of the acquirer during his education, study, or apprenticeship, always costs a real expence, which is a capital fixed and realized, as it were, in his person. Those talents, as they make a part of his fortune, so do they likewise of that of the society to which he belongs. The improved dexterity of a workman may be considered in the same light as a machine or instrument of trade which facilitates and abridges labour, and which, though it costs a certain expence, repays that expence with a profit" (38, pp. 265–66).

[17] See the important work on this subject by Theodore Schultz (34; 35; 36). See also (12).

per cent of gross national product between the years 1953–54 and 1960–61, and most of this has been financed by the federal government. In 1960–61 the federal government financed 65 per cent or $9 billion of the total outlay of $14 billion expended on research and development. Moreover, in the same period the federal government provided $745 million of the $1.3 billion spent upon basic research (27, pp. 134–142). Furthermore, government expenditures in the important areas of health and education show a secular rising trend and cross-sectional data indicate that such expenditures constitute a higher percentage of gross national product in high-income countries than in low-income countries (15, p. 10).

The growing importance of the role of the government sector is also confirmed by cross-sectional data, in addition to historical evidences of its growth in currently high-income countries. The available data indicate a high positive correlation between the size of a country's per capita income and government expenditures as a percentage of gross national product. The changing volume and composition of government expenditures may thus include a number of strategic, growth-inducing forces which increase in relative importance with the process of economic development itself (28; 15, p. 6; 22).[18]

Increases in per capita consumption within the household may play an important role in economic growth, not only through improving standards of nutrition, housing, and health, but also in the acquisition of skills and aptitudes; in improving the human agent's receptivity to certain learning processes and thereby raising his capacity to produce new knowledge, to innovate, and to adapt to change in his economic roles; and in changing the character of his motivations and aspirations which, in turn, modify his behavior in the economic arena. In short, the household must be examined as a "producer" of skills, aptitudes, and aspirations.

The sharp increase in expenditures on consumer durables, associated with rising per capita incomes, is an important case in point. With rising per capita incomes the household itself becomes increasingly mechanized as it builds up a stock of consumer durables associated with the performance of household tasks, with amusement and recreation for the leisure time which is increasingly available, and with the provision of private transport facilities — at lower levels, the bicycle and motor scooter, and at higher levels, the automobile.[19] Members of the household are, quite literally, immersed in an environment of considerable technological complexity. At these higher stages of per capita income the feedback from the consumption sphere to that of production skills and aptitudes may become extremely significant. For such surroundings

[18] For the historical experience of the United States see Fabricant (8) and Bator (2).

[19] See the data on the historical diffusion of the automobile in eight industrial countries in Rostow (33, pp. 84–85 and pp. 168–171).

both stimulate and, in some measure, compel a high degree of sophistication in the intricacies of modern technology and, in so doing, provide a socially costless diffusion of productive abilities. Consider furthermore the fearful array of children's toys of a mechanical and electronic nature, to say nothing of the specifically "educational" toys, games, and devices directed at the children's market, or the "do-it-yourself" kits with which it is now even possible for youngsters to build simple model computers. And, of course, the impact of the automobile has been strictly *sui generis*. It has been a source of fascination to generations of adolescents and adults and has played an immensely important role in the distribution of mechanical skills among the American population.[20]

Our final point encompasses feedbacks which may originate in both the consumption and production spheres. It is the practice of economists to assume that consumer wants are autonomous and determined independently of the process through which they are satisfied. The consumer is visualized as possessing an ordered structure of preferences and entering into market relations with the purpose of maximizing his satisfactions, subject to a budgetary constraint. By making this assumption it is possible to develop an important set of analytical relationships which illuminate the problem of optimum resource allocation. For purposes of analyzing the process of economic growth, however, this assumption is seriously deficient, since a major component of the growth process is a radical transformation of attitudes toward consumption and saving, and toward work and leisure. The changing structure of consumer wants and preferences, in other words, is itself a strategic variable in the growth process, as the classical economists recognized, since it is an important determinant of individual behavior and shapes the nature of his responses to economic incentives and opportunities. Yet our ignorance on this subject is almost total, and a systematic examination of the ways in which wants are shaped and modified as a result of participation in economic activities is urgently required. For, as Marshall insisted many years ago:

> . . . while wants are the rulers of life among the lower animals, it is to changes in the forms of efforts and activities that we must turn when in search for the keynotes of the history of mankind . . . although it is man's wants in the earliest stages of his development that give rise to his activities, yet afterwards each new step upwards is to be regarded as the development of new activities giving rise to new wants, rather than of new wants giving rise to new activities (21, p. 85, p. 87).

[20] It appears that, in recent years, the automobile has become too cumbersome and complicated and now requires equipment and facilities too elaborate to serve as extensively as it once did as a learning device. The growing interest in "hot-rods" may reflect an attempt to freeze the technical development of the automobile at a stage where it is still manageable without highly expensive and complex garage facilities. Alternatively, the motors of such devices as power-driven lawn mowers, particularly in suburbia, may provide a partial learning substitute.

BIBLIOGRAPHY

1. Abramovitz, Moses. "Resource and Output Trends in the U.S. Since 1870," *American Economic Review Papers and Proceedings,* Vol. 69 (May 1956), pp. 1–23.

2. Bator, Francis. *The Question of Government Spending.* New York: Harper and Bros., 1960.

3. Berg, Elliot. "Backward-Sloping Labor Supply Functions in Dual Economies — The African Case," *The Quarterly Journal of Economics,* Vol. 75 (August 1961), pp. 468–492.

4. Cairncross, A. K. "Economic Schizophrenia," *Scottish Journal of Political Economy,* Vol. 5 (February 1958), pp. 15–21.

5. Campbell, Robert. *Soviet Economic Power.* Boston: Houghton Mifflin Co., 1960.

6. Chi, Hoang Van. "Collectivization and Rice Production," *The China Quarterly,* Vol. 9 (January-March 1962), pp. 94–104.

7. Eckstein, Alexander. "Land Reform and Economic Development," *World Politics,* Vol. 8 (July 1955), pp. 650–662.

8. Fabricant, Solomon. *The Trend of Government Activity Since 1900.* New York: National Bureau of Economic Research, 1952.

9. Habakkuk, H. J. *American and British Technology in the 19th Century.* Cambridge: Cambridge University Press, 1962.

10. Hume, David. *Writings on Economics,* edited and introduced by Eugene Rotwein. Madison: University of Wisconsin Press, 1955.

11. Jevons, W. Stanley. *The Theory of Political Economy,* 4th ed. London: MacMillan and Co., 1911.

12. *The Journal of Political Economy,* October 1962, Part II, special supplement on "Investment in Human Beings."

13. Kindleberger, Charles. *Economic Development.* New York: McGraw-Hill Book Co., 1958.

14. Kuznets, Simon. *Economic Change.* New York: W. W. Norton, 1953.

15. Kuznets, Simon. "Quantitative Aspects of the Economic Growth of Nations: VII. The Share and Structure of Consumption," *Economic Development and Cultural Change,* Vol. 10 (January 1962), Part II, pp. 1–92.

16. Lewis, W. A. "Economic Development with Unlimited Supplies of Labor," *The Manchester School,* Vol. 22 (May 1954), pp. 139–191.

17. Lewis, W. A. *The Theory of Economic Growth.* Homewood, Ill.: Richard D. Irwin, Inc., 1955.

18. Machlup, Fritz. *The Production and Distribution of Knowledge in the United States.* Princeton, N.J.: Princeton University Press, 1962.

19. Malthus, Thomas Robert. *Principles of Political Economy,* 2nd ed. New York: Reprinted by Augustus M. Kelley, Inc., 1951.

20. Manners, R. A., and J. A. Steward. "The Cultural Study of Contemporary Societies: Puerto Rico," *American Journal of Sociology*, Vol. 58 (September 1953), pp. 123–130.

21. Marshall, Alfred. *Principles of Economics*, 8th ed. London: MacMillan and Co., 1948.

22. Martin, Alison and W. Arthur Lewis. "Patterns of Public Revenue and Expenditure," *The Manchester School*, Vol. 24 (September 1956), pp. 203–244.

23. Mill, John Stuart. *Principles of Political Economy*. London: Longmans, Green, and Co., 1909.

24. Moore, Wilbert, and Arnold Feldman. *Labor Commitment and Social Change in Developing Areas*. New York: Social Science Research Council, 1960.

25. Myint, Hla. "An Interpretation of Economic Backwardness," *Oxford Economic Papers* (June 1954), pp. 132–163.

26. Myint, Hla. "The Gains from International Trade and the Backward Countries," *The Review of Economic Studies*, Vol. 22 (2), No. 58 (1954–55), pp. 129–142.

27. National Science Foundation. *Twelfth Annual Report, 1962*. Washington, D.C.: United States Government Printing Office, 1963.

28. Oshima, Harry. "Share of Government in Gross National Product," *American Economic Review* (June 1957), pp. 381–390.

29. Ricardo, David. *Works, edited by Piero Sraffa*, Vol. 8. Cambridge: Cambridge University Press, 1952.

30. Rosenberg, Nathan. "Capital Formation in Underdeveloped Countries," *American Economic Review*, Vol. 50 (September 1960), pp. 706–715.

31. Rosenberg, Nathan. "Some Institutional Aspects of the *Wealth of Nations*," *The Journal of Political Economy*, Vol. 68 (December 1960), pp. 557–570.

32. Rostow, W. W. "The Take-Off into Self-Sustained Growth," *Economic Journal*, Vol. 66 (March 1956), pp. 25–48.

33. Rostow, W. W. *The Stages of Economic Growth*. Cambridge: Cambridge University Press, 1960.

34. Schultz, Theodore. "Investment in Man: An Economist's View," *The Social Science Review*, Vol. 33 (June 1959), pp. 109–117.

35. Schultz, Theodore. "Capital Formation by Education," *The Journal of Political Economy*, Vol. 68 (December 1960), pp. 571–583.

36. Schultz, Theodore. "Investment in Human Capital," *American Economic Review*, Vol. 51 (March 1961), pp. 1–17.

37. Singer, Hans. "The Distribution of Gains Between Investing and Borrowing Countries," *American Economic Review Papers and Proceedings*, Vol. 63 (May 1950), pp. 473–485.

38. Smith, Adam. *The Wealth of Nations*. New York: Random House, 1937.

39. Smith, Adam. *Lectures on Justice, Police, Revenue and Arms.* New York: Kelley and Millman, Inc., 1956.

40. Solow, Robert. "Technical Change and the Aggregate Production Function," *Review of Economics and Statistics,* Vol. 39 (August 1957), pp. 312–320.

41. United Nations, Department of Economic Affairs. *Land Reform: Defects in Agrarian Structure as Obstacles to Economic Development.* New York: 1951.

26

Bert F. Hoselitz

Economic Development and Change

in Social Values and Thought Patterns

I

In the last few years the study of economic development has gradually been pushed into wider and wider social, political, and cultural dimensions. Whereas in the early post-war phase of the concentration of social scientists upon problems of economic growth, communication between economists and other social scientists was quite limited, contacts have increased and the various participants in the discussion have given increased recognition to the fact that those coming from other disciplines in the social sciences have a genuine contribution to make to a general understanding of economic growth. When in 1951 a group of scholars representing the various social science disciplines met at Chicago to discuss, under the auspices of the Norman Wait Harris Memorial Foundation in International Relations, the problem of the progress of underdeveloped areas, one economist at the meeting clearly expressed his discouragement with the potential contribution of anthropologists to the problem of economic growth, by saying: "You are only interested in simple tribes like the Hopi; but you have nothing to say about the improvement of the lot of millions of downtrodden peasants in India and other parts of Asia, about the failure by Middle Easterners and Latin Americans to react constructively to more modern ways of production." To this one of the anthropologists answered that, he, in turn, was bewildered by the concentration on abstract models which economists were so fond of, and their failure to concern themselves with living people and their values and thoughts, rather than with bloodless mathematical formulas describing collective behavior of a kind no human society had ever experienced.

I am citing this exchange — and I will leave the two very distinguished participants in it anonymous — in order to show that a dozen years ago many social scientists still lived in secluded compartments and had little regard for each other's contributions to the understanding of economic growth. It was as a response to this contrast that the Research Center in Economic Development and Cultural Change was founded at the University of Chicago, and it was one of the chief purposes of its past activities in the 11 years of its existence to bring about a closer and better understanding of the contributions of the various social sciences to the problems of economic growth and development.

I present these remarks to explain why an economist has the temerity to attempt a paper on the role of societal values in economic development. This task is made a great deal easier by the development of interdisciplinary contacts and communications in the last few years. The model builders in economics have gradually come to recognize that in addition to economic changes, actual economic growth will only take place if social relations, cultural behavior, and patterns of values in developing nations are altered. The anthropologists have come to see that the cake of culture is not so hard that it cannot be broken, and have begun to study with increasing interest and frequency situations of change, of "modernization," and of acculturation. There is still a great area of ignorance and a good deal of mutual lack of understanding between persons representing different disciplines in the social sciences. But this mistrust and lack of communication is declining and we may look forward to a time when more general theories of economic development, not tied to a rigorous model composed of a few relatively easily measurable variables, will become the leading theoretical formulations in the study of economic growth. But even in broader-based theories the concept and analysis of social values is likely to form one of the most difficult and intractable variables. Hence, all I can do, here, is to present some very general and preliminary ideas on this topic, and I wish to express the hope at this point that further research and investigation will provide us with greater insights and more certain facts to cope more adequately with the problems in this difficult field.

II

In the analysis of social values, as in so many other fields of studying the process of economic growth, a convenient starting point is the delineation of widely distinct ideal types representing, on the one hand, the economically highly advanced and, on the other, the underdeveloped, societies. Another way of handling this problem consists of attempting to answer briefly the question of what differences may be found in the value and belief systems of Western and non-Western societies which may have decisive significance for the comparative rates of economic development in the two sets of societies. There are some societies which would fall outside this twofold classification. On the one hand some non-Western societies, e.g., Japan, have shown clear abilities for economic growth, and some Western societies, e.g., Portugal or certain Latin American countries, have exhibited an inability to pass beyond a very modest level of economic advancement. But, on the whole, the great division in the world today between economically advanced and under-developed countries coincides almost completely with the contrast between the Western and the non-Western nations, and it may be opportune to ask somewhat more insistently what are the value and belief patterns in the two sets of societies.

On one level this difference appears to have been extensively discussed already by Max Weber and some other writers who followed him in the study of the sociology of religion. Weber has shown, on the one hand, how Protestant (especially Calvinist) and other dissenting religious doctrines were instrumental in aiding in the growth of an economic ethic which was extremely favorable to economic advancement, notably under conditions of private enterprise and initiative. He has shown, on the other hand, how the religious doctrines of Eastern creeds, in particular, Buddhism, Hinduism, and Confucianism, failed to produce such an ethic and how, in spite of the often encountered greed and urge for gain displayed in market transactions in Asian countries, these motives were expressions not of a rationalized economic ethic, but of personal traits or magical beliefs (1, pp. 117–211).

The chief distinction in Max Weber's analysis is the difference between societies in which economic activity is subject throughout to rational calculation and those in which economic action is principally traditional. In fact, Weber extends the application of the principle of rationalism in modern societies to other sectors of social action, e.g., the political and, in some aspects, the integrative spheres of social action, to maintain the argument that he sees the overall process of economic growth as dependent upon an increasing imposition of rationalist modes of behavior and hence a growth of rationally determined systems of social values. For we must interpret his distinction between *Zweckrationalitaet* (instrumental rationality) and *Wertrationalitaet* (value rationality or purposive rationality) in this sense (14, p. 184 ff.).

But to many students of economic development this distinction has not been wholly satisfactory and has left unanswered several doubts, particularly since the contrast between rationalism and traditionalism, which forms the basis of Weber's distinction, constitutes only a partially closed system. For although one extreme of the dichotomy, that of rationalism, is extensively elaborated, the other extreme, the discussion of tradition and traditionalism, is left largely unexplored. Though Weber has not remained completely unconcerned with the content of traditional action, many of the finer distinctions between different types and roles of tradition are barely sketched in and often not discussed in any detail. In particular, Weber did not deal in any explicit fashion with the role of tradition in economically advanced societies, though it cannot be denied that, especially on the level of values, tradition plays an important role in these societies also. And once rational decision-making in a profit-oriented economy becomes widely generalized, it is impossible to deny that a good deal of social action in the adaptive sector of social behavior, i.e., in the realm of economic activity, becomes subject to many traditional norms and traditionally determined behavior patterns.

An example may make this clear. As I pointed out earlier, the main impact of the Protestant ethic has been the development of an economic spirit, which, in the words of Weber, created an "attitude which seeks profit rationally and systematically" (13, p. 64). Yet Weber admits elsewhere in his work that entrepreneurs in other societies also seek profit, in fact that "the people of Asia are notorious all over the world for their unlimited and unequalled greed . . . but the point is that this 'acquisitive drive' is pursued by all the tricks of the trade and with the aid of that cure-all: magic" (1, p. 207).[1]

How can we distinguish these two attitudes, the profit motivation based on greed and that based on a permeating rationality of the economic system? Weber himself tries to contrast rational and "traditionally" inspired entrepreneurship in a distinction he presents in *The Protestant Ethic*. He shows there that many of the men operating under the putting-out system were animated by traditions, "the traditional manner of life, the traditional rate of profit, the traditional amount of work, the traditional manner of regulating the relationships with labour, and the essentially traditional circle of customers and the manner of attracting new ones" (13, p. 67). In the business behavior encountered in Asian countries, this distinction is even clearer, though based on a different set of attitudes than those described by Weber for the putting-out system. Some of the relations of the businessman to others in these societies may also be regarded as based on tradition, but what matters most is his relation to the profitability of his enterprise and his calculation of its returns. The characteristic of the Western entrepreneur, both the modern capitalistic businessman and the merchant in the putting-out system, is that he considers the returns from his enterprise in terms of its appraisal in the long run and of its general position within the entire community in which he exercises his economic activity. The modern businessman is concerned with a particular transaction not as an end in itself, but as one of the many links in a large chain of events, the total impact of which

[1] The original passage may be found in Max Weber (15, p. 337).

is designed to yield a certain total profit. The bazaar-entrepreneur of Asia or the Middle East has a completely different attitude. For him each single transaction is an end in itself, and a calculation of his over-all returns is either not undertaken at all, or is only the incidental result of adding the profits made on each transaction by itself. In other words, when the modern entrepreneur is developing a plan for his enterprise, he estimates the prospective volume of trade, the various costs involved in performing the productive, merchandising, and service functions of his enterprise in this context, and he estimates a total return of his enterprise based upon these calculations. He may be in error on many points; he may estimate wrongly the demand for his output, the cost of its production, or the effect of the impact of his competitors. But though he may suffer losses, or unexpected profits, his rationalism is exhibited by his looking at his activity from the viewpoint of the system as a whole and the place of his activity within the system.

The bazaar-entrepreneur has no such concerns. He is interested in the profitability of a given transaction and disregards the long-run impact of his business activity and the general rate of return he may make. If he thinks that a given transaction may involve a loss, he will usually forgo concluding it, even if the loss in this transaction may produce sizeable profits in the long run. If he has publicly announced a price for a good or a service and finds that, in a given case, he would lose or have to forgo the expected profit by performing the service or selling the good at the published price, he will find some excuse for not having to fulfill the transaction. In brief, he will not act on the basis of an evaluation of his position in a social and economic system as a whole, nor on a calculation of his returns in the long run; he will be concerned with each transaction as a separate entity, and will disregard the long-run consequences and the "systematic" integration of each transaction in his economic activity as a whole.[2]

But if we make this distinction between the "rationally" inclined businessman in the advanced economies of the Western countries and the "traditionally" inclined businessman in the Orient, we find that the latter is operating on different principles even from those of the individual operating in a putting-out system. For the latter has a wider horizon than the merchant or producer in the Oriental bazaar. He may not develop the aggressiveness and the full-scale rationality of the modern capitalist business leader in charge of a large enterprise. But his outlook, though beset with a number of traditionally inspired attitudes, is influenced by a recognition of his activity as an outcome of the overall functioning of a total system. Rather than interpreting each transaction as a separate

---

[2] This evaluation of the principles of bazaar-entrepreneurship is based mostly on my personal experience in the bazaars and similar markets of Middle Eastern, African, and South Asian countries. But see also the discussion of bazaar-entrepreneurship by Clifford Geertz in (2, p. 390 ff.).

action unrelated to others and forming a self-contained entity, the merchant or manufacturer in a putting-out system regards his function as flowing out of the system as a whole. Hence though it lacks certain aspects of rationality it presents a very different type of traditional attitude than that of the greed-ridden bazaar-entrepreneur.

This discussion suggests that the more extensive exploration of traditionalism and its various forms of appearance may yield some further insights into differences in changes of attitudes and values in the process of economic growth in various societies. A more extensive discussion of this problem would be out of place here, particularly since I have attempted to indicate some of its dimensions in a paper published not very long ago (5, pp. 83 ff.). The views expressed in that essay constitute only a beginning in the fuller analysis of the differential impact of value systems on economic development, and more specifically on the question of what differences in Western and non-Western value systems appear to be crucial in the development of those economic motives and forms of economic behavior which are likely to initiate and support self-sustained economic growth.

An attempt to work out a general solution of this problem meets with great difficulties, because of the wide variety in cultural values and beliefs in different non-Western societies. One of the great advantages of the dichotomy between rationalism and traditionalism was the fact that it brought many widely diverse cultures into a relatively tight framework of analysis, in which emphasis was placed on the examination of a rather small, though crucial, set of variables which were considered the major determinants of the social system and the values of the system as a whole. Upon this general dichotomy between rationalism and tradition, Weber's followers have built somewhat more complex schemes, but apart from pointing more precisely to the selection of relevant variables, they have not extended the theory in an important manner. In other words, the general state of theoretical discussion of values affecting social change and economic growth is still founded upon some dichotomy such as that of the traditionalism and rationalism of Max Weber, or the folk-urban continuum by Robert Redfield, or other relatively simple dichotomies (9, pp. 293–308).[3]

III

One of the principal shortcomings of the Weberian analysis, and other theories of social change based upon it, is the implicit assumption of unilinearity, that is, the assumption that the destruction of tradition will lead gradually or abruptly to its replacement by rationalism. An example

---

[3] The theme has been discussed by Redfield in many other places and has been taken up in somewhat different form by several of his students. A full account of the literature based on the folk-urban dichotomy would fill a sizeable book.

of how Weber conceived of this change was touched upon earlier in this chapter when I showed how he considered the transformation within Western capitalism from the predominance of the tradition-oriented putting-out system to the rationalism-oriented factory system. The crucial phase in this process was considered to be the breakdown of traditional modes of belief and behavior influenced by this belief, and their change into rational ones under the impact of a new economic ethic. Yet it is reasonable to assume that the process of culture change is not unilinear, but multilinear, i.e., that the destruction of a simple traditional belief system does not always lead to the same outcome, but may produce quite different results. In the earlier discussion of two tradition-oriented patterns of business behavior, the one characteristic of the Western putting-out system and the other designated as bazaar-entrepreneurship, I have already shown that different varieties of belief and attitude systems, which all may be lumped together under the general designation "traditional," do exist. Hence the processes of change in these contrasting situations begin from quite different starting points, would show considerable variations, and it is now appropriate to stipulate that the outcomes of these processes of change may vary considerably.

In order to examine one possible set of alternatives in greater detail I shall attempt to discuss the variation in the Western and the non-Western pattern of change from traditional to rational forms of social values and attitudes. This analysis is assisted greatly by the work of F. S. C. Northrop, who upheld the view that, in addition to the Weberian dichotomy between traditional and rational action, we should consider also the difference between East and West. Northrop himself refers to the two related dichotomies in the following passage:

> Cultures with differing political, economic, aesthetic and religious ideals or values are grounded in differing philosophical conceptions of the nature of man and of the universe. These diverse philosophical conceptions fall into two groups: those which differ because they refer to different factors in the nature of things, and those which conflict because they are affirming contradictory things of the same factor. The philosophy of the Orient with its attention upon things in their aesthetic immediacy in contrast with the philosophy of the West with its emphasis upon the theoretically designated and inferred factor in things exemplifies the first group; the medieval and modern worlds or traditional communistic and democratic economic and political theory are instances of the second (7, p. 437).

What Northrop calls the difference between medieval and modern values is the contrast between traditional and rational action which we have traced back to Weber and his disciples. The other contrast between aesthetic and conceptual patterns of thinking, on the other hand, forms the new dimension which is added by Northrop's analysis. I shall not attempt here to discuss at length the meaning and significance of this difference, since Northrop's own work largely turns around this problem as a central theme. In very few words this point can be summarized as follows:

In the Western world, and as an outflow of Western philosophical tradition which emerged gradually in the Christian philosophy of the early Middle Ages, patterns of reasoning were evolved which tended to stress abstract, general, theoretical thought. Though these patterns of thought are most clearly displayed in the scientific and philosophical writings of Western authors, this thought has become so widely current that it penetrates all thinking, it affects attitudes toward and interpretations of things, and therefore it may be regarded as an underlying principle of all Occidental intellectual performance.

In the Orient a different basic value attitude is discernible which is in stark contrast to the theoretical orientation of the West. Northrop calls it the aesthetic orientation, but this concept requires explanation. Unlike Western thought, which contains a substantial ingredient of theoretical reasoning, Eastern aesthetic thought is directly empirical, and immediately self-expressive. Northrop uses as an example a comparison between the complex grammar in Western scientific exposition and Chinese writing in which each idea is expressed by a picture showing the general sense impression of an object in its original, primitive form with direct immediacy. The same contrast can be traced through Chinese and Western painting: the latter with its insistence upon providing the illusion of three-dimensional space, the rules of perspective, and emphasis on appropriate effects of lighting and color, and the former with its naive and direct expression of an immediately aesthetic principle characteristic of the object depicted. It finally can be studied by contrasting Western and Eastern philosophy, and through it Western and Eastern systems of beliefs.[4]

In this last area the contrast between aesthetic and theoretical approaches becomes more explicit, for here we deal with the actual methodological explanation of basic thoughts and ultimately determinative approaches to thought. It may be argued that no valid set of philosophical propositions is meaningful in purely theoretical or in purely aesthetic terms. In other words, a purely theoretical philosophy would rely on complete a priori reasoning without need to verify its findings by appeal to empirical validation. Some aspects of Hegelian philosophy come closest to this ideal, but the deficiency of this purely theoretical aspect of Hegelianism has quite appropriately been criticized often, most convincingly perhaps by Karl R. Popper.[5] In fact, Marx's argument of having placed Hegel's philosophy back on its feet is based on Marx's

---

[4] For a more extensive discussion of the "intuitive aesthetic character" of Eastern values, see Northrop (7, pp. 315 ff.).

[5] See the brief remarks in K. R. Popper (8, vol. 2, p. 26, pp. 38–39) on Hegel's philosophy of nature and on Hegel's doctrine of identity.

conviction that the empty "idealism," i.e., the purely theoretical approach, of Hegel is inadequate as a system of propositions designed to form the fundament of a structure for empirical scientific inquiry.

But if a purely theoretical philosophy, i.e., a philosophy which allows no appeal to empirical verification, is of no utility, a purely aesthetic philosophy also is of no value, for it makes impossible virtually by definition the elaboration of theoretical generalizations. But, in truth, neither Western nor Eastern philosophies are purely aesthetic or purely theoretical; they contain both elements mixed, though each of the two elements is present in different proportions. In Eastern belief systems and ways of thinking aesthetic tendencies prevail, whereas in the West theoretical tendencies prevail. Thus we may reinterpret Northrop's system as delineating a continuum with purely theoretical and purely aesthetic patterns at either end, with a series of intermediate stages, each representing a mixture of both extreme elements in different proportions. We may then attempt to represent the two dichotomies, one derived from Weber and the other from Northrop, in a diagram which in turn is based upon a fourfold table.[6]

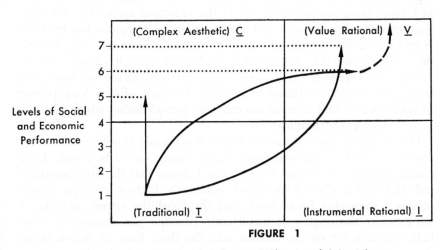

FIGURE 1

Degree of Change in Theoretical Orientation

The diagram is very simple; it is a rectangle in which each of the four sections represents a social system with one predominating value and thought system. In other words, societies which are dominated by a purely traditional value system would cluster around the lower left-hand corner, societies which respond to instrumental rational values in the

[6] I am indebted to Mr. H. Berringer of Northwestern University for having brought to my attention the possibility of combining Weber's and Northrop's analysis and of having devised originally a table from which the diagram is derived.

lower right-hand corner, and societies following purposive rationality as a predominant value in the upper right-hand corner. In Weber's system a movement was assumed which proceeded from Area T to Area I and from there to Area V in a more or less direct path. The line labeled A represents such a possible path of development and change of social values. The introduction of Northrop's dichotomy of aesthetic and theoretical orientations produces a fourth area in the diagram, which has been labeled "complex aesthetic" (C). We now can draw two more lines, B and C, the former of which ends in the same sector as A, but rather than passing through Area I, passes through Area C, and the latter of which only goes from Area T to Area C. At the same time, we can indicate what prevailing forces will determine the shape of the line tracing the change in values associated with progressive economic and social change. The path followed will depend, on the one hand, on the rate of economic and social change, but, on the other, on the rate of change from an aesthetic to a theoretical orientation. In the case of Lines A and B this change in philosophical orientation is clearly shown. It is strongest in the case of Line A, less so in the case of line B. These lines, especially Line A, represent schematically the change in social values in Europe from the pre-industrial to the industrial stage. But the more characteristic development of Eastern countries is represented by Lines B and C. In the second case a set of rational values does not become internalized, but the underlying attitude and thought patterns remain within a system of aesthetically determined values. In the first case a system of rationality is ultimately reached, but only after a long process of development, and after an intermediate period during which aesthetic thought patterns predominate.

One further comment on the level of economic development, which can be reached by different processes of change, might be made. Comparison of Lines A, B, and C in Figure 1 shows that the first (assuming only the solid portion of the lines) reaches the highest level, the second attains a somewhat lower level, and the third the lowest altitude. If we measure the degree of social and economic performance by some indicator or index on the vertical axis, the three lines, as drawn in the diagram, tend to show that different levels of economic development may be reached, depending upon whether a society can attain a position of internalization of a system of socially rational values, or whether its value system remains in the sphere of complex aesthetic values.

In other words, the diagram exhibits the proposition that different systems of social values may have different effects on the level of economic performance which can be achieved, and that the path by which value systems undergo change may have some impact on this result. This is shown by the solid portion of Line B which ends at a lower level of economic performance than Line A. On the other hand, it could be maintained that once a society has reached a system of socially rational values, the attainment of the highest levels of economic performance is not impossible and this is represented by the dotted portion of Line B. All these propositions, which are graphically represented in Figure 1, are, however, purely a prioristic and speculative. Whether they are accurate will depend on closer examination of value systems and their interaction with economic performance, and the more precise identification of the various components making up traditional, rational, and aesthetic systems of values.

At this point it may be useful to state more explicitly the mutual interdependence of the three main variables represented in Figure 1. On the horizontal axis the mixture between aesthetic and theoretical approaches is indicated according to some index. This means that any point further to the right in Figure 1 represents a situation in which the theoretical ingredient is greater and the aesthetic ingredient smaller in a society's system of thought. This means that if we wish to find a position along the horizontal axis for the thought systems of Oriental societies, especially at the time before their original cultural systems became subjected to a great extent to foreign influence, we would have to locate it on the left side of the diagram. Then as Oriental cultures adopted increasingly theoretical orientations from their contact with the Western world, their position shifted farther to the right. But the shift from left to right at a given level of scientific knowledge does not imply economic, social, or scientific progress. It merely shows a gradual change in the composition of thought patterns dominant in a society.

For example, a perusal of Joseph Needham's discussion of the origin of scientific thought in China would, I believe, show quite clearly how strong the aesthetic approach in early Chinese science was.[7] Yet it is well known that China experienced a more rapid and far-reaching scientific and technical progress than the Western world before the twelfth or the thirteenth century. The invention of such important objects and processes as gunpowder, porcelain, printing, and various more efficient methods of smelting and refining metals occurred much earlier in China than in the West. These facts are too well known to require extended discussion. In fact, it may be maintained that the inventions which can be accomplished on the basis of intensive practical experiments may be as readily, and perhaps more easily, possible in a civilization with predominantly aesthetic thought patterns rather than in one with principally theoretical thought patterns.

To this might be added that not all Oriental societies exhibited the same mixture of aesthetic and theoretical thought patterns in their original state. Though my acquaintance with scientific or pseudo-scientific thought in ancient Indian natural philosophy is limited, I have the

[7] See Joseph Needham (6, vol. 2, pp. 220–231 esp.), depicting the origin of scientifically relevant ideographic characters; but see also the subsequent presentation of the growth of basic scientific conceptions in China.

impression that it comprehended a somewhat larger element of theoretical orientation than Chinese philosophical thought of the Han or pre-Han period. Some supporting evidence for this may perhaps be derived from a study of the ideological and philosophical contrasts which arose as a consequence of the introduction of Buddhism in China. But a comparative study of either Indian or Chinese thought patterns with those of early medieval Europe shows that, in spite of the fact that scientific insights and technical performance of Europe in the eleventh and twelfth centuries were in no way superior, and in fact quite inferior, to the corresponding attainments in Asia, the Asian thought processes displayed a much less intensive theoretical orientation than the European ones. In fact the philosophy of early medieval Europe shows a strong deficiency in adequately confronting aesthetic approaches.[8] It might perhaps even be argued that the slowness of technical and material progress in early medieval Europe was not unrelated to the predominantly abstract a prioristic thought patterns of the tenth and eleventh centuries.

Hence, one of the variables related to different value systems represented in Figure 1 are systems of thought. The other variable related to them in the diagram is the level of economic and social complexity. Little needs to be said about this relation, for it will be quite commonly accepted that with an increase of some magnitude in economic and social complexity the system and hierarchy of socially relevant values change. Thus the diagram may be interpreted as presenting, in a very general way, the interrelation of values, economic performance, and patterns of thought, without any indication as to which of these variables are independent and which are dependent. We are concerned with a complex process of change often of long duration (i.e., lasting over decades and even centuries), and assigning the role of independence under all circumstances to any one of the three variables would constitute a highly one-sided interpretation. The transformation of value systems depends upon economic and socio-structural as well as "philosophical" variables, and changes in all these latter variables are partly dependent upon variations in social values.

The consequence of this mutual interdependence of several broadly defined factors is that each of the four boxes in Figure 1 represents a separate economic and cultural system exhibiting a particular combination of thought patterns, economic performance, and social values. But this conclusion raises the further question of what process of change takes place when a social system moves from one of the boxes to another. The three curves, labeled A, B, and C in Figure 1, show the path along which a society may move, and in view of the preceding propositions

[8] On the differences between the philosophical attitudes in India and China, see Needham (6, pp. 419 ff.), where the influence of Buddhism on Chinese science and scientific thought is discussed. On the development of western theory-oriented thinking see the very excellent exposition in R. W. Southern, (12, chapter 4, esp.).

presented, the crucial point on the path is that where a society passes from one box to the next one.

Now it should be stated that though in the diagram the lines between the boxes establish sharp boundaries, in actual fact each of the boundaries is a fairly fuzzy area. In other words, we may consider the passage from one box into the next as a historical process which may often take place during a long period of time. We may also consider it as a process in which the transition in values, economic performance, and thought patterns does not affect all social classes and sub-groups at the same time and that there are certain members of the society which perform the transition to new values, new thought patterns, and new forms of economic action faster and others slower. Hence the boundary areas between the systems represented by the four boxes should be interpreted as forming situations in which some members of a population adopt different attitudes and accept different values than others. I will discuss these points in somewhat more detail later in this chapter.

In view of what has been said so far it appears desirable to say, before concluding, a few more words on three topics which are raised by the analysis presented in the preceding paragraphs. First, some further explanation of the complex aesthetic sector of the diagram has to be given; second, a few comments should be made on the relationship between the diagram and my comments on it and Northrop's anticipation of the "proper" integration between Eastern and Western value systems in the form of what he calls "epistemic correlations."[9] Finally a few words may be in order on a problem which is also raised by the attempt to introduce thoughts derived from Northrop, i.e., the interrelation between systems of thought and philosophical speculation and systems of values. As we shall see, there is some interrelation between the first two topics, whereas the third covers a more general and independent set of propositions.

The stipulation of a complex aesthetic sector provides a fourth alternative to Weber's unilineal tripartite classification of tradition, instrumental rationality, and rationality in social values or purposive rationality. A brief examination of this fourth alternative shows that it is the result of economic and social progress, on the one hand, and the refusal to move away from the predominance of an aesthetic orientation, on the other. In other words, it is a system in which often complex and sometimes highly productive economic units or large complex social groups have become accepted and institutionalized, but in which individuals react and think in terms of immediate, strictly isolated issues and events rather than in response to an integrated system of abstract analysis of these

---

[9] See Northrop (7, pp. 440 ff., esp. pp. 442–443). Perhaps the briefest definition of this term given by Northrop himself is: "The aesthetic, intuitive, purely empirically given component in man and nature is related to the theoretically designated and indirect verified component . . . by the two-termed relation of epistemic correlation."

events or to a generalized schema of expectations. The differences which were outlined earlier between modern rationalized capitalist entrepreneurship, on the one hand, and bazaar-entrepreneurship, on the other, clearly show the basic mode of operation of a privately-owned economic unit in a complex aesthetic system of values. Though the typical bazaar-entrepreneur controls a small or at best medium-scale business, the principle of decision-making manifested by his behavior can also be applied to large-scale plants. This may be one of the reasons why, in spite of much lower unit costs of labor and some other services, total operating costs in many modern Asian firms are higher than in Western enterprises of comparable size. It may also be the reason why certain new fields of industrial development in Asia and other non-Western countries depend upon foreign investment or are left to the initiative of public agencies, though there are no legal impediments for the full display of private entrepreneurship.

This development is the outcome of a combined impact of the maintenance of complex aesthetic values and a growth in overall productive and general economic efficiency. But the decisive step is only taken when a society gradually passes beyond the aesthetic system of thought and achieves some compromise with the theoretical system of thought, i.e., when it moves to the right in Figure I. In more concrete language, once a society has, in terms of economic performance, reached a relatively high level of output, it finds itself in what I have called the complex aesthetic sector. As its system of values and thought gradually adopts characteristics of the theory-oriented Western societies, it is moving from the complex aesthetic to the value rational sector. This movement corresponds to what Northrop calls epistemic correlation, except that he disregards the level of economic performance at which this association between Eastern and Western systems of thought and values is attained. To Northrop the attainment of an epistemic correlation is due to adjustments in philosophy and rules of scientific inquiry, whereas if explicit attention is given to the conditions of economic growth, this correspondence between differentially derived systems of thought and values leads to the reflection that it is normally the result of social and economic progress on the one hand and the refusal or inability to abandon abruptly the predominance of a value orientation and adopt the other.

A study of the economic structures prevalent in social systems characterized by this correspondence of value and thought systems would show that some of the planned Asian economies have begun to incorporate more or less well integrated systems of epistemic correlation of thought. In practice this correlation is shown by the adoption of a multitude of theoretically derived strategies of economic planning, associated with frequent dismal failures in the execution of these plans owing to the imperfect penetration with theoretical attitudes of those who are called upon to execute the plans. An analysis of the experience of Communist

Chinese planning during the last few years yields results which could be interpreted in this fashion. A similar result would emerge from a study of the theoretical and concrete issues involved in the execution of development plans in other Asian countries. The dominance of an epistemic correlation in its initial, and as yet very imperfectly integrated, stage results in the fact that in spite of official efforts to impose rational plans, their implementation meets with very unequal success. Conflicts arise because each project is judged in its own terms, rather than as a fitting part of a whole, and these conflicts often lead to failures in execution, for the participants in a conflict situation tend to interpret each issue as an indivisible whole, circumscribed within its own dimension, rather than as part of a total system in which its function and place can be at least roughly estimated.

This discussion could be expanded from the analysis of economic performance to that of political behavior. The results in this sector of social action would differ from those arising in the economic sector, but here also a wide contrast may be expected between the interpretation of issues on the part of some, especially Western-educated leaders and that of the large mass of followers. This, in turn, will influence the practical exercise of political activity, the kind of propaganda employed, and the type of party organization preferred. This is not the place to enter into a full discussion of these consequences, but they would clearly be brought to light by an examination of the recent history of political movements in newly independent countries of Asia, especially in India, Burma, and Indonesia, where an effort for, or at least a semblance of, democratic political action was made. In these countries political developments, consisting either of widespread acquiescence to sudden changes in political objectives, frequent violent demonstrations, abrupt changes in leadership, and other forms took place, which can most easily be explained by the failure of epistemic correlation of values and thought patterns to have taken place on any other level than that of a small leadership group of intellectuals and members of a political and economic elite.

This discussion suggests that in the nations of Southern and Southeastern Asia, and possibly elsewhere, there exists a contrast of thought processes between persons on different levels of education, political power, and economic roles. The intellectual, political, and economic elites are sufficiently Westernized to understand, and to have integrated to a considerable degree, thought and even values based upon the Western theoretical approach. In other words, these persons have achieved, to a fair degree, the internalization of thought and value patterns exhibiting the epistemic correlation described in Northrop's work. But the large masses in these countries, though touched upon externally by the theoretical approach of the West — if in no other form, at least through contact with the former colonial administrations, businessmen, or planters, who came from Europe — have remained fully within the aesthetic thought and value patterns of their cultures. And it should be added that even the intellectuals and members of other elites, in spite of their adoption of theoretical approaches on the level of thought and scientific enquiry, have adopted them much less on the level of socially relevant values. This intermediate position of many members of the elites in Asian countries has been observed numerous times, and has been well described by Edward Shils in his various essays on the Indian intellectuals.[10] Though Shils maintains that the frequently asserted uprootedness and the suspense between two cultures of the Indian intellectual is based on a romantic and wrong conception of his role, he shows in the sphere in which explicit thought processes predominate, that influence of and commitment to European theoretical patterns is widespread, and that the impact of what we have designated as an aesthetic orientation predominates in the personal relations of these individuals, in their contacts with their families and friends, and in the general acceptance of social value systems. Anyone who, like this writer, has maintained close personal contacts with Indian intellectuals must have observed that many of them lead what might almost be described a Jekyll-and-Hyde existences, i.e., that in some contexts they act in a manner based almost exclusively on theoretical thought patterns, and in others, especially those relating to the ordinary performance of daily living and close personal relations, they revert to behavior ultimately inspired by aesthetically determined attitudes.

These views could be elaborated further. As a first step they may be regarded as providing some examples for the proposition made earlier in the chapter that the passage of a society from one box in Figure 1 to another takes place through a "fuzzy" zone in which different social groups or classes have contrasting and often contradictory values and economic attitudes. India and China may be assumed to be in such an intermediate position at this time. The impact of theoretical orientations in the thought patterns of these nations tends to increase the influence of rational approaches to various forms of behavior and to subject the intellectuals especially to a growing internalization of rational attitudes. In both India and China this differentiation in values and thought patterns and even in economic attitudes is apparently quite pronounced and is surely one of the reasons why some have observed a wide cultural gap between urban and rural areas in these countries; in other words, why they have regarded urban areas as social and cultural "exclaves" of the nations in which they are located.[11]

A more complete understanding of this problem of transition from one socio-cultural system associated with a particular level of economic performance and a peculiar mixture of thought patterns to an-

[10] See, for example, Edward Shils (10), and M. K. Halder and Robin Ghosh (3).
[11] I have discussed this problem in greater detail in (4, chapter 7).

other may perhaps be provided by a discussion of the economic and social history of Japan in the last 200 years. For in the pre-Tokugawa period, Japan, due to the far-flung adoption of cultural, intellectual, and even socio-economic traits from China, may be said to have been in an economic and cultural situation which would have placed it in Area T in the diagram presented earlier. During the Tokugawa period it gradually moved from Area T into Area C, and in the period since the Meiji restoration, from Area C into Area V. An extensive elaboration of this process would require too much space, but consultation of the more enlightened descriptions of Japanese social and economic history during the last 400 years shows that during the Tokugawa period, especially from about 1600 to 1800, there occured a substantial growth of the Japanese economy without a profound change in values. The social structure also changed; the actual or putative kinship groups which had formed the village, through which production was organized, and which were quite common at the beginning of the Tokugawa period, had come to survive only in highly isolated outlying villages. The use of technology, e.g., various improved fertilizers in agriculture, the growth of a middle sector, the great rise of urban populations, the establishment of a fairly widespread market system in which merchants, craftsmen, and middlemen of various kinds could be found, were developments which all took place in the period of Tokugawa rule, even though the basic traditional cultural and social values, though under stress and strain, fundamentally remained unchanged.

T. C. Smith has presented a good deal of support for this interpretation of social and economic, as well as cultural, developments in Tokugawa Japan. He explains that the stability of the system depended upon the loyalty and discipline of the peasants (who formed the vast majority of the population of Japan at that period), upon the "traditional language of loyalty and obligation," upon "old values," and upon the fact that while the Tokugawa regime "created conditions favorable to change; cities grew, communications improved, industry spread from town to countryside . . . government did its best to isolate the village from the effects of these and other changes." Traditional values in the villages and even among many of the more recent migrants to urban areas survived into the early Meiji period and the new masters of Japan in that period still attempted to use tradition, on behalf of change, and "the primacy of values of loyalty and obedience did not collapse; they were continuously reinforced by stronger, more efficient measures of indoctrination and thought control by the state."

Yet even though in the period after the restoration of the Meiji emperor the support of traditional values was used, the new developments in the economy and the political situation of Japan required the gradual transition to more rationally inspired patterns of thought. Smith describes this by pointing to the fact that "rational thought, which an educational system dedicated to the advancement of science and technology was bound to promote," grew and affected not only economic but also political and social relations. In fact the whole development of Japan in the period from the end of the nineteenth century to the outbreak of the Pacific war may be interpreted as a period in which the growing demand for the wider spread of rational values conflicted with the attempt to base the power of the dominant political elite on reinforcement of certain traditions, especially those relating to loyalty and obedience. In this situation, as Smith points out, "the groups in control of the state had no choice but to sustain orthodoxy. . . . There was no way to go ahead; but that way lay a further weakening of tradition which, the weaker it became, was the more needed to give stability and command effort. . . . The ultimate price the nation paid was to be led without enthusiasm into a war that could not be won."[12]

From this we may note that in the period roughly before 1870, the advance of the economy and the growing complexity of the social stratification system were associated with little change in values, but that with the new industrialization pattern and the development of new and much more far-reaching objectives in foreign policy, new thought patterns and with them gradually new values, based on more rational orientations, became the rule. It is in this sense that the historical development of Japan may be considered to have passed from the more simple and traditionally-oriented system of social order to the more complex and rationally-oriented one. I cannot produce a set of clear-cut explanations for the causes of this development. The regularization of political control, the successful enforcement of internal peace, and the strong and persistent leadership of a small conscientious elite in the early Tokugawa period may have been among the major causal factors responsible for the economic advancement of Japan. Similarly, the growing involvement in world affairs, the recognition of the need for rapid industrial development, improved armament, and modernization of production and administrative processes, again by a small, conscientious, and strongly devoted elite interested primarily in the advancement of their own country, may have been among the causal conditions bringing about a trend towards rationalization of thought patterns and the rapid adoption of intellectual, scientific, technological, and other characteristics of the Western world. The result is that at the present time even the last surviving traditional, chiefly aesthetically-oriented values tend to disappear completely in Japan and its overall attitudes and approaches to problems are almost undistinguishable from those of the Western world.

These reflections lead us to the final point, the relationship between values and thought patterns, and changes in each. In the work of Northrop there is no sharp distinction made between the two, and though

---

[12] The discussion in this and the preceding paragraphs is based on the excellent book of Thomas C. Smith (11, pp. 203–206).

sociologists following Weber have usually talked only of values, they believe that values influence patterns of thought. In societies with cultures in which change is slow, or in which strong traditions have developed which pass on the major framework of an existing value structure from generation to generation, there is a close correlation between values and thought patterns, and instituted aesthetic or theoretical thought systems will be closely associated with social values, since both are acquired through the same socialization processes. In other words, as children grow up in a society with well-established cultural traditions, they acquire in the course of their upbringing manifold parts of a system of cultural values and thought processes which already are integrated through tradition and the long-standing operation of various forms of mutual social adjustment.

But the situation is different in a society in which the socialization process and that of formal education are separated, as is true now for an increasing number of persons in Asia and Africa. This separation brings about conflicts in the underlying assumptions and understandings of persons who go through each of these processes by itself; conflict is likely to be stronger in those societies in which socialization requires close association with persons who are neglected or even treated as inferior in more formal schooling. It is not necessary to go into this point further, since its consequences are easily intelligible. It is a very rough description of what happens in Asian countries today, where the general process of socialization takes place in the homes of the people and is strongly associated with deeply tradition-bound women, and where education takes place in schools with a curriculum and a course content derived from a foreign culture. The persons who have only brief and relatively superficial contact with formal schooling are little touched by this experience and have therefore maintained value patterns and thought patterns basically derived from the aesthetic attitude. But those who have spent much time in schools, particularly those who have attended school in Western countries, and who upon returning home have been placed in jobs in which their knowledge acquired abroad is considered necessary, are in a serious dilemma. Their values were acquired through socialization in their homes subject to a prevalence of Eastern aesthetic inclinations, whereas their thought patterns were shaped powerfully by the theoretical orientations of the West.

One of the as yet unsolved problems is the question of how these two parts of the "educational" process influence one another. It is often maintained that the more advanced theoretical inclinations of Western-trained persons in Asia gradually bring about acceptance of these Western "values." It is also said that since the persons with the more strongly pronounced theoretical orientation occupy high positions of political or economic power, their "values" tend to exert an influence on those on lower levels in their societies. All these conclusions may be true, but

they may also be merely comfortable arguments without empirical support of those who favor political, economic, and intellectual "modernization." It is possible to cite quite a few historical cases in which an intellectual or even political elite had to accept the value system of the
population at large if it wanted to maintain its position in the societies
of which it was part.[13] In short, in nations in which the socialization and
the formal education processes are subject to principles derived from
different value orientations and different ingrained thought patterns, the
two systems of thought and values lead to different adjustments in persons, depending in part on the varying degree of exposure to the two kinds
of influences, and hence tend to produce a range of persons subject to
a variety of combinations of value and thought patterns derived from two
conflicting origins. Some do incorporate the epistemic correlation which
Northrop considers to be required for the whole society, if East and West
are ultimately to meet. But in the present period, the basic value orientations of many Asians conflict with their thought patterns to a considerable extent and the mutual impact of these conflicting attitudes is still in
doubt. For although, as already pointed out, the general assumption is
made that the Western-educated elite will bring about a change in the
general values, this is by no means certain, and the interrelation between
values acquired in early youth and thought patterns acquired principally
through formal educational experience requires a good deal more research. Only when we have looked more intensively and carefully into
this interrelation in the changing societies of Asia and Africa will we
have a more certain view on the role of values in social and economic
change.

BIBLIOGRAPHY

1. Bendix, Reinhard. *Max Weber, An Intellectual Portrait*. Garden City,
   N.Y.: Doubleday & Co., 1960.

2. Geertz, Clifford. "Social Change and Economic Modernization in Two
   Indonesian Towns," in Everett E. Hagen (ed.), *On the Theory of Social
   Change*. Homewood, Ill.: The Dorsey Press, 1962.

3. Halder, M. K., and Robin Ghosh. *Problems of Economic Growth*. Delhi:
   Congress for Cultural Freedom, 1960.

4. Hoselitz, Bert F. *Sociological Aspects of Economic Growth*. Glencoe,
   Ill.: The Free Press, 1960.

5. Hoselitz, Bert F. "Tradition and Economic Growth," in Ralph Braibanti
   and J. S. Spengler (eds.), *Tradition, Values and Socio-Economic Development*. Durham, N.C.: Duke University Press, 1961.

---

[13] A good example is provided by the political changes in Burma in the last
few years in which the more "modernized" and the more "traditional" factions held
each other in balance.

6. Needham, Joseph. *Science and Civilization in China.* Cambridge: Cambridge University Press, 1956.

7. Northrop, F.S.C. *The Meeting of East and West.* New York: The Macmillan Co., 1960.

8. Popper, K. R. *The Open Society and Its Enemies.* London: George Routledge and Sons, 1947.

9. Redfield, Robert. "The Folk Society," *American Journal of Sociology,* Vol. 52, No. 4 (1947), pp. 292–308.

10. Shils, Edward. "The Culture of the Indian Intellectual," *The Sewanee Review,* Vol. 67 (April and July), pp. 239–261, pp. 401–421.

11. Smith, Thomas C. *The Agrarian Origins of Modern Japan.* Stanford: Stanford University Press, 1959.

12. Southern, R. W. *The Making of the Middle Ages.* New Haven: Yale University Press, 1961.

13. Weber, Max. *The Protestant Ethic and the Spirit of Capitalism,* translated by Talcott Parsons. London: Allen & Unwin, 1930.

14. Weber, Max. *The Theory of Social and Economic Organization.* New York: Oxford University Press, 1947.

15. Weber, Max. *The Religion of India.* Glencoe, Ill.: The Free Press, 1958.

SECTION EIGHT

Special Areas of Institutional Change

The chapters in this Section are case studies of specific institutions, ranging from broad complexes such as education or science to more narrow confines such as railroads or philanthropic foundations. Regardless of the variations in scope, all these studies are sensitive to the multiple interaction between changes in the institutions focused upon and others which impinge upon them. If one reflects back upon earlier theoretical formulations relevant to these causal relationships, such as the Marxist, or the Ogburn "lag" concept, one is struck by their relatively dogmatic and simplistic quality. The present formulations tend to be tentative, "open-ended," avoiding premature closure. If the basic method of science involves, as Karl Popper has put it, "the successive casting out of error," then it would seem that the approach exemplified by the chapters in this section (and throughout the entire volume) would put us on the right track.

The general emphasis on the "relational" aspects of institutions can be quickly indicated. Cottrell treats railroads as "multifunctional" institutions; Marcus shows how trade unions adjust continually to both "internal" and "external" changes; Colvard points out that philanthropic foundations are both examples and instruments of social change; Duncan Mitchell looks at the British educational system in the light of changing class structure and technological developments; and Hirsch is concerned with the role of the scientific establishment vis-à-vis the industrial, political, and academic realms. To be sure, nothing could be easier than the reaffirmation of the tenet that everything in society is related to everything else. In this sense Kingsley Davis' assertion that sociology is identical with functional analysis can hardly be gainsaid. But the contributors to this Section go beyond "the painful elaboration of the obvious," as some wag has characterized the field of sociology, by asking whether and how and under what conditions some types of inter-institutional relationships are more deterministic than others. They are thus reopening the basic questions which have been asked by past generations of analysts, questions which for a number of reasons have been unduly neglected in more recent times, as pointed out by several of our contributors. Let us now glance at the substantive problems raised in the present Section.

Colvard analyzes the manner in which philanthropic foundations attempt to maintain their social legitimacy while at the same time fulfilling their functions as tax shelters for those who wish to go down in history as "benefactors" rather than "malefactors of great wealth" (a term used by Theodore Roosevelt to castigate the men who accused him of being a traitor to his class). Accomplishing this successfully requires that the foundations avoid being hung upon the horns of several dilemmas: they must show that the money they are spending could not be spent more equitably and intelligently by public agencies, yet they must avoid "controversial" causes which can be attacked as not being "in the public interest." Several foundations have been under double jeopardy; they have been accused on the one hand of subsidizing social research in safely established areas on the part of individuals and organizations which already get the lion's share of support; on the other hand they have been accused of subverting established social norms by supporting empirical research, such as Kinsey's study of sexual behavior. Furthermore, Colvard points out, in attempting to implement the goals of improving the work of scientific and educational institutions, the foundations necessarily are limited by their clients' legitimate assertion of autonomy from outside constraints, thus losing the freedom of action necessary for accomplishing their purpose. In a sense the foundations are committed to sowing the seeds of their own destruction; but since no organization can be expected to engage in such enterprise wholeheartedly we must expect them to build defense mechanisms to maintain their own autonomy and continued existence.

In his study of the changing structure and operation of American trade unions Marcus shows that Michels' "iron law of oligarchy" and its modification by Lipset and others tend to cut prematurely the chain of possible cause-and-effect relations inherent in institutional interaction. His own "dialectic" model stresses continuous adjustment of unions to changes occurring both within the organizational structure and in the outside environment, and stresses the interplay between the two sets of determinants. Thus he points out that changes in the organization of industry tend to produce increased centralization within unions, but this does not necessarily result in decreased control of union policies by the rank and file. Given certain circumstances it may bring about an increase in the members' decision-making powers vis-à-vis their own leaders and management as well.

Duncan Mitchell traces the stages of the "silent revolution" which has transformed the British educational system since the middle of the last century. He shows in some detail that the reforms — and the opposition to them — have been class-linked, but avoids reducing his explanation to class as the single or always most important determining factor. The insistence of a Matthew Arnold on the "cultural" functions of education demonstrated the existence of non-economic values and interests. It is plain that during the latter half of the nineteenth century the industrial bourgeoisie pressed for improvement and extension of technical education for the lower classes, in order to compete effectively with the productive power of their countries. But Duncan Mitchell points out that the Education Act of 1944, which struck at the traditional distinction between education for gentlemen and for plain people, was supported by a coalition of Conservatives, Liberals, and Socialists. It would be premature to assert that the recent reforms symbolize the death knell of the British class system or the successful construction of a "New Jerusalem" — evidence to the contrary is all too easily observable. While Duncan Mitchell is ideologically committed to the open society, as a sociologist he is aware of the need to strike a balance between the maximum development of skills and talents and the need to avoid the danger of overdeveloped aspirations among the lower social strata. The fact that the suicide rate among their representatives at Oxbridge seems to be rather high reaffirms the validity of Durkheim's conception of anomie.

The strategic role of science as a determinant of social change needs no documentation. It is equally plain that the state of education has an intimate connection with the viability of science as a social institution. What is still largely unexplored is the degree to which science depends on political and social institutions for its optimum development. The assumption that democracy is the best matrix for the flourishing of science is no longer as obvious as it was during the pre-Sputnik period. In his chapter Hirsch raises the question of the actual degree of freedom possessed by American scientists in order to clarify the basic problems relating to the autonomy of science in different social systems. If science is one of the major determinants of social change, are scientists aware of their role as potential "legislators of humanity," and if so, are they in a position to implement this role? The first question is raised for rhetorical purposes only in the present chapter. As to the second, Hirsch seeks to demonstrate that scientists operate typically within three major settings: the industrial, the political, and the academic. In the industrial and political settings the scientist must necessarily "integrate" his role as scientist with the requirements of organizations whose basic goals are non-scientific. As a result, the scientist is "co-opted" by the political and economic decision-makers, reducing his decision-making power and the autonomy of the scientific establishment. Furthermore the universities, traditional bastions of Lehrfreiheit *(freedom to teach) and* Lernfreiheit *(freedom to learn), are coming increasingly under the hegemony of the political and economic realms. Whatever countervailing power scientists seek to muster is seriously limited by the splintering of the scientific roles and the lack of consensus as to social goals within the scientific establishment.*

27

Fred Cottrell

Technology and Social Change,

on American Railroads[1]

Some theorists hold that man is inexorably driven by technology through specific kinds of social change to predictable forms of social organization. The orthodox Marxian, among others, holds this point of view. But, on both sides of the Iron Curtain, those who have tried to put knowledge about material things into operation have found no sure guide showing how to get innovations adopted with only the expected results.

The fact that technological change is always accompanied by social change is not in doubt. What is questionable is the nature of the relationship between them. Which is cause and which effect? What is the order of their appearance; must the social come before, simultaneously with, or after the technological? We cannot rely upon time sequence alone to reveal what is causal. Much of what a man does is done in anticipation of its consequences. In that case, which is causal, the thing supposed to produce the result, or the thoughts of the man who anticipated it? For this and still other reasons scientists have modified older concepts of causation. Instead the search is for propositions that will increase the accuracy of statements about the probability that, under certain conditions, prescribed events can be reliably expected to recur. The formulation of these propositions does not dispose of the necessity

[1] The author wishes gratefully to acknowledge the financial aid he received from the Social Science Research Council in support of the research upon which this study was based.

to observe facts and their order. It does raise a question as to the significance of sequence. All scientific law requires us to show that "under these conditions, when this occurred it was followed by this." In this sense history is a necessity. But in a laboratory the order in which the elements making up the required configuration are brought together can be altered and the discovery made as to whether order is significant. Often it can be shown that what are called "predisposing causes," to be set off by the introduction of "precipitating causes,"[2] can themselves produce the expected result if they are introduced into a situation where the other necessary factors already exist. It then becomes clear that in some cases what is required is not specific order but only the completion of a given configuration, in whatever order. It then becomes of little significance that a particular order was observed at the point where the law was first formulated.

Sometimes the same conditions hold in the development of social science. But many of the kinds of things we are trying to relate have happened in only a few places and not very many times. In these cases order may seem to be invariate. Moreover, since the bulk of social phenomena is carried from one generation to another as a single "bundle" of culture, it is hard to discover what is in a causal sense necessary for the persistence of a specific complex and what is only adventitious. As cultures are put under strain or become disorganized over time, we may find that often what seemed manifestly a causal connection to the actors involved at the time has later been shown to be dispensable. The historian reports what he sees, that all these things are going on, in this order. However, what the people involved thought necessary may not be important and they might not have even recorded the most significant factors later shown to have been inducing the behavior reported by the historian.

Until recently advanced technology was the possession of a limited number of Western peoples who had common origins, fairly similar institutional arrangements, and hierarchies of value. Since the technology had not been put into operation elsewhere it was natural for Westerners to assume that all the arrangements characteristic of these cultures were equally necessary to the achievement and perpetuation of scientific and technological advance. As more evidence came in, it became apparent that in the long past, where a very wide range of social systems experimented with a wide range of geographic and technical conditions, change

---

[2] This dichotomy has been widely used, particularly in the behavioral studies, since it was first enunciated by Edward Glover (6). Many economists use another dichotomy in which "all other things" are supposed to remain equal while there is variation in the factor whose causal influence they are examining. In both cases an assumption is made that one set of "causes" can vary independently of the others. This is a prejudgment that is frequently not demonstrable either theoretically or empirically and the assumption may introduce an initial error which invalidates all subsequent manipulation of the evidence.

did *not* always take place in a given order, a particular kind of technological change was not always associated with the same kind of change, nor were all of the particular institutional arrangements surrounding use of a particular technology the same. Stage theory broke down and for a time any kind of secular trend or ordered appearance of social change was denied. All kinds of evolutionary models were under attack.

But the practical necessity of doing something about technological change remains. Science and technology *are* dynamic and *do* have effects. Those who would use them have to develop some kind of idea about how they should proceed. They need to avoid the massive errors that might prevent success in the foreseeable future. They need to know what the social consequences of the technology they seek to use are to be, for inevitably the effects that technology has will also affect whether it will continue to advance and spread or be cut off. Those who hold values likely to be destroyed or downgraded in the hierarchy of a society as a consequence of technological change are as vitally affected as are those who hope to achieve more of their own values and upgrade them in the hierarchy by the same changes.

For example, small farmers, businessmen, and others with a stake in rural living make strenuous efforts to prevent the advance of technology which threatens their way of life. Some, like the Amish, attempt directly to prevent the use of the new technique. Others seek to impose indirect controls, as in limiting the size of the planting in tobacco, that have the effect of rendering machine technology unusable. In other cases the effort takes the form of using taxation to saddle the innovators with at least part of the losses suffered by those disadvantaged by the change. There are also many other types of situations where "conscientious sabotage," to use Veblen's phrase, takes place. These include "featherbedding" by unions and similar but not so widely recognized actions by management. Local government itself is retained in forms not suitable for the effective use of modern technology in areas like the maintenance of health, sanitation, fire and police protection. Very often the people who resist change are unable to verbalize in ideological terms the rationalization for what they are doing. What is important for the theory of change is the fact that they *act* on the basis of their feelings about the specific issues before them, often without knowing how these acts will affect some other conditions to which they will then have to react. It would be foolish for the theorist to expect that mere demonstration that something is "technologically superior" will automatically win the enthusiastic support or even the compliance of such people.

Nevertheless, the question as to just what *must* be done if the benefits possible only with the use of new technology are to be gained in a particular society becomes increasingly important at the same time that it is increasingly difficult to discover. If the people in the older industrialized states act on a melange of ideology, experience, rationality, and anticipation, those in unindustrialized areas must on the other hand try to find some theory on which to stake their own efforts. In other words, they must fight the battle along theoretical and/or ideological lines if they are not to depend upon blind trial and error in a situation where too many mistakes may prove fatal to their cause. So Westerners who would extend aid to them must be as concerned to know what will achieve the desired technological breakthrough as are the Marxists who insist they already have the answer. Under these circumstances, "stage" theory is again invoked, and evolution, particularly cultural evolution, is once more restored to intellectual respectability. (See, for example, [15].) We now know that recent efforts directly to reproduce in "underdeveloped" areas certain kinds of social organization that are already stable and regenerative in older industrial states have had results quite different from those anticipated. Whether or not specific sequence *is* required for innovation, it is clear that it is necessary for certain social and technological achievements to have been made before a viable industrial system can *survive* without outside support. In the absence of these technological factors tremendous ideological efforts to produce "advanced" systems turn out to be abortive.

Yet to determine just what the required technological conditions are for the achievement of given social values is not itself easy. There is great difficulty in classifying or typifying technologies without using criteria that are at least in part social phenomena. Without some means to categorize them which is independent of the social matrix within which they operate, there is constant danger of elliptical reasoning that gives no means to assess separately the influence of the ongoing technological, physical, or biological processes, as distinguished from that of social processes. We thus cannot say whether a given system succeeded primarily because it was capable of handling technological factors effectively or because the social arrangements met the expectations of the people who used them.

A Model Using Energy as a Factor in Change

It was to help break out of this cycle that I attempted in *Energy and Society* (4) to develop a model in which technology could be analyzed in terms of the energy conversion involved in its operation. The thought was that if we could show by measuring energy that *alterations in its flow* on a social system were correlated with *social changes* in that system, we might thus establish a means to know something about how dependent *were the appearance and survival of particular kinds of social phenomena on the material conditions necessary to secure and direct that flow.* It would be redundant to develop the whole case made there. Since the model used there will also be used now, I must outline it.

First of all, this is a feedback model. It has recently become popular to treat almost any kind of interaction as feedback. There is some justification for this position. But the model we are using is one which depends on instruments to trace and measure *energy flow* directly in *physical terms*.

In feedback systems a part, often a tiny part, of the energy being converted by a system is, through instruments, directed to "sense" some "outside" condition, and, in terms of its findings, redirect the flow being converted through the whole system. From energy derived from the larger source, what once was a tiny influence thus comes to be a major one. So one element involved in creating the ecological balance between man and his environment is the constant appearance of variables which, because they do or do not result in increased energy flow, do or do not have increased chance for survival in competition with other pre-existing variables.

Man's control over energy is always limited. The social arrangements that maximize energy flow from the physical and biological world *are by reason of that fact* provided with one advantage in survival vis à vis others that achieve smaller flows. This is not to say that all systems found at any point will be those that maximize the energy flow possible there. Social systems that achieve higher energy flows may at the same time use them less effectively to meet required conditions than do others that can convert only smaller flows. Before the probability that any system would survive in competition with another could be accurately stated, it would be necessary to examine all of the relevant conditions. But this does not deny the significance of energy flow per se. It means that to overcome the handicap of a lower energy flow a system must have some other offsetting advantage. Obviously there will be many situations wherein such offsetting factors do exist and energy differential is not sufficient to be overriding.

But the obverse is also true, and when the energy differential is very great it may lead to the survival of systems that are in almost everything else less conducive to survival than those they replace. That is, they may disrupt the functions of the family and community, undermine the authority of the religious, result in the destruction of old economic arrangements, and destroy the ability of a government long in power to rule legitimately, yet survive simply because the energy flow is sufficient to overcome these handicaps and simultaneously to provide through feedback the means to establish new institutions that better serve technology and sustain increased flow of energy.

The new arrangements in turn may subsequently be subject to competition with still other innovations that further increase energy flow or more effectively utilize it to achieve the values of those who control it. That which moves in the direction of the maximum flow a particular technology permits survives more often than does any other set of relationships which innovators have offered. For this reason the tendency to identify technological change with "progress" may be to a certain extent valid, if one means by progress, change sustained in a particular direction.

However, we must also recognize that many of the decisions made, which have this effect, were not consciously directed to this end. Energy flow is not per se the objective of many men. But what they do seek is usually to be obtained only with the expenditure of both time and energy. Increased energy may be used either to secure more things in the same time or to reduce the time which must be spent to secure things. The effects are not uniform. New technology in one field may permit the use of such an increase in energy that costs fall tremendously, while at the same time to do something else takes just as much time and energy from old sources as previously. If people contemplating the changed costs either decide to get the old ends by new means, or to choose as ends more of what has become less costly and less of what is now relatively more costly, they are altering their value hierarchies. They proceed to provide social sanction for the new roles necessary to make the new technology operative. Moreover, in providing new sanctions they create a new morality and value hierarchy that is then passed on to succeeding generations. What was originally to be secured through individual experience in adjusting to new technology is now obtained through cultural transmission.

Heuristically it is justifiable to study separately values, ecology, technology, and culture but those who study the behavior of men in changing situations will always find change going on in all of the categories of evidence they study.

Analysis of social structure or the institutionalized means to use particular kinds of technology will show that here, too, the existing arrangements are being reinforced by feedback from the system. As innovators produce new variables in order to use a particular kind of technology these variables are either reinforced by feedback because they enlarge the flow of energy or are put in jeopardy by their failures to do so effectively. For institutions that do permit increases in energy flow, simultaneously put into the hands of those who control them increased means with which to seduce, corrupt, or coerce those who would oppose them.

When we say that this is a feedback model we must of course recognize that it is not a complete explanation of social change. We do not go into the nature of the relation between the origins of specific innovation and its selection for survival or elimination, though obviously, as we have already pointed out, there is some relationship between what is anticipated to be the consequence of an act and the choice either to perform it or not. Nor does the theory attempt to deal with change not dependent on or responsive to changes in energy flow. The emphasis here is rather on the "law of effect." That is, we are concerned with classifying actions in terms of what happens *as a consequence* of man's having done some particular thing.

It is clear that some of what happens could only have happened because men reflected on what they had observed, speculated about it, and decided on the basis of their own values whether to repeat past acts or undertake new ones. Whether they are able to act in a particular way and still be within the limits permissible in their society, with social approval, or must violate norms to put new inventions into action will, of course, be part of the anticipated effects. It is not only technological gains or losses that affect the innovator's decision, nor are the effects of his acts confined to the realm within which the innovation is made. So, for example, an innovation which may in technological terms be fully justified may nevertheless be exorcised because of its putative social or religious consequences.

Obviously the historian who surveys what has occurred during a particular period may select any of a number of changes as being significant. He may choose a starting point and establish an order during which changes took place and indicate a preference as to which is "causal" in that sequence. It would be foolish for us to quarrel with those who cite an institutional invention, the emergence of a particular power structure, a new value hierarchy, or the juxtaposition of a man and a situation as the base from which to explain a particular change.[3] But if common factors can be shown running through some of these circumstances, these factors may provide a clue to understanding not otherwise provided. For this reason empirical studies of a large number of situations which have in common that they involved a particular kind of technological change may, when made, demonstrate the usefulness of studying the flow of energy as one important variable.

Railroads Provide a Historical Case Study

Analysis of changing technology and other change on and around the railroads of the United States should provide us with one example. Railroads were among the first organizations drastically altered by the introduction of fossil fuel. Because they have a longer history than most industrial organizations they may show more about longer-run relationships than do newer ones. The fact that it is transportation rather than,

---

[3] Adolph Berle and G. C. Means showed how the development of the corporation was instrumental in providing a framework which made the effective use of modern technology possible (2). Max Weber is an outstanding proponent of the proposition that the value system of a society has a great deal to do with technological and other forms of change (13). See also particularly the work of Pitirim Sorokin, Howard Becker, Talcott Parsons, and their students. Among those who emphasize power as a factor Bertrand Russell is a modern pioneer (12). Others prominent in this type of analysis include Felix Gross (7), Franz Neumann (10), and Hans Morgenthau, Barrington Moore, Jr., Richard Schermerhorn, Harold Lasswell, C. Wright Mills and many others. The "great man" theory of change is so ubiquitous that citation is redundant. As it relates to technology, biographers of men like Henry Ford, Andrew Carnegie, Thomas A. Edison, and their like would start their interpretation of change with the appearance of these innovators.

say, manufacturing, that is involved may render a good deal of what happens irrelevant.

The history of railroading occupies an enormous literature whose presentation and analysis would require too much time for the insights it provides. To make it meaningful without resorting to this heroic process we must find some things common to all the railroads and see what the recurring relationships between them are.

Let us now utilize the general theory outlined above to see if it aids in this endeavor. Let us see what changes in the flow of energy and in its source may have to do with the introduction and spread of the railroad.

The first railroads were *rail roads*. That is to say, they were roads on which, instead of paving the whole surface, a road bed was built with sleepers or cross ties supporting a rail, originally of wood or stone, later of cast or malleable iron, finally of steel. For quite a while the cross ties were buried deeply so the draft horses used as prime movers could find solid footing, without damage to the ties. The gains came in reducing friction between the rolling wheel and the surface it traveled upon. This permitted the horse, and later the locomotive, to move larger loads, at higher speeds. At first the means to produce tractive effort, the horse, remained the same as on other roads. Where a road was heavily traveled, decline in operating costs was great enough to more than compensate for the greater cost of roadbed and rails, but many roads, built to fit local needs, were more economical to use than was the more costly railway.

In fact, as one looks at the shift from road to railroad it is hard to see the advantages it offered. The engine was less efficient in energy terms than was the horse; the horse was able to deliver at the drawbar about 20 per cent of the heat value of the feed it consumed, while the steam engine was not often, in the same terms of fuel input and mechanical energy output more than one-half of one per cent efficient. The engines put more weight upon the rails, requiring that they, and the roadbed, trestles, and bridges supporting them, be more strongly built, at higher energy cost. The cost in terms either of the human time or the energy consumed in building an engine was considerably greater than that involved in raising a horse of equal tractive power, and the life of the engine was often less than the working life of a horse. The horse was far more versatile than the locomotive and its use could be shifted from railway to road, or into the field, as occasion might demand. And initially, and possibly even today, the cost of maintaining the kind of social organization required to use the locomotive effectively was greater than that involved in the more simple social structure adequate to exploit the horse fully as a prime mover. It is not surprising that there were many who could not see the advantage the locomotive offered. In terms of the economics of the day, little seemed to be gained by adopting it.

If the theory outlined above is correct, the solution is to be found in the difference between the sources of the energy used by the two techniques of propulsion. The power exerted by the horse originates in the radiant energy of the sun. Through photosynthesis in plants, this energy is made available to the animal's muscles, which convert it into mechanical power or work. This process is relatively inefficient. The best plants (in these terms) convert only a very small part of the radiant energy of the sun falling upon the land they occupy into forms of plant life that can be digested by men and plant-eating animals. Even a good system of cultivation on fertile land seldom yields more annually than ten times the energy required to sustain the cultivator and the offspring necessary to replace him. Very frequently the yield is just enough to sustain those who gather it.

The difference between the energy input involved in securing energy and the resultant energy output we call surplus energy. The excess is, in energy terms, free. We have gotten from nature more than we put in. There are very few kinds of human activity that have this result. Most of the time we put energy in, and have less than we formerly had. We do this because we value more highly the things we achieve or secure than we do the energy we expend in getting them. Thus a man might spend a great deal of energy to get a diamond weighing an ounce, far more in fact than he would to get coal weighing a ton. In value terms the surplus gained from the work spent securing the diamond is much greater than the surplus gained from the coal. But in energy terms the coal might represent thirty thousand times as much as the diamond. We must distinguish clearly between the two kinds of surplus. It is often because of failure to see the difference that men make what seem to be economically sound judgments which are in energy or survival terms disastrous. What Stephenson and the other pioneer builders of locomotives were up against was the difficulty in explaining why, in spite of the fact that it seemed uneconomical to those using the culturally approved system of thinking, the locomotive would replace the horse. Since costs and gains are measured in terms of value, the technological base for the productive system was often not clear to those using it. They measured inputs in terms of price and outputs the same way, and if they thought about it at all, generally assumed that the "just price" which had traditionally prevailed was something independent of or prior to technology and would always show man how to apportion the factors of production most efficiently.

What the steam engine did was to make it possible for man to get mechanical energy from sources hitherto not thought to be available. It could be used to turn the energy of plants like trees, which neither man nor horse could eat, into work. While in the long run this source was limited by the annual growth of trees, it was possible at first to cut them at a rate far in excess of replacement and so tap a new enlarged energy source. But far more importantly it made possible the use of coal to do work. Even when coal first came into use a miner could mine equivalent to a thousand or more times the energy he put into securing it. And with increasing efficiency in mining operations and the increasing tractive effort the locomotive was able to exert per ton of coal going into the firebox, the rate of energy return became, in comparison with that secured from plants, fantastic.

Even the driver of a ten-horse team, each producing less than a "horsepower" as measured in the terms used to establish the capacity of the steam engine, had to use a relatively large amount of human time in the care of the horses and while driving — as compared with the human time spent on the job by the engine driver. All the energy directed by the man holding the reins came from plants with their low yield of free surplus energy. On the other hand the man at the throttle controlled ever increasing amounts of free energy derived from coal, and even with the low efficiency of his engine, was able to secure more and more ton- or passenger-miles per working hour. By using steam man could get much more done in the same time — or do the same thing in much less time than was previously possible. Thus there now existed a potential way to secure transportation at less sacrifice of the other valued goods and services, since some of them could now be secured with the time freed from providing transportation.[4]

There was a great reward awaiting those who would change the existing social, economic, technological, or political arrangements that stood in the way of this achievement, and a corresponding penalty to be levied against those who resisted such change. The reward was a direct result of the increase in free energy. It need not be a result of heightened effort, superior motivation, or, except as such knowledge was instrumental to the achievement of the new technology, new knowledge. To that extent, then, we have an "outside" factor with which to account for much of what took place as railroading worked its miracles on the face of the earth. Note that this reward was available to whomever could make the necessary technological arrangements, and the social means to permit them to work, regardless of other aspects of their social system.

In a review of the railroad era we might look at evidence of the way the changes taking place were explained, we might talk about the changing value system that accompanied the change, we might look at the social structure growing up, in relation to the substitution of coal and wood for the energy sources previously used. And we need to discuss the specific social processes involved in making those changes.

Original Institutional Framework of the Railroads

The first American railroads were replicas of those found in England. It was there that the technology had its roots. Similarly, it was there

---

[4] An enlightening story of the early development of British railroads, built around the "great man" theory, but not confined to it, is L. T. C. Rolt (11). For an up-to-date view of what is now happening on British railroads see Geoffrey Freeman Allen (1).

that the first conceptions as to what were the desirable and necessary social and political arrangements for the operation of railroads originated. At the time the railroads were abuilding many aspects of American life were changing rapidly and theory borrowed from the old countries soon had to be altered to explain emergent social forms. What must not be forgotten, however, is that many of the same kinds of changes were being wrought in Britain and on the Continent. There, too, the struggle to control and use the rails was forcing a marked alteration in institutions. The outcome was often different than in the United States because of many factors, including particularly the ecological consequences of the ratio between land and labor and its location. It also was different because of the early military significance of railroads in European logistic arrangements. The interlacing of the Continent by railroads forced a realignment of power structures and the appearance of many new kinds of coordinating agencies that contravened the "fundamental" basis of European politics and economics. Some of these developments gave rise in the United States to new conceptions of the nature of effective and desirable organization. But for the most part it was British experience and institutions that came to characterize American railroads.

Of great importance to understanding these arrangements is the realization that the British had, over a comparatively long time, been shaping their system to encourage and support trade at a distance. The sailing ship reduced transportation costs far below those possible with any other existing means. Trade was the most effective way to use the wind, a form of free energy, to increase productivity by taking advantage of ecological differences. But to use it a whole host of changes in British culture had to be made. Perhaps greatest among them was the increase in the use of pricing to provide coordination between people at points distant from one another and sharing different cultures. They also needed new concepts making such relationships meaningful, and a set of rationalizations for their use. In an unpublished paper delivered at the Fifth World Congress of Sociology in Washington, D.C., in September 1962 Elias shows how new concepts of what was "economic" emerged (5). What were regarded by early British economists as being universal aspects of human nature were of course relatively recent developments confined to limited areas. Although they seemed to be unaware that this was so, what was going on in Britain had a lot to do with the models found to be acceptable to theorists there. In the meantime, however, technology was reinforcing the trading system through feedback. Pecuniary relationships replaced in large measure the economic arrangement common to manorial society or the self-contained village community. Pricing proved to be an effective way to reassess the worth of human services as men were forced from traditional roles into others made necessary by the new technology. What became dominant, at least in urban Britain and among the new elite, was the idea that it was not the new technology and increased energy flow which was responsible for the power and prosperity they enjoyed, but rather that these were due to the operation of the market, freeing men like themselves to make choices they found it profitable to make. They established to their own satisfaction that in pursuing profit they would be guided by an unseen hand to make choices that maximized the wellbeing of the people.

The common law came to represent this view. Monopoly was regarded as being dangerous and undesirable, even monopoly held by the state and operated "in the public interest." The doctrine of conspiracy provided a means to prevent the effective organization of labor, while the fiction that the corporation is a single person not dangerous to the operation of the law of supply and demand permitted the aggregation of great power in the hands of the managers of giant firms.

Many American businesses had their origin among British entrepreneurs, and for a long period of time American enterprise functioned in the framework of British law and culture. So it was not surprising that as railroading developed in the United States it operated under social forms sanctioned originally by British experience. Private ownership seemed to be the only natural way to run railroads. Railroad managers exercised the prerogatives typical in other private businesses.

The traditional logic of property required that the managers direct as large a segment of the increasing flow of goods and services as possible to the "capitalists" — those who had in fact put up the money to build the railroads. But it was not long before a new logic, which legitimatized the retention of the larger part of the new flow of wealth by the promoters, emerged. The actual investors were often paid only what was required to keep them investing in railroads rather than in competing enterprises. Since the bulk of the rest of economic activity was still dependent on energy from food, feed, and muscle power, the railroad promoted in America did not need to pay much more than could be gained from these enterprises in order to attract capital. Nor was it necessary to pay men whose other alternatives were to be found in tilling the land or working in less technologically advanced industries any large part of the product gained through their cooperation as laborers. Its abundance as compared with limited means of transportation made it possible to secure land free, or even to be paid to accept and use it.

What we are saying is that it was not necessary for a promoter to "exploit" any of the groups traditionally cooperating in enterprise in order to get rich building and running railroads. Each could be provided, in return for his services, reward greater than any he could secure elsewhere, while at the same time the shipper and the traveler could be given far better service at much lower cost than he could secure any other way. And the outcome would still leave enormous wealth in the hands of those who controlled the railroads.

This, put another way, is to say that the traditional value system in use prior to the railway age had no means for moral distribution of the wealth produced using the larger flow of energy which the new technology made possible. The old institutional arrangements often reflected an ecological pattern that could ignore energy brought from a distance. Once such energy was available, much of the justification for the old arrangements disappeared. Nor could the old system effectively decide *who* was to benefit by *how much* from the increased supply of free energy. Nevertheless, the old institutions persisted and their defense was rationalized by new arguments.

But almost as soon as the increased energy flow appeared there also appeared claimants on it and its product. Each claimant used some part of the traditional morality to justify his claim but none recognized as valid the "distortion" of tradition required to legitimatize the claim of the others. What we see if we look at developments over time is a continuing struggle among groups serving and served by the railroads — each trying to maximize what they value, at *their* least cost. The effectiveness with which they can do this is related to the strength of the structure through which they operate, their strategic location in the system, the position of others in the society, and the changing value hierarchies of the people living there. What must not be forgotten, however, is that effectiveness is also dependent upon the degree to which the decisions made by railroad management permit the exploitation of natural resources, science, and technology and so increase the flow of energy that they can use to obtain the objectives of the various contending groups.

Management performed different functions for each of the groups affected by the appearance and development of the railroads. For the traveler and shipper primary interest lay in fast, certain service at cheap rates. For the investor it was desirable to secure high dividends with little risk. The worker tried to maximize wages, fringe benefits, and security. Local and state governments came to look upon the railroads as a lucrative tax source through which they could claim for the polity its share of the wealth arising from the new technology. The military branches were more interested in the contribution a railroad could make to achieve the functions that were their primary concern. And finally, whether or not management could secure high returns for itself depended upon its ability to limit the success with which other groups achieved their goals.

Power Struggles Among Groups

If we look at the resulting arrangement we might usefully describe the railroad as the locus of a cluster of functions, or call it a multifunctional institution. Its workings depend at once upon conflict and cooperation among the groups for which it operates. Generally, in our society only the latter process is considered to be "good" and is given positive moral sanction. Conflict is generally regarded as being "bad" and it is assumed that, if possible, it should be extirpated. But since every group seeking to use the railroad to maximize its own returns comes into conflict with others who would have it perform differently, conflict can no more be exorcized than can cooperation. Instead, institutional means are developed to control conflict and limit it to acceptable forms. Social organization prescribes an arena, sets the rules, and determines the referee. At any moment these all reflect the past power of the contenders. But if, over time, there are important power changes among them they will seek to alter the arena, for it has much to do with the outcome.

It is, for example, important to know whether under the rules the vote of one man will equal that of another, or whether one dollar or a share of stock has influence equal to that of another. More commonly, some administrative arrangement is set up to weigh various kinds of consideration and determine at least tentatively what the outcome is to be. The determination as to who will select the referee to enforce the rules and perhaps declare the winner has a great deal to do with the way various groups fare. Similarly, the kind of strategy and tactics used and the effectiveness of various weapons will relate closely to the structure in which they are to be used.

The power struggle involved in the control of railroading has not often depended primarily and immediately upon the capacity of the contending groups to exercise brute force. This power has, for the most part, been relegated to government. What groups *have* done is to exert various kinds of influence in two directions: (1) to shift decision-making into an arena in which they have the maximum control; and (2) to persuade those who make decisions to make more favorable ones. In this latter endeavor they may depend upon deep-seated and widely held ideas and ideals, upon bargaining in terms of immediate and pragmatic propositions, or upon the self-interest of the decision maker and those who put him into his strategic position.

The Position of Management

In the case in point those who make decisions in the first instance are railroad managers. It is in their power to determine, at least tentatively, and within limits, the policies to be followed by the lower echelons. They will be selected by those who are legally in a position to choose them. Thus they can be expected to share the value hierarchy characteristic of the groups legitimately entitled to control. But this legitimacy is itself a function of the values widely shared in the society and the resultant sanction of the decisions made. So long and only so long as there is widespread acceptance of the legitimacy of the power they exercise can managers expect to manage effectively. As we indicated earlier, a part of the heritage from Britain included the idea that railroads "naturally" are to be treated as private property. In contrast (merely for example) the railroads in Germany were at the outset regarded as primarily public in nature for they served the strategic and political objectives of the emerging German state.

Given the idea that railroads are and should be private property, managers can rely on all the institutional means generally used to support and protect the prerogatives of the owner of such property. Like all other forms of "big business," railroad managements have benefited from the existence of this widespread belief. The identity of the corporation as a person and the use of the Fourteenth Amendment to the United States Constitution to guarantee such "persons" rights that originally were supposed to be vested only in a man with a "body to be kicked and a soul to be damned" has greatly affected what are managements' legitimate prerogatives. Similarly the development of securities with a government-guaranteed priority to earnings means that today on many railroads the prior claims of the bondholders leave little for other claimants on earnings to fight over.

Weapons of Shippers and Passengers

But if they are weak in the economic arena where law and tradition gave advantages to management and investors, other groups concerned with railroad services have developed strength in the political arena. For example, the rapid westward movement was dependent upon the use of railroads to carry farm products to the eastern seaboard and the docks from which ships could take them overseas. And as farmers and allied groups grew in numbers and in wealth they began to shape new institutions better designed to serve their own interests. That these movements brought them into conflict with the "moneyed interests" of the East and the courts that maintained the sanctity of these interests history has long since been demonstrated. Among the most significant determinants of Western prosperity were freight and passenger rates. Left in the hands of management to exercise this control as they saw fit, this power meant life or death to chosen commodities, communities, and firms. In response to what they considered to be the abuses of this power the legislatures of the Western states began to reshape the institution of property as it affected railroad operations. In spite of the drag imposed by tradition-minded judges who declared many of the newly proposed institutional arrangements sanctioned by farmer-dominated state legislatures unconstitutional, the prerogatives of railroad management were inexorably reduced, particularly as they related to the carriage of agricultural products and the serving of farmers' other interests. The Grange movement and the laws it sponsored were in part nullified by the actions of the courts, but in time the interests of other shippers induced them to enter political coalitions with the farmers at the level of the national government. The result was the creation of the Interstate Commerce Commission. Most of the shipper and passenger interest was thus entrusted to a new agency. The arena in which rates are set and schedules authorized, and the character of the services to be rendered was modified. No longer was it necessary to hold or control large blocks of stock in order to affect these policies. While management retained some initiative the veto power was found to lie elsewhere. If railroad owners and managers were to wield the kind of influence they once held they now had to overcome the political power wielded by their opponents in the United States Congress which set up the I.C.C. and the growing bureaucracy that actually performed most of its work. Short of doing that they had to face the fact that management's prerogatives were greatly reduced, and operate within these new limits.

Numerous studies have indicated how control over the I.C.C. has shifted and the consequences of these shifts. What concerns us here is that without changing the definition of property or modifying the values attached to the symbols representing it, the functions of property owners and managers were changed.

A similar movement which came to fruition later and was, at least until very recently, less complete, was set in motion by another of the groups for which railroads function, i.e., Labor. Later we will discuss in detail how this has affected management's prerogatives. At the moment we note that the social consequences of the use of power over new energy flows by those initially entrusted with its use were such as to alter greatly the future power and prerogatives of railroad managers. Nor were these social factors the only threats to be faced.

New Technology Alters Group Powers

As we indicated earlier, it was initially the rise of new technology directing greatly increased energy flows that, by feedback, strengthened social structure insuring the power of railroad managers. Further developments in technology have greatly weakened this influence. The initial development of steam power was most significant in the field of transportation. The economic gains resulted largely from the fact that with cheap transportation it was possible to take advantage of regional specialization, which in turn permitted more complete human exploitation of ecological differences. However, as the stationary engine was developed it became possible to use increased amounts of energy in local production, and sometimes the resultant reduction of costs made transportation of goods from a distance less attractive. The pattern of aggregating population in densely populated cities reduced considerably the necessity for railroad transportation relative to the volume of production. If railroad transportation cost too much the alternative was not, as in the past, to resort to muscle power, but rather to increase local use of energy from high energy sources. To serve the stationary engine some fuel was brought to the rising urban centers by rail but the electric grid, the pipeline, ship, and barge could often provide a cheap alternative. These new forms of transportation could also be substituted in other ways for the railroad. Of greatest importance was the appearance of the internal combustion engine and road traffic. Later other forms such as the airplane also provided new alternatives. This increased freedom of choice by passenger and shipper altered their power position vis à vis railroad owners and managers, railroad workers, and governments. But while the general effectiveness of the forms of control it could use was further reduced, it was still possible for railroad management to make certain decisions in response to the value hierarchies of those who had the power to select and remove them.

Nor were the effects of the new technology all of a character to reduce the choices which management could effectively make. Some of them opened up the possibility that management could, with their use, overcome the barriers imposed by the political and economic power of other groups. The diesel was borrowed from industries wherein it had reached a high state of technical efficiency, and with its use the employment of manpower was greatly reduced. Electronic data-processing offered further opportunities to escape the claims made by unions in behalf of men who now need no longer be hired. Automation in switching cars similarly provided a way to avoid the power of the unions. New forms of communication made it possible to dispense with people at places where their presence permitted local government to levy taxes designed to support the community.

What we have just been talking about are *technological changes* which served to modify the forms of social organization effectively used in railroading. We are saying that if technological factors only had been at work (and of course this was not the case), railroads would still have had to make great social alterations.

But the changes just cited did not occur overnight, nor were they independent of other factors in the railroad complex. Their continued development depended on continuous feedback from the results of their adoption. Many of them might not have occurred, or certainly would not have occurred in that order nor with such magnitude without this continuous process of interaction. Those who instituted change did so in contemplation of the opportunity costs involved in that change. They could, for example, greatly reduce costs by replacing manpower only if that manpower was expensive relative to the men and machines that replaced it. The more costly the man, the more it paid to find a replacement for him, and often the replacement was possible only if a new technological set-up could be made. Very often his cost to the railroad was as much or more dependent on the union to which he belonged, and the strategic advantage held by that union, as on any other factor. This advantage might in itself be related to many factors other than the possession of the technical skills necessary to do the work. Similarly, costs imposed by taxing authorities might in some cases make it profitable to replace men who, in order to carry on their expected functions, had to be located at a particular place, with technical equipment that did not require that the man in control be at the same place.

The list of conditions that might affect the judgment of the managers who decided whether or not to introduce technological change could be endless. The point we are trying to make is that technological invention is often created in the effort to lower costs. Some are a function of technological factors themselves, like the differences in engineering terms of efficiency between a reciprocating steam locomotive and a diesel engine, but perhaps as often the costs are socially imposed and technology is devised to escape these *sociological* barriers to the attainment of lowered cost. Moreover, we must not forget that technology is going to be put into operation only because some persons made the decision to do so. The factors affecting human judgment are seldom purely technological in nature. The resultant technology then can never be thought of as a "thing in itself," even though it may be true that over time refusal to make certain kinds of technological change will result in the disorganization or dissolution of the system rejecting it.

It is particularly important in the instant case that we see what were and are the *power of those who make the decisions* over technology, what are *their* primary interests, and what controls are exerted over them by other groups. If, for example, those who actually control the railroads have little to gain and much to risk from technological change, they are much less likely to accept or promote it than is the case of industries in which the rewards from such change are available in large part to those who introduce them. Similarly, there will be a different decision if those who might otherwise be inclined to introduce technological change are barred from doing so by others, who while they cannot themselves assume the responsibilities for management, can and do set limits to the time and place and manner in which change can be introduced, or can seize for themselves a large part of the reward for change which technology would make possible. So, again in the instant case, managers chosen by those who are, in the traditional definition of property, legitimately entitled to decide on technology, are faced with laws, administrative decisions, or union power resulting from choices made at the polls or as a result of union politics. They will in consequence make different decisions about technology than they might in the absence of control by the other groups contending for power.

As we have to a degree already indicated, railroad managers have been selected as a consequence of the evolving power structure controlling the firms for which they work. In time those who represent certain of the interest groups for whom the roads perform become more powerful than others, and as they do they maximize their return while minimizing that of other groups. Management composed of those who seek "profits" are concerned that the property be used in such a way that the "costs" of providing returns to all the other groups are kept to a minimum. They may be interested in liquidating an unprofitable service which is able to provide wages, taxes, cost of supplies, and adequate transportation to the traveling public. The other groups cannot rely on management to make judgments in *their* behalf and they have resorted to various means to maximize their own concerns. So, for example, when railroad managements repeatedly made decisions that forced their companies into bankruptcy they found that the only way they could get capital was through issuing bonds which the *government* guaranteed would have first claim on earnings. As the proportion of equity capital declined, the interest of the bondholder came to loom larger and larger in railroad directorates. Since the bondholder does not share earnings beyond his guaranteed return his representatives are less impressed with the opportunity to earn additional profits through new technology than a profit-sharing stockholder might be.

Some railroads have large holdings in real estate, some of which could bring in much greater profit if used for other purposes than railroading. Directors interested in maximizing the return to those whom they represent would logically seek to put these resources to this more profitable use. But the past abuses of railroad management has greatly limited what railroads may do. Diversification is not permitted to go very far. Thus it is more profitable for the railroads to dispose of their real estate than to preserve it in use. There is clear evidence that this is what has been and is being done.

To those who identify themselves as "the public," usually shippers and passengers, the idea that railroads should curtail service to them in the interest of anybody else is anathema. Since they do not, under the logic of property, have representation in management itself they resort instead to agencies over which they do have some control, such as the I.C.C. and the state public utilities commissions. But here their influence on technology is primarily negative. They do not have the means to induce innovation. Their activities, designed to preserve service at any cost, often deprive management of funds that might be used to innovate. The primary influence on innovation then is only to induce such changes as will reduce costs rather than create new services.

If the railroads themselves undertake innovations they have to share the profits with all those who have in the past established a claim on earnings, the bond holders, stockholders, pensioners, and tax collectors. But if a private company is set up to make innovation and sell to the railroads, the innovators can claim the profit for themselves. The result is of course that innovators have no particular interest in being represented on boards of directors, so long as the industry is healthy enough to pay their bills, and is willing to accept a rate of innovation that is most profitable. Consequently, the industry has fallen behind the rate that characterizes its competitors in transportation. This threatens the whole industry, so railroad suppliers, being no longer able to depend on the railroads as a market, must now themselves diversify or interest themselves in getting sufficient control of the roads to induce changes that would assure more successful competition. In their endeavor to make this kind of technological change they are faced with security-minded management concerned more with liquidating the unprofitable part of their business than in expanding. Some of the suppliers (like General Motors) have a large interest in the railroads as a market, as well as a service. One might anticipate that they would buy in or otherwise gain enough control to protect their interests. So far, however, they have apparently been content to improve the things they have to sell at a comparatively high profit and let existing management decide the future of the railroad industry.

Government has a great interest in the industry too. Originally it was an active partner but in more recent times it has not participated in railroading as it has in road traffic, marine shipping, barge lines, or air transport. Much of the original impetus it supplied through grants of land and other aids has for most railroads long since been dissipated. The military branch has provided and continues to provide a great direct aid to innovation in other forms of communication and transportation, but it has done little to supply research and development to the railroads. Nor does government policy offer incentive to those roads who seek to innovate. Through control over freight and passenger rates it often has the effect of penalizing efforts of those roads that try to gain new customers by providing better, faster, and cheaper service.

So management that holds the purse strings tight, enters no new ventures, eliminates marginal services, and accepts innovation not to gain profit from new service, but only to cut costs, is apt to be enthroned on all but a few roads, and so long as they serve the interests of those who select them, can be expected to operate this way. The way technology develops is affected not only by the value orientation of management but also by the way it has been structured. Like many other aspects of urban industrial society the railroads operate under very close limits in terms of time. Social structure must be so designed so as to assure that things and people are where they are supposed to be at the required moment. This is also characteristic of military action. Many American railroads were built and first operated by men who got their training as Army engineers. The military organization with its great emphasis on timing and discipline fits the requirements of railroad technology well enough that it generally has survived as the bureaucratic model for the industry. Not only are there structural evidences that this is so but the very language of the military has become a part of that familiar to rail-roaders (3). The table of organization, the relationships between line and staff, and many other parts of the system fit into a hierarchical pattern. It is difficult to innovate in such organizations. To change things means that new roles and statuses have to be created and new administrative arrangements made to sanction the behavior of the bureaucrats. The innovator is confronted on all sides by people with good reasons for "not sticking their necks out."

Not only is there resistance to change from individual railroads. The standardizing agencies like those of the Association of American Railroads have to take into account that rolling stock other than motive power is generally interchangeable over the whole of the United States. Nothing not acceptable in interchange can be sanctioned. This means that the less progressive and poorer railroads impose pretty much of a veto over the other roads. Many technological improvements must wait until these roads have earned enough to pay for them; but without these improvements the prospect for profits is bleak. The kinds of improvements that *are* adopted are likely to be those that reduce costs rather than generate new traffic. Here again social and technological considerations become merged in the minds of the decision makers.

We can now summarize the position of the various groups. Stockholders have initial legal control over management and can initiate policy. However, a large part of the control is exercised by banks, trust companies, and similar fiduciary agencies in the interest of those they represent. Control is exercised in the name of the shipper and traveler by various government agencies, and the alternatives provided by competing forms of transportation set further limits on managers. These leave them little range in which to maneuver. The result is that labor, the remaining large interest group, becomes a major element whose costs can be manipulated in the interests of those to whom management is responsible.

The Increasing Use of the Political Arena

As we have already indicated, the doctrine of conspiracy greatly handicapped the organization of unions in the United States. The individual worker was left "free" to bargain with the company. Very rapid growth of population, due both to natural increase and immigration, supplied labor in ever increasing numbers. If the native-born American, free to take to the soil or enter another enterprise, demanded too much it was always possible to turn to an immigrant who had fewer alternatives. So railroad wages need not be much — if any — higher than those in less technologically advanced industries. Efforts to create a powerful industrial union of all railroad employees were easily defeated. A few craft unions which had managed to gain power in other industries made successful efforts to organize their fellow craftsmen on the railroads, but for the most part these failed. The "operating" craftsmen, enginemen, trainmen, and switchmen, for whom there was no counterpart in other industry, could not even lean on so frail a reed. But they did manage to organize through an expedient not barred by law and the courts. They began with groups which were primarily insurance companies. The injury rate on the railroads was so high that most of the insurance agencies refused to accept employees as risks. So what amounted to "burial societies" were formed by various sets of railroad workers. This brought an organization into existence to serve their interests, and around this initial function new ones were joined as power and opportunity permitted. Finally, they reached the point that they could effectively threaten to strike. Collective bargaining based on economic considerations became possible, and theoretically, desirable. But those who felt themselves absolutely dependent on the services of the roads found such a threat intolerable. They resorted to their power in the legislature to minimize it.

In 1888 President Cleveland signed a law which provided for voluntary arbitration of railroad labor disputes. That failing, there was to be a public investigation. During the ten years' life of the law the provisions for arbitration were never used. During the Pullman strike there was an investigation but it will be recalled that this strike also led to intervention by the federal government. That the government would, if necessary, use troops showed that the public regarded the economic solution to railroad labor problems as one so endangering their interests as to be intolerable. The plain inference to be drawn was that if the unions were strong enough to cripple rail transportation effectively, government would intervene and remove the dispute from the economic to the political arena. In the aftermath of the Pullman strike, the Erdman Act was passed in 1898.[5] This act initiated the policy of having government conciliate and mediate labor disputes on the railroads. The Commissioner of Labor and the Chairman of the Interstate Commerce Commission were required to make themselves available for these purposes when called upon to do so by either management or labor. Failing to arrive at a solution through such means, the government was expected to provide a board of arbitration. Since only the operating unions could in fact effectively strike, the Act was made applicable only to them. It failed to satisfy any of the groups sponsoring it and was replaced when the Democrats came to power by the Newlands Act of 1913.

[5] The Erdman Act was approved June 1, 1898. It was signed by President McKinley. It is Public Law No. 115 entitled: An Act Concerning Carriers Engaged in Interstate Commerce and their Employees. It went out of effect when replaced by the Newlands Act which was approved July 15, 1913 signed by President Wilson. It is Public Law No. 6 (§ 2517) entitled: An Act providing for Mediation, Conciliation and Arbitration in Controversies between Certain Employers and their Employees.

This law created a permanent Board of Mediation and Conciliation and some full-time agents to act for it. To avoid the "one man rule" which occurred when two partisan and one "neutral" board members made decisions, the Boards of Arbitration were increased to include six members. A continuing interpretation of collective agreements was thus assured. During its life this Board was given rather wide use.

We note that between 1898 and 1916 a new arena for decision-making concerning railroad labor was emerging. Without any formal or ideological redefinition of its prerogatives, management was required to deal collectively with its employees where they belonged to unions and sought collective agreements, and to submit some of its administrative decisions to final judgment in terms other than those of success in the marketplace. The necessity to keep the technology operating had proved to be a more potent force than that of acting in conformity with ideological propositions about the rights of property owners. But we must also note that a similar transformation in the "rights" of labor was taking place. The bargaining power of labor "in the market" was clearly shown to rest on a framework of politics and resultant law, and the political functions of unions thus became as significant to their survival and success as were those called "economic." This became even more clear during World War I when government interest in transportation became more significant than that of either management or labor.

The Operating Brotherhoods took this occasion to press for an eight-hour day and a number of other gains. Acting under the Newlands Act, no agreement was reached. Faced with the threat of a strike, President Wilson succeeded in getting Congress to pass the Adamson Act which forced management to accede to some of labor's demands. The final adjudication of the dispute which led to the threatened strike was made by a special Commission enforcing a decision of the Council of National Defense. The supremacy of the law over the "rights" of management was fully demonstrated. Subsequently, because management was unable or unwilling to maintain a level of operations acceptable to the government, the railroads were taken over in December of 1917 and management was placed in the hands of a Federal Director.

During the period of government operation many of the current institutional arrangements came into existence. Government recognized some of the craft unions developed in other industries, such as the Machinists, unions composed of railroad workers exclusively, such as the Carmen, and of course the Operating unions and the Telegraphers that had already demonstrated on many railroads sufficient power to force their recognition. Since the unions were now to deal with government agencies they took on forms appropriate to these functions. Union structure thus became something quite different than it had been or might have become had the unions developed in response to the acts of private management only.

The Growth of Administrative Tribunals and Law

Of outstanding importance in this respect was the rapid growth of administrative law and its attendant tribunals. It became necessary to spell out in detail what management and labor could respectively do and what they were barred from doing. The interpretation of these rules became more and more crucial to the workers. Administrative decision now determined the lines between crafts, and so helped define the role and status they could occupy if they entered the occupation. Similarly, administrative law set boundaries to the kinds of disciplinary action that management could take. Seniority became the basis for establishing "property rights" in a job. A proposed modification of rules thus came to threaten the career pattern that induced men to enter and remain in railroad service. Because they were so vital, final decisions were no longer to be management's unilateral prerogative. Instead, Boards of Adjustment were created, which were composed of both management and union representatives, and sat to hear appeals from decisions made by management and contested by unions.

The resultant body of precedent, like the common law, was ill defined, at times illogical, and sometimes "irrational." In arriving at decisions the Adjustment Board was enforcing contracts that had been arrived at by bargaining. A particular rule might have been acquiesced to by management in return for labor's acceptance of another condition which they might otherwise have successfully opposed. When this rule, taken out of the context in which it originated, was interpreted by anyone not privy to knowledge about its origin it might appear to be totally unreasonable. With no independent judiciary to reform this kind of contract law derived from collective bargaining, and restate it in terms of general principles, there was a great accumulation of *ad hoc* decisions that defied generalization by the uninitiated. Nevertheless, like the common law itself, it proved to be more effective in keeping the system running than did the more "rational" proposals of those who would substitute statute and code for it. This was borne out by what happened after the emergency of the war was over and the country went back to "normalcy." Government control was ended and management regained some of its power and prerogatives. On the other hand, the power of the unions was greatly lessened. The decisions of government tribunals, once favorable, began to reveal that the new agents followed the election returns. Faced with their adverse judgments, the unions tried to exercise their economic power. In the defeat of the "outlaw" Switchmen's strike and the Shopmen's strike of 1922 their weakness was revealed. The operating unions refused to respect the picket lines and the strikes were lost.

In 1926 the United States Railroad Labor Board, no longer supported by either labor or the carriers, was scuttled. Efforts to re-establish the national Adjustment Boards were defeated. In their place were only some regional or system boards that more nearly reflected the desires of management than labor. With the advent of the New Deal the political climate shifted again. Labor had greater influence with the new administration than with that of President Hoover. Union leaders hoped to re-establish the power they had previously gained and add to it. As in 1920, there was a flurry over the proposal to nationalize the railroads, but no real continuing effort by any group with much political power. The pattern of control that developed for the railroads was somewhat similar to that which characterized the National Recovery Administration, but it took on characteristics that reflected the differences between railroading and other industry.

A federal coordinator was named to reorganize the railroads and bring them into some effective relationship with newly emerging forms of transportation technology (9). Obviously there were many kinds of interests involved here. To have responded effectively to their varied claims would have been a miraculous achievement. But most of the groups involved either had other interests to pursue or other ways to gain their objectives than to meet the well-entrenched power of the carriers and the unions before the coordinator. They pursued their objectives elsewhere or they were subordinated to the strategy of the two major contenders. The carriers organized and, in part, functioned through the new American Association of Railways and the unions built up the Railway Labor Executives Association, though this did not encompass all of them. The confrontation of these two sets of contenders resulted in a system reflecting the balance of power existing between them. The Railway Labor Act of 1926 was amended to provide the political and legal framework within which railroad labor relations have evolved since that time.

Management escaped many of the controls which once had seemed likely to be imposed on it "in the public interest." Labor got at least a modicum of protection against the arbitrary power of management. In the Washington Job Agreement labor gained compensation for part of the costs workers would bear if proposed mergers went through. They protected themselves to some degree from what appeared to them then as the more dangerous of the results of impending technological change. Once these objectives were obtained they dropped their support of the Office of Coordinator and of general legislation designed to rationalize the whole transportation system of the country. Insofar as I am aware, the Act of 1934 is the only law enacted in the United States that sets up an administrative tribunal which makes decisions in controversies arising out of labor contracts and which are enforceable by the courts. In this respect railroad labor is treated differently from any other kind.

The Railway Adjustment Board set up by the Act is composed of 36 members. Half of these represent the unions and half the railroads. It is divided into four "Divisions," each dealing with the problems of administering contracts with a particular set of unions. The First Division, for example, deals with the five operating unions, and it is by far the busiest. Cases come to these Boards as a result of failure to settle differences between management and labor on the systems they represent. The panel dealing with a particular dispute attempts to interpret an agreement or contract arrived at as a result of previous bargaining. When the panel deadlocks, as is frequent, it is usually along strictly partisan lines, all the members of management being pitted against all those on labor's side. Then a referee must be appointed to join in the making of a decision. Since he is usually unable to convince the proponents of either view that they are wrong he in effect becomes the sole judge of the dispute. It is possible for the members of the Division to agree on a referee, but they seldom do and the National Mediation Board has to name him. Thus the referees are selected by an agency which is part of a particular government in power and reflects its overall philosophy. The decision of these referees is binding on the parties, though they may and occasionally have appealed the decisions to the courts. The influence of politics thus extends down to the interpretation of the rules governing even the most minute detail of the railroader's work and life. The only way the interpretation can be altered is either through the appointment of a different set of referees or through bargaining for a rules change. The former is a long, slow, and uncertain process. The Adjustment Board is not a judicial body which respects *stare decisis*. It is an arena in which nothing is conceded to an opponent until the referee has ruled on each contest. Delay may be as effective as any other tactic and at the moment other than disciplinary cases in the First Division must wait seven years to be heard. In the meantime workers can wonder what will be their fate, and managers guess how much it will cost the company if the rulings they have made are not upheld by the referee.

To resort to the other alternative, bargaining, is not much more productive. Many of the rules now in operation were made when technology was different than it is now and when the power of the unions vis à vis the management of a particular road was not the same either. The rules which the unions are defending are often more generous than any that could probably now be negotiated, and they are not about to give them up. The lines between crafts and between seniority districts must be preserved to protect the rights of the members of the various unions. To alter them merely because technology would, if one were starting with a clean slate, justify a different structure than now prevails may seem rational to an outsider. But to the men whose only hold on the economic system is secured through these rules, to consent to such change would appear to be irrational in the extreme. So the unions have few or no concessions to make in return for new gains, and management is unwilling to concede anything without at least a *quid pro quo*.

The upshot is that after bargaining has failed management announces its intent to alter the rules unilaterally and mediation is attempted. That failing, arbitration is proposed, and when that medium is exhausted, the unions give notice that if the rules are changed they will strike. Then an Emergency Board is named by the President of the United States. While its findings are not legally binding, they indicate pretty clearly where the current administration stands. To secure compliance with the findings of the Emergency Board, presidents can use all kinds of pressure, even including threat of seizure of the roads and the drafting of workers into the armed services. So the fiction that collective bargaining (in the usual sense of the meaning given those words) is basic to the agreements administered by the Adjustment Boards finally breaks down and the stark reality of coercion is revealed.

The solution of grievances "on the property" becomes less frequent. Each of the proponents has some idea of where he would stand before an Emergency Board appointed by the president currently in office. Whichever thinks he will get more by using this expedient simply stands fast and waits till the machinery has ground out the specified procedures. In the meantime, day-to-day decisions must be based on rules that are increasingly vital, particularly to the men but in many cases to management also; but at the same time these rules become less and less defensible in terms of changing technology or to the outsider.

Slowly the differential between what management might hope to gain through rules change and what they must currently pay widened to the point that the American Association of Railroads decided to make a frontal attack on them. A prolonged attack on "featherbedding" was made in the press and from the rostrum. This was followed by taking an adamant position in bargaining sessions. The unions fought back with every kind of tactic available to them and the number of disputed rules grew enormously. Finally one of the Emergency Boards recommended the formation of a Presidential Commission to study the rules and make recommendations relative to them. The unions were reluctant to accede, but finally joined in asking for a Commission, which was appointed by President Eisenhower. It was composed of a man from each of the five Operating Brotherhoods, five representing the railroads, and five representing the public. To some who could see the situation of the industry the Commission offered hope for a constructive solution which would revitalize it. There might have been a thoroughgoing analysis of the industry. This would have related labor's position to that of management and the other interested groups. It would have analyzed management's practices to see which were in the public interest. It would have related the technological position of the industry to that of other industries. In short, it would have taken into account all the factors that impinge upon labor-management relations.

Instead, the Commission was limited to an adversary proceeding dealing with only such facts as seemed to have direct bearing on the narrow issues recognized as being in dispute, though there were staff studies showing how some other industries had attempted to deal with somewhat similar situations. In the end the Commission accepted the idea that it should be management's prerogative to initiate most of the changes it wished to make. Labor was in some ways protected. The individual worker was given compensation to offset some of the costs of change. But for the most part the effect of the proposed rule changes would have been to wreck the structure of the unions and set them one against the other.

The outcome was, of course, that the unions refused to accept the decision of the President's Commission as a basis for bargaining. When management in its turn attempted to proceed unilaterally to follow out the Commission's findings the unions turned to the courts and secured injunctions imposing delay. It had in the meantime become apparent that a really effective strike would not be tolerated. Sooner or later there would be a solution dictated by government.

What we will see next is, of course, not entirely clear; the social changes that will emerge as a result of the changing character of technology will be mixed with those arising from many other kinds of change which have also been taking place.

What is clear is that, in spite of broad general ideological support for "private ownership" and "freedom for the worker," technology has continuously altered alternatives in such a way that the social structure emerging resembles only slightly that which would allow the kinds of choices required to serve the "economic man" posited in classical economics. Instead we have a system that reflects the strength of many groups, operating in different arenas, utilizing different kinds of influence to achieve their goals. The outcome is not what would result from choices made in a "free" market, nor the pure influence of ecological variables, nor what would in technological terms be "most efficient." Neither is it a clear reflection of some value orientation. Methods of analysis that will reveal the extent and kinds of influence exerted by each class of variables in this particular situation will help if in turn they can be used to analyze what has taken place elsewhere. We may then learn whether or not certain quite specific sets of social relationships must accompany the use of specific technologies. The task of discovering how a particular system must be altered to achieve that relationship can then be approached with less probable error, and prediction as to whether this kind of change is likely to take place can more accurately be made.

BIBLIOGRAPHY

1. Allen, Geoffrey F. *British Railways Today and Tomorrow*. London: Ian Allen, 1960.
2. Berle, Adolph A., and G. C. Means. *The Modern Corporation and Private Property*. New York: The Macmillan Co., 1933.

3. Cottrell, Fred. *The Railroader.* Palo Alto, Calif.: Stanford University Press, 1940.

4. Cottrell, Fred. *Energy and Society.* New York: McGraw-Hill Book Co., 1955.

5. Elias, Norbert. "The Break with Traditionalism and the Origin of Sociology." 1962. (mimeo)

6. Glover, Edward. *War, Sadism and Pacifism.* London: Allen & Unwin, 1933.

7. Gross, Felix. *The Seizure of Political Power in a Century of Revolution.* New York: Philosophical Library, 1958.

8. Jones, Harry E. "Inquiry of the Attorney General's Committee on Administrative Procedure Relating to the National Railroad Adjustment Board." Eastern Committee for the National Railroad Adjustment Board. New York City, no date.

9. Latham, Earl. *The Politics of Railroad Coordination, 1933–36.* Cambridge: Harvard University Press, 1959.

10. Neumann, Franz. *The Democratic and the Authoritarian State.* Glencoe, Ill.: The Free Press, 1957.

11. Rolt, Lionel T. C. *The Railway Revolution, George and Robert Stephenson.* New York: St. Martin's Press, 1960.

12. Russell, Bertrand. *Power, A New Social Analysis.* New York: W. W. Norton, 1938.

13. Weber, Max. *The Protestant Ethic and the Spirit of Capitalism.* New York: Charles Scribner's Sons, 1930.

14. Zimmerman, A. F. Dissent to the Report of the Presidential Railroad Commission, 1962.

15. Northwestern University. *Social Science and the Underdeveloped Areas: A Revival of Evolutionary Theory.* Evanston, Ill., 1963.

16. Presidential Railroad Commission Report, Washington, D.C., 1962.

28

Richard Colvard

Risk Capital Philanthropy: The

Ideological Defense of Innovation

Many of the large philanthropic foundations established in ever increasing numbers in this country since the turn of the century (7, p. xiii) are both examples and instruments of social change. Collectively, they represent a new type of institution, evolved from an ancient model; individually, they are ongoing organizations committed to continual educational and social innovation.

As organizations, unlike many others interested in reform, these foundations' formal aim is to withdraw — to go on to something else — once the particular cause or idea they have supported (within a given field or location) has either gained considerable support from other sources or apparently proved abortive. Again, because they both represent and command considerable wealth, they have been perpetually deemed as having more potential power than many other organizations with analogous aims. For these and other reasons they have been constrained through the years to develop a circuitous style of operation aimed at what might be termed "innovation by indirection." Except as prominent advocates — and symbols — of the deliberate investment of surplus wealth in efforts at social improvement, their influence is exerted more through the giving of a wide variety of grants to other organizations than through the direct carrying out of operations themselves.

It is the distinctive and complex ideology which the large grant-making foundations have gradually developed — to explain their existence as institutions and justify their engaging-disengaging role as professional

728

foster parents of innovation — in which we are most interested here, and which we shall analyze as the "risk capital concept" in American philanthropy. Like "academic freedom," "free enterprise," and other ideologies intended in part to win public acceptance of considerable organizational autonomy, the risk capital concept is a cultural precipitate: in this case, a combination of ideas both drawn from many elements of the culture of Western civilization and variously interpreted by many groups in the American foundation environment. The three sources — both of support for and resistance to the risk capital concept — to be dealt with here are: a) Anglo-American law, especially that bearing on private wealth applied to philanthropy; b) political-economic theory, particularly American interpretations of the ancient ideas of self-help and voluntary enterprise; and c) the idea of progress, especially as amalgamated — in education and science — into the pragmatic theme of "progress through knowledge."

The guiding theses — to put them more specifically — are: 1) that the need to frame policies and programs justifiable to the courts, to the government and allied economic groups capable of affecting legislation — and also to the colleges and universities which have become their major "client" organizations — has been a major incentive to the development of the risk capital concept; 2) that the same mixture of encouragement and constraint has enabled the foundations to acquire considerable freedom of expression and action, but has also led them to engage primarily in efforts not only more indirect than those open to other institutions and reform organizations but less venturesome than the risk capital concept implies. The larger implication eventually developed is that, in the judgment of history, the risk capital ideology itself may be deemed a more important innovation than those stimulated by actual foundation grants. That is to say, the specific *structural* changes in medical education or university administration, for example, stimulated by foundation grants may prove less significant in time than the general *cultural* change represented 1) in the creation of a politically defensible rationale for continual research and reform, and 2) in the incorporation of that rationale in the ideological armory of government, industry, science, and education — as well as large-scale philanthropy. For the idea of systematically and continually putting surplus wealth to public purposes — of, so to speak, vaccinating the social system with weakened forms of the lively virus of change — has probably helped induce in American society an ability to tolerate the "creative destruction" endemic to both capitalism and science.

The Risk Capital Ideal

The risk — or venture — capital concept has been succinctly described in a historical passage by Andrews, who has done much to bring it into prominence in the foundation world:

Early in the twentieth century the foundation idea began to take deep root in American soil, but with this significant difference. Substantial endowments were set up, often in perpetuity, as in England; but frequently with wide latitude in their use. . . . The new doctrine asserted that the funds of foundations were largely the venture capital of philanthropy, best spent when invested in enterprises requiring risk and foresight, not likely to be supported either by government or the private individual. The usual purpose was not relief or even cure; it was research, prevention, and discovery. The very word "foundation" acquired in America connotations of freedom of action (5, p. 12).

And Keppel, a widely influential foundation executive of an earlier era, once elaborated it:

Though strictly limited in its scope, the foundation is nevertheless a factor of the first importance, for it has certain great assets. It is free to choose its objective, it can give when others withhold, it can give quickly, and if it keeps its funds free from obligations against future income, it can continue to give. Foundation support for any enterprise should be significant for its timeliness rather than for its amount, it should reveal imagination and courage. Incidentally, it needs nearly as much imagination and more courage . . . to stop support when the area of diminishing returns is reached. But only by so doing, can it continue to be creatively useful (48, pp. 593–594).

Support of the research of Goddard, Banting, Lawrence, Myrdal, and Kinsey; direct involvement in the eradication of hookworm in the South and the establishment of improved public health facilities and medical research and education in many parts of the world; sponsorship of such long-range efforts as the development of more liberal curricula in teacher education; acceleration of — to mention just two — the adult education and mental health movements: these and many other foundation activities are frequently mentioned as important examples of the carry-over into practice of this commitment to work on the frontiers of knowledge and preventive — not palliative — action (see, e.g., Embree [32, pp. 31–32]; Bremner [16, p. 136]).

But many critics both inside and outside the foundations have, with varying degrees of persuasiveness, persistently pointed out through the years that such examples are commitment-confirming exceptions to the more general tendency to support the politically "safe" field and the professionally "sound" project or person (1, pp. 227–228; 53, pp. 11–12; 3, p. 54; 32, p. 32; 80, p. 140, p. 214, p. 216; 52, pp. 37–38; but cf. 81).

Differing value judgments aside, the evidence bearing on both of these contentions is simply not clear. The existent statistics, for example, improving but chronically incomplete and imperfectly categorized, do not often detail individual recipients and specific proposals or otherwise provide a means of adequately dealing with the question of what might be "sound" and who might be most apt to break out of conventional patterns of thinking. On the matter of fields, such historical figures as are available do make it fairly clear that, although the purely palliative "welfare" types of programs have been pretty regularly avoided, the bulk of grants through the years have been concentrated in what we would consider the ordinarily politically "safe" fields of education and health (7, table 8, xxviii). The most recent year for which fairly comprehensive figures are available is 1957, and overall grant patterns that year, as is increasingly the case, were heavily influenced by grants from capital made by the Ford Foundation whose assets (market value) for that year were estimated at about $3-1/3 billion. But even if Ford's approximately $273 million in payments on appropriations for hospitals, medical schools, and teachers' salaries is considered atypical and removed from consideration, education and health got 47 per cent and 14 per cent respectively; social welfare 9 per cent; scientific research 13 per cent; humanities and religion 4 and 3 per cent respectively; and government and international affairs, respectively, 2 and 8 per cent of about $248 million in grants from 110 larger foundations in 1957 (7, table 9, xxxii). And of the approximately $33 million in grants for scientific research represented in the latter total, about 41 per cent went for life sciences, 31 per cent for the physical sciences, and 28 per cent for the social sciences (7, table 13, xxxix).

Given limited space as well as incomplete data, it is impossible to examine all the reasons why many would agree with Andrews that: "in their first half-century many foundations have chosen by preference non-controversial projects, but on occasions . . . have shown great courage and initiative . . ." (3, p. 54). Personality differences, the varying interests and influences of donors and officers, the generally conservative backgrounds of board members (53, pp. 32–46; 6, pp. 67–76), the natural scarcity of truly venturesome ideas in most fields, the definite limits to foundation assets in relation to costs and needs,[1] and a host of other factors are probably all important pieces of the puzzle. But much of the overall pattern, particularly the continuing support of education, may well be understood as a reflection of the foundations' efforts to arrive at a new way of working within a contradictory cultural heritage — a heritage whose internally conflicting legal, political-economic, and educational-scientific elements we will now take up in turn.

---

[1] Using reports mostly for 1956, 1957, or 1958, Andrews (7, xiv–xv) estimated the total market value of 5,113 reporting foundations (including Ford at over $3 billion and nine others at over $100 million each) as $11,518,019,000. These figures seem large in themselves but less so in the larger perspective of the American economy, or even of philanthropy in general in this country. The approximately $625 million a year Andrews (8, p. 161) estimates as available for grants in a normal year make up about 8 per cent of the total for all fiscal forms of private philanthropy.

Private Wealth and Public Purposes

Although the formalization of philanthropy can be dated back at least to the Pharaohs, highly organized grant-making guided by a risk capital ideal is almost entirely an innovation of this century and this society (41, p. 575). Legal support for the idea that philanthropic funds should be kept free to be spent in creatively constructive ways came in part as a long-developing reaction against early unsatisfactory experiences with charitable trusts. The latter often had narrow, specific purposes and were established in perpetuity, both trustees and courts being obliged to carry out the donor's wishes even when purposes and beneficiaries became obsolete (36, pp. 15–27). Establishment in perpetuity is still common, as are charitable trusts. But the philanthropic organizations of the sort established by Carnegie and Rockefeller deliberately coupled greater breadth of purpose with more administrative flexibility. Their trustees, to cite Andrews again, "spent less time in conserving money than in exploring new and enterprising ways of spending it" (5, pp. 11–12).[2]

Legal Supports

The frequently discussed doctrine of *cy pres* (14, p. 190), a method of attempting to counter "dead hand" obsolescence by approximating the donor's originally stated purpose, is one indicator of the increasing legal acceptance gradually obtained. But it is less significant, because weak and seldom applied (41, pp. 584–585), than the eventual general granting of broad powers to the corporate form of organization (73, p. 23) and the establishment of permissive tax laws. Of the latter development Chambers observed not long ago:

> Under long traditions of Anglo-American law, the State not only permits voluntary . . . charitable . . . associations to exist and operate with a high degree of autonomy . . . it also habitually encourages and aids them by various means, one of the most common of which is exemption from taxation (22, pp. 44–45).

And, as an even more recent and summary statement has it: "the law largely gets out of the way of individuals who want to transfer their assets to foundations in deference to the private property concept" (73, p. 23).

Legal Constraints

By 1950 it was being argued (15, p. 484) that the freedom of foundations to operate as they pleased had become virtually complete. But this was and still is a considerable exaggeration as far as the foundations of the sort with which we are concerned here, for there are definite ele-

[2] But cf. the comprehensive, somewhat less sanguine, overview by Curti (29, pp. 146–156).

ments of constraint as well as of support in the legal heritage affecting foundation ideology and operation. It has unquestionably remained true, for example, that federal and state regulations are often vaguely worded and weakly enforced.[3] But even the oblique language of the Internal Revenue Code can affect foundation deliberations in variously constraining ways.

One Code provision, for example, ordinarily (cf. 7, xvii) proscribes the unreasonable accumulation of income. As one recent statement explains:

> Federal laws regulating foundations require, among other things, that foundations must not accumulate out of income an amount that is "unreasonable in amount or duration." This is aimed at getting foundations to make their grants as soon as is practical after receiving their income and at preventing a foundation manager from using the charitable organization to build control of the business or businesses (56, p. 15).

While enforcement of this provision can presumably keep a foundation on a general philanthropic track, it may actually discourage the building of the main line, or even of spur lines, into new territories.

To mention two varying cases in point: one foundation was ruled as having forfeited its tax-exempt status for 1951 and 1952 because it had not spent more of its income during that period; the foundation's argument was that a new director had been taking time to develop plans for effective giving (56, p. 15). Another was led several years later, partly because of an unanticipated growth of assets and thus of income, to give huge grants for teachers' salaries, hospitals, and medical schools — an action highly praised by some but condemned by others as essentially palliative (54, pp. 141–142, pp. 117–137, pp. 166–171).

Another Code provision[4] restricts the claiming of tax-exemption where propagandizing or "otherwise attempting to influence legislation" constitutes a "substantial part" of the foundation's activity. But foundations not only find it difficult to avoid what some might consider propagandizing when supporting one kind of field or problem instead of another, but also sometimes find it necessary to get assurance of legislative clearance before certain kinds of demonstration projects, for example, can get started (23, pp. 147–160). By working through special advisory committees or even through grantee organizations themselves, program promotion and legislative clearance can sometimes be obtained indirectly. But even these tactics can bring criticism, e.g., that the foundations exert undue influence or abdicate social responsibility for acts of groups they support financially (81; 33, esp. pp. 14–30).

---

[3] See, e.g., Taylor (72). Another study of the enforcement of state regulations is currently being sponsored by the Russell Sage Foundation.

[4] For an interesting general discussion of "legal and taxation factors," see Andrews (4, pp. 254–261): subsequent quotations are from sections of the Code reproduced there (4, pp. 272–293). For a picture of bolder, earlier days, e.g., of the General Education Board and the allied Southern Education Board, see Fosdick and Pringle (34, p. 7, pp. 19–20, pp. 25–126).

Use of more direct tactics, however, can be even more suspect. As its director recently described the dilemma long confronting one of the few large foundations choosing to function as an operating rather than a grant-making organization in a controversial social science field:

> I have an old friend in Boston, an old professor, who says, "——, if you fail; if you don't do something controversial, you'll all be dispossessed like the monasteries in the sixteenth century." . . . [But] we foundations operate on a very thin legal basis. . . . There are many ways you can get harassed. . . . We testified before . . . [a] Congressional committee and had our tax-exemption removed for a year because they said that we were propagandizing. . . .
> [But] if you're not trying to influence legislation what are you trying to do? You're trying to do it at another level . . . trying to influence thinking (Interview with author; November, 1961).

For grant-making foundations, the most frequent result of the legal constraints of the sort just described has been the reinforcement of an attitude of circumspection about fields to enter and projects and organizations to support. As a spokesman for one of the larger foundations of this sort reported a few years ago, "Tax considerations have restricted us somewhat . . . we've not been able to go the route we would have preferred in some cases. But they haven't seriously impeded our activities — we're just being extra careful" (37, p. 1). In a specific case involving a grant for civic planning, the route chosen (29, p. 156), as the overall figures on grants cited earlier showed to be typical, was one leading through a campus.

That it is a university — rather than either a social work agency or a militant reform organization — with which the foundation has been most frequently compared through the years,[5] is thus partly a matter of foundation preference, partly one of legal constraint. In their efforts to break away from the traditional palliative model of philanthropy, the foundations have worked through universities and colleges partly because such organizations already have a degree of legal — and popular — support which the foundations are still only gradually acquiring. And as will be explained further below, in thus seeking acceptance for their new mode of giving they have become less private and more public, both more responsive and responsible to the organizations in which they have sought, and given, support.

Self-Help and Voluntary Enterprise

A society's legal traditions and innovations reflect its broader cultural heritage, including the political and economic theories held by groups

---

[5] Two of the best statements are those several decades ago by Keppel (46, pp. 9–12) and by Hollis (40, pp. 23–26).

creating (or influencing) actual legislation. If the legitimation of risk capital activity has been importantly dependent on interpretations made by the courts, it has been as much or more dependent on interpretations — and investigations — made by the Congresses. And if the major legal theme in foundation ideology has been that of the legitimacy of putting private wealth to public purposes, the major political-economic theme has been that of the importance of preserving the "American way" of limited government — of self-help and voluntary enterprise.

Political-Economic Supports

In our society, the idea of tax-exemption already mentioned is itself significantly based on a theory of the delegation of societal functions and a separation of powers:

> The theory underlying the whole [of the legal tradition supporting tax-exemption] is that to a considerable extent the voluntary institutions "relieve the burdens of government," that is, they perform functions which, if not so performed, might be considered mandatory or at least desirable for the state itself to perform. Thus the state delegates, in a manner of speaking, a variety of public functions to non-governmental agencies, which it encourages, assists within limits, and sparingly regulates and supervises (22, p. 45).

And, relying on this theory and related ideas, e.g., from Carnegie's "Gospel of Wealth" (20) which stressed the obligation of the rich to help the poor help themselves, many of the foundations' spokesmen have come to argue that their support helps individuals and organizations (sometimes including government agencies) do important research and experimentation they could not otherwise afford. Others go even further, arguing — and with considerable success, e.g., with the Cox Committee (75) — that foundations sponsor such work in ways state or national governments either don't attempt adequately, if at all; can't attempt effectively; or shouldn't attempt, because this would mean an ineffective expansion of the sphere of government. A related theme — frequently expressed, and as frequently criticized — is that risk capital philanthropy and economic free enterprise have a similar value (see e.g., 43, chapter 1; 27, pp. 107–108).

In general, Marts' contention (55, p. 149) that "the endowed foundation stands out, beyond question, as one of the great bulwarks of the American way," finds support in a lot of the foundation literature; as do Kiger's conclusions that:

> (1) American foundations are the result of the capitalistic system which, contrary to its European counterpart, allowed neither church nor state a monopoly on philanthropic activity.

(2) They were motivated by a concern for the secular well-being of mankind (51, p. 25).

Although religious themes — as Moe, for example, has shown (59, p. 143) — have traditionally influenced both the legal thought and the political-economic theorizing affecting philanthropy, the values of individual initiative and decentralization of power have become more integral components of this particular philanthropic ideology.[6]

Political-Economic Constraints

As was the case with legal themes and the courts, however, Congressional and public acceptance of these "American way" arguments, although substantial, has always been far from complete. From the efforts to get a federal charter for the Rockefeller Foundation, held up in Congress from 1910 to 1913, through the current rapid growth of foundations of many kinds, risk capital ideology and action have generated criticism from both left and right (45, pp. 22–24).

During the trust-busting era before World War I (74), and again in the Depression (53; 27), for example, critics argued that the foundations retained the most illiberal features of *laissez faire* economics. Then in the fifties, while being hailed by some (e.g., 43) as representing capitalism at its most responsible best, they were twice investigated by Congress as agencies subverting not only capitalism but democracy itself. The latter investigations repeated the pattern: the first (76) resulted in what was essentially a vote of confidence in the risk capital concept, the second produced a strongly condemnatory report (77; cf. 81). A third investigation just completed dealt more with the use and abuse of tax regulations, its central ideas being: (1) that foundation money is really public money because it has been derived from tax-exemption; (2) that more adequate government supervision is needed to make sure the money goes for valid charitable purposes — not to enhance further the power of large business firms (62).

Factors ranging from the suspicion of capitalism (27), and of wealth and power generally (16, p. 2, p. 119), to the maneuverings of presidential aspirants (57) have certainly been involved in all this through the years. But much of the general difficulty for foundations stems from the fact that the central political-economic elements of the risk capital concept are themselves extremely pliable; so pliable, in fact, as to be used to justify, on the one hand, support of scholarly studies based on the premise that capitalism "thrives upon a steady drumfire of criticism" (75, p. 183), and, on the other, the support of efforts to teach school children that the profit motive, free competition, and the idea of "government as protector, not as provider" (30, p. 1), are the fundamental bulwarks of our way of life.

[6] See especially the succinct rationale in Belknap and Mandel (11, p. 28).

The net result of this sort of ideological flexibility is to multiply the possible bases of external acceptance and tolerance and also of criticism and control. For incomplete Congressional acceptance of the foundations' "American way" arguments contributed to the establishment and more extensive enforcement of the legal restrictions already mentioned. And, both in the past and the present, fear of legislative retaliation has accelerated the tendency of some foundations to avoid sponsoring controversial activities. To mention just one prominent case in point: the Fund for the Republic has been described by its director as a "completely disowned subsidiary" of the Ford Foundation (54, pp. 69–70). Significantly, perhaps, one of the early efforts supported by this Fund was a study of Congressional investigating committees (54, pp. 70–71).

Lest we be misunderstood, the issue here is not that the Ford "Funds" or other foundations sometimes avoid controversy, for they have also been bold at times; neither is it simply that boldness and timidity are matters involving selective perception. Our contentions are, rather: (1) that, using the flexible self-help and voluntary enterprise components of the risk capital ideology, the foundations can incur criticism for almost any kind of grant; and (2) that foundation adoption of these "American way" arguments reflects not just the values of donors and trustees but the broader pluralistic political environment in which the foundations operate, and in which they have continually had to justify their existence and operation. Like the need to take legal stipulations into account, the need to develop and maintain a broader political-economic legitimacy has persistently limited the foundations' willingness and freedom to carry their risk capital commitment to all the sectors of society in which it might otherwise be possible to apply private wealth to public purposes.

Not at all incidentally, such constraint has been apparent even *within* some sections of what we would consider to be the generally "safe" fields of education and science — the foundations' record of approach-retreat-and-return in the social sciences being probably the best concrete case in point. The relative inability of social scientists to convince foundation officers and trustees of not only the objectivity but the relevance of their studies has also been involved.[7] But, as indicated earlier, the Walsh Commission Report before World War I (when the Rockefeller Foundation was considering the industrial relations field); the "tainted

[7] For a general discussion of factors limiting the development of the social sciences, see Young (83, pp. 325–335). We cannot resist citing these statements (interview with author, 1962) by one foundation official:

When it comes to social science: I got a letter once from [a prominent official of another foundation]. . . . He said, "I've kept my foundation out of that. It's too full of crackpots and I can't tell them apart."

My criticism of social science is that . . . [it] is not enough interested in social engineering. In imitating the hard sciences the descriptive approach won't hold water . . . [I mean, the attitude that] "Well, if my next-door neighbor over here can spend the rest of his life describing the protein molecule, I'll do the same thing of society." But society won't let you do that. You have to be willing to do something. The shelves are full of descriptive studies nobody has read.

money" criticism during the twenties and thirties (16, pp. 138–139); and the criticism of empirical social science made by the Reece Committee later on (77); all seemed to leave fairly clear marks on foundation programs.

Though even the data for the 1950's are imprecise and detailed comparisons with earlier eras very difficult to make with much accuracy, it is at least informative in this connection that the larger foundations' relative expenditures (including grants) for social science research, which had declined from 1939 to 1946 then increased again (6, Table 22, p. 270), dropped from 42 per cent of expenditures for all types of scientific research in 1953 to 28 per cent in 1957 — the years just after the Reece investigation.[8] Whatever forces were at work, probably a great many, it also seems pertinent here that Alpert's (2, p. 154) estimates of the annual rates of expenditures for social science research *performed* by various types of organizations in the United States in 1958 indicate that — of $215 million in such funds — private foundations spent $2 million or 0.9 per cent, independent institutes and the like 1.4 per cent, colleges and universities 16.3 per cent, the federal government 17.7 per cent, and industrial and commercial organizations 63.7 per cent.

Progress Through Knowledge

Whatever their record in the social sciences, and that is a history yet to be written, the foundations have, through the years, become significantly involved in supporting the research, experimentation, and teaching activities of persons in the interrelated social systems of science and higher education generally. And as this has happened, a third ideological component — itself a synthesis of elements from the idea of progress (17, pp. 278–349) and from what might be termed the scientific faith (cf. 13) and the pragmatic temper — has become another integral part of the risk capital ideology.

Educational-Scientific Supports

Taylor's argument (72, p. 6) that the freedom of private welfare enterprises should be protected because they have sponsored the research which has "set the pace of our social progress"; Rose's early (1923) assertion (cited in Fosdick 33, p. 141) that knowledge of the spirit and technique of modern science "affects the entire system of education and carries with it the shaping of a civilization"; and Kiger's explanation (51, pp. 118–119) that the pragmatic tendency to adopt better proce-

---

[8] For 77 larger foundations' expenditures (including grants) in 1953 and 1957, see Walton and Andrews (7, Table 13, xxxix). The interested reader should go to this source and to Andrews (6, pp. 270–273), being sure to note the bases of comparison, the qualifications, and the effects of large grants.

dures "permeates the foundations and our capitalistic society alike"; all are good illustrations of the various elements of this third line of defense of foundation existence and freedom. The foundations' creative synthesis of these ideas,[9] however, is most remarkably illustrated in Fosdick's explanation of a turning-point in the career of the Rockefeller Foundation:

> The decision in the late 1920's . . . to concentrate the work of the Foundation on the extension of knowledge was based on a growing conviction that the margin between what men know and what they use is much too thin. . . . Unless research is constantly maintained, the stockpile of knowledge becomes much too low for safety. There is a sense in which the practical applications of knowledge are the dividends pure science declares from time to time (33, p. 140).

By thus publicly linking their own efforts with the functions and traditions of prestigious and ostensibly "neutral" scientific professions and educational institutions, the grant-making foundations have helped enhance their legal and political-economic legitimacy, particularly in recent decades. In the Cox investigation (75) especially, for example, the record makes it clear that support for the risk capital concept from leading scientists and educators considerably increased the impact of the defense made by eminent foundation officials. Even more recently, an increasing number of industrial firms have adopted a similar "progress through knowledge" rationale in establishing their own "company" foundations (58, pp. 218–223). And similar lines of ideological argument are now increasingly visible in the writings of academic economists (67, pp. 571–583) and government officials (64, pp. 1–53; 39, p. 9), currently intrigued with the possibilities of spurring economic growth, both here and abroad, by accelerating investments in education, considered as a national resource.

Educational-Scientific Constraints

Such relative gains in legal and political-economic legitimacy have, nonetheless, come at a considerable cost in increased dependence on the educational and scientific organizations whose work the foundations have considerably stimulated and financed. This dependence, as we have argued in more detail elsewhere (24, pp. 167–184; 25, pp. 4–6), is reflected in the shift from the endowment to the limited-project method of grant-making, the increased use[10] of academic consultants, and the

[9] Akin to many of those in "educational meliorism," which Ballinger, in an important study (9, pp. 88–89) has traced, e.g., through Helvetius and Condorcet to Thomas Jefferson, Horace Mann, and John Dewey.

[10] Even several decades ago, as Keppel pointed out (47, pp. 13–14):

> At first foundations negotiated directly. Today there are advisory and supervisory groups of various kinds. For example, the first $2,000,000 given away by

addition of layers of specialists to many foundation staffs. For involved in the adoption of these and other administration methods is a
fundamental dependence — not always apparent to the man scrabbling
for a particular grant — on the creativity and the technical knowledge
and resources of the men actually conducting the work on the frontiers of
research, experimentation, and the dissemination of new knowledge.

Some of the innovative work of interest to the foundations has been
work done by these organizations themselves; more of it, plus a lot of
important but routine intellectual activity, has been carried out in the colleges, universities, and research institutes they have supported. And
these academic organizations (and the individual professions with which
they are both cooperatively and competitively linked) not only have
considerable contractual and moral control over the persons needed to
man foundation programs and projects; they also provide library and
laboratory facilities — necessary instruments of intellectual production
which even the wealthiest foundations could not permanently provide,
even if this were compatible with the risk capital commitment. And,
because most professions and many colleges and universities seek with
considerable vigor to protect and enhance their own legitimacy and
autonomy, these major clients' control over the human and material
resources which foundation grants must rent or buy is additionally
bolstered by their better institutionalized (and somewhat rival) ideology
of academic freedom (see, e.g., [34, pp. 150–171; 26]).

Thus in various cumulative ways — in publicly embracing the "progress through knowledge" rationale (which includes the idea of giving
credit[11] where it is due), in utilizing academically-oriented staff members and trustees, and in actually making grants to (and otherwise working with) educational-scientific clients, the foundations have acquired an
increasing obligation not to undermine the internal or external conditions protecting the general academic freedom to teach and do research.
As H. Rowan Gaither once described this obligation quite succinctly:
"If a foundation steps over the invisible line and encroaches on a grantee's
independence, the opportunity for service is transformed into a visible
and grievous disservice" (35, p. 23).

The perpetual paradox for contemporary grant-making foundations is
that the same vigorous advocacy of "progress through knowledge" which
has helped gain legal and political-economic support for their existence

---

the Carnegie Corporation was given wholly on the basis of direct negotiations between the Corporation and the institution concerned. Seventeen years later, 68
per cent of the annual program was based upon consultation with some representative advisory body. In a single recent year, the records showed that our
Corporation had been in consultation with no fewer than 68 national scholarly
organizations of one kind or another.

[11] Cf. Macdonald (54, pp. 97–98), but also West (78, pp. 54–62); on the incentive to shift the burden of both evaluation and responsibility to grantees, see
Colvard (25, p. 5) and Yarmolinsky (82, p. 83).

as complementary educational institutions has increased their dependence, as organizations, on the very groups whose effectiveness they have
sought to improve, both as a value in itself and in the larger interest of
social innovation. As Ross put it so well several decades ago, "Human
institutions and relations . . . glide insensibly into forms which would
not be assumed of intention (65, p. 471)."

Summary

As an important part of the effort to establish their collective legitimacy as a new type of institution and enhance their individual autonomy
as self-perpetuating organizations sponsoring educational and social
reform, the large grant-making philanthropic foundations of twentieth-
century American society have synthesized from a contradictory cultural
heritage a distinctive ideology — the risk capital concept. Because this
concept has proved to be a fairly successful rationale for minimizing
legal control, deflecting political-economic criticism, and engaging in
only temporary relations with specific educational-scientific clients, the
foundations have sometimes been able to conduct — and, more often, to
sponsor — widely acclaimed ventures on the frontiers of research, education, and social action.

Incomplete *legal* acceptance, e.g., of arguments for tax-exemption and
for freeing philanthropic funds from the "dead hand" of original donors,
however, has persistently tended to lead the foundation along two in-
tersecting paths somewhat off to one side of the risk capital route imprecisely indicated in their principal ideology. One path, difficult to
trace with certainty, is the support, in many locations, of activities more
conventional and palliative than innovative and preventive. The other,
more clearly marked and often overlapping the main route — but only
occasionally doing so in precipitous places — is a circuitous path skirting
many college and university campuses. For the larger grant-making foundations have concentrated on working through prestigious and politically
"neutral" educational and scientific organizations, and this has been a
matter partly of preference, partly of constraint.

The latter tendency, to adopt the foster parent role of "innovation by
indirection," has been intermittently accelerated through the years by
active *political-economic* opposition, stemming both from the political
pluralism of the broader society and the ideological pliability of the
"American way" components of the risk capital concept. To many Congressional critics — from Walsh to Patman, for example — the existence
and operation of large foundations has not been completely compatible
with the self-help and voluntary enterprise traditions.

Again, the fiscal and ideological support the foundations have given to
the "progress through knowledge" argument — that both industrial and
social progress are now continually dependent on technical and educa-

tional innovation — has helped the foundations gain access to, and legitimizing support from, many of their major *educational-scientific* clients. But the scientific professions, for example, and the colleges and universities which train and employ their leaders, are the vital centers of this new institutionalization of innovation, and they are also organizations competitively interested in enhancing their own legitimacy and autonomy. To gain acceptance and freedom for themselves, the foundations have thus over time become considerably dependent on their ability to stimulate their academic clients' creative potential without jeopardizing these grantee groups' own acceptance and freedom.

The foundations' leaders have not always balanced these delicate tasks as wisely or well as either they or their critics would prefer. But they have had the sometimes bittersweet satisfaction of seeing many of their interests acquired by and their methods adopted and improved upon by federal agencies.[12] And much of their risk capital ideology has returned as a new stimulus to the idea of progress and other elements of the cultural heritage from whence it came.

Broader Implications: Risk Capital and "Creative Destruction"

The foundations' contribution to the vitality of the American Dream[13] may prove to be their greatest achievement. For, as much of the overall analysis has probably made clear by now, the risk capital concept appears, to us at least, to be a striking example of the ideological affinity of capitalism[14] and science, and this affinity may help explain much of the history of American society in the years of its industrialization and urbanization.

For if the continuation of capitalism is dependent on continual obsolescence and innovation, the growth of science comes as much through the constant questioning and criticism (cf. 70, pp. 67–68) of old ideas as through the decisive proof of new ones. Science, that is to say, is a universal solvent of its own intellectual structure and substance as capitalism is of its industrial arrangements and products. Their individual organizations both appear to operate through what Schumpeter, in referring only to capitalism, aptly called a process of "creative destruction" (68, pp. 82–83); and, collectively — as institutions set in larger contexts — both must legitimize or market this inherently disruptive rationalizing process: the freedom it requires and the societal changes it brings, including the idea that change itself is the continuing condition of industrial-urban life.

It is difficult, as yet,[15] to know whether or to what extent the systematic

[12] See, e.g., Young (84, pp. 14–15), and Kidd (49, pp. 189–205).

[13] Cf. the perceptive appraisal in Polak (63, pp. 300–331, pp. 363–365). We are indebted to Gideon Sjoberg for calling this interesting work to our attention.

[14] On the affinity of science and socialism see, e.g., Bernal (12, pp. 32–33, pp. 221–231).

[15] See especially Jewkes *et al* (44, pp. 4–14), Sweezy (71), and Morrison (60).

investment of excess private profits in science, and education more generally, can actually yield knowledge and skill "dividends" capable of keeping the obsoleting-innovating process in motion while stimulating higher education and mobility. It does not, however, seem ridiculous to consider that, for better or for worse, such investments may have functioned to reconcile some American intellectuals (see 61, pp. 275–288) to some of the contradictions in capitalism, and also that the foundations' development and official advocacy of the risk capital concept may have functioned during persistent "times of troubles" to perpetuate public belief — not simply in foundations, but in capitalism, science, and the possibility of progress.[16]

To put these thoughts another way: both the theory and the practice of giving extensive private and public[17] support to education and science may be seen eventually as important factors in the relocation and perpetuation of the innovative industrial functions once much more dependent on the individual capitalist entrepreneur. For, in our own society at least, the creation of production techniques, the identification of new markets — and even the development of new ideological justifications for private enterprise — increasingly are activities involving professional research conducted with colleges and universities as well as within industrial firms themselves.[18]

If capitalism has indeed become both ideologically and operationally linked with science and higher education, and professionalism even more permanently "mated with progress,"[19] both the foundations and the federal government have helped with the matchmaking and the provision of dowries. These unions and their issues will probably receive

[16] As Chambers (21, p. 197) has noted in a valuable article, the "reaffirmation of this faith . . . in the midst of . . . an 'age of anxiety' was remarkable." For a broad view of such phenomena in general see Shils (69, pp. 60–83).

[17] Cf. the evidence and argument in Alpert (2, pp. 152–157). The changes here in less than fifty years would probably seem incredible to the men in the Walsh Commission, who pointed out with concern that:

Two groups of the 'foundations' namely the Rockefeller and Carnegie foundations, together have funds yielding an annual revenue of at least $13,500,000, which is at least twice as great as the appropriations for the Federal Government for similar purposes, namely, education and social service (74, p. 81).

Forty-four years later, Kidd reported that for research in universities and associated research centers alone:

During the year ending June 30, 1960, the Federal Government will spend somewhat more than $650 million . . . (50, p. 4).

[18] See, e.g., (31); also Carlton (19, esp. pp. 440–443). Halsey argues very generally that "The mark of the educational institutions of a technological society is that they are in a special sense crucial to its maintenance and, to the institutionalization of technological research, and to its further development" (38, p. 119).

See Barzun, however, on philanthropy as an "enemy of intellect" (10, chapter 1, pp. 6, 7), and Jaspers (42, pp. 871–884) on the various meanings of science, and the various historical attitudes toward it. For example:

Science left to itself becomes homeless. The intellect is a whore, said Nicholas of Cusa, for it can prostitute itself to anything. Science is a whore, said Lenin, for it sells itself to any class interest.

[19] The terms are Whitehead's (79, pp. 294–295); see also his important discussion of the invention of the method of invention, in the same work.

considerable attention by sociologists and historians of the future; they deserve far more attention now than they have yet been given[20] by contemporary students of social and cultural change.

BIBLIOGRAPHY

1. Allen, W. H. *Modern Philanthropy*. New York: Dodd, Mead & Co., Inc., 1912.

2. Alpert, Harry. "The Funding of Social Science Research," in Donald S. Ray (ed.), *Trends in Social Science*. New York: Philosophical Library, 1961.

3. Andrews, F. Emerson. "New Challenges for Our Foundations," *New York Times Magazine* (April 3, 1949), pp. 16–17, pp. 53–54.

4. Andrews, F. Emerson. *Corporation Giving*. New York: Russell Sage Foundation, 1952.

5. Andrews, F. Emerson. *Legal Instruments of Foundations*. New York: Russell Sage Foundation, 1956.

6. Andrews, F. Emerson. *Philanthropic Foundations*. New York: Russell Sage Foundation, 1956.

7. Andrews, F. Emerson. "Introduction," in Ann D. Walton and F. Emerson Andrews (eds.), *The Foundation Directory*, Ed. I. New York: Russell Sage Foundation, 1960.

8. Andrews, F. Emerson. "Growth and Present Status of American Foundations," *Proceedings of the American Philosophical Society*, Vol. 105 (1961), pp. 157–161.

9. Ballinger, Stanley E. "The Idea of Social Progress Through Education in the French Enlightenment Period: Helvetius and Condorcet," *History of Education Journal*, Vol. 10 (1959), pp. 88–99.

10. Barzun, Jacques. *The House of Intellect*. New York: Harper & Bros., 1959.

11. Belknap, Chauncey, and Philip Mandel. *The Federal Income Tax Exemption of Charitable Organizations: Its History and Underlying Policy*. Report prepared for the Rockefeller Foundation, March 8, 1954. (mimeo)

12. Bernal, J. D. *The Social Function of Science*. New York: The Macmillan Co., 1939.

13. Bernard, Jessie. "The Power of Science and the Science of Power," *American Sociological Review*, Vol. 14 (1949), pp. 575–584.

14. Beveridge, Lord. *Voluntary Action*. New York: The Macmillan Co., 1948.

15. Bittker, Boris I. "The Modern Philanthropic Foundation: A Critique and a Proposal," *Yale Law Journal*, Vol. 59 (1950), pp. 477–509.

16. Bremner, Robert H. *American Philanthropy*. Chicago: University of Chicago Press, 1960.

[20] See, e.g., the report of the Princeton conference, containing many recommended research topics (66), and Curti (28).

17. Bury, J. B. *The Idea of Progress*. London: The Macmillan Co., 1921.

18. Calkins, Robert D. "The Impact of Foundations on Higher Education," in *The Impact of Foundations on Higher Education*. Commission on Colleges and Universities, North Central Association of Colleges and Secondary Schools, 1954, pp. 1–13.

19. Carlton, Frank T. "Capitalism and Social Change," *Sociology and Social Research*, Vol. 28 (1944), pp. 440–451.

20. Carnegie, Andrew. *The Gospel of Wealth, and Other Timely Essays*. New York: The Century Co., 1900.

21. Chambers, Clarke A. "The Belief in Progress in Twentieth-Century America," *Journal of the History of Ideas*, Vol. 19 (1958), pp. 197–224.

22. Chambers, M. M. *Charters of Philanthropies*. New York: Carnegie Foundation for the Advancement of Teaching, 1948.

23. Colvard, Richard. "The Foundation and the Colleges: A Study of Organizations, Professions and Power in the Arkansas Experiment in Teacher Education." Unpublished Ph.D. dissertation, University of California, Berkeley, 1959.

24. Colvard, Richard. "Foundations and Professions: The Organizational Defense of Autonomy," *The Administrative Science Quarterly*, Vol. 6 (1961), pp. 167–184.

25. Colvard, Richard. "Foundations and Their Clients: Why the Project Method?" *The American Behavioral Scientist*, Vol. 5 (1962), pp. 4–6.

26. Colvard, Richard. "The Colleges and the 'Arkansas Purchase' Controversy," in Matthew B. Miles (ed.), *Innovation in Education*. New York: Teachers' College Bureau of Publications, 1963.

27. Coon, Horace. *Money to Burn*. New York: Longman's Green, 1938.

28. Curti, Merle. *The History of American Philanthropy as a Field of Research*. Mimeo. n.d., 17 pp., 1957 (?).

29. Curti, Merle. "Tradition and Innovation in American Philanthropy," *Proceedings of the American Philosophical Society*, Vol. 105 (1961), pp. 146–156.

30. Dugger, Ronnie. "Target: The Schools," *The Texas Observer* (December 18, 1959), p. 1, p. 3.

31. Editors of *Fortune*. *The Mighty Force of Research*. New York: McGraw-Hill Book Co., 1956.

32. Embree, Edwin R. "Timid Billions: Are the Foundations Doing Their Job?" *Harper's Magazine*, Vol. 198 (1949), pp. 28–37.

33. Fosdick, Raymond B. *The Story of the Rockefeller Foundation*. New York: Harper & Bros., 1952.

34. Fosdick, Raymond B., Henry F. Pringle, and Katherine D. Pringle. *Adventure in Giving*. New York: Harper & Row, 1962.

35. Gaither, H. Rowan, Jr. "The President's Review," in *The Ford Foundation Annual Report, October 1, 1955 to September 30, 1956*. New York: The Ford Foundation, 1956.

36. Gordon, Milton M. "The Girard College Case: Resolution and Significance," *Social Problems,* Vol. 7 (1959), pp. 15–27.

37. Grimes, John A. "Tax Crackdown," *The Wall Street Journal* (December 9, 1958), p. 1, p. 4.

38. Halsey, A. H. "The Changing Functions of Universities in Advanced Industrial Societies," *Harvard Educational Review,* Vol. 30 (1960), pp. 118–127.

39. Heller, Walter W. "Economic Growth: Challenge and Opportunity." Address to the Loeb Awards Fourth Annual Presentation Luncheon, New York, May 18, 1961. Cited in Luther W. Stringham and Earl E. Huyck, "Measuring Returns from Investments in Human Resources," a paper presented at 56th Annual Meeting of the American Sociological Association, St. Louis, Mo., August 31, 1961.

40. Hollis, E. V. *Philanthropic Foundations and Higher Education.* New York: Columbia University Press, 1938.

41. Hollis, E. V. "Evolution of the Philanthropic Foundation," *The Educational Record,* Vol. 20 (1939), pp. 575–578.

42. Jaspers, Karl. "Philosophy and Science," *Partisan Review,* Vol. 16 (1949), pp. 871–884.

43. Jenkins, Edward C. *Philanthropy in America.* New York: Association Press, 1950.

44. Jewkes, John, David Sawers, and Richard Stillerman. *The Sources of Invention.* London: The Macmillan Co., 1958.

45. Keele, Harold. "Government's Attitude Toward Foundations," in *Conference of Michigan Foundations.* Ann Arbor: Foster Foundation, 1954.

46. Keppel, Frederick P. *The Foundation: Its Place in American Life.* New York: The Macmillan Co., 1930.

47. Keppel, Frederick P. *Philanthropy and Learning.* New York: Columbia University Press, 1936.

48. Keppel, Frederick P. "The Responsibility of Endowments in the Promotion of Knowledge," *Proceedings of the American Philosophical Society,* Vol. 77 (1937), pp. 591–603.

49. Kidd, Charles V. *American Universities and Federal Research.* Cambridge: Belknap Press, 1959.

50. Kidd, Charles V. "New Government-University Relationships in Research," *Higher Education,* Vol. 16 (1960), pp. 3–6, pp. 18–19.

51. Kiger, Joseph C. *Operating Principles of the Larger Foundations.* New York: Russell Sage Foundation, 1954.

52. Lazarsfeld, Paul F., in collaboration with Sydney S. Spivack. "Observations on Organized Social Research in the United States: A Report to the International Social Science Council," 1961. (mimeo)

53. Lindeman, Eduard C. *Wealth and Culture.* New York: Harcourt, Brace and Co., 1936.

54. Macdonald, Dwight. *The Ford Foundation: The Men and the Millions.* New York: Reynal, 1956.

55. Marts, Arnaud C. *Philanthropy's Role in Civilization.* New York: Harper & Bros., 1953.

56. Merry, Howard. "Charity and Business: More Foundations Get Involved in Dealings of Their Own Officers," *The Wall Street Journal* (July 10, 1961), p. 15.

57. Miller, H. H. "Investigating the Foundations," *The Reporter,* Vol. 9 (1953), pp. 37–40.

58. Millett, John D. "Higher Education," in Beardsley Ruml, with Theodore Geiger (ed.), *The Manual of Corporate Giving.* Washington, D.C.: National Planning Association, 1952.

59. Moe, Henry Allen. "Notes on the Origin of Philanthropy in Christendom," *Proceedings of The American Philosophical Society,* Vol. 105 (1961), pp. 141–144.

60. Morrison, Philip. "The Innovation Industry," *Monthly Review,* Vol. 11 (1959), pp. 103–110.

61. Nomad, Max (pseud.) *Aspects of Revolt.* New York: Noonday Press (N212), 1959.

62. U.S. Congress, *Tax-Exempt Foundations and Charitable Trusts: Their Impact on our Economy,* Chairman's Report to the Select (Patman) Committee on Small Business, House of Representatives, 87th Congress, December 31, 1962. Washington, D.C.: Government Printing Office, 1963.

63. Polak, Fred L. *The Image of the Future,* II., Elise Boulding (ed.). New York: Oceana Publications, 1961.

64. Rivlin, Alice M. *Research in the Economics of Higher Education: Progress and Problems,* 1961. (mimeo)

65. Ross, E. A. *Principles of Sociology.* New York: Century, 1930.

66. Russell Sage Foundation. *Report of the Princeton Conference on the History of Philanthropy in the United States.* New York: Russell Sage Foundation, 1956.

67. Schultz, Theodore W. "Capital Formation by Education," *The Journal of Political Economy,* Vol. 68 (1960), pp. 571–583.

68. Schumpeter, Joseph A. *Capitalism, Socialism, and Democracy,* 3rd ed. New York: Harper & Bros., 1950.

69. Shils, Edward A. "The Macrosociological Problem: Consensus and Dissensus in the Larger Society," in Donald S. Ray (ed.), *Trends in Social Science.* New York: Philosophical Library, 1961.

70. Sjoberg, Gideon, and Leonard D. Cain, Jr. "Negative Values and Social Action," *Alpha Kappa Deltan,* Vol. 29 (1959), pp. 63–70.

71. Sweezy, Paul M. "Theories of the New Capitalism," *Monthly Review,* Vol. 11 (1959), pp. 65–75.

72. Taylor, Eleanor K. *Public Accountability of Foundations and Charitable Trusts.* New York: Russell Sage Foundation, 1953.

748 SPECIAL AREAS

73. Tunks, L. K. "Legal Basis for Foundations," in *The Impact of Foundations on Higher Education*. Commission on Colleges and Universities, North Central Association of Colleges and Secondary Schools, 1954, pp. 22–28.

74. U.S. Congress, Senate. *Industrial Relations: Final Report and Testimony Submitted to Congress by the (Walsh) Commission on Industrial Relations Created by the Act of August 23, 1912*. 64th Congress, 1st session. Senate Document No. 415. Washington, D.C.: Government Printing Office, 1916, 11 Vols.

75. U.S. Congress. *Hearings Before the Select (Cox) Committee to Investigate Tax-Exempt Foundations and Comparable Organizations*. 82nd Congress, 2nd session. Washington, D.C.: Government Printing Office, 1953, pp. 1–792.

76. U.S. Congress. *Final Report of the Select (Cox) Committee to Investigate Tax-Exempt Foundations and Comparable Organizations*. 82nd Congress, 2nd session. House Report No. 2514. Washington, D.C.: Government Printing Office, 1953, pp. 1–15.

77. U.S. Congress. *Hearings Before the Special (Reece) Committee to Investigate Tax-Exempt Foundations and Comparable Organizations*. 83rd Congress, 2nd session. Washington, D.C.: Government Printing Office, 1954. Part I, pp. 1–943; Part II, pp. 945–1241.

78. West, S. S. "The Ideology of Academic Scientists," *IRE Transactions on Engineering Management*, EM–7 (1960), pp. 54–62.

79. Whitehead, Alfred N. *Science and the Modern World*. New York: The Macmillan Co., 1941.

80. Whyte, William H., Jr. "Where the Foundations Fall Down," *Fortune*, Vol. 52 (1956), pp. 140–141, pp. 211–212, p. 214, p. 216, pp. 219–220.

81. Wormser, Rene. *Foundations: Their Power and Influence*. New York: Devin-Adair, 1958.

82. Yarmolinsky, Adam. "How to Run a Small Foundation," *Harper's Magazine*, Vol. 222 (1961), pp. 80–84.

83. Young, Donald. "Limiting Factors in the Development of the Social Sciences," *Proceedings of the American Philosophical Society*, Vol. 92 (1948), pp. 325–335.

84. Young, Donald. "Philanthropic Foundations, Sociology, and Human Betterment." Paper presented at the Annual Meeting of the American Sociological Association, Washington, D.C., September 2, 1962.

29

Philip M. Marcus

Organizational Change: The Case

of American Trade Unions*

In this chapter we should like to develop a model of trade union change. At first, we shall comment upon another general model of organizational change, the "Iron Law of Oligarchy," and then proceed to specify some of the variables we believe should be included in any system of analysis. Our model has two basic dimensions, an internal and external system. We postulate that solving problems posed by one dimension will give rise to new problems in the other dimension. Using trade unions as illus‑ trative of the model, we shall indicate how changes in the industry, technology, or legal system affect such internal variables as size and composition of membership, relationships between local and national organizations, as well as the total bureaucratic structure.[1] In the final part, we shall organize these basic variables and their relationships into a discussion of two aspects of union changes: centralization and control.

In a recent study of the literature on organizations, Blau and Scott concluded that organizational change should be examined in terms of

* This chapter was made possible by a grant from the Carnegie Corporation of New York to the Survey Research Center of the University of Michigan for the study of control in organizations. The author is indebted for many helpful suggestions and comments provided by readers of earlier versions. Among those who have been especially helpful are: Jerald G. Bachman, Dora Cafagna, Charles Perrow, Clagett G. Smith, and Arnold S. Tannenbaum, of the University of Michigan; Robert Perrucci of Purdue University. The editors, George K. Zollschan and Walter Hirsch, also helped clarify many parts.

[1] In this chapter we use the term "national" rather than "international" to refer to the central union administration.

dialectics, i.e., the solutions to one set of problems will in turn give rise to new ones (6, pp. 250–253). In this manner, organizations may be seen in terms of a constant evolution whereby a change in one part will effect some modification in another part. This certainly is consistent with much of the systems theory we use in sociological research today. What Blau and Scott specifically contribute is the suggestion that many of these changes will be unanticipated by the participants, and thus many of the new problems will actually be combinations of older problems and their solutions.

It is instructive to compare the Blau-Scott approach to the study of organizational change with another, more deterministic model. For example, Robert Michels has provided one of the most widely accepted theories of organizational change (27). Briefly, Michels stipulated an "Iron Law of Oligarchy," and attempted to describe many of the social conditions which would bring this about. He noted that, even in the very organizations whose goals were the expansion of democracy for its members, there tended to emerge a small number of men who gained control and retained it. This oligarchy developed primarily because of the separation of the membership from the leadership. Officials became specialists dealing with problems the membership could not comprehend. Membership frequently became apathetic, decreased its participation in the organization, and allowed the officials to select suitable policies and methods of attaining the goals. These leaders seldom faced elections, and even when they did, the incumbents frequently resorted to undemocratic methods in order to retain office. New leadership was co-opted from within the organization, and as the officials also controlled access to the top, divergent opinions were seldom discussed or entertained. The result of this oligarchy was a compromise of the organization's goals with the very environment that was to be changed by the organization.

Michels saw the development of oligarchy as inevitable, and most subsequent research of voluntary organizations has supported his analysis (e.g., [17]; [22]; [34]; [46]; [18]). Recently, Lipset has reformulated Michels' thesis and raised the question, "How is effective democratic control maintained?" ([23; 25]). He and his colleagues empirically studied a deviant case (the International Typographical Union) in which oligarchy did not develop. The continuation of a strong two-party system, Lipset found, was based upon historical circumstances which gave rise to a value structure legitimating opposition within the union. Membership tended to be highly literate and well paid, and the entire organization felt relatively secure in its operations vis à vis management. The many associations and clubs which formed within the union, independent of the hierarchy, provided sources for development of opposition leaders. Union officials could not control many of the activities and interpersonal relationships which developed in these clubs. Similarly, there were also various channels for the free exchange of ideas and communications among the membership, e.g., the opposition's easy access to the union newspapers, as well as the social clubs and other off-hour contacts. The leadership positions were tempered somewhat by virtue of salaries not high enough to prevent men from returning to the jobs they held prior to elections.

Lipset's analysis is a very important contribution for a number of reasons. First of all, he expands Michels' hypotheses and then proceeds to operationalize them for a more comprehensive theory. Historical and economic variables are skillfully interwoven with a sophisticated sociological analysis.

Secondly, Lipset suggests alternatives to oligarchy *within* the very framework that Michels originally proposed. In short, Lipset extends Michels to the limiting case where it is no longer an "Iron Law," and arises only under specified conditions. Thus, we are provided with a dynamic model of change whereby some conditions (the increasing demand for bureaucracy and the external pressures for hierarchical control), lead toward oligarchy, while other pressures (independent subgroups and legitimation of opposition) contribute greater democracy.

One limitation of Lipset's analysis, however, is the either/or model: democracy or oligarchy. It would appear to us that the very process of movement toward oligarchy is the result of attempts to solve specific problems (as Michels and Lipset so clearly state). But the emergence of an oligarchy will create new problems which an organization must solve if it is to remain viable and adapted to the environment in which it operates. New solutions are then sought which in turn will modify the oligarchical structure. The process of adaptation, then, is a never-ending one as the organization continually adjusts both its internal and external relationships.

In the remainder of this chapter we examine such a "dialectic" model, and then indicate how it is applicable to one type of organization, the American trade union. The primary focus of the last part of the chapter is on processes of change, and much of the material is drawn from social-historical data. However, we believe that the variables selected are easily quantifiable and the model may be tested for its general applicability. Use of the model also allows us to extend many of our present analyses and explore relationships an organization has with its environment, i.e., other organizations. In this manner we might begin to treat organizations as units of analysis which have properties different from the mere sum of individual components.

The Environment

In this section we specify some aspects of the total environment in which the union operates. We shall consider facets of the industry, technology, government, other unions, and the general public, and indicate their relevance to the analysis of union structure.

Industry[2]

To a very great extent, modern industry is dependent upon cooperative relations with labor unions. Because of its large-scale operations, industry aims to stabilize labor as well as continuity of production. Recognition of unions and willingness to negotiate is the price industry pays for workers who comply with overall management directives. In some respects, then, labor unions determine labor costs and "police" workers.

The gross structure of the union itself is shaped by the industry in which it operates. When the industry is widely dispersed, unions generally try to stabilize work rules as well as wages. Generally, we find such union constitutions are longer and include apprenticeship regulations, work rules, and other general standards against which locals are to measure their individual contracts (22, pp. 102–121). Unions in the more centralized industries, on the other hand, tend to have shorter constitutions and their collective bargaining agreements specify the working arrangements with management. This latter type of union obviously requires more complex contracts, and hence, we find the greater use of specialists and staff devoted to this purpose. Concentration of industry contributes to the bureaucratization of unions.

Dispersion of industry also affects the union's ability to organize the workers. Generally, the more dispersed the industry, the more difficult it is to organize. More stress is placed on the union communication and control structure as the union tries to coordinate its activities. The more dispersed the industry, the more likely it is that workers will live in small towns and work in small shops. Here community or work norms may mitigate against favorable union attitudes. Generally, unions formed in widely dispersed industries will have to offer more inducements to workers and will tend to become more multi-purpose organizations encompassing a wider variety of life activities for the membership.

Some industries are highly mobile, and this too affects the communication and control structure of the unions. For example, the sundry railroad, maritime, and teamsters unions are all affected by the fact that members are frequently away from their bases of operation. Some unions have tried to compensate for this by holding more than one meeting to discuss the same issues and then having representatives from each group arrive at a solution for the entire local.

The proximity of residence to work also affects the union. Those unions which operate where workers live nearby tend to have higher rates of participation at meetings (37, p. 240). Kerr and Siegel hypothesize that strike activity and overall union support are related to more homogeneous and isolated communities where work and residence are closely connected (20, pp. 191–195). In the maritime industry, where workers live part of the time on the job-site, living conditions become an important aspect of bargaining.

[2] This section draws heavily on the work of Dunlop (12).

The market position of the industry will affect the strategies a union employs in its adaptation. Unions in ascending industries tend to grow in strength as more workers are required for the tasks. But new workers may attract rival unions to organize also and this may lead to debilitating jurisdictional strikes. An industry in a declining market may try to diversify its product and this will also lead toward the admission of new workers. If a new technology is required, then workers traditionally employed may be displaced by others. Both diversification of products and changes in technology affect the union structure and its relationships with other unions. And also, we should mention the possibility of industrial migration to locations where resources, wages, and market might be more favorable. Should the company move without its workers, unions will be faced with the problem of finding jobs for those remaining, as well as attempting to organize the new workers employed. Generally, the latter is difficult to do, as industry has tended to move into areas relatively hostile to unions and where total union organization is very low. As Daniel Bell has noted, "many of these plants — and the town's welfare consequently — live on their ability to cut union wage corners. The political atmosphere in these towns makes organizing more troublesome" (3, p. 92).

Finally, we might mention the variability of the work force required in the industry as a determinant of union structure. For example, many unions strive for union shop agreements and prefer to maintain restrictions on admissions to the union. When employment is low, union members have the greatest opportunity to work; when employment is high, temporary permits can be issued to accommodate others. Perhaps an extreme case of this is the New York newspaper deliverers who issue temporary permits for the Sunday edition deliveries. However, if another union tries to unionize these temporary workers, who are denied admission but are still required to pay certain fees, membership rolls may have to be opened. This was the case with the Brewers who found the Teamsters encroaching upon their jurisdiction through the temporary members. The problem is complicated because the temporary workers are often of an ethnic group different from the one presently in control. Seasonal fluctuations always heighten this problem.

Technology

Although the technology utilized by members of a union is closely related to the industry, there still remain great differences that account for variations in union structure. For example, the actual job content may affect the success or failure of union organization. Dunlop has suggested that certain operations are more strategically placed than others, and if men in these jobs do not support union organizing, plant operations might be able to continue and a strike would carry little threat (11, p. 179). Ability to bargain is severely hampered if these strategic operations are not brought to a halt. A related factor, but distinct from the strategic position, is the workers' skill level and the ease with which they may be replaced. Generally, the higher skilled workers are more crucial to plant operations and their support greatly enhances the union's bargaining power. Many industrial unions had to recognize the inherent differences among skilled workers and their importance to the union. Provisions are frequently made for them to conduct their own bargaining and have special representatives within the union.

The hours of plant operations also affect internal union structure. Some industries with high capital investment in technology may become profitable only when operations are continuous. The plant may have to work 24 hours a day. Supervision tends to be more relaxed at night, social contact among workers may be greater, and interest in union affairs may be increased. Workers on night shifts also find it difficult to fit into the normal daily routines of their families and the union may acquire new importance for them as a substitute (25, pp. 135–139). In both cases, special bargaining concessions may have to be obtained for workers who handle peak loads, as in metropolitan transportation or other shift work (12, p. 56).

The size of the work group is determined largely by the technology utilized. Generally speaking, the larger the work group, the easier it is to organize. Employers have less direct access to large groups of workers and directives are mediated through supervisors and foremen. Status barriers are emphasized more, and there is more opportunity for horizontal identification and cohesion to develop. Anti-union opinions and supports for non-union membership may be given less weight because the individual worker is surrounded by his peers and social contact between levels is minimized. When work groups are smaller, the representatives of management and the employers have greater access to the workers and can proffer inducements for remaining independent of union organization.

As we shall see later, the growth of automation is greatly affecting union growth and structure. Manual workers are less in demand and higher skills are required. Whether or not unions can adjust their symbolic inducements and language to get white-collar and skilled technicians to join is still problematic. To date, they have made few inroads among these workers.

Government and the Law

Volumes have been written about labor law, and in this section we shall but suggest a few of the more relevant issues which have affected union development and internal structure.[3]

[3] The interested reader is referred to Gregory (16). For one of the rare sociological ventures into this fascinating area see Lipset (24).

The courts affected union development early in the nineteenth century. While unions were not usually declared illegal, or conspiracies in restraint of trade, their practices were subject to condemnation and punishment. Striking for higher wages was not punished as much as action designed to obtain a closed shop. The rationale for opposing the latter was based on the notion that it was illegal to force a man to pay union dues if he did not wish to do so. If a union's interests were not directly affected, as in the case of sympathetic strikes or boycotts, the intent of the strike was declared illegal. Similarly, traditional areas of misconduct were often widened to punish the union, e.g., unions attempting to break the "yellow dog" contracts were declared guilty of violating constitutional guarantees of freedom of contract.[4]

In most of these cases during the nineteenth century, the federal courts were not involved. However, state courts were generally hostile to unions, especially in states where industrial development was retarded. Injunctions restraining unions were issued freely in the 1880's and non-compliance was punishable as contempt of a court order. Both the injunction and its punishment could be issued without specifying individuals and without a jury trial (42, p. 371).

The Sherman Anti-Trust Act was interpreted by the federal courts as being applicable to unions and their members. This marked the first time the federal government entered the realm of industrial disputes and its attitude was essentially anti-union. If the unions thought they would be better protected by the Clayton Act (1914), they soon found the courts whittled their rights away. The hostile legal environment was only slightly ameliorated during the First World War, when the National War Labor Board was established and unions' rights to organize and help determine production policies with representatives of management and the public were insured.

Unions took little active part in government and did not turn to Congress for assistance or new laws. This policy did not change greatly during the Depression, and as late as 1931, the AFL remained opposed to proposals for unemployment insurance and the legislation of minimum wages and maximum hours (42, p. 398). Generally speaking, the AFL unions tended to support policies rather than parties, and major figures in the labor movement could be found in either political camp. This also held true of state and municipal elections and other political activities. On the other hand, CIO unions have been much busier in political activities, and as early as 1936 had formed the Labor's Non-Partisan League, and in 1943 the Political Action Committee. With the passing

[4] The "yellow dog" contract was an agreement the worker had to sign as a prerequisite to employment. By so doing, he agreed not to join a labor union while he was employed by a particular firm. The types of injunctions referred to here were issued by either state or federal courts, depending upon circumstances. They required the union to forbear further actions which might interfere with business rights.

years, the AFL has become more involved in political matters, but there has not always been agreement between the two major federations: they have often supported opposing candidates. Individual national unions have tended to be more active politically on both the national and local scene, e.g., the United Auto Workers, the International Ladies Garment Workers Union, Mine Workers.

Many of labor's barriers were removed by the Norris-La Guardia Act (1932), e.g., the injunction and yellow dog contract, but it was not until the passage of the Wagner Act (1935) that unions were able to advance their cause before the courts. The Wagner Act specified unfair labor practices which employers were to avoid, e.g., interference with union organizing, refusal to bargain collectively, and so on. The National Labor Relations Board was established for the adjudication of unfair practices.

The Labor-Management Relations Act (Taft-Hartley) in 1947 modified the NLRA to the extent of specifying some of the restraints applying to labor unions: unions were constrained not to coerce employers, nor were they to punish workers who would not join the union; closed shops were outlawed; unions could not refuse to bargain collectively; nor could they charge excessively high initiation fees if they maintained a union shop. Unions were also required to file financial statements and have their officers sign non-Communist affidavits. In some ways, this was the first attempt by the federal government to affect the internal government of unions.

Finally, we might mention the Labor-Management Reporting and Disclosure Act of 1959, which was the first major attempt to regulate the internal policies of unions. Following closely upon the McClellan Committee hearings of union (and sometimes management) corruption and moral turpitude, this Act provided for regular election of officers, membership participation in elections, rights of dissension, and the access to union machinery for opposition candidates. Restraints were also placed upon union officers' rights to take locals into "trusteeship." Interestingly, the "Bill of Rights" granted to union members contained no provision for removing discrimination on racial lines, although this is one of the issues which has frequently come before the courts (43, p. 472).

Perhaps we may best summarize our discussion of labor and the law by indicating some of the effects upon internal union structures. We have already noted how the participation in government during the First World War (and later during the Second World War) gave rise to union recognition and tended to decrease management hostility. During these wars, membership increased and unions were able to operate with less interference. Treasuries swelled, benefit programs increased, and in most cases, loyalty of members also increased. It was undoubtedly due to these periods of relative calm that most craft unions were able to maintain their membership during the depression following the First

World War and even increase in size in the 'twenties, when most unions lost members. Similarly, the increases in membership and the size of the treasuries undoubtedly helped unions sustain long and bitter strikes following the Second World War.

Secondly, most legislation has been enacted and prompted by the events of the preceding years. The Miners strikes in 1943 prompted the Smith-Connally Act, the strikes of 1946 led toward enactment of the Taft-Hartley Act, the investigations of the McClellan committee led directly to the Landrum-Griffin Act in 1959. Generally, we might say that Congress has not maintained a consistent attitude toward unions and is prompted to move when faced with specific issues and crises. (The depression obviously led to the passage of the favorable legislation during the 'thirties.) If there is any trend at all, it is probably in the direction of greater involvement with unions and their internal operations. The reader might wonder what effect legislation has upon a union's internal bureaucracy when, as Lipset has commented, most labor leaders do not require illegal means to maintain themselves in office. Certainly the notion that leaders did not represent the wishes of the membership has not been substantiated.[5] But Lipset does conclude, ". . . though legislation and juridically protected guarantees may seem relatively ineffective in enhancing the prospects for real union democracy, their importance should not be underestimated. The significance of a law does not necessarily lie in the extent to which it is obeyed: one of its major functions is to set a moral code or standard which society considers proper, but whose parts can be violated within certain limits" (24, p. 35).

Other Unions

Relationships with other unions also affect the internal structure of any given union. The two basic processes of competition and cooperation are clearly demonstrated here because unions have traditionally supported each other in some endeavors while competing for membership and the right to represent certain workers.

Jurisdictional disputes are the most common problems unions have with one another. Almost all constitutions specify which workers shall be included under the union's jurisdiction. However, even in the earliest days of union development, as well as in those industries where technology had developed the least, jurisdictional boundaries were frequently blurred and unions would contend for the workers and the job rights. In the first decade of the twentieth century, the AFL tried to set up a system for adjudicating disputes, but little progress was made: larger unions tended to win the disputes and the AFL was reduced to a position of

---

[5] For example, the Smith-Connally Act required that membership have a closed vote before the leader could call a strike. Invariably the rank and file supported their leaders, and their position at the bargaining table was enhanced (33, p. 190).

reconciling the smaller ones to "reality" (19, p. 5). Obviously, the emergence of industrial unions contributed to the problem as they organized all workers within the industry irrespective of skill level. Many of the power fights within the old AFL were directly related to the growing concern of the crafts over the invasion into their jurisdiction by industrial unions (42, p. 408).

Changes in materials and technology made existing boundaries obsolete and also created new ones. The creation of the NLRB placed the government in the role of deciding which unit should be the appropriate voting group, and in cases of jurisdiction, as well as representation, this determined to a very great extent which union would ultimately represent the workers. To some extent, we might say that Congress deprived unions of some of their power to determine their own structure. The emergence of the CIO, as well as the resurgence of the AFL organizing drives, created a power vacuum into which the NLRB moved in order that the public interest not be violated by long and frequently violent strikes (19, p. 5).

By the late 'forties, the costs and disadvantages of competition became readily apparent, as the rate of union growth tapered off, the public became impatient with strikes, and the Taft-Hartley Act was passed. Unions signed agreements that would curtail competition and allow resources to be used in other ways. Basically, these agreements dealt with not raiding other unions for members, joint organizing campaigns, machinery for adjudicating disputes, and agreements to negotiate jointly with management (13, pp. 103–108). It should not be concluded that all unions are mutually hostile and competitive. The very existence of the major federations and their merger in 1955 indicates the degree of cooperation and basic agreement which underlies the individual unions. On the local level, small independent locals frequently cooperate in strikes and boycotts, respect each others' picket lines, and form local trade councils. The very power of the Teamsters within the labor movement is predicated on their unwillingness to cross picket lines nor handle goods which might assist a company to continue operations while it is being struck by another union. Rival unions also cooperate during elections to secure officials who will be more favorable to labor interests.

The Public

The final variable we shall consider in a union's environment is undoubtedly the most amorphous and difficult to conceptualize. The public consists of those people and social units not ordinarily affected by labor-management disputes, but whose pressure is felt by the legislatures as well as by employers and union. For example, the public's refusal to cross a picket line helps a union obtain concessions from management when profits fall. Unwillingness to purchase goods without a union label and refusal to patronize non-union shops or contract with non-union workers can force employers to reconsider their hostility to union organization.

The social prestige of the workers is also another factor contributing to union organization. If the labor force is composed primarily of immigrants, then those who wish to organize may be considered somewhat foreign and possessing of alien ideas. Most union members work in occupations which fall in the lower part of the prestige hierarchy and thus, at least in America (with its emphasis on upward social mobility), it is hard to enlist support for their cause except under unusual circumstances, e.g., the Depression.[6]

We might contrast this situation of union members with that of management. The general picture is much more favorable, because management supplies goods and services to the general public and has higher prestige. Newspapers and other mass media consistently report their operations and contributions to community and national welfare. Unions, on the other hand, seldom receive publicity except during strikes, violence, or when under investigation. They are depicted primarily as "taking" something or making demands. (Unions always *demand* in the press, while management always *offers*.) Unions are seen as disrupting an ongoing, constructive process. It is never stated too clearly how the union organization operates for its members. The worker is frequently seen as an appendage to the large bureaucracy which operates not only against the members but also against the public for the perpetuation, profit, and power of frequently corrupted leaders. (The fact that most newspapers and other mass media are dependent upon advertising for revenue and are themselves business concerns undoubtedly contributes to their furthering this point of view.)

One other element contributing to the pressure the public exerts lies in the effect of the strike. Generally, the more inconvenienced the public is, the less support there is for the strikers. With the increasing interdependence of industry and other segments of the economy, it is virtually impossible for a strike in one industry not to affect a wide range of people. A steel strike may force railroads to lay off workers and auto plants to shut down. Strikes by machinists in airplane factories or electricians at missile bases are depicted as endangering the national welfare.

Because little is known about the operations of unions, and because of their low prestige, immoral acts discovered receive heightened importance and generality. Corruption found in unions tends to bring clamors for tighter control. Implications for the larger society and its relationships with business are seldom examined. There is national shock (but only

[6] In the study of occupational prestige based on a national sample by the National Opinion Research Center, it was reported that of those occupations traditionally considered as possessing union members, only three ranked in the top half of the scale: railroad engineer, electrician, and trained machinist.

back-page reporting) for scandal on the stock market; for corruption in unions there is public outrage and demand for additional legislation.[7]

The Union as a System

In this section we examine four general parts of a union's internal system: size, membership composition, locals, and communication channels.

Size

Size of an organization is always crucial in determining its operations and functions within the total external environment. Larger organizations tend to have more specialization, more problems with communication and coordination, more potential for the existence of subgroup formation, more potential for the differentiation of its population. The importance of unions' size is of additional significance because it is related to ability to operate within the industrial complex and obtain goals vis-à-vis management and other unions.

The more workers a union can pull off the job, the greater its bargaining power will be. If the union can immobilize the entire industry, then those companies most severely affected will place demands and pressures upon the stronger companies to yield to union demands. Larger unions may develop richer treasuries and survive more management pressure than smaller unions. Experts can be hired to assist in negotiating contracts and in the administration of union affairs. Expensive organizing drives require large resources of men and money; both are more available in larger unions. More pressure can be exerted upon government for favorable legislation when contributions of campaign funds or actual electioneering are available. Larger treasuries help build hospitals and medical facilities, or welfare and retirement plans, which help induce the unorganized to join unions, and reinforce membership loyalty.

Larger unions are also in a better position to win jurisdictional battles with other unions. Besides having more resources available, larger unions are capable of disrupting more operations within industry and exerting pressure upon management to negotiate with them rather than with smaller unions. Similarly, in most cases, larger unions can exert greater pressure upon "impartial" boards to award them jurisdictional privileges. For example, a threat to withdraw from the major federation by a large union poses a much greater problem than a small union's threat. The federation is more dependent for its own existence upon the larger union's support. Even government agencies seeking compliance for in-

---

[7] For a balanced report of corruption in labor unions and its implications for the political and economic system, see Bell (4). It might be interesting for the reader to compare this account of waterfront unionism with the more lurid movie, *On The Waterfront*, which covered similar material and certainly received wider distribution throughout the nation.

dustrial peace are more dependent upon larger unions whose potential disruptive influence is greater, and this is surely taken into consideration in the process of arbitration.

Large size creates internal problems of coordination and control. More workers and locals have to be contacted and considered when a strike is called, when a contract is negotiated, when changes in the constitution occur. To a very large extent, these problems are handled through the structure of the organization. The very problems created by large size, then, give rise to changes in the internal system of the union. More specialists are required to handle these problems and a larger bureaucratic staff tends to emerge (23, pp. 83–84).

Composition of the Membership

The problem of size is complicated somewhat by the type of people who are incorporated into the organization. In one sense, the labor movement was never totally disorganized; small groups of workers who had frequent contact and operated similar technology have always existed. Most older labor unions can be traced back to such small groups, their coalitions and cooperation. One problem confronting all these original small groups was how far to extend the boundaries of their organization, i.e., who else should be admitted? Some early unions adhered strictly to single craft lines within each shop, but joined with other crafts in city centrals. The emergence of the national union was usually along strict craft lines.

The more heterogeneous the composition of the workers within the union, the more complicated are the problems of communication and control. Various subgroups face different problems, and deriving one basic policy for all is frequently quite difficult. The workers differ in loyalties, needs, and goals. Variations occur by regions, skills, ethnic affiliation, and ideology. In the early years of union organization, one outstanding problem was the composition of the labor force which was highly heterogeneous and afforded a quick and easy supply of cheap labor and strikebreakers. Ethnic divisions within the total community could be exploited by employers as different groups were played off against each other. Then, too, when language barriers existed, communication among the subgroups was hampered and impaired. While it certainly was not the crucial determinant in losing the strike in 1919, the fact that the steelworkers' literature had to be written in seven different languages did not facilitate communication and coordination (7, p. 19). Even today such unions as the ILGWU print their journals in more than one language.

In order to reduce many of these internal divisions, many union constitutions have provided for the exclusion of certain types of workers. For example, some unions were restricted to white males, others contained provisions demanding that members be American citizens or at least have taken out first papers. Some unions provided for age limitations in order to restrict child labor; older workers were sometimes restricted because they would not contribute to benefit programs long enough before beginning to draw upon them. Union constitutions have also barred persons with certain political affiliations, women, or foremen. In almost every case, the reasons for exclusions were the same: the desire to have priorities on the job, the wish to protect the union from internal dissension, and the reflection of worker attitudes in the provisions (38, pp. 84–87).

Another method of restricting membership was to limit admission to only certain workers within a given craft. Jurisdiction for the union was drawn around the type of work performed. Most of these unions were for the highly skilled and the work required a period of training prior to admission. Some unions also required that a competency test be passed before admission. Many unions allowed the local to determine the apprenticeship policies and other qualifications for admissions. In this case, greater local control allowed discrimination against certain groups, even though the total union might not formally do so, and, sometimes, was actually against restrictions. We shall return to this aspect of admission restrictions below.

One reason for the emergence of strong union government was the geographic mobility of the labor force (41, pp. 49–152). A traveling member had to be admitted to the new local and a job provided for him. This would cause little trouble if there was enough work to distribute. However, if conditions were bad, newcomers would provide an oversupply of labor and might be willing to work for lower wages. Even when employment was high, employers frequently advertised for more workers from other cities in order to compromise the power of strong locals. It soon became apparent that if locals were not to suffer from national affiliation, they would have to arrange for central coordination of employment opportunities and some control over the placement of workers.

Another problem related to geographical mobility was the disciplining of workers. Members who violated local laws might relocate and hope to escape discipline. The new local, without sufficient knowledge of the misdemeanor, might accept the worker. Requests to punish the member through fines or expulsion were usually not respected nor reciprocated. Responsibility for the trial and possible punishment of the culprit was never explicit. Clearly some uniform law was required.

Quality of apprenticeship standards had to be standardized also. If workers wished to be admitted and nearby locals had lower standards or shorter periods of apprenticeship, they could move temporarily, serve the shorter time, and then return with full rights as a member. The entire problem of the traveling member was heightened by the expansion of industry, as well as the great improvements in transportation and communication in the latter part of the nineteenth century.

Locals

Generally speaking, the size and number of locals will affect the total operations of the union. Union size is highly related to the number of locals; larger unions have more locals. It is possible to conceive of locals in a similar fashion to nationals, i.e., as subunits of the larger system. Generally speaking, the locals tend to be more homogeneous than the union as a whole. Regional differences are eliminated, ethnic differences are mitigated, admission requirements are standardized. But if each local is more homogeneous internally, loyalty to the local may be much greater than to the national as a whole. Should the national advance a policy which does not conform entirely to a local's needs or preferences, membership loyalty will be somewhat divided, although probably more directed to immediate colleagues. The very number of locals, then, presents a problem to the communication and control structure in that relatively small, homogeneous groups may be operating at cross-purposes and have interests different from the national union.

This general point is illustrated by another aspect of coordination of locals. If national unions cannot control their locals, frequent wildcat strikes may occur. If the local is not supported, a rival national may appear more attractive and the local may secede. If the national supports the local, it may encourage other wildcat strikes and the national treasury will suffer. In short, the need to coordinate local decisions tends to give rise to a strong central government. One reason frequently given for the rapid decline of the Knights of Labor, the strongest union in the country in its time, was its inability to control strikes (5, p. 535).

Management may decide that recognition of unions is not effective if the grievance procedures are not utilized or if locals do not abide by collective agreements. Thus, there is some pressure from management for the national union to exercise control over the locals.

Not only is the number of locals a problem, but their size is also important (25, pp. 366–381). Larger locals tend to be more independent of the national than smaller locals. Small locals have neither sufficient funds nor manpower to draw upon for funds for their operations. They are more vulnerable to raiding from other unions and pressures from management. On the other hand, larger locals have treasuries which allow them to finance their own strikes, hire experts to assist in negotiating contracts, support their own benefit programs, publish their own newspapers, and so on. Some unions have a very high proportion of members concentrated in a few locals: Local 3 of the Brotherhood of Electrical Workers has about 5 per cent of the total membership and Local 6 has about 10 per cent of the Typographers' members. Should these locals refuse to comply with a strike directive, the strike may be totally ineffective. Similarly, refusal to return to work might vitiate a contract. These locals are sufficiently large that should they leave the national union, its entire bargaining power would be greatly affected. No small local can possess such power in the national union. Aware of their power, larger locals tend to exert greater influence on the national at conventions and with policy-making bodies. Faunce has shown that larger locals of the UAW tend to provide more diversity of opinion at conventions, and Seidman has discussed the competition among large locals for dominance within the national (14, pp. 291–299; 34, p. 33).

It should not be assumed, however, that larger locals are completely dominant in a union. There are many limitations placed upon them by industry as well as within the union. For example, most workers in a union belong to smaller locals and at conventions they may over-ride the larger ones. An indication of this is seen in those union constitutions which specify that amendments and referendums have to be initiated by locals in a number of states. Thus, the larger locals may not modify the existing structure at will. In fact, Faunce's study would indicate that, in the UAW, a coalition of small locals exerts more control than the larger locals. If this were not so, they would not be the ones providing the dissenting voices at conventions.

Communications

We have already noted some problems of communications and coordination within unions and they need not be repeated here. However, we might indicate some of the techniques unions use, as modifications in the communication system have great influence on the total organization structure. We shall deal with but two mechanisms of communication in unions: conventions and publications.

The convention may be considered one of the major mechanisms of communication from the rank and file to the higher levels. It is at such meetings that delegates vote on officers, amend the constitution, formulate new policies, and frequently act as a court of appeals for disciplinary problems. It should be obvious that control over the conventions may become essential if officials wish to maintain themselves in office or have their policies carried out by the membership. As Bromwich has shown, control over the convention committees is frequently tantamount to control over the union (9, p. 12).

The frequency of conventions is crucial for the operations of union government. If conventions are held infrequently, officials have a relatively greater control over policy formation because this check is not employed. However, infrequent conventions also prevent top officials from receiving information they require for their duties. Estimation of subgroups' support and attitudes toward certain policies becomes more difficult to ascertain. Changes in coalition formations may not be observed and the entire organization may become vulnerable to a rival faction whose dissatisfaction and power has increased sufficiently to secede. Similarly, changing problems that locals face will not come as readily to the attention of the leaders, whose ability to make appropriate decisions for the welfare of the entire membership will be impaired.

There are limitations on holding frequent conventions. They cost time and money. In order to curtail expenses, unions have tried various forms of representation. Many unions now have some form of proportional representation, e.g., one delegate for the first 200 members, another for each additional 500. Many constitutions allow payment of part of the delegate's expenses, which helps smaller locals whose treasuries are often so small they cannot afford to send representatives. There are also problems of finding appropriate times when all delegates are able to attend.

The union newspaper may be considered communication from the top down. It has many functions. If the union is large, the newspaper will communicate to workers the actions of the leadership and what part in them the rank and file have to play. Contracts and negotiations may be explained. The newspaper also may build loyalty to the national union when the benefits of union membership are explained. In addition, news coverage of "trusteeships" that the national undertakes to displace corrupt or incompetent local leaders also has the function of serving as a warning that too great a deviation from national policies may result in the displacement of local officials. Generally speaking, the size of the union is directly related to the frequency of its publications; in 1955, those unions which placed fewer restrictions on their admissions requirements tended to publish more frequently (26, chapter 5). To put the matter another way, if the union can create a relative homogeneity of workers prior to admissions, it will not require as frequent publications; if all workers are admitted to the union, then publications serve the same purpose as other more formal socialization mechanisms.

If larger locals tend to conform less to national policies, then the union publication may also serve another function. Locals tend to be more homogeneous than the national, and we may hypothesize that union newspapers will provide an alternative viewpoint to members within the larger locals. In short, the union newspaper may be one source of democracy within the larger locals because it provides a policy position different from that of the local. We might expect, then, that within larger locals there exist factions which tend to support the incumbent national administration as well as oppose it. The reason the opposition to the national usually wins is that reading the union newspaper is not as effective as personal social contact with local officials. The point is merely that the paper may provide information and an alternative explanation for policy which may be considered in the privacy of the worker's home.

The Impact of Environmental Change: Centralization

In this section, we should like to focus upon two major changes that have occurred in labor unions and indicate how they might be analyzed in terms of the variables previously discussed. The first change, centralization, was brought about primarily by changes in the environment. Internal control has also undergone change as a result of the unions' operations and interaction with the environment.

There has been an increased use of bureaucratic machinery for the solution of union problems. Lipset has suggested a number of reasons for this (23, pp. 83–86). The increase in size has created demands for greater efficiency in administrative matters. There are more workers whose dues and papers must be processed. Then, too, unions now undertake more programs (welfare and other benefits), which require staffs. Sometimes these involve merely the administration of money, but not infrequently, they also involve education and retraining programs for workers to learn new skills. In a world of changing technology, workers must develop the appropriate skills if they are to remain employed.

The concentration of many industries has led to the increasing centralization of some unions. If the union negotiates wage-setting agreements with but one or two companies in order to stabilize wages and grievance procedures throughout the industry, the union must be in a position to command the resources of its members. If the locals fail to comply, these contracts have little value. The interdependence of the total economy has also elicited more government arbitration. This has made it more difficult to negotiate on the local level and contracts are signed which set standards for the entire industry.

Negotiating for many firms in many parts of the country has led to more complex contracts. In one sense this has increased the use of staff men because specialists are required to understand the various aspects of the agreements. Thus, not only are lawyers required but time and motion men, economists, and so on. While this has led to the increased use of staff personnel, it has also given them more power within the union because top officials have come to rely upon their judgment and advice. Contracts made at higher levels, however, depreciate and deprive the lower levels of power within the union. Local officials have less expertise and smaller funds for hiring experts for negotiations; thus they become more dependent upon the national's administrative machinery.

Contracts have become more complicated for a number of reasons other than the wide variety of workers they cover. For example, contracts have become somewhat longer and cover greater periods of time than formerly (30, p. 30). There are a number of reasons for this. For example, longer contracts allow management to predict wage costs for longer periods of time. These costs become somewhat stabilized and management has more time to vary other aspects of production and technology in order to increase profits. With longer periods between wage negotiations, there is less likelihood of strikes, and both management and unions have to spend less of their resources in negotiations. For the union, this has the odd and dubious advantage of decreasing the amount of unfavorable publicity it would ordinarily receive at the hands of the mass media. But longer contracts require an administrative staff to help settle grievances and generally assist with the daily operations of running the union.

If negotiations do not occur as frequently, the probability of strikes will also decrease. Grievance patterns become established and the contracts require that they be observed until the next negotiation sessions. Many major issues are incorporated into a flexible contract. For example, wage negotiations, being tied to the cost of living index, may automatically raise and lower wages as the index fluctuates. Thus it is unlikely that many wage earners will find prices outstripping their incomes and be willing to strike before the contract expires.

While the number of wildcat strikes still remains high, they are growing less intense and unions as well as management have come to accept them as punishable. The unions find wildcat strikes embarrassing because they indicate the workers are not willing to accept the grievance procedures set up by negotiation. The impotence of the national union is visibly demonstrated. Management also has taken a stronger course of action against wildcat strikes because of the fear that precedents may be set if negotiations are undertaken or concessions are made (30, pp. 41–42). The overall effect of decreasing wildcat strikes is to decrease membership interest, as well as suppress dissidents within the union. Much of the glamor of action and personal involvement is lost when experts and leaders negotiate through grievance machinery.

Automation is also affecting the union's power to strike. Some unions have been forced to adapt themselves to less powerful positions because of the realization that they cannot affect productivity with strikes (32, pp. 63–64). In highly automated plants a few supervisors are able to keep production high even if workers have left the plant. Both the Communications Workers and the Oil Workers have found it difficult to make inroads in some areas because of the high level of automation and the new technology available. Automation also increases centralization because displacement and relocation become a problem which goes beyond the local. Resources necessary for retraining and other job placement are far beyond the average local's ability. Thus, automation calls for increased reliance upon the national offices.

The creation of the National Labor Relations Board has also decreased the use of strikes for the establishment of jurisdictional issues. We have already noted that unions found the cost of competition excessive and therefore turned to negotiations among the competing parties. Nationals merged, established joint organizing campaigns, and signed no-raiding pacts. Locals generally complied with the agreements. But the NLRB actually entered into inter-union relationships much earlier because it had to designate the size and structure of the collective bargaining unit. In short, many union elections held to determine which bargaining unit should represent a given group of workers were affected by the NLRB. Size of the bargaining unit, choice of workers to be included, and timing of the elections were all part of the NLRB's function. Such determinations by the Board greatly influenced the strict craft unions to become less restrictive and to admit more workers. Industrial unions almost always included the skilled workers and were capable of winning more elections. Although problems still arose if one union represented just a few of the highly skilled workers in the company, and another represented the remainder, the frequency of these conflicts was decreased.

The increasing legal control of unions' internal operations also contributed to greater centralization. The Landrum-Griffin Act of 1959 required that unions keep better records and file more accurate reports than they had in the past. Similarly, the unions were asked to issue statements to their memberships about financial matters as well as other happenings within the union. This Act also required that opposition within the union be allowed greater access to union newspapers and the membership rolls for election. The regular election of officials also demands that machinery be present for union government.

Increasing centralization tends to place greater strains upon the communication system. For example, more information is now required at the top, yet there is less information moving through traditional channels. There has been a tendency to decrease the frequency of conventions because of their expense. Information and knowledge which the top echelons may require for their operations are decreased further because of the many levels through which information must flow. The more levels in the hierarchy, the greater is the danger of distortion. This increases the chance that top echelons may undertake unpopular programs and miscalculate the amount of support they have.

Unions tend to use the centralized bureaucratic machinery for growth. For example, one noticeable change has been in the very manner of creating the union. Most early unions were formed from the bottom up, i.e., a number of locals joined together to improve their bargaining position. But later unions tended to form from the top down: organizing committees, frequently established by other unions, would move into an area, set up an organization, and try to enlist workers as members. When a union is organized in this way the bureaucratic machinery is established and the local officials become indebted to, and dependent upon, the national for their positions. Originally, the national helped organize the local, placed loyal officers in power, and supported its existence. The local officials usually realize that, should they wish to advance a career within the union hierarchy, they must be willing to support the incumbents.

Basically, there are two ways to admit new members: (1) incorporate them into existing locals; or, (2) form new locals and bring the members in. A union's choice of method may alter its structure. As suggested above, when a union creates new locals, and then admits workers, it has control over the local government prior to admitting new members. Many problems of coordination and communication are thus solved. The existence of many small locals usually means that none can attain too much power or influence and the dominant coalition can play one off against the other, co-opt the most threatening, and punish disrupters without fear of weakening the total union. As there are more small locals within the union, it becomes difficult to form coalitions against the incumbents. Dissidents have neither the finances nor access to communication facilities to coordinate their dissatisfactions into unified protest and action.

To sum up this part of our discussion then, we note that unions have moved from decentralized units to more centralized national control. Changes in the environment consisting largely of industry, technology, and legal system have affected strike procedures as well as contract negotiations. Problems which emerge can no longer be solved by the locals; they require the resources of the national administration. The locus of control, then, has shifted. But in the process, as we shall try to indicate below, there has arisen greater control over the internal as well as external environment.

The Impact of Centralization: Changes in Control

Changes in the locus of control tend to conform to the Michels-Lipset hypotheses of oligarchy: control tends to move from rank and file to leaders. However, as we shall try to indicate, in the process of centralizing control, the rank and file have also gained more control within the union as well as in their relationships with management.

Oligarchy has been described as a small group of men controlling an organization troubled with apathy and low participation among its members. It appears to us that such a conceptualization is essentially self-contradictory because apathetic workers are not being controlled: they may be in the organization, but are not part of it. Perhaps the analogy of the child misbehaving when the parent is not present would best fit this type of organization. It would appear to us, then, that another dimension of control must also be considered: the *amount* of control that is exercised as well as its distribution. In short, it is possible for the distribution to remain relatively constant but the total amount may vary.

There is really no evidence to indicate that management has lost any control over its functions because of the development and recognition of strong unions and the establishment of collective bargaining agreements with them. In fact, it would appear to us that management has actually increased its total amount of control. If wildcat strikes have decreased somewhat because unions have eliminated much of the un-savory aspects of work and improved general working conditions, if seniority privileges have given workers greater job security, and if the turnover rates have somewhat decreased (31, pp. 903–920), then it would appear that management is better able to realize one of its major goals: the predictability of labor costs and the stabilization of productiv-ity. The decrease of time and money required to train new workers may help offset the increases in wages and fringe benefits the unions have ob-tained.[8]

Automation is obviously affecting the amount of control both manage-ment and unions can exercise. Traditionally, unions have not been against the introduction of new machinery, but they have wished to con-trol its use. Recent agreements among the meat-packers and the West Coast shippers, with their respective unions, indicate that steps are being taken to establish procedures for the introduction of new machin-ery as well as for the retraining and relocation of displaced workers.

Lipset has indicated a number of reasons why the top union officials have been able to retain their offices, e.g., they control communication and avenues of mobility within the union. We might note in passing that influence of large locals has decreased along other lines. For ex-ample, if the larger locals provide most of the opposition at national con-ventions, then the pressures which are operative to decrease the fre-quency of conventions tend to operate against the larger locals; they have less opportunity to exert pressure upon top officials. Some unions have tried to change the representation of membership in hopes of creating a more manageable and less expensive convention. However, we might note that all such attempts will tend to operate against the larger locals. If the number of delegates tends to decrease arithmetically, the number of contacts they may make to influence others for support will decrease at a higher rate.[9] If there were just fewer delegates from the larger locals, then the smaller locals would be able to outvote them. And finally, with fewer members in their delegations, the representatives of larger locals would have less social support when defending their positions against a majority, and thus would be more susceptible to pressure from the larger group (1, pp. 476–483).

If the frequency of conventions tends to decrease with increasing size, then it would appear that rank and file members would have less control over their leaders: small locals are dependent upon the national and cannot oppose it, while larger locals have their power decreased by changing convention frequency. However, this is not necessarily the case. There are other alternatives available for membership expression,

---

[8] There is still considerable controversy over whether or not unions have actually been able to win wage increases for their members above what might have ordinarily occurred. The complexity of these arguments is given excellent treatment in Rees (30).

[9] Formulas for the varying rates of contacts available to different sized groups may be found in Caplow (10).

and these have derived from the changing nature of the union's composition and admission requirements.

Boulding has indicated that an organization tends to use up the favorable parts of its environment first (8, p. 22). In terms of union size, this would mean that workers disposed toward a union join first, while the remaining are more difficult to organize. At some point, a union may decide that the gain of additional workers is not worth the price of inducing them to join. To this extent then, if the unions wished to increase beyond their "natural" limits they would have to tap workers easier to organize but not previously considered eligible.

Secondly, if the unions did change their strategies and admit workers heretofore excluded, there would be internal repercussions as the existing distributions of dominance were disturbed. New members might form coalitions with some of the locals possessing little influence and then rise to a position of dominance. Or the number of new members themselves might grow sufficiently large to replace completely all other groups within the union. As we indicated earlier, one method for partially handling this problem would be to create new locals rather than admit workers to existing locals.

We have already indicated some of the admission policies for labor unions and the fact that restrictions were made to exclude various subgroups within the population. With the emergence of the CIO, however, it soon became obvious to the older craft unions that many of these restrictions were no longer functional and were even operating against them. For example, the advances in technology tended to blur many of the lines between craft and industrial unionism. Then too, the CIO was making rapid advances in growth and was emerging as the dominant force in labor relations. Since it organized both skilled as well as the unskilled, workers ordinarily eligible for the crafts might have become more favorably disposed to CIO unions. Perhaps reluctantly, the older craft unions began to remove many of the restrictions contained in their constitutions. The Second World War and the subsequent labor shortages brought more workers from the rural areas into cities and union-controlled occupations. With immigration severely curtailed after the 'twenties, new workers joining unions tended to be more homogeneous in background and many of the problems of language and other ethnic affiliations were decreased. With the passage of the Wagner Act, unions became stronger and could sustain some of the internal divisions. As unions obtained from the government a maintenance of membership guarantee which could be superimposed on contracts, membership rolls further increased. In short, the strength of the unions, the competition from other unions, and the war that curtailed management opposition enabled even the older, more restrictive craft unions to become more favorably disposed toward new workers.

One method of handling some of the internal divisions that arose was to let the locals decide which workers were to be ineligible for membership. Thus, although the national might be willing and able to admit new workers, locals could still refuse certain groups if they so desired. Even those unions such as the UAW, which contained clauses for the admission of all workers irrespective of race or religion, found it difficult to impose these provisions on some of their locals. Some of the older craft unions set up subsidiary locals for groups such as Negroes which were under the control of the nearby white local.

The magnitude of these changes toward opening union membership to previously excluded groups can be seen from the following example: in 1936, of the 148 unions listed by the Bureau of Labor Statistics, 27 contained some provisions barring certain racial groups (44, pp. 40–48). In a similar study in 1955, Bambrick and Haas report that of 194 unions, only five constitutions held some clause barring a racial group (2, p. 63).

Admitting these different groups of workers brought about changes in trade-union structure. These workers had to be provided with inducements beyond the wage and fringe benefits that might be obtained by belonging to other unions. Protection of their minority rights had to be assured also. In other words, these strong subgroups required some concessions from the union officials for their participation and support of union activities. We find a clue to such arrangements when we realize that many large unions had been willing to allow subgroups to form and negotiate their own contracts. Some industrial unions (e.g., the UAW) have allowed apprenticeship programs for some of their skilled workers. On the other hand, such unions as the Machinists, the Book-binders, and the Upholsterers, which were formerly pure craft unions, came to admit non-skilled and semi-skilled workers without their entering and participating in an apprenticeship program.

The structure of the executive board in unions is the clearest example of changes which have occurred. Originally created as a check upon the president and his power, the executive boards have grown in importance (41, pp. 286–301). They now assist the president in his duties, run the union between conventions, help negotiate contracts, and conduct strikes. Authorities are not quite sure whether or not executive boards composed solely of officers are more protective of rank and file rights than those boards with officers and membership representatives as well. In the early days of the CIO it was felt that membership representatives would be more democratic, but it has been pointed out that if the officers' salaries are stipulated, they may be more independent of the senior officers. Many membership representatives are also dependent upon the union president for their salaries and are incapable of exercising independent action.[10]

[10] There are very few empirical studies we know of union executive boards. The three that appear to deal most directly with this problem of structure are Bambrick and Haas (2), Seidman and Melcher (35), and Marcus (26).

Differences among subgroups within unions can be reconciled on the national executive boards. If the major subgroups, be they women, Canadians, those in geographic areas, or certain skilled trades, are provided representatives who are elected by the appropriate members and are responsible to them, major differences which arise in the negotiation of contracts or organizing may be taken into consideration. Some of the problems created by lack of frequent communication to the higher echelons will then be ameliorated and the interests of the subgroups will be protected.

Examining 77 constitutions of unions which existed from 1926 to 1955 shows that 46 have increased the size of their executive boards. In part, this is due to the greater amount of specialization and detailed knowledge required of larger organizations. The total amount of administrative work has also increased. But increasing the size of the executive boards also allows the union officers to maintain a favorable balance of power while allowing subgroup representatives to bring their electorates' interests to bear. Thus we find that unions which specify that executive boards shall contain representatives of subgroups have increased in number. This is apparent in the craft unions which existed from 1926 to 1955. Of the 25 unions changing the structure of their executive boards between 1926 and 1955, 15 which did not specify subgroup representation now do so.[11] While such data are far from conclusive, they do suggest that alternative mechanisms to free communication are available through formal channels.

Perhaps it is through the use of alternative mechanisms of communication that unions have actually increased their total control over the subunits. Admission of the subgroups had to be restricted when the labor force was very heterogeneous. But with the blurring of status lines, both ethnic and occupational, many of these differences could be reconciled. The larger unions, however, gave rise to greater problems of communication and, in order to compensate for these emergent problems, changes in the structure of the executive boards occurred. In this manner, many of the divergent factions were brought together and the union as a whole in the total society became more effective vis-à-vis management. The inroads of the law, industry, and technology made a more centralized union, but the opening up of admission requirements and their reconciliation allowed the union more total control over its members as well as over their environment. While the locus of control may have shifted from membership and the local, the total amount of control also increased.[12]

[11] Needless to add, most union constitutions did not change their provisions. Fifty-three unions did not specify subgroup representation in either 1926 nor in 1955; 16, however, did so.

[12] Tannenbaum and Kahn indicated that locus of control and total control are conceptually independent. See Tannenbaum and Kahn (39). In subsequent research, Tannenbaum demonstrated that these two variables are empirically independent.

Summary and Conclusions

The changes described here are most apparent in craft unions formed prior to 1930 and still in existence today. Being somewhat rigid in their adaptive strategies, they declined as influential forces in the American labor movement during the 'thirties and early 'forties. The emergence of the CIO, new technology, and new laws pressured them to change some parts of their internal structure which, in turn, affected their relations with their environment. It should be mentioned that not all of the older crafts were able to change, e.g., the Pattern Makers, the Horseshoers, the Fur and Leather Workers. Many of these unions have recently merged with larger unions, and, in effect, are no longer in existence except as separate bargaining units.

We should not over-emphasize the influence of the environment because there always exist internal pressures for change — existence of subgroups, for example, which strive for more influence within the union. Sometimes these subgroups may be the larger locals, but as we indicated, increasing the size of the union tends to have adverse effects upon their power: conventions are decreased in frequency, or the number of their delegates may be decreased. However, within a larger union, other subgroups will emerge and demand more influence in the power structure. We have tried to show how subgroups bound by ethnic, skill, or regional ties will be able to obtain representation on executive boards and contribute to policy formation and execution.

The determinism of the "Iron Law of Oligarchy" does not allow the researcher to understand change beyond a small and limited extent. Once oligarchy develops it becomes essentially static and, we believe, can exist only if the other elements within the total system remain constant. But as we have tried to show, external elements continue to vary because of the total environment in which they exist. The introduction of technology by industry was not merely due to its relationships with unions, but was more determined by the development of other market pressures. What we have tried to show is the development of oligarchy as well as some of the structural changes which follow from it.

Gouldner has suggested that theories tend to have a "metaphysical pathos" or a set of sentiments which will limit our observations and formulations (15, pp. 496–507). He suggests that selection of specific theories will lead to the neglect of alternative explanations of phenomena. Gouldner argues that social scientists tend to focus upon the negative aspects of human behavior rather than suggest some of the alternative approaches which might lead toward solutions and paths

---

For example, in a study of the League of Women Voters the correlation between distribution of control and total control was only .14. See Tannenbaum (40). Other relevant research in this area can be found in Smith and Tannenbaum (36). Zald, using a different terminology, arrives at very similar conclusions (47).

out of dilemmas. Gouldner specifically suggests there might be an "Iron Law of Democracy" as well as "Iron Law of Oligarchy." Hopefully, the dialectical model we have suggested would indicate certain neglected elements of membership influence and control over the policies of union government.

BIBLIOGRAPHY

1. Asch, S. E. *Social Psychology*. New York: Prentice-Hall, Inc., 1952.

2. Bambrick, J. J., Jr., and G. H. Haas. *Handbook of Union Government Structure and Procedures*. New York: National Industrial Conference Board, 1955.

3. Bell, D. "Discussion of Bernstein's Union Growth and Structural Cycles," in Walter Galenson and Seymour Lipset (eds.), *Labor and Trade Unionism*. New York: John Wiley and Sons, 1960.

4. Bell, D. "The Racket-Ridden Longshoremen," *The End of Ideology*, New York: Collier, 1961.

5. Birdsall, W. C. "The Problem of Structure in the Knights of Labor," *Industrial and Labor Relations Review*, Vol. 6 (1953), pp. 532–546.

6. Blau, P. M., and R. W. Scott. *Formal Organizations*. San Francisco: Chandler Publishing Co., 1962.

7. Bloom, G. F., and H. R. Northrup. *Economics of Labor Relations*. Homewood, Ill.: Richard D. Irwin, Inc., 1958.

8. Boulding, K. E. *The Organizational Revolution*. New York: Harper and Bros., 1953.

9. Bromwich, L. *Union Constitutions*. New York: Fund for the Republic, 1959.

10. Caplow, T. "Organizational Size," *Administrative Science Quarterly*, Vol. 1 (1957), pp. 490–495.

11. Dunlop, J. T. "The Development of Labor Organization," in R. A. Lester and J. Shister (eds.), *Insights into Labor Issues*. New York: The Macmillan Co., 1948.

12. Dunlop, J. T. *Industrial Relations Systems*. New York: Henry Holt & Co., 1958.

13. Dunlop, J. T. "Structural Changes in the American Labor Movement and Industrial Relations System," in Walter Galenson and Seymour Lipset (eds.), *Labor and Trade Unionism*. New York: John Wiley and Sons, 1960.

14. Faunce, W. A. "Size of Locals and Union Democracy," *American Journal of Sociology*, Vol 68 (1962), pp. 291–299.

15. Gouldner, A. W. "Metaphysical Pathos and the Theory of Bureaucracy," *American Political Science Review*, Vol. 49 (1955), pp. 496–507.

16. Gregory, C. O. *Labor and the Law*. New York: W. W. Norton, 1958.

17. Herberg, W. "Bureaucracy and Democracy in Labor Unions," *Antioch Review*, Vol. 3 (1945), pp. 405–417.

18. Howe, I., and B. J. Widick. *The UAW and Walter Reuther.* New York: Random House, 1949.

19. Kahn, M. L. "Recent Jurisdictional Developments in Organized Labor," in H. W. Davey, H. S. Kaltenborn, and S. H. Ruttenberg (eds.), *New Dimensions in Collective Bargaining.* New York: Harper and Row, 1961.

20. Kerr, C., and A. Siegel. "The Interindustry Propensity to Strike — An International Comparison," in A. Kornhauser, R. Dubin, and A. M. Ross (eds.), *Industrial Conflict.* New York: McGraw-Hill Book Co., 1954.

21. Landsberger, H. A. "Parsons' Theory of Organizations," in Max Black (ed.), *The Social Theories of Talcott Parsons.* Englewood Cliffs, N.J.: Prentice-Hall, Inc., 1961.

22. Leiserson, W. M. *American Trade Union Democracy.* New York: Columbia University Press, 1959.

23. Lipset, S. M. "The Political Process in Trade Unions: A Theoretical Statement," in Monroe Berger *et al* (eds.), *Freedom and Control in Modern Society.* New York: Van Nostrand & Co., 1954.

24. Lipset, S. M. "The Law and Trade Union Democracy," *Virginia Law Review*, Vol. 47 (1961), pp. 1–50.

25. Lipset, S. M., M. A. Trow, and J. S. Coleman. *Union Democracy.* Glencoe, Ill.: The Free Press, 1956.

26. Marcus, P. M. "Trade Union Structure: A Study in Formal Organization." Unpublished doctoral dissertation, University of Chicago, 1962.

27. Michels, R. *Political Parties.* Glencoe, Ill.: The Free Press, 1949.

28. National Opinion Research Center. "Jobs and Occupations: A Popular Evaluation," *Public Opinion News*, Vol. 9 (1947), pp. 3–13. Reprinted in *Social Stratification*, Bernard Barber (ed.). New York: Harcourt, Brace and World, 1957.

29. Parsons, T. "Suggestions for a Sociological Approach to the Theory of Organizations," *Administrative Science Quarterly*, Vol. I (1956), pp. 63–85, pp. 224–239.

30. Rees, A. *The Economics of Trade Unions.* Chicago: University of Chicago Press, 1962.

31. Ross, A. M. "Do We Have a New Industrial Feudalism?", *American Economic Review*, Vol. 48 (1958), pp. 903–920.

32. Ross, A. M. "The Prospects for Industrial Conflict," *Industrial Relations*, Vol. I (1961), pp. 57–74.

33. Seidman, J. I. *American Labor from Defense to Reconversion.* Chicago: University of Chicago Press, 1953.

34. Seidman, J. I. *Democracy in the Labor Movement.* Bulletin #39. Ithaca, N.Y.: Cornell University, New York School of Industrial and Labor Relations, 1958.

35. Seidman, J. I., and A. J. Melcher. "The General Executive Board in Na-

tional Union Constitutions," *Labor Law Journal,* Vol. 13 (1962), pp. 71–82.

36. Smith, C. G., and A. S. Tannenbaum. "Organizational Control Structure: A Comparative Analysis," *Human Relations,* in press.

37. Spinrad, W. "Correlates of Trade Union Participation: A Summary of the Literature," *American Sociological Review,* Vol. 25 (1960), pp. 237–245.

38. Summers, C. M. "Admission Policies of Labor Unions," *Quarterly Journal of Economics,* Vol. 6 (1946), pp. 66–107.

39. Tannenbaum, A. S., and R. L. Kahn. *Participation in Union Locals.* Evanston, Ill.: Row, Peterson and Co., 1958.

40. Tannenbaum, A. S. "Control and Effectiveness in a Voluntary Organization," *American Journal of Sociology,* Vol. 47 (1961), pp. 33–46.

41. Ulman, L. *The Rise of the National Trade Union.* Cambridge: Harvard University Press, 1955.

42. Ulman, L. "The Development of Trades and Labor Unions," in Seymour E. Harris (ed.), *American Economic History.* New York: McGraw-Hill Book Co., 1961.

43. Ulman, L. "Unionism and Collective Bargaining in the Modern Period," in Seymour E. Harris (ed.), *American Economic History.* New York: McGraw-Hill Book Co., 1961.

44. U.S. Department of Labor, Bureau of Labor Statistics. *Handbook of American Trade Unions.* Washington, D.C.: U.S. Government Printing Office, 1936.

45. Whyte, W. F. "Parsons' Theory Applied to Organizations," in Max Black (ed.), *The Social Theories of Talcott Parsons.* Englewood Cliffs, N.J.: Prentice-Hall, Inc., 1961.

46. Wilensky, H. *Intellectuals in Labor Unions.* Glencoe, Ill.: The Free Press, 1956.

47. Zald, M. N. "Organizational Control Structures in Five Correctional Institutions," *American Journal of Sociology,* Vol. 48 (1962), pp. 335–346.

30

G. Duncan Mitchell

Education, Ideology, and Social

Change in England

"My plan for instructing the poor is very limited and strict. They learn of weekdays such coarse work as may fit them for servants. I allow of no writing. My object has not been to teach dogmas or opinions, but to form the lower class to habits of industry and virtue."

Hannah More

When, at the beginning of the nineteenth century, Hannah More and her sisters began to teach the "wild children of the Cheddah Hills," as Ray Strachey (5) describes them, they were engaged in a novel endeavour. Their explanations appeared to be reasonable and they were certainly forthright and honest about them. It is doubtful if in recent years the educator is quite so forthright or honest, but this may be because he is much less clear in his mind as to what he is doing or wishes to do. His view is certainly different from that of Hannah More, whose ideas he finds quaint, and whose attitude he regards with mingled horror and fascination. Ideas about education have, of course, changed vastly — so has the social structure of England and people's attitudes to the stratified nature of English society. During the past 150 years England has become a highly industrialised nation, its population has multiplied many times, it has founded a great empire and emerged into a post-imperial era with a high standard of living, great sensitivity to international politics, and a desire to be distinguished for its social order and economic welfare.

Thus we observe much discussion about education, pressures for reform, greater provision at all levels of the educational process, and general emphasis on egalitarian ideals. We observe also a society divided into strata, albeit not very clearly defined, but with some degree of social mobility. Obvious also is the general concern over the nation's position in the international world of commerce and the implications of this position in respect to economic competition.

The purpose of this chapter is to examine some of the principal developments in education in England during the past century and to discern some of the shifts in ideological expression. The social changes in England that I wish to relate to both education and ideology are changes in the stratified character of the social order. The method adopted will be to trace the history of education over the past century, beginning with secondary education, continuing with primary and then technical education, and finally to consider the relationships between all the different levels of the educational process.

The Rise of the Middle Classes

On the accession of Queen Victoria in 1837, England was governed by a group of large landowners and the more prosperous of the country gentry. They conducted the business of the state themselves through Parliament, without a professional civil service. This aristocratic and amateur rule was much the same whether Whigs or Tories were in power. Even the Great Reform Act of 1832 did not materially alter a situation that had been in existence for some decades. To be sure, the growing bourgeoisie wanted some recognition, but they were very largely content with possession of the qualification to vote, which is what the Reform Act gave them. Indeed, what they most wanted, and succeeded in getting, was the recognition that there was property other than land which gave a person the right to vote. Although the new middle classes of the industrial era were enfranchised, they were unable to secure power for themselves as a class, even had they wanted it, for the country votes were gerrymandered in favor of the landowning classes.

The fact is that the middle classes gave little thought to government except when it interfered with their activities. Many subscribed to the view that government would diminish in importance as wealth accrued and science and technology advanced. But in any case their aim was less political than ideological. They wanted to secure recognition for their economic views, their moral values, and their social outlook; in short, the capitalist ethic. This they secured in the Joint Stock Acts of 1857 and 1859, which granted the status of limited liability to their enterprises and thrust on government the basic duty of maintaining the conditions for the success of the capitalist system, namely, the enforcement of contracts, the maintenance of law and order, and for the rest an absence of interference with trade and commerce. Thus the aristocratic outlook was modified by bourgeois attitudes. The national ideology altered a little so as to accommodate the new classes who now had a stake in the country. It is easy to speak of the upper, middle, and lower classes of the early nineteenth century.

In the more affluent Sixties of the nineteenth century the middle classes demanded that they be able to educate their children in a manner similar to that enjoyed by the upper classes. The latter had usually employed a tutor, normally a clergyman, or else sent their sons to one of the nine great public schools of the day.[1] The rising bourgeoisie wanted something like the public school, preferably without the residential element. They sought for this in the endowed schools, mostly grammar schools, some of great antiquity, which were scattered up and down the country, but situated mainly in the towns. Many of these schools had fallen into disuse or had been subjects of abuse for years. To put them in order it was necessary to revise their endowments. To this end the government was pressed to establish a Royal Commission, officially the Endowed Schools Commission, better known as the Taunton Commission, named after its chairman, the report of which was published in 1868.

Middle-class Education

Among the middle-class people who pressed for secondary education were the mill owners of Lancashire and Yorkshire, the wealthy shopkeepers, some army officers, farmers of various kinds, sons of clergy who had taken up a profession, and small businessmen who were making a profit but whose concerns could not expand further and so who were looking for new sources of investment. Their wants as regards education were not identical, and the Taunton Commission felt that, in deciding what kind of education a child should have, they would best consider parental requirements. The Commission assumed, probably correctly, that parental requirements as to type of education were indicated by the length of time a parent was prepared to send his son to school, for length of time did determine the nature of the education which was appropriate.

Thus considering education, as distinct from training for an occupation, the Commission argued that it was possible to classify schooling into

[1] The English Public School is a school providing secondary education, administered by a governing body, and depending on funds provided by endowment or the constitution of an incorporated company; the headmaster is salaried. In England, the term is used of those schools mainly financed independently of the state and whose headmasters are members of the Headmasters' Conference. In 1864 they were listed as Eton, Harrow, Rugby, Winchester, Westminster, Shrewsbury, Charterhouse, St. Paul's, and Merchant Taylors', but today there are 180 on the Headmasters' Conference list, and Whitaker's Almanack lists a similar number of Principal Girls Schools.

that which stopped at 14 years of age, that stopping at 16, and that which continued until 18 or 19. Clearly, they said, it is useless, if a boy is to stay at school only up to the age of 14 years, for him to begin subjects which need longer continuance for their proper study. On the other hand, if a boy stays on for a longer period he may safely postpone some subjects until later. "It is obvious," the Report says, "that these distinctions correspond roughly, but by no means exactly, to the gradations of society. Those who can afford to pay more for their children's education will also, as a general rule, continue that education for a longer time." The Commission quite frankly recognised the nature of the class structure of English society of the day and saw education as needing to be stratified accordingly. There was no question that this was anything other than just and proper. Thus the Commission sketched in outline the kind of system thought suitable. There were to be three grades of schooling.

Grade I would consist of education for two groups, those whose sons attended one of the nine great public schools — "men of considerable incomes independent of their own exertions, or professional men and men of business, whose profits put them on the same level," and "the great majority of professional men, especially the clergy, medical men, and lawyers; the poorer gentry; all in fact, who, having received a cultivated education themselves, are very anxious that their sons should not fall below them." The Commissioners added, significantly, that this second group wanted to cheapen education rather than widen it. "They have nothing to look to but education to keep their sons on a high social level. And they would not wish to have what might be more readily converted into money, if in any degree it tended to let their children sink in the social scale." The problem for this second group was that there was no alternative to the public school, for the local grammar schools were often poor and less and less inclined to offer a classical education; a classical education was being increasingly restricted to a few boarding schools, and boarding boys was expensive.

Grade II education also catered for the children of two groups, namely, those who could afford to keep their children at school after they were 16 years of age, but did not do so because they had to train them for their future employment, e.g., for the army, and all but the higher branches of the legal and medical professions, civil engineering, etc., and those who were compelled to take their children away from school to place them in employment so as to keep or part-keep them. The first of these two groups would, they said, have liked to keep Latin in the curriculum of the grammar schools, whilst the second group could barely tolerate it. It was by these latter folk that pressures had been brought to bear on grammar schools, most particularly in Lancashire, to abolish Latin from the curriculum.

Grade III was sharply differentiated from the first two, for the first two grades of education were for groups who were able to pay for it, whilst Grade III education was for the children of small tenant farmers, small tradesmen, and superior artisans who could not afford it. These people, said the Commissioners, want an education consisting of "very good reading, very good writing, very good arithmetic." And, they added, the small tenant farmers would not have wanted even this were it not that they did not wish to be left behind by the others and be outdone by the class below them.

It is quite clear that the Commissioners saw education as class-linked. Indeed, they felt it necessary to be quite explicit about the connection. For instance, they averred that parental views should carry weight and that an educational system imposed in defiance of these wishes would be ineffective.

> For much of the evidence tends to show that social distinctions cannot at present be altogether ignored. The education of the gentry has gradually separated itself from that of the class next below them, and it is but natural that this class in their turn should be unwilling to be confounded with the labourers whom they employ. It would be better that such distinctions, as far as education is concerned, at any rate in day schools, should disappear; but an attempt to obliterate them by superior authority might do mischief and fail in its object.

Such remarks display a gentle expression of their own upper-class prejudices and a nice understanding of the political power of the middle classes. Not only did the Commissioners appreciate the nature of the link between social class and type and length of education, but they also had a notion that the class structure was altering consonant with economic development and that this had implications for educational provision. "Education has become varied and complex. The different classes of society, the different occupations of life, require different kinds of teaching." Reflecting on former times and the educational ideas of those days, they saw that it was no longer possible to have a system of education which enabled the bright boy to move from a primary level to a higher level of schooling in a continuous manner. "It is useless to endeavour to restore what is plainly past," they argue. "It must be confessed — in confessing it we are but recording a plain fact — that it is no longer possible to keep all education in one groove, and by giving precisely the same education to all classes to make it easy for talent in every class to rise to its natural level."[2]

Thus by the mid-nineteenth century we see how in England men came to differentiate education both in terms of length and content, and to relate this differentiation to the stratified social structure of the country. The Bishop of Lincoln, giving evidence before the Commission, recommended what many thoughtful leading men of the time supported. He proposed that there be grammar schools to prepare boys for University,

[2] Report of the Endowed Schools, 1864.

the learned professions, and the civil service; upper-class Commercial schools teaching Latin, French, and perhaps German; lower-class Commercial schools teaching no Latin, but including mathematics, surveying, and bookkeeping in their syllabuses; and Primary schools giving basic skills in reading, writing, and arithmetic. The first two types of schools might, he added, be combined as two departments under a single head, and the second two types likewise under a head of their own, but the upper department would have staff paid at a higher rate. Here then was an attempt to do justice to occupational needs whilst recognising the significance of the stratified social structure of the country. In fact what the Commission did recommend, and what the government did in presenting the Endowed Schools Bill to Parliament in 1869, was to meet the demands of the new middle classes. To be sure the secondary schools needed to be reformed. Of this there was little doubt, but it had implications about which people were ambivalent. Earl Nelson in the House of Lords put his finger on the point, for he "thought the measure one likely to give improved education to the children of the middle classes, and, at the same time, admit a portion of the children of the working class to its benefits."[3] This last point had not been intended, and indeed to extend education at this level to the working classes, they held, might have been unwise as well as unnecessary. But some education they had to have, for the industrial bourgeoisie required a labour force that had been disciplined by the rudiments of education. No one thought in terms of an educational ladder, but provision of secondary education by the Act of 1869 to be followed by further provision for elementary education by the Act of 1870 raised the possibility of it. To this we now turn.

Elementary Education

Elementary education was introduced in England with the aid of financial support from the established church. Private philanthropy was advanced later by government grants to already existing private foundations. Thus 1846 saw the establishment of the teaching profession as the Treasury granted one pound sterling for every two pounds raised locally. As the Church was best placed to provide local funds for education, this meant that schools were mostly Church schools; teachers were selected and curricula chosen accordingly. However, when Macaulay defended the new grants he was successful in establishing the principle that primary education was a function of the state. As G. M. Young (6) puts it, once this was admitted it was clear that the radical view of education — universal, compulsory and secular — must prevail. It took a long time. Yet immediately after the middle classes obtained their secondary schools the first major step was taken to provide elementary education for all. The argument for it was succinctly given by W. E. Forster, the minister

[3] Parliamentary Debates (Hansard) June 28, 1869.

responsible for introducing the Elementary Education Bill in 1870. "It is no use trying to give technical teaching to our artisans without elementary education; uneducated labourers — and many of our labourers are utterly uneducated — are for the most part unskilled labourers, and if we have our work folk any longer unskilled, notwithstanding their strong sinews and determined energy, they will become over-matched in the competition of the world."[4]

The same year saw the Prussian armies decisively defeat the French, and the German Empire rapidly took shape as a military, industrial, and commercial power. Preoccupation with the problems of competition with the new German Empire on the one hand and the United States of America on the other led the English middle classes to review educational provision again and also in the last quarter of the nineteenth century.

It must not be supposed, however, that the Elementary Education Act was entirely the result of foreign competition. For some years the industrial and commercial bourgeoisie had been troubled by the lack of discipline among many of their labourers, their general lack of drive and initiative. The fact is that their own attitudes were shared by only a portion of the working classes. *The Times* commented in July 9, 1870 that "there is an increasing demand for juvenile labour. There is a still more increasing demand for intelligent juvenile labour. There is not a walk in life at this day in which a boy who can read and write has not a better chance than a boy who is ignorant." Those who preached self-improvement were not lacking or hesitant, for self-improvement for the industrious poor was welcomed if it led to self-improvement of the bourgeoisie. Contemporaries sadly commented that so few wanted to improve themselves. To provide schools was not enough, the children had to be made to attend them. *The Times* also noted: "If the lowest class of intelligent children are to be taken in hand, it must be independently of their parents," and hastened to add that compulsion must not apply to the respectable class. The position was indeed acute. In Liverpool, for instance, of the 80,000 children between five and 13 years of age, only 20,000, it was estimated, were receiving any schooling at all. The bourgeoisie were anxious to educate the lower class in middle-class virtues, but they did not want to create a rod for their own backs. Yet when a speaker in the House of Commons pointed out that in Germany all children went to school from the ages of six to 14, public opinion began to take the view that something must be done to improve the situation in England.

The problem rose again and again. In the 1880's the government was pressed to appoint a Royal Commission to examine the position in regard to technical instruction. This Commission sat from 1881 to 1884 and on the basis of their report the Technical Instruction Bill passed into law in 1889, laying the foundations of both technical training at the

[4] Parliamentary Debates, 1870.

secondary level and further training on a part-time basis. This particular development in education had no connection with the universities, for again there was no thought of an educational ladder; instead it was administered by local authorities. Various other Royal Commissions sat before the end of the century: the Cross Commission 1886–88 and the Bryce Commission 1894–95, but the next big development was the Education Bill of 1902.

Education and Ideology

As we have seen, English public opinion during the nineteenth century conceived education in functional terms, that is, except for a minority of people who received an introduction to a cultivated world of classical studies. Ideas about education were coloured by social class interests and there was frank expression of these interests. Hannah More's notion of what was fitting by way of education for the lower classes had altered, but essentially her attitudes were shared by most middle-class people until around the end of the century. But then we begin to see a change.

Rigid notions of differences in length and content of education, the lack of any idea of continuity and of an educational ladder began to dissolve, and ideas of continuity in education and of an educational ladder began to form. Thus A. J. Balfour, opening the debate for the Government on the Education Bill of 1902, which provided greater opportunity for secondary education, provision for the training of teachers and which endeavoured to rationalize the system, admitted that the 1870 Act had failed to put the primary system of education into any kind of rational or organic connection with the system of secondary education, and through this, with university education. He argued that higher technical education could only do its work on a sound basis of secondary education, and pointed to the increased recognition of a public demand. In presenting the Bill in the House of Commons, the Prime Minister went on to say: "It is only because we feel that the necessity with which this Bill is intended to deal is a pressing necessity, it is only because we are of opinion that it cannot with national credit be much longer delayed, that we have resolved to lay before the House our solution of the great problem which for so many years past, education has embarrassed the Legislature and the reformer." In this statement the pressure for greater provision is admitted, and was even more so when the 1906 Bill was debated four years later. Here is an indication that there was pressure from below for more provision. But in the House of Lords it was Britain's international position which claimed attention. The Bishop of Hereford compared the United Kingdom with Germany, to the former's disadvantage, for trade and industry had been lost because of the lack of continuation of education. Lord Tweedmouth spoke of Britain's rivals abroad and argued the case for an integrated system of elementary and secondary education. Back in the Commons a member spoke of "equality of opportunity," but he hastened to add, lest this appear too revolutionary, that it would be "tempered by selection, . . . based on relative capacity," but he too had been thinking of overseas competition. Another member, Mr. Seeley, came out boldly for the new principle when he described the Bill as providing "a carefully graduated system of education, whereby any children of sufficient intelligence will continue their education through secondary school up to the University."

But this was a rather rosy view of a bill which extended opportunity to only a very few. Dr. Macnamara, a powerful figure in the National Union of Teachers and editor of the *Schoolmaster,* spoke in the House of Commons for equality of treatment and rationality in organisation. "So long as each grade school is under a separate authority," he argued, "you cannot have that community of aim and purpose, that dovetailing of the curricula of various schools, which will enable a child of capacity but of humble parentage to move from one school to another without hindrance. From the point of view of the working classes, that is the most serious problem of this time."[5] The Bill was a move in the right direction, but it was only a short move, and yet it represented a partial acceptance of the principle of an educational ladder and hence stands as a landmark in the history of ideas; it denoted a shift in ideology on the part of both the landowning and the middle classes.

The Act of 1902 failed to provide a coherent system of education and it failed to provide free universal education at the secondary level. Indeed, despite the Bryce Report, the Act rejected the notion that secondary education might include technical instruction. But this was very largely the idea of Sir Robert Morant, the senior civil servant at the Board of Education. If social mobility through education was admitted as tolerable, it was nevertheless restricted to only the most intellectually able minority. Free places in secondary schools rose fast in number but the numbers were pitifully small. They rose from a tiny 5,500 in 1900 to a mere 25,269 in 1906. The idea of secondary education for all was in fact dropped until the Fisher Act of 1918 reconsidered it. Instead, the idea of compulsory part-time education gained favour. This proposal would have maintained early entry into employment whilst providing some opportunity for further schooling, and this in the end turned out to be optional, with the school-leaving age fixed at 14.

The fact is that the middle classes did not care for universal compulsory secondary education; for themselves there was sufficient provision. Hence there was little enthusiasm, but slowly the changing nature of English society, the interests of industry and commerce, and the persistence of educational reformers were altering the ideology. The Silent Social Revolution, as Mr. Lowndes calls it, (3) was in process.

Formal equality of opportunity came with the Education Act of 1944,

[5] Parliamentary Debate, March 24, 1902.

passed by a coalition government of Conservatives, Liberals, and Socialists. Mr. Arthur Greenwood, a Labour member, described the Bill as providing "a system of education offering full equality of opportunity for all, getting rid of class distinctions and realising, in the sphere of education, the principles of democracy to which we are pledged and for which we are fighting this war." The Parliamentary Secretary to the Board of Education, also a Socialist, claimed: "We have destroyed the old conception of elementary education being sufficient for nine-tenths of the population of this country." The minister, R. A. Butler, a Conservative, when presenting the Bill, described it as "providing variety of opportunity suitable to the age, ability and aptitude of the ordinary pupil," — a better description and more accurate. Parts of the Act have not yet been fully implemented, especially the provision of county colleges, and it in no way has impaired the private provision of education, or brought private schools into the state system; indeed, they thrive as never before. This is indicated by the difficulty of obtaining a place for a child in a school on the Headmasters' Conference list, and the higher standard of performance required generally in the Common Entrance examinations by such schools since the last war.

The foregoing is but a brief outline of the main changes in educational provision with some reference to the changes in educational ideas involved. We have said little about the content of education, of what should be included in the curricula, and what other extra-curricular activities are appropriate in schooling at different levels. We shall have to examine educational ideas further, particularly what is meant by a liberal education. To this end we shall briefly retrace our steps.

Ideological Accommodation

Our story began with the endeavours of a rising bourgeoisie to secure adequate educational provision for itself. This was a fitting place to begin, for the history of England during these years is of social change centering round this newly enlarged class. Whilst much is made of the progress of democratic ideas during the nineteenth and twentieth centuries, the fact remains that it was limited largely to middle-class enfranchisement. But to get the vote is not necessarily to acquire power, and whilst the working classes were largely admitted to the franchise in 1867, they had to wait until 1944 to acquire effective power, and even then their leaders were mostly middle-class men. Thus it was with the middle classes themselves a century earlier, for the 1832 Reform Act, momentous legislation though it was, failed to give them power. Yet having secured an acknowledgement of their own values — individualistic, *laissez-faire* and acquisitive — which occurred about the 1860's, the middle classes increasingly sought power.

This political movement was successful precisely insofar as they succeeded in establishing their values generally. The Duke of Wellington may have found their notions utterly distasteful in the 1830's, but by the end of the century trade and aristocracy were well mingled. But the newly arrived middle classes had to be accommodating, and it may be said that the fall of the upper class was broken insofar as the wider extension of a liberal education civilised the plutocracy. At least this was Matthew Arnold's hope and for years his principal aim, even as he also hoped to see England great, if not through her economic and political influence, at least through her culture. Few people understood as well as he did the nature of the middle classes and their needs. As a result of his inquiries in Europe, pursuant to his employment as H. M. Inspector of Schools, he had a right to assert: "Our middle classes are nearly the worst educated in the world" (1, p. 88). For Arnold it was middle-class education rather than working-class education that was most in need of reform, although he spoke of the two as secondary and elementary education respectively. "The great work to be done in this country at this hour," he wrote in one of his essays, "is not with the lower class, but with the middle; a work of raising its whole level of civilisation. . . ." For Arnold was a true democrat in that he wanted education for all; but he knew that until the middle classes had been educated, provision of elementary education, universal, compulsory, and free, would be lacking. The rising bourgeoisie knew they lacked culture and ideas, but their prejudices were strong. Education was not a little feared for what it might do to undermine their position if extended to the masses. Being fully conversant with the evidence supplied to the Taunton Commission, Arnold knew perfectly well the extent of the ignorance of the middle classes; he well named them Philistines. They remained such until internal changes took place in this stratum of English society and it became differentiated. This we shall turn to later in examining changes in educational curricula; for the present, let us return to look again at elementary education and the lower classes of English society.

During the first half of the nineteenth century England was little more than a police state. The upper and ruling classes were obsessed by a fear of revolution. The post-Napoleonic War years were times of repression. Organised labour was perceived to be a most dangerous development; Chartism in particular. Not until the 1850's did the fear of Chartism wane, then it collapsed rapidly. It was realized belatedly that much of the fear had been groundless. Only when this fear disappeared was the way open for the development of elementary education. Now, although elementary education was advanced by small Treasury grants, the annual expenditure rose fairly steeply. By the time the Crimean War was over retrenchment in Treasury expenditure was the order of the day and what had begun with some promise was suddenly afflicted as educational grants were cut. It was argued that the system was inefficient and that it was giving some children a better education than the children of the middle classes were receiving at fee-paying schools. Moreover, the last point was augmented by a general distrust of a system which might unfit the child for his place in society; for these were the days when men thought less in terms of an open-class society than a society of estates and orders.

In fact, of course, the middle-class child was getting an abominably poor education, and in the late 1840's and 1850's many middle-class people were justifiably angry that they should have to pay for inferior schooling for their own children and also pay taxes to support elementary schooling for the children of the lower classes. Thus when they obtained reform of the secondary schools they also pressed for a government inquiry into expenditure on elementary education. They secured the appointment of the Newcastle Commission in 1858. Already the government had been critical of some schools, which had been providing more than elementary education for some of their pupils. Indeed, inspectors of schools were advised to stress ability in reading, writing, and arithmetic to the exclusion of other and more advanced items as early as 1857. But after the publication of the Report of the Commission controversy was widespread on the subject of over-teaching children.

Elementary, Secondary, and Technical Education

The government was bent on retrenchment, strongly supported by middle-class opinion, and it was not difficult for them to draw up a Revised Code in 1861, which abolished all direct payments to teachers, retiring pensions, building and furniture grants, special grants for drawing, scientific study, evening schools, and so on. Instead, the Revised Code made grants on a *per capita* basis to school managers on condition children attended school a minimum length of time and satisfied the inspectors in an examination according to a fixed syllabus, no grant being given for children over 11 years of age. This system of payment by results was disastrous for the teacher, the child, and the development of both elementary and secondary education in the country. The Vice-President of the Committee on Education, Robert Lowe, made it quite clear what was in the government's mind. They had no intention of improving the quality of education in the schools with which the Committee was concerned. They did not "profess to give those children an education that will raise them above their station and business in life." Lowe argued that the government desired to fix "a minimum of education, not a maximum," but he added "we want not better schools, but to make them work harder." The three R's were all that were required for the lower classes; more was unnecessary, even dangerous.

To be sure, the publication of the Revised Code led to an outcry. There were protests in the press, many pamphlets and petitions, letters to newspapers, meetings, and much discussion. In the House of Commons, however, there was little interest. This was the middle-class reaction to working-class aspirations. As the *Daily News* leader of September 29, 1862, put it: "Very few members have spoken, the prevailing desire being to get a troublesome matter over as soon as possible, but the arguments have immensely preponderated in favour of the Revised Code." Not until 1897 was the Revised Code overthrown, but by then the damage had been done, and even today the teaching profession in England bears the marks of this setback.

Thus even with the coming of the Act of 1870, which filled the gaps in school provision, adding to the church schools and organising them under district school boards, elementary education was limited. It was limited by class interests despite the recognition of education as a national matter. The popularly held view that the 1870 Act was the result of the extension of the franchise following from the Reform Act of 1867, which gave the urban artisan the vote, is misplaced. To be sure, Robert Lowe said "We must educate our masters," but the masters were relatively few in number, they were not in power, nor was there any immediate likelihood of their being in power. Elementary education was provided by the state because prosperity depended on a labour force that had been given this basic training and discipline. What is quite clear is that it was developed with total disregard for its relationship to secondary education. This was not taken up until the bourgeois owners and managers discovered the lack of men skilled in technology, and their economic prosperity consequently in jeopardy. It will be noted that not only did the middle classes restrict the extent of education which the lower classes were to receive, but they determined the curricula of the schools to ensure it was restricted to education at the primary level only.

The political situation of England in the 20 years from 1870 to 1890 may not unjustly be described as an uneasy alliance of upper and middle classes, cooperating for national ends, providing more or less in turn Conservative and Liberal governments. It was a society which throve on an expanding economy served by a relatively unorganised and uneducated labour force. It was a situation which could not last. The advance of industrialisation brought with it demands for higher degrees of skill, and discussion took place during the 1880's as to how to meet this demand.

It led, as we saw, to the Technical Instruction Act 1889, but we must observe that views about technical instruction were very narrow. Sir Philip Magnus, Director and Secretary of the City and Guilds of London Institute, considered the purpose of technical education to be "to train persons in the arts and sciences that underlay the practice of some trade or profession." Professor Thompson, a physicist, defined it as follows: "Education is technical only so far as it is directed to the training of the individual in and for his business in life." These were the views which prevailed. They were opposed by people like T. H. Huxley and Matthew Arnold. The question was whether the artisan and his child should be instructed merely to perform their jobs or whether they should be educated fully to live a rich and fruitful life. Moreover, the interests of both elementary and technical education were ill-served if there was inadequate secondary education. For whilst the middle class had obtained access to reformed public schools and grammar schools, there was no suggestion that these schools should be related to technical instruction in any way. Arnold argued that technical education was not enough, for through such a system pupils learned the techniques of industry and the sciences, but they did not learn Science, which is "the aptitude for finding their way out of a difficulty by thought and reason." Furthermore, Arnold was cognisant of labour difficulties which for him reflected the poverty of the middle-class employers' education; a poverty of culture and education making them incapable of "creating new relations between themselves and the working class when old relations fail."[6] This prescient insight was scarcely appreciated at the time.

It might be thought from this account that the history of education in England is largely the story of a rising middle class seeking its place in the sun but denying a place to the lower strata. Yet this is not the whole story, for besides changes in the social structure of the country, which clearly had a strong influence on educational history, there were changes in ideology: in fact, there was a clash of ideologies. This may be seen in different attitudes toward education, for education at once reflects the changing social structure and the dominant ideas of the time. Moreover, education as a social institution is not without a measure of cultural autonomy. There are inherent forces working their way toward goals, and the ideas which give rise to them are from time to time brought into the forum of public discussion. Many of these ideas are not easily interpreted in terms of economic and social class interests. Such is the case with the discussion on what constitutes a liberal education. The older universities claimed to have an answer to this question; the more so as they were progressively reformed, following the Universities Commission of 1850–52, by the Acts of 1854 and 1856. This reform represented a move to render them more accessible to the middle classes. But whilst they opened their doors wider, they reaffirmed their devotion to liberal education of the traditional kind rather than professional education.

Ideas about Education

There was throughout the century periodic discussion as to what constitutes a liberal education, and this discussion took place against a background of argument about the provision of elementary, secondary, and technical schooling. Indeed, the interesting feature of the whole matter is the way in which the advocates of liberal education (themselves stemming mainly from the upper classes for many of whom this was the

[6] School and Universities on The Continent, A Report, 1868.

ideal) allied themselves with the democratically minded reformers, that is to say, those who favoured reform of institutions for the benefit of a wider population than just the middle classes. Thus we see provision of elementary and technical education together with non-public school secondary education criticised by the democratically minded, as being too limited, and by the educated elite, as being too narrow. The original curriculum of the public school was geared to that of the ancient universities. It emphasized the classical languages, ancient history, mathematics, and later on, included modern languages. Modifications to school and university curricula followed the introduction of examinations into the ancient universities, the establishment of open examinations for entry to the higher grades of the civil service in 1855, and the introduction of examinations into military training establishments. But the public school curriculum was further influenced by the religious and recreational disciplines which were overtly related to character building. All in all the ideal was to turn out the leisured, pious, and gentlemanly amateur. This kind of education was frequently contrasted with the "rigid erudition fostered by the German secondary school" and the "too purely intellectual tone of the French Lycée" (3).

Religion has always played a part in English educational history. Indeed, it may be objected that this account has so far avoided the topic. Even a casual perusal of Hansard debates and press comments on Educational Bills from 1870 to 1902, and even that of 1944, shows how much religious matters were in the public mind, and debates grow wearisome on the differences between the Established and the Free Churches. Yet genuine as were many of the positions taken, it must be added that the religious factor in educational policies obscures as well as reflects the class differences of the times. On the other hand the idea of a liberal education had strong connections with religion, as may be seen for instance in the work of Thomas Arnold at Rugby School. The gradual development of the idea of a liberal education is plain. This idea upheld the classical type of education, associated so long with a clerical tradition; it also included the study of modern subjects such as languages and literature of other European countries, the study of natural science and history. Its chief aim was to broaden the outlook of the pupil, improving his vision, and increasing the acumen of his thought. It was this, together with the traditional independence given to the scholastic profession, which raised the grammar schools to a high standard, that enabled the new civic universities[7] to avoid too narrow an interpretation of science

---

[7] Besides the medieval Universities of Oxford and Cambridge, universities at Durham and London were founded in 1832 and 1836, respectively, but the new civic universities began with the foundation of Manchester in 1880, followed by Birmingham 1900, Liverpool 1903, Leeds 1904, Sheffield 1905, Bristol 1909, and Reading 1926. Other bodies to receive Royal Charters did not obtain them until after World War II. These include the Universities of Nottingham, Leicester, Exeter, Hull, and Southampton.

and technology, and indeed helped them to develop professional schools without ceasing to give pride of place to liberal studies and research.

Yet the development of this liberal educational idea had one drawback, for unless educational provision was seen to lead toward it such educational provision was disvalued. Hence as secondary education developed, it bifurcated into that which led to university and that which ended at the age of 15 years. The former has always enjoyed high prestige and support; the latter has been neglected, indeed its curriculum has hardly yet taken shape. Thus we discover, for example, that in 1871, Huxley, as a member of the London School Board, failed to secure the teaching of liberal studies in the schools; Latin was deleted from the list of discretionary subjects that senior schools might teach, music (only vocal) after some difficulty was allowed to remain. The point was made that liberal studies were not for board-school children, and in fact by a High Court judgment in 1900 the ratepayers' money could not be spent on any form of secondary or higher education. Not until 1902 was secondary education provided by the state, and then it was hedged about with disabilities so that it remained for the 1944 Act to provide it free, compulsory, and universal, when it was differentiated into secondary grammar, modern, and technical. The curricula of these three are different, as is the quality of the teaching staff recruited. A measure of this is the continued provision of privately financed schooling, in particular the growth of "public schools" in size and number to cater for the children of those who can afford to pay and who shrewdly estimate the worth of the state schools in their locality.

Education Reflects Social Structure

That the educational system reflects the stratified social structure is fairly easily seen in nineteenth-century England. Not so readily discernible is the growing complexity of this structure toward the close of the century and in the beginning of the twentieth century. We are referring to the differentiation of the middle classes. The Taunton Commission noted the different strata within the middle class of the time, and the educational provision it recommended further enhanced these differences. Educationally, the main difference was between those who sent their sons away to boarding schools and those who did not. This partly reflected a family's financial circumstances, but partly it reflected different interests. Thus for the higher professions a public school and university education was desirable, but for a man who expected his son to join him in a family business it was better if the son stayed at home, developed an interest in the firm, and left school early. As for the minor professions, there was scarcely any encouragement to attend university, for there was no provision for training there, and as often as not no ability to pay for it had there been any. Moreover, whilst the religious disabilities of the dissenters had been removed as far as the ancient universities were concerned in 1871, these clerical institutions had not endeared themselves to the dissenting middle class, who had established their own excellent if short-lived academies in the middle of the century.

Attitudes toward the content of education varied greatly. Some middle-class people wanted modern subjects with an emphasis on their utility, others shared an older tradition which opposed this. Thus when technical education was being considered during the debates on the 1902 Bill it was excluded from a liberal educational context by those upper- and upper-middle-class people who saw the two as incompatible. The reason for this was that they viewed technical education as an extension of elementary education, and elementary education as being for working-class people; it was therefore isolated from the rest of the system. Yet a portion of the middle class found technical education of value, just as a section of the middle class had earlier found the more liberal studies of the grammar schools of value. The fact is that by 1902 there were different middle-class strata. It is not hard to distinguish an upper-middle class of professional and wealthy business families, a middle-middle class of minor professional people and tradesmen, and a lower-middle class of small shopkeepers, clerical workers, and some superior artisans. This differentiation of the middle class, whilst being partly and implicitly recognised by the Act of 1902, was not fully recognised until the post-war development of education authorised by the Act of 1944. In this last piece of legislation it is possible to discern the continued power of the upper class and the upper and middle elements of the middle classes, for public schools and boarding schools were left intact, and have since flourished more than ever. The middle and lower-middle portions of the middle classes were granted more opportunity for good free secondary education, and the lower or working classes were also given formal equality of opportunity. They were not granted, we should notice, full equality of opportunity in education, i.e., opportunity for all who desire it, but opportunity where there is equality of capacity to profit by it. The differences in content remain, although there are signs of attempts to reduce the differences. Liberal education, whilst offered with professional studies in the universities, has been in the past predominantly the education of the upper and upper-middle classes. It is recognised to be the education suitable for the elite. To be sure, recruitment is not limited to a section of the stratified structure. It is based more and more on merit, but opportunities are necessarily restricted to a few, socially if not legally. Political pressures today appear to emanate from the new class, the middle-middle class, which is growing rapidly. In this group we find the managers, executives, civil servants, and a host of new professional groups such as opticians, medical auxiliaries, social workers, personnel managers, and accountants. These are the people who press for more adequate secondary grammar school provision and who now send their children to the newer universities. As a class they are partly recruited from the lower-middle and working-class population, but increasingly they obtain a clear identity of their own. The establishment of seven new universities[8] during the past three years in a country which hitherto had only 17 such institutions is a significant measure of the political pressure being exerted by this new class.

Education, Ideology, and Social Change

The development of an industrial society involves the progressive development of a stratified social structure, but the stratification becomes less a matter of traditional socio-economic groupings than of occupational status groups. The picture in all highly industrialised societies displays differentiation in the middle class according to occupational status. Yet such groups tend to act in such a way as to maintain their existence against others both above and below them. Obviously, in nineteenth-century England there was an attempt by a rising bourgeoisie to take power from a traditional upper class and to defend class interests against a depressed working class. More recently this kind of process has become more complicated with the further differentiation of social classes. We have seen how one instrument of class struggle has been educational provision. However, what began as a frankly avowed policy has become covert and obscure.

The fact is that ideologies have altered; there is no Hannah More today. Ideologies have been affected by the economic and social changes of the past 150 years. To begin with, the ideologies of social classes have tended to give way to a national ideology. The nature of modern society is more unitary; the day of the "two nations" as described by Disraeli in his novel *Sybil* (2) is over, and a general identity of interests is essential as power becomes diffused. Next, internal and, more pertinently, international commercial competition demands the rational allocation of resources, including abilities and skills. Talent cannot be permitted to lie unused. The diffusion of power involves the introduction of egalitarian ideas, but the facts of competitive economic life support them too. Thus about the turn of the century we see the introduction of the notion of an educational ladder, hitherto explicitly disvalued. By 1944 it was institutionalised in the educational system.

However, it is at this point that we discern one of the main problems of modern society. A simple educational system with progression from the bottom to the top is not always functional for a complex industrial society. Some talent needs to be selected at an early stage for special help and special use. In the United States this is perhaps not so obvious as in

---

[8] Of these new universities, one at Keele is a former University College, now raised in status, as were others established in post-war years. The remainder are quite new and are still in process of formation, although Sussex admitted undergraduates in 1962 and York has announced its intention of doing so in 1963. The following are now acquiring staff and buildings: East Anglia, Essex, Canterbury, Lancaster, and Warwick.

the European nations. But we may note in passing that whereas in the latter, selection takes place at the secondary level, in America it takes place at college and university level; graduate schools are rigorous in selection and, varying in quality, are themselves rigorously selected. Selection, which is increasingly becoming a component of modern educational systems, runs somewhat counter to egalitarian ideas. It is here that obscurity acts as a cover for some dishonesty, but the dishonesty is built into the system. To be sure, individual rights of citizenship are recognised, and recognised in the English educational system. As the 1944 Act says, educational provision will not be adequate until it affords "for all pupils opportunities for education offering such variety of instruction and training as may be desirable in view of their different ages, abilities and aptitudes." But in practice, as T. H. Marshall points out, education is linked to occupation, and one of the values of education received is a suitable job afterwards. There are therefore strong social forces tending to bring educational provision into relation to occupational demand and the proportions of children receiving education of different grades cannot be fixed without reference to the proportion between jobs of corresponding grades. As Marshall says, "If a boy who is given a Grammar School education can then get nothing but a Modern School job, he will cherish a grievance and feel that he has been cheated. It is highly desirable that this attitude should change, so that a boy in such circumstances will be grateful for his education and not resentful at his job. But to accomplish such a change is no easy task" (4, p. 64). It is useless to argue that a continuous system of education with all children attending the same kind of schools will obviate this difficulty, for this merely creates the more serious one of avoiding a wastage of talent. The problem is unlikely to be resolved satisfactorily until the national ideologies of modern societies are totally freed of social-class biases, and this will depend on the degree of cultural autonomy enjoyed by existing educational institutions.

Social Change and Educational Autonomy

Social change is stimulated by economic, technological, and demographic factors, but it is also influenced by human purposes. If today we are less inclined than formerly to see these as the intentions of great men, we more readily acknowledge the influences of groups of men working within and shaping traditions of thought and practice. Such groups are to be found assisting the educational processes within a nation, for education both reflects and influences the course of historical development. Yet for social change to be even in part directed by educationalists there must be some degree of cultural autonomy for educational institutions. Upon what does this cultural autonomy depend?

The most obvious factor perhaps is financial independence. In the past this has been noticeable in England among the colleges of the older universities, also among the provincial universities, although to a smaller extent, and certainly among the great public schools. Yet the position alters as each quinquennium Parliament votes increasing grants to the universities; indeed the trend is toward greater state aid at all levels of the educational process. A second factor providing a foundation for cultural autonomy is formal self-government for universities and schools; this still obtains in the case of the former, and as for the latter there is still great power in the hands of head teachers in secondary schools, and in the public schools in particular the headmaster is still a strong commanding figure. A possible third factor may be found in the relationship between the leisured classes and the scholastic profession, for in England, in the past, aristocratic private patronage gave a scholar a measure of freedom and protection. But more pertinent is the long association of scholarship and teaching with gentlemanly activity, particularly at the secondary and higher levels of education. Paradoxically, this has sometimes meant an emphasis on class-free values in educational policy. The influence of the proponents of liberal education in the past 100 years may be cited as a case in point. The educated portion of a well-established leisure class is sometimes capable of freedom of thought and expression remarkable for its detachment from narrow class interests.

Yet when all this has been said, the most important factor is surely the growth of a critical tradition, maturing over a substantial period of time, which establishes criteria for judgment strong enough to remain unquestioned by partisans of the moment. Such traditions every nation has to develop for itself, and they vary in form and content. The erudite scholarship of the German academic, the clarity and power of expression of the French man of letters, and the sensibleness of the British empiricist are well known but different expressions of a critical tradition, which itself plays a part in shaping the educational structure of a country and, at all levels, upholds cherished values against the assaults of self-interested groups and classes as much as it combats the creeping mists of sloth and ennui.

BIBLIOGRAPHY

1. Arnold, Matthew. "The Popular Education of France," in *Complete Prose Works*, R. H. Super (ed.), 3 vols. Ann Arbor, Mich.: University of Michigan Press, 1962, Vol. 2.

2. Disraeli, Benjamin. *Sybil*. New York; Oxford University Press, 1946.

3. Lowndes, G. A. N. *The Silent Social Revolution*. New York: Oxford University Press, 1937.

4. Marshall, T. H. *Citizenship and Social Class*. London: Cambridge University Press, 1950.

5. Strachey, R. *The Cause*. London: G. Bell & Sons, 1928.

6. Young, G. M. *Victorian England: Portrait of an Age*. Garden City, N.Y.: Doubleday & Co., 1954.

31

Walter Hirsch

Knowledge, Power, and Social

Change: The Role of American

Scientists

The fact that science and technology constitute one of the major variables in contemporary social change needs no scholarly documentation. Our present inquiry will focus on the degree to which American scientists and engineers are aware of their actual or potential role as "agents" of social change, and on their ability to exercise significant decision-making power, vis-à-vis other agents.[1] In what ways do scientists[2] in a democratic society play a part in determining the nature of their "product," i.e., knowledge, and the uses to which it is put?

The proposition that a "democratic," as distinguished from a "totalitarian," social structure is the most conducive for the optimal development of scientific institutions is no longer as self-evident as it appeared less than a generation ago (6, pp. 105–7; 19). The Comtean dream (or nightmare) of a scientific elite running a society is not seriously entertained by any significant segment of the scientific community, even in

[1] We shall by-pass the "great man" vs. "cultural forces" controversy whose ancient flames have been lately fanned by Leslie A. White (50) and others.
[2] For the sake of brevity the term "scientist" will include engineers, unless the differences between the two categories need to be pointed up. For some of these, cf. Kornhauser (24, pp. 149–154). For that matter many generalizations about scientists will be shown to be of little utility in the discussion to follow.

the watered-down form of technocracy. There seems little evidence to support Veblen's post-World War I prophecy that the engineers, having been "thrown into the position of responsible directors of the industrial system," became organized for the "common purpose" of eliminating the "lag, leak and friction" pervading industry and are now the "arbiters of the community's material welfare" (46, p. 440). During the period following World War II, when the prestige of the physical scientists, and even of the "pure" scientist, at least in the field of nuclear physics, had risen to unprecedented heights, they were loath to translate their newly-found influence into the kind of power which some of their predecessors had vainly sought (42).

The reasons and feelings associated with this disinclination range from a "realistic" interpretation of the nature of the power structure through various assessments of the valid role of the scientist to a feeling of resignation. A poignant example of the latter is contained in a letter which Albert Einstein sent to a group of Italian scientists:

> The man of science, as we can observe with our own eyes, suffers a truly tragic fate — striving in great sincerity for clarity and inner independence, he himself through his sheer superhuman effort has fashioned the tools which are being used to make him a slave and to destroy him also from within. He cannot escape being muzzled by those who have political power in their hands (35, p. 144).

But others, especially among those who were directly involved in the creation of the atom bomb, were and are compelled to take their stand in the political arena, in part because, as Robert Oppenheimer put it, "in some sort of crude sense which no vulgarity, no humor, no overstatement can quite extinguish, the physicists have known sin, and this is a knowledge which they cannot lose" (32, p. 69). And to the extent that we can speak of prevailing opinion among scientists, the new sense of responsibility and urgency in their ranks is expressed by the Report of the Committee on Human Welfare of the American Association for the Advancement of Science:

> With each advance in our knowledge of nature, science adds to the already immense power the social order exerts on human welfare. With each increment in power, the problem of directing its use toward beneficial ends becomes more complex, the consequences of failure more disastrous, and the time for decision more brief. . . . At a time when decisive economic, political, and social processes have become profoundly dependent on science, the discipline has failed to attain its appropriate place in the management of public affairs. . . . Recent events have lent substance to the conviction of our Committee . . . and we believe to that of scientists generally — that scientists have a serious and immediate responsibility to help mediate the effects of scientific progress on human welfare (4, p. 68, p. 71).

The application of science to military uses and the impact of new devices on national and international politics is one area to which we will devote our attention. Another major area, less dramatic in its implications, but probably more salient for the "average" scientist, concerns the disposition of his product by industry and the scientist's position in the marketplace. It is, of course, evident that these areas are intimately related, but for our purposes we will treat them separately. Later on we will consider the role of other institutional settings for scientific activity, notably the traditional one of the university, which is being increasingly drawn into the orbit of the military-industrial complex.[3]

The Scientist in Industry

The industrial scientist's power position stems from his specialized knowledge and abilities. To what extent can he use his power to determine the goals to which his knowledge should be directed and the subsequent use to which it should be put? Even if he is engaged in "basic" research and has no personal concern about the "utility" of his product, he must find a sponsor willing and able to undertake the economic risks involved with the understanding that the research will eventually "pay off." He faces the dilemma which, according to Merton, is typical for intellectuals generally:

> If the intellectual is to play an effective role in putting his knowledge to work, it is increasingly necessary that he become a part of the bureaucratic power structure. This, however, often requires him to abdicate his privilege of exploring policy-possibilities which he regards as significant. If, on the other hand, he remains unattached in order to preserve full opportunity of choice, he characteristically has neither the resources to carry through his investigations on an appropriate scale nor any strong likelihood of having his findings accepted by policy-makers as a basis for action (27, p. 217).

It should be understood that the dilemma is more acute for some than for others. Not every scientist feels the need to exercise "policy-making" powers or the desire to have full control over the economic exploitation of his product. Thus one prominent aeronautical engineer and inventor, in discussing the putative powers afforded the scientist by the patent system, states that:

> . . . patent activities involve innovation, protection, and exploitation. Only exploitation has the possibility of directly producing returns of any considerable magnitude, and requires people who have the capabilities of the

[3] For an excellent treatment of the problems arising from this relationship, see Kidd (21). Our main reason for focusing on the scientists' position in the political and industrial areas is that it is easier to ascertain the decision-making powers there. As one sociologist has put it, "ideas are influential; they may alter the process of history, but for the sake of logical and sociological clarity it is preferable to deny them the attribute of power" (9, p. 732).

entrepreneur, the promoter, the businessman, the manager. . . . These people are not necessarily or even very often, the innovators or the patent negotiators who started a chain of events that culminate in successful exploitations.

. . . I have come to see clearly that rewards in our society go not to the people who make inventions but to the people who are able to exploit the knowledge and patent rights that have been created (11).

Rather than resenting this state of affairs, this scientist concludes that he is not bothered by it, since he's not interested in money but the "intellectual excitement" of research as is every "typical scientist or inventor." There exist few systematic data which would allow us to estimate the proportion of scientists who are typical in this sense,[4] but we do know that most people are not motivated by a single, overriding need, but rather by a hierarchy of needs which is rather fluid. In our society it seems that in many ways values are increasingly becoming "monetized"; thus the recognition of *professional* status depends to a great extent on the symbolic function of salary levels. Even though "money isn't everything," neither is the satisfaction of intellectual curiosity, and even if he's not "interested in money" the scientist is under pressure to maximize his income if he wants to exploit his status as a man of knowledge vis-à-vis other functionaries. One effect has been the success which industry has had in luring scientists away from academic and government employ, even though the economic incentive in many cases has turned out to be inadequate.

Let us consider further implications of the potential dilemma. As we have said, the scientist's power position entails two aspects: the ability to determine his research goals and working conditions; and the ability to dispose of his product in the market. To the extent that the conventional distinction between "pure" and "applied" research has any validity,[5] it is the "basic" scientist who should be most concerned with the former aspect. He typically works in a large firm, the kind which can afford the luxury of hiring him and of occasionally following up his hunches in the hope that they will pay off (29; 15). The available evidence leads to the conclusion that even in these firms economic considerations take priority, and that "typically, industrial scientists must be prepared to drop, or at least interrupt, projects in which they are professionally interested" (24, p. 69). The "applied" scientist has, of course, even less opportunity (and probably, it must be said, less motivation) for exercising his role as a searcher for knowledge. A study of six major industrial firms gives an indication of the degree and range of participation research scientists report having in major decisions affecting their work assignment:

[4] Some relevant empirical studies are Stein (45), who found that for his sample "scientific" incentives were lower than he had anticipated, and "administrative and monetary" rewards were higher; Opinion Research Corporation (31); West (48).

[5] The validity of the distinction is becoming increasingly questionable Cf. Kidd (22); Wolfle (49, pp. 210 ff.).

TABLE 1

	OFTEN PARTI-CIPATE	SOME-TIMES	RARELY OR NEVER	TOTAL	N
All scientists and engineers	41%	32%	27%	100%	622
Research administrators	56%	28%	15%	100%	90
With Ph.D. degree	52%	26%	22%	100%	186
With M.S. or B.S.	36%	36%	28%	100%	389
Company with highest participation	59%	26%	15%	100%	102
Company with lowest participation	28%	37%	35%	100%	102

Source: Kornhauser (24, p. 63).

The data indicate that holders of Ph.D. degrees have greater decision-making power than the rest, but not as much as the research administrators. The latter category represents a function typically found in large firms engaged in research and development ("R & D") and constitutes one of the major methods for integrating research into the organization. Does the research administrator operate mainly as a scientist or is he essentially an agent of management? Typically he would seem to be the latter, both in terms of the requirements of the job and of the capacities and motivations of the incumbents. "The dominant pattern in industry is not to select research administrators on the basis of scientific competence" (5, p. 31), and in one presumably typical company, "interviews show . . . that organizational incentives are more important for research supervisors and professional incentives for researchers" (24, p. 144). The recently created role of the research administrator tends to take the edge off the dilemma for those scientists whose commitments are to the organization rather than to their profession, but at the same time it tends to weaken the decision-making power of the "pure" scientist, since his communication to management is filtered through a "gatekeeper" whose orientations tend to make him take the side of management.

What other institutional devices exist by which the scientist can increase his power? According to the proponents of the patent system, one of its major functions is to provide for a continuous flow of scientific innovation by offering the incentives of economic rewards and public recognition to the innovator. Whether or not the patent system has been or is at present functional in these terms is a subject of considerable controversy.[6] Our specific concern is with the question of how patents can be utilized by the industral scientist to control the use of his product.

Management policies regarding patentable inventions vary. The em-

[6] For a review of the relevant literature and a test of the hypothesis which concludes that it cannot be accepted or rejected, see Machlup (26).

ployer may or may not pay bonuses, royalties, or other benefits to the inventor. Generally, "one condition of employment for engineers in most industrial plants . . . is the signing of a patent agreement in which the engineer guarantees to sign and execute all documents necessary to assign the employer the right to benefit from his invention" (47, p. 91). In the event that the inventor should retain his patent, "it seems safe to say that the average established corporation with its productive, financial, and marketing resources will be in a better position to make use of a patent . . . than will a private individual who lacks these resources" (10, p. 361). The majority of patents are held by large corporations (26), precisely those whose resources allow the greatest scope for the pure scientist in industry. Again we see another aspect of the dilemma: there is no positive relation between the scientist's chance to maximize his professional role and his ability to dispose freely of his product.

Undoubtedly, the fissioning process in such rapidly growing industries as electronics is indicative of some scientists' desire to participate more fully in the economic exploitation of their knowledge by combining the scientific and entrepreneurial functions. Non-economic motives are also involved, particularly the freedom from interference by non-professionals, for "in study after study, scientists and engineers in industry indicate that they think their special competence is not adequately utilized" (24, p. 139), and as Merton has demonstrated, the scientist has a legitimate need for recognition (28). The degree to which the scientist-entrepreneur is able to maximize both these roles and the extent and possible resolution of role conflicts are areas for intensive investigation.

One of the most important of the scientist's non-economic needs is that of communication with other scientists — a need frustrated by the firm's desire to maintain its competitive advantage, and, particularly since World War II, by the legislation affecting national security. The role of the latter has been sufficiently discussed in a variety of sources[7] for us to forego further documentation, especially since the differentiation between "military" and other aspects of research is becoming increasingly blurred. However, some general comments on problems involved in the freedom to communicate and some specific data recently made public warrant presentation here.

Even though most managers would probably agree with Charles F. Kettering's dictum that locking the laboratory door excludes more knowledge than it keeps in, the open-door policy is not generally maintained. Reliable data on industrial espionage are obviously unobtainable[8] but perhaps the most prevalent and efficient manner of conducting this operation consists simply of hiring one's competitor's "brains" away. Thus even if a process is patented the firm owning the patent may have no control

[7] For an incisive analysis of the causes and consequences of this phenomenon, see Shils (41).

[8] For one survey of prevailing attitudes and practices, see Furash (16).

over the knowledge possessed by the inventor. According to one legal authority, "the employee who departs with a trade secret is the most exasperating of all competitors," and in the United States there appear to be no effective sanctions for controlling this traffic in ideas (23). Here then is one possible way in which the scientist can dispose of his own knowledge (and incidentally that of his peers also) by selling it to the highest bidder. But again, unless he becomes an entrepreneur himself his freedom to dispose of the use of the product is out of his hands.

What of the scientist who has no such commercial ambitions but is simply motivated by the "natural" need to let others know what he has been doing? Very likely he will find that his professional papers cannot be published or will be censored before publication. A recent survey of company policies regarding publication of *basic* research findings shows the following:

TABLE 2

RESEARCH FINDINGS PUBLISHED	No. OF COMPANIES	PER CENT
Substantially all	24	14
Most	46	26
Some	77	45
None	27	16
Total	174	100

Source: National Science Foundation (30, p. 7).

Permission to write a paper for publication and preparation for its release in final form may require approval and revision by numerous functionaries, including representatives of the governmental or other agency supporting the research under contract, R and D directors, patent attorneys, and officials from public relations, sales and marketing, and security departments of the firm (30, pp. 11 ff.). In some instances as many as 12 officials will have had a hand in the publication process. No comparable data are available for publications of *applied* research, but there is no reason to believe that greater freedom of communication exists in that area.

Finally let us consider the role of unions and professional organizations as a source of power for the scientist. Like other professionals, scientists have been reluctant to participate in the kind of collective organization and bargaining typical of "ordinary" labor unions and generally have remained aloof from formal affiliation with the labor movement (47, p. 37). At the same time, they have been unable to use the sanctions employed by other professions, such as law and medicine, because of the nature of their industrial employment. According to one observer the "popular model of the professional . . . has to be distorted almost out of recognition if it is to include the members of the engineering department of a large firm. . . . In fact, the professional model is at such variance with the state of affairs in industry that a discussion of professionalism would seem irrelevant . . . if it were not for the fact that a large proportion of scientists and engineers in industry think of themselves as professionals" (40, p. 308). Nevertheless, the exigencies of industrial employment have produced a number of organizational attempts to maximize both economic and professional power on a collective basis, resulting in such federations as the Engineers and Scientists of America (ESA) and the Engineers and Scientists Guild (ESG).[9] How successful have they been in meeting their goals?

In a recent study exploring this problem Walton states that historically "the growth and rationalization of the engineering functions have deprived the individual professional of most of his influence over the many aspects of the employment relationship. He lost a share in the control of the job: the nature of the work assignment, the methods and pace of the specific task assignment, working conditions, pay and status" (47, p. 371). After having surveyed the impact of unions on management policy Walton concludes that "engineers need an independent mechanism for being heard that is influential at the level where decisions are made affecting the multiform terms of engineering employment" (47, p. 384). The results of his study indicate that this "independent mechanism" is available for only a small proportion of professionals in industry, and that its impact on managerial decisions is generally weak. The professional unions occupy a marginal position: while reluctant to engage in strikes and to enlist the help of other labor unions, and while far from engaging in "featherbedding" practices they press for full utilization of their members' capacities, they nevertheless incur management's suspicion and enmity because it is felt that they ought to identify fully with management (47, p. 353, p. 357, pp. 368–369). Recruitment of new members is inhibited by managerial identification among young professionals — college graduates and placement officials are suspicious of firms which are unionized (47, p. 244). The "company union" pattern is pervasive, since national technical and professional societies typically "are led by men who are the employers of those whom they represent" (24, p. 93).

In summary, it seems clear that in order to maximize their *professional* power potential, scientists must enter the managerial ranks; once having done so, their professional goals tend to become subordinate to or transmogrified into organizational ones. The possible impact of this process on the role of scientists as "agents" of social change is elucidated by one scientist:

[9] For a list of these organizations, see "Compilation of Unions Representing Engineering and Technical Employees," Walton (47, pp. 388 ff.).

Today an unusually able scientist, figuratively speaking, is on the scrap-heap sometimes at the age of thirty or forty; he becomes director of research of a large unit, or head of a large department, or dean, or an important committeeman oscillating between his home town and Washington, D.C. Not that he ceases to be useful, but he is doing work that many others could do equally well or better; and he has to abandon work, usually more important in the long run, in which there is no substitute for him. . . . If an outstanding scientist succumbs to the higher salary and prestige of an "executive" position, his opportunities for high-level work do not increase with the number of those under him; they probably diminish very sharply (34, pp. 237–238).

Scientists and Political Power

One knowledgeable observer recently made the assertion that "the plain fact is that science has become the major Establishment in the American political system: the only set of institutions for which tax funds are appropriated almost on faith . . ." (36, pp. 1099–1100). Apart from the questions of whether the appropriation of tax funds is a valid index for the power of an Establishment, and of whether faith does in fact precipitate the opening of the public purse for "science," our main concern will be with the degree to which the scientist *qua* scientist is able to dispose of his knowledge so as to influence decisions in the realm of politics.

Our discussion will in the main center on the circumstances attending the discovery and early utilization of atomic fission, since the historical record is becoming reasonably accessible.[10] (On the other hand, much of the current interaction of scientific and political variables is hidden in a miasma of classified information, e.g., the incidence of radioactive fallout, not to speak of problems of arms control and military strategy.)

The basic thesis which we shall attempt to elucidate and document subsequently runs as follows: scientists provided their professional knowledge and personal motivation to make atomic fission possible, but the use or disposition of their discovery did not remain in their hands. Rather than being decision-makers they were utilized to support decisions made by others while they (the scientists) may have been under the impression that the decision was theirs. In technical terms, they were co-opted by others who had the requisite power:[11] much of the glory —

[10] The most complete, and hopefully most objective source available at this time is Hewlett and Anderson, *The New World*. Whatever biases may inhere in the fact that this is the first volume of the official history of the Atomic Energy Commission is counterbalanced by the standing of the authors as professional historians and by their use of much hitherto classified information.

[11] "Co-optation is the process of absorbing new elements into the leadership of the policy-making structure of an organization as a means of averting threats to its stability or existence. . . . One means of winning consent is to co-opt elements . . . which in some way reflect the sentiment, or possess the confidence of the relevant public or mass" (39, p. 34).

and for some the "knowledge of sin" of which Oppenheimer speaks — remained for the scientists.[12]

Certain historical facts are not in dispute here — the exciting story of the realization that the atom could be split and that an atomic weapon could be constructed, and the successful enlistment by Szilard and other physicists of the prestige of Einstein and of the persuasive powers of the banker Alexander Sachs to convince President Roosevelt that he should set aside some funds to follow up the scientists' hunches. But what has often been overlooked is that the establishment and successful operation of the Manhattan Project required the enlistment and direction of forces which went far beyond the powers of the scientists. In the words of Hewlett and Anderson "it had taken the exigencies of war and all of [Secretary of War] Stimson's personal force and prestige to keep funds flowing to the Manhattan gamble" (18, p. 346). On the other hand, for those who believe that the decision to drop the atom bomb without previous warning on Hiroshima was imposed by bloodthirsty warlords on peace-loving scientists, the actual events may be disturbing.

In order to explore the future military and other uses of atomic energy President Truman had appointed an Interim Committee, chaired by Stimson and having as members three scientists (Bush, Conant, and Karl Compton), the Under Secretary of the Navy, the Assistant Secretary of State, and Truman's personal representative (James F. Byrnes). In order to help this Committee in its deliberations, Stimson set up a Scientific Advisory Panel, consisting of Arthur Compton, Lawrence, Oppenheimer, and Fermi — all of whom had been intimately involved in the atom bomb project. Conant had asked for the establishment of this advisory panel since "the government needed full support from the scientific community. There should be no public bickering among experts" (18, p. 345). An explicit statement of the functions of co-optation! When Stimson met with this group the question of the best military use of the atom bomb, about to be completed, was brought up. When it was suggested that a harmless demonstration of the bomb's destructive power should be considered, "Oppenheimer could think of no demonstration sufficiently spectacular to convince the Japanese that further resistance was futile. . . . Besides, would the bomb cause any greater loss of life than the fire raids that had burned out Tokyo?" Finally, "Conant suggested and Stimson agreed that the most desirable target would be a vital war plant employing a large number of workers and closely surrounded by workers' houses" (18, p. 358). This decision was, of course, implemented, after a number of desirable targets had been chosen from

---

[12] The glory had to be shared with engineers, the military, and businessmen. Thus in the 1947 Congressional hearings on the creation of the Atomic Energy Commission, Senator McKellar of Tennessee went on record that General Groves had "discovered the secret of atomic fission" (Dupré and Lakoff, 13, p. 138).

which Kyoto was specifically excluded because of its significance as a religious center.

The scientist's role in this decision is cast in an ironic light in view of Stimson's feeling that "[General] Marshall and he had convinced the scientists that they were thinking like statesmen, not mere soldiers anxious to win the war at any cost" (18, p. 359). This conviction was not shared by other members of the "scientific community," notably the Chicago group spearheaded by James Franck and Leo Szilard, who were concerned about the implications of the military use of the atom. Their attempts to influence the Scientific Panel and President Truman directly were in vain.[13]

Our aim is not to find scapegoats for the unleashing of the destructive powers of the atom. Rather, we wish to pose the question whether the members of the Scientific Panel were chosen because it was felt that their views would most likely be in accord with those of the military and political leaders, while the potential critics were left "outside." We have no direct evidence that this involved Machiavellian skullduggery on the part of Stimson and his colleagues, but in the context of the available data the hypothesis of co-optation is inescapable. To be sure, the agitation among the Chicago scientists caused sincere concern to their official representatives. Compton had asked that the scientists at the Metallurgical Laboratory of the University of Chicago be polled on the use of the atom bomb, and the results showed a considerable range of opinion. In forwarding them to Washington, Compton stated that "his own sentiment was with the 46 per cent that leaned toward a military demonstration," to be followed by "a renewed opportunity to surrender before full use of the weapons." But "nothing could have seemed more irrelevant to Stimson . . . than further exposition of scientific opinion. Scientists had been given an opportunity to express themselves, and the current arguments added nothing to what had already been said. The responsible authorities had considered how best to use the bomb and had reached a decision" (18, pp. 399–400).

The next episode to be investigated concerns the future functions and control of the Atomic Energy Commission (AEC). One of the major issues revolved around the role to be played by the military authorities in directing its policies and operations. After the surrender of Japan the feeling became widespread among many scientists that now, having completed their job for the war effort, their opinions were no longer in demand. In fact, the first version of the relevant legislation (the so-called Royall-Marbury bill) had been drafted by two War Department lawyers without consultation with the established scientific authorities, and scientists were not to see a draft of the bill before its introduction in Congress (18, pp. 421–422). In its later version, as the May-Johnson

[13] For a detailed account of the entire episode, see Smith (43).

bill, the matter became subject to long Congressional and public controversy during which occurred the establishment of a vigorous scientific lobby in Washington, and organization of the Federation of American Scientists with its medium, the *Bulletin of the Atomic Scientists.*

There is no doubt that the scientists engaged in lobbying and airing their concern over military control of the AEC were using their newly acquired prestige with considerable effect, thus helping in the eventual defeat of the May-Johnson bill. It is of interest that the members of the Scientific Panel had *supported* the bill when it came up for hearings, thereby further deepening the rift between themselves and the scientists who up to now had no direct access to the political decision-makers. But now the latter group of scientists suddenly found new allies — men like Senators Vandenberg and McMahon who wished to reduce the power of the military, and members of the executive branch, including the President, who became aware that their powers and prerogatives were severely limited by the proposed legislation. "A new alliance of scientists and senators had joined the issue" (18, p. 445). Could the May-Johnson bill have been defeated without help from the "scientific community"? The answer appears to be a "yes" rather than a "no," in view of the deep split within the "community." On the other hand, it is most unlikely that the scientific opponents of military control could have gotten very far without powerful allies in Congress and the administration, who had their own good reasons for wanting to establish civilian control. Once more the co-optation process was in operation, though a new group of scientists was now "on tap," if not "on top."

Our analysis could be further extended to survey problems of international control, the decision to produce the hydrogen bomb, and the like. It is our impression that the pattern is essentially the same as we have described it. Granted that "all but one of the major departures in American foreign policy toward nuclear weapons were initially conceived by scientists: the Baruch plan, the hydrogen bomb, the development of tactical nuclear weapons, the ballistics missile, and a nuclear test ban. Only the doctrine of massive retaliation originated elsewhere" (17, p. 37). But — "the mood of the nation lent support to the group of scientists [favoring a strategy of mass retaliation]. The attitude within the government invited advice from that group and excluded the others" (13, p. 123). Many of the latter lost their standing as "wise men" and in the case of Oppenheimer were even branded renegades and traitors — an ironic and tragic fate for one of the chief architects of the atom bomb.

According to Gilpin, who has made a thorough study of the role of scientists in nuclear weapons policy, "failure to maximize the potential benefits of the scientists' entry into political life has been both the cause and the effect of a lack of coherent and realistic American policy toward nuclear weapons" (17, p. 38). He concludes that "scientists must be utilized in a more realistic manner." But how can this be done in view of Gilpin's finding that "it was the assumptions of a political character and not simply technical judgment that divided the scientists over the hydrogen bomb" and several other issues? He advances a number of possible solutions, including better education of scientists in political matters and of politicians in scientific ones, and "integrated" studies involving various types of expertise (17, pp. 324 ff.). Similarly, C. P. Snow has called for a bridging of the existing gap between scientific and political know-how (44), but his own historical example (the Lindeman-Tizard controversy over the employment of the best weapons and strategy during World War II) does little to convince one that scientific expertise will carry the day in the arena of political decisions where a Churchill represents *vox Dei.*

In what ways then can scientists bring their special knowledge to bear upon issues requiring objectivity but which are entangled in "assumptions of a political character"? The American Association for the Advancement of Science, the organization most representative of the "scientific community," at least in terms of the range and extent of its membership, has charged its Committee on Human Welfare with answering this question. The Committee split the issues into two major categories: (1) Those where scientists have particular, esoteric interests and knowledge, namely, those relating to the development of science itself, such as legislation affecting the National Science Foundation or the establishment of a Cabinet post for science and technology; and (2) those issues of broader impact where the scientist figures essentially as the "informed citizen" on a par with other groups, as in the case of nuclear weapons policy (4). Assuming for the moment the possibility of drawing a line between these two categories, we are left with the question of how scientists are to become members of the "power elite."

One political scientist has some pertinent observations in this context, apropos the first of the categories we mentioned, but even more so for the second. He points out that "a policy with which the scientists are to be influentially identified requires the scientists to have leaders who can act as their representatives in that bargaining with public officials and other groups which accompanies the policy-making process" (37, p. 859). His historical survey shows that in the past the spokesmen of "science" have often been self-nominated or in many instances, as in the case of "advisory committees," the co-optation process has been the rule. At any rate it is not realistic to refer to the "scientific community" in view of the "pluralistic, fragmented and internally competitive attributes" which scientists share with other groups. If it should be possible to set up reasonably democratic methods of representation for scientists it becomes plain that more than ever before "the leaders of the scientists are perforce politicians" (37, p. 863). This means that, in order to be effective, they must enter alliances with other power groups and must be in a position to enforce sanctions. The choices involved will revolutionize the traditional status of the scientist, whether conceived in terms of the simple technician or of the sage hovering above the fields where "ignorant armies clash by night."

Knowledge, Power, and Social Entanglement

Fifteen years ago, Harold Lasswell characterized physical scientists as being "in a state of social entanglement without comprehension" (25, p. 141). It seems safe to state that the increase of "comprehension" has been substantially smaller than that of "entanglement" during the intervening years. However, the problems of "value-free" science, which had been mainly the concern of social scientists in relatively recent times, are increasingly coming to the forefront of the natural scientists' consciousness. While there is a relatively high degree of consensus among scientists as to their rights and responsibilities in an academic setting, their status in the industrial-military-political arena is far from having reached a state of crystallization among scientists themselves, not to speak of its legitimation in society generally.

Typically the contemporary scientist is operating at points of institutional intersections where new exigencies are created at an unprecedented pace. Thus on the top level of power and prestige a physicist may at the same time be a university professor, teaching courses in the more or less traditional manner, and doing and supervising research financed by university funds; a supervisor of research under contract arrangements between the university and an agency of the Department of Defense or an industrial firm which, in turn, may have sub-contracted its program; a researcher or consultant for a national laboratory such as Oak Ridge or Argonne, set up outside the framework of both the conventional university structure and the civil service of a federal department such as the Bureau of Standards; an owner or manager of a private firm engaged in research and production; a "private" consultant to several industrial firms; a member of the President's Scientific Advisory Board; an expert serving to screen applications and making recommendations for a variety of grants given by the National Science Foundation or a private foundation; a member of the board of directors of the American Association for the Advancement of Science and of the American Physical Society; an editor for a variety of professional journals; an author of textbooks affording royalties greater than all his other income; a writer of scientific articles for the mass media; and a teacher of a television program attracting a nationwide audience. The list of offices and titles could be easily extended, and is as long and resplendent as that of many a potentate cited in the *Almanach de Gotha* — and who today would not prefer the presidency of a professional society to an earldom?

What are the implications of such a variety of roles for the power position of the scientist? One possibility is that as the number of institutional intersections increases the degree of "leverage" available to the scientist increases concomitantly. What kinds of needs will be specified by those having such leverage at their command? Will the needs be individually or institutionally oriented, and which institutions will have priority? Consider a specific, and not at all hypothetical situation: suppose a physicist is able to negotiate a million dollar research grant from the Atomic Energy Commission for his department or institute. The desirable aspects of such funds are plain enough; but will he be able to foresee its impact on the existing balance of teaching and research on his department and the potential dangers to the "independence" of scientific investigation? The potential impact of the grant is greater than the often-expressed fears about "federal control of education," precisely because the controls are not "naked," and consequences often unanticipated.

Hence the strong possibility of an alternative effect of the increasing involvement of the scientist in a multiplicity of institutional arrangements — namely, the attenuation of his adherence to the ethos and institutions of science, an attenuation which functions as both cause and consequence of an increasingly successful co-optation by other institutions. As the scientist's "role set"[14] proliferates, whatever chance of common action among scientists may have existed is dispelled by the splintering of professional loyalties and responsibilities[15] — a contemporary version of what Benda called "the betrayal of the intellectuals." Benda was aware that the "true intellectual", whose values are not contaminated by the "realistic" needs of ordinary men, cannot exist in any society, except as an isolated case. But who can gainsay his prophecy that "the logical end of this realism is the organized slaughter of nations and classes" (8, pp. 154–162)?

The nefarious effect of totalitarian social systems on science has been delineated with considerable thoroughness (albeit not without important biases). Our present concern is with the paradoxical alternative possibility that in a democratic society the increased power of scientists in terms of their market position (i.e., demand for their services) may undermine the freedom of movement of the "scientific establishment." (An analogy with the history of organized labor in the United States may not be too far-fetched here.) By way of further illustration let us list a number of instances where freedom of movement is increasingly curtailed — instances which are particularly relevant to the scientist working in a university setting, where the degree of autonomy presumably is higher than in industrial or governmental employment:

1. Increasing dependence on large-scale government financing of university research, which may be dependent upon policy decisions regarding the priority to be given to certain weapons systems. Not only does

---

[14] For discussion of this concept relevant to the present context see Merton (27, pp. 368–384).
[15] For empirical data on the existence of role conflicts in specified organizational settings, see for example Evan (14).

this put emphasis on "applied" research, but scientists may be required to drop whatever they have been working on and shift to another line of inquiry.

2. Increased growth in the area of research *administration*, which tends to siphon off many able scientists whose *political* skills are then no longer available to support the interests of their former peers.

3. The prevalence of expensive machinery, which tends to inhibit gambling on experiments with a low probability of "pay-off" (38).

4. The creation of a "scientific proletariat" — researchers who are hired to meet the requirements of a specific grant, but do not become full-fledged members of the faculty and thus do not add anything to its political power vis-à-vis the administration (21, pp. 152–154).

5. Increasing specialization, which intensifies the difficulty of communication among scientists and thus tends to reduce the possibility of concerted political action.

What of the counter-forces which are available to maintain the relative autonomy of the scientific institution? There have been several recent instances of their mobilization. Thus a number of universities, including Harvard and Yale, refused to participate in the National Defense Education Act because of the "disclaimer affidavit" requiring recipients of loans or grants to swear that they do not believe in or belong to any organization that teaches the illegal overthrow of the government. Protests by scientists and organizations such as the American Association of University Professors, coupled with non-participation by universities, resulted in substantial modification if not complete repeal of the undesirable provisions by Congress.[16]

The amount of federal support for research accorded to different universities varies tremendously; during 1958–59, for example, Yale derived 16 per cent of its total income from federal support, and M.I.T. 58 per cent.[17] In the absence of systematically gathered data the hypothesis is plausible that institutions without federal tie-ins and with a sufficiently large private endowment or other sources of support are in a better position to maintain autonomy in research by their staff, and in the decisions affecting the training of their students. But does this necessarily mean that these "autonomous" universities are in a better position to influence decisions made on a political level? What are their channels of influence? Independence from governmental funds may leave freedom of action within the university, but it eliminates one possible channel of reciprocal interaction between the university and government.

The most logical device for exercising political pressures are the pro-

[16] For a detailed discussion of the protest against the disclaimer affidavit and its subsequent modification see (1, 2.).

[17] The data cited are taken from Hubbert (20). The author expresses strong misgivings about the effects of federally-supported research. The fact that even the definition of what constitutes "support" is highly problematical is indicated by the arguments and data adduced by DuBridge in challenging Hubbert, and by the latter's defense. See DuBridge (12).

fessional societies, but the heterogeneity of their membership and the lack of consensus regarding specific political action has kept their power position in a rather weak state, especially compared with that of the American Medical Association or the American Bar Association. There remains the possibility of a scientific organization devoted explicitly to political action, such as the Federation of American Scientists. It remains to be seen whether their kind of program will attract enough scientists to impose sanctions great enough to influence the power of the purse wielded by government and industry.

Granted that the ideal type of scientific establishment has never in fact existed, the choices facing scientists today require that we ask questions relevant to fundamental changes from a "traditional" to a "contemporary" stage in the development of the institution. Such an analysis has barely begun.[18] Social science has been indebted to natural science for over a century; it is to be hoped that some of the debt can be repaid so as to afford the natural scientist better insight into his social entanglements.

BIBLIOGRAPHY

1. American Association of University Professors. "Repealing the Disclaimer Affidavit," *Bulletin of the AAUP*, Vol. 46, No. 1 (1960), pp. 55–61.

2. American Association of University Professors. "The Disclaimer Affidavit: A Valedictory," *Bulletin of the AAUP*, Vol. 48, No. 4 (1962), pp. 324–331.

3. American Behavioral Scientist. "Science, Scientists and Society," (December 1962).

4. American Association for the Advancement of Science, Committee on Human Welfare. Report, *Science*, Vol. 132 (1960), pp. 68–73.

5. Anthony, Robert A. *Management Control in Industrial Research Organizations*. Cambridge: Harvard Graduate School of Business Administration, 1952.

6. Barber, Bernard. "Sociology of Science," *Current Sociology*, UNESCO, Vol. 5, No. 2 (1956).

7. Barber, Bernard, and Walter Hirsch. *The Sociology of Science*. New York: The Free Press of Glencoe, 1962.

8. Benda, Julian. *The Betrayal of the Intellectuals*. Boston: Beacon Press, 1955.

9. Bierstedt, Robert. "An Analysis of Social Power," *American Sociological Review*, Vol. 15 (1950), pp. 730–738.

10. Dernburg, Thomas, and Norman Gherrity. "A Statistical Analysis of Patent Renewal Data for Three Countries," *The Patent, Trademark and Copyright Journal of Research and Education*, Vol. 5 (1961), pp. 340–361.

[18] For a representative sample of the extant literature, see Barber and Hirsch (7); American Behavioral Scientist (3).

11. Draper, Charles S. "The Patent System From a Scientist's Point of View," *The Patent, Trademark and Copyright Journal of Research and Education,* Vol. 5 (1961), p. 72.

12. DuBridge, Lee S. "Letter," *Science,* Vol. 140 (1963), p. 573.

13. Dupré, J. Stefan, and S. A. Lakoff. *Science and the Nation.* Englewood Cliffs, N.J.: Prentice-Hall, Inc., 1962.

14. Evan, William M. "Role Strain and the Norms of Reciprocity in Research Organizations," *American Journal of Sociology,* Vol. 68 (1962), pp. 346–354.

15. Fisher, J. C. "Basic Research in Industry," *Science,* Vol. 139 (1950), pp. 1653–1657.

16. Furash, Edward E. "Industrial Espionage," *Harvard Business Review,* Vol. 37, No. 6 (1959), pp. 7 ff.

17. Gilpin, Robert. *American Scientists and Nuclear Weapons Policy.* Princeton, N.J.: Princeton University Press, 1962.

18. Hewlett, Richard G., and Oscar E. Anderson, Jr. *The New World, 1939–1946.* Philadelphia: University of Pennsylvania Press, 1962.

19. Hirsch, Walter. "The Autonomy of Science in Totalitarian Societies," *Social Forces,* Vol. 40 (1961), pp. 15–22.

20. Hubbert, M. King. "Are We Retrogressing in Science?" *Science,* Vol. 139 (1963), p. 887.

21. Kidd, Charles V. *American Universities and Federal Research.* Cambridge, Mass.: Belknap Press, 1959.

22. Kidd, Charles V. "Basic Research Description vs. Definition," *Science,* Vol. 129 (1959), pp. 368–371.

23. Klein, Herbert D. "The Technical Trade Secret Quadrangle," *Northwestern University Law Review,* Vol. 55 (1960), pp. 437–467.

24. Kornhauser, William. *Scientists in Industry.* Berkeley: University of California Press, 1962.

25. Lasswell, Harold D. *Power and Personality.* New York: W. W. Norton, 1948.

26. Machlup, Fritz. "Patents and Inventive Effort," *Science,* Vol. 133 (1961), pp. 1463–1466.

27. Merton, Robert K. *Social Theory and Social Structure.* Glencoe, Ill.: The Free Press, 1957.

28. Merton, Robert K. "Priorities in Scientific Discovery," *American Sociological Review,* Vol. 22 (1957), pp. 635–659.

29. National Science Foundation. *Funds for Research and Development in Industry.* Washington, D.C.: 1961.

30. National Science Foundation. *Publication of Basic Research Findings in Industry.* Washington, D.C.: 1961.

31. Opinion Research Corporation. *The Scientific Mind and the Management Mind.* Princeton, N.J.: 1959.

32. Oppenheimer, Robert J. "Physics in the Contemporary World," *Bulletin of the Atomic Scientists*, Vol. 4 (1948), pp. 69–72.

33. Orlans, Harold. *The Effects of Federal Programs on Higher Education.* Washington, D.C.: Brookings Institution, 1962.

34. Orowan, Egon. "Our Universities and Scientific Creativity," *Bulletin of the Atomic Scientists*, Vol. 15 (1959), pp. 237–238.

35. Piel, Gerald. *Science in the Cause of Man.* New York: Alfred Knopf, 1961.

36. Price, Don K. "The Scientific Establishment," *Science*, Vol. 136 (1962), pp. 1099–1106.

37. Sayre, Wallace S. "Scientists and American Science Policy," *Science*, Vol. 133 (1961), pp. 859–863.

38. Schwartz, Melvin. "The Conflict Between Productivity and Creativity in Modern Day Physics," *American Behavioral Scientist*, Vol. 6, No. 4 (1962), pp. 35–36.

39. Selznick, Philip. "Foundations of the Theory of Organization," *American Sociological Review*, Vol. 13 (1948), pp. 25–35.

40. Shepard, Herbert A. "Nine Dilemmas in Industrial Research," *Administrative Science Quarterly*, Vol. 1 (1956), pp. 295–309.

41. Shils, Edward A. *The Torment of Secrecy.* Glencoe, Ill.: Free Press, 1956.

42. Shils, Edward A. "Freedom and Influence: Observations on the Scientists' Movement," *Bulletin of the Atomic Scientists*, Vol. 13 (1957), pp. 13–18.

43. Smith, Alice Kimball. "Behind the Decision to Use the Atom Bomb," *Bulletin of the Atomic Scientists*, Vol. 14 (1958), pp. 288–312.

44. Snow, Charles P. *Science and Politics.* Cambridge: Harvard University Press, 1961.

45. Stein, Morris I. "Creativity and the Scientist," in Bernard Barber and Walter Hirsch (eds.), *The Sociology of Science.* New York: The Free Press, 1962.

46. Veblen, Thorstein. "The Engineers and the Price System," in Wesley Mitchell (ed.), *What Veblen Taught.* New York: Viking Press, 1936.

47. Walton, Richard E. *The Impact of the Professional Engineering Union.* Boston: Harvard University Graduate School of Business Administration, 1961.

48. West, S. Stewart. "The Ideology of American Scientists," *IRE Transactions of Engineering Management* (June 1960), pp. 54–62.

49. Wolfle, Dael (ed.), *Symposium on Basic Research.* Washington, D.C.: American Association for the Advancement of Science, 1959.

50. White, Leslie A. *The Science of Culture.* New York: Grove Press, 1949.

The Contributors

Ronald M. Andersen (Appendix to Part II and Chapter 22) holds a joint appointment with the Health Information Foundation of the University of Chicago and the National Opinion Research Center.

J. A. Banks and Olive Banks (Chapter 21) are, respectively, Senior Research Lecturer and Research Lecturer in the Department of Social Science of the University of Liverpool.

Homer G. Barnett (Chapter 14) is Professor of Anthropology at the University of Oregon.

James M. Beshers (Chapter 11) is Associate Professor of Sociology in the Department of City and Regional Planning at the Massachusetts Institute of Technology.

Alvin Boskoff (Chapter 8) is Professor of Sociology in the Department of Sociology and Anthropology at Emory University.

Kenneth E. Boulding (Chapter 1) is Professor of Economics at the University of Michigan.

Ronald Cohen (Chapter 19) is Associate Professor of Anthropology and Political Science in the Department of Anthropology at Northwestern University.

Richard Colvard (Chapter 28) is Associate Professor of Sociology at the State University of New York at Buffalo.

Fred Cottrell (Chapter 27) is Professor of Government and Chairman of the Department of Sociology and Anthropology at Miami University.

G. Duncan Mitchell (Chapter 30) is Head of the Department of Sociology at the University of Exeter.

Robert L. Eichhorn (Appendix to Part II and Chapter 22) is Associate Professor of Sociology at Purdue University.

S. N. Eisenstadt (Chapter 17) is Professor of Sociology and Chairman of the Department of Sociology at the Hebrew University of Jerusalem.

Frederick Elkin (Chapter 20) is Associate Professor of Sociology at the Université de Montréal.

Philip Gibeau (Chapter 6) is a Psychologist at the Veteran's Administration Hospital in Marion, Indiana.

Sidney M. Greenfield (Chapter 24) is Associate Professor of Sociology at the University of Wisconsin-Milwaukee.

Walter Hirsch (Chapter 31) is Associate Professor of Sociology at Purdue University.

Bert F. Hoselitz (Chapter 26) is Professor of Economics and Social Science and Director of the Research Center in Economic Development and Cultural Change at the University of Chicago.

H. David Kirk (Chapter 10) is Associate Professor of Sociology and Research Sociologist in the School of Social Work at McGill University.

Daniel J. Levinson (Chapter 12) is Assistant Professor of Psychology in the Department of Psychiatry at the Harvard Medical School, and Director of the Center for Sociopsychological Research at the Massachusetts Mental Health Center.

David Lockwood (Chapter 9) is a Fellow of St. John's College, Cambridge.

Philip Marcus (Chapter 29) is a Study Director in the Survey Research Center of the Institute for Social Research, and Assistant Professor of Sociology at the University of Michigan.

Don Martindale (Chapters 3 and 18) is Professor of Sociology at the University of Minnesota.

Robert Perucci (Chapter 4) is Assistant Professor of Sociology at Purdue University.

Nathan Rosenberg (Chapter 25) is Associate Professor of Economics at Purdue University.

Louis Schneider (Chapter 15) is Professor of Sociology and Head of the Department of Sociology at the University of Illinois.

Pitirim A. Sorokin (Chapter 16) is the Director of the Research Center in Creative Altruism.

Irving Sosensky (Chapter 2) is Assistant Professor of Philosophy in the Department of History, Government, and Philosophy at Purdue University.

Leon H. Warshay (Chapter 13) is Assistant Professor of Sociology at the University of Missouri at Kansas City.

Alfred Willener (Chapter 23) is affiliated with the Centre National de la Recherche Scientifique in Paris.

David Willer (Chapter 5) is a graduate student in the Department of Sociology at Purdue University.

George K. Zollschan (Chapters 4, 5, 6, and 7) is Assistant Professor of Sociology at Purdue University.

Index

Abelard, 462
Abramovitz, Moses, 652
Abse, D. Wilfred, 169–170
Acceptance of change, 345–366
Acceptance-rejection possibilities, 358–362; application of, 362–367
Accommodation: to alienative predicaments, 158–163; ideological, of education, 787–789
Action(s): personality systems of, 38, 39–40; social systems, 38, 40–41; cultural systems, 38, 41; theory of, 93; requisites for, 93–94; phases of, 95; collective, establishing patterns of, 104–107; collective, and division of authority, 109; communal, 140n.
Adams, Henry, 13
Adamson Act, 721
Adaptation, 187n.; assessing the means of, 274–279
Adaptive function, 220
Adjustment, 187n.
Adjustment Boards, 722, 725
Adler, Alfred, 332
Administrative tribunals and law, 722–726
Adoption Research Project, 267–274, 275
Adorno, Theodore W., 304
Advertising in French Canada, 522–523, 528–538; translation of, 538–540; adaptation of, 536, 540–541; separate campaigns, 541–544
Affiliation, as secondary goal, 166, 167
Africa, sociological and anthropological studies of, 495–496; Kanuri of Bornu (Nigeria), 499–520
Agencies of consensus and control, 114
Agricultural economy, prevalence of indolence and lethargy in, 655–656; and secondary benefits, 658, 661; skills generated by, 662–666
Albert the Great, 456
Alice in Wonderland, quoted, 152
Alienation, 154–158; institutional types of, 155, 271–272; problem of accommodation to, 158–163; conditions for, and the concept of rationality, 163–167; and the field of mental health, 167–172
Allport, Floyd H., 297n., 329, 335
Almond, Gabriel A., 300
Alpert, Harry, 738
American Association for the Advance-

ment of Science, Committee on Human Welfare, 799, 810
American Association of University Professors, 813
American Federation of Labor: and labor legislation, 755, 756; and jurisdictional disputes, 757–758
American revolution, 140, 144, 466
Analogy, 23–24
Analysis, functional, and the study of social change, 213–239
Andersen, Ronald M., 96, 493
Anderson, Camilla, 326
Anderson, Oscar E., Jr., 807
Andrews, F. Emerson, 729, 731, 732
Angelology, Duns Scotus, 293
Angels on pinhead, 293–294
Anthropologists, African studies by, 495–496
Anxiety, 160; reaction, and the sociopathic character, 170–171
Application, 93, 94; and cardiac patients, 205–206
Approval, as secondary goal, 166, 167
Aquinas, Thomas, 428n., 456, 463
Arendt, Hanna, 321
Argyris, Chris, 301
Aristotle, 47; notions of Substance and Being, 17, 30; on quality, 18; law of non-contradiction, 18–19; on precision, 53; readers of, excommunicated, 456; elevated to position of authority, 463
Arnold, Matthew, 697, 788, 790–791
Arnold, Thomas, 792
Arteriosclerotic heart disease. *See* Heart disease
Articulation of need, 90, 130, 153; requisites for, 91; as individual process, 93; phases of, 95; "false," 132, 168; of group interests, 136–139; progressive, 168; fixated, 169; regressive, 169
Artists, Renaissance, 459
Assimilation, 352–354
Association, categorical, 330, 331; formal, 330; traditional, 330; informal, 330–331
Association of American Railways, 723, 725
Athens, 82, 83; Periclean, 135
Atkins, Governor, 625n.
Atom, military uses of, 799, 807–810
Atomic Energy Commission, 806n., 807n., 808–809